55

THE MEXICAN REVOLUTION

VOLUME 2

THE MEXICAN REVOLUTION

VOLUME 2

Counter-revolution and reconstruction

〰〰〰〰〰〰〰〰〰〰〰〰〰〰〰〰〰〰〰〰〰〰〰〰〰〰〰〰〰〰〰

ALAN KNIGHT

Department of History, University of Essex

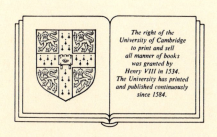

The right of the
University of Cambridge
to print and sell
all manner of books
was granted by
Henry VIII in 1534.
The University has printed
and published continuously
since 1584.

CAMBRIDGE UNIVERSITY PRESS

Cambridge
London   New York   New Rochelle
Melbourne   Sydney

Published by the Press Syndicate of the University of Cambridge
The Pitt Building, Trumpington Street, Cambridge CB2 1RP
32 East 57th Street, New York, NY 10022, USA
10 Stamford Road, Oakleigh, Melbourne 3166, Australia

First published 1986

Printed in Great Britain at the University Press, Cambridge

British Library cataloguing in publication data

Knight, Alan
The Mexican Revolution. – (Cambridge Latin
American studies)
Vol. 2: Counter-revolution and reconstruction
1. Mexico – History – Revolution, 1910–1920
1. Title
972.08′1   F1234

Library of Congress cataloguing in publication data

Knight, Alan, 1946–
The Mexican Revolution.
(Cambridge Latin American studies; 54–55)
Includes bibliographies and indexes.
Contents: v. 1. Porfirians, liberals, and
peasants – v. 2. Counter-revolution and reconstruction.
1. Mexico – History – Revolution, 1910–1920.
1. Title. 11. Series.
F1234.K65 1986   972.08   85–12798

ISBN 0 521 24475 7 (v. 1)
ISBN 0 521 26651 3 (v. 2)

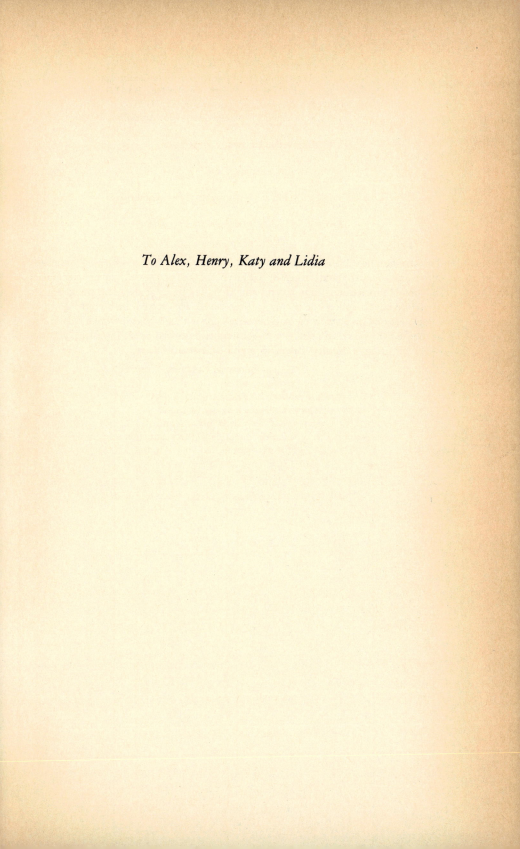

To Alex, Henry, Katy and Lidia

'Tezcatlipoca: he was considered a true god, whose abode was everywhere – in the land of the dead, on earth [and] in heaven. When he walked on the earth he quickened vice and sin. He introduced anguish and affliction. He brought discord among people, wherefore he was called 'the enemy on both sides'. He created, he brought down all things. He cast his shadow on one, he visited one with all the evils which befall men; he mocked, he ridiculed men. But he sometimes bestowed riches – wealth, heroism, valour, position of dignity, rulership, nobility, honour.'

Bernardo Sahagún, Florentine Codex, Book 1,

Contents

Preface

Like its subject, the Mexican Revolution, the two volumes of this book developed in a way that was unforeseen and unplanned. Indeed, it is unlikely that they would have been written at all had the conventional criteria which govern the production of academic history been followed. The work is unfashionably long, ambitious in scope, and, perhaps, narrative in form. It began with a commitment made years ago in days of post-graduate *naïveté* and financial constraint, when the proposed result was a succinct history of the Mexican Revolution, based on secondary sources. Already, however, my doctoral research (which focussed on the role of foreign interests in the Revolution) was generating a wealth of surplus material and prompting broader questions concerning the nature of the Revolution. In consequence, the book grew and grew; its 'data-base', primary and secondary, expanded; its objectives became more ambitious. Ultimately, I sought to write a history of the Revolution, during its armed phase, which, while it could not be called definitive (few if any histories are), was at least comprehensive, national, original and, perhaps, the closest to a definitive, unitary (i.e., single author) history that we have. Whether these aims have been achieved others must judge; but I would plead that the aims justified the considerable length of the work.

This undertaking required a combination of analysis and narrative, of primary and secondary sources. As regards the first — what Hexter terms the 'rhetoric of history' — I see no intrinsic superiority of one form over another. It all depends on the job in hand. I have therefore shifted from narrative to analysis and back again; I have made brief excursions into 'theory'; and I have ventured global comparisons with other revolutions and rebellions. In doing so, I have probably pleased no-one entirely, and offended everybody somewhat. The aggressively numerate, in particular, may regret the relative absence of statistical material. This is deliberate: I share Chevalier's scepticism about much of the statistical evidence for this period, and E. P. Thompson's belief that, especially as regards popular radicalism, the usefulness of statistical evidence is easily exaggerated. Cliometricians may therefore come away disappointed. So, too, may Mexican or Latin American historiographical nationalists (those, fortunately few in number, who believe that Mexican and Latin American history is best avoided by foreigners working from foreign sources). For the reader will soon appreciate that, while abundant Mexican primary sources have been used (especially national collections: Gobernación, Trabajo, the Madero, Robles Domínguez and Carranza Archives etc.) these are probably outweighed by foreign sources: the French Archives des Affaires Etrangères, the British Foreign Office and, above all, the American State Department. In part, this derives from the unplanned pattern of research: my doctoral work introduced me to consular reports which, it became clear, were a magnificent source not just for the history of foreign interests in Mexico, but also for the history of the Revolution, in all its facets. Accomplished local historians, like Falcón and Ankerson, have shown how consular reports – especially American consular reports – can provide a stream of valuable historical information. I have used the same sources (still relatively unexploited) to build up a national picture. Of course, this source, like all sources, involves bias, and must be used judiciously. But in many respects the bias of foreign observers (especially those based in the provinces, far from the high politics of Mexico City) is clearer, hence less distorting, than that of Mexican observers and participants who, of course, were rarely in the business of filing regular reports to some external agency. Similarly, I found the *Mexican Herald* to be, for all its rank editorial prejudice, more useful than the shackled Huertista press for the years 1913–14. If unplanned, therefore, my reliance on foreign sources is not regretted. Furthermore, the picture these sources reveal is corroborated, not negated, by the extensive Mexican archives I have also used. The two are complementary, not antithetical.

These primary sources form the basis for much of this study. But, in addition, I have tried to incorporate much, if not all, the published work on the Revolution, which has recently proliferated, and which makes the study of modern Mexican history so profoundly stimulating. The memoirs of old participants, the solid narratives of an earlier generation of historians (neither of which should be disdained as sources), have given way to highly scholarly monographs, many of them devoted to regional, local and 'micro' history. These have been immensely valuable and without their contribution (which I have all too briefly and partially recognised in the acknowledgements), this study would not have been possible. Yet, when all is said and done, the Revolution was a *national* phenomenon; it stretched from Tijuana to Tapachula, from the Río Grande to the Río Hondo; it touched the lives of all Mexicans. It therefore deserves a *national* history. And, without a national history, it is impossible to gauge whether local studies are typical or aberrant.

My basic aim, therefore, has been to write a national history which both takes into account local and regional variations, and also delves below the level of high politics and diplomacy. The latter cannot be neglected, but nor can they be understood *in vacuo*. There can be no high politics without a good deal of low politics. This is particularly true since, I believe, the Revolution was a genuinely popular movement and thus an example of those relatively rare episodes in history when the mass of the people profoundly influenced events. At such times, national politics are only explicable in terms of local and popular pressures. By a strange irony, this view seems to have become increasingly unfashionable, particularly in those recent monographs on which I have heavily relied. True, Marxist historians (of abstract bent) still assert the central role of the masses in the Revolution, but they often assert more than they illustrate. Many recent historians of the Revolution, on the other hand, have deployed their considerable research and learning to show that the Revolution was less an autonomous, agrarian and popular revolution than a series of chaotic, careerist episodes, in which popular forces were, at best, the instruments of manipulative caciques, of aspiring bourgeois or petty bourgeois leaders. For these historians, the Revolution is not the great and heroic popular movement typified by Zapata and described by Tannenbaum, but the more sordid vehicle of class and individual ambition driven by Calles and sketched by Jean Meyer. In all this, I am an unashamed conservative, or anti-revisionist. That is, I believe that Tannenbaum and his generation grasped the basic character of the 1910 Revolution as a popular, agrarian movement – the precursor, the necessary precursor, of the *étatiste* 'revolution' of post-1920. Of course, such interpretations are not entirely antithetical; they hinge upon questions of emphasis and degree; yet questions of degree which are not amenable to precise, positivist measurement. We cannot do a head count of 'agrarian' rebels, nor is it clear how many 'agrarian' rebels must be found before the Revolution counts as 'agrarian'. By way of defending my view of the 1910 Revolution as fundamentally popular and agrarian, I can only point to the evidence presented in these pages (itself a sample drawn from a larger stock of evidence) and hope that it convinces.

In presenting this view (and others) I have sometimes taken issue with other historians working in the field. Such arguments, I stress, are never *ad hominem*, and are designed solely to clarify my position *vis-à-vis* that of others. To the extent that particular authorities are 'interrogated', it is precisely because they present cogent arguments which demand serious attention. Vapid accounts can be more easily ignored. And, though I may convince myself that my arguments and evidence are superior, there will no doubt be many who disagree, many who, in turn, cap my arguments and evidence with their own. For, necessarily, I have had to skate over some topics (the diplomacy of the revolution, perhaps) and, in places, hazard conclusions which are tentative or downright risky. If these are seized upon and corrected, so much the better. A few hostages may be given, so long as the whole campaign is not thereby lost. As for the campaign itself, it remains to be seen whether subsequent history will absolve me.

ALAN KNIGHT

Alella, Spain, July 1984.

Acknowledgements

The origins of this work date back many years, and its final publication now affords an opportunity to thank those institutions and individuals who have helped me in its conception and completion (without, of course, any responsibility for its errors and defects, which are mine alone).

Professor Michael Cherniavsky first encouraged my interest in history, which was the initial step down the road, and the late Professor Jack Gallagher, while teaching me British imperial history in his inimitable fashion, pointed out the attractions and opportunities of the path I eventually took, that of Latin American history. That path taken, I undertook my doctoral thesis and did much of the preliminary research for this book at Nuffield College, Oxford, where I was a graduate student and research fellow. I therefore owe a large debt to the Warden and Fellows of Nuffield, especially the late Philip Williams and Lawrence Whitehead, who took a lively, constructive interest in my early Mexican studies. My second, major, institutional debt is to the History Department of the University of Essex, which gave me research time and resources to continue and complete the work; in addition, the Nuffield Foundation, the Twenty-One Foundation, and the British-Mexican Society generously gave me grants for travel and research in Mexico and the USA. Thirdly, I must thank the Cambridge University Press which accepted and carried through the publication of this unfashionably *magnum opus*. In particular, I would like to thank Malcolm Deas, under whose editorship the manuscript was first considered, read and accepted; his successor and my colleague, Simon Collier, who was a scrupulous and sensitive editor at the final stage; and Elizabeth Wetton and her staff, especially Sheila McEnery, who were unfailingly helpful and efficient.

Many individual debts have also accumulated. Over many years I have derived great benefit from both reading Professor Friedrich Katz's work on Mexico and, when possible, discussing our mutual research interests. Since our initial meeting over tea in Sanborns in 1970, these discussions, though infrequent, have been extremely valuable and remarkably unaffected by differences in our respective statuses or interpretations. I have also benefited greatly from the research, opinions and encouragement of many fellow-students of Mexican history: Leif Adelsen, Tom Benjamin, Romana Falcón, Javier Garciadiego Dantón, Linda Hall, Gil Joseph, Eugenia Meyer, Bill Meyers, Segundo Portilla and Asgar Simonsen. And I would particularly wish to acknowledge the support of the small but select group which has sustained the study of Mexican history in Britain in recent years: David Brading, Brian Hamnett, Tony Morgan, Simon Miller, Guy Thompson; and, above all, Barry Carr, whose help dates back to the beginning, and Ian Jacobs and Dudley Ankerson, whose sure grasp of local history has been invaluable. I have also, on my travels, benefited from the help and hospitality of the Grant-Suttie and Cherniavsky families of Washington DC; of the Granel and Portilla families, Enrique Márquez, Francisco Suárez, and Laura Salinas of Mexico City; and, last but by no means least, Juan and Lidia Lozano Martín of Alella, Spain, who allowed me unstinting use of their house, *bodega* and study, where most of the final version of this book was written up. Finally, I wish to thank those to whom the book is dedicated who – though they did not exactly speed its completion – certainly gave me valuable insights into what one author has called the 'revolutionary personality'.

Glossary

acasillado	resident peon
acomodado	privileged resident peon
adicto	unconditional supporter (of regime, faction)
administrador	estate manager
agrarismo	agrarian reform movement or ideology
alcabala	internal tariff
alcalde	mayor
Anti-Re-eleccionismo	see *Re-elección*
arriero	muleteer
atropello	outrage, abuse, arbitrary act (especially political)
ayuntamiento	town council
baldío	of land: lacking private title
barranca	gorge
barrio	quarter (of town, village)
boleta	(voting) slip
borracho	drunk
bracero	labourer; especially migrant labourer in the US
bronco	wild, untamed; hence, of the Yaquis, independent
burro	mule
cabecera	'head town'; seat of local government
cabecilla	local revolutionary leader
cacicazgo	example of cacique rule
cacique	local political boss
caciquismo	boss system of politics
cafetal	coffee plantation
campesino/campesinado	peasant/peasantry; rural labourer

xiv

canario	native of the Canary Islands
cantina/cantinero	saloon/saloon-keeper
capitación	head tax
capitalino	native of Mexico City
caporal	estate foreman (especially on cattle ranch)
cargadilla	addition made to a (peon's) debt
casco	main buildings of an estate
catrín	dandy; smart dresser; hence 'city slicker'
caudillo	political leader based on armed clientele
cerrado	dour, taciturn (usualy pejorative)
charro	of dress, appearance: relating to the typical
chegomista	adherent of the Juchiteco cacique, 'Che' Gómez
chilapeño	straw hat
chilero	native of sierra, especially Sinaloa/Durango
chusma	horde, rabble, gang
Científico	adherent and apologist of Positivism and Porfirismo; hence, a minion of the old regime
cofradía	confraternity; local, religious association of laymen
Coloso del Norte	'Colossus of the North': the United States
comerciante	merchant, businessman
compadre (compadrazgo)	God-parent; hence, friend, crony (relationship of)
compañero	friend, ally
congregación	small rural community; hamlet
Convencionista	supporter of the Aguascalientes Convention, 1914–15
Cristiada	Catholic revolt against the state, 1926–9
cuadrilla	work gang (of peons)
cuartel	barracks
cuartelazo	barracks revolt
Cuerpo Rural	rural corps: mounted police
cura	parish priest
curro	smart (gentleman); cf. *catrín*
Defensa Social	community self-defence force
disponible	available; 'up for grabs'

ejido	land corporately owned by community; hence land conferred under the agrarian reform programme
enganchado	worker hired, maybe held, by *enganche* system
enganchador	labour contractor
enganche	'hook': advance payment made to secure worker
entreguismo	handing over; hence, 'selling out' (of Mexico to foreigners)
extranjero	foreigner
finca (finquero)	rural property (owner), especially Chiapas
fundo legal	town or village site
gachupín	Spaniard (pejorative)
gallinero	chicken run; hence, backyard
gavilla	gang (of bandits, rebels)
gente	people, followers, rank-and-file
gente decente	respectable folk, middle and upper class
gente de razón	whites/mestizos; townspeople
gira (electoral)	(political campaign) tour
Gobernación	Ministry of the Interior
gobernador	state governor
gobiernista	supporter of the government
gringo	North American
guanajuatense	native of Guanajuato
guayule (guayulero)	rubber-producing shrub (collector of)
guerrillero	(military) irregular
hacienda (hacendado)	rural estate (owner of)
Hacienda	Ministry of Finance
hidrocálido	native of Aguascalientes
hijo (del país)	son (of the locality)
huaraches	sandals; peasant footwear
indigenismo	movement/philosophy advocating the protection of the Indian and Indian culture
infalsificable	'non-forgeable'; Constitutionalist paper currency
interinato	interim regime (of de la Barra, 1911)
jarabe	popular dance (especially western Mexico)
jefe	boss, leader
jefe político (jefatura)	political boss, prefect (prefecture)
juez (de paz)	justice (of the peace)

ladino	white/mestizo (as against indian)
latifundio (latifundista)	great estate (owner)
lechuguilla	fibrous plant, especially cultivated in San Luis
leva	press-gang
licenciado	roughly, graduate
machetazo	machete blow
macho	aggressively 'masculine'; violent; generally unpleasant
maestro	schoolteacher
manco	one-armed
manso	'tame', docile; of Yaquis, integrated into the mestizo state and economy (cf. *bronco*)
mapache	lit., racoon, a Chiapas rebel
máquina loca	'mad' locomotive: driverless locomotive, mined and used as offensive weapon
mayordomo	hacienda foreman
mesón	lodging house
mestizo	'half-caste', of mixed Spanish-Indian ancestry (but see vol. I, chapter I, People)
milpa	corn plot
mordida	bribe
Morelense	native of Morelos
muchachito	young lad
muera . . .	death to . . .
mujeriego	womanising
norteño	northerner
novio(-a)	fiancé(e)
obrero(-a)	(female) worker
oficial mayor	lieutenant-governor
ojo parado	wall-eye
paseo	walk, Sunday evening promenade
patria chica	'little fatherland'; i.e., local region eliciting quasi-patriotic allegiance
patrón	boss, patron
pelado	'skint'; hence, plebeian, uneducated
peon	rural labourer; sometimes endebted
peonaje	rural labourers (collectively); or the labour system, often associated with debt
poblano	native of Puebla
político	politician

Porfirian/Porfirista	adherent of Porfirio Díaz
Porfiriato	the regime of Porfirio Díaz; hence the period 1876–1911
porteño	port-dweller (e.g., inhabitant of Guaymas)
Potosino	native of San Luis Potosí
presidente municipal	municipal president; mayor
pronunciamiento	(military) rebellion
propietario	property-owner; or incumbent, usually of elected office (e.g., deputy; cf. *suplente*)
pueblo	village; or 'the people'
pulque	alcoholic drink obtained from maguey plant
ranchero	owner/tenant of *rancho*; smallholder
rancho	farm; sometimes implies homestead; but can also constitute a small hacienda
realeño	privileged peon (Morelos)
Re-elección	practice of repeated political re-election, hence *immobilisme*, associated with the Porfiriato (cf. *Anti-Re-eleccionismo*)
reivindicación	restorative demand, claim, act (usually agrarian)
reparto (de tierras)	distribution, share-out (of land)
rural(es)	member(s) of *Cuerpos Rurales*
sarape	heavy shawl, blanket
señorito	young gentleman (often derogatory)
serrano	mountain-dweller, highlander; adherent of local autonomist, movement (see vol. 1, chapter 3, The sierra)
sierra	mountain range
sinverguencista	shameless person; rebel lacking political credibility
sufragio efectivo	'effective suffrage', i.e., a real vote
suplente	stand-in for (usually elected) office-holder (cf. *propietario*)
suriano	southerner; specifically, adherent of Zapatismo
tapatío	native of Jalisco
temporal	rain-fed agricultural land (non-irrigated)
tequila	liquor distilled from maguey juice
terrenos baldíos	see *baldío*
tienda de raya	company or hacienda store
tierra caliente	hot country; tropical lowlands
tierra fría	cold country: high plateau and mountains
tierra templada	temperate, sub-tropical country; especially the valleys of central Mexico

tinterillo	'ink-pot'; hence, village intellectual/scribe/lawyer
torero	bullfighter
transacción	deal, compromise
vale	token, chit, issued by hacienda or company
vaquero	cowboy
vecino	'neighbour'; member of local community
vendepatria	one who 'sells his country'
yori	Yaqui term for whites/mestizos
zacatón	fodder grass; also used for brooms, brushes
zafra	sugar cane harvest
zócalo	main square, especially Mexico City

Abbreviations

GEOGRAPHICAL

Ags.	Aguascalientes	Mich.	Michoacán
Baja Calif.	Baja California	Mor.	Morelos
Camp.	Campeche	Oax.	Oaxaca
Chih.	Chihuahua	Pue.	Puebla
Coa.	Coahuila	Qro	Querétaro
Col.	Colima	Sin.	Sinaloa
CPD	Ciudad Porfirio Díaz	SLP	San Luis Potosí
Dgo	Durango	Sra	Sonora
Gro	Guerrero	Tab.	Tabasco
Gto	Guanajuato	Tamps.	Tamaulipas
Hgo	Hidalgo	Ver.	Veracruz
Jal.	Jalisco	Yuc.	Yucatán
Mex.	Mexico State	Zac.	Zacatecas

POLITICAL

CROM	Confederación Regional Obrera Mexicana
PCN	Partido Católico Nacional
PCP	Partido Constitucional Progresista
PLC	Partido Liberal Constitucionalista
PLM	Partido Liberal Mexicano

ARCHIVAL

AAE	Archives du Ministère des Affaires Etrangères
AARD	Archivo Alfredo Robles Domínguez
AFM	Archivo Francisco I. Madero
AG	Archivo de Gobernación
AJD	Archivo Jorge Denegri
ALB	Archivo León de la Barra
ARC	Archivo Ramón Corral
ARE	Archivo de Relaciones Exteriores

AVC	Archivo Venustiano Carranza
AZ	Archivo Zongólica
CRCFM	Convención Revolucionaria y Correspondencia con Francisco I. Madero
DDCC	*Diario de los debates del congreso constituyente* (see bibliography)
DEAS	Departamento de Etnologia y Antropología Social
DHRM	*Documentos Históricos de la Revolución Mexicana* (see bibliography under Fabela)
FO	Foreign Office
MCETA	Mexican Cotton Estates of Tlahualilo Archive
PHO	Programa de Historia Oral, Museo de Antropología e Historia
SD	State Department
SGIA	Samuel Guy Inman Archive
SRE	Secretaría de Relaciones Exteriores
SS	Serie Sonora
STA	Silvestre Terrazas Archive
WWP	Woodrow Wilson Papers

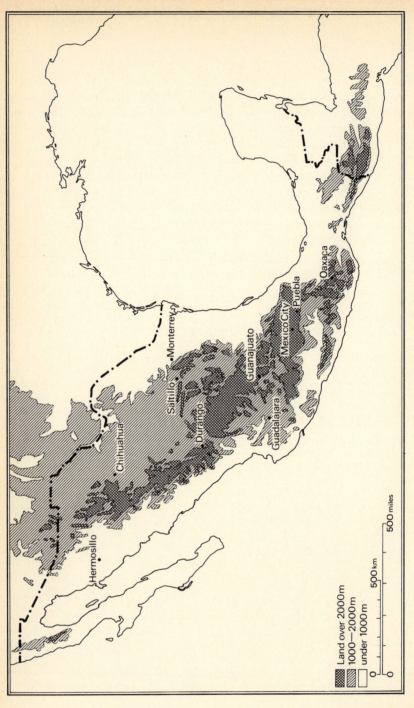

Map 1 Mexico: relief

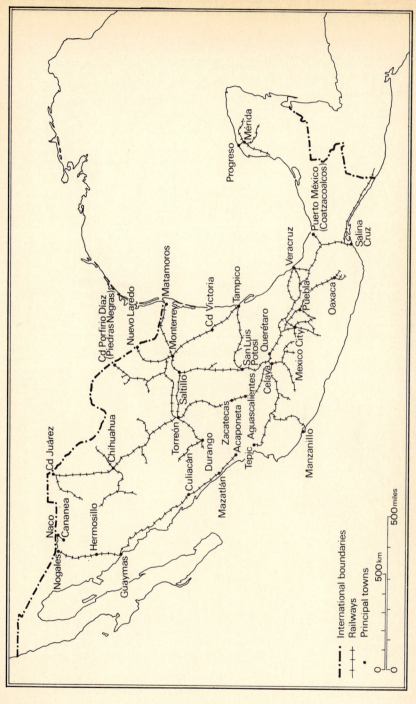

Map 2 Mexico: towns and railways (1910)

International boundaries
Railways
Principal towns

500 km
500 miles

Nogales
Naco
Cananea
Cd Juárez
Hermosillo
Chihuahua
Guaymas
Cd Porfirio Díaz
(Piedras Negras)
Nuevo Laredo
Matamoros
Monterrey
Cd Victoria
Torreón
Saltillo
Culiacán
Durango
Zacatecas
Acaponeta
Tepic
Aguascalientes
Mazatlán
San Luis
Potosí
Celaya
Querétaro
Tampico
Veracruz
Mexico City
Puebla
Manzanillo
Oaxaca
Progreso
Mérida
Puerto México
(Coatzacoalcos)
Salina
Cruz

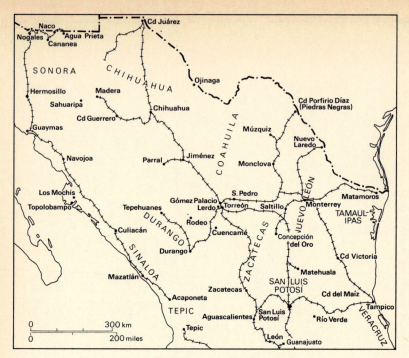

Map 3 Northern Mexico: towns and railways

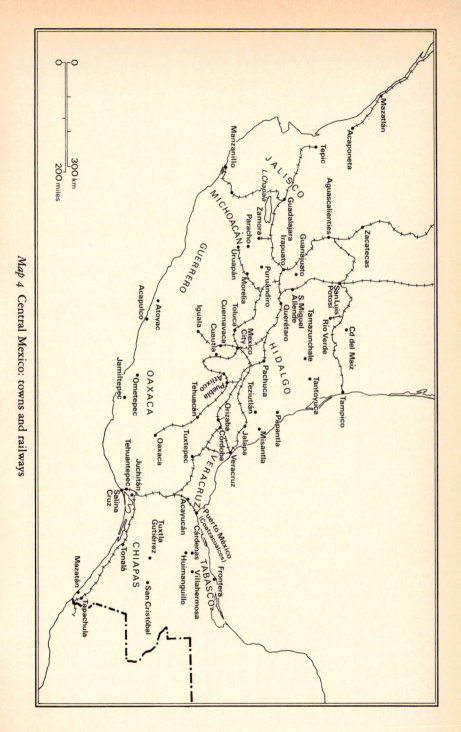

Map 4 Central Mexico: towns and railways

Huerta's
and forei
peace by
president
had gone
flattered
president
evinced t
and statu
that Hue
typical Se
for Hue rt
elicited th
the light
abundant.
business
administr
well-to-dc
accorded
relieved t
Cowdray's
country, t

The sar
standing
administr
Tampico,
with rejoi
general ob
rejoicing,

later recalled, the cathedral cantor 'danced the *jarabe* when Madero was assassinated'; in Oaxaca, 'a solemn religious function' was held at the Church of La Soledad 'to give thanks to the august patroness for having conceded the salvation of the Republic'.[7] Individuals like the Sinaloan merchant Antonio Caballero cabled their congratulations to Huerta for ridding the country of Madero (Caballero, unwisely keeping a copy in his personal archive, was later found out and executed for this act).[8] The Spanish businessmen of Acatlán (Pue.) were more prolix. Declaring that they were 'entirely separate from anything which relates in the least way to politics', they lamented the sad decline of the country since 'the change of government in the year 1911, which carried the country into an era of revolts and upheavals, and dragged it down the slope of a bottomless abyss', ruining business, destroying the fruits of thirty years' peace, threatening outright 'anarchy'. Then, providentially, came the *Decena Trágica*, which 'brought to the control of the country's destinies a Pleiad [sic] of persons who, by virtue of their background and deserved prestige, made us conceive hope of an imminent peace'.[9]

The relief of the 'better elements' (who, it should be noted, included Spaniards and clerics) was matched by serious misgivings on the part of the lower classes. As a radical later commented – with hindsight, but also with justice – 'to the simple man, the death of President Madero, that bloody blow to popular sovereignty, represented simply a return to military dictatorship, to the rule of hated *jefes políticos* and venal magistrates'.[10] However ill-informed about events in the capital, the common people soon came to appreciate the significance of the coup in local, concrete terms; lacking any capacity for prompt, organised resistance, they perforce accepted the new regime with sullen resentment; and they grieved for the death of a president who, for all his faults, was now seen 'as the one truly honest friend of the lower classes'.[11] Whether misguided or not, this popular reaction contrasted with the ostentatious celebrations of the well-to-do: the disgruntled *pelados* of *The Bosses* had their real-life counterparts in every state and city.[12] In the capital, the delight of the 'upper classes' was matched by 'a strong feeling in the lower classes of the population in favour of Madero', though it was not thought that this would be translated into action.[13] In Durango, 'the killing of Madero was celebrated with glee by the so-called better classes, but [there was] a dull resentment among the working class'; in Tampico, too, which had never been strongly Maderista, but where the workers had benefited from the new freedom to strike and organise, 'businessmen appear to want peace at any price but the masses will be slow to forgive the death of Madero who has become, in their eyes, a martyr to their cause'.[14] The traditional view – that the Huerta regime represented a return to Porfirian men and measures – though now questioned by historians, was certainly the view taken by contemporaries at both ends of the social scale.[15]

A major effect of the coup, therefore, was to accentuate class and political divisions: for, while Madero's *política de conciliación* had sought, with at least modest success, to bridge such divisions, his downfall and death re-emphasised their importance; and there were not wanting groups – like the Potosino 'upper class' – whose 'tendency to regard the late *coup d'état* as a class victory' greatly aggravated plebeian resentment.[16] It is therefore wrong to suggest that Huerta enjoyed broad, uniform support in 1913; on the contrary, his coup polarised opinion and radicalised politics – not so much by stimulating new, radical policies, but rather by exacerbating social conflicts, and ensuring that they would now be waged with unprecedented ferocity.[17] Even if the 'lower classes, the chief adherents of the fallen government' remained momentarily quiet, as they did at Córdoba and elsewhere, there was no guarantee – save the Federal Army – that they would continue to be quiet. The American consul at Mazatlán believed the prevailing calm to be illusory:[18]

after investigating it is found that great indignation exists and the situation is accepted as it is only because the mass of the people find themselves powerless and without means of resistance . . . If [however] a military dictatorship results . . . they will uprise [sic] and attempt another change of rulers.

This (Skocpol would do well to note) was broadly true. Irrespective of the regime's muscle, its palpable illegitimacy would soon generate serious resistance. And it was not the case that every potential opponent was powerless and overawed. There existed important concentrations of politico-military power apart from the Federal Army: anti-Madero rebels like Zapata in the north, Orozco's scattered forces in the north; Maderista *rurales* and irregulars; and dozens of lesser *cabecillas*, bandits and armed caciques. A lot depended on how Huerta handled these disparate groups; on how he utilised the brief political honeymoon the new regime might expect before more diffuse resentments crystallised into organised opposition. Not surprisingly, the great bulk of the Federal Army readily accepted Huerta; so, too, did the Mexico City bureaucracy ('a group not remembered for its zealous dedication to office', Meyer remarks; quite the contrary I would have thought).[19] There was the usual outburst of *empleomanía* following the establishment of a new administration: Félix Díaz (thought by many to be the man of the future) was 'overwhelmed' by supplicants.[20] But if, by mid-February, Huerta's regime was well established in Mexico City and the garrison towns of the Republic, the provinces remained political *terra incognita*. Here, the attitudes of three particular groups were crucial: the rebels in the field; the Maderista office-holders, who had come to power in 1911–12; and the Maderista *rurales* and irregulars, whose identity had always remained separate from that of the army.

The first act of the new Minister of Gobernación, Alberto García Granados, was to publicise an amnesty law which offered complete immunity for rebels who laid down their arms within fifteen days.[21] In response, Jesús ('Tuerto') Morales, the 'third or fourth ranking rebel general' among the Zapatistas, was amnestied along with several lesser leaders; in Oaxaca, Barrios and Oseguera, the captains of the Cuicatlán revolt, accepted terms, as did the *serrano* chief, Pedro León.[22] In Guerrero, Silvestre Mariscal went over to the new regime with 2,000 men; Juan Almazán surrendered; and the rebel Radilla converted his tacit liaison with the Federal General Reynaldo Díaz into an official alliance.[23] In the north the amnesty was even more successful. In Chihuahua, Orozco, Campa, Salazar, and Rojas entered into negotiations with the regime, holding out for a lump sum or a 'lucrative position under [the] new government'; while in the Laguna, terms were agreed with several leaders (Campos, Pedro Ortiz, Argumedo) who had harassed the region in 1911–12; indeed, in the case of Argumedo, 'a large sum of money was sent . . . to pay Argumedo's troops while they were actually committing depredations in the field'.[24] In San Luis, too, there were hopes that the Cedillos and their 800 men would reach a deal with the new regime.[25] By the early summer, therefore, the Huertista forces in the north had received a large transfusion of ex-rebel (largely ex-Orozquista) blood: at Zacatecas, for example, the bulk of the government forces (in May 1913) were 'ex-bandits or rebels who have lately surrendered'; while further north, in Durango and the Laguna, leaders like Campos, Escajeda, Emilio Campa and others, 'who a few months ago were looting, destroying and committing their outrages . . . are now at the head of their respective guerrillas and fighting for law and order'.[26] From the Mexico City and diplomatic viewpoint this was all very confusing. The British Minister noted the recruitment of Campos, Argumedo and others in some puzzlement: 'I had come to regard these bands as composed of pure brigands but it appears I was in error.'[27]

This confusion was understandable. The *condottieri* in question were veterans of 1910–11; they had rebelled against Madero under Orozco's banner; defeated but never annihilated by Huerta in 1912, they had since raided and robbed until, with the 1913 coup, they had an opportunity to revert to *gobiernista* status. Were they merely cynical time-servers? Did they throw in their lot with Huerta because he – as Michael Meyer has argued – offered genuine reformist policies? The answer, on both counts, must be 'no'. In explaining their conduct, four points should be borne in mind. First, the response to the amnesty should not be exaggerated. On paper, it looked impressive; but there had been amnesties before: some states, like Sinaloa, had seen several. Often, rebels used an amnesty to gain a respite, to restock with ammunition, perhaps to tend the fields during summer. Hence there were cases like that of the Zapatista Otilio Montaño who, having once been amnestied, repented and rebelled again; or Angel Barrios, amnestied in Oaxaca, who soon returned to the fray.[28] If well-known *jefes* could switch sides, it is all the more likely that anonymity gave the rank-and-file even greater freedom of movement. Though the evidence is skimpy, it seems probable that many amnestied rebels, veterans of 1910–13, drifted away from the Huerta camp in the course of

1913–14, reuniting themselves, in a sense, with the revolutionary mainstream. John Reed, in 1914, encountered one fourteen-year old who had been through all these gyrations.[29]

A second important consideration is the 'logic of the Revolution', already referred to.[30] The Orozquistas' rebellion against Madero had arguably obeyed revolutionary motives, quite consistent with those of 1910. When, in 1913, Madero was replaced by an appreciably more conservative regime, the Orozquistas – according to strict, 'ideological' criteria – should have fought on all the harder. But, no doubt, they were weary, they recalled that Huerta's campaign against them in 1912 had been slothful, even considerate, and they nursed a greater grudge against those Maderista irregulars and state forces (such as Obregón's) which had hunted them down more assiduously. Such feelings were also reciprocated. The personal, the immediate, the contingent thus overrode the dictates of ideology. Orozco, Campos, Argumedo and others opted to join Huerta *faute de mieux*: the logic of the Revolution required it.

But, thirdly, we must recognise the weakness of 'ideology' (itself usually a historian's invention; or, worse, a sociologist's) as an explanatory factor in the Revolution. Ideology was weak not so much because revolutionaries – including popular revolutionaries – lacked ideas which informed their conduct (I have argued against this assumption elsewhere), but rather because the basic objectives of many revolutionaries, being local and concrete, permitted the co-existence of apparently hostile ideologies, at least for the short term. To put it differently: ideologies which found practical expression in particularist terms, and which did not therefore claim universal application, were capable of a certain mutual toleration. And this was especially true when political authority was fragmented, and the state had perforce to accommodate ideological contradictions which in more normal times appear intolerable. In 1913, the 'centre' had to live with rival ideologies: liberal/populist, *agrarista*, *serrano*. In practical terms this meant that Huerta, keen for support, was prepared to offer tempting terms to rebels in the field: back pay, pensions, their enlistment as *rurales*, even a measure of agrarian reform: terms which Womack qualifies as 'remarkably generous'.[31] In Oaxaca, for example, Barrios, Oseguera and others were promised the recognition of their military ranks, government support for rural education, aid for villages devastated by the fighting, suppression of the *jefaturas*, and the employment of ex-rebels as local militias.[32] The sincerity of Huerta's offer is hard to evaluate: *pace* Meyer, it does not square with the general character of his regime. But, like the rebels themselves, he was resorting to expedients; maybe he intended to wriggle out of these commitments; and, above all, he could tolerate pockets of popular reformism, at least for the time being. Concessions of this kind are indifferent proof of Huerta's reformist intentions; but they indicate that even conservative regimes had to bend, and that popular rebels could – without reneging on their principles – take advantage of this reluctant flexibility. They could do so in particular, if, like Barrios and Oseguera (and unlike Zapata), they sought local benefits, rather than the acceptance of a universal, radical plan for the entire country (such as the Plan of Ayala). The deals struck between Huerta and revolutionary veterans in 1913 were not, therefore, final proof of the latters' unprincipled opportunism; rather, they showed how the sheer size and fragmentation of the country, combined with its current political instability, could persuade apparent incompatibles to conclude viable – if short-term and loveless – marriages; since, in most cases, the partners lived apart anyway.

A final point should help clarify the situation. While taking into account the factors just mentioned, it is worth noting that the amnesty achieved more success in the north than the centre or south. In the Morelos region a clutch of *cabecillas* surrendered: José Trinidad Ruiz, Simón Beltrán, Joaquín Miranda and his sons, and, the most important, 'Tuerto' Morales, the 'paunchy, blustery saloon-keeper from Ayutla'.[33] But Zapata and de la O would have none of it: they remembered the parts played by Huerta – and his new Minister of Gobernación, García Granados – in the repression of 1911–12; thus when Huerta's peace commissioners (including Pascual Orozco Sr) arrived at Zapata's headquarters they were arrested and subjected to a 'show trial', to indicate the *surianos'* total rejection of compromise.[34] Huerta, too, who knew Zapata as Zapata knew him, had little faith in these peace overtures. As he told the American Ambassador at the end of March: 'he was not at all optimistic about arrangements with Zapata and he frankly confessed that such men as he ought to be summarily dealt with; the best means to handle them with, he said, is an eighteen cents rope wherefrom to hang them'.[35] Quite what Huerta meant by 'such men as Zapata' cannot be known, but can be guessed; and Huerta's presumption of Zapata's intransigence was entirely correct. From 1911 to 1919, Zapata – and most of his lieutenants – would not be deflected from the path of autonomous agrarian revolution; though they made alliances (in later years, incongruous alliances, which defied ideological consistency) they never surrendered control of the Morelos rebellion, never entered government service, never became hired mercenaries. This fidelity to the Revolution (as conceived in Zapatista terms) grew out of a powerful allegiance to the village and its traditions: 'Zapata and most of his chiefs . . . had not lost their sense of who they were – the sons of the pueblo'.[36] The Zapatistas' strong, local, corporate, commitment deterred them from national alliances or official recruitment; like peasant movements elsewhere, they displayed a keen sensitivity to rights and obligations which made them appear – to those who would negotiate with them – foreign to compromise.[37]

There were northerners, too, like Contreras or the Cedillos, who revealed comparable characteristics; just as there were southerners, like the Figueroas, who lacked an *agrarista* base, and who shared the *serranos'* footloose flexibility and opportunism. It is perhaps significant that the two principal Zapatista defectors of 1913 were a saloon-keeper (Morales) and a Protestant preacher

(Ruiz): men of their stamp abounded in the north, unfettered by corporate ties, and their greater social and spatial mobility disposed them more to compromise and, perhaps, co-option. Orozco had teamed up with the 'Científicos' of Chihuahua in 1912; now, in 1913, he and his remaining colleagues joined hands with the victorious 'Científicos' of Mexico City.[38]

If, on paper, this accretion of strength bolstered the new regime, delighting the American Ambassador and justifying Huerta's amnesty policy, its practical results were less impressive. Now, the real character of these ex-rebels, and the nature of their surrender to Huerta, became apparent. Most of the amnestied irregulars were – like those of northern Zacatecas – as regards both 'troops and officers practically nothing more than peons'.[39] The rank-and-file were wild, disorderly and refractory to discipline; being typical ex-rebels, they showed a strong commitment to their own locality, and they persisted in waging local vendettas while in government service.[40] Regions which fell under irregular control often suffered more than those affected by rebellion: around Durango, Cheche Campos' forces 'move from point to point or remain idle at will . . . in many cases they have taken horses, cattle, etc., and have even had the audacity to re-sell them to their original owners'. The state governor and Federal military commander 'frankly admit that they have no control over these forces'.[41] When Campos' men finally quit Durango at the end of May 1913 their departure was 'accompanied by a great sigh of relief from the inhabitants': even if they were lapsed revolutionaries, they had not become servile gendarmes. In Zacatecas, too, the irregulars excited the distrust of the Federal commander; around Acapulco, Mariscal's and Radilla's forces, who controlled the region under a nominal adherence to the government, were seen as major threats to peace; and, even where irregulars, like Orozco himself, proved to be military assets, the inevitable friction between them and the regular army hampered operations.[42] In June, therefore, the government abandoned its policy of recruiting ex-rebel soldiers, save those with excellent credentials (who were few or none).[43]

In some troubled rural districts, the conversion of bandits (so-called) into policemen served only to legalise robbery. At San Dieguito, the American settlers exchanged unofficial harassment by rebel/bandits for semi-official harassment by *rurales* (which their persecutors had now become); and the local *jefe* was too scared to take action.[44] In the lowlands of Veracruz, the 'bad characters' recruited by the Huertista General Gaudencio de la Llave busied themselves tapping the rubber trees of the local plantations on a freelance basis; in the same state, eight *rurales* who bore a grudge against an American planter broke up the *zafra* celebrations, seized the *mayordomo* (a Spaniard), and forced him to walk barefoot to gaol at Playa Vicente. Only bribery, the planter complained, could induce these new policemen to behave as policemen should.[45] And such examples do more than simply illustrate the practical failure of Huerta's recruitment of ex-rebels and ex-bandits. They also suggest the continued social ferment which the country was experiencing. Converting bandits into *rurales*, rebels into official auxiliaries of the Federal Army, smacked of political alchemy: for the base metal of popular, plebeian hordes could not be transmuted into the pure gold of a disciplined police force. Those who had first risen against authority could not readily become its champions. Yet, in the long term, some conversion of this kind had to be achieved, if peace was to be restored. Sheer exhaustion and war-weariness would later help such a conversion. But, more important, a peace-making, peace-keeping regime would have to acquire some legitimacy in the eyes of the popular movement. It was not enough to purchase a fragile, mercenary loyalty, which of necessity would embrace only a fraction of the population. Many rebels – like Zapata – could not be bought; and, in the context of 1911–14, for every rebel who could be bought by the government (whether Madero's or Huerta's), there would be others to take his place and continue the struggle, so long as that government lacked a fundamental legitimacy. A viable regime would therefore have to combine military muscle with at least a measure of consent. Madero, in fact, came closer to the required formula than Huerta was to come: for Madero at least supplemented repression with certain constructive – albeit inadequate – policies; Huerta and his cronies mistakenly attributed Madero's failure to the inadequacy of the former rather than of the latter. So, like some obsessive callisthenic of the political world, Huerta continued the muscular build-up, neglecting political solutions to an even greater extent than his predecessor. Yet political, as well as military, solutions were essential for the restoration of peace: ultimately, even Zapatismo was co-opted as much as it was defeated. By placing its entire faith in militarisation, and by reversing even the tentative, reformist measures taken by Madero, the Huerta government most clearly revealed its 'counter-revolutionary' character, and most surely doomed itself to failure.

This priority was exemplified in Huerta's readiness to recruit ex-rebels (and worse) and his ruthless proscription of Maderista *políticos*. For, if the amnesty suggested a disposal to conciliate, the rest of government policy pointed in a different direction. Since, in Huerta's view, force was the crucial factor and politics an unnecessary indulgence, he believed in getting the gun-slingers on his side, rather than the effete civilians. 'Nada de política, la paz ante todo' was the apt slogan of the regime; and Huerta thought repression could secure peace more efficiently and promptly than politicking which – witness Madero's interference in Morelos in 1911–12 – only obstructed military operations.[46] Politicians were a liability; sturdy peon troops a necessity. And, having fought the northern rebels, Huerta was aware of their military accomplishments and eager to win them over, irrespective of the motives, attitudes and behaviour which characterised them. As for the politicians, they had to be shunted aside. Back in April 1911, Huerta had advised Limantour to quit parleying with the rebels at Cd Juárez and instead to hurl 2,000 cavalry at them; in August of the same year his advice to de la Barra, concerning Morelos, was similarly red-blooded.[47] Such attitudes (entirely consistent with the traditional image of Huerta) were evident throughout 1913–14, in aspects which will shortly be considered: the militarisation of government and society, the expansion of the army, the resort to assassination. And, even in these early weeks, when perhaps he was more disposed to compromise, it was the iron hand which Huerta favoured. In his first address to Congress on 1 April the presidential speech (read by an aide, because of Huerta's poor eye-sight) concluded with a passionate, personal pledge to 're-establish peace, cost what it may'.[48] Similarly, Huerta's declaration to Ambassador Wilson that the solution to Zapatismo was an eighteen-cent rope was more an article of faith than a chance aside. At the Embassy party which preceded Madero's killing, the new president had fallen into conversation with the Chilean and British Chargés in a manner which the latter recalled:[49]

we three went to the sideboard and helped ourselves. I drank to the success of his future government, while my Chilean friend stuttered something to the same effect. Huerta on his side stuttered, 'D-d-d-diez [y] O-o-o-ocho c-c-centavos una c-c-c-cuerda'. Between these two inarticulate individuals I was a good deal perplexed until I found out that all Huerta wanted was eighteen centavos to buy a rope to hang Zapata.

Peace, 'cost what it may', was in a sense the motto of the regime; and the eighteen-centavo noose its device.

Conversely, politics were to be avoided and adherence to the law could be waived 'where the public good is concerned', as Huerta's henchman Aureliano Urrutia put it.[50] This was initially evident in the government's treatment of Maderista office-holders, notably the state governors. When news of the *cuartelazo* reached the provinces, governors – and some lesser officials – were quick to cable their loyalty to the (Madero) regime, some of them offering reinforcements, some (like Cepeda of San Luis) their support 'hasta la muerte'. But they took no action; in Veracruz, Governor Pérez Rivera refused to issue arms to the Maderistas who clamoured for them.[51] And, once Huerta had taken power and demanded their allegiance, they readily submitted: some, like Barrientos of Puebla, with positive enthusiasm, others, like Cepeda, with face-saving formulae ('I will sacrifice all my patriotism for the reestablishment of peace and order').[52] Apart from three states which stood aside in the rush to embrace Huerta, most Maderistas accepted the new regime; and the men whom Madero had brought to power (for in most cases they had not fought for it themselves) readily acquiesced in his downfall. The Maderistas of Tabasco soon 'abandoned all hope', and the poetic young governor, who had vowed that he would not quit his post – save by due democratic process – before he had 'hurled the cream of the Tabascan political underworld head-first into the foaming Grijalva', now tamely submitted, promising to co-operate in the pacification of the country.[53] In Campeche, Governor Castillo Brito accepted

Huerta with self-styled 'eagerness'; Governor Leyva of Morelos rallied to Huerta and the state legislature voted its adherence; in Michoacan, Governor Silva recognised the regime and requested troops to put down rebellious Maderistas; Riveros of Sinaloa likewise disregarded Rafael Buelna's incitements to resist and cracked down on Maderistas who disagreed; even the hawkish Cepeda was said to have tried to bully or suborn dissident Maderistas into submission.[54]

Why this mass Maderista apostasy? Clearly, there were mitigating circumstances. Dr Silva, accustomed to saving lives, was reluctant to jeopardise them by resisting, it was said.[55] The Leyvistas of Morelos consoled themselves with the thought that Huerta was just a stopgap, and that civilian government was just around the corner.[56] Nevertheless, the absence not only of resistance, but also of resignations, demands further explanation. In the first place, Maderista governors were probably scared and certainly weak. The murders in Mexico City were soon followed by murders in the provinces: Governor González of Chihuahua, who was of sterner stuff than most of his colleagues (he had fought in 1911 and defied Orozco in 1912), declined to answer Huerta's demand for recognition; the local military commander loaded him onto a train for Mexico City and, *en route*, he was subjected to the *ley fuga*.[57] Lesser officials were also persecuted and the lesson was not lost on their superiors; it was generally supposed, after the deaths of Madero and Pino Suárez, 'that those of the late cabinet ministers and adherents of the Madero party who fail to come over to the new government stand a good chance of sharing the same fate'.[58] Most of the Maderista *políticos*, being well-intentioned, middle-aged, frock-coated liberals had not fought in 1910–11, and they had neither the desire nor the capacity to fight in 1913, when the odds were stacked against them. They could legitimately plead that the demobilisation of the Liberating Army and the build-up of the Federals made the latter the arbiters of the situation: the countervailing forces of Maderista volunteers and irregulars were confined to certain key states (of which more anon). Hence most state governors made their decision to recognise Huerta with a watchful garrison commander at their elbow: Silva, in Michoacán, was supposedly pressured by General Dorantes; and General Rábago's treatment of Governor González, in Chihuahua, illustrated the price of intransigence.

But some officials positively welcomed the new regime, or accepted it with a good grace. Individuals like Governor Bolaños Cacho of Oaxaca were Felicistas anyway; groups like the Cristobalense faction in Chiapas were glad to see Madero go; but there were also erstwhile Maderistas whose rightward drift had eventually brought them into harbour with Huerta.[59] This was a logical progression: for many of the respectable civilians of 1909–10 the subsequent fighting, social upheaval and dislocation of business hardly corresponded to their pipe-dreams of political reform; accordingly, they applauded and participated in Madero's more repressive policies and now welcomed the advent of Huerta. It was not difficult for a liberal Maderista sympathiser (of 1910) like Toribio Esquivel Obregón to denounce Indian barbarism, to treasure Mexico's European/Hispanic inheritance (embodying the values of family, property, religion and justice), and to conclude that 'republican institutions, if implemented by non-European populations, are destructive ... republican institutions and universal suffrage were the formula for Mexico's dissolution'.[60] Entertaining such beliefs, Esquivel Obregón was able to accept a cabinet post under Huerta, as was Jesús Flores Magón, Madero's one-time Minister of the Interior, and brother of the radical exiles. In assuming cabinet rank, they could hardly plead *force majeure*. Rather, they saw Huerta as a guarantor of order, who could hold the ring until elections restored the fabric of constitutional government.[61] Similarly, García Granados, an old opponent of Díaz and a minister in 1911, returned to his old post under Huerta.

Congress, too, with its Maderista majority, continued to sit, tacitly recognising the new regime. A few deputies – including Serapio Rendón – fled at the outset, but most followed Luis Cabrera's advice to remain in office, accepting the Huerta government *pro tem.*, and arguing (sometimes with the benefit of hindsight) that they could better serve the cause by legal, political opposition than by a difficult, dangerous escape. And, locally as well as nationally, names once associated with the old liberal opposition of 1909–10 could now be found lurking in the Huertista camp: Patricio Leyva, the Morelos gubernatorial candidate of 1909, and José Ferrel, his Sinaloan counterpart, who had promised to 'exalt the outraged rights of the poor and cast down the ill-fated tyrannies of the rich', and who now (1913) accepted an official commission to study, at first hand, the universities of Europe.[62] Nor is there any evidence that the judiciaries of the various states acted any differently from that of Zacatecas, which resolved to continue in office after the coup.[63]

THE OFFICIAL RESISTANCE

Within this prevailing picture of acquiescence only three states stood out against the trend: the three great frontier provinces of Sonora, Chihuahua and Coahuila. In Chihuahua, the murder of Governor González and the swift dismissal of lesser Maderistas robbed the state of organised leadership: its rejection of Huerta was therefore decentralised and popular, as will be seen shortly. Sonora and Coahuila, however, rejected Huerta 'from the top', the Maderista political elite taking the lead. As pioneers in the struggle against Huerta, the Coahuilans (notably Governor Carranza), and Sonorans placed their imprint on what was to become the Constitutionalist revolution, the year-and-a-half campaign to rid Mexico of Huerta, and the second great phase of revolutionary mobilisation. Allies and recruits soon joined them, but the Coahuilan/Sonoran hegemony went unchallenged, save by the upstart Pancho

Villa and his Chihuahuan hosts. Between them, Coahuila and Sonora supplied
four successive presidents, who ruled for fourteen years, during which time the
post-revolutionary regime was constructed. This northern pre-eminence can
be traced directly to the events of spring 1913; for, prior to that date, these two
states had played no such disproportionate role in the Revolution. Both, it is
true, were progressive, industrious regions, boasting high levels of literacy
and foreign investment, and a large middle class. Both were in the vanguard of
the 'new', mestizo, commercialised, dollar-hungry Mexico, as distinct from
the 'old', Indian, colonial and Catholic Mexico of the central plateau.
Coahuila, Madero's home state, had been prominent in the political phase of
Maderismo (1909–10); Sonora, if less specifically Maderista, had produced
vigorous movements of political opposition. But once the fighting started in
1910, these two lagged behind – certainly behind Chihuahua, which lay
athwart them. Only the south-western tip of Coahuila was virulently rebellious (and this, in terms of 'revolutionary geography', belonged with Durango
and the Laguna); in Sonora (apart from the Yaquis and a handful of troublesome Magonistas) the opposition was able to conquer power without extensive
fighting or social upheaval.

In fact, these hitherto socially passive entities took the lead against Huerta
partly because their very passivity enabled them to make a stand where more
war-torn, polarised states were paralysed. Administrations facing agrarian
revolt or banditry (like those of Morelos or Guerrero) were unlikely to bring
more trouble upon themselves by defying Huerta; rather, they could look to
Huerta for reassurance and military assistance. Socially stable, politically
homogeneous states like Sonora or Coahuila could afford the luxury of
resistance. Particularly in Sonora, elections had brought about a real renovation of the political elite, conferring power on Maderista cadres which – if
sometimes divided amongst themselves – at least stood in united opposition to
the old regime (the Torresista oligarchy), and furthermore counted on a good
deal of popular support. Two important results flowed from this. First, the
state administration (in Sonora more so than in Coahuila) was relatively
unencumbered by Porfirian caciques and left-overs, who might constitute a
Huertista fifth column, pressing for acceptance of the new regime.[64] Secondly,
though neither Sonora nor Coahuila had fought hard for the Maderista
revolution, they had both benefited from it, and were concerned to defend
these benefits. The newly ensconced cadres would resist any attempt to put
back the political clock: the Sonoran leaders were seen to be 'striving to get and
keep the state of Sonora in the hands of the men who gained control of the state
during the Madero revolution'; hence,[65]

'the object of the present Constitutionalist movement in Sonora is said to be merely to
retain for the people the right to choose their own state officials and conduct their own
affairs of government without military interference from the administration in Mexico
City'.

The experience of free (or semi-free) elections, the winning of a measure of freedom from the impositions of the 'centre', and the replacement of the Porfirian oligarchs by new men, were gains too valuable and too recent to be let slip without a fight. Thus the resistance of Sonora and Coahuila was basically defensive: it did not represent a radicalisation, a move towards social or economic reform, in advance of the old Maderismo; indeed, the absence of social conflicts and concerns was one factor making resistance possible. As Alvaro Obregón is said to have remarked: 'we have no *agraristas* here (in Sonora), thank God. We are all doing what we're doing out of patriotism and to avenge the death of Sr Madero.'[66] The Constitutionalist revolution was thus the offspring of an ensconced Maderismo, fighting for survival. But if, in terms of origins and ideals, its protagonists were Maderistas, the fight they undertook – fiercer and more sustained than the 1910 revolution – drove them to more radical measures, compelling them – in their quest for recruits, allies, and total victory – to go far beyond what Madero had done, and to implement and extend many of the ideas of the Maderista 'hawks'. Constitutionalism was, in this sense, an updated Maderismo, run by second-generation Maderistas; it was, in Córdova's telling phrase, 'la autocrítica del maderismo'.[67]

Though these factors made Sonora and Coahuila particularly antipathetic to Huertismo, all would have been in vain had they been unable to translate this antipathy into action. Here, they enjoyed a clear advantage over other states by virtue of their geographical remoteness (though, as the case of Yucatán – even more remote and also socially stable – demonstrates, this was maybe a necessary, but certainly not a sufficient condition for rebellion). Sonora was particularly favoured, in that it lacked a direct rail link with Mexico City, since the west coast line remained broken between Tepic and San Marcos (Jal.): a short enough gap, and one scheduled for elimination, but enough to hamper Federal deployment in the north-west, which was consequently dependent on maritime transport.[68] In addition, both states bordered the US. Remoteness thus gave them a breathing space before Federal troops could be shipped in, and proximity to the border facilitated arms smuggling. But, most important of all, both states had a non-Federal military force in being at the time of the Huerta coup, which enabled their leaders to defy the new government while others remained helpless and quiescent.

In Sonora, the state forces recruited to resist the Orozquistas numbered between 2,000 and 3,000, based in or near Hermosillo, Agua Prieta, Cananea, and the Yaqui Valley; they confronted Federal forces – who at once declared for Huerta – of about equal size.[69] Also important was the shared experience of action against Orozquistas, Yaquis and other subversives, which had created a certain mutual reliance and camaraderie among the officers and officials of the state administration: interim Governor Pesqueira, Alvaro Obregón, Plutarco Elías Calles, Benjamín Hill, Salvador Alvarado, and others. The existence of both an army and a politico-administrative superstructure enabled the Sonorans to resist Huerta in an organised, 'official', manner: their rebellion took the form, not of a spontaneous popular insurrection, but rather of a conflict 'between two distinct nations with parallel resources' – Sonora and the Federation.[70] In Coahuila, the state troops had already figured in the politics of the Revolution as a bone of contention between Carranza and Madero; and, though Carranza had been less successful than Maytorena in maintaining his private army, he was able to pull together his scattered irregular corps within days of the outbreak of hostilities in the capital – well before the overthrow of Madero. Pablo González, stationed under the watchful eye of General Rábago in Chihuahua, gathered his men (11 February) and marched east, arriving at Monclova towards the end of the month.[71] Jesús Carranza slipped away from the Federal forces commanded by General Aubert in the Laguna and, by means of stratagems, also made his way to Coahuila, to join his brother.[72] In Coahuila itself, Carranza could count on a nucleus of irregular officers and men: Cesareo Castro, Jacinto Treviño, Andrés Saucedo; and another, Miguel Acosta, was sent to San Luis to liaise with Carranza's crony, Governor Cepeda (a mission which proved abortive).[73] As regards numbers (less than 1,000) and cohesion, the Coahuilan forces were inferior to the Sonoran; but they were something, and they gave Carranza some scope for manoeuvre.[74]

But all these factors – the entrenched Maderista administrations, the remoteness, the military resources – would not have guaranteed rebellion had not Huerta's policy proved so wantonly provocative. Eulogists of Carranza and the Sonorans depict their revolts as the immediate, categorical responses of outraged patriots, rising up to defend the Constitution against a bloody usurper.[75] But others have pointed out (in my view correctly) that their defiance responded to more complex, grey motives. Indeed, granted Carranza's previous career, it is hardly likely that he would have embarked on a chancy rebellion out of spontaneous, moralistic indignation.[76] Rather, as a simple narrative of the events suggests, it required Huerta's intransigence to drive Carranza – and the Sonorans – into open revolt.

When Carranza received word of Huerta's succession to the presidency, he convened and addressed the Coahuilan state congress, arguing that Huerta could not legally assume the executive at the behest of the Senate (as Huerta's message seemed to imply), that Huerta had therefore – out of 'error or disloyalty' – usurped the presidential office and that he could not be recognised as president.[77] A circular was sent to other state governors putting this case and criticising this 'regression to our shameful and primitive period of *cuartelazos*', but Carranza appears to have received no encouragement from his colleagues.[78] Then, three days later, Carranza despatched two agents to Mexico City for talks, telling the American consul (officially) that 'he will conform to the new administration in Mexico City', admitting that he had 'completely changed his attitude', and arguing that the succession had, after all, followed constitutional norms.[79] This important decision (important in terms both of Carranza's historical status and of current Huertista policy) was later denied by Carrancista apologists; but the evidence for it is wholly convincing.[80] Furthermore, it fits the historical context. Carranza was no revolutionary firebrand; he was a shrewd, experienced politician; he was aware of his isolation both within Coahuila and the Federation as a whole; his attempts to raise a loan to bolster the state's – and potentially the revolution's – finances were encountering difficulties.[81] Thus his preparedness to negotiate was hardly surprising, and evidence of this disposition continued to mount. By mid-day on 21 February, it seemed certain that Carranza would submit, and the cable sent to introduce the Coahuilan envoys in Mexico City addressed Huerta as 'President of the Republic'.[82] The American consul at Saltillo reported that Carranza would soon publish his adherence, pending a telegraph conversation with Huerta.[83] But, once under way (Carranza later explained) this conversation was cut off, at Huerta's behest; and news reached the governor of the approach of Federal troops. The Saltillo consul urged the American Ambassador to restrain Huerta from aggressive moves against Carranza since, he stressed, 'he [Carranza] reiterates to me his conformity with the new administration . . . If the President deposes him he will lose the strongest man in northern Mexico and a serious mistake will have been made.'[84] The consul clearly believed that a *transacción* was possible, and that Huerta's intransigence, rather than Carranza's indignation, ruled it out; and there is no reason why he should have perjured himself to his superiors in Washington and Mexico City, had this not been the case. Certainly, the consul wanted peace – he was not therefore an entirely neutral observer – but there was no way in which his misreporting the situation would have furthered the interests of peace.

On 23 February, however, the news of Madero's death broke, forcing Carranza's hand. That evening he proclaimed his defiance of Huerta publicly, from the balcony of the governor's palace. His attitude was that of a man who had done everything that could be reasonably expected:[85]

his word for the Embassy and for Washington was that his overtures to the government at Mexico [City] had been ignored; that he did not propose to remain in Saltillo and meet the fate of Madero; that he would not resign but that he would go out into the open and fight. That the government of Mexico was responsible.

Though hopes of a compromise were still aired, Carranza now prepared for war. After reconnoitering the locality he returned to Saltillo, mustered his troops (they numbered 1,000), expropriated the public funds and raised a forced loan of 75,000 pesos on Mexican businesses (foreigners were exempt). Then he headed north as 1,000 Federals under General Aubert came up from the Laguna and occupied Saltillo.[86]

It has been suggested that Carranza's prevarications were designed to buy time, while funds and troops were collected: his appeasement of Huerta was cynical, not sincere.[87] Ultimately, this interpretation cannot be refuted, since it can dismiss any number of protestations of loyalty or offers of compromise as deliberate stratagems. But such duplicity does not entirely square with Carranza's dull, unimaginative, opinionated style. He would not readily demean himself, even in the interests of *realpolitik*. On the other hand, indecision had characterised his behaviour at critical moments in the past, notably in the spring of 1911. And there was every reason to display indecision in February/March 1913. Current opinion certainly inclined to this view: in Saltillo, the consul's belief in the possibility of compromise was general; and, some months later, Carranza's friend, ex-Governor Miguel Cárdenas, told John Silliman (also a friend of Carranza) that, although 'a great deal has been said about these negotiations being simply a pretext on the part of Carranza to gain time, it is the opinion of Governor Cárdenas, with whom this consulate agrees, that Carranza was entirely sincere in this matter'.[88] And, Silliman, who stuck with Carranza through thick and thin, did not depart from this view over the years.[89] At the very least, it should be noted that Carranza's rebellion – whenever it was actually decided upon – was essentially defensive and conservative: hence the moderate tone of the Carrancista Plan of Guadalupe; hence, also, the offer of leadership made to the old Porfirista and pillar of the north-eastern establishment, General Gerónimo Treviño.[90]

Over in the north-west a similar story unfolded. During the *Decena Trágica* Governor Maytorena and the other Sonoran Maderistas proclaimed their support for Madero.[91] But, with Madero's fall, Maytorena began to waver (as, like Carranza, he had in 1910), displaying what his critics called 'shameful womanly vacillations'.[92] Vacillations were only to be expected: the Sonoran Federals had readily gone over to Huerta and were now mobilising; Sonoran business interests recommended recognition of the new regime; and friends like Rodolfo Reyes – Bernardo's son, now high in the counsels of the government – urged Maytorena to support Huerta for the sake of peace and patriotism.[93] On 25 February, Maytorena's delegate, who conferred with Carranza, said that the Sonoran administration would acknowledge Huerta; next day Maytorena declared that the state was a 'spectator', pending the establishment of a stable regime in Mexico City.[94] Finally, Maytorena passed the buck and applied for six months' leave of absence on medical grounds. As the governor slipped away to the US, his interim successor, Ignacio Pesqueira, was left to make the crucial decision in conjunction with the state legislature. Still, they stalled: perhaps to gain time, perhaps out of genuine uncertainty; Pesqueira faced the same commercial pressures in favour of recognition, and, like Maytorena, he feared the possible social consequences of rebellion.[95] Lower down, however, among Maderista officials and military leaders, the groundswell of opposition grew until, with the news of Madero's murder, it became a flood tide. According to Consul Hostetter, at Hermosillo (who, like his counterpart in Saltillo, was involved in proceedings), the death of Madero aborted a probable recognition.[96] This, plus the 'centre's' provocative refusal to negotiate, left the Sonoran leaders 'very suspicious', fearful of a Federal military take-over and of the loss of their new political freedom. They told Hostetter:[97]

if they were guaranteed non-interference in state matters and that the Federal Government would continue paying the state troops, they would be satisfied. They claim that the Federal Government, as soon as it had the state in its hands, would replace all the officials with its own men, irrespective of those legally elected.

Indeed, there was a specific fear that the 'centre' would impose its own nominee as governor, in Porfirian style: namely, Manuel Mascareñas, the would-be sponsor of the Orozquista invasion of 1912.[98] Sonora's rebellion against Huerta, which could count on strong, majority support in the state, was thus premised upon the defence of local sovereignty, of states' rights, and of the political gains of the Maderista period. Only in mid-March, as Federal troops began to converge on Sonora, did defiance become official; and only then did 'national' demands – for the resignation of Huerta – start to figure.[99] In response, the central government took advantage of the rebellion's provincial origins and objectives by alleging secessionist intentions on the part of the Sonorans: 'Sonora would play the part of a twentieth-century Texas'; Maytorena aimed to dismember Sonora and Baja California from the Mexican Republic.[100] Nonsense though this was, it was an easy smear to cast and one which pandered to central Mexico's resentment of the distant, Americanised north. Before long, the government even began to make similar, irrelevant allegations about rebels in the south – who supposedly sought union with Guatemala.[101]

Two important features of these northern revolts can be projected nationally: Huerta's brusque treatment of Maderista office-holders, and the belligerent reaction of the Maderista irregular forces. As regards the first, Huerta's tough attitude – or, rather, the tough attitude of Huerta and Huertista sympathisers in the provinces – provoked a rash of revolts and left a legacy of bitterness. Many Maderistas who, like Carranza, might have agreed terms with the new regime were purged, humiliated, threatened and often goaded into armed opposition. Though this nowhere occurred on the same scale as in Sonora (usually, the Huertistas were too strong, the Maderistas too isolated and unprepared), it had the effect of placing in outright opposition many of the moderate, educated, civilian reformers who had staffed the Madero regime. In the main they did not want to revolt (revolts were personally dangerous, politically hazardous and socially risky, as Maytorena appreciated); they would have preferred to combat Huerta (if at all) by peaceful means, as the Renovadores in Congress attempted.[102] But, once forced into action, they provided the revolution – the Constitutionalist revolution, as it may now be labelled – with articulate, experienced cadres, who were determined to prevent popular, anarchic upheaval, and to impose coherent, national objectives. The still strong tide of popular rebellion could thus be harnessed, as it had been in 1910–11, to respectable urban leadership and aims. As in 1910–11, too, relations between these allies (the leaders and the led, the city and the countryside, the *gente decente* and the *pelados*) were constantly tense; but Huerta, crassly, gratuitously, and unwittingly, did his best to ameliorate them. Conversely, had Huerta conciliated and compromised, he might have confined opposition to the genuinely popular, agrarian rebels, binding the socially conservative civilian Maderistas to his cause. One likely casualty of such a policy would have been Victoriano Huerta, the symbol of military usurpation; but, had 'peace, cost what it may' been the overriding objective, such a sacrifice would have been in order. Instead, ambition and political *naïveté* conspired together. Huerta's drastic, draconian policy guaranteed the galloping inflation of rebellion and, by forcing men of order and moderation to take up arms against him, he achieved what Madero had sought in vain: the re-assembly of the old Maderista coalition of 1910–11, the urban civilians and the rural populists; a coalition of awesome power.

While most state governors secured a brief respite by their prompt adhesions to the new regime, those regarded as most doubtful in their loyalty were soon swept away, along with their minions. The death of González heralded a purge of Maderistas throughout Chihuahua.[103] By early March, Fuentes of Aguascalientes and Cepeda of San Luis (both associates of Carranza) were ousted, along with Riveros of Sinaloa, an ally of Maytorena.[104] The fall of Riveros and his replacement by General Legorreta was the signal for a mass turnover in the state administration, as the *jefe político* of Mazatlán and other leading officials were shipped to Mexico City, along with the deposed Governor. So too, in San Luis, with the fall of Cepeda,[105] 'a complete change [has] been made in the Federal and State officers in this district. In almost every instance the former officials who served under President Porfirio Díaz have been restored to office. In some cases the retiring officials have been arrested and humiliated. There has been no disposition to compromise'. And with Porfirian officials came Porfirian policies: Cepeda's reforms – including the abolition of the *jefaturas* – were repealed; the counter-revolution was in full swing. San Luis also witnessed political murders, as did Tlaxcala, where arrests and executions followed the fall of the radical Governor Hidalgo, and the imposition of a military regime.[106]

Throughout the country, purges, arrests and persecutions proliferated, as adherents of the old (Porfirian) regime, acting either officially or on a freelance basis, wrought vengeance on their Maderista enemies: again, Azuela presents a vivid yet realistic picture.[107] At Monterrey, the Maderista mayor (who happened to be Carranza's brother-in-law) was taken into custody, followed by the chief of police.[108] With Saltillo retaken by the Federals, numerous arrests were made on suspicion (the city was said to be riddled with Carrancista sympathisers) and imprisonment dragged on without trial.[109] Here in the troubled north-east, the government even went so far as to order the arrest of General Gerónimo Treviño – veteran of the French Intervention, stout Porfirista, and, though related to the Madero family, far from a Maderista – who was bundled onto a train and taken to Mexico City for questioning: an action which, even though the general's detention was brief, was seen as excessive by all, including many conservatives.[110] Treviño had, it is true, been mooted as a leader of the Coahuilan rebellion; but there was nothing to suggest that he seriously considered such a role; and his arrest was attributed by some to political spite, for Treviño was an old rival of Reyes in the north-east, and Reyista influence was strong in the new government.[111] Nor was this at all implausible: this was a time when political scores were being settled wholesale; when many 'new officials seem[ed] to desire peace less than revenge'.[112]

Certainly, political persecution reached into remote corners and affected all levels of the hierarchy. It touched the Puebla sierra and even distant Baja California (where the survival of a few Maderistas could hardly have endangered the regime). Yet, here too, officials were packed into the La Paz gaol until, by August 1913, it was full to overflowing and the military governor began sending inmates to the front line at Guaymas.[113] Local rancours, rather than national *raison d'état*, determined many of these measures – in revolutionary Mexico, as in revolutionary France. At Tampico, scene of some virulent political conflicts in 1912, 'two well-dressed men' called at the mayor's house one night and advised him to resign 'or accept the consequences'. He resigned. In the same town, the political gossip was that 'the plan of the new government is to make a complete change in the state authorities, municipal authorities, and military commanders, so that the people generally will realise the "complete" change'.[114] The gossips were right: the mayor of Tampico went; the mayor of Cd Victoria, the state capital, was removed by troops ('officials now say that he was a disturbing element and was attempting to arouse the lower classes against the present government'); employees of the State Treasury, in the same city, were arrested for allegedly 'mutilating pictures of President Huerta, General Díaz, General Mondragón, and others'; to the south, at Xicotencatl, all the local officials were ousted and charged.[115] And besides these direct victims, there were many Maderistas who prudently took the path of exile: such as those who arrived in Havana soon after the coup, telling the press that 'they had escaped from the capital because of the persecution suffered by those loyal to Señor Madero'.[116]

At the local level, this counter-revolution reversed the changes wrought by the Madero revolution or (probably less likely) by municipal elections during the Madero administration. Sebastián Ortiz, for example, we have encountered as a failed revolutionary, who fled to the Oaxaca sierra late in

1910; with Madero's triumph he became *jefe político* at Tuxtepec (thereby replacing the tough old *enganchador*, Rodolfo Pardo). But after Huerta's coup, Tuxtepec accepted the new regime, with only the local Maderista officials displaying opposition; Ortiz, as *jefe*, was reckoned to be 'hanging on by his eyelids' to office; and, within a matter of days, he was removed from his post and arrested.[117] So, too, at Zaragoza (Coa.), Madero's fall signalled the revival of the old caciques of the Porfiriato.[118] Higher up, those state governors who had achieved a stay of execution by temporising soon began to topple. The first crop (González, Riveros, Cepeda and Fuentes) went in March; they were soon followed by the governors of Zacatecas, Yucatán, Campeche, Chiapas, Tamaulipas and Mexico; by July, nineteen of the twenty-seven state governors were military officers.[119]

This decimation of the Maderista civilians stored up trouble for the future, but it did not produce much immediate armed resistance since, in 1913 as in 1910, this group showed little will or capacity to shoulder arms. But it was a different matter with the Maderista irregulars and *rurales*, those veterans of 1910 who had found a place – albeit a lowly one – under the Madero regime. They possessed weapons, discipline (of a sort), and organisation – a crucial prerequisite of revolt; they had also shown their readiness to fight against Díaz, so why not against Victoriano Huerta, Porfirio redivivus? Some veterans of 1910 figured among the Coahuilan and Sonoran forces, whose important role has already been mentioned. But, on the whole, these states had not been prominent in 1910 and their military leaders had gained their laurels not during the Madero revolution (when some, like Obregón, had not fought at all) but later, during the campaigns against the Orozquistas. In other states, however, there were other leaders who boasted a longer revolutionary pedigree, who had been early into the fray in 1910, and who showed – in conservative eyes – 'a congenitally rebellious spirit'.[120] It was not surprising that, in a more freelance, unofficial manner than their Coahuilan and Sonoran colleagues, they soon took up arms against Huerta.

In Durango, the *rural* commander Orestes Pereyra, allied with the Ocuila leader Contreras, seized the old trouble spot of Cuencamé, whither they brazenly summoned 200 Federal cavalry and shot them up. Both were, of course, well known in the locality and Contreras could count on his Ocuila following; as a result, the increase in their forces during March 1913 was 'little short of marvellous' and by the end of the month they commanded some 1,400 men, drawn from the 'many small garrisons of *rurales* who were composed of ex-Maderista revolutionaries', and reinforced by 'systematic recruitment of the labourers on the ranches through which they have passed'.[121] With the Arrietas resuming their rebellious ways in the sierra, in loose alliance with Pereyra and Contreras, the Federal government had, by April, lost control of most of the state (a familiar experience for Federal governments of all hues).[122] The rebellion – or, failing that, desertion – of *rurales* became a commonplace elsewhere too. Jesús Agustín Castro, whose 21st *Cuerpo* had been deliberately decimated by Huerta during the *Decena Trágica*, mutinied and led his forces on a three week trek from the capital to the north-east, where they linked up with Lucio Blanco; at Zacatecas, the 38th *Cuerpo* went over to the rebels when they attacked the city.[123] Gertrudis Sánchez attended a surreptitious junta on the banks of the Balsas, whence he launched an invasion of Michoacán; in Sinaloa, Macario Gaxiola, related by marriage to the deposed state governor, soon led 300 men against the new regime; later in the year, Agustín Portas (a follower of Tapia and Gavira in 1911) captained 100 rebels in the Atoyac district of Veracruz. All three were *rural* commanders.[124] As a result, one of the first priorities of the Huerta administration was to prevent such revolts: when General Díaz arrived at Mazatlán to take control, his first move − after arresting the civil governor − was to disarm the *rurales*; nevertheless, it was confidently expected that the disarmed men would soon take to the hills and secure new weapons.[125] Other measures were more severe and final: among the early victims of Huertista assassination were several ex-Maderista *rural* commanders − Rafael Tapia, Camerino Mendoza, Gabriel Hernández.[126]

The wholesale desertion, rebellion, or elimination of the *rurales* − especially when coupled with the failure of Huerta's ex-Orozquista recruits − meant that the burden of peace-keeping fell upon the Federal Army, which, despite unprecedented growth, was still chronically unable to tackle rural, guerrilla warfare. The ex-*rurales'* swift and effective mobilisation against Huerta also reflected a crucial feature of the 1913 campaigns: the Constitutionalist revolution was a re-run − or, better, a linear continuation − of the Maderista revolution; there was (*pace* several views to the contrary) no clear disjunction, no abrupt shift from the narrow, political revolution of Madero to the broad, social revolution of Carranza.[127] Carranza's revolution was to last longer, it had to achieve greater organisation and fight bigger battles; over time, it would adopt different (though not necessarily more 'radical') policies; but the same places, the same people, the same grievances and the same tactics were evident, establishing a fundamental continuity at the most basic level. In the early weeks, the parallels between 1913 and 1910 were less apparent: for the revolt *en bloc* of the state of Sonora was unprecedented (indeed, Sonora had played a minor role in the 1910 revolution). Equally, Carranza, a rebellious governor, had no 1910 equivalent. Between them, Carranza and the Sonorans imparted a degree of organisation, respectability and efficiency which the Madero revolution had never known. And, ultimately, this difference was to be of major importance. But the Constitutionalist revolution embraced vastly more than these two northern elements; under their nominal leadership, the old pattern of vigorous, decentralised, popular revolt, led, in the main, by unlettered, local *cabecillas*, reasserted itself. While the northerners undertook a national campaign, aiming ultimately for Mexico City, dozens of lesser, local movements softened up the Huerta regime, sapping its energy, penning its army in garrison towns, menacing the connecting railway links, continuing, in many cases, the struggle they had been forced to abandon in 1911.

This contrast – between the organised, white-collar revolution of Carranza and the Sonorans and the endemic, popular unrest elsewhere – was clearly evident to contemporaries, even if they described it in different terms. To some it seemed that only Coahuila and Sonora had produced true rebellions; the rest was mere banditry.[128] The British Minister affirmed that 'the socialistic spirit which permeates the whole Republic . . . presents far greater difficulties in its settlement than the northern revolution' ('socialism' – rather like 'banditry' – being diplomatic shorthand for popular rebellion, agrarian protest and the breakdown of traditional forms of social control and authority).[129] What was important was that these manifestations of continued social upheaval, though repressed even more fiercely by the central government, continued and were complemented by the organised rebellion of the north, a rebellion which, like Madero's of 1910, depended on such popular violence, of necessity encouraged and legitimised it, yet at the same time feared and sought to control or channel it in the right directions. Thus 1913 was a re-run of 1910 in that the old regime – then Díaz, now Huerta – faced a resurgent popular movement, a congeries of local, rural forces, legitimised by their participation within an 'official', organised, national revolution. The chief difference lay, not with the popular movement (whose consistency over time was remarkable), but the national leadership. Like Madero, the Constitutionalist leaders found themselves between the popular movement and the old regime (though in circumstances which, of course, had changed, and were changing): the question confronting them was the same one Madero had failed to solve: could popular forces be harnessed to pull down the old regime, without their threatening to run amok, subverting society and driving the revolutionary leadership into a fatal compromise with the old regime (e.g., the Juárez Treaty)? By simply posing this dilemma, a second new feature of 1913 is revealed: now, second time around, the principal actors were that much wiser; Carranza and the Sonorans had pondered the fate of Madero; they were resolved that history should not repeat itself, either as tragedy or farce.

The campaigns of 1913 clearly displayed the duality at the heart of the Constitutionalist revolution. We shall consider first the efforts of the Coahuilans and Sonorans (whose fortunes soon diverged); with the 'official response' to Huertismo outlined, we shall proceed to the 'popular challenge' which complemented it. Carranza was thought to enjoy a good deal of support not only in Coahuila but also in Tamaulipas, Nuevo León and even San Luis.[130] But it was not easy to translate this support into armed resistance. During March, as unrest and rebellion spread, Carranza 'marched and countermarched' in the Saltillo region, but did not chance a battle.[131] Múzquiz and Piedras Negras went over to the Carrancistas bloodlessly, but Carranza's first clash with the Federals – a skirmish at Anhelo – was a minor defeat. Bent on a dramatic counter-stroke, Carranza attacked a well-defended Saltillo: the assault was badly co-ordinated and after fifty-five hours of costly fighting the rebels withdrew to the north. For a couple of months Carranza remained, surprisingly unmolested, at Monclova, preoccupied with the problems of asserting his authority over other rebels in the field, while the Federals made a sluggardly advance north.[132] Possibly the central government did not regard Carranza as the chief threat (which, if so, was another reflection of governmental *naïveté*, for, while Carranza lacked military power, he had the political capacity to mount a more serious challenge than ever Zapata could, for all his stout peon troops).[133] Possibly other factors encouraged delay: it was rumoured that some of the Federal generals in the north were flirting with Carranza, and so dragging their feet; and certainly Huerta spent some of this time reshuffling army commands, promoting his own *adictos* at the expense of those more lukewarm.[134] At any rate, it took General Maass three months to progress from Monclova to Piedras Negras on the border, and by then Carranza was long gone. But if the Federal advance had been slow, it was apparently successful: since the spring there had come reports of disaffection in the ranks of the Coahuilan rebels; some had reached terms with the government; and by the time Piedras Negras fell in the autumn it was the 'consensus [of] opinion [at] Eagle Pass that [the] retreat of [the] rebels marks [the] virtual collapse of organised military operations on anything like [a] large scale by them in Coahuila'.[135]

Carranza did not witness the débâcle. Instead, he headed west, first to the battle-ground of the Laguna, then across the Sierra Madre to Sonora, where greater security and political opportunity beckoned.[136] If Carranza was a less than charismatic war-leader, he was a stout traveller (which, in the circumstances, was the next best thing: President Juárez, after all, had done more to defeat reaction by his peripatetic example than by his military contribution; and Carranza was fond of citing such historical precedents). So, spurning an easy train ride across the American south-west, he made personal contact with the *cabecillas* of Durango and Chihuahua (notably the Arrietas and Herreras) and then crossed the continental divide on horseback, with an escort of 100, braving the ascent in torrential rain, and descending into the Fuerte Valley to meet the rebel leaders of Sinaloa and Sonora. For a short-sighted, corpulent, middle-aged *político* – to his critics, then and now, 'mediocrity incarnate', 'a pettifogging country lawyer without great abilities' – this was some sort of achievement, which probably helped establish Carranza's shaky reputation and authority.[137] Though a civilian and a *político* (and all that that implied) he was at least prepared to show himself, in boots and leggings, sombrero and khaki jacket, to the troops in the field; to trek across country, discarding frock-coat, wing collar, and all the other accoutrements of the respectable bourgeois. It may be worth noting that when the revolution later bifurcated, and Carranza began to find out who his real friends were, both the Arrietas and the Herreras, with whom he had lodged on his overland trail in 1913, stayed loyal amidst mass defections: which may or may not be significant.

The situation Carranza encountered in the north-west was much more cheerful than that which he had forsaken in Coahuila. He was accorded a warm welcome; and he was delighted to find 'a disciplined, perfectly equipped army' in being.[138] Certainly, the Sonoran revolution had made impressive progress. Governor Pesqueira's repudiation of Huerta had been spurred and seconded by local insurrections, led by Maderista officials and irregulars: at Fronteras, Agua Prieta, Cumpas, Cocorit, Nacozari and elsewhere.[139] Hence Pesqueira, unlike Carranza, was able to carry almost the entire state administration with him: Pedro Bracamonte, *jefe* of Moctezuma; Juan Cabral, chief of customs at Magdalena; Plutarco Elías Calles, police chief of Agua Prieta; Aniceto Campos, mayor of Fronteras; Alvaro Obregón, mayor of Huatabampo; all, according to an American observer, 'honest, reliable men', who were supported by 'a pretty broad sentiment of sympathy throughout the state'.[140] Hence, good order and administration were maintained in the midst of 'revolution'; the men of Sonora were no wild, undisciplined hoodlums.[141] They prospered militarily, too, and here Alvaro Obregón had already emerged pre-eminent, securing promotion over those (like Hill, Alvarado and Cabral) who, unlike Obregón, had participated in the 1910 revolution.[142]

Obregón, who was to become one of the key figures in the Revolution, and the greatest of the many generals it produced, was just thirty-three when the Constitutionalist revolution began.[143] His father, a once prosperous land-owner who had married into the Sonoran oligarchy, fell upon hard times and died three months after Alvaro's birth, leaving his large family in straitened circumstances. They moved to Huatabampo – a hot, hard-working, irreligious sort of place – where Obregón was brought up by his three schoolmistress sisters and educated at the municipal school, run by Don José: an institution which Obregón's biographer has implausibly termed 'a rural Balliol College, with a rural Jowett as the chief pedagogue'.[144] But Obregón's education was practical rather than classical (a point later exemplified in his homespun political rhetoric): apart from acquiring a basic literacy, he picked up Mayo (and later learned Yaqui too), he worked part-time as a carpenter, while still at school, and he amused himself shooting rabid coyotes.[145] It was hardly the education of the middle-class *licenciado*, with its bias towards book-learning, the humanities and European culture. Rather, Obregón conformed to the stereotype of the northern 'self-made man': practical, mobile, opportunist, endowed with an eye for the main chance, a certain common touch, and a readiness to use both personal talents and social connections in the cause of self-advancement.[146] Though it could not have been foreseen at the time, this was an appropriate schooling for the ruthless, innovative, populist politics of the Revolution; it prepared Obregón for government much as Balliol did a succession of British prime ministers.

Obregón had various jobs: as a mechanic on his uncle's hacienda (where he showed a distinct technical flair), in a Navolato sugar mill, as a smallholder, first renting, then buying and expanding a farm dedicated to the lucrative chickpea. Bent on business, he avoided politics, even though his nephew, Benjamín Hill, was prominent in the local anti-Díaz opposition. When the Revolution broke out, Obregón – to his subsequent shame – did not participate; indeed, some of his family were strong for Díaz till the very end.[147] With the fall of Díaz, however, Obregón entered politics, securing election as mayor of Huatabampo by methods not untypical of the time, which have already been mentioned.[148] But he felt a nagging doubt about his failure to fight in 1910–11, and when the Orozquista invasion loomed on the eastern horizon, Obregón took the chance to redeem his reputation. Recruiting volunteers from around Huatabampo and Navojoa, he formed a detachment which joined the government forces at Agua Prieta (here Obregón met and began his long politico-military association with Calles) and fought at the battle of San Joaquín, at which Salazar's Orozquistas were decisively beaten.[149] By now, Obregón had acquired military expertise, reputation, and a strong personal authority over his men.

A colonel by the end of 1912, Obregón's promotion quickened when Sonora repudiated the Huerta regime in the following year. But his rapid rise to the leadership of the Sonoran forces was resented by some – notably Salvador Alvarado – who had done their bit in 1910–11 and who considered Obregón a novice and a latecomer; hence, through the campaigns of 1913, Obregón was clearly on trial, keen to consolidate his reputation, and acutely aware of rivals and critics within the Sonoran ranks.[150] The Sonorans' first priority was to capture the border ports, where customs could be levied and arms (illegally) imported. In mid-March, Obregón and Cabral took Nogales.[151] Next month, Sonoran forces including Obregón, Alvarado, Bracamonte, Calles, and the Yaqui leaders Buli, Acosta and Urbalejo moved against Naco, where the Federal General Pedro Ojeda, dug in behind trenchworks, spent his time terrorising rebel sympathisers and cruelly executing wounded prisoners-of-war.[152] Such conduct only heightened rebel *élan*, which already contrasted with the low morale and passive disposition of the Federals.[153] But Ojeda was confident: 'I will cut off my head with my own sword before I will surrender or cross into the United States,' he told the press. But days later, after some fierce fighting, Ojeda blew up the customs house, crossed the frontier and surrendered to the American authorities, leaving Naco in rebel hands (his head stayed on his shoulders, however, and he lived to fight another day).[154] Meanwhile, the towns of the interior also fell: Cananea and Moctezuma (both affording valuable mining revenue), and Alamos, where Benjamín Hill overcame the resistance of the prefect and 500 volunteers, who held out for Huerta.[155]

Now only Guaymas, of the major towns, remained in Federal hands, and the rebels could count on vital economic resources to finance their expanding military operations. They levied loans on business and real estate; they took over and exploited the properties of Huertistas who had fled the state; they established good relations with American mining companies, and with the Southern Pacific Railroad of Mexico, who appreciated Governor Pesqueira's 'zealous concern to guarantee property and order', and who, to the disgust of Huertista officials, readily paid taxes to the *de facto* Sonoran administration.[156] The Sonoran revolution, true to its origins, was thus efficient, orderly and pragmatic, given neither to popular disorder nor to Utopian reform. Pesqueira was not alone in seeing himself 'more as the representative of a constituted government than as the leader of a tumultuous, drastic revolution'; and, alone among the Sonoran leaders, Juan Cabral showed a concern for agrarian reform, which could make little headway in such an unfavourable environment.[157] Much more typical of the administration were the frontier 'brokers', whose crucial task it was to handle exports and customs, to negotiate covert arms deals, and to keep the American border authorities sweet. In men like Roberto Pesqueira (nephew of the governor), Ignacio Bonillas (prefect of Arizpe), Francisco Elías, Angel Lagarda, and, above all, Plutarco Calles, the Sonoran revolution – and later the Sonoran regime – found the required business acumen and administrative skill to complement the more famous military attributes of men like Obregón and Alvarado: they provided the sinews of war, which the generals flexed.[158]

By the early summer of 1913, Obregón was established as the leading military figure within the revolution. In Sonora, 6,000 men were now under arms, including a couple of thousand Yaquis (some directly recruited, some deserters from the Federal Army who had gone over to the rebels under Luis Buli in April). All Yaquis, however, recognised the old, overriding objective: 'our struggle can be reduced quite simply to the reconquest of our rights and our lands snatched away from us by brute force'; and to secure Yaqui co-operation, the state administration (like the Maderistas and others in the past) endorsed this aim.[159] But Yaqui *agrarismo* sat uneasily within a revolutionary movement which spurned agrarian questions, which abhorred disorderly popular mobilisation, and whose leaders were steeped in the traditions of the Yaqui wars. Hence there was constant tension between the local, agrarian and tribal objectives of the Yaquis, and the more grandiose, political and ultimately national ambitions of the Sonorans. Even in 1913, this tension broke out in sporadic violence, which hampered the joint effort against Huerta; but for the time being, it was contained, and the organised Yaqui contingents provided valuable services to the state leadership.[160]

As in Coahuila, the Federal counter-attack was slow; in Mexico City they compared it, complacently, to Huerta's slow but sure campaign against Orozco in 1912[161] Early in May, Federal reinforcements and two gunboats reached the Huertista redoubt of Guaymas. The hopes of the conservatives –

beleaguered in Guaymas, or exiled north of the border – at once lifted, especially since the Federal command was entrusted to General Luis Medina Barrón, who had campaigned in Sonora in 1909, and who carried a reputation of ruthless efficiency.[162] Sonora, thus far spared, was now to experience the rigours of the 'iron hand'. 'Disturbers of order' would be swiftly dealt with and left swinging from roadside telegraph poles, the general warned; fêted by the well-to-do of Guaymas, he promised that he would soon return the compliment with a victory banquet in Hermosillo. Next day, Empalme, the railway junction just outside Guaymas, was subjected to a gratuitously fierce bombardment (the rebels had already retired thence and only civilians were put at risk) and Medina Barrón began to advance north into rebel territory.[163] Obregón allowed the Federals to proceed across the hot, dusty country, pulling them out of range of the gunboats at Guaymas. But Medina Barrón would not be lured too far; and Governor Pesqueira grew edgy at the Federal approach towards Hermosillo. At the Hacienda Santa Rosa a three day battle took place, in which the Federals were sent packing back to Guaymas, losing up to half their men as casualties or deserters, and provoking criticism – among junior officers – of the leadership, equipment, and Federal rank-and-file.[164]

A new Federal commander was sent: none other than General Ojeda, who had just evacuated Naco, despite grandiloquent promises to the contrary.[165] Ojeda repeated the mistake of his predecessor. As he advanced north with 4,000 men, Obregón retreated; at Santa María, late in June 1913, the Sonoran army fell upon the Federals, who were again routed: 300 were killed, 500 taken prisoner, and a large stock of field-guns, shells, machine-guns, rifles and ammunition was captured. The Sonorans claimed twenty-seven killed and thirty-one wounded.[166] Thus Obregón twice 'made the Federals defeat themselves', in the sense of accepting battle on his own terms, on his own chosen terrain: a technique he used time and time again with unerring success.[167] All Sonora, save Guaymas, was now in rebel hands, and the Federals relinquished hope of recovering it. Ojeda huddled in Guaymas, under the protection of the gunboats, showing somewhat more skill and resolution in defending a fixed point than in sallying forth into hostile countryside (a typical Federal trait).[168] A brief attempt to ambush Carranza as he arrived on the west coast was thwarted by heavy rain and Carranza's Yaqui guides; otherwise, the Federals in Guaymas were subjected to a tight siege, though Obregón – wrongly, some said – declined to press home the advantage by a frontal assault.[169] Rather, he temporised, refusing to campaign during the late summer, and later undertaking an advance south, while leaving Guaymas still in Federal hands. The reasons for this delay, which was also the subject of criticism, were twofold: political and military.

On the political front, the summer of 1913 was one of uncertainty and internal conflict which, according to Aguilar's cogent analysis, paralysed rebel military operations.[170] Divisions now replaced the initial unanimity of the Sonorans. Some divisions – like the split between the Yaquis and the state leadership – were inevitable; it was a question of how long they could be contained and mitigated. The rivalry between Obregón and his supposed subordinate, notably Alvarado, continued; and Obregón, never lacking in *amour propre*, resented the fact that Carranza had appointed Pesqueira as chief of the Division of the North-West. After his victory at Santa María, Obregón broke off the campaign to visit the US for medical treatment, suffering, it was said, from heatstroke; he even talked sulkily of going off to fight in Chihuahua.[171] But the most serious dissension concerned the proposed return of Governor Maytorena, whose leave of absence expired in August. Though he had studiously avoided the action in Mexico, Maytorena had been busy in Arizona, liaising with revolutionary leaders – and not just those of Sonora – and exerting pressure on Washington to prevent to diplomatic recognition of Huerta.[172] In April, with the success of the Sonoran revolution evident, Maytorena announced his intention of returning to resume the governorship. This was his constitutional right, but the decision excited strong feelings for and against. Like any prominent *político*, Maytorena had his network of clients, centred on Guaymas and the south, who naturally supported his claim. He also enjoyed a longstanding connection with several of the Yaqui leaders, like Carlos Félix and Francisco Urbalejo. Finally, for all his vacillations, he carried weight as Sonora's ranking Maderista, the political symbol of the old civilian opposition, of *sufragio efectivo*, and of constitutional legality.[173] But he also had powerful opponents: the military, like Alvarado, contemptuous of Maytorena's hesitant behaviour in February; the 'brokers' of the northern frontier, remote from his southern fief and themselves products of the 1913 rather than the 1910 revolution; and, of course, interim Governor Pesqueira, reluctant to shrug off the post he had assumed in time of crisis and creditably occupied through to the happier days of the summer.[174] In addition, there were the deputies of the state legislature, who had crossed swords with Maytorena in 1912 and who now identified more strongly with the *interinato*.

Into this complex interplay of forces, which impeded the Sonoran revolution through the summer, one crucial, exogenous factor appeared: Venustiano Carranza, the self-styled 'First Chief' of Constitutionalism. On joining hands with the Sonorans and thus forming the nucleus of the movement, Carranza was clearly the weaker party, a defeated emigré from another state, hardly likely to receive a deferential welcome from the fiercely provincial Sonorans. Yet Sonora's internal divisions gave Carranza (whose only asset was his early repudiation of Huerta) a vital purchase, upon which he could build a *de facto* authority worthy of his grandiose *de jure* claims. The self-appointed First Chief could become an effective First Chief because he enjoyed a tenuous, external legitimacy to which the feuding Sonorans could appeal. Interim Governor Pesqueira began the process, sending two Sonoran delegates to meet with Carranza at Monclova in April, at which time they recognised his political leadership: the first explicit recognition that Sonora's local, states' rights rebellion had a national dimension.[175] Thereafter, Pesqueira was made commander of the Division of the North-West (the appointment which angered Obregón) and was accused of showing a 'total, even somewhat servile' loyalty to Carranza.[176] Pesqueira's allies, the northern 'brokers', likewise endorsed Carranza, while the Sonoran state deputies (also anti-Maytorenista) took the further step of investing him with the Federal powers in the state, which had fallen into default with the revolt against Huerta. Thereby, Carranza was voted control of customs, posts, telegraphs, Federal taxes and concessions.[177] Carranza's warm welcome in Sonora was not, therefore, wholly disinterested; and the anomalous situation, whereby the weaker partner in the alliance assumed leadership of the revolution, depended in large measure upon these internal Sonoran squabbles.

As for Maytorena, he returned as planned, and could not but be accepted; the 'Constitutionalist' revolution could hardly start off by sacking a constitutional governor. Once installed in the state-house, he wasted no time in building up his own power and party. An ambitious move to depose Calles and Bonillas – two of his key northern opponents – was thwarted; but subsequent measures, designed to revamp the state's fiscal machinery, place it in gubernatorial hands, and thus undermine the frontier 'brokers', were more successful. Maytorena also acted against his old enemies in the legislature, and sought to cultivate Obregón, whose position in these feuds remained (typically) uncertain and opportunistic.[178] One logical outcome of these clashes was a distancing between Maytorena and Carranza. The Sonoran governor had no intention of deferring to the Coahuilan First Chief; in June, at Piedras Negras, Maytorena had declined a post in Carranza's highly notional government; now, he disliked Carranza's arrogation of authority within Sonora, made possible only by Sonoran force of arms. He disliked it even more when, in October 1913, Carranza formed a cabinet including some of Maytorena's *bêtes noires*.[179] So far, these conflicts remained manageable, necessarily subordinated to the demands of the war against Huerta. The protagonists manoeuvred, moaned, sulked and denounced; though there was talk of fighting (Maytorena's Yaquis threatened drastic action against Esteban Baca Calderón, one of the governor's outspoken critics), it did not come to that.[180] But there was a real danger that, should the Constitutionalists win, the fall of Huerta would be the signal for these long incubating feuds (and alliances) to assume armed form. Often seeming petty in their origins, these early fissures within the core of Constitutionalism were in fact potentially explosive.

For the time being, however, their chief effect was to retard the military campaigns. But there were other retarding factors: the incidence of the rains and the planting season; Obregón's belief that Guaymas could not readily be taken; that an intensive siege would be too costly; and that too precipitate an advance south – with Guaymas still in Federal hands – was perilous.[181] Hence, through the summer of 1913 Obregón bided his time, and, even through the autumn and winter of 1913–14, he undertook only a gradual advance into Sinaloa (to be considered shortly). Meantime, rebel movements elsewhere were winning laurels, and the head start achieved by the Sonorans seemed to be gradually dissipated. To some, Obregón's extreme caution appeared reprehensible, even cowardly.[182] Yet there was an undeniable military factor which – if Obregón took it more seriously than some swashbuckling popular *cabecilla* – could not be ignored, and which increasingly determined the tempo of warfare in Mexico. As rebel armies got bigger, more sophisticated and committed to more extensive, ambitious campaigns, so the problem of arms supply became crucial, especially in the north, where such operations were now politically and geographically inevitable. Put simply, the Sonorans could not – like the Zapatistas – content themselves with guerrilla campaigns. Their forces, operating in open country, were built up methodically and professionally, with a view to ridding Sonora of Federals, then Mexico of Huerta. If the Zapatistas (and many lesser rebel movements) were still subject to the dictates of the harvest, the Sonorans (and other northern armies) were increasingly dependent on the supply of arms and ammunition from the US. And the crucial variable here was not so much the purchasing power of the revolutionaries (for, as the Sonoran 'brokers' had shown, it was quite feasible to milk the northern economy in order to nurture the revolution) but rather the availability of munitions north of the border. This raises the important question of American policy.

For a year (February 1913 to February 1914) the Constitutionalists were denied belligerent status by the US Government: this meant that shipments of arms to the rebels (though not, initially, to Huerta) were illegal, and had to be smuggled.[183] By now, it is true, smuggling was a major border industry. Not only was a majority of the border population – both Mexican and American – sympathetic to the rebels and therefore disposed to co-operate or at least turn a blind eye; in addition, the arms racket attracted plenty of active participants, including American officials.[184] As a frustrated American general observed, political interest and mercenary instinct conspired to unite the border population with the revolutionary factions in Mexico: hence, 'our border towns are practically their commissary and quarter-master depots' and hardware shops along the border (whose proprietors boasted of selling as much in a day in 1913 as in a year like 1911) 'have the appearance of a military arsenal'.[185] Arms consignments were shipped to the border in bulk and then transported to Mexico in small, clandestine loads – packed in barrels, driven in car-loads by night, even concealed in coffins.[186] The American border patrol, stretched over a huge, rugged terrain, could not hope to intercept all smuggling expeditions and the law regarding conviction was still such that the guilty party had to be caught *in flagrante delicto* for the charge to stick. There was also widespread offical complicity, which revolutionary agents, like the Sonoran 'brokers', naturally encouraged.[187] The Federal marshal of Nogales (Arizona) was arrested for carrying arms into Mexico; and at Naco rebel leaders met in the deputy sheriff's bar and concealed arms on his ranch.[188]

Hence, throughout the twelve month period when the export of arms to the rebels was illegal, arms nevertheless got through. But two points should be made about this illegal traffic. First, it cannot be inferred (as Huertista consuls and some later historians have maintained) that connivance and corruption on the border represented 'American policy', that Washington dictated or even approved this behaviour.[189] There is no convincing evidence to this effect; there were plenty of instances of the border authorities complying with the letter of the law, where they could; and, above all, it is difficult to see why Washington should have resorted to this devious and dangerous policy. Woodrow Wilson was quite prepared to halt arms shipments to Huerta (July 1913), and finally to recognise the belligerency of the Constitutionalists (February 1914): the evolution of American policy in this regard was logical, and suppositions of Machiavellianism are superfluous. It is not at all implausible, after all, to posit the existence of widespread illegality, in defiance of Washington's offical policy, especially where such strong vested interests were concerned: witness the subsequent failure of Prohibition or, even more relevant, the stream of illegal immigration since the 1940s.

The second point concerns the effect these arms shipments had on the course of the revolution. It is scarcely logical to argue that the US (unofficially in 1913, officially in 1914) determined the success of the Constitutionalist revolution by supplying it with arms.[190] Official policy favoured Huerta till July 1913, was neutral for over six months, and only swung behind the rebels in February 1914. For a year, American policy gave the rebels no disproportionate aid or comfort; and, throughout, Huerta had access to the arms markets of the rest of the world. Unofficial American help was important (though, as I have stressed, it derived from local sympathisers and profiteers, not from covert government favour). But this conferred no advantage which Huerta did not already possess, and smuggling, on whatever scale, cannot compete with free importation; it imposes its own additional costs and dangers. Figures of smuggled munitions are, of course, impossible to assess. FBI agents reckoned that 10,000 rounds a day were crossing via Douglas, Arizona, throughout the summer of 1913.[191] But despite these large figures, there were major problems and constraints. By no means all the American authorities were complaisant, especially when the Constitutionalists pushed their luck too far (for example, in May 1913, when Cabral's frontier agent tried to smuggle an airplane across the Arizona border).[192] Influential officials like Consul Ellsworth, at Cd Porfirio Díaz (Piedras Negras), were horrified at infractions of neutrality and did their best to stop them.[193] And there were certainly instances of arms consignments (and not just airplanes) being discovered and confiscated: according to a European, serving in Sonora, 'there were many desperate picaroons in America with the sporting instinct of skunks', who sold black market guns, cash in advance, and then tipped off the authorities. [194]

Thus the need to smuggle created risks and inflated the price of arms. Above all, so long as arms had to be smuggled, the demands of the growing rebel armies could not be met. Total rebel forces in northern Mexico were estimated to be 8,000 in March 1913, and 17,000 in August; if anything, the second figure errs on the conservative side. [195] While it was one thing to supply small mobile guerrilla bands by smuggling (and other forms of improvisation) it was quite another to provision fair sized armies – which by 1914 would run into tens of thousands. [196] Hence there is no doubt that arms shortages inhibited rebel operations throughout 1913. In Sonora, recruits outnumbered available weapons (a dilemma Huerta never faced) and some had to be turned away. Yaqui and Mayo Indians joined and fought with bows and arrows (though some sneered at this improvisation, Obregón persevered; and, when the Sonoran forces reached the bush country of southern Sinaloa and Tepic, the Indian bow proved its worth). [197] But for the reduction of towns like Guaymas, the rebels needed abundant small-arms ammunition as well as artillery, and, while these were in short supply, Obregón preferred to avoid an assault or intensive siege. Meanwhile, these problems were even more acute elsewhere in the north, where there was no real equivalent of the Sonorans' efficient commissary. In May 1913 a hundred rebels were easily driven out of Fresnillo (Zac.): their arms, which the Federals captured, consisted of old Remington carbines and 'antiquated rifles of all kinds', with only three Mausers among them; most rebels in this part of the country were 'very poorly armed and . . . short of ammunition'. [198] Operations in the Laguna were similarly constricted, while in the north-east, Federal superiority in arms (particularly their monopoly of artillery) proved decisive: 'in all recent engagements between Federals and the Constitutionalists', a report of August 1913 noted, 'the Constitutionalists have expended their supply of ammunition and have been forced to retire'. [199] Even if Federal artillery could be captured (as it was at Santa María, for example) the rebels had trouble securing the right shells for European guns; often they had to be manufactured locally, with considerable difficulty and no small risk. [200] Until the US government finally lifted the arms embargo in February 1914, therefore, Constitutionalist military activity – especially of a grand, conventional kind – was necessarily limited; not until then did Obregón shake off his apparent sloth and enter the race for Mexico City.

The preliminaries came with the gradual penetration of Sinaloa in the autumn of 1913. This was no major campaign; but it represented an interesting and significant fusion of two contrasting revolutionary modes: the organised, almost bureaucratic revolution of the Sonorans, and the more popular, chaotic, decentralised rebellion which characterised much of the rest of Mexico. Sinaloa became the first interface (if the term may be allowed) between the new, official revolutionaries and the revived popular movement of 1913. It thus provides a convenient bridge between the analyses of these two phenomena. In Sinaloa, the rampant unrest of 1911–12 (much greater than anything Sonora had experienced in these years) had died down in the latter part of the Madero presidency. Initially, Huerta's coup was greeted with sullen acquiescence; there was no organised resistance, and Governor Riveros sought to dissuade the bolder Maderistas from armed rebellion. But, as early as March, there came reports of *gavillas* resuming their activities around Concordia, Pánuco, and Rosario (all familiar names from 1910–12); and, by arbitrarily deposing Riveros in favour of a military governor, Huerta replaced a pacifying with a provocative influence.[201] The rebellion of Macario Gaxiola, a Maderista *rural* and relative of Riveros, was seconded by Cabanillas (once a carpenter), Carrasco (a *vaquero*), Gandarilla (blacksmith), and Iturbe (the revolutionary prodigy of 1911, just returned from California) – all veterans of the Madero uprising.[202] They were soon joined by Angel Flores, once a Mazatlán stevedore, Martín Espinosa, recently the Maderista *jefe* in Tepic, and ex-Governor Riveros himself who, arrested and then released by the government, proved more belligerent than most deposed Maderista governors.[203] These Sinaloan rebels lacked the cohesion, discipline, and logistical back-up of the Sonorans; they were 'poorly armed and short of ammunition'; Carrasco had a single field-gun but did not know how to use it; and, even when nominally subordinate to Obregón, he continued to act as a cavalier free agent. Altogether, the Sinaloan revolution was more popular, plebeian and anarchic.[204] But it was effective. By August 1913 there were reckoned to be 5,000 rebels in the state, and the Federals, outnumbered by two to one, were bottled up in a few towns, their superiority in munitions cancelled out by their immobility and low morale.[205] Hence, as the Sonorans began to inch their way down the west coast, they found Sinaloa ripe for the picking.

THE POPULAR CHALLENGE

As the first movers of the Constitutionalist revolution consolidated their hold on the north-west, endemic popular revolt – on Sinaloan rather than Sonoran lines – began to affect the rest of the country, its incidence closely following the pattern set in 1910–11. Once again, Chihuahua was to the fore. Despite the defection of Orozco and his lieutenants, the state still had Maderista *cabecillas* enough to take the lead; and the Huertistas' purge of Governor González and his officials ensured that these *cabecillas* would determine the character of the rebellion: popular, plebeian, disorganised, decentralised.[206] While the Sonoran revolutionary administration was already in being, that of Chihuahua had to be built from the ground up. Chief among the architects was

Pancho Villa, whose rapid rise from the common ruck of *cabecillas* to a position of outstanding power and prestige now began in earnest. Villa's decision to remain loyal to Madero at the time of Orozco's revolt (a maverick decision, based on personal and local loyalties and, perhaps, a certain political *naïveté*) at once set him apart from many of the 1910 veterans, especially Orozco, against whom Villa fought with enthusiasm in 1912 and again in 1913–14. As commander of a corps of somewhat wild Maderista irregulars, he fell foul of General Huerta who (for reasons not wholly concerned with military discipline) ordered him to be shot in June 1912. After a dramatic last-minute stay of execution, secured by Emilio Madero, Villa was consigned to gaol in Mexico City.[207] Here (Mexican gaols being remarkable for their capacity to collect and introduce to one another dissidents from different states and classes) Villa got to know Juan Banderas, 'The Sloucher', of Sinaloa; Zapata's secretary and chief of staff, Abraham Martínez (who tried to teach Villa to read); and even Bernardo Reyes.[208] Mexican gaols were also far from escape-proof and, from the start, Villa and Banderas planned to break out.[209] Using Villa's financial resources, they acquired moulds of the prison keys and assiduously cultivated the guards. But, when misguided well-wishers secured Villa's transfer from the Federal District Penitentiary to the Military Prison at Tlatelolco, the plan fell through. At Tlatelolco, Villa bribed and talked his way into the confidence of the young magistrate's clerk, Carlos Jáuregui, one of the horde of under-paid, petty-bourgeois, government drudges who populated the capital, who was flattered by the attentions of the fearsome northern *cabecilla* and gratified by gifts of suits, shoes, hats and ties, all in return for small favours. Eventually, Jáuregui himself suggested an escape plan; Villa suspected a police trap; but the plan advanced. Jáuregui filed the bars of Villa's cell and supplied the prisoner with two pistols, a hat and dark glasses. On Christmas Day 1912, Villa walked out of the prison, muffling his face with a handkerchief. None of the guards stopped him. Boarding a car laid on by his accomplice, Villa drove to Toluca; thence by train to Manzanillo and boat to Mazatlán; finally, still in the company of Jáuregui, he crossed overland via Hermosillo and Nogales to the US.

Apart from being a good story, Villa's escape was of real importance in the history of the Revolution. It antedated Huerta's coup by just six weeks; had Villa still been a prisoner in February 1913 (and had he not escaped – or been killed – in the prison mêlée following Reyes' break-out from Tlatelolco) it is likely he would have met the same fate as other Maderistas, like Gabriel Hernández, slain in a Mexico City gaol. The Chihuahua revolution would still have happened, but without Villa's charismatic presence. As it was, when the *Decena Trágica* broke out, Villa was hovering on the border, and ready to re-enter the revolutionary fray. He was a man of scant political subtlety, preferring the company of fellow-cowboys to that of smart politicians; but, as his career and recent escape demonstrated, he had a definite native cunning and a knack for survival. He neither drank nor smoked; he slept little (or so it seemed); and, when he did, he preferred to wrap himself in a *sarape* away from the tents and camp-fires. These legacies of his bandit days survived as he rose to become the greatest caudillo of the Revolution (so, too, did his rheumatism, which afflicted him as it afflicted other ex-bandits and ex-*vaqueros*, like Urbina and Argumedo).[210] He had, too, the capacious memory of the illiterate and the common man's impatience with political and financial complexities, which he treated as Gordian knots to be sliced through, rather than unravelled; he had no taste for flowery oratory (his own speech was colloquial and simple) and, like many popular *cabecillas*, he delegated the embarrassing task of speech making to the intellectuals and *licenciados*, who were only too keen for a job, a stage and an audience.[211] As a military leader, too, Villa drew on his bandit past and ignored the subtleties of strategy. True, he recruited artillery experts, surgeons and skilled railway officials; he built up a reasonably efficient commissariat (growing success made such sophistication essential); but his style in battle was all dash, verve and *élan*. His success came from the toughness, mobility and high morale of his men, recruited from the mines and villages of the sierra, the cattle spreads of the northern prairies; and Villa's chief contribution, once the early days of guerrilla skirmishing were over, was his own burgeoning prestige and indomitable confidence, which made up the Villa legend.[212] At moments in battle when the troops faltered – for example, during the bloody assaults on Torreón in spring 1914 – a stocky, mounted figure, in scruffy khaki and sombrero, would appear among the ranks, urging on his *compañeros* in direct, personal and effective terms: Pancho Villa.[213] And, as success followed success, so the myth of Villa's invincibility grew, endorsing his preferred tactics, swelling his popular appeal, but ultimately guaranteeing his military downfall.

If Villa lacked clear political principles he had, nevertheless, a fierce loyalty to individuals: in which respect he mirrored the popular attitudes now more openly revealed through the medium of oral history.[214] He fought for people, rather than for abstract principles; he remembered favours and repaid them, and did likewise with grudges; he carried the code of the *serrano* bandit over into revolutionary politics. In 1913, things were clear. Madero – to whom Villa had been scrupulously loyal – had been treacherously slain; so too, had Gustavo Madero, who had helped Villa when he had been in gaol. Emilio Madero's service gave him an additional obligation to the family.[215] No less important, Abraham González, his 'close friend', who had first recruited Villa for the Revolution, had been done to death by the Federals in Bachimba canyon.[216] At the head of the new usurping regime stood Victoriano Huerta, Villa's accuser of 1912; and alongside him the old enemy, Pascual Orozco. Villa's response was unequivocal and immediate. In March 1913, he crossed into Mexico from El Paso, with eight companions (they included Carlos Jáuregui), three horses, 'two pounds of sugar and coffee and a pound of salt'.[217]

At San Andrés, in the Sierra Madre, where the 1910 revolution had begun its triumphal march through Chihuahua, Villa made contact with his brothers, Antonio and Hipólito (kinsmen were often the first recruits to popular insurrections); with sympathetic groups like the *rancheros* of Ciénaga de Ortiz (where, Villa recalled, 'all the people were my partisans'); and with old *compadres* and allies – Maclovio Herrera and family, who had stood with Villa during the Orozco revolt, Toribio Ortega, from Cuchillo Parado, 'a lean, dark Mexican . . . by far the most simple-hearted and disinterested soldier in Mexico', old, white-bearded Rosalío Hernández, and Tomás Urbina, once a fellow-bandit, who had been among Villa's followers back in November 1910.[218]

Urbina's recent career also paralleled Villa's. Spurning Orozco in 1912, he had nevertheless found his way to gaol in Durango, where he languished until Emilio Madero took up his cause, protesting to his brother that Urbina had always been 'muy fiel al gobierno', and securing his release on bail.[219] The Maderos' solicitude for friends of the regime, even if it failed to prevent its downfall, at least ensured that it would be avenged. And a final point about Villa and his allies of 1913 might be noted. None came from the old Maderista and Orozquista heartland of the Sierra Madre: the Guerrero district (home of Orozco, Rojas and others) and Casas Grandes (whence came Salazar, Campa, Caraveo and Quevedo). Villa, it is true, had operated in the first of these regions in 1910–11, and did so again in 1913; but, like Urbina, he was a native of Durango and many of his exploits centred on Parral and the Chihuahua/Durango borderlands. The Herreras also hailed from Parral; Hernández from Santa Rosalía, a little to the north; and Ortega from the northern border, near Ojinaga. It was this geographical separateness – allied, in Villa's and Urbina's cases, to a certain political *naïveté* – which kept these leaders and their *gente* outside the mainstream of Orozquismo in 1912, thus enabling them to take the lead in 1913, when Chihuahua resumed its pre-eminent revolutionary role.

Villa's allies had already been active. Santa Rosalía had been captured; Maclovio Herrera (who had succeeded Villa in command of the Benito Juárez Regiment) left the sierra for Parral, taking Namiquipa en route; and Manuel Chao had thrown a scare into General Mercado, commanding at Parral, by launching a strong though finally unsuccessful attack on the town.[220] Villa's appearance accelerated the rebels' progress: hacienda peons flocked to the cause (like those of the Hacienda El Carmen, who were given guns and rose up against their despotic *administrador*) and, almost certainly, there were defections from the government regulars to the rebels.[221] But those irregulars (i.e., Orozquistas) who continued to fight for Huerta could expect no mercy from Villa and his lieutenants: over 100 who fell into their hands after the battle of Nuevas Casas Grandes in June 1913 were summarily but parsimoniously shot, lined up, three to a bullet.[222] By early summer, the Chihuahuan revolutionaries had free run of the countryside: Ortega threatened Ojinaga, where his troops were 'spoiling for a fight'; Hernández and Urbina prowled the southern marches of the state; and Villa himself controlled the North-Western Railway south of Madera. Only Parral, Juárez, Casas Grandes and Chihuahua City remained in government hands, protected by the Federals' invaluable artillery, and by late June the government forces were confined to Juárez and Chihuahua.[223] The latter city had become a virtual prison for the Terrazas family, who huddled within and dared not set foot outside without an escort – which they could not get.[224] Hence their great rural patrimony was given over to the rebels, and their massive herds went to sustain revolutionary armies and pay for revolutionary arms.

Meanwhile, the Federals' loss of Chihuahua had important strategic consequences. When Sonora and Coahuila had first pioneered the rebellion against Huerta, pro-government observers had taken comfort from the fact that Chihuahua stood as a Huertista bastion in the north, separating the two insurgent entities.[225] This was no longer the case: if anything, Chihuahua had outstripped the pioneer rebellions, loosening the government's hold on the entire north, including the strategic frontier, and forcing Huerta to extend his military commitments in that zone, much to the advantage of the Sonorans. Early in June, Pascual Orozco was sent up from Torreón to fight his way through to a beleaguered Chihuahua. This he did, harassed all the way by rebel forces; but short of reinforcing (and quarrelling with) General Mercado, there was little even Orozco could do to stem the tide of rebellion.[226] And this rebellion, it bears repeating, differed from the Sonoran movement in being built from the base up, in chaotic, cumulative fashion.

Now, as in 1911, the focus of activity in the north shifted down to Durango and the Laguna, to which first Urbina then Villa turned their attention. Already the Arrietas controlled the western mountains, Pereyra and Contreras the cotton country (where more orderly, organised rebels like Maclovio Herrera took a dim view of 'Contreras and his Cuencamé gang, swollen by a rabble from the Laguna').[227] Urbina and Trinidad Rodríguez now returned to their old stamping ground near Indé and El Oro; and the government's hold on the region was further weakened by the indiscipline of its own irregulars, and the disaffection of the local railwaymen, who were reluctant to co-operate with the new regime.[228] Dozens of lesser rebel bands sprang up, 'recruited from the worse elements of labourers on ranches and in mining camps' (at least where conditions forced the mines to close); by April, Torreón seemed threatened and Durango was surrounded by 3,000 rebels, who virtually held the city under siege.[229] The American consul at Durango, who did not conceal his dislike of the rural rabble outside (many of whose acts, he commented, 'are of a nature to make the average bandit blush for shame'), nevertheless had to admit that 'these rebel hordes are today in possession of by far the greater proportion of the state of Durango and claim to be fighting for the re-establishment of the

Madero regime, for which reason they will doubtless have to be considered as a political faction'.[230] But the political aims of this popular movement – loosely summarised as the restoration of a Maderista regime – rode on the back of social, notably agrarian, discontents. Cuencamé was not unique: in 1913, as in 1911 and 1912, observers reiterated that 'the main cause of the trouble has been and still is agrarian . . . the land is a burning question and nearly all the rebels have been drawn from the agricultural labourers'.[231]

In June, Tomás Urbina came south to take command of the decentralised guerrilla campaign which blanketed Durango and the Laguna (indeed, he would only contribute his services, and those of his *gente*, in return for the local command).[232] Urbina was a classic example of a northern popular *cabecilla*. He comes, an American reported, 'from the lowest element of the people, is illiterate, obstinate, vain, but has a certain amount of native shrewdness which easily makes him a leader among his kind'.[233] John Reed, who was more partial to such types, encountered Urbina some months later, when the general – 'a broad, medium-sized man of dark, mahogany complexion, with a sparse beard . . . wide, thin, expressionless mouth . . . gaping nostrils [and] shiny, small, humorous animal eyes' – was lording it over his newly acquired Hacienda of Canutillo, surrounded, like some feudal baron, by his retainers, his offspring ('in a corner . . .sat the General's baby daughter, chewing on a cartridge'), his animals ('a tame deer and a lame black sheep'), and his current mistress ('a beautiful, aristocratic woman with a voice like a handsaw').[234] Though no doubt embellished, Reed's depiction of Canutillo is convincing.

Back in June 1913, Urbina had not yet acquired the property; nor was he laid up with rheumatism, as he was when Reed encountered him; instead, he was engaged on the capture of Durango, the first major city to fall permanently into the hands of the rebels.[235] For this, Urbina gathered 4,000 men to support the 'holy cause' which his broadsheets proclaimed, and they launched a night attack which was 'exceedingly well-planned and executed'.[236] But the aftermath was chaos. Claiming that his ammunition was low, the Federal commander told the foreign consuls he would have to evacuate; the consuls, responding to a rebel offer, agreed to parley with Urbina to arrange a peaceful occupation. But the Federals perversely kept up their fire and the consular mission failed. When Urbina's men swept into Durango in the wake of the retreating Federals on the morning of 19 June, a riot ensued. Shops were sacked, the gaol was emptied and the city archive burned; the business section of the town was reduced to ashes; light, electricity and water supplies failed. The sack lasted two days, after which total damage was estimated – in the heat of the moment – at 10m. pesos.[237] It was the story of Torreón all over again, though without the xenophobic massacre. Clearly, the fears of the well-to-do concerning mob violence were not pure fantasy; for, though the rebels had instigated the sack, they were 'ably seconded in the general looting by the lower elements in the city' – who, during the Federals' flight, had also 'hunted the officers like rabbits'.[238]

The mob's propensity to riot, amply illustrated in 1911, had not faded away; and, as before, the people of property and status who (as victims, or just spectators) recoiled from such scenes included a good many Maderistas, even those of more radical persuasion, who condemned the 'lower orders' thirst for vengeance, destruction and rapine'.[239] They were thus reminded (if a reminder were needed) of some of the social side effects of revolution, be it Maderista or Constitutionalist, and of the paramount importance of keeping their plebeian recruits on a tight rein. A more unusual feature of these events was the apparent connivance of the rebel leaders who, in 1913–14 as in 1910–11, usually respected property and avoided looting (as, indeed, Urbina's pre-battle proclamation promised that they would). In part the abortive consular mission was to blame, for it left Urbina angry, feeling that his civilised gesture had been rebuffed; and Urbina, it must be said, was hardly the most decorous of Constitutionalist commanders. But it was also clear that he and his fellow-*cabecillas* were to an extent powerless: several told the American consul 'that the men had passed completely beyond the leaders' control'; which was probably not just a shamefaced alibi. The army which took Durango – if army it can be called – was a collection of disparate bands, lacking genuine discipline or unity of command; it had been recruited hugger-mugger from the cattle ranches and cotton estates, from the indigent villages and *serrano* communities of Durango and the Laguna. The experience of Torreón in May 1911, and now of Durango in June 1913, confirmed that the revolutionaries of this section – not to mention the sympathetic *canaille* of the cities – were a particularly wild as well as powerful force and that, unrestrained by a firm hand, and confronted by the wealth of a conservative city like Durango, they would behave as Boves' *llaneros* had behaved a hundred years before at Caracas.

Eventually, Urbina recovered control, posted guards on the streets, and ordered that all plunder should be handed over to military headquarters (there was a nice irony here: in the summer of 1915 Urbina 'retired' to Canutillo with an estimated half a million pesos of bullion and banknotes, mostly booty from the sack of Durango).[240] Forced loans on the city's commercial houses now replaced material plunder; prominent citizens were ransomed (the Archbishop for 7,000 pesos); and a train load of well-to-do citizens, desperate to leave revolutionary Durango, was allowed to do so at the cost of 500 pesos per head (they included the Archbishop).[241] When, after a month of such arbitrary government, Urbina went north again ('loaded with gold', it was said), Durango breathed easier.[242] Civilian Maderistas just released from gaol took on the business of administration and Urbina's Durangueño allies, Pereyra and the Arrietas, expressed their distaste for their recent commander and his brutish, self-interested behaviour. The Arrietas, in particular, set about creating an orderly regime; one which they would control, and which would soon constitute one of the first political fiefs of the Revolution.[243]

Meanwhile in Mexico City, where the fall of Durango caused a sensation and had repercussions in the highest political circles, chilling stories concerning the fate of the city began to circulate: some factual, some little more than the titillating inventions of street-corner gossip. Most dealt with the maltreatment of the *gente decente*, and harped on well-known themes: violence and disorder, deliberate humiliation, rape, robbery and sacrilege. To avoid persecution, it was said, the respectable people of Durango were obliged to wear *huaraches*, cotton drawers and cheap *chilapeña* hats; those who emerged onto the streets well dressed were attacked to cries of 'Mueran los curros' ('Death to the dandies/fops/nobs'); their wives' jewels and gowns were stripped from them and now adorned plebeian women.[244] If embellished, these stories were very probably founded on truth, for displays of this popular, arbitrary justice occurred regularly throughout the Revolution (as in other popular upheavals).[245] Other stories were more lurid and less credible. According to the American Ambassador, 'personal letters to individuals here state that over fifty young women of the best families [of Durango] committed suicide after being ravaged'. Church property was reported desecrated: if the incumbent Archbishop escaped, at a price, the bodies of his predecessors were said to have been disinterred, and banner headlines proclaimed that the Virgin's sacred mantle now clothed a *cabecilla*'s wife.[246]

Durango set the tone for atrocity stories, which accumulated as the revolution progressed. Some were wholly apocryphal; many were intensely cultivated from tiny seeds in the hothouse atmosphere of Mexico City and the other major towns. To the well-do-do, to foreigners and to supporters of the Huerta regime in general, they offered graphic, day-to-day proof of the evil of the revolution: they were the pabulum which nourished the myth of the 'iron hand'. For what other method was appropriate for barbarians who thus persecuted respectable people, who massacred women and children, who vandalised and desecrated churches?[247] As might be expected, it was the more popular, plebeian revolutionaries (not Carranza and the Sonorans) who afforded most opportunity for such scare-mongering. Eulalio Gutiérrez had erected a guillotine in the main square of Concepción del Oro to execute the rich; Villa and Zapata not only shot prisoners-of-war, but also resorted to more refined barbarism – cutting off prisoners' ears, gouging out eyes, even removing ears, tongues and 'other parts of the body'.[248] Again, elements of truth were blown up and distorted (Gutiérrez *did* perform executions at Concepción; Villa and Zapata certainly shot prisoners; Villistas were known to slice off ears).[249] Revolution, as Mao reminds us, 'is not a dinner party, or doing embroidery'.[250] And the Huertistas committed more than their fair share of atrocities too. But these the press (increasingly a controlled, *gobiernista* press) ignored, while revolutionary abuses were inflated, headlined and broadcast; thus they found their way into the foreign press, and into diplomatic reports, which in the course of 1913–14 began to exude paranoid fears of Boxer-like atrocities and anticipations of a Peking-style siege of the legations.[251] Such myths, even though they had a toe-hold in the truth, inhibited sound judgement on the part of both foreign and Mexican elites; they legitimised Huertista policy; and they carried over into common historiographical misconceptions.[252]

The loose alliance of Chihuahuan and Durangueño forces which took Durango repeated their exploit a couple of months later at Torreón, the railway junction at the heart of the Laguna, and the strategic key to north-central Mexico. An initial attack was made in July (coinciding with Carranza's journey through the Laguna) but, after ten days' fighting, the rebels, – numbering some 6,500 – were repulsed, their shortage of ammunition telling against them.[253] Now, in September, Villa came down from Chihuahua with 2,000 men (they included Federal prisoners-of-war, used to man the rebel artillery) and, with Villa replacing Urbina as commander, a second assault was mounted.[254] Reluctant to set foot in a hostile countryside, the Torreón garrison had sat immobile for months, with fears of an epidemic rising in the beleaguered city; now, when the attack came, the Federals were ill-prepared, reinforcements were still hundreds of miles away, and munitions destined for Torreón were still at sea in the Gulf of Mexico. A rout ensued. On 1 October the garrison evacuated amid an 'avalanche of soldiers, civilians, carriages and automobiles . . . which travelled in no semblance of order', one result of which was a speedy court-martial for the Federal commander, General Munguía.[255] But if the conduct on the Federal side was reminiscent of Durango, Villa proved a more responsible victor than Urbina. Only a handful of stores were looted (chiefly the clothing stores, whose managers collected piles of discarded rebel garments, 'not only filthy but amply crawling with vermin'), and the only gutted buildings were those fired by the retreating Federals.[256] A massive forced loan was imposed, though in orderly, businesslike fashion (Americans were exempted); the sale of liquor was banned and 'splendid order' maintained throughout. Within days of the city's capture 'business was being transacted under conditions approaching the normal'.[257]

The fall of Torreón represented an even bigger rebel triumph than the capture of Durango; indeed, it was the high point of rebel achievement in 1913, for Huerta, stung by these blows, came off the ropes fighting. Torreón also established Villa as the pre-eminent caudillo of the north (Obregón seemed dilatory in comparison, and Pablo González was about to be repulsed from the gates of Monterrey).[258] And, in contrast to Urbina, Villa had shown a cool, almost statesmanlike, awareness of his responsibilities, which foreigners commented upon with wonder and relief. Though 109 Federal prisoners were shot, Villa did not otherwise engage in violent reprisals (true, he was in benign mood, having just met, wooed and married Señorita Juana Torres, a cashier in one of the city stores). Nor did he plunder Torreón for personal gain. Rather, he extorted cash for the coffers of the revolution, and so that he could pay his men the customary victory bounty.[259] He also showed an awareness of the importance of foreign, especially American, goodwill, and (in his order to the Laguna peons to return to the cotton harvest) he anticipated the need to build a self-financing war machine, devoting the economic resources of the north to the defeat of the Federals. On both counts, therefore, he took pains to encourage American business, notably the mines within his zone of operations, to whom he extended guarantees.[260] There were, then, clear signs of forward planning and organisation, complementing the rapid growth of the rebel forces. How far Villa was personally responsible it is hard to say; but most of his 'grey eminences' (Angeles, Carothers, the Maderos) were not yet at his side, and John Reed believed that Villa made his own decision.[261] And it is not implausible that the cunning and shrewdness which had seen him through twenty years of outlawry now helped him to fashion a war machine which was as much his own as anyone else's creation. Banditry could provide an adequate base for short-term, military – though not, as I shall argue, for long-term political – revolutionary mobilisation.[262] When Reed met the ragged peons of Calixto Contreras' Briganda Juárez they told him: 'we are the real volunteers. The *gente* of Villa are professionals.'[263] This came six months later; but Torreón in October 1913 showed signs of an incipient Villista professionalisation, as the northern caudillo moulded his army – not always with the army's approval – into an efficient force capable of defeating the Federals.[264]

Organisation and professionalisation were the result of size, success and ambition. As Villa and his northern host took this path, most rebels retained a certain parochial innocence. They were ill-equipped, often isolated, and had little hope of taking a major town, let alone toppling Huerta. But they thereby retained a close rapport with the common people of the countryside and an appreciation of their grievances (still the chief motor of the popular movement); and they did not risk falling prey to national ambitions, power struggles, bureaucratic ossification and graft – risks which any large movement, like Villa's, soon had to face. The multitude of lesser rebellions which pullulated in the summer of 1913 cannot be treated in any detail. But a quick regional survey reveals not only how prolific, varied, and often disunited they were; but also how closely they derived – in terms of location, membership and *modus operandi* – from the revolutionary movements of 1910–12. When circumstances were favourable, and when an 'official' revolution (then Madero's or Orozco's, now Carranza's) conferred a degree of legitimacy, the old grievances surfaced, producing the habitual, violent responses: against landlords, caciques, Federals, sometimes clerics, Spaniards and Chinese (though rarely Americans). These familiar themes will therefore reappear. And, combined with the organised revolutions of the north – Carranza's, the Sonorans' and, increasingly, Villa's – these rebellions imposed an intolerable strain, now economic as well as military, on the Huerta regime, emphasising its limitations and forcing it to adopt new, drastic policies.

Northern Zacatecas was soon cleared of Federals as rebels bands sprang up:

Pánfilo Natera's, Patricio Martínez's, Esteban Robles', Tomás Domínguez's, Santos Bañuelos', Justo Avila's.[265] Rural grievances and recruitment were all-important. Avila, a small rancher at odds with the Lobatos hacienda, raised the latter's peons in revolt, recruiting 500 men in the Fresnillo/Valparaiso region: Lobatos was an hacienda with an absentee owner and, more important, a notoriously harsh *administrador*.[266] Other properties suffered: the huge, Spanish-owned El Saucillo, near Rincón de Ramos, was sacked; peons were reported to have taken over estates at Pinos, to the east, where the *rurales* had mutinied.[267] Soon, towns became rebel targets. At the mines of Los Tocayos the entreaties of the miners' wives prevented the triumphant rebels from dynamiting the company building; at Sombrerete the *jefe* and his men held off the rebels for a while, but finally the town was taken and sacked. Now, 'no-one of the better or middle-class people can be seen on the streets'.[268] Meanwhile, Pánfilo Natera, a canny *campesino* from the turbulent community of San Juan Guadalupe (Dgo), who had fought with the late Luis Moya in 1911, sought to establish some central command within the chaos.[269] In June 1913, rebel bands were assembled for a combined assault on Zacatecas (Natera ordered all Zacatecano *cabecillas* to report within five days or be declared bandits) and on 6 June the city was attacked and taken, the 38th regiment of *rurales* defecting to the rebels during the action. Like Villa, Natera ran a tight ship. Though there were forced loans, order was maintained. Zacatecas, whose fall preceded that of Durango by a few days, was the first major rebel conquest; as the 'northern gateway to the Bajío', its loss jolted Mexico City and the government more than events in distant Sonora.[270] And, on the rebel side, Natera acquired a sudden prestige: a jaded revolutionary intellectual, reviewing the dismal prospect in Coahuila, regretted that the state could not produce 'I won't say an Obregón, since *jefes* of that stature are rare, but at least a shrewd Natera or a bold (Calixto) Contreras.'[271] Before long, as success began to knit the disparate rebel forces together, and to pluck local leaders out of provincial obscurity, Natera was summoned north to help crack the border ports of Chihuahua.

The prospect in Coahuila and the north-east was dismal in that Carranza's 'official' revolution had failed, and its leader decamped to Sonora. But rebellion proceeded, following the familiar, gradual, guerrilla pattern, and displaying the continuity, as regards places and personnel, already mentioned. In the arid country which Gertrudis Sánchez had made his own in 1911, his old allies, the Gutiérrez brothers, now came to the fore (Sánchez himself was busy in Michoacán). Luis ranged down into northern San Luis, capturing Cedral and Matehuala; Eulalio, allied to Francisco Coss (one of Carranza's Coahuilan irregulars), took Concepción del Oro at the head of 700 men, who formed their so-called 'Army for the Restoration of the Constitution'.[272] At Concepción the mining company again suffered the fracas of a rebel occupation; but 'Don Eulalio', as the company chief clerk termed him, restored order and, apart from the inevitable forced loans, foreign interests were respected.[273] Other foreigners in the region faced petty extortions: such as the American businessmen visiting the Hacienda Agua Nueva (another familiar name from 1911) who had to pay twenty pesos for a revolutionary safe-conduct.[274] But these exactions, necessary for the financing of the revolution, were not 'xenophobic' – still less were they evidence of a rising tide of Mexican nationalism. With the important exception of the Spaniards and Chinese, the vast majority of foreigners, in this region as elsewhere, went unmolested, except by the inevitable, incidental annoyances of civil war. Consular advice to the Americans of Matehuala that they should remain politically neutral and avoid joining local defence forces was probably redundant; at any rate, they complied and were not troubled by the rebels.[275] But the Spanish miner and merchant José Pérez y Pérez thought differently, assisted in the unsuccessful Federal defence of the town, and had his house sacked by the mob as a result.[276] These events neatly reflected the contrasting roles and attitudes of Americans and Spaniards in Mexico: the former more alien, marginal, and reliant on their economic power within the community; the latter more tightly integrated into the local economy (often as a seller of goods rather than an employer of labour), more politicised, and thus more vulnerable to popular reprisals.[277] The fate of the Spanish (and, for somewhat different reasons) the Chinese communities thus contrasted with that of the American. A Spanish merchant's house was shot up at Valles (SLP); all the Chinese dwellings at Tamosopo, in the same state, were burned to the ground; yet, an American settler reported from Chamal (Tamps.), the two large rebel bands operating in the vicinity 'have treated me with every consideration, while taking horses, money and arms from native Mexicans, principally from the small part of the Mexicans who favor the present government'.[278] Many similar reports are extant, from the north-east alone.[279]

Along with the brothers Gutiérrez, Ernesto Santos Coy and Jesús Dávila Sánchez (also veterans of Gertrudis Sánchez's 1911 rebellion), returned to the fray: resisting Huerta's financial blandishments they began raiding the Saltillo–Concepción railway, and joined in the attack on Matehuala.[280] Federal counter-measures to these several revolts were ineffectual. True, the Federals enjoyed superior weaponry and a near monopoly of artillery, which made possible their gradual advance from Saltillo to the American border during the summer of 1913.[281] In contrast, the burgeoning rebel forces (at Concepción, for example, a contingent of 700 soon swelled to 2,000, probably through the recruitment of unemployed miners) were ill-equipped and thus incapable of mounting sustained, conventional campaigns.[282] But they could improvise: dynamite bombs were used to reduce Matehuala; and, within days of capturing Concepción, Eulalio Gutiérrez set his men to manufacturing cannons out of the available mining equipment.[283] In addition, the mobility of rebels like Santos Coy made Federal pursuit impossible; indeed, it is not at all clear that the Federals were at all interested in pursuit anyway, since it meant venturing into hostile territory, where their intelligence was poor, and where the conscript rank-and-file had the opportunity to desert.[284] The cities, too, offered more than just security. While the official press trumpeted fictitious victories, the army commanders kept their men in barracks, while 'young officers and some of their superiors [were] living an expensive and questionable life at the best hotels'.[285] A good deal of Federal effort was thus deployed in the cities themselves, as the army assumed a growing burden of administration, as suspects were rounded up, as forced recruitment was accelerated. Typical of Federal measures – of the desire to fight the civil war by proxy, on the cheap – was the practice of taking members of revolutionaries' families as hostage, even of loading them on pilot locomotives in the hope of deterring rebel attack: victims included the wives of Jesús Acuña and Ernesto Santos Coy (who had been denied asylum in the American consulate in Saltillo); the wife and daughter of Luis Caballero; and relatives of Carranza, Gertrudis Sánchez, Francisco Coss and the brothers Gutiérrez.[286]

But the war could not be fought by proxy, on the cheap. In effect, the Federals surrendered control of the countryside: by the summer of 1913 the governors and military commanders of Zacatecas, San Luis and Coahuila admitted that they could not police beyond the major cities, and they urged landowners to undertake their own self-defence.[287] Smaller towns, mines and villages, apprised of the incapacity of the Federals, gave up appealing for troops and made terms with the rebels instead. When the Mazapil Copper Co. requested protection, the Federal commander at Monterrey declined on the grounds that Mazapil lay twelve miles outside his zone of command; the management concluded that 'the rebels were complete masters of the situation', reached an agreement with Eulalio Gutiérrez, and were thereafter more fearful of a belated Federal advance than of continued rebel dominance.[288] The Federal withdrawal from the countryside was paralleled by a general exodus of the well-to-do: a move no more than prudent, since popular hatred of officers, officials, landowners, and merchants (especially Spaniards) had by no means abated. The *jefe político* of Matehuala was shot (though, at his request, the rebels sent his embalmed body to his family in the state capital); the *jefes* of four other Potosino towns fled to San Luis; Federal officers, especially those responsible for forced recruiting, were liable to reprisals if they fell into the hands of rebels or rioters.[289] So, too, were well-to-do members of *Defensa Social* organisations, like the *muchachitos* of Matamoros, lined up and shot by Emiliano Nafarrate, somewhat to the consternation of his more sensitive revolutionary colleagues.[290]

Soon, therefore, the major cities of the north-east were packed with refugees (though usually refugees of a respectable rather than destitute kind). Men from 'the smaller mines . . . plantations and the smaller towns' flocked to San Luis with their families; ranchers abandoned their properties and made for Saltillo;

by the end of 1913 (with 'phenomenal Spanish emigration' taking place from Laguna to the capital of Coahuila) there were also signs of an exodus to the US: 'a number of the wealthier citizens of Saltillo took occasion to visit the US before the line to Laredo was destroyed. It was plainly stated by them that they did not care to take the chance of having to put up either for the government or for the revolution.'[291] Haciendas were thus left in the hands of overseers (if they dared to stay) or of peons, sharecroppers and villagers; and the smaller towns were stripped of their caciques, officials and elite families. This was the case at Cerralvo (NL) where, by the end of April 1913, following a visit by rebel forces under Jesús Agustín Castro, 'all the prominent men have left the town, the police force has resigned, the Alcalde has gone to Monterrey, and there is no law and order of any kind as there is no-one left to enforce it'.[292] The result, once popular targets had disappeared, was not necessarily mayhem; life continued in the absence of the old authorities, in ways which will later be considered. But, multiplying the example of Cerralvo many times, it is clear that both formal political, and informal, cacical, authority was much undermined. Processes begun in 1910 thus continued, forming a vital element within the social revolution. And their significance lay not just in the fact that the agents and structures of Porfirian authority were tottering, but also in the fact that revolutionary leaders felt the need and the temptation to replace them.

The process of military and political dissolution cannot be easily mapped. Historians of the Revolution are wont to trace its advance with an eye on the major cities. But their fall came at the end of a long sequence, beginning with the mountains and remote hamlets, then the villages and scattered mining camps, finally the provincial towns and state capitals. The major revolutionary armies of the north, it is true, advanced on Mexico City in 1914 in a roughly progressive, geographical fashion. But long before – and also while – this advance took place, there was a complementary revolutionary advance which cannot be mapped, save metaphorically. This took the form, not of a tide sweeping across the country, but rather of an insidiously rising water level, which first inundated the rural areas, for some time lapped around the islands of Huertismo, and finally swamped these to cover the face of the earth like Noah's flood. The islands of Huertismo were the cities. In the north-east, these remained in Federal hands through 1913 and well into 1914. Rebel attacks on Saltillo and Monterrey were successfully beaten off by well-entrenched Federal forces. Here – and in other parts of Mexico too – the turn of the year 1913/14 thus witnessed a stalemate: the Federals held the cities, the rebels the rural hinterland, and neither side could break the deadlock without greatly augmenting its resources, efforts and losses. A Federal reconquest of the countryside was out of the question, but the rebels, granted their military limitations, were hard put to storm the cities; it was a repeat of the situation of May 1911, although now the forces involved were greater, and the disposition to compromise less. Thus, at Aguascalientes in November 1913, 'it would seem that both sides are adopting a waiting policy, each fearing the other'; and a similar situation prevailed in much of northern and central Mexico, with Chihuahua, as we shall see, the exception.[293]

This stalemate left the cities unconquered but by no means unaffected. Urban industrial workers, it is true, still showed no collective disposition to join the armed revolution: when the peons of the Mexican Crude Rubber Co. of Cedral quit to join the rebels, for example, none of the factory operatives followed their lead.[294] Indeed, with the massive build-up of the Federal Army in the towns, the chances of urban riot and revolt were even further diminished: such upheavals depended more than ever on the irruption of rural, revolutionary forces from outside. It was therefore the very military build-up, and the near siege conditions which often went with it, which most affected city life. Civilian administration was rapidly dismantled; forced recruits were taken off the streets; suspects were rounded up, and many were hung or shot — especially when the proximity of rebel forces made the military authorities edgy.[295] These features of Huertista rule will be considered shortly. But, in addition, the rising tide of civil war brought a general, growing insecurity, occasional outbreaks of panic and a gradual atrophy of economic life. Though the full effects of this malaise were not evident until 1914, preliminary symptoms were felt late in the preceding year. Where the revolution of 1910 had compromised the old political order, while leaving the economy intact, that of 1913 continued the work of dissolution such that the very economic fabric of the country was now being shredded.

Long before they fell, the major cities were subject to rebel threats and incursions. Carranza, as we have seen, mounted a sustained but unsuccessful attack on Saltillo in May 1913; in June, after taking Concepción, Eualalio Gutiérrez cheekily cabled Saltillo to warn of his approach; in the same month (despite a publicised Federal victory at Arteaga) Pancho Coss proceeded to raid the eastern suburbs of the same city.[296] Four months later Saltillo again awaited a rebel attack; garbled reports confused the city's inhabitants; and, following an alleged plot to blow up the governor's palace, twenty persons were arrested and four shot.[297] Monterrey experienced similar vicissitudes. When the Constitutionalist revolution began, the command of General Lojero inspired little confidence and 'the business element, both native and foreign, was constantly alarmed'; there were fears of an impending rebel sack, and Lojero did not allay the alarm by his wholesale arrests of political suspects (including the illustrious General Treviño). Subsequent commanders did better, but even they could prevent Pablo González — scarcely the most daring of rebel commanders — from mounting a sustained attack in October, which carried the rebels into the suburbs of the city.[298] Such incidents, the object of legitimate concern, were further magnified by rumour. In the pages of the official press revolutionary victories were studiously ignored, and Federal

victories systematically manufactured; mythical fortifications figured in fictitious battles.[299] Hence rumour – which sometimes exaggerated rebel successes – flourished, probably stimulated by the influx of refugees from the
countryside; and the prevailing insecurity was compounded by the anti-
American propaganda which the regime and its provincial supporters encouraged.[300]

A prime casualty was business confidence, already shaken by the breakdown
in communications and – though this was less serious – the material damage
occasioned by the revolution. Though by the summer fears of an imminent
attack on Monterrey had subsided, commercial conditions worsened: several
industrial plants had closed, businessmen were losing money, and the price of
staples was rising fast.[301] Saltillo was even worse hit (indeed, the unease here
prompted the National Bank of Mexico to shift its north-eastern branch to
Monterrey).[302] Already, the summer had seen food shortages, and one of the
city's largest business houses had gone bankrupt.[303] Exports from the Saltillo
district in the first half of 1913 were running at half those of 1912: the chief
contributory factor was the collapse in rubber exports, brought about by the
impossibility of harvesting and processing guayule: an apposite comment on
the agrarian significance of this late Porfirian boom crop.[304] By the end of
1913, therefore, business conditions in Saltillo were deemed deplorable;
pessimism prevailed, especially among the Spanish community.[305] In San
Luis, too, exports were reckoned to be running at no more than 60% of 1912
levels and 'local business [was] exceedingly depressed'.[306] This slowing
economic tempo in the north-east in fact marked the start of a general
rallentando which would soon affect the central government, and the country
as a whole.

The civil war which engendered these conditions in the north-east was
decentralised and chaotic, especially after Carranza quit the scene, ordering his
lieutenants to go their different ways, each 'making revolution on his own
account'.[307] No Sonoran-style revolutionary machine emerged, at least until
well into 1914. Instead, a congeries of rebel leaders and their *gente* harried the
Federals and jockeyed each other for regional supremacy. Even Carranza's own
lieutenants fell out. Lucio Blanco, a Coahuilan backed by fellow-Coahuilans
Cesareo Castro and Andrés Saucedo, established his hegemony in northern
Tamaulipas: Blanco – tall, dark, handsome and affable, lacking in formal
education but with a natural talent for guerrilla campaigning – acknowledged
the authority of Carranza and of his brother, Jesús, but would take no orders
from Pablo González, Carranza's appointed commander of the north-east, and
he took umbrage at the appearance within his domain of Jesús Agustín Castro,
the Lagunero veteran of 1910, who had fought his way up from Mexico City in
the spring of 1913.[308] Squabbles developed and in October 1913 a fight
between the forces of Blanco and Castro was only narrowly averted.[309] Some
attributed Blanco's waywardness to the presence of smart civilian advisers: for,

by mid-summer, his headquarters at Matamoros had become a haven for would-be *políticos* and administrators – 'men of education and intelligence' – deprived of jobs by the failure of the Coahuilan revolution to institutionalise itself, along Sonoran lines; and whom Blanco, unlike some commanders, readily welcomed, even though he was 'of quite a different type himself'.[310]

It was these civilians, and some of the more consciously progressive junior officers, like Francisco Múgica, who proposed and carried out the division of a large hacienda near Matamoros, Los Borregos, amid much speech-making, ceremony, and playing of stirring music, the Marseillaise included.[311] This has been seen as a highly significant act: the start of the revolutionary agrarian reform; and, even at the time, it attracted the attention of the great Jean Jaurès who, in the pages of *L'Humanité*, declared that he now understood what the Mexicans were fighting about.[312] What was particularly significant was the role played by civilians like Manuel Urquidi (who had been the first treasurer of the old Anti-Re-electionist Party) and Múgica, a student activist and journalist recently possessed of a somewhat decorative military rank; for it was these two, along with Guillermo Castillo Tapia, who undertook the administration of this inaugural land grant, and it was Múgica who delivered a speech 'full of patriotism and fine ideas' to the assembled *campesinos*. The orators, intellectuals and middle-class reformers (who in this case also included Ramón Puente, J. G. Hermosillo, Federico Gonazález Garza and Alberto Fuentes) were coming to appreciate not only the social justice but also the political utility of agrarian reform, and were losing some of the liberal inhibitions they had shown during the Madero presidency.[313] And there was an additional irony (not the last to be perpetrated in the course of the revolutionary agrarian reform): Castillo Tapia, who played a major role in these proceedings, had recently arrived from Havana as an emissary of Félix Díaz, whose affection for Huerta had much diminished of late; now keen for an entrée into the revolution, the tall, well-dressed Castillo Tapia set out to establish his political credentials by helping carve up Los Borregos: whose owner was – Félix Díaz.[314]

Both Blanco's espousal of agrarian reform and his propensity to feud with fellow-Constitutionalists earned him Carranza's displeasure and a swift transfer to Sonora, whither he was followed by lieutenants like Barragán and Saucedo.[315] While Blanco thus played a major part in Obregón's west coast campaign, Pablo González was left to direct strategy in the north-east, and to achieve some sort of unity among the rebels fighting in Tamaulipas, Coahuila, Nuevo León and points south. But González (a 'military dullard', according to one authority) found the reduction of Monterrey and Nuevo Laredo beyond him; and, despite the backing of Jesús Carranza, he could not unite his dissident subordinates who – like Antonio Villareal and Francisco Murguía – continued bickering to the detriment of the Constitutionalist war effort.[316] The impression of decentralised chaos (which some observers mistakenly took as evidence of an aimless, unprincipled revolution) thus remained strong; and, further south, in regions which González also sought optimistically to control, the fragmentation of revolutionary power, the absence of central direction, and the contrast with the orderly revolution of Sonora, were even more marked.[317]

In the region tributary to San Luis, for example, (comprising the state of San Luis, southern Tamaulipas and the Huasteca) ten different rebel bands could be discerned in May 1913; by the end of the year, their number had risen to thirty-three, totalling 5,000 men.[318] The Federals, torpid and fearful of desertions, clung to the state capital, leaving other towns and villages vulnerable, and compelling the local well-to-do, like those of Tula (Tamps.), to seek refuge in San Luis.[319] Local self-defence was difficult, since 'the majority of the population do not want protection against the Carrancistas. That part of the rural population which would be available for purposes of defence does not favour the Federal Government'; the peons, in other words, would not fight for Huerta against the rebels, unless compelled.[320] And *hacendado* recruitment of 'white guards', though attempted, was unsuccessful.[321] The pattern of revolutionary activity was confusing and chaotic; but its intensity was clear enough, and indicative of the widespread popular rejection of the Huerta regime and what it stood for, that is, 'a return to the old, Porfirian order which had protected the ambitions of expansionist landlords like the Espinosa y Cuevas'.[322] Amid the confusion, familiar names and places recurred. In the Cd Victoria/Xicontencatl region of southern Tamaulipas, the Nafarrete brothers soon led over 1,000 men; Vicente Salazar levied the oil companies of the Huasteca, where the *ranchero* families who had backed Madero now took up arms to resist Huerta's counter-revolution: Manuel Lárraga occupied Valles after the Federal garrison had mutinied and shot up the town; Pedro de los Santos, the young Maderista rebel and would-be governor of 1911, revolted near Tamazunchale, was caught, executed, and later personally avenged by his brother.[323] And the familiar victims of popular resentments were again sought out: the Spaniards and Chinese, military officers, officials and landlords; between September and December 1913 alone twenty-four haciendas in San Luis were attacked.[324]

Hence, in San Luis as elsewhere, the Constitutionalist revolution displayed the same internal ambivalence which had marked the Maderista: on the one hand, the recourse to civil war and the sustained attack on authority led to acts of popular violence and vengeance, perpetrated by 'mobs', 'bandits', 'alleged revolutionaries'; on the other hand, respectable, politically literate Constitutionalist leaders sought to maintain order, protect property, and weld together an organised military force capable of ousting Huerta. In San Luis, this ambivalence was represented by the division between the populists of Valle del Maíz, and the *rancheros* of the Huasteca; it was also personally embodied in the feud between the Cedillo and Barragán families.[325] As a student on vacation in his home town of Cd del Maíz, Juan Barragán had helped the local authorities resist an attack by Cedillo's forces at the end of 1912; for Barragán, scion of a rich landed family, the Cedillos were 'individuals without convictions or ideals', bent on making trouble and looting property. Both, however, were sucked into the Constitutionalist revolution in 1913: Barragán as a self-styled 'liberal and patriot', linked to Maderista interests in the state; the Cedillos as popular revolutionaries, continuing their struggle against local landlords (among whom the Barragáns figured).[326] Despite their common Constitutionalist affiliation, they were fundamentally antagonistic – just as Enrique Añorve and the Indians of Ometepec had been in 1911, notwithstanding their common 'Maderismo'. Accordingly, the Cedillos raided the Barragán ranch, El Carrizal, and were chased into the sierra; Barragán and his allies, including the itinerant martinet Castro, saved the owner of La Concepción hacienda from hanging at the hands of the Cedillos.[327]

As an ambitious, nationally aware young rebel, Barragán followed Castro north, and subsequently joined Carranza in Sonora. The Cedillos, true to type, stayed in San Luis. Following their 1912 rebellion, they had briefly dallied with the new regime; but they were under no illusions as to its character, their terms could not be met, and, with some 800 followers, they returned to the path of revolution.[328] Their national political affiliations had been – and to an extent remained – fluid. When they entered Cárdenas in February 1913 they carried a red flag and claimed to support Orozco and Vázquez Gómez. Now, these figureheads of 1912 had been superseded, and Orozco was about to throw in his lot with Huerta. Such national labels meant little anyway, and a surer guide to the Cedillos' politics was provided by their subsequent conduct in San Luis. Linking up with Alberto Carrera Torres, they harried the San Luis-Tampico railway line and soon came to dominate the country between Tula and Cd del Maíz.[329] There a form of 'simple communism' came to prevail: the Cedillos' peon troops were paid in kind rather than cash; families were issued with food, while artisans supplied shirts, *rebozos*, *huaraches* and palm-leaf hats. Meantime, the troops continued their peacetime work, cutting the *lechuguilla* fibre in the fields of abandoned haciendas, so that the Cedillos could sell the product and purchase arms.[330] Like Villa, they saw the need to maintain such local production to sustain the war; but their approach was more genuinely *agrarista* than Villa's. In their 'Executive Law for the Distribution of Land', issued by the Cedillos and Carrera Torres in March 1913, they denounced Huerta and promised the division of all estates belonging to Huertistas; these lands would be conferred on both rebel and Federal soldiers and their families; they would be inalienable and coupled with credit facilities to help cultivation. In addition, 'the Indians of all the Republic' were guaranteed the return of their lands despoiled by the 'Porfirista bandits'.[331] Copies of the new law were posted up in towns and villages: at first, the common people seemed incredulous, while the landowners laughed.[332] But the Cedillos' actions soon underwrote their promises. As the attacks on the landlord class mounted (with the Spaniards suffering most, Americans relatively little), it became 'obvious that the haciendas were the chief targets of the revolutionary movement'.[333] And the American consul in San Luis, dolefully reviewing what he termed the 'social warfare against property', predicted that repression would provide no answer, that 'readjustment is indicated', and that 'it must be at the expense of the landowners'.[334] As the landowners were driven out, estates expropriated, and peons' debts cancelled, the Cedillos and Carrera Torres created a popular agrarian movement that would endure for years, and survive the deaths of most of its leaders.[335]

Further south, where the Mesa Central tumbles down to the hot, coastal lowlands, such durable revolutionary movements failed to materialise. Here, closer to Mexico City, the Huerta government achieved greater vigilance (as Díaz had done in 1910), the local forces of order were stronger, and the plantations were no breeding grounds of rebellion. Veracruz witnessed sporadic revolts, involving familiar protagonists: Camerino Mendoza tried to raise the textile workers of Santa Rosa in protest at the killing of Madero but – again note the parallel with 1910 – to no avail; Mendoza was executed, as was the captured rebel leader Daniel Herrera, shot 'while trying to escape'.[336] Revolts led by Maderista officials at Zongólica and Acultzingo were summarily put down; indeed, the sole revolutionary success in the spring of 1913 came when the brothers Márquez, opportunist veterans of 1911, raised 200 men and took Misantla.[337] More typically, the old Porfirista, General Gaudencio de la Llave, deployed his thuggish retainers in the Atoyac region, shooting 'men of the peon class', and ensuring that the planters would enjoy peace and quiet during the rainy season.[338] Indeed, the rains themselves were a deterrent to rebellion, for in Veracruz – unlike Sonora – the practice of rebellion was still closely tied to the agricultural cycle, and thus subject to marked seasonal fluctuations.[339] Through the summer of 1913, therefore, rebellion was at a low ebb: debt-peons were still recruited in Veracruz and consigned to the Valle Nacional estates, where they were held 'as if . . . criminals, locked up in barracoons, ill-treated and abused'; while at Orizaba (unlike the industrial towns of the north) business continued to boom.[340] Late in the summer, the Veracruz state government – generalising its own feeling of confidence – informed local mayors that no military threat remained 'in the greater part of the states of the Republic', that the only infractions of order were the work of common bandits, and that *hacendados* should counter these with their own private forces.[341]

The same was true of Tabasco. Here, as in other states, observers noted a strong undercurrent of resentment at the killing of Madero; but this was not translated into effective protest.[342] True, the usual *municipios* of Cárdenas, Huimanguillo and Paraíso began to experience trouble: plantations were attacked, and scattered battles were fought with obscure marauders. A degree of leadership and organisation was provided by Carlos Greene and his allies, based on Greene's *rancho* San Pedro; but their capture of Cárdenas and Huimanguillo, in April 1913, was short-lived, and later attempts to take Cárdenas and Comalcalco all failed.[343] Attacks of this kind might involve 400 men; and there were reckoned to be some 2,000 rebels in the entire state in the late summer of 1913; but they mostly operated in small contingents of no more than 50 (a little above the optimal size of Hobsbawm's bandit companies), and to local observers they seemed no more than 'a rabble of Indian labourers without arms or competent leaders'.[344] By the end of 1913 the revolution in Tabasco was at a low ebb, and the Mexico City press pronounced its obituary.[345] But Greene's forces were still in being, desperate for arms and ammunition, and a second *foco* had been established under Luis Felipe Domínguez, in the eastern district of Los Ríos, whence the rebels launched raids into neighbouring Chiapas.[346] In the latter state, simmering discontent and sporadic rebellion were likewise evident, but could not break the control of army and planter; and Yucatán, too, remained generally quiet, its most notable contribution to the revolution in these years being Lino Muñoz's popular but highly specific revolt against the lecherous *jefe político* of Progreso.[347] Not least among the troubles of the Gulf states in this period were those imported from outside, as a result of the regime's policy of dumping rebel prisoners-of-war in the remote security of the insalubrious south. Over 100 prisoners, drafted into the army, and shipped to sweaty garrisons along the Gulf, rebelled against their officers at Frontera and seized a steamship, which at once capsized, drowning many of them; while at Mérida (Yuc.), 180 Zapatistas fought a two hour battle before they were subdued, and their leaders executed.[348]

Along the Gulf, peace and order roughly correlated with the plantation. Where the plantocracy ruled – typically in Yucatán – rebellion was at a discount. Conversely, in a more variegated state like Veracruz, rebel and bandit activity grew over time, especially in upland regions of peasant agriculture. By the late summer of 1913, the growing incidence of raids and robberies suggested a weakening of authority in the countryside; by the following spring and summer the condition had become chronic, with landlords in the cantons of Jalapa, Orizaba, Córdoba, Zongólica, Acayucán and Los Tuxtlas complaining of constant rebel/bandit demands – demands which had to be cautiously contested, haggled over, but ultimately met, at some agreed figure, since the Federals and *rurales* offered no protection.[349] A good deal of this was no doubt the work of (unsocial) bandits, or even irresponsible *rurales*.[350] But the harassment of landowners (seen by the landowners themselves and, thus, by many derivative commentators as pure banditry) was a necessary part of rural guerrilla warfare, as pursued by such irreproachable revolutionaries as Zapata. And there is sufficient evidence of genuine rural (and specifically agrarian) revolt in Veracruz to call into question the prevalent view, represented by Fowler and Falcón, whereby the vigorous peasant movement of the 1920s and 1930s leaps fully grown from the head of urban labour, owning no rural parentage, experiencing no gestation period during the decade of armed revolt.[351]

This is hard to credit. True, rural rebellion was localised and inarticulate; true, it often faced defeat, not just at the hands of Huerta and the Federals, but also more gradually and subtly at the hands of landlords and their 'revolutionary' allies (a process with which Fowler and Falcón are quite familiar). If, as E. H. Carr would have us think, only the success stories of history merit attention, then the Veracruzano agrarian movement of 1910–20 might be justly ignored; but Fowler makes a point of writing history (and good history) 'from the point of view of those who are the losers . . . those who are consigned to the dustbins of history'.[352] In that case, the neglect cannot be justified; and analysis of rural rebellion in 1910–20 might even suggest both a greater continuity over time, and a greater significance of autonomous, rural (as against exogenous, urban) factors in the long term evolution of the Veracruzano peasant movement after 1920.

The American consul at Veracruz was scarcely sympathetic to rebellion; he deplored the violence and economic upheaval occasioned by the Revolution; and, like most of his kind, he made much of banditry, highway robbery, and 'apolitical' attacks on persons and property. But by means of a network of contacts throughout the state he kept closely in touch with rural conditions and, if he failed to articulate his views in the deft analytical manner of his colleague at San Luis, he was nevertheless clear about the root cause of popular upheaval in the state:[353]

[the] agrarian question in fact has always been the cause of most of the unrest in this state. Tradition has taught these peasants [that] this acquisition of lands [by outsiders] is an ineffable injustice to themselves. Agitators may gain their ears and they may call themselves Zapatistas or Carrancistas; yet in the state of Veracruz the uprisings are purely local in their significance. The Indians do not bother themselves as to who may be in the presidential chair, if only they can gain the liberties their ancestors enjoyed. Sometimes they cannot tell for what principle they are fighting. Nevertheless, their raids are not made in a spirit of lawlessness; abuses exist and the realisation that they have suffered too long makes a reaction in such an extreme form seen lawful to this people. No changes in the central government will satisfy them, whatever promises are made, and until reforms have fundamentally altered the whole economic situation this discontent will continue to prevail.

Thus, an outside, unsympathetic observer neatly summed up the character of peasant protest in Veracruz (and, indeed, elsewhere): grievances were parochial, particular, poorly articulated, yet laden with moral sentiment ('ineffable injustice'); in the absence of peaceful, institutional forms of redress, they were now settled violently and directly; and would continue to be until some 'fundamental' reform – no mere nominal change of president – were undertaken. Concrete examples bore this out. At Aquila, where the municipal president had alienated the community's water rights to the town of Maltrata, the people revolted, burned the courthouse and killed the offending official.[354] When the Huertista authorities sought a truce with Bartolo Cabanzo, then leading a revolt in the canton of Zongólica, he[355]

gave them to understand that he is not a Carrancista, nor does he have any links with any contending party, but that what he desires is that the Indians of the region whom he leads be given possession of their lands, and likewise those who are said to have been despoiled by hacienda proprietors, and that they be left in complete liberty ... to name local authorities from among individuals of their own patch of land, and of their own estimation and trust.

This powerful amalgam of *serrano* and *agrarista* sentiment was most commonly found in those upland regions where the villages could better fend off the authority of state and landlord: in the Malintzi highlands of southern Tlaxcala, for example, where the revolutionary families of 1910–11 resurfaced and established themselves, initiating a conquest of the countryside which neither Federals, nor white guards, nor volunteer units could prevent.[356] In Veracruz, too, in the spring of 1914, peace-loving people trekked down from the troubled sierra to the relative calm of the *tierra caliente*.[357] Now, furthermore, the government's efforts at forced recruitment were providing an additional spur to rebellion. When forty rebels ('sin credo determinado') took Zongólica at dawn on 10 January 1914, they followed the familiar procedure, opening the town gaol, ransacking the *jefatura*, the municipal treasury and the courthouse, making a bonfire of the legal documents in the street, and looting five commercial houses. The mayor was wounded and the *jefe*, caught trying to phone for help, beaten up, the rebels telling him 'that they had put an end to his consignments to the army, the press-gang, and all the malpractices which had characterised his administration'.[358]

Indeed, the Huerta regime's indiscrimate use of the *leva* now served to generalise the very rebellious condition it was meant to curtail. Federal recruiting officers began to comb the Puebla sierra in mid-summer 1913, coercing the Indians into the army.[359] Hitherto, the sierra had been relatively peaceful: though he had fought long ago in the War of the Reform, the local cacique, Juan Francisco Lucas, was no war-monger; in 1912 he had been more concerned to get his son elected to the state congress, to which end he secured the good offices of President Madero.[360] When the *leva* began its work in the mountains, Lucas protested to the government, got no satisfaction, and finally rebelled in alliance with the local rebel veteran, Esteban Márquez: they fought to end conscription and to assert local autonomy; they were representatives, in effect, of a new wave of *serrano* protest, engendered by the Revolution itself. By mid-September, Lucas, riding in his old sedan chair, was leading 2,000 men in an attack on Teziutlán. After a week's fighting, with honours even, negotiations were opened, with the chief clerk of the nearby American copper company acting as intermediary (he alone was acceptable to both sides: an apt illustration of the neutral attitude of foreign companies in the midst of revolution). The rebels' 'complaints and desires were based entirely on local conditions', which the deal they finally reached fully reflected. The troops of Esteban Márquez would form the Brigada Serrana, to be paid by the Federal government for policing the region around Teziutlán, Zacatlán, Alatriste, Jalacingo, and Papantla; all Federal troops would withdraw from this territory, political prisoners would be released, and the Brigada Serrana would have the right to name all local officials. Pressganged Indians would be allowed to quit the army and join the Brigada, and all forced recruitment would cease. Finally, as from the beginning of 1914, free primary education would be provided for all.[361] The agreement was a *serrano* charter, indicative of the strength of Lucas' *cacicazgo*, and of the regime's belated recognition of the power of affronted provincialism. Accommodation was more feasible here than in the case of Zapata for, while the *serranos'* desire to be left alone was ultimately subversive of the state, it was a milder, less contagious form of subversion than the *agraristas'* assault on property rights; compared with Zapatismo, *serrano* protest was remote and inarticulate; furthermore – in this as in many other cases – the *serrano* rebellion was captained by traditional caciques of conservative mien.

Nevertheless, Huertista tolerance of *serrano* pretensions was grudging and potentially dangerous. In Oaxaca, a renewed *serrano* rebellion was discouraged by the pre-emptive arrest of the caciques of the Sierra Juárez, Hernández and Meixueiro (who happened also to be partisans of Félix Díaz); though there were reports of trouble in the spring of 1913, serious rebellion was postponed until the fall of Huerta and the release of these traditional leaders.[362] But in the Puebla sierra, the negotiated agreement – if satisfactory to Lucas and Márquez – did not placate all their followers, who perhaps fancied more fighting and spoils, or perhaps sought to go beyond the narrow, particularist aims of their leaders (Márquez, certainly, was a conservative opportunist). At any rate, by the autumn of 1913, Indian bands infested the sierra around Teziutlán, robbing local merchants, billeting themselves overnight in anxious towns and villages.[363] One day they rode into Aire Libre, crying 'Viva Zapata!' and 'exhibiting ample evidence of complete frenzy caused by intoxication'; their leader, who claimed to have fought with Zapata in Morelos, extorted some guns from the copper company. Meanwhile, as the revolution in the north slowly progressed, Lucas and his allies became concerned lest their local deal should brand them as Huertistas, invite the retribution of the Constitutionalists, and thereby revive the whole vexed question of alien interference in the sierra. They therefore contacted the American consul at Veracruz, asking him to 'approach the revolutionaries on their behalf and explain that they are not hostile'.[364] This required Washington's approval; and it fell to William

Jennings Bryan, the epitome of mid-Western parochialism, to turn his narrow mind to this distant problem, ponder the petition of the Teziutlán Indians, and authorise the good offices of the US on their behalf.[365]

The Lucas/Márquez rebellion reached as far north as the old trouble spot of Papantla, where the cultivation of vanilla had brought fortunes for a few, landlessness for many (notably the Indian peasantry), and a history of trouble and disaffection.[366] As was often the case in such situations, a long-serving *jefe político* became the focus of popular resentment.[367] In May 1913, a minor rebellion at Papantla was put down; a month later, Alejandro Vega and the Márquez brothers led a successful attack (described in one of the best *corridos* of the Revolution), advancing out of the rain from Coazintla, storming the town cemetery.[368] The local Indians were known to be sympathetic to the rebels; when the attack came, the Indians in the garrison at once deserted, the Federals dug in and manned the church tower, while the well-to-do (*los señores vainilleros*) hid in the cellars of their houses.[369] During the battle, the rain sheeted down, swamping the Federals' trenches and running in the pitted streets. By afternoon, the town was in rebel hands, the surviving Federals had surrendered, the *señores vainilleros* had emerged from hiding (to what unpleasant fate we do not know). At least, the *corrido* concludes, the common people of Papantla had proved they were 'of rebel stock, and no mere rag-dolls'.[370]

Of the men of Morelos, no such proof was required. In this panorama of popular rebellion, taking in most states of central Mexico in 1913–14, Morelos once again stood out, as it had in 1911–12. But it stood out less for the peculiarity of its grievances which (*pace* some analyses) were clearly evident in many other regions, than for their intensity and concentration, which were paralleled by the intense and concentrated activity of the Zapatistas. Hence Zapatismo became the pacemaker of revolution in south/central Mexico, affording an example and inspiration to popular movements from Puebla and Tlaxcala in the east across to Mexico, Guerrero, and the Costa Grande in the west. The revolution of the Mesa Central thus pivoted upon Morelos: it was here that Huerta faced his most proximate threat, and here that the northern Constitionalists encountered the most serious challenge to their revolutionary hegemony.

The Zapatista revival which marked the closing weeks of 1912 was given an extra fillip by the evacuation of Federal troops from Morelos during the *Decena Trágica*. When, therefore, Huerta began angling for the adherence of the Zapatistas, the latter were in a strong position, dominating the countryside and holding several provincial towns.[371] Huerta's overtures met with a limited response; and the new president soon committed himself to a policy of root-and-branch repression, appointing General Juvencio Robles – a man after his own heart – to continue where he had left off in 1912. Martial law was declared and Governor Leyva, 'who did not seem to be a decided supporter of the present government', was among the first of the state executives to fall. His constitutional successor, Benito Tajonar, was arrested along with the whole state legislature for refusing to sanction a military take-over of the state.[372] Robles became military governor, endorsed by most (though not all) Morelos planters, who readily placed their faith in peace, *cueste lo que cueste*; and Morelos' middle-of-the-road reformers – Leyva, Tajonar, Díez, Morales – became scattered fugitives and prisoners or, in some cases, grudging converts to hard-line Huertismo. As a result, 'the party of lawful reform in Morelos' disappeared, an early victim of Huertista government, and the ambiguous, three-way split in Morelos politics, which in 1912 had jeopardised the survival of a vigorous, belligerent Zapatismo, was resolved in favour of a clear dichotomy, from which Zapata and the guerrillas could not but benefit.[373]

Zapata's response to the establishment of military rule was swift. Jonacatepec was attacked and fell after thirty-six hours' fighting. The rebels acquired arms, horses and hundreds of prisoners; the latter were liberated on condition they undertook not to fight against the revolution in future; and one, the ancient veteran Higinio Aguilar, joined the Zapatistas, providing a useful and personally lucrative information service concerning corrupt Federals who dealt in contraband arms.[374] Rebellion in Morelos – unlike rebellion in the far north – directly affected Mexico City: Zapatista activity around Yautepec disrupted the marble quarries and halted work on the National Theatre and the new London and Mexico Bank.[375] Hence, with Zapatismo resurgent, with Cuautla and Cuernavaca threatened, and with the pampered metropolis sensing the tremors of proximate, popular rebellion, Huerta went to extreme lengths to suffocate the *suriano* revolt. While the Sonorans consolidated their position in the north-west, and the Federals undertook their dilatory advance into Coahuila, troops were poured into Morelos in an attempt to blot out Zapata: Morelos became the main priority. Within the cabinet there was criticism of this policy: Carranza, unlike Zapata, was *presidenciable*; a potential president and serious rival for national power, and the northern revolution, with its educated cadres and incipient professionalisation, posed a greater threat to Huerta than the rabble of Morelos.[376] But Huerta paid little attention to his cabinet anyway, and preferred to press ahead with his policy of repression in Morelos, using all the familiar techniques of primitive counter-insurgency campaigns, with which he was intimately familiar: the 'concentration' of the civilian population; the razing of disaffected *pueblos*; summary executions and mass forced conscription.[377] By 'the end of 1913', a villager recalled, '. . . you couldn't even step out of the village because if the government came and found you walking, they killed you'.[378]

It has been argued that Huerta's slow progress in Chihuahua in 1912 derived not from disloyalty to Madero, but rather from his prudent realisation, based on experience in Yucatán and Morelos, that 'the Mexican army was not equipped to engage in anti-guerrilla operations'.[379] Yet in Morelos in 1913

Huerta sanctioned the whole gamut of heavy-handed, counter-productive measures employed by Robles. This was Huerta's way of doing things; this was the quest for 'peace, cost what it may'. Even before Robles took up his command, Huerta was planning a major offensive in Morelos and talking of the forced deportation of 20,000 Morelenses to the plantations of Quintana Roo – the old Yaqui war policies, now to be applied to villagers just across the mountains from Mexico City.[380] And to the elite of the Jockey Club Huerta promised 'deeds . . . not words', called for the forbearance of the Morelos planters (those 'favoured of fortune') who would incur property losses, and intimated that 'the government [was] going, so to speak, to depopulate the state' in order to extirpate Zapatismo.[381] Huerta, as president, saw no virtue in a conciliatory approach and placed his faith in a Roman peace.

Furthermore a Roman peace was unattainable. Illusions persisted: throughout Morelos, village populations melted away at the approach of a Federal column, and the state came to resemble a desert, dotted with blackened skeletons of burned villages and small towns.[382] Eager for success and promotion, Robles drove on to the Zapatista headquarters at Huautla, in the southern part of the state, which, he resolved (if not in so many words) would be Morelos' Verdun, where Zapatismo would be cornered and bombarded into submission. But the Zapatistas were not the *poilus* of the Western Front. As three Federal columns converged on Huautla, the rebels dispersed into Puebla and Guerrero; the Federal artillery pounded a deserted site; and Robles staged a triumphal entry which pleased Mexico City and brought the desired promotions. In Huautla he claimed to find a large cache of arms and documents; he also found the bodies of Pascual Orozco (senior), and other Huertista envoys, who, sent to win Zapata's submission, had been summarily executed. For Robles, Morelos was now 'pacified', and, within weeks, as Huerta began to switch troops to the north, Robles was withdrawn along with several thousand Federals.

But Morelos had not been pacified. The vanished villagers and guerrillas made for the hills, and it was here that the 'concentration' promised by Robles' strategy was in fact achieved, in the burgeoning rebel encampments. Life in the hills was hard and hungry, but the operations of the *leva*, the deportations, the burning of villages, and the Federal embargo on food supplies only stiffened the resolve of the country people.[383] The minority of active Zapatistas in the state was now seconded by a host of new recruits and sympathisers, won over by the indiscriminate repression of the army. At Tepoztlán, hitherto on the fringes of Zapatismo, the villagers may have coveted neighbouring hacienda land, promised them by the rebels; but they ultimately joined the rebellion out of self-defence: 'were it not for the terrible abuses of the Federales it is probable that most Tepoztecans would have remained neutral'.[384] Hence the Zapatistas' numbers grew fast: they included even a women's battalion from Puente de Ixtla which 'under the command of a husky ex-tortilla maker

called La China . . . raided wildly through [the] Tetecala district', avenging
the deaths of their men.[385] Zapatista activity also spilled over into Puebla,
Guerrero and Mexico, and Zapata began to liaise with revolutionary leaders in
these neighbouring states.[386] Indeed, as his allies and subordinates became
more numerous, Zapata now found it necessary to plan, regulate, and organise
more than in the past. Though the Morelos revolution could never and would
never become professionalised, like that of Sonora, it needed to transcend the
parochialism and spontaneity of its early existence if it was to confront the
reinforced Federal Army and its obdurate leadership.

This process of organisation demanded talents which were in short supply in
Morelos; it therefore attracted a new breed of outsider – men who, at least, had
not figured in the early days of the rebellion. Successful *cabecillas*, pitched into
positions of military power and political authority, felt the need for orators,
secretaries, administrators, and political fixers, who might perform the
necessary, if unsavoury, tasks which the *cabecillas* themselves disdained; or, as
Lucio Blanco put it to Francisco Múgica (one of many such individuals who
made their way to Blanco's camp): 'in this campaign we're going to need words
as well as guns, and I want to get hold of one of those liars who knows how to
talk'.[387] Zapata's equivalent scribe, secretary and official spokesman was
Manuel Palafox, a 'short, spindly, pockmarked' young man, with a background in engineering, salesmanship and accountancy, and – so it was said –
unorthodox sexual tastes.[388] Having worked in different parts of the Republic,
acquiring experiences of places and practices (including 'the finer points of
hustling') denied the Morelos villagers, Palafox in 1911 was employed on the
eastern borders of Morelos; here, entrusted with conveying a bribe to Zapata,
he fell in with the rebels, who found his familiarity with the north useful in the
execution of political missions. When Pascual Orozco senior and his Huertista
colleagues were put on trial, Palafox was the prosecutor. And in 1913 he
emerged as the managerial spirit behind the new, organised Zapatismo.

First, the Plan of Ayala, overtaken by events, had to be revised. Zapata
replaced Orozco as the national leader of the revolution; Orozco and Huerta
were excoriated as traitors and usurpers. A Revolutionary Junta of the South
was set up, incorporating half-a-dozen prominent *cabecillas*, with Zapata as
president and Palafox as secretary.[389] What had hitherto been the spontaneous
decisions of local bands – concerning pay, provisions, forced loans – now
became subject to some central regulation. Leaders were enjoined to change
officials 'in accordance with the will of the people', and to offer 'moral and
material support' to villages demanding the restitution of their lands: this
generalised and codified existing Zapatista practice. In October 1913, with
Zapata's headquarters established in northern Guerrero, further directives
were issued, designed to co-ordinate the military campaigns: non-commiss-
ioned ranks were instituted, with the proviso that the *gente* of one chief should
obey the officers of another; the supply and distribution of pay were regulated;

desertion became a crime. These represented attempts – not altogether successful – to 'break down the clannish loyalties among the revolutionary forces and to consolidate direction and authority in a regular military hierarchy'.[390]

By the end of 1913, Zapata was concluding deals with rebel leaders as far afield as the Costa Chica, and husbanding every rifle and cartridge for a thrust into Guerrero which would be the prelude for a march on Mexico City. Guerrero, of course, had its own powerful revolutionary movement, dating from 1911; Julián Blanco in the central region of the state, the Figueroas in the north; Silvestre Mariscal on the Costa Grande, and Jesús Salgado in the *tierra caliente*.[391] Huerta's coup forced these leaders to take stock and reconsider – often in pragmatic, 'non-ideological' fashion – their relations both with each other and with the central government.[392] Initially, therefore, a fragile truce prevailed, and some rebels entered Huerta's service. But within weeks the situation began to change. Gertrudis Sánchez raised the standard of revolt at Coyuca in March 1913 and launched an offensive across the Balsas into Michoacán; through the summer he carried all before him, and the tremors of rebellion reached the far Pacific coast, where authority wilted.[393] Though an outsider and native of Coahuila, Sánchez collaborated with the local chiefs, whose fortunes varied. In April 1913, Rómulo Figueroa rebelled and briefly occupied Chilapa; facing a strong Federal counter-attack he had to seek refuge with Sánchez in Michoacan; meanwhile, his brother Ambrosio, Zapata's great rival of 1911, fell into Federal hands and was executed in June.[394] With the Figueroas' star in decline, other leaders could assert their predominance in Guerrero, and Zapata's quest for allies was advanced.

Already, Zapatistas from Morelos were spilling over into Guerrero, and operated even within the Figueroa bailwick of Huitzuco; and, late in 1913, as Huerta's grasp of Guerrero faltered, Julián Blanco went over to the revolution, accepting Zapata's leadership, as did the local *agrarista* Jesús Salgado.[395] Unlike many revolutionary affiliations, these were real and effectual: Blanco and Salgado, along with other Guerrero leaders, signed the Plan of Ayala, collaborated with Zapata militarily and economically, and fought alongside him in the grand joint action which brought the fall of Chilpancingo, the state capital, in the spring of 1914.[396] Of the major Guerrero leaders, only Silvestre Mariscal resisted the Zapatista embrace and remained loosely loyal to Huerta. But if the Costa Grande thereby seemed ostensibly secure, its security was deceptive and inspired little confidence among the well-to-do of Acapulco. Huerta's recruitment of the ex-rebel forces of Mariscal and Radilla (1,000 men, now armed with Mausers) merely gave power into the hands of local irregulars, in most respects indistinguishable from the rebels they were meant to suppress. Indeed, Mariscal showed no disposition to start the suppression; his men, it was noted, 'feel no grievance against their bandit brethren, they are never very enthusiastic in their pursuit'; Mariscal and Blanco were, for the moment, *compadres*, while Mariscal's chief *bête noire* remained the Spanish merchant community of Acapulco. As a result, 'the people in Acapulco seem to be more afraid of Mariscal and his men coming into town than they are of the rebels'.[397]

While Mariscal played his usual maverick role, dallying with Huerta, spurning Zapatismo, and thereby establishing a semi-independent political and military fief for himself, the bulk of the Guerrero rebels had clearly gone over to Zapata by 1914. By now, Zapata captained a genuine alliance of revolutionaries operating in Morelos, Guerrero, Puebla and Mexico, penning the Federals in the major towns, and prevented only by their chronic shortage of arms from assaulting these last bastions of Huertismo. The growth of the movement brought fresh demands and problems. It was felt necessary to make contact with the rebels of the north, and to plead the Zapatista case in the US – in the hope (illusory as it turned out) of securing belligerent status and arms supplies.[398] The veterans of Morelos – some of them disenchanted with Zapata's campaigning in Guerrero – had to be placated or disciplined. In all this (the broadening political horizons, the diplomacy, the expanded administration) the hand of Manuel Palafox was evident; but he did no more than fulfil a role necessitated by the steady, organic growth of the *suriano* rebellion, which still remained essentially the rebellion of Zapata and the villagers.

HUERTISMO: I CABINET, CONGRESS AND *COLOSO DEL NORTE*

Zapata, Carranza, and Huerta, too, all faced intertwined military and political problems, the result of an escalating civil war. Huerta – much as he might have liked to – could not abolish politics; and the political decisions he took, domestically and internationally, impinged upon his preferred military solutions. At the outset, his draconian policies had shoved Carranza and the Sonorans into outright rebellion. Subsequently, these rebellions were consolidated and popular revolts elsewhere began to coalesce. How did Huerta propose to cope with this deteriorating situation? The consistent thread which ran through the Huerta regime, from start to finish, was militarisation: the growth of and reliance on the Federal Army, the military take-over of political offices, the preference for military over political solutions, the militarisation of society in general. Even revisionist accounts, charitable towards Huerta, admit as much: the idea of 'pacification dominated Huerta's domestic policy'; Huerta came close to 'convert[ing] Mexico into the most completely militarist state in the world'.[399] But the revisionist view plays down the importance of Huertista militarism, seeing it as merely one aspect of a heterodox regime which recognised the need for a range of policies, which was at least as socially progressive as Madero's, and which was not therefore 'counter-revolutionary'. The evidence for this view (to be considered below) is not impressive.[400] In contrast, I would argue first that the Huerta regime was fundamentally militaristic (that militarism was its defining characteristic); and second (by no means an original argument) that it was fundamentally counter-revolutionary, in that it sought to end the liberal experiment, crush the popular movement, and get back to the good old days of the Porfiriato, in all of which it could count on the support of powerful conservative groups in Mexican society.[401]

However, within this argument (which is no less cogent for being familiar) there lurks a paradox which should be flushed out at once. The quest for a revived Porfiriato seemed to require militarist policies; yet these very policies implied a growing divergence from Porfirian practice, prevented Huerta's regime from becoming a carbon copy of Don Porfirio's, and ultimately lost Huerta the support of many of the Porfiristas who were initially his staunch supporters. For Huerta's militarisation had no parallel under Díaz. Even in his early days, Díaz had tempered military with political solutions; he had shown a gift for compromise and diplomacy; he had recognised the power of civilian caciques, guerrilla leaders, provincial oligarchies and Mexico City technocrats, as well as of the regular army. All these constituted limbs of the Porfirian body politic. Huerta's regime, in contrast, was one-legged, and where useful political crutches were available, they were cast aside. Inevitably, the regime soon began to totter. Where Díaz had systematically removed colonels and generals from government, preserving only those with political *nous*, Huerta re-inserted them regardless of talents other than the military ones (and some were even deficient there too). Huerta and his backers certainly wanted a return to Porfirismo; but in the heated atmosphere of civil war and social upheaval Huerta used means to this end which were foreign to Don Porfirio. This divergence had little to do with social justice or political progress. Huertista means – militarisation and repression – were unoriginal and inappropriate, even though unprecedented in their scale; and Huertista ends were no different from those which Díaz had pursued (with greater success) for a generation – the creation of a strong, centralised state and a dynamic capitalist economy, without any basic change in the socio-political status quo. In other words, Huerta sought to continue the Porfirian 'revolution from above' – a project whose inner contradications were becoming all the more evident, not least because of Huerta's chosen policies.[402] And, shifting from the grand and abstract to the human and particular, it is interesting to note that Huerta incurred far greater hatred than Díaz ever had. While it was possible for people – even Zapatistas – to feel a certain nostalgic respect for the patriarchal figure who had presided over Mexico's destiny for a generation and finally departed with dignity, Huerta, in contrast, was reviled and ridiculed as the brutish soldier who had assassinated Madero and attempted to bludgeon the country into submission.[403]

Early on, Huerta had shown his colours by eagerly recruiting ex-rebel soldiery while no less eagerly purging civilian Maderistas. A similar approach was evident in his relations with political allies. Huerta's first cabinet was a product of the Pact of the Embassy: it included renegade Maderistas (such as Toribio Esquivel Obregón and Jesús Flores Magón), Reyistas (notably the late general's son, Rodolfo), Catholics (de la Barra) and Felicistas, supporters of Félix Díaz like Mondragón and Vera Estañol.[404] These were, in the main, respectable politicans of the old school, who commanded widespread conservative support. But, in almost all cases, their tenure of office was short-lived. First, Huerta disliked cabinet government. He carried over into national politics the officer's preference for autocracy and obedience, refused to delegate authority, and addressed his ministers as if they were NCOs.[405] Secondly – over and above his general dislike of civilian *políticos* – Huerta resented the influence and pretensions of the Felicista party. In their eyes, Huerta was a stop-gap president, pending elections that would bring Félix Díaz to power. So, within the cabinet, they pressed for early elections; and, outside, they promoted a Díaz/de la Barra ticket (which would unite the Felicista and Catholic vote in a powerful bloc). Their banal manifesto, reiterating the usual concern for fair elections, decent government, and constitutional rights, was significant in two respects: it deferred to Catholic opinion by renouncing anticlericalism; and it admitted the existence of an agrarian problem, though it offered no real solutions and promised 'due respect for legitimate property rights'.[406] Felicista propaganda began; Felicista clubs were formed; and the workers of Mexico City again showed their willingness to be recruited by any promising political party, which might support their interests.[407]

In response, Huerta stalled over the question of elections, and began to prise the Felicistas out of their ministerial posts. As he confided to an ally in the Chamber: 'the present cabinet will have to go, and I need your collaboration to consolidate a regime which will be authentically mine'.[408] Hence, by April 1913, the capital was alive to rumours of a major rift between Huerta and Díaz, the two caudillos of the Ciudadela.[409] In his policy of delaying elections, Huerta found strange allies: the Renovadores of the Chamber, the legislative rump of Maderismo. Stunned by the fall of Madero, and persuaded of the necessity of recognising Huerta, the Renovadores continued to serve in Congress, believing (one of their spokesmen later argued) that they could best defend their principles and resist Huerta in this fashion.[410] But they were forced to make awkward choices. In their eyes it was preferable that Huerta should remain interim president rather than that Félix Díaz should receive a constitutional mandate until 1916; when, therefore, the Felicistas in Congress called for swift elections, the Renovadores and Huertistas combined in unholy alliance to defeat the measure.[411] With elections postponed *sine die*, Díaz petulantly withdrew his presidential candidacy, whereupon Huerta (following consultations with congressional leaders, including the Renovador spokesman, Francisco Escudero) declared that elections would be held in October.[412] The Felicista machine was thus stalled; and Huerta was given plenty of time to winkle the Felicistas out of office.

Indeed, the process was already under way. In April, amid rumours of cabinet splits and crises, the Minister of Gobernación, García Granados, resigned for 'health' reasons, and seasoned political observers began to discern the impending downfall of Felicismo.[413] They were not far wrong. Next month, de la Barra announced, first, that he would be taking 'an extended trip' abroad, then, that he would assume the governorship of the state of Mexico.[414] General Mondragón, after denying rumours of his imminent resignation late in May, resigned early in June and left for New York, breathing fire and brimstone against his ineffectual ingrate of an ally, Félix Díaz.[415] As for Félix Díaz himself (who had no ministerial post to lose), he was offered and meekly accepted a special ambassadorship to Japan.[416] Lesser Felicistas like Vera Estañol were also removed, and by mid-June 1913 the Pact of the Embassy was officially torn up.[417] As the Felicistas fell, Huerta rapidly introduced his own partisans into government: General Blanquet, his ally during the *Decena Trágica*, who became Minister of War; his personal surgeon, Aureliano Urrutia, a young man with more political ambition than experience, who received the post of Gobernación (which, by his own account, Huerta had promised him years before).[418] Huerta's *adictos* in Congress – Lozano, García Naranjo, and Querido Moheno – also got cabinet posts; and the President's old Reyista sympathies were evident in both the appointment of José López Portillo y Rojas as Foreign Minister, and the survival of Rodolfo Reyes as Minister of Justice until September 1913 – the longest term served by any member of the original Ciudadela cabinet.[419] In a short space of time, therefore, the executive became a nest of Huertistas; and some of the new appointments (such as that of the dissolute and brutal Enrique Cepeda as governor of the Federal District, or of Joaquín Pita, Governor Martínez's loathed henchman in Puebla, as inspector-general of police) not only revealed Huerta's personal tastes and ambitions, but also offended respectable opinion and soured relations with erstwhile allies.[420]

With the executive safely in Huerta's pocket, the focus of politicking shifted elsewhere. Three trends characterised metropolitan (as against local) politics during 1913: the deterioration of the executive's relations with Congress; the question of Huerta's standing with the Americans; and the campaign for the presidential election scheduled for October. These three interacted; and, given Huerta's preferred *modus operandi*, they pushed the regime into a stance of outright dictatorship. Though Congress – including the Renovadores – had supported Huerta over the postponement of elections, subsequent debates concerning a proposed government loan excited opposition, in which the Renovadores figured. Their defenders have since claimed that their policy of peaceful opposition (which required an initial acceptance of the Huerta regime) was designed to assist the rebellions in the north; their critics can point to their over-long dalliance with the regime (from February to mid-May) and can argue both that their display of congressional opposition only came *after* the rebels' military successes in the north, and that even thereafter their opposition was 'more feigned than real'.[421] Certainly, the Renovadores put up no resistance to Huerta until the loan debates in May; and it is not clear that even this resistance was particularly significant (the administrations itself was divided over the loan issue, and Huerta's interest in it was more political – the disgrace and removal of Mondragón – than financial).[422] The real break between the Renovadores and the regime awaited the new session of Congress in September and, here again, it does not seem that Congress's Maderistas went out on a limb to attack Huerta; rather, the policy of the executive forced them into a position where, like it or not, an outright break was unavoidable.

By now, too, the Constitutionalists were taking a hand. In August, Deputy Isidro Fabela, who had joined Carranza in the north, formally reproached Congress for recognising Huerta, castigated its members for giving the regime a semblance of legitimacy, and appealed to them to join Carranza: 'honorable gentleman', Fabela exhorted, 'you are either with Huerta or with the Revolution'.[423] But still the Renovadores did not budge. They were aware of the Constitutionalists' attitude; they discussed what their response should be; and they attempted, unsuccessfully, to send representatives to meet with Carranza. But they would not boycott the new session, and they would not decamp *en masse* to the north. At best (and as typical civilian *políticos*) they would 'provoke debates, present initiatives, and mount interpellations' in order to embarrass the government and mobilise public opinion in Mexico City.[424] Thus, when Congress reconvened after the summer recess (a period which had seen several revolutionary victories) it began to adopt a more belligerent tone.[425] First, Huerta experienced a minor rebuff when a Renovador/Felicista alliance rejected his appointment (made, either clumsily or provocatively, without the routine approval of the legislature) of a Catholic Secretary of Education.[426] This was hardly political dynamite; but Huerta fumed at the politicians' cheek. More seriously, a senator from Chiapas, Belisario Domínguez, launched a strong indictment of Huerta which, though it could not be pronounced on the floor of the Senate, circulated throughout the legislature and in the capital at large.[427] Domínguez alleged that Huerta had made conditions in the country worse rather than better; that he showed every willingness to 'cover the entire land with corpses . . . rather than to abandon power'; that it was the duty of Congress to depose Huerta in order to achieve a peace settlement. This was a new departure: Domínguez's outspoken attack was an example not only of individual courage, but also of the disenchantment and misgivings which had developed, even among respectable conservatives. For Domínguez was no radical, and not even a Maderista; he was a well-meaning doctor and *suplente* Senator who had entered the upper house only months before, following the death of the *propietario* in the *Decena Trágica*.[428] He expressed – with particular candour and courage – the growing belief that Huerta's promise of peace was spurious, that the continuation of the Huerta regime meant continued civil war, and that Huerta was 'the one who is least able to carry out the pacification which is the surpreme desire of all Mexicans'.[429]

Domínguez (who took care to provide for his small son before speaking out) was well aware that he courted martyrdom.[430] In this respect, too, he exemplified a general, not just a particular, plight. Huerta's regime had been inaugurated with political assassinations; and, during the summer, news of subsequent killings leaked out, causing a *frisson* in respectable political circles and further clarifying the regime's character. Gabriel Hernández, the young Maderista general who had entered Pachuca in fine style in 1911, was killed in a Mexico City gaol by the drunken governor of the Federal District, Cepeda, for reasons of personal vengeance – an act which even the conservative and Catholic press denounced.[431] More serious, if less gratuitously brutal, was the removal of several deputies (not parvenu young soldiers but respected members of the political establishment). Their alleged offences varied: Deputy Alardín had supplied cash to rebels; Gurrión of Juchitán was summarily executed for 'devoting himself to spreading pernicious propaganda' (the order came direct from Urrutia); Nestor Monroy, a teacher involved in working-class politics in Mexico City and a known opponent of Huerta, was picked up at a political meeting, taken to the outskirts of the capital, and shot; Serapio Rendón, a noted defence lawyer and close friend of Pino Suárez, was subjected to similar treatment a month later.[432] Not all Huerta's victims were *políticos*: officials, journalists, even the occasional dissident army officer were killed, contributing to a significant if uncertain total of political homicides.[433]

Hunting Zapatistas was one thing (the chief of the *rurales*, Rincón Gallardo, compared the Morelos campaigns to big-game hunting) but eliminating members of Congress in cold blood was another.[434] It begun to look, one observer put it, as though 'Huerta appears to care very little whom he shoots.'[435] It was hardly surprising therefore when, two weeks after Senator Domínguez's outspoken attack, four policemen – they included Huerta's son and son-in-law – paid an early morning call on the Senator's lodgings, dragged him into a car, drove him to a cemetery at Coyoacán, and there shot and buried him in a prepared grave.[436] Now Congress resolved to act. A committee was set up to investigate the Senator's disappearance; the Minister of Gobernación was summoned to answer questions; another such disappearance, it was declared, would force the Congress to remove itself to a safer part of Mexico. The resolutions setting out these intentions were the work of two Felicista deputies: fear and indignation had welded together Felicistas, liberals, and Renovadores in a common front against the executive. Flagrant Huertista repression had created union and opposition out of division and diffidence.[437]

Furthermore, Huerta's response to the gathering political crisis now assumed diplomatic importance. His inauguration as president had preceded by only a month that of the Democrat Woodrow Wilson in the US. Before long, the destinies of the two presidents became interlinked; Huerta's domestic actions found an international audience; and Mexican–American relations thus came to play a greater part in the Revolution. These relations have been closely studied by various scholars and it would be superfluous to replicate their work – especially since American policy had less direct impact on Mexico than has often been supposed.[438] However (if only to justify this last statement) a brief résumé must be made. Woodrow Wilson did not, at first, take great interest in Mexico: his chief concerns had always been domestic, and the first months of his administration were taken up with tariff and currency reform.[439] Inactivity, of course, constituted a form of policy; and Wilson's decision not to recognise the Huerta regime (a decision bequeathed to him by the outgoing Taft administration) clearly had important repercussions. Whatever the President of the US did – or did not do – would have some effect south of the border; recognition or non-recognition alike would count and would (for some) constitute interference in Mexican affairs.[440] The State Department's initial hesitation over the matter of recognition was pragmatic and unexceptional: it stemmed from the hope of settling some outstanding questions (such as the Chamizal territory dispute) while Huerta was still beholden to Ambassador Wilson and amenable to American pressure. And Huerta was distinctly compliant, going further than either Díaz or Madero had gone to satisfy Washington. There was no hint of anti-Americanism; indeed, it was the British who were subjected to gentle economic pressure, in order to hasten British recognition, which was soon forthcoming.[441]

As the major powers lined up to recognise Huerta, however, the absence of the US became conspicuous. Precedent suggested that the US would soon confer recognition; almost all the State Department officials favoured recognition; and Taft later affirmed that, had he continued in office, he would have recognised Huerta. But Wilson chose to delay. The motives for delaying – and, later, for opposing Huerta – were more complex than has often been supposed. They cannot be reduced to Wilson's narrow-minded Calvinism, or – at the other extreme – to his servile solicitude for American big business.[442] Certainly, his revulsion at the overthrow and death of Madero displayed a moralistic attitude to politics and a strong, perhaps undiscriminating, commitment to representative democracy. Both marked him off from the majority of Americans in Mexico, or of Mexico-watchers in the US, since for them (to take one example) the removal of Madero was simply 'the usual Mexican method of doing things [which] . . . shows the character of the people very clearly'.[443] For them, of course, the recognition of Huerta should have proceeded expeditiously. But there was more to Wilson's 'politics of morality' than righteous indignation. Like many Americans (and many mid-Victorian Englishmen) Wilson believed that liberal government was the best guarantor of political order, which, in the Latin American context, was good for

American trade and investment, and good for the maintenance of the Monroe Doctrine and the Roosevelt Corollary.[444] 'Moralism' and '*Realpolitik*' were not polar opposites. Wilson was not at all blind to the overseas economic interests of the US, but his policy – in some respects anticipating the Good Neighbour Policy – was conceived in grand terms, and required that, in some instances, economic interests be overridden. Thus, far from acting as a willing client of Standard Oil, Wilson was prepared to resist big business pressure, and repeatedly did so in his dealings with revolutionary Mexico. Yet his grand strategy had a distinct economic dimension. A stable, democratic Latin America was in the best interests of the US, as well as of the Latin Americans themselves: American goods, investment and political ideas would penetrate Latin America peacefully, consensually, and to mutual advantage.[445] Wilson's policy towards Latin America in general and Mexico in particular was thus more complex, subtle and necessarily ambiguous than has often been supposed. It was neither crude dollar diplomacy nor rank Calvinist humbug, even if some contemporaries – and some historians – preferring to deal in simple absolutes, have chosen to see it in these terms.

This was evident in Wilson's dealings with Huerta. It was not the case that Wilson blackballed Huerta from the start and resolved to drive him from office, 'cueste lo que cueste', as it were.[446] There was a long period of political groping, during which the US government liaised (unofficially) with the new regime and during which, had Huerta played his cards right, a settlement involving recognition would very probably have been forthcoming.[447] 'Up to August (1913)', General Leonard Wood noted, 'we virtually recognised Huerta as the *de facto* government'; had elections been held in July, Wilson's intimate, Colonel House, told Sir Edward Grey, 'our Government would have recognised Huerta's provisional Government.'[448] Voices were raised in favour of Huerta's recognition in the State Department (where John Bassett Moore discerned a 'strong tendency to recognise Huerta'), in the cabinet (where the Minister of War believed 'it might be well to recognise a brute like Huerta, so as to have some form of government which could be recognised') and, above all, among American interests in Mexico, be they miners, railwaymen, landowners, or journalists.[449] And Wilson was by no means deaf to such appeals: three months after the *Decena Trágica*, the American president could still discuss the question of recognition with an apparently open mind.[450] At about the same time, representatives of the Southern Pacific Railroad of Mexico, of the Phelps Dodge and Cananea Mining Companies floated a plan whereby the US would recognise Huerta on condition that early elections were held and Wilson was 'impressed' by the idea; Secretary of State Bryan welcomed a variant of this scheme whereby the good offices of the US would be employed to ensure a national election in Mexico.[451]

Recognition on such terms, of course, implied American interference in Mexican affairs. If the historian's task is to condemn 'interference' (a fairly futile activity), then Wilson deserves condemnation, as does Taft before him (for whom recognition was conditional not only or primarily on elections but also on the settlement of outstanding diplomatic and territorial claims), and as do most US administrations which have been confronted by such problems, in Mexico, Latin America, or the world at large. Recognition or non-recognition may each be construed as 'interference' and a great power like the US cannot but 'interfere' in the affairs of lesser neighbouring powers. Much more important are the criteria and effects of such 'interference'. Wilson's criteria differed from Taft's in that he resolved to recognise only a regime which had demonstrated a certain electoral legitimacy.[452] But this resolution by no means closed all the options: it guaranteed neither a crisis in Mexican–American relations, nor the overthrow of Huerta's regime. These events, which ultimately transpired, did not flow inevitably from Wilson's original, somewhat ill-defined position; and, of the several factors which intervened to bring them about, the actions of the Huerta government itself were crucial. It is therefore much too simple to say that Wilson 'blackballed' Huerta and thus determined his fall, *ergo* American policy was the key factor. Rather, there were many interlinked factors, some more important than American policy: Wilson's novel attitude presented Huerta with a reef to be circumnavigated, but the subsequent shipwreck was more of Huerta's own making.

The schemes floated in May (making recognition contingent upon elections) could not be implemented at once. Huerta had no desire for early elections, which would have played into the hands of Félix Díaz. And President Wilson, mistrustful (and with good reason) of his ambassadorial namesake in Mexico City, preferred to collect information from other sources. So he and Bryan began the practice of sending confidential agents to report on Mexico, independently of the diplomatic and consular staff: William Bayard Hale, Reginald del Valle, and John Lind in 1913; Leon Canova, George Carothers, Paul Fuller and John Silliman in 1914. Collectively, they were expected to transcend the common prejudices of diplomats and consuls (and these prejudices certainly existed). Individually, they were a mixed bunch, and have received a bad press, both from contemporaries and later historians.[453] Hale, the first, was a competent journalist, whose murky past excited critical – though irrelevant – comment, but whose reports from Mexico in the summer of 1913 were informative and broadly accurate – far more so than Ambassador Wilson's.[454] Hale argued (correctly) that while Madero had lost his early popularity by the time of his fall, the revolt against him had been a conspiracy rather than a popular rebellion; that resistance to Huerta was spreading apace; and that the US Ambassador, having nailed his colours to Huerta's mast, now felt compelled to file reports 'so exactly opposed to the truth as to be beyond all understanding'.[455] Less reliable was Reginald del Valle who, visiting Constitutionalist Mexico, reached the bizarre conclusion that the northern rebels were 'mainly bandits'; his mission was judged, not altogether wrongly, a 'disaster', and he was promptly recalled.[456] Such was the way with 'confidential agents': they avoided the familiar ruts of career diplomats and consuls (many of whom placed uncritical faith in the 'iron hand'), they could therefore break fresh ground, but they sometimes lost their way altogether. Wilson and Bryan, having paid their money, could take their choice. Sensibly paying more attention to Hale than to del Valle, they recalled Ambassador Wilson for 'consultations', after which consultations they relieved him of his post.[457]

During this long hiatus, the lack of American recognition was exciting hostile comment in Mexico. There followed a wave of anti-American agitation, which peaked in July 1913. Such waves were common during the Revolution: they represented officially-orchestrated reactions to crises in Mexican–American relations, and were used – generally without much success – to whip up support for incumbent regimes.[458] All political factions, left and right, were prepared to use this technique (already, in February 1913, fears of American intervention during the *Decena Trágica* had been exploited by Maderista officials to rally support and switch attention away from the fighting in the capital), but Huerta had more cause and better opportunity. Now, his administration turned the screw in the hope of forcing recognition. De la Barra protested at the prolonged stay of American warships in Mexican waters and hinted at discrimination in favour of European companies; the press (much of it government subsidised) alleged American connivance with the northern 'secessionists', predicted the prompt expulsion of the American Ambassador, and wrote up anti-American demonstrations with great emphasis. Such demonstrations – for example, that which welcomed the new Japanese Minister to Mexico City on 13 July – were dismal affairs, since anti-Americanism lacked deep roots; but their organisation revealed the drift of Huertista policy. The provinces were also affected – with a suitable time-lag – as copies of Mexico City newspapers and (one supposes) executive instructions were received, digested, and acted upon. Local newspapers took up the theme; orators spoke out in the plaza; the occasional desultory demonstration was mounted.[459]

While this aggressive anti-American policy held out hopes – albeit illusory hopes – of winning political support, and perhaps forcing recognition, it was not the only option. Powerful American interests advocated the recognition of Huerta, or failing that, of an alternative, elected administration; Wilson and Bryan were still uncertain and malleable (they had warmly received suggestions along these latter lines, and Wilson's confidant, House, regarded Huerta's betrayal of Félix Díaz as his chief blemish); the European powers had unanimously accorded recognition.[460] In this context, prompt, suitably controlled elections, as favoured by the Felicistas, would very likely have led to American recognition. But these would have opened the door to Félix Díaz, and closed it to Victoriano Huerta. So this option was rejected. Meanwhile, the longer Huerta delayed, the more the revolution spread, and the more American attention was focussed on his regime and its manifold failings.

With time, the American government's attitude hardened; yet it continued to seek a settlement. Early in August, Wilson's third emissary, John Lind, arrived in Mexico bearing fresh proposals. Quite suddenly, the anti-American campaign ceased.[461] Government officials became honey-tongued, and Lind's arrival in Mexico City went unnoticed.[462] Even more than his predecessor Hale, Lind carried the prejudices of Progressive North America into revolutionary Mexico. Physically, he was tall, blond, blue-eyed and gaunt, as befitted a Swedish immigrant; philosophically, he adhered to a stern Protestantism; politically, he was a loyal member of Bryan's mid-Western, populist clientele.[463] Honourable and idealistic, Lind was a faithful representative of the 'New Freedom'. But he was hardly at home among Mexicans, he regarded the Catholic Church as the whore of Babylon and, like many of his kind, he superimposed North American, Protestant values on disordered, dirty, revolutionary Mexico: 'the ways and customs of the Mexicans', an observer noted, 'irregular and reprehensible as they may be, are to him anathema, and he looks for real American ideals, cleanliness, morality and hygiene in the success of Carranza's revolution'.[464]

Lind proposed an armistice, elections (in which Huerta would not stand), and American recognition of the winner. Huerta's exclusion represented a further intrusion into Mexican domestic politics and the Mexican government played up the Lind mission for all it was worth, rejecting the 'strange and unwarranted' character of the proposal, ruling out an armistice with 'bandits', and pointing out that early elections were required by the Constitution anyway.[465] Rebuffed, Lind left Mexico City for Veracruz, there to be detained at President Wilson's pleasure, pining for the cool lakes of Minnesota.[466] Huerta – and, even more, his generals in the provinces – again resorted to the anti-American ploy in order to drum up recruits.[467] And Wilson himself, still optimistic, announced a policy of 'watchful waiting'. This involved doing nothing, save in one respect: a complete arms embargo was now placed on Mexico. This made little difference to Huerta, who could import as much arms and ammunition as he could pay for from Europe and Japan; but it indicated that the US government – notwithstanding continued support within its ranks for Huerta – had resolved on a policy of strict neutrality and *attentisme*.[468] Lind languished in Veracruz. Wilson watchfully waited in Washington. The initiative shifted to Huerta and the *políticos* of Mexico City.

American opposition to Huerta, *per se*, was now clear; but it was also clear that the US would recognise a regime emanating from elections, notwithstanding the state of the country.[469] 'Huerta's announcement that he will not be a candidate', Bryan declared, 'is the only thing necessary to the restoration of peace'; if legally elected, Bryan also pointed out, the Catholic presidential candidate, Federico Gamboa, would be approved by the US (Lind, meantime, showed a distinct preference for Félix Díaz).[470] Given Mexico's electoral traditions, and the particular circumstances of 1913, American readiness to recognise Gamboa or Díaz as 'elected' presidents was either naive or cynical, probably naive. At best, such a recognition would settle the Mexican–American squabble by removing Huerta; but it would neither guarantee democracy in Mexico, nor terminate the civil war, since the Constitutionalists would doubtless have fought on. To conservative groups in Mexico, however, a Gamboa or Díaz administration looked attractive: first, because it would be more broadly based – a more faithful copy of the Porfiriato – than Huerta's; second, because it could capitalise on American *naïveté*, secure recognition, and thus bolster its international reputation and credit. In my view, even these advantages would have proved inadequate to sustain such a regime, for it was manpower and legitimacy, rather than loans and diplomatic support, which the conservatives conspicuously lacked. Nevertheless, a civilian conservative regime, under a Gamboa or Díaz, now looked a better bet than Huertista militarism, and Mexico's conservatives, facing threats at home and abroad, quite rationally wavered in their support for Huerta and began to flirt with alternative solutions. It is therefore doubly mistaken to see American influence as primarily responsible for the revolutionary victory over Huerta: first, because American policy made a less than crucial difference either way (the revolution would have triumphed irrespective of American non-recognition of Huerta); second, because even after Huerta had been blackballed, there was ample opportunity for the creation – and recognition – of an alternative, fundamentally conservative regime, minus Huerta. And the chief obstacle to this course was not the doctrinarite do-gooder in Washington, but the single-minded soldier in Mexico City.

The hopes of the conservatives and the ingredients of such an alternative regime were evident in the carnival of conventions, parties and juntas which took up the summer of 1913. With Congress in recess and Huerta blowing hot and cold over Washington's attitude, the busy *políticos* of Mexico City (for this was largely a metropolitan sport) sparred and manoeuvred with their eyes on the October presidential elections. Though personal ambitions ran high, there was also a powerful, collective desire – reinforced by rebel victories at Durango, Zacatecas and in Sonora – to exploit the elections in the interests of a peace settlement incorporating – or leading to – American recognition. The millionaire Oscar Braniff, who had served as one of Díaz's representatives at Juárez in 1911 and who thus had experience of such political brokerage, journeyed to Washington, where he talked to the press and wrote to President Wilson. To the press he endorsed Huerta, while recommending moderate social reforms: the division of the great estates, the provision of agricultural credit, the creation of a rural middle class – all the familiar nostrums of enlightened opinion.[471] To President Wilson, he denied that the civil war was a simple polarisation between peon and *científico*; there were powerful groups in between, 'legitimate elements or [the] conservative class' ('middle Mexico', one might say), who rejected 'praetorian government' – revolutionary or

Huertista – and who sought a 'civil candidate, acceptable to the GENERAL [sic] social and political elements'; to which end Wilson was urged to bend his influence.[472] In Mexico City, meanwhile, Oscar's brother Tomás spouted similar proposals, incurred the wrath of the Huertista press, and assumed leadership of the National Unifying Junta, a Mexican Cave of Adullam, whence echoed cries of an all-party presidential candidate, who might, once elected, even win over the Constitutionalists.[473] Indeed, there was even a crackpot notion to get Carranza to run for the presidency.[474] The Junta attracted sacked cabinet ministers, Felicista deputies, and not a few Maderistas, all eager for the return of a civilian government which promised peace, stability, and jobs. Red-blooded Huertistas like Urrutia reviled them as professional opportunists, and the regime used threats and blandishments to try to break up this incipient civilian front.[475]

Meanwhile, individual parties proliferated: the still powerful Catholic Party, the Felicistas, the Grand Liberal Republican Party, even a rump Anti-Re-electionist Party. Several of their leaders were convened by de la Barra to form a Civil Political League which undertook to work for fair elections in October, on the grounds that the revolution sought 'nothing in the line of principles, but merely wanted a change of personnel', which elections could provide, thereby restoring peace.[476] For Huerta, the proliferation of parties was preferable to the creation of a solid civilian bloc; thus, while individuals were harassed, parties were allowed to organise (twenty-six eventually contested the congressional elections) and feelers went out to the Catholics, to detach them from their fellow-civilians.[477] And Félix Díaz, who had half-completed an erratic journey to Japan (delayed, halted and redirected by a stream of perverse government telegrams) was finally allowed back to Mexico, to complicate the picture further.[478] By October, the political situation was one of flux and uncertainty: among the elite there was a growing disillusionment with Huerta, and disgust at his strong-arm methods; Congress was squaring up to the president and the president showed every sign of relishing the impending confrontation.[479] Washington patiently awaited the outcome of the October elections, which the civilian *políticos* entered in a condition of disarray deliberately fostered by the regime. As for Huerta himself, though his precise intentions were unfathomable, it is clear that he intended to augment rather than to relinquish his power. Then, at the beginning of October, the news broke in Mexico City of the fall of Torreón, causing 'much depression'.[480] The stage was set for a series of dramatic events that would radically change and at the same time clarify the politics of Huertismo.

Congress convened in September, recalcitrant and determined to unravel the mystery of Senator Domínguez's murder. Backed by his close advisers Blanquet and Garza Aldape (War and Gobernación respectively), Huerta favoured an immediate dissolution of the legislature. Ministers of greater political experience argued against this, but the hard line prevailed.[481]

Indeed, Huerta went further: all deputies believed to be hostile to the regime would be summarily arrested. A list was compiled (it included a couple of Huerta's ex-ministers) and on the afternoon of 10 October, as Congress met, troops of Blanquet's 29th Battalion surrounded and entered the legislature; the deputies were told to rescind their offending resolution, which set up an official inquiry into the Domínguez case; they refused and the Congress was dissolved. As the deputies filed out 110 were arrested and taken to the Federal Penitentiary, where 74 were subsequently charged and the rest liberated.[482] The prisoners were soon to be seen engaged in a mock bullfight in the prison yard, cavorting in shirt-sleeves and braces, as bemused guards watched from the rooftop.[483] By way of justification, Huerta alleged that the deputies had been obstructing, even conspiring against, the executive; he laid down that a new Congress would be elected on 26 October (the day of the presidential election), when the voters might choose 'citizens whose only zeal, whose only ideal, is the reconstruction of the fatherland on a solid foundation of peace'.[484] But the coup against Congress ('the Mexican 18th Brumaire', as the British Foreign Office called it) did Huerta no good and played into the hands of his enemies.[485] It shredded the flimsy veil of legality which had been carefully woven in February, further alienating civilian and conservative opinion; and, though it did not excite much protest in the capital, it gave a further blow to business confidence following the fall of Torreón.[486] If European sensibilities were unruffled (the new British Minister, Sir Lionel Carden, presented his credentials to Huerta the day after the coup), the US Administration was 'shocked . . . and deeply distressed' by Huerta's 'lawless methods'.[487] In that the coup confirmed Washington's low opinion of Huerta it hardly mattered; more significantly, it brought home to Wilson's administration the fatuity of relying on elections to demonstrate genuine legitimacy. Any dwindling hope of compromise was eliminated and Washington and Mexico City were pushed into entrenched, antagonistic positions. Like Cortez's burning of his boats on the beach at Veracruz, the coup marked a point of no return.

The elections themselves confirmed this polarisation. Maderista elections, held under relatively free conditions, had excited dwindling interest and participation; those of October 1913 were even more anodyne affairs. In the capital, where parties and politicians had been active over the summer, the forced dissolution of Congress provided a cold douche for torrid ambitions, and little interest or preparation were evident.[488] In the provinces, too, where news of the dissolution had a mixed reception, fear and scepticism combined to discourage serious electoral activity. Some cities witnessed Felicista propaganda on a modest scale; in most there was a spate of arrests of supposed subversives. Apathy and resignation were universally reported.[489] Of the sundry presidential candidates of the summer, few now remained: Díaz had barely arrived at Veracruz and was under close police surveillance; de la Barra had renounced the Felicista vice-presidential slot; Francisco Vázquez Gómez and the Anti-Re-electionists had vanished from the political map. The Grand Liberal Republican Party argued that, since free elections were impossible under Huerta, their party's sole purpose, if elected, would be to hold more elections. Amid the gloom, apathy, and pointlessness of it all, some could only consider the impending elections with a wry smile.[490] Huerta could have let the farce run its course, annulled the result on one of several technical grounds, and remained provisional president, as many expected that he would.[491] But for obscure reasons he chose to do otherwise, at the last minute informing 'his confidants that he would respond favourably should the electorate give him a mandate to remain in office'.[492] Quickly, the word went round to *jefes políticos* and army commanders: Huerta–Blanquet was the official, all-military ticket. Appropriate placards began to go up on the streets, in Mexico City, Veracruz, and elsewhere; Felicista activists were bribed and intimidated into dropping their party; soldiers and government employees received their official instructions.[493] Yet, even as this went on, Huerta assembled the diplomatic corps, expressed modest fears that friends might press his candidacy and declared that all votes cast for him would be void.[494]

Election day, 26 October, was quiet and the poll pathetically low. An unenthusiastic 5% turned out at Cd Juárez (where the proximity of Pancho Villa aroused more interest than the exercise of the franchise); at Chihuahua City, similarly distracted, only the troops voted; throughout the country, apathy and corruption characterised the poll.[495] Soon, to the 'unbounded indignation of all parties' in Mexico City (though to the surprise of no-one), it was announced that Huerta had amassed a clear majority; but, since less than half the electoral districts had returned results, the outcome was annulled, with new elections set for July 1914.[496] Huerta's belated intervention had not secured him the constitutional presidency – if that is what he sought. But he had sown such fear, confusion and uncertainty that the Felicista threat had been headed off (though Felicismo still ran strongly in states like Oaxaca and Jalisco), and the vexed question of elections postponed until the following summer. Furthermore, he had rid himself of an obstreperous Congress and replaced it with one in which relatives, cronies and clients predominated. Among the senators and deputies newly elected from the Federal District, for example, could be found Aureliano Urrutia, two of Huerta's sons (one, Captain Gabriel Huerta, had been implicated in Domínguez's murder), his brother-in-law (a lieutenant-colonel), his close adviser and private secretary, Jesús Rábago, two members of the presidential staff (a colonel and lieutenant-colonel), and Blanquet's private secretary (a general).[497] There was now no danger of the executive tripping over the scruples of the legislature; representative institutions (even of an 'artificial' kind) and civilian parties had been eliminated from government to an unprecedented degree; and the elimination had been swift, callous, and arbitrary, calculated to cause deep offence, even to conservatives. Manuel Amor, scion of an elite Morelos family, complained that his 85% plurality in one electoral district had been ignored so that Huerta's nominee might be returned.[498] The Felicista party wound itself up, and Félix Díaz crawled across the roof of his Veracruz hotel to the American consulate, later to be taken aboard an American warship for safety.[499] The proscription of civilian politicians now even involved the Catholics, whom Huerta had tolerated longest. Gabriel Somellera, president of the Catholic Party, was arrested; *La Nación*, which like other Catholic papers had protested against Congress's dissolution and the rigged elections, locked horns with the official press and was finally closed down; *El País*, the main Catholic paper, survived for a time, but in a state of some bewilderment. 'Whither do we go?', it asked early in 1914, 'only the Lord knows and in Him we place all our hopes.'[500]

El País trusted in God; Huerta kept his powder dry. With civilian politics in abeyance, and a compromise with the US ruled out, Huerta could get on with the task he preferred: beating the rebels on the battle-field. After October 1913, the American Chargé commented, Huerta could 'be considered as an absolute military dictator': the first half of the Huertistsa slogan 'Nada de política! La paz ante todo!' had been accomplished; it was now time to deliver on the second half.[501] What Huerta and his hard-line advisers failed to appreciate was that their slogan was inherently contradictory – that, without an appropriate political strategy, peace could not be attained and that, as a result, their virtual abolition of politics made the task of pacification immeasurably harder, and arguably downright impossible.

HUERTISMO: 2 SOLDIERS AND LANDLORDS

Huerta's military strategy required that the militarisation of Mexico – already noted under Madero – be greatly accelerated. He had inherited a military establishment of some 45,000–50,000; thereafter, decree upon decree fixed new levels: 150,000 in October 1913, 200,000 early in 1914, a quarter of a million by the spring of that year.[502] These figures, furthermore, applied to the Federal Army, yet both the pay and the numbers of the *rurales* had been increased in the summer of 1913 and, if *rurales* and state militias are added to the spring 1914 figure, a total military complement of nearly 300,000 (or some 4% of the total male population) is achieved.[503] In fact, such figures represented a combination of fantasy, propaganda and corruption (padded payrolls were a favourite device in a graft-ridden army).[504] Official figures should therefore be deflated, perhaps by as much as 50%.[505] But, even allowing for exaggeration, these were hefty increases, and the scramble for manpower which they entailed had important consequences.

Huerta entertained none of Madero's quaint ideas as to the desirability of an impartial, all-embracing national service. And it was abundantly clear that he could not raise men on a voluntary basis, despite pay increases: 'the existing

Federal government can count on little popular support from the only classes
. . . which can or will bear arms'.[506] No clearer proof of the popularity of the
Revolution, and of popular disgust with Huerta and his regime, can be found
than the perennial refusal of the common people to serve in Huerta's army;
hence no Huertista organ dared assert – as the Constitutionalists' *El Demócrata*
did after the fall of Torreón in 1913 – that 'there is an abundance of men who
are clamouring for a rifle, but a rifle is lacking'.[507] Lacking volunteers, Huerta
fell back on old methods. Quotas were assigned to state governors who,
through the *jefaturas*, had to raise the appropriate 'contingente de sangre'
however they might. It was a hit-and-miss procedure: the governor of Sonora
was ordered to supply the full state quota when he held only the city of
Guaymas.[508] The chief result was unashamed and indiscriminate use of the
leva, now pushed to unprecedented lengths.

As early as May 1913 the *leva* was at work in the capital and in cities like San
Luis where it operated with 'unnecessary severity', and where the military
governor began to receive threatening letters from resentful citizens.[509]
Vagrants, prisoners, petty criminals, political detainees, captured rebels and,
in the last resort, innocent peons and *pelados* were all fair game for the *leva*.
Night-workers from textile factories in Puebla and Veracruz were snatched
from the streets in the small hours, on the grounds that they were vagrants; the
late-night customers of cinemas and cantinas were similarly impressed and
Mexico City night life – for the poor at least – ground to a halt.[510] The *leva*
operated in daylight too: 700 were said to be taken after one Sunday afternoon
bullfight (Belmonte was all the rage that month); and errand-boys disappeared
off the streets, never to be seen again.[511] At Veracruz, bootblacks, hired at 50c
a day to clean Federal equipment, were drafted into the army; in the capital,
the poor preferred 'to suffer and die in their nameless holes' rather than visit the
General Hospital, where 'the *leva* . . . always takes in a lot of men'.[512]

The policy caused bitter resentment. Conscription was the chief bugbear of
the common people, particularly in the towns: next to conscription, abuses
like rigged elections seemed venal. In Querétaro, said the governor, 'the lower
class look on military service with horror, even though it be legal'; in
Guanajuato, where 200 were being pressed per day late in 1913, it caused
'bitter feeling against the government'; the same was reported from Manzanillo on the Pacific coast.[513] Conscription on this scale affected many areas of
life. Men married in haste to avoid the draft.[514] At Aguascalientes the railway
shop workers began to quit, to avoid Federal recruitment; businessmen
complained of the loss of their labour force.[515] Problems were most acute
when, in its quest for the 'contingent of blood', the regime probed the
populated, Indian regions of central and southern Mexico, drawing off their
manpower for service in the distant, alien north. Again, this was a familiar,
Porfirian policy; but its prosecution on an unprecedented scale exacerbated old
grievances and jolted hitherto peaceful communities into outright resistance.

The Juchiteco Indians provided many forced recruits, as they had in the past.[516] Trainloads of Maya arrived at Mérida from the interior of Yucatán, and could be seen bidding farewell to weeping wives, amid 'heart-breaking scenes', before being shipped to the north.[517] In the Puebla sierra, as we have seen, the *leva* provoked a serious revolt, and in Veracruz too (particularly the Huasteca Veracruzana) conscription led to Indian uprisings.[518] Landlords found labour to be scarce as the *leva* carried off workers and forced others – such as the peons of Tabasco – to take cover in the woods and swamps of the interior; the planters of the Valle Nacional begged the government to desist from forced recruiting, which would prove 'fatal' to their enterprises, and produce 'alarms and upheavals', as it had in neighbouring Veracruz.[519] Thus Huerta's policy not only added to popular unrest, but also further soured his once happy relations with landlords and businessmen.

Since these recruits made poor soldiers, the policy also magnified the inherent defects of Díaz's conscript army. Governors preferred to shift new recruits out of their native locality and into strange, hostile surroundings as fast as possible, even if the troops had to be tied up in railway cars en route.[520] Many recruits, like those sent up from Mazatlán to Baja California in August 1913, were boys of fifteen and less; or they were 'pure riff-raff', who caused trouble in the quiet, businesslike peninsula and threatened mutiny when their meagre pay fell in arrears.[521] At the front, whole units of such troops had been known to desert, and officers were reluctant to lead platoons of sullen conscripts into open country. On both counts, therefore, the Federals preferred to sit in the major towns where they could more easily keep an eye on their own men.[522] Yet even there, mutinies and desertions occurred. Zapatistas – caught, impressed, and shipped to Yucatán – rebelled and fought a battle with local forces; detachments in the same state – where 70% of the army was reckoned to be ex-convicts and one entire 'volunteer' battalion consisted of impressed Yaquis – had been known to mutiny, desert, and murder their officers.[523] Such happenings were not confined to the distant south-east. In October 1913, elements of the 9th Regiment, mutinied at Tlalnepantla (Federal Distrct) and – 'crazed by alcohol and marijuana', it was said – killed two officers before making their escape. Next month an entire garrison at Iztapalapa, also in the Federal District, was placed under arrest. And at a crucial moment in the Morelos campaign, in March 1914, the 7th Regiment mutinied at Jojutla, undermining the whole Federal strategy in the south.[524] These were the dramatic incidents; no less important was the persistently low morale of the Federals, which contrasted with the *élan* and confidence of their revolutionary opponents.[525]

Faced by these problems, the Huerta regime had recourse to two expedients: it tried to get volunteers on the basis of a nationalist, anti-American appeal; and it relied on private volunteer forces, organised by towns, companies, and haciendas. For the first, Huerta could capitalise on his growing dispute with the US, and the fears of American intervention which it provoked, calling on his compatriots (in Emilio Campa's words) 'to spill their last drop of blood against the gringoes'.[526] Lind's mission triggered the first bout of Huertista anti-Americanism: at Guaymas, broadsheets warned of intervention and appealed for recruits; 100 volunteers were raised at Acapulco; the Federal commander at Cd Porfirio Díaz drummed up recruits and appealed to the local rebels to unite in a patriotic alliance.[527] Close by, an anti-American demonstration was mounted at Nuevo Laredo, General Téllez proclaimed that war with the US was imminent, and eighty volunteers came forward within twenty-four hours; it was rumoured that an invasion of Texas would shortly be undertaken.[528] In each case, the city in question lay in a rebellious region, extra troops were required to man the defences, and Federal commanders had no scruples about using patriotic volunteers to resist the revolution. The volunteers themselves soon became aware of this: 300 who came forward at Manzanillo were greatly indignant when the word went round that they would be sent north to fight the rebels in Sonora.[529]

The nationalist ploy met with minimal success. Its chief appeal was to the middle and lower middle class of the cities: groups of some education, who thus harboured nationalist sentiments, and who had not been drawn into the revolutionary camp.[530] Just as it was 'men of the better class' and 'prominent citizens' who were usually responsible for the anti-American propaganda (in newspapers, pamphlets and demonstrations), so it was the clerks, schoolteachers, students and journalists who were most likely to respond to nationalist recruiting drives – along with those unfortunates in government employment, such as the postal workers, who now had to join the colours, as in the past they had joined *gobiernista* rallies and polling queues. In the capital, recruits were drawn from the 'clerks and middle-class younger element'; at Zacatecas the 'Anti-Intervention Battalion' comprised 'young men of the better class'; and the same pattern was evident when nationalist recruitment was resumed – with more justification and greater vigour – in 1914.[531] All this did Huerta little good. As we have noted at several points, the urban middle class made poor soldiers; and, since they had joined up to resist the Americans, they had no stomach for fighting the rebels. Most of the volunteer forces – like the 250 men 'avowedly organised to repel foreign invaders' in landlocked Puebla – were 'very worthless'; they appear not to have engaged in combat; and their units melted away as if they had never been.[532] The rural population, meanwhile, displayed rustic indifference. For many, 'Mexico' remained an empty concept; for others, patriots though they might be, their patriotism could not override their ingrained fear and loathing of military service. The cool reception given Huerta's recruiting sergeants in San José de Gracia was thus typical of rural Mexico as a whole.[533] Huerta's cynical manipulation of the patriot cause (for there can be little doubt this is what it was) therefore paid few dividends. And again, in 1914, in even more propitious circumstances, the failure was repeated: in the year that millions of Europeans flocked to the colours, the common people of Mexico showed that their priorities and concerns were different.[534]

If national allegiances could not attract – and the Federal Army positively discouraged – mass recruitment, there remained the more local, personal, and proximate loyalties upon which the rebels built up their forces; and it must be asked why Huerta and the Huertistas could not capitalise on the clientelist networks within their own domain, why, for example, they could not convert *cuadrillas* of deferential peons into platoons of sturdy troops, and their *hacendado* masters into dashing, Chouan-style counter-revolutionary captains. By way of answer, we may develop an earlier argument.[535] Landlords – as well as merchants, businessmen, bankers and other men of property – did not lack incentive. The renewal of armed revolution in 1913, with its radical implications and incidental damage to material interests, was compounded by repeated reminders of the urban mob's capacity for mayhem and the newspapers' predilection for atrocity stories. Throughout the Republic (and especially after the fall of Durango) the well-to-do could not but realise that they faced a serious challenge; and they had welcomed Huerta as a potential deliverer.[536]

Yet, given the option of resistance or surrender, many chose surrender; and resistance, to the extent that it was channeled through the regime, proved largely ineffectual. This in turn had important implications for the survival of both the regime and the propertied classes who initially backed it. On paper, it is true, the story was somewhat different. The press teemed with reports of lavish private contributions to the Huertista war effort: loans, donations, recruitment drives, the formation of volunteer and vigilante groups. As early as May 1913 the government gave the go-ahead for factories and haciendas to raise volunteer forces for their own protection, and the summer saw the spawning of dozens of such organisations. In Jalisco, where the Agricultural Society advocated an additional land tax to finance recruits, 40 landowners met and agreed to raise 12 detachments of 100 men apiece; by September, 700 Puebla landowners were committed to field 10 men each; *hacendados* in Michoacán likewise began recruiting and offered a cash subvention to the government, which was seconded by landowners and chambers of commerce in seven different states.[537] Towards the end of the year, the government took a lead, ordering the formation of state militias, to be financed by landowners and businessmen; within days 12,000 men were reckoned to be enlisted – 2,000 in Michoacán, 2,300 in Guanajuato.[538] The Federal District had its volunteer corps, notably in the southern suburbs, which marched with Morelos (they included working-class elements, drawn from the factories of the capital); the *hacendados* of Querétaro organised a corps of cavalry; and old Próspero Cahuantzi, cacique of Tlaxcala, recruited two volunteer corps to patrol the Puebla/Tlaxcala borderlands.[539] Figures – as likely as not plucked out of the air – graced some of these reports: 200 volunteers were ready at La Paz (Baja Calif.); 1,000 at Azcapotzalco, in the northern suburbs of the capital; 1,000 policed the troublesome Mina district of Guerrero.[540] The cotton planters of the Laguna, among the hardest hit of all landlords, contributed lump sums to the government, raised volunteers, and undertook to pay a premium on every cotton bale shipped south.[541] Similar undertakings were made by the Morelos sugar planters.[542]

Reports of such fund-raising and recruiting efforts went on into 1914.[543] But the stirring promises were not matched by practical results. Some contributions were paltry (the landowners of Chiapas agreed to raise a force of fifteen men); other schemes simply foundered – in Puebla, for example where the Chamber of Commerce's plan for a volunteer corps collapsed for want of support, and the landlords of Huejotzingo failed to meet their agreed commitments.[544] The only Morelos plantations to receive a private guard (ten Japanese under a French officer: apparently no Mexican could be recruited) were those of the García Pimentel, two sons of which family remained in charge; but by April 1914 they, too, were forced to leave 'in great anguish', burying a few possessions in the plantation chapel and retiring to Mexico City, where their wives were busy organising sewing sessions for the Red Cross.[545] The relative tenacity of the García Pimentel contrasted with the supine attitude of most of the planters. 'As a class in crisis', Womack observes, 'the planters could not rally. Although they had been school chums abroad and had become Jockey Club cronies, polo team-mates, business partners and even in-laws, they could now summon no spirit of solidarity.'[546] Struggling to survive individually, they collapsed collectively.

Huerta – no scion of the aristocracy himself – began to lose patience. In May 1913, landlords and businessmen received permission and assistance to raise private forces; in August they were positively enjoined to raise men, releasing the Federal Army for more important tasks; at the end of the year, the state militias were launched – on paper, at least.[547] But the militias faced the same recruiting problems as the Federal Army and by 1914 the states of the Federation were experiencing severe financial troubles which curbed military efforts.[548] Certainly there is scant evidence of newly formed state militias playing a role in the battles of 1914. And by then Huerta's patience was at an end. At the Jockey Club he upbraided a Morelos planter for his family's failure to render active support; and, when the planter pointed out that he had lost 1.5m. pesos in the past year, Huerta's gruff comment was: 'lucky man to have it to lose'.[549] In March, forty of the 'richest businessmen and *hacendados* in the country' were summoned by the president and urged 'to take an active interest in the politics of the country' and to lend material aid to the government.[550] By now, however, it was too late, for many of the class to whom Huerta addressed his appeal had mentally ditched the embattled dictator and were flirting with possible political compromises, transactions, and even the drastic alternative of American intervention, as means to rescue their lost patrimony.

The urban equivalent of these volunteer and vigilante forces, the *Defensa Social*, had developed under Madero as a protection against external rebel/bandits and internal rioters or dissidents; now, under Huerta, it became ubiquitous. The most famous, that of Durango, comprised 500 volunteers, 'recruited largely from the most influential families of the state', who had come forward at a 'monster mass meeting' in April 1913, when the city was under threat of attack. Some participants sought no more than the defence of home and family; some went further, flaunting their fine new uniforms, attacking the revolution in the press and conducting a witch-hunt against rebel sympathisers in the city. For them, the *Defensa Social* was a powerful instrument for the preservation of order, stability and the status quo; and observers agreed that the 'moral effect . . . will be excellent in preventing disturbances on the part of the lower elements of the city'.[551] By the early summer, revolutionary sources numbered the Durango *Defensa Social* at between 700 and 1,000; its services were welcomed by the Federal commander, who ordered them to man the northern and eastern defences of the city, but who refused to carry out the summary executions of Maderista prisoners which the *Defensa Social* demanded.[552] When the rebels attacked, the *Defensa Social* made a real contribution to the city's defence, thereby incurring further revolutionary opprobrium; thus, when the garrison commander decided to evacuate, the *Defensa Social* preferred to flee with the Federals rather than await summary justice. They fought their way out of Durango amid considerable carnage: two prominent *hacendados* and many lesser members of the organisation were left dead on the fields of the San Martín estate, east of the city; and those who remained narrowly avoided being shot.[553]

This was not the end of the story. The Durango evacuees escaped to Torreón or Zacatecas and thence to Mexico City. In the capital, in collusion with the hawkish Huertista minister, Manuel Garza Aldape, they planned a *revanchiste* movement.[554] An expedition of 600 men (including several members of prominent Durangueño families) was kitted out; it assisted in the defence of Torreón late in July; and, against the advice of the Federal commander at Torreón, it set out across country to attack rebel-held Durango. At the Hacienda de Avilez the column was surrounded by a powerful rebel force including Villa, Urbina, and Calixto Contreras. Some escaped by swimming the Nazas; many were cornered in the big house of the hacienda, where the commanding general committed suicide; those taken prisoner were subsequently shot.[555] The Durango *Defensa Social* represented a serious effort by the local elite to resist the revolution by all the means in its power – military, financial and political. For this resistance its members paid dearly, in 1913 and again in 1914.[556] Lesser equivalents existed in other cities ('there are defence societies in many towns', a British journalist noted), but they made much less mark.[557] A mass meeting was held in San Luis to discuss the city's defence; a Monterrey banker set about organising a *Defensa Social*, to be trained by a Federal officer; the governor of the Federal District formed a *Liga de Defensa Social* to resist Zapatista incursions from the south.[558] None of these schemes bore results. At best such organisations might sally forth into hostile country to bring supplies to beleaguered cities: as did the *Defensa Social* of Torreón, formed by one of the Garza Aldape clan and composed of 'young men of the better class'; or that of Chihuahua City, sponsored by the Creel–Terrazas interests and dubbed the 'Millionaires' Corps', which managed to get to Juárez and back.[559] But it does not seem that the rebels were much perturbed by these deeds of derring-do, nor that these volunteers contributed much to the defence of Torreón and Chihuahua in 1914. Indeed, the twenty or so 'rich young things' (*jovenes ricachos*) of the Torreón *Defensa Social*, captured by rebels in April 1914, excited more ridicule than hatred.[560] Perhaps they were lucky: the irascible Emiliano Nafarrate had their Matamoros counterparts summarily shot.[561]

In such cases, involving large cities immediately threatened by rebel forces, the *Defensa Social* could act, at best, as an auxiliary of the hard-pressed Federal Army; like the Huerta regime as a whole, the *Defensa Social* stood or fell with the Army, which was the ultimate arbiter of the situation.[562] It represented, therefore, not an autonomous form of self-defence, but rather a secondary, auxiliary force, of very limited value; and its value was all the more limited by the internal politics of the big towns. The Chihuahua *Defensa Social* proclaimed its intention 'to defend with arms in hand within the city . . . the families and interests of all inhabitants without distinction'; but many such cities (as the *Defensa Social* members themselves were quick to point out) were riddled with revolutionary sympathisers, and prone to sharp internal conflicts.[563] Among those who bayed for revenge against the Durango *Defensa Social* was Juan García, the popular candidate who had lost the 1912 gubernatorial election to the conservatives in dubious circumstances; and the conservatives were, of course, prominent in the *Defensa Social*.[564] The major cities could now rarely produce that unity in the face of rural rebellion which had sometimes been evident in 1911–12; the *Defensa Social*, under Huerta, could not but appear as the vehicle of the conservative well-to-do; and, as such, it could do little to assist the war effort.

The same was true of two comparable movements which may be briefly dismissed. It has sometimes been suggested that foreign companies (notably the oil companies) made a significant contribution to the war against the revolution by sponsoring 'white guards'. Certainly, foreigners contributed to extraordinary taxes and levies designed to raise (government) forces; but they did so reluctantly and they sometimes resisted with success.[565] To some extent, too, they responded to the rising level of violence: ranchers armed their *vaqueros* to stop rustling; American residents acquired guns (if they did not already possess them) and, as in Mexico City, formed self-defence associations.[566] In the main, such groups were not overtly political, and did not involve direct support for Huerta or opposition to the revolution. But in the context of guerrilla war the defence of property and combating of 'banditry' (a notoriously fluid term, as we have seen) could easily assume political significance. At the Necaxa power plant, which supplied the capital with electricity, and which was a favourite Zapatista target, the company maintained a private, volunteer force of some seventy men; it is worth noting, however, that this did not impair the company's relations with revolutionary factions of different stripe.[567] The Aguila Oil Co. raised a similar force in the summer of 1913 but, when attacked by superior rebel forces, both the company guards and the Federal garrison ran away. The lesson was learned and the experiment was not repeated; not so much because the company had qualms about 'white guards' as such, but rather because they now grasped that protection was best secured by maintaining good relations with the prevalent military fashion in the neighbourhood, be it Federal or revolutionary.[568] Bribes, in other words, were more efficacious than bullets; and pragmatic, quasi-fiscal deals were as common, during the revolution, as 'white guard' recruitment and repression were rare. In fact, the fairly general abstention from this form of autonomous self-defence was further proof of the marginal role of foreign companies within the revolutionary process: they could rely on local military protection, in preference to armed self-help, because they were not cast as prime targets of the revolutionary forces, in the way that members of the *Defensas Sociales* were.

With the progress of the revolution, especially in the north, the task of would-be counter-revolutionaries became one of reconquest, rather than of self-defence. The veterans of the Durango *Defensa Social*, as we have seen, attempted a disastrous recovery of the city. In 1913–14, the press reported more successful counter-revolutionary movements. 'Rich *hacendados*' of Sonora were said to be captaining a movement of 'great proportions' in that state; Sinaloa boasted 900 armed counter-revolutionaries by March 1914; with 'guerrilla warfare' affecting Sonora and Chihuahua, it was claimed, the northern counter-revolution was an 'accomplished fact'.[569] By April 1914, the *hacendados* had begun a 'formidable counter-revolution' in the north-east too.[570] No doubt these stories cheered up the newspaper readers of Mexico City; but they reflected government control of the press rather than any genuine, counter-revolutionary tendency.[571] As usual, there was a grain of truth: in June 1913 'one of the most prominent *hacendados* and capitalists' of Sonora had visited the Huertista consul in San Francisco, urging a Federal recapture of Hermosillo and offering the material support of 'a group of capitalists' who, anxious to recover their properties, would furnish up to 700 men at their own expense.[572] Of course the Federals never recovered Hermosillo. Press reports of a counter-revolution in the Altar district of Sonora similarly derived from optimistic hopes rather than accomplished facts; and when, early in 1914, another Huertista consul looked into 'that very secret business, viz., the movement which the refugee proprietors of Sonora, despoiled by the revolutionaries, have for some time been thinking of undertaking on behalf of our government', there was nothing concrete to be reported.[573] Resentful and conspiratorial, the northern *émigrés* were evidence of the revolution's levelling tendencies; but the rebels were never seriously worried about being taken in the rear by a vengeful counter-revolution.

These various, abortive, counter-revolutionary groupings were concentrated in regions of intense rebel activity (Sonora, the Laguna, Durango, the outskirts of the Federal District) and were mounted in close co-operation with the Federal government and army. And they failed for much the same reason that the Federal Army failed: because in such areas of marked social polarisation the balance of forces favoured the revolution; indeed, the very existence of large revolutionary forces, mostly composed of *campesinos*, indicated the moral and political bankruptcy of the well-to-do, especially the landowners, brought about by a generation of Porfirian 'progress'.[574] Most, in fact, preferred flight to resistance. They relied on the Federal Army, and when the Federals failed they packed up and moved on: from Saltillo to the US, from San Luis to Mexico City (in a train chartered by ex-Governor Barrenechea), from Tepic ('all the rich men and their families') to Guadalajara, and thence, it was expected, to the capital.[575] A Protestant missionary in Coahuila had high hopes of winning converts in 1914, now that 'every community is disorganised . . . and the rich families who generally direct the community life are in the US'.[576]

Foreign observers – initially sympathetic – viewed the resignation and apathy of the Mexican elite with increasing impatience. It was, a British journalist thought, the 'refusal of responsibility by the better class' which encouraged rebellion; the 'wealthy classes', Lord Cowdray argued, lacked patriotism, despised their subordinates, and would not shoulder arms even against American invaders.[577] An American miner concurred that 'the high-toned Mexican of the 20% [sc. better-off] class' refused either to perform military service or to contribute significantly to the war effort, save under compulsion.[578] A Prussian commented (and who better to comment?) on the 'utter lack of patriotism and co-operation on the part of the better classes'; while the *Mexican Herald*, abandoning exhortation for ridicule, explained that the 'Plateros volunteers' would postpone campaigning until the rainy season ended, for fear 'of getting their patent leathers wet'.[579] This was not just another foreign prejudice; it was a recognisable feature of Mexican society during the Revolution. Back in 1910 Luis Terrazas had given up hope of arming his retainers and riding out to battle as he had against the Apaches in the 1880s; and his son Alberto, then governor of Chihuahua, had encountered an 'incredible egoism' among the state's *hacendados*, who contributed every excuse to avoid commitment to the government cause.[580]

Perhaps the successful *transacción* at Cd Juárez, the *interinato*, and the ultimate failure of Madero encouraged the elite's complacency. Though, throughout, they were prepared to deploy their political and financial power (for example, in the press and in elections), they avoided direct, violent confrontation: that was not their style. If violence was on the agenda, they deferred to the army, or tried to buy the services of disaffected rebels, like Orozco. And when Félix Díaz raised the standard of revolt on their behalf in October 1912, they did nothing: 'the upper classes, consisting principally of the big landowners ... almost as a unit regarded the situation with complete apathy'.[581] Landed elites are not, of course, incapable of vigorous – including violent – self-defence, or they would not have survived as long as they have. But the Mexican elite (or those large sections of it) which so readily succumbed in 1913–14 was neither a warrior nor an active ruling class, as many of their forebears had been. They were second-generation oligarchs, born into an opulent, urban life-style, shaped by the Porfirian 'order and progress dictatorship' rather than the rampant *caudillismo* of pre-1876, and therefore good for the law, high finance and diplomacy, if they were good for anything at all.[582] In Yucatán, for example, the dozen or so families of the 'Divine Caste', marketing their henequen internationally, supplanted the traditional henequeneros of the peninsula; in Morelos, the pioneers of the 1880s had given way to the educated, Europhile, sophisticates of the 1900s, who delegated to Spanish managers, passed their time in Mexico City or Europe, and – when called upon to govern, as Pablo Escandón was in 1909 – proved unequal to the task.[583] Like other Latin American rural elites, they gave up the right to command in return for the right to make money.[584]

Faced with growing rural rebellion, it was natural that they clung to Mexico City, where the good life continued with remarkable vigour well into 1914, and where they could still attend balls, dine at Silvain's and mix with the diplomatic corps. Some found other diversions: one adult male of the Escandón family, Mrs O'Shaughnessy notes, 'spends this revolutionary period peacefuly constructing small, perfect models of warships and locomotives'.[585] Enrique Creel, endowed with a shrewder grasp of reality, seemed a broken man, painfully conscious of his family's huge losses in Chihuahua; Azuela's fictional family, the Vázquez Prado, were similarly distraught.[586] But whatever the individual reaction – hedonism, withdrawal, dejection – each derived from a collective failure to resist the revolutionary challenge. These Porfirian landlords could negotiate contracts, litigate, play polo and grace drawing rooms, but they could not quell rebellion on or near their estates, still less arm their peons and tenants on behalf of the government. While the civil war raged, their talents and resources were virtually useless. A generation of agrarian commercialisation, absenteeism and polarisation had engendered popular revolt, while debilitating (even as it profited) the rural elite. By heaping spoils on the *hacendado* class, the Porfirian regime had, by a strange irony, led it like a sacrificial lamb to the slaughter.

A fundamental – though by no means unique – feature of the Mexican Revolution was, therefore, an agrarian rebellion against a landlord class which, for all its wealth, had lost its legitimacy in the eyes of the peasantry and was unable to defend its interests during the civil war.[587] The corollary and confirmation of this argument derive from those regions where popular protest was weak, and the landlord interest could defend itself, often without major Federal assistance: in the sierras of Puebla and Oaxaca, where landed caciques still ruled, with or against the revolution; in parts of the Bajío and the south-east, where ranch and plantation survived, and landlords would later display a capacity for mobilisation and resistance; and in provincial towns – like Azuela's Lagos – where the elite of landlord, merchant and cacique did not always have to depend on a massive Federal presence.[588] This divergent pattern cannot be explained solely or even primarily in terms of superior repressive power, which simply did not exist. It depended in part on the absence of popular grievances or organisational capacity, in part on the legitimacy of these elites, which was in turn nourished by ideology, cliente-lism, local 'patriotism', and even shared objective interests. The best examples would be those communities – rare in 1913–14 – which achieved genuine self-defence, and against rebels as well as bandits. In April 1914 the press reported the formation of yet another *Defensa Social*, at Moroleón, Guana-juata.[589] At first sight this looks like more *gobiernista* flannel: maybe the organisation existed only on paper; maybe it was an instrument of the town's elite; certainly it could not defend Moroleón against determined attackers. But in fact the Moroleón *Defensa Social* was vigorous, long-lived and successful, even though its leaders were clearly from the town's elite. As early as December 1910 the community gave notice of its spirit, refusing to hand over to the Maderistas two ancient cannon, used for fiestas.[590] In 1912, when the Pantoja brothers (*bona fide* rebels) demanded 20,000 pesos, the 'moneyed class' met with the *jefe político*, decided to resist, and with a hastily recruited volunteer force put the rebels to flight. Again, in the spring of 1914, when rebels of uncertain identity approached, the volunteers' leader – now claiming the rank of colonel – mobilised his men and drove off the attackers (they left Moreleón alone and joined Gertrudis Sánchez's forces in Michoacán). A third assault was beaten off in July 1914 and a fourth in February 1915; in 1917 Moroleón gave assistance to neighbouring Huandacareo, when it fell into bandit hands; and not until late 1918, when an internal feud over a lady's affections developed was the effective unity of the Moroleón *Defensa Social* impaired.

Perhaps there were comparable examples during the Huerta period (in June 1913 the mayor of Huachinango was reported to have driven off attacking rebels with a volunteer force); but not until 1916–18 did such stories become common.[591] This reflected a real shift in the socio-political climate. Local self-defence was rare under Huerta because, in regions where revolutionary activity made it necessary, the unpopularity of local elites all too often made it impossible. Only communities like Moroleón, which faced an external threat, yet enjoyed a certain internal cohesion (predicated on elite legitimacy and the absence of divisive social conflicts), could mount the kind of successful self-defence which – to take a counter-example – the Durango *Defensa Social* found impossible. The same applied to the landlord class: Terrazas and the Laguna planters had no hope of mobilising their *campesinos* against the revolution; after 1915 landlords in Veracruz, Chiapas, and Oaxaca readily won recruits in order to resist revolutionary incursions into their states. By then, the Federal Army had ceased to exist, yet the southern landlords proved capable of defending their own interests, autonomously and violently.[592] Hence the variety, and the apparent ambivalence, of the elite's response to the revolution: sometimes supine surrender, sometimes red-blooded resistance. It all depended on the time, place and character of local society, for landlord politics – no less than peasant politics – can only be understood in 'relational' terms.[593] Severe social polarisation – in Chihuahua, Durango, the Laguna, in 1910–14 – undercut the old elite while winning mass converts to the revolution; at Moroleón, San José de Gracia, in the sierras of Oaxaca and the Chiapas, 'social solidarity' (in Durkheim's sense) made collective resistance possible, even within inegalitarian communities, and under elite leadership.[594] In 1913–14, the Chihuahua/Durango/Laguna syndrome predominated in much of northern and central Mexico, dissolving traditional authority, abetting popular violence. The current ran for the revolution. Two years later the tide began to turn; the Moroleón/San José/Oaxaca syndrome became more common; traditional elites, hitherto so feeble, started to display a capacity for leadership, resistance and survival. But, in many respects, it was by then too late.

Meanwhile, during 1913–14, the militarisation of Mexico proceeded apace. Civil government gave way to military: independent parties were snuffed out, the Federal legislature was dissolved and its members consigned to gaol. The cabinet, stripped of Felicistas and other potential critics, became a tool and then an ornament. Ministers came and went like errand boys: nine ministerial posts had thirty-two different incumbents in seventeen months; Foreign Affairs and Fomento had five apiece. Garza Aldape, being briefly in Huerta's favour, went from Education to Gobernación via Fomento in three months, with an additional spell as acting Foreign Minister.[595] Undersecretaries moved just as fast. By 1914 the cabinet was a cypher, even if its members had all been issued military rank and uniforms.[596] Major decisions – such as the dissolution of Congress – were taken without ministerial discussion, or in the face of strong ministerial opposition. Meantime, the ministers quarreled among themselves (to Huerta's satisfaction) and grew fearful of presidential reprisals. Being Foreign Minister, Querido Moheno recalled, had been a 'small Calvary'.[597]

The press, too, was soon broken to Huerta's will. Initially, the bulk of the Mexico City press supported Huerta, just as they had opposed Madero; Huerta's private secretary, Jesús Rábago, edited *El Mañana*, and Luis de Toro, another close collaborator, edited *El Independiente*; both had been fierce critics of Madero.[598] But this consensus did not last, and Huerta soon resorted to direct methods of control. Ailing newspapers were subsidised and told what to print. Opposition papers – in the main small and insignificant – were forcibly closed. More important, the influential Catholic press fell foul of the government and began to experience harassment: *El País*, the pre-eminent Mexico City daily, was finally shut down in May 1914 for displaying 'veiled hostility to the government'. By then, only three (Spanish language) dailies remained in the capital: *El Imparcial* and *El Independiente* (neither aptly named and both run by de Toro) and the no less *gobiernista El Día*. And by the summer of 1914, even the editor of *El Imparcial* (a stout Porfirista and Huertista, Salvador Díaz Mirón) was concerned for his personal safety, 'expecting worse evils from the government than from the revolution itself'.[599] In the provinces, too, chosen newspapers (like *El Eco Fronterizo*, at Juárez) were financed, while others (*La Opinión* and *La Voz* of Veracruz) were suppressed.[600]

As a result, the press was 'entirely muzzled' and could print only what the government permitted or required.[601] The tone was set from the beginning, with the publication of the official version of the deaths of Madero and Pino Suárez, which was fundamentally implausible and believed by no-one (save those, like the American Ambassador, who had strong reasons of their own for believing it, or saying that they did).[602] Thereafter, the press concentrated on Federal victories, rebel defeats, inflated recruiting figures and recurrent, orchestrated bouts of anti-Americanism. By March 1914, the British Chargé (no enemy of Huerta) concluded that it was 'useless to seek in the newspapers for any true light upon the state of affairs. They contain nothing but accounts of victories over bandits and revolutionaries in every part of the country'.[603] And many of these 'victories' were entirely spurious.[604] Fictitious stories (for example, the US Navy's sinking of Spanish warship *Carlos V* off the coast of Veracruz) also characterised the anti-American campaigns which, a minister virtually admitted, the regime turned on and off as it chose.[605] Revolutionary victories, of course, presented problems: news was then delayed and distorted, encouraging wild rumour and speculation; and the fall of major cities was belatedly admitted to a shocked population. When the *Mexican Herald* of 9 October 1913 announced the fall of Torreón – over a week after the Federal evacuation and following 'several days filled with mysterious rumour' – it still managed a scoop.[606] Six months later, when Torreón again came under attack, in what was recognised to be the crucial battle of the war, Mexico City waited in an agony of uncertainty. Even individuals close to the government, like the

British Chargé, were baffled: it was 'quite impossible to obtain reliable news concerning events at Torreón'; 'no reliance can be placed on official reports'. Five days after Torreón fell an official communiqué dwelt on the 'very serious reverses' suffered by the rebels; after six days the Minister of War stated that the situation at Torreón was 'entirely satisfactory'. At the far end of this chain of misinformation, Whitehall officials minuted their profound perplexity.[607]

Maderista press freedom was thus thoroughly subverted and forms of control even more draconian than those of Díaz were imposed. Meanwhile, political changes – in state and local as well as Federal government – represented a willing return to Porfirismo, though to a crude, militarized Porfirismo. While Díaz himself prudently ignored conservative overtures, many of his old supporters were ready to re-enter the political fray.[608] Maderista governors swiftly gave way to regular soldiers, usually with long records of service under Díaz: 'old military men', Calero called them, 'of conservative bent, inured to order and discipline'.[609] In Durango, the Federal commander of 1910, Prisciliano Cortés, became governor; Rábago went to Chihuahua, Carlos García to Aguascalientes, Manuel Rivera to Campeche, and so on. Even states relatively untroubled by rebellion thus converted to military rule: by June, Gobernación Minister Urrutia was talking of a complete substitution of all civilian by military governors and by the end of the year this had virtually been achieved.[610]

Often, the transition was urged by local people – *hacendados*, merchants and businessmen, who believed that military rule was the best insurance against revolution (a view to which certain Maderistas, including at least one outgoing governor, also subscribed).[611] Deputations from Guanajuato preceded that state's conversion to military rule under General Rómulo Cuellar; Tlaxcala petitioned for a soldier in the state-house; in Chiapas, the Cristobalenses welcomed General Palafox; while the planters of Morelos 'lobbied constantly' for the return of Juvencio Robles, whom they eventually got.[612] On the coat-tails of the military came many old Porfiristas, eager both to resume their interrupted careers and to serve the new, congenial administration. 'The government', Cowdray's manager in Mexico City reported, 'is getting back into service officers of the old regime – men they can trust – who had retired during the Madero regime [hence] they are feeling more confident.'[613] The old *jefe político* of Salazar (Mich.) – also the nephew of the last Porfirian governor – returned to the district as military commander; both Próspero Cahuantzi and Joaquín Pita, Porfirian stalwarts of Tlaxcala and Puebla respectively, were restored to prominence.[614]

Once in power, the military ran things their own way. Most shared Huerta's objectives – though some were a little more scrupulous in the methods they used to achieve them. 'There is peace! There is peace!', Colonel Joaquín Maass had cried, galloping through the streets of Mexico City to celebrate the fall of Madero; and, if his proclamation was premature, it indicated the overriding concern of the military caste.[615] Generals took control of states mouthing unalloyed Huertista sentiments: 'I shall be inflexible', General José Legorreta warned the Sinaloans, '. . . in punishing with all energy those bad citizens who, by disturbing public order, prolong the state of anarchy and dissolution which we face.'[616] So the purges, trials, and executions began, and Porfiristas supplanted Maderistas down to the lowest levels of government. In Coahuila, a missionary noted, 'things are back to the same old state as in the time of the rule of Sr Garza Galán', even down to the clerks of the customs and post office; 'all the old crowd is back'.[617] General Eduardo Cauz, on assuming the governorship of Veracruz, cut a swathe through the *jefaturas* of the state.[618] Civilian institutions were brushed aside: General Cuellar suppressed the 'minor departments of [the] state government' of Guanajuato, following a 'policy of retrenchment'; and state legislatures which, like the Federal Congress, inflicted pinpricks on dictatorial soldiers were, like the Federal Congress, intimidated and closed down.[619] The civil–military friction which had characterised many states during Madero's presidency was thus resolved in favour of the military. Civilian politics were abolished. Only military solutions, effected by the military, were countenanced. And, as the military budget grew, uninhibited by civilian control, so military graft swelled, becoming 'a thousand times worse than it was under Porfirio and Co., and it was pretty bad then', and culminating in the arrest of a prominent general for misappropriation of funds.[620]

The process of militarisation went further: 'in the summer and fall of 1913 the area under Federal control was gradually converted into one huge military base'.[621] Military freight jammed the railways to the exclusion of other goods; non-strategic factories and stores were ordered to close on Sundays so that employees could receive military instruction; Minister of Gobernación, Urrutia, ordered a similar closure of the *pulquerías* of Mexico City (the decision for which he is most if not best remembered).[622] Students of the National Preparatory School, who had received horses and rifles from the government, could be seen parading through the streets of the capital, their uniforms mingling with those of the post office workers, the journalists, the bank employees, the telegraphists and all the other 'volunteers' called to the colours by the regime.[623] Despite protests, plans were pushed ahead to place all schools on a military footing, with compulsory training, parades and uniforms; in Puebla, primary schoolchildren were issued 900 wooden rifles for practice drill.[624] The police, too, were placed under military command and, by the spring of 1914, military uniform and three hours of military instruction per week were compulsory for all government exployees.[625]

'I do not believe that anyone has established a military Government comparable to mine. All the Mexicans were soldiers': Huerta's so-called memoirs may be apocryphal, but their sentiments, in this case, ring true.[626] These policies had the mark of a personal obsession. Soldiering had been

Huerta's life and, as president–dictator, he sought – so it seemed – to merge Mexico and the military, lavishing every attention on the army, ignoring politics and disdaining civilian politicians (even his own cabinet ministers). He toured the barracks of Mexico City incessantly (indulging his taste for large cars); decked in medals, he attended dozens of parades and ceremonies; he doled out decorations and promotions wholesale. His weekend cottage at Popotla he called his 'Division of the North', and his chosen companions during the long drinking bouts which occupied his evenings were 'old military cronies', whose talk was of women and war.[627] It was on this narrow circle of contacts and experience that Huerta drew for his ideas and inspiration for a year and a half.

Unlike Díaz, Huerta came to the presidency late in life and with scant political experience. In his view, politicians were rogues and trouble-makers, to be silenced forthwith or temporarily exploited until they became expendable: 'the art of government', he opined, 'lay in knowing the use to which each man for his period might be put'.[628] Government was personal and arbitrary: ministers and diplomats scoured the restaurants of Mexico City to find the itinerant president; and, in the president's closed, secretive and maybe superstitious mind, the distinction between public and private blurred – what was good for Huerta was good for the Republic.[629] We may discern here not only that equation between the military and the nation which has characterised a later generation of 'new authoritarians' (of whom Huerta was a notable forerunner), but also that hidebound, dogmatic incompetence to which career soldiers are prone.[630] In his diplomacy, both personal and international, Huerta was brusque and unsubtle. Ministers were sacked, with the minimum of courtesy, and they were not alone in serving as butts for the president's mordant humour. In his relations with the US Huerta blew hot and cold, aggravating a conflict that might well have been avoided.[631] Foreigners who met Huerta were often impressed (many of them, too, despised Mexican *políticos* and welcomed the 'iron hand'): Huerta seemed simple, unpretentious, stoic, canny; he had, the British Chargé noted, 'an air of firm resolution and determination'.[632] Some attributed this to Huerta's Huichol ancestry. Huerta was 'the old Indian', dour, inscrutable and tenacious. Mrs O'Shaughnessy, in one of those Lawrencian lapses to which even intelligent ladies in Mexico seem prone, found Huerta 'very canny . . . and full of vitality and a sort of tireless Indian perseverance'.[633] Other foreigners were more hard-headed and critical. A French entrepreneur came away from an interview with Huerta unimpressed: 'en effet, c'est un naïf'.[634] This was closer to the truth. Huerta was a competent and ruthless soldier, largely devoid of political talent, but who through a combination of military skill, luck, ambition and deviousness, came to occupy the presidency and embody the counter-revolutionary hopes welling up in Mexican society. He was Mexico's Kornilov: but it was his regime, not his *coup d'état*, which foundered in disaster.

REVOLUTION? COUNTER-REVOLUTION? WHAT REVOLUTION?[635]

Huerta was Mexico's Kornilov – or was he? Michael Meyer has deployed considerable research and learning to argue that, within the general framework of the Mexican Revolution, Huerta's regime was not counter-revolutionary, as often supposed.[636] This is an important question, central to any interpretation of the Revolution. Meyer arrives at his conclusion by setting out the 'basic goals of the Mexican Revolution', and then comparing both Huerta's and Madero's performance against these criteria. Since, he argues, 'Huerta's administration can be no more counter-revolutionary than Madero's was revolutionary', and since, on his criteria, the two are indistinguishable, therefore Huerta cannot be seen as an exponent of counter-revolution.[637] The 'basic goals' of the Revolution are listed as: agrarian reform, the protection of labour, education, economic and political nationalism, the defence and recovery of Indian culture – *indigenismo*. In these areas, it is argued, Huerta's policies differed little from Madero's, or were even more progressive and 'revolutionary'. The old Manichaean view of the Revolution – Madero good (or quite good), Huerta bad – is shown up as a primitive myth; the certitudes of revolutionary historiography are blasted; the new philosophy calls all in doubt. Such exercises in scepticism and revisionism are to be welcomed. But is the old Manichaeanism (in this instance) so flawed? Meyer is open to two kinds of criticism: first, that the evidence he cites concerning the Huerta regime is misleading; and second that the conceptual framework supporting the hypothesis is badly constructed.

Meyer cites Wilkie's budgetary analysis to show that Huerta's projected expenditure on 'social' items (education, public health, social security) was slightly higher than Madero's, and a good deal higher than that of the 'revolutionary' regime of 1917–20.[638] As regards education, which comprised the bulk of this expenditure, Huerta projected 9.9% of total expenditure for this field, compared with Madero's 7.3% and Díaz's 6.8%.[639] Ministers of Education, Vera Estañol and García Naranjo, both outlined broad schemes of educational reform during Huerta's presidency (though their approaches differed significantly, the first favouring rural, primary schools, the second seeking a revision of the secondary curriculum).[640] In agrarian matters, Huerta went beyond Madero at least to the extent of creating a separate Ministry of Agriculture, whose first incumbent, Eduardo Tamariz, looked to fiscal equalisation to effect land redistribution. 'The administration', Meyer concludes, 'was not opposed to the subdivision of the large estates . . . [and] was thinking in terms quite different from that [sic] of the Díaz regime'; hence, Huerta began to lose support among the landlord class.[641] In its treatment of foreign interests, too, the regime 'broke sharply with the past', with Huerta spurring Congress and cabinet to produce a plan for the nationalisation of the oil industry; and, on the international front, Huerta's defence of Mexican sovereignty in the face of North American interference, was the immediate, almost indistinguishable forerunner of the 'Carranza doctrine'.[642] Towards the Church, Huerta was no clerical lackey; and (more interestingly) his relations with organised labour were not wholly antagonistic. The new Department of Labour continued its work; strikes were tolerated; even the radical Casa del Obrero Mundial was allowed to operate in Mexico City until, following some outspoken attacks on the regime in the spring of 1914, its leaders were arrested and the foreigners among them expelled from the country.[643]

On closer inspection, however, Huerta does not emerge from this test of his 'revolutionary' (or, strictly, non-counter-revolutionary) credentials as well as is claimed – even assuming, for the moment, that the test is valid. To begin with, the budgets afford poor evidence. Even allowing for the vagaries of statistics, we still have only *projected* budgets for the Huerta period. Huerta's actual expenditure (for example, on education) is unknown, and it should be borne in mind that 1913–14 witnessed a soaring military budget and crumbling government finances. It was a period when non-essential – that is, civilian – projects were shelved, not expanded.[644] With regard to education, as well as other fields, accomplished facts would be no more persuasive than notional figures. Vera Estañol certainly drew up an ambitious plan for rural education; but he fell from power before anything significant could be achieved, and what evidence there is of new schools and an expanded school population must be culled from the dubious record of congressional debates.[645] No provincial reports attest the establishment of any of the 131 new schoools, allegedly set up between February and September 1913. Vera Estañol's successor, García Naranjo, undertook a reform of the secondary curriculum which, Meyer ventures, 'historians have had a difficult time [in] fitting . . . into the counter-revolutionary hypothesis of the Huerta regime'. But their silence on this subject hardly denotes embarrassment. As so often in history, it is a question of what is important and what is not. García Naranjo's reforms may be important within the evolution of Mexican educational thought (in fact, even this is debatable), but they are not important within an analysis of the Huerta regime and the Revolution. Huerta himself did not dictate every aspect of policy. Like any president, he delegated, and he delegated all the more in areas of policy which did not interest him. This did not detract from his ultimate autocratic power: examples are not wanting of autocrats who meddled incessantly in certain areas of policy (Mussolini in the press, Hitler in the armed forces) while neglecting others (in both cases, economic policy); Hitler's case suggests that dictatorial power could be enhanced, rather than diminished, by the delegation of responsibility, and the opportunities for factional manipulation which it afforded. Huerta lost nothing by letting his education ministers float schemes for reform: they sounded good in congressional debates, looked good in the press, and might

never come to fruition anyway. It was soon clear that Huerta could remove
ministers at will, that they and their pet schemes existed solely on presidential
sufferance; both the speed with which they entered and left office, and the
cavalier, even cruel treatment to which they were subjected while in office,
indicated the narrow scope of ministers' power. Huerta's overriding concern
was the prosecutiion of the war, which for him was a purely military question,
and the Huertista regime reflected this priority. To the extent that any
ministers counted, they were the ministers of war, finance, and the interior;
education lacked importance and the projects of ephemeral education
ministers offer no basis for an evaluation of the regime as a whole.[646]

The same was true of agriculture. Successive ministers produced proposals:
Toribio Esquivel Obregón, once a lukewarm Maderista, now Huerta's finance
minister, advocated the provision of government credit to enable the landless
to purchase holdings from the swollen estates; the first full minister of
agriculture, the conservative, Catholic Eduardo Tamariz, believed that fiscal
equalisation would make for a redistribution of land.[647] Both schemes, Meyer
concedes, were 'timid'; both had been scouted before (fiscal equalisation had
made real progress under Madero), and both were rejected by Congress anyway
– the second by Huerta's packed Congress. Individual ministers thus wrestled
with intractable problems in a deteriorating political, military and economic
climate, bereft of presidential support: it is in this light that González Roa (in
what Meyer calls an 'excellent analysis' of Esquivel Obregón's proposals) sees
Huerta's ministers tackling agrarian policy.[648] It is wrong to conclude from
these modest, individual, unfulfilled efforts that 'the Huerta regime was
thinking in terms quite different from that [sic] of the Díaz regime'.[649]
Indeed, if Moheno's version is true, the very creation of the Ministry of
Agriculture – the one genuine innovation of Huerta's regime – derived from
the president's desire to reshuffle the cabinet, introducing supporters and
demoting those he mistrusted.[650] Considerations of personal power, rather
than social necessity, acted as midwives of the new ministry.

So, too, with Huerta's alleged economic nationalism. As regards its
'relationship with foreign capital', Meyer writes, 'the [Huerta] regime broke
sharply with the past'. In fact the evidence advanced relates solely to the oil
industry which, despite its rapid, recent growth, still comprised only a
fraction of foreign investment in Mexico. Mines, railways, real estate and
public utilities were unaffected by Huertista 'economic nationalism', though,
like all property in Mexico at the time, they faced an increasing tax burden.
Indeed, it should be remembered that at the outset of his regime Huerta was
prepared to offer the US generous terms in the hope of securing diplomatic
recognition: there is not much economic nationalism there.[651] The increased
taxation of the oil industry came as companies began to realise handsome
profits, which were a standing temptation to regimes of all political hues:
Madero had already begun the upward revision of oil production taxes, which

Huerta and Huerta's successors continued; if mounting petroleum taxes were indicative of economic nationalism, then it was a trait which affected a series of politically diverse regimes, in evolutionary fashion.[652]

More dramatic was the proposal presented to Congress in September 1913 by Querido Moheno, who sought the nationalisation of petroleum reserves, which would be exploited by a state agency, in collaboration with private interests. Existing companies, merged into this 'giant company', would suffer no financial loss, though they would presumably sacrifice managerial independence; the scheme was reminiscent of Limantour's railway merger of a few years before and, as Moheno later pointed out, it involved nationalisation 'on bases and with objectives which were completely different to those pursued by the revolutionary regime' in subsequent years.[653] Still, like García Naranjo's educational reforms, this was a significant initiative. But it is not at all clear that Huerta or the Huerta administration backed it. The oil companies (whose intelligence in these matters was usually good) showed little anxiety over Moheno's nationalisation scheme: they were more worried about increased taxation and the immediate threat to property posed by the civil war.[654] Lord Cowdray, in a footnote, dismissed Moheno's scheme as 'absurd and impractical'.[655] Furthermore, for a plan supposedly concocted and supported at the highest levels of government, it met a sad and obscure fate. Moheno complained that the press ignored his proposal and, within days of making it, he was shifted out of Congress and into the cabinet.[656] This, Meyer reckons, 'indicate[d] that the threat of nationalisation enjoyed presidential support and was no idle bluff'; as Foreign Minister, Moheno could 'deal directly' with the companies' metropolitan governments. But there is no evidence that he subsequently locked horns with either companies or governments; his departure from Congress was considered the death-knell of the plan; and Moheno, apparently agreeing, could only promise to assist the legislature in this matter as a private individual and 'representative of the people'. These were hardly the words of a minister about to carry through a key item in government policy.[657] Furthermore, as Foreign Minister, Moheno found himself consistently ignored and thwarted, while his efforts – in respect of oil nationalisation and other issues – 'had an absolutely negative result'.[658] Like other Huertista ministers, he ploughed a lonely, ragged furrow, from which nothing sprouted.

There is finally the question of Huerta's relations with the labour movement.[659] As we have noted, the urban workers shared the general feeling of resentment at the fall of Madero. But, after their usual manner, they took no direct action and, instead, continued the day-to-day struggle for unionisation, more pay and better conditions. Strikes continued, and strikers were not treated as if they were urban Zapatistas. The docks, for example, were once again a focal point: five unions struck at Progreso in June 1913; the Department of Labour intervened to settle a similar strike at Tampico in the same month; in November, Veracruz was likewise affected and the govern-

ment urged employers to conciliate the stevedores and reach a settlement.[660]
Though it seems clear that the incidence of strike action declined in 1913–14,
compared with 1911–12, nevertheless, as these examples suggest, government policy was not one of indiscriminate repression.[661] Officials distinguished between economist union activity, which could be tolerated, and
revolutionary political commitment, which could not.[662] And, since the
latter was exceptional, repression was not widespread. Furthermore, Meyer is
quite right to point out, the government's attitude towards labour was not
purely passive. The Department of Labour remained in being and continued
its work of arbitration. In July 1913 the Huertista governor of Chihuahua,
General Mercado, approved an employers' liability law, a decision which was
locally interpreted as 'a bid by the present *de facto* authorities for the support of
the masses'.[663] Workers were drawn – or driven – into the nationalist
demonstrations and volunteer forces which proliferated in 1913–14. Thus the
Huerta administration was not unaware of the potential usefulness of the urban
working class, as a source of political and military recruits. In return, it offered
concessions: the authorities tolerated a huge May Day demonstration in
Mexico City in 1913; and the Casa del Obrero Mundial survived well into
1914, its organ, *El Sindicalista*, churning out attacks on the Catholics, harsh
employers and (unspecified) political demagogues, while avoiding reference to
the military campaigns in the north.[664]

A vague, rhetorical radicalism of this kind did not trouble the regime: let
the workers laud Rousseau and Ferrer, so long as they worked the docks and
railways and did not join Villa or Zapata. Direct opposition to the regime,
however, was soon punished. When Casa leaders convened a meeting in
Mexico City at which Huerta was denounced (not least for the murder of
Madero), they were arrested and several foreigners among them expelled from
the country.[665] Huerta's regime, like its predecessors and successors, saw the
advantages of encouraging a client labour movement; and the workers, for
their part, realistically recognised that they could make gains – albeit limited,
economic gains – by deferring to the government, invoking its protection, and
pitching their political radicalism at a suitably abstract and irrelevant level.
Thus, the May Day demonstrators respectfully presented their demands (for an
eight hour day and a six day week) to the Congress which had recognised
Huerta; workers' groups – some organised by a prominent Department of
Labour functionary – offered their support to Félix Díaz in his presidential
campaign; factory workers and railwaymen responded to Huerta's patriotic
appeal for volunteers.[666] Even allowing (in the latter case) for official pressure,
it would seem that elements of the emerging working class/government
detente, based on a shared urban environment, a shared stake in commercial
prosperity and a shared antipathy to the barbarians of both Gringo America
and Zapatista Morelos, survived during 1913–14, even when the worker was
an avowed anarchist, and the government was a military despotism.[667]

In his commitment to revisionism, then, Meyer seems to me to strain the evidence. It is correct to point out, if it needs pointing out, that Huerta was no lackey of the Church, and that he did not repress the labour movement root-and-branch. On the other hand, much of the mild reformism of 1913–14 (agrarian and educational policy, the oil nationalisation scheme, labour reform) was the work of individual ministers or officials, who faced – at best – presidential indifference, and whose projects often remained on paper. As Meyer puts it, in a telling admission, 'concerned as he was with the military and diplomatic engagements, [Huerta] failed to clearly perceive the potential significance of the series of measures emanating from within his government'.[668] If we were dealing with a puppet president, manipulated by over-mighty ministers, the revisionist thesis might have more to commend it; but it was the ministers who were the puppets, and Huerta who pulled the strings.[669] Hence Huerta's preferred policies of repression and militarism prevailed, and ministerial reformism went by the board.

These policies should be categorised as 'counter-revolutionary', and they were markedly more 'counter-revolutionary' than Madero's. In presenting this essentially traditional case, we come to the second aspect of Meyer's thesis: its conceptual framework. It is a highly selective piece of revisionism: it questions the inherited ideas about Huerta, but accepts all the old orthodoxies about Díaz and the Revolution; and these orthodoxies provide the criteria against which Huerta is judged. First, Huerta's – and Madero's – moderate reforms are compared with the reactionary Porfiriato, when 'the old stereotype system of nineteenth-century privilege and abuse' prevailed, 'hostile to all notions of twentieth-century liberalism'.[670] Huerta, it is argued, did not want to go back to that; his policies point in a different direction; he could not therefore play the counter-revolutionary. But this is a caricature of the Díaz regime. *Pace* much traditional history (of the kind Meyer questions when it deals with Huerta), Porfirian policies were not so radically different from those of later regimes. On Meyer's checklist of 'revolutionary' policies, only agrarian reform stands out as a revolutionary commitment for which there were no real Porfirian precedements (even here, a politically threatened Díaz had made some grudging, belated, reformist gestures, much as Huerta was to do). In other respects, the picture of a regime of black reaction is false: order *and* progress was the positivist slogan, and positivism itself was an authoritarian, technical version of liberalism; progress, rather than reaction, caused the Revolution.

Education, under Justo Sierra, did not stagnate; the educational budget doubled during the 1900s; and Vera Estañol, one of Meyer's Huertista reformers, had served as Díaz's last education minister.[671] Porfirian labour policy involved conciliation and co-optation, as well as repression.[672] In the realm of economic nationalism, it was Limantour who merged and nationalised the railways; it was Olegario Molina who, as Minister of Fomento, advocated and almost achieved a major revision of the mining code; and it was the Porfirian regime which began the nationalisation of the railways' labour force (a policy continued by both Madero and Huerta).[673] Even a kind of sloppy, rhetorical *indigenismo*, not so different from the sloppy, rhetorical *indigenismo* of 1913–14, was evident during the Porfiriato.[674] Finally, Huerta's opportunistic confrontations with the US cannot be taken as proof of a pioneering nationalism, contrasting with Díaz's *vendepatria* servility; this, in the case of Díaz, represents just the kind of cheap stereotype which, in the case of Huerta, Meyer seeks to eliminate. For, as Madero commented, 'if [Díaz] has governed us despotically, he has nonetheless always comported himself with patriotism in his dealings with foreign powers'.[675]

In many respects (agrarian reform was the prime exception) post-Porfirian regimes built on Porfirian precedents, particularly those of the 1900s. The parallels between the mature Porfirian regime and the Sonoran regime of the 1920s are striking, certainly in the areas upon which Meyer focusses. But here we enter the second area where revisionism is shelved in favour of bland orthodoxy. Meyer compares Huerta first with a stereotyped (reactionary) Porfiriato, then with a stereotyped (radical) revolution. Huertismo, by virtue of its reformism, departs from the first and aligns with the second. But if the new departure is, as we have suggested, empirically wrong, the revolutionary alignment is conceptually bogus. It is both true and interesting that several Huertista policies (those dealing with labour, education, foreign interests, for example) superficially resemble those of post–1917 revolutionary regimes (just as they also build on Porfirian precedent): they reflect the underlying continuity of government in its role as a state- and nation-builder, as well as the priorities of intellectuals and *políticos*, be they Científicos, Huertista reformers, or revolutionary administrators. The caste of mind – if not the careers – of Sierra, Vera Estañol, and Pani are in this respect comparable. But within this secular continuity the years 1910–17 mark a break and exception. Events, individuals and regimes falling within this period cannot be judged according to criteria imported from outside. The relevant criteria – of what is significant or insignificant, revolutionary or counter-revolutionary – must be 'endogenous', and cannot consist of a neat checklist of later, 'revolutionary' policies. In other words, they must be different from those employed by Meyer; and it is here that Meyer's conceptual framework, and with it the revisionist thesis, fall to the ground.

The appropriate criteria for evaluating the Huerta regime must derive from the Revolution itself – from, that is, the conflicts and allegiances (class, regional, ideological, ethnic and clientelist) which lent the Revolution its fundamental character in the years 1910–17.[676] These cannot be reduced to a checklist of governmental policies. Indeed, several of Meyer's indices (economic, nationalism, labour policy, *indigenismo*) were peripheral to the Revolution, especially in the formative years 1910–15; they became more important after 1915 precisely as popular mobilisation and social conflict (the defining characteristics of the Revolution) declined; they were features of *reconstruction* as much as of revolution. There is no evidence that thousands fought to expropriate foreign assets, enact labour laws, or rescue Indian culture. If, on the other hand, we eschew hindsight and revolutionary orthodoxy (both of which lead inexorably to this conventional checklist), we can safely generalise that the two most powerful forces fuelling the Revolution were the social and political liberalism of Madero and his urban, middle-class constituency, and the rural populism of the common people, both *agrarista* and *serrano*. The liberals initiated the onslaught upon the old regime, and ventured their alternative in 1911–13; the rural populists raised the people in arms and kept the armies on the march, and the country in upheaval, for years thereafter. Both were integral to the Revolution, and both – notwithstanding their mutual hostility and often commonplace ideologies – were 'revolutionary', in the sense it is used here. The criteria of being 'revolutionary' – and therefore of being 'counter-revolutionary' too – must derive from the actions, commitments and conflicts exemplified by these key groups; and, while formal policies comprise part of this total analysis, they may comprise only a small part, and they may not be the formal policies which with hindsight are often emphasised.

But, as the phrase, 'mutual hostility' reminds us, the Revolution was not monolithic. The city liberals and rural populists, briefly united against Díaz in 1910–11, soon fell out in 1911–13 (and the quarrel was further complicated by the 'logic of the Revolution' already referred to). Hence, legal, liberal reforms made only limited headway and, in its bid to suppress popular revolt and to uphold constituted authority, the Madero regime drifted closer to Porfirian precedents and practices, enlisting old Porfirian experts as it did. It is quite legitimate to see this as a form of counter-revolution: a concerted effort to halt popular mobilisation, reinforce existing authorities and curb local, often agrarian reforms. And, since this was evident – with the last-minute 'revolutionaries' of central Mexico or the Maderista negotiators at Juárez – as early as the spring of 1911, 'revolution' and 'counter-revolution' must be seen as virtually coeval, and even co-existing within individuals and within administrations.

At Juárez and after, Madero connived at counter-revolution? Here lies half the answer to Meyer's conundrum: 'Huerta's administration can be no more counter-Revolutionary than Madero's was Revolutionary.'[677] In repressing the popular movement, both Madero's and Huerta's regimes were counter-revolutionary; Huerta simply went further in eagerly applying the measures (massive recruitment, counter-insurgency operations, indiscriminate killing, military government) which Madero had reluctantly initiated. In this respect the coup of February 1913 was less a sudden U-turn than a switch to overdrive, as a diffident learner gave way to a fast-car fanatic who at once put his foot to the floor. And the fact that the one supplanted the other does not disqualify both from being 'counter-revolutionary': had Kornilov succeeded in supplanting Kerensky he would have been no less 'counter-revolutionary' for the fact of sharing some of Kerensky's attitudes to rebellious troops and peasants.

But this is not to say that Madero and Huerta were two of a kind. Their treatment of popular rebellion – an absolutely central issue in 1911–14 – was comparable; but with regard to the liberal strand within the Revolution they significantly diverged. Mexican liberalism, with its concern for civilian, constitutional rule, individual rights and the enlightened 'progress' of society, had deep roots; if, in practice, it had experienced many defeats and failures it could still raise high hopes and command strong allegiances. Liberal examples and aphorisms pervaded the discourse of the Revolution; revolutionaries (even of those of 'radical' stripe, who have often been seen as transcending these antiquated ideas) conceived of their struggle as but another episode in the 'secular battle between LIBERALS and CONSERVATIVES'.[678] Far from moribund, Mexican liberalism experienced a revival in the late Porfiriato, and Madero's political movement rode on this revival. Once in power, the Maderistas, like preceding liberal generations, found the implementation of their programme to be supremely difficult, especially in the context of continuing civil war. But they did not wholly renege on their liberal principles: the 'liberal apostasy', referred to above, was partial and patchy, and the result was a confused, ambiguous situation. Though the army swelled, martial law was introduced, and arbitrary shootings, press-ganging and election-fixing took place, nevertheless a form of civilian government remained (especially in the cities), legislatures functioned, political parties flourished, the press enjoyed unprecedented freedom, and the more extreme abuses of the military were held in check.

Perhaps this tension between civilian liberalism and military despotism had ultimately to be resolved. Towards the end of the Madero presidency some hard-line Maderistas – the 'hawks' – were developing policies which might adapt liberalism to its hostile environment. But these efforts (whose intrinsic 'liberalism' may be disputed) were cut short; the liberal experiment ended with the *Decena Trágica*; and Huerta came to power promising to restore peace by his own methods, untrammeled by liberal scruple. Notwithstanding the policies of enlightened education ministers, the oil nationalisation scheme, or the participation of police bands at *indigenista* ceremonies in honour of Cuauhtémoc, this meant one thing: an attempt to return, by Porfirian methods, to the Pax Porfiriana; or – if newer, tougher measures were required – by neo-Porfirian methods to a Pax neo-Porfiriana. It meant therefore, the repression of the popular movement and also the systematic dismantling of Maderista liberalism: on the one hand, counter-insurgency campaigns in the countryside, on the other, campaigns of political repression in the towns and cities. In short, it meant a wholesale counter-revolution. Huerta's ministers were largely Porfiristas, his governors were generals and Porfiristas, his provincial sympathisers and officials were ex-Porfirian office-holders, *políticos*, landlords and businessmen. Huerta's coup gave them hope and an opportunity to recover their old influence. It was not that they had disappeared under Madero; but they had perforce been more pliant and circumspect, seeking to defend their threatened interests by judicious involvement in the new politics – as the *Liga de Agricultores* did in Tlaxcala, or Braniff and Dehesa did in Veracruz. After the coup they could throw off the pretence: by April 1913, Dehesa was 'considerably mixed up in politics already', exemplifying the Porfirian *revanche* that was evident at all levels of government in 1913–14.[679]

Conversely, Maderistas were purged wholesale. Elected governors and local officials were turfed out of office. Persecution was thorough and sustained: 'now', noted an American, when Piedras Negras fell to the Federals in October 1913, 'begins the punishment for political crimes which will take many men who haven't fled'.[680] Sometimes, persecution culminated in assassination. Meanwhile, state and federal legislatures were closed at gun-point; elections were flouted more cynically than ever; newspapers and political parties – both enjoying a new-found vigour after the Madero period – were harassed and annihilated. The government of the country fell to the Federal Army – an army dependent on sullen conscripts and seconded by the ineffectual hirelings of landlords and businessmen. Huerta thus steamrollered the shaky edifice of civilian liberalism which the Maderistas had set up in 1911–13. He tried, at the same time, to steamroller the popular movements in the countryside. In the first undertaking he succeeded, in the second he failed: the Federal Army was better suited to political repression in the cities than to counter-insurgency campaigns in the countryside, and the Zapatistas were tougher opponents than the Renovadores of the Twenty-sixth Congress. That Huerta attempted this policy of dual repression is, however, important when it comes to the evaluation of his regime and its place within the Revolution. If Madero represented – forgive the cliché – a Janus-faced combination of liberal revolution and social counter-revolution, Huerta stood for counter-revolution on both fronts; and this is revealed not so much in formal policies as in the objective social and political conflicts which wracked the country. Huerta aimed to smash the city liberals as well as the rural populists. In this he terminated the ambiguities of Maderismo, harked back to Díaz, and stood in outright opposition to the two main currents of the Revolution. His regime was one of consistent, rigorous counter-revolution.

THE CONSTITUTIONALIST COALITION

In the north, meanwhile, we may discern the beginnings of a new political synthesis which, escaping the grosser failings of Díaz, Madero and Huerta, promised to find a way out of the cycle of rebellion, repression and instability.

Constitutionalism – or Carrancismo – was not simply Maderismo redivivus.[681] True, it recruited many old Maderistas, it made similar pledges, it was similarly infused with liberal ideas, and it honoured the anniversary of Madero's death every February. But Maderismo had failed in practice and experienced a tragic demise. Carrancismo was therefore the 'self-criticism' of Maderismo, refined and tempered in the furnace of 1913–14; it exemplified a 'new spirit and a new conception of political struggle', in which the old liberal idealism gave way to a 'ruthless, cunning, arbitrary' *realpolitik*.[682] Alternatively, it was the 'hawkish' Maderismo of 1912 grown to maturity. Some have interpreted this change chiefly in terms of a new emphasis on social reform, supplanting Madero's commitment to *laissez-faire* liberalism. Though there is some truth in this, it is easily exaggerated, especially if more weight is placed on words than on deeds. It would be truer to say that Carrancismo departed from Maderismo in respect of means, not ends. For, if we shelve for the moment the difficult question of Carrancista ends, it is certainly clear that the Carrancistas showed – in their pursuit – a flinty intransigence uncharacterist of Madero: they declined to compromise with the old regime and fought a war to the finish; they built up an army that confronted the Federals in open battle and ultimately annihilated them; they ruthlessly purged supporters of the old regime and systematically promoted their own. None of this necessarily made the Carrancistas more radical than Madero in their objectives (often, the general principles they espoused were similar); these policies were grounded in bitter experience rather than radical ideology; and they were carried through in the interest of survival. 'Political ideals', Córdova comments, 'were no longer the motor of political action; the prime mover was success for its own sake, this was the true objective.'[683] Ideals became less instigators of action than *ex post facto* justifications of actions taken from expedience (often in conformity to the 'logic of the Revolution'). Thus, with certain exceptions, the Carrancistas did not carry much ideological baggage to slow their advance: their prime concern was the defeat of Huerta, and what they would do once this was achieved remained a mystery. At any rate, if they won, they would win on their own terms, by their own efforts, and they would enjoy a measure of autonomous power denied Madero.

This was evident in the earliest days of Carranza's revolt against Huerta. After their abortive attack on Saltillo, Carranza and his followers retired north towards Monclova, spending the night of 25 March at the Hacienda de Guadalupe. Next morning, Carranza and his secretary, Alfredo Breceda, composed a political manifest which was presented to the governor's entourage – mostly young north-easterners, fifteen or twenty years his junior: Cesareo Castro, Jacinto Treviño, Lucio Blanco, Francisco Múgica.[684] It was a short, narrowly political document, which disavowed the Huerta regime, named Carranza First Chief of the Constitutionalist Army, and scheduled a return to constitutional government once Huerta was overthrown. It was concerned solely with the political here-and-now, and avoided all reference to socio-economic reforms – or, indeed, to political reforms of a general character. In this, it set a pattern which local Constitutionalist manifestoes – in Sinaloa or Tamaulipas, for example – also followed.[685] Carranza's young lieutenants were disappointed; they argued (it is recorded) for social and economic reforms, in particular for land distribution, for the abolition of peonage, for labour legislation.[686] Carranza doused their youthful ardour. The aim of the plan, he explained, was to facilitate the Constitutionalists' seizure of national power; an elaborate, radical plan would polarise opinion and foment opposition, while a short statement of political intent would not; did they favour a civil war of two or of five years' duration? Carranza's draft was – albeit grudgingly – accepted and signed. Known as the Plan of Guadalupe ('oft-mentioned and highly overrated', in Cumberland's words), it owed nothing to the reformist ideas evident in Madero's Plan of San Luis and, more strikingly, in Zapata's Plan of Ayala and Orozco's Plan de la Empacadora.[687] It carried no more ideological weight than Félix Díaz's plan of the previous October. What it aimed to do, above all, was to legitimise the Constitutionalist revolution and rivet Carranza's personal control upon it. For, after repudiating Huerta, his government and all state governors who did not reject Huerta within thirty days, it named Carranza First Chief and laid down that, when the Constitutionalists had taken Mexico City, the First Chief would assume the executive and, as provincial president, call elections 'as soon as peace has been consolidated'.[688]

In making this claim to national leadership, Carranza risked ridicule. His own Coahuilan forces – of, at most, a few thousand – had just been defeated at the gates of Saltillo. In all other states, save Sonora, Huerta enjoyed official recognition and controlled the Federal Army. Carried along by events, Carranza took a gamble unprecedented in his sober careful career. Over time, it paid off handsomely, conferring on Carranza undoubted prestige as Huerta's most prominent, elevated and constitutional opponent (Governor Maytorena of Sonora, his only potential rival, having ducked the issue and left for the US). Other revolutionary caudillos might excel in military power or popular appeal, but none could press a stronger claim to national leadership. And the revolution, however fragmented and factious, needed a national leadership to confer legitimacy, to deal with foreign powers, and to attempt some co-ordination among its diverse elements. This privilege was bestowed upon Carranza, the prize for his bold action in February–March 1913. With a firm belief in his own self-righteousness, and thus a readiness to assume authority far beyond what his material position warranted, Carranza was well suited to his new role. Some regarded it as silly or arrogant, as the First Chief fired off decrees, instructions and diplomatic notes from footholds in the far north – later on the Gulf coast. But Carranza survived, and his claims to national power – staked early and maintained through thick and thin – were ultimately made good, even as other caudillos, more powerful but also more diffident, ultimately failed. Like a coy virgin with a fat dowry but a horde of tiresome relatives, national power would only surrender to a single-minded suitor, sure of his own merits, undeterred by the responsibilities, and covetous of the prize.

This was apparent at the outset, as Carranza strove to assert his authority over the revolutionary coalition he claimed to lead. Representatives of Sonora and Chihuahua (the latter a solitary state deputy) met at Monclova and adhered to the Plan of Guadalupe; one of their number, brother of the interim governor of Sonora, was despatched to Washington to plead the Constitutionalist case, in the hope of securing recognition of the rebels' belligerency; and, notwith-standing his precarious situation, Carranza 'began issuing decrees of para-mount importance to the nation's future'.[689] Five million pesos of paper money were issued (the first ripple in a tide of paper than would eventually engulf the country); responsibility was assumed for all damages suffered by Mexicans and foreigners since the Revolution began in 1910; and a decree of 1862, promulgated by Juárez during the French Intervention, and laying down that all enemy prisoners, being rebels against a legitimate government, could be executed, was contentiously revived. It stood as an earnest of Carrancista determination and a riposte for Huertista killings, but it received a bad press, giving substance to press stories of rebel brutality and thus diminishing the broad appeal which Carranza hoped his cause might attain. And, like other Carrancista decrees, its implementation depended a great deal on the character and whim of local commanders.[690] Further decrees, published later in the year, regularised the collection of export and other taxes in rebel territory and legitimised the confiscation of property belonging to 'enemies of the Revolution'. In both cases, Carranza sought to control existing practices of *de facto* taxation and sequestration which – whether in a rough and ready, ad hoc manner, or according to the orderly, bureaucratic methods of the Sonorans – were already widespread.[691] Again, the First Chief's capacity to control and regulate was strictly limited. But such measures revealed Carranza's percep-tion that the war would be a long one, and that the revolution would require substantially more organisation and financial backing than the six-month wonder of the Madero revolt.

Carranza's most pressing problem was that of the revolutionary army. In fact, there was no army: rather, the state forces of Sonora and Coahuila (the latter in full retreat) and the scattered forces of dozens of *cabecillas* in a dozen other states. Like Huerta, Carranza's chief preoccupations were military; but whereas Huerta strove to strengthen an army which he surely controlled, Carranza had to impose his nominal authority over a powerful, expanding, but refractory popular movement. In return, he could offer only the imprimatur of legality and the promise of material support. The first weighed with some rebels more than with others: to the orderly, legalistic Sonorans, it afforded a means to settle – that is, to paper over – their internal squabbles, and Carranza thereby gained a political foothold in Sonora; but many rebels accepted Carranza's authority and the Carrancista label in a more cavalier spirit, while in some parts of the country, far from the north, local conflicts continued throughout 1913–14 in complete disregard of the Constitutionalist revolution.[692] As regards material support – arms and cash – Carranza had little to offer. Rebels had to raise money locally, by levies and taxes, robberies and ransoms; arms had to be imported or wrested from the Federals; in both respects, of course, the northerners had a marked advantage. But those who hoped that Carranza would come bearing gifts were disappointed. The Laguna and Durango rebels, who welcomed Carranza to their encampment near Torreón in July 1913, expecting that 'the First Chief would bring a sufficient number of men and a large quantity of ammunition', received no more than a request for 1,000 pesos to cover his travelling expenses (which he got).[693] The rebels of distant Tabasco, who dispatched emissaries to seek out Carranza 'or any other leader of the Constitutionalist Revolution in the north, so they may supply us with arms and munitions, which we totally lack' were similarly disappointed; the Tabascan revolution had to supply itself (it even tried to trade pigs for guns with the US Navy); and not until the summer of 1914 did northern assistance materialise, by which time it was far from disinterested.[694]

The authority of the First Chief was thus limited; he could not enforce strict obedience; and the Constitutionalist hosts were, in consequence, riven with dissension from the outset. This was true even in the two cradles of the revolution, Sonora and Coahuila. Huertista observers rejoiced at Sonora's personal and geographical rivalries which, despite Carranza's cooling influence, simmered until the summer of 1914, when they boiled over.[695] In Coahuila, too, prominent caudillos like Blanco, Castro and González were at loggerheads.[696] Further south, where the revolution was yet more popular and decentralised, conflicts persisted, especially as rebel forces expanded their area of operations, ran up against neighbouring 'allies' and vied for local supremacy. The old rivalries of Veracruz were reasserted; divisions among the rebels of Michoacán impeded their campaigns; and in some central states an incipient polarisation between Constitutionalist and Zapatista became apparent.[697] Carranza attempted to bring order and discipline to these heterogeneous forces. In July 1913 he decreed the creation of seven army corps, under which all rebel military activity would be subsumed. Three of these – the corps of the north-east, north-west and centre – had some genuine reality, and bore the brunt of the conventional campaigns in the north; but elsewhere, notwithstanding Carranza's efforts, rebel forces remained independent, parochial, fragmented and chiefly committed to guerrilla war.[698]

Thus, the First Chief often had little choice but to recognise the authority of a local *cabecilla*: blanket instructions were issued that 'the post of commander-in-chief in the state of Hidalgo should be assumed by the *jefe* who can count on the most support and [who] is in agreement with the Plan of Guadalupe'.[699] But this was no easy brief. Which *jefe* enjoyed 'most support'? What did 'agreement' with the Plan of Guadalupe entail? And did the 'state of Hidalgo' possess any significance in terms of 'revolutionary geography', which so often overrode political boundaries? Since local *cabecillas* were highly sensitive about their rights and authority, Carranza's attempts to create an ordered hierarchy easily gave offence and made enemies. The captaincy of the revolution in Hidalgo, for example, was strongly contested between local claimants, like Nicolás Flores (a *ranchero* from Pisaflores, who led a movement of fellow-*rancheros* reminiscent of the Figueroa rebellion in Guerrero), and a congeries of rivals, several of whom hailed from the Tres Huastecas: Francisco de P. Mariel, who had commanded a *rural* detachment here under Madero; Vicente Segura, a landowner, bullfighter and 'sportsman', who had sympathised – though not fought – with Madero, fled to Havana after Huerta's coup, and now returned, after buying with his own cash one of those arms consignments which had been repeatedly traded on the New Orleans black market; and Cándido Aguilar, a Veracruzano veteran of 1910, who, having commanded Maderista irregulars in Oaxaca and Durango, was now appointed Constitutionalist military chief in Veracruz, which for him included a watching brief over the Huasteca Hidalguense.[700]

By early 1914, the surplus of rebel leaders in this region was causing problems. 'Great divisions' existed among the Constitutionalists here, Aguilar told Carranza; Francisco Mariel was chiefly to blame; it was imperative that Carranza 'study the situation in this state and designate someone . . . capable of solving the many difficulties that crop up each day'.[701] Meanwhile, Aguilar took unilateral action, repudiating Segura's authority, retiring Mariel from his command, and lending his support to their local rivals, Cerecedo and Salazar.[702] The First Chief, riled by this insubordination, summoned Aguilar to Matamoros to answer for his actions. This time, Carranza's presumption of authority proved hollow. Revolutionaries in the field did not appreciate close supervision of their conduct, nor did they readily trek 300 miles to offer explanations for it. Pablo González, commanding in the north-east, was more sensitive to the foibles of his lieutenants: pointing out Aguilar's success in the Huasteca, he urged Carranza to go carefully, and to withdraw his peremptory order. Carranza was forced to compromise: Segura remained in command in the Huasteca Hidalguense, Aguilar's summons to Matamoros was postponed *sine die*, and González was left to sort out the future of Mariel. The story had a happy ending: Carranza and Aguilar were reconciled to the extent that Aguilar married one of Carranza's daughters (the ugliest, a critic said, who brought as her dowry the governorship of Veracruz) and he became Foreign Minister and one of the First Chief's closest partisans.[703]

Many similar disputes had less happy outcomes. Carranza's exercise of authority created grudges which rankled and were recalled in later times of crisis; hence in many regions there were potential divisions within the Revolution which, in appropriate circumstances, could be formulated in terms of support for, or opposition to, Carranza. In Sinaloa, for example, ex-Governor Riveros joined the Constitutionalist revolution a little belatedly, and found his authority clashing with that of the First Chief; some Sinaloan *cabecillas* objected to Carranza seeming to dictate to Riveros, and Carranza had to bow to local opinion.[704] In the same state, rebel leaders like Buelna and Pazuengo chafed at the authority of Carranza's west coast commander, Obregón.[705] And in tiny Tlaxcala the revolutionary divisions already apparent – and already productive of bloodshed – were exacerbated rather than soothed by Carranza's efforts to implant his authority and create a military hierarchy in the state.[706] For the time being the exigencies of the campaigns against Huerta kept rebel rivalries in check. But with Huerta gone, these centrifugal forces would be harder to contain.

Potentially the most serious challenge to Carranza's authority came from the state of Chihuahua. In terms of formal leadership, the Constitutionalist revolution was built around the Coahuilan–Sonoran axis. Despite its military importance, Chihuahua played virtually no part in higher level deliberations, such as the Monclova meeting of April 1913, and Carranza emphasised the fact by making the Chihuahuan forces subject to Obregón's command in the north-west.[707] Furthermore, in mid-1913 the First Chief installed as governor of Chihuahua Manuel Chao, a schoolmaster-revolutionary, one-time mentor of the Herreras, and the sort of educated, respectable figure who, in Carranza's eyes, ought to occupy such a post. All this rankled with Villa and the Chihuahuan rebels. Villa objected to being subordinated to Obregón: if Chihuahua lacked generals, let Chihuahuans be promoted. As for Chao, Villa would accept his political, but not his military supremacy. In order to secure Villa's adhesion to Constitutionalism, Carranza had to give way, and Villa was designated commander of the Division of the North, independent of Obregón and other generals.[708] But the problem of Chao remained. Late in 1913 a junta of generals – including Chao himself – named Villa governor of Chihuahua, but Carranza vetoed the appointment. Then, in the spring of 1914, when Chao disobeyed Villa's order to mobilise at Torreón, Villa ordered his execution. Such displays of *caudillista* pique were not uncommon: veterans of the Chihuahua revolution grew used to 'the rage of Francisco Villa which made men tremble', but which usually abated as fast as it had flared up. Homicide was generally – not invariably – averted, and Villa was quite likely to depart from his erstwhile victim with a fond *abrazo*.[709] So it was with Manual Chao who, thanks either to Villa's change of heart or to Carranza's prompt intervention, was allowed to go free and who remained a close ally of Villa for some time to come.[710]

But now another serious clash with Carranza occurred, concerning the killing of the British *hacendado*, William Benton, who had allegedly insulted or threatened Villa. The British colony in the capital was outraged; the British press took up the matter; questions were asked in Parliament.[711] Lacking representation in northern Mexico, the British government sought American good offices and the Americans elicited from Villa assurances that Benton had been formally court-martialled and executed, which was not true. When Villa was asked to reveal the body, by way of proof, he refused.[712] The Benton affair has been seen as an important episode in the high politics and diplomacy of the Revolution, as it was. Villa's impulsive and violent behaviour cast doubts on the rectitude of the revolutionaries; it gave Huerta valuable propaganda material; and it embroiled the Constitutionalist leadership with meddlesome foreign powers. Above all, it displayed the weakness of Carranza's control over his lieutenants.[713] In response, Carranza insisted that all foreign representations should be directed to him, as First Chief (a requirement which Villa gladly accepted, thereby extricating himself from an increasingly awkward situation); and he took advantage of the circumstances to press the British and other European governments, which had recognised Huerta, to enter into *de facto* relations with the Constitutionalist leadership.

But apart from its diplomatic ramifications – on which historians have lavished attention – the Benton incident was illustrative of the domestic character of the Revolution too. It revealed Carranza's limited control over his leading generals (a revelation the First Chief could well do without); and it also revealed contrasting concepts of revolution. For Carranza, the revolution should strive to be orderly and legalistic. Hence the stream of instructions – their number and repetitiveness a pointer to their inefficacy – ordering commanders to respect lives and property: Eulalio Gutiérrez is told to halt depredations in Zacatecas 'to avoid international difficulties'; Pablo González is given similar orders in the Tampico region; a Chihuahuan *cabecilla* is warned to desist from forced loans 'for the sake of the good name of the cause'.[714] That Carranza should be angry at the slaying of Benton is not therefore surprising. But Villa, and many like him, thought differently. Though he soon came to appreciate the value of American good will, his main concerns were domestic and parochial. For him, Benton was less a British subject, whose death would have international repercussions, than a Chihuahuan *hacendado* of notorious local fame (a point which diplomatic accounts usually overlook). As pre-revolutionary evidence shows, Benton was reckoned a harsh employer; he was engaged in a protracted conflict with the village of Santa María de Cuevas, which claimed land held by Benton, and whose inhabitants alleged that Benton fenced off his property, denied them transit and fined them for trespass. Benton, in turn, denounced the activity of local rustlers – anarchist enemies of property, in his words – and he summoned the *rurales* to protect him when threats were made on his life.[715] Not only was Benton a tough-minded, improving landlord of the kind likely to face popular reprisals; he was also known – by his colleagues – to be 'a little hot-headed' and quite capable of provoking Villa's proverbial temper.[716] His killing, apart from generating diplomatic activity and further cooling relations between Villa and Carranza, was yet another indication of the local social conflicts which underlay so much revolutionary violence. And while Villa and other popular leaders believed it right to engage in these conflicts in arbitrary, direct fashion, Carranza and the respectable leadership of the revolution felt qualms: such procedures were too anarchic, unrestrained and productive of international complications. But, while the war against Huerta remained the top priority, Carranza had to tolerate certain excesses and popular leaders like Villa had to put up with the nagging tutelage of the First Chief.

Carranza had established his court in Sonora in the autumn of 1913. His entourage was mixed. There were his young disciples from Coahuila: his personal secretary, Espinosa Mireles ('a very likeable fellow', thought Thord Grey; 'not unlike a barber's assistant', commented a British planter, 'and greatly proud of a certain amount of education in law'); his nephew, Alberto Salinas, an aviator; his Chief of Staff, Jacinto Treviño, one of the few with military training and, it was said, a martinet's mentality and a tetchy temper; young Francisco Urquizo, whose father, of the same name, had been an ally of Carranza in the 1893 rebellion against the Garza Galán interest in Coahuila.[717] All were in their twenties, unconditional clients of the First Chief, linked to him by ties of family, regional history and self-interest. There were other, more independent north-easterners, like Lucio Blanco, summoned to Sonora and now sulking in his tent like Achilles.[718] Then, there were the Sonorans, split into increasingly clear factions, but sharing (according to border gossip) a common antipathy to the Coahuilans, to whom Carranza had entrusted many key jobs.[719] Thirdly, the presence of the First Chief and the security of Sonora attracted civilian *políticos* who now risked open opposition to Huerta. Young Maderistas like Martín Luis Guzmán, Luis Aguirre Benavides, Juan Sánchez Azcona, and Alberto Pani found their way to Sonora by circuitous routes touching Cuba and the US; and experienced *políticos* turned up, several of whom had recognised Huerta, temporised, and finally fled north – the prominent Renovadores, Luis Cabrera and Francisco Escudero, state governor Miguel Silva, and ex-Minister Manuel Bonilla, who had made a dramatic escape from Mexico City after a period of asylum in the American Embassy.[720] And there was a single, high-ranking Federal officer, General Felipe Angeles, who had remained loyal to Madero in February 1913 and, after a spell in gaol, had left for Europe and returned to join the Revolution.[721]

From these elements Carranza constructed his cabinet in the autumn of 1913. In both form and content it resembled Madero's: there were no separate ministries of labour or agriculture; and civilians like Escudero, Ignacio Bonillas, and Rafael Zubarán Capmany occupied all the major posts save War which – to the disgust of several revolutionaries – went to the ex-Federal Angeles.[722] The more plebeian military were not represented, and Carranza's administration remained one of wing-collars, waistcoats and neckties.[723] As it got to work, however, regulating posts, customs, immigration and other day-to-day matters, the military campaigns were still the top priority; and the presence of the military could not be ignored, as rebel commanders (or their representatives) came to Sonora to pay their respects to Carranza, to legitimise their authority, to get arms and money, to co-ordinate military operations to the south. They included, for example, Señora Ramona Flores, so-called Chief of Staff to Juan Carrasco in Sinaloa, 'a stout, red-haired woman in a black satin princess dress embroidered with jet [and] with a sword at her side', who brought two gold ingots up from the south to pay for arms and supplies.[724] All such supplicants, records a complacent Obregón, went away satisfied.[725]

Accounts of Carranza's court during its sojourn in Sonora offer interesting though hardly consistent images of the individuals who were to form the nucleus of the later revolutionary regime. Martín Luis Guzmán, newly arrived from Huertista Mexico City, was warmly received; he met Carranza and was no more than moderately impressed; he noted the recreation of the Constitutionalist leaders – Luis Cabrera, the emerging ideologue of Carrancismo, playing billiards; Zubarán Capmany, one-time Reyista, now Carranza's Interior Minister, strumming his guitar; Isidro Fabela ('suave, courteous and very well educated', as John Reed observed), practising public speaking, when foreign relations and press interviews did not call; Angeles, 'a tall, slender, olive-complexioned, handsome fellow', riding, studying, meditating by moonlight.[726] They can be seen in the pages of Casasola, usually in three-piece suits, posing for group photographs in wickerwork chairs, or on the steps of public buildings. In Hermosillo and Nogales – for Carranza's court, like the old medieval courts, was peripatetic – they filled the hotels with their stenographers, telegraphists and adjutants, not to mention the 'political hangers-on . . . sleeping four in a room, on cots in the corridor, and even on the stairs'.[727] The inner circle dined regularly with Carranza (and fine meals they were) but in return the guests had to sit through Carranza's rambling monologues, drawn from his pet subject of history, and replete with schoolboy howlers. Diners who dissented from Carranza's opinions, as Angeles did, earned his patriarchal displeasure.[728] There was also an uncomfortably competitive atmosphere within the First Chief's entourage, as factions manoeuvred to get on and avoid being done down. In particular, the young military, like Treviño, were jealous of Angeles, a career soldier with a distinguished record. It is not clear if his military expertise, old regime connections, or personal character, offended most; Obregón complained to Carranza of Angeles' presence in his preserve, denied feelings of jealousy and alleged his genuine concern for the revolution – Angeles, said Obregón, dissimulates, hides his inner thoughts, conceals his true intentions.[729] Interestingly, Guzmán's impression of Obregón was similar; Obregón was a 'comedian' who affected an untidy, amiable manner, played to the gallery, and 'though convinced of his immense importance . . . pretended not to take himself seriously'.[730]

In the political hothouse of Sonora, cagey, circumspect, careerist politicans gathered and flourished. Meanwhile, amid their manoeuvring and posturing there emerged another factional division of great importance, which was superimposed upon the existing mosaic: a division between 'old' Maderistas and Carrancistas. Carranza and his Coahuilan and Sonoran allies had indifferent revolutionary records prior to 1913: their role had been marginal in 1910–11, limited and local in 1911–12. Driven into rebellion against Huerta on a defensive, states' rights issue, they were now determined to maintain their revolutionary pre-eminence. When veteran Maderistas – who had actively supported Madero between 1909 and 1912 – began to join the Constitutionalists, they received a mixed welcome. They were not repudiated: Guzmán was well received; Julio Madero was given a post on Carranza's general staff; Francisco Escudero briefly held a dual ministerial job.[731] But many old Maderistas felt a distinct chill, as it was made clear to them that times had changed, that a past association with the martyr president did not mean a meal-ticket for life, that indeed, such an association had a whiff of ancient history and political failure about it. For the arch-realists who ran the Constitutionalist revolution it was what you had done in 1913, not 1910 or 1911, which counted. Hence the Sonorans' antipathy to Maytorena and Angeles, who arrived late on the scene, brandishing their Maderista laurels; now, 'the capital and prestige acquired in the time of Maderismo was insufficient to establish anyone'.[732] Alberto Pani detected the same feeling, and was glad to quit Sonora for a commission in Washington; Aguirre Benavides was offended by the constant criticism of Madero in Carranza's circle; and Martín Luis Guzmán, increasingly disillusioned by what he found in Sonora, was relieved to be ordered to Chihuahua, to confer with Villa.[733]

This was not a purely Sonoran phenomenon. As a form of inter-generational political conflict, deriving from the 'logic of the Revolution', and pitting the Maderista generation of 1909–11 against its Carrancista successor of 1913–14, it occurred wherever the veterans of the first confronted the rising stars of the second; and the reception given the old Maderistas grew cooler the longer they delayed their conversion to Constitutionalism: Maytorena's six-month absence was enough to generate serious opposition to the governor on his return. But Carrancista exclusionist sentiments went further. After an impeccable revolutionary career in 1910–12 (which included a gaol sentence for political agitation under Madero), Gabriel Gavira narrowly escaped with his life from Mexico after Huerta's coup, and made his way to the north-east by way of Cuba. There he was at once struck by the 'hostility with which we who had made our mark in 1910 were received by those of 1913'; the Carrancista commander at Piedras Negras, Gabriel Calzada, 'made every effort to prevent those of 1910 entering [the revolution] anew'.[734] Exclusionism was most marked in Sonora, where the generation of 1913 was jealously entrenched; hence it was in Sonora that the disillusionment of the old Maderistas was keenest. The route taken by Guzmán, from Sonora to Chihuahua, from Carranza's court to Villa's, became a regular pilgrim's way for Maderista veterans who, tired of Carranza's tetchy manners, looked to Villa, the most spectacular of the northern caudillos, as a worthy alternative: thither went Aguirre Benavides, Manuel Bonilla, Felipe Angeles and several members of the Madero family.[735] Sonorans came too: Pedro Bracamonte, a veteran of 1910–11, and Anacleto Girón, 'the old guerilla fighter of Maderismo' who, significantly, was a close ally of Governor Maytorena.[736] There were signs already that Villa would be drawn into the factional squabbles of Sonora.

That these malcontents should turn to Villa was logical. For all his rough ways (and these could be mellowed), Villa was a devout Maderista, whose loyalty had been evidenced at the time of the Orozco revolt and again after Huerta's coup; he venerated the memory of Madero and Maderistas like Abraham González in a frank manner that was foreign to the spirit of Carrancismo; and he was beholden to the Madero family – as one of them reminded him – for his salvation from Huerta's firing squad in 1912.[737] Maderista politicians and intellectuals thus saw in Villa a counterweight to Carranza, and a vehicle which might carry them to power again: had not such rough-hewn *cabecillas*, 'modest sons of the people', carried them to power in 1911?[738] And it was a vehicle which, around the turn of the year 1913/14, seemed to possess more momentum than the sluggish Sonorans. An alliance with Villa, however problematic, was preferable to the Carrancista cold shoulder. 'We'll win now all right', as Vasconcelos put it, 'we've got a man.'[739] It was the recurrent dream of the impotent revolutionary intellectual: to play Plato to some powerful but pliant popular caudillo.

Villa's reaction was one of gruff tolerance. He was not politically choosy; it was military rather than political interference that he could not stomach. Some of Carranza's emissaries, sent to straighten out Villista administration, were positively welcomed.[740] And the Maderista malcontents, pampered civilians though most of them seemed, could fill posts in the burgeoning Villista apparatus, as secretaries, officials, administrators and propagandists.[741] Some had more practical talents: the young Federal officer Federico Cervantes, despatched to Chihuahua by Carranza, seemed to Villa 'a reactionary little dandy'; but he was broke, loyal to the memory of Madero, and knew about artillery – all of which endeared him to Villa and enabled him to rise rapidly in Villista circles.[742] Finally, there was Felipe Angeles himself, who chose to quit Sonora and Carranza to become Villa's artillery commander. On the one hand, Angeles brought valuable expertise to the Villista camp; on the other, he typified – in the eyes of suspicious Carrancistas – the perfidy of the old Maderistas, who were thought to be pitting Villa against Carranza to their own advantage. Angeles in particular, who rose high in Villa's estimation, was depicted as the 'grey eminence' who pulled the strings of the puppet caudillo of Chihuahua. The merit of the charge will be considered at a more appropriate point. For the moment, it is enough to note the gathering suspicions concerning Angeles' – and the other Maderistas' – purported influence over Villa.[743]

VILLISMO

Angeles arrived at Villa's side as the biggest campaigns of the Constitutionalist revolution got under way. In the heart of northern Mexico, along the axis running from Juárez down through Chihuahua and Torreón to Zacatecas, the decisive battles were fought. As Obregón inched his way down the west coast, and Pablo González kept up his inconsequential gyrations in the north-east, Villa took on and defeated the Federals, thereby opening the way to Mexico City.[744]

After a brief, business-like occupation of Torreón in October 1913 Villa headed north again with some 5,000 men, leaving Chao to supervise the cotton harvest in the Laguna.[745] Villa's aim was a final reduction of the Federal strongholds in Chihuahua – Juárez and the state capital – and the campaign was 'almost a classic in military improvisation and derring-do'.[746] Spurning the advice of his chief of staff, Juan Medina, who advised no more than a feint against Chihuahua City, Villa launched a full-scale attack; but the rebels, again short of ammunition, were beaten off by a strong garrison, the majority of them hardened Orozquista veterans.[747] General Mercado, commanding at Chihuahua, reported that the Villistas had been dispersed in confusion to the south; but this was not so. Villa's scattered forces were rapidly regrouped and force-marched around the city to a point on the Chihuahua–Juárez railway line, where Villa intercepted, stopped and unloaded a Federal coal train. The station telegraphist – a gun at his head and a Villista telegraphist at his side – tapped out a message to Juárez, indicating that the train could not proceed further south as the line was cut, and orders were received to return at once, reporting in from each station en route. The empty wagons were boarded by 2,000 Villistas and the train rolled north, leaving a big pile of coal by the side of the track. At each station the local telegraphist was compelled to cable the 'all clear' to Juárez; Juárez cabled back the code sign to proceed; and at midnight on 14/15 November, Villa's Trojan train rolled into an unsuspecting town, where the Federal garrison – believing Villa still to be licking his wounds near Chihuahua – had given themselves up to the delights of the frontier fleshpots.[748] Within hours, with little fighting and few casualties, the town was taken. Observers again commented on the good order and discipline Villa maintained. Most of the Federals were captured and, as usual, a large batch of officers was summarily executed; the Federal commander, however, was spared, since, in 1912, he had helped save Villa from Huerta's firing squad. Villa remembered his debts.[749]

Juárez was his by a stroke of daring; but it had to be defended *a fuerza y sangre*. Mercado – no doubt mindful of the recent court-martial of Torreón's ineffectual commander – despatched a strong force from Chihuahua to recapture the state's major border port. Since these were mostly Orozquistas, commanded by the veteran José Inés Salazar, a major Villista–Orozquista battle, with all the personal feuds and hatreds it involved, was now for the first time scheduled; it would also be a battle of comparable armies, for the Orozquistas (unlike the Federal conscripts) were redoubtable opponents, 'bold and battle-hardened, like our own *gente*' as one Villista put it.[750] Late in November the Federal force of some 7,000 approached Juárez and dug in at Tierra Blanca, twenty-five miles south, along the line of the railway.[751] Villa had no desire to be caught and shelled in Juárez (particularly as this might cause international complications) and so he decided to go out to meet the enemy. At dawn on 23 November, Villa's army – 'this ill-equipped little rebel force of about 5,500 men with bandoliers three-quarters empty' – moved out of Juárez.[752] There were Indians carrying machetes and bowie knives, young boys, and stoic *soldaderas* defying orders by their presence; few had uniforms, and only Villa's own regiment, the nucleus of the later *dorados*, showed signs of military discipline. The Villista artillery consisted of two Mondragon 75mm. field guns, recently captured from the Federals; their firing pins had been replaced in an El Paso machine shop only days before. For a day they marched across the cold, windy dunes south of Juárez, and bivouacked the night of 23 November. Next day they encountered the Federals at Tierra Blanca and battle was joined.

According to one account, Villa regarded Tierra Blanca as – if not the most important battle of his career – at least the most spectacular, and the one conducted most closely according to the rules of military science.[753] Such a view does not speak highly of Villa's military skill. In fact, Villa should have lost Tierra Blanca. The Federals, about equal in number to the rebels, were dug in and had superior artillery and abundant ammunition. Yet in a battle of reciprocal blunders, Salazar's uncertainty finally lost him the day. The Federal field-guns opened with a barrage to which the Villista artillery could make only a token reply: the Federal cavalry threatened to encircle the rebel flanks, pulling them ever wider; and Federal infantry, equipped with Mausers and machine-guns, raked the Villista lines from forward positions. The Villistas were everywhere on the defensive, concerned to husband their ammunition, their left flank stretched by cavalry attacks, their right reeling from sustained machine-gun fire. There was no reserve to call upon, and no apparent co-ordination among Villa's lieutenants; 'Villa relied, it seemed . . . on the various commanders to do the right thing without giving them definite orders. This was his usual practice when leading his guerrilla band.'[754] Had

Salazar launched a shrapnel barrage and an all-out attack, an experienced participant reckoned, Villa's army would have been shattered – for there was no line of retreat.

Instead, Villista *élan* saved the day. At a crucial moment, 300 cavalry, led by one of Villa's autonomous commanders, charged the Federal left wing.[755] Fearful of meeting the charge with gunfire, the Federals broke and scurried back to their defensive positions. For the rest of the day they stayed put, maintaining a desultory fire, surrendering the initiative. In the small hours, they contracted their positions further. For all their technical superiority, they were behaving like frightened men: as in so many encounters in 1913–14, revolutionary morale outweighed Federal *matériel*. Before dawn the next day, Villa pressed home the psychological advantage, ordering a general advance as well as covert flanking movements by the cavalry. Meantime, Rodolfo Fierro, Villa's vicious but intrepid lieutenant, was sent south to blow the railway tracks behind the enemy positions. The general advance stalled before withering machine-gun fire; but, about noon, the Villista cavalry appeared on the enemy flanks and the Federals began to evacuate their positions and make for the security of the troop trains. At this moment a tremendous explosion echoed from the Federal rear: Fierro – an old railway hand – had sent a runaway locomotive into the Federal sidings, its cowcatcher loaded with dynamite and percussion caps.[756] The old *máquina loca* trick, which had won the Orozquistas the battle of Rellano in 1912, thus helped them lose Tierra Blanca in 1913. The Federals panicked, broke and ran for the remaining wagons; the makeshift Villista artillery began to take its toll; some of the fleeing enemy broke out white flags, which were ignored. They were 'in a disgraceful retreat, abandoning guns and trains in their wild scramble to avoid Villa's wrath. It was a rout'.[757] There were over a thousand Federal casualties, as against some 300 Villista, and the booty was spectacular: four locomotives, eight field guns, seven machine-guns, horses, rifles, and 400,000 rounds of small arms ammunition.[758] Again, all the captured Federal officers were shot; and, back in Juárez, a massive fiesta was held to celebrate a victory that, perhaps, should never have been.

Villa now controlled Juárez and the valuable border traffic. General Mercado, in Chihuahua City, felt distinctly jumpy, and mounting disagreements between Mercado's Federals and Orozco's irregulars worsened the situation.[759] Despite the pleas of local merchants, Mercado decided to evacuate and head for the border, where Ojinaga remained in Federal hands, and the sanctuary of the US beckoned. With his army went numerous civilian refugees, including members of the Terrazas family and many of the Spanish community, who preferred not to await the arrival of Pancho Villa. Chihuahua was left undefended, with the bodies of political prisoners swinging from the poplars – Mercado's farewell gesture.[760] Since the railway track was torn up, the column went overland, on foot, by horse or by car, across 120 miles of

chilly, inhospitable desert; stores and ammunition were prodigally abandoned
in the pell-mell flight to the north, which was seen to mark the 'general
disintegration of [the] Federal forces in the state'.[761] After their weary arrival
at Ojinaga Mercado's army – much depleted by desertion – sat in the border
town for a month, amid shelled and blackened buildings, wandering animals
and piles of filth and fodder. Ragged and demoralised, they hardly bothered to
dig trenches, but eked out their scanty provisions, boiling corn husks and
dried meat in bombed-out billets. The only beneficiaries of this sad situation
were the people of Presidio, Ojinaga's twin town across the border, which
experienced the kind of boom conditions which made the Revolution such a
bonanza for border communities like El Paso, Douglas and Laredo.[762] But
Mercado's stay in Ojinaga was brief. After Tierra Blanca, Villa made his way
south and occupied the state capital unopposed. Despite the fears of the
Chihuahua merchants, Villa's administration proved orderly and efficient;
there was no looting, but rather deliberate arrests, fines and confiscations, the
remaining Spaniards being the chief victims.[763] Then, when Pánfilo Natera
bungled an initial assault on Ojinaga, Villa came north and comfortably drove
Mercado and his tattered army across the border, where they found peace – and
the US acquired 5,000 costly and embarrassing guests – in a refugee camp at
Fort Bliss.[764]

   The whole of Chihuahua was now in Villa's palm. His government was
personal and arbitrary, but orderly; and there was not, as yet, much evidence
that Villa was in the trammels of ambitious advisers and grey eminences.
True, the influx of experienced *políticos* and intellectuals, already noted, was
well under way, so that Villa could call upon a respectable Maderista like
Roque González Garza ('a very calm, serene man') to head the military tribunal
which assessed forced contributions at Chihuahua.[765] True, Villa happily
co-operated with the American consular agent detailed to shepherd him into
better ways; he was most amenable to the US consul at Chihuahua (who could
not abide him); and, when he met General Hugh Scott on the international
bridge at El Paso in February 1914, he took careful note of what he was told
concerning the rules of civilised warfare, which he graciously undertook to
observe.[766] Nevertheless, a critic commented, there were as yet 'few
intelligent and self-restrained persons around him' and, to the extent that
there were, Villa 'appears to dominate all of his associates'; Villa's sympathisers, from a different standpoint, reached similar conclusions.[767] The
regime which was constructed in Chihuahua in 1913–14 may, therefore, be
legitimately seen as Villa's own, even if its scope and complexity required
increasing delegation.

   In the midst of revolution, Villa imposed peace and order in Chihuahua.
The triumphant entry into the state capital was attended by none of the
outrages which had afflicted Durango; before long, in fact, Villa was
promising to bring 'peace and order out of chaos and anarchy – in Durango –

even if he had to execute one half of the revolutionaries of that section'; and, in Chihuahua, it was the 'general opinion that banditism [sic] will not soon appear under the severe treatment dealt them [sic] by Villa'.[768] So, too, in Villa's own army, where the theft of a pair of boots might be punished by public execution.[769] For obvious economic and military reasons, Villa was keen for railway traffic and business to revive as quickly as possible. Attention was at once given to the ravaged posts, telegraphs and railway lines, and as early as Christmas 1913 a 'noticeable improvement' was evident.[770] ASARCO agreed to rebuild the Chihuahua smelter, and Villista customs officials began to collect duties on cattle exports – Chihuahua's main source of dollars – in agreement with the big ranchers who remained; alternatively, confiscated estates were exploited directly, their cattle shipped to the US to raise cash for the Villista treasury.[771] Though no figures are extant, it is clear that this was big business; towards the end of 1913 the sheer volume of cattle exports threatened to glut the American market and Villista agents began to look elsewhere (for example, to Cuba) for markets; a year later Villista meat was being shipped, via Chicago, to the Western Front, where the herds of Terrazas now sustained the Old Contemptibles.[772] This growth in both Villista income and administration was evident in the detailed state budget drawn up by the military government for the financial year 1914.[773]

Despite this, the regime remained in many respects a personal and popular one, expressive of the desires and grievances of the common people. The rebels battened onto the local economy, flooding the cities with their paper money, forcing its circulation at par, and gaoling those who were reluctant to accept it. They commandeered the houses and properties of the rich, the 'enemies of the cause' who had fled in the face of the Villista advance; and some of those who stayed behind were shot.[774] The Spaniards came in for particularly harsh treatment – at a time when Americans were commenting on Villa's amiable and courteous manner. This, as has been said, was a persistent feature of the Revolution, and Villa was far from being the sole or even the outstanding revolutionary Hispanophobe.[775] Down in the Laguna, in the summer of 1913, before Villa arrived on the scene, the rebels had declared their intention of killing all the Torreón Spaniards; hundreds of Spaniards fled when the Federals evacuated; but this did not prevent Urbina from killing seven who remained, and it required American consular pressure to stop Villa taking action against the rest.[776] Again, in the closing weeks of 1913, there was 'phenomenal Spanish emigration' from the Laguna into Saltillo.[777]

Villa's conduct following the fall of Chihuahua was, therefore, part of a general pattern, common to much of Mexico and particularly of the northern states. He decreed the expulsion of all Spaniards and the confiscation of their property; he refrained from having them all shot, he said, because 'I am civilised and have been a humane man all my life.'[778] This expulsion order, which sent some 400 Spaniards trekking to the border, covered clerks, small shopkeepers and priests as well as the minority of merchants, landowners and their managers.[779] The same occurred later, after the (second) fall of Torreón.[780] Villa justified these extreme measures on the grounds that the Spaniards had involved themselves in the civil war, supporting Huerta with arms, money and exhortation; and there is certainly evidence, from Chihuahua and elsewhere, that they did.[781] But this political partisanship was only part of the story, and itself reflected the position of Spaniards in Mexican society: as merchants, grocers, pawnbrokers, moneylenders, foremen, estate managers and priests. It was the Spanish *administradores* of the Laguna plantations who, according to one source, particularly inspired Villa's Hispanophobia.[782]

With the expulsion of the Spaniards came the flight of most of the local elite. In January 1914 'few respectable people remain[ed]' in the Laguna towns, all the 'better classes' ('that is, all whom we were accustomed to know and do business with', a British planter explained) having fled at the prospect of further Villista victories.[783] The ripples spread, and alert observers in border towns like Piedras Negras could chart Villa's progress in the Laguna by the influx of 'the wealthy, polished, foreign-travelling class' who packed into the better hotels.[784] With the flight of the landlords, managers and businessmen, the rebels assumed the running of many commercial enterprises – though not, we should note, of those owned and operated by non-Spanish foreign interests, which were largely unmolested.[785] In both Durango and Juárez the slaughterhouses were run by rebel officials, in the interests of the cause; so, too, were the Juárez gambling dens and the trams, waterworks and electric plant of Chihuahua City.[786] While Chao was left to supervise the Laguna cotton harvest (valued at between 10m. and 20m. pesos), raw cotton, seized in the fields, was being worked in the factories of rebel-held Durango.[787] Such measures clearly responded to the revolution's need for organisation and income; but did they also indicate the social radicalism of Villismo and the regime's readiness to appropriate property – especially rural property – in the interests of the lower class?

On this important point both opinions and evidence are mixed. In his rosy portrait of Villa, as bandit-revolutionary, John Reed grants his hero strong, if inarticulate, reformist sentiments, in which *agrarismo* of a kind figures.[788] Villistas themselves claimed that confiscated estates were worked for the common good.[789] Before long, the American press began to talk of the 'socialistic experiments' being conducted in Villa's territory.[790] Sympathetic historians have developed this theme: Calzadíaz Barrera asserts that Governor Chao decreed the division of 25,000 hectares of hacienda land among needy *campesinos*, and established reserves of 10m. pesos in the new Bank of Chihuahua to supply credit to smallholders; M. N. Lavrov sees Chihuahua and Durango – along with Morelos – as the main centres of the 'revolutionary struggle of the peasantry', refers to Villa's division of the land among the peons, and calls Villa's army 'the army of the agrarian revolution'.[791] On the other hand, Marte

Gómez – perhaps the main authority on the subject – could not trace Chao's decree, and is sceptical that any actual agrarian reform took place in north central Mexico during Villa's rule.[792] Which way does the evidence point?

First, it must be recognised that two powerful factors militated against an agrarian reform along the lines of the classic *reparto* – the division of the great estates among peons and villagers – which Lavrov seems to believe happened. The pastoral economy of the north was hardly amenable to land division in the way that, for example, the fertile valleys of Morelos were. Here, as in highland Peru, the pattern of land use and the scarcity of water resources made division difficult, if not impossible; prairie and desert smallholdings would not work.[793] But, as I have already argued, the territorial dominance of the predominantly pastoral hacienda should not obscure the existence of villages and smallholdings in the river valleys, in the irrigated regions of the Laguna (which fall within the orbit of this inquiry), and in the folds and foothills of the sierra. Here, the monopolisation of land proceeded apace during the Porfiriato, generating social conflict and an ultimately rebellious outcome not dissimilar to that of central Mexico; witness, for example, the history of Cuencamé or the circumstances of Benton's death. But these northern land disputes – though more important than has often been recognised – could not generate a sustained movement for agrarian reform, on Zapatista lines. Given the nature of northern rural society, the classic village–hacienda conflict did not dominate the policy of revolutionary regimes, and it was more easily swamped by other concerns, to which I will turn in a moment. It was also the case that northern agrarian disputes frequently pitted villagers against caciques (rather than against *hacendados*), and often formed part of a more general, popular rejection of oppressive, centralised government. Thus, while agrarian factors were important in stimulating rebellion, they did not constitute the prime concern of revolutionary regimes, nor did they necessitate a general *reparto*, a division of the great estates. It was enough to evict the caciques (often, the clients of the Creel–Terrazas empire), demolish the Porfirian political inheritance, and recover land (private or communal) allegedly seized by caciques in former times. Once this was achieved, popular pressure for radical reform waned.

The second factor discouraging a general *reparto* was military and economic. The production of the great estates – the cattle spreads of Chihuahua, the Laguna cotton plantations – underwrote the Villista army. This precluded any official break-up of existing units, or shift from cash-crops to staples. In the case of the Laguna – where *agrarista* demands had been voiced, and where arable rather than pastoral farming was the norm – Villa retained the plantations intact, despatching Chao to supervise the 1913 harvest, and subsequently establishing a system whereby the land was rented out or sharecropped, with either rent or landlord's share accruing to 'the Revolution'.[794] Any possible *reparto* was thus forestalled. And to the extent that this was the norm for Villista Mexico – as it appears to have been – there could be no fundamental change in the agrarian system. If the structure remained intact, however, the holders of land were no longer the oligarchic *hacendados* of the Porfiriato. Some were Villista generals, in whose names managers, tenants and sharecroppers now worked the fields once owned by Creel, Terrazas or Luján. Though in some cases this represented a form of personal appropriation – witness Urbina's takeover of Canutillo – it could indicate simply the Villista method of running the agrarian economy and the revolutionary war. At a time of effective military rule, military control of farming came naturally. It does not follow that the Creel haciendas of Orientales and San Salvador, run by subordinates of the Villista commander at Ojinaga were seen (even by the commander himself, Porfirio Ornelas) as his own property.[795] Talk of a new 'bourgeoisie', composed of the Villista generals turned *hacendados* is, at best, premature, and probably unwarranted.[796]

This is all the more true since the properties run by or for Villista generals constituted a minority of those confiscated in the north.[797] The majority was controlled by state and local boards appointed to administer expropriated goods (*bienes intervenidos*), which they did by renting out land either for a money rent or on a shares basis; and the recipients of this land varied greatly, from rich tenants who rented whole haciendas, to 'poor sharecroppers', like those of the Rancho de la Concha y Anexas.[798] In reaching terms with their tenants, these boards were guided by prevailing 'local usages and customs', and thus they explicitly avoided any radical innovation.[799] Finally, it should be noted that only those estates abandoned by their owners (and tenants), or belonging to 'enemies of the cause' (i.e., supporters of Huerta), were marked down for exploitation on these lines.[800] What percentage of the haciendas of Villista Mexico this embraced is not known; but it is clear that there was no sweeping expropriation based on social need. Villista 'socialism' was a figment of the *Brooklyn Eagle*.

But while the character of northern society and the conduct of the war ruled out a grand *reparto*, this did not imply the complete preservation of the rural status quo. First, official statements and policies do not exhaust the question, for at the height of the Revolution agrarian reform could proceed locally, illegally, and – from the historian's point of view – unobtrusively. The common assertion that Morelos alone experienced significant agrarian *reivindicaciones* is false; the growing number of local histories suggest that land disputes were ubiquitous and often highly important in determining – or, at least, 'co-determining' – the incidence and character of revolutionary upheaval. But such disputes might not show up as 'official' agrarian reform. In the case of Chihuahua, it seems clear that the Villista regime did not go in for major, 'official' reform: such, for example, is the personal recollection of Villista veterans; but they also recall the flight of landlords (and managers), the *de facto* abolition of the peons' debts, the rise in wages, and the new freedom to come and go – all of which the Revolution brought.[801] In Durango and the Laguna, where agrarian demands and land seizures were a more marked feature of rural society, there was a measure of reform both official and unofficial. Pastor Rouaix, Constitutionalist governor of Durango, promulgated an agrarian reform decree in October 1913, promising the restitution of *ejidal* land and the expropriation and division of certain haciendas. This was not mere rhetoric: already, leaders in the field like Matías Pazuengo were distributing plots of land to the *campesinos* (work which, he recalled, 'stood us in good stead for the future'); and communities like the newly named Villa Madero – recently a community of hacienda peons – were among the first to receive official grants, stripped from local haciendas.[802] Again, during the Villista administration of the Laguna estates, there was a modicum of official reform, albeit no general *reparto*: a new Ley de Aparcería sought to mitigate some of the abuses of the sharecropping system, and there were individual cases of confiscated land being let on more generous terms than before.[803] In the late summer of 1914, a team of agronomists worked to produce an agrarian law – applicable in Chihuahua – which would facilitate the growth of smallholding and the fragmentation of the great estates, albeit in a gradual, bureaucratic fashion.[804]

Official policy was this modest in both its aims and its achievements. But the unofficial sphere – the sphere of the 'black' agrarian reform – cannot be ignored. Friedrich Katz, concluding his analysis with the question 'what changes really took place in the countryside controlled by the Division of the North?', and giving an answer which might be roughly paraphrased as 'not much', is no doubt right as regards basic, objective conditions: the large estates remained intact (even if ownership changed), wages and terms of tenancy underwent only limited improvement, and there was no revolution in the relations of production.[805] But the Revolution, in Chihuahua and elsewhere, wrought changes of historic importance which were neither 'objective', nor the work of official reform. These were changes of *mentalité*, to use the fashionable term, changes in the way individuals and groups saw their own position in society, and that of others. Such changes may be 'superstructural', but they were certainly not superficial, for they affected the ways in which social and political power was exercised and maintained. Indeed, with Gramsci so much in vogue, there is little need to belabour vulgar economic determinism, or to stress the importance of ideology, hegemony, and 'the necessary reciprocity between structure and superstructure'.[806]

As regards Villista Chihuahua, or revolutionary Mexico as a whole, this points up the need to analyse changing beliefs, attitudes and relationships, which did not directly reflect changing material circumstances or 'structures'. Under Díaz, the legitimacy of government was eroded and government came to rely increasingly on coercion. This was not readily perceived at the time; protests and rebellions – the most obvious though by no means the only indicators of illegitimacy – remained sporadic and manageable. It was a time, so one Chihuahuan *campesino* recalled, when 'the people were completely obedient'; when, despite harsh conditions, rebellion was suicidal rather than emancipatory.[807] Thus, even in the north, where peonage was weaker and the mobility of labour greater, the majority of the population remained 'obedient' to landlord, cacique, governor, and, ultimately, president. Now, many of these old totems had fallen. Suddenly, after 1910, the old order crumbled and wide-eyed revolutionaries experienced the 'amazing' transition from 'persecution . . . into power' which later astounded Lenin.[808] This did not usher in the millenium. The haciendas remained; the corn grew no quicker or fatter. Before long, in fact, the Revolution became associated in many people's minds with dearth, disease, and conscription – a new lottery superimposed on the old lottery of weather, harvest and family fortune. But even if material structures had not significantly changed since the fall of Díaz, things *were* different, just as things were different for the emancipated slaves of the American south who eked out a poor living during the years of Reconstruction.

It has already been argued that the 1910 revolution generated sentiments of equality – in the eyes of the elite an unprecedented and unwarranted uppishness on the part of the *gente baja*.[809] Porfirian habits of 'obedience' broke down, not least in Villista Chihuahua, and such developments were intimately bound up with the phenomenon of Villismo itself. In the summer of 1914, Silvestre Terrazas began letting out confiscated hacienda land to *campesinos* 'on very generous terms, and sometimes without their paying', a policy which Katz may rightly attribute to an 'acute labor shortage', but which surely also reflected the prevailing climate of opinion.[810] A labour shortage *tout court* might reinforce peonage – or some form of Barrington Moore's 'labor-repressive' agriculture – and it might herald labour conscription; but in Villista Chihuahua such options were never scouted. And it is not necessary to postulate altruism on the part of Villa's administrators (plausible though this might be); it was simply the case that labour could no more be dragooned than men could be successfully conscripted by Huerta. After 1910, dragooning was at a discount. The Villista regime depended on popular support, not just for recruits, but also for a range of back-up services, from provisioning to intelligence, and this support could not be lightly jeopardised. When General Matías Pazuengo, establishing camp at the Hacienda Cuatimape (Dgo) in 1913, proceeded to 'share out plots of land among the *campesinos*, along with teams of mules and oxen and sufficient seed for the agricultural year', he acted in a consciously pragmatic as much as an altruistic fashion.[811] The success Villismo enjoyed in the north, even in the bleak years after 1914, attested to its genuine, enduring popularity, which would be hard to explain had the rise of Villismo represented simply the exchange of one set of rapacious masters – one rural 'bourgeoisie' – for another. Even if material circumstances had not changed (and in some cases they had), the common people nevertheless regarded the Villista regime very differently from the Terracista; and the Villistas realised it was bad politics – as well as bad manners – to ride roughshod over the people who kept them in power. The prosecution of the war, while it inhibited certain grand designs, like the *reparto* or Villa's pet scheme for military colonies, also necessitated a certain regard for popular feelings.[812] Pazuengo's policy at Cuatimape guaranteed not only food and forage, but also a fund of local goodwill. 'Structural' changes there may not have been, but the reciprocal attitudes of governors and governed had changed significantly since 1910.

Some improvement in the lot of peon, tenant and sharecropper would thus have been quite consonant with the basic character of the Villista regime. The latter may be defined as institutionalised social banditry: a regime weak on ideology and studied 'structural' reform, but strong on generous gestures and hand-outs, and thus a regime enjoying genuine popularity and relying on legitimacy more than coercion. Like Samuel Gompers, Villa rewarded his friends and punished his enemies (defining both categories as he chose). His bandit peregrinations and lightning campaigns had left him 'familiar with the political history and commercial standing of every individual of prominence in every city and hamlet'; according to John Reed, some of this information was even codified in 'a black book in which are set down the names, offences, and property of those who have oppressed and robbed the people'.[813] Since, it was said, Villa's army contained men from every village in Chihuahua, some of whom now wielded considerable power, such a policy of instant, individual retribution – as against gradual, centralised reform – became the hallmark of Villismo as a whole, demonstrating its kinship with 'social bandit' movements in Europe or other parts of Latin America.[814]

While impersonal reforms were few, acts of retribution against specific landlords, officials and *administradores* were common. Soon after crossing into Mexico, Villa killed the *administrador* of the Terrazas Hacienda El Carmen, where the peons had complained of brutal treatment; and from a Terracista employee he worked his way up to Terrazas himself, using Fierro's persuasive methods to extort from Luis Terrazas (*hijo*) the hiding place of the family treasure.[815] Ultimately, all Terrazas property was confiscated, and earmarked by Villa for his post-war military colonies.[816] But *hacendados* did not suffer *per se*: Doña Luz Zuloaga de Madero, owner of the palatial Bustillos Hacienda, with its chapel modelled on St Sulpice in Paris, was beautiful, related to the Madero family and capable of charming Villa (not difficult, Villa being *muy mujeriego*); so she kept her lands.[817] By 1914 this selective persecution had become – like the whole Villista movement – more sophisticated. There were now codified lists of 'enemies of the people' who had supported Orozco and Huerta: politicians, businessmen, Spaniards, members of the Chihuahua *Defensa Social*, spies, informers, even teachers who had 'taught their pupils that (the revolutionaries) were bandits'.[818] But as the movement grew, so the application of social bandit principles became more difficult. In essence, these depended on first-hand knowledge: it was a common, generally valid belief that 'only the revolutionaries of the locality know who are the revolution's enemies and partisans'; hence, if the revolutionary organisation grew too big, or strayed too far from home, the touchstone of first-hand familiarity was lost.[819] In these circumstances, revolutionary leaders had to rely on second-hand information: while Gabriel Gavira followed a doctrinaire policy of sounding out the schoolteachers of any unfamiliar community, since these constituted 'good, liberal elements', many others were at the mercy of whoever gained their ear (a phenomenon evident as early as 1911).[820] When raising a forced loan at Saltillo – not that far from his homeland – Villa relied on the local knowledge of the Constitutionalist *político* Jesús Acuña; which he regretted, Acuña being corrupt and the outcome unjust.[821] By their very nature such problems expanded with the expansion of Villa's power, and had important consequences for the Revolution.[822]

The converse of robbing the rich was helping the poor. And, just as the rich were robbed in arbitrary, personal fashion, so the poor received their favours – like royal largesse – randomly, sometimes lavishly, usually at the whim of an individual benefactor. After entering Chihuahua, Villa sold meat at 15c. a kilo (15% of the old price); later, the Laguna Agricultural Commission allocated some of its maize harvest for sale to the poor at reduced prices.[823] Education, said Villa's sympathisers, was his great concern; though, once again, systematic reforms were absent, Villa reputedly filled the schools of the state with deserving orphans and poor, supplying them with free clothes. It was also said – plausibly – that he had personally adopted the orphans of dead revolutionaries, paying for their education; and that – less plausibly – he founded fifty new schools in Chihuahua.[824] Certainly he was capable of spontaneous acts of generosity, expressive of a *macho* character: when the destitute women in the Fort Bliss refugee camp (the *soldaderas* of Mercado's beaten army) appealed to the Huertista consul for relief, Villa sent them 1,000 pesos in gold.[825] Such stories soon got around. Villa, it was said, would give his shirt to a needy soldier; Villa, recalled a veteran, 'found us poor . . . if he had any money, he used to get it out and give us some; nobody gave us money, nobody looked after the poor, and Villa did'.[826]

Even allowing for hindsight and nostalgia, such reminiscences carry some weight. The poor received certain material benefits from the Villista regime, and not just the 1.50 pesos plus keep which the common soldier was paid.[827] But, in addition, there was a powerful psychic reward. After years of subjugation to Díaz, Terrazas or some local boss, the common people now saw one of their own in the saddle, humiliating the caciques of yesterday. Though (unlike Urbina) Villa kept good order, his occupation of a town could not go unnoticed either by the local *pelados* or the local elite – such as remained. No Durango-style atrocities marked the fall of Chihuahua City; but the state capital soon exhibited 'the anomalies of a city that has been turned upside down in a class revolution', with rebels billeted in the best houses, and a 'peon hackman' to be seen driving round the streets in an upholstered brougham.[828] 'Weeks before a town is taken', complained a British observer in the Laguna, 'the lower classes become expectant and ready'; and, if their lust for loot was increasingly frustrated, they could at least enjoy the discomfiture of the well-to-do who, for fear of reprisals, shed their starched collars and wore straw hats in the hope of merging anonymously with the masses.[829] It was, some remarked, as if the Magnificat had come true: 'the poor have been showered with riches and the rich have been left with nothing'.[830]

Of course, this was not so; but the impression prevailed, in the minds of rich and poor alike, giving the common people a profound admiration for Villa. He was one of them: the reverse of Orozco's disdain for the feeble Madero, or of Villa's contempt for 'pantywaists' like Carranza, was a strong, recipocral identification between the common people of the north and their rough-and-ready caudillo.[831] Crowds gathered to catch a glimpse of Villa as he passed through the northern towns (Carranza exerted no such appeal); he would rub shoulders with the *pelados*, attending dances, cockfights and *corridas*, mucking in and cracking jokes with his troops; and, like another dashing cavalry commander, in a different civil war, 'by stooping so low, he rose the higher in the common account'.[832] Needless to say, the contrast with the aloof, hated Federal commanders, with their gold braid and Kaiser Wilhelm moustaches, was acute. Thus, oppression, class allegiance, *machismo* and military success conspired to lift Villa to legendary status. Like other 'social bandits', he was endowed with great powers. He was 'very astute, very intelligent, very brave'; soon, in story and song, he became the 'centaur of the north', the 'untameable master of the sierra'. While Carranza was scarcely sung about – save in occasional, pejorative terms – Villa, like Orozco, became the subject of dozens of ballads. Many date from the post-revolutionary period, but they reflect the essence of the legend as it developed during the Revolution:[833]

> I am a soldier of Pancho Villa / of his *Dorados* the most faithful one;
> I shan't mind at all if I lose my life / to die for him is a job for a man

This legend was already in the making in 1913–14; it attracted disgruntled Maderistas from Sonora, it fired popular enthusiasm in Chihuahua, Durango and the Laguna, it caught the imagination even far from the Villista homeland. In February 1914 the relative calm of Yucatán was broken when 300 villagers rose in arms at Abala, killing the mayor and town council: 'Viva Villa!' was their war-cry.[834]

Popular support and adulation were compatible with graft and corruption, at least for a time. Eventually, the people might note the absence of significant reform, and wonder if they had exchanged one set of crooked masters for another. But meantime they were tolerant; indeed, a display of opulence, a flaunting of the wealth and property acquired by the sword and at the expense of the old regime, were positively welcomed and formed part of the myth. If peons had once identified with the wealth and ostentation of their *hacendado* master, how much more would they derive vicarious satisfaction from the same attributes when displayed by Villa and his generals, who had risen from the ruck of the common people?[835] A new legitimacy – charismatic, in Weberian terminology – was in the making. Anyway, the grafting side of Villismo took time to develop. Villa himself was not notable for his material acquisitiveness: he fought his campaigns in rough old suits and cardigans, a pith helmet or Yankee-style sombrero on his head; his travelling headquarters was a red caboose with chintz curtains, fold-up wooden bunks, and pictures of 'showy ladies in theatrical poses' tacked on to the dirty grey wall.[836] He was too busy running the campaign to graft and hoard systematically (he lacked the cash, Reed said, to send his son to school in the US), though he collected several wives en route.

Many of the minions, however, sought personal advantages within the burgeoning, loosely controlled Villista empire. This, while Villa and some of his more fastidious commanders contrasted with the Federals by shunning graft, the general trend was in the other direction. At Juárez, a town already noted for its saloons, casinos and brothels, and with a racy reputation which American Prohibition would soon enhance, the Villista Juan Medina took over the gambling houses and established an intitially honest regime: 'the officers and men of Villa's army', it was observed, 'do not . . . exhibit the selfishness and greed pecuniarly [sic] as did the Federals, who would not usually be in a town many days until a number of the officials [sic] would have an interest in a saloon or gambling house'.[837] But, as the main border port, Juárez soon became the focal point of Villista commercial enterprise, much of it legiti-mate: the collection of customs, the import of arms and supplies, the export of cattle. The pickings were rich, strict surveillance was impossible, and the rebels could not be expected to make a clean break with ancient, ingrained traditions of profit and peculation. When Martín Luis Guzmán arrived at Juárez, he found Hipólito Villa, Pancho's brother, running the poker, roulette and crap houses, and young Jáuregui, who had helped Villa escape in 1913, operating the city lottery.[838] Again, after Luis Terrazas had been sweated and the Banco Minero ransacked, the proceeds were handed out to the leading Villista commanders literally by the hatful; and, while this cash was meant to go – and maybe did go – for the purchase of military supplies, there was scant financial supervision.[839] Urbina, one of the recipients, certainly salted away loot from the sack of Durango, setting himself up at Canutillo like a feudal seigneur; other Villista commanders administered or rented confiscated properties, and it is impossible to know how far they thereby furthered the cause, or merely feathered their own nests.[840] Certainly the ubiquitous Arab merchants of northern Mexico battened on to the Villista army, forming mutually profitable relations with rebel jefes and trafficking in confiscated goods.[841] And, lower in the military hierarchy, there were Villista officers who installed 'women of ill repute' in confiscated private houses in Chihuahua.[842] Yet these were, if anything, only the advance symptoms of a disease that would later infect entire limbs and organs. Given the patient's pre-1910 case history, and the pestiferous atmosphere of 1910–20, it is hardly surprising that graft and corruption became chronic. No revolutionary group was immune; but while some – such as the Zapatistas and their kind – were protected by the antibodies of village tradition, corporate solidarity and *agrarista* sentiment, most northerners had no such resistance. The germs of corruption flooded in unopposed.[843]

Early in 1914, however, graft was only one incidental feature of a Villismo that was popular, powerful and on the march. Villa controlled all Chihuahua, while most of rural Durango, Coahuila and Zacatecas was up in arms. The Federals clung to the Laguna towns, blocking the railway line south. In the west, Obregón's advance was slow, sure and methodical; in the east, Pablo González's merely slow. The future of the revolution and of the Huerta regime hinged upon the campaign shortly to be mounted by Villa in the Laguna. In this respect, the spring of 1914 followed the pattern of revolutionary springs which, for rational as well as fortuitous reasons, were characterised by major battles, conquests and upheavals: the runaway success of the Madero revolution in 1911; Orozco's revolt in 1912; the several Constitutionalist rebellions of 1913. Now, in 1914, different factors conspired to produce one of those climacterics which historians love though history provides but parsimoniously. The most potent was Villa's advance on Torreón, the significance of which was generally appreciated at the time. But Huerta also faced mounting financial problems, a crisis of confidence within Huertismo, and an important shift in US policy. These provided the context for the great campaign in the Laguna.

Huerta's financial problems stemmed from a simple combination of rising expenditure and falling revenue (that is, revenue from traditional sources). The scale of the first is hard to assess, since after June 1913, when the last Maderista budget ended, the statistical record reveals yawning gaps. In the crucial area of military expenditure, Wilkie suggests that Huertista appropriations – at 31% of total expenditure – were some 50% higher than Díaz's, but only slightly higher than Madero's.[844] But Wilkie's figures again give *projected* expenditure, and it must be assumed that the prodigious growth of the Army – from 50,000 to a notional 250,000 in the space of a year – involved some upward revision of original estimates. In the summer of 1913, for example, 'troop payments' required 3.5m. pesos per month, averaging 42m. pesos per annum; by the end of the year, with the army increased to 80,000, Huerta needed 12.5m. per month (150m. per annum) to support the military: a 350% increase.[845] Furthermore, it is quite clear from the *ad hoc* and illegal methods used to raise cash in the provinces that a large slice of military expenditure was neither budgeted for in advance, nor accounted for afterwards. The projected military budget tells only a part of the story.

Expenditure rose while the government's tax base dwindled. It dwindled geographically, with the loss of rich areas like Sonora, parts of the north-east, soon Chihuahua and the Laguna, as well as the northern border ports, which alone supplied 20% of Mexico's imports and some 7–8% of government revenue.[846] But the revolution undercut government revenue even more by its gradual, deleterious effect on trade, industry and investment, even in regions where rebel armies had never set foot. In this respect, 1913–14 witnessed the first major erosion of Mexico's economic strength as a result of the Revolution. Though Madero's finances had wobbled in 1912, the underlying economy had remained strong, with exports high, the peso firm, mining and railway returns healthy, and the banking system still intact. Even in 1913–14 men marvelled at the resilience of the economy which – like other economies in times of devastation and upheaval – showed a remarkable capacity to produce in the face of adversity.[847] *Homo economicus* cocked a snook at the warring generals and politicians. Economic decline, when it came, was gradual and regionally varied. In this respect, the economy was – after the Catholic Church – the toughest of the institutions and structures tested by the Revolution. The decline of the economy, too, followed a different tempo from that of regimes, parties and political factions: economic collapse came one or two years after the political nadir (measured in terms of political chaos and anarchy) had been reached, and at a time when political authority was already resurgent. It was important for Huerta, however, that his presidency coincided with the first major economic reverses. For even this partial decline – so partial that the economy of early 1914 would appear vigorous compared with that of 1916 – had a multiplier effect on government finance, particularly the orthodox finance which Huerta, following Porfirian precedents, was expected to conduct. So long as Huerta relied on traditional sources of revenue – import duties, the stamp tax, foreign loans – a major downswing in the economy had swift, serious repercussions on government policy.

Economic decline varied regionally. The south and south-east were relatively unaffected in 1913–14: the chief problem faced by the planters of Yucatán, Campeche and Tabasco was a shortage of labour, a familiar problem now compounded by the operations of the *leva*. In December 1913, for example, Federal demands for recruits prompted such a flight of labourers into the woods and swamps of Tabasco that business was threatened and the demands had to be relaxed.[848] In most other respects, the southern economy flourished. The Mexico City–Veracruz Railway was unaffected and, in fact, benefited from the northern lines' loss of traffic, such that earnings per kilometre were 8% higher in 1913 than 1912; the Inter-Oceanic, serving the same route, earned more at the beginning of 1914 than a year before.[849] Meanwhile, henequen exports from Yucatán, which had dropped in both volume and value on the eve of the Revolution, forged ahead in 1911 and 1912, marginally increased in 1913, and shot up again in 1914. The long term fall in henequen prices was arrested: by the end of 1913 henequen was fetching 40% more per kilo than in 1908–10, and Yucatán's income was higher than it had been for a decade.[850] Even in the spring of 1914, the annual Mérida carnival could still be held at an estimated cost of half a million pesos.[851] And, while outsiders cast covetous eyes on the wealth of the peninsula, the Yucatecans themselves were all the more concerned to cultivate their henequen garden and avoid alien intervention. Finally, on the plus side of the economy, the oil industry had already begun to show its capacity to insulate itself from interference and disruption, despite its proximity to the revolutionary north. Production in 1913, a boom year, rose from 17m. to 26m. barrels.[852] Both sides in the civil war were concerned that oil production should continue, and oil magnates like Lord Cowdray were reasonably confident that neither would 'kill the goose which laid the golden eggs'.[853] Late in 1913 – despite the proximity of rebel forces – the Topila field was brought in; new companies were floated, attracting Mexican as well as foreign capital; and new shares issues were promptly snapped up and soon traded at a premium.[854] Though fighting in the oil district, culminating in the fall of Tampico in May 1914, curtailed further expansion, this was no more than a pause before production figures shot up again.[855]

The north presented a sharp contrast. While Sonora – safely in responsible rebel hands since early 1913 – remained prosperous, the rest of the north witnessed the major campaigns of the war.[856] The economic effects, as experienced in the north-east, have already been illustrated.[857] In general, economic decline was a by-product, not a direct result, of the fighting. Mines and smelters closed or cut production less because of direct threats or wilful damage (the strategic coal-mines of Coahuila were an exception) than because, with half the nation's railways affected by the revolution, they could not secure supplies (dynamite was particularly scarce) and could not ship out ore. Later, the breakdown of the banking system compounded the problems of business.[858] The major smelters of northern Mexico may be taken as indicators: in October 1913, Velardeña (near Torreón), Durango and San Luis had closed, chiefly for want of fuel; by December, Monterrey and Chihuahua had followed; while Aguascalientes survived a little into 1914, working at half capacity.[859] In the same period dozens of mines closed, many following precedents set during the 1908 slump: it was cheaper to keep the ore in the ground than to extract it and leave it at the mercy of uncertain communications and the hazards of warfare – witness the piles of coal which littered the mining towns of Coahuila for much of 1913.[860] The Batopilas mine, for example, closed along with the section of the Kansas City and Orient which cut through the Chihuahuan sierra to supply it; the manager, arriving in the US with $80,000 (US) of silver, stressed that he had left not because of revolutionary hostility, but because 'the war has upset conditions so that no-one can now make a living'.[861]

Thus mining production, so crucial to the economy and to government finance, began to drop significantly for the first time:[862]

Mining production (by weight), 1910 = 100:

	Silver	Gold	Lead	Copper
1910	100	100	100	100
1911	104	90	94	117
1912	104	78	85	119
1913	71	63	35	110
1914	34	21	5	56

Other sectors of the northern economy were also affected: guayule exports slumped; the lumber mills of the Chihuahua and Durango sierra closed; the cattle and cotton estates were fought over, and finally lost to rebel control. The loss of the Laguna forced textile factories in Nuevo León, Puebla and even distant Oaxaca to close for want of raw cotton and, though the Federal reconquest of Torreón in December 1913 allowed some cotton to get out, Huerta's control of the Laguna was neither complete nor prolonged enough to guarantee a supply to the major textile towns of central Mexico.[863] Mining, too, was affected by the loss of the country's principal dynamite factory at Gómez Palacio; while the fighting in the north jeopardised the supply of fuel oil from the Tampico region, forcing the government to impose an embargo on all non-military freight save food and cotton.[864]

Thus the ripples of revolution spread. Some commercial activities were unaffected: the mines of El Oro continued to work; the Mexico City–Veracruz rail links were busy; the capital's utility companies – mirroring life in Mexico City – seemed prosperous.[865] Indeed, in much of urban, central Mexico 'business as usual' was maintained, for the time being. But no individual or enterprise could entirely escape the gradual, inexorable economic consequences of the war. For breakdowns in the engine room of the economy soon had their effect on the bridge and on the crew as a whole. Goods became scarcer and prices rose: in Coahuila, one of the first victims of economic hardship, the prices of staples showed a marked increase as early as August 1913.[866] Interest rates rose, too, while stock prices – save those of the buoyant oil companies – began to fall. The peso also fell in a manner which alarmed old Mexico hands:

from its par value of 49.5 US cents in February 1913 it dropped to 42c. in the summer and 36c. in the autumn; by February 1914 it traded at three to the dollar, the worst rate 'within the recollection of the oldest bankers' in Mexico City.[867] Specie flew from the bank-vaults and – despite government counter-measures – from the country itself. A serious financial crisis was looming.

This crisis, generated by the decline of the 'real' economy, was bound up with Huertista financial policy, which helped to bring it on, even as it sought to avert it. Huerta himself was ignorant of financial matters; Limantour had no intention of returning from Europe; and the president depended on financial ministers who were less prestigious and, by all accounts, less capable.[868] One, Adolfo de la Lama, held office disproportionately long and enjoyed Huerta's confidence; his policies, a disgruntled colleague observed in a quaintly dated reference, 'could have demolished even the government of England'.[869] Certainly the government's desperate search for cash – evident in loans, both foreign and domestic, paper issues and increased taxation – contributed to the gathering financial storm and the mounting unpopularity of the regime. The quest for foreign finance, undertaken from the very start, was disappointing: American non-recognition made it virtually impossible for Huerta to raise loans in the US, and by no means easy for him to raise them in Europe.[870] Constitutionalist agents, assiduously lobbying in Washington, New York and Paris, added their influence to the natural caution of the international bankers.[871] A £20m. loan was raised in Europe in June 1913; but of the £6m. initially advanced, most went to cover outstanding obligations, leaving the Federal treasury with only 1.5m. pesos of disposable cash. And, as Huerta's position deteriorated, the European bankers declined to take up the option on the remaining £14m.[872] As well hung for a sheep as for a lamb, Huerta suspended payments on the national debt, thus saving the treasury 3m. pesos a month. This, as Meyer says, was a 'monumental decision', which elicited protests from the French government, marked a departure from Díaz's careful cultivation of Mexico's credit, and started once buoyant Mexican bonds down a long slide into oblivion.[873] Mexico returned to the lazaretto of bad debtors which she had so often occupied in the nineteenth century, and from which she would not emerge for thirty years.

Like the rebels, therefore, Huerta had to fight the war on the basis of domestic resources. Domestic loans proved more fruitful. The government negotiated an 18m. peso loan with the major banks and commercial houses in September 1913, half of which sum was handed over in the following month; by June 1914 the banks of issue had lent a total of 46.5m. pesos.[874] But, even as Huerta turned to the banks for help, the whole financial structure of the country was being shaken by the regime's second revenue-raising expedient: inflation. The currency and banking system had survived the fall of Díaz and Madero relatively unscathed.[875] But the summer of 1913 saw Mexico's effective departure from the Gold Standard and the beginning of a precipitate

descent into paper that would last until the end of 1916, and that would prove
not least among the engines of social change set in motion by the Revolution.
In successive measures Huerta relaxed the rules governing the relation of paper
to bullion, authorised the issue of paper by national and state banks, and –
when the bad paper drove out the good metal – decreed the forced circulation
of the depreciating paper. The total currency circulating in Huertista Mexico
doubled as compared with 1910. Since, at the same time, the Constitutionalists were churning out paper money (also on a fiat basis) the country was soon
flooded with competing paper currencies and a prodigious inflationary cycle
began.[876] Though the cycle did not reach its worst until 1916, its effects were
already evident in 1913–14. The flood of paper added to existing problems in
the north-east, prompting the mines and smelters of the Monterrey district to
close; in the Laguna, business was conducted with IOUs for want of sound
currency; the Federal commander at Saltillo shut down businesses which
refused notes issued by banks located in rebel territory.[877] Nor were such
problems confined to the north. Dredgers and oil-drillers on the Tabasco coast
had to stop work for want of silver to pay their workers; mining companies in
Hidalgo, Zacatecas, Mexico (state) and elsewhere met the wage bill with *vales*
(scrip).[878]

Vexed by these problems, business also faced an array of tax increases.
Import duties were raised 50% in October 1913; additional export taxes were
levied on a range of primary products (cotton, coffee, oil, rubber, henequen);
the planters of Papantla, already facing local agrarian troubles, now paid a
surcharge of two pesos per kilo on their vanilla exports.[879] The internal market
was loaded with additional taxes on tobacco, beer and other alcoholic drinks;
the stamp tax – which yielded 30% of government revenue – was doubled;
future tax income was mortgaged by the sale of revenue stamps at a
discount.[880] Land taxes were also increased, as they had been under Madero:
by 50% in the Federal District, 70% in rural Zacatecas; and some estates – like
those of Aguascalientes – were subjected to extraordinary levies.[881] Mortgages
and bank deposits were similarly levied (thus accelerating the flight of capital)
and a levy on the capital of public companies was planned, which Lord
Cowdray denounced as 'simply outrageous and downright robbery'.[882]

In the provinces, military commanders imposed loans, levies and taxes with
increasing frequency. Business was caught both ways: Silvestre Mariscal
mulcted the merchants of Acapulco for the Revolution, Joaquín Maass those of
Saltillo for the government.[883] Often, there was the strong implication that
refusal would leave property at the mercy of loutish rebels or – just as bad –
unpaid Federal conscripts. A Federal colonel paraded his 800 unpaid men
through the streets of Piedras Negras, emphasising the need for a local war tax;
at Tuxpán another colonel, short of 70,000 pesos to pay his troops and meet
old army debts, allocated sums to the major banks, merchants and oil
companies of the district, conveying 'the impression that whoever did not

subscribe would be extremely sorry for not having done so'.[884] 'It is', an observer at Tuxpán commented, 'simply another [example] of what has become known as "un préstamo voluntario forzoso"'; 'although', he added in an important aside, 'heretofore it has been supposed to be the exclusive patent of the rebels.'[885] This was important by way of indicating changing perceptions. Initially, the rebels were seen – certainly in Mexico City and the major towns – as thugs and vandals. While the Huertista press sedulously maintained this image, they could not prevent a growing awareness that it was false. Villa's transformation from the wild bandit of 1913 to the orderly caudillo of 1914 represented both a change in the character of Villismo and also a shift in public awareness and opinion. Conversely, Huerta had been hailed as the 'iron hand' of 1913, the champion of peace, order and property; the Federal Army had been apostrophised as the protector of society.[886] Now, on occasions, the roles seemed reversed: Villa policed Chihuahua, and Federal officers mulcted the well-to-do. This did not lead the well-to-do to desert Huerta *en masse* in favour of Villa. But it accelerated the process – already noted – whereby many erstwhile supporters of Huerta felt serious misgivings and longed for a solution to the civil war which eliminated Huerta without implying unconditional surrender to the revolution.

Mexico's financial problems exacerbated these misgivings. While Lord Cowdray denounced the capital levy, the French government protested against the suspension of foreign debt payments, and the Spanish against increased import duties.[887] American bankers with Mexican interests expressed their disquiet at Huerta's measures, and the shrill spokesmen of the oil companies deemed an increased petroleum export tax 'equivalent to confiscation'.[888] More important, Mexicans felt the same. The doubling of the stamp tax caused 'bitter feeling against the Federal Government' in Colima, which had already been hit by increased cotton taxes; when the government went further, demanding 100,000 pesos from local citizens, a protest demonstration was held, and the offending military governor removed.[889] Saltillo witnessed a similar, successful protest in January 1914.[890] In Tabasco, where the *leva*'s activities had to be relaxed for the sake of business interests, increased taxes were 'creating ill-feeling among all classes'; the landlords of Guanajuato complained of forced loans and the army's requisitioning of horses; even the Puebla textile workers, facing lay-offs, lamented that since the beginning of 1914 the government 'not only regulated the industry but [also] penalised it by imposing heavy contributions supposedly for war expenses'.[891]

Misgivings multiplied as it became clear that, despite additional taxes, the government's capacity was impaired by cash shortages. Contractors and employees went unpaid and public works were halted.[892] Funds for the sponsoring of patriotic demonstrations ran out. The consular service was starved of resources: at Laredo, the staff waited three months for their salaries; at Marfa the rent was owed; at El Paso the new consul found a mere $36 in the office safe.[893] Most serious of all, the troops' pay fell in arrears – and this, in a conscript army like Huerta's, was a recipe for rapid dissolution. By late 1913 reports came in of unpaid troops and anxious commanders. Many of the local levies and forced loans were imposed in order to avert desertion or even mutiny.[894] In 1914, the problems increased. The Eagle Pass consul could not pay for the upkeep of the 29th Cavalry Regiment, as instructed, since he had no cash and the Federals advancing on Matamoros were 'absolutely without funds'.[895] Usually, money eventually got through, or was raised locally. But away from the front line there was less urgency and less capacity to control restless conscripts. In January 1914 a large force – including 400 recruits newly arrived from central Mexico – mutinied at Ensenada (Baja Calif.), despite a whip-round among the merchants of the port; a fight ensued in which the loyalist artillery (whose pay had been scrupulously met) put down the mutineers; and nine of them were publicly executed – an act which 'caused very bitter feeling among the soldiers'. Still the situation remained tense: the townspeople were 'in a state of terror and some of the officers in a funk'; only the arrival of 49,000 pesos by ship staved off further trouble.[896]

Such extreme cases – where financial failure led directly to military collapse – were rare; they were concentrated in the latter months of the regime; and it would be wrong to attribute Huerta's fall primarily to economic factors, which only became acute after and because the regime had already failed in the political and military spheres. As an observer commented as early as May 1913, on reading of Huerta's initial success at raising cash: 'I don't think it will do a bit of good in the long run . . . they need money, but it will never do any good without union, wisdom, or justice.'[897] If the phrases were corny, the sense was right. Huerta did not fail for want of cash. But the want of cash and the fiscal expedients it provoked all added to the disenchantment of Huerta's supporters, some of whom already resented the rampant militarisation – and the elbowing aside of established families and cliques which went with it. Few doubted that Huerta was still preferable to the revolution (and doubts could be silenced by spine-chilling stories of revolutionary mayhem), but by 1914 the earlier enthusiasm had cooled, support for Huerta was grudging, and many of the well-to-do wished they could find an alternative to the stark dichotomy which confronted them.

Typical of this group was Miguel Cárdenas, ex-governor of Coahuila, protégé of Bernardo Reyes, and *patrón* of Venustiano Carranza. Though he had no time for Madero's 'socialistic democracy', he was equally sceptical of Huerta's attempted 'restoration of the old regime with its hopeless oppression'; he preferred a 'medium between the two views', a government both 'just and firm'. But in the summer of 1913 no *via media* presented itself; hence, Cárdenas confided to a friend, 'he supported the Huerta government because he considers it the choice [sic] of two evils'; for the revolution, already responsible for 'a long series of acts of vengeance, attacks on property, and all manner of excess', promised 'the ruin of the nation'.[898] 'There are', his interlocutor noted, 'many other Mexicans who share this view, not only civilians but [also] prominent army officers.' With time, Cárdenas grew more pessimistic. By November 1913 he was of the opinion that 'the government, apart from any question of legality or expediency, is beginning to show itself essentially unworthy as well as incapable'; yet the revolution's progress gave no cause for optimism.[899] General Peña, then governor of Coahuila, was of like mind. He found little satisfaction in his job, 'especially under present circumstances when everybody is under military direction'; he was 'not at all in sympathy with some of the policies of General Huerta', but dared not resist them; and he feared that the rebels, being aware of his Huertista affiliation, would take reprisals against his extensive properties in the Laguna.[900] These examples derive from Coahuila, where there were specific reasons why Huertismo should flag, while it still flourished elsewhere. But the sentiments were representative of a strong body of opinion, which despaired of Huerta, while it could still not stomach the revolution. At Acapulco, too, the 'better class of people' kept their heads low, 'fear[ing] to express their opinions'; few, outside the military, openly endorsed Huerta; and those keenest for peace – 'the merchants, businessmen and trades people' – had become political sceptics, assuming the 'role of curious spectators of passing and interesting events'.[901] By the end of 1913, then, the high hopes raised by Huerta's initial conquest of power had given way to scepticism and *attentisme*.

Disillusionment with Huerta prompted not acceptance of the revolution but rather the search for a third way, a negotiated settlement or even American intervention ('intervention' implying – as it did to contemporaries – anything from diplomatic pressure to military invasion). Hopes of a settlement were in the air during the politicking of 1913, described above; and, though this came to nothing, the hopes were still abroad, assuming different guises, conjured up by disaffected Huertistas, haunting the embattled usurper. Ex-President de la Barra, a specialist in such brokerage, now heading an emigré faction, communicated to the US government a scheme involving Huerta's replacement by a coalition of Catholics, Huertistas and Anti-Re-electionists; Limantour, from Paris, launched a similar scheme, contingent upon an American undertaking 'not only to recognise the new government but . . . also to persecute the rebels by all possible means within international law'.[902] The same sentiment began to crystallise in Mexico, and not in *sub rosa* conversations and quiet confidences. The new chairman of the (Huertista) Chamber of Deputies replied to the presidential message by urging everyone to 'relinquish with the most complete abnegation all ambitions . . . and to succeed in bringing about peace and union' – an exhortation which, for all its vacuity, displayed a different spirit from the draconian certainty of early 1913.[903] Now, Lind reported optimistically, 'sentiment is breaking away from Huerta in chunks'; the president's own private secretary inquired of the

American Chargé whether – if Huerta could be induced to resign – his government would accept Emilio Rabasa as successor; while prominent Mexicans like General Fernando González, son of ex-President Manuel González, called for a transitional administration to replace the 'moribund' Huerta regime – though this administation, it was stressed, should not be of revolutionary origin.[904]

For obvious reasons, much of this kite-flying took place in foreign skies, and involved foreign governments. Early in 1914 the Mexican Chargé in Washington sounded out the major European representatives, hoping to secure their pressure on Huerta to retire; this, he believed, would be more effective than the crude policy of the Americans.[905] The scheme was strongly reminiscent of the Juárez compromise of 1911 (even the same names surfaced: some 'fairly colourless man' like de la Barra was recommended as provisional president) and it appealed to the narrowly obtuse pragmatism of the Europeans, who were eager for a peace settlement that would salvage their Mexican interests. But any European *démarche* needed American approval, which was not forthcoming: Secretary of State Bryan (often depicted as a wordy, fundamentalist crackpot) told the British Minister that 'the moment [for such a compromise] had passed' and that 'the real cause of the trouble [in Mexico] was well-founded discontent and until this was quieted by legislative measures no real peace could be obtained'.[906] This viewpoint – 'inverted and false', 'quite impracticable', 'wrong-headed and inept', as the British, French and German representatives put it – was more realistic than that of most Europeans (and many Americans), who slated American policy, considered the revolutionaries a plundering horde, and advocated the 'iron hand' as the only solution'.[907] Years of active colonialism had left their mark. And this divorce between the American and European – the 'progressive' and the 'imperialist' – official minds became particularly acute at the beginning of 1914, since the former now experienced a significant shift, thus adding to the problems which beset Huerta.

In February 1914 President Wilson ended the policy of 'watchful waiting' and relaxed the American arms embargo in favour of the Constitutionalists. Henceforth, the latter could legally import all the arms they could pay for. This was a crucial decision, reflecting Wilson's definite commitment to the revolutionary cause. Again, it can be argued that this represented interference in Mexican domestic affairs; but, again, any policy on arms traffic implied 'interference'. It should not be forgotten that for six months after Huerta's coup the US had allowed arms to reach Huerta and not the rebels, and that for a further six months both sides had been denied (legitimate) access to the American arms market (during which time Huerta, unlike the rebels, could turn to Europe and Japan).[908] More pertinent than these normative questions, however, is that of causality, which has been less explored. Two individuals played salient roles in influencing the American decision: John Lind and Luis

Cabrera. Following the failure of his mission to Huerta, Lind sat in Veracruz, penning diatribes against the dictator and urging Wilson to take more urgent action. Many of his reports were garbled, ill-informed and naive, displaying a crude racism and a paranoid suspicion of Britain and British representatives in Mexico.[909] On the other hand, even Lind's Manichaean view of the war (rebels good, Huerta bad) was superior to the narrow colonialist mentality, with its abiding faith in the 'iron hand'. Furthermore, Lind had a grasp of American policy options: for him, the US was committed to the overthrow of Huerta which – if it was to be anything more than a spatchcocked compromise – required either American intervention or American aid for the revolution. Though Lind countenanced the first, the second was more palatable and appropriate: 'let this housecleaning be done by home talent', he advised.[910] This was a logical position, even if Lind allowed his eagerness for a revolutionary triumph to colour his reports and recommendations. Foremost among the latter was the lifting of the arms embargo, which he repeatedly urged around the turn of the year 1913/14. And, at the beginning of January, Lind sailed to the US to confer with Wilson, thus giving the president a 'splendid opportunity to see things . . . nearer at hand'.[911]

While Lind prodded the president towards recognition of the rebels' belligerency, the rebels were diplomatically active too. For months they had protested against the injustice of the embargo: Maytorena wrote to Bryan and Carranza to Wilson; Carranza raised the matter with 'confidential agent' Hale; and local commanders, like Gabriel Calzada at Piedras Negras, hinted at reprisals if it was maintained.[912] Throughout – and most explicitly in the talks with Hale – Carranza refused to accept a recognition of belligerency which carried with it conditions, such as a commitment to immediate elections, or permission for American troops to enter Mexico for the protection of foreigners; he sought recognition as a matter of justice, with no strings attached. Lobbying continued and, early in 1914, Luis Cabrera presented the Constitutionalist case to Wilson and Bryan in person. By then, the decision to grant recognition had been taken; but there can be no doubt that Cabrera's arguments – and those of preceding lobbyists – had carried real weight with the administration. When the British Minister to Mexico met President Wilson he 'could not fail to be struck with the identity of the views' of Wilson and Cabrera: that the revolution involved deep social forces, was more than 'mere political sedition', that Madero failed because of the strength of the Porfirian influences surrounding him, that genuine reforms – as outlined by the Constitutionalists – were necessary, and that the US should not 'seek to repress the will of a people'.[913]

Suave and articulate as he was, Cabrera not only reassured Wilson and guaranteed the lifting of the embargo, but also helped mould the American administration's thought, taking it well beyond the narrow constitutionalism of 1913. Then, a *transacción* between Huerta and the revolution would have been welcomed in Washington; now, Wilson regarded it as 'unthinkable'. Then, Wilson had insisted on elections; now, he and Bryan talked of 'well-grounded social discontent', which demanded serious reforms, particularly to correct 'inequitable methods of land tenure'. While the Europeans still harped on the old themes, likening the Mexicans to the Egyptian Fellahin and denouncing their political leaders as 'tainted with the personal ambition inherent in their blood', Wilson and Bryan had acquired a view of the revolution which, if simplistic and derivative, was nevertheless more profound and accurate. It is quite wrong, therefore, to dismiss Wilson's Mexican policy as a naive, obstinate and consistent attempt to export liberal democracy south of the Río Grande: compared with the policies advocated by many contemporaries, both American and European, it was sound, realistic and responsive to circumstances.[914] And this was particularly important in 1913–14, since it meant that the administration would not only lift the arms embargo, but also ignore the various deals, compromises and *transacciones* which conservatives were floating in the hope of sustaining the status quo and cushioning the impact of the revolution.

The arms embargo was lifted on 1 February 1914. Though Cabrera, in outlining the Constitutionalists' proposed reforms, had also provided certain informal assurances, there do not appear to have been any formal conditions attached. Carranza's obstinacy was vindicated.[915] The immediate effects were considerable, and illustrative of the constraints under which the northern rebels had previously operated (as recently as December 1913, the rebel campaign against Tampico had been broken off for want of ammunition).[916] Not surprisingly, they were jubilant. Villa was 'delighted'; at Durango, the rebels celebrated 'far into the night'; even down in Tabasco – where an influx of American munitions was neither likely nor imminent – it was seen as a pointer to an eventual revolutionary victory and, as a result, 'a noticeable inclination to sympathise [with] and covertly assist the revolutionaries has manifested itself among a large proportion of the inhabitants of this state'.[917] Now, in particular, Villa could prepare for his descent on Torreón. In the circumstances, Torreón represented much more than a key railway junction, the metropolis of the Laguna, and the chief barrier to a revolutionary advance into central Mexico; it would also be – as observers both inside and outside Mexico appreciated – the crucial battle of the Constitutionalist revolution, by which the ultimate fortunes of both sides would be determined. For Huerta, victory was essential: his finances were crumbling, his support was ebbing away, his army had begun to show mutinous tendencies, and the US had come out in overt opposition to his regime. Defeat at Torreón would be disastrous. 'Huerta's only hope', declared the *New York Times*, 'lies in vanquishing Villa at Torreón.'[918] Conversely, a Federal victory would regenerate the regime and deliver a stinging blow to American policy; though it would not end the revolution, it would – a rebel spokesman believed – set their movement ('now so flourishing') 'back a year'.[919]

Nor were the Federals lacking in confidence. The rebels had never taken a well-garrisoned and well-defended city. Villa had bluffed his way into Juárez; Chihuahua had been evacuated; attacks on Monterrey and Tampico had been beaten off. Earlier rebel successes (Durango, June 1913, and Torreón, October 1913) were partly attributable to the inept performances of Generals Escudero and Munguía.[920] Villa's own performance at Tierra Blanca could give the Federals (under the capable leadership of Refugio Velasco, 'Huerta's best general') grounds for cautious optimism.[921] Not that caution was always evident: the Huertista press claimed Torreón to be *inexpugnable*; the British Minister was confident that Huerta 'will whip Villa and Carranza [sic] at Torreón, and once this is done will have more energy to turn to the south'.[922] John Lind, stuck in Veracruz and dependent on the Huertista press, spent February–March 1914 in an agony of pessimistic anticipation: Torreón, he knew, was crucial, and a rebel victory would prove 'the turning point' of the revolution; but he considered the rebels to be inefficient and inactive, feared that Huerta might yet achieve 'substantial victories' here and elsewhere, and therefore urged the US government to take decisive action, even to the extent of mounting an expedition against Mexico City.[923] From their different perspectives, all observers agreed that 'everything seems to depend on the operations at Torreón'.[924]

TORREÓN AND ELSEWHERE

With Juárez in his power, and the embargo lifted, Villa could equip his army on a massive scale. Huerta's consul in El Paso reported a constant flow of supplies across the border: cartridges, shells, and Mausers (which by 1914 had ousted the old Winchester .303s of 1910); consignments of brown boots, gaiters, green felt hats (for the men) and *sombreros tejanos* for the officers.[925] In Chihuahua City, industry hummed in the service of Villismo: the La Paz textile plant was working flat out producing khaki uniforms; the shoemakers of the Barrio del Pacífico – mostly migrants from the south – worked overtime; the forges of the city churned out horse-shoes.[926] Flour, beans and forage were stockpiled in preparation. Meanwhile, recruits still poured in, many from Chihuahua, some from neighbouring states. One report suggested that Villa was equipping an army of 20,000; and it was certainly a force in excess of 10,000 which set out for Torreón, collecting more men as it went.[927] This army, the famous Division of the North, was a conglomerate, resulting from the merger of several *cabecillas* and their *gente* under Villa's leadership: the Brigada Benito Juárez of Luis and Maclovio Herrera, Toribio Ortega's Brigada González Ortega, Rosalío Hernández's Leales de Camargo, Eugenio Aguirre Benavides' Zaragoza Brigade, Trinidad Rodríguez's Cuauhtémoc Brigade. At the heart were Villa's own veterans, typified by the famous *dorados*.[928] The units took their names from liberal heroes of the past (Zaragoza, Juárez, Guadalupe Victoria), or from contemporary revolutionaries (Villa, Robles, Madero); and, while some proclaimed their place of origin in their title (Camargo; the Cuerpo Cazador de la Sierra), it was well known that all derived from regional as much as personal loyalists. The Zaragoza Brigade was made up of men from the Laguna, the Cuauhtémoc Brigade came from Huejotitlán: they could be distinguished by the clothes they wore (for American imports could not entirely swamp the heterogeneity of revolutionary apparel), even by the cigarettes they smoked.[929]

With the lifting of the embargo, they became a formidable, well-armed force. Felipe Angeles' 300 artillerymen had at their disposal twenty-eight field guns, including the two famous three inch cannons, El Niño and El Chavalito, each mounted on an armoured flat-car; the hospital train of forty boxcars with enamelled interiors was staffed by a hundred officers, nurses and stretcher-bearers.[930] Altogether, the army which rolled south from Chihuahua in March 1914 was the most impressive ever mustered in the service of the revolution: Villista professionalism had reached such a pitch that the rebels could now challenge a strong Federal force ensconced in a fortified position. And, by a certain irony, ex-Federal recruits were instrumental in this transformation: Angeles had licked the artillery into shape; Juan Medina had struggled against the waywardness of established *jefes* like Urbina; and Federal prisoners, permitted to join the Villistas, brought with them habits of discipline which rubbed off on their new colleagues.[931] By the spring of 1914, an unsympathetic observer admitted, the Villistas – with their new equipment, 'discipline and soldierly bearing' – 'for the first time resembled real soldiers instead of [the] unkempt ragged peons that one is accustomed to associate with revolutions in northern Mexico'.[932] But professionalism could only go so far. Some of Villa's Durango and Laguna lieutenants strenuously resisted the efficient organisation now demanded of them: though they collaborated with Villa, they still remained stubborn, independent, provincially-minded bushwhackers and *guerrilleros*, and their men – like the 'unpaid, ill-clad, undisciplined' horde of Calixto Contreras – felt primarily loyal to their own leader and the *patria chica* from which they sprang.[933] Thus, despite the pressing imperatives of professionalisation, Juan Medina found the task of disciplining Urbina, Fierro and others of that ilk to be insuperable; not least because Villa continued to show a fond indulgence to these, his oldest *compadres*.[934] Indeed, Villa himself bucked at the new constraints and burdens placed upon him. He was – Cabrera found – 'incapable of administrative labours'; he could be found 'in Chihuahua hopelessly perplexed with the piles of paper that were presented to him and longing to get back among his soldiers'.[935]

This uneasy balance between the popular and the professional persisted as

the Villista army headed south. The advance still had many of the characteristics of a 'folk migration'.[936] Sometimes, it seems, Villa toyed with the idea –
recently put into practice by the Federal General Mercado – of banning
soldaderas from the line of march; but this was the way the Mexicans (Federals
and, *a fortiori*, revolutionaries) made war, and the *soldaderas* stayed, perform-
ing as valuable a service as the Commissary or the Medical Corps, and
numbering possibly as many as the troops themselves.[937] So, as the trains
rolled south down the Mexican Central – that spine of revolutionary conflict,
where Orozco had driven González Salas to suicide, where Huerta had
pounded Orozco into submission, and where Governor González, Villa's
mentor, had been done to death in February 1913 – so, the women and
children encamped on the flat roofs of the boxcars, or even rode the cowcatchers
of locomotives, baking tortillas on fires of mesquite twigs, or hanging out
their washing to dry in the wind.[938] *En route* – in, on and under railway
waggons – babies were conceived and babies were born; beggars, musicians,
journalists, photographers, tumblers and whores tagged along. Associated
Press was there in force, along with an American film crew, their device a
winged clock and the motto: 'Mutual Movies Make Time Fly'. The Villista
officers and their fancy women rode in *carros de lujo*, Villa in his famous red
caboose with the chintz curtains; the forty hospital cars stood out with their
stencilled blue crosses on the sides.[939]

Through Villista territory progress was swift and safe; Villa could dance
away the night at Camargo, attending a *compadre's* wedding and rejoining the
army next day, 'his face . . . drawn into lines of fatigue'.[940] At Yermo, the
northern gateway to the Laguna, the trains halted on a flat, arid plain, spotted
with stunted cactus. To the east, stretched the sand desert of the Bolsón de
Mapimí; to the west, on the horizon, marched the peaks of the Sierra Madre;
and, seventy miles south, lay the Laguna towns, barring the route to central
Mexico. Here, Velasco was dug in with some 10,000 Federals – a formidable
garrison, even if largely composed of conscripts from the south, many of them
mere adolescents.[941] Federal detachments, including the tough *colorados* of
Benjamín Argumedo, defended the northern approaches at Mapimí, Bermejillo, and Tlahualilo, and these witnessed the first skirmishes in what was to be
'the most gruelling and bloody contest in the long annals of the Mexican
Revolution'.[942] Now, there could be no Villista subterfuges. Split into its
constituent brigades, the Division of the North was flung against the outlying
defences of the Laguna: Aguirre Benavides attacked Tlahualilo; Urbina
assaulted Mapimí; Villa, in the centre, swept into Bermejillo, the cavalry
pouring into the little town of adobe houses, driving the Federals pell-mell to
the south. The first ring of defences was broken. But as the trains crawled
forward in the wake of the army, receiving the wounded and probing the track
for mines, so the going got tougher.[943] A ferocious night attack – the fiercest
fighting he had even witnessed, Villa said – gave the rebels control of the

strategic Cerro de Pila, and with it of the outskirts of Gómez Palacio. But reinforcements failed to arrive and, at dawn, the Federals issued forth from Torreón and recaptured the position. In Mexico City the Huertista press boasted of 'complete and terrible' defeats suffered by the rebels.[944] This was wishful thinking. Fresh forces came up from the Laguna countryside (they included Calixto Contreras and his Cuencamé men); and Angeles brought the Villista artillery to bear on the Federal lines, personally cranking up and sighting the guns, having to contend with the defective shells shipped from the factories of Chihuahua.[945]

For four days the fighting continued unabated. John Reed's first-hand account – far removed from the neat manoeuvrings of military memoirs – conveys something of the mass confusion and chaos which marked this, like other battles of the Revolution: the *va-et-vient* of rebel leaders and their *gente*, linking up, dissolving, quarrelling, imposing their own spontaneous, tactical decisions on whatever grand strategy the commander-in-chief had conceived; the withering machine-gun fire, the devastating shrapnel, the artillery lighting the night sky like fiesta fireworks; the persistent hunger, sporadically assuaged by jerked beef and tortillas, the even worse thirst (the rains had not yet come, the irrigation channels – now military trenches – were dry and sunbaked, and the Federals had poisoned the wells); the brief lulls in the fighting when old friends met and parted, when soldiers brewed up coffee, played cards under a trestle bridge, sang old songs or improvised new *corridos* about a battle that was not yet over; the cool nights, misty dawns and torrid days; the inadequate first aid, the ghastly battlefield surgery; the ubiquitous movie team; the vultures gorging themselves on dead horses; the prolific executions of prisoners, the faint smell of corpses and the rising smoke of dozens of funeral pyres.[946]

In all this, Villa's role was less that of a conventional general, surveying the battlefield and implementing stratagems, than of talisman and rabble-rouser. According to Reed, Villa stemmed a rout at a critical moment during the attack on Gómez, urging his men to turn back, recover their discarded rifles and continue the assault.[947] Certainly the initial battle for Gómez was not won by superior tactics, weaponry or numbers, but rather superior morale. For, after five days, during which both sides suffered heavy losses, Velasco was obliged to evacuate Gómez and Lerdo, pulling his troops back to Torreón.[948] The artillery duel continued and the Villistas fought for control of the hills around Torreón. A Federal relief force of 2,000, heading from the north-east, was repulsed (Pablo González had been expected to prevent this advance; his failure increased Villa's doubts as to González's ability and good faith).[949] On 30 March Velasco requested a two day truce to attend to the dead and wounded; Villa, after consultation with Angeles, refused. Though rebel losses were heavy, Villa reckoned Federal morale was at breaking point: many superior officers had been killed and the failure of the Federal reinforcements to break through had been a bitter blow. Deliberately, Villa did not block off every escape route from the beleaguered city, but offered Velsaco an exit point along the railway line to Saltillo. On the night of 1 April the Villista artillery – which for two days had husbanded its shells – opened up a massive barrage. Next day the wind blew up a dust storm on the parched Laguna plains. Velasco took his chance and, in a 'masterly' move, evacuated his mauled army, in good order, to the east. The rebels saw smoke rising over Torreón: was it the incineration of more bodies or the departing Federals' destruction of munitions? It proved to be the latter. Early on the morning of Good Friday – 3 April – Villa and his army entered Torreón.[950]

In Mexico City the press reported Velasco's evacuation as a strategic withdrawal – as, in a sense, it was. But by now, Huertista strategic withdrawals had become something of a joke in revolutionary circles, and the explanation could not diminish revolutionary elation.[951] The price paid, however, had been heavy. Though suffering less than the Federals, the rebels had nonetheless lost over 500 dead and 1,500 wounded, the latter including prominent *jefes* like Calixto Contreras, Martín Triana, and José Isabel Robles; perhaps one in five of the Constitutionalists were thus casualties – an indication of the severity of the fighting. And Lerdo, Gómez and Torreón were left littered with corpses, evil-smelling, their trees bereft of branches and their buildings riddled with bullet-holes.[952] Despite the heavy losses, Villa gave his army no rest. Velasco had headed east, to link up with the Federal Army stalled at San Pedro, and Villa at once set off in pursuit, entraining his army and denuding Torreón of troops within days of its capture. Though the union of Generals Velasco and Maass at San Pedro created a force of up to 10,000, demoralisation and internal dissension made the Federals no match for the weary but enthusiastic Villistas.[953] After two days of facing Villista attacks from behind their cotton bale barricades, the Federals broke and fled in chaos, leaving a huge supply of arms and supplies, and putting much of the town to the torch as they went. While the battle of Torreón had secured the city, that of San Pedro – fought, appropriately, in Madero's home town – destroyed the Federal Army as an effective fighting force in the north.[954] After San Pedro the Federal survivors scattered eastwards, some dying in the desert, most straggling into Saltillo in disarray. An army of some 15,000 had thus been neutralised, and the rebels had shown their ability to deploy artillery, to shift and supply a large army in the field, and thus to defeat well-entrenched government troops in a sustained campaign. Federal morale in the north was broken; Villa now commanded 16,000 men; and 'man for man the Constitutionalist army was now considered by impartial observers to be a better fighting machine than the Federal army'.[955] These two weeks of battle in the Laguna revealed that Huerta's days were numbered and that Pancho Villa had emerged as the pre-eminent caudillo of the Revolution.

Despite Huerta's rigid censorship, these truths began to dawn in Mexico

City, sapping what remained of the regime's credibility and provoking 'great uneasiness'.[956] Conversely, there were noisy celebrations in rebel towns like Nogales, while down in Tabasco the revolutionaries perked up at the news of Torreón's fall and stepped up their military efforts.[957] But it was in the north that the effects of Torreón and San Pedro were most dramatic. While Villa battered the Laguna towns, González and his Coahuilans, benefiting from the influx of arms through Matamoros, moved against the 'much inferior' Federal forces holding Monterrey; and further south Luis Caballero invested the oil port of Tampico.[958] After six days of fighting, during which the rebels sustained only slight casualties (perhaps one in ninety, compared with one in five at Torreón), the Federals evacuated Monterrey, leaving a large quantity of supplies. Nuevo Laredo and Piedras Negras fell almost at once. González now moved on to Tampico, where the summer rains helped to flush the Federals from their outlying defences and force them into a precipitate overland retreat towards Puebla.[959] The final Federal *débâcle* in the north east centred on Saltillo, where the remnants of the army − still numbering 15,000, but lacking any will to resist − were concentrated. Villa maintained that González should clear up this detritus − it was, after all, on González's home patch. But Carranza, either doubting González's ability, or desirous of impeding Villa's progress south, insisted that Villa finish the job, even though this entailed a detour to the east. Villa, somewhat disgruntled, agreed.[960] Not deigning to wait for the promised assistance from González, Villa hurled his cavalry in a massed attack on the Federal positions at Paredón, north of Saltillo. An utter rout ensued: four Federal generals were killed, and hundreds of conscripts surrendered or deserted, throwing off their uniforms and kepis. Over 1,000 prisoners were taken, and over half the Federal force at Paredón was lost, either dead, wounded or captured/deserted.[961] The remainder fled to Saltillo, joined with the Saltillo garrison in firing a few buildings (now a regular feature of Federal evacuations), and then set off on an overland trek to San Luis Potosí to the south. The job done, Villa could recover the glory trail to Mexico City.

On the west coast, meanwhile, Obregón inched his way south with Fabian caution. As early as summer 1913 the Sonoran rebels controlled all their home state save Guaymas, which remained under siege, and had successfully linked up with the revolutionaries of Sinaloa. The city of Sinaloa fell in October 1913, after three days fighting; Culiacán was taken in November. Compared with Villa's campaigns, these were modest encounters: 1,000 Federals fled from Culiacán, leaving 150 dead and 100 captured; Obregón admitted to only 36 killed.[962] Now only the troublesome ports of Guaymas and Mazatlán remained in Federal hands; but, unlike Villa, Obregón could not surround and confine his enemy, and the perennial lack of ammunition and artillery held back this innately cautious commander from a risky assault (his caution, a qualified observer believed, was fully justified).[963] So Obregón spent the winter improving railway communications and preparing his men: he drilled his cavalry and artillery, tried to instill some discipline into his officers, laid on classes for NCOs, recruited more Yaqui and Mayo Indians.[964] Obregón's Division of the North-West thus went through the same process of pro-fessionalisation as Villa's Division of the North – which provoked similar protests from stiff-necked 'officers' and wayward recruits.[965] But circum-stances were somewhat different on the west coast. Both military and political apparatuses were stronger and more conventional (in the sense of conforming to a roughly bureaucratic, 'rational–legal' model); hence they could better constrain the centrifugal forces of popular rebellion. In this, Obregón's own role was typical, and highly important. While Villa tolerated professionali-sation – yet also impeded it by his fond indulgence of Urbina, Fierro and others – Obregón bent every effort to make his army efficient, orderly and responsive to central (i.e., his) direction. While for many prominent Villistas, including Villa himself, professionalisation was an irksome necessity, for Obregón and the Sonoran leadership it was the only safe, reputable and effective way to conduct the war. Their concept of 'revolution', to put it simply, was quite different from Villa's.

So, Obregón soaked up lessons in military science, studied contemporary campaigns (demanding 'more information on blockhouses, barbed wire entanglements and the light emergency trenches used in the Boer War'), and sought to apply these lessons in practice.[966] It was an uphill struggle: Obregón's officers chafed at military instruction; refused to take orders; omitted to place sentries or send out scouts; they quarrelled, alleged the insubordination of others, squabbled over women and griped about their overbearing commander. A sergeant, sent to Rosario to recruit for the cavalry, raised 300 men, promoted himself to general, and began to issue 50 and 100 peso notes printed on lavatory paper. Military justice caught up with him in the middle of a fiesta, whence he was dragged and subjected to the *ley fuga*.[967] Resistance to Obregón's discipline was naturally strongest among those who fell outside the original orbit of the Sonorans, and who regarded the latter as meddlesome interlopers: Durangueño rebels like Matías Pazuengo or – the classic case – the young revolutionary firebrand of Sinaloa, Rafael Buelna.[968] More tensions built up in the vitals of the revolution.

For the moment, these were contained, and with the lifting of the arms embargo Obregón began a cautious advance south, delegating the sieges of Guaymas and Mazatlán to Generals Alvarado and Iturbe respectively.[969] Though minor sideshows, these sieges were notable for the recourse – rare in the military history of the revolution – to naval and aerial warfare. In February 1914 the Federal gunboat *Tampico* went over to the rebels, giving them a chance to challenge Huertista control of the sea and to cut off supplies from Guaymas. But before this could be done, the two remaining Federal gunboats attacked, holed and disabled the *Tampico*. Obregón sought a replacement craft in the US, but his purchasing agent pocketed the cash and was not seen again.[970] Obregón, typically innovative, turned to aerial warfare. In April the biplane *Sonora*, piloted by Carranza's nephew Gustavo Salinas, bombed the Federal gunboats of Topolobampo, though to no effect. This Cumberland hails as the 'first aerial bombardment in history' (a not infrequent claim).[971] In fact, there had already been an earlier raid on the Federal trenches at Guaymas, which had resulted in [civilian] casualties.[972] And Mazatlán, during its prolonged siege, also suffered primitive air raids, when a Constitutionalist plane – nicknamed the *pájaro amarillo* – dropped a few 15lb bombs, killing four people (they included rebel sympathisers: such were the drawbacks of aerial civil war) and temporarily generating 'mortal fear' among the population. It was a new, strange threat which could not be countered: as a trigger-happy policeman discovered, the plane, flying at 2,000 metres, was outside the range of small arms fire. Foreign observers were scandalised by this additional evidence of Mexican barbarism. On 6 May 1914, therefore, Admiral Howard, commander of the US Pacific fleet, 'sent two of his staff to confer with the Constitutionalists protesting against this mode of warfare'.[973] *Autre temps, autre mœurs*. Fortunately for foreign sensibilities, and for the people of Mazatlán, Captain Salinas soon crashed his plane, the air raids ceased and life in the besieged post continued as usual, with movie shows and band concerts. Finally, in July 1914, a Federal evacuation was negotiated through the mediation of the American, British and German navies; over 400 terrified Chinese, who did not dare await the rebel entry, were taken on board ship; and HMS *Algerine* made a rapid departure, anxious to put distance between herself and the German cruiser *Leipzig*, which signalled a polite 'Good-bye'. It was 2 August 1914.[974]

Months before, the bulk of the Division of the North-West had gone south, traversing Sinaloa and entering the wild country of Tepic, where progress was slow. Compared with Villa's campaigns, these were small, scattered actions, in which the rebels successfully capitalised on the low morale and frayed nerves of the Federals. At Acaponeta (4 May 1914) 1,400 rebels – 400 without guns – attacked an equivalent Federal garrison, to the sound of Yaqui war drums; casualties were light, there was a rapid surrender and a useful haul of Mausers. At Tepic, a week later, 2,000 rebels deliberately raised a massive dust storm and told a Federal scout they were bringing up 5,000 men to attack the town, held by 2,000 Federals. After a brief, half-hearted resistance the garrison evacuated, leaving another large arms cache behind.[975] These were cheap, psychological victories, reminiscent of the facile Maderista triumphs of three years before, and they showed that the west-coast rebels were reaping the benefit of Villa's more costly success, and of the consequent collapse of Federal morale.

Villa's success had a secondary effect on Obregón's progress. The differences between Carranza and Villa, already mentioned, loomed larger as Villismo grew in strength and Villa eclipsed his fellow-generals. It therefore became

Carranza's policy to rein in the Division of the North, while spurring the progress of possible rivals: hence Villa's diversion to Saltillo. In particular, Carranza was reluctant for Villa to reach Mexico City first – an outcome which seemed very likely in the spring of 1914. Pablo González was hardly a serious competitor but Obregón, whose efficiency Carranza had witnessed first-hand, promised better. By May – if not before – Obregón had been instructed to hurry on down and beat the Villistas to the 'chief cities of the interior'.[976] Such instructions were neither unexpected nor unwelcome. Since February there had been talk in the Sonoran camp of Carranza's troubles with Villa; the news of the fall of Torreón had been 'received with mixed emotions by senior officers on this side of the sierra, especially by Obregón'; and the Sonoran leader had at once given orders to expedite the advance. Thord Grey was told 'to redouble [his] efforts to turn out new officers as we were going south as soon as possible to forestall Villa, apparently, from going to the Capital'.[977] So, now that victory seemed assured, allies became less comradely, suspicions surfaced, and Mexico City loomed like a prize on the horizon. The race for the capital was on.

There was, of course, one other major competitor who enjoyed the advantage of proximity. At the turn of the year, when attention focussed on Juárez and Tierra Blanca, Zapata was parleying with the rebels of Guerrero – Salgado, 'Chon' Díaz, Castillo, and Julián Blanco – and building a confederation which stretched from Morelos to the Costa Chica. Though these were not the only organised forces in the centre and south, they were the sole serious rivals to the burgeoning armies of the northern Constitutionalists. Unlike the latter, however, they derived no benefit from the lifting of the arms embargo, and they had still to rely on mobility, concerted action and overwhelming numerical superiority if they were to crack the garrison towns in their domain. In March 1914 over 5,000 rebels – including 2,000 Morelos Zapatistas and a congeries of Guerrero forces captained by Salgado – attacked Chilpancingo, drove the Federal garrison of 1,400 from the state capital and pursued them to destruction. Those many Federal conscripts who surrendered were allowed to go free and, as in the north, many at once joined the revolutionaries; but the Federal commander, General Cartón (who had recently won promotion burning villages in Morelos) was shot in the main square of the city.[978] After this concerted success, however, the rebel confederation dissolved, as unfinished business drew each leader back to his home territory: Salgado, now named governor of Guerrero, north to Iguala which he took on 7 April; Blanco to the Costa Chica and the environs of Acapulco; Zapata, loaded with captured ammunition, back to Morelos. Both the military exigencies and the natural disposition of the *surianos* went against the formation of large, permanent, professionalised armies, like the Divisions of the North or North-West.

Not least of these exigencies was the shortage of arms and ammunition. Hard put either to smuggle or – after February 1914 – to import arms legally from the US Zapata and his allies had to rely on stolen, captured, or bartered arms. The tempo of the Zapatista campaign therefore depended on windfalls like the Chilpancingo arsenal and, once this was spent reasserting control of rural Morelos, the Zapatista advance halted, leaving Mexico City as strategically distant as it was spatially close.

TAMPICO AND AFTER

Now, however, an additional factor emerged, bringing Zapata a sudden, fortuitous advantage, and affecting the campaigns elsewhere in Mexico. This was Woodrow Wilson's last determined effort to oust the Mexican dictator. Again, John Lind's influence was crucial. As already noted, he spent 1913–14 sitting in Veracruz, idle and disenchanted, filing reports imaginatively hostile to Huerta and the British. Gratified by the lifting of the arms embargo, he now expected results quickly, underestimating the logistical problems facing the northern rebels as they headed south. His reports exuded impatience: without decisive American action, he feared, 'the revolution may continue for years, both sides devastating . . . the country'; the rebels lacked 'competent gunners' and seemed incapable of putting Huerta's railways out of action – it was 'extremely unfortunate that [they] cannot bring some brains and a little efficiency to bear on this important work'.[979] By March, Lind was talking of the need for American intervention to topple Huerta, either by a direct expedition to Mexico City, or by helping the Constitutionalists take the oil port of Tampico. The appropriate maps were ready, he said; American casualties would be few or none; and 'the temporary taking of Mexico City', designed to rid Mexico of Huerta, 'should not be regarded as intervention in the offensive sense'.[980]

Lind's growing belief that, without American intervention, Huerta might survive and the revolution become a 'lost cause' was, of course, a sad misreading of the situation, probably influenced by the *gobiernista* press, and one which the fall of Torreón would soon invalidate.[981] But here timing was important. On 6 April, Lind left Veracruz to confer again with Wilson. Though Torreón had fallen (and Lind knew it) the full impact of this decisive event had not sunk in, and Lind carried with him to Washington the pent-up frustrations he had been feeling throughout the spring. He was thus influential in misinforming Wilson – by exaggerating the sloth of the rebels and the stamina of the government – and in spreading dangerous ideas concerning the necessity and the facility of American intervention.[982] The timing was particularly crucial since on 9 April a random incident occurred which gave an opportunity for Lind's strategy to be implemented. That day – it was grey and 'unseasonably cool' in the wake of a 'norther' – an American boat landed at Tampico to take on supplies.[983] This in itself was unexceptional: though rebels and Federals were skirmishing in the landward approaches to Tampico, this did not halt the port's business, and the sight of foreign warships off

Tampico bar was commonplace. But the proximity of the rebels made the Federals jumpy and, when the boat put in close by a strategic bridge, the crew were ordered out and placed under arrest. Within minutes, the mistake was rectified: the Americans were released and the garrison commander, General Morelos Zaragoza, issued a verbal apology. The incident could have ended there: the arrest – even the robbery – of foreign seamen by Mexican officials was nothing new at Tampico.[984] The only difference was that, in this case, the Americans had been taken off a ship flying the flag: technically, they had been arrested on American soil.[985]

The Mexican verbal apology did not satisfy Rear Admiral Henry T. Mayo, the obdurate martinet commanding US naval forces at Tampico. Without consulting his senior admiral at Veracruz – still less Washington – Mayo sent an officer in full uniform, complete with side-arms, to protest to the Federal commander and to demand an official apology, the punishment of the culprits and a 21 gun salute to the American flag.[986] Mayo's mental processes are not easily fathomed, especially since the evidence is scant. The case of Mayo's senior, Admiral Frank Fletcher, however, is somewhat clearer and suggestive of the predicament these American naval commanders faced in Mexico in 1914. They were unsympathetic to the basic premises of Wilson's Mexican policy; and they grew increasingly perplexed as to the specific implications of that policy.[987] 'After I had been here a month', Admiral Fletcher complained, 'I knew everything, now, after eight months, I find I know nothing.'[988] Yet the day-to-day responsibility weighed on him ('the man on the spot has only his judgement for a guide') and the strain of these long tours of duty in the Gulf also had its effect.[989] Early in 1914, when Fletcher's ships had taken off foreign residents from Tampico, the Admiral had seemed 'about ready to break down, getting tired', complaining of 'great responsibility, constant uncertainty, long telegrams, hot weather . . . naval vessels full of women and children, guns covered with diapers, and the Navy going to the Devil'.[990]

Admiral Mayo, who had done four months in the Gulf, may have been fresher; but he no doubt felt similar frustrations. Above all, there was the frustration of shackled power, of commanding capital ships to no apparent purpose: 'the Admiral has this big fleet there away on the horizon and the ordinary Mexicans are utterly oblivious to its presence'.[991] Frustration bred an itch for action. In December 1913, during the fighting at Tampico, Fletcher had seemed keen to land marines and 'most anxious to fire his guns up the streets. He was all for force, nothing for reason.'[992] Now, in April, Mayo showed a similarly rash spirit in making his demand to Morelos Zaragoza. It may not have been that Mayo or Fletcher actively sought American intervention (though they certainly did not shrink from it); but they clearly hungered for some sort of action to relieve the hot tedium of the tropics and justify their long-standing presence in Mexican waters.

Local decisions set the chain of events in progress, but the initiative soon shifted higher. Bryan reported Mayo's demand to the president with the fatuous comment: 'I do not see that Mayo could have done otherwise'; and Wilson, on vacation with his terminally sick wife, concurred and bade the State Department search out the relevant diplomatic precedents.[993] In Mexico, Morelos Zaragoza refused to comply with Mayo's demand without War Ministry approval, and Huerta would not let the Ministry approve. Both sides rejected compromise: Wilson because he saw an opportunity to hammer Huerta (Lind was present and influential during these critical days); Huerta because he believed a quarrel with the US would revive his flagging fortunes.[994] For days the cables hummed; Mayo's officers eagerly planned the punitive expedition against Tampico; and the ego of the young American Chargé in Mexico City swelled as the eyes of the world focussed on his feverish diplomacy. (In the end, it should be emphasised, all parties were disappointed: Wilson did not – contrary to the views of some historians – topple Huerta; Huerta did not reap a rich harvest of patriotic support; Mayo did not shell or seize Tampico; and Chargé O'Shaughnessy did not win praise or promotion – on the contrary, his diplomatic career promptly collapsed).[995]

For, as Huerta proved intransigent, Wilson claimed to see a pattern of 'studied contempt' towards the US on the part of Mexico; he showed no interest in a compromise proposal for simultaneous salutes to both flags; and he discussed with the cabinet and Congress the punitive options open to the US. The 'studied contempt' was essentially a pretext to move against Huerta and assist the Constitutionalists; but, as the administration became painfully aware, such drastic, presumptuous and unsolicited assistance could as much incur Constitutionalist enmity as gratitude. As Bryan was heard to moan: 'I want to help them, but I do not want it to appear as helping them.'[996] Meanwhile, more ships were sent to the Gulf. Typically, the denouement of the story came with yet another unforeseen factor. On 18 April, the American consul at Veracruz reported the imminent arrival of a German steamer carrying a large arms shipment for Huerta – again, nothing out of the ordinary. But Wilson and his cabinet resolved that the ship be intercepted and further arms deliveries prevented by a seizure of the Veracruz customs house. As for Tampico, the locus of the original 'insult' and the proposed victim of retribution, the cabinet now found reasons for a reprieve. If American cruisers went up the Pánuco River, they would be at the mercy of Mexican artillery; when the Secretary of the Navy 'timidly suggested' sending a destroyer instead, 'Admiral Fiske almost had a fit' at the prospect of half-a-million dollars' worth of warship coming to rest on the muddy bottom of the Pánuco. General Wood – seconded by Lind – pointed out that 'the whole miserable little town with its little tin fortifications' could easily be shelled by the main fleet standing out to sea.[997] But in the end, the Tampico operation was postponed, and the order went out for the seizure of the Veracruz customs house instead. Veracruz would pay for Tampico's bad manners. The landing was expected to be rapid, limited and virtually bloodless. It was in no sense a preamble to a full-scale intervention, which Wilson unequivocally opposed.[998] Lind even advocated the optimistic idea that the Americans 'occupy only the customs house and not the city'.[999] This optimism derived from the belief that the Americans would be seen as deliverers: as the presidential confidant, Colonel House, put it, in his sanctimonious style: 'I advised [Wilson] to stand firm and to blaze the way for a new and better international code of morals . . . If Mexico understood that our motives were unselfish, she should not object to our helping adjust her unruly household.'[1000] In 1914, Mexico; in 1919, Europe: the adjustment of unruly households was a thankless task.

Admiral Mayo and his men, itching to be at Tampico, heard with disgust that they were being sidetracked to Veracruz; worse, even before they got there, bad weather conditions forced Admiral Fletcher to effect the landing alone, with the forces at his disposal.[1001] Like his political bosses, Fletcher believed that the occupation could be achieved 'without any serious fighting or perhaps without any fighting at all'.[1002] They were all wrong. General Joaquín Maass, commanding 1,000 men, mostly raw recruits, and assured by the US consul that the Americans did not intend a full-scale attack on the city, decided to put up only token resistance. Thus, on the morning of 21 April, after boatloads of sailors and marines had poured ashore and occupied the wharves, Mexican soldiers resisted an assault on the customs house and battle was joined.[1003] It was a scrappy business. The Americans seemed to lack any preconceived plan and their action was 'dull and lifeless'.[1004] Facing sporadic resistance and sniping, their commander radioed for a 'heavy bombardment' from the navy but this, for the moment, was refused. Meanwhile, the Mexican troops pulled back to La Tejería, a few miles inland, leaving the fighting to civilians, liberated prisoners and the cadets of the Veracruz Naval Academy.[1005] By the morning of 22 April, 3,500 Americans had gone ashore, yet they still faced stiff opposition, especially from 'the little Mexican naval cadets' who, a British admiral reported, 'put up a gallant fight'.[1006] Then, however, the warships *Chester* and *Prairie* opened up at 'pointblank range' with their three-inch guns, training them on the Naval Academy and other pockets of resistance. These were soon silenced. By evening, Veracruz was securely in American hands and the Marines were scouring the streets for snipers, showing perfunctory respect for civilian life and property. The Americans had lost 19 dead and 47 wounded; casualties on the Mexican side, hard to establish precisely, were some 200 killed and 300 wounded.[1007]

For many Americans this was to be the first step in a general invasion of Mexico which would reduce it to colonial or semi-colonial status. The example of Cuba was often cited, by commentators as diverse as the American Ambassador to Britain ('we shall have to Cuba-ize the country, which means thrashing 'em first') and the racist radical Jack London ('we must pacify Mexico by force of arms and dominate it and police it as we did Cuba').[1008] Wilson thought differently; but one of the weaknesses of his Mexican policy was its ambiguity, which enabled quite different motives and objectives to be read into it – by historians as well as contemporaries. At the time, the occupation gave an unwarranted boost to interventionist and imperialist opinion, which welcomed Veracruz as the first step towards invasion, even annexation. Since this is a recurrent theme in US–Mexican relations, and one which some historians of the Revolution have stressed, it is worth pausing to consider its importance. Did revolutionary Mexico run the risk of American intervention, invasion or annexation? If it did, April 1914 was a critical time, for it was then that the most blatant violation of Mexican sovereignty took place, that American opinion was most stirred by the Mexican question, and that the anti-American backlash in Mexico was most pronounced.[1009]

Even so, the crisis was of fairly limited duration and severity.[1010] If the extensive correspondence in the Wilson archive is any guide, the pressure for intervention – though vocal and considerable – was more than matched by sentiments of pacifism or downright inertia. Most Americans shrank from war with a distant country over an obscure issue. Wilson received a barrage of letters opposing intervention in Mexico: above all, from socialist and pacifist groups, who denounced the machinations of big business and the service chiefs; and from religious and 'progressive' associations which took a similar, more moderate line, while stressing respect for Mexican rights and sovereignty.[1011] In addressing the president, most of these correspondents saw themselves holding up his arms against imperialism and militarism, not restraining a war-monger. The Texarkana lady who urged Wilson and his 'fat cabinet' to fight in Mexico in place of our 'poor marines, sailors and soldiers' was unusual in taking this line.[1012] But the 'peace' camp extended far beyond radical, progressive, or religious groups and in most parts of the country, it seems, public opinion was far from bellicose. In Connecticut 'sentiment . . . is strongly against war'; Andrew Carnegie, in Pittsburgh, heard 'not one voice in favor of war'; there was reckoned to be a 75% majority for peace in New Jersey; similar reports came from the mid-West, though rather less from the West and South-West.[1013] To the extent that the eastern seaboard favoured peace, the business community shared local feelings. Not only is there little evidence of big business pushing Wilson towards intervention; it also seems that business interests – logically enough – saw little to gain from such a move. As in 1898 they were cautious, and, unlike 1898, there were no spectacular victories to seize their imagination and excite their avarice.[1014] Carnegie, of course, was a special case, but there were other business spokesmen who rejected a forward policy in Mexico.[1015] Finally, the very racism and conservatism which so often consorted with jingo sentiments could have a paradoxical effect: an invasion of Mexico, one correspondent feared, would 'mean 15 millions more of black men to govern, less capable of self-government than the southern negro. I cannot imagine what greater calamity than this could come upon our country.'[1016]

Similar assumptions – leading to different conclusions – were evident in the rival camp, which called for intervention, even annexation. Indeed, it seems to have been the strength of such assumptions – rather than any rational, material interest – which was the hallmark of the war-and-annexation lobby. In other words, Americans advocated the conquest of Mexico because they thought it was right and necessary, rather than practical and profitable. Indeed, it is striking how far the advocates of conquest were ignorant of Mexico, the Mexican situation, and the immediate circumstances of the crisis. Americans with material interests in Mexico were much more circumspect; ignorance was almost a necessary condition for the strenuous advocacy of intervention. Many believed that the Veracruz occupation came as a response to outrages committed on American persons and property (an error which veterans' associations, who were well represented in this camp, shared with the yellow press). Many veterans thought that the American flag had been 'torn down and insulted'; they offered their services – or those of their sons and grandsons – to 'plant "Old Glory" . . . over the City of Mexico'; and they applauded this chastisement of those who sought to 'murder American citizens, to outrage American women, to torture American children [and] to wantonly destroy American property'.[1017]

Clearly, Wilson bore a responsibility for not clarifying his policy, and for thus allowing these misconceptions to flourish; as did the yellow press for sedulously cultivating them.[1018] Again it was the Hearst press which, in 1914 as in 1898, drummed up jingoist sentiment: not, I would judge, out of regard for Hearst's Mexican properties (which, being located in Chihuahua and Chiapas, would scarcely benefit from the intervention), but rather in order to make headlines, boost circulation, influence public opinion and, perhaps, further Hearst's own political ambitions.[1019] Whether Hearst mirrored or manipulated public opinion, it is clear that his own views tallied with those of many Americans who had no properties in Chihuahua and Chiapas – indeed, who had no stake in or knowledge of Mexico whatsoever. Their advocacy of intervention was irrational and emotive, deriving from beliefs of national and racial superiority and of imperial mission. They sought (by their own admission) to 'take up the White Man's Burden'; they quoted Kipling and called for 'a policy similar to the policy of Great Britain in Egypt'.[1020] Such attitudes coloured the thinking of individuals of widely different regions and occupations, who had in common only a non-proletarian background and a blithe disregard of Mexican realities.[1021] They differed in their emphases. A Cincinnati public speaker maintained that 'there will be no peace for any American in Latin countries unless the stars and stripes are planted there to stay'.[1022] The US must intervene, a Berkeley professer argued, since the 'task of restoring order is beyond' the Mexicans; half a million men should be sent, another stipulated, 'with a smile and a kind word for those poor illiterate people'; half a million men (and six to eight months), another agreed, would be enough, though the conquest would be followed by a 'few years of patient and forceful policing of their country [which] would turn the Mexican people towards us'.[1023] Both the protection of Americans and the 'uplift of Mexico's wretched people' would thus be served by intervention.[1024]

For some interventionists, however, altruism – even enlightened self-interest – took second place to crude sentiments of retribution. At best, these were expressed in boisterous, Boy Scout terms. 'Just take an example from old Johnny Bull', a Philadelphia piano-tuner advised the president: 'the best way out is for you to let Uncle Sam take off his coat, roll up his sleeves, and pitch into those Mexicans with all his might and main; and give them a good solid licking in a hurry and teach them to behave themselves'.[1025] Others displayed a mindless aggression. A Louisville railway clerk berated Wilson for his soft policy towards Mexico: 'Mexico is today and always will be, if left with free and unhampered licence, a madman with a razor; or, to use a simile from anatomy, a running sore in our side that can be cured only by cauterizing it with hot irons or by excision with the knife.'[1026] This was the tone of much interventionist opinion in 1914; crude, emotive, out of touch not simply with the realities of Mexico but also with the perceptions of American businessmen in Mexico, it welled up from middle and lower-middle-class groups who, perhaps, derived some satisfaction from the exercise of notions of racial, national and cultural superiority. If a tentative link were suggested between these and comparable attitudes evinced within domestic politics (attachment to status, 'traditional' American values, white supremacy, often with a fundamentalist veneer) it would not be far-fetched, since the correspondents themselves sometimes made this connection. If, argued a St Louis businessman, the US was to raise a Mexican expeditionary force of half a million (again, the magic figure) 'the training would do us good at home and abroad'.[1027]

Though these were the views of a minority, it was a significant and vocal minority, which had its educated spokesman, which drew comfort from the yellow press, and which commanded some political influence. Wilson's own brand of interventionism – hesitant, high-minded and, above all, highly circumscribed – was very different from the rampant, racist interventionism illustrated here; and, if the president deserved blame for giving such views a golden opportunity for publicity, he also deserved credit for thoroughly ignoring them in the subsequent conduct of policy. Unlike Huerta, he did not stoop to conquer the accolades of chauvinists. In this he was helped by a crucial factor: being 'ideologues' rather than active businessmen, these rabid interventionists had little in common with either American big business in general, or Mexican investors in particular. To the extent that Americans who knew Mexico first-hand sympathised with – or occasionally enunciated – such views, they were usually the vulnerable, small-time operators (family farmers, pioneer miners, retailers) rather than the big mining, oil and commercial interests.[1028] The latter, who clearly commanded more weight in Washington, were relatively pragmatic; they would call upon American diplomatic support and would occasionally countenance the use (or, better, the threat) of force *in extremis*; but they preferred more subtle, reliable and tested processes of negotiation and co-option, and unlike the interventionist ideologues, did not dream dreams of American territorial expansion 'from the lakes to Panama'.[1029] There is therefore little evidence that the Veracruz occupation responded to the intentions of either Wilson, or big business, to invade and annex Mexico. Strenuous interventionism derived from a domestic constituency which – to the advantage of Mexico and the Revolution – remained scattered, disorganised, and unable to mount a sustained lobby in Washington. The Revolution might be tactically 'intervened' by the US, but it was in no danger of being strategically overwhelmed.

For Wilson, the Veracruz operation had a limited, legitimate aim: to undermine Huerta, especially by cutting off his supply of arms from Europe. It cannot be said to have succeeded.[1030] The rebels neither welcomed nor benefited from the move and even the immediate trigger of the landing – the interception of the liner *Ypiranga* – went off at half cock, like so much of the operation. Prevented from docking at Veracruz, the ship eventually made Puerto México and unloaded its cargo late in May. The American intervention merely delayed delivery by a month – a modest enough achievement in view of the costs.[1031] It also had the effect of depriving Huerta of the Veracruz customs revenue, which had been running at about 1.5m. pesos a month.[1032] But these, the direct results of Veracruz, were hardly decisive: Huerta did not fall for want of arms or cash (note the large hauls of arms won by Villa at Paredón and elsewhere). Furthermore, the occupation similarly hampered the rebels, for it was now thought prudent to seal the American border against the traffic in arms; Villa now had to smuggle, or get shipments overland from the Gulf ports, to which the Americans – for no clear reason – allowed consignments to be sent.[1033] Shocked by the resistance encountered and the lives lost at Veracruz, Wilson had no intention of pressing on, or taking further aggressive measures against Huerta. The prickly reaction of Carranza – who denounced the occupation and called for an immediate evacuation – deflated any hopes of collaboration with the Constitutionalists.[1034] Lind's plans were shown to be bankrupt. So, despite proddings from the jingoes, Wilson refused to order American troops into the interior: instead, they stayed in Veracruz, cleaning the streets and city market, flushing them daily with sea-water, enforcing sanitary regulations, installing public urinals, exterminating mosquitoes, reorganising the city brothels and disinfecting the girls.[1035] Spitting in the streets was forbidden; and the famous *zopilotes*, the Veracruz vultures, went hungry and eventually flew away – for a time. Veracruz, if not Mexico as a whole, was thus 'Cuba-ized'.

Despite these good works, the occupation generated patriotic indignation upon which Huerta sought to capitalise, in order to revive his flagging fortunes. This tactic, as we have noted, was well-tried: Maderistas had used it in 1913, and Huerta at the time of the Lind mission. Now, of course, Huerta's need was all the greater; and the pretext – a genuine American invasion – afforded a better opportunity than previous diplomatic confrontations. Still, all the post-Veracruz phenomena – the speeches, riots, demonstrations and recruitment drives, which have been cited as evidence of a profound xenophobia – fell within a familiar pattern and had many precedents. [1036] Indeed, the sheer familiarity eventually bred contempt, for by 1915, if not 1914, people began to dismiss 'the old story of intervention' when they heard it. [1037] The Huertistas went through the usual motions, however. The press, which had avoided all mention of the crisis until the eve of the occupation, now launched tirades against the 'Gringo pigs' and promised a swift invasion of Texas. The Congress reverberated to cries of 'death to the thieves of 1848'. [1038] Cadets from the bombarded Veracruz Naval Academy were paraded through the streets of Mexico City to aid recruitment, and the mob stoned the American consulate, toppling the two-year-old statue of George Washington. Yet observers – both American and British – commented on the mild and ephemeral character of these demonstrations, which soon abated. [1039] Huerta's recruiting drive seemed to promise more tangible results, as April and May saw the culmination of the regime's militarist exhortations. All public employees were now subjected to two hours' military training a day; they received uniforms, were reviewed by the President and paraded up and down Reforma. A Civic Guard was established in Mexico City, in order to release regular troops for service at the front. Volunteer battalions proliferated: a Press Brigade, students' groups, dozens of (alleged) provincial detachments, and a Comité Civil de la Defensa Nacional, which set about propagandising and recruiting throughout Huertista Mexico. [1040]

Did this ostensible wave of support count for much? 'For the first time since he came to power', Meyer writes, 'Huerta had more recruits than he could actually use.' [1041] But the utility – and at times the very reality – of these recruits may be questioned. The military contribution of the grandly titled Comité Civil was, as Meyer admits, 'negligible'. [1042] The press talked glibly of volunteers corps being formed in Morelos, of the railway workers offering 150,000 men, of the militarisation of the beggars of Guadalajara. 'The pupils of the School of the Blind', thrilled *El País*, 'offer their bodies to build defences.' [1043] Even if such recruits joined the colours (which is often doubtful) they could contribute little, especially since they joined an army that was itself on the verge of collapse. The British Minister, visiting a Federal detachment at La Tejería – in the front line of a potential American advance – found soldiers who had not eaten for three days; according to one, recruited a week earlier in San Luis, 'no-one had ever taught him how to use his rifle, which, he said, he would be glad enough to use against the Americans'.[1044] At least he was in the right place. The enthusiasm of other recruits fast faded when they discovered they were destined not for a patriotic war against the Gringoes, but a grim fratricidal conflict with the Villistas.[1045]

Apart from the recruiting drive (which, for all its publicity, brought Huerta little practical benefit) two other phenomena were noteworthy in the aftermath of Veracruz: the outbursts of anti-Americanism (the worst of the Revolution) and Huertista attempts to win over the rebels to a *Union Sacrée* in defence of the fatherland. Contrary to common assertion, these also had little impact; it is their very insignificance which deserves comment, and which is illustrative of the dynamics of the Revolution. The anti-American riots which briefly affected Mexico City had their counterparts in the provinces. In most cases the chief victims were American consular representatives – the official agents of the US – rather than the exponents of American economic imperialism. If it was the latter which gave rise to anti-Americanism, as is often posited, it escaped retribution in an odd, inexplicable manner. In Mexico City, George Washington and the consulate suffered; at Guadalajara, the consular arms were torn down and the consul, fleeing with his 82-year-old mother, was insulted. A 'monster anti-American demonstration' confronted the Aguascalientes consulate, the coat-of-arms was ripped from the wall, and when troops arrived on the scene, their commander told the consul to hoist the Mexican flag over the building. 'I told them I would see them in hell before I would accede to their preposterous demand', the consul recalled, 'and for a few minutes it looked as if there would be no consul or consulate left.'[1046] In each case, however, the demonstrators dispersed, no serious injury was done, and feelings soon calmed. The Guadalajara consul, who fled in fear, returned in September to find that a 'complete revolution in sentiment' had taken place and no anti-Americanism was now evident.[1047]

For most Americans – that is, Americans who were in Mexico for economic reasons – the situation was delicate, but rarely dangerous. Save for two miners killed at the El Favor mine (Zac.), in somewhat obscure circumstances, there were no fatalities: most American residents came through the crisis unscathed, even when they declined to follow State Department advice to take refuge aboard ship.[1048] In at least one case (Acapulco), the Federal commander harangued the crowd, calling on them to resist American intervention, while warning against any assaults on local American residents who, he said, were there for legitimate commercial reasons.[1049] In many cases, harangues and verbal abuses were the worst Americans had to suffer.[1050] And the crisis soon passed.[1051] Americans who had stayed in Mexico City rather than join the rush to Veracruz reported 'complete apathy' by the first week of May; 'the feeling . . . changed in an instant' when news reached Mazatlán that the US–Mexican conflict would go to mediation; at Tampico (which Meyer says experienced the greatest 'hysteria') American refugees soon returned, found that their Mexican subordinates had coped admirably in their absence, and were welcomed by a city which desired a swift normalisation of business.[1052] On the rebel side, the reaction was similar, though even more muted. The fact that the occupation was designed to assist the rebels did not lead them to condone it. But particularly as they depended on the supply of American arms, they had no great incentive to make trouble for American residents. The mining camps of Sonora – supposed hotbeds of xenophobia – remained quiet and productive throughout; Americans who had quit them were urged to return, under guarantees, which they did.[1053] At Durango, the occupation was unanimously condemned; but American refugees were assisted in their departure, and a mob which formed outside the consulate was swiftly dispersed. For a few days the consul was subjected to 'the vilest epithets of which the Spanish language is capable' (though nothing worse than this), after which feelings subsided.[1054] At Laredo, the Constitutionalists remained 'very friendly' in their dealings with Americans.[1055]

There is, therefore, little evidence of a generalised, virulent anti-Americanism, nurtured by economic dependency. The reaction to Veracruz was short-lived and surprisingly moderate; it affected only a small minority of the population; it cannot bear comparison with genuine, popular xenophobia, such as Boxerism.[1056] To the extent that there were American victims, they were consuls, not businessmen: the crisis was an immediate, political one, not the result of long incubating resentment against American economic interests. Indeed, in the few cities where the outbursts were serious, it is clear that they responded to specific political and military factors, and to the encouragement of the (Huertista) authorities, not the levels of American investment. They were indicative of the attitudes and stratagems of the officer corps, who were offered locally – as Huerta was nationally – a chance both to win recruits and also to importune, divide and confuse their revolutionary opponents. Military commanders splashed the news across newspapers and billboards in besieged Mazatlán; in at least four northern cities, all threatened by the triumphal march of Villismo, American consuls were arrested and subjected to indignities, with official connivance. At Monterrey, patriotic broadsheets and demonstrators filled the streets; at San Luis, the consulate flag was torn down, 'torn into pieces and stamped on by Mexican soldiers and citizens and everyone who had a full bladder'.[1057] A reasonably neutral observer in Monterrey was convinced that the propaganda (including a false report of an American declaration of war) was deliberately aimed 'to get volunteers from among the citizens of the town and then force them to fight against the Constitutionalists . . . anti-American demonstrations were promoted by the Federal authorities evidently for the same purpose'.[1058] But, again, the response from the people was tepid.

Throughout northern and central Mexico, too, Federal commanders – sometimes embellishing reality – appealed to the rebels to join them against the Americans. General Téllez, besieged in Guaymas, tried to win over Alvarado; Villa rejected overtures from Generals Maass and Caraveo; Zapata, Mendoza, and de la O in Morelos, Caballero in Tamaulipas and Natera in Durango, all spurned similar offers.[1059] At Mazatlán, the rebels used their famous aeroplane to drop leaflets repudiating the Federal proposals and giving details of recent revolutionary victories (the first case of aerial propaganda in the world?).[1060] The Constitutionalists were, of course, just as sensitive to American violations of Mexican territory as any nationally-aware Mexicans, and they could not afford to appear as stooges of the US. Carranza was particularly concerned to emphasise his patriotism and denounce the American action – a response which in American eyes made him something of an ingrate.[1061] In Sonora, Constitutionalist officers seriously debated whether they should join with the Federals; Zapata was incensed at the American attack; and, as we have seen, rebel-held cities witnessed their anti-American protests, though the authorities here were more concerned to contain than to foment them.[1062] Villa, however, was something of an exception: he not only rejected Federal overtures but also gave qualified approval of the Veracruz occupation, in that it acted as an additional squeeze on Huerta. Perhaps this, the traditional version, exaggerates Villa's compliance. But certainly now, in the thick of the northern campaign, having just achieved the crucial break-through at Torreón, he could not conceive of changing partners and joining the Federals against the Americans; and, if such an alliance was out of the question, there was no point in jeopardising the new arms supply by a display of excessive, stiff-necked patriotism. On the contrary, Villa took steps to cultivate a favourable image in the American press, and was solicitous for American interests within his domain.[1063]

Essentially, this was a pragmatic response: the Sonorans, too, whose patriotism has never been called into question, were also keen to reassure American interests once the crisis had passed. But, assuming Villa's compliance was genuine, it could also have reflected a certain *naïveté*, a failure to transcend immediate, local concerns in favour of long-term, national commitments. Meyer suggests that Villa's response to Veracruz showed that 'he simply was not politically perceptive', and there is some truth in this.[1064] For, in general, touchy patriotism and a strict regard for national sovereignty went with an educated, urban, metropolitan outlook; they characterised lawyers, journalists, and *políticos*, rather than cowboys, bandits and peasants, many of whom lacked a strong national allegiance. Zapata, in whom traditional patriotism blended with fierce parochial loyalties, was uncomfortably cross-pressured; though the invasion made his 'blood boil', he was intransigent in rejecting Huertista overtures.[1065] Remote, rural communities (which, collectively provided a large revolutionary contingent) also scorned the nationalist appeal.[1066] In Sonora, where the officers seriously debated the question, the 'peon-soldiers' were more agitated over recent attempts to ban women from the line of march; while the Yaqui chiefs, for whom *patria chica* predominated over nation, spoke out against a Federal alliance.[1067] Carranza, on the other hand, had to stand firm on the national issue: since he both claimed a national revolutionary status, and also lacked a deep popular appeal. While Villa did not need to win plaudits by displays of patriotism, having already won them at Tierra Blanca and Torreón, the very fact of these victories made it imperative for Carranza to take a strong nationalist stance. This is not to doubt Carranza's nationalism, but rather to suggest that nationalism, like a party balloon, could be blown up for the big occasion. At the time, some Constitutionalists certainly believed that the First Chief was 'playing politics to keep his people in line'.[1068] And later, seeking to refurbish his international image, Carranza almost admitted as much: protesting his 'feeling of admiration and gratitude toward the American people and the Washington Administration', he pointed out that critics who made much of his 'haughty or . . . unfriendly' statements 'are far removed and do not realise what the local conditions are, nor do they appreciate that I have my own people to deal with and to satisfy'.[1069]

One consequence of Veracruz, therefore, was a further distancing between Villa and Carranza, and their respective factions. Villa, pragmatic and conciliatory towards the US, resented the potentially dangerous war-mongering and patriotic posturing of some of his fellow-rebels.[1070] In the press he was quoted approving the American action and criticising Carranza's stern protest; Carranza duly ordered him to avoid involvement in international questions; and Villa, publicly denying any rift with the First Chief, protested his absolute loyalty.[1071] However it prejudiced Huerta's cause, the Veracruz occupation certainly hindered the revolution by sowing dissension between Villa and Carranza, which in turn slowed the advance on Mexico City.[1072] In most respects, however, the occupation – like so much American policy – was notable for its irrelevance. It created a brief furore, but its net impact was very limited: it could do no more than modify, or marginally deflect, a course of events dictated from within, by the Mexicans themselves.

THE DÉBÂCLE

For, at the time of Veracruz, the writing was already on the wall: Huerta had been weighed and found wanting: his kingdom was being fast divided and given to the Carrancistas, Zapatistas, Villistas and others. Torreón and San Pedro had just fallen (2 and 12 April); Monterrey was under attack when Veracruz was occupied and fell three days after; May saw the Division of the North-West take Tepic and start to plough through the summer rains into Jalisco. In the north-east, Tampico surrendered in mid-May and Saltillo a week later. The Federal garrisons in Morelos were withdrawn because of the American attack (one of its few unequivocal results), enabling the Zapatistas to capture four towns unopposed. But the Federals were a spent force in Morelos anyway: when Jojutla fell early in May only 90 of the 1,200 troops 'staggered back to Cuernavaca', which now came under siege, the last Huertista redoubt in the state.[1073]

In each theatre, Federal morale and capacity had slumped. Even the initially resolute defence of Zacatecas – an eminently defensible city – gave way to a rout: as Villa closed in, 'panic seemed to go through the Federal Army and soldiers and officers who up to that point had fought bravely lost their heads completely and thought of nothing else but of saving their own lives'.[1074] This final débâcle at Zacatecas had many precedents. At Jojutla, in March, the garrison had mutinied, 'paralysing the defence of the whole southern zone'.; eye-witnesses of the Tampico campaign reported that 'the inefficiency of the Federal troops was quite extraordinary'; General Mier's order to the Federals to fight their way out of Guadalajara (July) resulted in panic, desertions, and consequently heavy losses.[1075] Mass desertions were now common, as the regime paid the price for its indiscriminate forced levies, and droves of conscripts quit the colours as ignominiously as they had joined them. As early as March there was talk of 'innumerable desertions' taking place at the front.[1076] During the Torreón fighting, 1,500 troops were reckoned to have deserted.[1077] This – antedating Veracruz – was the turning point: the British Minister, looking back in August 1914, ascribed the rapid collapse of the regime he had endorsed to 'the utter demoralisation of the Federal Army since the fall of Torreón'; and for once he was right.[1078] At Paredón and Saltillo, Federals deserted and/or surrendered in their hundreds; individual Villistas found themselves taking fifteen or twenty prisoners apiece.[1079] The officer corps, too, the main pillar of Huertismo, began to waver. Many officers had been killed – or captured and killed – in the Laguna campaign, and the arrival of defeated generals had become a common sight in Mexico City. As Velasco and Almazán returned from Torreón (via subsequent defeats in the north-east), and Morelos Zaragoza and Higinio Aguilar from Tampico, the reality of impending defeat was brought home to the inhabitants of the capital.[1080] Unlike their troops, Federal officers could not easily switch to the other side. By summer 1914 they had delayed their conversion too long and thus faced execution rather than welcome: the Constitutionalists were less tolerant of 'last-minute revolutionaries' than their Maderista predecessors had been. General Osuna, commanding the remote, neglected and troubled district of Baja California Sur, was luckier: in March, after a final, vindictive round-up of the 'leading citizens' of La Paz, he repudiated the Huerta regime, ransacked the town's business houses, seized the customs receipts and a merchant ship, and 'sailed for parts unknown'; he may even have bought his way into the revolution.[1081] Most officers lacked both the will and the opportunity for such an escape. Though there was talk of an anti-Huerta coup in Mexico City in May, nothing came of it.[1082] *Faute de mieux*, the officer corps stuck with Huerta to the end; unable to abandon ship, they went down with it.

Meanwhile, Huerta's military failure drove his erstwhile supporters to search even more frantically for an alternative. The army had not only failed to curb the revolution; it now represented a threat to order and property itself. In April 1914, it seems, Huerta ordered a 'modified scorched earth policy' to be followed by the beaten Federals in the north: the evacuations of Torreón, San Pedro, Piedras Negras, Nuevo Laredo, Saltillo and Zacatecas were all accompanied by the wanton destruction of public and other buildings.[1083] Much of Piedras Negras and Nuevo Laredo were put to the torch, and both here and at Monterrey the Constitutionalist occupation restored order and security to city life.[1084] At Zacatecas the fleeing Federals blew up the arsenal, killing and burying hundreds: a 'cowardly, dastardly act', commented the British vice-consul, which left him 'completely scared and nervous as a cat'.[1085] In the Bajío, meanwhile, there were reports of landlords taking up arms in protest at Federal depredations on their estates.[1086] The growing disgust with Huerta was paralleled by a growing, if grudging, respect for the rebels who – even unsympathetic observers had to admit – were not as bad as they had been painted, and who generally strove, with success, to keep order in the towns they conquered. Order prevailed at Piedras Negras, a missionary reported, and 'the Constitutionalists can't be nice enough to Americans'.[1087] Tampico was 'orderly [with] business in full swing'; it seemed unlikely, a British Admiral concluded, that a rebel entry of Mexico City would bring mayhem and massacre.[1088] At Monterrey, the American representative ransacked his vocabulary to describe the conduct of the Constitutionalists, whose actions 'are a credit to the civilised age in which we live', and whose treatment of Americans 'give[s] evidence of their love and respect for our country, our people and our flag'; compared with the Huertistas, 'they are as far apart and unlike as Zanzibar and Holland'.[1089] In the west, too, the occupation of Guadalajara was conducted with 'excellent discipline', incipient rioting – by the townspeople – was halted, and the rebel troops responsibly 'quelched [sic] an insurrection in the penitentiary'.[1090]

These examples of Federal collapse and revolutionary discipline gave further stimulus to the search for a negotiated settlement. Initial support for Huerta had earlier given way to a prudent *attentisme*; this was now replaced by wholehearted, if discreet, opposition. The transition preceded Torreón and Veracruz. 'The educated and property-owning classes', stated the *Mexican Herald* in March, 'will welcome any solution of the situation existing, whether Huerta will or not'; there was talk of invoking Panamerican mediation; and Huerta's Foreign Minister promised the president's speedy retirement, following elections, if the US suspended arms shipments to the rebels.[1091] But Torreón and Veracruz gave a great push to these efforts – and Veracruz, whatever else it did, at least provided a safe platform and a free press within Mexico which the disaffected could exploit. In May the Archbishop of Mexico passed through, en route to Europe, allegedly exiled for recommending – with papal support – that Huerta resign. Aureliano Urrutia, Huerta's one-time doctor, henchman and Minister of Gobernación, also stopped in Veracruz, declaring that 'the country can be saved the very minute that President Huerta and all those who are with him in power ... make up their minds to retire'.[1092] By prompting international mediation, Veracruz also raised hopes of a *transacción*. Within days of the occupation, the Washington representatives of the ABC powers (Argentina, Brazil and Chile) offered to mediate in the US–Mexican conflict, and the American government – which had quite probably conceived the plan in the first place – readily accepted.[1093] For Wilson, the mediation offered an instrument not only to extricate American forces from Veracruz, but also to prise Huerta from power in controlled, political fashion, rather than by the hazards of war. Huerta had misgivings: the ABC powers, like the US, had never recognised his regime; and informed opinion, he must have known, saw the mediation as a means to dump the president and talk the Constitutionalists – at least, the respectable Constitutionalists – into a compromise government. Pressured by the British Minister (among others), Huerta reluctantly agreed.[1094] And as the three Huertista delegates left for the ABC conference at Niagara, Mexico City 'breathed a sigh of relief'.[1095]

The delegates – Emilio Rabasa, Luis Elguero, and Agustín Rodríguez – were, in Grieb's words, 'devoted to Mexico rather than to Huerta'.[1096] Certainly they wanted American troops off Mexican soil, as virtually the whole political nation did; and certainly they were not unconditional Huertistas – but there were few of those left by May 1914 and, by the very nature of their mission, unconditional Huertismo would have been a major liability. But they hardly went to Niagara as high-minded, disinterested patriots. They were, as one report put it, 'men having the confidence of [the] educated and wealthy classes'; Rabasa, a prominent jurist, was also paterfamilias of the Rabasa clan of Chiapas; Elguero, who had close links with foreign companies in Mexico City, had held high office under Díaz and was, like Rodríguez, a ranking member of the Catholic establishment (his brother edited *El País*).[1097] They had no false modesty about participating in 'the most transcendental negotiations which Latin America has even seen' and no illusions about the point of their mission: 'the present occasion', wrote Rabasa, 'offers itself as the sole opportunity to subject the revolution to conditions, to save society'.[1098] Niagara, in other words, was to be the Cd Juárez of the Constitutionalist revolution.

If terms were to be reached with both the US and the rebels, the talks would have to proceed swiftly, while Huerta still had a position from which to bargain. Every Federal defeat would weaken that position and stiffen revolutionary resolve. A 'dignified retirement' of Huerta would only be possible,

Rabasa said, while the president still had an army at his back and 'could not be supposed to act under duress, but out of disinterested patriotism which all the world will applaud'. Thus, the talks must be expedited, they must cover internal as well as international arrangements, and the campaign against the rebels must meanwhile be prolonged, even if victory were out of the question. The somewhat surprisingly dogged defence of Zacatecas in June can be traced back to tactical instructions issued from the Niagara conference table. 'Victory at Zacatecas is crucial', Rabasa cabled, 'it will decide the fate of the nego-tiations'; he even pleaded, optimistically, for a Federal counter-offensive. [1099] The carnage at Zacatecas – where 6,000 Federals died – thus stemmed directly from the desperate, rearguard strategy of the Niagara delegates, men 'devoted to Mexico'.

They were not playing a lone hand. The ABC powers were sympathetic; the Argentine Minister in London tried to enlist European support; and the British Minister in Mexico, having cajoled Huerta to the conference, urged London 'to strengthen the hands of the mediators' and to persuade the US to restrain the rebels while a settlement was reached. [1100] Prominent Mexican *émigrés* preferred similar advice: since 'it can't suit England in any way that Villa or any of his followers should get to the presidency', the Foreign Office should 'exert some pressure upon Wilson . . . [to] consent in having some moderate man, of advanced ideas, but not a revolutionary, put at the head of the government'; for 'if not, we are lost'. [1101] Oscar Braniff, a professional fixer, bombarded the State Department with arguments to show that the mediators must replace Huerta with a compromise president who would be acceptable to 'the reasonable elements of the revolution', but who would not espouse 'ultra-radical doctrines'. [1102] But Europe refused to budge: American sensitivity over Mexico ruled out any *démarche*; and, as the Niagara talks petered out, the Sarajevo assassination and its ramifications shouldered aside these peripheral diplomatic concerns. The onset of the First World War, however, merely confirmed and reinforced European deference towards the US in Mexican affairs. [1103] And Wilson, closely advised by Lind, saw the talks as a means not to arrest and compromise the revolution, but rather to facilitate its orderly assumption of power. 'The object of our conference', as Bryan said, 'is to find a method by which the inevitable can be accomplished without further bloodshed'. [1104] Granted the correctness of the premise – that Huerta was doomed – this policy was more practical than pig-headed; it certainly made more sense than the elaborate schemes being floated by the Huertistas and their *émigré* sympathisers, in which old presidential names (Limantour, Lascuraín, Lauro Villar) were combined with new governmental formulae (Huertistas, Constitutionalists and 'Neutrals' – whoever they might be). [1105]

In all this fruitless diplomacy, the Huertistas were aided by the ABC representatives who, Rabasa said, 'have conducted themselves with unsurpass-able loyalty and sympathy'. [1106] But they collectively insisted that any deal was conditional on an armistice, and this Carranza would have none of: he, no less than the Huertistas, remembered the lesson of Cd Juárez. Indeed, it is unlikely that the First Chief – even had he tried – could have halted the headlong progress of the revolution. So Carranza refused either to participate in the talks or to call a truce while they proceeded. The US government, for its part, respected this decision and refrained from exerting pressure (as it could have done) to force Carranza to the conference table. 'We get the impression', Wilson observed, with a certain acuity, 'that the Mexican representatives are chiefly anxious that we should by some means intervene to prevent the complete success of the revolution now in progress. We on our part cannot afford in right or conscience to do that.'[1107] The Niagara conference therefore failed. Or, rather, it succeeded as regards the narrow, formal issue for which it had been convened: protocols were signed on 1 July dealing with the Tampico incident, and resolving the specific, somewhat spurious conflict between Huerta and the US government. But the real issue – the political future of Mexico, which the Huertistas hoped to co-determine – was left unsettled. There would be no political fix, no repeat of the Juárez Treaty. The revolution would go on until Huerta capitulated unconditionally. Foreign mediation having failed, the last best hope of the conservatives now lay with foreign intervention.

The fall of Huerta was now just a matter of time. But the time-schedule depended upon vicissitudes within the revolutionary camp. In May, Carranza had side-tracked Villa to Saltillo. This proved a brief excursion; but, meanwhile, the First Chief visited newly conquered Torreón (where the Villista leaders received him coolly) and Durango, where he conferred with the Arrietas – now somewhat distanced from Villa – and the revolutionary caudillo of Zacatecas, Pánfilo Natera.[1108] They assured the First Chief that they could take Zacatecas alone, without Villa's help, which was music to Carranza's ears.[1109] The last major obstacle on the road to Mexico City would be dismantled by loyalist forces. But the Federal position at Zacatecas was strong, and the Federals outnumbered Natera's forces by two to one. After two days fighting, Natera admitted that the task was beyond him.[1110] Carranza, who wanted the military victory without paying the political price, ordered Villa to send reinforcements, though not to lead them in person. But trying to detach *gente* from caudillo in this manner was tricky and provocative (ironically, Villa's squabble with the Arrietas happened for precisely the same reason, with Villa the offender); in protest, Villa resigned his command, and the fifteen generals of the Division of the North backed him up, reproving Carranza for his jealous and authoritarian ways, his bad faith and his diplomatic ineptitude.[1111]

This was strong stuff. As the cement of Huertismo crumbled, the breach between Villa and Carranza gaped. Two weeks later, an attempt was made to plug it, when representatives of Villa and of González's Division of the

North-East met at Torreón and reached agreement on several points, military and political. Villa recognised Carranza as First Chief and was confirmed as commander of the Division of the North, which was guaranteed greater military independence and adequate supplies of ammunition and coal (hitherto withheld, Villa complained).[1112] Joint suggestions were made for cabinet posts and for the social reforms to be enacted by a future revolutionary government.[1113] Most important, the Torreón agreement stipulated that, once Mexico City had fallen, a revolutionary convention would be held, at which representatives of the entire army would discuss a programme of reforms and decide on the date of elections. The agreement thus amended Carranza's Plan of Guadalupe and sought to give the army a controlling say in the creation of the new regime. Just as the lessons of the Juárez Treaty had sunk into revolutionary thinking, so too the military of 1914 – particularly the Villista military – were determined not to be passed over as their predecessors had been in 1911. Faced with this challenege, Carranza played a typically foxy role: he accepted the Torreón agreement 'in general', including the idea of a revolutionary convention; but he would not commit himself as to the convention's make-up (whether, for example, it would be purely military), nor would he endorse the proposed labour, agrarian, and anticlerical reforms, which, he said, went far beyond the original purpose of the Torreón conference.[1114] The differences between Villa and Carranza were thus temporarily, imperfectly, papered over. Whatever the caveats and conditions, however, one thing was clear: some kind of general, representative convention was now on the agenda of the revolution.

While the politicking went on, Villa did not remain idle. Ignoring the dispute with Carranza, he led the Division of the North – over 20,000 strong with its redoubtable artillery – against Zacatecas.[1115] As at Ojinaga in January, he would finish the job that Natera had begun and bungled. In a couple of days the outer defences were reduced; the Federal commanders pulled back in trepidation; and when the final Villista assault was launched on 23 June the result was a 'hecatomb'.[1116] While at Torreón Villa had deliberately left a bolt-hole for the beaten army, at Zacatecas the rebels stoppered every outlet and subjected the fleeing Federals to withering enfilade fire. The defeat became a rout and the rout became a massacre. Maybe 6,000 Federals died: some killed when the public buildings and arsenal were dynamited; some who fell headlong into the disused mineshafts which pitted the surrounding mountains; some – the officers – who, once captured, could not escape summary execution by ripping off their gold braid and claiming to be common soldiers.[1117] Droves of conscripts joined the rebels, and only a handful of officers escaped. One was the wily old Orozquista Benjamín Argumedo who, dressed in rags with a blackened face, drove a team of mules through the Villista lines posing as a charcoal burner.[1118] But then Argumedo, a veteran *guerrillero*, looked the part; most Federal officers were instantly recognisable, even without insignia. All told, only a few hundred of the Federal garrison of 12,000 reached Aguascalientes: of the rest, maybe half were killed and half taken prisoner.[1119] For days, a foul stench hung over the devastated city; typhus broke out and claimed the life of the Villista general Toribio Ortega; finally, the unburied corpses were soused in petrol and burned. Felipe Angeles was jubilant: 'I saw the event', he wrote at the end of the battle, 'from the artistic point of view, as a master work terminated.'[1120]

Angeles has been deservedly criticised for this callous aestheticism; but in a sense he was right. If Torreón had been the crucial turning point, Zacatecas – the last stand of Huertismo, urged by the Niagara delegates – was the end, the most costly defeat of the entire war, which revealed the utter collapse of the Huerta regime. Two weeks later, Obregón annihilated another, weaker Federal army at Orendaín, near Guadalajara.[1121] In Morelos, Cuernavaca alone remained in Federal hands, its inhabitants hungry, the poor slipping out to join the Zapatistas, the Federals 'proving themselves traitors by running away whenever they could'.[1122] Cuernavaca in fact held out until August, when the garrison, accompanied by several hundred townspeople, beat a harassed retreat to Mexico City. Long before that, however, the Zapatistas began mopping up the sierra villages on the outskirts of the Federal District: from the roof of La Hormiga textile factory, Federals and Zapatistas could be seen skirmishing betwen Puente Sierra and San Gerónimo and 'as a result, great excitement, anxiety and fear reign throughout that region'. Some factories were forced to close, and houses at Contreras and La Magdalena were put to the torch by the rebels (though where prudent residents had displayed notices proclaiming their revolutionary sympathies, no damage was done).[1123]

Last-minute attempts by the government to talk the Zapatistas into an armistice – 'to trick the southern rubes into a deal' – came to nothing.[1124] On all fronts, the revolution advanced. Gertrudis Sánchez led an army of Guerrero and Michoacán rebels across the Balsas against Huetamo; the Márquez brothers invested Tlaxcala; Jesús Carranza and Pablo González advanced on San Luis, while Cándido Aguilar moved south from Tuxpán and, by July, was approaching the Veracruz state capital of Jalapa, as the Federals, unpaid and dispirited, fell back and deserted *en masse*.[1125] There was only one significant contrary movement. Dallying only briefly at Zacatacas, Villa decided not to race for Mexico City, but to pull back to the north. Some attributed this to American pressure, in that the US government preferred to keep Villa out of the capital.[1126] But Villa's stock was high in American circles, and it seems doubtful either that the US urged a retreat, or that Villa would have heeded such urgings, if made. Rather, the move indicated the fragility of the Torreón agreement: Villa feared Carrancista incursions into his home territory (chiefly from the Carrancista forces around Saltillo) and was reluctant to stretch his lines of communication from the border to Mexico City. Anyway, the capital lured Villa less than it lured ambitious claimants for national power.[1127]

The way was therefore open to Obregón. Carefully mopping up pockets of Federal resistance, he headed south-east from Guadalajara, through the Bajío, until at the beginning of August his army of some 18,000 stood at the gates of Mexico City, where they could link up with the advance guard of González's north-eastern division. In Mexico City, the foreign diplomats wallowed in Peking-style paranoia, anticipating robbery, rape and pillage.[1128] And the Huerta regime began to collapse from within. Since the spring, the government had been in disarray: the cabinet had not met since April, and the conduct of policy – as regards Tampico, Veracruz and Niagara – had been personal and arbitrary.[1129] At the end of June the cabinet plucked up courage to call for Huerta's resignation; it was 'the first occasion on which they have shown any independence or solicitude to work together'. A week later, the British Minister counselled resignation, urging that a 'neutral' successor might be able to negotiate with the Constitutionalists, and adding 'other arguments, mostly of a personal nature which I adduced in order to influence his decision'.[1130] Huerta was persuaded: on 9 July the President of the Supreme Court, Francisco Carbajal, was appointed Foreign Minister; six days later Huerta resigned and Carbajal succeeded – constitutional niceties being observed at the death as they had been at the birth of the regime. Accompanied by his old crony and War Minister, Blanquet, Huerta made the risky rail journey to Puerto México and there boarded the German battle-cruiser *Dresden*, which took him to Jamaica. Thence he sailed, by way of England, to Barcelona, where he settled with his family into the life of a weary exile. But not for long.[1131]

Though Huerta had gone, and with him many of his old allies, his political executors survived another month, striving for a conditional armistice which would avert the anticipated bloodshed and upheaval of a total revolutionary triumph. Delegates went from Carbajal to Carranza bearing proposals: that the old Twenty-sixth Congress reconvene and appoint a provisional president; that there should be an armistice and general amnesty; that the rump of the Federal Army remain in being, existing ranks being recognised. These were wildly optimistic terms and, despite American exhortations, Carranza spurned them.[1132] On 12 August Carbajal and his cabinet gave up the diplomatic struggle and quit the country, leaving the governor of the Federal District in charge of Mexico City. The Hobbesian fears of the foreigners were not realised and, in the absence of government, anarchy did not break loose. Governor Iturbide met with Obregón at Teoloyucán, on the city's outskirts and, along with military representatives, signed terms of surrender: Obregón would take control of the city, guaranteeing order; the Federal garrison of 25,000 would evacuate to the east, taking only their rifles, billeting themselves along the Mexico–Puebla railway; throughout the country, Federal forces would surrender to the appropriate authorities.[1133]

The Treaty of Teoloyucán was significant in two respects. First, the surrender was unconditional, in that it involved no acceptance of Carbajal's terms: no amnesty, no recognition of the Federal Army, no political strings. Unlike Madero in 1911, the Constitutionalists entered upon a free and disentailed inheritance. Second, in ordering the Federal evacuation, Obregón stipulated that the detachments on the southern flank of the city, facing the Zapatistas, should remain in position until relieved by Constitutionalist forces.[1134] In the political sphere, therefore, the Constitutionalists claimed to be the masters, establishing a new regime from scratch; and, in the military, there was already the anticipation of new conflicts to come.

2

The Revolution in power: (1) The great schism

In August 1914 the capital of the Republic experienced its first revolutionary occupation. Fears of riot and massacre were soon dispelled: the Carrancistas' 'assumption of power' commented the British Minister, 'has been effected in greater tranquillity and order than the most optimistic could have anticipated'.[1] Martial law was proclaimed, cantinas were closed, a few looters were shot and their bodies exhibited for public edification. A week later, huge crowds turned out to witness Carranza's triumphal entry: 300,000, it was reckoned, compared with the 100,000 who had greeted Madero in 1911.[2] Not that numbers – even assuming them to be remotely accurate – were an index of popularity. Motives other than warm enthusiasm impelled the *capitalinos* on to the streets; not least, an anxious curiosity to see the khaki-clad northerners, and Obregón's fearsome Yaqui contingents.[3] One observer – who had reason to feel jaded – was 'struck by a lack of enthusiasm' in the crowds.[4] These indifferent feelings were reciprocated by the Constitutionalists. Addressing the governor of the Federal District, Carranza warned that Mexico City, 'the cradle of coups', untouched by violence (he forgot the *Decena Trágica*), could no longer expect privileged treatment: 'it is only just that it should pay for its faults, and we are going to punish it severely'.[5] Obregón, too, visiting the tomb of Madero, made pointed comments about callow non-belligerents (a theme to which he was much attached); his hostility to Mexico City became a constant.[6] The old sentiments of northern federalism thus surfaced and, from the outset, relations between the Constitutionalists and what they saw as the corrupt, conservative capital of the Republic were unhappy.

Whereas in 1911 Madero's arrival had provoked genuine enthusiasm, tinged with relief at the onset of peace, in 1914 the mood – on both sides – was sourer, a good many 'well-to-do people' were slipping away to Veracruz, and Constitutionalists and Zapatistas were already skirmishing in the environs of the city.[7] There were further parallels and contrasts between 1911 and 1914. Madero and Carranza were both northern (indeed, Coahuilan) leaders, who had rebelled against conservative regimes on the basis of narrow, politico-constitutional programmes. In both cases, the written commitments of the rebellion (free elections; the restoration of the Constitution) implied no more than a new political order, within which 'social' reforms might or might not be achieved. But the struggle against Huerta had been long and bloody; it had, as we shall see, demolished much of the old Porfirian system; and it had provoked a novel commitment to a general revolutionary convention. Thus, while Madero's rebellion produced the *interinato* and subsequent elections, Carranza neither established a provisional presidency, nor resurrected the constitutional authorities of 1913. Fifty deputies of the Twenty-sixth Congress met with a view to reconvening, but they were ignored – Carrancista contempt for the Renovadores was pronounced – and rumours of a provisional presidency were soon scotched.[8] For the time being, Carranza's authority remained that of the First Chief of the Constitutionalist revolution – a misnomer, in that it derived from military victory and was unchecked by representative institutions. As Obregón pointed out, he and his followers were really 'anti-constitucionalistas', since their prosecution of the war had involved so many anti-constitutional acts and 'if we had stuck to the Constitution we would have had to recognise Huerta, for the law required it, as Huerta had been sworn in before Congress'.[9] The Constitutionalist revolution and regime cannot therefore be understood in terms of their 'constitutionalism' and 'legalism'.[10] In practice, Carranza, his cabinet and generals governed by decree; many of them anticipated – and with enthusiasm – a period of tough, authoritarian rule, not a swift return to the Constitution. Mexico needed at least a year of 'pre-constitutional' military government, declared the new governor of Colima, the Sonoran General Eduardo Ruiz; even civilians argued for a 'moderate, conscientious tyranny'.[11] And military rule was what the country got: government by decree in Veracruz, under Governors Jara and Aguilar; 'absolute militarism' at Guadalajara.[12]

But if the form of rule was roughly standard, the content could vary, since there was no fixed set of policies to which all were pledged. The British consul at Tampico, who had sounded out several prominent Constitutionalists, including Carranza, concluded that 'none of the Constitutionalists ... appear [sic] to have any fixed party platform. The elimination of Huerta having been accomplished [they] are rather at sea as to what they ought to do next'.[13] Though, as I shall argue, Constitutionalism displayed distinctive policies and attitudes, it is still true that in the summer of 1914 these remained imperfectly developed, codified and enacted. The widespread – if not unanimous – recognition that a rapid 'return to normalcy' on the lines of 1911 was impossible or undesirable marked the most important contrast between the Maderista and Carrancista revolutions; it derived from changes wrought by both revolutions, and from the political implications of these changes. Since neither Madero nor Carranza elaborated blueprints for social reform and, in their respective manifestoes, concentrated on political issues, their revolutions have often been seen as tame, tepid affairs, which neither projected nor achieved important changes in Mexican society. There was fighting aplenty; but, as Ruiz chooses to put it, no 'revolution'.[14]

As regards 1911, I have already argued that the ostensibly mild political reforms of the Plan of San Luis carried radical implications; and that the Madero revolution encouraged and drew upon profound social tensions which contributed first to the fall of Díaz, then to the ferment which the country experienced under Madero. Madero's pronouncements afford poor criteria for assessing the radicalism of the 1910 revolution, especially when viewed from the perspective of late twentieth-century industrial democracies (where liberalism is easily taken for granted) rather than of early twentieth-century agrarian dictatorships (where it was not). So, too, with Carranza. The Plan of Guadalupe, which probably excited less interest than the Plan of San Luis, was, as Carranza intended, a rallying point for all anti-Huerta forces, urban and rural, liberal and *agrarista*, middle class and plebeian.[15] Its great virtue was that, apart from repudiating Huerta, it said virtually nothing: paraphrasing Thiers, it was the Plan that divided Mexicans least. In subsequent statements too – such as his address to the revolutionaries of Sinaloa, at San Blas – the First Chief was studiously vague about future policies.[16] But it would be wrong to infer from this that Carranza was a blinkered conservative, concerned only to oust Huerta; and even more wrong to infer that the Constitutionalist revolution as a whole was a movement of blinkered conservatism, concerned only to oust Huerta.

On the first, individual, and much less important question, it should be noted that Carranza admitted the need for social reform: in his famous Hermosillo speech he talked of the impending 'struggle of classes', which would go beyond the specifics of effective suffrage, agrarian reform and education, and would seek 'justice . . . equality . . . and the elimination of the powerful'; in the same speech he promised a major legislative overhaul and the provision of a new constitution.[17] Córdova's interesting gloss on this speech – in which he categorises it, and Carranza's liberalism in general, as a form of Jacobin *étatisme*, bent on abolishing privilege while controlling the masses – clearly absolves Carranza of conservatism; and it makes Carranza's subsequent policies – notably the revisions of the Plan of Guadalupe decreed in December–January 1914–15 – more explicable and less the sudden, opportunistic U-turn which they have often been considered.[18] Indeed, we may lengthen the perspective: Carranza can be seen as one of the intransigent Maderistas who in 1912 feared that Madero would fail for want of decisive measures that would both conciliate the masses and neutralise the power of the Porfiristas – agrarian reform, for example, on the one hand, and the maintenance of Maderista military forces on the other. This brand of thought was scarcely orthodox in 1912; but two years later, after the failure, fall and death of Madero and the prolonged struggle with Huerta, its adherents had multiplied exponentially. More than ever the masses had to be conciliated, and more than ever the power of the Porfiristas had to be irrevocably broken.

Even Carranza's stated position, therefore, was not one of narrow political liberalism. He distinguished between the necessarily narrow provisions of the Plan of Guadalupe and the broader revolutionary demands (many of them 'social') which lay behind the Constitutionalist revolution; and in the right time and place – like Chihuahua, April 1914 – he could sound postively populist. 'My repudiation of the so-called central government', he conceded, was not a revolutionary plan'; but 'the Revolution has welled up from the people themselves, who wish to redeem themselves before a return is made to constitutional order, and it is the people who, by their own efforts, are carrying out the great work of redemption'.[19] Of course, this was revolutionary flannel (in a different time and place Carranza would sound very different). But it serves – as revolutionary flannel sometimes does – to dust down and polish up a profound truth about the Revolution. And here we come to the second, more important count against the view which sees the Constitutionalist revolution as a primarily political movement, neglectful of 'social' issues.[20] At the level of high policy, it is true, there had been few verbal commitments and fewer practical concessions to 'social' demands. The prosecution of the war against Huerta had been the overriding concern. But, as in 1910–11 – but more so – official policy was only part of the story and perhaps not the main plot. Once again, armed, popular revolution brought change *nolens volens* – change, sometimes of a radical kind, but unsanctioned by national plans and programmes. This was the way of the Mexican Revolution as a whole, at least in the period thus far considered. A cursory review of the state of the nation in the summer of 1914 reveals the extent and significance of this change, which had not been debated, legislated or codified, but which had sprung from the soil of Mexican society, germinated by the sun and rain of revolution, and which was all the stronger for its organic, unplanned genesis. The major changes wrought by the years of revolution, 1910–14, derived from local impulses, inarticulate groups, and their complex, obscure interaction, which often produced unforeseen results; they did not derive from the rational plans of individuals or elites. In this sense the Revolution was – if the paradox is permissible – a Burkean rather than a Jacobin phenomenon; though after 1914, as we shall see, Jacobinism increasingly reared its head, as planned, 'official' reform supplanted local, popular *reivindicación*. It is for this reason that many historians, their ears attuned to the 'importunate chink' of Jacobin grasshoppers, have neglected the large, taciturn ruminants of the field, and thus misinterpreted the course of the Revolution.[21] For they have seen the climacteric of 1914–15 as the radicalisation of Constitutionalism and the birth of the 'social' revolution, when in fact the striking-up of the grasshoppers' chorus marks less revolutionary triumph and advance than defeat and retrocession. And this was because the paucity of official, Jacobin reform prior to

1914 coincided with significant social change, while the plethora of such reform after 1914 often implied the reversal, nullification and containment of the change thus far achieved.

THE END OF THE OLD ORDER

What manner of change? The most general, apparent and important was the destruction of the old Porfirian system, at least in northern and much of central Mexico (the south was different: change would soon come, but it would be imported, planned, typically Jacobin change). The Madero revolution had begun the process, but Madero had backed up and the process was arrested. In 1913–14, with the *guerre à outrance* against Huerta, the process was accelerated, pushed along by an anonymous multitude. Official, Constitutionalist policy played its part too; but official policy came later, and was as much imitative as innovative: it appropriated certain popular demands in its own interest, it frowned on others, and it sought out victims – such as priests – against whom the multitude often bore little animus. The 'official' and 'unofficial' attacks on the Porfirian order thus obeyed different rhythms and priorities; they diverged as much as they converged; yet, taken together, they constituted a formidable onslaught.

To the 'better elements' who had applauded Huerta's coup – to *hacendado* and *jefe*, merchant and prelate – the revolution brought fear and flight. At Zacatecas, as early as May 1913, the 'better people [were] frightened to death'; by October, it was reported from Mexico City, 'the property-owning classes . . . dread the violent expropriation of their property, their being forced into exile, and the reprisals which will inevitably result if the northern revolutionaries conquer'.[22] Sometimes, these fears were irrational or exaggerated. The apprehensions of the diplomatic corps, who feared a siege of the legations when the rebels came to town, were unfounded; so, too, were fears of indiscriminate Zapatista rapine.[23] The scare stories which emanated from Durango and elsewhere were often greatly inflated and embellished: rebel forces – especially the larger armies – were usually disciplined and rarely riotous. But what the elite (rightly) feared were not so much wanton, arbitrary abuses, as specific, often predictable attacks on their property, persons and status; attacks which followed regular patterns and which, even when they were perpetrated by the mob rather than by military commanders or revolutionary courts, still showed some rationality and discrimination.

The expropriation of property – particularly of the large estates – was the most important line of attack, which will be considered separately in a moment. So, too, will anti-clerical measures. But these should be seen within the general context of popular uppishness and elite apprehension which prevailed. In Villista Chihuahua, we have noted, adherents of the old regime like the Terrazas family and the Spanish community were driven from the state, their property was seized, and commentators were struck by the social *bouleversement* which accompanied Villa's rise to power. In the southern provinces of Villa's kingdom, these phenomena were even more marked. Durango experienced the worst sack of the Constitutionalist revolution; thereafter, the rich (who had not got away) were gaoled, mulcted and ransomed; their estates were confiscated and their town houses seized; in 1914 a second bout of arrests − of ex-*Defensa Social* members − ensued, by way of reprisal for Huerta's *leva*.[24] In the Laguna towns, meanwhile, 'extortion . . . has extracted the last cent from nearly all the professional and well-to-do people' so that − for reasons of poverty or prudence or both − they discarded their starched collars and took to wearing old clothes and shoes in the street. And it was not simply the rebels who were to blame. There was now ample evidence of the vengeful, criminal disposition of 'the non-combatant lower classes in these towns [who] were considered before the revolution broke out as being, comparatively speaking, quiet and orderly'. To what pitch had society sunk when, for example, manservants revealed to the rebels where their masters had concealed the family valuables?[25]

The rot soon spread. After the fall of Guadalajara, 'former employees avenge[d] themselves by pointing out their old masters as Huertistas', thus incurring their imprisonment and sometimes the sequestration of their goods.[26] In the same city, long spared the trauma of rebellion, houses and cars were seized (chauffeurs, though ordered to resist, refused to do so, pleading that they were the worse for drink); Federal officers were shot and their families subjected to persecution.[27] A year later, with 'the proletariat in the saddle', Guadalajara was no better off. The traditional, elegant, flirtatious *paseo*, which filled the main square on Sunday evenings, was now a travesty of its old self: 'ever since the beginning of the revolution the *plaza de armas* has been practically abandoned by the *gente decente*'; in their place 'there is only to be seen a conglomerate mixture of the proletarian element, from the passably decently clothed to the dirty and ragged'. Meanwhile, parvenu rebel generals toured the city in their sequestered limousines, while their men, swathed in bandoliers, swaggered and brawled in the streets.[28] At times like this, respectability could be dangerous: in the state of Mexico a mob lynched an excessively smartly dressed couple.[29] And, in several instances there were deliberate attempts to humiliate − and not simply to expropriate − the well-to-do; to give almost theatrical proof that the world had been turned upside down. After the fall of Culiacán prominent Huertistas were made to sweep the streets to the accompaniment of a band and to the delight of the people; in the same town the *jefe* was subjected to a mock execution before he fled to the US.[30] At Zacatecas, leading citizens were expelled and 'other prominent men were to be seen sweeping the streets'; here the *jefe* was subjected to a real execution, at the hands of Melitón Ortega.[31]

Popular hatred of officers and officials, merchants and landlords, evident at the outset of the Revolution, was thus still vigorous in 1914. Now, it paralleled official purges and proscriptions, sometimes blending indistinguishably with them. But usually it had a style of its own. The four days looting suffered by Acapulco – chiefly by the Spanish merchant houses – at the hands of Blanco's men and the 'local riff-raff' hardly typified the way Carranza or Obregón sought to extirpate Porfirismo and privilege; rather, this was the tradition of Durango, Torreón, Concepción, and many lesser episodes.[32] Even less typical of official policy was the behaviour of the 'ignorant, brutal General Quintanilla', said to be a Zapatista, who 'on the night of his arrival [at El Oro] . . . ordered a dance [to be] given and obliged the best families to appear (not foreigners) and their daughters to dance with his drunken soldiers of the worst peon class. The following day his men looted the stores.'[33]

Such, if we may borrow Azuela's phrase, were the tribulations of respectable families. In reply, few put up a stout defence (the reasons for which have been mentioned). Many, instead, opted to leave; hence one of the most striking and general effects of the Revolution was the disappearance of local elites which had dominated Porfirian society. In some regions this was evident in mid-1913, as the well-to-do quit the smaller provincial towns for the state or national capital.[34] There was a general exodus out of the Laguna so that by the end of the year 'few respectable people remain[ed]'.[35] The landlords of Durango – some of whom had returned to their estates, reassured by Huerta's coup – first congregated in the threatened city, then chose to leave, even though it meant the certain confiscation of their property by the rebels.[36] There were similar movements from Tepic to Guadalajara; from Saltillo and San Luis to the US and Mexico City; while Villa's triumph in Chihuahua brought a mass exodus of 'the better class of civilians'.[37] States and cities further south experienced the same phenomenon months later. Ninety-two 'Huertistas' left Mazatlán by boat shortly before the port surrendered, sailing away with the departing garrison; in Veracruz it was noted that 'as the rebels advance the richer families flee while the poorer classes usually seize any weapon at hand and join the Constitutionalists'.[38]

The experience of small towns like Cerralvo (NL) – stripped of its officials and elite families as early as April 1913 – was thus replicated throughout northern and central Mexico.[39] At Chalchihuites (Zac.) 'no-one of the middle or better class people can be seen on the streets'; in the state of San Luis 'the country towns (were) . . . largely abandoned by the class who supply employment and who have served as patrons [sic] of the poor' (this was especially true of Valle del Maíz); while an American, touring Mexico early in 1915, noted 'that in Chihuahua . . . and in all other portions of the country there was an absence of persons of education. Crudely put, "the man in the white shirt had apparently disappeared".'[40] True, this is impressionistic evidence: the social mortality of the old order cannot be quantified. True, it comes largely from foreign observers, trying to describe the state of the country in broad terms:

extant Mexican sources, such as newspapers and official correspondence, being concerned with specifics, rarely comment on such gross matters (which were presumably familiar to writer and reader alike; and which in some circumstances were best left unsaid). True, also, that many foreigners were over-fussy when it came to dealing with revolutionary parvenus in place of the familiar old Porfiristas; they perhaps exaggerated the coarse, plebeian character of the first, and overlooked the discreet survival of the some of the latter alongside or even within the revolution. In many cases, however, this survival only became apparent in later years, as these persons floated to the top again. Even allowing for possible bias, however, the evidence for 1913–15 clearly points to a major – if in some cases temporary – eclipse of the old Porfirian elite.

Nowhere was this clearer – and here some figures may be thrown into the pot – than at Veracruz during the American occupation. This provided a convenient bolt-hole at a crucial juncture, when Villa and his revolutionary colleagues and rivals were bearing down on central Mexico. Within weeks of the occupation, General Funston found the influx of refugees already 'assuming alarming proportions', at the rate of some 200 a day; in August, the fall of Mexico City signalled 'a very large exodus of the well-to-do people to Veracruz'; by the end of the summer, 15,000 refugees had crowded into the port.[41] Not all were rich and prominent: there was a large Spanish contingent (and Villa's persecution had revealed that the middle-class Spaniard suffered along with the rich) as well as 300 priests and nuns, fearful of revolutionary reprisals.[42] But what was clear was the high concentration of Porfirista and Huertista elements, many whom passed – like Francisco Carbajal 'very depressed' – through Veracruz on their way to exile. Passengers leaving on one ship in September 1914 included; José Elguero, one-time editor of *El País*; three ex-governors of Veracruz (Dehesa, de la Llave, and Cauz); Generals Juvencio Robles, the butcher of Morelos and Alberto Rasgado, the grafter of Mazatlán; and two bishops.[43] After Veracruz the next stop was usually New Orleans, Southampton, or Santander – above all, the first. By the end of 1914, therefore, a large emigré community existed in the US, many of its members officially proscribed by the revolutionary regime and liable to execution if they returned. Enrique Creel had joined his father-in-law Terrazas; Félix Díaz was there, contemplating revolt; there was a clutch of Huertista cabinet ministers and a dozen or so Federal generals. Some plotted; some wrote their memoirs; Aureliano Urrutia, once Huerta's close confidant and Minister of Gobernación, wisely kept out of politics and built up a thriving dental practice in San Antonio, where he died, a respected citizen, in 1975.[44] But though many got away, hundreds remained in Veracruz and, as the prospect of American evacuation drew closer, they besieged the American consulate, begging for transport and salvation from revolutionary justice.[45]

Theirs were no idle fears, for revolutionary justice could be swift and draconian. And what was 'revolutionary justice'? 'Rapid justice', was Gabriel

Gavira's confident answer, 'justice without delays, justice informed only by an honourable conscience at the service of a sound judgement.'[46] Commanding at Papantla, Gavira ordered several executions and expulsions from the country ('it must be borne in mind', he explains, 'that in those days it was not feasible to gaol people'): of an hacienda administrator known to be a Huertista spy; of a mayordomo guilty of rape; of oppressive Spanish landlords and collaborators of the hated Papantla *jefe*.[47] Gavira was an honest, if somewhat self-righteous man, who lived up to his high ideals better than most. Others were less scrupulous; and under the rubric of 'revolutionary justice' were subsumed acts of popular retribution and jacquerie, calculated political purges, personal vendettas and criminal self-advancement. Indeed, the initial thrust of the new regime was less in the direction of concrete reforms (of the kind which are supposed to lie at the heart of Constitutionalism: labour, agrarian, economic nationalist measures) than of political revenge and renovation. Carranza's regime, a plantation manager concluded, 'has as its fundamental principle the punishment of any and everybody that ever had anything to do with the Porfirio Díaz government'.[48] If this was an exaggeration, it nevertheless encapsulated a feature of Carrancismo which sober scholars have also stressed: its rejection of Madero's old 'politica de conciliación' and its firm belief that 'victory never comes by halves and that for it to be complete it is necessary to destroy the enemy'.[49] And, though there were Villistas who preached and practised this doctrine, it is worth noting – without at this stage explaining – that it was the men around Carranza who were the most consistent exponents of this revolutionary exclusivism.[50]

In Mexico City, promises of punishment were soon honoured. Known Huertistas like Francisco Olaguibel, of the 'quadrilateral', were gaoled; at least one, Alberto García Granados, was later shot after a disreputable trial; and rumours flew that there would be a massive levy on 'those who had despoiled the country', that is, the Científicos. Limantour's properties alone, it was reckoned, would yield 6m. pesos.[51] Certainly, the grand town houses of the old elite were soon taken over: Rafael Buelna now played billiards in Tomas Braniff's; Ignacio de la Torre's went to Pablo González; Lucio Blanco billeted himself in Joaquín Casasús', where the fine library was plundered and the new occupant reconciled himself to drinking Casasús' wine, rather than leaving it to be stolen.[52] Sour observers talked of champagne being sold off at a peso a bottle and of 'nightly orgies' taking place in these once refined homes.[53] Meanwhile, the same critics went on, cars were seized and there was much aimless joyriding around the city, to the accompaniment of celebratory gunshots.[54]

The denigration and proscription of the old regime went further, at both a rhetorical and practical level. Obregón paid homage at Madero's tomb; the bloodstained clothes of Madero and Pino Suárez were unearthed and paraded for the benefit of the press; even the remains of Huerta's victims – including

Serapio Rendón and Gustavo Madero – were disinterred and solemnly reburied.[55] Further to stress the iniquity of the old regime, the Constitutionalist press delved into the Urrutia archive and – it repeatedly declared throughout October 1914 – found evidence of clerical intrigue, linking the Archbishops of Mexico, Puebla and Michoacán with Porfirian *políticos*.[56] This muckraking was supplemented by polemical attacks on the 'thirty accursed years' of the Porfiriato; by eulogies of Madero, Belisario Domínguez and other revolutionary martyrs; and by rhetorical celebration of the demise of the 'Científico Mafia'.[57]

At a more practical level, the Constitutionalists riveted their control on key institutions. Editors of Huertista newspapers were arrested, their presses confiscated, and their publications – in the jargon of espionage – 'turned'; in the space of one week in September three new revolutionary phoenixes rose from the ashes of the conservative press, each bearing a suitably fresh, revolutionary sort of name.[58] Carranza had no intention of being pilloried in the press as Madero had been; and he saw no reason to pussyfoot about with discreet subsidies when outright expropriation would do as well or better. The Constitutionalists also mounted an onslaught upon the civil service, which Madero had spared. A clean sweep was made of the diplomatic corps: diplomatic Vicars of Bray, like the Mexican Minister at Rome, who had served twenty-four years under every successive administration, now found themselves out of a job.[59] Government departments in Mexico City also came under attack. By November, Cowdray's manager reported, 'the administrative machine is now completely smashed and the civil service finally dispersed'.[60] This was an exaggeration. There is evidence of continuity in departments like Labour, which maintained operations under Carranza as it had under Huerta, and of sustained friction between revolutionary leaders and supposed conservative elements in the civil service after 1914 (the Ministry of Hacienda in particular was said to be steeped in reaction).[61] This theme will be taken up later; but it is worth noting its inception in the 1914 purges.

As the revolution progressed, too, much of the railway system had come under *de facto* military control. With the capital in their grasp, the Constitutionalists now sought to extend and legitimise this control, rather than to relinquish it. September saw wholesale changes in the railway administration; and, three months later, Carranza decreed the confiscation of the entire system, placing it under the directorship of Alberto Pani.[62] Again, the implications of this extension of state power will be considered later. Another species of confiscation was of less practical but great symbolic significance. The Jockey Club, the Mecca of metropolitan high society, was taken over and given to the capital's newspaper sellers; while Obregón saw to it that the Casa del Obrero Mundial received both the confiscated convent of Santa Brígida and the printing press of the Catholic *La Tribuna*.[63] Thus were the aristocrats and clericals humbled, to the advantage of the working people of Mexico City, and to the credit of the Constitutionalists.

Similar scenes were enacted in the provinces. Forced loans and other financial penalties were imposed on 'enemies of the cause' on a regular basis: at Monterrey, after an impeccably orderly occupation; at Tampico, where business still boomed; and at Mazatlán, where José María Cabanillas demanded 200,000 pesos from the rich, exempting all foreigners save the Spaniards.[64] The revolutionary net trawled fine and deep: in small communities like Zaragoza (Coa.) known conservatives were fined sums of 200 pesos.[65] Urban property was seized: the town house of ex-Governor Dehesa in Jalapa; of ex-Governor Espinosa y Cuevas in San Luis (now occupied by the plebeian *jefe*, Eulalio Gutiérrez); of prominent Porfiristas/Huertistas in lesser towns like Puerto México or Piedras Negras, where the confiscated houses of 'the enemies of our holy cause' provided an additional administrative headache for the municipal authorities.[66] At Guadalajara up to 400 cars were sequestrated by the revolutionaries, ostensibly for military purposes, in fact – said one observer – for the personal amusement of 'very dirty people, officers and joyriders'.[67]

People, as well as property, suffered Constitutionalist retribution. Purges, arrests and occasional executions occurred throughout Mexico. After the fall of Oaxaca, known conservatives were proscribed, their property was seized.[68] At Puerto México, Jesús Carranza arrested prominent Huertistas and – ran one account – fomented a local witch-hunt: 'everyone with a grievance supposed or real is now trying to have it rectified'.[69] In Guanajuato, the new governor gaoled state and national deputies, an ex-*jefe político*, and an ex-Supreme Court magistrate, who had served as secretary to Huerta's military governor: all, of course, 'very respectable men'.[70] So, too, in Aguascalientes, where another 'respectable gentleman' reported a 'reign of terror' in which twelve members of the city's best families were shot; in San Luis, where Javier Espinosa y Cuevas was one of the notable victims; and at Mazatlán where, following the forced loan, forty-three Huertistas – 'a squad of businessmen, lawyers and engineers' – were arrested. One of these, the manager of an iron foundry, was gaoled for seven years for attending a banquet given by the Huertista military commander; while Francisco de Sevilla, a bank manager and brother-in-law of the Spanish Minister to Mexico, was sentenced to death for having applauded the fall (or the death) of Madero. Sevilla, 'a quiet, well-educated, unassuming man', was shot before an audience of 2,000.[71]

In some towns and cities, revolutionary justice proceeded by committee – indicating, perhaps, the fondness of Constitutionalist intellectuals for French precedents. A Committee of Public Safety was established at Piedras Negras to flush out local reactionaries; Gavira set one up at Papantla (though after he had passed his draconian sentences); another met in the main theatre at Jalapa, where it heard denunciations and ordered at least one execution.[72] By 1915, in fact, some revolutionary *enragés* even advocated the erection of the guillotine in

Mexico.[73] Such examples suggest the mood of the times. There was no chance of the guillotine operating in Mexico; no doubt its advocate hoped, with this rhetorical flourish, to alarm those Huertistas who skulked in safe obscurity. And, no doubt, many of the reports – often rumours – of arrests, confiscations and executions were exaggerated. The American consul at Guadalajara, who wrote aghast of 'hundreds – perhaps thousands – of executions and assassinations' in the city, could offer only four definite cases.[74] But the evidence (not just from foreign sources) of a sustained campaign of retribution, both official and unofficial, is overwhelming; and, if the numbers were inflated or the details embellished, this no doubt thickened the miasma of apprehension which hung in the air, and sickened the well-to-do.

Running like a constant thread through these episodes was the persecution of the Spaniards. Villa had expelled them from Chihuahua and, despite his susceptibility to American suggestions, remained 'absolutely uncompromising' on this question when it was raised.[75] Spaniards flocked to Veracruz (where the resident Spanish community watched the revolution's progress with mounting anxiety); they bore the brunt of the looting of Acapulco; and they even suffered at the hands of Huerta's disintegrating forces – such as Argumedo's irregulars, whose association with Huerta could not mask their popular, revolutionary origins.[76] On the west coast, a US admiral noted, 'there is a strong prejudice against the well-to-do people, especially against the Spanish'; at Tampico, Luis Caballero threatened 800 Spaniards with expulsion if they did not take out Mexican citizenship.[77] Many of the acts of persecution already mentioned – at Papantla, Mazatlán and elsewhere – involved Spanish victims; and often they alone of foreign communities were singled out for harsh treatment.[78] In Tehuacán and Puebla, for example, the Spaniards suffered persecution, while 'throughout this entire region the rights and property of Americans seem[ed] to be respected'.[79] Again, Argumedo's men and other dispersed irregulars joined with Zapatistas and the nominally Constitutionalist forces of Máximo Rojas of Tlaxcala in a series of attacks on the local textile mills, in which Spanish commercial and industrial interests were major targets: an example of 'worker–peasant' militancy, perhaps even of revolutionary Luddism.[80]

Spaniards were also well represented among two groups which merit special attention: the landlords and the Church. Both suffered seriously from revolutionary retribution, but in different ways. Attacks on landlords were coeval with the Revolution: they dated from 1910–11, and they demonstrated the central importance of the agrarian question in the Revolution. Particularly in the early years, they were often localised, violent, and 'spontaneous', in that they derived from popular resentments requiring no outside encouragement. Madero's or Carranza's rebellion might afford an opportunity for agrarian protest, but it did not need to clap spurs to the sides of a sluggish, inert *campesinado*. The *campesinado* could move of its own volition, as it had in the past. Attacks on the Church, however, were initially rarer and only became commonplace during the Constitutionalist revolution. And, while it would be wrong to deny the existence of popular anti-clericalism, analogous to popular agrarianism, nevertheless the great bulk of anti-clerical sentiment and policy was imported from outside the popular movement, and derived from urban, educated, middle-class groups. Agrarianism welled up from the depths of rural society; anti-clericalism radiated out from the cities. Agrarian reform was imposed upon the Revolution's middle-class, educated leadership, while this leadership, in turn, foisted its anti-clericalism on the countryside. The terms of trade – scarcely equal – will be evaluated in the final chapter. Here, we simply note the origins of the exchange. For if, on the one hand, 1913–14 saw the launch of anti-clericalism into the mainstream of the Revolution, it also saw, on the other, the establishment of agrarian reform not just as a popular, 'spontaneous' demand, but also as a conscious, even cynical official policy. Certain Constitutionalist leaders recognised that a degree of agrarian reform was not only unavoidable (it was happening already: the task was to guide it) but also productive of political advantage, in that it served to win popular support and weaken the power of the landed class. This is also a theme to be pursued in the final chapter.

In analysing the agrarianism of 1913–14, however, two important, related problems must be recognised. First, the problem of sources. The city is always better reported than the countryside; much of the agrarian protest of the early years of the Revolution is only dimly and imperfectly perceived. The evidence is, in my view, sufficient to show the importance of agrarian factors in the Revolution, as well as the major turnover of landownership which the Revolution brought about, even before 1914 (I am referring to immediate, *de facto* landownership: the long term outcome was a different matter). But many questions (who obtained what, on what terms, and for how long) remain unanswered.[81] With the growth of 'official' agrarianism there are more sources, but sources – indicating governmental action or intention – which tell the story from the top, often suggesting a lack of energy or initiative on the part of the *campesinos* themselves. But peasant resistance to 'official' reform cannot be taken as proof of resistance to all reform. Furthermore, it would be wrong to infer from the greater volume of sources (especially those clearly packaged and labelled 'Agrarian Reform') a profound change in the character of the revolution, around 1914, as 'political' demands gave way to 'social', 'liberal' to 'agrarian'. For this would be to follow in the footsteps of our urban, educated, middle-class predecessors, for many of whom agrarian reform was a discovery made around 1914 – whether as a joyous revelation or a grudging recognition of the inevitable. Like the New World, agrarianism existed long before it was discovered by newcomers. Indeed, as the analogy suggests, the discovery and appropriation of the agrarian cause by newcomers were by no means unqualified benefits for the natives, who could not always recognise in the new agrarian slogans, policies and myths the old objectives for which they had fought.

The second problem follows from this and concerns motivation. Why did the newcomers take up and prosecute policies of agrarian reform? Indeed, where is the line to be drawn (if it is to be drawn at all) between the 'spontaneous', particularistic, agrarian demands of the *campesinos* – demands for specific *reivindicaciones* in the locality – and the more calculating, instrumental, and universalistic agrarian policies of the revolutionary leaders – policies providing for agrarian reform in grand, national, impersonal terms? Were these leaders cynical opportunists; or genuine converts to agrarianism, whose revolutionary experience (like Che Guevara's in the Sierra Maestra) opened their eyes to the legitimate demands of the *campesinos*, which they now disinterestedly endorsed?[82] The problem is compounded by the fact that, with time, the pioneer, popular agrarians transcended their original, particularistic concerns and framed general, potentially national programmes: Zapata's defence of the fields of Anenecuilco led to the Plan of Ayala and a spate of subsequent manifestoes; the Cedillos' conflict with La Angostura was the first step towards a general, solemn commitment to settle the agrarian problem by 'the distribution and breaking up of lands monopolised by the caciques, which supreme ideal will alone make our beloved country great'.[83] The programmes of mature agrarian rebels like these do not sound so different from the equivalent statements of the 'new agrarians', the *políticos* who may have boarded the *agrarista* bandwagon for the most cynical motives. Yet there were certainly *políticos* whose conversion was genuine, and whose involvement in specific, local agrarian issues derived from sincere concern rather than shameless self-interest: Múgica at Los Borregos, for example, or some years later, Gildardo Magaña in his championship of the *surianos*.[84] And, a final complication, it may not always be that intention and outcome correspond: the cynical manipulator may bring real benefits; the disinterested idealist may prove a liability.

In other words, 1914 may be taken as the year when 'official', revolutionary agrarianism became established, superimposed upon – often subtly blending with – the older, popular agrarianism out of which it had developed. Though analytically valid, and vital for an understanding of the post-revolutionary settlement, this distinction is not always easy to draw in practice. There were clearcut cases: compare, for example, the Yaquis' inarticulate but temporarily successful struggle to recover their homelands with the gimcrack agrarianism displayed by plausible conservative *émigrés*.[85] In many cases, however, official and unofficial reform intertwined. And it would be simplistic to label specific acts of reform (such as Borregos or Gavira's *reparto* in Tlaxcala) as belonging neatly to one or other category. Rather, these categories denote ideal-types which, while remaining analytically distinct, may be seen to inhere and co-exist in actual historical circumstances; they are useful since they enable the great welter of facts which may be subsumed under the heading of 'Agrarian Reform' to be better organised and understood.

It is clear that in northern and central Mexico the revolution had a decisive effect on the countryside, driving out a large proportion of the landlord class, of the managers and *mayordomos* who worked for them, and of the officials and police who had previously sustained them. The scope of this turnover is evident in the land grants recorded in Zapata's correspondence (which go far beyond Morelos), and in the requests for the restitution of confiscated land which crowd the Carranza archive.[86] But how did this turnover affect the relations of production? Sometimes the departure of the landed elite simply left a vacuum, and the fields went untilled.[87] But, given the prevalent demand for land, food and revenue, it was usual for new owners, managers and cultivators to take over. In the case of Villista Chihuahua, as we have seen, there was an extensive confiscation of large estates, to the value of 200–300m. pesos.[88] But the nature of Chihuahuan agriculture and the exigencies of the Villista war effort precluded any massive *reparto*; many of the estates were sublet or taken over by Villista generals, 'as to the effectiveness and honesty of [whose] administration, opinion differs'.[89] Though the Villista Governor Fidel Avila prepared for a genuine land distribution, and a team of agronomists began the work of surveying, the fortunes of war turned against Villismo before anything was accomplished.[90] It does not follow, however, that the agrarian changes effected in Chihuahua in 1913–15 were therefore irrelevant. The replacement of Porfirian oligarchs and caciques by ex-bandits and ex-vaqueros was a change of some social consequence; and it seems likely that in both Chihuahua and the Laguna the era of Villista rule saw a shift in the climate of rural labour relations and of tenancy or sharecropping arrangements.[91] Katz notes the absence of 'land occupations and jacqueries' in Villista territory, and is right to attribute this (in part) to the absence of a powerful, land-hungry peasantry (Villismo was, in origin, a movement of *serrano* protest, whose *agrarista* content was limited, though not negligible); but the absence of (known) land seizures and jacqueries may also reflect the relative contentment of the rural population in these years, now that the old elite had been ejected and conditions had improved.[92] How many jacqueries were there in Zapatista Morelos?

Elsewhere in the north, agrarian change was also bound up with the prosecution of the war. It was not that agrarian demands were absent; rather, they were of secondary importance and could not determine the course of policy as they could in Morelos. While in Morelos *agrarismo* dictated the character of the civil war, in the north the civil war dictated the character of *agrarismo*. Committed to a long, conventional war, the northern leaders needed a continuous supply of men and resources; they could not halt cash-crop production; and they would not jeopardise their mass armies by exposing them to the lure of land distribution. So, throughout the north, confiscated estates were often kept intact, and worked for the good of the cause, either directly or through commercial contracts. In Sonora, this was evident from the early days of the Constitutionalist revolution, and it proceeded in typically efficient, Sonoran fashion, with no hint of populist agrarianism.[93] Though the Sonorans were later to become expert practitioners of official, instrumental agrarian reform on a national scale, this was still some way off, and, during these years of unofficial, popular *agrarismo*, the Yaquis alone championed its cause within Sonora. When, in 1914, Villa sent an engineer to Sonora to 'cut up [the] big farms and divide the land among the peons', Governor Maytorena politely informed him that his visit was 'premature', and Villa's emissary had to sell his valuables to buy a ticket back to Chihuahua.[94] Even if apocryphal, the story contains a neat moral: despite their superficial resemblance, popular and official agrarianism could stand poles apart; it was one thing to carve up estates in the midst of social revolution, quite another for the state to preside over a gradual, controlled reform, when peace prevailed and due process of law could be followed.

Even in Sonora, mestizo leaders had been obliged to offer agrarian concessions to the Yaquis. And in states where resistance to such demands was weaker, the extensive confiscations clearly involved measures of distribution and reform, not just exploitation for the benefit of the war. In Durango, confiscated estates were placed in 'public' hands and haciendas were either worked 'directly for the benefit of all' or parcelled out among friends and retainers of rebel commanders, notably the Arrietas.[95] Some haciendas were specifically divided up; and, as early as the summer of 1913, an observer reported that 'what planting is done will mostly be by the *pelados* working independently of the owners'.[96] For this, the Arrietas received the distant commendation of the Magonistas.[97] In Zacatecas too Pánfilo Natera established a Department of Agriculture of the Division of the Centre to supervise the running of confiscated estates – said to number nearly 150 in the region.[98] Natera's policies raised the hopes of 'lots of ignorant peons who think the millennium has arrived', with the prospect of land for all.[99] No doubt most were disappointed; but it is hard to imagine that a rudimentary, populist regime like Natera's could have maintained a strict, bureaucratic control over such extensive holdings. Zacatecas was not Sonora; it was not even Chihuahua. The need to export cash-crops and cattle was less exigent thus far south, and the very physical appearance of the rebels in this region indicated their lower level of organisation and professionalisation. Even if Natera was against agrarian reform – and there is no evidence that he was – it is unlikely that he could have prevented its *de facto* occurrence in the circumstances. It may be that the phenomenon was so clear and irresistible by traditional methods that a dozen Zacatecas landowners were reported as offering their lands for division in the summer of 1914.[100]

There was no millennium; Zacatecas did not become a land flowing with milk and honey (no more did Morelos). But this switch from hacienda to peasant production – from commercial farming to '*pelados* working independently of the owners' – was a significant kind of agrarian reform. And, even in the north, it was a familiar phenomenon. The 1916 corn harvest was a 'peon' crop, 'planted by the peons in patches on other people's land, by sufferance or as tenants of the military chiefs'.[101] It is worth noting, too, that in those parts of the north where the revolution displayed less plebeian virulence than in Zacatecas, and where land confiscations were as much political as social measures (in that the chosen victims were 'hostile to the Constitutionalist cause'), still the beneficiaries might be 'entirely poor people', who thereby gained access to land they would not otherwise have enjoyed.[102]

In much of Mexico, of course, the agrarian question was central to the revolution: it was what the protagonists were fighting about. But the fight, as we have noted, could be conducted on different scales and at different levels of sophistication. Around Cd del Maíz (SLP) the Cedillos and their ally Carrera Torres had built up a formidable force, which drove landlords and Federals from the region and instituted their 'simple brand of communism'. In other words, haciendas were confiscated, land was distributed, and a form of control was established over artisan manufacturing and retailing.[103] Again, some estates were commercially exploited for the sake of the war; but – as in Morelos – this was compatible with extensive, popular agrarian reform.[104] The fact that the chief beneficiaries were either *rancheros* and smallholders, like the Cedillos themselves, or labourers whom the Cedillos liberated from oppressive conditions and debt-bondage, rather than 'communal' villagers; or that the Cedillos preferred to grant land in fee simple (especially to their retainers) rather than as *ejidos*, cannot detract from the significance of the reform.[105] No less than *ejidal* restoration, private grants strengthened the peasantry at the expense of the landlord, especially when they were backed by the Cedillista regime, and the landlords themselves were in no doubt that they were cast as victims, as one of them put it, 'just because we are *hacendados*'.[106] To limit agrarian demands and reforms to the communal sector alone is to present a distorted picture, in which the absolutely central importance of rural class relations within the Revolution is lost.

For, even in Morelos, the classic case, there was more to the conflict than the recovery of communal [sic] land.[107] Here, by 1914, the regime of planters and bosses was over. Huerta and the Federals had been defeated and driven out. Yet, despite their size and military success, Zapata's forces had not become an autonomous army, had not sundered the bonds which tied them to the villages. They did not, in other words, go the way of Villista professionalisation, and this for a variety of reasons: their geographical isolation, the absence of a vigorous adjacent market and, above all, the fundamental character and social origins of their revolt, which differentiated them from the northern *serranos*.[108] Try as he might to revive the devastated sugar mills,

Zapata could only get four back in operation, and the contribution they made to Zapatista funds was 'meagre'.[109] Instead, sugar gave way to corn and beans – a reversal of the secular trend of the Porfiriato. Radicalised by three years of war, the Zapatistas refused to allow the planters back, dropped any idea of peaceful co-existence with the plantation, and confiscated all haciendas without indemnity. Under the dynamic administration of Manuel Palafox the existing, *de facto* gains of the villages were extended and legitimised: agrarian commissions staffed by young agronomists from the National School of Agriculture were recruited to survey the lands, and a hundred or so pueblos received officially delimited land grants. By early 1915 Palafox was ready to despatch similar commissions into Guerrero, Puebla, Mexico and Hidalgo.[110]

Thus, while in Chihuahua the big houses of confiscated haciendas fell prey to Villista parvenus, and while in the capital Constitutionalist chiefs commandeered the town houses of the Científicos, in Morelos it was the young agronomists – some of whom, like Felipe Carrillo Puerto and Fidel Velázquez, would later enjoy spectacular political careers – who occupied the deserted mansions of the southern planters.[111] The land surveys which these – the '*ingenieritos*', as the villagers called them – carried out formed part of a programme that was 'official' in that it proceeded rationally, peacefully, according to legal title and Zapatista agrarian legislation. But the bureaucracy served the agrarian cause, not vice versa, and the reform was intimately linked to the needs, traditions and peculiarities of each community. Due respect was given to the 'custom and usage' of each village; decrees harked back to 'the time of the viceroyalty'; and it was stipulated that both state and federal government would refrain from interfering in municipal agrarian matters.[112] Zapatista agrarian reform, though self-consciously legal, thus allowed for local particularism and independence, and was no charter for the creation of labyrinthine and impersonal bureaucracy.

Political and agrarian independence went together. Municipal self-government was essential to preserve newly recovered lands. Hence, local authorities were elected, to whom the Zapatista military deferred; *jefes* who encroached on civilian powers were admonished by Zapata himself; law and order remained the prerogative of the village councils. 'The result', Womack writes, 'was the real possibility of local democracies.'[113] The real possibility; but not yet the actuality. The survival of Morelos' civilian power would depend not only on the self-denial of the Zapatista military, but also on outside events and forces, and their impact within the state. But for the time being, the Morelos revolution went its own way, reasserting traditional rights and values – a statement which, in the light of previous observations, need not be contradictory.[114] In the three years since its inception, Zapatismo had grown more powerful, articulate and – in that it now denied the plantation a place in Morelos, which it had not done at the outset – more radical. But the movement's fundamental continuity, evident in its agrarian aims, in the paramountcy of traditional, civilian authority was impressive, and contrasted with the changes which had overtaken Chihuahua's popular revolution in the same period.

At the most general, comparative level, the Zapatistas still sought to dissolve their 'subordinate relationships to a group of controlling outsiders' and to pursue their ultimate goal, 'the utopia of a free association of rural clans'.[115] And in doing so, they necessarily repudiated the Porfirian–Científico vision of a progressive, centralised, urbanised, capitalist, exporting Mexico. It is remarkable to what extent the Zapatistas had, between 1910 and 1914, imposed their own counter-vision upon Morelos. The planters and caciques had been driven out, and with them went the opulent life style which exemplified the polarisation of Morelos society. Balls gave way to bullfights and the highlight of the season was the Yautepec *corrida*, held in a contrived *plaza de toros* and attended by rebel chiefs from the whole state, Zapata included. Save for the few *jefes* who sported *charro* outfits, the *campesino*'s baggy white drawers were now *de rigueur*; sartorial sanctions had changed since the days when Díaz's officials tried to enforce the wearing of respectable trousers, and the well-dressed now risked physical assault. Save for the *ingenieritos*, whose efforts earned popular respect, outsiders and city folk were not welcome in Morelos. Nor were the railways, those key instruments of Porfirian centralisation and development: the villagers prevented train crews from taking on water, or cutting timber for fuel and sleepers.[116] Most important of all, as sugar gave way to staples, food became plentiful and the standard of living rose higher than it had been for years. For Morelos, these were the fat years of the revolution; but prosperity, like village democracy, depended on a degree of isolation from the harsh world outside.[117]

Zapatismo, meanwhile, spread beyond Morelos to neighbouring states, merging with indigenous rebel movements. In Guerrero, the battle between village and hacienda was less significant: though there were land seizures (at Chilapa, for example, where Señora Eucaria Apreza's property was placed 'at the disposition of the Revolution, to be worked by the needy'), it was the refusal to pay rents which represented the most common form of rural protest.[118] This was enough to alarm the state's landlords, especially since by 1915 something like two-thirds of the state (by area) and five-sixths (by population) were reckoned to be under 'Zapatista' domination.[119] This Zapatista territory, a well-to-do Constitutionalist observed, looked 'fine and prosperous', with a rich harvest of corn and other crops.[120] The Zapatista *reparto* also spilled over into the Federal District, Mexico state (where Iñigo Noriega's Chalco property suffered), Hidalgo and, above all, Puebla.[121] In the latter state, there was extensive land distribution around Tepeji, while in the Matamoros valley 'work patterns changed dramatically as peasants from the villages invaded the haciendas and cultivated subsistence crops of corn and beans on the former [sugar] cane lands'.[122] Even if managers stayed put, they sometimes did so by conniving at peasant demands. Cristóbal Sosa, left to manage the Hacienda San Pedro Coxcotán, 'turned it over to the Indians, dividing the profits with them', such that the owners received nothing.[123] Throughout 'Zapatista' Mexico, therefore, agrarian demands and solutions varied; but it cannot be doubted that there was a major transfer of power and resources away from landlord and cacique, and in favour of the peasantry – and not just the 'communal' peasantry.

In Tlaxcala, too, a vigorous agrarian movement was under way, and 'control of the countryside was slipping out of the landowners' and authorities' hands'.[124] *Hacendados* began to pull out of the Atoyac Valley as early as 1911; by mid-1914 most had gone, and those who left managers in charge soon found that – as in Puebla – they reached deals with the local *agraristas*. They had no choice. The peasantry controlled the Atoyac Valley – though their control was vitiated by constant squabbling. Rival rebel leaders competed in urging and sanctioning *de facto* agrarian reform: Arenas in the south west of the state, Máximo Rojas around Chiautempán (these two both local men, as were 80% of the Tlaxcalan revolutionary elite), while around Apizaco the Veracruzano Gavira sought to establish good relations with local villagers, arming them and making a land grant to San Cosme Xalostoc.[125] With this case we run full tilt into the problems of interpretation already mentioned. Gavira was operating away from home (he was no peasant himself) and he needed backing against the Zapatistas. His grant to Xalostoc was not necessarily cynical, but it promised political advantage over and above its intrinsic, social merit. In some other examples, the pursuit of advantage seems to have been paramount. Late in 1914 Ramón Iturbe commanded a fractious garrison at San Blas (Sin.): it was a time of political crisis, his troops were deserting, and his own factional allegiance was out of line with local opinion; Iturbe therefore started carving up the nearby haciendas, beginning with the American Sinaloa Land Company. 'It is probable', noted an observer, 'that this move is purely political on the part of those in authority, to stem the tide that is gradually sweeping them down.'[126]

Many other *repartos* were promised and undertaken between 1913 and 1915: by Cándido Navarro, shortly before his death; by Francisco Carrera Torres (the first *reparto* in Guanajuato); by Gertrudis Sánchez in Michoacán and Francisco Múgica in Tabasco. By the spring of 1915 'parts of several estates and lands in the Canton of Veracruz [had] been taken to be divided among the lower classes in accordance with the programme for agrarian reform'.[127] In many cases, the evidence is skimpy and even suspect. At best it indicates that *de facto* agrarian reform was being talked about, promised, and perhaps carried out. The uncertainty is unfortunate since, taken together, these cases represented – pardon the expression – the interface between official and unofficial, guided and 'spontaneous' agrarian reform. It was here that the new revolutionary leaders got to grips with the fundamental agrarian problem; and whether they did so as disinterested redeemers of the dispossessed, or smart manipulators of the gullible, cannot be established without much more detailed research. No doubt, the truth varied from person to person and case to case; and, at our current level of knowledge, it is hard to say whether the manipulative, politically-inspired reform of the 1920s, represented a departure from, or a consummation of, the localised, pioneer reforms of the previous decade.[128]

As individual *cabecillas* faced the problem in the localities − dispensing social justice or building political capital, or both − so the Revolution's intellectuals, journalists and high *políticos* developed their own, official *agrarismo*. A month after Múgica's stirring speech at Los Borregos, Pastor Rouaix, revolutionary governor of Durango, promulgated the first state agrarian law − the work, it should be noted, of a qualified engineer, not originally a native of the state, and a governor whose exercise of power was much inhibited by the popular *cabecillas* who surrounded him.[129] In Washington, Cabrera convinced President Wilson of the importance of the agrarian question (for which Wilson soon earned Zapata's warm commendation); and at Torreón the old PLM activist Antonio Villareal saw to it that the agreement between Villa and Carranza contained a commitment 'to emancipate the *campesinos* economically, making a fair distribution of land, or by other methods which tend to a resolution of the agrarian problem'.[130] Sniffing the wind, Emilio Vázquez Gómez resumed his vocal championship of the agrarian cause.[131] Conservative emigrés, as we have seen, joined the chorus; so did a few Sonorans, who had hitherto guarded a discreet silence in these matters. First Juan Cabral then Eduardo Ruiz (an educated man, native of Cananea, now Governor of Colima) declared their commitment to agrarian reform policies which would better the lot of the poor; Salvador Alvarado soon carried the word to Yucatán.[132] Men began to con Carranza's speeches, to discover whether a similar commitment could be found, and of this Carranza was no doubt aware.[133] When, early in 1915, Carranza came out with such a commitment, he was not so much making a violent U-turn, as easing himself out into the flow of traffic. *Agrarismo* − of the official, rhetorical, orderly kind − was now fashionable. As an eloquent conservative put it:[134]

the Agrarian Reform has revived in my memory some fond recollections. In my rustic youth I could notice after the first spring rains, with the bursting forth of the green grass and the formation of the first puddles, innumerable toads of unknown origin coming from all directions. There was something fascinating in the exquisite nastiness of these animals: an emerald, bright and resplendent, in their foreheads ... The revolutionary puddle has done just that: it has thrown out on the Mexican soil the most hideous beings which, however, carry on their foreheads a bright idea: Agrarian Reform.

Thus, the toads of the Revolution besported their new, coruscating acquisition − at once talisman, adornment and badge of revolutionary rectitude. But, as these manifestations of the new, official *agrarismo* proliferated, so the older, unofficial, popular variety continued its course, now sometimes in tandem with official sponsorship and legitimation, still often spontaneous, isolated, and obscure. Indeed, so long as political chaos prevailed and faction contested with faction, legitimation had no certain basis, and communities which had received land under one official aegis reverted to 'unofficial', even 'rebel' status once that aegis was removed.[135] And legitimation was often superficial and arbitrary: a mask clapped onto the features of old agrarian quarrels. *Which* mask was chosen would depend as much on considerations of local expediency as on a careful study of the agrarian programmes of Carranza, Villa, Zapata and others. In some cases, the tail very clearly wagged the dog: in other words, it was not the grand programme which pulled in recruits (as is often supposed, for both 1910 and 1915) but rather the immediate prospect of securing the aid and comfort of a powerful, national caudillo, for the furtherance of a local, agrarian struggle. The programme was not irrelevant: it showed that the caudillo's heart was in the right place; it was a statement of intent; and it legitimised *de facto* change, so long as his writ still ran in the region. But it was the caudillo's power – his capacity to deliver the goods – rather than his agrarian prospectus which really counted. Few if any local *reivindicaciones* were couched in terms of Molina Enríquez's Plan de Texcoco – a Plan eminently popular and *agrarista* but lacking all political muscle; conversely, Carrancistas could win support, even within Zapata's orbit, and despite Carranza's indifferent agrarian record, if they lent their muscle to local agrarian causes.[136] Like the urban working class (and like peasants elsewhere), the Mexican *campesinos* were necessarily practical-minded; the delivery of the goods, even in a slightly shop-worn condition, counted for more than the glossy pictures in the prospectus.[137] And now, as in 1913, the political fragmentation of the country encouraged numerous alliances and allegiances which, though arising from basic economic – especially agrarian – conflicts, were determined by clientelistic expedience, rather than ideological consistency.[138]

Francisco Puertas, for example, led a revolt at Aticpac (Ver.) in 1914, captaining a crowd of 'unknowns'.[139] Before long he was styling himself a Constitutionalist colonel, claiming allegiance to Pablo González, and had acquired an ascendancy over the local authorities. This influence was put to the service of a kind of crude *agrarismo*. Among several local landlords against whom Puertas campaigned, the chief victim was Vicente García. In 1914, Puertas and his men ransacked García's house, making off with his land titles, alleging that García 'considerably maltreated' his tenants, and promising that if he did not stop he (Puertas) would 'personally come and get Sr García, tie him to his saddle-horn, and carry him into the presence of General Pablo González, who was his *jefe*'. The feud continued. In 1916, Puertas demanded of the local authorities why García's family was exempted from the *faena de caminos* (road repairs) and said he would be glad to make them break rocks. In

1917, backed by the authorities, Puertas expropriated and divided up García's land, alleging that it had been illegally acquired in the first place and that 'the principles of the revolution carry as a consequence the distribution of land'. The properties of other families were also affected. It is unlikely that many permanent changes resulted: before long, Puertas was languishing in gaol. But for three years he had waged a vigorous, parochial, agrarian campaign, counting not on the plans and programmes of revolutionary administrations (though these afforded a certain legitimacy), but rather on local influences, *de facto* power, and the alleged support of a mighty *patrón* (of minimal *agrarista* commitment).

A final example, similar in character but with the official labels reversed, is worth mentioning. Back in 1911, Ometepec (Gro) had been the scene of a classic jacquerie, which affected several communities on the Guerrero–Oaxaca borders, causing a number of deaths. Among the victims was the commander of the town guard at Pinotepa Nacional, José Santiago Baños; and his brother, Juan José Baños, served as captain in the Maderista forces of Enrique Añorve which put down the rebellion, restoring stolen titles to the landlords and administering summary justice.[140] Baños, a cattle rancher, returned to his home town of Jamiltepec (Oax.) and became military commander. But the troubles continued, and Baños and his Jamiltepec forces found themselves engaged in a running battle with a congeries of 'rebels', 'bandits', or 'Indians' (they were variously described), whose headquarters was Poza Verde, but who also hailed from villages involved in the 1911 uprising, such as Huehuetán. Now, their prime targets were Jamiltepec and Pinotepa, and their chief opponent was Baños. Through 1912 and 1913 they rustled cattle and raided; in the autumn of 1913 a full-scale rebellion was anticipated but averted by Baños' pre-emptive arrests and executions.[141] In the summer of 1914, however, the Pozaverdeños mounted a successful coup against Jamiltepec, seizing power, sacking some properties and setting up their own authorities in the town – to which end they got the support of the new state authorities of Oaxaca, led by Guillermo Meixueiro. Baños reacted precisely as revolutionary logic required: he repudiated the Oaxaca authorities, recognised the Carranza regime and the Plan of Guadalupe (eighteen months after its promulgation) and set about organising four companies of 'Constitutionalists of the South' to drive out the Poza Verde rebels. Baños recovered Jamiltepec in September, lost it again in December, and successfully defended Pinotepa against his old enemies early in 1915

On the face of it, this was simply another of the complex family and community feuds which littered Mexico during the Porfiriato and Revolution. As such, it has attracted little interest: it scarcely impinged on state, let alone national politics, and – to the extent that anyone has tried to make sense of what happened – it has been seen as a story of law and order, police and bandits.[142] But it is clear even from the pro-Baños account that there was more to it than this, and that the Jamiltepec troubles closely paralleled the Ometepec events of 1911, with Constitutionalist nomenclature replacing Maderista. As so often, the national labels are misleading: the Pozaverdeños affiliated to Meixueiro and his 'reactionary' regime in Oaxaca; they attacked Jamiltepec with cries of 'Viva Félix Díaz!', hurling insults at the Carrancista 'cockroaches'.[143] Conversely, Baños published Constitutionalist decrees on political and social reform, and put out his own manifesto endorsing agrarian reform and a measure of economic nationalism.[144] Affiliation and ideology should not deceive, however. In terms of social background and material interest Baños was a well-to-do rancher, and the Pozaverdeños were popular, agrarian rebels. It was Baños who protected the 'well-off families' when they were driven from Pinotepa; it was the merchants of Jamiltepec who financed his garrison, and the 'honourable people' who applauded his summary executions; it was the artisans and merchants of the town who beat off a rebel attack in January 1915.[145] It is clear, too, that the conflict between the feuding pueblos represented more than simple territorial rivalry (of the kind which affected even the Zapatista villages of Morelos).[146] Jamiltepec was the political and economic centre of the region, inhabited by well-to-do ranchers and merchants. The Pozaverdeños were different people with different concerns: this may be inferred not simply from their propensity to raid and rustle, nor from their alliance with the Zapatistas of Guerrero (from whom they received their military ranks), but rather from repeated instances drawn from the (pro-Jamiltepec) history of the conflict.[147] Most were illiterate – only a quarter of the 186 signatories of their July 1914 Plan could sign their names – and they repeatedly gave out that their grievances against Jamiltepec were agrarian: they called for a 'reparto de las tierras', inveighed against the *ganaderos*, and, in another, ill-written manifesto, laid claim to 'the lands of our fathers [which] were seized'. They fought, so they said, to free the people from the 'yoke of *caciquismo*', now represented by Baños and his Constitutionalists.[148] And, apart from Baños, they bore a special animus against rich landlord–merchants like the Spaniard Dámaso Gómez of Jamiltepec, whom they persecuted 'for reasons concerning lands', rustling his cattle and finally sacking his store when they occupied the town. Robbing the *ganaderos* was in fact one of their main activities: they stole fifty head of cattle from one ranch, 'telling the mayordomo who looked after the animals that he, too, could sell them ... since the Zapatista cause conceded this right'.[149]

Here, then, was a local conflict on the periphery of a state that was peripheral to the Revolution; a conflict which, from the national perspective of then and now, seems insignificant. For the locals, it was different: for several years after the original 1911 outbreak, the whole region from Río Ometepec to the Río Verde was kept in a state of agitation by these inter-pueblo battles, fought to maintain or eliminate the politico-economic dominance of the merchant–landlord elite. In origin and character this struggle was not so different from that waged in staunchly Zapatista pueblos like Tepoztlán. The difference lay in the fact that Tepoztlán was sucked into the vortex of a more extensive, organised revolutionary movement, while the Poza Verde rebels remained – despite their loose affiliation with Meixueiro or Julián Blanco – isolated, inarticulate and largely anonymous. Their agrarianism was not translated into ringing phrases and enduring laws; they occupied the extreme end of the *agrarista* spectrum, far removed from the official, incipiently bureaucratised *agrarismo* of the educated *político*. Indeed, there is both a lesson and an irony – though not necessarily a contradiction – in the conduct of Baños, who stoutly defended the interests of the Jamiltepec *ganaderos*, while espousing the official *agrarismo* of the Constitutionalist programme. One final point emerges. Here was a sustained, if parochial, agrarian conflict, which historians of the nation have entirely ignored, and even historians of the state (of Oaxaca) have neglected – dismissing the rebels' activities as meaningless 'actos vandálicos'.[150] How many other such attributions – of vandalism, robbery, brigandage, vendetta and so on, which strew the pages of books, newspapers, consular reports and official documents – conceal the underlying conflicts of which these were the outward expression? How many communities had a Dario Atristaín who, painstakingly recording the events he had participated in a few years before, left clear if unintentional insights into what happened at Jamiltepec during the Revolution – and why?

LANDLORDS, PRIESTS AND OFFICERS

Facing agrarian revolt, Baños and his allies mounted a successful resistance, ultimately under the Constitutionalist banner. Landlord resistance to such threats was a notable feature of 1914 and after, and it indicated two things: first, that the threats were real enough (few landlords would have dismissed the Constitutionalist revolution as a mild, political upset), and second, that some landlords now possessed both the capacity and disposition to resist. So far in this account, it has been the feeble response of the landlord class which catches the eye – its failure, for example, to aid the Huerta regime beyond the provision, and that sometimes grudging, of funds and *matériel*. After 1914, however, we note the quite sudden, increased incidence of successful landlord resistance to the revolution. The craven emigré of 1913 gives way to the doughty counter-revolutionary of 1915; hitherto effete grandees, the land-lords of Mexico start behaving like Carlists. The explanation is quite simple: the locus of the revolution has shifted; above all, it has shifted from north to south. In 1913–14, rebellion had flared in those regions where the power of landlord and cacique was most resented and precarious: in Chihuahua, Durango, the Laguna, eastern San Luis, Morelos, Tlaxcala and parts of other central states. The pattern was hardly surprising, given that hatred of expansionist landlords and oppressive caciques provided the main fuel of popular revolt. In contrast, the Bajío and centre–west, Oaxaca, southern Veracruz and most of the south-east were relatively quiet, affected by banditry or by isolated agrarian protests (at Naranja, Jamiltepec, Acayucán and so on) which were insufficient to undermine the status quo. The records of one of Hidalgo's big pulque haciendas show no marked hiatus in 1914; San José de Gracia lived through the period without major upheaval; and pockets of *agrarismo* like Naranja could be forcibly dealt with. Indeed, on the hacienda as in the mine, the revolution could reinforce the dependence of labourers on their employer.[151]

By the summer of 1914, however, with the descent of the Constitutionalists on Mexico City, many of these central and southern regions faced their first encounter with a powerful, organised revolutionary movement, which both posed an intrinsic threat and also stimulated hitherto weak, indigenous revolutionary causes into greater activity. Local *cabecillas* like Julián Medina in Jalisco, Nicolás Flores in Hidalgo, Luis Felipe Domínguez in Tabasco, now became Constitutionalist generals (of Carrancista or Villista stripe) and thereby acquired both a certain legitimacy and a quantity of coveted American weaponry.[152] Landlords and caciques who had coped hitherto were now in a quandary. But they did not capitulate as their counterparts of 1913 had in Chihuahua, Morelos or the Laguna. Their very survival so far – the very success, for example, of the Naranja landlords in repressing local *agraristas* – bespoke a degree of political influence and military muscle which Terrazas, for all his banks and broad acres, had lacked. Indeed, survival had little to do with money and acreage: minor landlords – like the ranchers of the Sierra Alta de Hidalgo – survived more lustily than grand potentates like Terrazas or the Morelos planters.[153] Survival indicated at least partial control over rural society, exercised in a variety of forms: force, clientelism (perhaps 'paternalism'), economic power (for example, strategic control of limited resources, rather than lavish capital), even 'ideological hegemony'; and the obverse of this control was the quiescence or deference of the rural poor. The peons of Yucatán, to take an extreme case, were very different from the *bronco* Yaquis or the *campesinos* of Morelos.

Furthermore, the irruption of the Constitutionalists had diverse, unpredictable results. True, they were bent on purging 'enemies of the cause', and many landlords fell into this category. But such purges, though collectively significant, were often arbitrary and ineffective. Two outcomes in particular were both common and unanticipated, and they permitted the landlord class to survive, even to prosper: first, as pseudo-revolutionaries, colonists of Constitutionalism, 'revolucionarios de la última hora'; second, as outright counter-revolutionaries. In the first case, Constitutionalists – and Villistas in particular – allied with local landlords in search of political or military advantage. Cynicism perhaps played its part, but there was a common factor which made cynicism understandable. The Constitutionalist invaders burst upon *terra incognita*: they were poorly acquainted with the line-up of local politics (Villa's little black book did not list the undesirables of the whole Republic); and, at best, they could only rely on rough rules of thumb (like Gavira's: teachers good, clergy bad) when it came to taking advice, purging enemies, or promoting friends. Sometimes these friends were people who, back home in the north, they would have shunned; sometimes they were people whom the indigenous revolutionaries, their wishes overriden, would have preferred out of the way. The problem, incidentally, was not new; but the scope of the revolution greatly increased its significance. [154]

In addition, there was the question of timing. The landlords of Chihuahua, Morelos or the Laguna were forced into a stark choice in the course of 1913: for the revolution or against. Many ducked the issue and fled to the US, having 'plainly stated that . . . they did not care to take the chances of having to put up either for the government or for the revolution'. [155] Racing for the border guaranteed their lives and liberty, but not their lands, which were at once forfeit. In fact, most northern landlords (or, more strictly, landlords in regions of early, intense revolutionary activity including Morelos, Tlaxcala, parts of San Luis) opted to support Huerta, directly or indirectly. Hence, they were marked men long before the Constitutionalists triumphed, and no amount of repentance or recantation could remove the stigma. There was no way that Terrazas could make his peace with Villa, the Pimentels with Zapata, the Espinosa y Cuevas with the Cedillos. Of course, the landlord class was not entirely unrepresented in the ranks of Constitutionalism: witness Carranza himself, Barragán, Urquizo, Maytorena, and the Pesqueiras. But these were present by virtue of an early, risky, and sometimes reluctant adherence to the cause (it is no coincidence that all these hailed from Coahuilan and Sonoran official circles); they had established their revolutionary credentials where so many of their class had failed. [156]

Where, in contrast, the revolution had lagged behind, landlords and caciques had been spared the agony of decision; or, at least, the dilemma had been posed less starkly. If local rebellion was limited or non-existent, there was less pressure to form *Defensa Social* units, or platoons of white guards. The planters of Yucatán, for example, had contributed as much as any group to Huerta's war chest, but they were not yet compromised by an active, anti-revolutionary stance – for the good reason that there was no powerful revolutionary movement in the peninsula against which to take such a stance. Many lesser landlords in central and southern Mexico thus enjoyed a certain political anonymity, at least so far as the invading Constitutionalist captains were concerned. Some therefore had the option of a tardy, tactical conversion to the Constitutionalist cause – an option all the more feasible where the rebel commander was tolerant, unsure of himself, and keen to build up local support (the classic example, at national level, was Villa himself). The tardy converts became the 'revolucionarios de la última hora' of 1914. The breed was rarer than in 1911, since by now political affiliations were better known and more deeply etched. In staunchly revolutionary regions like Chihuahua, Durango and Morelos, in fact, 'revolucionarios de la última hora' scarcely existed. But in the centre and south they blossomed.

Indeed, it may be suggested as a general rule that the best strategy for a landlord to follow in 1914 was to acquire, if possible, a foothold and even a military rank in the revolution; to colonize Constitutionalism. Baños, with his belated adherence to the Plan of Guadalupe, managed it. So, too, did the Méndez brothers of Apam (Hgo) – well-known landowners of the region – and the Márquez brothers of Puebla, opportunist 'revolutionaries' of long standing; in these two cases it was the genial tolerance of Villismo which enabled them to pitch their tents in the rebel camp.[157] But there were fresh recruits to the Carrancista wing of the revolution, too, drawn from 'enemy' families who sought to safeguard their personal interests.[158] The best examples cropped up in the strife-ridden state of Guerrero. Here, the landlords and merchants of Acapulco and its hinterland faced a barrage of threats: the sheer fragmentation – or absence – of political authority, the welter of competing *cabecillas*, the agrarian demands of Salgado and other 'Zapatistas', the prevalent hatred of the Spaniards. Some tried self-help: the Acapulco Spaniards recruited Santiago Nogueda (himself a landowner whose plantation had been looted) to captain 500 men for the protection of their estates.[159] But such freelance operations – comparable to that of the Kennedy family in Tlaxcala – were risky, especially in revolutionary regions.[160] Other Guerrero landowners more prudently took shelter under the wing of a national revolutionary faction. The redoubtable Señora Eucaria Apreza of Chilapa, a veteran of the anti-Díaz opposition, but also a landowner, and victim and 'bitter enemy' of Zapatismo, received official recognition and a considerable quantity of money and ammunition from Carranza's envoys, thereby maintaining a sizeable (1,000) and effective force in the field.[161] (Students of the role of women in the Revolution would do well to focus on Sra Apreza and her kind, rather than the marginal, urban intellectuals who seem to populate such studies).[162] In Apreza's case, the anti-Díaz record provided a convenient passport to official recognition. This was hardly true of the Uruñuela family of Acapulco, one of the three big Spanish clans which dominated the economy of the port. Nicolás Uruñuela ran a 10,000 acre estate outside Acapulco, where Zapatista raiders had carried off the cattle and destroyed the cotton mill and ice plant, prompting Uruñuela and his brother to take 'an active part in the campaign against the Zapatista brigands'.[163] By the end of 1915 they had secured commissions in the Carrancista forces, one as captain of engineers, the other as a major and army surgeon: their expertise and antipathy to Zapatismo thus overcame the well-known anti-Spanish sentiments of the Carrancista commander, Silvestre Mariscal.

Colonising the revolution – through personal involvement or liaison with a friendly revolutionary *jefe* – represented the landlord's optimal strategy.[164]

But more common, and sometimes in the long run successful, was the path of outright resistance – resistance, that is, on the part of landlords whose local influence had not been undermined by indigenous rebellion. Hitherto secure, such men now witnessed the southward spread of the revolution, with its attendant purges and upheavals. As it threatened to engulf them, they fought back, just as the old *serrano* caciques had fought to roll back the tide of Porfirian centralisation. Indeed, it is important to note this kinship: while some landlord revolts after 1914 were clearly, ideologically conservative, in that they resisted the radical change (including land reform) implied by the revolution, there were many in which this element was secondary or absent, and where the rebels, counting on a broad basis of support of a 'polyclassist' kind, represented a collective, parochial protest against revolutionary invasion, control and centralisation. And, as revisionist scholarship now stresses, revolutionary centralisation was not always radically different from its Porfirian predecessor. In many cases, therefore, the landlord rebels of post-1914 fell within the *serrano* tradition; and the fact that they fought as nominal 'conservatives' against nominal 'revolutionaries' does not negate this kinship with earlier *serrano* movements: Tomóchic's revolt against Díaz (1889), de la Rocha's against Díaz (1911), 'Che' Gómez's against Madero (1912), Lucas' against Huerta (1913). Only a mistakenly rigid acceptance of national labels, ideologies and orthodoxies (whereby all anti-Díaz revolts must be 'revolutionary', all anti-Carranza revolts 'conservative') prevents recognition of the underlying socio-political realities which determined all such movements. Certainly Constitutionalist commitments to social reform stimulated some landlord resistance; so, too, did the behaviour of a rapacious, alien soldiery. But, more consistently and significantly, resistance derived from the Constitutionalists' firm intention to impose their control on the country, and to brook no rivals in the exercise of power. It was Hobbes' 'perpetual and restless desire after power', rather than profound differences over policy, which set Constitutionalist against landlord; and agrarian reform – far from being the cause of the conflict – was often a weapon devised to bring advantage once the conflict had already begun.

West-central Mexico (from Tepic to the Bajío), Veracruz, and the states of the south-east were the three main areas of landlord rebellion; but consideration of the last will be postponed for the moment. West-central Mexico, hitherto spared major upheaval, entered the crucible in 1914; thereafter it faced major conventional campaigns, landlord and religious revolt, endemic banditry and dearth. Landlords in the Bajío had resisted Federal depredations in the summer of 1914, and there was talk of shadowy 'private armies' being organised in Guanajuato.[165] By the end of the year, the Constitutionalists had so antagonised the people of Jalisco that 'a strong movement [was] on foot [sic] to create a revolutionary party among the wealthy *hacendados*'.[166] No organised rebellion ensued. But landlords certainly figured in the anti-Carrancista (hence nominally 'Villista') forces which operated in the centre–west thereafter: in Tepic the Natividad brothers armed local ranchers in a self-defence movement directed against Constitutionalism; *rancheros* took to the hills in protest at Carrancista abuses in Guanajuato; and in Michoacán General Moreno, 'reportedly a very wealthy man before the revolution', led several thousand troops in 1916.[167]

In Veracruz, the evidence is better and the resistance was stronger. In the canton of Misantla, a centre of coffee production and of political support for the old Porfirian cacique Teodoro Dehesa, the depredations, demands and purges of the Constitutionalists provoked a rebellion by the Armenta family, whose paterfamilias, Manuel Armenta, the owner of extensive properties, had been gaoled and mulcted by the revolutionaries. Armenta tapped a well of local support:[168]

all the owners of property . . . rushed to the active support of the movement, the result being that the army of Sr Armenta includes large and small property-owners, people farming on rented land, and people who follow other occupations, all having been victims . . . of the oppression of the Constitutionalists.

Different reports concurred that the Misantla rebellion – which by 1915 dominated the region, printed its own money, and could allegedly put 5,000 men into the field – was captained by local landowners, whether 'very wealthy planters' like Armenta himself, or *rancheros* of 'modest fortunes', all of whom bore a grudge against the revolutionaries, and whose prolonged military success indicated a significant level of local support. This – and the fact that some Misantla rebels were labelled Zapatistas – warns against too neat an equation between the rebels and agrarian reaction, between Constitutionalism and radical reform.[169]

The Misantla rebellion was not an isolated affair. Salvador Gabay, 'of a good Veracruz family', led a powerful rebel movement in the Huatusco–Córdoba region; Cástulo Pérez, a Minatitlán rancher, was active on the Isthmus. These and other rebels, operating the length of the state of Veracruz, mounted a sustained challenge to the Constitutionalist regime; and if, by 1916, they came under the generic label of Felicismo, the origins of their revolts were local, and dated back to 1914–15, well before Félix Díaz tossed his hat into the ring (yet again).[170] But the most powerful of the landlord rebels of the Gulf – so powerful that he could remain aloof from Díaz and Felicismo – was Manuel Peláez of the Huasteca Veracruzana. Like Armenta, Peláez has been depicted as a 'gangster', or a paid hireling of the oil companies.[171] His relations with the oil companies, and the general character of the 'mature' Pelaecista movement, must await the final chapter; here, it is necessary to indicate its origins, its initial independence of the companies, and its place within this broad and important category of landlord rebellions.[172] The Peláez family owned land in the oil-rich Huasteca; they had co-operated with the oil companies as landlords, attorneys and labour contractors.[173] But Manuel Peláez ('a splendid type of Mexican', as an American oil-man termed him) was driven to revolt by Constitutionalist practice in the Huasteca, rather than by any foreign incitement; indeed, though Peláez later reached a working agreement with the oil companies, this was not the result of deliberate company policy, and there is no reason why the oil interests should have set out to achieve this objective back in the early days of Peláez's rebellion, when their relations with the Constitutionalists were satisfactory.[174] Rather like Félix Díaz (in 1916) the companies came upon an existing, flourishing rebellion, which happened to suit their interests; but even then (and again like Félix Díaz) they could not play the puppeteer to Peláez's puppet.[175]

Peláez, it is true, had flirted with Felicismo in 1912.[176] But his revolt did not get under way until late 1914, and it was a year or more before his forces swelled to enable him to dominate the region between Tampico and Tuxpán. By 1916–17 he led a formidable force, numbering as many as 5,000, all drawn from the locality. 'Fear of confiscation', it was said, 'drove many of [Peláez's] soldiers . . . to take up arms'.[177] Oil company money certainly helped sustain the campaign, and Peláez no doubt acted as a 'protector of the propertied classes in the region'; but it cannot be sustained that his tenacious control of the Huasteca Veracruzana depended primarily on 'the use of terror', nor can it be denied that he enjoyed a wide measure of popular support, extending beyond the 'propertied classes'.[178] And Peláez was not alone: Alfonso Sánchez, 'a prominent merchant [of Tuxpán who] . . . had suffered greatly from *atropellos* from the Carrancista authorities' rebelled late in 1914; and Peláez was seconded by other prominent landlords, including the son of an ex-state governor and the ex-*jefe político* of Tuxpán.[179]

The landlord rebellions of 1914 thus represented a strong, collective rejection of Constitutionalist – especially Carrancista – authority; they mobilised broad support in regions, like Peláez's, where indigenous *agrarismo* was weak; and, under different factional labels, they caused the aspiring national government serious problems.[180] They also represented a back-handed compliment to the thoroughness of Constitutionalist – especially Carrancista – policy, for these were rebellions provoked by official purges, fines, confiscations (the work, in other words, of an ambitious, expansive admin-istration), not by popular insurgency. A similar distinction is evident as we turn to Constitutionalist anti-clericalism, a phenomenon which derived chiefly from the educated leadership rather than the rural rank-and-file, and which in the course of 1914 became a key item of policy. Thereby, it evoked protests and even armed resistance: the clerical equivalent of the landlord rebellions just mentioned (occasionally the two went together), and a har-binger of the great Cristero rebellion of the 1920s.

The social and ideological roots of Constitutionalist anti-clericalism are by no means easy to explain. Attempts at a general explanation will be postponed for the moment.[181] The point to establish here is that the triumph of the Constitutionalists in 1914 marked the entrance of anti-clericalism – hitherto a minor, shadowy figure – to the centre of the official revolutionary stage. In this – as in the case of 'official' agrarian reform – Luis Cabrera is the best bellwether of changing revolutionary opinion.[182] Two secondary points must also be made concerning the rather sudden take-off of Constitutionalist anti-clericalism, and they run counter to the prevailing current of present historiography.[183] The first is that anti-clericalism was not wholly absent from the popular movement: while it is true that the waves of anti-clericalism spread from the cities to the countryside, and from the educated elites to the rural masses, nevertheless there were instances, which will be mentioned, of popular anti-clericalism. Compared with popular agrarianism, it was a frail plant; but it was there. Secondly, the argument that Constitutionalist anti-clericalism derived from the Church's support for Huerta is by no means as threadbare as the (new) orthodoxy would suggest. Once again, revisionism has gone too far, and the traditional interpretations, though somewhat battered, still have some life left in them.[184]

As regards clerical opposition to the revolution, it is true that much of the (familar) evidence dates from 1914 and after: it can thus be depicted as a response to revolutionary anti-clericalism, which is the aggressor.[185] Certainly, there was an interplay between revolutionaries and Catholics: the former spurred Catholic support for Huerta, later Villa, which in turn cranked up (Carrancista) revolutionary anti-clericalism. But it is too arbitrary to give causal precedence to one side without firm evidence. Catholic support for Huerta was sufficiently early and enthusiastic to constitute an autonomous rather than a purely reflex action: Catholics, for example, welcomed the fall of Madero, and this was well before Constitutionalist anti-clericalism had reared its head. The Te Deum sung 'in Huerta's honour at the conclusion of the *Decena Trágica*' was neither an isolated nor a 'natural', politically neutral act; it was paralleled by the welcome which individual Catholics gave the new regime, by the political backing of the PCN (which was reciprocated), and by the Catholic press's denunciation of Zapatismo and other revolutionary movements (not just those of anti-clerical stamp).[186] Catholic–Huertista relations were further illustrated in the dedication of Mexico to the Sacred Heart, which the regime allowed in January 1914. Thus, even if unprovable allegations of clerical financial help are discounted, there is sufficient evidence of Catholic and clerical support for Huerta which cannot be dismissed, nor parried by Jean Meyer's uncharacteristic evasions, errors, and rhetorical questions: 'everybody, or almost everybody, supported Huerta, and the Catholics probably did so less enthusiastically than the others . . . It is true that eminent members of the PCN . . . participated in Huerta's government, but who was not a Huerta supporter?.'[187]

The Catholic constituency, of course, was heterogeneous. *El País*, the PCN, the episcopate, represented the Catholic, urban establishment: in the 1910s, as in the 1920s, this was far removed from popular, rural, Catholic sentiment. In its extreme form, this rift was exemplified by the vandalistic anti-clericalism of rebels who wore Virgin of Guadalupe badges in their hats.[188] And it is certainly true that there were parish priests – and not just in Morelos – who followed in the tradition of Hidalgo, espousing the popular cause, winning popular respect and affection.[189] But there were also priests in the provinces who opposed the revolution, usually from the pulpit, occasionally on the battle-field.[190] Even if exceptional, such cases gave credence and some justification to the rebels' assertion of clerical Huertismo. Nor was the assertion wildly implausible. No-one doubts that Catholic groups underwent political mobilisation before and during the Revolution (this is one of the main themes of the revisionist school); priests and bishops backed the PCN in the time of Madero; local *curas* exercised political as well as spiritual influence in their parishes.[191] At San Miguel Allende, the *cura* quelled a riot; at San José de Gracia, the parish priest was the community's leading figure and, in the case of Padre Juan González, 'far from being apolitical. He was a Maderista and in the end a keen Villista'; after him, however, came two priests from Sahuayo, remembered as being 'prejudiced against the Revolution'.[192] Perhaps their 'prejudice' was the result of revolutionary persecution; on the other hand, Azuela's portrait of the *curas* of neighbouring Jalisco suggests a degree of clerical antipathy to the Revolution even in Madero's time, before dogmatic anti-clericalism infused revolutionary practice.[193] In addition, priests were not independent of local, material circumstances. The Indian rebels of Igualapa killed Padre Rafael Salmerón, subsequently mutilating the body, because the priest had acquired a portion of their erstwhile communal lands, which they sought to recover.[194] Salmerón was not a martyr to the faith; yet his case illustrates how – just as some priests identified with popular protest – others were compromised with local elites or (a common situation) with unpopular Spanish communities, and they could not then expect the cassock to exempt them from retribution. If such retribution can be classified as anti-clericalism, it did not imply a general, abstract, liberal vision, nor a thorough-going Jacobinism; it could co-exist even with traditional Catholic beliefs and symbols – hence the paradox of priest-baiters who wore the Virgin of Guadalupe. Popular anti-clericalism, like popular agrarianism, was the parochial, inarticulate, often violent alternative to the 'official' anti-clericalism which emanated from the educated Jacobins of the towns. And (the parallel with agrarianism holds again) it was a very different alternative.

The evidence for a brand of popular anti-clericalism thus exists, but its relative slimness suggests that this was a minor theme within the Revolution. Jean Meyer, showing a reasonable but perhaps exaggerated diffidence towards John Reed's account, exempts Villa from the charge of anti-clericalism: the anti-clerical acts of Villismo were few, concentrated in the early months of his campaign, and perpetrated by subordinates anyway; 'in Villa's territory there was never any religious persecution'.[195] But the evidence of Villa's hostility to priests (Quirk goes so far as to call him a 'deep-dyed clerophobe') goes beyond Reed, and resides in incontrovertible acts, as well as the jottings of an imaginative radical journalist.[196] Spanish priests and nuns were expelled from Chihuahua; the priests of Saltillo were rounded up and forced to leave; after the fall of Zacatecas the bishop's palace was gutted and two priests were shot. All these events occurred in or after December 1913, the Zacatecas incidents in June 1914, eighteen months after Villa's initial revolt. This was not the first fling of a nascent rebellion: this was mature Villismo.[197] How far Villa was personally responsible may be debated (actually, it seems that he was); but the fact that his subordinates acted in similar fashion merely illustrates that Villa's antipathy to the Church – like his more marked and thorough Hispanophobia – was shared by many of his followers. In rebel Durango, churches were desecrated, priests arrested, and the 'few priests who remain at liberty are beaten and insulted at every turn'. Sacristans were kept busy ringing church bells 'in celebration of the saint's day of some petty leader'.[198] In the pious city of San Luis, Eulalio Gutiérrez – a leader of Villista type, though not affiliation – confiscated church property, expelled thirty-four priests, took over the bishop's palace, and ransacked the seminary library.[199] No doubt some of these stories were exaggerated; but there is little point in dismissing these, while maintaining a 'willing suspension of disbelief' when it comes to Carrancista excesses. By their very nature, acts of anti-clerical violence invite publicity, denunciation, exaggeration. In trying to apply some sort of deflator, the historian should aim for consistency, and not explain away those acts which seem to occur in the wrong place, perpetrated by the wrong people.

Jean Meyer is quite right, however, to argue that 'Villa never shared the outlook of the Jacobins'.[200] As with agrarian reform, the difference lies not so much in specific acts (for specific acts, like the physical take-over of a church, could be the work of popular or Jacobin anti-clericals); rather, it depends on the general context of action. Villista anti-clericalism was a part – only a minor part – of plebeian rough justice, of social banditry writ large; it did not derive from a calculating, cerebral Jacobinism, complete with formal ideology, approved texts, coherent, national policies and, above all, a grand vision of secular progress and development. It took reprisals against priests who were considered enemies of the people – because they were Spanish, accumulated land, or aligned themselves with hated elites – but it entertained no plan for the elimination of the Church or of the Catholic religion, as some of the Jacobins did. For this reason, Villismo could easily trim its sails and emerge, after 1914, as the protector of the faith. By then, after all, Villa had flushed out the foreign priests he particularly disliked in the north; and, since he did not cleave to a doctrinaire secularism, it was no great apostasy (and it promised political advantage) to defer to Catholic opinion in the centre.

Other revolutionaries thought differently. By November 1914, the Catholic hierarchy was complaining that sporadic anti-clerical outbursts had given way to conscious, directed policy: recent attacks on the Church 'obeyed a pre-arranged plan', worked out in concert with Mexican Freemasons and North American Protestants.[201] It was hardly as conspiratorial as that.[202] But the national triumph of the Constitutionalists and their victorious descent on Mexico City certainly produced a quantitative and qualitative change: 'by mid-1914 the tempo [of anti-clericalism] increased and the direction changed'.[203] Now, not only were priests arrested, mulcted, ransomed, sentenced for political offences and exiled from the country; they and their churches were also subjected to deliberate humiliation, hostile propaganda and close regulation. In place of sporadic, sometimes violent attacks, in which the clergy suffered along with other members of the propertied elite, there were now systematic policies directed against the Church as an institution, and Catholicism as a set of beliefs. Where popular anti-clericalism vented itself against specific priests – the Spaniard, the landlord, the cacique's crony – the new, official variant was no respecter of persons: it attacked the clergy *qua* clergy, stigmatising them as the collective enemy of the Revolution.

This is not to say that policy was uniform throughout the country: that would have been impossible in the chaos of 1914.[204] But there were clear, common features of Constitutionalist policy. The Church was mulcted: Rafael Buelna ransomed the Bishop of Tepic; Obregón ransomed the clergy of Guadalajara, then (with rather less success) the clergy of Mexico City; Gertrudis Sánchez imposed a massive forced loan at Morelia.[205] For many priests, especially foreigners, this was the immediate prelude to expulsion from the country.[206] Ecclesiastical property was confiscated wholesale – church buildings, monasteries and convents, colleges and seminaries, schools, episcopal palaces, and rural real estate. This was justified on the grounds that all church property was nationally owned and thus fell under the jurisdiction of the government.[207] During the campaigns of 1914, confiscated churches served as barracks and stables; but soon – and increasingly over subsequent years – they were put to less squalid, more symbolic use. In Mexico City, Jesuit property was given to the Casa del Obrero Mundial, and similar facilities were later provided for Casa branches in the provinces.[208] Other church buildings became schools (such was the case with the archbishop's palace in Mérida), libraries, hospitals or municipal offices. Gabriel Gavira, one of the most dedicated, deliberate anti-clericals, cut a swathe through ecclesiastical property from Veracruz through San Luis to Durango: at Papantla the *cura*'s house was given over to the municipality and church valuables were sold to pay for a new market; at San Luis, a convent became a hospital (receiving the confiscated mattresses and sewing machines, while furniture and pianos went to the Schools Department); a convent was likewise converted into a hospital at Durango, where old church buildings were razed to accommodate Gavira's town-planning schemes.[209]

Throughout Constitutionalist territory – at Guadalajara, Jalapa, Monterrey, Mexico City – churches and church schools were closed down. Some commanders advocated the total abolition of Catholic schools (though this was not achieved); and, when the churches were reopened, it was often under the 'strictest regulations', as at Monterrey.[210] Some authorities went further, limiting the number of priests to a fixed (and low) percentage of the state's population.[211] Gavira enforced the Reform law which forbade the wearing of clerical garb in public; Governor Martín Triana of Aguascalientes (a young, chubby, cherubic ex-priest himself) restricted the ministry to 'Mexicans of irreproachable conduct' who refrained from 'meddling in any way in local or national affairs'.[212] Along with these measures of confiscation and regulation went attempts to ridicule, humiliate, denounce and undermine the Catholic Church. Images were smashed – not solely in the frenzy of the moment, but as deliberate policy. Antonio Villareal, the veteran PLM anti-clerical, maintained excellent public order at Monterrey; but he had the cathedral's colonial statues smashed, and the confessionals piled in the plaza and burned.[213] Incidents of this kind occured in metropolises like Monterrey, and in minor pueblos like Milpa Alta.[214] Though the massacres alleged by Catholic propagandists did not take place, it is possible that the mock executions described in these accounts had more basis in fact.[215] Certainly the Constitutionalists took their opportunities to belittle and demean the clergy. Obregón did not conceal the fact (who knows, he may have invented it?) that of 180 priests arrested in Mexico City in February 1915, 49 were certified to be suffering from venereal disease.[216] The Constitutionalist press, too, in its repeated exposés of old regime politics implicated the Catholic hierarchy and spoke in awe of the 'monstrous crimes committed under the guise of corrupt clerical rites'.[217] Clericalism was lumped together with Cientificism and Militarism as the baneful Trinity of the Porfiriato. And, it was now alleged, intransigent defenders of the old regime like Almazán, Argumedo and Higinio Aguilar, were fighting on under the ancient, reactionary banner of 'Religión y Fueros'.[218]

There was something of the self-fulfilling prophecy in this allegation. Like the embattled landlords, the Church and its supporters looked to their defences. They could – pursuing the analogy – colonise existing revolutionary movements, and there is some evidence that this happened.[219] Or they could mount their own independent resistance. Granted the nature of the institution under attack, this was often done peacefully, in the city, with women in the front line. At Monterrey, where 'the dissatisfaction of the people with the anti-Catholic policy of the government' was said to be 'very pronounced', the 'families of the better class' boycotted dances and public functions, pending a relaxation of anti-clerical measures.[220] There were peaceful protests at

Querétaro, too; while Gavira's closure of convents in San Luis provoked petitions, an appeal to Carranza's wife, and a visit first from a committee of 'elegant ladies' then from 1,000 poor women who trooped into the governor's palace with their children, begging Gavira to reverse the decision. The convents gave education to 500 poor girls, they pointed out. Gavira was inflexible. His own mother, he said, would have behaved like them: 'the poor old girl couldn't see further than the end of her own nose, since she was ignorant, like you'. The nuns were mere instruments of that 'rascal', Bishop Montes de Oca, who sought to deprive these girls of 'true education', so they would grow up to become '500 mothers as ignorant as you'. Gavira remained inflexible when, some months later at Durango, the clerical lobby tried to soften the general's hardline policy towards the Church by means of the blandishments of a beautiful widow ('a true temptation which put my will to the test', Gavira recalled).[221]

Some scenes were uglier and ultimately violent. When Obregón gaoled 180 priests in Mexico City, demonstrators – mostly women – took to the streets in large numbers and had to be dispersed by Yaqui troops. Next day, pro- and anti-clerical demonstrators clashed in Avenida Juárez, the police were summoned, and two participants died in the fray.[222] But it was in west-central Mexico that Catholic indignation and resistance were most profound. In July 1914 the British consul at Guadalajara reported how 'the acts of vandalism, of barbarity, of iniquitous blasphemy have made a horrible impact on my mind'; and, in subsequent months, similar impressions, loosely based on stories of murder, persecution and rape which could rarely be authenticated, were continually reported from the same city.[223] Whatever the truth, it is clear that the anti-clerical acts of the Constitutionalists – first Obregón, then Diéguez and Murguía – won them an evil reputation in Jalisco. Since the perpetrators were Carranza's men, Jalisco's Catholics logically inclined towards Villa: Villismo seemed the 'antidote' to anti-clerical Carrancismo.[224] Some of the more militant began to recruit armed brigades, with a view to violent resistance. And, by the autumn of 1914, there were reports of actual – albeit small and obscure – revolts, mounted by outraged Catholics: the first shots in the Church/State struggle that would culminate in the great rebellion of the 'twenties.[225]

Militarism ranked with clericalism in the Constitutionalists' blacklist of Porfirian abuses. Both allegations were somewhat unfair, for Díaz's regime had been no more militarist than clericalist. When it came to Huerta, however, the militarist – if not the clericalist – tag was indisputable. Indeed, since 1910 the power of the Federal Army had constantly grown and by 1913–14 most Constitutionalists had reached the firm conclusion that the influence of the army had increased, was increasing, and ought to be diminished, if not annihilated altogether. As early as Februrary 1913, one of Sonora's shrewdest leaders, Plutarco Elías Calles, argued that the rebels should have no truck with

Federal officers, and that they should create their own army and officer corps from scratch.[226] There should be no repeat of Madero's 'política de conciliación'. Soon possessed of the most efficient army of the Revolution, the Sonorans spurned Federal defectors, save for deserting conscripts: they had less need of Federal expertise, and no intention of sustaining potential rivals for power. Carranza, too, was adamant that a deal with the army, on the lines of 1911, was unthinkable.[227] The army, he declared, 'has besmirched itself serving the usurper and most of its elements are corrupt'; it could not expect generous treatment.[228] Thus, after entering Mexico City, Obregón arranged for the evacuation and disbandment of the capital's garrison: each soldier received a few pesos and a rail ticket home; and most of the 30,000 troops involved drifted away, their arms and ammunition falling into rebel hands.[229] In subsequent weeks, too, as recruitment restarted in anticipation of renewed hostilities, Carranza and Obregón still blackballed ex-Federals.[230]

Already, of course, the Federal Army was in a state of collapse. During 1913–14 it had suffered a series of unprecedented defeats; it had been dislodged from the cities of northern Mexico, *a fuerza y sangre*, not by political arrangement, as in 1911. Huerta, by pumping men and money into the army, had not necessarily strengthened it as an institution: too rapid expansion had undermined its *esprit de corps* (Villa had done his bit too); widespread graft and speculation had tarnished its image; ultimately, in defeat and disarray, it had even forfeited the reputation it enjoyed in some circles as the defender of life and property. Discipline had cracked and towns had been ravaged in retreat.[231] Meanwhile, losses had been heavy – at Torreón, San Pedro, Zacatecas, Guadalajara. And the carnage was not confined to the battle-field; Villa's prolific executions of Federal officers were seconded by the Sonorans following the unconditional surrenders of Guaymas and Mazatlán in the summer of 1914.[232] By now, the Federal Army was finished as a unitary organisation, capable of maintaining or overthrowing regimes. This alone was a major consequence of the Constitutionalist revolution.

But so many men – a quarter of a million according to Huerta's notional figures of March 1914 – could not be so easily neutralised; nor could the accumulated beliefs and personal loyalties of the Federals (particularly the officers) be removed by revolutionary fiat. Though the army no longer existed as a unitary organisation, some of its constituent parts survived. Like the landlords, some fought on independently, while some chose to colonise the revolution. Both alternatives were eminently feasible. Supposedly 'demobilised' Federals terrorised parts of Tlaxcala, acting as freelance *condottieri*.[233] The Isthmus, still free from Constitutionalist control, acted as a magnet to such free companies. General Joaquín Téllez, having quarreled with his superiors in Manzanillo, sailed to Salina Cruz, dumped his men there, and proceeded with a haul of guns and money to El Salvador.[234] All told, perhaps

5,000 Federals were congregated on the Pacific coast of Oaxaca in the late summer of 1914: a force large enough to cause anxiety, and possessed of sufficient weaponry to excite envy. Constitutionalist emissaries – Gabriel Gavira, Jesús Carranza – were sent to arrange their demobilisation, which was ostensibly carried out, their arms being shipped to Mexico City.[235] It was not purely coincidental, however, that the Isthmus and southern Veracruz soon became the main focus of ex-Federal military activity. Here, several ex-Federal officers led sizeable forces, ultimately under the broad umbrella of Felicismo: General Eguía Liz and his son in Oaxaca; a nameless captain, 'once a good Federal officer and an equally good bandit', at Playa Vicente (Ver.); a high-ranking naval officer, Arturo Solache, who in 1916 came up from the Isthmus to join Gabay's Huatusco rebels, leading – it was said – 1,000 men.[236]

The most successful ex-Federal freelance, however, was Esteban Cantú, who operated at the other end of Mexico, in Baja California. Cantú, a major in 1913, emerged from the Federal collapse as the dominant figure in the peninsula and rejected a Constitutionalist demand for his surrender in August 1914. Subsequently – since no-one cared overmuch about events in this remote section; still less could they spare troops to do anything about it – Cantú was allowed to maintain a vigorous but judicious independence, avoiding direct involvement in mainland conflicts and adopting different factional camouflage to suit circumstances. 'He will', reported the Mexican consul at Tucson, 'recognise Carranza or whatever other government which leaves him in power and lets him carry on robbing as up to now.'[237] Though true, this was misleading. Cantú and his collaborators may have robbed by lining their own pockets; but the robbery was conducted in a brisk, businesslike and orderly manner. Under Cantú, peace and prosperity reigned in Baja: taxes and duties were levied (in gold or dollars), local businessmen praised the General's acumen, and – at the price of accepting the political hegemony of Cantú and the economic hegemony of the US – the local people suffered less than their compatriots on the mainland. Not till late 1915 did Cantú finally reach terms with the triumphant mainland faction, after a year and a half of splendid and successful isolation.[238]

Particular circumstances favoured Cantú's enterprise (not only was Baja California remote; it was also – compared with, say, Yucatán – an indifferent prize; and Sonora, the necessary springboard for invasion, was itself riven with conflict). For most ex-Federals, splendid isolation was impossible; if they were to survive, they had to colonise the revolution. While Carranza and Obregón opposed any wholesale incorporation of the Federal rump into the Constitutionalist armies, some of their subordinates, tempted by this source of manpower and expertise, were less exclusive; and some of their rivals were positively ecumenical. In Sinaloa, the young (pro-Carranza) leader Ramón Iturbe recruited 200 ex-Federals, including artillerymen (the newcomers were not popular with Iturbe's revolutionary veterans: when they arrived aboard the gunboat *Guerrero* in March 1915 they were greeted with hoots of derision). Numerous ex-Federals were also said to have joined up with Pablo González's Division of the East; and, when the Carrancista Manuel Diéguez led an army from Jalisco to Sonora in October 1915, 'many of the troops that arrived at Guaymas . . . were recognised as being men who had previously served with the Huerta army at Guaymas, including the entire [military] band'.[239] Expertise counted. Trombone-players, like artillerymen, were rare in the ranks of the revolution.

To the extent that this recruitment was confined to rank-and-file soldiers, it was not hugely significant: it gave the footloose Federals a place to go, and it showed that many Constitutionalist commanders anticipated further hostilities. Where Federal officers were concerned, however, and particularly where officers and men moved as one, the matter was more serious; here, perhaps, was a devious process of conservative 'entryism', whereby the ex-Federals, the Myrmidons of Díaz and Huerta, still true to their cause, infiltrated and manipulated the victorious revolution. Felipe Angeles, Villa's ex-Federal grey eminence, thus becomes a stalking horse for dozens of his old Federal cronies. Certainly the Federal generals were keen to reach a deal with Carranza which would give them a foothold in the new regime.[240] Perhaps this represented a devious policy of entryism, pioneered by Angeles; perhaps it indicated the officer corps' belated conversion to democracy and social reform;[241] certainly it reflected the fact that ex-Federal officers had no real alternative, save, at best, the abrupt termination of their careers or, at worst, disgrace, persecution, gaol, exile, even execution. Embracing the leper of the revolution was no doubt distasteful to most of them. But they had little choice: like so many groups, they found that the 'logic of the Revolution' pushed them in strange, unwelcome directions. Hence in 1914–15 many of Díaz's and Huerta's old servants (police, officials and irregulars, as well as Federals) entered incongruous alliances with revolutionaries chiefly (and significantly) Villa and Zapata. Circumstances and survival required it:[242]

> The time misorder'd doth, in common sense,
> Crowd us and crush us to this monstrous form
> To hold our safety up.

The choice of Villa and Zapata was determined by the simple but significant fact that, unlike Carranza and Obregón, these leaders were flexible in their attitude towards ex-Federals. It was not that they were greatly enamoured of their recent enemies: Villa complained of indiscriminate Zapatista recruiting and 'feared that Zapata has been influenced by the reactionary elements in Mexico City'; while Zapata noted rumours of ex-Federal infiltration of Villismo, and of Angeles' devious role therein.[243] But despite these misgivings, the process went on. Villa, though responsible for the execution of a good many Federals in 1913–14, had also been prepared to accept conscripts into his army and had, on occasions, welcomed defecting officers too. Angeles thus managed Villa's artillery, just as the ex-Federal Elías Torres managed Maclovio Herrera's; other ex-Federals were evident in Villista ranks even before the summer of 1914 and, it is suggested, Angeles saw to it that their number increased.[244] After the fall of Huerta, the trickle became a stream. Villista agents were down in Veracruz in September 1914, 'conferring with ex-Federal officers and furnishing them with funds'; Federals washed up in the American border states leaned towards Villismo and, in some cases, joined the movement; Villa was keen that the Federal troops – if not the Federal generals – interned at Fort Wingate should be allowed to return home 'as there is a great demand for labourers [sic] in the northern part of Mexico'.[245] Ultimately, early in 1915, Villa published an amnesty for all Federal officers who were not directly implicated in the death of Madero.[246]

Meanwhile, Villa's subordinate commanders were not, like Carranza's, subject to any restraint in the matter of recruiting ex-Federals, and they took their cue from their leader. In Sonora, Maytorena was said to have incorporated captured officers into his forces, allowing them to retain their old ranks; Rafael Buelna, in Sinaloa, counted many ex-Federals among his men; Rosalío Hernández, commanding at Piedras Negras, amnestied and recruited ex-Federals from across the border.[247] Such alliances, however, had their drawbacks. There was 'no love lost' between ex-Federals and revolutionary veterans at Aguascalientes; rumours of dissension flew about, at a time of crucial military action and, it was reported, 'dark hints are heard that in the coming fight there may be some casualties not resulting from exposure to the enemy's fire'.[248] The expediency of the moment could not wholly subdue the old enmity between Federals and Villistas; and, against the yet deeper enmity of Orozquistas and Villistas, it could scarcely prevail at all: Huerta's irregular allies of 1913–14 – Orozco, Argumedo, Salazar, Campa, Canuto Reyes – could expect no welcome from Villa and had to turn south to Zapata if they were to find any immediate outlet for their proven military talents.[249]

This Argumedo did after his improvised flight from Zacatecas. But he was not alone in linking up with Zapatismo: though reports of 'many thousands' of ex-Federals joining Zapata were exaggerated, they had a basis in fact.[250] Old Higinio Aguilar, who had flirted with Zapatismo in 1913, when taken prisoner in Morelos, now went over to the *surianos*; Trinidad Ruiz, one-time Zapatista turned Huertista, returned to the fold; and Juan Andrew Almazán, weaving one of the most tortuous of all revolutionary careers, appealed to Zapata to recall his past services and to overlook his recent apostasy.[251] Though only months before Almazán had bitterly attacked Zapatismo ('it is the black banner which deserves complete extermination'), this did not stand in the way of reconciliation and alliance.[252] Weeks later, when the *surianos* occupied Mexico City, their tolerance was again exhibited. Far from purging those remnants of the old regime which Carranza and Obregón had not eliminated, they called on the services of Porfirian *políticos* and officials to organise the police and administer the city. Where, only weeks before, the police and the Carrancistas had engaged in gun-battles, Zapatistas, police and ex-Federals seemed to work in happy union.[253]

This drew a variety of comment. The city's well-to-do, notably the foreigners, observed with surprise, relief and delight how the Zapatistas 'welcomed the assistance of ex-Federal officers and employees', kept order and showed no penchant for the purges, fines and imprisonments which had characterised Carrancista rule.[254] The Carrancistas, in return, began to depict the Villistas and Zapatistas as tools of reaction.[255] This required a quick turnabout: in November 1914, Carranza's press alleged, the Zapatistas entered the capital (the 'corrupt and venal metropolis') 'amid general fear and stupor', leaving city 'wrung dry and profaned'.[256] This, of course, was pure invention. Now, Carranza's journalistic hacks woke up to the fact that the old 'Attila of the South'/'Zapatista Cossacks' theme no longer applied, at least not in Mexico City. Instead, they began to stress Zapata's liaison with the old regime, the well-to-do of Mexico City and, above all, the clergy: Zapata became the leader of deluded Indians, obeying murky 'instincts of rebellion', but now in the trammels of Reaction. 'Behind Zapata stand the priests'; Zapata is 'the man of the clergy'; Zapata has many 'partisans among the pseudo-cultured classes of the ex-capital'.[257] Eventually, reaching a *reductio ad absurdum*, the hacks put it about that the planters of Morelos had 'suborned the Zapatista hordes in such a way that they have come to constitute a kind of army sustained by those very planters'; Zapatismo was therefore a 'faction dependent on the reactionary landlords of Morelos'.[258] And Zapata's new allies, like Aguilar and Almazán, readily fitted into this interpretation, given their Huertista and Federal antecedents.[259]

Villa's recruitment of ex-Federals laid him open to similar charges. The view which sees Villa as an instrument of the reactionary Angeles is as old as the events it seeks to explain. If Zapata stood for 'clericalism', Villa and Angeles represented 'Porfirismo'; or 'Maderista reaction'; or 'the last redoubt of reaction'. At any rate, something particularly nasty.[260] How valid were these charges? It was certainly true that Carrancista exclusivism encouraged, and Villista/Zapatista tolerance permitted, a significant movement of ex-Federals, irregulars and even some Porfirian *políticos* towards the Villista–Zapatista forces. But the very factors which facilitated this movement also assured that its effects would be limited and transitory. In the case of Zapatismo, which is the clearer, old regime *políticos* and officials performed functions which most Zapatistas spurned. Zapata had no wish to administer Mexico City; he had no wish even to stay there. To a patronising foreigner, the Zapatistas were 'pure country Indians, but men of common sense and with no exaggerated ideas as to their own merits or importance' – quite different, in other words, from the pushy, parvenu, meddlesome Carrancistas.[261] They knew their place, and it was not inside the courts, ministries and police stations of the capital. Their leader, Zapata, had never been seen as *presidenciable*, and they showed no desire or capacity to make a determined grab for national power.

But in all this, observers mistook indifference for deference. The Zapatistas did not consider themselves inferior and subservient to the urban well-to-do (witness the contemporaneous lynching of *catrines* in Mexico state; or the supremely confident advocacy of the Plan of Ayala): it was out of indifference, not deference, that they allowed others to run Mexico City, or entered into apparently anomalous alliances with 'reactionaries'. These did not represent major concessions, still less successful 'reactionary' attempts to suborn Zapatismo. Morelos, along with extensive neighbouring regions, remained securely Zapatista, immune to 'reaction', so long as military defeat was staved off. Allies like Almazán and Aguilar were kept at arm's length and meanwhile performed a useful function, providing a *cordon sanitaire* behind which the Morelos revolution (which they neither penetrated nor perverted) could survive. As this form of words suggests, these were hardly warm, comradely alliances. Relations between the allies were difficult; military operations (notably at Puebla) were thereby prejudiced, and the ensuing defeats produced recriminations.[262] As we shall see later, the character of Zapatismo was scarcely altered by its 'reactionary' liaison; and, if the failure to purge all remnants of the old regime, swoop on the cities, and set up a sound Zapatista government is to be regretted, this failure cannot be attributed to reactionary wiles and blandishments. The reactionaries did not co-opt, suborn, distort, or arrest the *suriano* revolution. On the contrary, the *surianos* did what they wanted to, and in 1914–15 they were, to an unusual extent, masters of their own destiny. If Zapatista parochialism – the narrow horizons, local concerns and indifference to national government – is to be blamed for ultimate Zapatista failure, this parochialism cannot be attributed to the dubious alliances of 1914. It existed from the start. Zapata's reactionary allies did not make him a parochial; rather, parochialism made the reactionary alliances possible.

The same was true, though less completely, for Villa. The 'reactionaries' (a Carrancista catch-all including ex-Federals, ex-Porfiristas, ex-Maderistas) penetrated Villismo with more success: Villismo was a broader, bigger, looser movement than Zapatismo; it was less 'closed' (*cerrado*) and more tolerant of new converts. Pre-1914 Villismo already contained groups – the old Maderistas, the Madero family, Federals of liberal inclination like Angeles – with whom the reactionaries could combine to form a nationally aware, articulate lobby, opposed to radical social change and plebeian rule. In this respect, Villismo might indeed appear to have been co-opted, suborned, distorted or arrested. But, we shall argue, this take-over was imperfect, short-lived, and often illusory.[263] The reactionary converts of 1914 were ill-received; they found that they could not control Villismo (which, to the extent that it was controlled, remained in the hands of Villa and his old military veterans); and their sojourn in the Villista camp was therefore frequently brief. Defeat and disillusionment soon flushed them out. By admitting such 'reactionaries', Villismo and Zapatismo displayed political characteristics which differentiated them from Carrancismo, and which will later repay analysis; they also provided these 'reactionaries' with a continued foothold in the civil war which they might otherwise have lacked. But neither Villismo nor Zapatismo – nor the Revolution as a whole – underwent significant change as a result.

THE NEW REGIME: POPULISTS, PAROCHIALS AND PETTY BOURGEOIS

By the end of 1914, then, the much-praised, stable structures of Porfirian Mexico lay in ruins, at least north of the Isthmus. The network of patronage and mutual support which had stretched down from the 'centre' through the state oligarchies, caciques and *jefes políticos* was irretrievably ruptured. Much of the personnel of the old regime was gone, and many of the victorious revolutionaries were committed to the extirpation of those who remained. The Federal Army – Huerta's instrument for the re-creation of the Pax Porfiriana – had been broken up, as had the *Cuerpos Rurales*. Landowners faced the dual threat of official and unofficial agrarian reform. The *modus vivendi* between Church and state had come to an end and the clergy confronted the biggest challenge to their position since the 1860s. Capitalism – or whatever mode(s) of production had prevailed before 1910 – survived (we will consider what manner of survival in conclusion); but the changes accomplished in these five years were real, extensive and significant – even if, in many cases, unplanned and unforeseen. But if the old order had been subverted, what had taken its place? Who ruled, by what means, and in whose interest? Answers will not only suggest the degree of change, but also lay the basis for an analysis of the final bout of civil war, the 'war of the winners'.

Whatever policies were pursued by the new regime – liberal, conservative, radical, *agrarista* – it was a new political elite enacting them. This elite, furthermore, derived from markedly inferior social origins than its Porfirian predecessor; and it was a good deal younger.[264] To ruined but philosophical Mexican oligarchs, this was yet another of the violent renovations of the political elite which the country had periodically experienced – with Independence, the Revolution of Ayutla, the Reform.[265] In fact, though the comparison is hard to draw, the social upheaval and political renovation of 1910–15 were probably greater than those of the 1870s, the 1850s, even, perhaps, the 1810s. Those who were ousted naturally complained bitterly of their displacement by men 'of low cultural and moral level'.[266] 'Socially, morally, and mentally', observed one conservative, the new rulers 'were in the great majority [drawn from] the garbage and underworld of the cities and country-side'. Most of the new military had held posts no higher than that of corporal of *rurales* – and that in Madero's time, when 'the winds of revolution had already stirred up so much rubbish'. With more precision, the same writer (author of the 'best conservative account' of the Revolution, we are told) identified the 'cream' of the revolutionary elite as one-time 'sharecroppers, drug-store assistants, mine foremen, railway workers, dairymen, policemen, carpenters, saddlers, tram-drivers, not to mention many farm workers and day labour-ers'.[267] Carranza himself (who had of course been a *político* of the old regime) was over-fond of commenting on the illiteracy of prominent rebels like Villa and the Arrietas.[268] For their part, the illiterates, plebs, and parvenus wrote and said less. Though the more articulate might declaim about reform, revolution and progress, they rarely dwelt on their social origins: some, like Obregón, boasted of being self-made men; some, like the Arrietas admitted their intellectual limitations; most presented the revolution as a crusade against abuses, rather than a wholesale renovation of the political elite.[269]

Foreign observers, however, almost unanimously stressed the rise to power of new groups, of low social origin. Leon Canova, President Wilson's representative, was characteristically rude: 'it is a case of dregs boiling to the top'.[270] Hohler, the British Minister, agreed that the 'country is in the control of the very scum of the people'.[271] London and Washington reached the same conclusion: Wilson's Minister of the Interior (a Mexico-watcher, who served on the 1916 Mexican-American commission) spoke of the 'Marats of Mexico' who now held power – one-time 'grocers and longshoremen, butchers and bakers'.[272] In the heart of provincial Mexico, foreigners lamented that they now had to deal with inept, inconstant boors. The US consul at Tampico, 'worn out' by the exertions of his office, was 'offended at being compelled to do business with a whoremonger and a drunkard who is habitually discour-teous'.[273] But even such tetchy comments could be revealing: Puebla, the American consul complained, was now ruled by 'illiterate men without the least capacity for helping the country . . . but only capable of ruling a sufficient number of men to keep them in the field'.[274] The criteria of political advancement (to put it another way) had drastically changed since the days of Díaz. Naval captains, usually less sensitive to punctilio than resident consuls, reported along the same lines. Illiterates 'from the lowest class' now governed Campeche.[275] And the Sonorans – often depicted, not unreasonably, as 'bourgeois' or 'petty-bourgeois' leaders, a cut above the rustic *cabecillas* of Villismo and Zapatismo – were included in these observations. 'Practically all the present military leaders in the various factions', ran a report from Sonora, 'have sprung from the lower and poorer classes.'[276] An Englishman, meeting Obregón while the general bathed at Guadalajara's Hotel Fénix, observed him as he might a beast in captivity: 'the man Obregón', he noted, 'gave an impression of superb health and excellent animal vitality'; but that Obregón and his lieutenants were unsuited for political office was beyond doubt: 'among officers high and low I have yet to find one who seemed in any way intellectual or imbued by any degree of honest appreciation of the cause of the revolution'.[277]

These were, of course, blind prejudices. But they were revealing prejudices, which reflected the old Porfirian – and Maderista – assumptions about who was fit to govern; they fed on the belief (still strong, but beginning to fade) that politics was the preserve of the educated, the well-to-do, the cosmopolitan. The populist leaders who now collectively controlled Mexico were none of these; their conquest and retention of power showed that the prejudices of the Porfiriato were not immutable laws of political science. Men whose political credentials consisted of 'ruling a sufficient number of men to keep them in the field' could, as it turned out, make capable political leaders. Urbano Angulo, to take one obscure example, was recently a ranch foreman near La Paz (Baja Calif.); by 1915 he had risen to become military commander and governor of the territory, which now enjoyed firm government and brisk trade, making it, the British vice-consul reckoned, 'the paradise of Mexico'.[278] We will note many similar examples in the final chapter. The metamorphosis of despised plebeians into capable *políticos* not only subverted the assumptions of the mature Porfiriato; it also implied a democratisation of the Mexican polity – not in the middle-class, Maderista sense of promoting parliamentary democracy, but rather in that it overturned and expanded the political elite, breaking old barriers, stimulating social mobility, forging closer (if informal) links between rulers and ruled, and obliging the rulers to pay closer attention to what the ruled wanted. The trend of Porfirian politics towards narrow, self-perpetuating oligarchies was decisively reversed: revolutionary politics involved more people (one might choose to call them 'mass politics'), they distributed power more broadly, with less regard to status, and they thus proved capable of producing novel, radical policies. If the final chapter emphasises some of the conservative aspects of the final revolutionary settlement, it must be remembered that this settlement was the work of new, young, parvenu leaders. It cannot be doubted that there had been a major *political* revolution in the country by 1915, and that this facilitated later, radical, social policies.

A fleeting survey of the new leaders of 1914 illustrates something of their character and heterodoxy, of the problems of political union and national integration which the regime faced, and of the partial truth of the foreign stereotypes just quoted. Many have already been introduced: from Zapata, loved and trusted in Morelos as 'the champion who would right all wrongs' to Cantú and his Chapultepec Military Academy graduates, running Baja California Norte as if it were a subsidiary of General Motors.[279] These two occupied different ends of the spectrum: one, the dedicated, popular *agrarista*, sprung from the traditional peasantry of the Mesa Central; the other, a career soldier, practitioner of *realpolitik*, operating in the dynamic, commercialised borderlands of the north. These distinctions – no mere random, individual attributes – will be clarified shortly; the 'spectrum' referred to here is a useful concept for understanding this final phase of the Revolution. But most of the *cabecillas* to be paraded here combined elements of both: Zapata's popular appeal (often his *agrarista* commitment, too), Cantú's shrewd instinct for survival and advancement; Villa, whose regime in Chihuahua has already been sketched, is a case in point. But whereas the regimes of Villa and Zapata – and now Cantú[280] – have been investigated, those of the many lesser leaders have not; in the absence of sound local studies, this roll-call of *cabecillas*, though important, must be as cursory as that of the captains of the Danaans in the Iliad's second book.

In Sonora, where rebel rule had been longest established, the portly, opportunist *hacendado* Maytorena (successively Reyista, Maderista, Constitutionalist and Villista) had at last achieved his family's ambition of controlling the state, even if his enjoyment of power was jeopardised by a rival faction dating back to early 1913. Maytorena's cause was helped, however, by Sonora's remarkable export of revolutionary leaders. Of the Pesqueira brothers (also of notable lineage) Roberto represented the revolution in Washington, while Ignacio had left the state to serve in Carranza's cabinet; Obregón, of course, had gone south at the head of his army, accompanied by Hill and Diéguez.[281] Two leaders remained to challenge Maytorena's rule – one briefly, the other consistently, doggedly and ultimately successfully. The first was Salvador Alvarado, a shopkeeper son of a shopkeeper, native of Potam and Cananea, activist, intellectual, and veteran of 1910. Though he played his part in the incipient factional violence of 1914, he was soon whisked away from Sonora to serve the revolutionary cause at the other end of Mexico.[282] There remained Plutarco Elías Calles, who in 1914–15 vied with Maytorena and his Yaqui allies for control of Sonora.

Of the many leaders thrown up by the Revolution, Calles was to prove the most adroit, successful politician. The revolutionary state which emerged when the fighting ended bore his mark more than anyone else's. Yet, notwithstanding Aguilar's excellent regional study, Calles' personal history remains somewhat obscure, and the lack of a good biography of this great revolutionary figure remains one of the major lacunae in modern Mexican historiography. Since his illegitimate birth in 1887, Calles' life had been 'roving, disordered and marked by irregularity'.[283] His father, a wealthy *hacendado* of known family, had looked out for his bastard son and helped him through his chequered career; but his mother died when he was a child, and it was his step-father, a modest Hermosillo saloon-keeper, who saw to the boy's upbringing (consideration of the effects of such a childhood – reminiscent, perhaps, of Eva Perón's – must be left to future psycho-historians). By the age of seventeen, Calles was a 'dour, energetic, somewhat alcoholic' schoolteacher; thereafter – and thanks often to his paternal family connections – he managed a bar, a hotel, became secretary of the Fronteras town council and finally a tough, efficient police chief at Agua Prieta. Calles was neither an active Maderista oppositionist, nor an active Maderista rebel; he came to prominence, as did Obregón, during the Orozquista invasion in 1912, when Agua Prieta became a centre of Sonoran mobilisation.[284] There, despite the growing suspicions of Governor Maytorena, Calles built up an effective administration, and forged links with both the local landowners (to whom he was related) and with the rising Sonoran military – Obregón, Hill, and Alvarado. When they headed south in 1913, Calles was left the dominant commander in northern Sonora. Already, in 1913, Maytorena had tried to dismiss Calles from his post; now, in 1914–15, open war ensued.

It was a conflict tinged with ironies. Maytorena was a fat, rich, educated landowner; Calles, despite his paternal blood, a footloose parvenu, literate and talented, but lacking his rival's breeding and status (even in the 1920s, when he was the most powerful man in the land, he remained 'a rather quiet and somewhat austere figure . . . not yet entirely at home with all the rules of etiquette called for in . . . top official circles').[285] Yet Maytorena's military power depended on the support of Yaqui chiefs and contingents, and when the crucial choice had to be made in 1914, Maytorena allied with the plebeian Villa, while Calles went against him in support of Carranza. What is more, Calles (later qualified as a rabid nationalist, radical, even Bolshevik) excited the warm admiration of Americans in Sonora and along the border: he was a man of 'decided spirit, of confidence and determination' who ran his district with rigorous discipline, closing the bars and brothels of the border towns, executing looters and guaranteeing peace and order for American mining interests. Under Calles, 'the town of Agua Prieta is a model, so far as police and sanitation are concerned'; 'should he command [all] Sonora', thought an American army officer, 'and instill these methods throughout peace would result'. And the US consul at Hermosillo, witnessing Maytorena's Yaquis rampage through Sonora, feared that 'unless Calles and his people take possession of the state, I cannot see any chance for betterment'.[286] Eventually, Calles 'and his people' took possession not just of Sonora, but of Mexico as a whole.

Calles' mixed background gave him a foothold in different social sectors, while his education and career imparted a broad, urban, businesslike outlook. Americans who dealt with Calles were impressed and reassured, not appalled; even sensitive ladies praised his style of government and were flattered to accompany him to the shops.[287] He contrasted, therefore, with the dour, rustic, rebels who inhabited much of the country; and he was the kind of leader for whom a career in high politics – involving ministries and bureaucracies, *sindicatos* and companies, intellectuals and diplomats – was eminently feasible. In this respect, in 1914–15, he was the exception. Closer to the contemporary norm were the Arrietas, who had descended from the Sierra Madre to fasten their control on the city and state of Durango, which they now governed even in defiance of the mighty Pancho Villa. Domingo Arrieta was an illiterate, endowed with a 'phenomenal memory'; but he and his clan – he was said to have nine brothers and, beyond that, 'the family relations are extensive' – had no misgivings about assuming the government of Durango. When they clashed with the civilian governor, the erudite young engineer Pastor Rouaix, it was Rouaix who had to give way. By the late summer of 1914, the Arrietas commanded some 5,000 men; their appointees filled all the state administration; and, as a result, 'Durango is entirely under the control of the Arrieta brothers.'[288] Theirs was a jealous, local, popular regime. The Arrietas' army was a top-heavy, ramshackle organisation (by 1916, shrunk to 2,500 men, it still had 15 generals, not counting the Arrietas themselves); it was entitled, significantly, 'the Division of Durango'; and the leaders' chief objective was to retain local power in local hands, in defiance of interlopers. Unusual among northern commanders, the Arrietas successfully defied Villa and, thereafter, they quarrelled with their (supposed) Carrancista allies who encroached on their domain.[289]

National affiliations did not carry much weight with the Arrietas. They fell out with Villa over questions of local command. Though this inclined them towards Carranza, it did not demand a doctrinaire enmity towards all local Villistas (of whom there were a good many in Durango). They had no quarrel with Tomás Urbina, who had carved out a small empire around Nieves, to the north; and their relations with the hordes of the Laguna – Villistas to a man – were mutually respectful and at times cordial. There appears to have been a *de facto* demarcation between the two factions, which prevented hostilities even when they seemed likely. Domingo Arrieta and Calixto Contreras were, despite their rival national allegiances, *compadres*, and *compadrazgo* took precedence. In 1916, it was noted, Arrieta and Contreras 'have never been able to have a battle during the last three years, although at one time their forces were in immediate contact for more than a month and on opposite political or revolutionary sides'.[290] Contreras, himself, of course, was a classic, popular rebel – indifferent not only to national power but even to the prospect of storming the local metropolis of Torreón. Through 1913–14 he built up his army around Cuencamé, campaigned with Villa more or less when it suited him, and encouraged *de facto* agrarian reform in blithe disregard of the orders of the First Chief; for 'the forces of General Contreras which are encamped at Pedriceña, Asarco, and Velardeña are in absolute control of that section of the state and General Contreras will not brook the interference of another authority whatsoever in matters which pertain to his own little kingdom'.[291]

To the south, Pánfilo Natera ruled in Zacatecas. Natera, Leon Canova generously conceded, 'is not a bad man as Indians go. [But] he is uncouth, ignorant, and easily misled.'[292] By way of supporters, Natera had the usual educated secretary at his elbow, and a gaggle of plebeian lieutenants at his back. Among his entourage – another critic noted – Lieutenant Colonel Acuña Navarro was 'the only man holding an executive position capable of giving an intelligent answer to any question of importance . . . or with culture enough to receive anyone wishing to make representations to the local powers'.[293] More typical and more influential were officers like Colonel Melitón Ortega, or Generals Tomás Domínguez and Santos Bañuelos – violent, unshaven 'drunken loafers' (in Canova's description), who accompanied Natera on his tours of the red-light district, and against whom the young, weak, agreeable state governor, Carlos de la Vega, was powerless. Ortega was supposedly responsible for shooting the Zacatecas *jefe político* in between the acts of a play; he ordered all shops shut on the afternoons of bullfights, in which he and Bañuelos participated as picadors.[294] No doubt foreign prejudice embellished these stories; but they call to mind scenes from *Los de Abajo*, which was set in just this time and place; and they bear comparison with reliable (Mexican) accounts of drink, bullfights, and revolutionary mayhem.[295]

To the west, Sinaloa fell under the loose hegemony of the Sonorans. But it had produced a variety of vigorous, indigenous rebellions under the leadership of Riveros (ex-Governor and *hacendado*), Buelna (student), Iturbe (clerk), Flores (docker), Cabanillas (carpenter) and Carrasco (cowboy). These, and their respective followers, were split by feuds and united by friendships; before long, their national allegiances bifurcated in a manner reflecting these local, clientelistic patterns. Collectively, however, they comprised the new rulers of the state – rulers distinctly younger and more plebeian than their predecessors, the Redo *camarilla*. Riveros alone represented the old, civilian Maderista constituency: it was not surprising that he allied with Maytorena, another landlord veteran of the anti-Díaz opposition.[296] Nor was it surprising that both ultimately failed in that role which the civilian Maderistas rarely assumed and yet more rarely accomplished: that of warlord–caudillo. Like Maytorena, Riveros never created an effective, personally loyal force: he lacked the grassroots popularity, the common touch, the military prowess. Obliged – if he was to survive as a credible *político* – to engage in the fighting, Riveros, like Maytorena, tried to fight by proxy and failed; while the war continued, purely civilian skills were at a discount.

Buelna and Iturbe – two of a kind, despite their rivalry – were of a different type. Buelna had been a young, baby-faced law student, a dabbler in opposition journalism, before taking up arms with Martín Espinosa in Tepic in 1911. Two years later he became one of Obregón's chief commanders: he led his troops in exemplary fashion, kept good order, and could mouth the right phrases – his cause, he declared, was that of constitutional government, for which he deserved 'the moral support of mankind'.[297] Iturbe, once a clerk in Culiacán gaol, also on the fringes of opposition politics, won his spurs in dramatic style in Sinaloa in 1910–11. Now he, too, emerged as one of Obregón's dynamic lieutenants during the advance south.[298] Both were young: Buelna in 1914 was twenty-four, Iturbe a year older. Youth, prestige and ambition were enough to stimulate rivalry, and the Buelna–Iturbe quarrel became a central feature of Sinaloan politics. This was further compounded when Buelna fell out with Obregón, and Iturbe, predictably, backed Obregón.

Buelna and Iturbe belonged to that small, significant group of young veterans who managed, unusually, to combine orthodox political talents (evident in their early Maderismo) with military capacity, that is, with the capacity to raise and lead men during the guerilla and conventional campaigns of 1910–11 and 1913–14.[299] (They might also be loosely described – in contrast to the landlords Maytorena or Riveros – as 'petty-bourgeois'; but this problematic term must await clarification in a moment). The three remaining Sinaloan *cabecillas* were of more plebeian stock (and, had Banderas not joined up with Zapata by now, his presence would further have lowered the pedigree of the Sinaloan rebel leadership): Cabanillas, an ex-carpenter, veteran of 1911, and 'a well-meaning man, but ignorant'; Angel Flores, previously a docker, now (according to Olea) an illiterate, provincial caudillo; and Juan Carrasco, once a *vaquero* on the Redo estates, a fine horseman, qualified by an American naval officer as 'an uneducated man, given to many excesses . . . and a hard drinker'. More sophisticated Mexicans who encountered Carrasco during the west coast campaign did not disagree.[300] Apart from his fondness for alcohol, Carrasco was in other respects a Sinaloan version of Pancho Villa. Like Villa he was brave and popular, celebrated in *corridos* as 'Juan sin Miedo'; like Villa, too, he lacked education and went accompanied by a bright young secretary, Ernesto Damy.[301] And, as he advanced from southern Sinaloa into Tepic, so his progress, like Villa's, wrought changes symbolic of the transformation taking place in much of northern and central Mexico. For fifty years, ran a report of 1915, Tepic had been under the economic and political sway of the Aguirre family, landlords of Spanish stock whose estates produced cotton, tobacco, sugar, cattle and horses. The family was favoured by Díaz; local officials did its bidding; and the Aguirres 'lorded it over the people worse than the feudal barons of the Middle Ages'. Then came the revolution:[302]

today the scene has shifted and the peon, personified by General Juan Carrasco, an illiterate, drunken debauchee of the lowest type of manhood now rules where the house of Aguirre once held sway. Their cattle are being taken, their plantations stripped, and their stores levied upon. Spain will no doubt protest as the family is powerful at the Spanish court. [But] while conceding the injury and the technical verity of the protest, one familiar with Tepic's history and its Spanish overlords cannot refrain from believing that the inexorable law of retribution is in the process of fulfillment.

Such telling transitions – Tepic passing from the Aguirres to Carrasco, Chihuahua from Terrazas to Villa – were effected, if less dramatically, throughout northern and central Mexico. In San Luis, the Cedillos, allied to

Carrera Torres and (in 1915) aided by Tomás Urbina, dominated the eastern section of the state. Confronted by this phalanx of popular leaders, the civilian state governor, Emiliano Sarabia (the tippling Maderista governor of Durango in 1912) was reduced to impotence, and the Cedillos ran their Valle del Maíz fief as they saw fit, effecting what an intellectual observer described – inappropriately but suggestively – as 'a return to the Indian *cacicazgo*'.[303] To the north west, Eulalio Gutiérrez dominated the Zacatecas/San Luis/Coahuila borderlands which Gertrudis Sánchez (allied to the Gutiérrez family) had controlled in 1911, and which had produced dozens of rebel bands in 1913.[304] 'Stolid, honest and slow-thinking', Eulalio had, like his brother Luis, worked in the local mines; to the US consul at San Luis, who was polite and sympathetic, he seemed 'somewhat inexperienced'; an ex-employer considered him a good foreman of fifty or so peons, but quite unsuited for further responsibility.[305] Gutiérrez was soon to be President of the Republic. In 1913–14 he had shown a certain expertise dynamiting trains (a point made by the Mexican City press in 1913, seized upon by Canova in one of his rude reports, and since rehearsed by generations of historians); the local mining companies, whom Gutiérrez knew at first hand, found him to be an efficient, orderly, if somewhat corrupt commander, of independent mind.[306] And to revolutionaries elsewhere, it was to Gutiérrez's credit that he had put the Church in its place, 'shot many of the old caciques and made prisoners of the rest' and, it was said, raised a guillotine in the main square of Mazapil, to dispense revolutionary justice.[307] More to the point, he had also promulgated, in September 1914, a law fixing minimum wages for peons, abolishing *tiendas de raya* and debt peonage, and regulating the terms of sharecropping agreements.[308]

Gutiérrez was soon to be plucked from provincial obscurity and placed in the national limelight. Thereafter, his career was less typical than tragic, as he wrestled with problems for which he was ill-prepared, and which would have taxed the abilities of consummate statesmen. Most provincial caudillos were luckier and did not have greatness thrust upon them. In Tlaxcala, for example, the political inheritance of Cahuantzi passed to a group of *cabecillas* – Máximo Rojas, Isabel Guerrero, Pedro Morales, Domingo Arenas (who succeeded Felipe Villegas after the latter's death in the summer of 1914) – all from 'worker-peasant' families in the state.[309] Allied with the Zapatistas of western Puebla, and with Lucas and his *serrano* Indians, they forced the capitulation of the last Federal garrison in August 1914, and proceeded to arrest the Huertista state governor, the military authorities and the leaders of the Liga de Agricultores. In rural areas, they undertook the agrarian reform already mentioned; while their depredations in the industrial zone of Puebla/Tlaxcala carried Luddite overtones.[310] Across the border in Hidalgo, too, Zapatista agrarianism made headway.[311] But the Sierra Alta fell under the sway of Nicolás Flores – 'who has always been a great enemy of the Plan of Ayala' – and for whom agrarian reform was chiefly a manipulative device. Nonetheless, here (as in parts of the Huasteca Potosina, controlled by the Lárraga and Santos clans) power had shifted to a new *ranchero* class (a rural petty-bourgeoisie?), capable of mobilising popular support on the basis of clientelistic relations and, in some cases, their rough-and ready, rustic manners.[312] They might resist genuine *agraristas* (Lárraga opposed Cedillo, as Flores did Hidalgo's Zapatistas) but their rise to power marked a significant change, in terms of political personnel and *modus operandi*, from the days of Díaz, Cravioto and Fidencio González.[313]

To the south east, the state of Veracruz displayed a bewildering variety of rebellions, which defied the claim to central authority of Cándido Aguilar. At Misantla, a supposed Zapatista rebel co-existed with Armenta and his fellow-landlords; along the Papaloapam River, Raúl Ruiz sustained a freelance rebellion of several years standing, he 'having been in arms against all the different governments of Díaz, Madero, Huerta, and Carranza'; yet further south, around Los Tuxtlas, the cattle-thief Pascual Casarín – said to be illiterate, popular with his men, but solicitous for the plantations of the district – fought on under various factional labels.[314] And these were but a fraction of the whole; other Veracruzano leaders, who contested the political inheritance of Dehesa, will appear later.[315] West of the capital, Michoacán and Guerrero were no less fractured and anarchic. In the former, the authority of the Coahuilan Gertrudis Sánchez (himself an ex-*guayulero* of modest origins) was only imperfectly imposed on a congeries of local leaders: the deviously ambitious Joaquín Amaro, son of an hacienda foreman; the violent, hard-drinking Alejo Mastache; the Pantoja clan of Puruándiro, also *rancheros* of 'scant culture', captained by Anastasio, an ex-*arriero*.[316] In Guerrero, mean-while, the eclipse of the Figueroas brought the eastern and central parts of the state into the Zapatista orbit. But the hot country to the west enjoyed a different revolutionary identity, linked to that of coastal Oaxaca, which revolutionary commanders, like their nineteenth-century predecessors, dis-covered to their cost when they sallied forth from Acapulco into the interior, leading troops reluctant to enter the mountains and liable to swift defeats and retreats.[317] The coastal revolution hinged upon the rivalry between Julián Blanco and Silvestre Mariscal. Blanco, old and illiterate, was a nominal Zapatista, though in 1914 he also acquired Carrancista status. He led a 'rabble' which, having dominated the countryside during 1913–14, occupied and looted Acapulco in October 1914, singling out the Spanish merchant houses for special attention. Blanco was a *campesino*, his chief lieutenant, Manuel Villegas, an *arriero*; but they enjoyed the usual services of a glib, young, educated secretary, and were allied to Canuto Neri, scion of an established family long active in Guerrero politics (we have, therefore, a classic trinity of plebeian *cabecilla*, revolutionary intellectual, and 'out' *político*). Their rival, Mariscal, traced a tortuous career through the revolution: once a schoolmaster, he fought for Madero in 1911 and Huerta in 1913; now he declared himself a partisan of Carranza. An American considered him 'much the cleverest leader that has come under my observation'; a man 'very ambitious [who] professes to be always with the existing central government'.[318]

Though for a time Blanco and Mariscal boasted the same (Carrancista) allegiance, their contest for power continued, punctuated by skirmishes and complicated by the activities of Zapatista invaders and the Spaniards' mercenary forces.[319] However, 1915 saw a trend away from decentralised chaos towards unitary political control. In May, Mariscal pulled off a coup, securing a large arms shipment from Carranza; the rivals fought over its distribution, but Mariscal retained the lion's share.[320] Three months later an affray between the Blanco and Mariscal forces in Acapulco – numbering some 500 apiece – developed into a pitched battle (during which the official commander of the port raised the Red Cross flag over the garrison fort, indicating his neutrality). The Blanquistas lost; Blanco, his son, Villegas, Neri and others were executed. Mariscal now commanded the Costa Grande; his methods, the US Consul reported, with evident satisfaction, 'may be exactly the means necessary to restore order'; and he was now free to undertake the tempting but tricky task of conquering the hinterland.[321]

It would be possible, but tedious, to prolong the list. It is already clear that, north of the Isthmus, the Constitutionalist victory had shifted power on a massive scale from the old elites into the hands of new, local, popular leaders: *campesinos* and *rancheros*, muleteers and miners, clerks, peons and schoolmasters. Equally clearly, power had shifted down a generation or more: where 60- and 70-year old generals and governors had recently ruled, men in their 20s and 30s now held authority; it was a 'revolución de mozos'.[322] Beyond stating that these men were newcomers, young and often of low social origin, is it possible to present any more satisfactory analysis of their character and values? To categorise, as it were, the fundamental nature of the regime which has supplanted the Porfiriato? Some attempt must be made, so that the significance of both the revolutionary upheaval of 1910–14 and the revolutionary schism of 1914–15 may be understood; the one follows from the other.

Marxist historians of the Revolution naturally employ class as the fundamental category of explanation. Whether they explain anything is another matter. Some achieve a successful blend of Marxist categories and empirical data which is a tribute more to their skill and research than to the explanatory power of the categories used.[323] In other instances, where the theory dominates and determines the data, the outcome is less happy. Individuals are labelled (Carranza: 'bourgeois'; Obregón: 'petty-bourgeois') and complex social movements in turn acquire the labels of their leaders.[324] Other scholars – *marxisant*, liberal, even those apparently dedicated to the old-style, 'value-free', Rankean history – borrow these terms when they venture general statements about the Revolution; then, striking out from the shallows of empirical or narrative history, they instinctively clutch at the life-belt of Marxism.[325] Pages of detailed, scrupulously footnoted dates, events and prosopography, suddenly give way to the 'grand, impersonal forces': the 'bourgeoisie', 'petty-bourgeoisie', or '(semi-) feudal aristocracy', who make a brief, walk-on appearance that bears little relation to the rest of the plot. Having done their bit, they retire as quickly as they entered, leaving the rest of the cast to continue as if nothing had happened. The matter is, of course, more serious when the 'grand, impersonal forces' play a significant role in the analysis. History is much the poorer without broad generalisations and syntheses, and, for the former, the choice of basic categories or 'organising concepts' is crucial. It is in this respect that the almost automatic deployment of conventional Marxist terms can prove stultifying; it is 'to choose intelligibility and coherence in describing a myth, and then to baptise the myth as history'.[326] There are only two alternatives: to abandon broad generalisations altogether, which would be a pity; or to evolve more satisfactory 'organising concepts', which is not easy. Nevertheless, a tentative attempt will be made.

The almost reflex use of Marxist terms in this context may be criticised from three angles: methodological, definitional and theoretical. The first criticism has already been suggested: the proof advanced – to demonstrate, for example, that Obregón represented the 'petty-bourgeois' wing of the Revolution – is often narrowly individualistic and inadequate; the analysis leaps from the leader's personal origins to the class identity of an entire movement; rarely is an attempt made to link leader and led, or to relate class identity to ideology and practice in a coherent way.[327] Also, the sample of individuals who are taken as representative of broad social movements is exiguous: the host of lesser *cabecillas*, whose inclusion in the sample would help consolidate – or wreck – the hypothesis, is ignored.[328] In its extreme, but not uncommon, form, this analysis reduces the Revolution to a quadrille danced by Carranza, Obregón, Villa and Zapata, with occasional partners thrown in to make up the numbers.

Secondly, the definitional premises which lie behind these ubiquitous but contentious concepts (bourgeois, petty-bourgeois, proletarian, feudal) are rarely spelled out, and they are used as if their meaning was straightforward, rather than the subject of endless argument.[329] Thus, not only are the identities of specific classes left obscure (who were the Mexican petty-bourgeoisie?); it is not clear either what concept of class itself is being used (how should this or any other class be defined? What are the criteria?). Are these good, old-fashioned Marxist classes, defined according to their relationship to the means of production?[330] In the absence of clear exposition, it might seem reasonable to adopt this, the classic formulation, as the (unacknowledged) basis of such analyses. In the hands of today's sophisticated Marxists, of course, such a definition is often stretched, rolled, kneaded and larded with additional ingredients: ideologies, conjunctures, class fractions, blocs, and articulated modes of production. There being no good study of the Revolution (1910–20) couched in these terms, it is difficult to know whether the theoretical flexibility gained by this method justifies the loss of clarity and rigour which may equally result. Anyway, it might be presumed that even this Marxism *à la mode* shares certain fundamentals with 'classic' Marxism, which demarcate both from the alternative approach suggested here (that is not really for me to judge). And the same presumption would apply, if it were taken in isolation, to Weber's concept of class (a concept which finds no place in the historiography, and which has sufficient in common with Marx's – a common focus on developed capitalism and a common emphasis on the ownership of property as the chief criterion of class – to hit the same problems when applied in this contexts); Weber, however, placed class alongside, and not above other explanatory concepts – status, party, and, above all, forms of domination.[331]

We broach the third, final and most important criticism of the Marxist or *marxisant* approach; this is a twofold, theoretical criticism, relating, first, to its Eurocentricity and, second, to its unsuitability for middle-range, historical analysis, such as is attempted here. Both Marx and Weber concentrated on the development of capitalism in Europe, and evolved their basic concepts accordingly. Marx's notion of class derived from a fundamentally dual model: the peasantry, petty bourgeoisie and lumpenproletariat might constitute classes, but they were secondary to the primary, bourgeois/proletarian 'dichotomous axis'.[332] Such secondary classes are therefore 'marginal', 'intermediate' or 'standing in a relationship of functional dependence on one of the [primary] classes'. Under capitalism, they are also terminal cases: 'peasants were interesting for Marx when they held no promise of survival'.[333] Such analysis presents problems even when applied to developed capitalist societies.[334] Given its level and pattern of development, revolutionary Mexico is even more intractable. If it was capitalist at all, it was imperfectly so: there remained a large, non-market sector, a significant – and possibly growing – servile (peon) population, a still vigorous attachment to communal forms of property. Industry and the industrial proletariat were concentrated in a few cities (and the proletariat's numbers were declining, in absolute terms). Above all – according to certain criteria of capitalism – the direct producers had been only partially dispossessed from the means of production. These factors inhibited the growth of both market relations and free wage labour; whatever the criteria of capitalism, therefore, they were far from fully realised. Even if it is argued that capitalism was the dominant mode among several, it must be noted that the revolution arose in precisely those regions and sectors where capitalism was less entrenched and archaic modes were still strong. Peasant rebellion, *serrano* revolt, lumpenproletarian riots: wherever we look, there are essential features of the social conflict of 1910–20 which cannot be accommodated within the 'dichotomous' Marxist scheme; the Revolution is too often the work of 'secondary' classes, acting autonomously, in no sense as surrogates of the big two.

As these cases suggest, and as much of this book tries to show, these (secondary) classes were engaged in a form of class struggle; the reality of that struggle pervades the history of the Revolution. But it is one thing to analyse class struggle *in situ* – where, for example, peasants confront landlords – quite another to erect a general model of *the* Revolution, in which classes and political factions are conflated. If it is conceded that Porfirian and revolutionary Mexico was too 'backward' to fit the Marxist model of developed capitalism, there are at least two ways of trying to rescue the grand theory. It may be argued, quite simply, that it was feudal; hence the peasantry, far from constituting a secondary class, ancillary to the bourgeois/proletarian dichotomy, was the motor of a class revolution, directed against feudal landlords (the bourgeoisie now becomes the ancillary spectator). Taking into account the points already made – in particular, the incomplete dispossession of the direct producers – this argument is neither empirically implausible nor theoretically illicit.[335] But telling points can be made against this, too. Market relations and free wage labour were extensive, if not clearly dominant; in some regions, peonage was certainly on the decline; the dispossession of direct producers, though incomplete, was proceeding apace. Furthermore, the popular movement itself was tainted with capitalist ideas and practices (according to some definitions thereof): the Zapata and Cedillo families were rural entrepreneurs, of a modest kind; their communities possessed clearly defined notions of private property; they participated in – and often produced for – the market. *A fortiori*, this may be argued for northern *serranos* like Villa, Orozco, de la Rocha and others. Such popular leaders and the rural communities from which they sprang, and from which they drew inspiration and support, had adapted to capitalism, and themselves practised a form of 'penny capitalism'.[336] It will be objected that this is to follow Frank and define capitalism at the level of circulation, ignoring the relations of production. Popular rebels, after all, had often rebelled precisely to resist proletarianisation; market involvement *per se* (i.e., 'penny capitalism') was old, familiar, and tolerable; it was the new imperatives of the voracious Porfirian market – its demands for land and labour – which now provoked revolution. All this is historically valid. But what is now left of the 'feudal landlords', who must figure centrally in a dichotomous feudal class struggle? They are following market signals, accumulating capital, and dispossessing the peasantry for all they are worth. And while some may resort to servile labour systems, many – like the planters of Morelos – may not.[337]

Whether Porfirian and revolutionary Mexico is theorised as capitalist or feudal, therefore, the theory runs into serious trouble. There remains the final escape route of those doggedly committed to this terminology: the flight into the transitional. Mexico is in transition between the two poles; hence anomalies are bound to occur. The period 1876–1920 was certainly one of important transition, if 'transition' is taken simply to mean social change (all periods, of course, are transitional; but it is quite valid to argue that some, like the Porfiriato, witnessed particularly rapid, profound change; hence the Revolution).[338] But the transitional theory goes much further, incorporating a notion of *teleological* change in the direction of capitalism. On a strictly Frankian interpretation, this is untenable, since Mexico had already been capitalist for three centuries and no transition was necessary. Yet on anti-Frankian lines (where relations of production are stressed at the expense of market activity) the transition continues and is still incomplete; indeed, the Revolution, by instituting the agrarian reform, has delayed the transition *sine die*. For this reason, Goodman and Redclift (reluctant to follow those who have seen *ejidal* peasants as 'concealed proletarians') are happy to talk of a 'permanent transition' (sic).[339] Nor is this bizarre usage unique. The route from feudalism to capitalism is constantly being stretched: in England, it has been measured over six centuries of 'transition'.[340] And, as the case of India suggests, it is not clear what instruments should be used in the measurement; we may not even know, in other words, when the transition has been completed, when we have got to where we are meant to be going.[341]

This brings me to the final observation. If grand models of the transition from feudalism to capitalism have any utility, it must be in the analysis of the *longue durée*. They must encompass societies and centuries, not individuals and decades. Revolutions – even major, social revolutions like the French and Mexican – do not necessarily revolutionise the mode of production. Thus, while class conflict may be crucial (though not always causally anterior to other forms of conflict: ideological, ethnic, regional and clientelistic) the revolution cannot be comprehended within an epochal teleology, whereby classes, factions, even individuals become automatic vehicles of dialectical progress. Historical research, Hexter warns, 'must not . . . prostrate itself in unholy worship before the altar of the materialist, mystical three – feudal, bourgeois, proletarian'.[342] Or, indeed, petty bourgeoisie. Inappropriate, Eurocentric terms, casually imported from the warehouse of grand theory, should not be allowed to serve as the 'organising' (i.e., distorting) concepts of historical analysis. The historian of the Revolution – tackling an ambitious but chronologically finite theme – should rather deal in middle-range concepts and arguments, framed within the specific historical context; he should engage (as one historian – as it happens a Marxist – has put it) in 'that exciting dialectic of making-and-breaking, the formation of conceptual hypotheses, and the bringing to bear of empirical evidence to enforce or break down these hypotheses'.[343]

The weaknesses of the grand theory are particularly evident at the present juncture, when the 'petty bourgeoisie' claims attention. With the triumph of the Constitutionalists and/or the Sonorans, many historians assert, the petty bourgeoisie occupies centre stage. Given the definitional laxness already mentioned, this process is not described in identical terms, nor is it possible to make precise equations between, for example, Lavrov's 'petty bourgeois left wing' of Constitutionalism, Lobato's 'progressive petty bourgeoisie', Barry Carr's 'prototype petty bourgeoisie of Sonora'.[344] Nevertheless, it is clear that many historians agree that an important development, along these general lines, took place after 1913–14. The petty bourgeoisie, the doomed, dependent victims of developed capitalism, become the high-flyers of revolutionary Mexico. Meanwhile, landlords, businessmen, and merchants – who must have claims to constitute the bourgeoisie over and above the petty bourgeoisie – prove feeble and decadent. What is not clear is why the petty bourgeoisie's entrance has been so delayed. There are, after all, strong theoretical presumptions for including the peasantry under this label; Zapata's reforms have been described as being of a 'radical petty bourgeois nature'; the *ranchero* rebels of Hidalgo have been termed a rural 'peasant bourgeoisie'.[345] I have no brief for the use of this label, preferring, like Córdova, an alternative terminology; but the label is so widespread that it demands clarification. At the methodologically individual level at which it is often used, it could be asked in what fundamental respects the small farmers Obregón and Nicolás Flores differed from their counterparts Zapata and Cedillo; or the teacher Calles from the teacher Carrera Torres; or the lawyer Espinosa Mireles from the lawyer Liborio Reyna. Yet in each case, the former – the Constitutionalists – are conventionally termed 'petty-bourgeois', while the latter are usually considered something else. Extending the argument to their respective followers does not help either: Obregón and Flores, like Zapata and Cedillo, led predominantly peasant forces; and, as already suggested, there are theoretical grounds for subsuming the peasantry into the petty bourgeoisie anyway.

Nevertheless, the triumphant petty bourgeoisie of 1914 *are* seen as qualitatively different from their 'peasant' predecessors of 1910–13, and historians are right to stress this new development. They are wrong, however, to capitulate to a readily accessible, but inappropriate terminology, which leads to conceptual confusion. The prime differences between the 'petty bourgeois' revolutionaries (like Obregón) and the ('peasant'?) revolutionaries like Zapata cannot be reduced to class differences, determined by their contrasting relationship to the relations of production; nor even (though this is more plausible) by their differential access to economic resources. Rather, the term 'petty bourgeois', readily applied to Obregón – and to Alvarado, Calles, González, Múgica and others – while (usually) denied Zapata, describes a *mentalité* more than a class relationship; it is shorthand for a bundle of cultural attributes possessed by the former, largely absent from the latter; attributes which, though linked to class, are in no sense determined by it (otherwise one would expect a culturally homogeneous petty bourgeoisie) and which relate to education, religion, place of origin and location within the revolutionary process. Finally, there is not much typically 'petty bourgeois' about these attributes, many of which were shared by other classes, just as they were absent from the (petty bourgeois) peasantry.

The so-called 'petty bourgeois' revolutionaries displayed certain 'relational' characteristics[346] which marked them off from the pioneer popular movement: an emphasis on national as against local concerns; a familiarity with urban life, associated with a commercial, entrepreneurial spirit and an awareness of the role of organised labour; an indifference, or more often a hostility, to the Church; and a capacity for bureaucratic organisation – of army or civil institutions – which was apersonal, universalistic and meritocratic. Thus the ideal-type (for we are dealing with abstractions from and accentuations of reality) was nationalist, urban,[347] literate, secular, bureaucratic, achievement-oriented; where the popular movement was parochial, rural, illiterate, Catholic, personalist and ascriptive. The first emerged from the cities or commercialised farming regions; it sought national power by means of an organised, quasi-mercenary army, backed by an efficient civilian bureaucracy; in the process, it trampled on the Church and other rivals for power, and displayed a brash confidence in its ability to govern, at all levels. The popular movement, in contrast, was the child of the countryside, especially the partially commercialised and integrated villages and haciendas; it was dedicated to the locality and indifferent to national power; its forces, though sometimes capable of limited professionalisation, were based on personal prestige and popularity – bureaucratic back-up was weak or non-existent, and rapid growth could bring dissolution; jealous for power in its own locality, it was genially tolerant of rivals elsewhere, including Church, old Porfiristas and foreign economic interests.

These attributes consistently correlated: despite exceptions, nationalism (a concern for national power and issues) usually went with anti-clericalism, bureaucracy, and a lively interest in the labour movement. To designate these attributes 'petty bourgeois' is misleading (and, in the current jargon, 'class-reductionist'). Though class (in the sense of differential access to economic resources) played its part in their formation, other factors were present, even predominant: culture, education, religion, place of origin, revolutionary history. The choice of an alternative nomenclature, however, presents problems. It will be noted that these attributes are closely akin to those beloved of modernisation theorists ('participant political cultures . . . open, achievement-oriented systems . . . secular ideologies');[348] and these pygmy theorists stand on the shoulders of giants like Maine, Toennies and Durkheim, who developed concepts relevant to this analysis – Toennies' *Gemeinschaft/Gesellschaft* polarity, for example, and Durkheim's mechanical and organic solidarity.[349] But there is little point escaping the Marxist frying-pan in order to be consumed in the fires of modernisation theory. Both models are laden with Eurocentric, teleological implications (both, of course, derive from teleologically-minded, nineteenth-century, European thinkers); and, since our task is the analysis of an historical problem, there is no need to pledge allegiance to any grand theory, especially one (like modernisation theory) with strong normative overtones, a tendency to posit rigid, unilinear sequences of development, and an emphasis on phenomena, like industrialisation, which are peripheral to this analysis. Discarding the theory – and avoiding the key words 'modern' and 'modernising' – we should nevertheless keep in mind some of the central concepts of this school, especially of its founding fathers, for later reference.

With this theme introduced, we should return to the *explananda*. As the revolution progressed, the 'petty bourgeois'/popular cleavage was revealed in different ways. Now, with the fall of Huerta and the Carranza–Villa schism, it was the nationalist/parochial polarity which emerged most clearly. In this context, it is appropriate to term Obregón and his ('petty bourgeois') kind 'nationalists', not just in the sense of defending Mexico's political and economic sovereignty against foreigners, but also, and more important, of transcending the local concerns of the popular movement and seeking national power on the basis of national policies. Later, in analysing the final phase of revolutionary reconstruction (1916–20), other emphases – on anti-clericalism and 'developmentalism' – will emerge.

Revolutionary movements may be located on a nationalist/parochial axis, which corresponds neither to class location, nor to positions on a conventional radical/conservative axis. Most leaders of the popular movement were local boys made good whose power derived from popular support, often of an intense, personal, parochial kind. Their authority fell in the tradition of old-fashioned *caudillaje*; their forces came from a particular valley, region or cluster of villages; their extended families often provided members of the 'officer corps'; they were personally known and admired by their followers.[350] This was the case with the Arrietas in Durango; in Tlaxcala, where Arenas, Rojas and other were all from 'worker-peasant' families in the Zacatelco and Xicohtzingo districts; and, on a grander scale, in Morelos where women and children prayed for Zapata and 'a religious faith and a "military" faith united all the people to their leader'.[351] A similar local, personal commitment (the two went together: the larger the political unit, the weaker the personal commitment would become) sustained the Cedillos in San Luis, now and years after, and also Ceniceros and Contreras in the Laguna, where – first as a village lawyer, now a military commander – Ceniceros was seen as 'representing the Indians, just the regular Mexican Indians', while around Cuencamé 'all the people liked Contreras'.[352] And such fervent localism, allied to clientelism, bolstered caciques like 'Che' Gómez, Lucas of the Puebla Sierra, and Meixueiro of the Sierra Juárez.[353]

The commitment was reciprocal: parochial leaders were indifferent to national power, regarding it, at best, as a means to guarantee the *patria chica*. Many ignored it altogether; some even disdained opportunities to seize state capitals. Zapatismo, the most consistently powerful of popular movements, displayed such inhibitions throughout: the occupation of Mexico City was hesitant and partial; and the Zapatistas declined to go east of Puebla (not, as has been argued, because they lacked ammunition, for they were well provided at the time) but because they disliked quasi-foreign expeditions. After a brief occupation of the city, 'the troops from Morelos that [Zapata] had taken on campaign followed him home, uninterested in the glory of conquest'.[354] Again, Zapatismo was typical rather than unique. Julián Blanco displayed no interest in national politics, save to the extent that they directly impinged upon the Costa Grande (hence Mariscal was able to steal a march on him); Juan Carrasco of Sinaloa dismissed the idea of a national convention of the military as a waste of time (a 'nest of scorpions' was his phrase) and preferred to get on with the fighting in his home state.[355] Repeatedly, such localist forces refused to divert their energies outside the *patria chica*, at the behest of a distant, tenuous authority, like Carranza's. The Cedillos scarcely budged out of Valle de Maíz between 1912 and 1916, but went their own way, adopting a succession of national labels, obeying 'superior' orders when it suited them, reverting to guerrilla war if they were threatened by interlopers.[356] In such circumstances, political allegiances reflected local expedience rather than shared ideology. The Cedillos repudiated Eulalio Gutiérrez because he planned a campaign into Coahuila involving Cedillo's forces; similarly, it was the Arrietas' refusal to leave their own patch for the siege of Torreón which engendered their quarrel with Pancho Villa; 'throughout the five years of revolution', it was noted in 1916, 'the Arrietas have always refused to leave the state'.[357] And lower still in the hierarchy, elusive to the gaze of historians, there were lesser leaders whose concerns were entirely local and whose 'national' allegiances were tactical, ephemeral and meaningless. Miguel Canales of Muleros (Dgo) commanded 500 men in 1915: he had been a Maderista (1911), Orozquista (1912), Carrancista (1913), Villista (1914) and now, in 1915, was again a Carrancista.[358] His operations were wholly confined to the remote, south-eastern corner of the state, where his forces lived off the local haciendas, like San Juan de Michis. It need hardly be added that such leaders evinced little interest in or grasp of foreign relations. Calixto Contreras, who had dragged his feet even for the attack on Torréon, believed that Villa's impressive stock of American ammunition was a personal gift from Villa's *compadre*, General Hugh Scott.[359] International relations, like national politics, were mediated through familiar, personal concepts, like *compadrazgo*.

In contrast, there were revolutionary leaders who displayed outstanding spatial – and, as a result, social – mobility. Cutting loose from local ties, they pursued their politico-military careers according to national exigencies, travelling, fighting, governing like revolutionary conquistadores. Inevitably, this breed grew in numbers and importance. For, despite the intense localism which helped generate the initial popular insurgency, the revolution over time worked to break down parochial commitments: a congeries of local rebellions gradually fused into something resembling *the* Revolution of official rhetoric and historiography. It was another example of the ingrate revolution devouring the parents who had brought it into the world. Maderista liberals, *agraristas*, die-hard parochials – all made major contributions before 1914; but decisive, permanent gains eluded them; and, ultimately, they all lost out for a similar, simple reason – because, unlike the eventual victors, they looked backwards, evoked a lost past, and stood against the main trends and pressures within Mexican society, which, whoever ruled in the National Palace, had an irreversible dynamic of their own. The *déraciné* nationalists (the misnamed 'petty bourgeoisie' of many accounts) collaborated with these trends and pressures, hence over the years their power waxed, even though they had played little part in the genesis of the Revolution. Precisely in 1914–15 – the high point of decentralisation, chaos and warlordism – countervailing tendencies towards national integration were set in motion. For, just as the campaigns against Huerta in 1913–14 had forged guerrilla bands into revolutionary armies, so the contest for national power in 1914–15 encouraged the formation of broad political coalitions with pretensions to national power. Parochial *cabecillas* went on cultivating their gardens; meantime, nationalist elites were bidding for power and the mobile, opportunist, *déracinés* of the revolution became key weapons in this final bout of civil war.

This must be seen in a national context. By 1914 the revolution was becoming a powerful solvent of local particularism, impinging on remote, introverted communities which had hitherto been immune to national conflicts: San José de Gracia, where inhabitants had only read about the Maderista revolution, now had first-hand experience of Villista and Carrancista warmongering; Tilantongo, in highland Oaxaca, where Independence and the Reforma had passed by unnoticed, was now for the first time affected by national politics.[360] War, economic dislocation, and the pressgang had uprooted families and individuals, taking them to unknown parts of the country, even abroad, widening horizons and breaking down particularist sentiment.[361] Some military leaders (military leaders being easiest to trace) etched complicated patterns across the face of the country – and not just the national caudillos whose lengthy peregrinations ('8,000 kilometres on campaign', as Obregón's autobiography boasts) were only to be expected. Lesser leaders shuttled to and fro over the years: Gertrudis Sánchez from Coahuila to Guerrero and Michoacán; Cándido Aguilar from Veracruz to Oaxaca, the Laguna, and back to Veracruz; Gabriel Gavira from Veracruz to Oaxaca to Cuba (after Huerta's coup) to Tamaulipas, Veracruz, San Luis, Durango and Chihuahua. Even quintessentially popular leaders were forced to roam: Juan Banderas, brought under arrest from Sinaloa to Mexico in 1912, was freed, joined the Zapatistas, attended the revolutionary convention at Aguascalientes (October 1914), acted as a broker between Villa and Zapata, fought in

Hidalgo, and finally returned to Sinaloa, where he fell in with a guerrilla band including Sinaloans, Orestes Pereyra's Durango veterans and Angel Barrios, the Oaxaqueño *agrarista*, once a Zapatista, now translated by the fortunes of war to a new, northern environment.[362] Nor was this mobility purely individual: detachments – like Gavira's much travelled, ultimately decimated, Juchitecos – followed their leaders around the country.[363]

Much of this mobility was forced, not voluntary. But it indicated that mobility in general had increased, as local gave way to national campaigns, and this inevitably favoured the careers of readily mobile, nationalist rebels at the expense of their parochial rivals. The former really became prominent with the Constitutionalists' descent on central Mexico in 1914. Prior to this, military fiefs had been created almost organically, subsequently being ratified by caudillos, like Carranza, who sought to trade recognition for allegiance, and to smooth the multitude of inter-revolutionary rivalries which by 1914 were reaching critical proportions.[364] Now, further south, it was a question of inserting loyal Constitutionalists into the political shambles occasioned by the fall of Huerta – establishing a new political order, obedient to the First Chief. Like Madero in 1911, Carranza in 1914 had political debts to pay, and creditors clamouring for payment, but where Madero had somewhat grudgingly tossed a few *rural* commissions to the young, revolutionary military, Carranza promoted them lavishly and extensively; above all, the mobile, administratively competent nationalists. Many of these – the Sonorans for example – had strong local roots themselves, but these did not commit them to a limpet-like localism. On the contrary, the Sonorans mobilised their domestic resources for the descent on Mexico City; and, as they won power, they 'nationalised' their local base by the wholesale preferment of fellow-Sonorans.

In Veracruz, for example, a 'clean sweep' was made of all officials, even down to the lighthouse keepers and the personnel of the Mexican Railway.[365] In the northern part of the state, new Constitutionalist officers even superseded 'those who have been doing the active fighting', causing resentment and the threat of further revolts in this already turbulent region.[366] By late 1914, all the official military commanders (though not, of course, the perennial local rebels, the insurgent landlords, and the intrusive Zapatistas) were northern newcomers.[367] In neighbouring Puebla, too, the Carrancistas replaced 'all the office-holders from the humble clerk to the bosses, irrespective of their antecedents or affiliations . . . the majority of the military commandants [sic] in substitution of the *jefes políticos* . . . being selected from among the northern element'.[368] In remote sierra districts, where particularism ruled, such thorough political renovation was extremely risky, if not impossible. It antagonised indigenous revolutionaries, like those of Tlaxcala, who were now subordinated to northerners like Francisco Coss and Alejo González; it stimulated the landlord rebellions already mentioned.[369] And it was all the more galling when the northerners rode roughshod over local interests: when they abused local saints, or the Church in general; when they ransacked businesses (Coss, evacuating Puebla in December 1914, was said to have done 2m. pesos of damage); when, like the high-minded Gavira, they closed cantinas and brothels and steamrollered insalubrious parts of town.[370]

Such actions were often premised on notions of northern cultural, even racial, superiority. John Lind's belief that the 'men of the North' were alone capable of regenerating a decadent society was shared by *norteños* themselves: Ciro B. Ceballos, one of Carranza's intellectual hacks, included Lind among those 'most enlightened people' who believed that 'the northerners (*los fronterizos*) are summoned to be the rulers of all the inhabitants of the country in the future'; but Ceballos had misgivings, since[371]

by placing themselves in close contact with the rest of the Mexican population, especially that of the central plateau, the former [northerners] may acquire the vices of the latter, leading to the degeneration if not the transformation of the essential conditions of their present, undisputed, racial superiority.

If such outspoken racialism was unusual (a subtler form can be found in Salvador Alvarado's writings), there was always the cogent argument of political success: in a competitive world, the triumph of the northerners indicated that they were the revolutionary elect. It was only right, argued one, that 'a son of Tamaulipas, Sonora or Sinaloa' should govern Yucatán, or any southern state, since these were states 'thoroughly reactionary in the political struggle . . . [lacking] sufficient elements of strength and intelligence to direct public opinion'.[372] Therefore, northern carpetbaggers would have to assume the responsibility.

The classic examples of Constitutionalist carpetbagging came – appropriately – in the deep south, in Tabasco, Oaxaca, Chiapas and Yucatán. These instances showed nationalist (alias 'petty bourgeois') leaders operating in their purest form. It was, first of all, significant that Carranza should order a *coup de main* on southern Mexico: Villa, though advised to this effect, made no attempt to despatch Villista proconsuls to the south.[373] There were immediate, tactical reasons for Carranza's decision: a desire to tap the economic resources of Yucatán; the need to demobilise the Federals congregated on the Isthmus; and the possibility that the south could provide a sanctuary, if Villismo swept the rest of the country. Hence the southern missions of Jesús Carranza, Gavira, Pascual Molina y Morales, and even Obregón, who briefly considered traversing the Isthmus to open up a campaign against Villa on the familiar west coast.[374] But these were but preambles to sustained politico-military campaigns, undertaken to impose Constitutionalism on the south, if necessary by force. To this end, Carranza was not content – as Villa often was – with the token allegiance of *de facto* independent generals and governors, of varied political hues. Seeking to govern the south in reality as well as name, Carranza had to rely on nationalist proconsuls who, like him, were keen to incorporate the benighted, provincial south into Constitutionalism. 'Chiapanecan cowards', as one addressed his new subjects, 'I will teach you to feel the effects of the Revolution.'[375]

Three deserve particular mention: Francisco Múgica, Jesús Agustín Castro, and Salvador Alvarado – soon to be governors, respectively of Tabasco, Oaxaca and Chiapas, and Yucatán. Múgica, alone of the three, came from central Mexico: he served his political apprenticeship as an opposition journalist in Michoacán, where he had been born into a staunchly liberal, anti-clerical professional family. He did not take up arms in Michoacán in 1910 but travelled to the US, linking up with the Maderista national leadership early in 1911. His military exploits were not notable. Defeated at San Miguel Camargo (Tamps.), he crossed back to the US, where, for the first time, he encountered Venustiano Carranza.[376] Múgica did not return to his home state until June 1911, when he came as a 'Peace Delegate', charged with demobilisation and pacification – the work of a politician and administrator, not a military caudillo. This completed, he joined the long queue of job-hunters outside the Mexico City ministries; but, finally, it was through his recent northern contact, Carranza, that he secured a post, as Director General of State Statistics in Coahuila, which he retained until 1913. Múgica was therefore in Coahuila, on Carranza's payroll, at the time of the Huerta coup. He readily slotted into the First Chief's staff, signed the Plan of Guadalupe and fought alongside the northerners Blanco, Saucedo and González during 1913. Despite his new military rank, Múgica was more administrator and propagandist: one of those 'civiles militarizados' whose numbers swelled as the revolution progressed; he came into his own with the famous land grant at Los Borregos.[377] And, though a Michoacano by birth, he was a northerner by inclination and political adoption: liberal, anti-clerical, educated, articulate and efficient, he was a natural choice for preferment when the Constitutionalists came to power. Accordingly, Múgica was placed in charge of the Veracruz customs, of the port of Tampico, and finally of the state of Tabasco.[378]

Castro came from the Laguna: but from the urban, industrial Laguna, typified by Torreón, rather than the rural hinterland of Contreras and Ceniceros. Born into a 'modest family' of Cd Lerdo in 1887, he had a reasonable, if interrupted, schooling, at least to the age of fourteen; thereafter, like Calles, he held a succession of jobs – metal-worker, carpenter, builder, cashier, tram foreman – which took him to Santa Barbara, Gómez, Chihuahua City, Parral and finally Torreón, where he was working for the tram company at the outbreak of the revolution.[379] His subsequent military mobility was no less marked: after leading the initial attack on Gómez in 1910, he fought elsewhere in Coahuila and Durango during the Madero revolution, distinguished himself during the *Decena Trágica*, and then undertook a long odyssey to the north-east, where he again showed himself to be a capable, strong-willed commander.[380] While the great majority of the Laguna rebels inclined to Villa, Castro – a different type of Laguna rebel – threw in his lot with Carranza in 1913–14; hence he was chosen to export Constitutionalism to Chiapas late in 1914.

Alvarado, finally, was a native of Sinaloa, born in 1880.[381] As a child, however, he moved with his family to Potam, in Sonora's Yaqui Valley, where his father established a store. After a decent schooling – evident in his prolix writings – Alvarado worked as a pharmacist's assistant in Guaymas, before setting up his own store at Potam, and later Cananea. There he moved in opposition circles and was among the first Sonoran rebels to challenge Díaz in 1910–11. Though he and Juan Cabral had claims to revolutionary seniority in the state, Alvarado witnessed – with some disgust – the return of Maytorena and the rise to power of Obregón. To the latter he was reconciled, becoming one of Obregón's leading commanders; but the feud with Maytorena smouldered and finally flared up in the summer of 1914. Then Carranza plucked him from the flames and sent him to govern Yucatán.

Múgica, Castro and Alvarado were all personally known to the First Chief; the first, though not a northerner, had been Carranza's political client. More important, all were highly mobile, nationally-conscious men – literate, if lacking the humane, impractical, formal education (the 'enseñanza libresca') of the *licenciado*.[382] All three had moved about in search of jobs, preferment, and – later – military victory. Their assets were not local connections and popular support, so much as personal talent and a powerful blend of idealism and ambition. They were cast in a different mould to Zapata, Contreras or the Cedillos; equally, they boasted more plebeian origins and more practical abilities than the educated, refined, civilian *políticos*; they were better suited to establish a dialogue with the common masses. They were, therefore, peculiarly suited to the proconsular role. But this begs the question: how did they differ from these other socio-political groups? Class *per se* explains little: it is arguable that nationalists, rural populists and even some civilian *políticos* fell into the capacious 'petty bourgeois' category; which, in turn, must be disaggregated along lines which cannot be class-derived.

Clearly, education was important: Castro, like a good many (urban) manual workers of his generation, had received a basic education; he was able to assume managerial tasks; to an American naval officer he seemed 'fairly well educated' (and, incidentally, something of a ladykiller).[383] But this was not education in the classical curriculum (Latin, philosophy, history, theology), to which – of the three – only Múgica had been subjected, and against which he had youthfully rebelled.[384] Alvarado was something of an autodidact, for whom the reading of Samuel Smiles had been a revelation; his own writings are larded by references to Spencer, Victor Hugo and Henry George, and pervaded by a Puritanical, social Darwinist progressivism, tinged with racialism.[385] All three chased jobs in restless, ambitious fashion and, though they counted on some paternal support, none enjoyed access to the privileges or favour of the Porfirian oligarchy. They were not (like Madero) close to the Científico elite, nor (like Palavicini) recipient of government stipends; they did not (like Cabrera) enjoy lucrative contracts with foreign companies.[386] They were, in Barry Carr's phrase, 'self-made men' (*Self-Help* was Alvarado's bible) and, as such, they were enemies of privilege, hierarchy and entrenched officialdom. Resentment against the latter impelled Alvarado to revolution; Múgica, having bucked the intellectual tutelage of the Church, turned to journalistic assaults on the Porfirian oligarchs of Michoacán.[387] Castro, crossing Chiapas in 1914, was shocked by the action of an Indian woman who prostrated herself before him: descending from his car, he raised her up and explained that now, with the Revolution, all men (and women) were equal.[388] Whether true or not, the episode caught something of the nationalists' ideology: one that was couched in universalistic, liberal terms, which admitted no ascriptive hierarchies and which − while endorsing order, property and centralised government − was hostile to tradition and privilege, both secular and clerical.

Such an ideology compares closely with Carranza's 'Jacobinism'.[389] But, in the case of the proconsuls (and of Obregón, Calles, Gavira, Murguía and others), it was allied to a distinct revolutionary experience: that of military recruitment, organisation and campaigning, which, apart from providing administrative experience, also brought them in close contact with the common masses, made them aware of popular grievances, and developed in them a capacity for populist leadership. Meanwhile, their background and careers differed from those of popular rebels (like Zapata) in obvious respects. All were products of an urbanised, commercial milieu, which had most fully developed in the north. They were products of dollar capitalism rather than penny capitalism. If Obregón was a farmer, he was a mobile, innovative farmer, familiar with other lines of business, and dedicated to an export cash crop.[390] If Alvarado hailed from a small community (Potam) it was precisely one which had grown thanks to the influx of go-ahead, mestizo ranchers and traders, like Alvarado's father, and at the expense of the dispossessed Yaqui Indians.[391] Such men had no personal experience of − or empathy with − the traditional peasant community, with its corporate ethos, self-regulating mechanisms, and resistance to external pressures, political and economic. What therefore distinguished the (petty-bourgeois) Múgica, Alvarado and Castro from the (petty-bourgeois?) Zapata, Cedillos and Contreras was less class than contrasting world-views: one literate, urban, individualist (*gesellschaftlich?*), inculcated by school, newspapers, jobs and the entire experience of commercial, city life; the other illiterate, rural, corporate (*gemeinschaftlich?*), moulded by the traditional, closed patterns of village and hacienda. It was a difference inexplicable in Eurocentric, Marxist categories, being one that derived − rather like the Church–State conflict of the 1920s − from the whole concatenation of Mexico's social, economic and cultural development at national and regional levels.[392]

THE NEW REGIME: THE PROCONSULS

Through 1913–14, Oaxaca had remained fairly quiet. Scattered revolts against Huerta had never coalesced into a powerful movement. Governor Bolaños Cacho was unusual in that he survived, a civilian governor, through the year and a half of Huertista militarism; an indication of the peculiar, self-contained character of Oaxaqueño politics. But the *serranos*, who had descended from the mountains to lay siege to the state capital in 1912, were by the summer of 1914 growing restless again. Typically, their grievances were against the state government (Bolaños Cacho was a valley landlord) which had been obliged to respond to Huertista demands for men and money to combat the revolution. By July, with Huerta tottering, the *serrano* leaders decided to put an end to the tax increases and (they alleged) the graft, political murders and other abuses of the Bolaños Cacho regime; they also wished to stake their claim to power as political crisis loomed.[393] The moving spirit behind the Plan de la Sierra was Guillermo Meixueiro, cacique of the Sierra Mixteca, staunch supporter first of Porfirio then Félix Díaz, whose Felicismo had brought his arrest by Huerta in October 1913. Released the following July, Meixueiro met with his allies at the hacienda of Rodolfo Pardo, the old Porfirista *enganchador* and *jefe político*, near Tuxtepec where, it was well known, they were planning a descent on Oaxaca.[394] So it turned out: denouncing Bolaños Cacho, they swept down from the mountains, following the same route of 1912 – via Etla, Tlacolula and San Felipe de Agua – meeting scant resistance on the way. Bolaños Cacho was overthrown a matter of days after Huerta and, with the *serranos* triumphant, the state legislature appointed a new, conservative, civilian governor, Francisco Canseco. Oaxaca was now, in effect, a self-governing entity, claiming a somewhat spurious legality; and, despite a brief co-existence with the Constitutionalist regime through the autumn of 1914, its leaders no more welcomed Carrancista incursions into the state than they did those of the ex-Huertistas Almazán, Argumedo and Higinio Aguilar, then prowling its north-eastern borders.[395]

For reasons already mentioned, Carranza could not tolerate Oaxacan autonomy. On the Isthmus, his brother Jesús saw to the demobilisation of Federal forces and began appointing new, Constitutionalist officials, to local disgust.[396] This was not the only affront to Oaxaqueño sentiment. When the Meixueiro faction sent a delegation to the military convention, they were reviled as reactionaries; and, even worse, General Luis Jiménez Figueroa – a maverick Oaxaqueño revolutionary of chequered past – staged a briefly successful coup in the City of Oaxaca itself, claiming to represent Carranza and the central government.[397] But the city could not stand against the sierra; and in the sierra itself Jiménez Figueroa and the Carrancistas could only count on the support of inveterate enemies of the Meixueiro faction, like the Ixtepejanos – whom, it is no surprise to learn, Jiménez Figueroa had captained in earlier times. His coup offered another example of the constant redefinition of local rivalries in national terms; and it also reinforced the *serranos'* control of Oaxaca and suspicion of the rest of the Mexico. As an observer noted: 'some idea of [Meixueiro's] hold upon the people may be had from the fact that when Figueroa captured the capital, Meixueiro made his escape, fled to the mountains, and within four or five days returned with an army at his back'.[398] Recovering power, Meixueiro built up a state militia and, in December, secured the election as governor of José Inés Dávila, an old Porfirista *político* and ally. While Carranza – short of friends and not lacking enemies – now sought to placate the controlling interest in Oaxaca, disowning Jiménez and justifying his brother's presence on the Isthmus as a military necessity, it was nevertheless clear that Oaxaca and the Constitutionalists were out of step. Under Governor Dávila, the state government sought to immunise itself from the revolutionary contagion: its aim was to maintain 'the Federal laws and national traditions of the Porfirio Díaz government' and its philosophy was outspokenly Burkean, dismissive of Constitutionalist Jacobinism: 'the customs and manners of peoples are not modified by legislative fiat, but by measures that are slow and well considered'.[399] Oaxaca seemed 'a restored paradise of the old order . . . surrounded by a revolutionary hell'.[400]

Before noting the outcome of this strained relationship, the focus must shift to Chiapas, where a similar situation prevailed. In September 1914, Castro and 1,200 men arrived to effect the demobilisation of the Federal garrisons there.[401] An old political fief of the Rabasas, under the economic control of prosperous, *ladino* landowners, Chiapas presented the Constitutionalists with a clear choice: 'either to reach deals with the established interests, or to try to subjugate them. Jesús Agustín Castro chose to destroy the political domination of the Rabasistas and to abolish the rights and privileges of the landlords.'[402] In other words, he embarked on a range of proconsular policies, designed to break the power of the Chiapaneco elite and integrate the state into the national revolution. *Jefes* were purged and replaced by Constitutionalist appointees; notorious Porfiristas were executed; in October, peonage was declared abolished and minimum wages were set; in December, church property was expropriated and convents were closed down; a programme of land reform was initiated.[403] Irrespective of any inherent social justice in these measures, they represented a clear assault on the landlord class, and an attempt to prise the peons from their dependence on and control by the *finqueros*. The first produced a predictable landlord rebellion, the second proved largely fruitless. Late in 1914, Tiburcio Fernández Ruiz, the young scion of a landed family of Chiapa, led a rebellion in protest at the 'vandalistic acts of the Carrancistas'; it was a carbon copy, albeit on a grander scale, of the landlord rebellions of Veracruz, taking the same form and obeying similar motives. And like the Veracruz rebellions, this counted on widespread support, not only from landlords (many of whom stayed neutral, while a few turned Carrancista) but also from peons, Indians, and Chiapanecans in general, who resented outside interference.[404] The initial core of revolt, in the southern foothills of the Sierra Madre, thus included 'frontier landowners, ranchers, hacienda foremen, cowboys, ex-soldiers and *rurales*'; the rebels were termed *mapaches* since, like racoons, they ate raw corn in the fields when campaigning.[405] Outgunned by Castro's forces, they made slow progress. But by the summer of 1915, Fernández had been seconded by numerous supporters across the state: Angel Pérez and other *ganaderos* of Soconusco (whose commitment was short-lived); Tirso Cantañón of Comitán, who became rebel governor; Manuel Robelo Arguello and Flavio Guillén, both ex-governors of the Maderista period, the latter now a nominal Villista; and a clutch of ex-Federals. Most important, in 1916 Alberto Pineda, son of the Cristobalense leader of 1911, raised forces in the highlands and on the Chiapas/Tabasco borders, and threw in his lot with the rebels. Again, Carrancista abuses had helped provoke rebellion, and had even achieved a temporary resolution of the old conflict between San Cristóbal and Tuxtla. Long after Castro was sent to Oaxaca to retrieve the perilous situation there, the Chiapas rebels sustained a powerful challenge to the central government, soon attracting to their encampments the Porfirian pretender, Félix Díaz.[406]

Castro shuttled back to Oaxaca in July 1915 as Oaxaqueño disenchántment with Carrancismo crystallised into open rebellion. Several factors acted as catalysts. From his base at Jamiltepec, Juan José Baños – a bitter enemy of Meixueiro – urged Carranza to move against the *serrano* reactionaries. And on the Isthmus, the other locus of Carrancismo in Oaxaca, the Tehuantepec cacique Alfonso Santibáñez captured and executed Jesús Carranza, the First Chief's brother. The facts of this case – like the revolutionary politics of the south in general – are highly complex. Santibáñez, often wrongly termed an ex-Federal or Huertista, was a veteran of 1911, whose assumption of power at Tehuantepec, described above, followed family tradition.[407] Though he may well have arrested Jesús in order to extract concessions from the central government, as conventional accounts suggest; and though he may well have executed his hostage when the First Chief, showing Roman fortitude, refused to bargain; nevertheless, the episode was not quite the morality play it seems. Like most local leaders, Santibáñez (though briefly a Carrancista himself) resented the wholesale political changes wrought by the Carrancista interlopers, and he particularly resented it when Jesús Carranza lined up a client to usurp his hard-won Tehuantepec command.[408] Nor was Jesús' the first blood to be shed. Santibáñez's two brothers had been executed when he broke with Carrancismo; Jesús Carranza was reckoned to be responsible for the death of Carbajal – a nominal 'Zapatista' and, like Santibáñez, a veteran of the 1911 revolution in the south.[409] It is entirely likely that considerations of personal revenge, linked to the current, fierce, political strife, were enough to determine Jesús Carranza's death, irrespective of his brother's stoic stance. Isthmus politics – as 'Chato' Díaz, 'Che' Gómez, now Jesús Carranza, soon his killer Santibáñez, and later many others found to their cost – were treacherous, violent and bloody.[410]

At any rate, by mid-1915, Oaxaca and Carrancismo had rudely parted company. The state government repudiated the national regime, denounced the legal fiction of the 'pre-constitutional' period, and declared that Oaxaca 'resumed' its sovereignty, breaking the federal pact and asserting its independence. Fundamentally, this was a 'states' rights' movement, as yet unaffected by political liaison with Félix Díaz (beyond the loose, personal link between Díaz and Meixueiro); but there could be no doubt of the conservatism of the movement's leaders and philosophy, nor of the boost given Oaxaca's traditional autonomist leanings by the fact of a radical government in Mexico City.[411] Yet the rupture was popular, and received with 'great enthusiasm' by many Oaxaqueños: because it promised an escape from revolutionary violence, a defence of local interests against the demands of the central government (for men and money) and, yet again, an opportunity to pursue old, local vendettas under a new set of labels.[412] It would be wrong, therefore, to underestimate the strength of such provincial sentiment, and its capacity to unite diverse classes against a presumed common enemy. In Oaxaca, Chiapas and, it will be seen, Yucatán, 'provincialism and local roots' provided a firm base for multi-class, 'vertically integrated' rebellions, directed against alien, centralising forces.[413] Once again, the Revolution, like the Porfiriato, raised up *serrano* rebellions which proved tough opponents.[414] And, though the circumstances of 1914 made for different emphases – *serrano* rebellions were now formally 'conservative', harking back to Díaz, Juárez, and the Constitution of 1857 – the underlying socio-political reality remained. Such movements were genuinely popular and, though often captained by caciques and landlords, embraced a wide section of society, for whom the external enemy posed a bigger (subjective) threat than internal exploiters. Proconsular promises of reform and progress made only limited headway against such sentiments.[415] It is finally worth noting the nostalgia for the past, and the antipathy to forced change, which these (conservative) *serrano* movements shared even with the (radical) popular rebellions of the centre and north. 'These men', a critic pointed out, 'have only taken up arms to defend the past, and have not proceeded in the manner of the men of the north, who took up their arms to hurl themselves towards the conquest of the future.'[416] The 'men of the north' were, of course, the Constitutionalist Jacobins, against whom Meixueiro polemicised; and the observation, though made by a Oaxaqueño against his fellow-Oaxaqueños, could also have been applied to the Zapatistas. The past which these respective rebellions sought to defend was not identical, nor were the threats against which they reacted the same. Zapatismo, as a classic, agrarian movement, resisted *economic* change, confronted an innovative, expansionist landlord class, and necessarily pursued – in rhetoric and practice – a form of class conflict. *Serrano* rebellion, political and anti-centralist, contained no such radical, class-conscious dynamic. But in the right circumstances (and there were plenty of these after 1914) it could display greater strength and stamina, and make a bigger historical impact, than the radical, agrarian movements, whose superiority is often arbitrarily assumed. And, despite their clear differences, both found a common enemy in the swaggering, obtrusive Jacobins of the north.

In July 1915, one of these, Castro, quit Chiapas for Oaxaca, landing at Salina Cruz to begin a conquest of the interior. It was a scrappy but fierce campaign, as the well-armed northern veterans confronted numerically superior but poorly armed local levies.[417] In March 1916, the City of Oaxaca fell to the Carrancistas and Governor Dávila, Meixueiro and their lieutenants took to the mountains, where, formally allied with Félix Díaz, they maintained a stout resistance throughout the year. An American, observing the fighting around Tuxtepec early in 1916, was struck by the 'great animosity' shown by the rebels – 'simple Oaxaca Indians', as he called them – against the Carrancistas; he commented, too, on the good marksmanship of the *serranos*.[418] Despite this, and their undoubted numbers (some said 25,000), their cause declined. They lacked artillery and ammunition; they suffered dissensions within the leadership (which have been traced back to primordial divisions between Zapotec and Mixtec); and their fragmented, local forces, however numerous, could not cohere for joint action. The Carrancistas, too, could exploit local rivalries, winning to their cause communities like Nochixtlán (which promptly paid for its apostasy).[419] Late in 1916 the rebel headquarters of Ixtlán fell to the Carrancistas – who found the town's stock of grain laced with cyanide – and it became clear that Oaxaqueño separatism had gone down to defeat.[420] Yet such movements were notoriously hard to eradicate. Despite further defeats in 1917, the *serranos* sustained their guerrilla struggle into the following year.[421] As governor, meanwhile, Castro had pursued the same policies here as in Chiapas: he purged and propagandised, carried out a cadastral survey and undertook land reform, patronised the infant labour movement and bullied the Church. Oaxaca, as he put it, could no longer 'exclude itself from the struggle'; the burdens and benefits of the revolution were to be shared, like it or not.[422]

Francisco Múgica's transfer to Tabasco in the summer of 1915 derived from similar causes: a situation of fragmented local factionalism, in which resistance to Carrancista central control – even on the part of local 'Carrancistas' – was marked, and a succession of governors had failed to bridge the gulf between local opinion and central demands – for men, money and obedience. Luis Felipe Domínguez, landlord and leader of a rebellion against Huerta in the far east of the state, slipped into the governorship in 1914, but proved too much of a *transaccionista* – too soft, some thought, on local 'reactionaries' and Huertistas (which was strange, since his campaigns had earned him the gratitude of peons, freed from the notorious *monterías* of the highlands).[423] He was succeeded by Carlos Greene – the pig-dealer of 1914 – and the pre-eminent Constitutionalist commander in the state. But by mid-1915 Greene was also out of favour with Carranza: he was summoned to Veracruz to face charges of indiscipline; fresh troops were brought in from Campeche; and Greene's own forces were gathered at Frontera to be neutralised. They[424]

will eventually be subdivided in small detachments and incorporated with the Constitutionalist forces in northern Mexico. It appears that it has been found necessary to adopt this plan in order to avoid an uprising among those troops who do not wish to leave or be far away from Tabasco, which is their home.

Indeed, the Constitutionalist command hoped to settle this tricky – but familiar – problem by sending Greene's troops first to Yucatán, which at a pinch they would tolerate, and then to the battle-fields of the north. Thus, it was hoped, local revolutionary particularism would be broken down; and, while the north supplied governors and generals for the south, the south could at least provide cannon-fodder for the north.

Governor Greene's career seemed 'to have come to an end'; a new Carrancista appointee, Aquileo Juárez, took his place; and there was a brief illusory calm. But Juárez, another native of Tabasco, also took the line of least resistance; like his predecessors and like his equivalent in Yucatán (Eleuterio Avila), he identified with local interests at the expense of his loyalty to the national regime – priorities which were natural enough in view of the national regime's evident shakiness. Previously confiscated property, for example, was returned to its owners. Probably for this reason, Juárez was 'accused of being a Spanish sympathiser'; he was considered 'generally not in accord with the Carrancista'; there was talk of his being a covert Villista – another way of saying that he was at odds with Carranza.[425] So Carranza rang the changes again and Juárez was replaced by Pedro Colorado. This provoked further resentment and, within days, a serious rebellion. Local troops, led by José Gil Morales (and, it was said, tacitly backed by Aquileo Juárez) revolted at San Juan Bautista, killing the new governor and several of his officers and family. Gil Morales, the author of this fresh piece of Isthmus violence, was a colourful character: a 'revolution-ary of Indian type', said to incline towards Villismo, a natty dresser with a big local reputation, who had only recently been released from gaol after killing a man in a dance-hall brawl.[426] To the central government, Gil Morales stood for 'reaction', Villismo, and contagious provincialism. To Gil Morales himself, this was a purely Tabasqueño affair, lacking national significance: 'our uprising', he declared, 'is not against the First Chief of the Constitution-alist Army . . . being simply local'.[427]

For Carranza, the distinction did not apply. Such localist insubordination clashed with the grand objectives of Carrancismo; and, if generalised, it would convert the country into a patchwork of semi-autonomous military fiefs. Furthermore, there was a real danger, in the summer of 1915, that a rebellion in Tabasco might coalesce with similar provincial movements in southern Veracruz, Oaxaca and Chiapas, jeopardising Carrancista control of the entire south. Recently, Oaxaqueño rebels had strayed across the Isthmus into the historically troubled districts of Huimanguillo and Cárdenas, there to be joined, it was said, by 'a number of prominent citizens [of Tabasco] who were exiled and their properties confiscated'; these may well have been the 'sons of Tabascan landlords' who were soon to be implicated in Pineda's revolt, on the Chiapas/Tabasco borders.[428] The spectre of landlord and provincial rebellion had to be exorcised – and Carranza now realised the folly of relying on indigenous revolutionary forces to impose his will. Fortunately, at this moment events elsewhere meant that forces could be released for campaigns in the south. From Campeche and Veracruz Carrancista troops converged on San Juan Bautista, and in their wake came a new governor, Francisco Múgica, who had no compromising links with the state he had been sent to rule.

At San Juan, Gil Morales had imposed the usual levies on business and ordered a big fiesta to celebrate the new regime. The celebrations were premature. Despite rumours of a sympathetic mutiny at Frontera, the San Juan rebels remained alone, unable to resist the Carrancista invaders. In a matter of days the town fell and Gil Morales' forces – depleted by desertion – fled into the steamy rain forests around Palenque.[429] Múgica proceeded to govern Tabasco for a year. His biographer praises the governor's enlightened reforms: improved education, public works, the beginnings of agrarian reform.[430] But it was also a governorship characterised by a strong, sometimes doctrinaire, extension of Constitutionalist power and ideology, and one which (*pace* the same biographer) did not endear Múgica to the hearts of the Tabasqueños. Perhaps they were stupid, misguided and retrograde not to applaud Múgica's measures more than they did; but the fact remains they did not. And Múgica, for his part, had no intention of repeating the soft *política de transacción* of his predecessors: Gil Morales' supporters were hunted down and summarily executed (they included several prominent revolutionaries of 1913–14); San Juan Bautista recovered its old, secular name of Villa Hermosa; the cathedral was used as a barracks and its main altar destroyed. Old *jefe políticos* were removed and replaced by new administrative committees, equally named by the executive. The main road out of San Juan was completed by requiring all travellers who passed along it to push a wheel-barrow full of earth. Tabasqueños also witnessed the new revolutionary phenomena of Pedagogic and Feminist Congresses. Radical this may have been; popular it was not. When Múgica quit Tabasco in February 1916, it was to the boos and jeers of the San Juan crowd.[431]

Múgica's sojourn in Tabasco was too brief to convert the state into a true 'laboratory of revolution'; that was to come ten years later, when Múgica's one-time protégé, Tomás Garrido Canabal, carried Constitutionalist policies to their extreme conclusion.[432] But proconsular rule could prove effective. The sequence of events in Yucatán followed a familiar pattern: a Carrancista bid for power, disturbing a relatively tranquil polity; local resistance and near-secession; finally, the defeat of particularism and a period – in this case longer and more constructive – of progressive, proconsular government. Dominated by peonage and plantocracy, Yucatán had been barely touched by Madero's reforms.[433] Resistance to the Huertista authorities came late, and in the guise of a vendetta against the libidinous *jefe político* of Progreso. Meanwhile, export earnings from henequen were rising: 1914 was a 'bumper year'; and this encouraged first Huerta, now Carranza, to look to the peninsula for hard cash. For Yucatecan henequen was, along with Tampico oil, the richest, most concentrated resource which might be exploited to sustain the Constitutionalist revolution.[434] Thus, while the events in Yucatán paralleled those in other southern states, the ultimate prize was bigger, and winning or losing could have major repercussions outside the peninsula itself.

September 1914, when Eleuterio Avila was appointed governor by Carranza, was the date, some said, when the revolution came to Yucatán.[435] Certainly it was from this date that important political changes – as opposed to sporadic revolts and riots of uncertain significance – took place, and they came from the top, from the new elite, rather than from popular pressure. Though a native of Yucatán, Avila had been away for years; he was coolly received by the people of Mérida (only a reception committee of railwaymen displayed any enthusiasm); and he soon began to act like a typical Constitutionalist governor. Martial law was imposed, the remaining Federals were disarmed, the courts suspended, and political prisoners freed. A forced loan of 8m. pesos was decreed: 'we are now shareholders in the Revolution', Yucatecos commented wryly. More important, as far as the planters were concerned, was a decree of 11 September 1914 which annulled the peons' debts and freed them from existing contractual obligations: it was part of a package of Constitutionalist decrees against alcohol, gambling, prostitution and similar anti-revolutionary pursuits.[436] Analysis of the significance of these measures must await the final chapter; here, it is the Yucatecan reaction which demands attention.

Within weeks, Avila began to waver. In late September the decree against peonage was revoked, and the henequeneros proffered a 6m. peso loan to the Constitutionalist government. A Yucateco himself, Avila had – like Aquileo Juárez in Tabasco – succumbed to the blandishments of the local elite; he was seen as the 'planters' errand boy'.[437] If the loan was the price the henequeneros paid for the retention of the status quo, the bargain did not hold. Perhaps they felt the price was too high; that it might prove the first of many instalments; that Carranza might fall, and with him Yucatán's insurance policy. At any rate, by November, with the loan as yet unpaid, there was widespread talk in Yucatán of the need to dissociate the state from Constitutionalism; and, true to the historical tradition of the peninsula, this even included advocacy of outright secession.[438] An additional goad was Carranza's demand for men, in addition to money: late in 1914 the Cepeda Peraza battalion (named after a Yucatecan hero, commanded by an ex-Federal, and including native Yucatecos as well as Yaqui deportees) refused to sail to Veracruz when ordered, rebelled, and marched eastwards out of Mérida, defying the authorities.[439]

Carranza, who could ill afford the loss of either face or finance involved in a Yucatecan secession, resolved to send a more committed Constitutionalist carpet-bagger, with a team of fellow carpet-baggers, to take control of the dissident state. At the turn of the year, therefore, Toribio de los Santos (a Potosino) was sent to Yucatán with a thousand troops and a clutch of top Carrancista propagandists: Isidro Fabela, Jesús Urueta, Alfredo Breceda, all loyal civilian supporters of the First Chief. These eloquent men set up shop in the Peón Contreras theatre in Mérida and began to enlighten the Yucatecos about Revolution, Constitutionalism and Social Justice; they took over the *Revista de Yucatán*, with similar intent; and, early in 1915, they set up a Mixed Agrarian Commission, to supervise the process of (official) agrarian reform. These measures, coupled with increased taxation, jolted Yucatecan complacency, and complaints against Governor de los Santos' 'severe socialistic ideas' and 'anti-capitalist' reforms began to circulate – the first of many such canards and hyperboles which were to emanate from affronted vested interests in the years to come.[440] 'Socialism' and 'anti-capitalism', properly understood, had little in common with these policies, which were the stock-in-trade of a new generation of nationalist reformers, infused with liberalism, bent on 'progress' and committed to a capitalist pattern of development.[441] It is true, nonetheless, that they were often seen in their starkest forms in such quasi-colonial contexts: where, that is, the more radical northern reformers confronted – as they saw it – the more backward society of the south, desperate for political redemption. Pitched into an alien environment, the proconsuls were less inhibited by local connections or by the inertia of long familiarity than revolutionaries in their home states; hence they often waxed more radical – and gave greater offence to vested interests – the further they were from home.

The planters – especially the Casta Divina, the top dozen families of the plantocracy – were shocked. Taxes were going up; agrarian reform, successfully averted under Governor Avila, had begun; and there were sporadic revolts in the interior, indicative of the growing unrest. Observers noted 'a strong public feeling of anxiety with an expectancy of trouble from the agitation and the lower classes'.[442] Colonel Abel Ortiz Argumedo, sent to chastise the rebellious Cepeda Peraza battalion, rebelled instead; ex-Federals, ordered to sail to Veracruz, refused and joined the revolt; so, too, did some opportunistic 'Carrancista' forces (the Sosa brigade) and detachments of Maya Indians. Finally, Ortiz Argumedo and his army returned to Mérida, driving Governor de los Santos and his entourage in flight to Campeche. Yucatán had thrown off the Constitutionalist yoke.[443] With its appeal to Yucatecan provincialism and its overt attack on political outsiders, the rebel movement enjoyed wide popularity, which transcended class and ethnic differences. Ortiz Argumedo received a hero's welcome in Mérida; the Constitutionalist governor of Quintana Roo pledged his friendship; and even Mérida's traditional rival, the port of Progreso, readily accepted the new regime. Meanwhile, a junta of prominent Yucatecos was appointed to assist the new governor (Ortiz Argumedo) and the state government set about raising volunteer forces to defend their new autonomy. The planters put up the money and agents left for the US to purchase arms. The appeal for recruits enjoyed marked success: though many – like Julio Molina Font and his fellow 'Voluntarios del Comercio' – came from well-to-do families, there was a more general response, cutting across class lines (though, it would seem, confined to the coastal, Ladinized region). 'Unusual interest' was shown 'by the people at large, namely, employees, mechanics, and sons of planters in this new demand for the rights of the state of Yucatán to manage its own affairs, which has been the trend of all public discussions and manifestations since Governor Ortiz Argumedo assumed control'.[444]

Like Meixueiro in Oaxaca or Gil Morales in Tabasco, Ortiz Argumedo asserted that his rebellion was not a challenge to the central government, merely an expression of legitimate states' rights.[445] This might have washed with a Villista administration, but not with a Carrancista. Seeing a second Constitutionalist governor end in failure, Carranza took tougher measures: gunboats were sent to blockade the peninsula and halt the export of henequen; and a second military expedition – the Army Corps of the South-East – was kitted out under the command of Salvador Alvarado. The first ploy had mixed results: the gunboat Progreso – blockading its namesake port – was blown up when an intrepid Yucateco, delivering fresh vegetables to the ship, planted a bomb aboard; and Woodrow Wilson, displaying a concern for American interests which was not untypical, protested to Carranza regarding the harm done to US buyers of Yucatecan henequen as a result of the blockade. To the delight of Cyrus McCormick, Carranza was forced to climb down.[446] This was of little consequence, however, so long as the Carrancista land forces met with prompt success.

They did. Alvarado's army numbered some 6,000 (its size a tribute to the political and financial importance of Yucatán); it included many southerners from Veracruz, Tabasco and Campeche, as well as Italian and Rumanian pilots, who helped Alberto Salinas Carranza fly the expedition's biplane; it was, compared to the Yucatecan host, an organised, professional force, reasonably equipped, experienced, and held together by a proper administration. Most of its members – in contrast again to their opponents – had no personal stake in the conflict, and they fought because they were ordered to and paid to.[447] It was, we might say, a contractual, *gesellschaftlich* army – the kind which, Quesnay notes, will carry on till the cash runs out.[448] Against this, the Yucatecan forces had only a nucleus of veterans (such as the Cepeda Peraza battalion) and a horde of volunteers of all ages, who lacked experience, and whose initial high spirits evaporated as they marched out of Mérida, through the henequen fields, to meet the invaders. A common provincial sentiment bound them together; but provincialism was not enough. As Alvarado advanced into the peninsula, the Sosa brigade, garrisoning Ticul, reneged on its opportunistic commitment to the state government and joined the Carrancistas.[449] In mid-March, the Yucatecos attempted to halt the Carrancista advance at Blanca Flor and, after a fierce battle, were roundly defeated. Again, aerial bombardment played a part (though an indiscriminate one: the bombs hit both sides); but more serious were the Yucatecos' almost total lack of artillery and the poor quality of their small arms. Days later they suffered a second, definitive defeat at Halacho.[450]

Governor Ortiz Argumedo and his government quit Mérida and fled inland to Valladolid, where they were finally routed in April.[451] After a brief hiatus, while prominent citizens took charge of the city, Alvarado made his triumphal entry into Mérida (29 March 1915). There followed the usual spate of revolutionary measures. Members of oligarchic families, like the Molina, were hunted out, a number of Yucatecan volunteers were executed, prominent 'reactionaries', like the former Mérida chief of secret police, were gaoled; Alvarado approved of gaoling landlords in order to emphasise that they were mere mortals.[452] After this initial onslaught, however, he proved a lenient proconsul, as much concerned to win over as to punish the errant Yucatecos.[453] But he was a tireless legislator: during his three year governorship, it was reckoned, he passed over 1,000 laws and decrees – abolishing peonage and the *jefaturas*, reconstituting municipal government, establishing labour tribunals, promoting education and agrarian reform; he also launched 'a blitzkrieg on the region's manners and morals', campaigning against drink, gambling and prostitution.[454] The chief, direct beneficiaries of all this were the infant labour movement and the burgeoning revolutionary bureaucracy – together constituting a tiny minority of the state's population. But, conspiring with world economic trends, Alvarado also revamped the old Henequen Regulating Commission, centralised and controlled marketing, and thus forced up the state's export earnings. Between 1915 and 1918, when Alvarado left Yucatán, the price of the fibre had risen threefold, and Yucatán's earnings had doubled. This greatly sweetened the pill of proconsular rule: it brought healthy profits into the pockets of the planters (some of whom served on the Regulating Commission); and it paid for Alvarado's new schools, libraries and other public works. Wages rose and urban taxes were cut. So long as the henequen trade boomed (which meant so long as the First World War continued), there was something for everybody, and the Alvarado regime, unusual among proconsular regimes, was buoyed upon a 'consensus of popularity'.[455] Evidence of northern domination – mariachis playing 'La Cucuracha' in the courtyard of the governor's palace in Mérida – could be borne with fortitude while the times were good.[456] Alvarado's proconsulship thus proved more durable and constructive than Castro's or Múgica's. Meanwhile, it faithfully served the interests of the central government: Yucatán contributed a million pesos a month to the hard-pressed treasury during the boom years when Alvarado ruled.[457]

THE BATTLE FOR PEACE[458]

The question of Constitutionalist relations with the south will recur in the final chapter. The preceding analysis, focussing on the Constitutionalist proconsuls and their policies, exemplified this new breed of revolutionary leaders, mostly northerners, who fought and governed in distant, alien environments, lacking local, popular support, but backed by professional armies and bureaucracies; a breed which, as the character of the Revolution changed, usurped the central role of the old, parochial popular leaders and thus came to play a key role in the construction of the post-revolutionary state. Their activities can be seen in clearest, pristine form in the south in 1914–15; but in later years similar missionary work would be undertaken elsewhere in Mexico, and resistance would stem from 'revolutionary' as well as 'reactionary' provincials.[459] For the time being, however, revolutionary provincials – the traditional, populist leaders – held sway throughout much of the country. Carranza could not count on them for prompt obedience, as he could with his hand-picked proconsuls; indeed, to one observer, the Constitutionalist revolution seemed 'only a number of semi-independent chiefs loosely associated under the nominal leadership of Carranza'.[460] In some cases, Carranza had perforce recognised and legitimised the authority of such chiefs (Mariscal in Guerrero, Flores in Hidalgo, Rojas in Tlaxcala) and in most he exercised only a distant, limited authority. Besides filling the political vacuum in the south, therefore, Carranza also faced the intractable problem of securing the loyalty and union of entrenched revolutionary forces in the rest – the great part – of the country. Some were conditionally loyal; some were hostile; most felt a primary allegiance to themselves, their followers and their *patria chica*; hence national allegiances were secondary and expedient. There could be no question of subjecting them to imposed, proconsular rule (not yet); but neither could Carranza in every case defer to their particularist pretensions, or he would end up a First Chief with no Indians. The supreme task for Carranza, or any would-be national authority, was the integration, by force or cajolery, of these scattered leaders and movements into a sound, legitimate, national regime.

This provided the central theme of the years after 1914; a theme played to the staccato rhythm of renewed civil war in 1914–15, and to the ponderous adagio of political and economic reconstruction after 1915.

According to the Torreón conference of July 1914, which papered over the growing Carranza–Villa rift, the First Chief was required to summon a convention of revolutionaries 'to discuss and determine the date on which elections shall be held . . . and other topics of national interest', once Huerta had fallen.[461] The proposed convention assumed added importance when, during August, talks between the Constitutionalists and Zapatistas revealed not only the cultural gulf which separated them, but also Zapata's profound suspicion of outsiders and uncompromising attachment to the Plan of Ayala; 'the intransigence of Citizen General Zapata and his people', Carranza was warned, 'will not be overcome either by wisdom or threats'.[462] But Manuel Palafox, who now did most of Zapata's talking for him, favoured a national convention and, since Carranza would hardly adhere to the Plan of Ayala – as Zapata stipulated – a convention seemed to offer the best hope of peace and co-operation.[463] Within a couple of weeks of entering the capital, therefore, Carranza set a time and place for the convention's first session: 1 October in Mexico City.

It was touch-and-go, however, whether the convention met before the centrifugal forces within the revolution blew it apart. Not only was Zapata suspicious and instransigent; Villa and Carranza viewed each other with deepening mistrust; and, of the many local conflicts gnawing at the vitals of the revolution, that of Sonora was proving critical.[464] Sonoran and national interests became inextricably linked, as local contenders sought external allies, Obregón, working assiduously for a settlement, met and negotiated with Villa, with Maytorena, and again with Villa, and early in September it seemed that the two pre-eminent generals of the revolution had reached agreement on not only the Sonoran question but also a programme for a return to civilian government. Juan Cabral would go to Sonora as governor and military commander, superior to the rivals Calles and Maytorena; Carranza would either assume the provisional presidency and supervise elections (in which he would not run), or he would retire in favour of an alternative provisional president. And Carranza, if he did not explicitly endorse this agreement, at least allowed it to go forward for discussion and approval at the scheduled convention.[465]

Much of this was shadow-boxing. Old jealousies and rancours worked against a tidy, rational solution. Sonora continued to seethe, Villa to take Maytorena's part. Both sides were recruiting as hard as they were politicking: Villa, as we have seen, welcomed Federal troops wholesale, and Villista recruiting officers were active, for example, in Zacatecas in early September.[466] When Obregón came north to Chihuahua to confer with Villa in the same month, he was treated to a four hour Villista march past and a sight of

Villa's huge arms dumps.[467] Even as the convention met, amid general protestations of peace and good will, the military preparations in the Villista camp were unmistakable.[468] Not that the Carrancistas were doves: they, too, were busy recruiting in Veracruz and Mexico City (where recruits were offered 1.50 pesos a day, in dubious paper currency); and the grand haul of ex-Federal munitions retrieved from the Isthmus was speedily brought up to the capital.[469] Here, too, the Carrancista authorities made precautionary arrests of prominent pro-Villa *políticos* (though their incarceration was hardly arduous).[470] Carrancista and Zapatista troops meantime skirmished on the fringes of the Federal District; and throughout the country rival *cabecillas* were looking to their defences, manoeuvring for position, forging alliances, and generally preparing for the day when hostilities were resumed.[471] Not that they were, on the whole, keen to start fighting again. No bellicose fever gripped the land.[472] But in a situation of tremulous uncertainty, it was only prudent to take precautions; the logic of the Revolution required it. The outcome depended on the leadership exercised at the top: a firm, co-operative union of the major caudillos – Villa, Carranza, Obregón, Zapata – could have stifled the uncertainty, generated confidence and, by means of example, persuasion and force, kept the secondary *cabecillas* in line. Disunity at the top, however, would breed disunity at the base.

As it was, no strong commitment to peace existed among the major leaders, Obregón excepted. Carranza was, at best, cagey and non-committal; Zapata suspicious and obstinate, though with good reason; Villa, true to character, downright belligerent. As the recruiting and re-equipping suggested, Villa was spoiling for a fight; or, at the very least, he had no intention of effacing himself for the benefit of Carranza; and, if this provoked reciprocal intransigence, so be it. Like Orozco in 1911, he was not yet ready to hang up his six-gun and *sombrero tejano*. He looked forward, he told Soto y Gama in November, to 'a few more shootings' and his cavalier attitude towards negotiations – and negotiators – helped ensure that the final decision would be made on the battle-field. And his educated advisers, confident of victory, tended to agree.[473] The forthcoming Mexico City convention, Villa declared, was a Carrancista front and he would have none of it. Obregón, a tireless political broker, came north again to confer with Villa and was threatened with a firing squad (rather as Chao had been the previous year); then, as was the way with Villa, the quarrel was resolved and ended with a warm *abrazo*.[474] So far, Villa thought – or gave out that he thought – that 'they could arrive at an agreement without further fighting'.[475] He agreed to send delegates to the Mexico City convention, on condition the Zapatistas were also represented; but his spleen against Carranza ran high, and he pointedly dropped the 'First Chief' form of address in his cables to the capital.[476]

Now Carranza did his best to avert peace. Fearing – it was said – that Obregón had walked into a trap and that Villa would soon be bearing down on

Mexico City, Carranza ordered the railway line between Torreón and Aguascalientes to be cut. Villa was furious and Obregón, still in Villista clutches, twice came close to execution again. But he survived to attempt one more, important, political mission in Zacatecas, where he conferred with Villa's representatives and other Constitutionalist generals who shared his desire for a peaceful settlement: Triana, Gutiérrez, and delegates of the Mexico City 'Permanent Pacification Committee'.[477] They agreed that all troop movements should cease, and that a new, enlarged convention should meet at Aguascalientes (on 'neutral' ground) on 10 October. There the revolution's collective leaders would thrash out a generally acceptable peace plan, independent of – but, they hoped, satisfactory to – the rival national caudillos. A personalist struggle between Villa and Carranza would be avoided; the Aguascalientes convention, following immediately on the heels of the convention already scheduled to meet, minus Villistas, in Mexico City on 1 October, would provide a forum in which the middle-of-the-road revolutionary consensus would emerge, swamping individual ambitions.

The decision to meet at Aguascalientes upstaged the Mexico City convention (or junta, as some preferred to call it) which met, as planned, on 1 October. Indeed, the chief task of this first gathering was to decide its attitude towards the second: should its members recognise its legitimacy and attend? And, if so, who should be eligible? The Mexico City convention included Constitutionalist generals and governors, many of the latter being civilians; it had been convened by Carranza and boycotted by committed Villistas and Zapatistas, who regarded it as a pliant instrument of the First Chief. But, different authorities agree, this was not the case.[478] Though die-hard Carrancistas were present – and vocal – the majority genuinely sought a middle way; and there were leaders, like Rafael Buelna, whose independence placed them closer to the Villista camp. And the debates and decisions, though confused, make it clear that the Mexico City convention/junta was no Carrancista rubber-stamp. While confirming Carranza's executive power, it resolved to attend the Aguascalientes convention, whose sovereignty, it believed, Carranza would also recognise. This, however, was a misconception, deriving from the complexity of the debates, and the subtlety, or deviousness, of one of Carranza's civilian backers, Isidro Fabela; it showed, Amaya points out, that 'in parliamentary matters the[se] valiant generals were scarcely average apprentices'.[479] In reality, Carranza regarded the impending convention with profound misgivings, and the Carrancista press was at pains to stress the limited powers of the Mexico City gathering. Die-hard Carrancistas (a small but active minority) were reluctant to see the First Chief stripped of his power to the advantage of a large, factious, populist assembly.[480] Meanwhile, Villista die-hards in Chihuahua were issuing propaganda linking promised reforms to bitter condemnations of Carranza, who, they said, had assumed 'the role of Dictator' and whose prompt removal from power was imperative.[481]

Clearly, the search for a *via media*, begun at Mexico City and soon to be resumed at Aguascalientes, faced major obstacles.

The Mexico City convention reached one decision – after acrimonious debate – which was of great practical and even more symbolic significance: that, as the original Torreón agreement stipulated, the Aguascalientes convention should be confined to the revolution's military leaders, or their appointed delegates. Civilians, in other words, could only appear as delegates of the military: the revolutionary army was the fount of legitimacy. Led by Luis Cabrera, the civilians protested: lawyers like Juan Néftali Amador lamented the rise of a 'new militarism'; the schoolteacher David Berlanga maintained that 'the future of the country . . . should not be discussed solely by the military'.[482] But the military were in the majority and they were adamant. Obregón, fond of parading his war record, slapped down Cabrera and reminded the civilians that 'we [the military] knew how to be patriotic, not like some others . . .'; Eduardo Hay, expounding on the same theme, asserted that mere civilians could not appreciate 'the hopes of those who suffered thirst and hunger and risked their lives on the battle-fields'; now, he concluded, the military had triumphed 'without the help of the civilians and, if the triumph was theirs, it is to them exclusively that the resolution of the country's affairs must be entrusted'. Against such numbers and strength of feeling the civilians could not prevail, their parliamentary expertise and Cabrera's 'implacable logic' notwithstanding.[483] They conceded that Aguascalientes would be a military gathering.[484]

This was a telling reversal of the Maderista policy of 1911. Then, the civilians had collected the spoils and the military had been sent home, or fobbed off with minor posts. Now, following the great upheaval of the interim, civilian respectability was no longer a *sine qua non* of government office; so long as civil war raged, the capacity to recruit, organise and campaign (a capacity that went beyond narrow military expertise) was at a premium; while civilian qualifications (education, oratorical and literary skills, professional and formal political experience) were at a discount. By sitting out another revolution – or, at best, by participating as advisers, scribes and diplomats – the respectable civilians had forfeited their right to rule, if not in their own eyes. Obregón, showing a sound grasp of recent history, rubbed home the point: when Huerta ousted Madero, he reminded his listeners, the civilians declined to act: 'they pleaded: "I'm neutral." "I have too many children." Or "it would hurt my business." We, on the other hand, have restored, or tried to restore, their liberties. Now we are going to represent them again. The people are behind us.'[485] Allowing for a certain rhetorical licence, it is clear that Obregón had hit upon a crucial point: between 1911 and 1914 the balance of power had shifted decisively and a new group, the revolutionary military, were the preponderant power in the land. Even if the civilians possessed talents which guaranteed them a role (and a role which would grow in years to come) this role was for the time being dependent, not dominant. It was also significant that the military, or some at least, now appreciated their new power, which they attributed, grandiloquently but not altogether unjustly, to 'the people'. Such expressions of crude populism contained a measure of truth: in times of upheaval and rebellion, such as the English or Mexican Revolutions, it was the army which came closest to representing the ill-organised, inarticulate common people.[486] To attribute the exclusivity of the military, their desire to freeze out the civilians, to some 'reactionary' plot to 'deprive the Revolution of its intellectuals' is to entertain too rosy an opinion of the revolutionary intelligentsia, and too credulous a notion of the powers of 'reaction'.[487] The revolution's intellectuals had hardly distinguished themselves by their outstanding contribution or unswerving fidelity to the cause; a good many resembled the fictional stereotype, most starkly represented by Luis Cervantes, whose 'revolutionary ardour and idealism are feeble from the very beginning [and who] soon relinquish[es] the struggle to change society or, at least, waver[s] indecisively between periods of revolutionary activity and of defeatist lethargy'.[488] It is not at all clear that the civilians' exclusion from the Aguascalientes convention (an exclusion which in the event was far from complete) was either such a loss for the 'revolution', or such a coup for 'reaction'.

On 10 October 1914, Aguascalientes played host to the Convention which – Carranza's reluctance and Villa's belligerence notwithstanding – many hoped would achieve a peaceful, political compromise. It was a smart, prosperous town of some 45,000: a thriving mining and railway centre (the National Railway workshops were sited here); in a state where rural property was subdivided and rural rebellion had been rare. Reformist politics had flourished here, fighting had been frowned on; the arrival of the Convention marked only the second, and more serious, disruption occasioned by the revolution, following the troubles of Fuentes' governorship back in 1912.[489] Now, *cabecillas* and their variegated forces crowded into the town, jamming the streets, packing into cantinas, bringing undreamt-of profits to pedlars and street-vendors, and profound anxieties to respectable families, especially those with desirable daughters.[490]

All told, some 150 delegates came, of whom 37 were classified as Villistas, 26 as Zapatistas. Most of the rest were, to varying degrees, independent; die-hard Carrancistas were rare, not least because the criteria for membership excluded those civilian *políticos* who were strongest for Carranza.[491] The criteria stipulated that delegates should be recognised revolutionary generals or governors, or that they be selected at the rate of one per thousand soldiers; all were to display a revolutionary record at least antedating the battle of Zacatecas. There were to be no 'revolucionarios de la última hora' at Aguascalientes. In theory, these criteria guaranteed a rough cross-section of the revolution's military leadership; and, to an extent, this was the case – the

Aguascalientes Convention came appreciably closer to being a representative assembly of revolutionaries than any other body, including the Twenty-Sixth legislature and the Constituent Congress of 1916. Popular leaders of rudimentary education, like Pánfilo Natera, attended and spoke (though the location of the convention made Natera's attendance virtually obligatory; and he took no pride in his oratory); Eulalio Gutiérrez — bluff, simple and inarticulate — played a prominent role in proceedings.[492] Observers commented on the prevalence of inexperienced, uneducated, tough characters; in the opinion of the British Minister, whose natural prejudices were nourished by reports in the Mexico City press, 'the convention at Aguascalientes ... appears closely to resemble the parliament of monkeys described by Mr Kipling in the *Jungle Book*'.[493]

The impression of a rustic, Rousseauesque gathering should not, however, be overdone. Many archetypal popular leaders showed no interest in attending: Zapata and his leading generals stayed in Morelos; Juan Carrasco dismissed it as a waste of time.[494] A favourite recourse of absentees was to send accredited delegates, which the rules of the Convention permitted and, it must be stressed, nearly two-thirds of the participants were of this kind.[495] Indeed, some of the most wordy contributors were the civilian spokesmen of absent *cabecillas*: Samuel García Vigil (Magdaleno Cedillo's delegate), Alejandro Aceves (Anastasio Pantoja's), Enrique Paniagua (Agustín Galindo's). In addition, both criteria and inspection of credentials were sufficiently vague for a large number of 'generals' to appear, despite doubts as to their rank or military experience. Already, in Mexico City, Buelna had referred to 'generals' created by the purchase of insignia at five pesos a set; in Tlaxcala, one delegate pointed out, thirteen men had been known to fight under the command of four 'generals'.[496] Thus, efforts to exclude civilians from the proceedings were only partially successful: they flocked to Aguascalientes as delegates or newly created 'officers'; and it is not clear that the delegates carried or fulfilled mandates from their military sponsors. Any such national forum provided a stage which the civilians, intellectuals, orators and fixers could not resist. They came to Aguascalientes just as they congregated, in even greater numbers, at Querétaro in 1916. This was politics as they understood it. And, though *bona fide* soldiers attended in large numbers too, it was the more politically aware, nationalist leaders who were most vocal and influential: Obregón, Hay, Villareal, Angeles, Alfredo Serratos.

As regards the first group — the civilians — the lure of Aguascalientes was most apparent in the Zapatista camp. When Felipe Angeles rushed to Cuernavaca to coax the Zapatistas to the Convention, it was 'the secretaries, men of the pen, the number and the word' who conferred with him and showed most willing; 'except for Zapata himself, no important Morelos chief took part' in the exchanges, shying away, it seemed, from national entanglements;[497]

the only responsible course, they apparently believed, was to let those who proclaimed themselves experts in grand dealing do the grand dealing; meanwhile, they would try to defend the little places that were their own. Afraid, like Zapata, of betraying their people, they turned over the chances for doing so to the intellectuals they had always at heart despised.

Hence, of the twenty-six Zapatistas who finally arrived at the Convention, most were *ersatz* colonels, created for the purpose of attending; 'civilians who had never led troops in any form'. Only one was a native of Morelos (and he was a lawyer); two were doctors; and another, Alfredo Serratos, was an ex-Federal, 'a man of political and military mark in Hidalgo', and possibly a Villista secret agent. To Villa, Zapatistas like Antonio Díaz Soto y Gama and Paulino Martínez were 'men of great culture and knowledge'.[498]

Most of the talking was done by such 'militarised civilians': Soto y Gama, Berlanga, José Inocente Lugo (a Maderistas veteran of 1910), Roque González Garza, and the delegates already mentioned. The vocal military, less common, were either those who stood on the borders of civil/military status (like Villareal, a schoolmaster, PLM veteran, indifferent general and, in Guzmán's phrase, a 'civilian hero of the revolution') or those genuine soldiers who displayed a nationalist awareness, a certain political flair, and some oratorical confidence: like the worldly-wise Obregón, or the young Villista commander José Isabel Robles, who read Plutarch in his spare time.[499] This latter breed, rare enough, was particularly lacking at Aguascalientes since Carranza, by disdaining the Convention, deprived it of the services of several competent, articulate generals: Gavira, Aguilar, Murguía, Jara, Múgica and Castro.

Verbal contributions, of course, may not indicate political influence (though it is suggested that the Convention was swayed as much by orotund philippics as pithy argument; Silva Herzog, present as a journalist, later analysed it in terms of Le Bon's crowd psychology).[500] And certainly the Zapatistas were particularly prominent, vociferous and influential. Angling for a Villista/Zapatista alliance, Angeles had led a deputation to Morelos, whence the Zapatistas were persuaded to come, a little grudgingly, disputing the size of their delegation, and preaching their agrarian doctrines 'as though they bore the truth and the gospels'.[501] The Villistas smoothed their path, and the Convention was persuaded to endorse the Plan of Ayala's agrarian provisions. Some delegates, like Hay, cavilled at the Plan's proposed expropriation of legally acquired land; others, like Villareal and Berlanga, found the Plan excessively moderate and limited – neglectful, for example, of administrative, educational and penal reform.[502] In general, however, the Convention's acceptance of both the Zapatista Plan and Zapatista delegation was warm, even effusive, representing a political coup for the *surianos* and for Angeles, their benign but crafty sponsor. And, whatever motives lay behind this endorsement, it certainly indicated that Mexico's new political leaders accorded a high priority to agrarian reform. In the four years since 1910,

Womack points out, official neglect of – even hostility to – agrarian reform had given way to grudging consideration and now keen acceptance.[503] This was one of the salient effects of the revolution, attributable to the strength of agrarian movements – not just Zapata's – during the civil war.

At this moment of political triumph, however, Zapatismo revealed something of its growing schizophrenia; a condition shared, actually or potentially, by many popular rebellions, and brought about by the need – recognised but simultaneously resisted – to transcend the local struggle and establish a foothold in the national arena. Such a foothold was necessary – the more perceptive *cabecillas* increasingly appreciated – if local gains were to be consolidated. But if the championship of local, popular interests at national level required oratory, administration, lobbying and fixing, who would be the champions? Not the local leaders themselves: witness the composition of the Convention itself, which was as popular and plebeian a 'regime' to emerge in the course of the Revolution.[504] National champions would have to be recruited elsewhere, according to different criteria. Hence the Zapatista political campaign at Aguascalientes contrasted pointedly with the military struggle in Morelos: the first articulate, flamboyant, overweening; the second dour, dogged and taciturn. When the Zapatista delegates first mounted the rostrum, they brimmed with confidence and initiated a 'deliberate drive . . . for control' within the Convention: if Dr Cuarón was suave and to the point, and Paulino Martínez forthright and rousing, Antonio Díaz Soto y Gama soon established himself as the most radical, outspoken and histrionic orator of the Convention.[505] It is worth pausing momentarily to consider this champion of Zapatismo.

Díaz Soto 'knew nothing of the battlefield; his forte' – Robert E. Quirk says – 'was the quintain of parliamentary oratory'.[506] At Aguascalientes he was in his element. But he was an odd Zapatista. A lawyer, in his early thirties, Díaz Soto came from a 'modestly middle-class home' in San Luis.[507] He had moved, with the PLM, from conventional liberalism to an ill-defined anarchism, becoming involved in student politics (that breeding-ground of opportunism) in the 1900s. In 1904, however, family commitments forced an early retirement from political activism; and in 1910 Díaz Soto declined to join Madero's revolution – a decision later explained, or rationalised, in terms of Madero's excessive moderation.[508] Though he had not participated in the fighting, Díaz Soto resurfaced in 1911, active in Potosino politics, and, for all his simon-pure radicalism of the previous year, active in reformist, electoral politics and critical of the PLM's continued commitment to violent revolution. His forty-two point manifesto to the people of San Luis offered something for everyone, including an implied promise that San Luis should evolve into 'the Chicago of Mexico'; and, until April 1912, he opposed Zapata's revolt against Madero.[509] *El País* regarded him as 'a young man full of impetuosity and error'.[510] As a reformist liberal, Díaz Soto achieved little;

later in 1912 he appeared in Mexico City, working with the nascent anarcho-syndicalist movement. In June 1913 he co-wrote the Casa del Obrero's manifesto, evidence that he now 'accepted the PLM radicals' critique of political activity' which, since there was not much popular political activity in Huerta's capital city, was just as well.[511] It was from this springboard that Díaz Soto launched himself into the mainstream of revolution, joining the Zapatistas in the spring of 1914. He therefore formed part of the urban diaspora in Morelos, the 'citified radicals' who brought to Zapatismo a new, articulate militancy and 'a theory, in the latest jargon, of "Land and Liberty"'.[512]

Díaz Soto was a natural for Aguascalientes, which gave him providential opportunity to escape from the long shadow of Manuel Palafox, and to spread his rhetorical wings in a more buoyant atmosphere than that of rustic Morelos.[513] Hence the Zapatistas' verbal assault was led by a young Potosino lawyer who, dressing for the part, appeared in *charro* trousers and sombrero, radiating an 'affected plebeianism' and trying, so it seemed, 'to act as a symbol, an allegory of Zapatism'.[514] Treating his audience with disdain, he told the northerners that they could not understand the aspirations of the Indian, and taunted Eulalio Gutiérrez for his ignorance of history; he presented a synthesis of global history (embracing Buddha, Marx and Zapata), excoriated Carranza, insulted the Mexican flag, and was nearly shot for doing so.[515] For a moment, the Convention was in uproar; then calm returned, some speakers making acid comments about socialists 'who simply talk'.

Like much of his political career, Díaz Soto's verbal pyrotechnics were several stages removed from reality. They lent a certain bravura to the occasion and illustrated the radical ideas that sprouted in the fructiferous climate of revolution. But, in a political culture where artificial democracy was entrenched, where constitutional facades and rhetorical flourishes often concealed an antithetical reality (and where revolutionaries as well as conservatives were influenced by these traditions), it would be wrong to take such rhodomontades too seriously. This is not to impute insincerity so much as irrelevance to Díaz Soto, Berlanga, and other civilian orators. For the crucial task of the Convention was one of political brokerage: to find a workable political settlement that would satisfy enough people to avert a major revolutionary schism and another bout of civil war. And it seems clear that, while some, like Angeles, schemed and some, like Díaz Soto, sermonised, the majority bent its disinterested efforts towards this practical goal. Furthermore, in stressing immediate, pragmatic – over distant, ideological – goals, it should not be overlooked that the former, involving questions of war and peace, were no less legitimate, humane and creditable than the latter; it could be argued that a successful resolution of the first favoured a successful resolution of the second.

Certainly, hopes were high that the Convention could provide the necessary 'third force' between the emergent Villista and Carrancista factions.[516] To this end, it sought to establish itself as a legitimate authority, independent of the First Chief or any other revolutionary caudillo. A convention president was elected (the able, ambitious Antonio Villareal); a general truce was declared throughout the country (in some areas it went unheeded); and, most important of all, the Convention declared itself a sovereign body – an arrogation of power which, in Carranza's eyes, was not justified by the original terms of the Convention and which the First Chief therefore rejected.[517] Pressed to retire in the interests of peace, Carranza cagily replied that he would do so only if Villa and Zapata also retired; meanwhile, the Carrancista press in Mexico City lampooned the Convention's claim to sovereignty and the Carrancistas continued recruiting.[518] So, too, did the Villistas, while Angeles lobbied to line up an anti-Carranza majority in the Convention; at this juncture it cannot be doubted that his directing influence within the incipient Villista coalition was of great importance.[519]

Undeterred by Carranza's intransigence, the Convention heard out the Zapatista delegation, approved the Plan of Ayala (in part), and elected a new provisional president, who would wield the executive power in place of the First Chief: Eulalio Gutiérrez, the bluff ex-miner of Concepción, described above.[520] Having demoted Carranza, the Convention evenhandedly removed Villa from his military command: a decision which the northern caudillo – his reply orchestrated by Angeles – gracefully accepted, further offering that if the Convention saw fit to have both him and Carranza shot for the sake of peace, he would readily comply.[521] The Convention appeared to be groping towards a solution: despite some acrimonious debates, the mood of harmony and good will had not entirely evaporated; group antagonism and individual ambitions had been contained; a genuinely popular president had been elected.[522] Ultimately, however, the third force did not have time to crystallise. Neither major caudillo trusted the other (with good reason) and neither would retire unless the retirement of the other was certain. In this stalemate, the moral will and collective muscle of the Convention were crucial; the third force, the independent majority, had to cohere and deploy its united strength to impose a compromise on the recalcitrant rivals. This it failed to do, because the bonds of personalism and ambition which tied the minorities to their respective caudillos proved stronger than the tenuous, recently woven threads which stitched together the broad centre.

The Villista minority must bear the greater responsibility for this failure. For the Convention, above all, needed time: to consolidate its new executive, its ample forces, and its doubtful legitimacy. This Villa denied it. His fair words were almost at once belied by his forceful actions. From the outset, indeed, the physical proximity of Villista troops gave rise to charges of intimidation: though these were few and possibly exaggerated, the Convention could not ignore the presence of Villista forces just outside the city, or of

Villa and his army at Guadalupe, some seventy-five miles up the railway to the north.[523] In contrast, Mexico City, then the seat of Carrancista military power, lay over 300 miles to the south-east. Late in October, furthermore, a Villista build-up began in and around Aguascalientes, exerting pressure on Carrancista sympathisers and prejudicing the Convention's neutrality; and at the beginning of November 7,000 Villistas, including Angeles' formidable artillery, blatantly entered the city.[524] President Gutiérrez gave out that they came with his permission, to obtain supplies and that they would soon leave; Villista officers declared they were there to forestall a Carrancista move on Aguascalientes.[525] Neither explanation sounded very convincing – especially as the build-up continued until, by 7 November, 30,000 Villistas were billeted in Aguascalientes and its environs.[526]

Not only did this constitute a troop movement in violation of the Convention's own ruling; it also undercut the Convention's claim to neutrality, letting it fall like a ripe fruit into Villa's hands. The Carrancista response was swift and predictable. Several pro-Carranza delegates left at once; generals, like Pablo González at Querétaro or Jesús Carranza on the Isthmus, at once cabled their delegates to quit.[527] Carranza himself, fearing a Villista advance on the capital, slipped out of Mexico City – ostensibly to visit the pyramids at Teotihuacán – and headed east to the Puebla/Córdoba region, where the loyal forces of Coss and Aguilar were based.[528] From Tlaxcala he cabled the Convention, refusing to retire unless Villa and Zapata also retired; last-minute attepts at mediation by González and Obregón – who caught up with the First Chief at Córdoba – proved unavailing.[529] On the evening of 10 November, the Convention declared Carranza to be in 'open rebellion'.

Meanwhile, in Aguascalientes, the Villista vice tightened. In theory, Villa had surrendered his command, placing himself at the orders of the Conventionist Minister of War; but the latter was the Villista General, José Isabel Robles and, within days, Villa's arbitrary assumption of the new title 'General-in-Chief' was effectively ratified by Gutiérrez, who named him Chief of Operations to lead the Convention's forces against the Carrancista 'insurrection'. It is hard to disagree with Cumberland that Villa's actions displayed a bellicose spirit, only briefly, inadequately camouflaged during the early days of the Convention; and that Gutiérrez's capitulation was the result of either prior agreement or sheer impotence.[530] At any rate, by mid-November it seemed – from the Villista point of view – that Carranza had been successfully ditched, without any equivalent effacement on the part of Pancho Villa. And now the shooting Villa had looked forward to was about to begin.[531]

For Carranza showed no disposition to give in. He scattered telegrams throughout the country, boasting the breadth of his support and appealing for loyalty against Villa and the Convention.[532] His cabinet packed their archives and entrained for Puebla and points east. Meanwhile, the roster of generals who had repudiated the Convention, withdrawn their delegates and declared for Carranza continued to grow: Manuel Diéguez, Pablo González, Jacinto Treviño, Francisco Coss, Máximo Rojas, Luis Caballero, Franciso Murguía and others.[533] At Aguascalientes, the Convention became a rump of Villistas, Zapatistas and their sympathisers. In this critical situation, Obregón's conduct was crucial. The second most successful revolutionary general, a popular figure and a shrewd politician, Obregón had worked hard to achieve a peaceful settlement through 1914.[534] Now he could side with Carranza, or stay with the Convention in the hope of moderating Villa; as it was, when Carranza ordered him to join the retreating Carrancistas on the road to Veracruz, Obregón complied and cast in his lot with the First Chief.[535] On 13 December 1914, the Convention confirmed Gutiérrez as Provisional President, pending elections, named a Permanent Commission of twenty-one delegates to draw up a programme of reforms, and wound itself up. Gutiérrez, his cabinet, and the Permanent Commission, prudently retired to San Luis, as Villa began to advance on Mexico City.[536] The Convention had briefly postponed, but failed to avert, the armed clash between Villa and Carranza and their respective forces; the 'battle for peace' gave way to the 'war of the winners';[537] and the last major bout of civil war in the Revolution began.

THE WAR OF THE WINNERS

Previous bouts of civil war had involved distinct opponents: Madero's loose revolutionary coalition against the forces of the Porfiriato; the Constitutionalists against a vastly expanded Federal Army and its allies.[538] Notwithstanding the revolutionary professionalisation of 1913–14, each conflict pitted volunteer guerrillas against regular army officers and conscripts; like did not fight like. Now, it was a different matter. Formally, the struggle was between the Convention, led by Gutiérrez and supported by Villa, and the 'rebel' Carranza and his forces. Within weeks, however, the authority of Gutiérrez and his cabinet dwindled and Villa emerged supreme within the Conventionist camp. A final break between Gutiérrez and Villa in January 1915 produced a brief trichotomy: Villismo, Carrancismo, Convencionismo.[539] Though the Convention survived – an itinerant debating chamber – under Zapatista protection, its authority was defunct; hence the civil war crystallised into what, in essence, it had always been: a battle between Villa and Carranza and their respective adherents. Born in hope and optimism, commanding real and widespread sympathy, the Convention had failed to create an independent, alternative regime and, once this was apparent late in 1914, the revolution fissured along the old Villa–Carranza fault line, where so many prior tremors had predicted upheaval.

Analysis of this last conflict may therefore legitimately focus on the Villista–Carrancista quarrel, even if, for a few months, Villismo wore a Conventionist mask. But this analysis – of a bifurcation in the mainstream of the revolution itself – presents problems clearly distinct from that of previous confrontations (Madero–Díaz, Carranza–Huerta). Some have seen this as a struggle between 'peasantry' (Villismo) and 'bourgeoisie' (Carrancismo); even at the time, Zapata's literati called Carranza a 'bourgeois'.[540] Others, retaining the 'bourgeois' label for Carrancismo, are reluctant to consider Villismo a 'peasant' movement: Jean Meyer distinguishes between Carranza's supporters – 'proprietors, petty bourgeois, politicians, military, town and city bureaucrats' – and Villa's 'frontier horsemen . . . pioneers, vaqueros, Mexican and foreign'; as it extends south, Villismo further recruits 'the uprooted, the young men and bachelors'.[541] Given the different social bases (whether defined in terms of 'primary' classes, or loose, secondary categories) it is to be expected that commentators also discern 'radically different political philosophies' behind Villismo and Carrancismo. Quirk sees the Villistas (and Zapatistas) as radical agrarians, while the Carrancistas, representing liberal, middle-class groups and supported by the 'order-loving' elements of society, 'always aspired to legality, to the creation of a stable government'.[542] In addition to these two interpretations, which overlap at points, there is a third which also posits a major difference between the two factions, but in quite different terms. To contemporary Carrancistas, Villa represented conservative policies and was 'backed by reaction'; Zapata was often seen in similar terms; hence it was their enemies who were the genuine radicals.[543] There are, then, at least three analyses which argue for a fundamental social and political distinction between Villismo and Carrancismo: the first two, differing as to terminology and the nature of Villismo, but agreeing on the 'bourgeois' character of Carrancismo; the third reversing the roles, seeing Carrancismo as radical, Villismo as conservative (and 'bourgeois'?).

In complete contrast, some writers reject such sweeping categorisations and attribute the war to purely personalist factors: it was, for them, a battle for power between rival caudillos, lacking clearcut social or ideological significance.[544] This view, inherently unattractive to those who prefer to see history in terms of 'social forces' rather than 'great men', has the added disadvantage of making the last – and quite possibly the most bloody – bout of civil war also the most pointless.[545] While the three 'social' interpretations see the conflict as a mighty struggle of rival classes and ideologies, ending in either tragic defeat (Gilly) or creative compromise (Quirk), the fourth school implies that the carnage was in vain: like the Lion and the Unicorn, Carranza and Villa fought for the crown and, had the historical result been reversed, it would have made no more difference than if the fabulous Unicorn had skewered the mythical Lion. There are, therefore, two important, related but tricky questions to consider: in what respects did Villismo and Carrancismo differ? And were these differences such that the outcome of the struggle significantly affected the outcome of the Revolution? Putting it simply: what was at stake in the war of the winners, and did it matter that Carranza won and Villa lost?

The initial answer to the first question is a historiographical cliché: it depends. It depends on the perspective taken, on the precise phenomena under scrutiny as 'Carrancismo' and 'Villismo'. When viewed at the level of individual leaders or narrow, national leaderships (a common perspective), the differences are plain, even if their analysis is not as simple as often supposed. But seen from a broader, nation-wide perspective, the picture changes, the differences recede, the two movements increasingly resemble one another. The degree of difference therefore depends on whether the focus is narrow (leaders and their entourage) or broad (national coalitions). Furthermore, there is a temporal as well as a spatial perspective. The Villismo of March 1913 differed from that of November 1914, which in turned differed (less markedly) from that of March 1915; all differed from the Villismo of 1916–17. Similarly, an analysis of Carrancismo in 1914 will emphasise different features from an analysis encompassing 1914–20. This will become clear as we proceed; for the moment, the temporal perspective is essentially that of late 1914, the moment of the revolutionary schism.

Depending on perspective, Villismo and Carrancismo blur together, or are thrown into sharp, contrasting relief. The secret of this *trompe l'oeil* picture is simple enough, and can be explained by switching to a scientific metaphor. Each national faction contained a solid nucleus, geographically, historically, (to some extent) socially distinct; around it, however, whirring particles revolved, in different orbits; some so close that they might – permanently or temporarily – fuse with the nucleus, some so far away that they easily flew off when subjected to a counter-attraction. Each faction was thus inherently unstable: it could swell or collapse with the accretion or loss of dependent particles; and this process affected not only its weight, but also its properties, for, though the simple nuclei differed, the acquisition of particles and the development of bigger, more complex atomic structures, produced a kind of elemental convergence. The bigger each factional 'molecule', the more they looked the same.

We must begin with the nuclei, or cores. Despite Carranza's nominal authority, Villa had by 1914 built up a separate political, economic and military machine in north-central Mexico: 'there General Villa holds an imperium in imperio. He has installed his own officials and has by force thrown out the Carrancista occupants of office . . . He is a law unto himself.'[546] The revolution thus contained two rival authorities which might aspire to national government, and which had already clashed over several issues: Chao's appointment as governor of Chihuahua; the Benton case; the Veracruz occupation; Carranza's retardation of the progress of the Division of the North.[547] Apart from the important international questions, which were peculiar to the Carranza/Villa rivalry, these differences – over military co-ordination and political appointments – were typical of intra-revolutionary squabbles at all levels. Carranza and Villa feuded in the same manner as petty *cabecillas* in the backwoods of Guerrero or Tlaxcala. Their feud was of vastly greater importance, of course, because they aspired to national – not local – supremacy; hence no revolutionary participant could escape its consequences. But did profound social or ideological polarity underlie these elevated but all too familiar quarrels?

The Carrancista nucleus, first, derived from the fusion of Coahuilan and Sonoran elements in 1913; though these did not always cohere as fast as they might, nevertheless the nuclear bonds were sufficient to keep them together in 1914 (notwithstanding Maytorena's defection) and for six more years. On the Coahuilan side, Carranza's closest allies – who were with him in 1912–13, gave unconditional support in 1914, and were rewarded for their steadfastness after 1915 – were the young soldiers and officials from his home state, the 'protoplasm', in Calero's phrase, of the Constitutionalist revolution. These included military elements drawn from the Coahuilan state forces (which had resisted the Orozquistas in 1912 and were the subject of Carranza's long wrangle with Madero): Francisco Coss, Jacinto Treviño, Cesareo Castro, Andrés Saucedo, Pablo González, Francisco Murguía. Coss, Treviño, Castro and González all fought in the initial abortive campaign against the Federals in 1913; González, rising to command the Division of the East, was seen as Carranza's 'special pet'.[548] Also in the First Chief's entourage were his brother, Jesús. Young, civilian secretaries like Alfredo Breceda and Gustavo Espinosa Mireles, and equally young, 'military' leaders like Múgica and Barragán, whose talents were as much political and administrative as soldierly.

Though youth was a common denominator of these pioneer Carrancistas (only Carranza and his brother were over forty), there was no common class affiliation. Carranza, Barragán and Francisco Urquizo came from landed families; Urquizo and Treviño were career soldiers; Andrés Saucedo's father was an old political ally of Carranza, active in Coahuilan state politics in the mid-Porfiriato (so, too were the fathers of Urquizo and Gustavo Salinas).[549] All could be classified as well-to-do, or 'bourgeois'. Lower in the scale (petty bourgeois?) were a group of Carrancistas who emerged from the mining districts of northern Coahuila/Nuevo León; Pablo González (who, for all his later prominence, still retains a certain anonymity of origin); and Francisco Murguía, later González's 'right-hand man', a native of Mexico state, who moved to Coahuila, became a professional photographer in the mining town of Sabinas, and progressed through opposition politics and Maderismo to become a prominent Carrancista commander in 1914–15. Lampazos (NL) alone produced González, Antonio Villareal, and Fortunato Zuazua, the latter born into a well-known local family of longstanding liberal commitment.[550] Lower still (proletarian?) came Francisco (Pancho) Coss, reckoned an 'ordinary labourer'; and Luis Gutiérrez, brother of Eulalio, once a 'humble miner', a man, like his brother, of 'no culture' but a certain innate shrewdness. When Gutiérrez ran for the Coahuilan governorship in 1917, it was noted, 'the lower classes [peons] were his strong supporters. In fact, he himself came from that class.'[551] The Coahuilan half of the nucleus, therefore, enjoyed no common class identification, spanned a range of occupations and backgrounds, and shared only a common geographical origin (by birth or adoption) and a common loyalty to Carranza, based on kinship, *compadrazgo*, or recent, clientelist experience.[552]

In the Sonoran half, too, status varied, perhaps less markedly (the 'middling' origins of Obregón, Calles and Alvarado have been mentioned; Hill, related to Obregón by marriage, was a prosperous landowner; Diéguez a mining employee – not a miner – who had participated in the Cananea troubles). Again, geography and shared revolutionary experience provided the common denominator. Although this group gravitated into Carranza's camp following their row with Maytorena, and gave immensely valuable service in 1914–15, their loyalty to the First Chief was less personal, more conditional, than that of the Coahuilans. In 1920 the presidential succession split the old Carrancista nucleus along these lines; and great was the explosion.[553] Together, these Coahuilans and Sonorans constituted the Carrancista elite, who recruited, fought, governed and set their stamp upon the entire movement. Obregón and González led divisions; others fought for Carranza in home territory (Calles in Sonora, Gutiérrez in Coahuila), in recalcitrant central Mexico (Diéguez in Jalisco, Murguía in Mexico and Michoacán), or in the hostile south (Múgica in Tabasco, Alvarado in Yucatán). They were primarily responsible for defeating Villa and assuming the government of Villista Mexico. As Carranza learned to his cost in 1920, they were the key men of Constitutionalism.

This nucleus captured a host of orbiting particles. The method of capture will be explained shortly, but, first, two important aspects of these dependent forces should be noted. Like any nationally aspiring movement, Carrancismo needed its administrative and intellectual cadres; hence it recruited intelligentsia and *políticos*, who usually possessed a record of Maderismo but no military experience or local attachments: Fabela, Cabrera, Pani, José Macías, Luis Rojas – Carranza's scribes, ideologues and polemicists. Quirk stresses the importance of their role, linking it to the brand of civilian liberalism which (he says) stamped Carrancismo. But not only is this ideological categorisation of Carrancismo open to question; it is also the case that Carranza's liberal intellectuals and *políticos* were balanced by an equivalent group – men of similar type, background and philosophy – who adhered to Villismo.[554] Their presence, on either side, cannot therefore be used as a criterion of differentiation. Furthermore, the course of events does not suggest that their influence was determinant: intellectuals, speechwriters and lawmakers were eventually necessary for the creation of political institutions; but this task, later to be central, was still secondary to the business of recruiting, fighting, and winning. For the moment, intellectuals (conventionally defined) had only a limited, dependent role to play.[555] Real power within the Carrancista coalition lay with the military.

The second point is that Carranza's dependent forces – those orbiting the nucleus – were in some real sense dependent and in some real sense Carrancista. Again, as a nationally aspiring movement, Carrancismo recruited extensively throughout the country, co-opting and legitimating local rebel groups. Veracruz in particular provided a clutch of Carrancista converts: Gavira, Millán, Jara, Portas and (soon to be Carranza's son-in-law) Cándido Aguilar.[556] To one suspicious northerner, addressing Carranza in July 1914, the Veracruz connection threatened to tip the balance within Carrancismo away from its *norteño* centre of gravity; and it was not simply from a desire to emulate Juárez that the First Chief chose Veracruz as a refuge when Villa threatened Mexico City late in 1914.[557] Carranza's sojourn on the Gulf reflected – and reinforced – *jarocho* participation in the Carrancista coalition. Indeed, the Veracruzano revolutionaries could be regarded as sub-particles in the core; or, at best, as the closest, most powerful of the dependent satellites. Other dependents were more fully dependent, in that they exercised no individual control over the national nuclear leadership: Carrasco (Sin.), Mariscal (Gro), Rojas (Tlax.), Amaro (Mich.), Baños (Oax.), the Arrietas (Dgo), the Herreras (Chih.). These, we shall note, were local men, leading local forces, who adopted a Carrancista label for immediate, proximate local reasons. There were many – indeed, more – Villista equivalents. What distinguished the two rival groups was less any instrinsic attributes than the nature of their relationship to the respective nuclei; which distinction is to be explained, not by looking at the peripheral particles, but by examining the nuclei themselves.

Essentially, the Carrancista leadership – because of its nationalist perspective – exercised greater discrimination in its choice of recruits and greater control over their subsequent activities. It recruited selectively, not wholesale; it purged as well as co-opted; it despatched its proconsuls to conquer and govern hostile provinces. It could attract to itself like-minded nationalists, like the Herreras of Chihuahua.[558] Carrancismo's national vision, and the crucial ability of the Carrancista military to realise it, ensured that the Carrancista coalition enjoyed – not homogeneity – but at least coherence. Despite its diversity, it hung together, it was no fiction. That it did so is testimony to the national awareness and efficacy of the Carrancista core, especially the military, who provided the real bonds of the movement. This, rather than any clear, class affiliation, was the hallmark of Carrancismo; and it meant that the Carrancista core deferred neither to the revolutionary intellectuals in their midst, nor to their dependent allies in the provinces. For Carranza, Obregón, Alvarado, Calles, Múgica, González and the rest, there would be no abdication of power. This is a vital point, to which we will return.[559] But it is first necessary to point the contrast with Villismo, for it was in this respect, rather than in respect of class origin and allegiance, that Carrancismo and Villismo basically differed.

The Villista nucleus, too, shared a common geographical origin: the sierra districts of Chihuahua and Durango, known for their rebelliousness both before and after 1910. Some of the leading Villistas of 1914 – like Colonels Baca and Luján – had ridden with Villa in his bandit days in the 1890s; others, like Urbina, Avila and the Rodríguez brothers, Trinidad and José, had certainly known Villa in the 1900s.[560] Some rose to commands in their own right – the Rodríguez brothers captained the Cuauhtemoc Brigade, from their home district of Huejotitlán – while others, like the Durangueño Nicolás Fernández, achieved prominence in Villa's personal escort, the *dorados*.[561] Even as Villismo embarked on its prodigious expansion, this regional and personal identity remained. 'Aquí somos todos de Chihuahua', Carranza's envoy, Vicente Dávila, was told when he came to parley with Villa in 1913; and it was from the original Chihuahuan/Durangueño forces of a few thousand that the massive Division of the North was built up. Natives of Chihuahua who followed the troop trains as they rolled south in 1914 were forever meeting old friends, friends of friends, and ex-neighbours amongst their fellow-Villistas; which no doubt helped bolster the movement's *esprit de corps*.[562] Not every Chihuahua veteran became a Villista, of course: Orozquismo had siphoned off many, whose commitment to Huerta placed them beyond the pale, at least for the time; in 1914 the Herreras sided with Carranza (which was all the more surprising in view of their old liaison with Villa).[563]

But the remnants of Orozquismo could achieve nothing, and the bold independence of the Herreras was soon curbed.[564] By later 1914 all north-central Mexico, from Juárez to Zacatecas, was solidly Villista; only the Arrietas, driven into their remote Durango mountain retreats, maintained a precarious defiance. As a resident of Torreón commented:[565]

here in the north we have almost forgotten what active revolution means . . . for this section of the republic is so solidly for General Villa that, for the present, no other faction would stand a chance in the popular favour and without popular favour it would not attain any success.

But who comprised this all-powerful faction? Observers stressed its plebeian character: 'Villa's triumph in northern Mexico has brought to the top a lot of men like himself – cowboys and ranchers, tough and illiterate and ignorant of any niceties of moral conduct, but fully straightforward and dependable men.'[566] Others concurred, though were more critical. Villa's entourage lacked 'men of the high order of morality, mentality or education or patriotism . . . necessary to establish and maintain a stable government'; such a government could not emerge from Villista circles.[567] Historians have categorised Villismo in similar terms: 'out for kicks and spoils were the rowdies, whose hero was Pancho Villa'; Villa's captains were 'untutored men who lived by the law of the jungle'.[568] This category included Villa himself; his fellow rheumatic bandit, Urbina; the cruel, ex-*ferrocarrilero*, Rodolfo Fierro; Nicolás Fernández, once *caporal* on the Agua Zarca Hacienda (Dgo); and Fidel Avila, herd boss on the San Andrés estate (Chih.), who looked a typical '*ranchero*' figure.[569] These were not peons or peasants; neither were they men of learning, wealth or sophistication. As regards early origins and objectives, they may be analysed in terms of the *serrano* concept already introduced.

Though prominent, the plebeians did not monopolise the Villista core. Apart from the civilian intellectuals who rapidly colonised the movement (whose role will be considered shortly), there were also 'respectable', military Villistas, high in the leadership: the well-to-do Eugenio Aguirre Benavides, the schoolmaster Manuel Chao, old, white-bearded Rosalío Hernández, young José Isabel Robles, who read Plutarch and quoted the classics.[570] These (we shall later argue) were not typical of core Villismo; their presence did not change its basic, popular character; nevertheless, they negate any stark distinction between plebeian (or peasant/proletarian) Villismo and bourgeois Carrancismo. Villa had his well-do-do intimates, just as Carranza had his plebeians (Coss, Luis Gutiérrez); and we may note that Carranza's chief Chihuahuan recruits, the Herreras, were modest, uneducated ranchers. Most foreign evaluations of Carrancista personnel, furthermore, were comparable to those of Villista leadership just quoted.[571]

It is therefore hard to sustain – even at the 'nuclear' level – that Villismo and Carrancismo differed according to some fundamental class distinction. The differences were more subtle and only secondarily (if at all) related to class; they derived rather from place of origin, location within the revolutionary process, and education, broadly defined. The most notable of these distinguishing characteristics was Carrancista nationalism, which contrasted with Villista parochialism.[572] Such a characteristic, uncontentiously applicable to Zapata and the *surianos*, may seem inappropriate for the freewheeling military chiefs of the Division of the North. And, to be sure, they did not display the static obduracy of Zapata (here, *serrano* and *agrarista* rebels differed).[573] But what they shared with the Zapatistas and popular rebels generally – and what set them off from the nationally conscious Carrancistas, plebeian and patrician – was a failure to transcend their limited, local political commitments, and to make a serious bid for national power. In the absence of such a bid, requiring administrative as well as military expertise, even Villa's local conquests would remain vulnerable.

Unlike Carrancismo, which was itself a creature of the Revolution, born in 1913 of 'official' parentage, Villismo traced back to the pioneer, popular rebellions of 1910 – and beyond; on the basis of popular support, displayed then and again in 1913, it established a powerful regime which enjoyed 'popular favour'. After Torreón it seemed likely that Villa, the pre-eminent caudillo of the Revolution, would trounce the First Chief and convert his regional into national hegemony. In fact, Villismo had reached the limits of its charisma. Outside north-central Mexico, Villista military operations were markedly less successful (and this was not due solely to the change of opponents). With the significant exception of Angeles, a career soldier, Villa's lieutenants performed poorly away from home. Urbina, a fine *guerrillero* in the foothills of Durango, botched the command of 15,000 men at the siege of El Ebano, where he confronted the young Carrancista general (and military graduate) Jacinto Treviño.[574] Fierro and Contreras, sent on a foray into Jalisco, met with severe defeats at the hands of Diéguez and Murguía in January and March 1915; despite local sympathy, they lacked – Villa lamented – 'the aptitude to defend the territory . . . entrusted to them'; not that Villa himself was above criticism, in view of his later campaigns against Obregón in the Bajío.[575]

These were not purely *military* failures. They were also failures of political will. Villa and the 'core' Villistas did not set much store by establishing themselves as a national elite with claims to govern all Mexico, as their Carrancista rivals did: they were more interested in thrashing their rivals on the battle-field (which was almost a *macho* end in itself), and in hanging on to their north-central domain, especially those bits of it now converted into the private estates of Villista generals. Urbina's enthusiasm for distant campaigns dwindled as his hankering for Canutillo grew; finally, to Villa's displeasure and his own cost, Urbina opted out of the war and went home.[576] Villa himself showed no desire to establish a stable regime in Mexico City and, it may be presumed, Calixto Contreras' forays into Jalisco were as grudging as they were ill-executed. Despite Silvestre Terrazas' urgings, there were no Villista equivalents of the proconsular expeditions to the south: civilian overtures to the labour movement were not backed up.[577] Such *political* stratagems foundered because the Villista military lacked the wit, purpose, and personnel to carry them through. A resumé of the revolution reveals that all the Villistas' great victories were home wins: Tierra Blanca, Torreón, Zacatecas. Their away record was far inferior. In contrast, the Carrancistas – the proconsuls most of all – depended less on the support of their home crowd; they were natural professionals who performed as well – often better – away from home.

This difference between the rival cores proved crucial in respect of recruitment – the process whereby the grand, national coalitions were built up. Both coalitions were highly disparate; both included a range of social groups, such that they cannot be differentiated by their components. For it was not the bricks that differed, but the cement holding them together: Villismo threw its materials together with no ground plan and little regard for structural cohesion or longevity; sheer size and volume were the chief criteria; Villismo was built for effect, not to last. The Carrancista edifice, initially less imposing, was more carefully conceived and constructed, with architectural direction; unsuitable bits were discarded or pounded into shape; it was to be no nine-days wonder. This was evident in regard to both regions and social groups. Villismo recruited casually and indiscriminately: in Jalisco – a rich prize, seemingly up for grabs in 1914–15 – Villismo combined indigenous forces and their allies, who enjoyed local sympathy in their battle against the Carrancista interlopers, Diéguez and Murguía. The 'so-called Villistas', noted an observer, 'are really local people ready always to take any name under which robbery can be cloaked'; that is to say, they were bandits, social bandits, popular rebels, or some combination of the three.[578] And the chief Villista leader in Jalisco was Julián Medina 'a very stupid, simple man', an ex-blacksmith, whose revolutionary career – even in this un-revolutionary state – dated back at least to 1913.[579] Medina confronted the Sonoran invader Diéguez,[580] a man also of low social origins, but who had emerged from the cosmopolitan environment of Cananea politically educated and possessed of a radical anti-clericalism. Both, according to some simple class analysis, were working class; but they were on different sides, they conceived of the revolution and its objectives in different terms, and they fought, propagandised and governed accordingly. While Diéguez offended local sensibilities by his attacks on the Church – and other vested interests – Jalisco's Villistas, and their transient allies, Fierro, Contreras, briefly Villa himself, were more genially tolerant.[581] Hence they were more popular, though not more effective.

The same pattern was repeated in many parts of the country. In neighbouring Michoacán, local forces were 'Villista', since Villismo was seen as the 'antidote' to unpopular Carrancismo.[582] Villismo also provided an umbrella for the proliferating landlord rebellions of central and southern Mexico: for the Márquez and Méndez brothers in Hidalgo, Peláez in the Huasteca (where he was styled 'General-in-Chief of the Villa forces'), for perennial rebels like Pascual Casarín and Raúl Ruiz on the Isthmus, for Gil Morales in Tabasco, and a minority of Chiapas' landlord rebels.[583] Meantime, many *bona fide*, popular, often agrarian leaders declared themselves Villistas: Arenas and Morales in Tlaxcala, the Cedillos in San Luis, Contreras in the Laguna, the Yaqui and Mayo Indians of the north-west. Of course, Carrancismo, too, was a diverse, ill-assorted coalition. But while the Carrancista leadership strove – with some success – to control the process of recruitment and incorporation, Villismo displayed a rampant eclecticism, a readiness to tolerate any local power or interest which pledged its name and promised short-term advantage: landlord, *agrarista*, ex-Federal, bandit, cacique, cleric. Purges and impositions were foreign to its easy-going, parochial nature. When Villismo held sway in Carranza's home state it undertook no sweeping political renovation, made no attempt to colonise it with Villista *adictos*. A local peon, Santiago Ramírez, became governor; and in towns like Múzquiz the incumbent authorities remained in office.[584] Monetary policy offers a parallel: while – in San Luis and elsewhere – Villa allowed rival currencies to co-exist, Carranza decreed the forced circulation of Constitutionalist paper only.[585] With its systematic purges, decrees and impositions, Carrancismo multiplied disaffection and opposition, driving dissidents into the arms of Villismo; and Villismo, amiably tolerant, welcomed them all. As a result, Villismo swelled into a vast, amorphous coalition, bound together by anti-Carrancismo as much as anything else. In many regions it was negatively conceived and constituted, as an anti-Carranza force, rather than as one endowed with its own positive attributes or programmes, and the war of the winners took the form of a struggle between (Villista) locals and (Carrancista) outsiders, between natives and proconsuls, parochials and nationalists.[586] But this pattern of recruitment, while it enabled Villismo to make ostensibly great strides in 1914, denied it strength and stamina in 1915. Promiscuous local recruitment, uncontrolled by a determined, nationally-aspiring elite, afforded only a shallow, short-lived popularity, inadequate for winning the war or seizing power.

The hostile coalitions of 1914, then, were built along different lines, reflecting the contrasting organisational practices of the respective cores or nuclei. But if their molecular cohesion differed, their component particles were substantially similar. Outside the nuclei, Villismo and Carrancismo were largely indistinguishable. As we broaden the perspective, shifting from core to coalition, it is worth making a preliminary distinction – not uncommon in political sociology – between active and passive members; which, in this context, corresponds roughly to military and civilian constituencies.[587] The military – the dozens of *cabecillas* and their *gente* for whose allegiance Villa and Carranza competed – were, though numerically fewer, much the more important; so long as war remained the arbiter of political success, their actions and decisions were crucial; and, as the history of the Convention had shown, they claimed – and could enforce – their predominance over the civilians. The latter embraced the rest of the 'political nation': from administrators and polemicists, through local officials, (non-military) caciques and influential notables, down to the ordinary *pacíficos* of city and countryside, whose collective views constituted the shifting mirage of public opinion. Though far more numerous, and variously endowed with cash, influence and powers of persuasion, the civilians – like civilians throughout the revolution – could not translate their political opinions into direct action; short of exchanging civilian for military status (a daunting, if feasible, undertaking) the best they could achieve was a kind of proxy influence, through the medium of a friendly *cabecilla*. And some civilians (such as Palafox) did achieve 'active' participation thereby. But – as the classic case of the Madero family shows – this was not easy to sustain.[588] For the time being, therefore, the civilian majority followed the military minority, and it was the latter which – irrespective of majority opinion – would decide Mexico's fate, on the field of battle. In this respect, the war of 1914–15 was essentially 'undemocratic', compared with those of 1910–11 and 1913–14. For while in previous years public opinion – broadly defined and mediated through guerrilla war – had contributed to the military outcome, this was no longer the case. The war of the winners was no guerrilla conflict; it was fought by professional armies in conventional battles; and there was no guarantee that the more popular side would win. Ironically, this last phase of the civil war, which would decide the ultimate victors and the shape of post-revolutionary Mexico, was the one in which popular preference and support would count for least.

This becomes evident if we compare the military and civilian consti-tuencies;[589] for the two were built up quite differently, and displayed a marked incongruence. The military coalitions were 'Namierite' associations: they derived chiefly from personal allegiances and rivalries, from the vicissitudes of personal careers, from opportunistic local decisions. It was for this reason that – apart from the 'insider/outsider' distinction already mentioned – the two coalitions looked the same and displayed no class or ideological polarisation. *Cabecilla* and *gente* went one way or the other according to local, proximate, pragmatic considerations. The civilian constituency, on the other hand – larger, looser, and less effective – did display patterns of ideological and group loyalty. Villismo exerted a genuine appeal to particular groups, transcending local, personal, 'Namierite' allegiances: it offered protection to the Church and the well-to-do; at the same time it gave hope to the common people, and to traditional, nineteenth-century liberals. The contradictions here are obvious, and they provide further warning against any neat identification of Villismo with either 'conservative/reactionary' or 'radical' interests *tout court*. Villismo, as already suggested, was a broad church: it exerted both a general, but contradictory, appeal to particular social groups, based on collective, civilian interests and ideology; and also a specific attraction to military factions, related to *ad hoc* expedient and clientelistic considerations. Any analysis of the totality of Villismo – or Carrancismo – must include both aspects, both modes of analysis (one loosely 'Marxist', the other typically 'Namierite'). Yet ultimately, it was the second form of (military) recruitment which was crucial; thus, any explanation of the war of the winners must give priority to the respective military coalitions.

With some exceptions, the revolutionary military were not keen on a renewal of hostilities. The 'battle for peace' – the attempt to avert another civil war – had attracted general support and sympathy.[590] And when the major caudillos failed to agree, the minor *cabecillas* did not at once rush headlong into the fray. Like some Puritan divine, Gabriel Gavira wrestled with his con-science, tossing sleeplessly in a 'state of indecision'; finally, he saw the light – Villa had been snared by 'reaction', while Carranza stood for 'liberal consti-tutionalism'; he therefore made his choice, threw in his lot with Carranza, and afterwards slept soundly.[591] For some, the light never dawned. From El Paso, Juan Cabral wrote to Carranza, affirming that he could not, in all conscience, take part in a renewed civil war; four months later he could be found in

Douglas (Ariz.) 'as ever, sitting on a fence . . . struggling with his conscience as to whether he should be a Gutiérrez [sic], or Villa, or Carrana, or whatnot'.[592] Cabral's indecision – which his uncharitable critic put down to boyish immaturity – was shared by many revolutionary leaders, and the feeling was not necessarily expunged by a commitment – often made under pressure – to one side or the other. Gavira might cast the conflict in Manichaean terms and eschew second thoughts, but others were more open-minded and perplexed. Having fought and defeated Villista forces in Michoacán, Fortunato Zuazua admitted:[593]

to tell the truth, neither the men [*gente*] nor I knew exactly what the object of the new struggle was, nor in whose interest it was undertaken, [and] according to their own statements the defeated party found themselves in just the same circumstances as ourselves – that is, completely bewildered.

Zuazua, it seems, had been prodded by his crony, the Carrancista *adicto* Murguía. And so it was in many cases: the broad majority of waverers was subjected to the pressure and cajolery of a handful of enthusiasts – not least Villa and Carranza themselves. Important *cabecillas* like Pánfilo Natera, who had misgivings as regards both factions, were assiduously courted.[594] Thus, although local conflicts and rivalries were legion, it was the national schism between Villa and Carranza (and their respective nuclei) which proved the determining factor, and it was the national leaders who took the initiative, with their competitive recruiting and propagandising. With few exceptions, the leadership whipped an uncertain rank-and-file into renewed hostilities, not *vice versa* (in which respect the war of the winners was again different from previous revolutionary conflicts). Indeed, at the grassroots, a feeling of war-weariness was already making itself felt, restraining the belligerence of local leaders.[595] As the Villista Aguirre Benavides put it, he and his men 'are tired out and do not want to continue fighting . . . they had considered the revolution settled and finished . . . [and] they will not continue indefinitely to take part in a personal conflict between Villa and Carranza'.[596] The sincerity of this opinion was borne out by the speaker's prompt defection from Villa and departure for the US; a path to be followed by other confused, uncommitted *cabecillas* who, ground between the millstones of Carrancismo and Villismo, chose to opt out of the conflict altogether.

But, short of complete withdrawal, it was not easy for revolutionary leaders to maintain a neutral position; only those who enjoyed the luxury of isolation and unchallenged local hegemony (as Cantú did in Baja California Norte) could avoid implication in the fighting. In many regions, there was much watchful waiting and tactical switching of sides – the result less of duplicity than genuine bewilderment. Hence the apparent inconstancy of worthy revolutionary veterans like Gertrudis Sánchez in Michoacán; the suspicious manoeuvring which observers noted in Zacatecas and Aguascalientes; the prevarication of *jefes* unsure of their troops' loyalty, of their rivals' strength, above all, of the likely outcome of the national schism.[597] Vicente Dávila, for example, commanding at Piedras Negras, was a nominal Carrancista, but his men, mostly *laguneros*, were sympathetic to Villa. When the Sonoran – and committed Carrancista – Eduardo Hay stopped by en route to Veracruz he delivered a strongly pro-Carranza speech, to which Dávila had to reply. His response, cordial but non-committal, was symptomatic of the dilemma facing local commanders in 1914–15: he 'stated that he was in sympathy with General Carranza, if the General was in sympathy with the people'; and, as for 'the people' themselves – at least, those of Piedras Negras – they were no less circumspect, seeming 'very indifferent and reserved'.[598]

Some *jefes* went beyond prevarication and sought local pacts with potential enemies which might preserve peace. Severino Ceniceros and the Arrietas respected each other's contiguous fiefs, despite their antagonistic affiliation; in the north-east, where 'no bitter party feeling' was evident, the military commanders of Saltillo and Monterrey reached a similar non-aggression pact.[599] But these were exceptional. Similar attempts in Sinaloa failed.[600] Given a lead from the top, this disposition to compromise might have prospered; as it was, the national caudillos had a vested interest in averting compromise and fomenting conflict, in order to secure recruits. To this end they played on the local rivalries endemic in revolutionary politics, and compelled allegiance (albeit a skin-deep, expedient allegiance) from *cabecillas* who feared for their own local positions if they did not link up to a national coalition. Many individuals had no choice in the matter: past actions, old debts, and ingrained enmities tied their hands. Carranza's chauffeur – to take a whimsical example – 'had to join Villa because he stole Carranza's automobile and all the spare tyres when Carranza left Mexico City'.[601] Many more important actors were also prisoners of their past; and there were few who could decide their course of conduct in detached, rational fashion – say, by comparing rival programmes. Again, the logic of the Revolution dictated action; individuals went where the gusts of the hurricane blew them.

The Carrancista and Villista military coalitions were thus chiefly constructed according to local, personal, *ad hoc* rivalries, lacking coherent class or ideological consistency. The most important of these – the one which attracted most national attention – occurred in Sonora.[602] This has been well rehearsed by historians; but most of them, dwelling on its national significance, have lost sight of its local typicality; of its membership of a genus of provincial squabbles, great and small, which displayed common origins and characteristics. Even in well-ordered Sonora, Maytorena's return precipitated a factional division, deriving in part from regional loyalties.[603] The polarisation was gradual; Salvador Alvarado struggled, in typically honest fashion, to avert a complete breakdown; but in Sonora as in the nation the 'battle for peace' was lost, and the third force proved unable to contain mounting personal rivalries.[604] By the spring of 1914 the Sonoran rift was openly visible, as Calles, the leading anti-Maytorenista, purged the border towns of uncongenial officials (following, it should be added, a precedent set by Maytorena at the time of his return to Sonora in July 1913).[605] For a time, Calles and his military allies seemed to prevail; and, as the national schism developed in parallel to the Sonoran, he nailed his colours to the Carrancista mast. By the summer, rival newspapers were locked in logomachy; Maytorena's newly acquired *La Libertad* expressed itself in scurrilous terms about Carranza; and the quarrel became the big talking point in Arizona's border towns, always centres of gossip and speculation.[606] More important, Maytorena – militarily the weaker – began to recruit, arming Yaqui forces from the south of the state, where his lands and influence lay.[607] Alvarado, then Bonillas, sought to mediate. Calles tried – and failed – to disarm Maytorena's new recruits; when Alvarado made a similar attempt – the first overt violence of the conflict – he was defeated and arrested.[608]

Now, the pendulum swung towards Maytorena and the south; Calles went onto the defensive; and the third force was effectively eliminated. Alvarado, having languished in gaol through the summer, was released to come to Mexico City, and thence Yucatán; meanwhile, Maytorena suborned his men and incorporated them into his own forces. Most significantly, a Villista delegation – including the 1910 veteran and old crony of Maytorena, Anacleto Girón – crossed the mountains and conferred in cordial fashion with the Governor.[609] State and national conflicts thus meshed together: Carranza backed Calles (and vice versa), Villa gave his support to a resurgent Maytorena, who reciprocated. There was no class or ideological rationale behind this alignment. Maytorena was a rich landlord (as were some of his Callista opponents, like the brothers Pesqueira) and he had no affinity with Villista populism. His political platform of 1914 was one of legalism, states' rights (a favourite Sonoran slogan), and opposition to 'militarism', supposedly represented by Calles.[610] The only conceivably rational or 'ideological' justification for this arrangement was Villa's known predilection for ex-Maderistas: as an anti-Porfirian *político* and Maderista governor (antecedents stressed by his commitment to 'legalism'), Maytorena could expect better treatment from Villa; just as the political parvenu Calles, a non-combatant in 1910, lacking Maderista credentials, stood to gain from Carrancista exclusivism.[611] *Some* form of national affiliation was necessary; political expedients, relating to recent, revolutionary careers, rather than broad class or ideological loyalties, determined which it would be. Thus Maytorena, with his keen eye for the main chance, hopped on the Villista bandwagon in 1914 as he had the Constitutionalist in 1913, the Maderista in 1909, the Reyista in 1908.

As the Sonoran war developed – an important sideshow of the main conflict – Maytorena quested for support and found three principal allies: Villa, labour, and the Yaquis. Each alliance reeked of opportunism. The first has been mentioned: as early as August 1914 Maytorena was openly stating that 'in case there were difficulties between General Carranza and General Villa, he would side with General Villa'; somewhat prematurely belligerent talk.[612] At the same time, he made a determined bid for the support of the Sonoran miners. This was an interesting development, soon to be paralleled at national level: it showed how, in the context of continued civil war, the working class – for all its small size and non-revolutionary record – was now cast as a desirable ally. And in Maytorena's case the conversion came overnight: he had no reputation as a friend of labour; his was a 'sudden *ouvrièrisme*'.[613] Nevertheless, he set about inciting strikes at Cananea and La Colorada, publicising labour's grievances in his newspaper, *La Voz de Sonora*, thus winning supporters and causing trouble in the northern mining camps – which fell within Calles' sphere.[614] Fermín Chávez, one-time president of the miners' union at Cananea, was now 'a staunch supporter of the Governor'; and, it was said, Maytorena had issued arms to contingents of sympathetic miners.[615] Calles, it seems, attempted a similar form of recruitment, but with less success: it was harder for the military commander *in situ* to parade his radicalism, back strikes, and win recruits.[616] Finally, most important of all, Maytorena won the support of the *manso* Yaquis under Urbalejo, Trujillo and Acosta, to whom he 'made great promises', and who bore the brunt of his campaigns in the north: of the Maytorenista force of 1,300 which attacked Naco in October 1914, seeking to dislodge Calles, 600 were Yaquis and 300 miners from the Cananea region.[617] It was, in other words, a blend of old and new cannon-fodder: the Yaquis, who had turned out to fight in the white man's wars for decades, always to return home disappointed; and the proletariat, new to the game, and just beginning to abandon its hitherto circumspect, peripheral role in the armed revolution.

But none of Maytorena's allies fulfilled their promise; and his grand coalition failed. Villa had no intention of diverting men or supplies to Sonora which was of scant strategic significance. After the protracted negotiations of 1914 broke down, and the Calles–Maytorena war intensified, Villa paid little attention to the north-west. As for the miners, they never provided a reliable military force: a succession of defeats at Naco disillusioned them; their pay (and it was pay, not 'land and liberty', for which they fought) fell into arrears; and, most important, their military commitment to Maytorena never embraced a majority of their number.[618] While one Cananea faction, led by Chávez, was strong for the governor, the majority favoured Juan Cabral – a neutral or, at best, a half-heared Maytorenista – for military commander. The reason, which was revealing, was that Cabral, who had a reputation for honest efficiency, 'would force the company to resume operations', which had been suspended during the fighting.[619] The majority wanted to get back to work, and a union delegation told Cabral as much. Maytorena, on the other hand, had a vested interest in continued disruption (which is perhaps why he had incited strikes in the first place). In May 1915 he refused to allow the Cananea Co. to resume smelting, 'giving as his reason that the men in his army would desert him in order to go back to work and earn money'.[620] The belated participation of industrial workers in the armed revolution thus depended greatly on the economic dislocation and unemployment which accompanied the later stages of the Revolution; and on the opportunism of leaders like Maytorena, anxious to win mass support. As never before, caudillos sought to wheedle the proletariat out of their mines and factories; and, as the latter were closing or cutting production on a big scale, these attempts at recruitment were bound to achieve some success. In addition, in Sonora and elsewhere, the appeal could sometimes be couched in nationalistic, anti-American terms. This partly reflected the almost reflex resort to nationalism at times of political crisis: by desperate Huertistas in 1913–14, schismatic Constitutionalists in 1914–15.[621] But in Sonora in particular, opportunist leaders could tap the miners' anti-Americanism; a sentiment which, though well-grounded and well-known, was not typical of the Mexican proletariat as a whole. Now, for the first time during the Constitutionalist revolution, Americans noted a genuinely hostile feeling welling up in mining camps like Cananea, deliberately impelled by (Maytorenista) political authorities.[622] It is crucial to remember, however, the timing and novelty of this agitation, undertaken by one faction, at a time of political and economic upheaval, before grand but shaky conclusions are drawn concerning the anti-imperialism of rebels, workers, or the northern 'national bourgeoisie'.

Finally, as regards the Yaquis, they behaved as the Yaquis always had. Despite their proven aptitude for war, they were uncertain allies for white or mestizo leaders like Maytorena. Marching north to drive the Callistas from Sonora, their rowdy conduct alarmed the towns en route; the Chinese, as usual, were singled out for especially harsh treatment; and, in the stray shooting which accompanied their passage through Hermosillo, a young lady had a narrow escape when a Yaqui bullet lodged in the steel stays of her corset. Maytorena's control of his Yaqui *jefes* – notably Francisco Urbalejo, recently promoted to brigadier-general at Villa's orders – was tenuous: the Yaquis now seemed 'very impertinent where formerly they were respectful'; and they boasted, as they went north, that 'their chief will be Governor when they return'.[623] On the border, they captured Nogales and besieged Naco. But the rains came (the defenders were issued with waterproofs – not so the Yaquis); successive reverses affected morale; and it was surmised that the Indians were keen to 'leave and go home to their homes on the river again'.[624] This did not happen at once. But as 1915 progressed and Maytorena's star faded, so his control of the Yaqui troops attenuated; and, once again, a quasi-autonomous Yaqui rebellion emerged from the cocoon of a *yori* civil war, and took flight across Sonora.

Maytorena claimed to govern as an elected Maderista governor; so, too, did

Felipe Riveros of Sinaloa, who shared with Maytorena his civilian, landed background, his US exile (1913), and his commitment to Villismo (1914–15). Indeed, it was Riveros' intimacy with the Sonoran governor, coupled with his dislike of Obregón, Pesqueira and the Sonoran military, which drove him into Villa's arms: in Sinaloa, as in many states, Villismo went with an assertion of provincial independence and a rejection of Carrancista centralism.[625] But Riveros, like most Maderista civilians, made a poor caudillo, and the burden of the Villista war effort in Sinaloa fell to Rafael Buelna, in opposition to the Carrancistas, Iturbe and Carrasco. Again, no class or ideological polarisation was evident. Riveros was a landowner; Buelna a young, ex-student, 'hardly over twenty years old, retiring, quiet, and not at all fond of notoriety' – hardly a typical Villista. A quarrel with Obregón over the supply of arms and an accumulating antipathy to both Iturbe and Carrasco determined that he would turn Villista.[626] And his two opponents hardly conformed to type: Iturbe displayed a most un-Carrancista religious piety; while Carrasco was a hard-drinking, rough-riding *vaquero*, a quintessential Villista fighting under the banner of the First Chief.[627] Here, as in Sonora, questions of political patronage and recent revolutionary history determined the division of forces. In one final respect the Sinaloan conflict copied the Sonoran: the Mayo Indians, under Felipe Bachomo, took to the warpath, designated as Villistas, robbing and raiding in the northern part of the state until a dual policy of repression and conciliation enabled the Carrancistas to restore control.[628]

Across the mountains in Durango the Arrietas had always striven to run the state as they saw fit, with the minimum of outside interference. This had irked Carranza; but, even more, it irked Villa, who, as the neighbourhood caudillo, compiled a list of typical grievances against the Arrietas arising out of the prosecution of the war: they had disobeyed his orders, declining to appear at the siege of Torreón; when Villa had sent Urbina to Durango to 'guarantee order' (!), they had protested to Carranza, who countermanded Villa's disposition. Indeed, it was the Arrietas' feud with Urbina – dating back to mid-1913 – which most fouled their relations with Villa.[629] And the Arrietas stoutly maintained that they were in the right, that Villa did not treat them as true *compañeros*, that – to take an example which rankled – he had disarmed and appropriated 800 of their men, commanded by the great lieutenant, José Carrillo, during the Laguna fighting.[630] The Arrietas' position was gravely threatened by the near-unanimous Villismo which prevailed in the Laguna and the rest of Durango, where Contreras, Ceniceros, Pereyra, Urbina, Robles, Emilio Madero, Aguirre Benavides and their motley forces, early recruits to the Division of the North (in most cases 'nuclear' Villistas) were solid for Villa in 1914.[631] Thus, by the end of summer, 1914, as their quarrel with Villa sharpened, the Arrietas and their 4,000–5,000 men were left isolated and vulnerable. At Villa's orders, the Durango railwaymen pulled out of the state capital with all their rolling stock. Contreras moved south from the Laguna and – a last-minute attempt at reconciliation having failed – occupied Durango. The Arrietas did the predictable thing: they headed south west into the Sierra Madre whence they had come in 1911; they linked up with the Carrancistas of Sinaloa (who also had their backs to the wall); and they spent the period of Villista supremacy on the west coast, safely out of reach. By spring 1915, however, they were back in their local patch (this, too, was predictable) and they drew on their strong local support to conduct a successful guerrilla war against the Villista authorities.[632]

The Arrietas were simple, *serrano* revolutionaries, in most respects typically 'Villista'; yet, in defence of their local satrapy they sided emphatically with Carranza (whom they had no reason to love).[633] So, too, did the Herreras of Parral (Chih.), whose defiance placed them in an even riskier position (the two clans were aware of this unenviable political kinship).[634] The Herreras were a large – though diminishing – family of revolutionary veterans: José de la Luz Herrera, the paterfamilias, directed policy; his sons Luis and Maclovio, both in their thirties, did the fighting (Maclovio's disposition of his forces at Tierra Blanca was likened to Capablanca's chess-play). They had fought against Díaz in 1911, Orozco in 1912, Huerta in 1913; they were the stuff of which *corridos* are made.[635] In the two latter campaigns, furthermore, they fought as staunch allies or subordinates of Villa: in 1912 they had together manned the last bastion of Maderismo in the state of Chihuahua.[636] Why, then, was the old alliance ruptured in 1914? There was no great social antithesis: modest farmers and muleteers by occupation, the Herreras fitted snugly within popular Maderismo and Villismo; General Pershing, encountering Luis Herrera in 1916, thought him uneducated and illiterate.[637] Their defection from Villa was acrimonious (more so than the Arrietas', whose position had always been more ambiguous) but it produced no clear statement of rival principles. The Herreras denounced Villa (and Urbina) as 'bandits', driven by 'ambition to rule and thirst for gold'; at the moment of their defection they got an orator to stand up in the plaza at Parral and make a 'most bitter and hostile anti-American speech', calling on the Mexican people to hurl the gringos from Veracruz and 'if necessaray [to] fight the traitorous countrymen who were giving them succour and encouragement' – that is, Villa and his supporters.[638] Villa himself blamed Herrera *padre* and Manuel Chao for poisoning the young Herreras' minds against him; he also believed (more plausibly) that Carranza's visit to the Herreras' camp back in the summer of 1913 had laid the groundwork for their defection.[639] Observers sympathetic to Villa looked no further than 'personal jealousy' (which might be interpreted to mean 'rivalry for political control of Chihuahua') to explain the Herreras' conduct.[640]

We are left with a welter of virulent, personal accusations, largely devoid of class or ideological content. Only one avenue of 'ideological' interpretation –

the Herreras' affronted nationalism – remains open; but even this, on closer inspection, proves a blind alley. Even if the Herreras split from Villa in disgust at his pro-American stance, evidenced at the time of Veracruz, this would constitute proof not of factional allegiance following class identity, but rather of 'cultural' attributes – such as nationalism – distinguishing Carrancistas from Villistas. As it is, the evidence only weakly supports this hypothesis. The problem is the familiar one of cause and effect: did the Herreras split from Villa *because* of their affronted nationalism; or was affronted nationalism a symptom of the split? There may be truth in both hypotheses, but the second appears more plausible. As early as May 1914 observers in Chihuahua were 'look[ing] for a serious break any time between the Herreras and Villa' – though they did not suggest that Veracruz or the Herreras' nationalist sensibilities were the causes.[641] There had been no prior differentiation of the Herreras on this score; Villa himself, in later years, would give vent to virulent nationalist sentiment, when provoked; furthermore, as we have seen in other cases, the nationalist appeal was often instrumental, designed to win popular support in a political struggle which derived from quite different [domestic] issues. 'La patrie en danger', invoked by Huerta and the hard-pressed Federal generals of 1914, now became a revolutionary slogan, a weapon in the factional struggle of 1914–15. If this interpretation is correct, the Herreras were not alone; nor, across the country as a whole, were Carrancistas necessarily more 'nationalist' (in this conventional sense) that their opponents.[642] Villa, after all, claimed to repudiate the First Chief, who 'has not the smallest atom of patriotism in him'.[643] Maytorena, apart from his trail-blazing alliance with labour, was also the first Sonoran revolutionary to exploit a 'nationalist', anti-American appeal: when his *Voz de Sonora* started prodding the so-called 'sleeping and latent hatreds which we [Mexicans] have always felt against that exploiting nation' and making pointed comparisons between Veracruz and Guantánamo, observers stated that these were the first anti-American outbursts in a state where 'we have never had any open expressions against Americans [before]'.[644]

Maytorena, of course, was a Villista; yet an almost identical article appeared, at the same critical juncture, in the newspaper *Tamaulipas* edited in Tampico, and controlled by General Luis Caballero – a Carrancista.[645] When the going got tough, when popular support was at a premium, the temptation to play the nationalist card was overwhelming; and it affected revolutionaries and conservatives, Villistas and Carrancistas alike. Those who succumbed were not necessarily the most inherently 'nationalist'; they were quite likely those who were more desperate, or who nursed the most recent, acute grudge against the US: the Federal generals of 1914, Pancho Villa in 1916. It was quite natural for the Herreras, at odds with Villa and facing daunting local opposition, to convert the 16 September celebration into a propaganda stunt and recruiting drive.[646] Others had done the same before, and others – Villa included – would do the same again. None, it is worth noting, drew much advantage from the ploy.

Personalism and pragmatism, rather than principle, governed the conduct of minor *cabecillas* as well as major caudillos. South of Sahuaripa, in the mountains of Sonora, the old feud between Rosario García and Jesús Hurtado – both veterans of 1910 – was now redefined in new terms: García became a Villista, Hurtado a Carrancista (and so it went on, even after the Villa/Carranza schism had passed into history: by 1916 García had sloughed off his Villismo and was operating – in the manner he had always operated – under a 'Felicista' label).[647] Similar, arbitrary decisions were made in central Mexico, where the Villista and Carrancista cores appeared as alien, but powerful, forces with which local revolutionaries had to come to terms. Michoacán, for example, was the scene of tortuous alignments and treacherous acts. Gertrudis Sánchez, sometime a Conventionist, was pressured into a Carrancista commitment by Francisco Murguía (and his 20,000 men); soon after, Sánchez was attacked, wounded, captured and executed by his erstwhile lieutenants, now Villistas.[648] Murguía, meanwhile, passing through Michoacán, was treacherously attacked in the rear by fellow-Carrancistas; Anastasio Pantoja, wrongly blamed, was unjustly executed; his *gente* – *rancheros* of Puruándiro – logically declared for Villa under the leadership of José Inés Chávez García (of whom more anon). Meanwhile, the plebeian Joaquín Amaro, chief architect of the treachery, emerged as the ranking Carrancista in the state.[649]

In Tlaxcala, meanwhile, the local peasant leader Máximo Rojas, had been named military governor by Pablo González on behalf of Carranza; Domingo Arenas and Pedro Morales, however, veteran revolutionaries of similar origins and agrarian commitment, were recognised simply as colonels.[650] At the same time, with Huerta and the Federals beaten, divisions began to fissure revolutionary unity in the state. And the apparently arbitrary decision of González – itself part of the nationwide rationalisation of the Constitutionalist revolution then taking place – exacerbated local rivalries and rancours. While Rojas supported Carranza, solicitously escorting him through Tlaxcala en route to Puebla and the Gulf, Morales and Arenas moved into the Convention's camp, and openly rebelled against Rojas in November. After a brief imprisonment, Rojas raised the Carrancista standard, first in Puebla, then back in Tlaxcala. As Buve makes clear, personal rivalries and ambitions determined the Tlaxcalan alignment in 1915: there was no discernible difference between the protagonists with regard to social origins or political aims.

The same was true of the *rancheros* of the Huasteca Potosina, where the Lárraga declared for Carranza, their rivals, the Santos family, for the Convention;[651] and of the *ranchero* rebels of northern Hidalgo, where Nicolás Flores had – courtesy of Carranza – assumed the governorship in May 1914 and taken effective control by August.[652] But Flores, too, had to compete with local rivals who, in view of his fidelity to the First Chief, pledged their allegiance to

Villa and the Convention, while some groups, like the *serranos* of San Andrés Miraflores, rejected Flores and Carrancismo in favour of Zapata, also for local, *ad hoc* motives.[653] The *ranchero* rebellion fragmented (its unity had always been fragile) and Flores was forced out of the state: among his enemies could be found 'his own half-brother and many former friends from the sierra'.[654] (Such family rifts, rare in 1910–11 and 1913–14, became more common in 1914–15, and constitute further evidence against class polarisation: divided families included the Madero, Triana, Medina, and Gutiérrez; Francisco Urquizo found himself in the opposite camp to his kinsmen, the Aguirre Benavides.)

Tlaxcala and Hidalgo boasted fairly homogeneous revolutionary movements, composed of 'worker-peasants' and *rancheros* respectively. Any major bifurcation would lack clear socio-economic significance; on the other hand, the fact that such a bifurcation occurred – and with some vehemence – shows that class polarity was certainly not *necessary* for the revolution to fragment into warring factions. Furthermore, even in regions where no such homogeneity prevailed, the resulting factions displayed no consistent, appropriate allegiances. On the coast of Guerrero, the wily Silvestre Mariscal (who 'professes always to be with the central government') opted for Carranza, thus securing a valuable arms supply. So Santiago Nogueda, Mariscal's old enemy, and a supposed mercenary of the Acapulco Spanish, declared for Villa. Julián Blanco, the other major caudillo of the Costa Grande, hovered between Carrancista and Conventionist/Zapatista affiliation.[655] Further down the coast in Oaxaca, Juan José Baños made his tardy conversion to Constitutionalism and rallied the local well-to-do behind Carranza, while his assorted, *agrarista* opponents were for Villa and Zapata.[656] Here, at last, factional allegiance and social class seem to fit; and the fit may not be random (as it certainly is in other cases), since Zapatismo exerted real influence in these southern regions, and Zapatista agrarianism was sufficiently well-known to attract like-thinking agrarian rebels, while alarming embattled landlords. Villismo, on the other hand, displayed no such precision and elicited no such response: it was remote, diffuse, ideologically vague while militarily powerful; above all, it was hostile to Carrancismo, which had now invaded the south to the detriment of the status quo ante. Hence many of the landlord/provincial rebels of 1914–15 readily adopted a superficial Villista label: Peláez, the brothers Márquez and Méndez, Ruiz, Casarín, Gil Morales, some of the Chiapas insurgents.[657] Yet even where – partly under the influence of Zapatismo – class and faction seem to fit, as they do at Jamiltepec, closer examination reveals anomalies. Baños' opponents might be *agraristas* pledged to the cause of Villa and Zapata; but their more proximate, important allies were the *soberanistas* in the City of Oaxaca – hardened old Porfiristas, led by Meixueiro. What is more, in yet another neat reversal of the situation which pertained at Parral, the 'Villistas' (or 'Zapatistas') of Jamiltepec laid claim to the mantle of affronted nationalism:

they fought, one of their leaders maintained, against the 'covert treason of Carranza', who sought 'to make of our Republic a "gringo" protectorate'.[658]

To sum up: the broad military coalitions of 1914–15 were not based on clear class or ideological identification. In some regions, such identification was absent; in others, though it existed and had been crucial in the development of the revolution, the redefinition of local class or ideological conflicts in Villista/Carrancista terms followed no coherent pattern. It obeyed instead immediate, tactical, personal imperatives. As a military coalition, Carrancismo was no more 'bourgeois', 'petty bourgeois', 'legalist', 'liberal' or 'conservative' than Villismo. Mexico's ancient political fragmentation, now exacerbated by the revolution, ensured that factional labels – as adopted across the country, beyond the respective 'nuclei' – were superficial, especially in the case of Villismo; and that they could be assumed and discarded according to expedient, without suffering ideological trauma. It followed from this that the national, military coalitions, Villismo especially, were ricketty structures, combining odd materials, thrown together in haste. The war of the winners can only be understood in these terms: as a Namierite conflict, fought by shifting factions, led by suspicious *cabecillas*, who campaigned in opportunistic, often half-hearted and perplexed fashion. Hence, as Urquizo noted, the war lacked some of the *fiereza y rabia* of previous conflicts – those against Díaz and Huerta, where the issues had been clear, the commitment certain; it was a confused, scrappy, but no less bloody *pelea de gallos*.[659]

The military factions collectively determined the outcome of the war; and, despite hypotheses to the contrary, they were still largely autonomous, they had not become the pawns of vested interests; hence Mexico, a mosaic of factional fiefs, was clearly in the hands, or under the heel, of the revolutionary military. But there were vested interests, and there was a vague but perceptible groundswell of 'public opinion'. The civilian constituency was huge and diverse, ranging from businessman to beggar, latifundista to *milpero*; but it had in common a relative powerlessness, since property and numbers carried no weight unless converted into military muscle, and this conversion was no easy matter. Over time, some landlords, some exasperated *pacíficos*, took up arms in self-defence.[660] But most did not; and those who did confined their activities to the locality. Meanwhile, the military did not lack for recruits (they were operating in a buyer's market) and they controlled enough of the economy to fund their fighting. Civilian influence over the course of the revolution was therefore exiguous. But the character of the war of the winners cannot be grasped without some reference to civilian opinion. And here we return to the apparent paradox, whereby the last, conclusive bout of civil war, fought by revolutionary veterans and determinant of the country's future, was in fact the least 'democratic', the least responsive to the broad currents of popular opinion.

For popular opinion favoured Villa. That this should be the case in

Chihuahua is hardly surprising.[661] But, if consular records can be trusted, Villa's popularity extended far beyond. There was a 'strong pro-Villa sentiment' in northern Sonora; border ports like Piedras Negras and Nuevo Laredo were for Villa; even Coahuilan towns like Monclova and Cuatro Ciénegas, Carranza's birthplace, displayed similar leanings.[662] So, too, further south: at Aguascalientes, Mazatlán, Guanajuato and (though the reporter was somewhat *parti pris*) Jalisco and Michoacán.[663] Different factors conspired to produce this general inclination towards Villa. Perhaps the most important, which transcended class and region, was the belief that Villa would win. Few doubted that Villa, the hammer of the Federals, would win a shooting war with Carranza; Villa's record of uninterrupted success won him an aura of invincibility, while, in the course of 1913–14, his army had become strikingly professional (by early 1915 he was showing off a new biplane, he was 'much pleased with the machine', and talking of buying two more).[664] Observers were impressed; the Villista bandwaggon rolled on; and opportunists – who within months would reveal the shallowness of their Villismo – leaped aboard. Around the turn of the year, opinion of all shades anticipated a swift Villista victory, and the belief was infectious. In the capital (November) 'all are expecting Villa as a saviour'; 'unless [Villa] is killed', ran another report, 'there is every reason to believe in the success of his party'.[665] This was also the opinion of President Wilson's representative, Canova; of General Pershing, watching events from the border; of Lord Cowdray in London, Landa y Escandón in Biarritz, and Thomas Hohler, the British Minister in Mexico City.[666] 'Villa may be the man of the hour', thought Pershing; Cowdray anticipated that 'Villa or rather his nominee will be fairly firmly in the saddle by the end of the year and that Carranza will, by that time, have been eliminated'. What with Cowdray's weighty opinion, and Hohler's conviction that 'the whole country appears to be going over to Villa, even with enthusiasm', it was understandable that the British Foreign Office considered Carrancismo dead and buried, omitted to answer diplomatic notes from Carranza's Foreign Minister (since, a clerk minuted, 'the Carranza government has vanished'), and began to debate whether Carranza should be allowed to flee aboard a British ship, if he so requested.[667] The foreign press in Mexico (the only press free of factional commitment) thought similarly. As early as July 1914 the *Mexican Herald* detected 'a growing sentiment that the Villa element rather than the Carranza faction . . . will not only control eventually in Mexico City but that a government with Villa at its head, or at least its dominating spirit . . . offers the only possible opportunity for Mexicans to restore peace'.[668] By the end of the year, *Le Courrier du Méxique* was anticipating Carranza's imminent flight to Central America.[669]

Foreign sources, then, are rich in endorsements of Villa.[670] And though they perhaps exaggerated the mood – and certainly misconstrued the realities – they did not give an entirely false picture. Villa's might and military record spoke for themselves. Luis Aguirre Benavides – a 'respectable' Villista – chiavalrously warned Obregón 'in all sincerity' of Villa's military superiority; while Obregón, for his part, looked back to the turn of the year 1914–15 as 'the most difficult moments for the Revolution and for the First Chief' when defeat was generally anticipated.[671] In modest pueblos, too, the belief took root not just that Carranza was doomed, but that he had already retired.[672] For the superstitious, finally, there was additional proof: La Madre Matiana had, on her death-bed 200 years before, uttered prophecies of the usual sombre, safe variety ('wars, mass exterminations and invasions'); but, more specifically, she had foretold that four Franciscos would govern Mexico, the first three of which would be deposed. Hence Francisco Villa, succeeding Francisco León de la Barra, Francisco Madero, and Francisco Carbajal, received sibylline endorsement of his claim to power.[673]

Villismo's past record and future expectations thus lent it great appeal, enabling it to recruit in the eclectic manner already described. Indeed, the eclecticism of the movement was such that it could simultaneously appeal to different – and antagonistic – groups within the same region. In Sonora, for example, where 'the better class of people at Guaymas . . . all seem to be favourable to Villa rather than to Carranza', the Yaqui chiefs likewise backed Villa, and Maytorena rallied a section of the Cananea miners to the cause.[674] Nor was this case unique. Unlike Carranza, Villa could excite the hopes, sympathy and support of the entire civilian constituency; common people and well-to-do alike. This unique ambivalence demands some explanation. For the well-to-do, Villa promised the 'iron hand', the despotism necessary to bring peace and order to the country. Huerta, eliciting similar hopes, had failed; perhaps a caudillo of revolutionary provenance would prove more successful. The Terracista flirtation with Orozco in 1912 offered a precedent and, indeed, Luis Terrazas *hijo* was said to be in the market, looking to buy off Villa, just as his family had previously bought off Orozco.[675] More generally, a chorus of voices hailed Villa as the new man on horseback, almost as Porfirio redivivus. Foreign voices were prominent, but again they echoed the sentiments of the Mexican elite. Villa was 'the only man in sight who can redeem Mexico from its present plight and restore order'; 'the only possible scheme of salvation from complete anarchy', wrote Hohler, a reluctant convert to this viewpoint, 'lies in the bloody, ruthless methods of Villa'.[676] Carranza, an old, indifferent caudillo, could not compete with Villa on this score; and it was Carranza's ostensible weakness, as much as his supposed radicalism, which cost him the support of well-to-do groups in 1914–15.

From this point of view, Chihuahua was Villa's showpiece. Protected by the Pax Villista, foreign companies returned and resumed profitable operations; the employees of mines and railways attested to the benefits of Villa's rule; and elsewhere in the north people hoped and expected that a Villista victory would bring similar advantages.[677] Sure enough, the Villista occupation of Piedras

Negras revived business confidence, brought lower taxes and fewer confisca-
tioins, and delighted the town's business interests.[678] At Monterrey, the best
barometer of northern commercial opinion, the Villista 'entrance inspired a
feeling of welcome'; Felipe Angeles eloquently guaranteed order and liberty;
and Raul Madero organised meetings between Villa and local businessmen
which 'had an excellent effect, greatly improving the feeling of these businessmen towards the General'.[679] The Villista occupation of the Huasteca
oilfields also received a good press; while at Cd Victoria and Xicontencatl
(Tamps.) several 'Mexicans of good standing in the community', including
'one of the wealthiest merchants of Victoria', were executed by Carrancistas 'on
the charge of being in sympathy with the Villistas.'[680] North of the border,
meantime, well-to-do emigrés (including members of the Terracista and
Torresista clans) were reported to be meeting in Los Angeles to raise huge sums
for the Villista cause.[681]

In the eyes of northern businessmen, therefore, Villa the bandit became
Villa the guarantor of order and prosperity – a transformation evident, if less
dramatically, in the rest of the country.[682] Villa also became, especially in
west-central Mexico, the defender of the faith. Two factors made this change
possible: the character of Villa's earlier anti-clericalism; and the extension of
Villismo into regions where Carrancista anti-clericalism had already given
offence and where Villismo appeared as a welcome 'antidote'. Unlike some of
his rivals, Villa was no doctrinaire anti-clerical and, perhaps under Angeles'
influence, he saw some advantage in appeasing the Church. Hence, where
Carrancista anti-clericals like Diéguez and Murguía were earning evil reputations, Villismo was represented by local bands who wore the Virgin of
Guadalupe in their hats, and who showed a seemly deference to the cloth; and
when Villista outsiders – Contreras, Urbina, Villa himself – joined them, they
avoided the anti-clerical excesses of their Carrancista enemies. Two successive
Villista occupations of Guadalajara were well received: during the second
many of the 'best families' of the city could be seen on the streets (they had lain
low during the Carrancista occupation), joining in the general enthusiasm; in
March 1915, Villa was personally invited to Guadalajara, came, and was
feted.[683] Elsewhere in the Bajío, Villista respect for the Church, coupled with
the rough but effective methods of the Pax Villista, won Villa many
friends.[684] Nor was Catholic sympathy for Villismo confined to this region: in
Monterrey, which had suffered Villareal's hard-line anti-clericalism, Angeles
promised to respect the faith, churches were reopened, and were soon thronged
with 'happy, thankful people'.[685]

All this was grist to the mill of Carrancista propaganda. Having recruited
ex-Federals and allied with rebellious *hacendados*, Villa was now deferring to
priests and businessmen. As the civil war intensified, therefore, Carrancista
denunciations of 'reactionary' Villismo became more shrill; and there were not
wanting American radicals who – repudiating their fellow-radical John Reed –

resorted to the kind of simple-minded syllogism beloved of the left (and sometimes the right), equated Villa with Wall Street, and concluded that Villismo must stand for reaction, Carrancismo for revolution.[686] Such an argument was sloppy, partial and ultimately highly misleading. For while ex-Federal, Catholic, landlord and business support for Villa was important, and while the appeal of the 'man on horseback' was integral to Villismo (as it had been to Porfirismo and Huertismo), this was by no means the whole picture. The latter must also take in the ideology espoused and influence exercised by these well-to-do Villistas; their relations with popular Villismo; and some counter-factual consideration of how a victorious Villismo might have evolved. Without the last of these, the real significance of the war of the winners cannot be assessed.

Among the droves of recruits brought to Villismo by opportunism and dislike of Carrancismo, was a small but significant group: the old Maderistas, the civilian *políticos* of 1908–13 who had supported the Madero movement and regime: Manuel Bonilla, Miguel Díaz Lombardo, Francisco Escudero, Miguel Silva, the brothers González Garza and the Madero family itself. To these could be added the cases, already mentioned, of ex-governors like Maytorena, Riveros and Guillén; and of Felipe Angeles, the 'spiritual heir of Madero', who, if his point of departure had differed, ultimately took the same path, from Maderismo to Villismo.[687] This group, historians and Carrancista apologists have both argued, exercised an insidious, conservative influence upon Villismo; and, whatever the truth of this, it is clear that their recruitment affected the movement's character and appearance. Like the pro-Villa landlords and businessmen, they came from the upper strata of society. They were educated and usually propertied. But their adherence to Villismo (which was more prompt and positive than that of the businessmen or landlords) derived from specific, political, rather than general, socio-economic considerations. Since 1910 the Maderista civilians had played the part of chiefs without Indians. Despite their opposition record, they had not contributed greatly to the ouster of Díaz; and, though they collared the spoils during the Madero administration, serving as ministers, deputies and governors, they did not initially oppose Huerta (note the long heartsearchings of the Renovadores, the ambivalent conduct of most Maderista governors). With Huerta in power, militarism in the ascendant, and civilian politics in decline, many sank out of sight. Some, converts to Huertismo, never rose again. Others surfaced and were rescued – looking somewhat shamefaced and bedraggled – by the Constitutionalist lifeboat. But the Carrancistas, many of them new men from Coahuila and Sonora, representing a different political generation, gave them a frigid welcome. Hence many of the Maderista civilians found their way to the Villista camp, even before the great schism of 1914.[688]

This lateral move could be construed in idealistic terms. According to Martín Luis Guzmán, who himself made the transition, the Maderistas sought in Villismo a 'democratic and impersonal' government, close to what Madero had intended; 'under Carranza's leadership' – they believed, or said they believed – 'the revolution was headed for the most unbridled and unrestrained absolutism': a betrayal of all that Madero had stood for.[689] José Vasconcelos concurred.[690] Often exaggerated, often hypocritical, the point was nonetheless valid.[691] Carrancismo, with its practice of *realpolitik* and preference for 'pre-constitutional' rule (i.e., *force majeure*), broke decisively with Maderista precedent. Not only were elections deferred; they also no longer figured as the crux of the revolutionary programme. While the (minority) ex-Maderistas who joined Carrancismo took their cue from the top and avoided trumpeting this issue, the majority – cold-shouldered into the Villista camp – carried with them the refrain of free elections and constitutional government, which they converted into a distinctive Villista theme.

Thus, the Villista manifesto of September 1914 which paraded the charges against Carranza, called for the 're-establishment of constitutional order through proper elections', alleged that Carranza was assuming the 'role of Dictator', and imputed that he had 'throttled the courts', done away with the cabinet, and 'dispensed with all counsel'.[692] At a time when both factions were mouthing *agrarista* and other 'social' slogans, and were not easily distinguishable in those terms, Villista 'constitutionalism' represented one of the few, clear points of ideological differentiation.[693] Predictably, it was seized upon by American observers, like special representative Paul Fuller, who noted the 'radical difference' between Villista advocacy of constitutional rule, and the Carrancista – in this case Villareal's – preference for 'an interim . . . called a "pre-constitutional period" during which all the changes in existing laws desired by those in control should be made by military decree'.[694] This reinforced the Wilson administration's belief that 'Villa represent[ed] the forward movement in that so-called [sic] republic' – that Villa was, in other words, a progressive force, attuned to American values and solicitous of American interests; and, for a time, the US government was, if not a passenger, at least a benign spectator of the rolling Villista bandwaggon.[695] Indeed, some Americans, even at the highest governmental level, were capable of seeing Villa as, simultaneously, both the 'man on horseback' *and* the champion of democracy; as Napoleon and Lincoln rolled into one.[696] For the Carrancistas, on the other hand, Villista constitutionalism was yet another ploy of 'reaction', which preached the 'restoration of Maderismo' for its own, conservative ends.[697] Whatever the merits of these beliefs and accusations, it is clear that, at the level of rhetoric and propaganda, Villismo had the edge in claiming the mantle of Madero and adherence to the Constitution. It is therefore difficult to maintain that Carranza stood (firmly, consistently, and in opposition to Villa) for legal, civilian government.[698] However relevant to the Carranza/Obregón split of 1919–20, this argument cannot be backdated to explain the Carranza/Villa schism of 1914–15; for constitutionalism was then a Villista, not a Carrancista slogan, vaunted, in particular, by Villa's ex-Maderista supporters.

But the basic question again is not the propaganda and rhetoric, but the real character of the regime: who controlled Villismo, in whose interests? Many – not just Carrancista polemicists – doubted the sincerity of Villista constitutionalism, and its ex-Maderista proponents. The Madero family, in particular, were seen as time-servers who, denied lodgings *chez* Carranza, decided to board with Pancho Villa, in the hope of turning a bordello into the Ritz. 'Their object', it was said, 'is to get in the new government on the shoulders of Villa;' they were reckoned to be infiltrating friends, clients and relatives into key positions.[699] This was plausible. The Carrancistas had denied them preferment; and – bearing in mind the Orozquista precedent – there were *prima facie* reasons for believing that the *serrano* caudillo Villa, ideologically pliable and ignorant of the ways of government, would welcome the help of well-to-do, educated men, especially if they were linked by blood or personal history to the martyred President Madero.[700] And, of course, the rapid growth of Villismo, in terms of both territorial extent and administrative complexity, created a strong demand for *políticos* and officials, which the Maderos and their kind were eager to meet.

Whether impelled by self-interest or idealism, such men saw in Villa an instrument to be used: the alliance was a calculating move, rather than a warm embrace; and towards Villa himself their feelings were often mingled fear and contempt. The crucial question, Guzmán wrote, was whether Villa ('who was too irresponsible and instinctive even to know how to be ambitious') could be controlled and pointed in the right direction, whether he could be made to serve 'principles which either did not exist for him or were incomprehensible for him'.[701] Vasconcelos was no less calculating: 'the revolution now has a man', he exclaimed after Villa's impressive victories; yet he considered Villa to be 'an ignorant, ferocious type, already going crazy with the power of commanding'.[702] Much depended on whether the Maderistas could control their man, and whether Villa would play the part assigned him. Eugenio Aguirre Benavides (a Maderista who, unusually, commanded troops in the field) likened the role he and his colleagues assumed *vis-à-vis* Villa to that of nurses tending a 'sick, fretful child', who must be humoured and gently brought along; difficult though this was, it was more than could be achieved (another agreed) with the obstinate, opinionated First Chief.[703]

Meanwhile, the preferment went on. Apart from the well-known Maderistas who provided the top flight of Villista government (examples will soon follow) there were also lesser recruits, to varied positions. Feliciano Tavera, an old employee of the Madero interests, was put in charge of the expropriated soap factory at Torreón; civilian advisers like Lázaro de la Garza and Roque González Garza figured as administrators or recipients of *bienes intervenidos*; while Eugenio Aguirre Benavides, whose family owned property in the region, controlled the huge Laguna confiscations.[704] As Villa's army headed south, new opportunities opened up. In September 1914, Ernesto Madero took aside the Aguila Co. manager (who was an old contact), intimated that 'the people from the north will be the dominating factor very soon', and recommended useful lobbyists – also civilian Maderistas – whom the company might employ to gain Villa's ear.[705] In some quarters, even those sympathetic to Villa, there were misgivings: 'Villa seems to be a strong man and may be the man of the hour', thought Pershing, '[but] I question the motives of some of his advisers.'[706] And Silvestre Terrazas, veteran of the anti-Díaz opposition and early adherent to Villismo, was dismayed by the recent, questionable conversion to the cause of 'professional politician[s]', like Andrés Molina Enríquez.[707]

Such converts supplied the literate, educated, respectable, 'nationalist' elements, which contrasted with the original, plebeian, parochial *serranos*; they could, to a great extent, make common cause with ex-Federals like Angeles and Medina, who bent their efforts towards disciplining and professionalising the Villista forces. Observers therefore distinguished between two contrasting wings within Villismo. Enemies, like Obregón, divided Villistas into 'moral' and 'amoral' elements (the latter corresponding to Urbina, Fierro and the original *serrano* veterans); apologists like Fuller stressed the quiet influence of 'good' or 'decent' Villistas, like Dr Miguel Silva, men 'who must be encouraged in every way'.[708] But did these latter elements determine the course of Villista policy in 1914–15 – and would they have emerged as the new elite following a hypothetical Villista victory?

On the face of it, the Maderista civilians performed valuable tasks. Of the three-man Villista cabinet named after the split with the Convention in January 1915, two were well-known *políticos* of Maderista origin: Francisco Escudero (Finance) and Miguel Díaz Lombardo (Foreign Affairs).[709] Díaz Lombardo and Miguel Silva (a doctor, briefly Governor of Michoacán under Madero, whose feebleness earned him general approbation and scant political power) advised Villa on legal matters; Silvestre Terrazas, Manuel Bauche Alcalde and Roque González Garza collaborated on Villista propaganda; Abel Serratos (failed revolutionary of 1910) and Emiliano Sarabia (Governor of Durango in 1912) assumed gubernatorial posts, in Hidalgo and San Luis respectively.[710] More important, there was Angeles, and lesser ex-Federals like Medina. Angeles, an old-style liberal with a social conscience, was certainly influential: he planned Villa's campaigns, recruited ex-Federal colleagues, and played a prominent role cultivating the Zapatistas and mollifying church, business and foreign interests. Both Angeles and José Isabel Robles – the young, cultured Villista commander – exerted influence over their leader, and for Angeles in particular Villa was said to display a 'superstitious admiration'.[711] At one point, he intimated that Angeles was being lined up as provisional president.[712] Medina, 'a man of military profession, educated, and very knowledgeable of the arts of war', joined Villa in 1913 and took command in Juárez the following year, halting confiscations and diverting proceeds from the city's casinos to municipal needs (which Villa approved).[713]

Thus the collective influence of the 'responsible' Villistas, ex-Federals and Maderistas alike, gave Villismo a glossy veneer of respectability in 1914–15. As already noted, favourable reports of Villa, the guarantor of peace and property, began to multiply: Hohler, the cynical British Minister, commented on Villa's 'progress in the paths of civilisation, of which one hears such satisfactory accounts from American sources'.[714] Indeed, Americans like Fuller and, *a fortiori*, George Carothers helped propagate the image of a reformed, respectable, responsible Villismo.[715] Not that the image was wholly false. The respectable Villistas worked hard: Angeles wooed the Americans; Terrazas patiently explained the rationale behind Villista confiscations; Maytorena went out of his way to avoid giving offence during the protracted siege of Naco.[716] Villa himself, long aware of the importance of the American arms market, played his part to perfection. He approved Medina's clean-up of Juárez, 'the port through which the foreign countries approach to behold us'.[717] He pandered to American fears of Japan and declared, with 'unquestionable' sincerity, that 'the people of the US were his friends and that in case of a war with any other country excepting Mexico the resources of Mexico would be at the disposal of the US if he, Villa, had anything to do with the government at the time'.[718] But Americans were not the only beneficiaries of the reformed Villa. In October 1914 the British vice-consul at Zacatecas (a miner) personally requested Villa that two railway cars be made available to shift timber to the Bote mines. Villa at once exuded co-operation; he ordered Aguirre Benavides to supply the rolling stock; he removed some troublesome troops from the Unión mines; he chatted about mining (drawing on his own experiences) and promised that 'when the time came for him to put his hand on the state of Zacatecas . . . the mining industry would flourish more than it had ever done before'. He concluded with a polite reference to the Western Front, which left the British representative delighted: 'you will see that I have been quite successful in arranging my business with the General; he is quite nice to talk to and takes a great interest in our war, expressing his desire for the allies to win'.[719]

Symptomatic of this mellowing was Villa's changing attitude to the Church. The sporadic, popular anti-clericalism of 1913–14 petered out. By the end of 1914, Villa was issuing statements guaranteeing the freedom of priests, so long as they abstained from politics. Angeles, doyen of the 'respectable' Villistas, took it upon himself to reassure Catholic opinion – not only in Mexico but also in the US, where Father Francis Kelley was mounting a noisy campaign on behalf of Mexico's persecuted Catholics. Advisers like Felix Sommerfeld quite deliberately orchestrated Villa's pledges to the Church, in the hope of securing American goodwill.[720] And the hope was not without foundation: by February 1915 Kelley was describing Villa – in correspondence to the State Department – as something of a reformed prodigal; 'I am well aware that nothing is to be expected of Carranza', he wrote . . . but I do believe that Villa can be reached.'[721] By early 1915 this refurbished image was being publicised in the US by priests and newspapermen, lobbyists and generals.[722]

Had the respectable Villistas therefore roped and corraled the plebeian Villista veterans: Villa himself, Urbina, Fierro, and the many lesser leaders of popular provenance? Historians too readily assume that they had; and they do so, perhaps, because of attitudes which they share with, and even derive from, contemporary observers. For them, rough-and-ready, illiterate caudillos needed respectable backers, advisers and string-pullers; such caudillos were the instruments of their scribes and secretaries, not vice versa. Thus, Enrile manipulated Orozco, Palafox Zapata, Angeles Villa and so on.[723] Clearly, these grey eminences exercised power; but they exercised it at the behest, not at the expense, of the caudillo they served; the caudillo called the tune. Thus, Zapata's revolutionary career began well before and continued well after 'little Manuel Palafox' enjoyed his brief tenure of power, which he did precisely in those areas where Zapata was most reluctant to involve himself. Even if they were illiterate, caudillos were no fools – or they would not have got where they were. Villa oozed a kind of plebeian cunning ('his intelligence', General Scott noted, 'is most apparent'); Urbina, though 'illiterate, obstinate and vain', displayed a 'native shrewdness'.[724] In the light of this, one is tempted to see in Villa's wry comment – 'how strange: me, working for the peace and quiet of others' – an ironic awareness of his new role, and the careful grooming which went with it; while the follow-up: 'as for me, one day they'll kill me', suggests neither complete acceptance of this role, nor complete faith in its permanence.[725] On the other side, there were advisers like Martín Luis Guzmán who were also aware of the falsity of their position; or like Vasconcelos, who were surprised to learn, *ex post facto*, that they had served as grey eminences to caudillos, with whose independence of mind they were fully acquainted.[726] Popular revolutions are, after all, strange and rare events, when, to an extent, the world is turned upside down. Historians, being, usually, literate and educated, may find it hard to envisage situations in which literacy and education were subordinated to military prowess, *machismo* and popularity with the mass. They may, particularly when dealing with Mexico, find it hard to credit that these latter attributes were at a premium, while conventional political talents were at a discount. Yet this was the case, at least for a few years between 1910 and 1920. Thereafter, the world righted itself; the literati recovered their birthright; and the plebeians sank to the bottom. But it would be wrong to assume (common though the assumption is) that more recent circumstances – associated with a stable, bureaucratic, 'bourgeois' Mexico – had always pertained, or that the plebs had always known their place. On such an ahistorical assumption it is impossible to understand Villismo or the events of 1914–15.

First, the continued popular character of Villismo must be emphasised. Growing professionalisation had by no means eliminated it. Hence the Villismo of 1914–15 was riddled with contradictions. The calculating, grudging, or patronising Villismo of the well-to-do was matched by the more emotive commitment of the common people – emotive, not because the people were unable to appreciate their own interests in rational manner, but rather because, in most regions, Villa's capacity to serve those interests in practical fashion still had to be taken on trust. If in Chihuahua the Villista record of social reform was ambiguous, elsewhere it was virtually non-existent. True, some Villistas were genuinely popular – even agrarian – rebels, who expressed popular demands; but so, too, were some Carrancistas.[727] Nationwide, the two factions were indistinguishable according to class or ideological identity. At the level of official, national policy (a somewhat ethereal level in 1914–15) Carranza outdistanced his rival in reformist decrees and promises; and in the provinces, the feverish reformism of Castro, Alvarado, Múgica, Gavira had few Villista parallels. The Villista Convention legislated with gusto, but its members were increasingly impotent civilians, not generals who could make their policies stick.

Written laws and decrees, however, were not everything. Though, as we shall see, they could buy support, they could not guarantee popular esteem – a more intangible sentiment which grew spontaneously, unplanned, 'irrationally', and which Villa enjoyed, notwithstanding his indifferent legislative record. As one historian of the revolution has put it: 'naive popularity is generally won by personal exploits, brave gestures and generous impulses, theatrically displayed, and not by decrees and diplomatic notes'.[728] Or, we might rephrase it, 'affective' and 'pragmatic' allegiances were distinct, both analytically and – in that they governed different historical relationships – empirically. By way of evidence, it is not necessary to rely on Villa's own account of rapturous popular receptions.[729] 'The peon believes in Villa', an American mining engineer observed, 'he is one of their own and he has a good deal of their confidence.'[730] Reasons have already been suggested: with his plebeian origins, bandit past and revolutionary record, Villa appealed to the poor – laws and decrees aside – as a *pelado* who had bucked the bosses and come out on top; he was, save in his abstinence from liquor, the epitomy of the *macho*. He had, and never lost, the common touch, the ability to appeal to the populace, even in defiance of their own 'objective interests' (whatever they might be). This he shared with Zapata, with the Cedillos, with many popular *cabecillas*, and even with some old Porfirian *políticos*, like Morelos' Governor Alarcón.[731] On this score, Carranza could not compete: not simply because he was an old Porfirian worthy (witness the case of Alarcón), but because his character and manner – ponderous, austere, reticent – failed to stir popular sympathy.[732] People who thronged the streets to get a look at Villa remained unmoved by Carranza; the First Chief's travels through northern Mexico were dull affairs compared with Villa's triumphal progresses. Alighting from the train at Ramos Arizpe in June 1914, Carranza shook a few hands while spectators 'stood regarding each other with that dumb expression on their faces like so many cattle'.[733] Only in the cynical, time-serving capital did Carranza – and his army – get a big welcome, and even here the sincerity of the demonstrators was doubted.[734]

That Villa should outdistance the First Chief in popularity in Chihuahua was to be expected; but in Coahuila, too, Villa was 'certainly a popular chap' and 'on the haciendas and outlying districts the Mexican cowboys and other labouring class [sic] idolise General Villa'; yet the same cowboys, 'when questioned about General Carranza, have nothing to say'.[735] The same was, of course, true in Morelos, where 'First Chief Carranza sparked not the faintest sympathy among ... farmers and field-hands.'[736] Hence there were no Carranza legends or *corridos*; Carranza figured in revolutionary songs chiefly as a butt for Villista humour, notably in the famous *La Cucuracha*:[737]

> I'll take old Carranza's whiskers / And make a cockade out of
>   them:
> And then I'll stick it in the hat / Of his master Pancho Villa.

And hence Carranza had to rely on written, official reforms to manufacture an *ersatz* (pragmatic) support, in default of a natural, homespun (affective) popularity. Hence, too, at the height of Villa's appeal in 1914–15, nominally 'Carrancista' troops seemed to waver in their allegiance to the First Chief; for, even if their *jefe* declared for Carranza, the Villista undertow threatened to pull the rank-and-file into the opposing camp. Frequent reports indicated that the Carrancistas of Sinaloa – Carrasco, Iturbe, Cabanillas – were having difficulty retaining the loyalty of their men, and that a 'substantial [Villista] victory' would produce widespread defections.[738] Hostetter, no admirer of Villa or Villismo, noted a similar phenomenon in Sonora, which made Alvarado fear an imminent mutiny among his troops.[739] In Jalisco, too, Manuel Diéguez, playing his dangerous anti-clerical game, 'doubted the loyalty of some of his subordinates'; Dávila had problems at Piedras Negras; while at Monterrey it was questioned whether the Carrancista commander could count on his men if they were ordered to fight against Villa.[740] In fact, there were few major defections. The links of proximate, personal loyalty which, along with self-interest, bound together *jefe* and *gente*, which had often been forged years before and hardened in subsequent campaigns, ultimately proved stronger than the more general, diffuse enticements of Villismo. Like the Europeans then engaged in their own civil war, soldiers were motivated by loyalty more to their own, immediate military unit, than to any grand, national cause or abstract ideology.[741] So, narrow, Namierite allegiances prevailed. But for a while the matter hung in the balance, and any resounding Villista victories would certainly have produced the swift dissolution of many Carrancista armies.

With Villismo's sustained popular support went a sustained popular–plebeian leadership which stayed substantially independent of vested interests. In other words, theories about grey eminences are greatly exaggerated: the respectable Villistas could not control the movement as they had hoped; on the contrary, its elemental, unpredictable, wayward character drove them to desperation. Though they run counter to many authorities, these conclusions are hardly surprising. The Maderista civilians were, in the main, a feeble crowd: worthy, earnest, humane and civilised, but feeble. Having failed to dominate, even to participate in, their eponymous revolution of 1910, they could hardly be expected to crack the whip over the hardened Villista veterans of 1914–15. Nor could it be expected that liberal worthies like Dr Miguel Silva ('a scholar but no politician . . . patriotic, generous and good . . . a wise medic and great philanthropist') or Roque González Garza (of 'incredible ingenuousness . . . unlimited generosity and unfailing good will') would win over the likes of Urbina and Fierro by exhortation and example.[742] On the contrary: they found their *mission civilisatrice* an uphill struggle. In 1914–15, as in 1910–11, they could not sustain a common cause with the plebs and rabble. Civilisation and barbarism would not mix. Between Guzmán and Villa yawned a 'social abyss'; a 'gorge' separated González Garza from the military leaders he sought to contain and moderate.[743] On the one hand, the military tended to regard the civilian *políticos* (as Orozco had regarded Madero in 1911) as meddlesome *curros* and *catrines* – as fixers who, yet again, were trying to collect the spoils won by the sacrifice of others (were they so wrong?). Banderas cursed devious *licenciados* just as Villa, in conversation with Obregón, cursed his intellectual advisers; Villa and Zapata warmed to each other in a bitter, mutual denunciation of 'opportunistic politicians', rogues (and worse) who sought only place and preferment and whom, Zapata boasted in forthright terms, he had 'busted' and sent packing.[744]

On the other side of the great divide, civilians like Guzmán despaired.[745] Vasconcelos' flirtation with Villismo – carefully played down in his auto-biography – came to a tearful end: 'these men are beasts, not human beings', he confided to his beautiful mistress, '. . . I can't forgive myself for running with this kind of people.'[746] Pani's prediction – a reasoned statement of middle-class prejudice – thus came true: Vasconcelos, he had foretold, would experience 'the same as any civilised man in his position: he would find it intolerable to be in contact with and above all subordinate to a primitive human being [General Villa] who was ignorant, cruel and bloodthirsty'.[747] Emiliano Sarabia, striving to govern San Luis in the name of Villa, found Urbina just as incorrigible as he had been in 1913; González Garza, as chief executive of the Convention, came to consider his job a 'very Calvary', for all the notice that was taken of his orders by the Villista and Zapatista military.[748] Up in Chihuahua, things ran better: but Chihuahua's peace and prosperity were partly attributable to the departure south of many of the 'disorderly elements', who were rampaging elsewhere, leaving *'puros pacíficos'* to run the Villista heartland.[749] But even here the respectable Villistas faced serious problems. Juan Medina, the sober, reflective ex-Federal, found himself locked in 'perpetual struggle with Fierro, Banda, José Rodríguez and others' – representatives of veteran Villismo.[750] Lázaro de la Garza, a well-to-do Torreón businessman, prominent in Villista financial circles since 1913, was undermined by the mixed corruption and ineptitude of Hipólito Villa, Pancho's brother.[751] Even those individuals whose advice Villa was supposed to heed most carefully were disappointed: by his own admission, and to his own cost, Villa ignored Angeles' advice; while, José Isabel Robles concluded, Villa 'doesn't need us, except as a sort of emblem'.[752] Far from showing Villa (and his military veterans) as the pawns of respectable advisers, these accounts strongly suggest that it was the advisers who were sacrificed, and the veterans who made the moves.

This conclusion is borne out by Villista policy – or the lack of it. Respectable Villistas like the ex-Federal Cervantes continued to prate about constitutional government; but it was never implemented, not even in Chihuahua, where circumstances were most favourable.[753] Despite Terrazas' urgings, Villa made no attempt to take control of Yucatán; and, despite the openings created by Chao, González Garza and others, Villa showed no interest in recruiting urban labour to his side, as Obregón was soon to do. There were also sins of commission. Guarantees to the Church were forgotten when Villa chose to resume his vendetta against Spanish priests.[754] Likewise, his solicitude for American interests and opinion was soon revealed, as some predicted it would be, as a fairweather phenomenon, just as capable of drastic change as Huerta's initial benevolence.[755] As Villista public relations faltered, as the respectable Villistas were ignored, so Villa's old, military *compadres* called the tune: a wild, dithyrambic revel. Their occupation of Mexico City was marked by rapes, gun-fights and murders, the victims including fellow-revolutionaries (Carrancista and Zapatista) as well as Porfiristas and Huertistas; these were killings dictated less by *raison d'état* than by personal vengeance.[756] In Mexico City, as in Guadalajara and San Luis, the early promise of orderly government, which had so captivated the well-to-do was brutally broken. At the moment of its greatest power and territorial extension, Villismo again resembled banditry – rank, rowdy, criminal banditry – writ large.[757] For, on a national as on a local scale, social banditry was a poor traveller.[758] And, however this phenomenon might be qualified, it hardly responded to the machinations of conservative controlling interests. The respectable Villistas recoiled in horror; American observers began to suffer doubts; and once sympathetic *pacíficos* (especially the better off) were bitterly disappointed.[759]

This was no 'iron hand', still less a champion of constitutional rule. Here, rather, was a brand of *caudillaje* at once arbitrary, violent, and personal, combining the ruthlessness of Huertismo with the deep prejudices and waywardness of *serrano* populism.

Before leaving this analysis of the rival factions and resuming the narrative of their conflict, a moment of speculation is appropriate. Since Carranza won, the nature of a Carrancista regime can be straightforwardly examined. But, Villa having lost, the hypothetical character of a Villista regime remains obscure, and (to my knowledge) there have been no counter-factual speculations as to how it might have turned out. Yet this is no idle, might-have-been question; it is a useful re-formulation of the basic problems already posed; for, if Villismo represented popular/peasant forces – or, alternatively, 'reaction' – a Villista regime would have differed radically from that which in fact took power. On the other hand, if the two factions were fundamentally similar, engaged in a personalist struggle for power, the outcome made little difference and the losses were in vain. This speculation is all the more valid since the decisive military conflict, which determined the outcome, was a close-run thing.

A hypothetical Villista regime, arising from a hypothetical Villista victory, would certainly have differed from that which emerged, but not by virtue of any greater social egalitarianism or revolutionary fervour. Two scenarios might be sketched: not black and white alternatives, but variations along an axis, the precise position depending on the relative strengths of the two wings of Villismo, the respectable civilians and the plebeian military of the 'core'. Had the latter dominated (as they appeared to do in 1915); had Villa, avoiding defeat, sloughed off his educated advisers and deferred to his rough-and-ready *compañeros*, the Villista state would have become a cypher, a *fainéant* Mexico City regime weakly presiding over dozens of local, largely independent fiefs. Villa showed no personal appetite for the presidency; his occupation of Mexico City had been brief; he had seemed 'anxious to get away from here as he . . . found the multitude and complexity of the problems here too much for him'.[760] The same was *a fortiori* true of Zapata and many other popular leaders. National power would have been delegated to proxies – to Angeles, or effete civilians like Dr Silva – while Villa and his generals retired to their newly acquired northern estates, lording it over Chihuahua, living in the primitive seigneurial style anticipated by Urbina in 1913 and later emulated, with evident satisfaction, by Villa after 1920.[761] Perhaps Villa would have run for governor (and been elected); perhaps he would not have bothered. Elsewhere in a Villista Mexico local regimes, derivative of the civil war, would have ruled in relative independence: populist caudillos like Cedillo in San Luis (a factual, not counter-factual example); an agreed nominee – if they could agree – of the Laguna leaders in Durango and Coahuila; possibly Julián Medina, or his proxy, in Jalisco; young Rafael Buelna in Sinaloa; Maytorena and his clique in

Sonora; Peláez in the Huasteca; a government of Zapatista provenance in Morelos; representatives of vested interests in the south – Meixueiro in Oaxaca, a *finquero* regime in Chiapas, a provincial plantocracy in Yucatán. The sheer diversity of this notional Villista polity is obvious (though the Carrancista/Sonoran reality was diverse, too). But the Villista scenario would not only display greater diversity, but would also lack any powerful, countervailing, integrating force: a characteristic deriving from the most basic difference separating Villismo from Carrancismo, *viz.*, the parochial, popular Villista core, and its nationalist, centralising Carrancista counterpart.

Of course, the respectable Villistas, ensconced in state and national government, would not have been content with their futile roles. Over time, the populist generals would have conceded ground to their civilian proxies: as the former perused their estates, patronised bullfights and put on weight, so the latter – invested with cabinet portfolios, governorships, legal and financial positions – would grapple with the problems of post-revolutionary reconstruction: rebuilding the shattered state, reducing the swollen armed forces, restoring the economy and currency, securing foreign recognition and investment, striving to legitimise the new regime on the bases of formal laws and parties. Over time, therefore, as the caudillos aged, as the politics of civil war gave way to the politics of reconstruction, as new talents and forms of authority emerged, so the power of civilian *políticos* and bureaucrats would wax, that of the Villista veterans wane. All this, of course, is a scenario drawn from reality; if valid, it suggests that any post-revolutionary regime, Villista or Carrancista, would have evolved according to certain patterns (de-militarisation, reconstruction, bureaucratisation). There is no reason to doubt that the respectable Villistas would have pursued ends broadly similar to those pursued by their victorious Carrancista equivalents; they were similar people.

But that is not to say that all would have been the same, even assuming that the Villista civilians made at least some headway against their military partners. For a regime of this kind would have proved less tough, tenacious, and stable than the reality which emerged. Whereas the Carrancistas (in particular the Sonorans: Obregón, Calles, Alvarado) combined political and military skills, alternatively governing or fighting as circumstances demanded, Villismo (and by extension the notional Villista regime) embodied a clear division of labour, based on the military's reluctance to govern and the civilians' incapacity to fight. The parochialism of the Villista caudillos gave the ex-Maderistas and ex-Federals their chance to exercise power; but, such was the pedigree of that power that it lacked muscle and stamina, rather as the Madero regime had in 1911–13. They would have constituted a national elite which had not fought its way to the top (a process requiring not just military skill, but also popular support and legitimacy, and all that these implied), but which had had power conferred upon it, by default, by those who had done the fighting. Hence it would have been a flawed, precarious power, only conditionally conferred: for the Villista caudillos, though they might not want to run the government themselves, did not want the government to infringe their new parochial rights and properties. They would relinquish (formal) power to aspiring, nationalist civilians so long as the civilians left them alone; but this condition at once set tight limits on the reconstruction of the state and, in many respects, condemned the state to impotence. The Villista caudillos – which includes the whole roster from Villa to Meixueiro – would not govern, but they would not allow others to govern either.[762] Policies of reconstruction, demilitarisation, centralisation, state-building, bureaucratisation and mass political mobilisation would all run into the brick walls of entrenched local *caudillaje*. In reality, as the history of the twenties and thirties shows, these were formidable obstacles. Under a Villista regime, characterised by stronger caudillos and a weaker, insecure national government, they might well have proved unbreakable. It is hard to envisage a Silva, a Díaz Lombardo, even a Felipe Angeles, successfuly curbing army and caciques in the manner of Obregón and Calles.

It is particularly hard, given the character of the respectable Villistas. Arguably, they would have paid more homage to the past than their Carrancista rivals for, as well-heeled, cultured, liberal *bien-pensants*, they had a closer affinity to the Porfirian status quo (in terms of education, property, jobs, foreign contacts, even age) than the young Carrancista parvenus. They would be more inclined to conserve and conciliate than to innovate and proscribe. Already constrained by their limited power, they would have been further held back by their bulky ideological baggage, and their inherited contacts and *compromisos*. Would a President Silva or Angeles have battled against the Catholic Church or foreign oil companies? Would they have dragooned *agraristas* and labour unions into these battles on behalf of the revolutionary state? And even if they had tried, which is doubtful, would they have carried the caudillos with them? Cedillo, perhaps the best, real example of a 'Villista' survivor, necessarily participated in these policies; but in his own fief he resisted them, and was ultimately ousted by them.[763] A hypothetical Villista regime would have less resembled (real) post-revolutionary Mexico than post-revolutionary Bolivia, where weak civilian *políticos*, somewhat fortuitously installed in government, struggled, but failed, to establish a dependable power base, where the state abdicated control over large sections of political society, and where the outcome was eviction from power and a legacy of instability and praetorianism.[764] If this argument holds, then much of the political development and stability which characterised post-revolutionary Mexico must be attributed to Carranza's triumph over Villa; and, had the battles gone the other way, as well they might have, then the political outcome would have been quite different: no CROM, no Cristero war, no PNR, no Callista state. Note that we are talking of *political* outcome. Villa's defeat in no sense enshrined capitalism or averted socialism; either way, capitalism was on the national agenda, and the Villistas – civilian and military – had no intention of taking it off.[765] Modes of production were not at stake during the war of the winners. But as these alternative scenarios suggest, plenty was. It was not an inconsequential conflict. Whether, on the other hand, the outcome was worth 100m. dollars and 200,000 lives is a question for moral philosophers, not historians.[766]

The war of the winners differed from previous revolutionary conflicts by virtue of the shifting loyalties which underlay it. Leaders affiliated to national factions in cautious, tactical fashion, sometimes conscious (if they were Carrancistas) of the popular Villista undertow which might drag them down. Only a minority (in each core) was strongly committed; yet it was upon these minorities that the outcome depended. A telling victory for either side would initiate a landslide, as the waverers and time-servers (who were often wavering and time-serving for perfectly good reasons) rushed to join the triumphant faction. For this reason, maps drawn depicting Villista and Carrancista spheres of control are partly meaningless, and certainly likely to exaggerate Villa's real strength.[767] Head counts of total factional forces are only slightly less misleading. The crucial factor was the size and competence of the armies which the respective nuclei could field against each other; for the outcome of this – what might be called the 'hegemonic' conflict – would determine the outcome of the many, lesser, contingent conflicts throughout the country.

The war of the winners also differed analogously from previous wars by virtue of the strategy involved. The campaigns of 1910–11 and 1913–14 had pitted initially raw, poorly armed, rebel troops against well-equipped regulars; first in guerrilla skirmishes, then unbalanced wars of attrition, in which the rebels dominated the countryside, the Federals controlled the fortified towns. Now, revolutionary fought revolutionary, like against like. Two professionalised armies, leavened by Federal recruits, endowed with experience, *esprit de corps*, artillery, and logistical support, faced each other in conventional battle. Neither side could claim superior morale (the general belief that Villa would win does not appear to have undermined the morale of the 'core' Carrancistas). And the prime object of the war was not, as in previous campaigns, the occupation of territory, but – following Clausewitz's injunction – the destruction of the enemy's forces, thus of his prestige and power. This, quite clearly, was Obregón's aim in forsaking Mexico City (which under the terms of the war could be occupied and abandoned at will) and marching to meet Villa on the plains of the Bajío. Here, in a region of no great strategic significance, one hitherto spared major conflicts, the final, decisive battles of the Revolution were won and lost through the spring and early summer of 1915. These weeks formed a brief hiatus in the usual pattern of revolutionary warfare; a hectic interlude of pitched battles after which – the crescendo over, the chords resolved – the old, familiar themes (urban garrison, rural rebellion, guerrilla skirmishing, repression, *reconcentración*, and stalemate) reasserted themselves and became the motifs of the long, funereal finale of the Revolution.

This gathering and collision of forces can only be conveyed by conventional narrative. In November 1914 the Division of the North, detained from its triumphal march on Mexico City earlier in the year, was heading south through the Bajío towards the capital. Towns fell without resistance and Carranza evacuated Mexico City heading east towards Puebla and the Gulf.[768] Dropping his original idea of a west coast expedition against the Villistas, Obregón followed the First Chief eastwards.[769] As they decamped from the capital, the Carrancistas ransacked the mint and the government archives, loading the spoils, along with horses, munitions and supplies, on railway cars which soon jammed the Mexican Railway; and, as they made their escape through Tlaxcala, they hitched a locomotive to the track, ripping it up behind them.[770] Just in time, the Americans ended their futile occupation of Veracruz, leaving the port clean, scrubbed and vulture-free for the Carrancistas to enter, which they did enthusiastically, installing in their new offices the archives, typewriters, furniture and even the ink-pots they had brought from Mexico City; while Carranza billeted himself in the lighthouse building. It was clear that the Carrancistas did not consider themselves politically defunct, and that they intended getting down to business.[771]

The Carrancistas held Veracruz, but within days their enemies held Mexico City. Lucio Blanco, whose long association with Carranza and the Sonorans had not made him an *adicto*, and who had been strong for Gutiérrez and the third force, remained in the capital with his troops, loyal to the Convention. Attempts to inveigle him to Veracruz failed.[772] He therefore policed the city as the first Zapatistas began filtering into the suburbs. Fears of pillage and rapine, the legacy of three years of press scaremongering, were soon dispelled. Though the Zapatistas appeared 'the roughest of the rough', they were orderly, even deferential; their behaviour, noted the *Mexican Herald*, was 'attentive, courteous, and modest and made a very favourable impression'.[773] *Capitalino* spirits rose, and crowds even gathered along Avenida San Francisco to behold 'the southern revolutionaries about whom such hair-raising stories have been current during the last four years'.[774] Zapata himself paid a brief, unenthusiastic visit to Mexico City and promptly returned to Morelos.

On the last day of November, Villa, too, arrived and went to meet his southern ally in a Xochimilco schoolhouse, on the outskirts of town. Here, in a famous encounter, the two plebeian caudillos ate, drank – Villa, a teetotaller, politely forced down a glass of cognac – and, after the initial shyness had worn off, fell to cursing Carranza and planning their joint campaign against him.[775] To this end a loose military alliance was established and Villa undertook to supply the *surianos* with weapons. They agreed publicly on a joint triumphal entry of the capital and privately on a list of political executions. Accordingly, on 6 December, some 50,000 Conventionist troops – infantry, cavalry, and artillery, northerners in khaki and stetsons, southerners wearing the loose white cotton and broad sombrero of the *campesino* and carrying banners of the Virgin of Guadalupe – filed through the streets of Mexico City to be reviewed by President Gutiérrez in the Zócalo.[776] And, later in the month, there was a general, bloody settling of old scores.

At first, however, the new regime seemed orderly and benign. The Zapatistas roamed the streets 'like lost children'; they knocked on doors, asking politely for food and displayed a quaint rural *naïveté* by attacking a fire engine, which they took to be a hostile machine of war. They did not share the predatory ways of the Carrancistas: the only houses singled out for sequestration were those of prominent Morelos families; other properties taken over by the Carrancistas were returned to their owners. Zapata himself, instead of appropriating a luxurious town house, 'holed up in a grimy, gloomy little hotel a block away from the railroad station where trains left for Cuautla'. Here reporters found him unhelpfully laconic.[777] Compared to the Carrancista occupation, then, there were few confiscations and less speeches (Zapata even declined to appear before the crowds outside the National Palace), and all this the anxious people of Mexico City perceived gratefully, acquiring a sudden, patronising affection for the 'clean, well-built Indians' who seemed 'a very much better type of men than the Carrancistas'.[778] From the Zapatistas' point of view, Mexico City was the great wen, its occupation a painful necessity dictated by the strategic needs of Morelos. They did not therefore throw themselves into the task with gusto; they did not amass urban real estate or political offices; they were happy to allow old Porfirian officials, like the chief of police, to resume their jobs in the interests of public order.[779] In practice, Zapatismo had no brief to revolutionise Mexico City; it lacked the will to centralised control which characterised Carrancismo.

The same was true, *mutatis mutandis*, of the Villistas, who shared the Conventionist occupation of the capital. Initially, they, too, won the approbation of the inhabitants.[780] But disillusionment soon set in. Villa's concern for responsible, constitutional government depended a good deal on skilful public relations, and on the precarious influence of what Luis Aguirre Benavides called 'el grupo civilizado' – the respectable ex-Maderistas and ex-Federals.[781] In the summer of 1914 they had done a good job, guiding Villa's policy and pronouncements, turning towards interested observers the movement's best profile; hence Villa's reputation soared. But in Mexico City, around the turn of the year, their influence faltered: several, including Angeles, were busy in the north, depriving Villa of their steadying restraint; the prospect of imminent victory had, perhaps, a similar liberating effect; and the big city presented raw, *serrano* leaders with unprecedented problems and temptations. As they succumbed, Gutiérrez and his civilian cabinet lost control. But Villismo did not so much go off the rails, as revert to type. For the 'lapse' in Mexico City fell squarely within the old tradition of *serrano* banditry and rebellion, out of which Villismo had grown; and it gave a bitter foretaste of the Villismo of 1915–20 which, bereft of sophisticated advisers, recovered its old, violent, wayward character. The real lapse, or aberration, had come in 1914, as Villismo was artificially schooled and sensitised, in the illusory hope that it would emerge as a serious candidate for national power.

During his brief sojourn in the capital, Villa was surrounded by his old boon companions: Womack's 'rowdies . . . out for kicks and spoils'; the 'two or three fellows with pistols' who, Vasconcelos noted, 'were never far from the side of the guerrilla chieftain'.[782] In their company, Villa took in the sights of the capital, frequented the San Cosme cockpit, and abducted the wife of a French hotelier. Old *compadres* like Fierro 'were having full swing . . . and [Villa] heeds their baleful advice as his good counsellors are not now at his side'.[783] Nor was Villa the only sinner. Tomás Gutiérrez, of Natera's forces, tried to rape the wife of an oil company manager; Juan Banderas did 1,500 pesos damage, smashing furniture and windows in the Hotel Cosmos, possibly on the occasion when he shot to death General Rafael Garay (Banderas was involved in another fracas two months later at Tepepám, in which his adversary, the Zapatista Antonio Barona – 'a malign bully', much the worse for *pulque* – brought into action an 80mm. field gun).[784] Killings became commonplace. Some victims were old Porfiristas and Huertistas, like Generals Munguía and Ojeda (for Ojeda the revolution had been a catalogue of personal miseries); but others were fellow-revolutionaries, embroiled in political or personal vendettas. David Berlanga, the tactlessly outspoken schoolmaster, was dragged from Sylvain's Restaurant by Fierro and José Rodríguez and done to death in the Panteón de Dolores. Most considered this a political assassination, ordered by Villa, though some said Berlanga's fault was to have reproved Fierro for paying his restaurant bill with an IOU.[785] More serious, the prominent Zapatista, Paulino Martínez, was murdered by Villista officers, and it was reported that Díaz Soto and Palafox were also on the assassins' list.[786] Not that the Zapatistas were entirely blameless: despite the protests of President Gutiérrez, they persuaded Villa to hand over Guillermo García Aragón, a serving member of the Convention, so that he might be summarily executed.[787]

All told, up to 200 people were murdered in Mexico City during these weeks.[788] And the provinces, too, came to know the feral side of Villismo. Angeles and Raúl Madero could still inspire confidence at Monterrey; but at Guadalajara and San Luis it was a different story.[789] True, the citizens of Guadalajara preferred almost anyone to the hard-line anti-clerical Diéguez, but their initial enchantment with Villismo soon faded: 'all the raised hopes on the part of the public at a change from a Carrancista government to that of Conventionists have vanished . . . hence a state of complete and thorough demoralisation exists here'.[790] Catholic spokesmen were also disillusioned. Soon after Villa's whirlwind, well-received visit to Guadalajara in December

1914, 'feelings of deception set in, anxiety returned, and most of the good elements who had helped Villa against Diéguez drifted away'.[791] The *tapatíos* could no more rely on the likes of Julián Medina to protect life, property and church than the *capitalinos* could on the likes of Villa and Fierro. San Luis faced a similar experience weeks later, when Urbina's arrival initiated 'a reign of terror', during which property was confiscated, drunken troops brawled in the streets, and there were arbitrary arrests and extortions.[792]

Observers, allies and respectable Villistas were shocked. Dr Silva was reported 'horrified'; Robles, the Conventionist Minister of War, voiced his disgust at recent events and promised a full investigation; Díaz Lombardo and others urged Gutiérrez to declare a political amnesty.[793] Even the Zapatistas undertook to curb their ally.[794] But none of this had much effect. When Gutiérrez spoke out, deploring that the population was 'gripped by panic because of the continual disappearance of individuals seized by night . . . for the purpose of ransom or assassination', Villa's response was to place him under house arrest.[795] Respectable Villistas who attempted their mollifying role were ignored, or worse. Vasconcelos, having protested in vain again the killings to the impotent president, was sent to see Villa, whom he found sleeping ('"sorry . . .", said the officer, "but I have orders not to wake him; he went to bed very late last night"'.); and the response of Villa's officers to the protest was incredulous: '"What the devil . . .! This seems important to you: that a few more or less should die? After all, this is a revolution. A lot more will die before it is over, including ourselves, today or tomorrow perhaps." And while they were talking, I could hear the shots.'[796] The account – Vasconcelos' own – may be embellished; but it convincingly calls to mind the macabre *corrido*, the amoral, sanguinary heroes of Azuela.

These events, apart from baring the soul of Villismo, also contributed to immediate political developments. Faced with arbitrary killings by his subordinates, President Gutiérrez could only 'exhort' and 'admonish'.[797] Individuals committed to the Convention, rather than to Villa personally, began to regret the Villista liaison and to talk of the desirability of Villa's retirement as commander-in-chief. Even one-time Villistas like Robles and Felicitas Villareal, the Convention's Minister of Finance, became 'so disgusted with Villa's conduct during his last sojourn in the capital that they were resolved to break with him'.[798] Hence in January 1915, as the Convention re-assembled in Mexico City and resumed its interminable phillipics, there was an attempted re-formation of the third force, as Gutiérrez and his middle-of-the-road supporters tried to dump Villa and open up negotiations with the Carrancistas. The third force could still recruit some big names, across a range of opinion: *cabecillas* like Blanco, Robles, Gutiérrez and Mateo Almanza, respectable Villistas like Eugenio Aguirre Benavides and Felicitas Villareal, intellectuals like Vasconcelos. But Obregón showed no disposition to parley and when Villa, then in the north, got proof of Gutiérrez's manoeuvres, he ordered the execution of the president and of any other members of the Conventionist government who tried to leave the capital. Fortunately for Gutiérrez, the order came via Robles, who was privy to the plot. Forewarned, the conspirators slipped out of Mexico City in the early hours of 16 January, taking with them several thousand troops and the contents of the National Treasury, leaving behind a surprised, agitated city, fly-posted with manifestoes denouncing Villa and Zapata.[799] There followed a sad, winter Calvary through the mountains as Gutiérrez headed towards his home territory of San Luis, harassed by Villista forces, never receiving the flocks of adherents he had hoped. Denied a foothold even in San Luis, he set up his token administration at Dr Arroyo (NL) 'and from that point issued orders to which no-one listened and sent to the US agents whom no-one heeded'.[800] At the end of May he bowed to the inevitable, resigned, and made his peace with Carranza. Many of his colleagues were less fortunate. Almanza was caught by vengeful Villistas and shot; Aguirre Benavides, despite a Carrancista safe-conduct, was killed by Carrancistas on his way to the US; Robles, surprisingly amnestied by Villa, survived only one more year of factional conflict before he, too, faced the firing squad in Oaxaca. Vasconcelos, of course, survived to disport himself in America with the beautiful Adriana, visiting the opera and studying in the New York Public Library ('what', he wondered, reading Plotinus, 'did the Mexican revolution and all its wickedness matter in comparison with that immortal world of the spirit?').[801]

With Gutiérrez's flight, the Convention's executive collapsed. The sovereign assembly, however, remained, recently reconvened in Mexico City and still, to its own collective mind, the legitimate government of the Republic and mouthpiece of the revolution. But the history of the Convention itself in 1915 was a Calvary comparable to that of its departed president – though with more light relief along the way. In the wake of Gutiérrez's sudden departure, the Convention's president, Roque González Garza, declared martial law and assumed control of the executive; but he did not replace Gutiérrez as provisional president (of the Republic) and, indeed, the Convention debated long and hard the merits of presidential as against parliamentary government, before finally resolving on the second.[802] A welter of other topics absorbed the delegates' attention: the immediate problems of finance, appointments, public order and military strategy; grander questions of legislative reform in the fields of agriculture, labour, mining, foreign investment and the electoral system. In the course of these debates, the divisions between north and south, Villista and Zapatista, became more obvious, acrimonious and ultimately violent. González Garza clashed repeatedly with Palafox over the allocation of funds and jobs, railway arrangements and the campaigns against the Carrancistas.[803] Ideologically, the northern delegates – led by González Garza, Nieto and the ex-Federal Cervantes – inclined to more cautious, liberal positions: they favoured a strong executive, rather than government by assembly; they defended private property rights, including those of *hacendados*; they trod carefully in the field of labour legislation. The southerners (which does not mean Zapatistas so much as *zapatisant* intellectuals like Palafox and Díaz Soto) were for root-and-branch policies of Conventional sovereignty, radical labour and agrarian reform, and a thorough purge of the old regime.[804]

Out of the verbal maelstrom emerged a comprehensive programme of reform – the Proyecto de Reformas Politico-Sociales de la Revolución – which the delegates debated late in February.[805] Both Proyecto and debate are of interest, in that they closely mirrored equivalent plans and arguments then emanating from the rival, Carrancista camp. Indeed, the Convention was well aware of Carrancista reforms and sought to compete with them. 'Just because Don Venustiano Carranza has introduced divorce', complained one delegate during the debate on civil marriage, 'we feel we must adopt it in order to say that we, too, are revolutionaries.'[806] Thus, across the great factional divide, the revolution's intellectuals and *políticos* spoke, if not with one voice, at least with comparable, competitive voices: the same liberal/radical debates which wracked the Convention were also taking place, if less flamboyantly, in the opposite camp. To conservative foreigners like Thomas Hohler, there was little to choose between the radicals of either side: Palafox was a 'sea-green incorruptible' whose agrarian ideas were 'utterly impractical [and] threaten[ed] dire ruin to the Mexican Republic'; while 'it is hard to see how even insanity could go to greater lengths' than Dr Atl's socialistic rhodomontades.[807] More temperate observers also found it difficult to distinguish between the plans and pronouncements of the two factions.

The crucial thing about the Convention, however was that it increasingly dealt in plans and pronouncements rather than constructive policy: it became a mere talking shop, a forum for Díaz Soto's *enragé* speeches (which finally drove delegates to request that he be medically certified); a sustained opportunity for orators to air their knowledge and polish their phrases, while outside the ultimate fate of the revolution was being decided on the battle-field.[808] Indeed, some of the delegates grew uncomfortably aware of the contrast between their own wordy impotence and Obregón's dour commitment to action.[809] But, in Mexico City in 1915 – as in Aguascalientes, 1914, or Querétaro, 1916–17 – the men of the pen and spoken word strained to make themselves heard above the din of battle. As it was, reference to global history and philosophical systems crowded out discussion of mundane Mexican problems: the French Revolution (sometimes the Third Republic) supplied criteria of political rectitude; Lic. Borrego discussed *latifundismo* with learned references to Pliny; delegate Zepeda, on divorce, cited 'Voltaire . . . the greatest sage of England.' But Cervantes, a most literate soldier, carried off the palm with a speech on labour reform which cited Rousseau, Spencer, Darwin, Cornejo ('that noted sociologist') and 'the anarchist Nietzsche'.[810]

The rhetoric became emptier as the Convention receded, literally and figuratively, from the centre of power. In January 1915 it had to quit Mexico City for the security of Cuernavaca (where the military continued brawling on the Convention's doorstep); it returned to the capital late in March, only to leave, definitively, for Toluca in July.[811] Well before this, González Garza had confessed to the futility of his position and tried, unsuccessfully, to resign.[812] The major caudillos ignored or abused him, much as they had Gutiérrez. Villa set up an independent government in the north, revealing his 'Conventionist' allegiance for the sham it was. When González Garza pleaded for reinforcements in Mexico City, Villa 'replied that the capital might go to ruin'; months later, when González Garza's successor Lágos Cházaro sought to join Villa in the north, his entreaties were ignored.[813] Zapata, though closer, was no more helpful. Despite the growing preponderance of Zapatista radicals within the Convention, Zapata ignored the assembly when it suited him. He extracted cash and leaped to the defence of Palafox, but he gave no constructive assistance and he flouted González Garza's authority at every turn.[814] The Convention's attempts to make something of the Villa–Zapata alliance, to knit together the diverse forces of north and south, came to nothing. Within the Convention itself, the Villista minority, including the hard-pressed president, was increasingly overridden by the radical Zapatista minority. Even before the exodus to Toluca, as military and economic crises piled up, the Convention had 'virtually ceased to exist'.[815] Thus, with the fall of Gutiérrez and the decline of the Convention, the two 'legitimate' authorities deriving from Aguascalientes foundered. The brave attempt to achieve union and democracy had failed. In contrast, the two factions built squarely on personal and regional commitments, in the best traditions of *caudillaje*, lived to contest the political succession.

For three months after Gutiérrez's flight from the capital, preparations were in hand for the impending, ultimate conflict. And the subsequent three months witnessed fighting of unparalleled intensity. During the first period, Villa gave priority to military campaigning, on a lavish scale, while the Carrancistas, militarily more cautious, concentrated on the political prerequisites of the struggle; though this did not ensure a Carrancista victory, it was illustrative of the contrasting characters of the two factions. On the military front – which we shall mention first – early 1915 witnessed several sideshows, but no Western Front. Mexico City changed hands twice; but these successive occupations (by the Carrancistas in January, the Zapatistas again in March) were of greater political than military significance, for neither side regarded Mexico City as the main prize: the Carrancistas had different, immediate priorities, their enemies spurned the seat of national government. But it showed that Carrancismo was still in business. Back in December, all had seemed lost, with the First Chief beleaguered in Veracruz and Puebla falling to the Zapatistas; this latter blow, reported one Carrancista sympathiser with a gift for tautology, 'will further weaken the already hopeless cause of

Carranza. He should know that it is impossible for him to regain what he has, in many ways, irretrievably lost.'[816] Many now expected Villa to swoop on Veracruz – indeed, Angeles' advice was to chase the Carrancistas down to the coast, 'plunge them into the sea and drown them'.[817] But Villa, according to the same account, was reluctant to encroach on Zapata's theatre of operations; he would attack Veracruz only if Zapata proved unequal to the task. Zapata proved unequal, but by then it was too late. Meanwhile, Villa preferred to direct his attention to enemy activities elsewhere, particularly in the north-east where Maclovio Herrera, the Chihuahuan renegade, and Antonio Villareal posed a threat to Torreón, the pivot of Villa's northern empire. This territorial commitment – which the freewheeling Carrancistas could more readily ignore – cost Villa dear. Carranza was given a respite in Veracruz and his cause rallied. Villa dispersed his energies in campaigns in the north-east, the Huasteca, and the centre-west.

At the turn of the year, Obregón resumed the offensive. The Zapatista garrisons facing him showed no disposition to resist, either at Puebla or the important railway junction of Apam (Hgo). Promised Villista aid never materialised and the Zapatistas, disillusioned with both their Villista and ex-Federal allies, preferred to pull back closer home.[818] Their ready surrender of Puebla, it was surmised, showed that 'Zapata has neither the soldiers to fight nor the men to govern outside the confines of his customary ambuscades and surprise attacks in the hot country, his own stronghold.'[819] For their part, the Villistas were disgusted by their allies' feeble prosecution of the southern front; the northerners in the Convention criticised the military failings of the *surianos*; Villa soon began to blame Zapata's evil counsellors (now, Benjamín Argumedo) for leading him astray.[820] Indifferent to Puebla, Zapata was no keener to cling to Mexico City. Hence, with Villa busy in the north, Obregón was allowed a second occupation of the capital, from late January to mid-March. This served further to sour relations between Carrancistas and *capitalinos*, who now faced food shortages, unemployment, strikes, new taxes, inflation and persecution of priests and businessmen (of which more anon).[821] Militarily, as Obregón told the press, the capital was expendable: 'whether to hold this city or not is all the same to us.[822] The main point of the occupation – apart from underlining the revival in Carrancista fortunes – was to recruit and prepare for military action against Villa. For, unlike Huerta in 1913, Obregón ignored Zapatismo (insofar as he could) and concentrated on the more formidable, conventional threat from the north; and, unlike Villa, who had been busy tackling lesser Carrancista forces in Jalisco and the north-east, he went straight for the enemy generalissimo and his army. As Angeles had recently advised, when Villa set off in hot pursuit of secondary opponents: 'those *jefes* are like hats hung from a hatstand who is Venustiano Carranza'; the main target should be the hatstand, not the hats.[823] That was Obregón's plan as he squared up to Villa himself. Railway communications were prepared northwards into the Bajío and, at the end of March, Carrancista troops began to entrain for Querétaro and the big showdown, allowing the Zapatistas to walk back into Mexico City.

Elsewhere, brisker fighting was taking place, though the chief significance of these peripheral campaigns was often the way they drew men and munitions from the impending battle in the Bajío. Some have already been touched upon. In Chiapas and Yucatán, Castro and Alvarado were battling against local resistance. In Sonora, Maytorena and his Yaquis had Hill and Calles penned up in Naco; but such were American fears for its Arizonan twin that a neutralisation plan was agreed, permitting the Carrancistas to retire eastwards to Agua Prieta. Villa's initial interest in the Sonoran imbroglio soon cooled. Troops sent to help Cabral overcome Calles were recalled for fear of Cabral's connivance with Gutiérrez and the third force; thereafter, 'Villa was forced to write off Sonora from his campaign plans.'[824] The Sonorans themselves realised that the epicentre of the civil war lay far to the south. Sonora was a sideshow, and it was prudent to await the result of the main bout. Thus at Nogales in the spring of 1915, 'both the political and military situation is suspended awaiting the result of the impending action between the armies of Generals Villa and Obregón'; and Urbalejo, the Yaqui leader of the largest force in the state – nominally a Villista/Maytorenista, essentially an Urbalejista – paused in his campaigning, 'awaiting the result of the battle now preparing between Villa and Obregón: Urbalejo will throw the weight of his forces with whichever side wins'.[825]

Greater action was guaranteed in the three theatres where committed Villistas were operating, and where Villa himself took a direct interest: in the north-east, the Huasteca and centre-west. Angeles, Villa's most skilled lieutenant, was deputed to lead the Villista campaign in Coahuila and Nuevo León, neutralising any Carrancista threat to the Villista heartland. Leaving Torreón in December, Angeles thrashed Villareal at Ramos Arizpe and occupied Monterrey, where people, church and commerce could now bask in the warm rays of a benign Villismo.[826] In March, Piedras Negras fell, leaving in Carrancista hands only three imperilled border ports along the whole northern frontier: Agua Prieta, Matamoros and Nuevo Laredo. And sallying out to defend the last of these, the doughty Maclovio Herrera was slain, in dubious circumstances, in mid-April.[827] The Carrancistas of the region were dismayed and demoralised: they undertook to split their cavalry into mobile guerrilla forces, and to send their infantry to Veracruz, where it might be of more use than in the lost north-east.[828] The Villistas thus acquired control of the coal mines of Coahuila (the conquest of strategic resources – coal, oil, henequen, chickpeas – was seen by both sides as vital prerequisites of victory, for the conventional armies of 1915 consumed quantities of pay and supplies).[829] This lent particular importance to the battle for the petroliferous Huasteca and the oil port of Tampico; and, if the Carrancista position in the north-east was disastrous, at Tampico it was dire. Here, some 15,000 Villistas under Chao, and later Urbina, joined with indigenous 'Villistas' like Peláez in a sustained action to dislodge the numerically inferior Carrancistas from the port.[830] As the attackers closed in, El Ebano became the focus of the conflict: it came under fire on 21 March 1915 and was besieged for over two months; yet, despite their superior numbers and the prevailing belief that they could not lose, the Villistas made no further headway. Frontal assaults were unavailing against entrenched defenders, and neither the schoolmaster Chao nor the bandit Urbina possessed the military ingenuity to vary the tactics (nor, of course, did contemporary military experts on the Western Front). Urbina, a successful bushwhacker in the Sierra Madre, proved an indifferent commander of 15,000 troops in a war of positions. On the other side, Jacinto Treviño, commanding at El Ebano under Pablo González, was a young military graduate; and El Ebano was the kind of battle in which expertise and organisation outweighed numbers and *élan*. The defenders employed trenches and aerial reconnaissance; they inflicted losses as much as seven times greater than those which they suffered; and by the end of May they were able to take the offensive against the weary, depleted Villista forces.[831] Urbina retreated in disgust to terrorise San Luis.[832]

The campaigns in Jalisco and Michoacán were much more fluid, thus more congenial to Villista taste and conducive to Villista success. Large Villista forces entered these states late in 1914, linking up with local allies like Julián Medina and Jesús Cíntora, easily dislodging the garrisons left by Obregón earlier in the year. Gertrudis Sánchez was sent scuttling towards Guerrero (the same route he had taken in 1913); Manuel Diéguez evacuated Guadalajara, to the delight of the inhabitants. But Medina, Contreras and (Melitón) Ortega, all plebeian to the core, could not maintain their positions. Notwithstanding their 10,000 men, and Villa's order to stand firm, they surrendered Guadalajara to the enemy in January, infuriating Villa and giving Diéguez another chance to blacken his local reputation.[833] Events in Guadalajara roughly paralleled those taking place in Mexico City: the Carrancistas were seen as avaricious, imperious anti-clericals; the Villistas were welcomed (not least by the 'best families' of the city) as guarantors of order and defenders of the faith.[834] But this did not last. Ugly incidents, coupled with repeated military failures, revealed the true nature of Villismo; *tapatío* enthusiasm for the cause waned; and Diéguez, it seems, mellowed. By spring 1915, as Villa was forced to draw reinforcements from Jalisco, disillusionment set in. The news that Fierro, retreating before Diéguez, would enter Guadalajara, petrified the city; and when Diéguez finally marched in towards the end of April, the people 'received and cheered him . . . heartily'.[835]

Early 1915 therefore saw Villismo dominant but not triumphant throughout northern and central Mexico. It had secured most of the border; it controlled, in a loose sense, the greater part of the west, from Sonora down through Sinaloa and Tepic to Jalisco and Michoacán.[836] Carrancista forces had not been eliminated – hence black-and-white maps of the respective military zones are misleading – but they were generally weaker, on the defensive, with morale faltering. Most of the north-east was lost, though Tampico still resisted bravely. If the oil port was to be relieved, local Carrancista resistance encouraged, and a spate of potential defections averted, Obregón had to move against Villa and join battle promptly; he reasoned like Marshal Foch a few months before ('my centre is giving way, my right is in retreat; situation excellent. I shall attack.'), though he put it more prosaically: 'in such circumstances it was vital to speed our advance into the centre, to resolve a situation which was daily worsening'.[837] To this end, Obregón enjoyed one major advantage: while Villa dissipated his forces in far-flung, if successful, campaigns, the Carrancistas could devote their primary attention to the main theatre in the Bajío. Thus, even while Villa was despatching troops from centre to periphery, Carranza was recalling men from the north-east and south-east to Veracruz, while Obregón was winning new recruits in Mexico City and elsewhere. As Villa expended blood and treaure with some profligacy, Carranza and Obregón schemed, prepared and politicked: such were their respective styles.

It was now, according to many accounts, that the Constitutionalist revolution made its decisive 'social' breakthrough: with Carranza's decree of December 1914 and the law of January 1915, promises of sweeping social, especially agrarian, reform were extended; and, under the aegis of these pronouncements, he garnered sufficient popular support to defeat Villa – *in hoc signo vinces*.[838] The December decree (the Additions to the Plan of Guadalupe) gave a general commitment to implement, even while the war continued, 'all those laws, dispositions and measures leading to a resolution of the economic, social and political needs of the country, enacting reforms which opinion demands as vital for the restoration [sic] of a regime which guarantees equality among all Mexicans'.[839] In particular – though without specific detail – Carranza promised the dissolution of the latifundia and the protection of small property, the restitution of illegally seized land, fairer taxation, labour reform, revisions of the civil, penal and commercial codes and of the laws governing the exploitation of natural resources, judicial and divorce reform, and respect for the anti-clerical provisions of the 1857 Constitution. In the law of 6 January 1915 he went further, sanctioning the restoration, expropriation and distribution of land, through the agency of Constitutionalist governors and military commanders, backed by local, state and national agrarian commissions.

This was not quite the dramatic *démarche* it has sometimes been seen as. There were many local precedents for such reforms: revolutionary *jefes*, Carrancista and Villista, had sponsored agrarian and labour reform, abolished debt peonage, revised taxes and economic concessions, and enforced the

Reform Laws.[840] Though a comprehensive, national statement, emanating from Carranza, was important, it was not a bolt from the blue; Carranza had already granted vague recognition to the 'social' dimension of the revolution; and his collective national antagonist, the Sovereign Convention, was at the same time discussing and promulgating substantially similar measures.[841] Together, these trends indicated the convergence of 'official' and 'unofficial' reform; they illustrated the revolutionary leadership's awareness of popular *agrarismo* and the need to placate or co-opt it; and they implied some greater incorporation of the 'masses' into the political process.[842] But these were cumulative trends, and it would be misleading to single out one (or two) measures, issued by the national leadership of one faction, as momentous events.[843] Still greater scepticism must be exercised as regards the effects of Carranza's proposals. It was hardly coincidental that they came at the very nadir of Carrancista fortunes, and the unanimous opinion that they represented deliberate ploys to win support is certainly valid.[844] But it is quite another matter to argue that 'with an agrarian programme more advanced than the Zapatista, Carranza was in a position to attract the mass of the Mexican peasantry to his side'; or that 'in effect, this single law was decisive in tipping the balance of the war in favour of Constitutionalism'.[845] At best, this argument is one of *post hoc ergo propter hoc*: Carranza won (soon after the measures in question), therefore they played a crucial part. No causal connection is proven and, indeed, such proof would be hard to find. It is scarcely credible that, within a few months, a general commitment to reform could work its way through popular consciousness to be translated into effective military action (for it was military action, undertaken by revolutionary veterans, rather than any – notional – popular sympathy which achieved Carranza's victory in 1915). These were soldiers' battles; they were not to be won by some spontaneous, peasant *levée en masse* – even assuming that Carranza could raise one.

Official *agrarismo*, which antedated January 1915, was to become a powerful weapon in the hands of the revolutionary leadership. But it took time to be tempered and honed. As they stood, Carranza's measures were statements of intent, to be evaluated in terms of many other factors, not least Carranza's own political future. Though the peasantry knew of them, they could not pay dividends in the short term.[846] More relevant were the actions (as opposed to the commitments) undertaken by the Carrancistas early in 1915. These followed the precedents of 1914; but in one respect there was genuine innovation. Once again, the Church came under the harrow.[847] On re-entering the capital in February, Obregón ordered the clergy of the archdiocese to hand over half a million pesos for relief measures. They protested, made an undisclosed counter-offer, but failed to produce the sum demanded; Obregón therefore ordered them to appear at the National Palace, where 167 were arrested.[848] Diplomats protested, women marched on the streets, Catholics and anti-clericals met in violent clashes.[849] As in most Church–State conflicts, there were no clear winners; most of the priests were soon released, on payment of a sum much inferior to that demanded. A similar, inconsequential confrontation took place between Obregón and Mexico City's businessmen. Bracketed along with the clergy as exploiters of the poor and allies of reaction, the businessmen were ordered to pay a large (unspecified) capital levy. When they met to protest, they, too, were arrested, pending some payment to the authorities.[850] In both cases, however, the Carrancista occupation of the city was too brief for the conflict to be resolved.

Essentially, these were not conflicts over cash. A large subvention in hard currency (the capital levy was to be assessed in dollars, not depreciated pesos) would have been welcome – but that was asking a lot. And, as regards Constitutionalist paper, Obregón had all the money the presses could churn out. Rather, both conflicts, and any pay-offs involved, were about power and popularity. The Carrancistas' dislike of Mexico City could only have been exacerbated by the capital's recent, warm reception and write-up of the Conventionists. And, while Obregón sought to pillory the Church and the well-to-do, there was also the mass of the people to consider. For them, 1915 brought hard times: the currency was in chaos, food could not reach the city and prices were rising by leaps and bounds – maize flour was dearer than it had been in living memory.[851] The incidence of smallpox, typhus and gastric illnesses rose; and – sure proof of hard times – theft overtook drunkenness as the most common cause of imprisonment in Belem gaol.[852] Faced with these problems (which some cynics alleged Obregón encouraged out of political interest) the Carrancistas set up a Revolutionary Junta for Aid to the Public, which distributed food and money to the destitute.[853] The onslaught on Church and business, even if it raised little money, served to identify the true culprits, to exonerate the Carrancistas, and even to drum up some active, popular support. In the short term, Obregón's persecution of the rich may have done as much as Carranza's reformist declarations to help the war effort. For it was conducted in classic, populist style: Obregón was out to get the approbation of the poor as much as the money of the rich. The Church, he declared, 'which gave forty millions to the execrable assassin Victoriano Huerta . . . today has not even half a million for our needy classes'.[854] Hoarders and speculators who profited from the misery of the poor need expect no mercy; in the event of food riots, he warned, his army would quit the city rather than fire on 'the hungry multitude'; for – here Obregón assumed his favourite man-of-the-people role – 'if my children had no bread I would go out and look for it with a dagger in my hand until I had found it'.[855] No efforts were spared to humiliate the victims. Detained Spanish merchants were made to sweep the streets; and much play was made of clerical venereal disease.[856] Here, two major themes in revolutionary social history blended: the deliberate humiliation of the rich and powerful, for which there were many precedents in recent years; and the blaming of hoarders, speculators, profiteers and counterfeiters for the massive economic hardships generated by the revolution, which was to recur incessantly in the years to come.[857]

In one important and novel respect, Obregón's rabble-rousing had practical results: he was able to forge an alliance with the Mexico City labour movement, which immediately produced useful military recruits. Since this represented the outstanding political coup of Carrancismo in 1915 (a coup which the Villistas had signally failed to pull off) it deserves passing attention. Constitutionalist overtures to organised labour had followed swiftly on the fall of Huerta. In August 1914, the Casa del Obrero Mundial re-opened with official blessing, and Obregón soon inaugurated the fashionable, double-edged policy of making over church buildings to labour unions. Catholic opinion was affronted as the new tenants hurled sacred objects onto the streets.[858] In several states, Carrancista leaders (Diéguez in Jalisco, Aguilar in Veracruz) issued labour decrees, often fixing minimum wages; in Aguascalientes, Alberto Fuentes continued the reforms he had begun as Maderista governor; Múgica, in charge of customs at Tampico, promised the stevedores direct control of dock labour, breaking the monopoly of the Rowley Co.[859] But the Carrancistas were far from having it all their own way. The Convention also showed a lively interest in the labour question: it included among its delegates Casa members like Rafael Pérez Taylor, Luis Méndez, and Díaz Soto; its Proyecto of 1915 contained what was probably the most comprehensive package of labour reforms of any revolutionary statement.[860] Under the Convention, the Department of Labour continued its work, as it had under Maderista, Huertista and Carrancista auspices; Roque González Garza (once an aspiring artisan himself) was keenly sympathetic to workers' demands; and Chao, as Governor of the Federal District, had called for a 'sane radicalism' in pursuit of workers' interests.[861] There is also clear evidence of working-class support for Villa and Zapata. Villa enjoyed support among the railwaymen and the Mexican Miners' Union, which was strong in the north; Zapata won recruits from the Atlixco textile region. In March 1915 the Mexico City schoolteachers' union organised a demonstration in support of the Convention which, according to the press, brought 10,000 people on to the streets.[862]

Carrancismo did not, therefore, enjoy a monopoly of working-class support, either before or after the celebrated pact with the Casa. Rather, both factions had a (dependent) working-class wing; both demonstrated concern for working-class grievances and an interest in working-class support; both pitched their appeals to the workers in decrees, manifestoes, speeches, *veladas* and newspapers. How, then, could the courtship of the Convention be weighed against Carrancista solicitude? And why should the Casa abandon its apolitical, anarcho-syndicalist stance – its fear of a 'new dictatorship' and contempt for the 'bastard ambitions' of politicians – and commit itself to one faction?[863] As it was, ideological appeals and stances were compromised by pressing circumstances and proximate motives. As already noted, economic conditions in the capital were fast deteriorating. The year 1915 came in with dearth, disease and destitution. Jobs, food, fuel and water were in short supply. There were long queues outside food shops and street demonstrations against the annulment of Villista currency; water had to be drawn from artesian wells (the Zapatistas had cut off the supply at the pumps) and, in the absence of coal, trees were hacked down to provide fuel.[864] The offer of government succour and patronage, in return for services rendered on the battlefield and the hustings, was tempting as never before. Indeed, the text of the Casa's agreement with the Carrancistas, ruefully noting that it represented a departure from anarcho-syndicalist practice, virtually admitted as much: 'faced with the terrible loss of life caused by fighting and hunger, which weighs directly upon the exploited masses of field and factory', the workers should confront the 'single, common enemy: the bourgeoisie and its immediate allies, professional militarism and the clergy'.[865] Opponents of the agreement were confounded by the belief, prevalent among their fellow-workers, that 'in order to escape from the hunger which . . . afflicted us, it was necessary, vital, to follow the tracks of Constitutionalism'.[866] Or, as one bitterly disappointed Casa leader put it, the Casa sold itself 'in a pitiful manner, for a scrap of bread, tossed to them by the barbarian of Sonora, Alvaro Obregón'.[867]

But this does not explain why it should have been Obregón and the Carrancistas, rather than their rivals, who lured the Casa from its apolitical retreat and concluded the deal. It has been suggested that the leaders of organised labour in Mexico City felt a closer affinity for the Constitutionalists than for the Conventionists. The suggestion is valid, so long as it is not cast in terms of the conniving Constitutionalist bourgeoisie (or petty bourgeoisie) seducing the infant proletariat away from its (objective) peasant ally. The secretaries, orators and intellectuals of the Convention were not so different from their Constitutionalist equivalents: Díaz Soto and Dr Atl cut similar postures; each side had its radicals, eager for social reform, and its conservatives, fearful of demagogy and upheaval. Carranza, for example, was not at all keen on the pact with the Casa.[868] And, within the murky realm of 'objective interests', it is not at all clear that the workers would have been worse served by a Conventionist alliance (bearing in mind the counter-factual hypotheses already presented). The crucial difference lay, rather, with the respective, controlling military elements; which difference, it has been suggested, related to culture more than class. The Carrancista military (not just Obregón but also González, Múgica, Alvarado, Diéguez, Jara) were alive to the potential of organised labour and readily cultivated relations with the unions. Civilian spokesmen like Pani or Atl thus had the backing of the real holders of power. On the other side, things were different. Gutiérrez, an ex-miner, legislated in favour of labour, but he was soon rendered impotent.[869] The good intentions of Chao and González Garza, the quixotic radicalism of Díaz Soto, the proletarian commitment of Pérez Taylor, were all in vain so long as the Conventionist caudillos – especially Villa and Zapata – ignored these civilian spokesmen and took no interest in their reformist projects. As already noted, Convention delegates dolefully contrasted their own wordy inactivity with the decisive, if contentious measures taken by Obregón to tackle the food shortage and punish speculators; soon, Zapatista generals took up the cry, lamenting that 'the enemy is growing, winning the sympathies of the People, on account of our apathy'.[870] So, too, when it came to the labour movement, Carrancista practice, sometimes sharp practice, contrasted with Conventionist rhetoric. Orators might declaim and *políticos* legislate, but those who held real power – Villa, Zapata, Urbina, Fierro and others of that ilk – showed no interest in recruiting organised labour; just as they showed no interest in marching to Yucatán or despatching imperious notes to the White House.

The explanation lies in the nationalist/parochial distinction introduced earlier. Obregón, Calles, Alvarado, Múgica had a better grasp of political options, a broader, national vision and a greater awareness of the potential of organised labour; these attributes derived, not from some specific class location, but from a shared urban, commercial, literate milieu, which the Conventionist leaders (whose class location was not manifestly different) had not enjoyed. It may be noted that, apart from the intellectuals and *políticos* of the Convention (Palafox, Méndez, Pérez Taylor, González Garza), the Villista leaders who showed most interest in the labour unions were Chao, a schoolmaster and Maytorena, the opportunist *hacendado*. Furthermore, the nationalist outlook which gave Obregón, and others, an insight into the world of urban labour was shared by the urban workers themselves. These were not 'worker–peasants'.[871] On the contrary, the Mexico City proletariat (certainly that part which formed unions and joined the Casa) was well-established and often skilled or semi-skilled. Prominent among the early unions were the bricklayers, plumbers, metal-workers, printers, mechanics, and tramworkers; many of them artisans, who worked in small shops, proud of their craft, status and literacy.[872] They had formed mutualist associations, dedicated to self-help and education, and now boasted unions whose leaders preached anarcho-syndicalism, anti-clericalism and rationalism.[873] Some, like Luis Morones, wrote lyric poetry; they attended civilised *veladas* (of the kind Obregón sponsored), complete with classical music and political speeches; when they gathered, as they often did, for group photographs, they wore neat jackets and ties.[874] And for some years past they had shown an awareness – not only in Mexico City but also in other industrial cities – of the role of national government; they had participated in national politics, parties and elections.

Thus, whatever their differences with the Carrancistas, which could prove considerable, they were at least on the same wave-length. Urban middle and working class shared certain common political and cultural proclivities: 'self-help' was the motto of the 'self-made man' of Sonora, as well as of working-class mutualism; Atl appealed simultaneously and successfully to 'workers, students and middle class' to join Constitutionalism.[875] Zapata's rural hordes, Villa's boorish veterans, were culturally distinct. This was not the case in Mexico as a whole: in many regions (Sinaloa, Tlaxcala, Hidalgo) the rival factions were indistinguishable, hence there could be no generalised polarisation of the working class on this basis and, as already noted, the workers leaned both ways. But in Mexico City in 1915 the workers were confronted with a clear choice: between the simple, Catholic *campesinos* of Morelos, their diffident leader and wild northern allies, on the one hand; and the worldly-wise, priest-baiting Carrancistas on the other. The latter could pitch a progressive, racist, anti-clerical appeal which chimed in with the workers' own attitudes: Zapatismo (and to a lesser extent Villismo) represented Indian barbarism and benighted clericalism; radical papers carried cartoons of Zapatistas flaunting the Virgin of Guadalupe, while the official press told stories of Zapatista atrocities against defenceless workers.[876] Talk of Indian barbarism struck a sympathetic chord, since Zapatista activities were now affecting workers' livelihoods: the building of the Bellas Artes building had to stop (not, unfortunately, for good) when the Zapatistas cut off the supply of marble; the closure of La Magdalena and Santa Teresa textile factories, also because of Zapatista depredations, threatened to make 2,000 families destitute; it was the Zapatistas who denied the city its water – and later its electric power.[877] Nor were such conditions confined to the capital: in Puebla, Zapatistas made off with machinery and clothes from the Metepec and La Molina factories and local textile workers showed no affection for the Zapatista cause.[878]

If these factors predisposed the workers of central Mexico towards Carran-cismo, it was nevertheless the positive initiative of the Carrancistas – and the corresponding apathy of the Conventionist military – which produced the alli-ance. Where the Conventionists had deferred to the Church and the city well-to-do, Obregón cracked the whip: bosses and clerics were being arrested, ran-somed, humiliated.[879] More practically, the Carrancistas distributed relief (and gave a specific subvention to the Casa); following a strike at the Mexican Telephone and Telegraph Co., they expropriated the firm and placed it under the management of the electricians' union, led by Morones; church buildings and a Catholic press were given to the Casa. This last move was deft as well as symbolic. It gave organised labour formal recognition and a stake in the new, Carrancista regime; as the secretary of the mechanics' union put it – sounding rather like a German Social Democrat of the period – the workers now had something to fight for, they had their own *patria* to defend.[880] Or, putting it another way, the workers thereby gained an enclave within the bourgeois state: a real, tangible gain which any amount of talk about co-option and betrayal could not wipe out.[881]

Nevertheless, even when Pani and Atl came bearing gifts, the workers were diffident and did not precipitately abandon their tradition of peaceful, pragmatic politicking (a tradition suitably rationalised in anarcho-syndicalist terms). Prudence as well as ideology held them back. And it required sharp practice on the part of the Carrancistas, and certain sympathetic labour leaders, for the deal to be struck. At the first meeting where Atl – the 'mysterious agitator' who executed Carrancista labour policy – met with Casa members, the proposal to ally with Carranza was shouted down; it took a secret session of chosen Casa leaders to accept and formulate the alliance.[882] In return for official recognition of the Casa, a reaffirmation of the December 1914 decree in favour of labour, and an undertaking to listen to workers' grievances, the Casa promised to supply recruits and to propagandise for the Carrancista cause.[883]

This was far from a blanket commitment of (organised) labour to Carrancismo. There was dissension within the Casa itself; and the Casa, though growing fast, by no means embraced all the capital's, still less all the nation's, proletariat. Better-off artisans were disproportionately represented in its ranks, and large groups like the railwaymen and the miners were not privy to the agreement. On the other side, Carranza and more conservative advisers like José Macías showed no enthusiasm for the pact; at the very time of its conclusions, Palavicini – also on the right of Carrancismo – was telling the capital's schoolteachers that the government disapproved of its employees forming unions.[884] Equally, the immediate results of the pact should not be exaggerated. The Casa, claiming 52,000 members, undertook to provide 15,000 military recruits.[885] In fact, the Red Battalions which were actually recruited, hastily trained and sent to the front, numbered about 5,000.[886] Though this figure did not represent total Carrancista recruiting in Mexico City (Pani claimed additional contingents, plus even greater untapped potential) it must have represented the major part, if only because of the constraints of time, training and arms supply.[887] The First Red Battalion undoubtedly fought bravely at El Ebano, as the Third and Fourth did at Celaya; but in the two battles they comprised only 12% and 9% respectively of the Carrancista forces.[888] In neither case were they the only fresh troops (an equivalent number of Tabascans reinforced the position at El Ebano; 'Red' troops similarly represented half the reinforcements at Celaya); and, though their prowess was extolled – the First Battalion receiving 'extravagant praise' for its deeds at El Ebano – it is hard to believe, and it has never been proved, that they swung the course of these battles.[889] Gabriel Gavira, who had every reason to sympathise with their efforts, recalled how he and his Juchiteco veterans had to support the Carrancista right at Celaya, 'since the workers commanded by General Juan José Ríos, untried in battle, did not inspire confidence'.[890] And, granted that these were raw recruits, facing the repeated charges of Villista cavalry, this is hardly surprising (nor is it depreciative of the individuals concerned). It does call into question, however, the bold and unsubstantiated assertion that the Red Battalions 'played a decisive part in the defeat of the combined forces of Villa and Zapata'.[891] They helped; but even without their help Villa and Zapata would not have won.

But the pact was of great significance in the long term. It advanced the subtle rapprochement of government and labour which had tentatively begun under Díaz and progressed with Madero; it illustrated the government's appreciation of organised labour as a useful, manageable political client, as well as the unions' awareness of the advantages – granted their inherent weakness – of official patronage. At the time, critics discerned the imbalance in the relationship and predicted, correctly if too apocalyptically, that the Casa's reliance on the government entailed a surrender of working-class autonomy. It was 'useless [for the unions] to inject an artificial strength which derived from government circles, since this would do no more than weaken them and place them, with their hands tied, in the grasp of the government, bringing about their ultimate ruin'.[892] A Zapatista manifesto put it more succinctly: 'la Casa del Obrero Mundial ... no es sino una Casa de Enganche'.[893] But the one-sided nature of the relationship, perhaps inevitable in view of the immaturity of working-class organisation, was not yet clear to all; the Casa was riding high, Carranza fighting for his political life; there would have to be mutual tests of strength to determine the division of power and influence within the alliance.

THE BATTLES OF THE BAJÍO

The Red Battalions were created just in time to play their small part in the impending showdown between the major Villista and Carrancista armies. Only by advancing boldly into central Mexico and tackling Villa himself, Obregón reasoned, could the flaccid fortunes of Carrancismo be revived. It was as though he had read (though he certainly had not) Clausewitz's dictum: 'everything is subject to a supreme law: which is the *decision by arms* ... therefore the destruction of the enemy's armed force, amongst all the objects which can be pursued, appears always as the one which overrules all others'.[894] Sideshows and quasi-colonial expeditions were put on one side; economic warfare assumed a secondary priority; Mexico City was tossed to the Zapatistas. Obregón spurned Carranza's timid advice to pull east to Ometusco, and resolved to head north, forcing Villa to a major encounter while his forces and lines of communication were extended.[895] The advance guard went north at the beginning of March; the Carrancista garrison evacuated the capital on the tenth and ploughed through heavy rain to Tula, San Juan del Río and Querétaro.[896] Reinforcements were summoned and integrated en route; by the time Obregón's army reached Celaya on 4 April it included some 6,000 cavalry, 5,000 infantry, 86 machine guns and 13 field pieces. Villa was kept well informed of both their numbers and progress.[897] Celaya was a pretty, prosperous town, famous for its textiles, strawberries and paté, and, commented a radical from Orizaba, 'conservative like the rest of the interior'; it stood on a plain by a river and local *hacendados* had spent large sums irrigating their fields, so that the countryside was criss-crossed by canals and ditches.[898] Here, the major encounter began and observers, far away on the northern border, eager for the garbled news which filtered through, rightly anticipated that it would be of crucial importance: 'I look for a death struggle there', wrote Villa's friend, General Scott, 'that is going to decide the future fate of Mexico.'[899]

Villa took up the challenge. Arguably, he need not have. Angeles advised that Obregón's advance was aimless, designed to force a battle, and that Villa should let him come on, harassing his army, while consummating Villista domination of northern Mexico.[900] The strength of this argument became apparent later, when questions of supply became crucial and Obregón's initially shorter and notably efficient lines of communication proved invaluable. For, though – to Villa's disgust – the Zapatistas failed to cut Obregón's supply lines from Veracruz, nevertheless every kilometre he advanced up the Mexican Central stretched those lines, carrying him further into Villista territory, augmenting the task he faced.[901] Hence, Villa could have drawn the Carrancistas on, until the time, place and balance of forces favoured the Villistas. Instead, he decided to check the advance: perhaps he feared Obregón would gain recruits and reinforcements en route (as he later, rather implausibly, maintained); more likely because it was not in his nature to stall and defend – as Obregón well knew – and his string of previous victories derived from sustained, reckless aggression. What had worked before would work again; innovations, at this stage in his career, would only cause consternation. 'If I fell back before Obregón', Villa reckoned,

or clung to what's called the defensive, the prestige of my troops and my own reputation would suffer in the eyes of the enemy. After all, when . . . since our first attack on and capture of Torreón in September 1913, have we let the enemy tire himself out looking for us in our territory? When have I not gone out to fight him, shattering him with my momentum, putting him to rout?[902]

So, cabling his brother at Juárez for more ammunition, Villa left the north-east and hurried south to take command at Irapuato, thirty-five miles west of Celaya.[903] The size of his forces is hard to establish. His own claim of only 8,000 is tinged with bravado, and contradicted by his jactatory statements to the American press; on the other hand, the rival estimate of 20,000 has perhaps been too generally and uncritically accepted.[904] Though Obregón was pretty certainly outnumbered, it was not, perhaps, by so large a margin as sometimes thought.

The figures may never be fixed; and, over subsequent weeks, they fluctuated considerably on both sides. For the ensuing conflict was not decided in a day's encounter: it spread over three months and 150 miles, involving over 50,000 men, and perhaps 20,000 casualties.[905] Four principal engagements occurred: the two battles of Celaya (6–7, 13–15 April) which, somewhat, mistakenly, are often accorded all the attention; the long-drawn-out, ultimately crucial battle of León (more accurately, called Trinidad), which lasted through May; and the *coup de grâce* at Aguascalientes in July.[906] And, irrespective of arguments as to their relative importance, it cannot be doubted that collectively they decided 'not only the destiny of Constitutionalism, but also the fate of the revolution'.[907]

Celaya began badly for the Carrancistas. Expecting that they would not come under fire until they approached the Villista headquarters at Irapuato, their advance guard – cavalry commanded by Fortunato Maycotte – ran into overwhelming Villista forces at El Guaje and Obregón himself, steaming out of Celaya in an armoured train, had to cover their retreat. By the end of the first day's fighting, as the Carrancistas dug in at Celaya, they had suffered serious losses; their cavalry had been badly mauled; and Obregón's evening telegram to Carranza had a backs-to-the-wall sound to it.[908] But he resisted advice to pull back to Querétaro – a retreat in open country would put his army at the mercy of Villa's formidable cavalry – and he resolved to hold Celaya, where the surrounding canals and ditches would facilitate a strong defence, yet from which there would be little thought of an easy retreat. There would be no alternative but resistance: 'even if our courage failed us, we would make do with the instinct of self-preservation, perhaps to our advantage'.[909]

Suitably encouraged, the Villistas pressed on, hurling massed cavalry charges against the Celaya defences; on the morning of 7 April, thirty charges were made between dawn and midday.[910] There was little skill or science involved: the Villista cavalry strove to take Celaya *a fuerza y sangre*, without infantry support, carried away (Villa confessed) by their success in scattering the Carrancistas the previous day.[911] The old tactics, so successful against a shaky Federal Army in 1913–14, nearly paid off. At crucial moments during the long morning of 7 April the Carrancista line seemed to waver: once, Obregón threatened the execution of his artillery chief for effecting a retreat without orders; once, a ten-year-old bugler, sounding the *diana* at Obregón's orders, confused the attackers and enabled reinforcements to fill the breach (the infant was commended by the First Chief and promoted to corporal).[912] Ultimately, however, the old tactics failed against resolute troops and sound generalship; and Villa's military limitations ('fortunately', Obregón reported back to Veracruz, 'Villa directed the battle personally') were cruelly exposed. By the afternoon of 7 April, Villista *élan* was spent and Villista ammunition exhausted. Attacks were getting bogged down in flooded fields and piles of dead horses obstructed the charge.[913] Obregón now executed his favourite pincer move, sending his carefully husbanded cavalry to fall upon the Villista flanks. Incapable of further combat and lacking a prepared reserve, the

Villistas fell back and beat a disorganised retreat to Irapuato. They had lost over 2,000 men, dead, wounded and captured. In Mexico City, the Conventionist press reported the 'overwhelming defeat' of the Carrancistas.[914]

Second Celaya, a week later, followed an identical pattern, and suggested that Villa, like the Bourbons, had learned nothing and forgotten nothing. After the predictable rejection of his 'humanitarian' offer to fight outside the town in open country, Villa renewed his assaults on the Carrancista positions on 13 April. Both armies had grown: Obregón's reinforcements included the two Red Battalions and Amaro's men from Michoacán (who, for want of proper uniforms, wore striped convict outfits); now totalling at least 15,000, his troops were freshly supplied with munitions which arrived on the eve of the second battle. Though Villa later claimed his forces were inferior to the enemy's, save in artillery, this does not seem likely: estimates of 30,000, even 42,000, are probably inflated, but it is doubtful that he fielded less than 20,000.[915] These, too, were adequately supplied: if – according to one of his purchasing agents on the border – Villa's 'cries . . . for ammunition were something piteous', the fact is they were met: 'Villa had got, or is getting, plenty of ammunition now and is . . . about to roll up Obregón'.[916] More serious were the waverings and dissensions in the Villista camp. Orders were disobeyed, and reinforcements failed to appear: Urbina seemed to tarry; Natera never came.[917] There was evidence of growing discord between the veteran Villistas and their ex-Federal allies.[918] Some of the latter – experienced professionals – pointed to the strength of Obregón's position at Celaya and advised caution; but Villa, still harking back to the triumphs of 1913–14, ordered another full-scale assault.

At first, the old methods again seemed to work. Despite heavy losses, the Villistas dislodged the Third Red Battalion from its position on the Carrancista right; and, more from their own momentum than any preconceived plan, they encircled the enemy's position. This was enough for the Mexico City press to announce another Villista victory, the decimation of Obregón's Yaquis, and an imminent Carrancist retreat to Morelia.[919] But again Obregón bided his time and the line held. Veterans reinforced the weakening Red Battalion on the right; the Villista artillery – whose role, granted the enemy's entrenched position, was crucial – failed to do its job, hitting the town of Celaya rather than the Carrancista trenches; and, again, rain and mud hampered Villa's assaults.[920] So far the Carrancista infantry had borne the brunt of the battle (indeed, Villa believed that the enemy cavalry had dismounted, as cavalry of the day often did, to fight in the trenches). This was partly true; the striped men of Amaro had.[921] But it was not wholly true: Obregón had stationed a large cavalry force, 6,000 men under the Coahuilan Cesareo Castro, in woods near Apaseo, five miles east of Celaya, behind the lines. At dawn on 15 April, when the Villista impetus seemed spent, this cavalry was launched in a major counter-offensive, which the infantry supported: the exhausted Villistas, again short of ammunition, were swept from the field, leaving thousands of men dead, wounded or captured, along with large numbers of horses, small arms and field guns. Carrancista losses (even allowing for Obregón's understatement) were remarkably light.[922]

Celaya was a crushing blow for the Division of the North: its losses had been heavy, its charismatic commander had been out-generaled, his reputation for invincibility forfeited. As news filtered through to Mexico City, hopeful uncertainty gave way to gloom, pessimism and the search for excuses.[923] But Villa's army was by no means a spent force. It retreated in reasonable order, the cavalry keeping in touch with the Carrancista advance guard. Reinforcements were summoned from the west, and from the heartland of the north (where Carothers reckoned 15,000 fresh troops were available); munitions continued to pour across the border.[924] And, it is important to note, Villista morale remained high; there was still everything to play for. Celaya had left the military options open and its chief importance lay in the fact that Obregón had not been crushed (as so many expected, and so many Federal generals had been in the past), that he had lived – his reputation and experience enhanced – to fight another day. The real reckoning came in May, in the long, hard, fluctuating battle of Trinidad (León): the battle in which Obregón lost an arm, and Villa the war.

Trinidad was the revolution's Waterloo: a conflict in which dour resistance and near defeat were ultimately converted into an outright victory of momentous consequence. Like Waterloo, it was a near-run thing, cool generalship finally triumphing over *élan* and charisma; but, unlike Waterloo, which was consummated in a day, Trinidad stretched – a mosaic of fragmented encounters, defeats and victories – over thirty-eight days (29 April–5 June) and a hundred miles, where at least 5,000 men died in the dry, desert land between Silao and León. At the end of April, Obregón's troop-trains began to move north-west into the broad, arid valley, flanked by sierras, which led to the Villista-held city of León. At the very outset, as at Celaya, Obregón walked into trouble. Reconnoitring by train within four miles of León, escorted by only 500 tired horsemen, Obregón encountered 6,000 Villista cavalry, whose attacks were only just beaten off as the Carrancistas fled back to their main force. Here, helped by the timely arrival of a munitions train from Veracruz (the punctuality of these trains, which still had to fight their way through Zapatista territory, was crucial for Obregón's success), the Carrancistas were able to establish a defensive position – a solid square – astride the railway at Trinidad station. The tactical and strategic risks were considerable. The formation was static, offering limited opportunity for manoeuvre. Nevertheless, despite protests, Obregón stuck to his battle plan with almost aesthetic conviction, determining 'no perder la figura' ('not to lose the shape'), possibly foreseeing how the encounter would develop.[925] Additionally, there was a risk of the Carrancista army being cut off in the middle of a pastureless desert, far from its home base. Again, Angeles counselled Villa to fortify Aguascalientes and let Obregón advance, so that time, distance and continual harassment would weary his forces and lure him into battle on unfavourable terms.[926] But Villa yearned to even the score after Celaya; and he was reluctant to abandon León, where he had been well received in 1914 and again after Celaya, into the hands of the enemy.[927] 'I came into the world to attack, even if my attacks don't always achieve victory', Villa told his mentor, 'and if, by attacking today, I get beaten, by attacking tomorrow I shall win.' It was the philosophy of the cockpit and the poker table. Again, Angeles was overruled. Early in May, Villa committed his army, now some 35,000, to all-out attack.[928]

After several days skirmishing in the surrounding foothills, there came the familiar Villista charge which Obregón was expecting – even willing. It was the biggest the Carrancistas had yet faced; and, though it forced back the right flank, it incurred heavy losses, particularly from concealed snipers; in five minutes of furious action a Villista rider fell every second.[929] Fighting continued for several days, the Villistas replenishing their supplies from León, the Carrancistas on the trains steaming up from the Gulf. Again, on 22 May, four massive Villista assaults were repulsed, and Villa's cavalry was beaten off as it fell upon the Carrancista rear. Then for a week the main battle cooled, as hostile forces skirmished on the periphery – Dolores Hidalgo, San Miguel Allende, San Juan del Río. This did not prevent the arrival of a Carrancista munitions train on 29 May, which enabled a distribution of cartridges next day. Now, the Carrancista command began to discuss a counter-attack; but Obregón favoured waiting a couple more days. Thereafter, events moved rapidly. On 1 June a Villista force swept behind the enemy, took and burned Silao. Counter-attack was now out of the question; the Carrancistas were surrounded, fighting for their lives; but their morale remained high.[930] Crucial to their position was the Hacienda Santa Aña, which not only protected the left flank and formed the pivot for Obregón's proposed counter-attack, but also offered forage and shelter for the cavalry. Santa Aña, like La Haie Sainte, had to be held. In the face of fierce attacks, infantry reinforcements were rushed to the position; and, at dawn on 3 June, Obregón and his general staff, planning their counter-attack, mounted the hacienda tower to command a view of the battle-field. Suddenly, the position came under close-range artillery fire; as Obregón and his colleagues rushed for the trenches, a shell exploded in the patio, blowing off Obregón's right arm. Losing blood fast, convinced that the injury was fatal, Obregón drew his pistol and tried to shoot himself, 'seeking to complete the job which the shell had failed to finish'.[931] But there was no bullet in the chamber: Obregón's adjutant had removed it, while cleaning the gun the day before. Now, his colleagues took the gun, bound the bleeding stump, and rushed their commander to the army headquarters at Trinidad.

Had Obregón died and the battle been lost; or had he lived, thanks to his adjutant's fortuitous carelessness, and, by living, snatched victory from the jaws of defeat, there might be cause to philosophise on the role of chance in history. Obregón's pistol joins Cleopatra's nose in the museum of momentous trivia. But (and the point is important) the drama of 3 June made no difference to the outcome.[932] The Carrancista army was too professional to collapse with either the death or temporary discomfiture of its commander (had the victim been Villa, the case might have been different); equally, the battle was too far advanced, too finely cast in the familiar mould of Celaya for Obregón's absence to be decisive. The counter-attack had been agreed and planned. With Obregón on the surgeon's table, his second-in-command – also his second cousin – Benjamín Hill took control without delay, fuss or contention (thus maintaining a family tradition: his grandfather had fought for the Confederacy before emigrating to Mexico; his uncle had died fighting the Yaquis; his father, a famous gambler, had survived a gun-battle with the celebrated bandit Heraclio Bernal).[933] At dawn on 5 June, Hill ordered a concerted offensive: the cavalry of Murguía – who played a major role – rolled back the Villista right; Diéguez's infantry, for whom the Villistas had a healthy respect, attacked the left; the enemy broke and scattered, leaving the way open to León. In the aftermath of the battle, Carrancista forces marched into neighbouring Silao and Guanajuato. Another massive arms haul fell into their hands: 300,000 cartridges, 3,000 rifles, 6 field-guns, 20 machine-guns. All told, in the month's fighting which constituted the battle of Trinidad, Villa had listed over 10,000 men, dead, wounded, or dispersed; the Carrancistas, so Obregón claimed, under 2,000.[934]

The *coup de grâce* was delivered one month later at Aguascalientes. Fast recovering from his injury, Obregón continued to advance north. Now, his army had to carry all necessary supplies for, while Villa and the bulk of his forces retired to Aguascalientes, fast-moving cavalry detachments (a Villista speciality) went south to cut the Carrancistas' comunications with Veracruz.[935] Obregón risked marooning his troops in a hostile desert. Paradoxically, it was this very situation, and Villa's growing belief that Obregón had overreached himself, that finally decided the outcome. Instead of sitting behind his defences in Aguascalientes, denying Obregón succour from any quarter, Villa was again seduced by the prospect of outright victory. Despite evidence of faltering morale in the Villista army, its generals remained confident; ammunition still flowed from the border and, throughout June, fresh recruits were being drilled in Aguascalientes.[936] On 8 July, the Villistas checked the Carrancista advance outside the city, forcing the enemy to form a familiar, defensive square. Next day the Villistas poured out and surrounded the square. The Trinidad pattern was repeated, but more briefly. Once the Villistas were stretched, their impetus spent, Obregón chose the time and place to counter-attack. Early on the tenth, Hill's infantry broke through the Villista lines at the Hacienda El Maguey, Murguía's cavalry swept wide onto the Villista flanks. Villa's army, now acquainted with rout, broke and fell back, with more heavy loss of men and matériel; many of the infantry surrendered; others bolted from Aguascalientes, 'leaving pans full of stew on the fire, after the manner of the Federals'.[937] There could be no more telling comment: Villa's army reduced to the condition to which it had reduced Huerta's in 1914. The celebrated Division of the North was thus eliminated as a capital military force. Fragmented into *guerrillas* it could still cause plenty of trouble; but its days of concentrated, conventional battle were over; for no force could now stand against Obregón's army of operations, and there could therefore be no serious pretender to national power, which Carranza securely enjoyed, thanks to Obregón.[938] One other consequence of the battles of the Bajío was clear to some: as Villa's star declined, Obregón's was in the ascendant; El Manco de Celaya – who was soon telling jokes about his lost limb – usurped El Centauro del Norte as the revolution's pre-eminent caudillo.[939] Once again (recall Orozco in 1911, Huerta in 1912) military victory created a potential heir, rival, or over-mighty subject. At Veracruz, Palavicini's advice to the First Chief sounded a sombre note amid the rejoicing: 'Villismo dies at Celaya; but there rises up a new caudillo and with him a new faction, Obregonismo. This is something against which precautions must be taken.'[940]

3

The Revolution in power: 2 Reconstruction

While the first lustrum of the revolutionary decade (1910–15) had been crowded with incident – major rebellions and battles; active politicking and febrile diplomacy; the birth and death of regimes – the second (1915–20) displayed a different character. The main politico-military question – who would govern Mexico – had been resolved; Carranza had won and Villa was no longer a serious pretender to national power. This, the US Government somewhat grudgingly acknowledged, with its *de facto* recognition of the Carranza regime in October 1915.[1] Now began the task of 'reconstruction' (a phrase in constant use);[2] a slow, painful, unspectacular process, as the weak, infant regime struggled to overcome enormous problems. Major battles now gave way to endless skirmishes, ambuscades and punitive raids; where five or six presidents had, *de facto*, governed between 1910 and 1915, Carranza now remained in office, somewhat precariously, for five years. Save for the promulgation of the new Constitution in 1917, the period lacked great highlights and climacterics; and even the new Constitution, for this very reason among others, has often been given too much attention, invested with too much contemporary significance.[3] The period is also less well studied than its predecessor. It gets relatively short shrift in many standard works on the Revolution. Increasingly, international attention was turned towards Europe's civil war.[4] Yet this was a period of great importance, in which the foundations of the post-revolutionary regime were laid; and many of the key attributes of the Callista state can be discerned, in origin, during the years 1915–20.[5]

Given its character, this period requires thematic rather than narrative treatment. But the thematic breakdown is important. Many histories exaggerate the new regime's control of its own destiny: the Carrancistas become the assured, far-sighted victors, methodically undertaking the great constructive, redemptive work of the Revolution. Teleology is again evident: just as we know Porfirio Díaz is going to fall (and this knowledge clouds analysis of the Porfiriato), so, because we know the revolutionary regime will survive and prosper, its actions are invested with more certainty, decisiveness and purpose than they in fact possessed. By the same token, it is the regime's purposive political action (especially its creation of the new Constitution) which absorbs attention. In this final chapter, however, the analysis will proceed – as it did with Madero's regime – in a different direction: from the military and material conditions of the country to the composition and policies of the regime; from the intractable realities with which government wrestled, through the practical, messy business of government, finally to the familiar rhetoric and legislation which embellished reality. Along this path, we shall consider first the fundamental problem of order: the continued rebellions (often underestimated), rural banditry and urban crime; the related questions of economic collapse, inflation, dearth, disease, strikes and riots; then – the context established – the government as it actually governed (its personnel, policies, failings and abuses); finally, the 'ethos' of the new regime, its dominant ideas, their pedigree, and their implications for post-revolutionary Mexico.

THE PROBLEM OF ORDER: I VILLISMO

'To govern is to command. In what way is Mexico, a heterogeneous country, governable, and who exercises the *imperium*?.'[6] Like their Maderista predecessors, the Carrancistas faced great problems in validating their claim to national power and in liquidating the *damnosa hereditas* of armed revolution. There might be no serious rival for national power, but there were plenty of groups dedicated to the circumscription and, if possible, the annihilation of Carrancista authority; and these the Carrancistas, with their *étatiste* commitment, could not ignore, and could not but combat. Foremost among them were the Villistas, and here the regime's problems were compounded by the strange trajectory Villismo traced after 1915. Obregón's victories had immediate repercussions throughout the north. The Villista coalition – always something of a paper tiger – began to crumple. Already, with Celaya in progress, it was clear that the Villista bandwagon had ground to a halt; in Sonora, Urbalejo paused to await the outcome; at Durango, behind Villista lines, pessimism lurked behind a confident exterior; on the west coast, Villismo showed signs of premature dissolution.[7] The battles with Obregón, furthermore, compelled Villa to withdraw forces from north-eastern and west-central Mexico, to the detriment of local campaigns. At the beginning of May, the advanced positions at Pánuco were abandoned, affording evidence of Villa's 'already waning prestige'; the siege of Tampico was progressively eased and finally lifted, enabling the Carrancistas to break out. Urbina retired to San Luis in a black mood and, at the same time, Saltillo, Monterrey, and Monclova were evacuated (not all permanently), thereby releasing troops for service in the Bajío.[8]

Yet more serious was the tightening of Villa's economic tourniquet on the north. The prodigal expenditure of ammunition at Celaya and León had to be met by the export of hides, meat, cotton, cattle and minerals; the Villista north also had to feed, clothe and service the front line. So far, Villa's resource base had served him well: though Carranza's oil and henequen probably gave him the edge economically, it does not seem that Villa's defeats derived from financial constraints. But defeat soon produced constraints, as the resource base shrank, production dropped and the Villista peso depreciated. By June the writing was on the wall. 'The country behind', observed O'Hea in the Laguna, 'is being drawn upon to the point of exhaustion to obtain the necessary elements for the sustained conflict.'[9] The demands placed upon foreign companies, the better-off Mexicans who remained, and even the common people, became more onerous. Forced loans and a special war tax were imposed on the Laguna cotton estates, with threats of execution for those who failed to comply; merchants' stocks were confiscated and major enterprises, like the Torreón smelter, levied. Villa's Finance Minister, Escudero, demanded a 300,000 peso (gold) loan from American miners, to be credited against future taxes and freight charges. If they did not comply, the miners feared, their properties might face expropriation.[10] Villa's brief honeymon with northern business thus ended. Business could not actively resist; but it could stall, dissimulate, invoke diplomatic protection and, if necessary, suspend operations. Merchants concealed their stocks; General Scott, on behalf of the miners, resumed his cajolery of Villa, with some success; at the same time, many American mines closed, their managers prudently absenting themselves during the death agony of Villismo.[11] As resources and revenue shrank, Villa's voluminous paper currency depreciated fast; indeed, the value of Villista paper during 1913–15 provides a fair barometer of the movement's headlong progress from dubious origins through brief respectability to precipitate decline. At the turn of 1913/14 the Villista peso was traded at 18–19c. (US) in the banks of El Paso; by the summer of 1915 it was down to 2c.; by the autumn it was worthless.[12] Hence, Villa's arms supply was jeopardised. Late in July it was touch and go whether he could raise the cash for a consignment of a quarter of a million cartridges awaiting delivery at the border; in the event, he could; but this was the last of the big transactions which had proved so lucrative for the arms dealers of the border towns.[13]

Increasingly, therefore, the Villista army had to live off the land, and Villa had to rely on arbitrary, forced exactions. These might sometimes exhibit a certain radical populism: the Laguna Soap Co. of Gómez was expropriated since, Villa declared, it belonged to 'Mexicans of the scientific and reactionary party, enemies of our democratic cause'; the merchants of Chihuahua had long exploited the people 'in a scandalous manner' and deserved the rough treatment they now got.[14] The rhetoric was indistinguishable from the Carrancistas', but the actions were reminiscent of Villa's Robin Hood days. At Chihuahua the public market was looted and goods sold off cheap to the citizens; people and horses were turned loose to forage in the gardens and truck-farms of the long-suffering Chinese of Torreón; at Durango, where a dozen or so *ricos* were arrested and ransomed, the manager of the electric light company was 'ordered to give free electric light to everyone in the city for one month'.[15] But in the straitened circumstances of 1915, such hand-outs could not be sustained; they were outweighed by abuses and exactions, which now affected the poor as well as the rich. Hence, despite the fund of goodwill which Villa undeniably retained in the north, the character of his moribund regime and later campaigns soon alienated the exhausted civilian population.

This was first evident on the periphery of Villa's sprawling empire. At San Luis, Urbina extorted and sequestrated, such that the inhabitants 'wish[ed] the troops [were] disarmed and eliminated'.[16] The Villista flying column of several thousand which swept through the Bajío in the rear of the advancing Carrancistas left a trail of destruction at Silao, Irapuato, Salamanca and Guanajuato. Gaols were opened (another return to primeval revolutionary practice), shops were sacked, at Irapuato the railway station was burned down. As in 1911, the mob seconded revolutionary pillage, or took advantage of Fierro's incursion to settle old scores and make off with what they could. Carrancista soldiers and officials were attacked, and as the Villistas tore up the railway track, the sleepers were filched, presumably for fuel.[17] Less characteristic of the community were the 'terrible riots' which afflicted Monterrey on the occasion of the Villista evacuation in May, or the looting which Parras suffered at a similar juncture in September.[18] Thus, as dissolution set in, Villa's forces reverted to the bad old ways which had characterised their conduct in the early days of the revolution, and which they had learned to moderate with the increased size and success of their operations. But the chastened *pacíficos* were now less prepared to applaud or second attacks on property which were no longer confined to the well-to-do (an increasingly tiny minority), and which seemed increasingly to represent wanton rather than social banditry.

Soon, the Villistas began to prey on their own people. In Durango, where the Arrietas posed a constant threat, the Villista forces quit the outlying districts, stripping them of food, commandeering mules, and shipping provisions to the north: 'the movement is described as being more like that of an invading army looting the enemy's country rather than a mere movement of troops within the territory already dominated by this faction'.[19] Durango and Chihuahua, once the showpiece of Villismo, now presented a dismal aspect. Chihuahua City seemed 'full of wounded men'; there was little corn to be had, no fire-wood and no trams on the streets. The once prosperous towns of the Laguna were strewn with wrecked locomotives and redolent with the stench of dead horses; in both regions the poor rioted, looting shops in search of food.[20] And Chihuahua, too, faced sequestrations, kidnappings and killings. Estates like Bustillos, owned by Villista sympathisers and hitherto immune from molestation, now had their cattle seized; 'they are now devouring one another' was the sour comment of an observer once favourable to Villismo.[21] The poor also suffered. Villages in the sierra were stripped of maize and other provender as the Villistas passed by; and, since mobility demanded the abandonment of the army's camp-followers, rape became more frequent than previously.[22]

By the late summer of 1915 Villista morale had cracked. An American surgeon who spent two busy months in Chihuahua left at the end of August believing that Villa's army was 'practically whipped'.[23] At Durango (July) the Villistas were 'baffled and demoralised'; at Torreón (August) there was 'a great deal of discontent' in the ranks; at Juárez (September) the 'Vill[ist]a troops [were] ragged, lousy and dispirited, officers in conversation expressing hopelessness of [the] situation and opposition to further fighting.'[24] Though accurate, these reports were also misleading. It was not, as they thought, the terminal illness of Villismo which these observers were witnessing, but rather its cathartic transition from conventional to guerrilla status; a chaotic, painful transition, which involved sloughing off the newly acquired habits of order and discipline and reverting to old practices. It demonstrated yet again that Villismo lacked the institutional bonds and central direction which had held Carrancismo together during its recent hour of crisis. But once the transition was complete, the new Villismo, or, better, the old Villismo *redivivus*, would survive, even flourish. There was an early intimation of this in October 1915 when, amid teeming reports of Villa's military collapse, it was noted that the Villista forces were indeed disintegrating 'but not as rapidly as they should'.[25]

What is more, Villa himself was still full of fight. Even as his outposts to south and east (Monterrey, Saltillo, Torreón, Parras, San Pedro) were surrendered amid scenes of rout and pillage, Villa was confidently planning a counter-offensive to the west. For the second time, a Chihuahuan caudillo, defeated in conventional battle, posed a threat to Sonora. In October, at Juárez, Villa talked openly and cheerfully about his plan, promising that, even if the US Government recognised Carranza, 'the revolution would be far from ended, as he would fight until killed'.[26] He planned to cross the Sierra Madre, join up with Maytorena's forces, and assault Agua Prieta (American objections were dismissed: 'Calles attacked Nogales', Villa declared, 'and only God Almighty will stop me attacking Agua Prieta'); then the combined Villista forces would march down the west coast, seize Guadalajara, and – ultimately and very optimistically – re-enter Mexico City, where they could renew the old alliance with the Zapatistas. Meanwhile, Villista forces from Durango, led by Banderas and Pereyra, would execute a similar move to the west, into Sinaloa.[27]

In October, Villa's army, numbering some 13,000, headed into the mountains. But, like the Orozquistas of 1912, he found the invasion of Sonora to be a stiff task. Maytorena's forces were already in disarray; the 'tactiturn Indian' Urbalejo, now the real power in the state, declined to give Villa his full assistance until too late.[28] Though numerically inferior, the Carrancistas were well placed: they had been 'greatly encouraged' by the news of Obregón's victories; and Calles had carefully prepared both the moral and material defences of the state against Villa – digging in at Agua Prieta, promising an amnesty for recent enemies, calling on all Sonorans to help resist the invaders. As in the past, this was a cogent appeal: the Sonorans no more wanted Pancho Villa in their state than they had Pascual Orozco.[29] Reinforcements were brought up by ship from the south and – following American recognition of Carranza – by train across the US.[30] Agua Prieta now contained a garrison of some 3,700, well provided with artillery, machine guns and ammunition; it was thought to be impregnable from the Mexican side 'on account of its excellent trenches and barbed wire entanglements'.[31] Calles took the further precaution of stripping the country between Bavispe and Agua Prieta of food, thus preventing the Villistas from living off the land while they mounted a siege.

Unaware that Carrancista reinforcements had reached Agua Prieta through the US – unaware even of American recognition of Carranza – the Villistas attacked the town on 1 November, expecting to take it inside the hour. The result was a predictable, costly defeat which, following the battles of the Bajío and the exhausting traverse of the Sierra Madre, left them 'stunned' and lacking the stomach for another encounter.[32] Desertions became common and, as men made their way back across the mountains into Chihuahua, Villista numbers fell by two or three thousand. Now, too, Villa's troops learned of Carranza's recognition by the US (Villa probably knew of it earlier) and despondency grew. But Villa did not abandon his west coast strategy at once. He moved south against Hermosillo, recently reinforced by Manuel Diéguez, and launched a 'slashing, determined attack in the old Villa style', which was beaten off, with the defenders' machine-guns and artillery taking a heavy toll. Twice more, as the Villistas retreated to the east, they were mauled by the advancing Carrancistas.[33] Meanwhile, the second prong of the western offensive was blunted. At El Fuerte and Jaguara the Carrancistas won resounding victories; Orestes Pereyra was caught and shot, Banderas and the Mayo leader Bachomo surrendered.[34] The west coast strategy was bankrupt, and Villa headed back to Chihuahua. En route, his forces dwindled further: some Villistas drifted north towards the border, pillaging as they went; forced to ditch his artillery west of the divide at Suaqui, Villa led the remnants of his army across the snowy mountain trails, usually frequented only by *arrieros*, during the worst of a cold winter.[35]

The abortive Sonoran campaign hastened the transition of Villa's forces from a conventional army to a congeries of guerrillas, committed to local, irregular action. The most obvious transition was quantitative. At the height of the Bajío battles, Villa had personally led over 30,000 troops, which represented at most half of total Villista strength.[36] Somewhat over 10,000 Villistas had marched into Sonora: the hard core of veterans, disciplined, loyal and still paid.[37] But the rest of the massive División del Norte was melting away. Since the retreat from the Bajío, desertions had been frequent.[38] Thousands of Villistas were mustered out at Juárez at the turn of 1915/16 when the Carrancistas opened recruiting offices for their ex-enemies who either exchanged uniforms, or collected the cost of their fare home. By the end of February 1915, nearly 8,000 Villistas had been officially demobilised.[39] Since many – lacking an alternative livelihood – at once joined the Carrancista army, the subsequent campaigns pitted ex-Villista defectors against their old colleagues.[40] In 1912, a similar arrangement (whereby ex-Maderistas combatted the Orozquistas) had proved successful; now, with opportunism and war-weariness rife, these new recruits were no great military asset, though at least their recruitment gave some guarantee against a revival of Villismo on a grand scale.

It is easier to chart the subsequent progress of Villista leaders than of the great, anonymous mass of Villista soldiery.[41] Some made their way home, still displaying the typical rancours of popular rebels. Two hundred of Calixto Contreras' men, deserting from the Villista cause, killed the administrator at the Las Huertas Hacienda, south-east of Durango; Contreras himself, rebuked by Villa for his failings at the battle of León, sloped off to Cuencamé to resume his preferred career as a local *guerrillero*.[42] Tiburcio Cuevas, veteran of 1910, took to freelance operations in the Durango sierra, became known as a 'famous bandit' and in 1917 contrived to capture the French vice-consul on the road from Durango to Mazatlán. He was finally run to earth and killed by Carrancista forces later in that year.[43] Miguel Canales, also a Maderista veteran of numerous factional allegiances, deserted at Aguascalientes and, with 500 men, returned to the Hacienda San Juan de Michis (Dgo) and began to pick it clean; a smaller ex-Villista detachment billeted itself on the Hacienda Guichapa in the same state.[44] In Chihuahua, meanwhile, as the Pax Villista crumbled, the mines renewed their acquaintance with banditry, and observers noted 'the appearance of lawless bands acknowledging loyalty to neither of the factions now in the field'.[45] Thus the grand Villista coalition, rapidly assembled to fight the war against Huerta, now just as rapidly disassembled into its component parts, many of which reverted to the local guerrilla and bandit actions characteristic of the earliest phase of the Revolution.

Many *cabecillas*, encouraged by the offer of amnesty, chose to go over to Carranza rather than to maintain a perilous independence.[46] After prevaricating through the summer, Pánfilo Natera accepted the offer; but his lieutenants Bañuelos and Domínguez preferred to fight on; and Natera's defection started a series of hostage-taking in Durango, a sign of the uncertainty of the times.[47] Individual garrisons also acted independently, sizing up the situation, negotiating with the (recent) enemy, sometimes defying their officers. The Villista garrison at La Paz revolted against their commander at the end of May; by August the canker was affecting the Villista heartland in Chihuahua and causing anxiety on the border. Palomas, for example, 'has certainly turned against Villa'; for this, Villa blamed 'Huertistas'; but it was also reckoned that the Palomas commander 'recognises neither Villa nor Carranza [but] . . . Gutiérrez'.[48] Such situations were dangerous as well as uncertain, particularly when a major prize like Cd Juárez was at stake. Here, the Villista commander, Tomás Ornelas, dickered with the Carrancistas for weeks before deciding to switch sides; by then, Villa, having got wind of his intentions, sent General Medina Veitia with orders to execute Ornelas; but Medina Veitia instead tipped him off, and Ornelas escaped to El Paso.[49] The fall of Juárez was thus postponed till December, when Fidel Avila and Joaquín Terrazas negotiated its surrender, along with that of other local garrisons.[50] As for Ornelas, he enjoyed only a stay of execution: returning to Mexico under the aegis of the Carrancista amnesty, he was caught and killed by vengeful Villistas early in 1916.[51]

Other, minor Villistas also paid the supreme price for trying to extricate themselves from the moribund coalition.[52] But the most famous casualty was Tomás Urbina, Villa's old *compadre*, the veteran *cabecilla* of Durango. After his failure at El Ebano – which aroused Villa's wrath – Urbina decided to quit the revolution and retire to his newly acquired hacienda, probably with the loot he had collected from the sack of Durango in 1913. Though this was the typical aspiration of a *serrano* bandit/rebel (one that Villa fully understood and later fulfilled himself) Villa could hardly tolerate such premature, unilateral retirements among his chief lieutenants, at a time of rapid Carrancista advance. Thus, despite his many pressing concerns, he gave the matter high priority. When Urbina ignored a summons south, 800 men were sent to track him down at Nieves; he was seized and taken aboard a train bound for Parral; en route, as was often the custom in these events, he was bundled off the train and shot, probably by Fierro.[53] Urbina's death, which snapped one of the principal, personal bonds within Villismo, was reported in shamelessly sanctimonious fashion by the Villista press. It did not figure as evidence of the movement's internal disintegration; nor as the violent denouement of an old, once close relationship which had turned sour; it was, rather, 'a further proof of General Francisco Villa's love of order'.[54]

Thus, 1915 was a year of outstanding revolutionary mortality. Those who escaped death in battle or factional feud now risked execution at the hands of their erstwhile comrades – if not of their erstwhile enemies, who did not always honour the guarantees of the amnesty.[55] Facing such dangers, many prominent Villistas had the wit to plan for retirement in the US. In particular, the respectable Villistas – the Maderista civilians and ex-Federals – preferred exile to either ignominious (and possibly dangerous) surrender or prolonged, guerrilla resistance. Angeles and Juan Medina both crossed to the US; so did Robles, Raúl Madero, and the Pérez Rul brothers, Villa's private secretary and cashier.[56] Lázaro de la Garza got away, probably with a haul of dollars.[57] Other northern allies also trod the stranger paths of banishment: Cabral,

Buelna, Maytorena. The more prudent bided their time, protested their abstention from active politics, and were eventually able to return to Mexico. By the end of 1916, Luis Aguirre Benavides, once Villa's trusted secretary, was allowed back to Mexico City, where he set up in business; Cabral waited six years before resuming a distinguished military, political and diplomatic career; Maytorena spent twenty-three years in Los Angeles before returning to Sonora, where he passed the last decade of his life.[58] But at least Maytorena, in his usual way, managed to survive. For many Villista exiles, the taste of power, so briefly savoured, could not be forgotten, nor the lure of revolutionary politics resisted. Mixing with the ex-Federals, ex-Orozquistas, ex-Huertistas, and other malcontents in the American border towns they dreamed and plotted *revanche*, encouraged by the evident failings and unpopularity of the Carranza regime. And some, like Robles and Angeles, eventually returned to the fray, with fatal consequences.

The border towns thus harboured a latent opposition – in the main articulate and respectable, much of it ex-Villista, but prepared to assume different labels in the crusade against Carrancismo. Within Mexico a more plebeian opposition survived, led by *cabecillas* who had little taste either for exile or for submission to Carranza, and who maintained their local guerrilla operations in the Micawberish hope that something would turn up. The Villista 'General' Leocadio Parra, for example, led his famished army of 2,000 from Durango into the mountains of Jalisco, where they planned to hole up and harrass the Carrancistas; as regards the amnesty, they were sceptical, believing that they would nevertheless be killed 'under one pretext or another'; so they would fight on, hoping[59]

that maybe matters might shape up differently after a while, when they could come out and be received by those who were not so recently their deadly enemies, or join some 'opposition' crowd with some hopes of success – that they had no faith whatever in the promise of the Carrancistas, as matters now were.

Many rebel leaders thought like Parra: they knew they could no longer sustain conventional campaigns; but surrender was shameful and dangerous. Even if they reached terms – as many did – that was not always the end of the story. Parra surrendered but was later executed for involvement in a revolutionary plot.[60] The Villista veteran Rosalío Hernández retired to his ranch in the mountains west of Santa Rosalía in the autumn of 1915 but returned to the revolutionary fray in the new year.[61] Another Chihuahua veteran, Julio Acosta, surrendered to the Carrancistas, but rebelled again and embarked on three years of mayhem.[62] Indeed, surrenders and parleys were sometimes set up as bait for Carrancista forces: the garrison commander at Jiménez was killed by such a ploy in the summer of 1916 (the Carrancistas, of course, used similar tricks).[63] Even generous terms could not exorcise the old devil of rebellion. Hilario Rodríguez, a Villista captain based at the trouble-spot of San Juan

Guadalupe, was amnestied along with 600 men: they were set to police 'an extensive region between Torreón and Zacatecas'; and the Carrancista commissary took pains to pay Rodríguez well ahead of time. But, as in the days of Madero, when similar arrangements were attempted (for example with Calixto Contreras), they did not last: before long, Rodríguez was again in open rebellion, proclaiming Villa's cause, and allied to Villa's old lieutenant, Medina Veitia.[64]

It was this phenomenon which made possible the strange death and rebirth of Villismo in 1915. In the summer, observers confidently predicted the movement's demise (as they had that of Carranza the previous year). The 'Villistas are a thing of the past', believed an American miner at Guadalajara; 'we have practically resolved the military problem', asserted a Carrancista general early in 1916.[65] Both were mistaken. Villismo changed but did not die: its leader's decision to break up his remaining forces, abandon the *soldaderas*, and 'go off to the sierra to live like a bandit' represented not surrender, but a commitment to fight on in a fashion that was old, familiar, and potentially more effective.[66] Hence, by early 1916, with their conventional forces fragmented, the Villistas got their 'second wind'; the old rebel districts of western Chihuahua and northern Durango, where Villa had once robbed and from which 'were drawn many of Villa's most loyal followers', were now infested with Villista guerrillas; and the old pattern of government-controlled towns and rebel-dominated countryside, the pattern of 1910–11 and 1913–14, reasserted itself.[67]

Villismo's 'second wind' might also be termed its 'second childhood': for in defeat the movement reverted to its infant origins. Villismo began and ended a local, popular movement, rooted in the sierra, led by plebeian chieftains, and displaying considerable consistency and stamina; the prodigious expansion and sophistication of 1914 proved to be superficial, short-lived, and untypical. Now the bandwagon had stopped, the passengers could alight (they cannot necessarily be blamed for inconstancy: many had never wanted to get on board in the first place). Across the country, local rebels who had tactically adopted a Villista label (Carrera Torres and the Cedillos, Peláez, a handful of Chiapanecos, a host of Michoacanos) now fought on independently, discarding the Villista label.[68] Closer home, Laguna rebels like Contreras – more genuine 'Villistas' – went their own way. And, in the Villista heartland, the respectable Villistas (Angeles, Medina, Chao, Robles, Raúl Madero, Díaz Lombardo, Escudero and so on) deserted in droves, convinced that Villa could no longer serve as the 'instrument' they had sought to defeat Carranza and mould the political future of the country. Indeed, some had reached this conclusion even before military defeat made it inescapable. In June, 'one of the best characters' of the Villista movement dilated on his 'disgust with the mistakes and excesses of Villista officials'; in July, it was reckoned that Díaz Lombardo, Angeles, 'and others of the better Villa element have practically no power or influence under present conditions and that Villa is beyond reason'.[69] Further defeats and 'erratic acts' during the Sonoran campaign merely confirmed this growing disenchantment.[70]

In defeat, of course, Villa lost his only claim to political capital. An angry, beaten, rheumatic bushwhacker was no substitute for the pliant national caudillo which the respectable Villistas had sought; they now found themselves victims of both Villa's evil temper and Carranza's intransigence (the recent amnesty covered only soldiers); and they did not fancy the life of the *guerrillero*. So Villa witnessed a *trahison des clercs* on a grand scale, as his advisers, administrators and orators quit the movement and joined the swelling emigré community in the US.[71] Their prompt disengagement reflected upon the basic character of Villismo and acted as both cause and effect of Villa's apparent brutalisation. They did not like the direction the movement had assumed even before the great defeats of 1915: not because it pointed towards a more radical egalitarianism,[72] but rather because it threatened a rough, arbitrary, personal regime; and their disengagement removed the chief restraint on its momentum. By August 1915, Carothers reported, 'Villa's ministers and diplomatic agents have been practically set aside except in name and Villa is handling all matters himself according to his ideas.'[73] By the autumn, even the pretence had been abandoned; most respectable Villistas had retired (Federico González Garza, though not yet in retirement, was pondering the history of the French Revolution to see where they had gone wrong); and *serrano* populism ruled.[74]

Villa now found himself predominantly – and probably gratifyingly – in the company of men of his own kind: the 'criminal elements', as they were termed, most of them from the old rebel heartland of western Chihuahua.[75] Though mostly veterans of 1910, these were *cabecillas* of second rank, since death and defection had robbed Villa of many of his leading lieutenants. Urbina had been assassinated by Fierro; Fierro in turn drowned in a quicksand on the road to Sonora; others, like Agustín Estrada, from the rebel district of Guerrero, had died in the holocaust at Celaya.[76] Leadership therefore devolved: Estrada's brigade was divided between Cruz Domínguez, whose *serrano* veterans fought a rearguard action against the advancing Carrancistas from the Laguna north, and the López brothers, Pablo and Martín, from the staunchly Villista pueblo of Satevo, who were to play a key role in the final years of Villismo.[77] Julio Acosta, an ex-*arriero* and another Guerrero veteran, still commanded 1,500 men in the district at the end of 1915; his officers were all local men, and their forces represented one of the major obstacles to Carrancista control of the state.[78] Once again, a deal was struck, involving Acosta's surrender, but in the new year he returned to the fray, leading a guerrilla band in the San Andrés region, the focal point of the 1910 and 1913 rebellions, the scene of Villa's bandit exploits, and now territory 'infested with Villistas'.[79] It was from this region, too, that Villa now drew his ammunition, from arms caches concealed in better days, as well as recruits for his Sonoran expedition or his raid on Columbus, New Mexico.[80] Acosta was still at large in the hills around Cd Guerrero when Pershing led his forces in pursuit of Villa in 1916; he teamed up with Villa towards the end of the year, entered Guerrero, forcibly recruited some surprised peons, and 'ruined all the places he had a grudge against'.[81] He behaved, in other words, much as *serrano* rebels had throughout the revolution: operating locally, recruiting local men (now, more forcibly), satisfying private grudges. The chief difference between 1910–11 and 1915–16 was less the method of operation than the general climate of opinion which, after five years of warfare, was less supportive of guerrilla forces, and sometimes even given to outright resistance.[82]

The same was true of the García brothers of Sahuaripa, just across the mountains in Sonora. They had campaigned as allies of Orozco in 1910. But they had no intention of quitting the locality in search of distant plunder or prestige: they fought to control the *patria chica*, to resist incursions, and to prosecute private feuds (hence they opted for Villa/Maytorena when their enemy, Jesús Hurtado, declared for Carranza).[83] Though Carranza triumphed nationally, the Garcías held their own at Sahuaripa and continued operations long after Villa was defeated and Maytorena driven into exile. Early in 1916, Alberto García led 200 men near Sahuaripa, 'most of whom were residents of that district and [who] whenever pursued ... scattered to their homes'; Sahuaripa also offered the Villistas aid and comfort on their mountain expeditions into Sonora and back.[84] Later in 1916, Alberto surrendered, but his brother Rosario carried on – now labelled a mere 'bandit' – and gave sufficient trouble for the Carrancistas to prepare a campaign against his Sahuaripa redoubt in the summer of that year.[85] This could not have been successful, for Rosario was still at large that winter, allied to another *serrano* veteran of 1910, Francisco Reina, who kept up the struggle at least until 1917.[86]

The survival of these old veterans into the final, grim phase of the northern revolution is further illustrated by the case of the Orozquistas. Prominent in 1910, they had sided with Orozco against Madero and were thus driven into an odd alliance with Huerta and a bitter, fratricidal struggle with the Madero loyalists – later Villistas. But the *gente* of Orozco and Villa came from the same region, exhibited similar attitudes, and were the same kind of popular rebels; there had always been some degree of mobility between the two camps, at least at the base; and it was natural – albeit difficult, given the 'logic of the Revolution' – for them gradually to sink their differences, especially when confronted by a Carrancista invasion of their common *patria chica*. José Inés Salazar, for example, followed the Orozquista trajectory through 1910–14; with the fall of Huerta, he crossed to the US, was gaoled, and escaped; by 1915 he was back in Mexico, fighting alongside the Cedillos in San Luis.[87] Again, he was captured and, somewhat imprudently, consigned to gaol in Chihuahua

City. When the Villistas attacked the town in September 1916 they freed Salazar along with other ex-Orozquista prisoners like Silvestre Quevedo.[88] Within weeks, it was reported, Salazar – a man of tough, *serrano* stock, but with a smattering of education and old PLM connections – 'acquired great control over Villa'.[89] This may be treated sceptically: yet again, observers were keen to discover grey eminences behind Villa, particularly when the fortunes of Villismo were on the rise. But certainly, and despite their history of conflict between 1912 and 1914 (Salazar had commanded against Villa at Tierra Blanca), the two veterans now collaborated successfully during the final guerrilla phase of Villismo. In the autumn of 1916 they mobilised 5,000 men; Salazar rode with Villa and Acosta when they entered Cd Guerrero; in the winter of 1916–17, following the path he had taken in 1912, Salazar led 800 in a raid deep into Coahuila.[90] Meanwhile, ex-Orozquistas elsewhere (Argumedo in the Laguna, Caraveo in Puebla and Oaxaca) were also able to live down their association with Huerta and reunite with fellow-rebels in opposition to Carranza.

The adherence of such men, some old allies, some new converts, enabled Villismo to survive with remarkable resilience after 1915. Predictions of Villa's military demise provided premature; the switch from conventional to guerrilla campaigns suited Villa's particular talents, and also recreated the familiar scenario in which an inept, static, regular army (now, the Carrancista) vainly sought to combat fluid, mobile, guerrilla bands, operating on home territory.[91] Under such conditions, Villismo was virtually unbeatable. Sizeable Villista armies (numbering several thousands) were assembled for attacks on towns, even cities, but for much of the time the Villistas operated in small groups, elusively dispersed through the mountains and foothills of Chihuahua. Dispersal began after the abortive Sonoran campaign: Villa himself led a mere 100 men in the sierra; Acosta maintained a small force north of Guerrero; Pablo López commanded 200 at Santa Isabel; Miguel Hernández and some 400 were reported south-west of Minaca.[92] Such scattered forces acted in arbitrary, irresponsible fashion (since they entertained no pretensions to government, there was no need to pose as potential governors, for the benefit of Mexicans or foreigners); hence, forced loans, robberies, intimidation and pressganging were common. The Villista *leva* was a new but soon familiar phenomenon, used in particular to gather men for sporadic, large-scale operations. Both Villa and lieutenants like Acosta forcibly recruited in the Guerrero region – threatening, at Bachíniva, to burn the houses of those who resisted; and they applied a crude martial law in the sierra, summarily shooting supposed spies or deserters.[93] Atrocity stories circulated again (perhaps with more justification than in the past) and there can be no doubt that Villa now inspired fear as well as respect among the common people of Chihuahua.[94]

Yet the old charisma remained. For some, Villa could still do no wrong; he still treated them well; and stories of Villista abuses were dismissed as lies, or explained away as legitimate acts of vengeance (which perhaps they sometimes were).[95] Villa's brief occupation of Torreón in December 1916 neatly illustrated the ambivalence of latter-day Villismo, which could still stir popular admiration, even as it incurred popular fear and disgust. Here, some 2,000 recruits were raised by a combination of 'fear and goodwill'; and, in one revealing incident, 'when a big crowd of "pelados" were standing outside the Hotel Francia, waiting to see and admire Villa, he came out with a pistol in hand and ordered everyone arrested and from the crowd he picked out the ablest men, forcing them to be enlisted in the army'.[96] And, even as such incidents undermined Villa's popularity, so the ill-judged policies of both the Carrancistas and the US Government came to his rescue, restoring Villista prestige even in the face of Villista abuses. For the latter were outweighed by the Carrancistas' own; while the invasion of Mexico by Pershing's Punitive Expedition created – certainly at the outset – a wave of genuine sympathy for the gringos' quarry. Whether out of 'fear or friendship', Pershing noted, the rural people of Chihuahua lent their support to Villa; the expedition therefore faced the initial 'opposition of the whole people who were generally proud of Villa's daring raid and who, to hamper our progress, intentionally spread misinformation of all sorts regarding his whereabouts'.[97]

Freelance Villismo was, therefore, altogether more rough, arbitrary and uninhibited than its organised predecessor of 1914.[98] And its victims now included Americans who remained in Villista territory. Overt anti-Americanism, unusual amongst the revolutionaries as a whole, had been particularly rare in the Villista north, where the leadership had been well aware of the importance of American trade and investment, both for the short-term war effort and the long-term development of the region. But Villa's benign attitude towards the US began to change in 1915, and did so for one simple reason (unrelated to any awakening anti-imperialist conviction): he was losing the war. Like embattled generals and *políticos* before him – Maderista, Orozquista, Huertista – Villa resorted to anti-Americanism as his military and political fortunes faltered: it was a shallow, inconsistent anti-Americanism, lacking genuine, popular roots or coherent, practical expression. Nor can it be attributed, in origin, to American opposition to Villa, or support for Carranza, since it antedated these developments (though they in turn stimulated it). As early as May 1915 the Villista paper *El Combate* (Ags.) published a series of articles denouncing the 'criminal work' of the US (Yanquilandia) against the Conventionist government, imputing American intentions to 'seize our land and prostitute our race', and alleging Carranza's connivance with these policies. 'Mexico', concluded one article, 'must not be another Nicaragua.'[99] At the same time, the paper devoted a good deal of attention to the impending battle of León. Thereafter, anti-American reports and rumours flourished at Aguascalientes (the Villista military headquarters), alarming American residents.[100] To the north, Durango witnessed the first expropriation of an American hacienda, said to be at Villa's personal order; the local *jefe*, when asked for an explanation, put it down to 'anti-americanism' – it was 'the only means of getting even with the Americans'.[101]

By midsummer, Villa had a pretext for his new-found anti-American line. In June, Woodrow Wilson drafted a statement deploring the continued civil war in Mexico, offering 'active moral support' to anyone who could 'rally the suffering people of Mexico' behind a constitutional regime, and appealing to the belligerent factions to compromise and unite, on pain of some vague, unspecified American sanctions.[102] As an exhortation to people as much as to leaders, this foreshadowed Wilsonian diplomacy in Europe; it was about as successful; and, like the botched occupation of Veracruz, it represented a clumsy intervention in Mexican affairs just when those affairs were achieving some internal clarification. The presidential advisers of 1914 (Lind especially) had misled Wilson into precipitate action designed to topple Huerta, who was about to fall anyway; those of 1915 (notably the State Department 'expert' Leon Canova, who looked to some conservative, American-backed solution to the civil war) urged this general overture, backed by vague threats, even as Obregón's forces were winning the decisive battles that would settle the issue.[103] In this respect, the Carrancistas were the offended party, and Carranza repudiated Wilson's *démarche* in lofty yet confident terms: 'History furnishes no example in any age or any country of a civil war terminating by the union of the contending parties. One or the other must triumph.'[104] Villa's reply was more co-operative: he was prepared to participate in a conference of revolutionary groups; he urged factional unity upon Carranza; he paid tribute to the respect the Mexican people felt for President Wilson.[105] But this – the necessarily suave response of a fading faction – contrasted with the growing anti-Americanism within Villista territory. *El Combate* referred to Wilson's statement under the headline: 'towards intervention'; and from Aguascalientes to Chihuahua, American interests began to face novel abuse, extortion, and intimidation.[106]

Villista anti-Americanism was therefore born as Villa's military fortunes slumped, at a time when US policy was scarcely hostile to the Villista cause.[107] But thereafter, as the US recognised Carranza, prevented arms reaching Villa, and even allowed Carrancista troops to be shifted across American territory, such anti-Americanism necessarily increased, becoming a staple feature of 'late' Villismo. After his repulse from Agua Prieta, Villa issued a manifesto which circulated along the border (and even in the US mail) denouncing American recognition of Carranza which, it argued, was contingent upon American acquisition of Magdalena Bay, the Tehuantepec Railway, and the Gulf oil-fields, as well as an American loan, a lien on Mexican government revenue, and a veto on key cabinet appointments.[108] This was nonsense, though fairly traditional nonsense.[109] But it reflected real Villista resentment. The US recognition of Carranza came as a 'great blow' to González Garza and left Villa 'indignant and defiant'; there was talk, among El Paso's Villistas, of the opportunities which a US–Mexican conflict would afford for Villa 'to get himself into the limelight again as a popular hero'; and, after the disastrous Sonoran campaign, a Villista deserter reported, Villa swore to 'get even' with the US possibly by raiding the border.[110] Indeed, the summer of 1915 had been rife with rumours of Mexican aggression across the border, and there had been sporadic incidents, including a Villista raid in the vicinity of Columbus, New Mexico.[111]

These did not add up to much. American fears of a full-scale Mexican invasion, coupled with a revolt of Mexican–Americans and aimed at the recovery of the south-western states, were ill-founded and short-lived. They were quite enough, it is true, to provoke a fierce backlash against Mexican–American communites, which resulted in over 100 deaths. But it is not clear that the 'Plan of San Diego' and the associated border plots and violence influenced the course of events inside Mexico.[112] The Carrancista press followed the established tradition of publicising both the grievances of the Mexican–Americans (which were real) and the calamities which afflicted the US (which were often imagined: negro revolutions and rebellions by defeated presidential candidates); it therefore made a lot of the supposed conspiracy, even while Carrancista commanders on the border voiced diplomatic assurances.[113] It has been suggested that this double game speeded US recognition in the autumn of 1915; but, equally, the ability to police the border was one of the tests the US applied before granting recognition in the first place; and it may be that the apparently contradictory statements and policies of Carrancismo reflected not Machiavellian statecraft but fragmented authority.[114] And, though the Carrancista military knew of these plots (they had their spies across the border just as the Americans had), and though a few were more directly implicated, it is inconceivable that any invasion of the US was seriously contemplated, save in the event of full-scale war provoked by American intervention. Carrancista flirtation with agitators in Texas was, perhaps, a contingency plan, rather than a first step in a war of aggression which – with domestic victory in their sights – the Carrancistas would have been crazy to undertake.[115] As for the war-weary Mexican population, they showed no desire to pursue such chimeras, which, according to one report, they regarded more as a joke than anything else.[116]

More serious, from the domestic point of view, was the growing anti-Americanism of the Villista rump, an anti-Americanism not confined to rhetorical denunciations and fabrications. After the recognition of Carranza, the Villistas of the Huasteca began to display an 'ugly disposition' towards American settlers; Villistas in the Laguna robbed Asarco, stating that 'in accordance with policy . . . all Americans were to be killed'; another band attacked ranches around Sierra Mojada (Coa.), acting, so they said, upon Villa's order that all Chinese, Arabs and Americans were to be slain. For the first time the gringos were bracketed with those ethnic pariahs who had borne the brunt of revolutionary xenophobia in previous years.[117] But the most serious incident came at Santa Isabel (Chih.) where, in January 1916, seventeen American mining engineers, returning to their company at Cusi-huaráchic, were caught and shot by the Villista Pablo López. López, soon captured and executed, claimed that Villa himself had been close to the scene of the killing, which had been done at his orders.[118] This Villa later denied. But not only is it quite likely that he was in the vicinity; it is also clear that some kind of general orders had been issued, sanctioning attacks on Americans.[119] The nature and severity of these attacks might vary from place to place, but patently American companies still operating within Villa's dwindling territory ran a serious risk, following US recognition of Carranza; there were some – red-blooded patriots too – who felt that the Cusi miners had asked for what they got.[120]

It is against this background – border unrest and intrigue, Villista resentment and retribution – that Villa's famous raid on Columbus must be seen.[121] The events of the night of 8/9 March 1916 are tolerably well known; but the motives behind and the general significance of the attack are more murky and conjectural. During February, Villa had lain low; when, early in March, he was reported to be heading towards the border, there were some who believed that he planned to cross peacefully to the US to put his case to President Wilson in Washington.[122] Perhaps this was deliberate camouflage. At any rate, at 4 a.m. on 9 March, several hundred Villistas attacked the garrison town of Columbus, a couple of miles across the border into New Mexico. Though the attackers, crying 'Viva Villa!', appeared familiar with the local terrain, and caught the garrison off guard, they were beaten off by the Americans (among whom the cookhouse staff, then preparing breakfast, distinguished themselves with 'potato-mashers, kitchen knives [and] butcher's cleavers'); and, as the Villistas retired, leaving several dead, an American detachment set off in pursuit, harrying them back across the border and several miles into Mexican territory.[123]

The motives behind the attack have been much discussed and often embellished. In particular, Villa has been cast as a servant of Wilhelmine *Weltpolitik*: Villista provocation of the US was, it is said, prompted by German agents, in order to embroil the Americans in Mexico, deter their involvement in the European war, and deflect the flow of American arms away from the Entente.[124] Certainly the Central Powers welcomed Villa's raid and the American counter-measures it elicited: 'so long as the Mexican question remains in this state', wrote the German Ambassador in Washington, 'we are, I think, fairly safe from aggressive moves on the part of the American government'.[125] Just as certainly, the US government was anxious to avoid military involvement in Mexico, which would curtail its freedom of action in the more crucial area of Europe. The new Secretary of State, Robert Lansing, who entertained a profound suspicion of German intentions, evolved a fundamental item of policy: 'Germany desires to keep up the turmoil in Mexico until the United States is forced to intervene; *therefore, we must not intervene*.'[126] But it is illicit to infer from these hopes and fears – or from the presence of a few Germans in Villa's orbit – a direct German involvement in the Columbus raid. Indeed, it is clear from the German documents that neither the German Ambassador in Washington nor the Mexican specialist at the Wilhelmstrasse knew anything of it; and the evidence that they were by-passed by the military, though not inherently implausible, is too skimpy to warrant such a conclusion.[127] At times, it seems, adherents of the *Weltpolitik* thesis are won over less by hard evidence than by the perennial attraction of conspiracy theories, allied to the somewhat patronising assumption that the key determinants of events lay outside Mexico: in the White House, the Wilhelmstrasse, or the offices of Standard Oil. Here, too, we encounter another kind of Villista grey eminence: the devious Teuton, in the shape of Felix Sommerfeld (who at least had some claim to influence) or the ludicrous Dr Lyman B. Rauschbaum, 'perhaps the most influential man on Villa's general staff'.[128]

In fact, while like any good conspiracy theory this one cannot be disproved, there is no logical need to introduce these exotic characters and distant ramifications. Local, proximate, and personal causes are quite sufficient to explain Villa's action. For several months Villa had been incensed against the Americans – for their recognition of Carranza, for their connivance at his defeat at Agua Prieta. The practice and rhetoric of Villista anti-Americanism had grown more extreme, and both Villa and his lieutenants spoke of taking the war to the US.[129] Given the border troubles and recent raids in the lower Río Grande Valley, this would not have been a radical new departure (indeed, a group of Villistas raided near Columbus six months before the big attack of March 1916).[130] And it was a matter of open comment that, by provoking a conflict with the US, Villa might recover some of his waning popularity and prestige. As early as May 1915, some had perceived a 'danger that [Villa] will make a grandstand play against the US, intending to boost himself'.[131] It did not require devious Teutons to stoke the fires of Villa's wrath, or beguile him with crafty stratagems; to believe that is to discount both Villa's bandit *machismo* and bandit cunning.

There were particular reasons, apart from proximity, why Columbus was chosen. For years the American border towns had served, much to their own profit, as entrepots for the supply of the revolutionary forces. There was great scope for chicanery, especially when the US banned the free transit of arms to Mexico: dealers undertook contracts and then tipped off the authorities; or they failed to deliver consignments, knowing there could be no legal redress. Such was the case with an ammunition consignment purchased by Villa from Sam Rabel, a well-known arms dealer of Columbus.[132] Retaliation against the

US thus combined with specific revenge against a gringo swindler: when the Villistas attacked Columbus they knew precisely where Rabel's property was (there had been preliminary reconnaissance and the attackers followed a clear plan) and they shot up the property before being forced to retire.[133]

The American response was to despatch troops to pursue Villa inside Mexico. This action, too, has been surrounded in a nimbus of conspiracy. But the despatch of the Punitive Expedition obeyed no devious plan to subvert the government of Mexico, still less to annex chunks of Mexican territory. It was a hasty, ill-prepared, muddled and – from the perspective of American domestic politics – unavoidable response to Villa's aggression. On the border, General Funston argued, with justification, that unless Villa were pursued the US would risk further raids; for, despite the bombastic claims of the Carrancista press (which attributed the Columbus raid to the 'tenacious persecution' of Villa by Carrancista forces), it was clear that the Carrancistas were unable to police large sections of northern Mexico.[134] Indeed, the honest Gabriel Gavira, commanding at Cd Juárez, admitted as much.[135] There was no guarantee, of course, that the Americans would do better: their forces were ill-equipped for a Mexican campaign; they embarked on the operation 'at a moment's notice'; and the expedition revealed many military failings.[136] They realised, too, that the active pursuit of Villa inside Mexico would 'add to the tendency already created ... to make him a national hero'; and they appreciated that serious involvement in Mexico would leave Germany a *tertius gaudens*.[137] On the other hand (a point not always recognised, especially by proponents of the German connection), Wilson had to do something in response to this provocation: to do nothing, House argued, 'would not only destroy him in the US but it would destroy his influence in Europe as well'; and in Latin America, too, some thought.[138] A weak administration, apparently indifferent to lesions of American sovereignty like Columbus would be less able to deter German aggression, at a time when unrestricted submarine warfare was under consideration; it would, in modern jargon, lack credibility. Just as important, a feeble response to Columbus would present the Republicans – historically the party of the 'big stick' – with abundant ammunition for the presidential election of 1916.[139]

Wilson's cabinet virtually unanimously pressed him to take decisive action; his secretary, 'argued with the President desperately, saying if he did not send our troops after Villa, or if he hesitated a moment to act, he might just as well not contemplate running for the presidency, since he would not get a single electoral vote';[140] even Bryan, whose pacifist leanings had recently cost him his post as Secretary of State, was said to favour such action.[141] Still, Wilson was reluctant to intervene, and he consented to do so only on the understanding that the Carrancistas accepted such intervention, and did not intend to resist it.[142] This condition was fulfilled, or so it seemed: apprised of the raid and of the American intention to pursue Villa into Mexico, Carranza cited the precedent of the Indian troubles of the 1880s, when the Mexican and American governments had agreed to mutual rights of pursuit across the international boundary; and he 'recommended strongly that such an agreement be effected again'.[143] Carranza intended this to cover future eventualities; the US Government – whether out of design or (more likely) oversight – took it as Mexican approval for the armed pursuit of Villa, preparations for which were already under way. But consultations did not stop there; hence it is hard to believe that any initial misunderstandings survived unnoticed. On 13 March the US Secretary of State made it clear that the US conceded reciprocal rights of pursuit to Mexican government forces; he praised the Mexicans' spirit of co-operation; and his communication was apparently well received by his Mexican counterpart, Jesús Acuña. At the same time, the objective of the expedition and the strict constraints under which it would operate were spelled out: to the military, who were ordered to treat Mexican government forces with courtesy and co-operation and the Mexican people with 'justice and humanity'; to the press, which was informed that the dispersal of Villa's band was the sole aim; and to the Carranza administration, which was assured that 'the military operations now in contemplation . . . will . . . in no circumstances . . . be suffered to trench [sic] in any degree upon the sovereignty of Mexico or develop into intervention'.[144] In response, Silliman reported from Mexico, the Secretaries of War and Foreign Relations communicated their 'approval and acquiescence', and Obregón ordered his commanders to co-operate with the American expedition.[145] All this – the invocation of the old agreement, the amicable exchanges – was promptly reported, if not in great detail, in the Mexican press.[146]

On 15 March therefore, General Pershing led three brigades into Mexico, anticipating correctly, as it turned out, that Carrancista forces on the border would not resist, and planning, though without success, to encircle Villa's band in the immediate vicinity. When encirclement failed, Pershing pressed on: he passed by the Mormon settlement at Colonia Dublán (where 'knees bent in gratitude' at the appearance of American troops), and advanced into the Villista heartland of western Chihuahua.[147] The terrain was difficult, the local population unhelpful or antagonistic, the supply of food and forage uncertain. There was, at the outset, a general refusal to sell goods to the Americans or to offer directions. 'The populace', Pershing reported from Namiquipa, an old revolutionary pueblo where Villa was well-known, 'at every critical stage in this campaign have circulated misleading information concerning [the] whereabouts [of the] Villa band and [have] assisted in [their] escape'.[148] In time, as the expedition became a more familiar feature of the Chihuahua scene, these attitudes changed, and the Americans were able to buy supplies and win a measure of co-operation; still, however, the expedition's task was daunting, and the limitations placed upon it galled the commanding officers.[149]

Sporadic skirmishes with Villista bands occurred, in one of which Lieutenant (later General) George Patton shot the Villista captain Julio Cárdenas, much to his own satisfaction ('I feel about it just as I did when I got my first swordfish. Surprised at my luck').[150] But Villa himself was never located. Recently wounded in a fight with Carrancista troops, he holed up in a mountain cave, from which (according to a popular story, which may have a basis in fact) he could watch the Americans meander past on their fruitless quest.[151] And even the covert offer of $50,000 (US) for any Mexican 'guide' who would betray Villa achieved no success.[152] The American officers itched for more uninhibited military action and, in Patton's case, verbally vented their frustration on Woodrow Wilson – who 'has not the soul of a louse nor the mind of a worm. Or the backbone of a jellyfish.'[153] Wilson, for his part, showed no inclination to extend the operation or to release it from its tight restrictions, and it was said he felt a sneaking admiration for the rebel–bandit who was leading his high-mettled officers such a dance through the wilds of Chihuahua.[154]

With Villa lying low, the chief threat to the expedition came from the growing hostility of the Carrancistas. Carranza's initial, somewhat ambiguous complaisance soon wore out. Though he had no interest at all in incurring a war with the US, he could hardly let himself appear a supine collaborator, while Villa became a national hero.[155] Every day the Punitive Expedition remained on Mexican soil, Mexican national sovereignty suffered a slight; and Carranza, a champion of Mexican nationalism throughout his revolutionary career, was obliged to adopt an increasingly querulous tone – one that responded to domestic exigencies and could be easily relayed through the controlled press. Carrancista reactions to the expedition therefore offer another example of government manipulation of 'patriotic' opinion, and, at the same time, of the superficiality of supposed Mexican 'xenophobia'.[156] Initially, Carranza kept the press under wraps: throughout March the newspapers remained silent, omitted mention of the expedition's progress, and even referred to Pershing as if he were commanding in the vicinity of Columbus itself.[157] In some parts of the country the wraps stayed on until April, several weeks after Pershing had crossed the border.[158] As a result, as numerous consular reports indicate, public opinion remained ignorant and indifferent.[159] In addition, Carrancista authorities, like Governor Enríquez of Chihuahua, seemed keen to quieten rumours and maintain calm.[160] But, as one observer in the capital pointed out, a change in official policy could produce a swift change in the climate of opinion; and this proved to be the case later in 1916.[161]

For, as the weeks went by, the expedition showed no sign of prompt success and every sign of a long sojourn south of the border. Now, Carranza's patience wore thin. There were limits to the powers of censorship; Carranza, like Wilson, had a domestic political constituency to consider; and, if the presidential election of 1917 was a less than urgent matter, maintaining the loyalty of the Carrancista military – some of them, like their American counterparts, red-blooded patriots, scornful of civilian politicians – was an immediate, pressing problem. Though many of the military (Obregón in particular) backed Carranza's cautious policy, there were others, noisy patriots like Emiliano Nafarrete and the Herreras, who soon began to question Carranza's apparent tolerance of foreign invasion. Luis Herrera objected to orders requiring co-operation with the American forces; he issued a statement recalling the stand he and his brother had taken against the Veracruz occupation; it was rumoured (without, it seems, much foundation) that the Herrera clan would go over to Villa.[162] By the end of March it was clear that 'Carranza's enemies in Constitutionalist circles [were] already seeking to make capital against him by overt criticism for his weakness and lack of patriotism in yielding permission for our [American] troops to enter'.[163] Now, spokesmen like Cabrera stressed that a prompt American withdrawal was expected; and official denunciations of American 'bad faith' began to appear.[164] In the US, meanwhile, several member of the cabinet concluded that the expedition had outlived its usefulness and that, in the words of the Secretary of War, 'it was foolish to chase a single bandit all over Mexico'.[165] Withdrawal seemed to be the only answer.

Then, on 12 April, a column of American cavalry approached Parral (the home town of the Herreras) seeking foods and forage, claiming that they had received prior permission. A crowd gathered, shouting abuse, and shots were exchanged. Two American soldiers and rather more Mexicans were killed.[166] The clash at Parral lent greater urgency to Carrancista demands for an immediate withdrawal; it led also to more widespread anti-Americanism, which, in a few cases, was translated into active persecution.[167] But these cases were still few and far between, and observers in many parts of the country, including the north, continued to report an atmosphere of calm, even indifference.[168] In this respect, governmental policy was crucial; and it is clear that, while the regime was ready to orchestrate patriotic campaigns when it saw fit, it avoided agitation at critical moments such as these. The official tone, therefore, was firm but moderate. Cándido Aguilar, recently installed as Foreign Minister, regretted the killing at Parral, gently chided the Americans for causing it, and called for an immediate withdrawal which would maintain the 'good and cordial relations' existing between Mexico and the US.[169] Carranza, whose attitude the Americans found 'exceedingly satisfactory', urged calm, and his urgings appeared in printed proclamations on the streets of Parral.[170] And on the border, Obregón, as Minister of War, speedily issued a circular explaining the Parral events in sober terms, which contrasted with the inflammatory style of the American press in El Paso.[171]

In the wake of the Parral crisis, Pershing was ordered to halt operations, and Obregón met with General Scott to discuss the delicate situation. The US hoped to secure Carrancista co-operation to eliminate Villa; the Carrancistas sought a definite date for American withdrawal.[172] As the talks – though amicable – dragged on into May, the US suffered a second border raid at Glenn Springs, Texas, in response to which American troops again crossed the border in pursuit of the raiders.[173] Now, with the Parral crisis receding, Carranza adopted a tougher position. Any attempt to send additional troops across the border would be resisted; the original punitive expedition must be immediately withdrawn; the motives of the US were imperialistic and bellicose. The 'diplomatic politeness and tone of conciliation' evident in Carranza's previous communications were replaced by an 'aggressive and recriminatory' style.[174] At the same time – roughly from the end of May – Carranza lost no opportunity to parade his patriotism, and to increase the pressure on Washington, on the stalled Punitive Expedition, and on Americans resident in Mexico. Pershing was bluntly informed that any move he made, save in the direction of the American border, would be resisted.[175] Anti-American demonstrations were held in Saltillo, Chihuahua, Mexico City and elsewhere.[176] Carranza's rude note to the American government was published, along with all its stirring rhetoric, in the press, and it set the style for newspaper comment throughout June.[177] Meanwhile, rumours of war and talk of invasion flourished. Some said that Jacinto Treviño was about to attack the US border towns; others that Villa and Carranza would unite against the gringos.[178] In ports like Veracruz and border towns like Piedras Negras, fears of American intervention quickened, particularly after Wilson ordered the mobilisation of the militia in the middle of June.[179] In Mexico City the mood was nervous, expecting war; and General Scott – more diplomat than fire-brand – anticipated a Mexican attack on the Pershing expedition, which would precipitate a full-scale conflict, for which he duly prepared.[180]

By late June, therefore, that kind of situation had been reached where, as historians love to say, only a spark was needed to ignite the powder; only a push to send everyone into the abyss; now, Haley writes, 'war came close. With the proper incident as midwife it would arrive.'[181] Yet the spark or push or midwife came; and there was still no war. On 21 June a sizeable American patrol, heading east in defiance of the Mexican ultimatum, encountered a Carrancista garrison at Carrizal, fifty miles south of Juárez. The respective commanders conferred and, for no very clear reason and despite a warning to the contrary, the American, Captain Boyd, insisted on passing through the town. When this was attempted the Mexicans opened fire, which was returned; there were several deaths on both sides (including those of both commanders); the Americans were driven off, leaving behind some prisoners.[182] That this did not, despite the preceding tension, result in a major war, of incalculable consequences, may be attributed to several factors. First, the tension which preceded Carrizal was partly illusory. It was screwed up by the Carranza government with the understandable objective of pressuring the Americans out of Mexico; it did not represent wanton belligerence;

still less did it derive from a powerful, popular hatred of Americans. The anti-American demonstrations of June 1916, like those drummed up by Huerta, were tame affairs. The Monterrey demonstration seemed 'very mild'; that held in Mexico City 'did not amount to much'; at Veracruz the US consul knew many of the 150 demonstrators and 'they smiled as they passed'.[183] While protestors marched in the streets of Saltillo, the state governor remained 'extremely friendly' and, taking the American representative aside, assured him that the patriotic posters now covering the walls were 'not to be taken too seriously'.[184] At Durango, where the authorities waved the flag without such disclaimers, 'the fact is that . . . the great mass of the people and especially those of intelligence and some education are not much interested [in] or put out over the fact that American troops are in Mexico'.[185] Some attributed both the indifference of the people and the patriotic agitation of the government to the same causes: the collapse of the currency, the parlous state of the economy, and the threat or actuality of dearth.[186] In such circumstances the authorities were as keen to invoke patriotism as the populace was prone to ignore it.

Perhaps these consular reports erred on the side of optimism (though there is no clear reason why they should have). Certainly many people, Mexican and American, anticipated a war in the wake of the Carrizal incident, as anti-American demonstrators marched again and, in a few places, Americans were subjected to attacks or abuse.[187] But, in this second crisis, too, the Carranza regime showed no desire to provoke a serious backlash; indeed, it is doubtful if such a backlash could have been provoked. Anti-American propaganda again failed to quicken a response; and even the demonstrations seemed half-hearted affairs, held to prove patriotic credentials, perhaps to distract attention from other problems, and lacking genuine, xenophobic content. At Puebla, for example, only 400 turned out, of whom half were reckoned to be soldiers and a quarter government employees.[188] And the genuine fears of war and intervention, where they had been raised, soon subsided.[189] To this end, the pacificatory policy of the Mexican government – which contrasted not only with its own stridency in previous weeks but also with the bellicosity of prominent Americans, like the Mayor of El Paso – was crucial in defusing the situation and ensuring a peaceful outcome.[190] The military command in Chihuahua was apparently ordered to avoid further clashes; it was announced that American prisoners would be handed back; and an offer of Latin American mediation was accepted, in the hope of averting 'a war [which] would cause grave wounds to both sides'.[191]

Thereafter, the peak of the crisis surmounted, the pace of reconciliation quickened. Carranza undertook to police the border more effectively; the staunchly anti-American General Emiliano Nafarrete suffered, it seems, a cautionary reproof; and the press began a policy of referring to the Punitive Expedition only in respect of its imminent withdrawal.[192] Though there were no further armed clashes, however, withdrawal took time. A joint US–Mexican commission began negotiations at New London, Connecticut, in September, but from the outset it stalled over a fundamental point. The US government sought to link an agreed withdrawal to guarantees concerning Mexico's domestic affairs: the protection of foreign lives and property, religious tolerance, the relief of hunger and disease, the establishment of a Mixed Claims Commission.[193] Whatever may be thought of either the source or the legitimacy of these demands, they clearly represented a major intrusion in Mexican domestic politics, at a time when the Querétaro Congress was about to meet to draw up the new Constitution.[194] As Haley puts it, with only a touch of hyperbole,[195]

the Wilson administration plainly sought to bargain the withdrawal of the Pershing expedition in exchange for sweeping promises from the Mexican government that touched the core of Mexican life and the Mexican Revolution. From a justified expression of self-defense the presence of American troops in Mexico had been twisted into a vehicle for controlling Mexico's future.

In other words, though Pershing had not initially entered Mexico at the behest of American material interest and *grosspolitik*, it was for their sake that he now languished south of the border through the autumn and winter of 1916–17, his men cold, bored and homesick.[196] Though determined (to the disgust of his muscular chauvinist critics) to avoid war, Wilson grew impatient at Carranza's refusal to accept policy recommendations which were so demonstrably reasonable. As in Europe two years later, the president found the world obstinately blind to truths which he held to be self-evident. In the case of Mexico, however, it should be noted (since it is often overlooked) that it was the Mexicans themselves who at first encouraged the idea of making the joint commission a forum for wide-ranging discussions of their country's problems; and it may be presumed that this encouraged Wilson to attempt a grand, composite settlement which would at the same time benefit Mexico (as he saw it) and place US–Mexican relations on a stable footing, thereby strengthening America's hand in Europe. For Cabrera had initially favoured a conference which 'would open [the] whole Mexican question and establish [a] good basis for [the] future'; the Carrancista press talked of the 'vast plans of reforms' which the Mexican delegates outlined, to the 'effusive applause' of their American counterparts.[197]

At least some weighty members of the Carrancista government thus favoured a broad dialogue, particularly with a view to securing American financial help in Mexico's reconstruction: in effect, they reversed Wilson's stance and sought to use the beleaguered Punitive Expedition as a lever to extract American aid.[198] But Carranza was sceptical, preferring to limit the talks to the question of withdrawal, *tout court*; and, after a period of ambivalence, evident in the Carrancista press, his view prevailed and the

Mexican delegates dug in their heels, refusing to discuss other matters until withdrawal had been unconditionally conceded.[199] Their position was now formidable. Pershing's value as a bargaining counter was fast depreciating; neither the American government nor American public opinion would countenance war with Mexico; the Mexicans could mark time, confident that the expedition was more of a nuisance to the US than a threat to Mexico. Indeed, it was increasingly the economic power of the US — its capacity to provide food, arms and cash — rather than its military strength, which gave it most leverage *vis-à-vis* Carranza's government.[200] By the end of 1916 it was clear that the US could extract no concessions in return for withdrawal; so — to Wilson's chagrin — the withdrawal became unilateral.[201] At the end of January 1917, the expedition broke camp, literally, for the American company on whose land the troops were billeted feared that the soldiers' huts, if they remained up, would attract Mexican squatters, and to the cheers of the Carrancistas of El Valle the Americans headed north, accompanied by a stream of refugees and 'two waggons full of painted whores'.[202] On 5 February the last American quit Mexican soil.

The Punitive Expedition had not proved very punitive. It had failed to catch Villa, the first begetter of all these troubles; and, though Clendenen argues that this was not its chief aim, it can hardly be doubted (and the offer of a fat reward indicates) that his capture would have been a real achievement.[203] True, the Americans had contributed to the dispersal of Villa's forces, but such dispersal was in the nature of Villista guerrilla warfare, and it did not prevent Villa regrouping and successfully renewing the offensive late in 1916. By then, the expedition was stalled: Pershing believed that had he continued Villa would have been caught and Villismo extirpated.[204] This is doubtful. Villa's eclipse in the summer of 1916 coincided with his recovery from a serious wound (sustained in combat with Carrancistas, not Americans); and, while the expedition took the war to Villa and possibly deterred him from future border raids, it could not permanently police Chihuahua; that was a task for the Carrancistas alone. Finally, the achievements of the expedition (of which perhaps the most notable was the help it gave Wilson's re-election) must be set against the ill-feeling it generated, ending Wilson's brief honeymoon with Carrancismo, and the fillip it gave Villa's fortunes and reputation; for, in both its initial active phase and its later, long travails, it allowed Villa to assume the role of a daring patriot, eluding the meddlesome, maladroit *gringos*.

The expedition's effect upon Mexico must be set in a wider context. Apart from the obvious headache it caused for the Carranza regime, as it struggled to establish its legitimacy, it must also be recognised that Villismo extended beyond the borders of Chihuahua (to which the expedition had been confined) and that Villismo survived well after Pershing's withdrawal. Both spatially and temporally, therefore, the punitive expedition overlapped with latter-day Villismo only to a limited extent; and there was much more to the Villismo of these years than its inconsequential duel with the Americans. At the time that Villa moved against Columbus, detachments of Villistas had fanned out from western Chihuahua: Ceniceros back to the Laguna to help his old ally Contreras; Juan Vargas and Miguel Hernández to Zacatecas, José Rodríguez and Carlos Almeida to Sinaloa; while others scattered into the sierras of Chihuahua and Durango – Uribe, Ocaranza, Pablo López.[205] Through the winter of 1915–16 they operated as guerrillas, ready to reunite when the occasion might be more propitious in the spring.

With the northern sierras in the grip of winter, and the Americans soon reinforcing the Carrancistas in Chihuahua, so the focus of rebel activity shifted south, to Durango and the Laguna: it was the old revolutionary counterpoint of 1910–11 and 1913. Now, in 1915–16, Contreras, Argumedo, Canuto Reyes, Domínguez and Bañuelos kept the Carrancistas in constant anxiety: Gómez and Lerdo were briefly captured and looted in January 1916; Torreón nearly fell; and the familiar old trouble-spots – Cuencamé, Pedriceña, Yerbanis, Rodeo, San Juan del Río – were all at the mercy of elusive Villista war parties.[206] Zacatecas, where the Carrancistas 'recognised [the] prevalence [of] Villista sentiment', was also overrun.[207] Government troops were rushed in; and the capture and execution of Benjamín Argumedo, the 'Lion of the Laguna', and one of the most durable of revolutionary veterans, dealt the rebels a severe blow. Furthermore, with the spring, the rains, and the prospect of a good cotton crop, the situation calmed and several rebel chiefs – Contreras, Ceniceros, Reyes – began the old, familiar round of tongue-in-cheek nego-tiations with the authorities.[208] While 'the demands of Calixto Contreras and his Cuencamé Indians [were] considered [to be] rather large', in most cases a deal was struck, giving both government and rebels a breathing space.[209] Hence, as the campaigns abated, it was reckoned there were 'several thousand former Villa soldiers . . . working in the cotton fields' of the Laguna in spring 1916.[210] But such deals rarely lasted. Canuto Reyes, having surrendered and secured supplies for his men, rose in revolt again in June.[211]

But no sooner had the Laguna quietened than the Villistas of Chihuahua, less constrained by the exigencies of the planting season, effected their planned reunion. Insistent reports of Villa's death were disproved as the old cam-paigner emerged from his cave, or whatever mountain hide-out he had inhabited, now bearded, limping, using a walking stick, and travelling wherever possible by car rather than horse.[212] In July 1916, a series of raids around Jiménez culminated in an attack on the town by 1,000 Villistas who, descending from the mountains, looked 'a verminous crowd, half-naked and half-starved like savages from the hills'. The Carrancista garrison, though equal in number, was in no mood to resist: morale was low and the commander, General Ignacio Ramos, had just been killed, along with his entire staff, in a Villista ambush. The rest of the garrison fled, and the Villistas swarmed into Jiménez. The days of orderly occupations were over. The town was looted, and Carrancista prisoners were either killed, or allowed to go free with their right ears clipped off. So, at least, went the story, which attributed the mutilations to Baudelio Uribe, one of Villa's close *serrano* lieutenants, who thus acquired the nickname of 'ear-clipper'; months later, by way of corroboration, travellers from Torreón reported seeing one-eared Carrancista soldiers returning from the north. And while the mutilation went on, the mob applauded.[213]

Despite Villa's gammy leg, his forces had to keep on the move. From Jiménez they rode to Parral, where an attack was repulsed.[214] Then, after a pause, several Villista columns began to converge on Chihuahua City, which was attacked on 16 September, the Villistas penetrating as far as the governor's palace before being driven off.[215] Though short of ammunition and supplies, and thus unable to capture and hold the cities of the plain, the Villistas could still undermine the government's tenuous hold on Chihuahua, and call into question its legitimacy throughout the north. The Villista revival in Chihuahua, for example, stimulated rebellions by disaffected garrisons in Zacatecas.[216] The Carrancista forces, meanwhile, were in a parlous state: unpopular, unpaid, ill-clad, depleted by desertion, clinging to the towns and railways, incapable of implementing the martial law which had been proclaimed in Chihuahua following the attack on the capital.[217] Like the Federals of 1910–11 and 1913–14, they also found that attempts to carry the war to the rebels in the mountains were disastrous. Often, therefore, no attempts were made: prior to Columbus, Villa had been allowed to move and camp as he pleased en route to the border.[218] After the repulse from Chihuahua City he retired to the Santa Clara cañón with some 500 men, and the Carrancistas sent in pursuit – mostly men from the south, who went 'filled with fear of Villa' – could make no headway.[219] Nor was Carrancista morale helped by the crushing defeat of the Coahuilan forces of Carlos Zuazua, who were driven from the Laguna in a headlong retreat across the arid Bolsón de Mapimí, arriving back in their home state starving, half-naked, and vowing never to return to the fray.[220]

With a secure, if uncomfortable base in the sierra, Villa could raid as he chose. As 1916 ended, with the Constituent Congress deliberating at Querétaro (a scene often depicted as one of serene statecraft) the Carrancista commander in Chihuahua, Jacinto Treviño, was bottled up in the state capital with a demoralised garrison, wrangling with his colleagues and conceding Villa free run of the sierra. Here, Villa was busy installing sympathetic authorities at Guerrero, San Isidro, Minaca, Temosáchic (the names and practice straight out of 1910), as well as forcing recruits. He was also capable of lightning raids, seizing Santa Rosalía, Jiménez (again) and Parral (again) in November 1916.[221] Government forces soon re-entered these towns (they rarely took them *a fuerza y sangre*) and they managed to repulse Villa from Chihuahua again at the end of the month. These were hailed as decisive victories: the Villista attack on Chihuahua was a 'great failure', which left Villa only a handful of men; it was a final and decisive repulse', a 'fatal blow' to Villismo.[222] A month later Villa returned and captured both Chihuahua City and Torreón, the two strategic keys to northern Mexico. Torreón's experience also conjured up memories of 1911. Like the Federals of that year, the Carrancistas pulled out with indecent haste, even leaving some of their men in the outlying trenches, as Villa's tatterdemalion army approached. There followed a 'brief reign of terror'; a number of Chinese and Syrians were killed; and the 'inevitable looting of the stores by the "pelados" took place right away'.[223] After this brief fling the Villistas rode off, leaving Torreón 'quiver[ing] with the horror of [their] visitation.[224] The effects of these two rapidly successive Villista coups were not confined to the vicinity. Down at Querétaro, a shiver went through the *constituyentes*; and, despite the silence of the official press, news of Villa's resurgence got about, stimulating recruitment elsewhere; in Toribio Ortega's old patch near Ojinaga, for example.[225]

So it continued through 1917, as the northern campaign became a dogged duel between Villa and the tough, corrupt, but capable Francisco Murguía. Repeatedly, Murguía flushed Villista raiders out of the lowland towns (most occupations lasted only days, or hours; the purpose was to collect food, money, recruits, and to embarrass the government); and repeatedly these skirmishes were reported as great victories. In March 1917 Villa was 'completely defeated' near his old home town of San Juan del Río; hence, he was 'eliminated as a leader in Mexico for [the] present or ever again'.[226] But repeatedly, too, the Carrancista follow-up was feeble, or a failure. On this occasion, Murguía, pursuing Villa west of Parral and believing him beaten, walked into a carefully prepared ambush near Reforma.[227] Badly wounded, he retreated to Parral, then Jiménez and Chihuahua. The pendulum swung, and within days Villa was again at the gates of the state capital, though this time he was denied admittance.[228] The arrival of Joaquín Amaro with massive reinforcements gave the government a respite; scattered groups of Villistas headed for the mountains or got jobs in the slowly reviving mining industry.[229] Another false dawn rose: 'military activity is quite a thing of the past in the state of Chihuahua', an observer hazarded in May 1917. Almost at once, Villa captured Ojinaga – hoping to get ammunition across the border and, perhaps, to capitalise on local support – and, though he could not hold the port, he recaptured it again later in the year.[230]

Minor skirmishes and raids continued through 1917–19.[231] In addition, Villa regularly raised sizeable forces – between one and two thousand – for attacks on major towns. Parral fell in July 1917 and again in June 1918; Jiménez, Moctezuma, Ahumada and Santa Eulalia were captured (Jiménez twice in quick succession) during the winter of 1918–19; and in the spring of 1919, Villa, now with Angeles again at his side, raised a well-equipped force which took Parral and occupied most of Juárez, before being dislodged, in some disarray, by American troops.[232] This was a dirty, inconclusive war. The Carrancistas, plagued by desertions, behaved rather as the Federals had before them; after his successful defence of Chihuahua City in 1917, Murguía ordered the 'wholesale' hangings of Villista prisoners and sympathisers.[233] The Villistas were hardly above reproach themselves. In order to save bullets, it was said, Villa ordered Carrancista prisoners to be beheaded; and, more certainly, his brief occupation of towns was often marked by the summary executions of personal enemies: the González family of Jiménez, an anonymous 'well-known Mexican citizen' at Santa Eulalia, and, above all, members of the Herrera family, once Villa's staunch allies, now his bitter foes.[234] Luis Herrera who, following the death of his brother Maclovio was the family's ranking general, was killed after the fall of Torreón in January 1917 and his body suspended outside the railway station with a paper peso in one hand and a picture of Carranza in the other. Six months later, when Parral fell, his brother Ascención was caught and hung, Villa stating that 'he would get the entire Herrera family. He has now put them all away except the father and one brother, the mayor of Juárez.'[235] And such selective violence was not without practical effect. When the authorities sought to ring the City of Chihuahua with barbed wire early in 1919, the Chamber of Commerce refused to foot the bill, fearing it would make them prime targets for Villa's wrath.[236]

But if the pendulum continued to swing – Villa descending from the mountains to the plain, the Carrancistas faltering then, reinforced, driving him from the scarred cities back to the sierra – nevertheless its swing tended gradually to shorten. The scope and ferocity of the fighting could not be sustained. The Carrancistas, for all that their troops were lacklustre and prone to desertion, could count on a flow of mercenary recruits, who did not usually want for munitions. Villa, however, faced problems on both counts. Something like half his ammunition had to be captured, stolen or bought from the enemy, the rest being smuggled in from the US.[237] From 1916 on, the phenomenon of the half-armed Villista army – quite different from the well-equipped professionals of 1914 – became common.[238] Even more significant, Villa lacked manpower. The high mortality of his chief lieutenants continued. Pablo López, perpetrator of the Cusi massacre, was executed in 1916; his brother Martín, El Güero Martín, who had followed Villa since the age of twelve and was 'almost a son' in Villa's eyes, was killed in 1919; Uribe, the cutter of Carrancista ears, perished in a fight with a hacienda defence force in 1917; and Angeles, returning to Mexico late in 1918, survived less than a year before being captured, court-martialled (a tribute to his prominence and respectability: plebeian Villistas were shot out of hand) and executed by firing squad in November 1919.[239]

More important, Villa's popular base had atrophied. Though the *pelados* of Chihuahua felt no love for Carranza, his grafting generals and indifferent but rapacious soldiery, they saw there was now little to be gained by backing

Villa.[240] They might applaud Villista daring – and brutality; they might take advantage of his attacks to loot; but they would not volunteer to fight for Villa – hence the Villista *leva* remained sporadically active – and they would sometimes join local defence forces, hence the proliferation of the latter throughout Chihuahua, and their significant military successes.[241] Villismo could not be extirpated, but it was no longer buoyed up by the great popular tide which carried it forward in 1913–15. O'Hea, a perceptive observer, noted that 'there exist no longer in this part of the Mexican Republic the same facilities for uprisings against the central power as caused disturbances of this nature to prosper in previous years'; but this did not indicate general satisfaction with the state of affairs, on the contrary, food was short (even the rebels were 'half-starved'), and 'extreme misery and suffering are almost universal'.[242] This bred, not rebellion, but a dull apathy, which reigned among a 'people . . . whose spirit has to a great extent been broken and whose illusions in regard to the benefits they may derive from rebellions have largely vanished' (an outcome consonant with some general theory).[243]

Thus, the popular insurgence of 1910–11 and 1913–14 gave way to the popular quiescence of 1916–20; a change signalled, for example, in the shifting seasonal pattern of warfare, which went through three successive phases. In the early years of the revolution, the summer – the period of planting and harvesting – marked the low point of military activity, when the *campesinos* returned to the fields; major campaigns were usually fought between November and April.[244] During the years of greatest military professionalisation (1914–15), when the major armies had emancipated themselves from such constraints, no pattern emerged. Now, after 1915, Villismo and comparable movements obeyed a different pattern, though one also linked to the agricultural cycle. While some of their forces found summer employment (e.g., in the Laguna cotton fields) the hard core remained 'professionals', detached from village and hacienda life; for them, summer was the time for campaigning, since climatic conditions were favourable and, in the absence of an efficient commissariat, food and forage were readily available.[245] Campaigning thus followed the schedule of the mercenary, dynastic armies of pre-industrial Europe. From this it followed that dearth or drought at least had the beneficial side-effects of inhibiting military activity; while a good harvest offered both opportunity and incentive; the seasonal imperatives of 1910–13 and 1916–20 were thus reversed.[246]

Mortality, military attrition, dearth, and war-weariness all damped down the fighting. But it could not be extinguished. Old rancours, typified by Villa's hatred of Carranza, kept the struggle going: 'we shall fight on', as Villa is supposed to have said, 'until Don Venustiano is swinging from a tree'.[247] The logic of the Revolution, which had created and deepened these schisms, debarred proud men like Villa, or Leocadio Parra, from accepting defeat and surrender. But pride and personal rancour could not sustain an indefinite civil war. The mood of the people (typified by the Villistas who exchanged guns for picks and shovels to work in the mines at Villa Ahumada) set limits to the caudillos' costly concern for personal honour.[248] So, without showing signs of stopping altogether, the fighting gradually subsided, sometimes, it seemed, lapsing into a routine which satisfied honour, preserved reputations, and incidentally gave opportunity for profit.[249] Ultimately, with another twist of history in 1920, the logic of the Revolution gave Villa and many lesser leaders a chance to secure peace with honour; a chance which they readily seized, thus bringing a sudden resolution of the long, military discord of 1916–20.[250]

THE PROBLEM OF ORDER: 2 ZAPATISTAS AND OTHERS

Had Villa's northern campaigns been isolated military phenomena, they could have been more effectively dealt with. But throughout much of Mexico these years witnessed guerrilla campaigns paralleling those of Chihuahua. In each case, the Carrancista victories of 1915 weakened and divided the opposition, creating a rash of defections, surrenders and defeats. But, as 1915 gave way to 1916, as Villa and Zapata remained in the field, so many lesser rebel bands perked up and took the fight to Carranza's regime, multiplying the military problems it faced. Individually, even collectively, they stood no chance of wresting control of the national government from Carranza, or of posing as plausible national alternatives, in the eyes of Mexicans or foreigners. But they were locally tenacious, and could severely impair the government's capacity to govern.

Three kinds of guerrilla movement may be distinguished in these years: first, the still vigorous survivors of the early popular (often agrarian) rebellions, most evident in central and parts of northern Mexico; second, the defensive, autonomist campaigns of more recent vintage, largely confined to south-central Mexico; and third, the endemic banditry which, in west-central Mexico, developed into a military problem of unprecedented dimension. Members of the first group usually assumed Villista or Zapatista labels, those of the second Felicista; as in previous years, these labels were superficial and often misleading. More to the point was the question of ancestry. Both Felicismo and the rampant banditry of west-central Mexico were products of, or reactions to, the revolution itself, and could not trace their genealogy much beyond 1914 at the earliest. In contrast, a striking feature of the first group was the way they followed the regional, personal and morphological patterns laid down five years before, at the outset of the revolution. The same sectors which had pioneered the revolution against Díaz and contributed most to the fall of Huerta now constituted the tough, gnarled knots of resistance to Carrancismo.

As with latter-day Villismo, there were of course changes: in leadership, due to the high mortality of the old *cabecillas*; in the prevailing political climate, as the war-weariness of the common people and sometimes the arbitrary behaviour of the rebels prised these erstwhile allies apart. Nevertheless, popular support, reinforced by popular antipathy to the Carrancistas, was strong enough for local guerrilla forces to sustain protracted struggles against the regime, which, somewhat ironically, found itself in the position once occupied by its old opponent, the Federal Army of Díaz, Madero and Huerta, fighting costly and seemingly interminable counter-insurgency campaigns in the countryside. The British Minister had advised Huerta to defend his vulnerable railway network with armed blockhouses, as the British had done during the Boer War; the Carrancistas later carried out the recommendation.[251] In Morelos, the Carrancista González followed precisely in the footsteps of the Huertista Robles – possibly he overstepped them.[252] Even though they could not win, the popular rebels of 1915–20 set the terms on which the new regime had to operate.

Events in the Laguna – with Chihuahua the main pole of northern rebellion – have already been touched upon. In mid-1915 the retreating Villistas swept through, leaving the region quieter, though economically prostrate. Carrancista forces followed in their wake: Murguía advanced from the east, taking Parras, Viesca, San Pedro, Torreón and, it is worth noting, Cuencamé, late in October 1915; Contreras, the Cuencamé *jefe*, seemed beaten (several members of his family had been captured); while down in Durango the Arrietas had come out of the mountains to seize the state capital in the name of Carranza.[253] But this rapid Carrancista take-over was deceptive. In the winter of 1915–16 the old actors and activities were again prominent. Argumedo, Ceniceros and Contreras captained rebel bands, repeatedly defying Carrancista forces at Yerbanis, Pedriceña, Cuencamé and, to the north-west, Rodeo and San Juan del Río. Like their erstwhile Villista allies to the north, the Laguna rebels gathered large, conglomerate armies to attack major towns (Contreras alone led 3,000 men against Gómez and Lerdo in January 1916); but these armies soon disintegrated, since the rebels had neither the desire nor the capacity to mount large, conventional attacks on fixed positions. When Carrancista reinforcements arrived, the rebels scattered for the higher country around Rodeo and San Juan, where forage was abundant and pursuit reluctant and ineffective.[254] Hence numbers, even assuming reports to be correct, fluctuated greatly. In the early summer of 1916, as the seasonal lull began and negotiations with the government were undertaken, Contreras, Ceniceros and Reyes had only 600–800 men quartered at San Juan.[255] The negotiations followed the pattern of 1912: the rebels wanted to retain their arms and receive positions in the state government; Contreras' demands were thought to be excessive; Reyes dallied with the authorities throughout the summer without reaching a definite deal.[256] Meanwhile, many of their men returned to work on the cotton estates, and military activity was confined to hit-and-run raids on trains running through the Laguna.[257] Notwithstanding this pause, it was clear that the rebels still enjoyed local support, especially around Cuen-camé, and that there were regions, like San Juan, which they fully dominated.[258]

Then, in winter, as Villa headed south from Chihuahua, and the Laguna plantations lay fallow, the scattered rebel bands began to coalesce for the attack on Torreón, accomplished in January 1916. It was in winter, therefore, that harassed hacienda managers renewed old acquaintances. Contreras and Argumedo, for example, returned to the Hacienda San Fernando (Contreras' headquarters in 1913–14); now defeated, they were in a meaner mood than previously; but an ex-peon of the hacienda, now a colonel in Argumedo's forces, gave the manager a fond *abrazo*.[259] Next winter, as the rebels again campaigned in the lowlands, two employees of an hacienda near Viesca – ordered to be shot for being implicated in the Carrancistas' hanging of local peons – were reprived, since 'many of the people of the same hacienda where these men worked were among the Villistas [and] they prevailed upon the [rebel] authorities to let them off'.[260]

A conflict of this kind – pitting a demoralised, static, but well-equipped regular army against more daring, mobile guerrillas, lacking arms but closely associated with the rural people – was bound to be protracted and inconclusive. The rebels could no more capture and hold Torreón or Lerdo than the government could Rodeo or San Juan del Río. At best, they could raid, loot and devastate their respective bases, chiefly to the detriment of the *pacíficos*. It was a war of attrition, though one of the decreasing tempo. Continued Carrancista abuses ensured continued popular sympathy for the rebels, but this could not tip the military balance decisively in their favour.[261] And, however inefficient and predatory the Carrancista army, it could keep going 'so long as the central government can dole out to its half-starved troops a pittance at least'.[262] Losses could be made up almost indefinitely. But, as hunger, disease and unemployment worsened, the rebels had no such pool of reserves. Their own leaders suffered a high mortality: Argumedo, 'an exceedingly courageous general and a good strategist' was wounded, captured and summarily shot early in 1916; Calixto Contreras died of wounds later in the year (though the government had placed a large price on his head, the body never came to light); Tiburcio Cuevas met his end at Llano Grande. But Lucio Contreras succeeded to the leadership of his father's forces and, like Canuto Reyes, was still under arms and causing trouble in 1918.[263]

By then, however, the Laguna was quieter: the common people were chiefly concerned to secure employment on the revived cotton estates, to avoid the ravages of disease (1918 was the year of the Spanish influenza), and to earn enough to cover the inflated prices of foodstuffs. The peace which descended on the Laguna by the end of 1918 was thus a Roman peace; it indicated neither popular contentment nor popular support for the regime. The common people of the Laguna still prayed to old gods and remembered recent triumphs; their quiescence,[264]

does not imply for one moment that they . . . have anything but hatred and contempt for the present governing regime or that they have ceased to hold in their hearts Villa as their idol . . . this leader occupies indeed in their sentiment and imagination probably a similar place to that of Zapata in regard to the poorer classes of the south and they still look back with longing at the days when, before the country was exhausted, Villa gave them loot and a primitive kind of justice.

So, too, in San Luis, it seemed that the Carrancista victories of 1915 had condemned the Cedillos and their fellow-Villistas to oblivion. Towards the end of the year, the Carrancistas were making 'great headway' in eastern San Luis; Alberto Carrera Torres, losing men fast through desertion, had united with the Cedillos at their old headquarters, Cd del Maíz; and it was thought that they might reach a deal with the government.[265] But neither annihilation or co-option occurred – at least, not for several years. True, the Cedillos' numbers fell and their operations contracted from major campaigns to local guerrilla war; but this suited them well, since 'all of the Cedillo forces are familiar with the territory in which they are operating and as soon as they are attacked by a superior force they scatter into small bands and hide in the mountain retreats'.[266] Hence, through the winter of 1915–16, they survived and next spring there were still about 1,000 rebels in the rugged country of eastern San Luis, most of them badly armed and divided into groups of less than 200.[267] And this was not just a pause in an inexorable decline: the disintegration stopped, and the Cedillos and their allies bounced back. Through 1916–17, it was reported, 'banditti [sic] are creating a reign of terror between San Luis and Tampico'; the rail link between these cities (important for transporting men and supplies from the Gulf to the north) was under constant attack; and Valle del Maíz became a no-go area for Carrancista troops.[268] The 'banditti' label, though predictable, was hardly justified. The Cedillos' *agrarista* commitment was longstanding; and they still put out political manifestoes, orotund and indignant, in the name of the 'Convention-ist Army of the Centre', denouncing Carranza and his 'pack of Iscariots' alleging, with justification, Carrancista connivance with caciques and land-lords, and calling for a genuine, sweeping agrarian reform.[269]

Their numbers were variously reported (the variety no doubt reflecting objective changes, as well as inevitable errors). Some 400 in the spring of 1916 became 800 in the autumn; in 1917, when they had 'completely overrun' their district, they were said to command over 3,000; though these were 'bearded, long-haired, half-naked men'.[270] Their local support was crucial for survival: 'the native sentiment [is] in favour of the bandits out in the mountains. When once within their mountain homes guns are discarded and each member of the band returns to his home until such an opportune time as when other raids are planned by the leaders.'[271] Even so, the risks were high. Cleofas Cedillo was killed in 1915; Alberto Carrera Torres was captured and shot early in 1916; both Homobono and Magdaleno Cedillo perished in 1917.[272] But Saturnino's death, ultimately similar, was postponed for twenty years; meanwhile, what he and his kind awaited – if not consciously – was a political opening, by which to reintegrate themselves in the 'official', victorious revolution, without sacrificing their local interests and supporters. Such an opening could only come from outside, from the official revolution itself: local *cabecillas* like Cedillo could not whistle one up and therefore had to wait upon events. When a gubernatorial election split the Carrancista elite of neighbouring Coahuila in 1917, Cedillo was thought to be aligning himself with the leading dissident, Luis Gutiérrez – a particularly rough-and-ready, plebeian sort of Carrancista, with Potosino connections, but nonetheless an 'official' revolutionary, on whose coat-tails an ally might come to official recognition.[273] Nothing came of this. But in 1920, with another, more serious Carrancista schism, Saturnino was providentially accorded his re-entry to the national revolution, on terms which he and his staunch followers could stomach.

The classic example of this pattern, however, was to be found in Morelos. Here – in a case too often viewed as unique – the same characteristics were evident: remarkable stamina, which sustained rebellion through 1911 to 1920; dogged resistance to Carrancista repression; a necessary contraction from extensive conventional to local guerrilla campaigns; and, finally, a search for allies and contacts that might help the movement pursue its objectives under the aegis of the new regime. Until mid-1915, the Zapatista position in Morelos was impregnable, enabling the 'pueblos [to] carry out a revolution'.[274] But, like other anti-Carranza movements, Zapatismo depended on the counterweight of Pancho Villa in the north; and, as Villismo wilted, so the Zapatistas were forced onto the defensive. In August 1915 Carrancista troops under Pablo González occupied Mexico City for good and in November, with Villa beaten, a 'definitive' campaign against Zapata was planned.[275] Revolutionaries round about, in Puebla and Hidalgo, inclined with the wind and reached terms with the Carrancistas.[276] These were not necessarily sell-outs: Zapatismo itself reached terms five years later; but in 1915 the pressure to concede worked chiefly on the weak (as well as the opportunist) and Zapatismo was still too proud and strong to treat with the enemy. But the bandwagon effect weakened the Morelos rebels. Accommodations reached elsewhere enabled the Carrancistas to tighten the noose around Morelos; recent Zapatista recruits, 'commissioned in droves' and sent to garrison the northern entry to the state, deserted at the promise of amnesty; and among Zapata's leading generals fears of defection and betrayal bred conflict. The old feud between Pacheco and de la O was rekindled by rumours of treachery; Pacheco took exception to de la O's suspicions and demonstrated his displeasure by evacuating Huitzilac, allowing the Carrancistas to advance almost to Cuernavaca. For this, Pacheco – caught by de la O's troops in March 1916 – was summarily shot.[277]

Militarily, however, the Zapatistas were still formidable, especially now they were fighting on home ground. Late in 1915 the Carrancista advance ground to a halt and Zapatista counter-attacks were launched into Mexico, Puebla and the Federal District. To the south-west, de la O repulsed a Carrancista move through Guerrero, drove the enemy back to their base at Acapulco, and raided the Costa Grande, leaving the Carrancista position in that state 'greatly weakened'.[278] But sheer mobility could not offset the Carrancistas' quantitative superiority in men and munitions. Raiding exhausted the Zapatistas' exiguous supply of home-made cartridges, while the Carrancistas, with their oil and henequen resources, could field an army of some 30,000 well-armed, if poorly motivated, soldiers.[279] In April–May 1916, in a concerted campaign which included aerial attacks, the Carrancistas powered their way into Morelos, seizing the major towns, Cuautla and Cuernavaca (they looked, said the press, like large rubbish dumps), and leaving only Jojutla and Tlatizapán, Zapata's headquarters, in precarious rebel control.[280]

Like Villismo, Zapatismo now made the transition from conventional to guerrilla status. Its complement of some 20,000 shrank to 5,000 by the end of 1916; these were split into groups of one or two hundred, based in remote mountain camps, where they were 'intimately familiar with the terrain and people of their respective zones'; most were led by veterans who 'had been with Zapata from the first'.[281] The Carrancistas might hold the towns, but the guerrillas could concentrate on hit-and-run raids, aiming at vulnerable targets, avoiding static defence.[282] Hence arose the illusion – soon to be dispelled – that Zapata was beaten. In the summer of 1916 Pablo González, commanding at Cuernavaca, announced that 'the Morelos campaign is almost finished'; Zapatista agents, reviewing the national scene, were as pessimistic as their opponents were hopeful.[283] Both were wrong. Even as these opinions were expressed, large, well-armed Zapatista forces were active around Jilotepec (Mex.) and haciendas in Tlaxcala and Puebla were suffering 'constant incursions' from Zapatista bands, who carried off even the farm animals and implements.[284] In the autumn, the Morelos Zapatistas took the offensive: they raided the southern suburbs of the capital and put the Xochimilco pumping station – which supplied Mexico City's water – out of action; in November, two trains were dynamited on the Mexico City–Cuernavaca line.[285] As Carrancista confidence crumbled, and their troops, billeted in the hot valleys of Morelos, sickened, Zapata launched attacks on the lost Morelos towns: late in 1916 their garrisons were driven out and forced to make desperate, harassed retreats to Mexico City.[286]

The year 1917 dawned with the Zapatistas again in control of Morelos. This reconquest, too, was more durable than Villa's fly-by-night occupations of

Parral or Ojinaga. But the Zapatistas still lacked the military hardware to hold out for long against a determined, solvent government. In the autumn, a Carrancista offensive regained Cuautla, Jonacatepec and other towns, but in 1918 the government advance stalled in the summer rains. When these abated, the Carrancistas pressed ahead, now with somewhat more method: they repaired the railway network, systematically garrisoned the state, and created a facade of civilian, municipal authority. Once again, the Zapatistas were driven into the hills or neighbouring states.[287] But for the government it was like grappling with an inflated balloon: pressure at one point (like Morelos) was redistributed elsewhere, thus creating new excrescences which had to be contained. As González advanced into Morelos in 1918, he pushed the Zapatistas into Puebla; at their approach Carrancista garrisons stationed in the Chiautla and Matamoros districts fled, leaving only local defence forces to bar the way into the Poblano heartland.[288] And in Morelos itself there was no certainty that González's 1918 campaign would achieve the knock-out blow which had eluded previous generals, or that Zapatismo, rolling with the punch, would not come off the ropes fighting yet again.

Militarily, therefore, the years 1915–18 witnessed a stalemate: though fortunes fluctuated, neither side could achieve outright victory. It was the same situation which prevailed in Chihuahua, the Laguna, eastern San Luis, and other regions yet to be mentioned. Morelos and Zapatismo were not unique. And there were further parallels. On the Carrancista side, these campaigns were conducted with a combination of ruthlessness, inefficiency and graft reminiscent of Huerta's Federals. Some pushed the comparison further: 'never did anyone believe', a Zapatista wrote in 1917, 'that there would be ruffians who surpassed Huerta's ... [yet] Robles, damned a thousand times, is little in comparison'.[289] Confronted by an infuriating, elusive enemy, backed by indifferent, unhealthy troops, González resorted to the usual easy counter-insurgency methods. Villages were burned to the ground; food, goods and animals were confiscated; there were wholesale killings and deportations of the civilian population.[290] In November 1916 a draconian form of martial law was imposed upon Morelos, Guerrero, Mexico, Puebla, Tlaxcala and four districts of Hidalgo: under its terms, anyone found helping the Zapatistas, straying outside the authorised 'concentration points', treading the roads without a pass, or approaching a railway line without 'a satisfactory explanation of their presence', would be summarily shot.[291] González was not alone in following Huertista precedents. Other Carrancistas, including 'radicals' like Heriberto Jara, threatened to burn entire villages for sheltering rebels; and in some instances, threats of this kind were carried out.[292] But González, facing particularly tough opposition, fearing for his political future, and as devoid of scruples as he was of skill, carried repression to its limits. 'This is not the time to talk of reconstruction ...', he told Rosa King, 'the work of destruction is not yet completed'; 'extraordinary severity' would be shown in response to Zapatista outrages; even the total evacuation of Cuernavaca in February 1917 (a military admission of defeat) was converted into a grandiloquent verbal victory. 'For the first time in our country's history', González told Carranza, 'the total removal of a town's population has been achieved.'[293]

Meantime, González and his officers grafted for all they were worth, and grafting reinforced their zeal for repression, even if it did not improve their military effectiveness.[294] In Mexico City the official press, also following Huertista precedent, endorsed González's methods and justified them with the usual, racially tinged references to Zapatista atrocities and Zapata's 'reactionary' commitment. Prisoners and *pacíficos*, it was said, suffered tortures applied with 'Oriental imagination'; Zapata was the instrument of landlords and clerics, gulling the simple *campesinos* with a spurious, illegal, agrarian reform; Zapatismo was 'a gangrene which would only be extirpated with a hot iron'.[295] An occasional voice of dissent was raised within the political establishment.[296] And, more important, González's policies often seemed to aggravate more than quell Zapatista insurgency; hence, not for the first time, a Mexico City government had to cool the ardour of its commander in Morelos. In 1916 Benjamín Hill suggested that Zapatista prisoners might be deported to the Islas Marías, 'to avoid the frequent shootings of those who are taken prisoner'; a year later, Carranza vetoed González's scheme for deporting Zapatistas – like the Yaquis of the Porfiriato – to Quintana Roo.[297] Certainly these policies, like those of Robles, often redounded to the rebels' benefit. The Carrancistas were generally loathed. 'The Carrancistas were owls', one villager recalled, 'they were devils. They stole our chickens, pigs and food. If they caught us eating they carried away all the food, together with the tortillas and dishes, leaving us without anything to eat.' In addition, they abused priests and defiled churches and shrines.[298] As in the past, indiscriminate repression bred further resistance, active and passive. While the campaign against Villa was furthered by local, volunteer forces, this was never the case in Morelos; indeed, such forces were organised by the Zapatistas themselves.[299] Rather, the Carrancistas complained, with a hyperbole bred of frustration, 'every settlement, every hamlet, every municipality, every head town is a centre of active conspiracy [and] an inexhaustible source of men ready to mobilise at the harsh sound of the war-horn which calls to mind that which the Indian prince wound to muster his hosts'.[300]

But this was too pessimistic. The *suriano* revolt was no irrational, atavistic caste war; nor did the fighting gratify those deep, dark Indian urges which Carranza's journalistic hacks discerned, a little in advance of D. H. Lawrence. The *surianos* fought for tangible objectives; their fight was essentially defensive; and the fighting itself was a bloody, costly chore. Over time, they grew sick of war, and questioned its utility. 'The people', Pedro Martínez recalled, 'were tired. They didn't want to fight any more'; Martínez himself 'saw that the situation was hopeless and that I would be killed and [my family] would perish'.[301] In 1916, he quit the struggle and migrated to Guerrero. Over time, too, the revolutionary movement tended to sour, fragment and weaken (a tendency Womack perhaps underestimates). For reasons of humanity and pragmatism alike, Zapata urged his forces to respect the villages and their civilian authorities; he strove to mitigate the effects of the ceaseless campaigns on the lives of the *pacíficos*; and he took tough measures – 'the law of the 30–30' – against bandits or predatory rebels.[302] As these measures suggested, there was a real danger that the bond uniting army and village would be snapped, or attenuated; that, as González bludgeoned his way into Morelos, and the state fell on hard times, the army would prey on the villages more than protect them. As early as the spring of 1915 – and 1915 was a good year in Morelos – the provisioning of the Zapatistas placed a heavy burden on the villages, there was a reported decline in public order, and an increase in crime and flagrant banditry.[303] Bandits operating on the fringes of Zapatismo merged with the more irresponsible *guerrilleros* who, despite Zapata's orders, placed the victualling of their men above the well-being of the villages.[304] Complaints came in, like those of the villagers of Tecapixtla who, already short of food, 'complain of having suffered great losses of corn . . . at the hands of the armed forces'.[305]

In response, some communities, acting with Zapata's approval, equipped themselves for self-defence. At Ameca, villagers shot up a party of rebels who came soliciting food: though the victims were not Zapatistas (but nominal Felicistas under Marcelo Caraveo) the incident took place in Zapatista territory and, the local Zapatista commander perceived, carried implications for the Zapatistas too: 'they will do the same tomorrow with our forces'.[306] Local defence forces sprang up rapidly within Morelos, as well as in Puebla, Tlaxcala, Oaxaca, Guerrero and Mexico.[307] Their activities were important and revealing. Within Morelos itself, Zapata sanctioned this new development; veteran Zapatistas captained the local forces; and they played a major role protecting communities during these final, bitter years of the revolution, as the fighting wound down and the search for a political settlement proceeded. Ultimately, as a veteran recalled, it was not the government but 'we, the Zapatistas ourselves, who re-established order' in Morelos.[308] At the same time, there were examples of these local forces combating the Zapatistas themselves, especially when the latter strayed into neighbouring states. Village forces barred the way into Puebla when government troops fled; they likewise guarded the entrances to Oaxaca; at Buenavista de Cuellar (Gro) the ranchers fought to resist Zapatista exactions.[309] Such cases would no doubt repay closer investigation; but it cannot be argued that the defenders were invariably hacienda guards or government dupes; and they reveal, again, the temporal and territorial limitations which constrained popular rebellion and its close cousin, social banditry. The popular champion of 1910–14 could become the military tyrant – the revolutionary *reyecito* – of post-1915; a transformation wrought as much by changing conditions as by intrinsic, individual degeneration.[310] And the popular rebel or social bandit of Morelos could easily relinquish this status if he roamed too far afield, driven, perhaps, by Carrancista repression.[311] Zapatista parochialism had its rationale. Hence the enforced mobility and war-weariness of these years affected Zapatista–peasant relations; complaints against and even resistance to Zapatista forces became more common; and, for the historian, it becomes difficult, impossible, or even pointless to distinguish between rebels and marauders, 'social' and 'unsocial' bandits.[312]

Even as Zapata urged moderation upon his lieutenants, he had also to bind them together, since feuds, suspicions and Carrancista blandishments threatened to prise them apart.[313] He was largely successful: the Zapatista leadership of 1911 and 1918 showed relatively little change, indicating further the stamina and constancy of the movement.[314] But, after 1915, defections, scandals and executions could not be avoided. As already noted, the Pacheco – de la O feud was resolved with the shooting of Pacheco in March 1916; Lorenzo Vázquez, dismissed for 'cowardice' in August 1916, rebelled against Zapata in 1917 and was executed along with his civilian mentor, Otilio Montaño; thus perished one of the chief architects of the Plan of Ayala.[315] Meanwhile, Manuel Palafox, another leading Zapatista 'intellectual', receded from the centre of the stage, 'sidetracked' by Zapata; reduced to a pathetic, posturing role, he made overtures to Carranza and narrowly escaped execution in 1918.[316] Among the plebeian Zapatistas some, like Valentín Reyes, became gun-happy (Reyes shot prisoners like a Carrancista); some sought out the limited opportunities for graft available in Morelos; others turned to drink. Eufemio Zapata, Emiliano's brother, was shot after a drunken brawl, his killer defecting to the Carrancistas with his entire force, who were to prove valuable allies of the government in their Morelos campaigns.[317]

But the most serious loss to the movement came in April 1919 with the death of Zapata himself. 'In practice as well as theory', Hobsbawm notes, 'bandits perish by treason'; there is no other way for them to go, for they are 'invisible and invulnerable', protected by their identification with and immersion in the peasantry.[318] So, too, with Zapata.[319] The winter of 1918–19 saw another government offensive, as hunger and disease conspired with Carrancista arms to subdue Zapatismo. Zapata retreated into the mountains with his loyal lieutenants; he gathered reports of Carrancista movements in the state (not least from the whores and bartenders of Cuautla, where González had pitched his headquarters); and he defied Carrancista attempts to corner him. 'The popular protection he had earned was inviolable. No-one would turn him in despite gossip of gigantic rewards.'[320] It was the same, we have noted, with Villa. Carranza and González, each with strong, immediate reasons for wanting Zapata out of the way, resorted to subterfuge. Colonel Jesús

Guajardo, a dashing young Coahuilan cavalryman, known to be at odds with González, whom Zapata sought to lure to the rebels' side, was ordered to play along; on 9 April 1919, he declared himself in rebellion and, with a ruthless concern to establish his credibility, he ordered the execution of fifty-nine Carrancista troops against whom the Zapatistas bore a special grudge.[321] Zapata was convinced. He met with Guajardo, they conferred, Zapata accepted the gift of a sorrel horse. On 10 April they were to meet again, at Guajardo's headquarters, the Hacienda Chinameca. Zapata came with a small escort (most of his men were encamped outside, or scattered on patrol), while Guajardo commanded 600; as the *suriano* chief rode in to the strains of a welcoming bugle, Guajardo's troops opened fire, at point-blank range, with two crashing volleys. Zapata was killed instantly. His men fled and were not, it seems, actively pursued. Guajardo quit the scene of betrayal and conveyed the body as fast as possible to the Carrancista headquarters at Cuautla, where it was identified, displayed and buried – with a film crew in attendance. A shiver went through the people of Morelos. Pablo González exulted: 'Zapata having disappeared', he declared, 'Zapatismo has died.' The Carrancista press echoed his sentiments.[322] But the *campesinos* thought and behaved differently: when Zapata's lieutenants vowed to fight on and launched a spate of attacks on Carrancista authorities in the state 'they went on receiving protection, supplies and information from country folk'; among whom it was soon rumoured that Zapata had in fact tricked his betrayers, that a substitute had died, that Zapata still lived, that he had been seen galloping into the mountains of Guerrero, still mounted on Guajardo's sorrel.[323] It was the classic resurrection of bandit myth, following the classic death of bandit reality.[324]

The deaths of Zapata and his many lieutenants weakened the movement over the years. But the movement declined less for want of leadership than by virtue of the extreme deprivation which the Morelenses were now suffering and which, well before the trauma of Zapata's assassination, had left Zapatismo 'drastically weakened in numbers, health and reserves of men and supplies'.[325] This decline went back longer than may be supposed: its origins can be discerned in the happy days of 1914–15, before González's brusque and bloody irruption into the state, when the pueblos were 'carrying out their revolution'; it responded to the general economic dislocation of the country, as well as specified military campaigns. As early as October 1914 'a truly sad poverty' reigned in the region of Jonacatepec; from Tochimilco, in March 1915, Fortino Ayaquica reported that 'the anguished cry which hunger begins to draw from the poor villages of this zone' had forced him to fix food prices and halt speculation; Ayaquica, in Morelos, thus behaved much as Obregón in Mexico City.[326] Matters got worse, not better. Food prices were exceptionally high (at least double those of the 1900s).[327] After August, González's depredations began; soon, eleven Zapatista generals appealed to their leader to curb the prevalent poverty and hunger, pointing out the inadequacy of peons' and soldiers' pay, the 'fabulous prices' demanded by retailers, and the Carrancistas' ability to win popular support by price-fixing.[328]

Any amount of price-fixing could not offset the callousness of Carrancista policy in Morelos. But the constant fighting further undermined the local economy and, here as in the Laguna, poverty, hunger, unemployment and disease engendered apathy or migration, not armed resistance. By 1917–18 many villages were empty shells, the fields stood bare, cattle, pigs and chickens were nowhere to be seen; to a quirky American observer, Morelos seemed like Flanders fields.[329] As a final scourge, late in 1918, came the Spanish influenza which – to the gratification of the Carrancista authorities – turned towns into hamlets, decimated villages, and prompted further out-migration to Guerrero. In 1918 alone, Morelos lost a quarter of its population through death and emigration.[330] When, a year late, Pedro Martínez returned home after a three year sojourn in Guerrero he was appalled at the prospect: 'when we arrived at Azteca there was nothing here. The streets were completely deserted. It was like a forest, all the streets were choked up with weeds.'[331] As the revolutionary decade drew to a close, the population of Morelos was only three-fifths what it had been at the outset.[332]

The mounting privation, which undercut Zapatismo's active support, and the relentless if inept Carrancista campaigns, forced the leadership to look to outside allies and political solutions. The carapace of parochialism, carried by Zapatismo from its birth, was shed. Tenuous links were established with Felicista rebels in the south and with Peláez in the Huasteca; the old alliance with Villa was briefly, notionally resurrected; overtures went out to Arenas in Tlaxcala, to the Cedillos, to even more distant dissidents.[333] Zapata now took an uncharacteristic, and misinformed, interest in relations with the US, convinced (Womack argues) that only a speedy resolution of Mexico's troubles, through some kind of revolutionary unification, could avert American intervention once the European war was concluded.[334] And he issued novel appeals to the industrial workers of the cities.[335] But the stream of manifestoes, appeals, and paper alliances which flowed from Zapatista head-quarters after 1916 had little tangible effect; they reflected a Zapatismo grown somewhat desperate, down-at-heel, and at the same time worldly-wise. The proud, intransigent demands of 1914 could no longer be sustained. But the business of backing down, compromising and politicking was wearisome; it no doubt contributed to Zapata's 'dark, crabbed, irascible' mood; it also produced rifts and arguments between protagonists of different strategies: compromise with Carranza, alliance with the Felicistas, or continued, splen-did isolation.[336] By 1918, Zapata was prepared to stomach the first: he offered submission in return for local control of Morelos – a deal similar to that sought by Contreras in the Laguna, but which involved an abandonment of Zapatista claims to national *agrarismo*. Carranza, however, did not respond. In the same year the Plan of Ayala, the old shibboleth, was quietly superseded by a bland, general appeal, designed to unite all dissident groups and regions in a common front against the government.[337]

The most significant and realistic of the several strategies mooted by the Zapatistas was that of Gildardo Magaña – an outsider, a young, educated liberal from Zamora (Mich.), whose anti-Porfirian stand had taken him to Morelos in 1911. Through the middle years of the revolution Magaña had operated, in Morelos and the north, as one of that breed of secretaries, advisers, brokers and polemicists which habitually surrounded successful caudillos. But unlike many of that breed, Magaña placed peace, conciliation and principle before personal ambition. Emerging as Zapata's key adviser after 1916, he was designated leader of the movement in the crisis following Zapata's death.[338] Magaña discerned the best way forward: one which avoided abject surrender, heroic self-immolation, or flimsy, futile alliances with alien rebellions. Rather, he argued, Zapatismo should seek allies within the national revolution, establishing contact with potentially sympathetic Carrancistas, who were not *adictos* of the president, and whose political lives might prove longer. Thus, as the fighting continued – if more scrappily and sporadically than before – Magaña skilfully lined up allies, in particular the political heir-apparent, Alvaro Obregón. When the Carrancista press applauded Zapata's death, papers sympathetic to Obregón were notably more restrained.[339] Like rebels elsewhere, Magaña and the Zapatistas waited on national events, anticipating an upheaval from which they might draw advantage.

When such an upheaval occurred, in 1920, it enabled a host of veteran revolutionaries to achieve some sort of *modus vivendi* with the national regime. Weary of fighting and reduced in numbers, they conceded to the government on terms they would have instantly rejected five years before; but the government, in turn, had to recognise revolutionary demands, not least in the sphere of agrarian reform. The compromise thus achieved was ambivalent and unstable; yet it was at least grounded on the broad, shared assumption that a revolutionary regime was in power, committed to a variety of reforms. The revolution, in other words, created a loose consensus – a consensus, to be sure, which was often fudged, blurred and mythologised – within which Carrancista and Cedillista, Obregonista and Zapatista could co-operate, and conflict. A large chunk of the popular movement thus, eventually, fell into the political mainstream, affecting its direction. Some elements, however, were denied access. In particular, the more independent Indian rebellions were regarded with fear and suspicion, and were repressed more often than co-opted. Here the regime behaved paradoxically: it was eager to integrate the Indian into the nation state and revolutionary polity; but it was happier freeing the meek, deferential Indian from the (alleged) shackles of *caciquismo* and clericalism, than embracing the insurgent Indian of the sierra. The Indian who knew his place could be redeemed, the Indian who did not would first have to be forcibly reminded. 'To nationalise this state', wrote Alvarado from Yucatán, 'the only course is to organise the Indians, creating for them real interests which they owe to the Revolution' – this to be done by propaganda, education, political recruitment and, above all, agrarian reform. 'Giving them lands', Alvarado concluded, 'we bind them to Mexico.'[340]

But Alvarado's shrewd paternalism contrasted with the fierce repression visited upon the Yaquis of his home state of Sonora. And though the Yaquis waged the most important Indian rebellion of the period, they were not entirely alone. They were seconded by the Mayo of Sinaloa; they were paralleled by smaller, weaker Indian groups, like the Santa María Indians of the Huasteca Veracruzana, who maintained that region's tradition of popular revolt with fierce independence, even during the years of Pelaecista dominance.[341] But such movements, intensely parochial, inarticulate and remote, elude national and often local histories. Only the Yaquis posed a major problem for the Federal government, as they had in the days of Díaz.

After Villa's defeat in Sonora, many of the Yaqui contingents who had fought for him and Maytorena – notably those of Trujillo and Urbalejo – surrendered to the Carrancistas.[342] To the south, the Carrancistas raised the siege of Navojoa and defeated the Sinaloan Villistas, thus breaking the power of the Mayo Indians and forcing the surrender of their chief, Felipe Bachomo.[343] But the Yaquis presented a more intractable problem. In December 1915, Obregón conferred with the Yaqui chiefs: of the several peace missions undertaken by this tireless revolutionary broker (with Villa in 1914, General Scott in 1915) this was the most difficult and the least successful. Himself the archetype of the progressive, commercial mestizo farmer, Obregón was scarcely sympathetic to the Yaquis' claim to absolute dominion over their extensive ancestral lands; a claim which would have involved the wholesale expulsion of *yori* settlers. To accede to such a demand, Obregón wrote, would be to sanction 'the perpetuation of barbarism . . . even where civilisation had now been implanted' – a retrograde step, 'which would demean the aims of the Revolution, making them malignant where they had been well-meaning.'[344] So, no deal was struck, and, while many of the *manso* Yaquis surrendered, the *broncos* fought on.

By the end of 1915, therefore, the Yaquis represented a powerful, independent force in Sonora, hostile to the Carrancistas in particular, but also to the *yori* in general. There were 6,000, including women and children, at large in the Yaqui Valley, pressing their claim to their tribal lands and receiving covert assistance from Maytorenista deserters; while as far north as Ures and La Colorada the country was 'infested' with roaming Yaqui bands.[345] The situation was hardly new: recruited to fight in a mestizo civil war, the Yaquis again took advantage of the chaos to establish an autonomous military force, as they had in the nineteenth century. And similarly, the government took tough measures, which followed old precedents. Large forces were channeled into Sonora from the south; a draconian Callista decree briefly deprived all Yaquis and Mayos of Mexican citizenship (a ploy never considered, certainly never implemented, with regard to rebels like Zapata or Cedillo).[346] By the early spring of 1916 this policy seemed to be working. The Yaquis took to the mountains where, destitute, they lived off mescal bulbs; and, as the campaign eased up, Carrancista troops were diverted to Chihuahua.[347]

But, like previous lulls in previous Yaqui wars, this was a mere respite. The Yaquis retired to the mountains to regroup; in the late spring they began to launch sorties in the central valleys of the state; by summer they were pushing north again, up to and beyond the Sonora River, which marked the rough limit of their territorial claims.[348] Calles, commanding in Sonora, promised to 'settle the Yaqui question for good' (he was not the first to make such a promise) and he planned the construction of defensive lines running east–west, from the mountains to the Southern Pacific Railroad: Hermosillo–Ures, Torres–La Colorada–Tecoripa, and Ortiz–La Misa–Punta de Agua.[349] Notwithstanding, by the autumn of 1916, Yaqui raiders had reached as far north as Carbo, Pequeira, Cucurpe and Magdalena; an Indian 'reign of terror' reportedly enveloped the villages of the Sierra Madre foothills; and the fall of Merichichi, a trading station half way between Hermosillo and the border, showed that the Yaquis could capture defended townships, despite their shortage of ammunition and their alleged hunger.[350] And, though the general trend of Yaqui activity was northwards, the Yaqui Valley itself and the Southern Pacific south of Guaymas were also seriously affected.[351]

Late in 1916, perhaps short of supplies, perhaps hoping to capitalise on their success, the Yaquis showed a disposition to compromise. Some *broncos*, promised food, clothes and land, surrendered to the government; Calles drew up plans for Yaqui reservations in the lower reaches of the valley; a bold Carrancista general, ignorant of history, proclaimed the Yaqui war at an end.[352] But in the summer of 1917 the fragile peace was shattered again and the amnestied Yaquis – following the seasonal cycle of these years – rebelled, burned their settlements and prompted Calles to promise severe retribution.[353] The old practices revived: the Yaquis pursued their guerrilla tactics; the government impressed vagrants into the army (few volunteered to fight the Yaquis) and required travellers venturing into the disaffected areas to carry passes.[354] So it continued into 1918, when an American observer – comparing the Yaqui to the Riff War in Morocco – noted the ineptitude of the Carrancistas, and the combined valour and cruelty of the Indians.[355] By 1920, with another agreement scheduled, the Yaqui question became bound up with the contentious issue of Federal–Sonoran relations and the related presidential succession (of which more anon).[356] The result was another, longer, but illusory period of peace. In 1926, the old duel was resumed, with Calles now in the presidential chair. Congress voted a million pesos to quieten the Yaquis 'forever'; deportations were resumed, after the style of Torres and Díaz; but now planes could hunt the Yaquis into the hills and strafe their villages.[357] This time, the repression proved to be permanent.

During, and even beyond, the decade of revolution, the Yaqui revolt showed the stamina characteristic of popular, agrarian movements; but if, in this important respect, it resembled (say) Zapatismo, it was in other respects distinct, and peculiarly resistant to peaceful settlement. Though there were cases of individual land grants (like those of 1916), the Yaquis would not be so readily appreased as other agrarian rebels; conversely, the government was less ready to appease. The Yaquis' cultural separateness and lively sense of self-identity distanced them from the national political arena, and made them resistant to the promises, appeals and bargains traded within it; they had (unlike Zapata) been unmoved by the American occupation of Veracruz, and they had not heard of Carranza's 1915 agrarian decree.[358] Though their struggle merged with that of mestizo revolutionaries (and many Yaquis, uprooting themselves from home, became the mobile janissaries of Sonoran generals) their protest was fundamentally traditional, built on the examples of Cajeme and Tetabiate, led by indigenous leadership, and dedicated to the complete recovery and untrammelled enjoyment of their old tribal patrimony. These elements of separateness and utopianism – shared, to a lesser degree, by other popular movements – made compromise difficult; and there could be no question of the mestizo revolutionaries fully conceding Yaqui claims, dispossessing *yori* farmers, and conniving at the triumph of 'barbarism' over 'civilisation' which Obregón deplored. There was no place for independent tribal enclaves – as opposed to North American style Indian reservations – within the new revolutionary state; hence the Yaquis would have to be bludgeoned into submission, forcibly integrated into the Mexican nation, of which they were not yet truly members.[359] Only after miliary submission could the Yaquis expect – or could they themselves contemplate – the rewards of deference: agrarian reform mediated through the revolutionary state, a very partial restoration of their lands, the assimilation of bits of their culture into the great folkloric jamboree of revolutionary *indigenismo*.[360] In this, the Yaquis represented the extreme case of a more general, popular surrender.

THE PROBLEM OF ORDER: 3 FELICISMO

In addition to these veteran popular movements, Carranza's regime also faced serious 'Felicista' rebellions, which cut a swathe down through Veracruz to Oaxaca and Chiapas, encroaching on Puebla and Tabasco, and jeopardising communiciations between the central plateau and both the Gulf coast and the Yucatán peninsula. Here, in regions where the classic agrarian revolt had never flourished, provincial sentiment had fuelled the Juchiteco rebellion, the troubles in Chiapas, the campaigns of the Oaxaqueño *serranos*. The descent of

the Constitutionalists in 1914 greatly amplified this provincialism; furthermore, it directed provincial hostility away from Porfirian centralisation
towards the new, revolutionary version, which shared features of the old, but
which operated on different lines, exerted different kinds of pressure, and
selected different victims.[361] This outraged provincialism – now a specifically
anti-revolutionary provincialism – was at the heart of a loose congeries of
rebellions collectively termed Felicismo. Yet, like so many portmanteau
labels, this was applied *ex post facto*, that is, after most of its components were
already in being, or at least in formation. Félix Díaz no more created Felicismo
than Pascual Orozco did Orozquismo; both, rather, lent their name and
leadership (Orozco rather more decisively) to rebellious movements that were
already under way, impelled by local political forces.

The defensive revolts of 1914 – the major states' rights movements of
Oaxaca, Tabasco, Chiapas and Yucatán, the lesser landlord rebellions of
Veracruz, Puebla and elsewhere – met with mixed results. The Carrancistas
fought long and hard to control Oaxaca; they retained Yucatán more easily,
though the old elite still displayed a 'bitter enmity' and a 'spirit of antagonistic
aloofness' towards the new, *norteño* regime; after initial success, much of
Tabasco and yet more of Chiapas slipped from their grasp.[362] The landlord
rebels – Armenta, Peláez, Gabay, Cástulo Pérez – were no easier to subdue.
Despite their common antipathy to Carrancismo, however, the rebels of the
south lacked unified leadership or a joint programme. These deficiencies Félix
Díaz undertook to fill in 1916; but to grasp how this came about, we must
briefly go back to 1914 and the fall of Huerta; and make a rapid digression via
Veracruz and Barcelona, Berlin and El Paso, New York, New Orleans and
Havana. With the triumph of Constitutionalism, a crop of illustrious exiles –
generals, governors, ministers, bishops – headed for Europe and the US.[363]
Huerta himself settled in Spain. When the victorious revolutionaries fell out
among themselves, the *émigré* community took note and began to make plans.
In the US, in particular – in San Antonio, El Paso, Los Angeles and New
Orleans – frustrated *políticos*, defeated generals and dispossessed landlords
met, conspired, hoped and dreamed, churning out protests, plans and
polemics, all under the watchful eye of Mexican and American intelligence.[364]
Apart from naked ambition, of which there was plenty, or disinterested
patriotism, of which there was some, the *émigrés* had pressing reasons for
seeking a return to Mexico: many of them – army officers or officials – were
unemployed and destitute, in a 'pitiable' state, and ready to consider 'any kind
of adventure' which offered hope of improvement.[365]

Many of the names and nefarious activities involved can be passed over,
since their impact on events south of the border was minimal. But in
1915–16, two prominent *émigrés* hatched plots of greater significance. The
first, centring on Victoriano Huerta, received sufficient attention from both
contemporaries and later historians (who have again succumbed to the lure of

German intrigue). Though it made its contribution to border anxiety and had fatal consequences for some of its participants, this plot came to nothing. The second, involving Félix Díaz, was to have greater consequences for the revolution; and, since our conceern lies here (rather than with events or non-events in the Wilhelmstrasse, the bars of El Paso, or the bugged hotel rooms of New York) we shall deal cursorily with the first, before proceeding to the second.

In the spring of 1915, as Villa engaged Obregón in the battles of the Bajío, Victoriano Huerta took ship from Spain to the US and made his way – with considerable publicity – from New York to El Paso. There he assumed the central role in an *émigré* plan to make a counter-revolution in Mexico.[366] Some have argued that German intrigue lay behind this plan, as it did behind Villa's Columbus attack.[367] While it may be that the German military flirted with a Huertista liaison (again, the German Ambassador to the US did not), this liaison was not consummated. Much of the evidence for this thesis derives from the autobiography of Franz von Rintelen (the 'Dark Invader'), a work more picaresque than reliable, in which exaggeration of the hero's exploits necessarily involves an exaggeration of German influence.[368] Assertions that German officials met frequently with Huerta in the US, and that German cash and munitions were supplied in large quantities have not been substantiated; the US records reveal no evidence to this effect.[369] It is also worth noting that the German Foreign Office showed little interest in the closely related revanchist project put to them by Gonzalo Enrile (Orozco's old ally) in 1916.[370]

It is clear, however, that the Mexican *émigrés*, once the holders of power and property in Mexico, latched on to Huerta in 1915 as they had in 1913. Again, he was the strong man promising salvation. The *émigrés* included old Científicos like Creel, ex-Huertista Ministers like Querido Moheno and the Catholic Gamboa, Orozquistas (including Pascual Orozco himself, a key figure), and many ex-Federal officers who, no doubt, recalled the days of army supremacy with nostalgia.[371] As in 1913–14, however, Huerta could not deliver the goods. American agents kept a close watch on his movements and meetings; late in June 1915, as he met with Orozco in New Mexico prior to their planned invasion of Mexico, the plotters were arrested. Orozco escaped, remained at large for two months, and was finally tracked down and shot in Texas; thus ended the career of the first major, popular caudillo of the revolution.[372] Huerta survived him five months, awaiting trial in detention at Fort Bliss, increasingly drunk, morose, and sick. In January 1916 he underwent two operations and died – poisoned by the Americans, some said, though the accumulated ravages of jaundice, gallstones and cirrhosis were explanation enough.[373] Huerta was buried alongside Orozco in Concordia cemetery, which thus brought together two central figures of the Mexican Revolution, successively enemies and allies: the pioneer, *serrano* rebel and the self-appointed restorer of Porfirian stability; both, in their ways, rough, unsophisticated men, lacking the political guile which, for success and survival in the Revolution, had to supplement military valour.

The other prominent emigré, more guileful and less valorous, was Félix Díaz who, unlike Huerta, made it to Mexico and became a more significant factor in the last years of the Revolution than is often supposed.[374] Unlike Huerta, too, he had a territorial base to make for (the state of Oaxaca) and he was more favoured by the turn of events south of the border. While Villa and Obregón were slugging it out, the chances of a third party making headway, of recruiting dissident rebels or conservatives, were limited; but with the defeat of Villa and the disintegration of his movement, new alternatives opened up, especially as it became clear that Carranza's popularity was low and his control of the country patchy. Villa's ex-Federal allies were thought to hanker after a more congenial, conservative leader; and their services were now available.[375] The decline of Villismo, therefore quickened rather than depressed *emigré* hopes: 'as soon as Villa began to have difficulty beating Obregón', noted an observer in the *emigré* capital of El Paso, 'all the opposition parties around here at once began to look up and get busy'.[376] Huerta, gaoled and dying, was in no position to take advantage of these developments, but Félix Díaz was.

Díaz's personal history had touched the grander story of the Revolution at several points. A career soldier, he had served as Inspector-General of Police (1904–11), in which capacity he had helped snuff out the initial Maderista revolts of 1910; for a matter of weeks he served as governor of Oaxaca, before quitting political life in the summer of 1911. Next year he chanced a rebellion at Veracruz, which was put down; and in 1913 he collaborated in Reyes' coup *manqué*, looked to have the presidency lined up, but lost out to Huerta, who had Díaz driven into exile late in that year. He followed a familiar *emigré* route: Havana, New York, New Orleans. When the Huerta conspiracy got under way, Díaz, not surprisingly, would have none of it; he also had no time for German liaisons.[377] Now, with the failure of Huerta and Orozco, Díaz and his cronies (they included Gamboa and the ex-Governor of Veracruz, Gaudencio de la Llave) planned a descent on the southern Gulf coast, where they could link up with partisans in Veracruz and Oaxaca.[378]

So, six weeks after Huerta's death, Díaz set sail from Galveston, making for southern Veracruz. Like his previous efforts, this *pronunciamiento* soon ran into problems. The filibusters' boat foundered as it crossed the Gulf and they were forced to swim ashore barely south of the Texas/Tamaulipas border.[379] Hungry and thirsty, their box of decrees and documents lost at sea, they were arrested and taken to Monterrey, where they narrowly escaped identification by the Carrancista authorities. But they lied their way out of trouble and made for Mexico City. The objective was still the south, where ex-Federal rebels and the sovereign state of Oaxaca were in arms against Carranza, and where the name of Díaz still carried weight and excited hope.[380] After a tortuous journey from the capital, Díaz linked up with Almazán, Higinio Aguilar, and the Oaxaqueño authorities at their Tlaxiaco headquarters in the summer of 1916. He now led some 3,000 armed men, and planned a descent on the valley and city of Oaxaca, as *serrano* forces had attempted in previous years. But the *serranos* were cautious about committing themselves to Díaz: times were hard, they could not provide supplies (though they would trade food for guns), and they made it clear they would resist sequestrations. 'Respect for the rights of others', as a witty Felicista put it, parodying Juárez's famous slogan, 'has us dying of hunger.'[381] Worse was to come. The Felicistas were beaten in several encounters with government forces, who now began to pick off the *serrano* garrisons, and Díaz decided to head south-east, where he could acquire allies and assert his authority over the rebels of the Isthmus and Chiapas.[382] But the journey through the hot jungle lowlands was a disaster: the Felicistas were reduced to eating dead horses and monkey meat; and of 3,000 men, only 100 reached the temperate, safer highlands of Chiapas.[383] The Carrancista press gleefully announced the annihilation of Felicismo, and both Díaz and Almazán were reported to have crossed to Guatemala. This was true of Almazán who, stricken with disease, made his way to New Orleans, then back to northern Mexico.[384] But Díaz found shelter with the Chiapas rebels who, in 1917, were on the offensive; he was active on the Chiapas/Tabasco border in the spring of 1917; and he returned to lead sizeable forces in Oaxaca and Veracruz later in the year.[385]

From 1916 to 1920, it was Díaz's prime task and partial achievement to provide leadership, co-ordination, and respectability to a host of disparate rebel movements in southern Mexico: in this respect he sought to do what Carranza had done in the north in 1913–14. Lacking, as he did, any personal military following (or any great military talents) Díaz nevertheless conferred three advantages on the heterogeneous southern rebellions: a political programme, an international connection, and – most tenuous of all – integration into a national movement. The Felicista programme, rehearsed in the Plan of Tierra Colorada (February 1916) and other pronouncements, was one of classical liberalism, which endorsed the 1857 Constitution – 'the symbolic and sacred code which saved the Republic in its struggle with the monarchy and the homeland in its struggle with foreign invasion' – and repudiated the new Carrancista Constitution of 1917.[386] It maintained that constitutional legality had terminated not in February 1913, with the ouster of Madero (Carranza's old claim, which Díaz, as co-architect of that coup, could hardly repeat), but rather in October 1913, with Huerta's dissolution of Congress; thus as liberals and patriots, the Felicistas sought to restore the constitutional order. They promised something for everyone: individual rights and guarantees; toleration for the Church; the reconstitution of the Federal Army (ex-Federals were a prime target of Felicista propaganda); fair and fraternal treatment for the luckless Spaniards, who had been 'iniquitously harassed and

criminally abused'. This reassuring, liberal conservative approach, appealing to the propertied, Porfirian elements in society, was suggested in the
official title of the Felicista forces – the 'National Reorganizing Army' – and
summed up in the Felicista motto, 'Paz y Justicia.'[387]

But there was more to it than this. First, on the international plane,
ideology and interest both inclined the Felicistas towards the Allied cause:
they denounced the Carranza regime as pro-German and plangently
addressed the 'Governments of the Allied Nations in the war which they
sustain to save the most sublime interests of Humanity against the Central
European Empires.'[388] The Europhile (which generally meant Anglo- and
Francophile) sentiments of the Porfirian elite, forged by education, travel
and commercial association, were thus sharpened by the ostensible pro-
German stance of the Carrancistas and this polarity (paralleled elsewhere in
Latin America) created an additional, if secondary, division between Felicismo and Carrancismo, between the old, liberal oligarchs and the new,
nationalist parvenus, between civilians and soldiers.[389] This international
alignment, however, merely reinforced the primary division, which derived
from domestic issues; issues which, in turn, were neither neatly ideological,
nor clearly encapsulated in rival programmes. The battle between Felicismo
and Carrancismo in other words, was fierce and protracted, eliciting strong
loyalties on both sides; it had its ideological dimension, in which the rival
claims of conservative liberalism and jacobin nationalism, of the 1857 and
1917 Constitutions, were fought over; but, as so often in the Revolution,
ideology masked material and local interests. It was not therefore irrelevant;
it could even attain a certain 'relative autonomy' of these interests; but it
was not the prime mover, and any analysis of Felicismo must match the
national programmes and pronouncements with local personnel and
practice.

The Felicistas, for example, gave an explicit, detailed commitment to
agrarian reform.[390] Their programmes provided for the restitution of despoiled village lands; the formation of agricultural colonies of revolutionary
veterans; the expropriation of hacienda land in response to popular need; the
legal protection of sharecroppers; appropriate taxation of large estates; and
government action to further irrigation projects. True, they ruled out
unconstitutional confiscations and land seizures: but in this (and much else)
the Carrancista leadership thought no differently.[391] Apart, perhaps, from
its greater stress on constitutionality – which accorded with the whole ethos
of Felicismo – this programme did not differ radically from Carranza's, following his belated recognition of the agrarian problem. It demonstrated yet
again (as did the agrarian proposals of the Mexican Peace Assembly) that
manifesto agrarianism was now *de rigueur*; that any political appeal had to
pay lip-service to this issue, which the Revolution had shown to be central
to Mexican politics.[392] The sameness of Felicista and Carrancista (formal)

agrarian commitments serves as a warning against too stark a separation of the two factions, as regards explicit ideology and policy.

With respect to agrarian reform, the Felicistas also pitched a negative appeal, echoing Zapata's, which could not but elicit sympathy, and perhaps support. 'As regards the division of the land', declared a manifesto of September 1917, the Carrancistas 'have already begun to divide it up among themselves.'[393] This shaft was loosed off amid a flight of similar accusations, aimed at Carrancista graft, corruption and profiteering. 'The Carrancista revolution', it declared, 'has no other objective than the enrichment of its chiefs'; the Carrancistas had 'taken possession of the country as if it were an individual patrimony, belonging to them, with the absolute exclusion of all Mexicans and foreigners who are not Carrancistas'; and their 'agrarian promises have been nothing more than the bait whereby the popular masses were induced to help them to victory' – since which time, 'the urgent and patriotic solution of this important problem' had been forgotten.[394] Hence the sad state of the country: the people hungry, factories ruined, railways destroyed, fields barren, homes in mourning, life cheap, rights and liberties lost, foreign credit exhausted, banks robbed, commerce pillaged or monopolised by Carrancista crooks. There was justice in these accusations; they accorded with contemporary Zapatista propaganda; and they were presumably appreciated by those who still bothered to read political manifestoes.[395] They were echoed, too, by other Felicistas: Peláez in the Huasteca, Meixueiro and Dávila in Oaxaca, José Isabel Robles, one-time Villista, who now fought against Carranza under a different banner, in a different region.[396]

But in Felicismo, as in other movements, personnel and practice counted for more than formal statements. For all its balanced reformism and commitment to *agrarismo*, Felicismo mobilised many adherents of the old regime: it was the last hope (short of colonising Carrancismo) of those who had grown fat under Díaz, and sought salvation with Reyes, de la Barra and Huerta. Whether their new combination of constitutionalism and social reform represented cynical opportunism or genuine conversion it is impossible to say. But the old Porfirians were there, backing Porfirio's nephew inside Mexico and abroad. Landowners and Federals were prominent in the 'National Reorganizing Army'; General Luis Medina Barrón (one-time scourge of the Yaquis, defender of Zacatecas and darling of the conservatives) now commanded the 'Félix Díaz Brigade'; General Aureliano Blanquet, a key figure in the ouster and death of Madero, travelled from Cuba to join Díaz, the two plotters of 1913 coincidentally meeting at the Hacienda Ciudadela, on the Veracruz coast.[397] And there were others of similar pedigree, allies of Díaz from the start of his campaign: the brother of the bishop of Sonora, who perished in a *barranca* on the hard march into Chiapas; the two sons of Mucio Martínez, the old cacique of Puebla, who were among Díaz's closest companions.[398] Abroad, the roster of Felicista agents, apologists and well-wishers, active in both the US and

Europe, read like a *Who's Who* of the Porfiriato: more generals, like Mondragón
and Eugenio Rascón (Madero's Minister of War); Rodolfo, son of Bernardo
Reyes (and a Huertista Minister); García Naranjo, Manuel Calero, and Jesús
Flores Magón (all Huertista Ministers); the Spanish millionaire Iñigo Noriega
and the last Huertista Governor of the Federal District, Eduardo Iturbide;
Científicos like Emilio Rabasa, Landa y Escandón and Pimentel y Fagoaga.[399]

These relics of the old regime looked to Díaz – a smart *político*, patriotic,
nationally conscious and, above all, *presidenciable* – to create a broad movement
capable of challenging and ousting the insecure Carranza regime. Díaz set to
work with a will: by the end of 1918 the 'National Reorganizing Army'
boasted ten divisions, with a complete hierarchy of officers; Felicista commanders had been appointed for most states of the Federation.[400] But much of this
– the chain of command, the manifestoes, the *émigré* propaganda – was mere
paper; and reality was less impressive.[401] Though there were Felicista
movements in northern Mexico, their impact was minimal: Almazán and
Caraveo caused a ripple in Nuevo León; Evaristo Pérez sank without trace in
Chihuahua.[402] The Felicista contingents active elsewhere, if not outright
fictions, were often long-established rebels, at odds with Carranza, conveniently dubbed 'Felicista' with or without their consent: Mariscal in Guerrero or
Cíntora in Michoacán, both of whom were on the way down anyway.[403] Even
Peláez, who was closer to Díaz, was no Felicista *adicto*.[404] In terms of numbers
and activity, the real Felicista heartland lay in Veracruz and Oaxaca, with
powerful associated allies in Tabasco, Chiapas and Puebla.[405] Here Díaz
commanded – not altogether fictionally – forces that were extensive and
formidable, capable of sustaining a guerrilla war as tenaciously as many
popular rebels. And an analysis of these forces suggests that Felicismo was not
simply, or even primarily, a movement of disaffected conservatives, hostile to
Carrancista social radicalism and typified by the suave, articulate *émigrés* of
Paris, New Orleans and Los Angeles.

For one thing, Felicismo was much more variegated – and hence fissiparous.
It embraced landlord caudillos like Peláez, Cástulo Pérez (Minatitlán) and the
Gabay brothers (Huatusco); Federals like Medina Barrón, Blanquet, Higinio
Aguilar, Rafael Eguía Liz; *serrano* caciques like Meixueiro and Pineda; lowland
caciques like Santibáñez; ex-Orozquistas like Caraveo, Almazán and (briefly)
Canuto Reyes; ex-Villistas like Robles; perennial local rebels like Raúl Ruiz,
rustler/bandits (Pascual Casarín), and Indians (Gerónimo Dávalos). Maintain-
ing co-ordination among these forces was a major problem, with which Díaz
wrestled persistently, with only modest success; missions like that of General
Gaudencio de la Llave, who in 1917 was ordered to 'get the different bands of
rebels to work together more' were virtually impossible.[406] The tough, old
Federal, Aguilar habitually disobeyed, skirmished with fellow-Felicistas like
Pedro Gabay, and finally drifted back into the Zapatista camp; Raúl Ruiz
feuded with Pascual Casarín, and probably contributed to Casarín's defection

to the Carrancistas; Santibáñez had Eguía Liz and his son shot, in return for which Díaz arranged the court-martial and execution of Santibáñez, his brother and top aide.[407] Even Peláez, who was in close touch with Díaz and whose rebellion displayed classic Felicista features, proved to be a lukewarm and ultimately inconstant ally. Meanwhile, as military and political upheaval afflicted the south, the old scourge of banditry reappeared with renewed vigour. Bandits – whom observers carefully distinguished from 'the regular rebels' – molested the river traffic of southern Veracruz, extorted payment from the Misantla coffee pickers, raided the railways, plantations and ranches of Chiapas.[408] To be sure, the boundary between Felicismo and banditry was blurred; but the Felicistas were not, as is sometimes suggested, simonpure bandits, who preyed professionally on local people; on the contrary, they elicited local support and were anxious to distance themselves from such predators. Felicistas like Cástulo Pérez of Minatitlán took drastic measures to rid their territory of brigands.

From the local, Mexican – as opposed to the elevated, international – perspective, therefore, Felicismo shared a common *modus operandi* with popular movements like Zapatismo. But its *raison d'être* differed, necessarily, since it arose in different regions at a different time. Beneath the froth of official pronouncements, paper commands and *émigré* propaganda, Felicismo drew on a reservoir of popular support, without which it could not have sustained its activities over so long a time and across so wide an area. The common denominator which loosely united the varied Felicista forces – and for which the proclaimed adherence to the 1857 Constitution was a kind of political shorthand – was a rejection of alien, northern interlopers (whose generals were callous and whose troops ill-behaved) and an assertion of local opposition and resistance. Indeed, this confrontation between north and south was evident in the very bosom of Carrancismo: for many northerners, typified by the proconsuls, wanted to herd the recalcitrant south into the revolutionary fold without delay; while southerners, even those enjoying a foothold in the Carrancista establishment, denounced the abuses of the military, their disregard for local rights and property, their profiteering (goods were extorted from the south and shipped north), and their intention of converting imposed, military commands into imposed constitutional governorships.[409] In Chiapas, this conflict was epitomised by the struggle between the appeasing Chiapaneca Governor, Villanueva, and the adamantine Sonoran commander, Alvarado.[410]

But if, in contrast to Zapatismo, and despite its ideological facade, Felicismo was fuelled by provincialism, rather than agrarianism (or anything else), and was often captained by men of property and status, it could still count on popular support. Peláez's forces 'somewhat resemble[d] a "Home Guard" working their little farms and reporting for immediate duty when called to "arms" – 'arms', because less than half Peláez's 6,000 available men had guns, the rest had only machetes.[411] Like Peláez, other Felicista leaders were propertied: Armenta was a Misantla coffee planter, the Gabay brothers, Pedro and Salvador, came from a 'good Veracruz family' (though it seems they had early revolutionary connections); Cástulo Pérez was a rancher (his cousin, too, was in arms in the Minatitlán region); while in Chiapas, as already noted, the irruption of the Carrancistas provoked a rebel movement of 'ranchowners and other citizens of property [who] took to the field in self-defence' and remained there until 1920.[412] Despite the leadership, it is mistaken to regard these rebellions simply as species of counter-revolutionary resistance to Carrancista radicalism. Certainly the conflict was depicted in these terms in the press and Carrancista manifestoes; Salvador Alvarado delighted in the declaration of the Chiapas Indian delegation which came 'saying that they are ready to do anything for their *Tata* Carranza, who has freed them from the slavery in which they have always lived'.[413] But Carrancista rule was often less emancipatory than predatory: reforms were outnumbered by extortions, and the latter were certainly more evident to the local population, both rich and poor. It is clear, too, that it was the initial Constitutionalist invasion (antedating any definite social reform) which provided the spur to provincial resistance in the south; that, with the significant exception of Yucatán, subsequent Constitutionalist rule provoked rather than mollified the population; and that resistance was broadly based, not confined to the elite.[414] Meixueiro could whistle up an army of *serranos* without having to dragoon the peons off his estates; and the *serranos* (witness their cool reception of Díaz in 1916) were nobody's puppets.

Perhaps the rank-and-file followers of Felicismo would have done better to collaborate with the progressive northern invaders against their own native exploiters (as some, like the Ixtepejanos did). But more was at stake than calculable material interest: provincial sentiment, attachment to the *patria chica*, concern for local customs and mores (however backward, obscurantist and hierarchical) were all offended by the Carrancista incursion. And if these values are to be discounted – as the impedimenta of 'false consciousness', perhaps – then the same argument and conclusion could apply in the case of Zapatismo or the Yaquis: *viz.*, that rational material self-interest, stripped of normative encumbrances, demanded collaboration with, not resistance to, Mexico's new rulers. It should finally be added that the southerners' consciousness was not altogether 'false' even as regards material self-interest. Landlords and caciques were not the sole victims of Carrancismo, which brought severe privations and persecution for the common people too (outside Yucatán). In Chiapas, we have noted, *finquero* and *campesino* had certain shared, material interests; in Oaxaca, agrarian conflict pitted village against village more than village against *hacendado* (it was no coincidence that Zaachila, 'one of the few large valley towns chronically short of land' was also one of the few 'revolutionary' communities).[415]

And the bonds uniting landlord and *campesino*, cacique and client were often strengthened by Carrancista abuses: by the corruption of commanders like Aguilar, Millán and Portas in Veracruz; by speculation in foodstuffs on the Isthmus; by the depredations committed by supposed railway escorts; by the military's seizure of municipal funds (at Chicontepec, Ver.).[416] As in Morelos, the Carrancistas took tough measures against rebels, real and supposed. Salvador Alvarado was a model commander, a wholesome contrast to military tyrants like the Veracruzano, Guadalupe Sánchez; yet – perhaps inevitably in the circumstances – his expedition through the troubled Isthmus in 1917 resembled Sherman's progress through the defeated south in 1864. True, Alvarado delighted in emancipating enslaved Indians; but, at the same time, as towns and haciendas were occupied by his forces, the civilian population was reported as having 'received worse treatment than at the hands of the rebels', some of them being driven to flee from their homes, abandoning their crops.[417] The following year, Alvarado's 'reconcentration program, more than any other single action of the revolution, destroyed the economy of Chiapas and brought starvation to the state'.[418] It was not surprising that Felicista rebels in the south included leaders like Gerónimo Dávalos, an illiterate Indian, 'driven to become a rebel by [the] Carranza government'.[419] Impeccably Carrancista sources concurred: in May 1916 the pre-eminent Veracruzano revolutionary, Carranza's son-in-law, Cándido Aguilar, wrote to his old colleague Agustín Millán, who was about to assume military command in Veracruz; admitting that, in many of the richest parts of the state, 'reaction and banditry reign in alliance', he stressed that armed resistance to the government obeyed different motives. 'Certainly', he argued,[420]

there are in our state many groups up in arms who are quite clearly delineated as reactionaries, but there are also not a few who have rebelled out of self-preservation, goaded by the loss of their interests (I do not refer to the reactionaries) and by virtue of the deadly reprisals or infamous robberies of the military chiefs, who have become caciques even more hated than the *jefes políticos* of the Porfirian dictatorship.

Local revolutionary leadership, Aguilar therefore stressed, must be held responsible for the rash of (Felicista) revolts agitating Veracruz: 'honourable revolutionaries are very few, and if we do not eliminate our *compañeros* who only dream of satisfying their personal ambitions, they will be responsible for the debacle which the Revolution will suffer'.[421]

The classic Felicista revolts of 1916–20 were thus extensions of the defensive movements of 1914–15, mounted in opposition less to Carrancista social radicalism than to Carrancista military invasion and political oppression; hence they bear comparison with the popular *serrano* rebellions of the earlier Revolution.[422] They elicited popular support within a defined territory, which they sought to preserve independent of Carrancista centralisation: Peláez who could count on an existing clientelist network in the Huasteca;

Gabay, who bolstered his popularity around Huatusco with occasional hand-outs; Pérez, whose plantation near Minatitlán served as headquarters, where his men returned to stack their rifles and work during interludes in the fighting.[423] These, along with Ruiz, Dávalos, Pineda, Martínez, all local men, were the backbone of Felicismo; outsiders like Almazán and Robles, for all their revolutionary experience, achieved little success in the south.[424] The Felicista *modus operandi* – closely akin to that of the classic popular movements – may be illustrated by taking an example which, though exceptional in some respects, was typical in many more: the rebellion of Peláez in the Huasteca, the origins of which have already been touched upon.[425]

In 1914, as the rebellion began, the oil companies were busy conciliating Carrancismo (and Villismo); there was no question of them initiating the revolt and, as it gathered strength in 1915, they had to come to terms with it.[426] Peláez's relations with the companies therefore developed in the same fashion as many rebel–company arrangements: as *de facto* commander, Peláez levied taxes; and the companies, appreciative of an orderly regime, paid up, albeit under protest. Similar relationships had been established previously with Carrancista commanders like Aguilar and Caballero. The companies did not finance revolutionary outbreaks; rather, successful revolutionaries won the right to extract cash from the companies. Lesser companies, meanwhile, were forging links with lesser caudillos. Casarín exacted regular tolls from the landlords of Los Tuxtlas, offering protection in return for pay ('he is now friendly to the plantation', reported an American manager, 'but it has cost a lot of money'); Cástulo Pérez collaborated with the plantations east of Acayucán; while the Motzorongo estate made monthly payments of 400 pesos to Panuncio Martínez; Ponciano Vázquez – like all these, a Felicista – charged a regular 6% property tax to support his forces.[427] The existence of such working arrangements was, in the eyes of property-owners at least, one of the key factors differentiating 'rebels', who were orderly and regular in their demands, from 'bandits', who were violent and arbitrary. But even where the relationship was regularised, the rebel did not therefore become a mercenary, with its connotations of dependence and obedience. Peláez commanded junior officers who scarcely behaved as mercenaries should towards their employers.[428] And Peláez himself squeezed the companies for all he could get. By early 1917 he was taking 10,000 pesos a month off each of the two biggest operators, the Aguila and Huasteca Companies; a year later, facing a Carrancista offensive, he demanded 30,000 from the latter. This was hardly the conduct of a faithful retainer; nor was the company's response that of an all-powerful sponsor: its manager would 'confer with Peláez and resist [his] demands to a point consistent with [the] safety [of its] interests'.[429]

In this respect, Peláez's case was exceptional only as regards the duration of the arrangement and the economic, political and strategic significance of his financial backers. This significance was enhanced after 1917, as Carrancista plans to tax and regulate the oil industry came to fruition, and American entry into the World War brought growing fears of German sabotage in the Mexican oil-fields.[430] Now, the local hegemony of Peláez offered not only security and order, but also protection from Carrancista economic nationalism and German threats. Peláez realised this well enough and his political statements – in tune with Felicista thinking – denounced the expropriatory aspects of the new Constitution and asserted his commitment to liberal values and to the Allied cause.[431] The companies, for their part, warmed to Peláez, whom they now regarded less as a necessary evil and more as a positive asset in their struggle against the revolutionary regime, its nationalist reforms, and its supposed German sympathies; hence, though their liaison with Peláez created an 'anomalous situation', it was nevertheless 'in every way a situation which should be preserved'.[432] What is more, the metropolitan governments, concerned to protect the Allies' oil supply, were now prepared to go much further – further even than the companies – to keep the oil-fields in friendly hands and prevent destruction by either German or Carrancista sabotage.[433] For neither the first nor last time, grand strategic thinking outstripped local, economic interests in its commitment to imperialist aggression.[434] Thus, the State Department was prepared to let the companies supply arms direct to Peláez (an option which the companies declined); voices within the Department were raised in favour of military intervention; and certainly there existed a contingency plan for American seizure of the oil-fields, to prevent their destruction – a plan in which it was expected that Peláez would collaborate.[435] On the British side, too, some argued that it would be a 'fatal error' to allow Carranza control of the oil-fields, and some flirted with wild ideas of kitting out an *émigré* expedition to help Peláez in his resistance to Carranza.[436]

Such schemes, though intrinsically interesting and potentially momentous, in fact came to nothing. The Americans prepared for intervention in 'an eventuality which they hoped to avoid'; and they managed to avoid it. [437] Neither Carranza, nor the Germans, nor even Peláez, got round to sabotaging the oil-fields, whose output rose throughout these years.[438] The voice of rabid interventionism in the State Department (Canova's) was ignored; at the end of the day, the American records reveal no evidence of direct, official American support for Peláez.[439] The companies themselves had always been more pragmatic; and, true to their traditional policy, they wished neither to commit themselves unequivocally to Peláez, nor to foul their nest irremediably with Carranza. As the manager of the Huasteca Co. told Peláez in February 1918, though he might sympathise with Peláez's cause, 'it would not be right for me to lend him any support either moral or physical'; increased payments were impossible; and 'the moment we considered our relations with him were onerous to us, we would discontinue the payment of any money'.[440]

Peláez could have been under few illusions as to the loyalty of his oil company allies. The relationship was entirely conditional and contractual. At that very time, as the Carrancistas mounted an offensive into the Huasteca, the companies' enthusiasm for Peláez cooled, for they now faced increased Pelaecista demands and suffered material damage from Peláez's rearguard actions.[441] Falling back before the Carrancistas, Peláez complained that certain companies were doing nothing to help him, though he 'accepted with pleasure' the idea of collaborating with an American intervention force.[442] The companies, meanwhile, were also paying extraordinary levies to sustain the Carrancista troops (hence Peláez's chagrin); and Lord Cowdray was urging a reluctant Foreign Office to grant recognition to the Carranza regime.[443] The Huasteca campaigns did not end in 1918, and Peláez still had a function to fulfill; but the companies and, more gradually, their metropolitan governments were coming round to favour a deal with Carranza (one in which the financial power of the US could be used to extract favourable terms).[444] The conclusion of the World War and the end of the German threat thus ushered in a phase of diplomatic wrangling, while the spectre of armed intervention receded, and Peláez's utility diminished.[445]

The fortuitous combination of oil and World War invested the Pelaecista rebellion with these grand, politico-strategic implications. And, though the implications were never realised – the oil-wells went on pumping, there was no sabotage, no intervention, no prototype Bay of Pigs – they have tended to distort analysis of Pelaecismo, wrenching it out of context and locating it in a different world of black gold and *grosspolitik*. That world existed, impinged on the Mexican Revolution, and deserves analysis. But the analysis often suggests the limits rather than the extent of its local impact.[446] As regards Pelaecismo (and the same might be said of Irish republicanism or Indian nationalism) its domestic roots were more interesting and revealing than its international ramifications. Globally, Peláez was an expendable pawn; locally, he led one of the strongest, yet typical, southern rebellions, bearing certain comparisons with the classic popular movements of Villa or Zapata. He had a well-defined territory from which he had never strayed: the strip of country inland from the Gulf between Tampico and Tuxpán, from the Pánuco River in the north to Papantla in the south.[447] His forces were drawn entirely from this region (hence their 'Home Guard' character), and they had no contact with up-country rebels like the Cedillos of Valle del Maíz which, though close enough on paper, was sundered from the Huasteca by traditional divisions between highland and lowland, fief and fief.[448]

The Pelaecistas were local men; but it is not clear what kind of local men. Peláez's 'force consists of . . . inhabitants and labourers of the oil-field districts'; and, though it included oil workers, there were (and would have to have been) many others besides.[449] One report, already quoted, depicts the Pelaecista soldiery as *campesinos*, working their 'little farms' between campaigns.[450] Certainly they fought a classic guerrilla war. Facing Carrancista offensives, they fell back for want of arms (company, even British, largesse failed to meet that deficiency); but the Carrancistas' superior fire-power could not guarantee a definitive victory.[451] In early 1918, for example, a big government offensive was launched, which led to the 'silly' claim of General Acosta that Pelaecismo had been annihilated (how many times had similar illicit claims been made about Zapatismo?).[452] But the Pelaecista army simply melted away, returning to farms, villages and oil camps, permitting a series of Carrancista 'victories' and 'advances', then regrouping when the opportunity arose and ammunition was available again. After the big push of 1918, it was noted,[453]

[the] government claim of control of Pelae[cista] territory is true only in that its forces operate at will. No battle has been fought. Peláez has not been defeated nor forced to a general retreat. His forces also operate at will in scattered bands with little opposition, using guerrilla war tactics.

Hence, later in 1918, Peláez's forces swept back, took Pánuco, and even threatened Tampico.[454] Not till 1919 – when, nationally and globally, new factors were at work – did the government make real progress in the Huasteca campaign.[455]

Carrancista operations in this theatre were marked by the same ill-discipline and inefficiency which affected other counter-insurgency campaigns, alienating local people and enabling the enemy repeatedly to escape, regroup and strike back. Government troops in the Huasteca, numbering some 3,000 early in 1918, against Peláez's roughly equivalent force of 'regulars', were a 'ragged lot', many wearing *huaraches* rather than boots, many of them young boys; at times, detachments were reported to be 'unpaid and hungry, demoralised and beyond control'; and, despite the Huasteca's fine pastures, their horses were spent and emaciated.[456] Though the retreating Pelaecistas took it out on company property (in a mild sort of way; but it showed their ambivalent feelings about the hand that fed them), the Carrancistas, sparing the companies, took it out on the villages: Amatlán and San Antonio Chinampa, for example, where they were said to have executed *pacíficos*.[457] And, if such measures bolstered Peláez's local support, the behaviour of some Carrancista commanders (they came and went in swift succession) also gave him aid and comfort.[458] While the travails of counter-insurgency campaigns encouraged extreme caution, even sloth, on their part, the economic opportunities prompted a good deal of fraternisation with the enemy: gun-running (not unknown in Morelos too) flourished and, in one instance, the Carrancista garrison at Huejutla sent a prize fighting cock with a 500 peso bet to participate in a Pelaecista fiesta being held two miles away. Obviously enough, some 'sort of understanding' existed between the two sides, and it was the indifference and demoralisation of the Carrancistas which made it possible.[459] They had no stomach for a fight in these circumstances: the high-mettled revolutionary forces of 1913–14 had become the sullen regular army of

1916–20, engaged not in heroic rebellion, but long drawn out, static repression.

Thus, all the malpractices of the old Federal Army reappeared. Ammunition, for example, could not be sold to the rebels without some pretence of military action, which justified the shortfall: and, as a Carrancista colonel explained, 'to lend colour to this story it was necessary now and then to sacrifice a few of his men'.[460] Connivance between government and rebel forces was well established while Luis Caballero commanded the Carrancista forces in the Huasteca. Caballero was then involved in a fierce contest for the Tamaulipas governorship, and it was common knowledge that electoral defeat would lead to military rebellion; hence it was in his interest to stall the campaign against Peláez, so as not to alienate a potential, neighbouring ally by an excess of aggressive zeal.[461] Carrancista divisions and failings thus perpetuated the struggle. Though by 1919–20 the tempo of the fighting had dropped, this did not indicate a definitive government victory; on the contrary, it reflected rifts within the national administration from which obdurate rebels like Peláez might derive advantage.[462]

Peláez's relations with Félix Díaz and 'official' Felicismo were shaky. He endorsed Díaz's political programme and, in the summer of 1918, welcomed Díaz to his headquarters at Potrero del Llano.[463] But some of his lieutenants, it was said, disdained the Felicista connection; and there was little Díaz could offer Pelaecismo (which was thriving on its own resources) save a veneer of legitimacy. No concerted strategy evolved and, two years later, it served Peláez's purpose to make a complete break with Felicismo.[464] It is nonetheless valid to see Pelaecismo as an illustrative case of the southern rebellions – broadly based, defensive reactions to the northern invasion – which were loosely grouped under the Felicista label. Stretching down from Peláez's fief to southern Veracruz, Puebla, Oaxaca and Chiapas, they presented the Carranza regime with insuperable problems – insuperable in the strict sense, for many were never defeated but politically co-opted after Carranza's fall. Though little confidence can be placed in numerical estimates, the figures are impressive, and borne out by the scale and success of Felicista operations. The *mapaches* of Chiapas numbered at least 2,000, the rebels of Tabasco somewhat less; the Veracruz rebels – including those of Armenta, Cejudo, and others north of the Inter-Oceanic, the Gabay, Galán and Vidal contingents inland from the port of Veracruz, Ruiz and Martínez near Minatitlán, and the Isthmus bands of Pérez, Dávalos and Nájera – totalled 8,000 in 1916 and 15,000 in 1917.[465] Even if such absolute figures are unreliable, it cannot be doubted that the Felicista forces grew in strength between 1916 and 1917, and that in each state they outnumbered government troops (in Veracruz by as much as two to one).[466]

Figures aside, there is ample evidence of the military pressure which the rebels exerted on the precarious Carrancista authorities throughout this large, rich region. By mid-1915 (before Díaz's arrival) Orizaba was virtually besieged and, to the south, 'the entire rural district of the state [of Veracruz] is out of the control of the present government [and] only a few of the important towns and railroads are controlled by the Carrancistas'.[467] Early in 1916, only three of Oaxaca's thirty-one districts were reckoned to be under government control; most of Chiapas and much of Tabasco were imperfectly held.[468] Railway communications were at the rebels' mercy, with recurrent attacks, derailments and robberies; eventually the Carrancistas built blockhouses and applied the same draconian measures as they had in Morelos.[469] Local trade suffered: the coffee industry of Veracruz stagnated and, further south, river traffic was suspended and plantations ceased work, adding to the prevalent unemployment and poverty; in Chiapas, goods travelled in convoys of ox-carts, under military escort.[470] Bad conditions were aggravated by Carrancista repression. The 'small mountainside farmers' of the Orizaba region were driven to rebel against the predatory Carrancistas; over 400 men were recruited by an elderly cacique, who received a ready welcome in the Indian villages; and in response, it was reported, Cándido Aguilar set to burning villages thought to be sympathetic to the rebels.[471] The same happened down near Los Tuxtlas, when the Carrancistas captured a rebel headquarters at Arroyo Largo: the rebels 'following their policy of avoiding contact with the Carrancistas wherever possible retired as soon as the Carrancistas appeared [and] the latter burned the dwelling huts of the peaceful inhabitants of the town, charging them with having helped the rebels'.[472]

With Carrancistas like the 'beardless and bloodthirsty' Guadalupe Sánchez commanding in the state, such abuses were to be expected.[473] But even enlightened commanders, like Alvarado, took harsh measures. Leading an expedition of 7,000 to the Isthmus in 1917, Alvarado imposed an economic blockade of rebel zones, banning all commerce, confiscating all goods emanating from these zones, and outlawing all 'who might be caught in liaison with the rebels, whether concealing them, supplying them with victuals, munitions or information'.[474] Alvarado also applied the *reconcentrado* here and, even more thoroughly, in Chiapas the following year.[475] The results were mixed. By guaranteeing the plantations and promising funds from the full coffers of Yucatán, Alvarado restored a degree of peace and confidence on the Isthmus; men returned to work, the rebels retired to the remoter hill country, and trains chugged from cost to coast unmolested.[476] In Chiapas, the economic cost was greater, the resistance more dogged. The year 1918 ended in the familiar stalemate: 'the government could not pacify the countryside and the rebels could not hold the cities'.[477]

While Tabasco, Oaxaca and the Isthmus gradually grew quieter, the Felicista heartland on the borders of Veracruz, Oaxaca and Puebla remained rebellious. Major towns were threatened, and the 'appalling . . . boldness' of the rebels, noted in 1916, continued until 1918–19.[478] Jalapa, the state

capital of Veracruz, was a favourite target. In the spring of 1916 the forces of
Roberto Cejudo occupied a warehouse on the city outskirts to hold a *baile*; a
year later they entered the city on a foray, terrifying the inhabitants; Cejudo
'took' Jalapa again in March 1918 and a concerted Felicista attack, mounted by
Gabay and Medina Barrón, penetrated to the heart of the city the following
October.[479] Orizaba was similarly beleaguered, from 1915 to 1918; people no
longer dared picnic in the surrounding countryside, the city's power was
intermittently cut off, and rebels raided the outer suburbs.[480] Soledad, the
first stop on the railway inland from Veracruz, fell late in 1916, and the people
of Veracruz itself, hearing the cannon-fire close by, feared that the port might
fall to the Felicista forces 'just beyond the hills'.[481] Certainly there were rebel
leaders, like Blanquet, who favoured a direct attack on the town.[482] Meanwhile, lesser towns continued to fall: Minatitlán to Panuncio Martínez in May
1918, Huatusco to Cejudo and Aguilar two days later, Teocelo to Cejudo in
March 1919.[483]

By then, however, some of the steam had gone out of Felicismo. Death and
defection had taken their toll. Aureliano Blanquet, Huerta's ally in the ouster
of Madero, died within weeks of returning to Mexico from Cuba in 1919:
pursued by Carrancista forces, he was killed falling into a *barranca*, whence his
severed head was taken to be exhibited in Veracruz.[484] In the same encounter
the Felicista General Francisco Alvarez was captured, later to be shot. Soon
after, José Inés Dávila, the secessionist governor of Oaxaca, was run to ground
and executed; his ally Meixueiro reached terms with the government, forcing
Díaz to name new, largely fictitious, Felicista authorities in the state.[485] In
Chiapas, the rebel leadership split, and appalling economic conditions
conspired with Alvarado's campaign to weaken resistance.[486] In 1920,
Gaudencio de la Llave was captured and Ponciano Vázquez killed; Cejudo, the
leading Puebla Felicista, agreed terms with the government.[487] To the south,
a Carrancista gunboat cruised up the Coatzacoalcos River to shell Cástulo
Pérez's headquarters, while Raúl Ruiz, a perennial revolutionary for ten years,
sank without trace and was not heard of again.[488] By then, Félix Díaz's sphere
of operations was reduced to the central Veracruz region controlled by the
well-organised troops of Pedro Gabay. But at the same time, the gaping
divisions within the Carrancista national elite offered the surviving Felicistas
an opportunity to secure peace, and even peace with honour.

THE PROBLEM OF ORDER: 4 BANDITRY AND CRIME

The popular movement remained strong, even in defeat; Felicismo, gathering
to itself the defensive revolts of southern Mexico, constituted a second,
powerful challenge to political stability; the third threat to Carrancista control
came from the endemic banditry which afflicted much of the country and
against which the authorities often seemed powerless. Now, more than ever,

the distinction between rural rebellion and banditry – 'social' and 'unsocial' – is difficult to draw. Not only were Villa and Zapata now considered 'bandits' by the central government; their *modus operandi* was also typically 'bandit', for they now avoided sieges and conventional battles in favour of hit-and-run, even 'terrorist' tactics. If the nature of the armed struggle thus affords a poor criterion for distinguishing rebels from bandits (I am assuming that, say, Zapata was not in fact a 'bandit'), it does not follow that formal political statements and commitments – the criteria favoured by contemporaries – serve any better. The absence of an extant political manifesto should not be taken as proof of 'banditry' (if it is, the entire Revolution was populated by 'bandits'); conversely, there were genuinely bandit movements which (I would argue) by selecting one of the superficial factional labels off the shelf, laid claim to political, 'rebel' status. More significant, but no more straightforward, is the distinction between 'social' and 'unsocial' bandits: between those who, however inarticulate, have a genuine popular base, and those – seen as the scourges more than the champions of the common people – whose activities benefit the bandit group and its small network of clients, while prejudicing the livelihood of the mass. Social banditry, virtually indistinguishable from popular rebellion during a period of social revolution, depends for its success on broad support, in the absence of which it may rapidly decline; 'unsocial' (or 'professional') bandits are socially autonomous – though they may possess a secure headquarters, and may purchase or compel a degree of popular connivance, they are fundamentally self-seeking and mercenary, uninhibited by the reciprocal ties uniting social bandit and peasant. The presence of popular support – or its antithesis, popular resistance – thus affords a useful criterion, since it offers a roundabout way of probing the motives and priorities of bandit/rebels (whose diaries, memoirs and collected letters are in short supply).

But, as already noted, 'popular support' is not an objective datum. All bandit groups, even the most cynically criminal, had their beneficiaries, clients and relatives (sometimes, too, their patrons in the upper levels of society). Where a community, like Pijijipam, Chiapas, benefited from the activities of its highwaymen, they no doubt enjoyed popular support: were they not hard-working artisans with a dash of *machismo*? On the other side of the hill – or in this case the lagoon – opinion probably differed.[489] If the concept of social banditry is not to be excessively diluted, therefore, a practitioner must be seen to transcend narrow social and spatial boundaries, and display some broader commitment to the wellbeing of the common people, which is in turn reciprocated. Of course, social bandits, like most popular rebels, were parochial animals; but this did not prevent their reputation stretching beyond their native community, generating a fund of popular sympathy far more extensive than the personal clientele of the 'unsocial' professional. As has also been noted for both banditry and popular rebellion, there is a temporal as well as a spatial axis to be considered.[490] The social bandits or popular rebels of today become the professional brigands of tomorrow. Many made this transition after 1915, as, with mounting economic hardship and government repression, the common people were less disposed to support – and more to resist – those who remained in arms. Once genuine revolutionaries could find themselves seen as outlaws by the people as well as the government, hunted down by irate villagers as well as Carrancista regulars. In these circumstances, a proud refusal to surrender was no great virtue, since it led erstwhile popular rebels/bandits to prey upon their old supporters: as Villa did, seizing food and men from the villages of Chihuahua; or as renegade Zapatistas did, to Zapata's disgust.[491]

If sense is to be made of the endemic banditry of 1915–20, a typology must be found which fits both the empirical data (murky though they are) and the social bandit hypothesis already advanced. Three forms of banditry (again, ideal-types) are discernible. First, there is the clear case of the 'social' bandit or popular rebel degenerating into 'professional' brigandage; the sad decline of movements for whom the times are out of joint. Second, there are 'social' bandits of more recent vintage: men driven to banditry by the actions of the new regime, who thus constitute the 'bandit' (i.e., the small-scale, inarticulate) equivalent of the defensive rebellions of the south. While the first group had relinquished much of their earlier popularity – hence their transition from 'social' to 'professional' banditry – the second, fighting in protest at recent, keenly felt injustices, often counted on extensive local sympathy (hence their 'social' prefix). Finally, there were out-and-out professionals: bandits for whom banditry was a way of life, a lucrative, perhaps exciting occupation, devoid of 'social' implications. And this third category, of limited significance in the early years of the Revolution, leaps to prominence after 1915; it is no great exaggeration to say that the period 1915–20 saw the development of a wholly new form of professional banditry, the product of the revolutionary upheaval, which created enormous problems for the Carranza regime.

In France, Russia, China, banditry and great revolutions go together, if only because revolutions brutalise and impart military skills wholesale. So, too, in Mexico. The decline of the major popular movements produced a crop of rebel/bandits, engaged in the painful transition from popular champions to footloose brigands. They were the flotsam left by the ebbing tide of social revolution; hence, as one *político* put it, they were not to be considered, strictly speaking, as criminals, but rather as 'the fag-ends of revolutions, the residual revolutionaries whom it has proved impossible to extirpate at one blow' – like Villa and his hordes, who still rampaged in the north, despite the crushing defeats of 1915.[492] In central Mexico, too, and not just in Morelos, banditry grew out of once strong, popular agrarian movements. The Malintzi region of Tlaxcala was infested with bandits in 1916; the mayor of Ixtenco reported almost daily rapes and robberies. Military patrols were sent repeatedly through the neighbouring pueblos, but without success, whence it was concluded that 'the individuals who commit these abuses are inhabitants of the self-same villages'.[493] Banditry of this kind – the 'fag-end' of revolution – was more of a nuisance than a major threat to the authorities. In particular in regions like Morelos, where genuine popular movements survived, and eventually were integrated into the official regime, banditry lacked a firm purchase in the villages and was constricted in scope and power. The Zapatistas themselves took the lead in extirpating (unsocial) banditry, first as rebels, then, after 1920, as allies of the central government.[494] The best guarantee of public order in Morelos was a Zapatista mayor in every pueblo. Thus, the very village-based structure which underpinned the classic popular movements made widespread, predatory banditry – divorced from and hostile to village interests – difficult to sustain.

Conversely, it was in regions where the traditional village was weak, where classic popular movements were unknown, where more 'anomic' rural relations prevailed, that banditry made most impact. In many such regions, the banditry of 1915–20 correlated negatively with previous revolutionary activity; it was not the 'fag-end of revolution', but a fresh phenomenon, responding to new conditions. The best example is afforded by the Bajío: chiefly Guanajuato and Michoacán. Here, haciendas and *ranchos* dominated; traditional villages of the Morelos type were rare; many rural communities were of recent creation, some created from the fragmentation of haciendas. Though there had been agrarian protests of some importance, notably in Michoacán, and though these conflicts sometimes simmered on, they did not cohere into an organised movement like Zapatismo or Cedillismo.[495] Perhaps the most impressive revolutionary movement produced by this region was that of Cándido Navarro, which did not survive beyond 1913.[496] Subsequently, the Bajío grew acquainted with banditry; this, however, remained a limited, local phenomenon until 1915, when it swelled to the proportions of a national problem, with reports of bandit raids, escapes and victories emanating from the borders of San Luis across Guanajuato into Jalisco and Michoacán. 'A great many small bands of bandits' were noted in Guanajuato, especially around San Miguel Allende, in 1917; bandits were 'very numerous' in Michoacán at the same time; the rural districts of Jalisco were reported to be infested.[497] These may have been exaggerations, but the impression that banditry was a greater problem in the Bajío than elsewhere is confirmed by frequent press reports of the elimination of bandit *chusmas* ('gangs') in the region.[498] Landowners in Guanajuato were prepared to put up even with rapacious Carrancista soldiery in preference to the local bandits.[499]

Some Bajío bandits had a revolutionary past (hence correspond to category one); but in the absence of a powerful, previous revolutionary movement in this region, the majority must belong to categories two and three. Defensive banditry – a reaction to Carrancista abuses, analogous to the southern rebellions – did exist. Carrancismo was certainly not welcomed in the Bajío. Archbishop Orozco y Jiménez led a revolt on the Michoacán/Jalisco border in 1917, protesting at Carrancista anti-clericalism; the men of Luciano López attacked Ahualulco (Jal.) in 1918, with cries of 'Viva la Religión!'.[500] More typical, and more truly analogous to the southern rebellions, was the banditry provoked by the 'normal' exercise of Carrancista military power in the region; by the day-to-day extortions and abuses. This was to be expected: the Bajío had a large population of *rancheros*, uncommitted to the Revolution, and vulnerable to economic extortion; hitherto spared major campaigns, the region became the main battle-ground of 1915, and the passage of Carrancista forces, both then and later, provoked the armed opposition of outraged farmers. One example is well documented: it is impossible to say how typical it is, but it clearly illustrates the existence of a vigorous defensive (as against predatory) banditry in the Bajío. By early 1918 there were reckoned to be as many as 1,000 bandits operating in the hills around Irapuato, whence they emerged to raid haciendas, to ransom the rich, even to launch surprise attacks on the city itself. A British rancher who was captured, held for a time, and finally ransomed, has left a detailed account of his experience: a rare description of the internal workings of a bandit outfit in these final years of the Revolution.[501]

The group, led by Juan García, was but one component of a loose association nominally commanded by 'General' Alfaro. Like most alleged 'bandits' García repudiated the label, claiming – with typical vagueness – that his men 'were not bandits but Villistas and Felicistas and were just preparing to join the army when the time comes'. Their British victim, Charles Furber was seized as he rode cross-country by car; the bandits manhandled him a little, haggled over a suitable ransom figure, and finally released him in return for a payment of 6,600 pesos, giving him a safe-conduct, a horse and an escort to get home. Before then, Furber noted their activities carefully. Their headquarters was a ruined 'mountain village', situated 'amongst natural fortresses of great strength and vast extension'; their targets were the lowland haciendas and their managers; their chief sport seemed to be skirmishing with Carrancista troops and hacienda guards, neither of whom put up much resistance when confronted by the bandits. Furber himself witnessed one encounter in which thirty hacienda guards briefly faced the bandits and then ran away: 'the chief laughingly told Furber that is the way they always do [sic]'. As for the Carrancista regulars, the bandits 'had absolutely no fear of the soldiers and treated them as a sort of joke'. Hence the bandits would ride with impunity to the outskirts of Irapuato, cut down the bodies of *compañeros* who had been caught and hung, and take them back to the mountains 'to give them a Christian burial'.

Most interesting, however, are the origin and motivation of this band. Though some were criminals on the run, most claimed to be local farmers driven to rebellion by Carrancista excesses. It is worth quoting the analysis

Furber gave, after listening to the bandits' version over several days: perhaps his captors tried hard to justify their behaviour; yet Furber, who in the circumstances was hardly an indulgent reporter, certainly came to believe them. 'During my stay with the bandits', he recalled,

I endeavoured to inform myself of their reasons for being in arms and I found that they seemed to have been driven to it by the government. The region is largely composed of little villages and surrounding holdings of land. At the beginning of the revolution the inhabitants lived in comparative comfort with their own houses and cattle and animals and tilled each his piece of ground. The villages had their little shops and their church and the people lived contented and happy.

Then the Carrancistas entered Arcadia; and the results were the same as in other parts of central and southern Mexico:

the government troops went up there and began stealing the animals, goods, chattels, the owners resisting were called bandits, their homes were burnt, everything was stolen and many were killed. These that were left took to the hills, got a rifle and did their best to defend about all that was left to defend, their lives. When they finally banded together and became too strong for the government they were offered an armistice. A few accepted, were disarmed, and shot. The present situation of these people today is one of extreme difficulty, they cannot surrender because the government kills them, they cannot work in the hills as they have no guarantees or money, and if they come down to the plains and find work they would soon be denounced and killed. The great majority of them are tired of the life that they live, with all its privations and dangers, and would gladly lay down their arms and go to work if only the government would afford them some protection and means of working.

Clearly, banditry of this kind closely paralleled the defensive revolts elsewhere; and, granted the prevalence of Carrancista abuses, it is plausible that a significant part of the banditry afflicting the Bajío was of this type. In Michoacán, 'diverse social sectors' shared a common antipathy to their new rulers, and there were specific examples, for example, in the southern part of the state, where Jesús Cíntora led a successful rebellion for several years, of pillaged *rancheros* supporting the rebels.[502] But it also seems clear that a more mercenary, committed, vicious, and wide-ranging banditry (category three) flourished, sometimes recruiting these malcontents, but absorbing them into a movement which was qualitatively as well as quantitatively different, and which presented the authorities with far more serious problems. The development of this essentially new phenomenon is linked to the career of one famous but obscure individual: José Inés Chávez García. He was by no means the only bandit leader operating in the Bajío; but he established himself as the most powerful, and he knitted diverse bands together until they constituted a veritable army, which greatly transcended the usual numerical norms of banditry.[503] Whereas latter-day Villismo – and, *a fortiori*, latter-day Zapatismo – represented a phase in the decline of once popular movements,

Chavismo was a new phenomenon, the birth and survival of which depended less on broad popular support than on the weakness and ineptitude of the government, and on the social upheaval and deprivation consequent upon the years of revolution. In this respect, Chavismo resembled the endemic banditry which afflicted Germany in the wake of the Thirty Years War, or the Rhineland in the 1790s.[504]

After Obregón's capture of Aguascalientes and Fierro's welcome departure from the region, a form of peace descended on the Bajío; at least, there was 'no true political enemy' competing with the Carrancistas by the autumn of 1915.[505] But already – at Pénjamo, Piedra Gorda, Otates and Yuriria – bandit groups were active, indifferent to offers of amnesty and untroubled by the regime's military counter-measures.[506] These bands were small, numbering less than a hundred apiece, but in the following years of dearth and drought their numbers multiplied (economic factors were clearly important; whether more so in the Bajío than elsewhere it is difficult to say).[507] By autumn 1917, eight of the forty-five municipios of Michoacán failed to render accounts to the governor, being grievously afflicted by banditry; a year later, a Carrancista general reported, 'almost all the state of Michoacán is effectively overrun with bandits', chiefly Chávez García and his allies Cíntora and Altamirano, but also a multitude of auxiliaries ('sin fin de segundos').[508] Some prominent leaders, like Cíntora or Chávez García himself, were revolutionary veterans; and it is generally asserted that the dispersal of Villista forces after the defeats of 1915 made a large contribution to the later epidemic of banditry.[509] Yet many of the leaders of 1915–20 were also obscure, lacking a known revolutionary past; they also led sizeable forces in regions which had previously witnessed only limited military activity.[510] The continuity between earlier revolutionary and later 'bandit' movements, evident, for example, in Chihuahua, is therefore lacking, and it must be presumed that many of the bandits were recent converts to a violent way of life.[511]

Their numbers, too, were considerable. In 1917–18 Chávez García was consistently reported as leading up to 2,000 men; his ally Altamirano led 1,000; several other chieftains maintained a couple of hundred, joining up with larger forces for a major campaign. Hence, Chávez García could stand up to the regular army in pitched battles, like that fought at the San Miguel Hacienda, near Acámbaro.[512] Here, he counted on the support of his second-in-command Manuel Roa (like himself, a native of Puruándiro); of Macario Silva and Rafael Núñez of Valle de Santiago (an old centre of banditry); of Manco Nares of Peribán; of three sets of brothers – the Cenejas of Villa Jiménez, the Morales of Tendeparacua, and the Barriga of Quiroga; of Pedro Vázquez of Chucándiro and Fidel González of Las Cañadas de Villa.[513] There were other, important leaders who did not fight at San Miguel: Altamirano, Enrique Zepeda and Trinidad Avalos; Cíntora (a bandit/rebel of some entrepreneurial flair who, from his base in the tierra caliente, shipped in arms from the Pacific coast); and others best, or only, known by their rustic nicknames: 'El Tejón' (the badger), Luis Gutiérrez, 'El Chivo Encantado' (the charmed goat).[514] To the west, other gangs were active, from Colima through Jalisco up to Tepic, which was said to be 'overrun with bandits'.[515] But, while names and localities can be established, origins are more obscure: some leaders were known to be ex-peons, several were shepherds, and most were of plebeian origin; but there were also some *rancheros*, and some, like the Landeros brothers of Jalisco, who were landlords; as for Chávez García himself, he was born of a poor family – and an Amazon mother – and progressed through the *rurales* and the revolutionary forces of Anastasio Pantoja before achieving prominence after 1915.[516]

Their *modus operandi*, on the other hand, is clear enough. The most seriously affected region – Chávez García's own patch – lay athwart the borders of Guanajuato and Michoacán. Here, between 1916 and 1918, he took – that is, entered and held long enough to loot, kidnap and abduct – Tacámbaro, Zamora, Cotija, and many lesser pueblos in Michoacán; as well as Abasolo (a favourite victim), Acámbaro, Cd Manuel Doblado and Pénjamo in Guanajuato. He cut the electricity supply feeding Morelia (a carbon-copy of Zapata's interdiction of Mexico City's power, or the Felicistas' of Orizaba's); he raided haciendas, robbed trains, and ransomed the rich; he kidnapped an entire military band and force-marched them across country with him, requiring them to play for hours on end for his delectation.[517] Several thousand troops were despatched to Michoacán (they included a large Yaqui contingent); by autumn 1917 the Carrancista commander, Norzagaray, had 10,000 men at his disposal; and a year later the government was spending 10,000 pesos a day (not counting the cost of ammunition) on the campaign against Chávez.[518] Indeed, Chavismo probably represented the most serious threat to the Carrancista authorities after Villismo. For, unlike Zapata or Peláez, Chávez (who was a capable tactician) could hold his own even in open battle. But in general he preferred hit-and-run tactics (even with Cíntora as an ally, ammunition was hard to come by). His speed of movement was notorious – and reminiscent of Cándido Navarro's campaigns in the Bajío in 1911: Carrancista generals found themselves pursuing the bandits for weeks on end without success; it was said that Chávez, a superb horseman, could even sleep in the saddle.[519] The unfortunate, hijacked military band suffered more from sheer exhaustion than outright brutality: 'what tortured them most were the long and incessant marches from Guanajuato to Jalisco and from there to Michoacán, without stops anywhere'.[520]

But brutality there undoubtedly was, and on a large scale. Rape, murder and pillage followed Chávez's tireless itineraries across country. And if the well-to-do – townspeople and *hacendados* – suffered the kidnapping and ransoming, all classes appear to have fallen victim to indiscriminate violence, sometimes committed with a certain sadistic panache. Baudelio Uribe, the

Villista clipper of ears, was mild compared with Chavista thugs like Fidel González, who rejoiced in slitting throats (the machete of the *tierra caliente* was a favourite Chavista weapon); or with Chávez himself who, after the fall of San José, killed twenty men to the sound of music, asking each in turn what final request he would like.[521] Whole populations, terrorised, sought refuge in the larger towns: nine-tenths of the people fled from San José, the inhabitants of nearby Jiquilpam decamped to Zamora; yet even in larger towns they were not necessarily safe from Chávez's depredations.[522]

How should Chavismo be categorized? Granted that it did not represent the rearguard action of an older popular rebellion, was it an example of extensive social banditry?[523] Certainly the tactics were typical of guerrilla warfare; the leadership was mostly plebeian; and there was evidence of 'bandits' returning to the fields as *campesinos* after a foray.[524] Some Chavistas had been revolutionary partisans, and their leader was adamant in his claim that he was a rebel – not a common bandit – and that he posed a political challenge to Carranza, whom he cordially hated: to this end he styled himself governor of Michoacán.[525] He was also sufficiently *au fait*, and witty, to tease one of his Italian victims about the recent disaster at Caporetto.[526] Finally, it may be noted that some Chavistas later cropped up in the ranks of the Cristeros, defending the Church against Callista anti-clericalism (at the time, the Chavistas' treatment of the Church was generally, though not uniformly, respectful; some parish priests were associated with the movement; however, any interpretation of Chavismo as a reaction to Carrancista anti-clericalism has to explain the absence of any statement to this effect).[527]

There is some evidence, therefore, that Chavismo transcended professional banditry. But the bulk of the evidence points the other way. It may be, indeed, that the ambivalence of the evidence derives from points already made. First, Chavismo changed over time: its leader is said to have undergone a transformation – from ordinary *guerrillero* to brutal bandit – as a result of a bout of typhus; and certainly the movement, beginning as a localised guerrilla, whose members still tilled the fields, had by 1917 established itself as a bigger, wide-ranging, permanent and predatory association (which, for example, campaigned and did not return to the fields in summer).[528] This may relate to the economic question: systematic banditry paid – perhaps more in the Bajío than elsewhere. There was a spatial as well as temporal variable: some communities (the larger ones; and those whose resistance incurred Chavista wrath) suffered disproportionately, while some were favoured; Michoacán, it seems, suffered less than Guanajuato or Jalisco.[529] This selectivity, however, may not be incompatible with a form of professional banditry, which would also pick particular targets and exempt others. In addition, the widespread use of terror, much more marked than in the case of Zapatismo, tells against a revolutionary or social bandit interpretation of Chavismo. While the rich were among Chávez's main victims – being killed, mulcted and ransomed – this may be explained in terms of the movement's practical necessities, rather than its social aims. This may also explain the harsher treatment meted out to larger towns, and the attacks on haciendas which, in the absence of any evidence of *agrarista* commitment, look more acquisitive than retributory.[530] As many incidents attest, the poor were not spared either; and where communities resisted, they appear to have done so as units, with no sign of Chavismo mobilising plebs against patricians.

The apparent lack of a secure home base is also significant. Chávez's own family remained at Puruándiro, while his campaigns covered some 7,000 square miles; favourite bolt-holes are mentioned (this, too, would be compatible with professional banditry); one was an hacienda in the Zinapécuaro district, where the bandits planted corn, fished and collected firewood; but this was more a self-made military encampment than a popular base.[531] It was sheer speed, endurance and fire-power, not local protection and sympathy, which enabled Chávez to elude capture and avoid defeat. This was reflected in Chávez's recruitment policy, which was highly selective. He would only accept robust young men into his band and, at one hacienda where recruits were sought, he rejected thirty-eight out of forty men as being 'too old, weak or sickly'.[532] Full-time fighters, not part-time peasant *guerrilleros* were required. Finally, it is worth noting the opinion of Primo Tapia – later a foremost *agrarista* and no stranger to violence – who roundly denounced the banditry which afflicted his home state of Michoacán, and who applauded the death of Chávez García, 'that old bandit . . . [and] exploiter'.[533] Like other (professional) bandits, Chávez had charisma in life, and was mythologised after death; but the scale, character and impact of Chavismo make claims to social banditry, at best, non-proven. The best sociological alibi for what, on the face of it, became an unprecedented form of brutal depredation, is that the movement derived from the specific conditions of west-central Mexico after 1915: years of drought and dearth, political and military instability, when (particularly with a few revolutionary veterans to offer a lead) violence offered as good a means to survive as any other, and professional bandits could recruit on a scale which created an illusion of broad popular support.[534]

Chavismo thus depended for its success on the weakness of genuine popular movements, which might channel popular grievances and, as in the case of Zapatismo, provide local structures of authority. While Zapatismo was rooted in traditional authority, Chavismo was fundamentally anomic: a contrast between the central plateau and the Bajío which had been evident a hundred years before at the time of Hidalgo's revolt.[535] Chavismo also depended for its success on the incompetence of the Carrancista forces, already evident in many theatres. They could not be relied upon to stand firm; garrisons ran away at the approach of bandits; their generals were unpopular, inept, and given to constant feuding.[536] As elsewhere greater resolution was shown by local defence forces, recruited within pueblos or haciendas, which by 1918, as the regular army progressively withdrew from smaller communities, became common.[537] At San José, Apolinar Partida's dozen men twice put up a stout resistance to Chávez's hordes, beating off 100 attackers, it was said, in December 1917, before succumbing to a much larger force (800) in May 1918.[538] Prudencio Mendoza maintained his *cacicazgo* in the mountains of western Michoacán, repelling bandits, some of whom, like Mendoza himself, had briefly borne a Villista label.[539] Moroleón, too, continued to man its defences.[540] But such local resistance was often hampered by internal disputes; and local forces sometimes turned their aggression on rival pueblos, rather than hostile bandits. The San José force feuded with that of Del Valle, even though both were commanded by members of the Partida family.[541] And the presence of a local strong man could prove a mixed blessing: Jerónimo Rubio ('Mano Negra'), the tall, fair, bibulous commander at Teocuitlán spent less time pursuing bandits than, it seems, terrorising the people under his supposed protection: 'he did not let a week go by without hanging someone'.[542] So, in a situation of great complexity and confusion, local forces were gradually able to wear down, eliminate, and on occasions co-opt the bandits afflicting their region.[543] In 1918, a new Carrancista commander – Lázaro Cárdenas, of local origins – began to prosecute the campaign with greater success; Chávez García began to suffer defeats; and at the end of the year he died, neither in battle nor 'a la pared', but from the combined effects of wounds, pneumonia, and influenza.[544] Unlike Zapatismo, which had the institutional strength to survive its leader, Chavismo never recovered. Altamirano, too, fell victim to the influenza epidemic, and Cíntora was defeated (by Cárdenas) and driven into the mountains.[545] A year later, when the famous Italian tenor Caruso toured Mexico, he wrote to his wife, with evident relief, 'there are no brigands in Mexico'; if the report was somewhat sweeping and premature, it reflected the fact that by 1919–20 banditry was more a limited, local, than a major, national problem.[546] But the evil that men did lived after them: apart from the destruction of life and property which it brought about, the rampant banditry of 1915–18 also left a legacy of violence and political *pistolerismo*. Banditry, and local resistance to it, made the careers of a new generation of 'revolutionary' strong men, typified, in the case of Michoacán, by 'Don Melchor' of Paracho, who forged a 'new rural dictatorship' based on guns, liquor, and political clientelism.[547] Soon – here as in Chihuahua – state governors would emerge from the ranks of the para-military forces of the late Revolution.[548]

Chavismo reflected both the weakness of social control and a new predisposition to crime and violence introduced by the Revolution. In this, it was symptomatic of the times. The years 1915–20 were marked by high levels of crime, urban and rural, which mirrored contemporary privation and poverty, and contrasted with the good old days of the Porfiriato. Rural crime was the unescapable corollary of rural revolution; and, no doubt, perpetrators of such 'crime' (officially defined) were often ex-rebels or social bandits who could not adjust, or were not allowed to adjust, to the new, post-revolutionary state of affairs. Robbing a train or rustling cattle – acceptable, commendable acts in 1913–14 – were capital offences by 1916. But over and above this category of 'crime', which occupies the same subjective, intermediate position as the social banditry already mentioned, there was also abundant 'professional' crime, committed for personal gain and lacking political significance, which reached epidemic proportions after 1915, and for which severe economic conditions, rather than revolutionary objectives, afforded the only justification. Indeed, this wave of varied, sometimes ingenious crime may be seen as part of the general post-revolutionary ferment, an economic *sauve-qui-peut*, in which life and property lost some of their sanctity, and people were driven to explore and exploit new ways of making a living in difficult, unfamiliar circumstances.[549] In this sense, crime might be seen as part of the 'revolutionary entrepreneurialism' which characterised society after 1915; and in which the new rules of the country set an example and gave a lead to the people they governed.

As already suggested, rural crime was endemic, and reports of robberies and depredations were legion. Robbers afflicted the wild country of Tepic, where the Acaponeta region was infested; they stole from the sharecroppers of the Hacienda de Xico (Mex.) as did the Carrancista troops; while all along the railway from San Luis to Querétaro, ran a report of December 1916, 'it is no longer possible to support the robberies which are being committed on all the haciendas and *rancherías*'; cattle, goats and cereals were all disappearing, and this while the Constituent Congress was beginning its sage deliberations at Querétaro.[550] Rustling, which the Porfirian authorities had managed to curtail, enjoyed a great resurgence. It was commonplace in Chiapas; at Lampazos (NL) people dared not let their cattle forage far from the town limits; and the problem was so severe in the north that the death penalty was imposed for those caught rustling and illegally exporting cattle to the US.[551]

The marauders did not confine their activities to the hinterland. The Lampazos bandits were to be seen, from time to time, in the town; one brazenly entered and shot the mayor (he was caught and executed within days).[552] And it was urban crime and violence which spread most rapidly and attracted most concern after 1915. This urban crime was new and pervasive. It was the work not of professional criminals but of ordinary people, 'simple delinquents', as the Mexico City police chief called them, who were often driven to crime by poverty, and whose activities were facilitated by the ineptitude of the police.[553] Statistical evidence is hard to come by and, where available, unreliable; it is therefore difficult to make fair comparisons with the Porfiriato.[554] But the authorities' opinion that crime had greatly increased was shared by many observers. In Mexico City, the police complained of a plague of robberies; there was a spate of kidnappings; car thefts (often resulting in accidents) were a new problem, possibly stimulated by the revolutionary confiscations and joyriding of 1914.[555] As in the past, crimes against persons – rape, assault, homicide – figured prominently, and Mexico City night life suffered accordingly (the greater incidence of rape reflected, in the countryside, the changing character of rural revolt and banditry; and, in the country as a whole, the relaxation of sexual mores produced by the revolutionary upheaval).[556] Observers in the capital linked the rising crime rate to popular destitution: the high levels of 1918 came at a time when 'beggars and vagabonds infest[ed] the city'.[557]

The same was true of the provinces. At La Paz (Baja Calif.) 'lawlessness and disorder are the order of the day'; repeated robberies were reported at Veracruz; at Orizaba an observer commented on the 'frequent and serious burglaries and breaking into houses usually occurring at night'.[558] Again, crime correlated with destitution. At Durango 'robberies and housebreaking in the town are frequent and highwaymen ply their vocation in the outskirts'; the city itself was 'overrun with beggars, burglars and footpads, and robberies are without end'.[559] A similar correlation was noted at Piedras Negras where, in midwinter, wages had plummeted and there was 'much discontent among the general populace', manifesting itself in frequent robberies: foreigners complained that their clothes were being pilfered from the washing line.[560] The railways, already facing enormous problems, were especially vulnerable. Some robber gangs specialised in railway thefts, operating with the connivance of employees: railway cars were cleaned out as they waited in sidings; goods left at stations promptly disappeared.[561]

Police as well as railwaymen connived at crime. Among a gang arrested for a series of thefts at Guadalupe Hidalgo, on the edge of Mexico City, was a policeman, the brains ('autor intelectual') behind the operation: he was shot on the site of his felonies and his body left on display 'as an example for delinquents'.[562] Carrancista troops also dabbled in crime, as they virtually had to, granted the meanness and uncertainty of their pay. But whereas rural sequestration could go unnoticed and unpunished by superiors, urban pilfering was more culpable, especially if it involved arms dealing. In one week of March 1916 alone, the press reported – with a certain careful, didactic detail – three separate cases: at Tehuantepec three soldiers were shot for robbery (they comported themselves bravely, asking for food and brandy before their execution); a sergeant, convicted of robbery at Pachuca, was executed before an audience of 4,000 ('it's not bulls you have come here to see', he exclaimed to the spectators, after his last coffee and cigarette); while in the capital 300 troops, picked from all the garrisons and joined by a 'multitude of the curious' witnessed the execution of two soldiers at the School of Marksmanship, where one of the victims made a final speech urging his fellow-soldiers not to engage in robbery and arms dealing as he had.[563] Such incidents continued through 1916 and after; two years later the suburb of Mixcoac suffered a spate of robberies – thirty occurred in one week – which was attributed to poor policing and the presence of a large garrison.[564]

It may be that some criminal activity was mistakenly ascribed to Carrancista soldiery, since by 1916 some Mexico City thieves had taken to wearing military uniforms and conducting robberies under the guise of official searches. This technique – another opportunistic adjustment to the times – was the chosen *modus operandi* of the famous Grey Automobile Gang, whose exploits represented the professional, up-market end of the current crime wave. The gang began their activities in the summer of 1915, towards the end of the Zapatista occupation of the capital, where they specialised in daring robberies of fashionable houses (notably those of prominent exiles), impersonating police or troops and gaining access with phoney search warrants. Their hauls were impressive, and added to the gold, jewels and pictures being traded in large quantities in the 'black' economy; their personnel – both men and women, several of them Spaniards – acquired a certain mystique; and an extra *frisson* derived from the fact that their original grey getaway car (they later boasted three) was said to be the same limousine which had taken Madero and Pino Suárez to their place of midnight execution in February 1913.[565] The gang survived the Zapatista evacuation and continued operations under Carrancista auspices, enjoying, it was plausibly suggested, the protection of some high-ranking officers. In September 1915 some were arrested and executed, though the alleged ringleader escaped; three years later a second narrow escape led to renewed allegations of complicity in high places.[566] Now, indeed, with the name of the presidential aspirant Pablo González being mentioned, the gang acquired a certain political topicality. Their chief historical significance, however, was as an indicator of the rampant city crime of the period, and of the connivance of the authorities – police, generals, *políticos* – in its commission and cover-up. In this, as in the wider field of entrepreneurial initiative, the new revolutionary elite set the standards which others followed.[567]

The authorities also encouraged crime by their sheer inadequacy. The police of Aguascalientes – and before 1910 Aguascalientes had been a smart, well-run town – were said to be few, disorganised and illiterate.[568] The maintenance of order at Tampico, a booming sea-port on the edge of the oil-fields, had never been easy; now (1916) it was a rough place to live, with a high incidence of violence and frequent brawls between police and troops, especially in the red light district. In response, the authorities employed drastic measures: there were summary executions (the body of a forger was exhibited for public edification); and one observer reported 175 deaths, from casual as well as judicial violence, in the space of ten days.[569] Summary executions were now common practice. A spate followed the riots occasioned by Fierro's violent passage through Salamanca and Irapuato in the autumn of 1915.[570] And often the executions were public, drawing large crowds. Often, too, the victims were not homicides: robbery, forgery, and trafficking in arms were sufficient cause for a swift execution 'as an example for delinquents'; in Veracruz, theft became a capital crime and executions followed at once.[571] In the capital, alternative, draconian sentences were instituted: inmates were shipped from the Federal Penitentiary to the notorious Islas Marías, in an attempt to curb the 'plague of robbers which has been let loose on the city'.[572] Even as Mexico's new rulers met at Querétaro to debate the new Constitution, the problems of crime and violence impinged: though they talked, in somewhat jocose and sexist fashion, of the 'present epidemic' of rapes being experienced, they could not ignore the insecurity of the railways, or the *cantina* shootings which, in one celebrated case, brought a death sentence for a *constituyente*'s brother.[573]

ECONOMY AND SOCIETY

Crime and banditry mirrored the destitution of the country. After five years of continued upheaval, Mexico was economically shattered. Economic rhythms, as already noted, followed a different, slower tempo compared with their political and military counterparts: not until the turn of the year 1913/14 did the accumulated effects of political conflict begin seriously to undermine the robust Mexican economy.[574] By then, production had dropped, inflation set in, bankruptcy and unemployment joined the tribulations of the people. But still, even as the fighting against Huerta reached its peak, there was adequate food, and economic decline was far from reaching economic collapse. But the war of the winners, apart from demanding further human sacrifice, also placed an additional, intolerable strain on the economy; the collapse of which probably led to greater mortality than the fighting itself. For, even as the major conventional campaigns of 1914–15 gave way to the protracted guerrilla warfare of 1916–19, the economic decline continued, reaching its nadir a year or more after the definitive triumph of Carrancista arms. Hence, among the dominant problems and constraints facing the new regime were those created by the parlous state of the economy: these bulked larger than the epiphenomena of political decrees and declarations, certainly in the purview of the common people, probably in the eyes of the elite too. For without economic recovery, the decrees and declarations were so much rhetorical froth, and the very existence of the regime was jeopardised. In this respect, 1916–19 was characterised by the primacy, not of politics, but of economics.[575]

The Porfiristas had prided themselves on the creation of a national railway network and a sound currency, pegged to gold after 1905. Both, however, were sabotaged by the Revolution, with important consequences for the country's economic life. The railways served as the arteries not only of Porfirian economic development but also of revolutionary warfare: the tributes paid by victorious generals to their railway managers were not hollow courtesies.[576] But the line suffered, and after 1915 still suffered, both inevitable neglect and disinvestment and direct physical damage: the ripping up of track (at which the Carrancistas were adept), the conversion of locomotives into *máquinas locas* (a Chihuahuan speciality), the frequent bombings of trains, bridges and culverts which went on, especially in the south, well after 1915. Hence the railways were a mess. Across the plains of northern Mexico, where the bleached bones of cattle lay scattered and human skeletons marked the site of old battles, there was an estimated 50,000 tons of iron and steel awaiting salvage (in the south, too, some Zapatistas were doing a brisk trade in scrap metal).[577] Even after a year of reconstruction, many of the northern lines were in poor condition: Saltillo and the Laguna were joined by a 'frail link', with bent rails, rusted spikes and rotten sleepers; and the government's failure to pay the railway workers did not speed repairs.[578] On the Inter-Oceanic between Veracruz and the capital – still the victim of repeated attacks in 1917–18 – the rolling stock had sadly deteriorated: the woodwork had rotted, cars lacked roofs, and only twenty-seven serviceable locomotives remained in operation.[579]

These shortages were compounded by the military's near monopoly of rolling stock, which was only gradually broken after 1915 (a difficult, unpublicised piece of de-militarisation, which almost cost its chief protagonist, Alberto Pani, his life).[580] Even where military priorities and graft could be circumvented, the resulting service was poor. The trains ran slowly, often burning wood for want of coal and oil: the journey from Acámbaro through Morelia to Uruapán (a little over 100 miles) could take as long as the regular trip from New York to Mexico City.[581] Passengers, prepared for long stops, possible bandit attacks, and the constant risk of derailment, were sometimes given a rousing send-off as they left the station; and they travelled in an adventurous, if not apprehensive spirit, very different from the blasé confidence with which railway trips had been undertaken during the Porfiriato.[582] Justly, perhaps, the Director-General of Constitutionalist Railways had his own narrow escapes from attacks and bombings.[583] For the economy as a whole, the deficiencies of the railways hampered commerce and aggravated the growing problem of food supply. Merchants anxious to ship goods had to pay hefty bribes and, in some cases, appeal to the highest authority in the land.[584] And, in the absence of alternative forms of bulk, long-distance transport, the failings of the railways constrained economic recovery and encouraged introverted, local production and marketing.

An even greater problem facing regime and people alike was that of the currency. By early 1916 it was reckoned that 'the money question . . . is the ruling factor in the establishment of a permanent government in Mexico under General [sic] Carranza'.[585] This was neither an exaggeration nor an isolated opinion: in regions like Campeche, relatively free from military troubles, the vicissitudes of the currency provoked riots and the view was expressed that Carranza was 'committing suicide' with his monetary policy; the currency was likewise seen as the most urgent question facing the government in San Luis.[586] Certainly, the collapse of the peso brought extreme economic dislocation, unemployment and hardship; it generated riots and protests; it threatened to dissolve the Carrancista army and regime. It was a problem that had to be solved. Its origins were obvious: in the course of the Revolution different factions had printed money to finance their campaigns; it was, as one Constitutionalist put it, echoing Benjamin Franklin, the fairest way of sharing out the cost of the fighting among the population.[587] Huerta, too, increased the note issue, driving gold out of circulation and contributing to the peso's slide against the dollar. Prior to 1914, Constitutionalist paper had been issued with some degree of prudence: the total issue may not have much exceeded 30m. pesos.[588] But with the fall of Huerta and the renewal of civil war between Carranza and Villa prudence was cast to the winds. By September 1914 total Constitutionalist paper had – according to Finance Minister, Felicitas Villareal – reached 60m., and Villareal, a sober northern businessman, was driven to resign in protest at the accelerated printing (a decision perhaps influenced by a recent incident in which Villareal, dining in a Mexico City restaurant, had a Constitutionalist banknote refused).[589] His protest, however, did not staunch the flood, and the currency soon became a weapon in the war of the winners; both sides printed apace; and both (though the Carrancistas were the more determined) tried to invalidate their rivals' currency while decreeing the forced circulation of their own. Zapata, too, entered the monetary fray.[590] The result was hyper-inflation. At Mazatlán, money was being churned out 'by the basketful' early in 1915.[591] Figures of total output confirm this: by September 1915 the Carrancista issue (including the miserly 33m. pesos of 1913–14) reached nearly 300m.; the official Villista issue (June 1915) stood at 176m.[592]

With this profligate printing, the country was swamped by a polychrome tide of paper money: national and local bills, cardboard *cartones*, notes of the Henequen Regulating Commission, company *vales*, revolutionary IOU's, and the bizarre, improvised, *bilimbiques* which ranged from toilet paper to shin plasters.[593] Often aesthetically pleasing, and now of antiquarian interest, their contemporary effect was to condemn Mexico to that form of traumatic hyper-inflation historically associated with political crisis – France in the 1790s, Germany in 1923 – and to the social stresses, the arbitrary windfalls and penalties which accompany it. Metal was driven from circulation. By 1915, only foreign companies and ships offered a supply of gold or gold-based notes in most parts of the country.[594] Though – at the price of unpopularity and sporadic riots – the Carrancistas invalidated Villista currency in the regions they controlled, they could not sustain the forced circulation of their own at par; at one point, indeed, Mexico City appeared to be without any 'official' currency at all.[595] Villista money, as already noted, spiralled down to worthlessness during 1915: by the autumn, 20,000 Villista pesos would not buy a tortilla in the Laguna.[596] But, though they could beat Huerta and Villa, the Carrancistas could not beat the laws of the market, and their own currency fared little better than that of their defeated rivals'. The peso's gradual slide in 1913–14 gave way to precipitate collapse thereafter: from a value of 49.5c. (US) in January 1913 it fell to 43c. in July 1913 and 37c. in January 1914, to stand at 31c. at the time of Huerta's fall; by January 1915 it was down to 14c.; July 1915, 7c.; January 1916, 4c.; May 1916, 2c.[597] By the turn of the year 1915/16, the situation was critical; Carranza and Obregón were said to be at loggerheads over the monetary question, since Carranza favoured a repudiation of the currency, while Obregón believed that this would jeopardise the loyalty of the army.[598]

Eventually, Carranza's view prevailed. In an attempt to make a fresh start the government brought out a new 800m. paper issue in May 1916: the so-called *infalsificables*, printed in the US, and designed to eradicate the evils of forgery, then common.[599] At once, the value of the old currency crashed to zero. The new *infalsificable* peso was officially rated at 10c. (US). But through 1916 it steadily fell, becoming valueless by the end of the year:

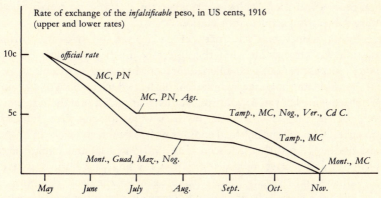

Rate of exchange of the *infalsificable* peso, in US cents, 1916 (upper and lower rates)

(Source: US consular reports, Mexico City, Piedras Negras, Aguascalientes, Monterrey, Guadalajara, Mazatlán, Nogales, Tampico, Veracruz, Cd Carmen).

By the end of 1916, therefore, this great pile of paper was worthless, and Mexico went over to an economy based on barter, foreign notes, the few, scarce metal coins, and improvised tokens backed by some company or authority which inspired confidence.[600] Desperate, above all, to retain the loyalty of its troops, the government seized the bullion deposits of the major banks in September 1916; it authorised the free importation and circulation of American note and coins; and it set about introducing a new, metallic currency in 1917.[601] Through 1916–17, wages and prices were fixed in terms of silver or gold and American notes circulated freely: along the northern border 80% of business was transacted in dollars.[602] Inevitably, the fluctuations in the currency and, by 1916, the sheer shortage of coins, hampered commerce and economic revival.[603]

Apart from the practical measures mentioned – which were thrust upon it – the government could do little to halt the inflation; hence it took to exhortation instead. With the issue of the *infalsificables* the public was urged to place its confidence in the new currency, oblige traders to accept it at par, and retain, for the moment, old notes, which remained legal tender for tax payments till the end of 1916.[604] Meanwhile, hoping to drain away the flood of old paper and bolster confidence in the new, the government took in and destroyed earlier issues – a policy carried out with similar exhortation and publicity. The Ministry of Hacienda proudly consigned 46m. pesos to the flames in one mighty holocaust; *El Demócrata*, the official newspaper, sold food to the poor and undertook to burn the half million near-worthless paper pesos it received in return.[605] Patriots responded to these official initiatives: the schoolmasters of Mexico City celebrated the national holiday of 5 May by burning bundles of the Veracruz (1914) issue; the Governor of Veracruz participated in a similar fiesta at Orizaba 'with the aim of amortizing the national debt'; and the famous actress Virginia Fabregas publically burned 15,000 pesos at Saltillo.[606] Next year, when the *infalsificables* collapsed, they too were subject to patriotic immolation.[607]

If burning money was the mark of patriotism in 1916–17, currency speculation was treasonable, and the object of much official attention and publicity. Just as hoarders were blamed for food shortages, so speculators were held responsible for the runaway inflation (both of which evils were, of course, social consequences of the Revolution, rather than individual delinquencies). Indeed, the speculators – or *coyotes*, as they were called – were branded as reactionaries, who sought political ends, as well as profiteers, seeking financial advantage; they joined the pantheon of revolutionary villains (what sociologists might call 'negative integrating symbols') along with Porfiristas, Huertistas, Villistas and clericals. 'There is no reason for the decline of our paper money', declared a brazen front page of *El Demócrata*, 'the abuses of our bankers and businessmen are now intolerable.'[608] The present shambles in the currency, Cabrera explained, represented 'a phase in the struggles of commercialism against the revolution'.[609] Rooting out speculators became a patriotic duty: those who clung to their grubby old paper notes, said the Governor of Tlaxcala, did so in the expectation of an imminent triumph of 'reaction'; in Veracruz, the accomplished witch-hunter Heriberto Barrón located currency speculators among the judiciary.[610] Later in 1916, *coyotes* were said to be prowling the barracks of Mexico City, trying to get their hands on the precious silver pesos, which emerged into circulation through the army payroll.[611] Exemplary punishments were handed out. Forty *coyotes* were rounded up on the streets of Mexico City in one day; they were, the press emphasised, 'for the most part bourgeois, above all that kind of supercilious rake who lives on his wits'.[612] If foreign, they were deported; Mexican *coyotes* followed convicted robbers to the Islas Marías; while in the provinces they were consigned to the army – a suitable chastisement for corrupt, city shysters.[613]

Such measures may have been politically effective; but they did not solve the chronic problems associated with hyper-inflation. In the longer term, inflation was important because of its capricious redistribution of wealth within the context of existing social upheaval. Savings were wiped out, pensions and fixed incomes collapsed, goods were hawked, bartered and pawned in a market where old values had been thoroughly subverted. Once affluent people sold off the family jewels for a pittance; foreigners, or anyone with access to hard currency, bought them up with alacrity.[614] The inflation thus contributed significantly to the social change set in motion by the Revolution, whose effects were generally redistributive and levelling; certainly it helped further erode the position of the old, propertied, Porfirian elite, already buffeted by five years of civil war. Inflation, and the opportunities which went with it, also stimulated the entrepreneurialism and economic innovation of these years.[615] In the short term, however, it hit the poor hardest of all.[616] The rural population might, to some extent, insulate itself from inflation by means of subsistence farming, in village or hacienda (at least so long as harvests were adequate and the cultivator could retain the fruits of his labour). But these conditions did not apply in much of the country and even in Morelos (where they did) inflation was a serious problem by 1915.[617] Urban workers, who could rarely resort to subsistence,[618] had to rely on the growing, but still puny, power of their *sindicatos*, on sporadic government charity (more evident in the towns than the countryside), and on the largesse of those companies, chiefly foreign, still doing business; companies, that is, whose income accrued in hard currency, who could afford to maintain their labour force through these hard times, thus reinforcing the clientelist relations which often antedated 1910.

Company charity came cheap. A large west coast mining enterprise (which had operated throughout the revolution) was 'purchasing food at high prices and selling it to employees at a loss' in 1915; but 'this loss has been greatly overcome by paying the miners in their old wages but in paper'.[619] Through 1915 and 1916 ASARCO provided rations of corn and beans for over 1,000 workers in Aguascalientes, selling them a less than half wholesale price; but, again, there was method in this charity, which was thought 'preferable to affecting the wage scale' (money wages, in other words, were upwardly 'sticky'; it was better to give subsidies in kind than pay rises).[620] Company charity, of this prudential, self-interested kind, was not confined to big corporations like ASARCO.[621] Nor did it guarantee the good life. But it helped avert the worse features of dearth and privation: at Los Mochis, for example,[622]

practically all of the *gente* are, in some degree, retainers of either the United Sugar Co., or of the colonists, and independent of [the] general Mexican disorganisation and discredited money and they are maintained at an even average of destitution (!) which, if one may judge from their apparent contentment, is above the present general average for Mexico.

During the hard winter of 1916–17, the wages, taxes and customs duties paid by the American mines in Sonora (Cananea, Nacozari and El Tigre) carried 'the burden of feeding and financing the whole state'; American enterprises bolstered the economy of Campeche; while, more generally, it was the maintenance of high levels of exports and foreign income which enabled Tampico and Yucatán to escape the worst destitution after 1915.[623] It is not surprising, therefore, that local people welcomed the return of foreign companies which had suspended operations and, on occasions, actively sought to prevent rebel/bandit attacks on working enterprises. In Sonora, sometimes depicted as a hot-bed of economic nationalism, people 'appear[ed] anxious [to] see foreign-controlled industries revived'; in Coahuila – where people were 'elated' at the prospect of the Southern Pacific repairing and running the line between Piedras Negras and Torreón – the 'populace in their need of employment gladly welcome[d] foreign interests for their own betterment and needs'.[624] Though there were also occasional demonstrations of antagonism towards foreign companies, usually on the part of officials rather than the population as a whole, these were clearly outweighed by the examples of welcome, dependence and clientelism illustrated above; indeed, it was during these final years of the Revolution, as economic nationalism of an official kind first became prominent in revolutionary politics, that popular dependence on and appreciation of foreign investment and employment were most marked. Foreigners might not be loved but, now more than ever, foreign companies constituted islands of higher employment, wages and consumption in a sea of destitution. The benefits were relative, and stemmed from company calcula-tion, not altruism; but they were real enough, did not go unnoticed, and helped ensure that economic nationalism evoked little sympathetic response from the masses, in the way that (say) agrarian reform did.

The beneficiaries of foreign investment were a minority, albeit a significant one. Most of the population remained at the mercy of monetary and economic fluctuations. Inflation and dearth thus became the two jaws of a fearsome vice which squeezed the common people, urban and rural, even as their leaders were daily promising reform and improvement, while (if the pages of Casasola are anything to go by) attending banquet after banquet.[625] Harvests were inadequate; the transport system had partially broken down; and the vagaries of the currency made it additionally difficult for many people to maintain 'an even average of destitution'. To be sure there were big regional variations. But evidence drawn from places throughout Mexico shows that the general trend after 1915 was remorselessly unfavourable, as food production and supply failed to meet demand, as prices shot up, as hunger stalked the land. Such a trend might have been predicted (in some quarters it was). In the late

Porfiriato Mexico had to import grain from the US, especially after the bad harvests of the years immediately before the Revolution.[626] Fortunately, though quite fortuitously, the early years of the Revolution coincided with good harvests. By the turn of the year 1913/14, however, the growing economic dislocation was beginning seriously to affect food prices: in the north-east, where it was clearly evident, flour sold at more than 50% above its 1910 price; rice and potatoes were up 40%; meat and sugar nearly 30%.[627] But these increases were only a harbinger of what was to come. By spring 1915, observers in Mexico City predicted famine within six months, not least because of the decline in cultivation in the Bajío, then the chief battle-ground of the revolution.[628] Such predictions were not far wrong; furthermore, though there were partial recoveries in some regions after 1915, these were neither typical nor permanent; hence dearth remained a feature of Mexican society until the end of the revolutionary decade, revealing again the divergent rhythms of politico-military trends on the one hand, socio-economic on the other. In summer 1918 it was reckoned that the country's total corn crop was no more than a quarter to a third of its usual 150m. bushels, and that over 100m. would have to be imported to avert starvation; in 1919, times were still hard, with corn production below 1906–10 levels, which were themselves low.[629] Well before this, the State Department had arrived at the firm (though largely mistaken) belief that it could use Mexico's food shortage as a lever to control the Carranza regime; and there were not wanting Carrancista *políticos* who agreed that only American financial help could save the country from starvation.[630]

Through the intervening years came a stream of reports of steeply rising prices, shortages, dearth and privation. In Aguascalientes – by no means the hardest hit region – the price of corn rose from 0.40c. at the end of 1915 to 1.00c. in February 1916 and 2.50c. in September of that year.[631] In Mexico City, between July 1914 and July 1915 food prices in general rose fifteen-fold.[632] Increases on this scale reflected poor harvests, the rapid depreciation of the currency, and the breakdown of communications and market mechanisms, which created acute shortages in some places, while others got by. While Tepic, like most regions, suffered an 'extreme rise' in the price of staples late in 1916, Mazatlán, not far up the coast, experienced increases of only 20% above normal.[633] There were also big fluctuations over time: in Tabasco, the price of corn shifted as much, in three weeks of 1917, as it had over twenty years in Mexico City prior to 1909.[634] As a mass of reports from different sources and regions indicate, food prices went up in real as well as money terms (they were not covered by rising wages) and the secular trend of the later Porfiriato was thus greatly accelerated. In the early 1890s (the high point of popular living standards under Díaz) an agricultural daily wage bought something like seventeen litres of corn. By 1908 this had fallen to 9–10 litres.[635] In October 1914, a Mexico City gardener could buy only 7 litres with his daily wage.[636]

But 1914 was the turning point: at the beginning of the year, times were difficult but not desperate; at the end, destitution was evident and growing. By 1916, a Tampico stevedore earned the equivalent of only 4 litres of corn per day.[637] Possibly this was a pessimistic estimate; but there is abundant evidence that the real cost of staples had risen to something like this extent. A peon's daily wage in the Laguna (1916) bought 4–5 litres of corn; in Zacatecas, 5 litres; in San Luis between 6 and 8.[638] These figures suggest a doubling or tripling of the real cost of staples since the 1890s and a steep rise even upon the high levels of 1908. A report from Guanajuato agreed that, for the peon, the real cost of corn had tripled in the past twenty-five years.[639]

The Revolution forced up prices by means of inflation and rural devastation. After 1914, climatic factors conspired with human agency to depress production further. Already, the war had taken its toll: in parts of Durango still infested by Villistas in 1916, only 10% of the usual crop could be planted; in Zacatecas it was no more than 20%. A year later, there had been only a very limited recovery.[640] But the north was not exceptional. In Aguascalientes many estates were abandoned and uncultivated; around Jalapa, less than half the fields were sown; rich and poor alike had quit the valleys of western Chiapas, where fighting continued and where, it was feared, the 1916 harvest would be lost as the 1915 had been.[641] Indeed, even where cultivation was possible, the harvest was often at the mercy of hungry troops or marauding bandit/rebels. Farmers in the Laguna harvested their crops and shifted them to the nearest town at top speed.[642] Nevertheless, the urge to plant and harvest, especially when prices were high, was strong enough to surmount these human obstacles and, as the fighting dwindled and grew more localised, crops were soon brought in with surprising success. During 1916 – the first year of relative peace – planting proceeded apace around Saltillo; the Laguna estates were busy; the Aguascalientes state government laid down that those 'many people [who] at present desire and demand to invest in agriculture' could cultivate abandoned land, paying the (absent) owner 20% of the value of the harvest; much more generous sharecropping arrangements than had prevailed in the region before 1910.[643] Hence, here and points north, the 1916 harvest was by no means disastrous. Drought in the spring and floods in early summer limited the wheat harvest; Guanajuato, Aguascalientes and, above all, Zacatecas were hard hit. But the basic staples of corn and beans survived better, much of the 1916 harvest being a 'peon crop', grown by squatters, tenants or sharecroppers who had taken their chance to acquire the usufruct of land during the years of revolution.[644] On the border, too, from Sonora to Coahuila, production kept up during 1917, and the food situation was less acute.[645]

But the border was unusual in enjoying relative plenty well into 1917. In much of the country the partial recovery of 1916 gave way to a downswing and consequent dearth in 1917. It is quite wrong, therefore, to see 1915 as the trough of agricultural production, followed by successive annual increases. It may be, indeed, that this misconception derives from the familiar, urban bias of much revolutionary history: for by 1917 conditions in Mexico City appear to have improved, while the countryside, including the north, suffered its most acute shortages.[646] Coahuila, Durango and the Laguna were hit by drought which, according to one estimate, ruined three-quarters of the crops.[647] The Bajío and central plateau escaped the drought only to suffer a freak frost at the end of September: this, it was reckoned, wiped out 50% of the corn crop in Michoacán and Mexico, 75% in Guanajuato, 90% in Querétaro. By October, corn was selling at six times its usual price in Aguascalientes.[648] O'Hea, reviewing the situation from the vantage point of Gómez Palacio, late in 1917, believed that 'there is no doubt but what [sic] the coming winter [the poorer classes] will face worse conditions than have existed within the memory of the present generation'.[649] Thus 1917 went down in popular memory not as the *annus mirabilis* of the new Constitution, but as the 'year of hunger'.[650]

The hardships of the years 1915–18, outstripping anything known in the earlier years of the Revolution, are conveyed by a range of evidence which is nonetheless revealing for being 'impressionistic'. Hunger was ubiquitous: it affected even the mining towns of Sonora, where the Calles–Maytorena struggle had halted production, even though 'the people at Cananea are hungry and would like to go to work'; it affected Zapatista Morelos, too, where, though the land had been given to the tiller, there was no guarantee he could conjure plenty from the ravaged countryside.[651] By mid-1916, one third of the population of Veracruz were reckoned to lack food.[652] Even well-heeled foreigners resident in the new, temporary capital of Querétaro felt the pinch: 'I nearly starved there', reported a diplomat after a brief visit.[653] And for Mexicans, hunger reinforced the growing political quietism of these, the lean years of the Revolution. This was a moral and psychological as much as a crude biological question. The high ideals and naive hopes of the early Revolution, dashed by Huertista militarism and Carrancista *realpolitik*, guttered out amid what one revolutionary – for whom private and public misfortunes coincided – lamented as the 'general crisis' of 1917.[654] By then, disillusionment was widespread. Captain Mendoza, a member of Cabral's Sonoran forces and 'a man of unsavoury reputation', was only a little ahead of his time when, with tears in his eyes, he declared that 'he was sick and tired of revolution; he was ready to quit . . . when children had to rob horse troughs to live'.[655]

This was no hyperbole. People ate what they could get. Armies on the march stripped the locality clean: during their 1915–16 campaigns the Villistas lived off meat (tortillas were a luxury for the officers); in some dire cases they butchered their own mounts for horsemeat.[656] The common people had no such option; indeed, they were the victims of the marching armies, Villista, Carrancista, Chavista. In Zacatecas they ate cactus leaves and soup made from prickly pears; in Nuevo León and Sonora, mescal stalks and bulbs; in Nuevo León and Puebla, the maguey afforded food as well as *pulque*.[657] Near Orizaba, Stephen Bonsal saw Indians searching horse dung for undigested kernels of corn.[658] There were other signs of extreme destitution. Cans were used and re-used; when leather bridles wore out they were replaced by rope; and, notwithstanding Mexico's booming oil production, candles replaced oil lamps.[659] In Jalisco – a state unfamiliar with abject poverty – the peons now wore gunny sacks with holes cut for head and arms.[660] Beggars, it seemed, thronged the streets of cities like Saltillo; 'hordes of beggars' were still evident in the capital late in 1918.[661] They were blamed for the growing incidence of urban crime, already noted, and they presumably contributed to the rising tally of deaths from what was politely known as 'inanition'. Thirty-eight persons died of 'inanition' at Aguascalientes in one week in July 1916; the miners of Guanajuato were reportedly dying of hunger, a *constituyente* complained in January 1917; people perished in the streets of Mexico City a year later.[662]

Queues and food riots were also signs of the times. Mexico City, victim of the *va-et-vient* of rival armies, was among the first to suffer, early in 1915. Shops and markets were looted; two Spanish saloon-keepers were nearly lynched; to carry a full sack in the streets was to invite robbery. When food became available – sometimes thanks to government relief measures – the result might be more violence. A child was crushed to death in a bread line; over 200 women fainted when a crowd of 10,000 gathered to receive rations in May 1915; finally, the police had to disperse them with gunfire.[663] By 1916–17 the provinces witnessed similar scenes. At Mazatlán huge queues formed outside shops even before dawn; at Monterrey, businessmen closed and barred their shops for fear of the mob; the same fears were evident in Sonora, where an attempt by the Guaymas Chamber of Commerce to import 85,000 pesos worth of food from Sinaloa was foiled by the collapse of the *infalsificables*.[664] Elsewhere, the anticipated food riots actually occurred: in the interior towns of Yucatán and at Frontera (Tab.), where the mob looted Spanish and Chinese stores, the local authorities – against whom the people displayed 'intense bitterness' – declining either to prevent the attack or to recover the stolen goods.[665]

In such situations, the authorities sometimes cultivated a rather spurious radicalism, after the manner of Obregón during his second occupation of the capital. Perhaps Governor Múgica, who 'defended the action of the mob' after the Frontera riot, was genuine enough.[666] In other cases, populist rhetoric was a substitute for positive action. While to the outside world the government denied the facts of dearth and starvation, to its own citizens it held up the hoarder and speculator as the authors of these evils.[667] Speculation, not outright scarcity, drove up food prices, declared the press; the poor suffered from the 'speculators' lust for gain'.[668] Practical measures to combat speculation and shortages were, however, limited and largely unsuccessful. Frequent attempts at price-fixing failed; the authorities lacked either will or capacity to regulate the market; sometimes they found themselves – as the Mayor of Piedras Negras did in June 1916 – fixing prices for food which was unobtainable anyway.[669] In emergencies, the government intervened directly: Obregón created a relief junta to distribute food to the hungry of Mexico City, but its budget represented only a 'drop in the ocean'; yet smaller droplets were distributed to indigent states like Guanajuato in the summer of 1916.[670] But, as the governor of that state complained, it was extremely difficult to control the grain market. Richer states (like Sonora) traded nationally, bidding up prices to the disadvantage of the poorer; and though governors might impose extraordinarily taxes (a return to the old nineteenth-century *alcabalas*) or even prohibit all grain exports, such measures were of limited effect and duration.[671] In particular, the Federal government favoured a free market and regarded controls as temporary, regrettable expedients. The wives of Constitutionalist Ministers might distribute charity to the orphans of Mexico City, but there was to be no permanent institutionalised system of relief.[672] Indeed, the relief centres and public kitchens established in Mexico City in 1915 were wound up early in 1916 on the grounds that the food supply had now improved and that such establishments encouraged vagrancy.[673]

An additional factor was perhaps the defeat of Villa: for there can be little doubt that relief measures in Mexico City had been undertaken in a certain spirit of competition with the Convention, and with an eye to winning political and military recruits.[674] Such considerations now carried less weight; and, while the alleged improvement in food supply was largely spurious, the fears of vagrancy were real enough, and indicative of Constitutionalist ideology.[675] It was not the job of government to sustain the poor or regulate markets; there would be no War Communism in the Mexican Revolution. Food shortages would be eliminated only by hard work and initiative. The official press exhorted the country 'to abandon the apathy and indolence with which it is now possessed and to dedicate itself to work, so that the problem of hunger might be resolved'.[676] Exhortation of this kind was typical of the 'official mind' of Constitutionalism.[677] In the absence of sustained government intervention, food production would be revived by hard work and market forces; meanwhile, American supplies were severely limited by war-time controls, and the State Department's perverse attempt to link economic relief to a favourable settlement of outstanding differences.[678] Choice and necessity therefore both required that recovery would be autonomous, largely unregulated, and slow. Published statistics, for what they are worth, suggest that corn production in 1918 was the same as in 1910, while that of beans had fallen by a third.[679] It is unlikely that these figures err on the side of pessimism. What is more, while the production of beans picked up after 1918, corn production remained static until the mid-1920s.[680] Cumberland concludes, on the basis of 'impressionistic' evidence, that 'all parts of Mexico recorded a gradually deteriorating situation until 1918, and then a renewed degeneration after 1921'.[681]

The regime's culpability in the matter was not confined to resolute inactivity (which for some economists would be no sin anyway). Besides such debatable sins of omission, there were also abundant, incontrovertible sins of commission, aggravating shortages and hampering recovery. In 1915, the demands of the war against Villa overrode considerations of relief: food was exported to secure foreign exchange and arms; food exports continued into the years of dearth, although there were emergency prohibitions at times of greatest need.[682] Throughout, however, the profiteering of the authorities themselves constituted an insuperable obstacle to the rational organisation of food supplies. As early as 1915, the governor of Guanajuato complained that the Supply Committees set up in other states to buy and sell grain (whose activities were forcing up prices in Guanajuato) were in fact composed 'of out-and-out businessmen, who speculate in the poverty of the poor'.[683] Thereafter, as the new Constitutionalist elite consolidated itself in power, matters grew worse rather than better. Allegations of graft and corruption were constant, emanating not only from censorious foreigners, but also outraged Mexicans, high and low, civilian and military. Trafficking in foodstuffs – grain, flour, beans, chickpeas, meat and cattle – was one of the most commonly cited abuses, and the alleged practitioners embraced a wide section of the elite: Iturbe in Sinaloa, Treviño, Murguía and the Herreras in Chihuahua, the Arrietas in Durango, Triana in Aguascalientes, Diéguez in Jalisco, González in Morelos.[684] If these were the big names, there were many lesser grafters, too: Miguel Acosta, who shipped stolen cattle up from Papantla and points south to sell in Tampico; Luis Freyría, who controlled the confiscated hacienda of San Nicolás Chaparro (Mich.) and the branch line to Irimbo, dealing in wheat and other crops.[685] Freyría claimed his actions were legitimised by a letter of authorisation from Carranza – though it seems he interpreted its terms somewhat liberally. The situation, however, was far from unusual: Carranza – and his regime – regularly empowered individuals to manage rural properties, run railways, supply foodstuffs to towns, cities, railway work gangs and garrisons.[686] Privileged individuals were also exempted from export duties or controls temporarily placed on the internal movement of goods.

Such privileges – a legacy of the armed revolution, and an index of the weakness of revolutionary bureaucracy – in no way constituted a rational system for the production and distribution of food; and they illustrate how far removed the real economy of 1915–20 was from a perfect market, ideology notwithstanding. It was, rather, a chaotic, *ad hoc* system, free in the sense of being unplanned, but subject to constant, 'non-economic' inputs ('non-economic' in the sense of being economically irrational), which in turn responded to local political priorities, personal avarice, debts, favours and patronage. Of these varied inputs, graft was the most significant; indeed, graft, rather than any high-minded social engineering, was probably the most widespread, effectual form of government intervention in the economy during these years. Market forces, in other words, were bent more often in the pursuit of personal or sectional gain, than of revolutionary social justice. And this was particularly true of food production and distribution, for so long as the military remained in control and the economic situation encouraged shortages and speculation, abuses were endemic. It may also be presumed that, of the many forms of graft practised by the Carrancista elite, that associated with food-trafficking incurred most popular resentment. Meantime, the carapace of graft inhibited the development of rational policies (whether of *dirigiste* or free market rationale) to avert dearth and famine. Viewed from this angle, Carranza's regime loses much of its alleged social radicalism and related economic *dirigisme*, and assumes instead the features of Weber's 'decentralised patrimonial authority', in which 'governmental authority and corresponding economic rights tend to be treated as privately appropriated economic advantages' and, in consequence, 'the development of markets is . . . more or less seriously limited by irrational factors'.[687]

This is an important point, to which we shall return. For the moment, we should note how graft – and its associated economic irrationality – aggravated shortages and blocked solutions. Meantime dearth, poverty and malnutrition combined with the filth and squalor brought on by protracted warfare to produce epidemic disease on a scale unknown for generations. Many observers (not just fussy, hygiene-conscious Anglo-Saxons, with their olfactory obsessions) commented on the prevalent squalor. As a result of the Revolution, the Tepic *jefe político* reported, public hygiene and sanitation had been neglected and urgent remedies were now needed.[688] At Aguascalientes, a more prosperous community, the streets were not cleaned for eight months in 1915; the pavements were unrepaired, the street lights deficient; beggars roamed the streets and the police were inadequate to handle the situation. Typhus started, and further epidemics were feared.[689] Similar problems afflicted Mexico City, where the deficiencies of public hygiene, familiar enough during the Porfiriato, were greatly compounded by the Revolution.[690] Poverty drove destitute families to scour the huge rubbish tips on the plains of San Antonio Abad, to the south-east of the city, whence they brought scraps of food or old clothes, for their own use, or for sale in the more plebeian markets of the city – Tepito, Candelaria and Santo Tomás.[691] The threat to public health was transparent; in one incident, a man, woman, three children and a mule were overcome by the noxious gasses and seized with fits of vomiting as they prospected the rubbish piles. But if the capital was an extreme case, its problems were reflected throughout the country, in both urban and rural districts. Veracruz, scrubbed and disinfected by the Americans, was back to its familiar, fly-blown self a year later; the towns of Chiapas were filthy and lacked sanitation; the villages of Morelos, like Azteca, displayed ruined houses and overgrown streets.[692]

Hence conditions were propitious for epidemic disease. Observers did not doubt that disease stemmed from dearth and destitution. In Chihuahua, the notable increase in gastric fever, smallpox and measles was attributed to 'the condition of revolution which the country is suffering'; the smallpox which ravaged Tepic was blamed on the 'neglect and state of physical destitution suffered by the majority of the inhabitants of this region'.[693] Statistical evidence confirmed these impressions. From Durango (May, 1917) came a report of 'great suffering among the poor, much hunger, sickness, and many deaths from inanition, typhus, fever and smallpox'; some country people, unable to buy corn, were subsisting on grass and suffering intestinal sickness; the death rate stood at 160 per thousand, five times the average for 1900–10.[694] Not that Durango was the worst afflicted: the typhus epidemic of 1916 pushed the death rate in Guanajuato up to 300 per 1,000.[695] In states like Guanajuato and Zacatecas, such epidemics – correlating with poverty and stimulating out-migration – produced large falls in population. During the years of armed revolution (1910–17) the population of the city of Guanajuato fell by about two-thirds, from some 35,000 to 13,000; that of Zacatecas even more, from 26,000 to 8,000.[696] After 1917–18, which represented a nadir, came a partial recovery: nevertheless, the 1921 census still showed a net fall, compared with 1910, of 16,000 (45%) in the case of Guanajuato, over 10,000 (40%), in that of Zacatecas; in their eponymous states, the fall was some 20%.[697] Not all this decline was directly brought about by disease (Zacatecas had been the site of one of the bloodiest battles of the Revolution, in which civilian as well as military lives were lost). But disease, apart from being the single biggest killer, also contributed to the redistribution of population, as people quit poor, hungry, unhealthy regions in search of something better.[698] Thereby, they spread disease – the greater mobility as well as the greater destitution of the revolutionary years ensured that these epidemics would outstrip their Porfirian predecessors – and they joined that great army of *déracinés*: migrant workers, refugees, soldiers, deserters, bandits, beggars, which represented one of the main human legacies of the Revolution.

Typhus, the classic disease of wars and dearths, was the main killer in 1916–17.[699] There had been premonitory outbreaks in 1914: 'much sickness' was reported among Villa's army at Zacatecas, where the veteran Toribio Ortega had succumbed.[700] Vague reports of increased mortality from gastric illness emanated from Mexico City early in 1915.[701] By the end of the year the epidemic had struck in earnest. In the capital 30,000 cases were registered (the city gaols were particularly affected) and, notwithstanding some diminution in the spring of 1916, when illusory hopes were raised that the epidemic was spent, it revived again in the winter of 1916/17.[702] At its peak, the epidemic claimed 1,000 victims a week in the capital; not till well into 1918, when the rate had fallen to 20 per week, could it be said that normal conditions again prevailed.[703] Meantime typhus began to ravage the provinces. Aguascalientes was affected by the end of 1915, Pachuca and Toluca by the following spring.[704] Those who could, fled infected cities, like Zacatecas, for healthy retreats; fugitive peons carried the disease north, even to the American south-west; typhus, it was said, warped the once benign character of Chávez García.[705] Now, typhus (or typhoid) was a feature of much of northern and central Mexico, from Veracruz to Jalisco; disease of 'epidemic proportions' flourished in San Luis (plague and *mal de pinto* as well as typhus); and the early months of 1917 saw no real improvement.[706] Guanajuato and Zacatecas were worst hit: at its height, in the summer of 1916, typhus claimed the lives of 200 people a day in Zacatecas; over a period of five months, a *constituyente* observed, 5,000 were thought to have perished.[707]

If typhus was the main killer in 1916–17, other diseases seconded its attack on a weary, weakened population. The Porfirian regime had made headway against smallpox, but with the Revolution and the decline in preventive medicine which it provoked, the trend was reversed: smallpox revived in Morelos in 1912, in Mexico City in 1915, and in many parts of the country in 1916–17.[708] It was noted in Chihuahua, the Laguna and Veracruz, and in the latter case it conspired with malaria and yellow fever, the endemic diseases of the tropical lowlands. Malaria came to Mexico City with the Zapatistas in 1915; and, as the people of Morelos succumbed to typhus, the Carrancista invaders of Morelos fell prey to malaria: 'the streets were full of corpses and the women who followed their men in the army searched among the bodies to find their dead'.[709] At the same time, malaria was 'decimating' Carrancista troops who campaigned in Veracruz without adequate supplies of quinine.[710] Malaria, and the more dreaded yellow fever, were also reported in Chiapas and Yucatán.[711] And – since humans were not the only victims of disease – in 1915 the boll-worm attacked the Laguna cotton plantations.[712]

By early 1918 it seemed that the worst epidemics were over. Then, later in the year, the influenza pandemic – the 'Spanish influenza' which was already ravaging the Near East and Europe – arrived in Mexico, again encountering a war-weary, hungry population. Unlike typhus, influenza came and went rapidly: it swept through Chihuahua in a few weeks.[713] But its incidence and mortality were greater, especially in northern and central Mexico.[714] A healthy middle-class youth like Alfonso Taracena could tuck himself in bed with a glass of lemon and recover virtually overnight; but for the poor – now a greater majority of the population than ever – it was a different story and in much of Mexico, as in Morelos, 'there were the perfect grounds for an epidemic – prolonged fatigue, starvation diets, bad water, continual moving'.[715] Hence, although many Mexicans, like Taracena, contracted influenza and recovered, mortality was also high; much higher than in healthier industrial societies like England. Though a greater proportion of the English population contracted influenza, the total mortality was only about 4 per 1,000; one estimate of Mexican mortality is as high as 20 per 1,000; and, if the equivalent Indian figure is borne in mind (over 60 per 1,000), this is not at all implausible.[716] Unfortunately, statistics for the period are lacking and those which survive do not inspire confidence. No doubt San Pedro suffered heavily from the epidemic, but the figure of 1,400 deaths in one day (about 10% of the population) is hardly credible.[717] Nearby, in the Laguna towns, 300 were said to have died in 2 days: mortality on this scale, spread over no more than a week, would produce a death rate of some 20 per 1,000, which fits the national estimate.[718] With a little juggling, the Chihuahua statistics suggest a comparable figure; while those for Querétaro (state) reveal 25 per 1,000.[719] Further south, the figures tend to be lower: 8 per 1,000 in Veracruz, only 2 per 1,000 in Puebla.[720] If the national estimate of 20 per 1,000 – or a total mortality of 300,000 – is too high, it may not be radically too high.

Such a conclusion is borne out by impressionistic evidence. The medical and sanitation services could not cope: there were insufficient doctors, medicines, hospital beds and burial places. At Zacatecas, corpses piled up unburied (here, perhaps because of the extreme conditions, influenza returned in 1919); at Juárez the sick were billeted outside the town in the race-track; in Mexico City, the authorities closed public buildings and mass was held in the open air.[721] Nearby, in Morelos, emigration and influenza brought a 25% drop in the state's population; a demographic collapse which the Carrancistas hoped would undercut Zapatista resistance. Whole villages were abandoned and towns, like Cuautla, shrank to the size of villages.[722] Nor was Morelos altogether exceptional. 'In many districts close to Mexico City', it was reported, 'the population of villages have been decimated and in some cases practically annihilated.'[723] For war-weary Mexico, as for war-weary Europe, the winter of 1918/19 was a bitter time when, Jesús Romero Flores recalled, 'a feeling of sadness and fear seemed to envelop everything'.[724] Or, as his fellow-Michoacanos from San José opined, looking back at 1918, 'a worse year than that there had never been'.[725] However, 1918 did extend one favour to them, when the Spanish influenza carried off Chávez García, the bandit scourge of those regions.[726]

The recrudescence of epidemic disease – typhus, smallpox, malaria, influenza – spurred the government to action. The Porfirian regime had shown a lively concern for and achieved some notable success with preventive medicine, which was seen as a legitimate area of government intervention (had not progressive, capitalist metropolises like Birmingham and Vienna permitted a certain 'collectivist' modification of liberal *laissez-faire*?).[727] And, even before the major epidemics began, local authorities, like those of Huertista Tampico in the spring of 1914, grew alarmed at the mounting health risks, realising that 'the unsanitary conditions were more to be feared than the rebels'.[728] When such fears were borne out after 1915, the revolutionary authorities took prompt, if not always effective, action. The Consejo Superior de Salubridad campaigned extensively to clean and disinfect foci of contagion: churches, theatres, barracks, gaols, stations, schools, libraries and trams.[729] Teams of experts were despatched to the provinces: to Pachuca, Toluca, Veracruz and Oaxaca; local health committees were established in some states, medical police (who could also serve as useful government spies) in others.[730] Disease became another subject of public exhortation: during the typhus epidemic the Consejo Superior de Salubridad held a 'patriotic junta' at Guadalupe Hidalgo, near the capital, at which songs – including a 'hymn to progress' – were sung, films shown, and speeches delivered, one being a 'talk about hygiene concerning several animals known to be injurious to man'.[731]

Such efforts were to be expected as the incidence of disease mounted. But these were more than mere *ad hoc* measures; indeed, the energy of the authorities in the field of public health contrasted with their supine acceptance of hunger and destitution. Money was more readily spent and programmes more boldly conceived; furthermore the administrative mechanisms for combating disease were more organised, efficient and classically bureaucratic.[732] A cynic might attribute this to the fact that public health offered less opportunities for graft (than, say, food distribution); and that the authorities themselves were more at risk from typhus or influenza than hunger and destitution; disease, after all, had claimed prominent *cabecillas* like Ortega and Chávez García, while few revolutionary leaders (witness the plethora of banquets) actually went hungry. But the concern for public health went beyond narrow, sectional interest and followed Porfirian and European precedents, of which revolutionary intellectuals and bureaucrats – additionally spurred on by circumstances – were well aware.[733] Indeed, the ideology, or 'ethos', of Constitutionalism was particularly conducive to such public health and hygiene campaigns, which figured as prominent elements in a set of related, mutually reinforcing, 'developmentalist' policies, including education, temperance, anti-clericalism and so on.[734] During the typhus epidemic, for example, the import of *pulque* into Mexico City was banned (*pulque* was probably as nutritious as it was noxious); in Yucatán, Alvarado attributed the decline in pellagra to his anti-liquor laws.[735] Churches were closed (a legitimate preventive measure, perhaps) but they were also bulldozed, and the faithful were enjoined not to kneel during services – advice which, the health authorities stressed, was given in order to combat disease, not religion.[736] Even if the disclaimer was sincere, advice of this kind suggests the mental connection which revolutionaries readily made, perhaps unconsciously, between religion, superstition, dirt and disease; and it implied priorities which were unacceptable to most of the population, for whom it still made more sense, when disease threatened, to bend the knee than to visit the doctor.

LABOUR

A rough picture has been given of social conditions between 1915 and 1920. Rebellion, banditry, crime, poverty, hunger, squalor and disease were rife. Yet, though conditions were objectively far worse than in 1910–15, social protest declined. There were food and currency riots, and continued support for popular rebellions like Zapata's or Cedillo's. But the military challenges to the regime increasingly emanated from defensive, landlord rebellions, usually draped in the flag of Felicismo, and the kind of banditry associated with the name of Chávez García. The *campesinos*, the vanguard of the early Revolution, returned to their *milpas*, disillusioned, or persuaded that they could only secure gains through the official revolution, especially its official agrarian reform. The urban working class – or, at least, that fraction of it represented by the Casa del Obrero Mundial – seemed to have arrived at a similar conclusion in 1915, with the pact which created the Red Battalions. But, in fact, the path which led from mutualist self-help and syndicalist militancy to the mass, manipulative unions of the 1920s was sinuous and rutted; above all, it wove its way through the ravaged no man's land of 1915–18, affording those who travelled it an experience they would not forget and which would inform their subsequent conduct. The later detente between government and labour (or, some would say, the surrender of labour to the government's stifling embrace) must therefore be seen within the context not only of the armed revolution and 1915 pact, but also of the economic collapse and destitution which followed, and which affected urban labour more profoundly.

In 1915, Carranza and the Casa enjoyed a brief honeymoon. If the Red Battalions did not swing the civil war, Casa propaganda was unstinting. Its newspaper, *Revolución Social*, applauded the Carrancistas for combating clericalism and reaction, for giving land to the peasants and freedom to the proletariat.[737] Casa spokesmen went to the provinces, recruited new members, set up new branches and publicised the Constitutionalist cause: by June 1915 the Casa claimed 52,000 members.[738] The fortunes of these proletarian emissaries were mixed. At Córdoba they were denounced from the pulpit and excommunicated; in the benighted Oaxaca of Meixueiro and Dávila they were harassed and killed; two lost their lives when Zapatistas attacked their train in Tlaxcala.[739] Elsewhere they were welcomed, by the Constitutionalist authorities at least, and were able to organise unions, establish local headquarters, recruit, parade and propagandise. Enlightened governors like Elizondo in Michoacán and Alvarado in Yucatán were cordial and helpful; glad, no doubt, of the support these similarly enlightened activists offered to regimes struggling in hostile environments.[740] Here, the Casa faithfully performed its allotted role as client, ally, and beneficiary of Carrancismo.

But no less significant was Casa activity in the industrial heartland of Mexico around Orizaba. Here, at a time of dearth and unemployment, Casa representatives set out to radicalise and recruit the workers.[741] The usual appeals were made: the Red Battalions were fighting clericalism and reaction; behind Villa stood an unholy trinity of bishops, ex-Federals and American big business.[742] By way of appealing to the indigenous trade union tradition, Casa activists joined in a 'spectacular commemoration' of the 1907 Río Blanco strike.[743] But these activists, it was clear, were no Carrancista stooges: they went far beyond what Carranza, or even Obregón, expected from their new, proletarian allies; to some, they seemed bent on closing the region's factories. In reality, the Casa sought to use the pact – and the opportunity and legitimacy it conferred – to win support among the largest proletarian group in the country, in a region where hitherto the Casa had not been strongly represented. Local businessmen were appalled and Carrancista military commanders, backed by the Department of Labour, took steps to counter Casa propaganda.[744] As a result, within weeks of the pact being signed, one of the Carrancista signatories confessed, 'the government is having great trouble with the labour unionists from the City of Mexico who have lately joined the Constitutionalists'.[745]

The reactions of the workers themselves – for whom militancy, even in the context of revolution, was a risky stance – were varied. Some responded favourably to the Casa's appeals and some, though not many, joined the Red Battalions; others, including a majority of the textile workers, displayed a certain suspicion of Casa interlopers and a preference for existing, local associations; some sought the protection and patronage of Carrancista generals, even enrolling as soldiers in local garrisons.[746] It may be presumed that (as with the original Casa – Constitutionalist pact) enrolment in the military represented a final capitulation in the face of unemployment and hardship. The great majority of workers stayed at work while work was available (some even developed a profitable sideline selling food to the troops): in March 1915, for example, 90% of the Río Blanco operatives were still in employment and a recent pay rise meant that wages were now sufficiently high, 'that the pay offered in the army is too low to be tempting'.[747] Through the summer of 1915 the workers continued their long-standing, largely defensive struggle to maintain jobs and pay, especially as conditions deteriorated and more lay-offs occurred.[748] Furthermore, the rival Casa and Carrancista appeals did not exhaust the workers' options. Some (like the workers of Atlixco in 1914) could count on company paternalism; others – in the Puebla–Orizaba region, as in Mexico City and elsewhere – looked to the Convention, or more specifically to Villa or Zapata.[749] A carpenter's apprentice from Atlixco reported that eighty workers had joined the Zapatistas 'in view of the shortage of work . . . or out of ignorance or sympathy'.[750] Though, we have noted, there were general reasons why the Carrancistas, rather than their main political rivals, struck an alliance with organised labour, there were also many specific, local factors inclining labour in other directions.[751]

Nevertheless, the chief contest in what Ruiz calls the 'struggle to control labor' was fought between the Carrancistas and their supposed Casa allies. The Casa's quest for an independent proletarian base was bound to elicit fierce resistance from the Carrancistas, whose military leaders and labour bureaucrats wanted a docile Casa and labour movement (desiderata which, it may be noted, the conservative elements of the Convention also entertained).[752] Carrancistas and Conventionists (and we are dealing, in both cases, with northerners) saw the need to make concessions to labour; but these were designed to buy adherence and deference, not to create a syndicalist hydra. Assertions of working-class independence were, at best, grudgingly and temporarily tolerated while the civil war lasted. Ultimately, a showdown was inevitable. Indeed, within weeks of the pact, Casa–Constitutionalist rivalry was plain to see, as the Labour Department battled with the Casa for proletarian allegiances in Veracruz and Puebla, denouncing Casa subversion and strikes, urging arbitration, forming 'resistance groups' in direct competition with the Casa's *sindicatos*.[753] For the time being, therefore, the department orchestrated Constitutionalist policy towards the working class: it offered tangible benefits (such as wage rises), it outbid more radical, rival appeals, and it strove to establish that social equilibrium which was the guiding principle of Constitutionalist thinking with regard to labour relations.[754] In what was an updated version of Don Porfirio's *pan o palo*, the Department of Labour supplied the *pan*.

So, too, did many Constitutionalist leaders, at least on paper. Never before had the Mexican working class been the object of such solicitude. Apart from the well-known demagogic appeals of Obregón in Mexico City or Maytorena in Sonora, there were many other instances where political leaders threw their weight behind working-class demands – or, disgruntled business interests alleged, even provoked them in the first place.[755] The oil and dock workers of Tampico – proletarian groups of proven muscle – were particularly favoured. When the oil workers struck in summer 1915, they were reported to 'have the solid backing of the local military authorities'.[756] In cases large and small, the Constitutionalist authorities arbitrated in industrial disputes: involving the Tampico oil workers again in summer 1916, the Frontera dockers, the miners and railwaymen of Coahuila, the *zacatón* workers of Tlaxcala.[757] Arbitration did not necessarily imply a fierce attachment to proletarian interests (Díaz, after all, had arbitrated in industrial disputes); nevertheless Constitutionalist arbitration, even while it placed social equilibrium above proletarian emancipation, favoured the workers' interests to an unprecedented extent. It was for this reason that the regime acquired a black reputation in business circles, while it struck more sympathetic observers as 'a reforming movement of international importance'.[758]

This reputation was enhanced by the Constitutionalists' formal labour legislation: the establishment, on paper at least, of maximum hours, minimum wages, accident compensation and sick pay, workers' training schemes. 'In myriad ... helter-skelter ways', Cumberland observes, the regime 'indicated support for the laboring man and the labor movement.'[759] It would be tedious to cite such legislation in detail, for in 1914–17 it covered the greater part of the country: Pablo de la Garza decreed a minimum wage for Guanajuato in September 1914; Diéguez followed suit in Jalisco two months later; even as the battles of the Bajío got under way Obregón extended similar measures to three more states.[760] And, with the civil war won, legislators could embark on more complex, comprehensive schemes of labour protection and arbitration: as Martín Triana did in Aguascalientes, Calles in Sonora, both early in 1916.[761] This reformist drive culminated, of course, in Article 123 of the new Constitution.[762]

Many of these, however, remained paper reforms; and they must be seen in their context of economic upheaval, unemployment, inflation and destitution. The years 1914–17 witnessed repeated strike action, which affected the railways, oil camps, mines, docks, trams, electric plants, textile factories, big commercial houses as well as small artisan workshops, schools, even the police. Though many blamed subversive influences – chiefly the Casa and its international counterpart, the IWW – it is clear that inflation and the falling standard of living lay at the root of the incessant industrial action. Though some groups, such as the Tampico workers, were ready and able to mount industrial offensives, looking to real improvements, the great majority strove to defend existing, modest standards, at a time when real wages were slipping and, a Constitutionalist official admitted, 'were insufficient to maintain the subsistence of the proletarian classes'.[763] Hence the most common demand in 1915–17 was that pay should be pegged to gold, silver, or hard foreign currency – that, somehow, the worker should be protected against the dire consequences of inflation. Such was the demand of the miners of Pachuca and of the Dos Estrellas Co. (Mex./Mich.); of the Mexico City printers, the machine shop workers of Aguascalientes, and the employees of the Monterrey smelting industry.[764] Veracruz faced a general strike over this question in February 1916, and further action in May; nearly forty commercial houses in Mexico City were closed by strikes; the railwaymen of Chihuahua struck for silver pay in spring 1916, while, later in the year, the engineers at Juárez refused to shift a locomotive until a gold-based pay scale was introduced.[765] 'Economist' though these protests were, they sometimes threatened public order. At Veracruz, some feared that the 'continuous state of unrest due to strikes' would eventually lead to the underpaid garrison taking strike action; at Nuevo Laredo the police had already struck; while, late in 1916, there were riots in the capital when the government tried to pay off striking police and tram workers in near worthless paper.[766]

In other respects, too, the industrial action of these years was defensive, even desperate, rather than confidently aggressive. The urban workers suffered greatly from high prices, hunger and disease, all of which militated against the creation or development of strong unions, or even viable mutualist societies. A bout of illness, scarcely avoidable in these pestiferous times, could mean destitution; yet, at Orizaba certainly, management strongly resisted demands for sick pay.[767] Not surprisingly, some unions seemed to surrender the battle over wages to concentrate on the war on prices: his workers would not respond to a strike call, declared a union leader in the Puebla/Tlaxcala region: 'their sole desire is that the government turn its attention to the abuses being perpetrated by the majority of merchants on account of the excessive increase in prices'.[768] Like Hobsbawm's 'primitive rebels' (urban variety), these workers appealed to the government in times of dearth and unemployment, locating their grievances in the field of consumption, not production.[769] Whether or not this represented an archaism of mind, it certainly reflected the weakness of union bargaining on the factory floor. And this weakness, greatly exacerbated by current conditions, can be readily imagined and sometimes illustrated. The slow accumulation of union funds and members was easily jeopardised by sickness, unemployment and poverty. The Aquiles Serdán Workers Mutualist Society (Cananea) suffered from the 'frightful' fluctuations in the currency: 10,000 pesos were lost and the society's capital, built up since its foundation in 1911, plunged after 1915. A branch of the society established at Santa Rosalía (Baja Calif.) in 1916 also fell on hard times, being particularly hit by the influenza epidemic.[770] At Orizaba, the membership of a mutualist society set up at the Río Blanco and San Lorenzo factories traced a similar curve: foundation in 1913, growth in 1914, collapse in 1916 (after which recovery began).[771] Assuming (and there are good reasons for making the assumption) that similar trends affected working-class groups elsewhere, it becomes evident that labour was in a particularly weak, disorganised state between 1914 and 1917; and that the strikes, paper reforms and repression of these years coincided with proletarian retreat, not advance.

The response of companies, as of politicans, varied. Some firms, selling overseas for hard currency, could afford wage rises, just as they could afford charitable good works. Indeed, companies which could master domestic upheaval while catering to the voracious international demand stimulated by the World War enjoyed an enviable position. Labour was cheap, abundant and one, observer commented, unusually 'respectful'.[772] Companies, like Real del Monte at Pachuca, could undertake major renovations on the cheap, thanks to the depreciation of the peso.[773] Thus, while production of precious metals slumped, and recovered slowly if at all (silver did not reach its 1910 level until 1922), copper and zinc bottomed out in 1914–15 and then rose sharply:

Production by weight of	gold	silver	lead	copper	zinc
1910=100	100	100	100	100	100
1914	22	36	5	55	44
1915	17	51	16	46	322
1916	29	38	16	59	2083
1917	59	54	52	106	2511
1918	61	80	79	146	1150
1922	56	104	89	56	339

Meanwhile, between 1910 and 1919, the US price of silver doubled, that of copper rose by two-thirds.[774] In addition, oil and henequen experienced a war-induced boom. Between 1915 and 1918 the price of henequen tripled and Yucatán's export earnings doubled; what did not go in profits to the planters and remittances to the central government was used to underwrite Alvarado's 'burgeoning welfare state': the schools, libraries, unions, wage rises and emergent bureaucracy.[775] In the case of oil there was no *dirigiste* institution comparable to Alvarado's Regulating Commission (though the economic nationalist policies of these years, deployed with particular vigour in respect of oil, obeyed similar objectives).[776] As production shot up – from 3.6m. barrels in 1910 to 26.2m. in 1914, 63.8m. in 1918, and 193.4m. in 1921 – the chief benefits accrued to the companies.[777] But their tax bill rose, and they were able to meet wage demands, albeit grudgingly, so that real wage levels were maintained. The oil workers were accordingly less militant than, say, their comrades on the Tampico docks, and strikes, though common, were usually settled rapidly, without the shipment of oil being affected. 'At present', reported the US military attaché in January 1918, 'the workmen and employees of the different petroleum companies are well paid and in the confidence of the officials of the companies.'[778] Paid on a gold basis, the oil workers had spurned Casa agitation in 1916.[779] For the companies, therefore, government regulation and taxation posed a greater threat than the militancy of their labour force.

The position was very different for enterprises serving the domestic market, which were seriously affected by the peso's collapse and the rupture of internal communications: notably the railways, public utilities, textile industry and coal-mines. In these sectors conflicts over wages were more acute and, for want of resources, less capable of negotiated settlement; confrontation and repression were more likely (and less damaging to the employer). Paradoxically, the employer was often the government. Thus, even as the Carrancistas promulgated their fine labour decrees and codes, they were locked in battle with their own employees, and resorting to frequent repression: 'in labour . . . as in all else Mexican', Gruening comments, 'things are often not what they seem or what they are declared to be'.[780] In the Coahuila coal mines, for example, a typical defensive strike occurred in May 1916: the miners protested against a wage cut, which took away half a pay rise conceded two months earlier; they offered to return to work, however, if the price of corn were cut by one-third.[781] The gouging employer in this instance was the government, in the shape of the General Administrator of Coahuilan Mines, while the company's chief customer was also the government, *viz.*, the Constitutionalist Railways, which were heavily dependent on Coahuilan coal. Faced with a drop in coal output, which had military as well as economic implications, the government had to reach a settlement, rescind the wage cut, and bring wages back in line with inflation.[782] Later in 1916, however, as the peso spiralled down, there was renewed trouble; and it was probably with some relief that the mines were returned to private ownership in December.[783]

The case raises an important point about government intervention in the economy during the Revolution – which has often been seen as indicative of radicalism or economic nationalism. The regime found itself – willy-nilly, without any ideological or practical preparation – running large sectors of the economy: mines, estates, railways and public utilities. Intervention on this scale derived from political and military, rather than economic, imperatives; and, after 1915, as these lost some of their force, while the economic burdens often grew more onerous, the regime was eager to shed some of the load (to 'hive off', in modern jargon, elements of the swollen 'public sector'). We shall note this particularly in the case of real estate.[784] While profitable interventions, in oil or henequen, justified themselves, many were loss-making and contentious. It was, for example, embarrassing for the government when their employees on the Tampico docks – who were on the Constitutionalist Railways' payroll – called a strike, demanding parity with the waterfront employees of a private, American contractor; ultimately, the American company had to keep its wages in line with the (lower) level set by the government.[785] Further anomalies were created when, as income slumped and labour disputes mounted, the regime sought to return 'intervened' public utilities (such as tram companies) to their private owners, only to find the latter reluctant to resume operations in the circumstances.[786] The picture which emerges, therefore, is not one of a bold, *dirigiste* regime, dominating the commanding heights of the economy; but of harassed authorities, ideologically committed to free enterprise capitalism, but bent under a burden of randomly accumulated economic commitments which, until the day they were gratefully shed, presented constant problems.

As regards labour, one solution was repression. Unlike the oil companies, the government lacked the cash to meet working-class demands; but it had the troops to silence them. Repression derived not just from innate conservatism or a cynical intention to cripple the labour movement now the civil war had been won, but also from feelings of impatience, frustration and resentment.

The revolutionary leaders had been in the field for two, three or more years; they had suffered the risks and privations of campaigns; so, too, had their troops, who now subsisted on low and irregular pay. The urban workers, who in the great majority had never fought, now clamoured for better pay and conditions, contesting government authority, subverting public order, sometimes criticising the regime in vituperative terms. One such critic denounced the authorities — especially the military — in the pages of *El Insurgente* (Orizaba): 'this gentleman overlooking the fact', a Constitutionalist general fumed, 'that it is precisely thanks to the "brass-hats" (*soldadones*) that the workers now receive just treatment; yet not only do they attack us, but they even resort to insult'.[787] Sentiments similar to those which spurred Obregón's — and others' — denunciations of middle-class non-combatants now encouraged brusque treatment of the working class, even on the part of progressives like Alvarado. Docile, co-operative workers would receive their due from the revolutionary state — arbitration, wage rises, labour reforms — but dissidents would be brought to heel; for the first, *pan*, for the second, *palo*.

The stick became increasingly evident during 1916–17. Affiliates of the Casa (or IWW, as American observers termed it) were among the chief victims; but the repression was not simply aimed at this organisation — rather, it sought to contain working class protest in general, in the interests of political stability and economic production, and the Casa figured as the main, organised embodiment of proletarian disaffection. At Tampico, always a focal point, the military commander, Emiliano Nafarrete, now emerged as a flail of the labour movement. In spring 1916, as demands for gold-based wages and strike action increased, the local Casa called for a general strike, and summoned a meeting of working-class groups at which this, the brightest and best weapon in the anarcho-syndicalist armoury, would be prepared for action; whereupon, 'the military with infantry and cavalry charged the meeting and broke it up. A number of leaders and others were arrested. Some were severely handled. Two or three were reported killed.'[788] With rumours flying that the workers would respond with rioting and looting, Nafarrete banned further gatherings, closed the town's saloons, summoned reinforcements and put patrols out on the streets. He then convened a meeting of employers and union leaders, urging the former to pay 'a proper wage', while lecturing the latter in 'stinging' tones: 'General Nafarrete told them they were disloyal to the Government and . . . that the paper money was backed by the Government, while there wasn't anything back of the gold.'[789] The employers agreed to consider a new pay scale — no more; meantime, a union leader complained, the workers would starve; 'go to work' was Nafarrete's final riposte. In American circles, his conduct met with 'hearty approval'. The reaction was no doubt similar when, a month later, Nafarrete warned strikers that he would shoot trouble-makers, and police again broke up a gathering of protesting workers.[790]

Nafarrete, though a particularly tough and fearsome character (one who, incidentally had a reputation for 'anti-Americanism'), was not atypical.[791] His successor at Tampico, General Guerra, was a 'loyal Carrancista' who, in 1917, 'assisted in every way to put down the IWW agitation'.[792] At Monterrey, too, Jacinto Treviño followed precedents and cracked down on the Casa.[793] More surprisingly, Salvador Alvarado took stern measures when faced with a strike by railway mechanics, stonemasons (they were building the new Escuela Normal), printers and newspaper workers. The redemptive work of Constitutionalism in Yucatán could not be jeopardised: the strike leaders were arrested and threatened with death; the headquarters which the Casa had received during the honeymoon period was taken from it and turned into a museum of Yucatecan life and customs.[794] Another progressive, Calles, closed down the Cámara de Obreros at Cananea, Nacozari and El Tigre, where its agitation ran counter to Calles' own brand of labour reformism.[795] Elsewhere, repression was often crude, but usually effective: Luis Caballero, commanding in Tamaulipas, threatened to shoot the leaders of striking railwaymen if they did not go back; at Nuevo Laredo, where police and railway mechanics went on strike, they were told by the local commander that 'they would either go back to work or go to the cemetery'.[796] Troops were brought in as strike-breakers on the Veracruz trams and the Tampico trains, where they 'apparently regarded the matter as a great joke, resulting in several accidents'.[797] But perhaps the outstanding example of governmental overriding proletarian interests was afforded by Manuel Diéguez. Diéguez, prominent in the Cananea strike of 1906, was now a leading Carrancista general: having earned the hearty dislike of the people of Jalisco, he was sent to direct operations against the Villistas in Sonora; and he did so as a paladin of Constitutionalism, not an armed tribune of the working class. The businessmen of Guaymas received a pleasant surprise (they were struck by Diéguez's 'willing[ness] to concede much to business interests'); but the workers of Cananea faced a shock. Here, in an economic imbroglio typical of 1916, government officials, including the customs service, had struck in protest at the decline of their (paper money) wages; the Cananea Co., meantime, continued paying its workers in silver, contributing to the local depreciation of Constitutionalist paper; and the miners strenuously resisted the political authorities' attempts to force the company to meet its wage bill in paper. Diéguez showed no sympathy: 'they are agitators', he was quoted as saying, 'and do not want to conform to our governmental wishes; I am afraid they [will] have to be disciplined presently.'[798]

His attitude chimed in with Constitutionalist policy at the highest level. Local repression of labour proceeded at the direct instigation of the Federal government. Carranza himself had reacted coolly to the pact with the Casa; as early as summer 1915 it was rumoured that he had fallen out of love with his new troublesome allies.[799] Certainly by 1916, with the civil war won, the regime was ready to mount a counter-offensive against labour in general, and the Casa in particular.[800] Orders went out to halt strikes, silence Casa propaganda and arrest agitators.[801] The official press roundly denounced Casa activity, while subventions to radical papers were withdrawn.[802] Carrancista agents shadowed known activities – especially foreigners like Krum Heller and Eloy Armenta – and filed reports on their supposed subversion: the 'erroneous ideas' they propagated, the 'absurd liberties' they enjoyed, the influence they wielded not only over 'workers of very slight intellectual training', but also over children, whom they taught in sordid rooms, lacking portraits of the First Chief. The authorities must persuade such subversives of the folly of their ways; but 'if by persuasive methods they cannot be got to desist from their harmful propaganda, then there remains no alternative but to bend every effort, at whatever cost, so that the authority and respect which . . . the ideas of the First Chief deserve shall be made to prevail'.[803]

A pale, autochthonous, Stalinism *avant la lettre* pervaded these times. The revolutionary elite, beset by political challenges and economic problems, took refuge in purges, repression and censorship. With regard to the labour movement, they could not allow an autonomous challenge to their newly acquired, still precarious power. The Red Battalions were, therefore, dispersed or merged into regular army corps.[804] The harassment and arrest of labour leaders continued until, in the summer of 1916, a general strike in Mexico City prompted a showdown.[805] The strike leaders were arrested, the military took over the affected power plants, the offices of the Casa and its affiliated unions were occupied, in Mexico City and the provinces alike. Even sellers of Casa newspapers were arrested; and it was now, according to one account, that the Casa library and archive were destroyed by Carrancista troops.[806] More dramatically, Carranza invoked the old Juarista law of 1862, which laid down the death penalty for treason; treason now encompassed sabotage, striking and incitement to strike; the workers of 1916 merited the same draconian treatment as the Huertistas of 1913.[807]

The general strike was broken. The voice of Grub Street – the one-time Porfirista, Reyista, *agent provocateur*, now revolutionary convert, Heriberto Barrón – praised Carranza's prompt action, denounced anarchist subversion, and recommended further curbs on political freedom (especially freedom of the press). Barrón undertook to pen laudatory articles in *El Pueblo*; he warned against publishing news of strikes in the US, which might act as a stimulus in Mexico; and he rejoiced in the 're-establishment of the social equilibrium, which was beginning to be jeopardised by the repeated, growing demands of the working class, egged on by agitators of bad faith'.[808] The theme of 'social equilibrium' – central to Constitutionalist ideology – now reached a crescendo. In the preamble to his August 1916 decree, Carranza denounced the 'anti-patriotic' and 'criminal' activity of the unions and warned that 'if it is true that the Revolution had, among its chief aims, the destruction of the tyranny of capitalism, it was not going to permit to arise another tyranny, so prejudicial to the good of the Republic, as the tyranny of the workers'.[809] In this, Carranza echoed an earlier proclamation of Pablo González, condemning the demands of organised labour, their detrimental effect on 'legitimate' rights, and the workers' assumption that their 'organisations are a kind of official institution, enjoying almost governmental authority'. This was a dangerous illusion; social harmony must prevail over sectional interest.[810] Others, more progressive and eloquent, took a similar line. The state might throw its weight behind workers' organisations, compensating for their initial weakness, but this implied neither hostility to capital, nor commitment to class struggle. Capital, wrote Alvarado, was a 'sacred inheritance of humanity'; it was 'accumulated work'; as such, it was in complete accord with labour – for they were mutually supportive – and the role of the state was to supervise this fructiferous relationship.[811] His fellow-proconsul Castro, embarking on social reform in Oaxaca, affirmed his respect for property and his intention to 'promote perfect harmony between capital and labour, such that their respective functions, though performed by distinct organs, may contribute to the supreme function of industrial prosperity'.[812] Implicitly, and sometimes explicitly, class conflict was denied.[813] The official press droned on in similar, sonorous style.[814] In practice, the repression went on, while the Department of Labour, seconded by reformist governors, provided the positive lubricants: arbitration, subsidies, protective legislation, which would smooth labour relations and conciliate the workers.[815]

But, especially while times were hard and repression continued, the doctrine of social equilibrium found a sullen audience in the working class.[816] 'The working class and the worker', riposted the paper *Germinal*, 'has nothing in common with the other classes which form society'; along with other radical papers, it cited cases of harassment, arrest, and protest at government measures; it argued for an autonomous working-class struggle and opposed collaboration with the regime. 'Those very gains which the worker makes which have not been the product of his own effort, his own work, those gains the worker should reject.'[817] In a sense, *Germinal* made a virtue of necessity. It took two to collaborate, and between 1916 and 1918, the regime often ignored *pan* in favour of *palo*: it had more sticks than loaves at its disposal. Meanwhile, the radicals published their skimpy, ephemeral newspapers, and took refuge in the contemplation of global events: the Russian Revolution, strikes in the American copper mines, labour agitation in Barcelona and Madrid.[818] These harbingers of world revolution brought solace, it seems, at a time of domestic hardship and impotence.

The readership of these radical papers was no doubt tiny; but they expressed views that were at odds with the populist pabulum of the official press, and which certainly coincided with an opinion much broader than the readership. 'People have grown weary commenting on how the real beneficiaries of the revolutionary triumph have been the ones who least deserved it', stated one such paper.[819] In this, it reflected a strong, perhaps a prevailing mood. Feelings of disillusionment, at best grudging acquiescence, did not have to await some long-term 'betrayal' of the Revolution in later decades. The working class, in particular, entertained no illusions about the regime (no more, of course, did the peasantry, whose 'betrayal' had been all the greater). The workers of Veracruz – now thoroughly familiar with the threats, abuses and strike-breaking of the authorities – were reckoned to have turned against the administration; in Coahuila, railwaymen published an open letter blaming the regime for low wages and for 'attempting to put government on the principles of [the] Díaz administration'.[820] Workers from Orizaba even appealed to Villa – an unlikely champion – listing the abuses of the regime and asserting their readiness to overthrow it by strike action.[821] This, assuming the letter to be genuine, was syndicalist braggadocio; the unions' weakness ruled out any Sorelian strategy. But there was no doubt that the brief honeymoon between Constitutionalism and organised labour had come to a recriminatory end. As the *constituyentes* gathered at Querétaro to draw up the new Constitution, which would contain, in Article 123, the 'Magna Carta' of Mexican labour, labour itself was in sullen, defensive, semi-defeated mood, confronted on the one hand by harsh economic realities and on the other by a regime bent on economic reconstruction and determined to hold the line against supposedly excessive working-class demands. At the congress itself, labour exercised little influence: few workers attended and the denunciations of government policy uttered by Nicolás Cano ('it's more sure we get bad governors than good ones') were rare and untypical.[822] Article 123 descended from on high, like a Mosaic tablet conferred by a stern deity on a chastened, disgruntled people: at best, it offered future salvation, conditional upon present good behaviour. Meanwhile, the regime's chief rival for working-class allegiances, the Casa del Obrero Mundial, had been fatally weakened. And, before long, the regime would feel sufficiently secure, and discern sufficient advantage, for it to pick up the pieces of the alliance forged in 1915 and shattered in subsequent years, and for it to refashion them in the shape of a better-tempered and more malleable weapon.[823]

THE CARRANCISTA MACHINE: INTERNAL WORKINGS

Like any government of Mexico – Hapsburg, Bourbon, Porfirian or revolutionary – Carranza's faced basic problems created by size and poor communications, class, ethnic and geographical divisions, and provincial antipathy to central rule. And like any government of this decade, Maderista, Huertista, Villista, it also confronted the specific problems engendered by the Revolution: agrarian conflict, popular protest, *caudillismo*, regional and personal vendettas. Finally, Carranza's regime had to tackle the more recent problems occasioned by economic collapse, inflation, dearth and disease. How did it cope and survive, where others had failed? And what was the character of the 'national synthesis' it achieved – in succession to Porfirismo, and as a foundation for the modern state?[824]

In general, the regime's freedom of manoeuvre and power to command have been exaggerated. The Carrancista state was certainly not the 'Leviathan' state which some have discerned in the 1920s.[825] The parameters within which it could act were narrowly set by forces beyond its control: not least the socio-economic conditions just outlined. Yet if, on the face of it, these conditions were inimical to sound government, they nevertheless assisted the stabilisation of the regime in a crucial respect. With regard to popular mood, Carranza enjoyed a definite advantage over his predecessors. In 1910–14 the tide of popular rebellion had run strongly, buffeting Díaz, eroding Madero, dragging down Huerta; by 1915, however, it had begun to ebb; it dashed itself against obstacles with diminished force; and dykes could now be built to contain it. Though popular rebellion of the kind which had been coeval with the Revolution (agrarian seizures, *serrano* revolts, social banditry, popular riots) continued, it was now past its peak. The high hopes and quasi-millenarian expectations of earlier years gave way to disillusionment and a collective *sauve-qui-peut* which greatly facilitated the task of government. The forces of protest now faced an uphill struggle: Villa had to pressgang recruits in the north, and even the Zapatistas feared an erosion of popular support. Where, a few years before, reports continually stressed the uppishness, the 'espíritu levantisco' of the common people, contrasting it with their deference in the days of Díaz, the emphasis was now on war-weariness, resignation and apathy. Men no longer itched to 'ir a la bola ('join in the fun'); they preferred to stay home and cultivate their gardens, often literally. This was a significant, subtle psychological change, impossible to quantify; but it is arguable that only this changed mood enabled the Carrancista regime – in many respects a ramshackle regime, wracked by divisions and submerged in an economic morass – to survive and gain strength. It was this more congenial climate, as much as any innate vigour, which enabled Carrancismo to take root, where Maderismo and Huertismo had withered. Like many of the success stories of history, the Carrancistas prospered less because of their rare, intrinsic qualities, but because they were in the right place at the right time.

Throughout the Revolution there had existed a *pacífico* constituency, keen for peace and stability, sceptical of or downright hostile to rebellion: most landlords (including *rancheros* as well as *hacendados*); many city-dwellers, including merchants, artisans and industrial workers, especially in larger, prosperous towns. Though often politically aware and active, they had deplored violent rebellion and inclined to the established government, be it Madero's or Huerta's.[826] Now, with jobs, business and livelihood under greater threat than ever, their commitment to peace and reconstruction was all the stronger. A French observer noted the townspeople's 'favourable disposition . . . towards anything which would herald a return to order and normal life'; in Sonora, it was the 'planters, merchants, and artisans who feel the pinch of war . . . and who are eager for peace'.[827] Now, these attitudes were more common, and shared by the rural population. The rebel/bandit counted on less covert assistance or active support; the forces of order (not necessarily the army) incurred less hostility. A corrido captured the mood:[828]

> Let it be an example to all / whom ambition guides;
> That the people no longer support / any old revolution.
> They want only work / and also guarantees,
> No matter whether Juan or Pedro govern / a civilian or a
> general.

Such sentiments were evident throughout the country. In Tabasco 'everybody is weary of the revolution' and eager for work; at La Paz (Baja Calif.) 'the people do not care which faction occupies the place but desire only to be left alone' (Cantú reflected peninsular feelings).[829] So, too, in more troubled regions: Veracruz, Zapatista Morelos, Aguascalientes – after the battles of the Bajío were under way.[830] And the same was true of revolutionary Durango and Parral, where the people were 'sick of revolutions and . . . anxious to obtain a peaceful living by honest work'.[831] Such general statements are suggestive (of not only a desire for peace but also an appetite for work and reconstruction); but they are not conclusive. More solid evidence is available in the proliferating examples of military self-help in the years after 1915. Previously, communities widely supported, sympathised with, or at least tolerated local rebel bands. Successful resistance was rare, not because it was impossible (note occasional exceptions like Moroleón), but because it was unpopular. People did not resist rebels because they did not want to. The *Defensa Social* movements created to defend certain towns, notably Durango, were rightly seen as being narrowly representative of the urban elite.[832] After 1915, however, local military self-help became common: communities banded together to beat off rebels, bandits, even, sometimes, rapacious government troops. The turnabout is so marked that it must indicate a shift in popular mood, evidenced in practical, effective action (as well as indicating the gross failings of police and army).

Local defence forces fought the Chavistas in Michoacán, resisted marauders entering the sierra of Hidalgo from Veracruz, and guarded the northern approaches of Oaxaca, where fourteen pueblos formed a self-defence league, protesting that they were apolitical and concerned solely to maintain peace in the vicinity.[833] Villagers in the Tehuacán valley, complaining of the inadequacy of the army, similarly formed 'regional corps in each pueblo to help the Government defend our lives and interests' (so, too, did Italian colonists at Chipilo, also in Puebla); in Guerrero, the ranchers of Buenavista de Cuellar drove off Zapatista raiders, setting a precedent which the Carrancista authori-

ties sought to encourage in later years.[834] Military self-help also received
official sanction and support in Mexico state, and Veracruz, where demands for
'armed ranchers' to be recruited to resist 'bandits' were realised with the
creation, in 1918, of a civil guard of 1,000.[835] Meantime, some local forces
were actively resisting Carrancista depredations. 'Embattled farmers' combined to oppose government troops near Orizaba (such movements were akin
to the 'defensive' rebellions mentioned earlier); in the Huasteca, the inhabitants of San Nicolás defended their village against a gang of army deserters;
villagers in south-western Tlaxcala attacked and disarmed troops marauding
in their locality – for which they were denounced as Zapatistas.[836]

In the north, too, where the problem of order was acute and the tradition of
military self-help stronger, there were many comparable examples: in Zacatecas, the ranchers of Dolores caught and belaboured bandits who troubled the
district; local people collaborated with the army to flush out bandits around
Nochistlán.[837] General Nicolás Morales, one of the Arrietas' lieutenants who
operated in freelance fashion in the mountains of Durango, met an obscure
end, presumed to be at the hands of 'the mountain ranchers and their people,
who put an end to Morales and his escort because they did not propose to be
robbed any further'. Morales was a nominal Carrancista, but local antipathy to
the military ignored tenuous factional labels: 'the sentiment on the ranches is
getting so strong against all the so-called soldiers of all factions that their small
bands are no longer safe'; one-time *guerrilleros*, in other words, now risked
being picked off in the countryside as if they were Huerta's Federals.[838] But it
was in Chihuahua, afflicted by the long death agony of Villismo and the
outstanding military incapacity of the government, that local self-defence,
following an old tradition, was most extensive.[839] Volunteer corps – entitled
defensas sociales, though they clearly differed from their namesakes of 1913–14
– were set up throughout the state, especially in pueblos like Bachíniva and
Namiquipa which, though once of revolutionary inclination, had recently
suffered Villista depredations. These were not necessarily 'counter-
revolutionary', nor even class-based movements.[840] And, though it was the
government who supplied their arms, 'if government people came along and
tried to commit abuses too, defence had to be mounted against them as
well'.[841] Over the years, these groups notched up numerous successes. The
Villista, José Rodríguez, was slain by hacienda workers at Babícora in 1916;
the *defensa social* of the Hacienda de Rubio, between Chihuahua and Ojinaga,
put an end to the sanguinary career of Baudelio Uribe – 'Mocha Orejas'; the
ranchers of Cusi, high in the sierra, helped in the pursuit of Villa mounted by
Diéguez in 1919.[842]

Indeed, it was only by enlisting such local support that the army, now
displaying so many of the faults of its Porfirian predecessor, could undertake
offensives in the remote country districts. Here, as in Morelos, pacification
involved some co-option of the parochial, popular tradition. Indeed, so

powerful had the *defensas* become by 1918, that Villa issued specific threats against them; they aligned themselves with rival Carrancista factions; and in some cases they became predators themselves: they 'simply take everything they can lay their hands on'.[843] Even after they had outlived their original purpose – the battle against Villa – they remained in being, given official sanction by a law of 1922: *defensa* leaders enjoyed great political influence and could, in the case of Jesús Almeida, attain to the state governorship; here, as in Michoacán, Veracruz, San Luis, and elsewhere, such local irregular forces contributed to the legacy of political violence and *pistolerismo* which the Revolution bequeathed to the 1920s.[844]

But, if Mexicans showed a growing desire for peace, antipathy to rebellion, and disposition to work – all of which served the interests of the regime – this did not indicate popular support for the regime, which was tolerated *faute de mieux*, rather than embraced enthusiastically. 'The present (Constitutionalist) revolution is not popular in Mexico', observed an unusually candid Carrancista, 'the majority of the Mexican people is still against the revolution ... [and] we are still the minority.'[845] At the top, Carranza inspired no more confidence or affection in 1915–20 than he had in 1913–14. His recognition by the US inspired mixed feelings: devout Carrancistas like Governor Berlanga of Jalisco might weep for joy, hug the American consul and order church bells to be rung, but the celebrations were sourly received.[846] This was not surprising, perhaps, in Catholic Guadalajara; but elsewhere, too, the mood ranged from (at best) cautious optimism through indifference to outright dismay. There was certainly no collective jubilation.[847] Furthermore, 1916 witnessed general, growing scepticism about the First Chief's capacity to govern. No serious national rival emerged, but criticism and disillusionment were common, and it would be wrong to see Carranza, and his regime, progressively consolidating their popularity and winning new recruits after 1915. The official press reported the First Chief's rapturous receptions in different parts of the country; that was its job.[848] But foreign observers detected a 'marked decline' or 'continuous eradication' of Carranza's prestige.[849]

This was partly, but not wholly, foreign prejudice. The state of the nation – hungry, bankrupt, and sick – hardly reflected credit on the regime, even if there was little the regime could do about it. And Carranza himself had never been and never became a genuinely popular, charismatic leader. As a sympathiser admitted: 'General Carranza is not what might be termed an easy, approachable man, or one who might inspire any considerable devotion of personal loyalty'; Richmond's bold assertions to the contrary: 'Carranza enjoyed a mass support rarely before witnessed in Mexico', remain unconvincing details in a generally unconvincing portrait.[850] Carranza's image as president was staid: with his broad hats and sombre jackets, patriarchal beard and tinted glasses, his strict work routine, abstinence from drink and tobacco, and preoccupation with his respectable, middle class family, he resembled an English Nonconformist mayor more than a president of revolutionary Mexico.[851] Few individuals who met Carranza came away impressed. The Spanish writer Blasco Ibáñez was critical, just as John Reed had been five years before; the French Chargé found conversations with the ponderous First Chief hard going.[852] To the revolutionary rank-and-file, Carranza seemed remote and cool – not one of them. Of course, Carranza was not one of them; he was a well-to-do civilian; and, though he could inspire loyalty in a narrow group of intimates, he lacked the *don de gente*, the ability to establish a rapport with a wider range of heterogenous followers. Villa had commented on Carranza's aloofness; Villa and Zapata warmed to each other dissecting Carranza's 'high and mighty' character.[853] But the Carrancista rank-and-file thought the same; just as the Maderista rank-and-file had regarded Madero as a feeble civilian in 1911. To Captain García de la Cadena, an officer in Natera's command and a nominal Carrancist, the First Chief was a 'bewhiskered old goat', who feared men of mettle, like Natera; indeed, it would seem that Carranza's abundant whiskers were his only attributes to be celebrated in popular songs and jokes, and then in satirical, mildly obscene terms.[854]

This cool response was evident in the country at large, despite the tireless efforts of the press to build a legend around the 'Hero of Cuatro Ciénegas.'[855] His lacklustre personality and modest prestige could not offset the prevailing unpopularity of his regime; his triumphal progresses were, in contrast to Madero's of 1911, desultory affairs. At San Luis, late in 1915, he received a 'very cold welcome', which left him 'much displeased'; as he rode to the governor's palace not a cheer was to be heard, and the lower-class crowd which formed to witness the sight was 'a curious, playful, disinterested gathering, not a group of ardent admirers'.[856] So, too, in the west in 1916: *pace* Obregón's loyal assertion of the First Chief's popularity among the masses, such enthusiasm as there was appears to have been carefully orchestrated. At Guadalajara, Carranza's 'reception was a "frost" as to the civil public'; apart from the bunting displayed by the perpetually prudent foreign community, no decorations were displayed until orders were given to break out the national flag wherever possible.[857] Time did not wither Carranza's unpopularity. Novelists and balladeers passed him over: save for a few, contrived, 'official' songs, Carranza scarcely figures in revolutionary *corridos*, save as a butt for Villista humour (as in *La Cucaracha*); among the heroes of revolutionary myth, Carranza 'is worth mentioning . . . only as the non-legend.[858]

This is not to deprecate Carranza, who was neither 'politically obsolete' nor 'mediocrity incarnate': he was a reasonably able and certainly a conscientious leader, who did not lack courage, fortitude and conviction, and who displayed a staunch, consistent patriotism.[859] His political achievements between 1913 and 1920 were considerable. But he clearly failed to generate popular sympathy in the manner of some local and national caudillos; his administration survived in spite, rather than because, of his personal reputation. The final onset of peace in the Laguna, an observer reckoned, owed nothing to the virtues of Carranza and his regime, for whom the people – still 'idolizing' Villa – had nothing but 'hatred and contempt'.[860]

Nationally, the picture was not so black and white as this; but Villa's popular appeal certainly dwarfed Carranza's; and, even in defeat, it retained some of its power, far beyond regions of continued Villista resistance. Indeed, there was a sense in which Villismo, now representing a remote, hopeless cause, exerted greater sentimental appeal than in its heyday of 1915; for then the Villista myth, like other bandit myths, had suffered by its translation into harsh reality, while now it swelled as reality receded and the bandit became once again a mere symbol, in particular of popular resentment against the regime. After 1915, Villa could no longer tarnish his image with practical reminders of the ugly side of Villismo (except, of course, in Chihuahua and its environs); Villismo stood, not for violent, capricious, politically naive caudill-ismo, but for bold resistance to Carranza and the US. Hence the old cry 'Viva Villa!' came to denote dislike of Carrancismo more than any positive commit-ment to the defunct cause of the northern caudillo.[861] Food rioters, mostly women, who 'ran amok' in Torreón cried 'Viva Villa!' (so did the well-fed young blades of San Luis); the same slogan could be seen chalked up on walls and railway cars in Tampico.[862] In the noisy cantinas of Aguascalientes (where people could remember Villa's brief descent on the city late in 1914) piano-players picked out the Villista *corrido* 'Tierra Blanca' far into the night, to the chagrin of Carrancista listeners.[863] Through 1916 and 1917, as Villa not only refused to surrender but even seemed to revive, challenging the might of the US as well as the government, so his popularity remained buoyant: in Chihuahua, where Pershing encountered initial hostility; in the Laguna, where 'the lower classes . . . in their hearts are Villistas one and all'; in Sinaloa ('very strong Villista sympathy'), Colima and Tepic.[864] This residual Villismo has the appearance of a psychological salve. It was something to sing about in the cantina, during years of austerity and disillusionment; it was a way of cocking a snook at the authorities, if only by daubing furtive graffiti on walls. But Villismo offered no real alternative to the incumbent regime; no more did Zapatismo or Felicismo; they resisted less out of rational expectations of seizing national power than from a proud refusal to bow the knee to Carranza; in which they were sustained, though decreasingly, by the regime's unpopularity.

This unpopularity was part inevitable, part gratuitously earned. And it derived from the character of Carrancista rule: not the formal decrees, policies and speeches (which sought to offset it, are well known, and will be mentioned later) but the informal, often more important, structures of organisation and authority. Carrancismo, we noted, developed from the alliance of Coahuilan and Sonoran forces of 1913. Thereafter, the Carrancista 'core', attracting recruits and allies, fought ceaselessly, and ultimately successfuly, to retain central control over an expanding, national coalition. Carranza, as First Chief, later president, still headed the movement; Obregón and González, the leading generals of 1913–14, were still the military (though at loggerheads with each other); northerners in general, and Sonorans and Coahuilans in particular, still dominated the movement and much of the country: Castro in Oaxaca, Alvarado in Yucatán, Murguía and Treviño in Chihuahua, Diéguez in Jalisco, González in Morelos, Cesareo Castro in Puebla.[865] These Carrancistas enjoyed a loose collective loyalty, a legacy of the critical days of 1913 and 1914–15 when, in Benjamin Franklin's words, they had to 'hang together or, most assuredly . . . all hang separately'. Their quickly forged armes were annealed in the campaigns against Huerta, then Villa. In power, they displayed a narrow exclusiveness, almost a sectarianism, which contrasted with the promiscuous political tolerance of Villismo. The initial purges of 1914 were not isolated, impulsive acts, committed in the flush of victory: they were the start of a consistent, calculating policy, which aimed at the political elimination not only of ex-Porfiristas and ex-Huertistas, but also ex-Villistas, ex-Zapatistas, and ex-Conventionists, and which became one of the hallmarks of Carrancismo.

In one sense, the Carrancistas' motives were clear enough: they would not repeat the mistakes of Madero's 'política de conciliación' they would root out 'reactionary' opponents (and revolutionaries like Villa were readily assimilated to this category) rather than mortgage their own political future. This was the logical development of the emergent 'hawkish' Maderismo of 1912. But, like many Constitutionalist policies, this exclusivity went beyond strict pragmatism: it became an end in itself, a work of necessary purification, the political equivalent of the social redemption which the Revolution promised. Indeed, as the Querétaro debates revealed, many revolutionaries regarded this political clean-up as more important than any social reform. Nor was such an emphasis 'conservative', confined to the 'moderate' wing of Constitutionalism. On the contrary, 'radicals' like Alvarado and Gavira saw this political renovation in Manichaean terms, as a chapter in the 'secular struggle between LIBERALS and CONSERVATIVES' which would go on until the definitive defeat of 'REACTION'. Thus Alvarado, the quintessential proconsul, was the 'purifying action' of the revolution in Yucatán.[866] Gavira, too, governing San Luis and Durango, thought similarly. In San Luis he purged the state administration, the town councils, the judiciary, the Scientific Institute, and any organisation which he believed harboured enemies of the revolution: the Bullfighting Club was closed down, since it was frequented by the *jeunesse dorée* of the city, who antagonised Gavira not only by their existence, but also by their raucous cries of 'Viva Villa!'[867] All this was done, not with covert stealth, but self-righteous, rhetorical indignation. Potential sympathisers, like the city schoolteachers, were dressed down for their passivity and urged to 'do good liberal work and undertake the new task of regeneration with zeal'.

Waverers who called for a political amnesty, citing a recent precedent in Querétaro, were told that that amnesty, 'so inopportunely' conceded, was the work of 'moderate liberals' who were 'unsuitable for revolutionary work which, to be fruitful, must be intransigent'.[868]

Thus, intransigence, resolution, hostility to compromise, became tests of political integrity, and purges proof of revolutionary virility. Alvarado and Gavira were sincere, if somewhat self-important; they believed in the virtue of their cause and acted accordingly and consistently. The repeated claims to intransigence of other revolutionaries (including Carranza) rang more hollow: they were often ignored in practice and could sometimes afford alibis for acts of private vengeance and self-gratification.[869] Over and above this, it may be that denunciations of 'reaction' and purges of political enemies responded to a desire, conscious or not, to affirm the ideological unity and validity of the Revolution: a desire felt all the more keenly as military heroics gave way to mundane reconstruction, and fissiparous tendencies began to crack the facade of Constitutionalism. Purges and witchhunts raised morale and reinforced revolutionary unity, reminding the new elite not only of their historic destiny, but also of the threat of reaction, which still stalked in the wings. We do not advocate the persecution of *all* our enemies, *El Demócrata* declared magnanimously, but ('and this is a colossal but') 'only by means of revolutionaries can the revolution be transformed into a government distinct from the dictatorships of the past'; to this end the revolutionaries must maintain their unity and avoid the reprisals of their enemies; it was a reminder, especially to Carrancista dissidents, that, once again, if they did not hang together they might all hang separately.[870] The spectre of 'Reaction' was no mere stage ghost – it assumed corporeal form in the emigré groups, the Church, the hosts of Félix Díaz – and the revolutionaries were right to feel a frisson of apprehension at its activities. When, however, it assumed the grand proportions of Milton's Satan, as it often did in Constitutionalist imagery, 'Reaction' became less reality than symbol; a 'negative integrating symbol'; or, in more straightforward terms, a bogeyman to keep the restive children quiet.

Whatever its motives, Carrancista exclusivism was thorough, sometimes draconian. Army officers and civilian politicians accused of participation in the Huerta coup were arrested, court-martialled and executed; some alleged that this summary justice was guided by personal malice.[871] Well-known names were involved. Joaquín Pita, once *jefe político* in Puebla, was seized in a police raid, charges of complicity with Felicismo were preferred, and, after six hours interrogation (prolonged by the 'casuistry with which Pita evaded responsibility'), he broke down and confessed all.[872] More cruel and celebrated was the case of Alberto García Granados: now old and seriously ill, he had held ministerial office under both Madero and Huerta, after which he had gone to ground in Mexico City, emerging in public only in disguise. In September 1915 he was arrested, court-martialled (being 'very weak' he collapsed several times during the trial, and had to be supported by two soldiers), and finally executed, dying 'without recriminations, praying to God that [his] blood would be the last to be spilled in this horrible fratricidal struggle'.[873] The elimination of 'Huertistas' obeyed a certain rationale (in 1917 all participants in the 1913 coup who had remained in or returned to Mexico were declared liable to expulsion); it may even have been popular.[874] But Carrancista purges went further, to include Villistas, Zapatistas, Conventionists, all lumped together as 'reactionaries'; indeed, one honest revolutionary complained that the regime showed more enthusiasm persecuting these heretic revolutionaries (such as the worthy Dr Miguel Silva, one of many Maderistas turned Villista) than dyed-in-the-wool Huertistas like Franciso Olaguibel.[875] Victims included Bordes Mangel (a veteran, if unsuccessful, rebel of 1910, latterly a Villista); Heriberto Frías, the old opponent of Díaz, now blind, who faced imprisonment for editing the Villista *El Monitor*; and General Lucio Blanco, co-author of the Los Borregos land grant, who had been prominent in the search for a middle way during the revolutionary schism of 1914.[876]

But these were the big fish; and the Carrancista net trawled deep and fine. Frías, an old, revered revolutionary precursor, served only seven months of his twelve years sentence before being released; a more obscure and unfortunate journalist languished two years in gaol at Veracruz on account of articles he had written for the Constitutionalist press in 1914; again, personal animosity was hinted at.[877] A prisoner in Mexico City had been arrested in the small hours on the grounds that he was a Zapatista and had served in the police reserve under Huerta; the first he denied, the second, he claimed, brought a living and implied no political sympathy; he had never arrested a revolutionary and had even tipped off suspects in advance. Personal spite, not revolutionary justice, lay behind the charges.[878] It is surprising neither that such minor characters were caught up in the purges, nor that allegations of private vendetta were so common. Government, national and local, spurred on the processes of inquiry, denunciation and arrest. At the end of 1915, the Minister of Gobernación ordered all governors to dismiss ex-Huertistas and enemies of the Revolution; employers of the Ministry of Hacienda (said to be a hotbed of reactionaries) received an elaborate questionnaire, which sought to ascertain whether they had served the Díaz, Madero, Huerta, Conventiontist or Villista administrations, or participated in Díaz's 1912 revolt or the *Decena Trágica*.[879] Meanwhile, magistrates and policemen lost their jobs in the Federal District; a secret agent denounced reactionaries holding positions in the Census Office; even employees of that office, parading their revolutionary virtue (and looking for promotion?), demanded that reactionary colleagues, whom they named, be investigated and removed.[880] The provinces followed suit. Castro, governing Oaxaca, ruled that all ex-Federals quit the Constitutionalist army, and circulated a questionnaire to state employees, requiring details of their careers and political affiliations; Gavira, though inhibited by the flaccid compromises of his predecessors, purged Porfiristas and ex-members of the *Defensa Social* in Durango; in Puebla, a Junta Depuradora set to work winkling out Huertistas and Martinistas (partisans of ex-Governor Mucio Martínez).[881]

No doubt the success of such measures varied. For Gavira, San Luis was a triumph of political purification, Durango a sad disappointment.[882] A year after the Hacienda employees received their questionnaires, 80% of them were still reckoned to be 'Huertistas'.[883] And governors like Pablo de la Garza of Nuevo León, determined to purge government of 'elements hostile to the cause', found state archives barren of information and local informants reluctant to denounce municipal officials; still, de la Garza hoped that 'from day to day [information] will assuredly be unearthed and will serve to remove them from their posts'.[884] But, whether wholesale dismissals took place or not, the climate was one of surveillance, denunciation, and proscription: a mild version of the political house-cleanings which have accompanied other great revolutions. Minor officials trembled at the prospect of a capricious dismissal based – if not simply on personal animosity – then on the victim's supposed indifference (not necessarily hostility) to Constitutionalism. A Veracruz customs official, whose assiduous search for preferment got nowhere, was alarmed to receive one of the career questionnaires which government departments now delighted in compiling: 'I am not able to reply', he besought Carranza's secretary, 'and I beg you to take into account that I am head of a family and it would be very sad for someone . . . to lose their job, simply for being unable to prove that they had done something for the revolution.'[885] Establishing proof of service to the (Constitutionalist) revolution thus became a major concern. Fernando Cuevas had been unable to follow the Constitutionalists to Veracruz in 1915, because of his sick mother; but twenty colleagues attested that he 'undertook verbal propaganda . . . during the time of trial (*época de prueba*)', which proved his loyalty.[886] Moments of doubt, apathy, or downright opposition were quickly forgotten; episodes of revolutionary commitment were embellished, if not created *de novo*. Even as the manufacture of grand, national, revolutionary myths got under way, myriad individuals, great and small, began mythologising their own pasts – some with mild exaggerations and distortions, some (like Azuela's fictional but illustrative General Xicontencatl Robespierre Cebollino) with grotesque fabrications and soaring, pseudo-radical rhetoric.[887]

As already noted, this political exclusivism – the denunciation of 'enemies of the cause', the manufacture of spurious political credentials, the cult of revolutionary orthodoxy – all smacked of a mild Stalinism.[888] As in revolutionary France or post-revolutionary Russia, the informer flourished: indeed, the official press carried anonymous advertisements appealing to readers to report on known reactionaries and offering to buy photographs of such persons; 'the object is simply that of co-operating in a general revolutionary purification . . . [since] bitter experience has shown the need to be scrupulous in the

extreme'.[889] Spies, officials, journalists and private individuals (whose existence is scarcely recognised in most histories) bombarded the regime with
reports on 'dangerous elements' who, from right or left, threatened the
Revolution.[890] If some celebrated trials and executions were thought to stem
from private grudges rather than sound evidence, this was probably all the
more true in lesser cases. After a conversation 'of little importance', a
Monterrey official was denounced by the governor's brother, Juan de la Garza,
for having 'defamed the state and local government', for which he was arrested;
the victim claimed to be a loyal Constitutionalist, whose words had been
misreported by 'Don Juan [who] is not motivated by the best will in the world
towards me.'[891] Another victim was arrested for 'having insulted the First
Chief of the Army, Venustiano Carranza, on an electric tram [going] from San
Angel via Churubusco', in the Federal District; the charge, it later transpired,
had been trumped up — the tram service had been suspended the day the
alleged offence took place. The prisoner was released after two months in
gaol.[892]

Behind the welter of denunciations, arrests and complaints lay an additional
factor of great but unquantifiable magnitude: the question of the *bienes
intervenidos*, the property confiscated by revolutionary authorities since 1913.
According to Constitutionalist practice, such property was seized for basically
political, not socio-economic, reasons; that is, to punish enemies of the cause
and fund the revolution, not to achieve an egalitarian redistribution of
property. Whatever important social side-effects they may have had, these
seizures were political acts, whose victims suffered *qua* Porfiristas, Huertistas
or Felicistas, not *qua hacendados*.[893] This policy gave great scope to the
arbitrary will, and cupidity, of revolutionary leaders, whose eagerness to snap
up town houses, automobiles and landed estates has been noted, and will bear
further examination.[894] Of 175 'urban' properties seized in the state of Puebla,
for example, the majority (134) belonged to the Church and the rest were
listed as belonging to an 'enemy of the cause', 'wife of an enemy', or one who
'has protected enemies of the cause'.[895] Clearly, there was an important
material dimension to the policy of 'purification', in that proscription, often a
subjective decision, led to confiscation, which in turn created a vested interest,
public or private, on the part of ranking general or humble tenant, in the
maintenance, even the extension, of such confiscations. Hence, well after
Carranza's triumph, confiscations went on, and the devolution of property was
similarly blocked, on the grounds that the recipient remained an 'enemy of the
cause'.[896]

Constitutionalist sectarianism derived from the ideological principle that,
if a loose translation from the official press may be allowed, 'the Government
has a monopoly of revolutionary thought'.[897] This principle governed the
running of the press itself. The short-lived freedoms of the Madero period,
abruptly terminated in 1913, were not revived. Rather, the presses which had

served Huerta were placed in the political service of the revolution and the *de facto* controls then established were later codified into a Ley de Imprenta which fixed penalties for any expression of opinion, whether in newspapers, photographs, films, drawings, songs or speeches, which aimed to ridicule, deprecate, or undermine the nation or its fundamental institutions.[898] Even before these ample legal sanctions were available, however, the regime had closed down critical papers and arrested editors and journalists.[899] The rationale was the familiar one (it has been urged on Madero by Maderista hawks back in 1912, with little success): press freedom would benefit reaction and jeopardise the revolution. As General Diéguez reputedly asked a group of dissident journalists, sent under arrest to Chihuahua so that their 'misreporting' of Villa's revival might undergo 'rectification', 'do you conservatives really believe that we are going to hand over power to you?'[900] Books and plays, as well as newspapers, came under the censor's scrutiny.[901]

Meanwhile, the regime followed Porfirian precedent in running its own subsidized press, which retailed approved news and official opinion; indeed, *El Demócrata* spoke proudly of the 'heroism' with which it continued publication while losing 70,000 pesos a week and incurring prodigious debts.[902] Papers like *El Demócrata* and *El Pueblo* thus operated almost as minor departments of government (the point was neatly illustrated when *El Pueblo's* editor left to assume high office in the Ministry of Gobernación; and one journalist recalled how pay-day was signalled by the return from the Ministry of Education of an employee carrying bags of silver coins). They also maintained the old tradition of reporting phoney victories and fictive triumphs.[903] Conversely, they sat on embarrassing stories. Pershing's progress into Mexico went largely unreported; *El Universal*, Taracena notes, preferred to cover the banalities of Carranza's trip through Jalisco than to comment on the Zimmermann telegram.[904] Not that the European war was ignored; on the contrary, it often crowded domestic matters off the front pages of Mexican newspapers. In part, this reflected the subsidies then being paid to large sections of the press by belligerent powers, especially Germany – which the Mexican government, steering a devious course between the contestants, could divert to its own, domestic propaganda needs.[905] In particular, the official press laboured to build political reputations, most of all Carranza's. In reports of Carranza's travels through the Republic, 'huge crowds' thronged the streets of tiny pueblos boasting a single thoroughfare and a few dozen inhabitants; the journalistic hacks of Constitutionalism strove to build an imposing facade from the simple bricks and mortar of Carranza's stolid character.[906] Antonio Manero harped on Carranza's austerity (a theme attuned to the times and to the Puritan strain in revolutionary thought, but hardly likely to enthuse the masses): Carranza was the 'austere caudillo' (and the 'caudillo of redemption'), he was 'austere like Cato' (Salvador Alvarado, by the same pen, was 'Cato redivivus': Manero stuck to a good idea when he thought he had one).[907] Gregorio Velázquez, in a sustained eulogy

(1918), likened the 'extraordinary figure' of Carranza to Gratian, Carlyle and
Emerson (an unlikely trio); Carranza was 'the *alma mater* [sic], apostle, and arm
of a general movement for the renovation of Mexico'; he was 'Revolutionary
. . . Reformer and, finally, the great spiritual Caudillo of the Race, the happy
successor of Bolívar and, like him, well-deserving of Humanity.'[908] Such
attempts to create a Carranza personality cult, however, came to nothing: the
personality was unprepossessing, the cultists were uninspired, and, as already
noted, popular attitudes to Carranza were wan and indifferent. But the
Constitutionalists took the fourth estate seriously. 'By its invocation', declared
one, 'old institutions fall and are reborn, beliefs are reformed . . . and public
opinion is fashioned, as if in a mould'.[909] Though not all would have gone so
far, most shared this middle-class, Maderista belief in the power of ideas in
general and the written word in particular; unlike Madero, however, they
sought to exploit this power by illiberal manipulation. 'Make sure', a friend
advised Alvarado, 'that the *Voz de la Revolución* has a great deal to say about the
First Chief, at every possible opportunity . . . that pleases him a lot.'[910] Some
Maderista hawks had thought along these lines in 1912; Madero certainly had
not.[911]

But while – in contrast to Madero's conciliatory policy – Constitutionalist
victory encouraged a policy of *vae victis*, it also weakened revolutionary
cohesion. In the absence of serious challenges to national power, the Carrancistas could indulge in the luxury of internal squabbles. The press offered good
examples of this dissension: while almost all papers dutifully toed the official
line, lauding the revolution and lambasting reaction, they also became the
incisors of the new factionalism gnawing the vitals of Constitutionalism. The
press thus played an ambivalent role: ideologically it stood for revolutionary
unity, orthodoxy and intransigence; practically, it served the interests of
emergent, intra-regime factions (and, to an extent, their foreign backers).
Civil and military factions counted on their newspaper outlets: Palavicini,
editor of *El Universal*, became a key ally of Carranza and the *bête noire* of the
military.[912] Rival aspirants to state governorships warred in the pages of the
local press. Yet higher in the hierarchy, ministers and would-be presidents
manipulated the press: Pablo González, it was said, got Barrón the editorship
of *El Pueblo*; Obregón tried the same with Dr Atl; Acuña's slide from power in
1916 was signalled by his loss of control over the press.[913] Over time, the
forces of factionalism overcame the fragile unity of Constitutionalism, personal allegiances overrode ideological. By 1919–20 'reaction' had been seen off
and the Constitutionalists wrestled with each other, no holds barred, under a
blanket of bland ideological consensus. In the press, and in electoral politics,
this internal dissension guaranteed a real measure of genuine political debate
and mobilisation. By 1919, some newspapers were printing violent attacks on
Carranza himself and the president 'seem[ed] afraid to suppress them'.[914]
Time had changed: the threats of the past had receded, the temptations of the

future beckoned. The evolution of the press between 1915 and 1920 neatly exemplified the shift from enforced, sectarian unity, to a more uninhibited, faction-ridden pluralism.

The strengths of Carrancismo, I have suggested, lay in the shrewd opportunism of its leaders, their aptitude for national power, and ability to transcend the narrower world of traditional relationships (those of village, hacienda and *patria chica*) and to operate in the arena of mass impersonal, associational politics: the politics of bureaucrat, *sindicato* official, career officer, diplomat, and newspaper editor.[915] This arena offered great scope for advancement, political and economic; for, though the revolution had not subverted the relations of production, it had ousted the old Porfirian elite and opened the way to a generation of newcomers, hungry for power, influence and profit. Thus, even more than in 1911, a bitter struggle for advancement followed the triumph of the Constitutionalist revolution. At the top of the tree glittered the presidency. While Carranza was a safe choice for the first presidential term (1917–20), the second looked more open; and, as early as 1916 the long-term skirmishing – in which Obregón and Pablo González figured prominently – was already under way.[916] The battle began in earnest, and was violently resolved, in 1919–20.[917] Meanwhile, ample areas of political contention remained. Nationally, Carranza's cabinet weathered a major crisis in June 1915 (even as Obregón was advancing on Aguascalientes; and Obregón made sure of cabling his views to Carranza at Veracruz); a crisis simmered through the summer of 1916, associated with the financial collapse and the rival policies propounded for its solution; and the feuds initiated during these episodes recurred during the Constituent Congress (Nov. 1916–Jan. 1917).[918]

Local squabbles were legion, and often linked to these national divisions. In Veracruz, the promotion of Cándido Aguilar to the cabinet opened the way to Governor Heriberto Jara and military commander Agustín Millán who (to Aguilar's dismay) bitterly contested the succession; both, however, agreed on their antipathy to Gabriel Gavira, who returned to his home state to run, a second time, for the governorship in 1917.[919] Jacinto Treviño, who held the unenviable command in Chihuahua, engaged in a running battle with Obregón, who blamed the young Coahuilan for Villa's success: Carranza defended his protégé, whose brother-in-law alleged that Obregón was 'crowding him [Treviño] to the wall', deliberately withholding ammunition; when Treviño relinquished his command late in 1916 he did so breathing retribution and declaring – it was said – that he would 'kill Obregón or get himself killed'.[920] In addition, Treviño feuded with his fellow-Coahuilan, Francisco Murguía, who took Obregón's part and succeeded to the command in Chihuahua. Treviño's denunciation of Murguía – directed to Carranza himself – revealed not only the animus involved in such disputes, but also the kind of charges readily, vigorously preferred, even by one Carrancista *adicto* against another. Flattery, Treviño alleged, made Murguía imagine himself some kind of Napoleon; but the public, well aware of his military failings, discounted stories of victory published 'in big letters and hugely magnified solely in the pages of the official press'; Murguía, in short, was a 'human stain on Constitutionalism – his hands drip blood and his guts distill alcohol'.[921] Revolutionary camaraderie was not much evident, either, in Calles' squabble with Diéguez in Sonora; in Gavira's impatient criticism of Luis Gutiérrez's incompetence or Francisco Bertani's insubordination; in the wrangling between Carranza's central government and local commands like Flores' in Sinaloa and Mariscal's in Guerrero.[922] In this last case, Mariscal's efforts to emulate Juan Alvarez and establish himself as cacique of Guerrero were only foiled by his arrest, in Mexico City, in 1918, and at the cost of a serious local revolt.[923] And yet lower in the hierarchy, in Tlaxcala and the perennially fragmented Costa Chica, minor *cabecillas* fought for their share of the revolutionary inheritance.[924]

Such divisions were to be expected in the wake of revolution, as the primary struggle for national power gave way to the secondary process of institutionalisation; which involved the promotion of some caudillos, the passing over of others. In particular, the spate of gubernatorial contests which began in 1917 was marked by fierce conflicts, violence and outright rebellion: evidence not only of the superfluity of ambitious Constitutionalist leaders, but also of their determination to convert informal military fiefdoms into legitimate 'elected' posts within the formal political order.[925] Relations within the elite, therefore, were hardly those of fraternally united comrades – the dutiful generals and dedicated reformers of Carrancista myth (which still has its adherents today);[926] rather, they displayed a Hobbesian character – 'a condition of war of everyone against everyone', a 'restless striving after power which ceases only in death'; and not least among the tasks of revolutionary myth, rhetoric and exhortation was to contain Hobbesian conflicts, lest they tore civil society apart. The Leviathan of the 1920s, it could be said, grew out of the 'state of nature' pertaining in 1915–20. But the endemic conflict of these years did not lack meaning or pattern. Some squabbles were certainly personal – the dour Gavira could not abide Diéguez's preening and ostentation – or based on military failures and disagreements (Obregón against Treviño).[927] But two recurrent patterns were evident: a primary conflict between civilian and military authorities; and a secondary contest between 'insider' and 'outsider' Carrancistas; both had important consequences for the Carranza regime.

The civil–military rift ran from top to bottom of the political nation. It has been given due recognition in the context of the Constituent Congress where, it is usually asserted, the polarisation was ideological, the civilians favouring moderate, liberal policies, the military more radical, nationalist, *dirigiste* alternatives. The merits of this argument will be considered shortly.[928] It is worth appreciating, however, that the polarisation at Querétaro was only part of a grander, almost ubiquitous division which dichotomised civil society; one so general that it cannot be reduced to some anterior (e.g., ideological) polarisation, of which the ostensible civil–military split was an external manifestation. In other words, civilians did not contend with soldiers because they espoused a moderate liberalism in opposition to military jacobinism, even if this was in some cases true; rather, the civilians asserted the need for civilian government, which the military resisted; two sectional groups, defined by career and life-style (rather than class and ideology) competed for political supremacy, invoking appropriate ideological legitimations. Such a revolutionary polarisation was not confined to Mexico.[929] Nor was there anything very new about it. Civilians still believed, as they had in Madero's day, that it was the prerogative of the *licenciado* to govern; the military argued, as Obregón and others had in 1914, that those who had fought and won the revolution should determine its outcome.[930]

This sentiment was pervasive after 1915. When municipal elections were held in west-central Mexico in 1916, there were violent affrays and arrests, especially where 'non-revolutionary' civilians (who had not shouldered arms against Huerta) had the temerity to take part: 'the army took exception to these outsiders, as they termed them, for an attempt to take from the "patriots" the fruits of the revolution'.[931] Alvarado denounced the *politiqueros* of Yucatán, old cronies of Pino Suárez, recently 'Platonic Villistas.'[932] On the other hand, as the military brandished their laurels and sneered at effete politicians, civilian orators stood up to denounce military rule, and journalists observed that a cull of revolutionary 'heroes' would be no bad thing for the country: 'it must be recognised', Félix Palavicini commented, after Obregón had suffered an accident, 'that if a few of the heroes of the Revolution were to disappear, it would be a great advantage to Mexico'.[933] Obregón, of course, had his own views on journalists like Palavicini.[934] Indeed, the latter was a classic example: an archetypal civilian, cabinet minister and newspapermen, he championed the civilian cause and earned the cordial hatred of the military. 'In the face of the portentous power of the press', he declared, 'even armies themselves are secondary powers'; what is more, he behaved as if he believed such fanfaronades.[935] He stood at the centre of the cabinet crisis of 1915 when, it was thought, Carranza sought to rid himself of excessive military influence.[936] On this occasion, despite Obregón's efforts, the pro-military elements lost ground (Zubarán Capmany, co-architect with Obregón of the pact with the Casa, left the cabinet) and Palavicini survived.[937] But not for long; losing his ministerial post (Education) in 1916, he was constantly pilloried by the military and their spokesmen at the Querétaro Congress and other political gatherings; in spring 1917 his anti-military declarations led to his arrest and the temporary closure of *El Universal*. 'I believe', a British observer wrote, 'the military authorities are most anxious to shoot Sr Palavicini and I have no doubt they will do so if they can find an opportunity'; late in the year, with Mexico City agitated by rumours of an impending military coup, Palavicini deposited his valuables in the British legation and went into hiding.[938] In 1918, he was forced to quit Mexico altogether.[939]

Palavicini's anti-militarism, though strident, was not unusual. Carranza sympathised, gave him support, and sought to clip the military's wings: the debacle of 1920 was signalled well in advance.[940] Speakers at Querétaro – echoing Madero – deplored the 'military Caesarism' of Mexico's past, expressed fears that the revolution, though anti-militarist in origin, had spawned a new military caste, and pointed to recent examples of the military's arrogation of power.[941] They also returned to the old theme of the civilians' – the educated civilians' – greater aptitude for government: no doubt, conceded one orator, the military possessed merits,[942]

but those merits do not enable [the] military to legislate in the Chamber. The military are the least qualified to discuss laws and yet, now, are we going to make them deputies on the strength of their abilities in the field? That's what it comes down to . . . There are many revolutionaries among the civilians who could replace them in Congress. They [the civilians] are more civilised and more capable, since they consider matters from the civilian point of view, devoid of all military spirit.

The press, too, took up the cry: the Catholic *Excelsior* recalled that the army should be the servant, not the master, of the civilian government; Vasconcelos, writing in *ABC*, alleged that the revolution had served simply 'to enrich a new oppressive class of crooks with the rank of generals'.[943] International alignments reinforced the domestic: while the pro-military press were sympathetic to, and subsidised by, the Central Powers, Palavicini's *El Universal* linked together pro-Ally and civilian sentiments, making pointed references to the 'barrack life' of the militarist Teutons.[944]

The military did not ignore these goads. Palavicini was forced out; Vasconcelos' barbs provoked General Juan Merigo (recently implicated in the Grey Automobile scandal, and particularly sensitive to slights to his and the army's honour) to attack the editor of *ABC*, striking him over the head with a rubber truncheon; during a chance meeting in a Mexico City *pastelería*, General Juan Banderas traded insults with one of his congressional critics, attacked him, and was instantly shot dead.[945] Such incidents must be understood in terms of the contemporary level of casual violence, and the mutual dislike, even loathing, which civilians and military displayed. Civilian repudiation of corrupt praetorianism was mirrored by the military's contempt for feeble, devious, condescending civilians. After Palavicini it was Cabrera, the smooth diplomat, propagandist and financier, who most raised military hackles: partly because he was blamed for the currency crisis of 1916 (which threatened army payrolls); partly, perhaps, because he was expert in those fields where the military were least qualified; but mostly for what he was – a highly articulate, influential lawyer with a record of political opportunism, an attachment to civilian rule, and a total lack of first-hand military experience.[946] Back in 1915, the rumour went, 'Pancho' Coss, one of Carranza's more plebeian generals, lost the governorship of Puebla after threatening Cabrera's life; and certainly Cabrera excited fierce dislike among the military, as an oil company manager discovered when he dropped Cabrera's name in conversation with General Acosta, then commanding in the Huasteca. In response, Acosta 'mentioned the canine epithet and remarked that while Cabrera was a very smart man, his father had not been too careful in choosing a breeding partner, suggesting that Cabrera's mother was able to scratch the fleas off her back with her hind foot'.[947] A year later, Cabrera emerged as the main spokesman for a civilian presidential succession, in open opposition to Obregón.[948] With such strong feelings and group loyalties in play, it is not surprising that rumours of military coups were recurrent, especially at the end of 1917, when the government made a show of force on the streets and there were rumours of summary, pre-emptive executions.[949]

Locally, the civil–military split was no less marked: civilians, especially civilian authorities, would have endorsed Palavicini's views; and, like other ranking Carrancistas, Palavicini was no doubt aware of this pervasive feeling. Military garrisons were a heavy burden, the more so as the threat of rebel attack diminished. Already, in 1915, there were complaints of Constitutionalist troops appropriating property, declining to pay rent to the municipality, even renting out houses or converting them into bordellos.[950] Thereafter, troops were blamed for imposing forced loans (Ags.), butchering milch cows (Chih.), robbing villages (Tlax.), drinking and brawling (Ver.).[951] An observer in rural Jalisco noted 'the absolute state of terrorism that the civilian inhabitants are held in by these military ruffians'.[952] Even Carrancista spokesmen admitted – in correspondence, political debates, and the press – that abuses were committed, alienating the common people from army and regime.[953] Municipal authorities, in particular, found themselves lorded over by military bosses: 'feuds and bad blood' characterised local civil-military relations in the Laguna; and at Monterrey and elsewhere troops and police clashed in street battles.[954] Even communities of impeccably *pacífico* past thus suffered military extortions, robbery, forced recruitment and, above all, graft. Civilian authorities, of course, were not above lining their pockets; but the presence of a large, usually alien, garrison drained local resources faster than the run-of-the-mill peculation of municipal officials. Hence civil authorities, like those of Coahuila, longed to see the back of Murguía; and the restoration of civilian control at Piedras Negras had the immediate effect of 'do[ing] away with so much grafting that had always run hand in hand with military control'.[955] Of that, more anon.

Parallel to this civil–military friction ran the conflicts between Carrancista 'insiders' and 'outsiders'. While Carrancismo had exported cadres of officers, mostly Sonoran and Coahuilan, to govern conquered territory, it had also come to terms with local forces, legitimising their local control: Mariscal in Guerrero, Baños in Oaxaca, Flores in Hidalgo, Rojas in Tlaxcala, the Arrietas in Durango and Herreras in Chihuahua. The process did not stop in 1915: in later years (above all, 1920) ex-Villistas, ex-Zapatistas and ex-Felicistas were reintegrated into the ruling coalition. Many of these converts differed from the 'core' Carrancistas in two respects: all were local men, dependent on local, largely rural support; and many were populist leaders, uneducated, rooted in 'old' Mexico, and as indifferent to national power as they were committed to the *patria chica*. Hence there were conflicts. Silvestre Mariscal, forcibly evicted from his Guerrero fief, was succeeded by Francisco, then Rómulo Figueroa – similarly 'a military cacique whose dependence on a regional political base placed him firmly in the traditionalist camp'.[956] Having dumped Mariscal, however, it did not take the central government long to dislodge the Figueroas, who were supplanted by civilian *políticos* 'who looked to Mexico City rather than the local army for assistance in their political careers'.[957]

A similar conflict but different outcome ensued in Durango, which the Arrietas had dominated for the best part of five years. Their extensive, family-based forces ('in some respects a horde rather than an army'), lacking payrolls or archives and top-heavy with officers, contrasted with the organised, mercenary Carrancista forces, recruited largely in the south, dependent on the flow of cash from Mexico City, and led by the Coahuilan generals Murguía and (Arnulfo) González. Since 'he controls the purse-strings' – and the ammunition supply – Murguía called the tune. But it was not to the Arrietas' taste, especially when they were demoted from their governorship and military command. Murguía claimed that pacification was impossible with Mariano Arrieta 'secretly working against him'; Mariano was arrested on a charge of embezzlement and moves were afoot to get his brother Domingo posted outside the state (such attempts had been made before, even by Villa, without success).[958] Meanwhile, the Arrietas' forces – notionally hunting down Villistas in the Laguna – gave their old *compadre*, Calixto Contreras, an easy time; and when the government tried to disarm some of these troublesome troops, a fight started in which Mariano's son was wounded.[959] In May 1916, Obregón, as Minister of War, had to take remedial action: Murguía was recalled, a Durangueño (Miguel Laveaga, from a well-to-do *serrano* family of San Dimas, up in the Arrietas' part of the state) was brought in to defuse the situation, and some of the Arrietas' forces even consented to serve in Chihuahua.[960] But these local *cacicazgos* were notoriously hard to eradicate, even by a remorselessly centralising regime. In the Durango gubernatorial election of 1917, Laveaga, the official candidate, confronted Domingo Arrieta who, though illiterate and 'opposed by the central government in his candidacy', remained 'very popular with the masses' and won a resounding victory, going on to serve as governor until 1920.[961]

In Chihuahua, too, the Herrera family were rewarded for their daring but costly opposition to Villa. José de la Luz Herrera became mayor of Parral; his son, Melchor, mayor of Juárez; Luis and Asunción Carrancista generals. But they remained a refractory family, cavilling at Carranza's orders in the critical months of 1916 when Villa was on the rampage and Pershing was advancing; giving rise to fears that they might go over to Villa or launch a unilateral attack on the Americans; subsequently feuding with the Carrancista military comm-nader, Treviño, who tried, but failed, to blackball Melchor's appointment as mayor of Juárez.[962] Treviño's squabble with the Herreras in Chihuahua thus perfectly replicated Murguía's with the Arrietas in Durango: the young Carrancista interloper quarrelling with the entrenched 'Carrancista' natives. But where the Arrietas survived, the Herreras experienced a terrible mortality, the price of their defiance of Villa. Of the father and six sons, only the old man and one son were left by mid-1917.[963] Thus depleted, the family could not sustain the political pre-eminence its record deserved. Mortality on this scale, meanwhile, eased the regime's difficulties. But enough 'local' Carrancistas survived the decade, and were then reinforced by dissidents – ranging from the Zapatistas of Morelos to the *mapache* rebels of Chiapas, from Villa to Cedillo – who presented the post-revolutionary state with comparable problems, and contributed to the recurrent tension between the centralising, revolutionary regime, and the centrifugal forces of revolutionary caudillismo; a tension best evidenced, and in a sense finally terminated, in the career and death of Saturnino Cedillo.[964]

Against them stood the 'core' Carrancistas, generally outsiders (like Alva-rado in Yucatán or Murguía in Chihuahua), lacking local support, imposing a form of order, regulation and taxation which was resented both for the fact of imposition, and because the imposition was frequently harsh, heavy-handed and corrupt. To have their way, these Carrancistas could use force – which meant the maintenance of a loyal, efficient army – or cajolery; and the latter could work through individual, clientelistic hand-outs, or through broadly based, universalistic reforms, such as labour and agrarian laws. The latter, important in the long run, have attracted disproportionate attention, at the expense of more informal mechanisms of control and recruitment; for, at the time, they represented pious hopes, or even cynical window-dressing; and they belonged to an area of government where maximum freedom was attainable. Carranza could, up to a point, decree what he liked; the Constituent Congress could incorporate into its draft whatever radical innovations it desired; such ideological chickens would only come home to roost later. Meanwhile, in the real world of day-to-day politics – a world still governed by the old vice-regal motto: *obedezco pero no cumplo* – the constraints on government were greater, and the regime appeared less as a Mosaic authority, dispensing new laws to a grateful people, than a diplomatically harassed, financially embarrassed, militarily embattled administration, whose chief concerns were to maintain itself, curb internal dissension, and compel obedience throughout the fragmented territory it claimed to rule. Here social reforms might help, but they were far from the whole story.

In this, the role of the army was central. Carranza depended on it for the maintenance as he had for the establishment of his regime. Hence the disproportionate military budget and the notional complement (1917) of 150,000 men: about 1% of the total population, or ten times the Porfirian military establishment.[965] But these figures are probably misleading: they exaggerate the fighting strength of the Carrancista forces, while underestimating the real burden placed on the civilian economy. As in the days of Huerta, padded payrolls redounded to the benefit of corrupt commanders: like the Arrietas, accused of embezzling 100,000 pesos of troops' pay; General Carlos Vidal, who claimed for 400 men when he had 208; or Mariscal, alleged to be 'doing nothing other than getting drunk and trafficking in his soldiers' supplies'.[966] The continued success of rebel/bandits like Villa, Chávez García, Zapata and the Cedillos thus partly derived from the fact that the forces opposing them were not as big as they were cracked up to be. But Carrancista troops were also intrinsically poor: for as Carrancismo metamorphosed from a loose coalition of rebel bands into a Federal army, committed not to overthrowing but maintaining a national government, so it acquired many of the characteristics of the old Federal Army – one based on pay, forced recruitment and compulsion, rather than the voluntary commitment of *gente* to *cabecilla*, united in a political cause. This transformation strained the loyalty of troops already questioning the purpose of continued fighting. Dr Atl recounted a soldier's lament after one encounter: 'and what was it all for? All that running, all those frights, all that hunger – what for? For the colonel to have rides in his motor car with a girl he calls his wife.'[967] Pockets of the old voluntarism survived: with the peasant recruits of Rojas in Tlaxcala, with the forces of Zapata or Cedillo, which would be later incorporated into the regime, or with local *defensas sociales*. But increasingly the norm was set by the Coahuilan/Sonoran 'core', which had pioneered a form of mercenary revolutionary army.[968]

For them, mobility was a key factor. The army was autonomous, not anchored in the community. The Carrancista regime, like the Porfirian, 'has followed the policy of stationing detachments in territory remote from their recruiting zone or ultimate points of origin'.[969] While northerners came south to govern, southerners were sent north as rank-and-file, or cannon-fodder. Many of Murguía's troops which garrisoned Durango and Chihuahua in 1916 were men – or boys – from the south, ill at ease in their new environment, unused to the cold, and scared of Pancho Villa; the Villistas disdained these *changos* ('kids'), who were short, bad horsemen, and enervated by the climate; a neutral observer considered 'these starvelings, these boys and stunted men . . . [to be] poor stuff to put up against Villa and the men of the northern sierras' (though Villa, too, was now recruiting adoloscents).[970] Life in the Carrancista army had most of the drawbacks of Federal Army service, which the *pelados* had traditionally loathed, and only extreme poverty and unemployment gave Carranza's generals the edge in attracting men to the colours.[971] Still, those who came were often too young, opportunistic, and irresolute to make up into good soldiers; only the lure of payday – a highly movable feast – kept detachments in being. Murguía's forces included many boys under sixteen; on the Isthmus they were recruited from twelve up; in Baja California the ranks were swelled by 'mere boys', pearl fishers whose industry had collapsed.[972] Obregón, proudly reliving his battles with Villa, dwelled on the courage of youth (and of women): the ten-year-old trumpeter, mentioned above; the twelve-year-old he encountered during the battle of Trinidad, burying his father, alongside the corpse of a Villista, the father's killer, whom the 'pequeño luchador' had himself slain.[973]

Apart from the young, there were the urban unemployed, already tapped to provide the Red Battalions, now taken off the streets by Calles to combat the Yaquis.[974] And there was the plentiful supply of ex-Villistas, who – with Villa's blessing, it seems – took advantage of the Carrancista amnesty and the 'good money' the Carrancistas paid.[975] Of course, these did not become fervent Carrancistas: many deserted, and some went back to Villa at the time of Pershing's expedition.[976] Like their Federal predecessors, Carrancista commanders lived in constant anxiety as to the loyalty of their troops (especially those who had passed, as entire units, from one side to the other) and anti-guerrilla operations were consequently inhibited – the men did not want to go into the hills and their officers did not want to go with them into the hills either.[977] As in the past, too, spatial mobility, which was intrinsic to Carrancista strategy, undermined morale, even health. The southerners' reluctant participation in the campaigns against Villa was but one example. Men from the *tierra templada* soon succumbed (as they had in the days of Santa Aña) when required to campaign in the tropics: two-thirds of the forces of Manuel Lárraga, fighting in Morelos, went down with malaria; the general appealed for extra doctors and 6,000 men from the *tierra caliente* who could withstand heat and humidity.[978] Conversely, *costeños* wilted as they pushed inland into the high country of Guerrero (and what affected men often affected mounts too).[979] These constant, sizeable troop movements greatly facilitated the spread of epidemic disease – not only those already mentioned, but also the venereal disease which was reckoned to be endemic in the country, and particularly the army, by the end of the Revolution.[980] Even if they remained healthy, troops disliked serving far from home (and had been known to mutiny in protest); 'detachments supplied by forces from outside my state', complained the governor of Guanajuato, 'cannot be counted on to campaign vigorously, and are always at odds with the civil authorities'; hence, the local preference for self-defence forces, recruited in the state, which campaigned more effectively but aroused the suspicions of a jealous central government.[981]

In the last analysis, the entire Carrancista war effort depended on cash (thus, indirectly, on oil, henequen, garbanzos, minerals and so on). Without pay, the army would dissolve. As it was, notional pay scales were, despite some optimistic Villista anticipations, low and, like all cash wages, vulnerable to the wild fluctuations of the currency. Facing the same problem, industrial workers organised and struck; soldiers deserted or stole. In the commander's eyes, stealing was the lesser evil, and it was generally accepted that the soldier's meagre, depreciating pay (1.75c. plus 0.75c. for a horse in 1916) forced him to live off the land; Carrancista troops, Pershing reported, are 'obliged and expected to take what they want in the country through which they operate, even the clothes off the backs of the peons'.[982] Carrancistas themselves concurred: troops stationed at Texmelucán (Pue.) were robbing the villages for want of pay; General Andrés Bautista had to appropriate the municipal funds of Chicontepec (Ver.), his commanding officer agreed, since he was surrounded and had no money to pay his men.[983] Hence, as the Carrancistas stole and sequestered, they were often seen as 'a worse menace in some respects even than the rebels themselves'; the civil population refused to co-operate; at Ures (Sra) they would prefer to take their chance with the Yaquis than retain a rapacious garrison.[984] Some civilians threatened to rebel in protest, and some did: joining 'defensive' revolt, setting up as bandits, or taking freelance military action against the soldiers.[985]

As Minister of War, Obregón sought to rationalise this shapeless, conglomerate army, regularising the chain of command, establishing hospitals and training programmes, developing aviation.[986] But these reforms were the military equivalents of the civilians' paper radicalism: significant for the future, but marginal or ineffective in the present. A school of aviation was a luxury when the army was on the verge of collapse. For by late 1916 the situation was critical. For over a year there had been recurrent local crises (like that at Chicontepec), forcing commanders to extort goods or money. For want of food, 300 troops threatened to mutiny and sack Guaymas in May 1915 (in such situations, the effect of drink on empty stomachs could be fearsome) and the authorities had to distribute corn and beans.[987] In February 1916, a bankrupt commander 'borrowed' 40,000 pesos from the merchants of Mazatlán to pay his men; across the mountains in Durango, pay was six months in arrears.[988] By the end of the year, as the Constituent Congress met, the paper peso had collapsed; the campaign against Villa was going badly, with increased desertions; troops in the Laguna were 'starving and unpaid'.[989] Drastic policies were devised. The banks' bullion reserves were seized and the troops' wages converted to metal: Obregón issued a new pay scale, designed to 'avert the distressing situation with which the selfless Constitutionalist Army has been struggling'. Paid in metal, troops need no longer sequester provisions, the military commander of Veracruz advised.[990] Providentially, 100,000 silver pesos arrived to pay the garrison at Aguascalientes, and

Murguía received a million which, it was thought, would stem the flow of deserters.[991] By the end of 1916, this supply of hard currency to the troops was, like the annual injection of bullion into Hapsburg Spain, essential for the survival of the regime. And though the major crisis had been averted, nagging local problems continued. Murguía had to levy the merchants of Chihuahua early in 1917; Carrancista commanders in the Huasteca depended on *ad hoc* loans from the oil companies to pay their men and prevent desertion; in the Laguna (1918) the Tlahualilo Co. was a mainstay of the local garrison.[992]

Government disbursement of cash and goods was also crucial in regard to army officers. Put crudely: they, like their men, had to be allowed to steal, if their loyalty was to be retained; but officers stole less to survive than to get on. Loyalty was at issue not so much for fear of defection to Villa or Díaz (though these occurred) but because of intra-Carrancista feuds, which gathered strength and even threatened the survival of the regime. Under the 'decentralised patrimonialism' which prevailed, graft offered the central government a means of buying off generals that was cheap and convenient; graft, therefore, was not some innate feature of human or Mexican nature (though, of course, it was rooted in Mexican social mores) but a vital part of the political system. Nor did 'predatory self-seeking', as one critic called it, constitute a form of deviance but, rather, the normal way of doing things; 'without this peculiarly characteristic detail [Carranza's] rule becomes an almost unintelligible phenomenon'.[993] Official corruption also swelled, here as in other societies, with the sheer, unchecked growth of the functions of government;[994] and it merged with the vigorous entrepreneurialism which the revolution stimulated.[995]

Contemporary images of Carrancista corruption thus reflected not minor blemishes but major, objective facts, no less important than laws and decrees. Graft deserves as much attention as, say Article 123. To the common people, Carrancista rapacity was proverbial, expressed in world-play: *carrancear*, 'to steal'; *Constitucionalistas = con las uñas listas* ('with fingernails at the ready'). Rebel manifestoes, Zapatista and Felicista, hammered away at Carrancista greed and corruption.[996] Friends of Carrancismo, too, like Lincoln Steffens, admitted the extent of the problem; as did many Carrancistas themselves.[997] Civilian critics of the military were outspoken, in the Chamber and at the Constituent Congress; Roberto Pesqueira denounced speculators in *La Vanguardia*, as Cabrera did in *El Universal* and Vasconcelos in *ABC*.[998] 'Nobody deplored more than Mr Carranza himself', a Minister explained, 'the gross dishonesty and immorality which existed among the military element, but this could only be remedied in the course of time.'[999] But generals, too, grappling with a recalcitrant civilian population, realised the scope of the problem. Murguía, who was not above suspicion himself, lamented that in Durango 'there are many humble people who work in agriculture and who have been despoiled of what little they have by the military chiefs'; and it was

Obregón, later to have years of experience of buying off generals, who came out with the famous quip: 'no Mexican general can resist a cannonade of 50,000 pesos'.[1000]

This awareness served the regime well. For graft not only bought loyalty in moments of crisis but also gave successful generals – now settling down, thickening in girth and, like Obregón, turning from the battle-field to the market-place – a stake in the regime which they were reluctant to jeopardise. Defrauded of the Coahuilan governorship in 1917, Luis Gutiérrez was restrained by the inertia of affluence: 'General Gutiérrez was reminded of his immense property holdings over the state, recently acquired by the proceeds of the revolution [and] that an overact [sic] might serve to revert these holdings to the Federal Government by executive decree' (though Gutiérrez paused for thought, he rebelled in the end).[1001] In other cases the outcome was different. In Morelos, Pablo González rented out plantations to his generals, binding them to the status quo; and in 1918 another potential rebel, Murguía again, was supposedly 'restrained from such a [rebellious] line of conduct by the extensive investments he has made of recent years'.[1002]

But while graft might serve the interests of central government, its chief function was to enrich the revolutionary elite (chiefly, though not solely, Carrancista); and, while some allegations may be mistaken, they are so common and implicate so many revolutionary leaders that they must indicate an endemic problem. Mariscal grafted in Guerrero; Aguilar 'lived like a prince' off his dealings in hides; Millán and Portas, also of Veracruz, were grafters; Acosta dealt in cattle in the Huasteca; Treviño and his uncle in foodstuffs in Chihuahua, making large deposits, it was said, in an El Paso bank; Murguía stocked his Laguna ranch with stolen cattle, traded in guayule, and engaged in the illicit export of silver.[1003] Obregón, turning full-time to business in 1917, made over $50,000 for himself, handling the sale of the entire 1918 chickpea harvest in the north west (here the line between graft and politicised big business becomes impossible to draw).[1004] Ignacio Pesqueira – notwithstanding his brother's denunciations of corruption – was involved in shady land deals; Alvarado's invasion of Chiapas served 'to fill the pockets of the government generals and their lieutenants'.[1005] Invasion and *reconcentración* similarly served the interests of the revolution's biggest grafter, Pablo González, for whom 'the Morelos campaign was a great chance for patriotic boodle, the most irresistible kind'.[1006] Already, González held the Mexico City bullfight concession and was engaged in shipping sugar from Oaxaca to the capital.[1007] In Morelos, he and his officers compensated themselves for the travails of war, exporting coal, dynamite, sulphur, copper, hides, printing presses, cattle, sugar, alcohol and foodstuffs for sale in Mexico City. Even bathtubs, looted from a Cuernavaca hotel, were retailed in the capital; and the prospective buyers, also army officers, brazenly asked their previous owner to identify them, in order to guarantee their quality.[1008]

This was organised, wholesale, governmental profiteering. But corruption covered a range of activities and factions. Of the leading Sinaloan revolutionaries, the Villista Buelna found consolation in San Francisco where, by the end of 1915 he was living the good life, 'having feathered his nest during his period of control'; his old rival and victor Iturbe was said to be dealing in hides, chickpeas, corn, beans and tequila.[1009] Further south, in the revolutionary chaos of Michoacán, all factions grafted. The Carrancista Freyría we have encountered, controlling the Hacienda Chaparro and the branch line to Irimbo, trafficking in wheat and other crops and defying the landowner's efforts to get the property restored.[1010] An American, passing by Lake Chapala and looking to do business (and perhaps to offload a pile of depreciating Villista paper), met the Villista – later Chavista – General Luis Gutiérrez at Los Reyes (now, but not then, at the foot of Paricutín); Gutiérrez, said the American, declared that 'he could sell us anything we wanted and in any quantity . . . [and] he expressed himself as being "the owner of everything we could see with a telescope from the top of the biggest mountain in the state"'; so, for 7,500 pesos (Villista) the American got three tons of sugar and a safe-conduct.[1011] But, in circumstances typical of the time and place, the deal fell through. Back at Los Reyes another Villista, Jesús Cíntora, commandeered the American's mules, dumping the sugar on the ground (Cíntora specialised in kitting out massive caravans, up to 600 mules, to ship rice and other goods down to the coast, whence the rebels imported arms).[1012] But at this point, the Villistas were attacked and scattered by Amaro's forces; Cíntora's mules and the American's sugar fell into the hands of another grafter; and – not to miss a trick – Amaro held Los Reyes' Spanish merchants to ransom.[1013]

Among these many – often, no doubt, distorted – accounts lie certain recurrent patterns. Graft was common to all factions: some Villista examples have been given, and more will follow; there were, even among the Zapatistas, 'cowards and egoists who have retired . . . enjoying [the] wealth they have taken over in the shadow of the revolution'.[1014] But the Carrancistas – the winners, often interlopers in alien territory and, certainly at national level, active entrepreneurs – were the most sustained, insatiable grafters. They engaged in four main lines of business which, taken together, represented a large slice of the economy: food, transport, city vice and real estate. The traffic in foodstuffs was a key area since, at a time of dearth and inflation, it guaranteed certain profits, as high as 300% on the west coast.[1015] The alleged practitioners were legion: the Arrietas in Durango; Martín Triana, governor of Aguascalientes; Diéguez in Jalisco; the second-in-command at Piedras Negras; Murguía, Treviño and the Herreras, who were all involved in Chihuahua's food trade.[1016] Even the Juntas Proveedoras, set up to ration and distribute food, served the interests of speculators and their military partners.[1017]

Closely, in some reports explicitly, linked to this was corruption on the railways, now largely in military hands. Some stretches of railway – like Freyría's at Irimbo – had become patrimonial privileges; Lieutenant-Colonel Castillo Tapia controlled the lines running east out of Mexico City, disposing of rolling stock to his own advantage.[1018] Foreign interests, dependent on rail transport, were free with their complaints: the Southern Pacific Railway had to contend with Calles' arbitrary and corrupt trainmaster; ASARCO, and others, complained of the backhanders necessary to get freight shifted throughout the north; 'petty graft prevails in every branch of the railway service', concluded a planter, trying to transport coffee from Jalapa to the coast.[1019] Merchants, desperate for access to rolling stock, bid up the cost of freight and the inevitable, associated 'gratifications'.[1020] Military escorts – essential in much of the country – also took their cut from the goods they were supposedly protecting. And the peculation of the military was seconded, in a minor way, by that of the railwaymen.[1021]

A third area of profit, clearly important, though harder to penetrate, involved city vice and entertainment. Again, there was nothing new in politicians or policemen running cantinas, casinos and brothels; but now it became more blatant (and probably more extensive); and it revealed a fundamental contradiction between Constitutionalist theory and practice which, though rarely discussed, is of central importance. For Constitutionalism had a strong Puritan streak: evident in repeated denunciations of the evils of drink, vice and bad hygiene, which crowded the press, political debates and the writings of key figures. In practice, too, there were frequent attempts to ban liquor, close brothels, eliminate gambling and bloodsports, inculcate health and hygiene, and generally to bring about a 'social regeneration' of Mexico.[1022] But, in practice, this moralising campaign collided with the immediate imperatives of profit – and taxation. Before looking briefly at the collision, it is worth noting that the tension between Puritanism and peculation was much less obvious within Carrancismo's rivals. Villa, though teetotal, did not try to convert others; his abstention from drink was personal and prudential, unrelated to any ideological commitment; while Zapata – fathering children, attending bullfights, drinking beer and spirits – embodied most popular vices. Indeed, one of his disillusioned intellectual spokesmen blamed Zapata's political failure on his excessive love of 'good horses, fighting cocks, flashy women, card-games and intoxicating liquors'.[1023] In Morelos, however, both the desire and the opportunity to extract profit from these vices were limited. Villista Chihuahua was a different matter. Here, officers filled confiscated houses with 'women of ill repute' (whether for personal or pecuniary advantage is not entirely clear); Hipólito Villa controlled the crap table of Juárez; and the Chinese proprietors of gambling houses and opium dens – among others – paid retainers to the military.[1024]

When the Carrancistas triumphed, they began a clean-up of Juárez; while at

Piedras Negras the drive for municipal morality involved prohibition, a ban on cockfights and bullfights, the closure of saloons and beer gardens, and the arrest of Americans who crossed from Eagle Pass 'to enjoy an evening of lustful pleasure'.[1025] There were many comparable cases, throughout the country. But these blasts of clean, Puritan reformism lasted no longer than the Americans' dutiful clean-up of Veracruz. At best, bans (on liquor in Quintana Roo or brothels in Baja) gave way to regulation and taxation.[1026] Often, in the border towns, for example, where profits were outstanding, vice made a rapid comeback. At Piedras Negras a 'saloon party' emerged, protested vociferously against tax rises (which were destined for education), and campaigned for the return of bloodsports.[1027] Francisco Serrano – himself a notorious gambler and dabbler in the liquor trade – took command in Sonora and promptly repealed Calles' systematic prohibitionist measures, even sacking the prohibitionist state treasurer, Ramonet.[1028] In the 1917 gubernatorial election, Calles clung to the temperance ticket (and won, not for that reason): his opponent, Obregón's brother, José, campaigned for the re-opening of the cantinas.[1029] Already, at Mazatlán, a prohibition order had been relaxed (a matter of days after one unfortunate had been executed for selling liquor).[1030] San Luis experienced a sudden transition from the Puritan Gavira to the dissolute Dávila, who consorted with the well-to-do (landlords, Spanish merchants and Huertistas), trafficked in confiscated goods, and helped his friends corner the market in grain (he could be seen daily in their company, 'tippling in different establishments of the city'). His military subordinates, too, kept bad company; one had been seen 'in an embarrassing state' at a San Luis theatre, cracking bottles of champagne, which were shared with 'an actress [*artista*] who at the time was dancing in a suggestive manner'.[1031] Dávila and his corrupt crew will return in a moment. Meanwhile, San Luis' sad decline, continued under Barragán's governorship, was typical. Despite bans, gambling still flourished in Mexico City, especially at the traditional centre of Villa de Guadalupe; by 1918, gambling joints were 'springing up in great profusion' in the capital, and the regime, keen for revenue, turned a blind eye; had not the police organised horse-races to raise money for the amortisation of the national debt?[1032] Bans on bullfighting and *pulque* were also lifted; in the latter case after much debate over principles of free trade and the nation's need for revenue.[1033] The *pulque* trade was essential to the economy of central Mexico, stated Gerzayn Ugarte, Carranza's personal secretary; fiscal necessity argued against a ban on *pulque* and other liquor, a *constituyente* agreed (but, since he owned the Saltillo bullring, he was of Satan's party anyway).[1034] By the end of the decade, therefore, revolutionary Puritanism, though far from defeated, was on the retreat, the victim not least of revolutionary corruption.[1035]

The triumph of profit over principle was even more starkly and significantly evident in the matter of agrarian reform. The regime's official agrarian reform

– the decrees, legislation, and meagre distribution of land – will be considered shortly; here, it is necessary to sketch the back-drop (which is sometimes left, as in avant-garde Shakespearean productions, bland and empty, leaving the actors to comport themselves *in vacuo* and the audience to concentrate on the text). But this exaltation of the word, justifiable in the case of the bard, is positively harmful in the study of the revolution; for it elevates rhetoric above deeds, and conveys an impression of masterful legislators, transforming reality; where, more often, reality refused to be transformed or, indeed, transformed the legislators themselves.

The revolution produced a transfer of property as well as political power (though the latter was more obvious and complete). Confiscation of 'enemy' property was extensive and, by 1915, included not only Porfiristas and Huertistas but also Villistas and Conventionists; these latter groups, indeed, were now persecuted with even greater alacrity.[1036] If the rebels' takeover of city houses and limousines was the most overt, symbolic manifestation of the arrival of a new elite, the transfer of property in the countryside – the locus of the popular revolution – was more significant. But it is hard to evaluate this transfer: the extent of the old, Porfirian landlords' decline and their replacement by revolutionary parvenus (or even peasant communities) remains unquantifiable.[1037] But it is possible to show how, in some cases, the alienation of land was either reversed, or allowed to affect the character of the new, post-revolutionary political elite.

The war against Huerta resulted in numerous confiscations of property, some of which, in Sonora or the Laguna, were worked for the 'benefit of the revolution' (though with graft thrown in), while some were privately appropriated.[1038] Urbina enjoyed Nieves – and the loot which went with it – as a private patrimony until Villa tired of his old partner's selfish retirement; in San Luis, too, while supposedly directing the campaign at El Ebano, Urbina had dabbled in mining enterprises, allowing his relatives to make off with ore.[1039] Urbina was unusual less as regards his urge to self-enrichment, than the bare-faced, suicidal – bandit? – way he set about it. Others, particularly the Sonorans, behaved more like archetypal Weberian capitalists. Indeed, in Sonora, the take-over of Porfirian property, and the rise of a new, revolutionary landed elite was more complete than in any other state.[1040] Obregón, devoting himself to business after 1917 and handling the entire north-western garbanzo crop in 1918, began building up an economic empire which by the 1920s included 3,500 hectares (he had begun with 150), 1,500 peons, a mill, cannery, soap factory and bank.[1041] Other Sonorans, like Hill, acquired property and business, to their own – and, they argued, the nation's – advantage.[1042] Many Carrancistas did likewise. Murguía, grafting assiduously, acquired a hacienda in Zacatecas, whence he exported cattle and guayule. Of his fellow-Coahuilans, Coss, also of modest origins, was running a ranch by late 1916, and Cesareo Castro, Obregón's dashing cavalry commander, had leased a cotton plantation, which he worked on a share basis (without, it seems, paying his share). And there were other examples of obscure leaders, like General Santiago of Tepic, who had settled down with 400 retainers, who worked his land and protected his person (a precursor of Cedillo's military colonies of the 1920s).[1043]

This acquisition of land by revolutionary generals has often been seen as the rise of a 'new bourgeoisie'; or, as Córdova puts it, more cautiously, the Constitutionalist army was the 'seedbed . . . in large measure, of the new capitalist class'.[1044] Confronted by yet another rising bourgeoisie, sceptics may reach for their revolvers. That there was a turnover of land, and that revolutionary leaders benefited, is beyond dispute; but, as already suggested, the turnover cannot be quantified, and the evidence of a 'new bourgeoisie' remains equivocal. In fact, an analysis of the relations of production (which is what talk of a 'new bourgeoisie' is all about) suggests that the most significant changes lay, not in the pattern of ownership, but in the changing pattern of production, employment, and socio-political relations (to which we will turn in a moment). For, as regards ownership, it is clear that many old landlords survived or recovered; and that the new revolutionary elite merged with them, as well as usurping them. Landlord recovery is no more quantifiable than landlord dispossession. But it was certainly considerable – Katz talks of their 'tremendous' recuperation – and many examples can be cited.[1045] In Sinaloa, landlords were recovering confiscated land (at a price) by the end of 1915; two years later an observer noted the 'unexplained return of Científico families' to their Sinaloan haciendas.[1046] In Aguascalientes, 'haciendas and other real property [sic] which were confiscated [were] being returned to their lawful owners' late in 1915, and it is clear that the state experienced no major upheaval in landownership.[1047] So, too, in upland San Luis – not in Valle del Maíz or the Huasteca – 'the majority of the large properties and town houses have been returned to their owners', who included old Porfirian oligarchs.[1048] Elsewhere, Díaz's sister-in-law and widow both recovered property (Madero's widow, ironically, remained dispossessed); as did María Luján de Terrazas, who linked two of the richest families of Chihuahua and the Laguna, and whose lands, seized by Villa in 1914, were returned in 1916.[1049]

Politically jealous, the Carranza regime thus showed itself to be remarkably forgiving as regards property rights. Old Porfiristas could return to their estates, so long as they eschewed politics. Of course, this policy – urged from the 'centre' – incurred criticism. Smart operators, who had battened onto confiscated property, saw their livelihood endangered: the devolution of the Hacienda El Salado and 'certain others' in San Luis to the Arguizoniz family, hit one speculator, involved in the *guayule* trade; his problems were compounded by the 100,000 pesos of worthless *infalsificables* he held.[1050] More seriously, revolutionary leaders also opposed this policy. Múgica was disgusted to be ordered to return confiscated land, already distributed as *ejidos*, to a Tabasco company (composed of '*Gachupines* and Yanquis'): the regime's agrarian policy, he concluded, was a 'complete fiasco'.[1051] Múgica and the recipient *ejidatarios* managed to stall, resisting devolution; in the Laguna, too, it was reported that, 'Carranza has ordered the governor of the state at least four times to deliver certain Spanish properties to their lawful owners and each time a positive refusal was given.'[1052] From Hidalgo, Governor Flores – no *agrarista* firebrand – complained that restitution of the property of 'reactionaries' ('amassed with the tears of innumerable familes'), 'has caused so bad an impression among the state's inhabitants that some have come to see it as a deal between the Revolution and the Científicos'; furthermore, 'posterity would judge this devolution very severely considering that the Revolution was defrauding the interests of the people'.[1053] Posterity may now judge. In neighbouring Tlaxcala, too, embattled landlords now took advantage of national policy to attempt a come-back: some villages lost control of lands they had recently acquired, and others found legalisation of *de facto* possession difficult; the struggle continued into the 1920s.[1054] But the clearest case was Morelos, where the decline of Zapatismo encouraged a revival of the planter interest; which offended not only the villagers, but also the Gonzalista generals who had staked claims in the state.[1055] Battles within the Carrancista elite, coupled with official concern for commercial agriculture, enabled many planters to recover their estates and re-start cultivation. By requiring land-titles to be ordered and registered, the government facilitated 'not the protection of the pueblos, but their destitution and the resurgence of the planters'.[1056] This was by no means the end of the story; but at the beginning of 1920 it seemed that the plantocracy was on the way to regaining its landed possessions and local prominence.

Clearly, this was a policy of great significance. Whatever the scope of Carrancista agrarian legislation, the regime's practical policies were conservative, even 'counter-revolutionary'. Very little land was distributed, and a great deal more was handed back to landlords, reversing the *de facto* reform of the revolution, and creating further barriers to future redistribution. There was a basic contradiction, even cynicism, here: grand, egalitarian gestures (like Article 27) contrasted with specific, regressive measures, like the wholesale devolution of land just mentioned. Why did the Carrancistas take away with one hand what they appeared to be giving with the other? First, it may be inferred – though it is not easy to prove directly – that agrarian promises had been wrung from a reluctant regime, or would-be regime. Carranza, who may be seen as representing a strong element within Constitutionalism as well as the individual leadership, was at best equivocal on the agrarian question: capable of a certain political radicalism – in his proscription of opponents, infringement of constitutional rights – he remained socially conservative; he was a leader who, by 1916 at any rate, 'appealed to a certain class of people who had property to protect'.[1057] Hence his hostile attitude to labour, and his poor

record of agrarian reform. Carranza actively encouraged the devolution of land
to dispossessed landlords; he restrained reformers like Múgica in Tabasco and
Alvarado in Yucatán; he presented a draft constitution in which the agrarian
reform proposals were modest and limited.[1058] So, too, were the official land
grants – totalling some 200,000 hectares – made during Carranza's presidency.[1059]

The political exigencies of the civil war, coupled with the pressure of more
sincere Carrancista reformers, had induced Carranza to adopt stances which,
over time, proved uncomfortable; once in power, he could relax his contorted
ideological limbs. By mid-1917, a foreigner reported, 'a tendency towards
conservatism is observable now that the government is well established . . .
undoubtedly Carranza is doing his utmost to free himself from the extrem-
ists'.[1060] Under Carranza, complained peasant leaders from Durango, the
agrarian reform had been 'betrayed'; the Agrarian Commissions established to
carry it out, argued a Carrancista critic, 'have been nothing more than entities
set up to defraud the villages'.[1061] This conservative approach was reinforced
by the regime's concern for economic recovery (without which the regime itself
would be jeopardised). Since War Communism was not under consideration,
revival demanded economic orthodoxy, and ruled out radical agrarian experiments – quite the opposite conclusion to that reached in the 1930s, when
collectivism and *dirigisme* had become globally fashionable. Now, with food
shortages and even famine affecting the country, and valuable foreign
exchange going on grain purchases in the US, agricultural, which meant
hacienda, production had to be stimulated; the 'Dumont effect' had to be
conjured.[1062] Landlords, not peasants, became the beneficiaries of Mexico's
NEP. And these included landlords facing *agrarista* threats. Alvarado's
modest agrarian reform in Yucatán was aborted; the henequen plantations
remained inviolate.[1063] In Michoacán, haciendas which produced staple crops
(like Cantabria) or timber for the railways (like Santiago Slade's) could count
on official protection.[1064] In addition, states trying to balance precarious
budgets needed revenue from land taxes and agricultural production; landlords, like those of Tlaxcala, could use their fiscal power (even to the extent of
calling a tax strike) to pressure the authorities.[1065] And, like the urban
workers, the *campesinos* themselves could be driven by circumstances to forego
militancy, to go back to work on the hacienda, even to take refuge in *hacendado*
paternalism.[1066]

But the landlords' recovery and the frustration of reform must also be seen as
part of the rapprochement between *hacendado* and revolutionary, which formed
a crucial feature of reconstruction. Not that the Carrancista elite was predominantly *agrarista* to start with; but it had been pushed towards reform, and it
had ridden roughshod over the landed interest in its conquest of power.
Sonora, where *agrarismo* was weak, saw the most complete transfer of property.
Now, in power, many revolutionaries succumbed to *hacendado* blandishments;

many became fellow-landlords; others connived at landlord recovery to their mutual advantage. This connivance, it has been suggested (and the examples given here tend to confirm the suggestion), was most noticeable in central Mexico, where the *agrarista* threat was greater and where the Carrancistas – often outsiders – preferred economic collaboration to usurpation.[1067] The classic cases are to be found in fiction: in Azuela or Fuentes' *La Muerte de Artemio Cruz*; but there were also plenty of factual examples. In San Luis, Villa de Reyes had fought a long battle, productive of much litigation and some violence, with the Hacienda Gogorrón. Under Madero, the hacienda was confirmed in possession of the community's former *ejidal* land; this decision, however, was reversed by Gabriel Gavira during his brief governorship of 1915.[1068] But Gavira was sent north and replaced by Vicente Dávila, a Coahuilan engineer and devout Carrancista ('whose role in Mexican politics has been no more than the harmonious complement of the public conduct maintained by Venustiano Carranza').[1069] Dávila soon made connections in Potosino high society and, in particular, became a boon companion of Enrique Závala, the owner of Gogorrón. Acting through a corrupt official in the Confiscated Properties Office, he had Gavira's *ejidal* grant reversed, and the land returned to the hacienda. As in many such cases, however, this was not the end of the story.[1070] But it was Dávila rather than Gavira who set the tone for later Carrancista policy in the state. The constitutional governor, Barragán, another *adicto* of the president, was himself a landlord, and a bitter enemy of the Cedillos; he governed in arbitrary, selfish fashion, promoting friends, purging enemies, maintaining a 'startling' level of corruption, and setting his face against agrarian reform.[1071]

Similar deals were hatched in Puebla, where, it was alleged, 'reactionaries' successfully defended their interests in part by suborning the Carrancista military commander, Cesareo Castro.[1072] When villagers in the Tehuacán valley petitioned for the return of lands, waters and *montes* lost in previous years the State Agrarian Commission ruled that the village titles were deficient, and that the present landlord could not be dispossessed. But the commission, the villagers complained, worked hand-in-glove with the landlords and local military; *hacendados* refused to provide work or did so paying old, inadequate, Porfirian wage rates; the *jefe de las armas* calumnied them, calling them Zapatistas when, in fact, many had fought for Carranza.[1073] The alliance of landlords and military was intimate: troops were used to keep the villagers out of the woods; timber, charcoal, and stoves had been seized by the soldiers, and the villagers had been ordered not to trespass on the *monte* on pain of death. The local colonel's rebuttal of these charges, and his justification for defending the haciendas, was a classic exposition of Constitutionalist theory: one that, while it did not reject agrarian reform outright, nevertheless balked at *de facto*, illegal, populist assaults on property, and conceived of the revolution in quite different terms. The colonel spurns us, the villagers explained,

> telling us we are so many scoundrels (*sinvergüenzas*) who, on the strength of the Revolution, want to strip the Hacendados of their lands, which have cost them so much, and that we ought to understand that the Revolution is working to establish a government, not to give land to bandits, and that for these claims we have no right, still less laws or decrees to protect us.

It was the voice of Añorve, five years on, with a different factional label.[1074]

This was far from an isolated case. Other villages in the same valley made identical complaints: of poverty, lack of work, starvation, agrarian usurpation, and the connivance of landlords and military.[1075] It was in Puebla, too, that Rosalie Evans had to win the support of the military in her dogged efforts to recover her hacienda and evict the *campesinos* who had appropriated it.[1076] Similar connivance was evident in Michoacán, where one threatened *hacendado* enlisted the support of an ex-Porfirian magistrate, now a high-ranking functionary in the Constitutionalist army; by the 1920s, such relationships had become commonplace in the state, as landlords, officers, and *agraristas* mobilised their forces, fought and politicked.[1077] Indeed, as Hans-Werner Tobler has shown, these conflicts were endemic in the 1920s, by which time the army had become primarily a force for agrarian stabilisation, its generals – some of whom, like Guadalupe Sánchez, were notorious in this regard – acquiring property and collaborating with landlords in opposition to peasant demands.[1078] Thus, in Veracruz, Zacatecas, Michoacán, Puebla, Guerrero, Hidalgo and Tamaulipas (to name but the states from which Tobler's examples are taken), military units guarded haciendas, repressed *agraristas*, victimised their leaders, and resisted land distribution. That landlords should survive and prosper in, say, Chiapas – where the post-revolutionary *mapache* administration (1920–4) was composed of landlords and 'concerned itself primarily with the welfare of the landed class' – was hardly surprising; but the same occurred in Zapatista Morelos, though to a lesser extent and at a later date. Zapata's nephew, allied to a 'clique of generals', sought to wrest the best lands of Anenecuilco from the *ejidatorios*; his own son (who as an innocent infant had dozed during his father's famous meeting with Villa at Xochimilco) acquired land, became mayor of Cuautla, and 'learned the rudiments of politics, which rotted his sense of obligation'; he ended up a client of the planter interest.[1079] *Corruptio optimi pessima*.

THE CARRANCISTA MACHINE: IN MOTION

The ostensible paradox between Carrancismo's radical discourse and conservative practice should become clearer as we turn from the internal workings of the machine to its external appearance and progress (which are more familiar).

In many accounts, the 1917 Constitution is seen as the consummation of revolutionary aspirations (sometimes tautologically, in that the Constitution also furnishes proof of what these aspirations were), as well as the blueprint for Mexican development in the post-revolutionary period. As regards the second claim, judgement is waived; as regards the first, there are major objections. The new Constitution only imperfectly represented popular, revolutionary hopes: it was conceived without direct popular participation; it was drawn up in haste and chaos, rather than calm deliberation; and its limpid provisions contrasted with the murky reality which existed outside the Querétaro Palace of Fine Arts.

There had been talk – on Carranza's part – of a new Constitution as far back as 1913; Cabrera referred to the need for one during the Mexico City junta (October 1914); and during 1915, as the war with Villa spread and the Carrancista social conscience flowered, the idea received extensive press coverage.[1080] Certainly by spring 1915, Carranza was committed to calling a congress that would 'raise to constitutional precepts the reforms dictated during the struggle', and in September of the following year, it was officially convoked. The timetable was ambitious; elections in October, deliberations in November–December, promulgation on 1 February 1917, after which congressional and presidential elections could be held under the new constitutional order.[1081] The *constituyentes* of 1916 could not afford the deliberate tempo of their predecessors of 1824 and 1857, when the making of a new Constitution had taken almost a year. But this rapid return to constitutionality, it was hoped, would bring a speedy improvement in the political and economic situation, both domestically and internationally.[1082] The Constitution served an immediate, pragmatic, as well as long-term, ideological interest.

The task was accomplished and the Constitution emerged, one of the most radical of its time. It incorporated many political features of its 1857 predecessor – a federal system, separation of powers, no re-election, provision for individual rights, restrictions on the Church – but it added new socioeconomic reforms, granting the state greater powers in the ordering of society. Of the two most celebrated innovations (Articles 27 and 123) the former asserted the nation's prior right to property which could justify expropriation (e.g., of latifundia) in the public interest; it also reserved subsoil deposits to the nation, so that mineral and hydrocarbon exploitation could take place only by government concession, and with foreign concessionaires adopting Mexican citizenship. Thus, communities were given constitutional rights to the restoration or award (*dotación*) of land, which might be expropriated from large landowners, who would receive bonds by way of indemnity; thus, oil and mining companies would have their freehold properties converted to leasehold; and no foreigner might acquire land within frontier or coastal regions.[1083] Article 123 'constituted the most enlightened statement of labor protective principles in the world to that date': it required state and federal governments to produce labour legislation, including minimum wage laws, laid down a maximum eight-hour day, regulated child and female labour, stipulated a range of measures to ensure safe, healthy work conditions, abolished debt peonage, and recognised the right to strike (save for government munition workers, and in cases where a majority of workers engaged in acts of violence).[1084] Differences between capital and labour would be arbitrated by government juntas combining workers, management and officials: a means to secure the 'social equilibrium' which was central to Constitutionalist thinking, even of a 'radical' kind. Here, indeed, we come to the philosophical heart of the Constitution (and we touch on themes to be developed in the next section). Despite denunciations of its 'Bolshevik' character, the Constitution was not even socialist. By contemporary standards it was certainly radical; but it conferred powers on the state not with a view to achieving a planned economy, still less a classless society, but rather to mitigate abuses and arbitrate between conflicting groups.[1085] The themes of social equilibrium and common, productive effort – seductive to government during a period of reconstruction – resounded at Querétaro.[1086]

The implementation of these measures, however, was to be slow and incomplete. And, at the time of their formulation, there was an air of unreality about the whole procedure. To grasp something of the actual, contemporary (as against the retrospective, mythical) significance of the Constitution, it is necessary to consider the circumstances of its birth, the character of its progenitors, and the manner of parturition. The first is hardest to fathom. As the Congress met, Villa was descending on Torreón, Zapata was still supreme in Morelos, the Felicistas were at the peak of their strength. Few newspapers, and few *constituyentes* dwelt on these topics.[1087] As they debated – one heretic pointed out – people were dying of hunger in Guanajuato.[1088] And the upheaval affected representation: Chihuahua 'elected' only one *constituyente* of the six to which it was entitled; Guerrero send only three out of eight; Morelos, strangely, sent its full complement of three. People in Mexico City were cynical: they expected the Congress to rubberstamp the draft presented to it by Carranza; and some high-up Carrancistas agreed, anticipating an obsequious farce.[1089] The Congress was less consummatory proof of victory, peace and stability than a means to these as yet unattained ends; a means to confer legitimacy on a shaky regime. Though some participants entertained sincere, radical ideas – and a few even implemented them – the very pliability of the government, in its acceptance of certain of these ideas, suggests that what Carranza and his colleagues chiefly wanted was *a* Constitution, the hypothetical contents of which could later be reviewed, rewritten and ignored (all of which happened). Hence, as Carranza's original draft, which closely followed 1857, was drastically revised and supplemented by the Congress, so his supporters bowed to the wind and, on occasions, ran before it. Indeed, they had signalled their intention well in advance: a year before, as Macías and Rojas got down to preparing the government's draft, they indicated that it would 'serve as a basis or starting point for the *constituyentes*' discussions', that approval or modification might result, and that, while they had taken 1857 as their model, no-one should lose sight of the 'profound change taking place in our fundamental institutions'.[1090] It was the same tactic that had been used before, in response to popular agrarian demands: promises and resolutions, after all, were easily compiled. Thus, as one *constituyente* pointed out, Article 123, with its magnificent array of pro-labour measures, was drafted in a country where living standards were suffering a marked decline, where strikers were being pilloried, and where the very weakness of the labour movement pointed up the Utopian character of such provisions. It was not so 'incredible' that an advanced labour code saw the light of day in a poor, agrarian country like Mexico: rather, the very insignificance of industry and organised labour made such exercises in Utopian legislation – or, in some cases, Orwellian Newspeak – all the more feasible; promises could be flaunted before a weak labour movement with reasonable confidence that their implementation would depend on government, not union, initiatives.[1091]

This raises the crucial but difficult question of popular awareness of the Congress and its work. Elections were held in seven-eighths of all national electoral districts: they were quiet, subject to a considerable degree of official control, and generally failed to excite much enthusiasm. Niemeyer asserts that 'voter interest and turnout were substantial' but his own evidence hardly bears this out; Cumberland's 'widespread lethargy' seems nearer the mark.[1092] Police supervision and control, which guaranteed the election only of approved Carrancista candidates, were well attested; there were many complaints of fraud (Palavicini alleged a bloc, garrison vote in the Federal District); and some results looked distinctly odd.[1093] In one district of Chihuahua, for example, a candidate secured 94% of the vote.[1094] Average turnout, Cumberland suggests, was around 30%; but the evidence furnished to the credentials committee, dealing with 76 of the 215 delegates, suggests a lower figure of 20–25%; this, furthermore, reflects votes counted, not votes genuinely cast.[1095] It also indicates wide variations: the average vote (in constituencies of 60,000 population) was a little over 2,000; but while 8,227 voted for Manuel Aranda at San Francisco del Rincón (Gto), Antonio Gutiérrez was elected for Cd Lerdo (Dgo) with only 145 votes. Of Guanajuato's 17 districts, 10 polled an average of over 3,500, while 5 of the 12 Federal District districts averaged barely 1,000, confirming that in the capital 'voting was very slight due to lack of political cohesion'.[1096] Contemporaries, Mexican and foreign, agreed that the elections were held 'without enthusiasm and without any interest'; that – at Aguascalientes, one of the few places where consuls saw fit to comment – the election was quiet and 'very few people cast their votes'.[1097] The sheer speed of the process inhibited organisation (hence the lack of 'cohesion' in Mexico City) and even official groups were kept under police surveillance.[1098] There was, therefore, no scope for independent mobilisation. The labour movement, for example, which was to receive the gift of Article 123 from on high, did not involve itself in the presentation or selection of candidates.[1099]

Once under way, the Congress excited more interest. But it figured less as a sovereign, democratic assembly, than as a power to be petitioned, another manifestation of the 'centre', whose influence might be brought to bear on a particular problem. For the great majority of petitioners to the Congress were concerned, not with major issues of policy, but minor questions of abuse, corruption and, above all, political geography. They wanted prisoners released, politicians investigated, and new administrative units created: a state of Zempoalla, in the Puebla sierra, or – a demand emanating from numerous town councils – a state of Tehuantepec on the Isthmus (one sycophant advocated the elevation of Tepic to statehood under the name 'Carranza').[1100] Apart from indicating a neglect of the ideological issues supposedly prominent in 1916–17, these examples testify again to the strength of provincial sentiments – disappointed though they were. The only exception was the labour movement which, once the Congress was well advanced, yet again displayed its awareness of national politics, at least in Mexico City and the north (Tampico, Saltillo, San Luis, as well as Orizaba), whence came petitions on behalf of specific unions and, in particular, deferential acknowledgement of Article 123.[1101]

The Constituent Congress, therefore, excited neither popular participation nor enthusiasm. Certainly it inspired no *corridos*.[1102] And its detachment from broad, national realities is borne out by an analysis of its members. It was not full of popular caudillos or radical agrarians, as sometimes imagined.[1103] On the contrary, all the *constituyentes* were Carrancistas (that, we shall see, did not guarantee unity, or even fraternity) and most, 85% according to Peter H. Smith's estimate, were middle class, compared with 11% lower class and 4% upper class.[1104] As in most political gatherings of this sort, therefore, middle-class professionals predominated: over half the delegates (53%) had professional qualifications, just over a quarter being *licenciados*; nearly half had had a university education. There was, too, the usual indigestible lump of legal expertise: of 220 delegates no less than 62 (28%) were lawyers; this compared with 18 teachers, 16 engineers, 16 doctors (their importance will be noted) and 14 journalists. The middle-class character of the Congress was, perhaps, reflected in the generous expenses the delegates received (60 pesos a day); and in delegate Lizardi's comment that 'it was agreed that all young men had their first sexual experience with the cook or the maid'.[1105] 'Popular' delegates were rare: 5 have been classified as 'labour leaders', 3 were railway workers (a good deal has been made of this fragment; we should note that the Congress also included Colonel Aguirre Escobar, who chaired the court-martial of strikers in the munitions industry); 19 delegates were considered 'farmers'.[1106] Delegates were, therefore, somewhat removed from the world of industry, commerce and agriculture, educated in the humanities, and predominantly urban (Niemeyer's assertion that they were 'from rural areas' and 'provincial in outlook' seems misleading). Like previous revolutionary assemblies, too, the Congress failed to reflect the military realities of the country. At a time when revolutionary generals were the true wielders of power, the Congress was disproportionately civilian. Of the delegates, 30% held military rank (10% were generals, 12% colonels) but the military delegates were of secondary, or lower, rank (generals were common enough in 1916): only Aguilar, Jara, Múgica, and Nafarrete could qualify as important military, and, of these, only Nafarrete ('an ignorant peon') was a real man of the people who owed his prominence to military prowess; Jara and Múgica were, in some senses, politicians in khaki; Aguilar, whose social origins are open to debate, was rarely present anyway.[1107]

Thus, though Jara and Múgica played important roles, they did so as somewhat untypical, politicised generals – not as popular, local caudillos; and even the behind-the-scenes influence of Obregón, once thought to be the prime mover behind the congressional 'radicals', was perhaps not as decisive as has sometimes been imagined.[1108] While, in the provinces, generals fought, governed and grafted, the civilians held the stage at Querétaro, as they had at Aguascalientes; in this respect, too, the Congress had a somewhat unreal quality about it. For what good were pious resolutions on agrarian and labour reform when their implementation lay in other, callous, bloodstained hands? Telling revolutionary generals to read Tolstoy was a counsel of perfection.[1109] Generals might espouse social reform – Obregón was a pioneer – but they would do so from considerations of *realpolitik* or, perhaps, from their populist rapport with the rank-and-file, not out of deference to the loquacious civilians at Querétaro. These included many old, familiar faces. Prominent among the so-called 'moderates' were Maderista civilians and Renovadores like Palavicini, Nieto, Rojas, Macías and Cravioto – professional men, who supported stock liberal measures and usually recoiled from the flamboyant radicalism of the 'jacobins'.[1110] Other erstwhile *políticos* now recaptured the limelight: Rafael Cañete, once (1912) governor of Puebla, who chipped in with his Juarista anti-clericalism; Antonio Hidalgo and Rafael Cepeda, ex-governors of Tlaxcala and San Luis; Martínez, editor of *El Demócrata*, and Ceballos, Carrancista journalistic hack; Dorador, the Durango artisan and town councillor of 1912; the tireless agrarian theorist Nicéforo Zambrano, the old polemicist Molina Enríquez.[1111] Most important of these, however, was Pastor Rouaix, whose influential role at Querétaro contrasted with the embarrassingly ineffectual position he had held as civilian Governor of Durango under the thumb of Urbina and the Arrietas. These civiliams now enjoyed a novel prominence, revelling in their rhetoric and legal know-how, imputing ignorance to others, and parading their knowledge of the American

Constitution, the French Revolution, Rousseau and Spencer, Hugo and Zola – all the intellectual impediments of the *licenciado* (the prize must go to Hilario Medina who, in one speech, cited, among others, Marx, Taine, Dante, Shakespeare, Beethoven, Michaelangelo, Maeterlinck, Emerson and D'Annunzio).[1112]

What they did at Querétaro has, in retrospect, acquired a justified celebrity. But it was often the result of haphazard events, in which the protagonists were not altogether clear about their role. Like Britain and her Empire, it might be said, Mexico acquired her Constitution in a fit of absence of mind. The myth of 200 sage legislators sedately deliberating their country's needs requires correction; but so, too, does the standard image of moderates and jacobins clashing in fierce ideological debate, the jacobins' triumph determining Mexico's future radical course.[1113] It may be, indeed, that this image essentially derives from a contemporary interpretation, which is itself vague, polemical, and strongly influenced by the immanent precedent of 1857.[1114] It is true that Carranza's original draft, presented at the beginning of December, was taken up, mauled, supplemented and thus transformed from a modest restatement of 1857 to the prolix, more radical document of 1917.[1115] But the process was not as neat, and Manichaean, as sometimes supposed. The 'moderates' responsible for the first draft expected changes, and did not stonewall when they were proffered.[1116] The two crucial articles (crucial as they were later seen) 27 and 123 emerged from a small committee which, because of the accumulating pressure on the Congress's time, played a central role preparing draft articles. Under Rouaix, this committee compiled Article 123, drawing on the labour research of Macías (a supposed 'moderate') and the help of José Inocente Lugo, one-time Maderista Governor of Guerrero, and now chief of the Department of Labour; other 'moderates' like Cravioto endorsed the article.[1117] After its progress through two committees, the draft article reached the Congress floor on the evening of 23 January 1917; by 10.15 p.m. – notwithstanding a brief recess – the Congress was ready to approve the measure; only one paragraph elicited real debate, the rest being rushed through to cries of 'adelante'. The vote was unanimous.[1118]

Article 27, which redefined property relations, had an even swifter passage; it appeared late and, like Article 27, depended on behind-the-scenes preparations. In this case, Molina Enríquez produced a first draft. But (he was a sociologist) his arid theorising appalled his listeners. Again, Rouaix chaired an *ad hoc* committee of some twenty delegates (half of whom had participated in the compilation of Article 123); they debated for ten days, the Congress's First Committee for four; the fledgling article then proceeded to the floor where (by candlelight, the power supply having failed) the first six paragraphs went through on the nod; number seven elicited a confused debate; eight to twelve, which contained the bulk of the agrarian reform provisions, scarcely caused a ripple.[1119] All told, the plenary discussion of what was arguably the most important article in the Constitution stretched from the afternoon of 29 January to the small hours of 30 January; it was passed after a disjointed debate, whose participants had not, in the main, read or, it was admitted, understood the draft, and whom the Congressional secretary had to warn not to doze off during proceedings.[1120] 'Did the delegates fully realise the significance of their handiwork?', Niemeyer asks; 'many probably did not.'[1121] The debate on Article 27, Cumberland comments, 'give[s] a strong impression that the great majority of the delgates were prepared to vote in the affirmative without explanation or discourse'.[1122] Certainly, though a few recognised its importance, others focused on quite different questions (like militarism); and there were not wanting 'radicals' like Hilario Medina who, in a long farewell speech, lauded Articles 3, 5, 24 and 129 (those dealing with Church-State relations) and made no reference to Articles 27 or 123.[1123] Indeed, these anti-clerical provisions – not to mention lesser trivia – had excited much longer and more acrimonious debate than the 'revolutionary' articles.[1124]

The speed and confusion of these proceedings, the emphases of debates, the decisive influence exercised by a handful of *constituyentes* – moderates as well as jacobins – make it hard to accept the standard images of the Congress as either a collective representation of social revolutionary aspirations, or an ideologically polarised assembly in which left wrested victory from right.[1125] The computer, too, bears out the relative flexibility of the supposed 'moderate' and 'radical' blocs, and casts doubt on the neat correlations previously assumed between 'moderates', middle age and civilians on the one hand, 'radicals', youth and the military on the others.[1126] The only ideological correlation revealed links 'radicalism' to certain state delegations: those of Chihuahua, Sonora, Sinaloa, Nayarit (sic), Zacatecas, Hidalgo, Veracruz and Yucatán, which seem to have displayed more consistently jacobin tendencies; and which Peter Smith explains in terms of these states' socio-political characters – their distance from the centre, the strengths of their labour movements. But these are *ex post facto* rationalisations drawn from small samples (one delegate in the case of Chihuahua) and assuming an identity between state and delegation which often did not exist. A minority of delegates were not natives of the state they represented; more important, many were imposed by the dominant local authority, in accordance with its, rather than the state's, wishes. The radicalism of Yucatán's delegation reflected the radicalism of the proconsul Alvarado, not of the peninsula; in Oaxaca, Castro hand-picked delegates (and not in accordance with local wishes); the delegation from Chiapas, a state no less remote, consisted entirely of landlords, consonant with the 'home rule' character of the Villanueva administration.[1127]

The correlation between region and ideology may reflect a genuine causal relationship in some cases, for example, Sonora.[1128] But it may be that in this, as in other revolutionary episodes, the search for ideological consistency is fruitless (albeit encouraged by the latter-day rationalisations of the participants themselves). Equally, Namierite explanations may serve better. It is clear from the debates that ingrained personal hostilities lay behind many bitter exchanges; and that, to the extent that these conformed to any pattern, it was the old civil–military polarisation which prevailed (and which, though it sometimes assumed ideological form, cannot be reduced to a prior ideological basis).[1129] Again, the Renovadores – Palavicini in particular – were pilloried for their dalliance with Huerta; but – no strangers to abuse – they gave as good as they got, 'with bitter attacks on the military element in general and Obregón in particular'.[1130] This familiar polarisation was enhanced by a certain regional split between north and south. Southern delegates advocated that only *hijos del país* (natives of the state) should assume governorships; thereby military impositions – of the kind recently perpetrated 'machete in hand' in Puebla, and anticipated in Mexico state – would be averted, and the perverse ambitions of the military frustrated.[1131] Meanwhile, lesser Namierite squabbles, often of local origin, added to the impression of raucous, unprincipled verbal brawling.[1132] Jara, on behalf of Veracruz, repudiated the supposed territorial ambitions of Oaxaca.[1133] Samuel de los Santos, fighting his family's old Huasteca feuds on the Congress floor and, it was said, grooming himself for the San Luis governorship, denounced both Rafael Cepeda and Enrique Medina (the second of whom was implicated in the death of Samuel's famous brother) as Huertista collaborators.[1134] Medina, though not Cepeda, was cast out of the Congress. The government's initial exhortation that the Congress should display 'a single interest and a single ideal: Achieving National Tranquility' was hardly acted upon; yet more energy and acrimony were devoted to personal and factional disputes – or, secondarily, to ideological issues of long standing, such as Church–State relations – than to the new, 'social' questions for which the Constitution is famous.[1135]

Such disputes, national and local, assumed major importance after 1916–17. On 31 January 1917 the new Constitution was signed (Carranza's pen inauspiciously broke during the signing) and the Constituent Congress, having spent 150,000 man-hours and 2m. pesos, dispersed, the participants rushing for souvenirs before leaving for home.[1136] The new Constitution was now in force and Carranza could live up to his Constitutionalist title and restore legal government to the country. This was a rapid, confused, but important process, in which certain key features of the post-revolutionary regime began to emerge. The return to legality in fact antedated the Congress, since municipal elections had been held in many states in the autumn of 1916; these were followed by national elections for president and congress in March 1917, and a spate of gubernatorial elections in 1917–18. The clearest, least contentious outcome of these was the choice of Carranza himself as constitutional president for 1917–20, after an election in which, facing no serious opponents (Obregón had wisely decided to wait his turn), he claimed 800,000 votes against 15,000 (though some alleged he got only a quarter that total).[1137] At any rate, Carranza peacefully took office, wryly commenting, in private, that 'the task before him was as difficult as the day when he initiated his revolution'.[1138] Indeed, the Congress simultaneously elected, though thoroughly Carrancista in make-up, was – like the Constituent Congress itself – given to factional dissension and independence; despite his efforts to the contrary, the president found it to be an intractable partner in government, increasingly critical of the executive, and far from the rubber stamp of Porfirian times.[1139] In gubernatorial elections, too, which were arguably more important, the 'centre' did not have things all its own way.[1140] And this raises the whole question of elections and political mobilisation during the post-constitutional phase, which deserves analysis.

Many elections were still conducted on Porfirian lines, with scant participation and much central direction. That this should be so for the presidential election was hardly surprising: Carranza was determined and expected to win, he faced no serious opponent, and the Partido Liberal Constitucionalista – a loose, official party, founded in 1916 to support Carranza – grouped the major Constitutionalist generals and *políticos* in temporary union, at least for the duration of the presidential and congressional elections.[1141] The time was not ripe for a squabble over the national leadership (that was postponed for three years) and, for the time being, Carrancista feuds were concentrated at local level. Here, as in the days of Díaz and Madero, local candidates still sought to link themselves to the 'centre' and the guaranteed national winner, notably by using the 'Carranza – X' formula, a device even amnestied Conventionists assumed in the hope of forgiveness.[1142] Since – now as in the days of Díaz – it was divisions within the political elite which fostered popular participation and real political conflict, the official consensus over the presidency ruled out both, and the election was conducted amid quiet and apathy. In Mexico City 'no elections in the real sense of the word took place'; the British Minister reported that 'my chauffeur could not conceal his amusement when I told him that I wished to go and see the elections'. Similar reports emanated from the provinces: Chihuahua, Sinaloa, Colima.[1143]

The same indifference had been apparent in many – not all – of the municipal elections, notwithstanding official claims of electoral enthusiasm.[1144] Only Carrancistas could stand (General Lauro Villar, though a hero of the *Decena Trágica*, had not been allowed to run for mayor at Veracruz) and there was tight control by the authorities, usually the military.[1145] Since all this had been expected, turnout was low.[1146] At Veracruz, 5% of the electorate voted; at Frontera (Tab.) 10% voted and 'most of the Mexicans seemed to regard the elections as a joke'; at Manzanillo voting was so low that the new city officials were effectively chosen by the votes of the outgoing officials.[1147] These reports cannot be dismissed as the fabrications of supercilious foreigners: they conformed to Mexican electoral history (local elections had often been anodyne affairs); furthermore, the same foreigners reported more vigorous electoral conflict in certain cases.[1148] At Aguascalientes, in September 1916, most polling booths remained deserted, attracting only a handful of votes apiece (typhus was prevalent and no doubt kept people indoors); but further elections in October were better attended, and the city's subsequent electoral activity was, true to its character, brisk and eventful.[1149] After the municipal elections came the usual spate of protests and allegations of imposition, from Mexican as well as foreign sources. Unpopular officials had been imposed at Lampazos (NL); the *jefe político* had imposed his candidates at Atzalán (Ver.); carpetbaggers, lacking local support, were imposed in Durango.[1150] But the protests remained verbal, for there was little people could do about such impositions, even assuming that, in the current economic climate, after years of revolution, they still felt inclined to involve themselves in local politics.

But, even at the municipal level, there were exceptions. Carranza's control over the country was too loose to guarantee universally smooth, managed elections. Margarito Ríos won the mayoralty at Cananea, despite being declared 'ineligible', and was forced to take to the mountains for a time to escape official retribution.[1151] The official candidate was also defeated at Veracruz, in what was a fair, if numerically insignificant contest.[1152] Upsets of this kind depended not simply on the 'objective' level of discontent and opposition, but also on the degree of dissension among the Carrancistas themselves. If, at the extremes of national and municipal elections, they maintained a common front and presented a united ticket, the chances of popular participation and electoral upset were slight. Carrancista dissension, however, created an *apertura democrática*. This occasionally happened in municipal elections, chiefly in larger towns, where control was harder, the spoils were bigger, and politicisation – especially of the working class – was more marked; it happened even more often in gubernatorial contests. The reasons are clear: the *municipio* was usually under the thumb of the military boss and his cronies, who would brook up no competition; the state, however, was too large to allow such personal domination – indeed, it usually embraced the political fiefs of two, three or more generals and their clients. These members of the new elite did not dare set their sights on the presidency, hence the unanimous election of Carranza, but they longed to convert military *cacicazgos* into constitutional governorships. It was, therefore, in a few major cities, and in many states of the Republic, that political feuds were translated into active, participatory, even violent electoral conflicts.

As in 1911–13, the Gulf states of Veracruz and Tamaulipas were politically effervescent. In the city of Veracruz, we have noted, even the 1916 municipal election produced a defeat for the official candidate (at Tuxpán elections excited less interest, but even there candidates disbursed cash and entertainment to woo voters).[1153] Through 1916/17 political interest was sustained by a campaign against the incumbent officials at Veracruz (legal charges were preferred and the case went to the Supreme Court) and by a struggle for power in the statehouse, in which several leading Carrancistas – notably Gavira and Aguilar – participated. When municipal elections were repeated at Veracruz in 1917, the campaign was intense: Professor Alarcón ran on the Gavirista ticket, Captain Izaguirre, commander of the San Juan de Ulúa arsenal, was supported by Aguilar – and, it was said, a clique of German businessmen (note, again, the civil–military split, with an international veneer). Posters adorned the port, and Izaguirre even put up two electric signs in the Alameda. Alarcón, representing the 'popular party' polled 1,220 votes to Izaguirre's 840; but the total poll – in a community of 60,000 – was over 4,000, a turnout approaching a third, and a six-fold increase over the previous year.[1154] (This may be compared with the result in the west coast port, Mazatlán, where state politics also encouraged an active campaign and, in an election which was considered a 'fair expression of the people's choice' a merchant was elected mayor in a 25% poll.)[1155] Tampico, true to form, also experienced active politicking, with allegations of corruption being hurled at incumbent officials; but here one of the protagonists in the impending gubernatorial election, Luis Caballero, exercised such tight control that the municipal election was a non-event (heavy rain helped his ploy).[1156] At Orizaba, too, there was vigorous participation, especially on the part of the factory workers: people 'took considerable interest in the [electoral] proceedings, at any rate crowds surrounded the different polling booths during the day' and, to the disgust of local businessmen, Salvador Gonzalo García, 'a vigorous supporter of the labouring element' was elected mayor.[1157]

In these Veracruzano communities, municipal politics were galvanised by the gubernatorial contest between Gavira and Aguilar. Through early 1917, political clubs cabled their support for Carranza, linking his presidential candidacy (a foregone conclusion) to their preferred gubernatorial candidate.[1158] Both candidates had their contacts with urban labour: Gavira was a political veteran from Orizaba; Aguilar had produced pro-labour legislation as governor and now spoke fondly of the working class as a candidate on the stump.[1159] It may not be coincidental that, that summer, the Orizaba workers won a favourable pay deal – political conflict and involvement advanced economist action.[1160] No less decisive for the outcome, however, was the support Aguilar received from Carranza, his new father-in-law (from whom, Gavira remarked, he now received the state of Veracruz as a dowry); for, yet again, Gavira was credited with a majority of the votes, but Aguilar was declared elected.[1161]

The appeal to urban labour, already noted during the new politics of 1911–13, again became common. Elections were decided in the towns (one aspiring governor, in Tabasco, was believed to allow the Felicista rebels free run of the countryside since it conveniently restricted the area in which he had to campaign) and in the larger communities the labour unions were the most effective vote-getters (workers' political clubs greatly outnumbered peasants'; and national political parties were still embryonic).[1162] At the same time, unions were in a weak position, thus eager to fasten on to political patrons who promised assistance. As the organiser of the Partido Obrero Veracruzano (the grandiloquence of the title will become apparent) wrote to Aguilar, whom he was backing for the governorship, the party was in a mess, meeting sporadically, usually inquorate; no proper accounts were kept and one official had defrauded his colleagues; the financial plight had been exacerbated by the attempted general strike against the Veracruz tram company, which had been easily broken, leaving some of the participating unions, like the electricians, shattered.[1163] Morale was as low as funds and the workers' interest in politics had flagged (expenses incurred in the congressional elections had also depleted resources). Plans to send propagandists into the countryside so far remained on paper. This weakness, reflected in other, and more 'advanced', industrial sectors, predisposed union leaders to seek political allies, who might compensate for the unions' current, economic plight. After 1916, the tide of 'militancy', typified by the Casa, receded, and unions increasingly opted for political participation (even of a dependent, deferential character) in preference to syndicalist action. Strikes – which were easily broken – had to be supplemented by political horse-trading.

These and other emergent facts of political life became evident in the gubernatorial contests of 1917–18. Many proceeded quietly, centrally controlled, though not necessarily lacking genuine interest and participation. Carranza secured the 'election' of *adictos* in several states: Ricaut, as provisional Governor of Nuevo León, ensured the succession of Nicéforo Zambrano; Emilio Salinas, the president's nephew, got Perrusquía elected in Querétaro; Breceda warmed the bed for Barragán in San Luis.[1164] Such exercises naturally elicited protests: Samuel de los Santos (of course) complained of Barragán's imposition and subsequent heavy-handed policies; popular indignation at the 'election' was also evident, though short-lived and ineffectual (there was a 'near-riot' at San Luis, where Barragán was barracked in the city plaza).[1165] 'Little interest' – but no doubt plenty of surreptitious grumbling – accompanied the election of the anti-clerical Diéguez in Jalisco; electoral abuses helped Alfonso Cabrera, brother of Luis, to the Puebla governorship; and in Michoacán, Múgica was allegedly robbed of the election in favour of Ortiz Rubio.[1166] Thus, in something over half the states of the Federation, Carranza managed to tag his loyal followers into the statehouse, though at the expense of some popular resentment.[1167] It is also worth noting that about half the state governors, and a higher proportion of Carrancista *adictos*, were either outright civilians, or *civiles militarizados* – honorific generals (like Ortiz Rubio) who had no claim to revolutionary pre-eminence, and no record of populist recruitment.[1168]

In some cases, however, the 'centre' failed, or incurred serious opposition.

As in 1912, Aguascalientes was ready to buck the national trend and elect a conservative Catholic (in a quiet election).[1169] In another civil–military confrontation, in Zacatecas, Dr Moreno was defeated by General Enrique Estrada (no Carrancista *adicto*).[1170] In Durango, Domingo Arrieta beat off the electoral challenges of Jesús Agustín Castro and Miguel Laveaga: all were local men – Laveaga, finally the official candidate, was a sierra landlord; but Arrieta, who enjoyed 'a sort of tribal leadership . . . of the inhabitants of the Sierra Madre', won a convincing victory (7,020 votes to Laveaga's 2,454). The new governor was reported to be 'very popular with the common people by whom he was elected and amongst whom he still finds his favourite diversions'.[1171] Sonora, factious but politically sophisticated, also witnessed a genuine battle, in which Carranza was unwilling or unable to meddle. Here, Calles, the Sonoran who had stayed at home, thus establishing a strong local base, confronted José Obregón, Alvaro's brother (Alvaro did not, however, throw his weight behind his brother's candidacy: Calles' power had to be respected).[1172] As usual, conventional ideological distinctions were blurred, while geographical and personal clientelism played a major role. Within Sonora, Calles was a northerner, Obregón had the backing of the south; the old division, dating to Porfirian times and carried through the revolution, was maintained.[1173] The principal ideological difference has been mentioned: Calles stood for prohibition, anti-clericalism, and a stricter, 'moral' regime, while Obregón angled for the clerical and *cantina* vote; what is more, both his previous record and his campaign statements made Calles the candidate of strong, efficient government – one which the mine-owners could rely on, and which the miners (for all Calles' labour reformism) might have occasion to fear.[1174] Obregón, one suspects, had the more appealing programme (Richmond's comment that 'Governors who permitted the production of beer . . . were . . . often unpopular' is an extraordinary flight of Puritan fancy); but Calles controlled the local machine, and won.[1175] Once elected, he embarked on a policy of financial retrenchment (de la Huerta had been prodigal during his provisional governorship), raising taxes, promising the mines fair treatment and a favourable modification of the labour laws already enacted; the new governor, an American commented, 'inspires confidence for the future prosperity of the state'; but some of Sonora's miners, such as the Cananea union, were unhappy at the election's outcome and protested to the government.[1176] Carranza was no more enraptured at Calles' victory, but central control of Sonora – distant, independent and highly politicised – was impossible; Calles' campaign had been conducted 'in the most approved American fashion', with extensive propaganda (and kickbacks?); and a 'very heavy vote' was polled in the election itself.[1177] Not only could the 'centre' not impose its will on Sonora; before long, Sonora would impose its will on the 'centre'.

If there were certain states where central imposition was feasible, even facile

– while in Sonora it was impossible – there were several where it was achieved only at the cost of fierce conflict, politicisation, and violence. Again, key features of the post-revolutionary state emerged in these instances, of which three – Sinaloa, Tamaulipas, and Coahuila – deserve brief attention. Of the six candidates who figured in the run-up to the Sinaloan gubernatorial election three, the leading military *políticos*, were prominent: Angel Flores, Ramón Iturbe and Manuel Salazar.[1178] Flores, on bad terms with Carranza, briefly fielded a front-man before entering the fray himself; apart from being the 'unofficial' candidate, he was popular at Culiacán and in the north, and was thought to enjoy the backing of the 'commercial houses and the better class of people'; this despite his lowly origins (he had been a stevedore), and perhaps because of their antipathy to Carranza and Mexico City.[1179] Iturbe, veteran of 1911, who had militarily seen off Buelna in 1915, emerged as his main rival; he derived his support from the south, around Mazatlán, and from the lower classes; nevertheless, he enjoyed Carranza's favour (which did not follow any neat class lines) and had plenty of money at his disposal.[1180] The electoral skirmishing was fierce, with the rivals running newspapers and campaigning hard.[1181] Hence, in summer 1917, the situation became tense and Obregón – who was thought to be sympathetic to Flores – came to perform his familiar mediating role. He met Flores and Iturbe at an official banquet, but the love-feast became a brawl, with Iturbe pulling a gun on his opponent.[1182] The following month, Iturbe was elected: there were protests and demonstrations, especially in Culiacán; six of the state's fifteen *municipios* repudiated the result; Iturbe and his family had to flee to Mazatlán for sanctuary.[1183] But these were gestures, rather than serious revolts, which were hard to sustain in the circumstances of 1917. Obregón returned to conciliate and Iturbe entered upon an uneasy tenure of power. Flores sulked in his tent until a new call to arms came in 1920; then, in Sinaloa and elsewhere, it turned out that the victors of recent elections were swiftly ejected, and their victims consoled by a belated, but more durable, access to power.

In Tamaulipas and Coahuila, as in Sinaloa, political conflict was based on a clear polarisation of interests – but not along the traditional (class) lines often supposed. These were not struggles between left and right (conventionally defined); programmes and principles did not ostensibly differ as between factions; and class alignments, though sometimes evident, did not follow clear patterns. Urban labour – a key participant – lent its support to both sides; and the 'centre' supported the supposedly 'popular' candidate in Sinaloa, his opponent in Coahuila. Indeed, the most revealing alignment (evident in Tamaulipas and Coahuila – and Durango, though not Sinaloa) was created by the involvement of the 'centre', which highlighted a central feature of Constitutionalism, already evident during the conflict with Villa and the proconsular expeditions to the south. For in these two states the Carrancista candidate, backed by the 'centre' was a young, educated, *adicto*, endowed with political rather than military skills and national rather than local connections; while his opponent – and the dichotomy is clearer in the case of Coahuila – represented local, popular forces, and derived his prestige and influence from his revolutionary past.

In Tamaulipas, Cesar López de Lara, recently Governor of the Federal District, confronted Luis Caballero, who 'had given magnificent service during the revolution . . . spending most of his time in his native state or its immediate environs. Extremely popular, he enjoyed the full support of most important municipal officials as well as of the majority of the military'.[1184] The contest was bitter, with both sides mobilising strong support.[1185] Caballero was certainly the more popular, especially in rural districts, 'among the lower classes', and in the south of the state (he hailed from Victoria), which had been traditionally more rebellious. López de Lara, from Matamoros, on the border, needed the backing of imported troops and provisional state governors (Osuna, then Ricaut, both agents of Carranza); but since force alone would not suffice, he cultivated support among the labour unions, the most available, manipulable allies.[1186] Tension rose: Caballero, campaigning against Peláez, was said to be treating the Huasteca rebel as a potential ally; the authorities vainly tried to curtail meetings and demonstrations, and the election was deferred, in the hope of inducing calm. But violent affrays began: a bootblack was killed during political brawls in Doña Cecilia, the working-class suburb of Tampico; a more illustrious victim was General Emiliano Nafarrete, a strong supporter of Caballero, who was shot by police in the same town.[1187] There were troubles, too, at Victoria and Villagran, and, after the election, as the result hung fire for months, rival supporters clashed in faraway Mexico City, leaving two dead.[1188] The general view in Tamaulipas was that, as expected, Caballero had won; one account credited him with victory in thirty-two of the state's thirty-eight districts.[1189] But his opponent disagreed, and the Caballeristas, defying both the governor and the central government, declared their candidate elected and forcibly occupied the state legislature.[1190] In April 1918 Caballero was declared in rebellion against the regime, which he defied until 1920.

In Coahuila, finally, a similar imposition prompted revolt, and even more neatly typified contemporary modes of conflict. Here, Luis Gutiérrez, an ex-miner, veteran of 1911, and brother of the Conventionist President of 1914, confronted a fellow-Coahuilan, Gustavo Espinosa Mireles, a young man, recently provisional governor, formerly Carranza's secretary and still 'one of his most devoted followers'. Espinosa Mireles was the subject of a harsh but revealing portrait by a perceptive foreign observer, who contrasted men of this new Carrancista breed with the more earthy, rugged, uneducated leaders – like Domingo Arrieta – whom they now confronted (though the contrast is drawn with Arrieta, Gutiérrez is referred to as another 'popular idol of the type of Arrieta').[1191] Espinosa was young, dapper and cleancut, 'not unlike a barber's assistant'; he worked hard and was 'free from the vulgar vices' which characterised Arrieta and his kind (vices which, however, 'make the latter rather human'); he was 'greatly proud of a certain amount of education in law, chiefly self-acquired'. With his vaunted expertise and connections in high places, he combined arrogance, a supposed commitment to 'socialist' ideals, and an eye for personal profit. The portrait is drawn in broad, emotive strokes; Arrieta, the painter admitted, was 'an excellent friend of mine'; and foreigners often tended to patronise the rustic, popular rebels (at least when they were not on the rampage; recall the eulogies of Zapatismo), while they sneered at literate, nationally conscious parvenus and their programmes – these were the *babus* of the Revolution. Espinosa, of course, was no socialist (Cumberland calls him 'a dedicated Carrancista of somewhat conservative bent'), nor were his peers the 'demagogues, socialists', IWWs and Bolsheviki' the writer claimed them to be. But the comparison, though badly defined, was valid, highlighted contrasting types, and suggested how they operated in the new political environment: one relying on local popularity, linked to a revolution-ary (military) record, the common touch, and some personal rapport with (especially rural) people, the other displaying a shrewder grasp of the new, national political reality, of the potential of social reforms (conceived in universalistic, not parochial terms), and of the emergent power of the state. The same polarity would be evident in San Luis, between Cedillo and Manrique; or in Guerrero, between the old and new generations of the Figueroa family.[1192] Both had a place in the heterogeneous Constitutionalist coalition, whose strength derived from a blend of local populists and nation-alist *políticos*. But, over time, the latter tended to predominate. The central government would tolerate the pretensions of local caudillos out of short-term expediency; but as the Revolution and revolutionary modes of conduct receded into the past, the caudillos' local base tended to atrophy, while the resources of the state, and thus of the nationalist *políticos*, expanded; this process, determined by the victory of Carrancismo in 1915, culminated in the corporatist structures of Cardenismo.[1193]

In Coahuila, in 1917, the sides were evenly matched, and their contest transcended local significance. Espinosa was at once branded as the 'official' candidate: an ex-governor, succeeded in the statehouse by an ally, who had the upper hand as regards control of the state's machinery. Troops allegedly intimidated Gutierrista supporters and controlled the vote in certain dis-tricts.[1194] But official status had its disadvantages. Espinosa was judged on his record as governor: while the recovery of border trade redounded to his benefit, the low level of wages caused resentment, especially among the railway workers, who were strong for Gutiérrez.[1195] And, more generally, Gutiérrez was thought to 'control the lower element'; 'the lower classes (peons) were his strong supporters'.[1196] Hence the campaign was lively, at times violent. Espinosa campaigned extensively, speechmaking and setting up political centres. Propaganda on both sides tended to be personalist and polemical, containing 'very few proposals [and] consisting largely of past acts and criticisms of opponents' utterances'.[1197] In default of broader support, Espinosa looked to the unions, especially the miners, whom he urged to enter politics (on his behalf), and who complied.[1198] This vigorous gubernatorial campaign, meanwhile, contrasted with the apathy in which congressional elections were coincidentally held, with 'practically the entire Carranza ticket [being] elected without opposition'.[1199]

At election time, troops were moved into the state, chicanery was rampant, and the state electoral college declared Espinosa elected, though it was common knowledge that Gutiérrez had polled more votes. Carranza reminded the loser of his newly-acquired property and held out the prospect of promotion elsewhere, away from Coahuila; but the bait, if indeed it was proffered, was not taken; as Madero found with Figueroa, and Cárdenas would find with Cedillo, local caudillos spurned preferment which detached them from their home base.[1200] In short, the whole election was redolent of 'the method followed by President Díaz'.[1201] But these were no longer the days of Díaz: popular participation was much greater, the 'centre' was less secure, and the defeated candidate had powerful allies. As Espinosa was inaugurated, talk of rebellion increased. The mayor of Torreón rejected the result and threatened resistance in the Laguna, which had never loved Carranza.[1202] At the end of 1917, Gutiérrez and Pancho Coss – a congenial, popular ally – rose in revolt; Múzquiz and Monclova were briefly occupied; and there were fears of a full-scale rebellion in the north east.[1203] This did not ensue. Despite their undeniable resentment, people were not disposed – or not able – to take up arms against the regime. Rumours of a Gutierrista alliance with Cedillo to the south, however socially plausible, proved unfounded; the great weakness of such leaders had always been their reluctance to cohere in supra-regional blocs.[1204] Once again, the 'centre' could, with some difficulty, isolate and eliminate pockets of resistance. Early in 1918, Gutiérrez and Coss were driven into the hills. But this was by no means the end of their involvement in Coahuilan politics.[1205]

Nor was this the end of the story; the best – the most significant – is yet to come. Young, civilian, unpopular, dependent on the 'centre' and its indifferent troops, Espinosa entered on a fragile political inheritance, desperate for reinforcement. His patron, Carranza, too, felt increasingly insecure as would-be successors jockeyed for position in the presidential race. In March 1918, therefore, they collaborated on a project that would redound to their mutual benefit: a national convention of labour unions convened in the Coahuilan state capital, with all expenses paid by the Federal government. For Carranza, this was an about-face; not simply because, since 1916, he had taken a hard line against strikers and 'subversives', but also because he had never been keen on the formation of a nationally-organised, politically active labour movement.[1206] For Governor Espinosa, who had courted labour during his election campaign, and who was now associated with the new Partido Cooperatista, the initiative was more characteristic; and, though it has been argued that Carranza broached the idea, relying on his protégé to host the convention, it is clear that Espinosa stood to gain significantly from the venture (enemies accused him of 'prostituting' the labour movement; the participant unions, of course, were adamant that they were not being manipulated).[1207]

On the workers' side, indeed, where hard times and industrial defeats had instilled a mood of tired realism, the offer was soon taken up, and 120 delegates, representing 18 states (though with a heavy concentration from the north-east), a wide range of industries, and conflicting ideologies, met in Saltillo for a fortnight of rumbustious debate and intrigue.[1208] Apart from practical demands for better wages and conditions and the protection of trade unions, the resolutions and rhetoric still reflected the old anarcho-syndicalist philosophy: the class struggle polarised society, direct action was preferable to political participation, the working class owed no allegiance to the bourgeois nation state.[1209] Nor was the prevalence of this philosophy surprising, granted the prominent presence of old Casa leaders like Huitrón. But the underlying reality was quite different; and both this philosphy and its adherents were rapidly being supplanted by rivals more attuned to that reality: Huitrón, the anarcho-syndicalist, like Gutiérrez, the popular rebel, was giving ground to a new breed of leader, and a new style of leadership. In the radical press, meanwhile, the old battle between political pragmatists (favouring workers' participation in bourgeois politics, in pursuit of concessions) and doctrinaire anarchists (who rejected participation, denounced corrupt government, and placed their faith in autonomous organisations and direct action) was still being fought out, though with the latter sounding increasingly proud but *passé*. The miners' union (UMM), which had pioneered the alliance with Espinosa, was keen for collaboration and, like miners' organisations elsewhere, was sceptical about anarchist strategy; socialism, declared a spokesman, 'recognises honourable men of government, whom it feels obliged to help in effective fashion'.[1210] Others still clung to the old anarchist vision whereby 'every region, city, village or hamlet will govern itself according to its own lights, without ignoring universal solidarity': a vision which, in the context of the emergent centralised revolutionary state, appeared increasingly anachronistic and Utopian.[1211]

More consonant with reality was the new, national workers' association, the Confederación Regional Obrera Mexicana, established at Saltillo under the leadership of Luis Morones. Morones had risen to prominence in the Mexico City printers' union; he had not fought in the revolution, but his name was to be seen at the foot of rousing articles and lyrical poems in the radical press of the time. Despite his literary bent, he had a firm grasp of reality and an eye for the main chance; he took to heart the examples of Samuel Gompers and the AFL (with whom he collaborated); and he sought to further the Mexican labour movement – and his own career – by adopting similar tactics.[1212] His aim was to 'pursue fewer ideals and more organisation'; it was the labour boss's adaptation of the quintessential Constitutionalist political philosophy – deeds, not words, workmanlike successes rather than glorious defeats.[1213] He would allow the anarchists their rhetoric (he, too, had once declared himself against all government), while he cultivated key members of the political elite, and gathered real power in his own hands (through, for example the semi-secret Grupo Acción).[1214]

The course the CROM would take under Morones was not immediately obvious. The recruitment of members was slow; major groups like the oil and railway workers remained indifferent; by 1920 it could claim – and it was only a claim – 50,000 members.[1215] Meanwhile, Carranza's continued repression of labour agitation made further rapprochement between the CROM and the regime difficult. Like its more radical predecessor, the Casa, the CROM found itself competing and clashing with the Department of Labour, and in 1919 CROM leaders were arrested for their involvement in strikes. Paradoxically, however, Carranza's failure to cement the alliance initiated at Saltillo in 1918 ultimately benefited the CROM – and even more Morones. As the regime entered its twilight period, and the presidential succession absorbed growing attention, Morones was happy to play a clandestine waiting game. Behind the scenes, he made contact with Obregón, who sought the support of organised labour for his presidential bid (possibly Calles, known for his labour reformism, acted as broker).[1216] In August 1919, a pact – a peaceful, electoral version of the pact which had created the Red Battalions four years earlier – delivered the CROM into Obregón's camp, in return for solid concessions.[1217] Out of this pact grew the Partido Laborista, the political wing of the CROM, which was to help Obregón to the presidency, Morones to new heights of power and wealth, and the Mexican labour movement into the trammels of the revolutionary state.

The progress of the Carrancista machine in 1916–20 was, therefore, uncertain and ambivalent, rather than straight and purposive. After the manner of Díaz, the central government sought to control elections, achieving greatest success in the *municipios* or in states where the revolutionary elite – perhaps because they were an unpopular minority – stuck together and avoided dissension. But success was elusive, or purchased at some cost, in states where the revolution left a legacy of competitive caudillismo. Here, too many feeders jostled at the trough and, until they were culled, or the central government acquired more control, conflicts and rebellions would continue. In the process, political participation, which the regime scarcely welcomed, would increase, evidenced in new parties and politicised labour unions. Meantime the losers, like Flores in Sinaloa, constituted a reservoir of dissidence which could be tapped by Carranza's opponents. In this respect they were only one fragment in a mosaic of opposition which, by 1919, was nearing completion, and which would include popular rebels – Villa, Cedillo, the Zapatistas; the Felicistas of the south, from Peláez in the Huasteca down to the *mapaches* of Chiapas; the unions, disgruntled with Carrancista ambivalence; individuals, familes and communities tired of the slow pace of economic recovery, the absence of promised social reforms, the graft and corruption of the revolutionary leadership. And in 1920 this variegated coalition of dissent fell into shape.

Of course, the dissent was not wholly Carranza's fault. Many problems were beyond his limited power, and he became a scapegoat for evils, particularly of an economic kind, which neither he nor any rival could claim to cure.[1218] But the buck stopped in the National Palace, and the judgement of those presidential aspirants who had passed up 1917 in preference to 1920 (after which times might improve) was amply vindicated. But Carranza made mistakes too. It is a commonplace that the reforms promised in early decrees or in the Constitution itself were slow in coming. By the summer of 1917 it was noted that 'everywhere among the revolutionists murmurs are heard against [Carranza] and he is already freely accused even in the Chamber of becoming a reactionary himself'.[1219] Despite Article 123, strong-arm methods were used against strikers, and the foundation of the CROM suggested only a partial, grudging and opportunist recognition of labour's right to organise nationally.[1220] The agrarian reform promised in Article 27 scarcely made an appearance. While some governors and officials achieved modest progress locally, the national government dragged its feet: by mid-1918 there was still no enabling legislation on the statute book, and barely 100 villages had received official grants. When, in autumn 1918, Rouaix produced a draft bill, it was couched in traditional liberal terms, it ignored communal property and it contained 'completely unrealistic' provisions for the payment of such grants. It never became law anyway.[1221] Though even the halting beginnings of reform were significant (the Porfirian trend towards concentration and monopoly was reversed; the principle of the *ejido* was explicitly recognised) the Federal regime could claim little credit; and history was to show that central government alone could provide the thrust for a major *reparto*.[1222] Meanwhile, Carranza's conservatism went further, with plans to rewrite offensive sections of the new Constitution. He signalled this intention – though pleaded inability – in talks with foreign interests in 1917.[1223] He soft-pedalled the Constitution's anti-clerical provisions.[1224] And, pursuing what has been seen as 'a policy of reconciliation not only with the mass of *hacendados* but also with the leading members of the Científico oligarchy', he ordered the return of Luis Terrazas' huge northern properties.[1225]

It would be simplistic – and sentimentally radical – to assume that Carranza's conservatism sealed his fate. In some cases – such as the clerical question, or even the assertion of national control of subsoil deposits –

ignoring the Constitution offered peace and quiet, without necessarily alienating powerful sections of opinion. Agrarian and labour reforms were a different matter (here, the devolution of real estate, even to the likes of Terrazas, may have offended no less than the absence of reform) and Carranza's innate social conservatism, previously masked, overrode expediency. But a stronger regime could – and stronger regimes did – ignore the Constitution with impunity. Popular resentment (even assuming it is provoked by conservatism, which is not always the case) is not automatically translated into active resistance, least of all in circumstances like those of 1920. Though these questions deserve consideration, the fact is that Carranza's crucial errors were committed in the political arena, alienated less the broad masses than specific organised groups, and were avoidable. Indeed, the story of 1920 bears a strange resemblance to that of 1910, when an old president, out of touch with a changing political reality, sought to perpetuate his own rule in defiance of public opinion and jealous competitors for power. By 1919, Carranza was politically on the defensive, suspicious of rivals, the subject of attacks in press and Congress.[1226] With the presidential election a year away, Obregón now threw his hat in the ring, even without receiving the presidential endorsement he had hoped for. In a long-winded manifesto (June 1919) he indicted the government, proclaimed his adherence to Liberalism, invoked historical precedent, and avoided concrete commitments.[1227]

The content probably did not matter much. Just as Carranza had been the logical choice in 1917, Obregón now established himself as the favourite for 1920 (hoping, it seems, to force Carranza's reluctant endorsement). After the manner of Mexican politics then and now, people scrambled to board the bandwagon, to hitch their fortunes to the heir-apparent, *el tapado*. A powerful 'reversionary interest' was created.[1228] Political incumbents, anxious to survive, turned to Obregón, as did those in limbo, looking for a way back. Congressional representatives pledged their allegiance, further weakening executive control of the Chamber; the pact with Morones won over the CROM; negotiations began with the Zapatista rebels. Even Carranza's hope of playing off González against Obregón failed, when González reached terms with the heir apparent.[1229] Reason and *realpolitik* demanded that the president, too, give his blessing to Obregón's candidacy, thus ensuring peace and continuity. But like Díaz, confronted by Reyes ten years before, Carranza disliked the prospect of a popular military figure succeeding to the presidency and he cast about to find a more docile, congenial, civilian candidate. He found Ignacio Bonillas, a Carrancista *adicto*, then ambassador in Washington; a civilian *político* 'of respectable but unspectacular reputation ... largely unknown to Mexicans'.[1230]

Why? Ideological sympathy may have counted. More important, Carranza was keen for a civilian succession (and civilian can no more be equated with conservative than military with radical); he was well aware of the abuses and obstructions endemic in a militarised administration which, he hoped, a civilian president would counter. In his propaganda he made much of civilian virtues and the threat of praetorianism, a theme also developed at length by Cabrera in a sustained polemic with Obregón in 1919.[1231] Carranza probably still entertained ideas of who was – and was not – *presidenciable*; and the self-made, self-taught general could not measure up to these old, if fading, stereotypes; while the civilian graduate of MIT, 'Meester Bonillas', plainly could.[1232] And, finally, like almost every outgoing president, Carranza hoped not only to select but also partly to control his successor. This alone provoked opposition: had not the Revolution begun under the slogan 'No Re-election'? But if public opinion jibbed at this apparent imposition of a political client, the revolutionary elite – above all, the generals and their associated political cadres – were acutely sensitive to Carranza's civilian commitment. An old dichotomy reappeared: Madero, demobilising the Liberating Army and consoling its leaders with no more than a few commissions in the *rurales*, had provoked widespread rebellion in 1911; in 1914, the civilians' claim for representation at Aguascalientes had been brushed aside by a more confident, powerful, politicised military. If, with civil war raging, Carranza had condoned the eclipse of civilian government, five years later he was less inhibited in his opposition to praetorianism, which was in turn grounded in his ideological antecedents and personal history.

But, as in 1911, the decision was premature. The *ultima ratio* of armed force had only somewhat receded from centre-stage, and it could easily return; furthermore, to the extent that force had been replaced by finance, persuasion and peaceful mobilisation, it was principally because the leading generals now clothed their naked military power in decorous economic assets and political clienteles. Over time, this diversification would produce a brand of civilian-bureaucratic politics in which, though many of the protagonists would still be generals, they would govern without directly depending on military prowess and power (the *ultima ratio* now conforming to the usual image of a veiled sanction, lurking in the wings); and during this process, it was precisely the most adept politicised generals (Obregón, Calles, Amaro) who, in their own interest, slimmed down the swollen army and disciplined its troublesome leaders.[1233] The demilitarisation of politics, in fact, could only be achieved over time, by the military themselves; Carranza, a civilian, seeking to prefer other civilians, had little hope of success, certainly not in his premature, ill-judged and fatal attempt to force a civilian succession in 1920.

Furthermore, compared with the days of Díaz, the centre's ability to 'make' elections was much lessened: popular participation had increased, and the revolutionary elite comprised a body of relatively independent, realistically ambitious *políticos* which had no parallel in the mature Porfiriato. Carranza resorted to the old methods in new circumstances. As early as January 1919, Obregón was publicly warned off; as the campaign developed, the official press backed Bonillas, its rivals were harassed; Obregonistas were systematically intimidated. [1234] Sonora, the pillar of Obregón's regional support, was subjected to intense pressure from the 'centre'. The president cultivated Calles, decreed the Sonora River a Federal property, refused to ratify a pact with the Yaquis negotiated by Governor de la Huerta, and, switching Federal commanders, sent troops to impose central control. [1235] But the old methods would not work. When the state governors were summoned to Mexico City to receive instructions, ten refused to go. Sonora would no more accept Carranza's imposition in 1920 than it had Huerta's in 1913. Enjoying overwhelming local support (including Calles'), de la Huerta resisted Carranza's pressure until a complete rupture between state and federation ensued. On 23 April, the Sonorans issued the Plan of Agua Prieta, calling on the country to overthrow Carranza.

Carranza's faltering attempts at a neo-Porfirian imposition contrasted with Obregón's deft use of new political techniques. Ill-health and good judgement encouraged him to postpone his presidential bid until 1920, by which time he had put together a winning coalition. [1236] The PLC – the loose, Obregonista grouping of 1916 – established itself solidly in Congress, and was soon seconded by lesser (equally loose) parties which, for pragmatic as well as ideological reasons, hitched themselves to Obregón's wagon (the Partido Nacional Cooperatista, Morones' Partido Laborista, and others); the candidate, true to his 'Liberal' discourse and consensual strategy, chose to regard them all as components of a great, amorphous Partido Liberal. [1237] In similar fashion, minor labour associations followed the lead of the CROM. Meanwhile, Obregón – unlike Carranza – showed great flair in presenting himself to this mass audience. He already enjoyed the charisma of victory; he cultivated a bluff, joking, populist style; he toured the country tirelessly, meeting workers and *campesinos*, *políticos* and veterans, risking intimidation and even assassination. [1238] Mexico had seen nothing like it since Madero's campaigns ten years before.

Meanwhile, more important, he enlisted key groups and individuals: disaffected intellectuals like Vasconcelos (even Palavicini saw which way the wind blew and made his peace); defeated *políticos* and rebels still in the field; above all, the Constitutionalist army – in many respects his own creation – which now polarised into Obregonista and Carrancista commanders, the latter threatened by a popular undertow, as they had been back in 1915. [1239] Thus, when the Sonorans made their public defiance, the Carrancista regime collapsed. Obregón himself – charged to appear in court in Mexico City – escaped from the capital in disguise, fled to Guerrero, and endorsed the rebellion. The majority of Carranza's generals followed suit. So did many rebels: Peláez in the Huasteca, Fernández Ruiz and the *mapaches* of Chiapas, Almazán and most of the Veracruz Felicistas. [1240] When Pablo González 'joined the stampede', Carranza faced certain defeat. [1241] True to character, however, he would not surrender but, as in 1915, set off for Veracruz, encouraged by protestations of fervent loyalty from Guadalupe Sánchez.[1242] Sánchez promptly rebelled; the governmental train was repeatedly attacked and finally forced to halt: Carranza and a few supporters headed into the Puebla sierra on horseback. On the night of 20 May 1920, Felicista rebels attacked the group as they slept at Tlaxcalantongo, and Carranza was killed.[1243]

With the triumph of the Agua Prieta revolt and Obregón's overwhelming victory in the presidential election of September 1920, the revolutionary decade is conventionally and correctly seen as ending. Though it was not the last major revolt (others were to ensue in 1923, 1927, and 1929) it was the last to succeed; though sporadic revolt and endemic local violence persisted, political and economic reconstruction had emphatic priority. Agua Prieta therefore marked a major transition from violent to 'institutional' revolution. It did so, partly, in the longer term, because the Sonoran dynasty was more disposed to social reform than Carranza, and more capable of demilitarising government; but also, more immediately and significantly, because it afforded an opportunity for wholesale deals, surrenders and submissions, which achieved, within months, a degree of pacification the country had not known for years.

A handful of die-hard Carrancistas were added to the long list of revolutionary dead and exiled; but a host of rebels took advantage of this twist in the logic of the revolution to reach terms. Virtually all the Felicistas laid down their arms: Díaz himself went into exile, but Peláez became, albeit briefly, Tampico's military commander, while the *mapaches* of Fernández Ruiz took political control of Chiapas.[1244] Villa at once entered negotiations and surrendered, to enjoy three years affluent retirement at Canutillo.[1245] Magaña shepherded the Zapatistas back into the national fold, enabling them to achieve place and power in Morelos, where some sponsored a major agrarian reform and some feathered their nests.[1246] Like the Zapatistas, the Cedillistas of San Luis settled down, received land, and assisted in the pacification of their state.[1247] In consummating the armed revolution and bringing peace, Agua Prieta thus left – beneath the broad umbrella of Sonoran rule – a varied political patchwork: landlord rule in Chiapas; varieties of 'socialist' mobilisation – the legacy of proconsular rule – in the Gulf states, Yucatán, Tabasco and Veracruz; populist agrarianism in Morelos and San Luis; landlord, military and *agrarista* conflict in much of central Mexico; CROM agitation in the cities and, soon, Church–State antagonism in the countryside. In the 1920s, as in the 1900s, there were 'many Mexicos'. But the 'many Mexicos' of the Sonoran dynasty were different from those of the Porfiriato. The generic changes which society had undergone are the subject of the final section.

THE GHOST IN THE MACHINE

We have moved from the inner workings of Carrancismo to its overt motion; now, penultimately, we consider the movement's ethos: the ghost in the machine. So far, the analysis has stressed proximate, *ad hoc*, silent factors at the expense of explicit ideological principle: graft rather than nationalism, civil–military dissension rather than liberal–jacobin conflicts, Namierite rather than Marxist (or Hegelian) explanations. But ideology played an important role too, sometimes legitimising actions that, at root, derived from other motives, sometimes directly determining action in 'relatively autonomous' fashion. In the first case, ideology drew strength from its practical application – or functional relevance (the best example would be official *agrarismo*). In the second, ideology determined policies which were arguably 'dysfunctional', that is, they went against the grain of reality and expedience and incurred a high opportunity cost. Sometimes (we will return to the example of revolutionary Puritanism) policies therefore failed; sometimes (as with anti-clericalism) they achieved only modest success, at disproportionate price. Whatever their success or functionality, however, these policies all derived from a common ideological matrix, which constituted the ethos of Carrancismo and which, despite its diverse pedigree, displayed a certain unity and coherence. This matrix, furthermore, contained important ideological elements which have since been overlooked, in favour of others of less contemporary significance.

During their rise to power the Carrancistas had formulated a range of reformist policies designed to curtail the power of the Church, to further lay education, to promote agrarian reform, to protect labour, and to extend governmental control over economic resources, especially those in foreign hands. In their general character, these reforms clearly departed from Maderista precedent. Though the old commitment to 'Sufragio Efectivo, No Re-elección' remained on paper, and though the political foundations of the new Constitution (taken from the rubble of 1857) were impeccably liberal, these were more often honoured in the breach. Elections, however rowdy and participatory, were scarcely free; and the specifically 'political' provisions of the Constitution were no longer the cynosure they had once been. Madero's liberal experiment was, therefore, never repeated. Indeed, Porfirian theory and practice were revived. Carranza's stern commitment to strong government, and scepticism as to Mexico's democratic potential – shared by most of his followers – echoed Porfirian positivism.[1248] The optimistic Maderista belief that, given a free democracy, social problems would be capable of gradual, consensual solution, was superseded by a more pragmatic, even cynical, reliance on government direction and control, which the experience of the Revolution had itself fostered. Just as the positivist generation of the 1880s, keen for 'order and progress' and appalled at Mexico's chronic instability, rejected Juarista liberalism, so the generation of the (Constitutionalist) revolution, witnessing yet greater national upheaval, spurned Maderistas laissez-faire in favour of *étatisme*. In the political field, at least, the commitment was to an active state; one that – often in unquantifiable ways – would govern, control, repress, purge, guide, educate and uplift. Hence the narrow political exclusivism already mentioned and hence, too, the selective resort to social policies which – apart from promoting natural justice – also created docile clienteles. In the wake of revolution, 'politics' could not be eliminated; but there were plenty of Carrancistas who, like Obregón, echoed Porfirian sentiments in their preference for 'administration'.[1249]

This is sometimes hailed as a new radicalism, an advance on the narrow liberalism of Madero. It is not clear, however, that this comforting teleology is valid, or that a reversion to more authoritarian rule – mixed with modest social reform – constituted any advance. Arguably, genuine liberal democracy (even a reasonable approximation to it), by devolving power to the masses, threatened greater change and upheaval than the guided paternalistic reformism of the Carrancistas; a reformism which, as Córdova and others have argued, aimed not at the emancipation but the control of the masses and the concentration of power in the hands of the state.[1250] Nor is this a *post hoc* rationalisation; contemporaries (winners like Obregón and Alvarado, losers like González Garza) had witnessed the power of the masses, mobilised in the revolution, and grasped the need for directive control.[1251] Perhaps the pursuit of liberal democracy was an illusion (certainly it incurred strenuous opposition – from conservative groups – and probably a 'successful' outcome would have differed from the western European model espoused by Madero and others). But illusory (or 'Utopian') policies are not necessarily – and, in fact, are rarely – conservative. The consistent pursuit of liberal democracy was no exercise in tepid conservatism. Conversely, the Carrancistas' demotion of, or downright disregard for, liberal practices, and their espousal of modest social reform, cannot be seen as typically 'radical', especially in the light of their poor record in the subsequent implementation of those reforms. Bismarck and others have shown how social reforms (of a limited *étatiste* kind) may underpin authoritarian regimes; should a socially interventionist, undemocratic Bismarckianism be seen as more 'radical' than a socially passive liberalism – like Peel's or Gambetta's? Social reform may deflect popular demands and may even integrate mass organisations into the state, laying the foundations for more durably authoritarian regimes. Indeed, discussions of relative 'radicalism' and 'advances', though common, may be misconceived. The liberal-democratic 'path' to the 'modern world' can be as radical, in its time and place, as the 'revolution from above'. The most important and uncontentious fact is that they differ; that Maderista liberalism and Carrancista *étatisme* offered contrasting policies, notwithstanding their common northern, and perhaps 'bourgeois' origin, and their common claim to the mantle of Juárez.

The Carrancistas eschewed the optimistic liberalism of 1911. They purged opponents, controlled the press and fixed elections. New bases of power, which Madero had never enjoyed, bolstered their regime: a professional revolutionary army, a fresh administrative cadre, client labour unions, an official *agrarismo*. And where Madero had posed no challenge to the US or to foreign economic interests, and had muted the anti-clerical tones of Mexican liberalism to the extent of applauding Catholic political mobilisation, the Carrancistas were prepared to hector the US, put pressure on foreign companies, and bully the Church. Here, comparing Carrancismo with Maderismo, was a certain radicalism of means or temper; but these policies implied no fundamental change in Mexico's social organisation; rather, I shall shortly argue, they derived from traditional liberal ideology, refracted through the prism of revolution. The ideological inspiration was old, but the circumstances and pragmatic responses were new.

Among these responses was official *agrarismo*. This ostensible 'advance' of Carrancista over Maderista practice reflected the strength of popular demands, which perforce had to be recognised. Equally, the regime was compelled to incorporate popular elements into its governing coalition (the Herreras and Arrietas; after 1920, Cedillo and the Zapatistas), thus compromising earlier, elitist assumptions about who might rule.[1252] And the discourse of the new regime was larded with references to the 'people', whom the Revolution had supposedly emancipated.[1253] But these populist concessions, important though they were in bolstering the regime, hardly satisfied popular demands. While the agrarian reform brought benefits, these were not usually of the anticipated, restorative kind; nor were the revolutionaries necessarily the beneficiaries; and they were dispensed, sometimes grudgingly, often cynically, by politicians for whom *agrarismo* represented a slogan and an instrument rather than a cause.[1254] Demands for local autonomy, which lay at the heart of *serrano* rebellion, were even less capable of satisfaction under the new, power-hungry revolutionary state; while – as the gubernatorial conflict between Gutiérrez and Espinosa Mireles exemplified – popular *cabecillas* would, over time, lose out to a new generation of more educated, city-based *políticos*. The pressure of the popular movement, in other words, left its mark, especially in the agrarian field: no future regime dared disregard popular feelings as blatantly as Díaz had; the Revolution had brought the masses into the political arena, albeit shackled, weaponless and vulnerable. But the 'revolutionary consensus' school (which posits that all groups contributed to and benefited from the Revolution) is too blithely optimistic: the sacrifices of the popular movement greatly outweighed the patchy, often rhetorical, rewards which its members (or even their children) would receive in later years.

But if Carrancismo inherited relatively little from either Maderista liberalism, or the popular movement, where did it acquire the political genes that would determine the regime's physiognomy, its robust character and longevity? From Porfirismo (though the paternity would not be admitted) and from the Revolution, whose quintessential child it was. It was not that the Carrancistas consciously aped Díaz; rather – and the point is hardly abstruse – successive regimes, for all their mutual hostility and proclaimed differences, displayed a marked continuity, at least as regards the broad trends of policy. Since 1917, of course, under the impact of a severe ideology, example, and often mentor, revolutionary change (in the world at large) has been more traumatic and far-reaching: the Cuban Revolution – a backyard scuffle compared with its Mexican counterpart – led to faster, greater, 'structural' change. But the Mexican Revolution was virtually consummated before this internationalisation of revolution took place: it was the last of the 'great' revolutions which, following a Tocquevillean rather than a Leninist model, remained essentially national, produced no ideological blueprint or vanguard party and, above all, served to reinforce – rather than to subvert – many of the features of the old regime it overthrew. We may echo Tocqueville more precisely: 'the Revolution had . . . two distinct phases: one in which the sole aim . . . seemed to be to make a clean sweep of the past; and a second in which attempts were made to salvage fragments from the wreckage of the old order'; hence the outcome was 'a government both stronger and far more autocratic than the one which the Revolution had overthrown'.[1255]

For, though the Carrancista/Sonoran regime usually – not always – sounded very different from Díaz's, and though, in the important area of political mobilisation and institutionalisation, it broke new ground, yet its broad goals were neo-Porfirian – capitalist economic development and state-building. Hence it encouraged the growth of commercial agriculture, industry, exports and the infrastructure (railways with Díaz, roads with Calles); it greedily gathered political power at the centre, breaking down local particularism, 'forging the fatherland' (*forjando patria*) in Gamio's arresting phrase. Both regimes, in other words, saw the creation of a strong nation state and dynamic capitalist economy as their prime objectives and, in pursuing them, were prepared to demand heavy sacrifices (of a kind familar enough in such drives towards 'modernisation'), which precluded either liberal democracy or egalitarian levelling. More specifically, I will suggest, both regimes pursued a 'revolution from above', as Barrington Moore has termed it. The key difference was that the post-1915 'revolution from above' was built on the ruins of a prior (1910–15) 'revolution from below', which the Carrancistas were ultimately able to contain and co-opt; they were, in a sense, successful, populist equivalents of the Chinese Kuomintang. And this success is all the more remarkable, in that their policies, redolent of Porfirismo, clashed with those of Maderista liberalism (which subscribed to similar ends but willed them by different, arguably impractical, parliamentary methods); and, yet more violently, with the objectives of the popular movement, whose very commitment to the revolution derived from hostility to political centralisation and rapid, unfettered, capitalist 'development'. The Carrancistas' special genius lay in their ability to harness the revolution – albeit a tired, broken-in revolution – to antithetical, neo-Porfirian ends.

It was in this respect that they were quintessential children of the Revolution; unlike most Maderistas and popular rebels, they were products, not initiators of the revolutionary process. Their action was informed by the experience of the Revolution as it unfolded: hence their celebrated opportunism, pragmatism, and cynicism; qualities which Obregón, with his growing mastery of new military and political techniques, best exemplified. Glorious the Revolution might have been, but political upheaval was costly, bloody and undesirable. Now, the job was one of reconstruction (a term in constant use) and Obregón waxed lyrical in praise of hard work and effort; 'revolutions', he reminded listeners, 'are not springs of good fortune; they are upheavals which cause peoples great loss, and their fruits are only gathered by succeeding generations'. [1256] They had seen the Revolution; it was up to them to make it work. Hence they avoided sacred texts (like the Plan of Ayala) and panaceas (like free elections). Instead, they cobbled together a broad, eclectic, inconsistent programme, which paid lip service to liberalism, even 'socialism'; which appropriated the middle class as part of the proletariat, while attacking the bourgeoisie; which preached the harmonious mutual interest of capital and labour; which welcomed foreign capital to the country while denouncing capitalism. [1257] And which, of course, was capable of all manner of practical implementations. Experience governed their political evolution: but what experience, with what results?

In very general terms, the experience of governing Mexico – and, like Díaz, governing in the wake of endemic civil war – encouraged political centralisation and a degree of economic *dirigisme* (which, given the Carrancistas' conventional commitment to capitalist development, followed conventional lines). But historically specific problems and solutions, arising from the revolution itself, gave Carrancismo its distinctive character, setting it apart not only from Maderismo or Zapatismo, but also from Porfirismo, whose broad objectives it might share, but whose methods of achieving them necessarily differed. The initial Constitutionalist revolt of 1913 was improvised, defensive, and ideologically vague. The policies since associated with Constitutionalism, and enshrined in the Constitution, grew cumulatively and chaotically over time, in response to immediate pressures, acting upon a general, shared, Constitutionalist ethos. The historian who searches for their origins in early revolutionary manifestoes, or in the publications of the Precursor Movement, though he may sometimes find arresting parallels, deludes himself if he believes that these early utterances (to be found among many which have been forgotten) profoundly influenced later revolutionary practice.

The belated, opportunist conversion to *agrarismo* is well known. But other policies – rightly seen as central to government after 1915 – also evolved in convoluted fashion, did not represent unequivocal revolutionary commitments, and owed a sizeable debt to the old regime. The two classic cases are anti-clericalism (which must be seen as part of a broader, 'developmentalist' philosophy) and economic nationalism. The marked incidence of anti-clericalism after (not before) 1913 has already been noted.[1258] Priests were gaoled, ransomed, exiled and executed; Church property was confiscated wholesale; a variety of local anti-clerical decrees presaged the constitutional provisions of 1917, which separated Church and State, legalised divorce, banned clerical parties and the political participation of priests, and conferred on the state extensive powers to regulate the numbers, nationality and activities of the priesthood. Some Carrancistas had wanted to go further, prohibiting all Catholic education.[1259] Furthermore, the clerical question absorbed much greater time and attention at Querétaro than did 'social' questions; even radicals like Múgica considered it on a par with labour and agrarian reform.[1260] There was an element of paradox, here, as in so much of the Congress's dealings. Though they claimed to represent the people and have been seen as carriers of popular, revolutionary aspirations, the *constituyentes* were clearly out of step with majority sentiment; anti-clericalism (as one admitted) was not a popular cause.[1261] For, though sporadic acts of popular anti-clericalism punctuated the Revolution, there was no sustained, popular jacobinism – of the kind evident at Querétaro, or later, in the Tabasco of Garrido Canabal. Still less did the mass of the people, whose opinions of the hierarchy and local *cura* might differ from place to place, wish to ditch their old beliefs for some new, cerebral abstraction, be it Gallicanised Christianity, Protestantism, or the religion of humanity.[1262] Like economic nationalism, therefore, anti-clericalism filtered down from the top, and did not well up from below.

The 'top', in this case, was not an exiguous elite, however. Anti-clericalism (of a milder form) had long characterised the urban, professional middle classes, especially in the north; it had played its part in the gestation of the PLM. But, while anti-clericalism was a feature of the civilian Maderismo of 1909–13, it was a minor, unobtrusive one. Individual Maderistas might rail at the Church, but official policy was benign and in several states an incipient liberal–Christian Democrat political polarity emerged – peacefully and consensually.[1263] Huerta's coup changed all that. The Church now complained of systematic persecution (which many revolutionaries warmly encouraged). Cabrera, who omitted all reference to the Church in his 1911 catalogue of Porfirian abuses, was, by 1915, penning 'a reasoned but bitter indictment of the Church'.[1264] As already argued, revolutionary allegations of Catholic support for Huerta were by no means groundless;[1265] and, of the abominated reactionary trinity, the Church remained an obvious, institutional (and propertied) target, while the Army was defeated and dispersed, and individual

Porfiristas had fled, gone to ground, or colonised the revolution. But there was much more to it than the Church's alleged – and exaggerated – 'reactionary' politics. The Church, after all, was far from monolithic: there were plenty of 'social' Catholics, Catholic democrats, and popular *curas*; revolutionary anti-clericalism, condemning the Church as an institution and, often enough, Catholicism as a creed, recognised no such distinctions.

Two additional factors must be noted by way of explanation. First, many Carrancistas had a sincere, deep-seated detestation of the Church which formed part of a complex of related ideas concerning the problems of Mexican society and the solutions they demanded; this complex, though far from new, was powerfully stimulated by the Revolution, which seemed to offer a fresh opportunity to implement these ideas. Putting a name to this complex is not easy. Previous analysts, usually taking a partial view of this totality, have applied various labels: 'nationalism', 'populism', 'jacobinism'.[1266] The first two, as conventionally applied, are inappropriate; the third, though nearer the mark and derivative of contemporary usage, is too specifically Eurocentric.[1267] Since, *au fond*, we are seeking to describe an ideology of development, political and economic, the ugly but apt term 'developmentalism' will serve; what is important is the content of the term. Revolutionary 'developmentalists' sought to make Mexico a progressive, modern, capitalist society, broadly along the lines of Western Europe and North America; they favoured a dynamic, exporting economy (again, foreign precedents could justify a measure of state intervention to achieve it); they looked to create an efficient state, staffed by a competent bureaucracy and professional army; they believed that state-sponsored, secular education could produce a literate, numerate population, loyal to the revolutionary state, contributors to and beneficiaries of the progressive capitalism which would prevail. This was an old vision, which harked back, explicitly, to the Reform; and, implicitly, to more conservative theorists from Alamán to Limantour.[1268] But the failures of the Porfirian and Maderista regimes (both of which were infused with similar notions) forced the vision into new perspectives. The benefits of free suffrage and federalism receded from sight; those of centralised government, mass politics, bureaucratisation and *dirigisme* came to the fore. In particular, I would suggest, the condition of Mexico, prostrate, bankrupt, ravaged by want, sharpened the developmentalist viewpoint, which now accorded with more general yearning for work, reconstruction and recovery. Never had the work ethic seemed more appropriate. It was a time, a fictional revolutionary commented, when 'we had to decide to begin to build and construct even if it meant tarnishing our consciences'.[1269] Hence the appeals for reconstruction, hard work, social equilibrium and shared effort: Obregón's eulogies of honest sweat, the 'vehement exhortation[s]'[1270] of the press that all citizens should 'work for national reconstruction'. And, we shall note, here as in other post-war societies, such appeals did not fall on deaf ears.[1271]

The Church and Catholicism obstructed progress in two respects. In a specific sense, they placed rival claims on individuals, which clashed with those of the revolutionary state. As we shall note, in its attempts to overcome national diversity – to bind together those 'various groups which still cannot fully collaborate in a shared objective', and to create a 'national type' – the regime was bound to clash with the Church, be it reactionary or progressive.[1272] But more generally, Catholicism clashed with developmentalism because it was bracketed with other fundamental evils: economic backwardness, sloth, illiteracy, ignorance, superstition; and, perhaps paradoxically, with social vices – drink, prostitution, gambling and filth. As the *constituyente* Salvador Guzmán, a young doctor from Puebla, put it: 'the Republic will be saved when the Mexican people learn to read before they learn to pray, know the road to the workshop before the one to the saloon, and get used to the plough before the censer'.[1273] Here, the associated stigmata of backwardness are explicitly linked; often, the connection must be inferred, since the revolutionaries sniped at their different targets separately (and this separation has carried over into historical analyses). The Church acted as a brake on economic development not just in the old liberal sense of monopolising resources in its 'dead hands', but also through its obscurantist control of minds, exercised through the school, pulpit and confessional. Thereby 'antiquated and backward ideas' were imparted, to the detriment of science and prosperity. Schools should instead supply rational education, 'scientifically based on the truth'.[1274] Not only the economy, but also national, even racial, vigour would thus be enhanced: 'the diffusion of education, especially secular, will mould the strong spirit of the race and, with the economic betterment of Mexicans, their devotion to the country will be strengthened'.[1275]

The persecution of the Church was therefore paralleled by a renewed stress on the role of education, which followed Porfirista and Maderista precedents, but now in more militant fashion. Even 'moderate' civilians, like Palavicini, saw the schoolteacher as a politico-cultural missionary, as in Republican France; the closure of schools was 'a crime of lèse-civilisation'; 'our first effort', Obregón stressed, 'must be towards the enlightenment and education of our broad masses'.[1276] Education would politicise, nationalise, uplift and counter pernicious clerical influence. And, if secular education saved youth from the trammels of the Church, patriotism and the rights of the state could be furthered by rejecting the authority of Rome and fostering a Church – granted that some sort of Church might be necessary – on Gallican, regalist lines. Thus was born the idea of the Mexican schismatic church, later attempted in the 1920s.[1277] Little of this was new: precedents may be found in Maderista concern for education; in Porfirian critiques of clerical obscurantism or attempts to inculcate, through education, the 'religión de la patria'; even in Bourbon regalism.[1278] Moreover, parallels with developmentalist ideologies elsewhere are easy to find. The most obvious is with European Protestantism, which similarly rejected papal supremacy and the Catholic state-within-the-state, while linking anti-Catholic, anti-clerical thought to ideas of economic progress, efficiency, morality and the work ethic. The northern revolutionaries, Jean Meyer observes, 'made their Jacobinism the vehicle for a pragmatic and very effective illustration of the theories of Max Weber'. [1279] And the inference receives support from the evidence of Protestant influence in the ranks of the rebels, which in turn was used to fabricate myths of American-Protestant-Freemason plots to subvert Mexico's historic Catholic culture. [1280]

But this is to mistake symptom for cause. Protestantism exercised a – limited – appeal in revolutionary circles for much the same reason as it did in other, developing societies: it fitted in with, and reinforced (i.e., in the classic formulation, displayed an 'elective affinity' with) modes of thought and behaviour which were already emerging. [1281] Protestantism, and 'Protestant' values, rationalised emergent forms of deviant, hence 'revolutionary', practice in twentieth-century Mexico as in seventeenth-century England. [1282] Indeed, there was no need for a formal Protestant commitment. As other examples confirm, the 'Protestant' values of hard work, sobriety, individual initiative and thrift could be inculcated and rationalised by other (secular) ideologies. Apter has noted the recurrence of 'a form of contemporary Puritanism [which] . . . emphasises social thrift, hard work, the dignity of labour and selflessness', particularly in 'new states' engaged in 'bootstrap economic operation[s]'. [1283] Post-revolutionary Mexico was not post-colonial, but it faced comparable tasks of political integration and economic development, which encouraged similar ideological appeals, drawn from the repertoire of traditional liberalism.

The evils of drink (another Maderista theme) were constantly rehearsed. Drink rotted the body, burdened the economy, and encouraged violence, homicide and mental disease, declared one *constituyente*; it 'degenerated the race'; it led to 'degenerate offspring, of low intelligence, useless as far as social and political questions are concerned'. When the workers were weaned off alcohol, as in 'dry' Sonora, they saved instead of boozing. [1284] Furthermore, it was assumed, a twin attack on drink and Church fiestas would eliminate the old, inefficient practice of San Lunes. [1285] These reforms were practised as well as preached: Calles campaigned assiduously against alcohol in Sonora; *pulque* was banned from the Federal District; Piedras Negras experienced 'wonderful changes' in the direction of municipal temperance and sobriety. [1286] Similar campaigns were waged in Tepic, Tlaxcala and, above all, the Gulf states, where proconsular rule encountered the traditional vices of tropical ports. [1287] Again, there were Porfirian precedents (as well as abundant foreign parallels) for this condemnation of alcohol. [1288] But it is important to note how 'revolutionary' temperance was recurrently associated with other 'Puritan' concerns. Drink, gambling, prostitution and bloodsports flourished together (it was said) and had to be extirpated together. 'Vices, savage amusements and [religious] fanaticism' maintained the Mexican people in 'a state of barbarity', and 'a great and strong citizenship' would not emerge until they were eliminated.[1289] 'Social regeneration' required measures such as those taken in Jalisco, as well as many other states, to stop bullfights and gambling; Calles' clean-up of Sonora reflected official concern to uplift the 'moral level of the people, by means of the suppression of vices which degrade man, and the encouragement of education'.[1290] Disease, then rampant, was attributed less to malnutrition than to excessive drink and inadequate personal hygiene: the new Constitution, one *constituyente* proclaimed, should be inscribed on tablets of soap.[1291]

Examples could be multiplied almost indefinitely; and they could, of course, be drawn from the 1920s and 1930s, when the ideological complex of progress and Puritanism, of anti-clericalism, temperance and *étatiste*, secular education continued to flourish, reaching its apogee in the 'laboratory of the Revolution', Garrido Canabal's Tabasco.[1292] Then, as before, reality and rhetoric diverged. Temperance, we have noted, could not be enforced with any sustained success: official graft, fiscal needs and popular cussedness conspired to thwart the anti-drink lobby. So, too, with gambling, bloodsports and prostitution; at best they could be sanitised and regulated, for extirpation was impossible. By late 1916, the Mexico City police were (legally) organising horse races, with betting, supposedly to raise money for the amortisation of the National Debt.[1293] Alvarado's boast, that he had stripped Yucatán clean of brothels, casinos and bars, proved hollow.[1294] But the relative failure of such policies should not detract from their importance, in that they formed a key element of the Constitutionalist ethos, and claimed a great deal of political time and attention – much more than, say, agrarian reform. Furthermore, while temperance (largely) failed, other aspects of this ideological complex – more attuned to reality – proved capable of realisation, as we shall note.

Anti-clericalism, of course, endured as a central feature of the Revolution until the late 1930s. It throve – despite the bitter opposition it elicited – because the Church was now seen not just as a general brake on social progress, but also as a specific rival of the revolutionary state; and its rivalry was all the more serious in that (revolutionary myth to the contrary) the Church embraced reformist as well as reactionary elements, both of which were capable of mass mobilisation. Church–State conflict, muted by Díaz, and channeled in a peaceful, consensual direction by Madero, now broke out with unparalleled ferocity. The *constituyentes* were hypnotised by the threat of political Catholicism. 'The manifest intention of the clergy to dominate education is nothing but a step towards usurping the powers of the State', declared one; it was the secular schoolmaster's task to curb this influence and work for the 'formation of the national soul'.[1295] Allied to the landlord interest, the Church represented a force for reaction, especially in the countryside (one *constituyente* therefore advocated restricting the vote to literates).[1296] But, more serious, the Church competed with the revolutionary state for the support of politicised groups, particularly in the towns – the middle class, workers, youth – and could do so by virtue of the appeal of social Catholicism, which the revolutionaries might ignore in public rhetoric, but had to consider in their private counsels. The Catholic Association of Mexican Youth (ACJM) founded during Madero's honeymoon with the Church, prospered after 1915, recruiting young urban Catholics, establishing branches in west-central and northern Mexico, receiving papal benediction in 1917.[1297] With militant commitment, the ACJM protested against anti-clerical measures, lampooned the government in its publications, demonstrated on the streets, and sought to resist the confiscation of church buildings; these last two activities involving physical clashes with government supporters. If the ACJM was based on one of the most readily mobilisable groups, urban middle class youth, it did not take long for Catholic workers' groups to pick up where they had left off in 1913. While the bishops condemned the CROM, rival Catholic unions were established which, in 1919, convened a national convention at Guadalajara. By 1922 the CNCT (National Catholic Labour Confederation) claimed 353 affiliated unions and 80,000 members (the CROM claimed 400,000 members, but had perhaps a quarter that number); plans were soon afoot for a Catholic peasant league.[1298]

Even in the political field, a Catholic comeback was attempted. Though the Catholic candidate in the 1920 presidential election predictably flopped, the Catholics achieved local successes in states like Aguascalientes; this was enough for official organs to denounce the rebirth of the 'fateful PCN', and to warn that 'a political Catholic is and always will be an enemy of the Revolution'.[1299] By now, most of the exiled bishops had returned to their pastoral role and, if they did not always welcome the militancy (and reformism) of the ACJM, they spoke out against anti-clerical measures, especially those enshrined in the new Constitution.[1300] This, in Jalisco, led to outright confrontation, a foretaste of the Church–State conflict of the 1920s. For, when the combative archbishop of Guadalajara returned from the US and – in hiding – denounced the offending Constitutional provisions, the state governor took drastic action.[1301] Churches in which the archiepiscopal protest had been read were closed; all priests were required to register with the Ministry of Gobernación; Jalisco's priestly population was restricted to one per 5,000 laymen. The archbishop himself was arrested, and again exiled; some of his supporters took to the hills; there were mass demonstrations (which the police dispersed), a boycott of trams, buses and newspapers, and finally a suspension of all church services. The Catholic protest succeeded. Facing other problems, Carranza lacked the stomach for a fight with the Church. The Jalisco state government was obliged to climb down, the offending decrees were rescinded, the Archbishop returned. It was a famous victory, but a dangerous precedent, and certainly not the end of the war. Nine years later, when radical anti-clericalism was again ascendant, the Catholics resorted to similar measures and, this time, the outcome was not a government surrender, but a protracted and bloody civil war. For, as this preliminary skirmish indicated, the Catholics would resist revolutionary anti-clericalism, not just as an inert 'reactionary' block, but also utilising new forms of mass mobilisation of 'revolutionary' character, and this infringement of its monopoly the state would not suffer gladly. Hence the revolutionary anti-clericalism which stood in the forefront of Carrancista policy and debate after 1915 was not simply a cyclical revival of the old liberal conscience; much less was it the consummation of popular aspirations; above all, it marked the beginning of another story – that of the new state's struggle for its supposed birthright.

Like anti-clericalism, economic nationalism was a recent, revolutionary emblem: it was largely absent from Maderismo; it elicited no popular enthusiasm; yet it became a major theme of the 1920s and 1930s. Indeed, not only were Madero and the Maderistas content with the broad pattern of foreign investment created during the Porfiriato;[1302] their Constitutionalist successors, too, were seen as posing no threat to foreign interests to begin with. During 1913–14 the rebels – above all the 'nationalist' Sonorans – received glowing tributes from American businessmen, who discerned little hostility, and dwelt on the good order, responsible administration and friendly relations which the northern leaders maintained.[1303] Within a couple of years, these same leaders would be excoriated as radicals, xenophobes and Bolsheviks drawing their inspiration from 'Trotski's Russia'.[1304] In fact, though times and perspectives had changed, the leaders in question had – in this as in so many areas of policy – shown remarkable consistency. Time brought change as local caudillos seized national power and sought to implement policy during a period of economic collapse; they needed revenue, they were driven to more drastic solutions, they appeared, in foreign eyes, as radical, power-hungry Bolsheviki, rather than as the compliant, responsible caudillos of yesteryear. Foreign interests, desperate for peace and order in 1913–14, and suitably gratified when it was provided, could afford to be more critical four years later when, with a national government established, they expected a renewal of Porfirian complaisance (this was especially true of the oil industry, the source of the most vocal complaints) but were disappointed.

As this suggests, the revolutionary leaders necessarily changed with time and advancement; it was one thing to deal with the Southern Pacific Railroad as a Sonoran commander, another to tackle the oil industry from the point of view of the national executive. But the underlying ethos was constant. The Constitutionalists had no deep affection for foreign (principally American) business, though many had a deep admiration; however, they believed it to be necessary both for the short-term needs of the revolution (hence the ready collaboration of the Villistas, or Sonora's frontier brokers), and for the long-term needs of the country. Like Díaz, they sought capital for development, and they especially sought European capital to offset American pre-dominance; and, radicals as well as moderates, they believed in the fructiferous partnership of foreign and domestic capital, as had the Científicos.[1305] Salvador Alvarado – a 'radical', whose policies cost the International Harvester Company dear – was explicit that Mexico could not erect 'Chinese walls' against those external 'economic and social forces which ought to help us achieve progress and well-being'; rather, they should be welcomed, assisted, channelled; immigration should be encouraged (but energetic Basques or Lombards should be preferred: on no account Chinese, who would neither 'improve our race nor increase our wealth'); and production would best be served by 'a team consisting of the state, Mexican citizens and foreigners'.[1306] Obregón agreed: Mexico's reconstruction demanded a progressive, capitalist economy, with a major, though controlled, foreign sector. Foreign invest-ment, even immigration, were welcome, so long as they came on the terms laid down by the state.[1307] Meanwhile, ideology conspired with circum-stances to grant foreign business a warm reception, even as economic nationalist provisions began to appear on the statute book. Murguía and Treviño sought to revive American mining activity in Chihuahua; the Governor of Aguascalientes was keen for smelting to restart; throughout – despite major wrangles – the oil kept pumping from Tampico.[1308]

It is quite clear, therefore, that the Constitutionalists conceived an impor-tant role for foreign investment (and for Mexican exports). The question was the terms on which these would operate. And here, practice evolved not in response to some clear revolutionary blueprint, still less to satisfy popular demands, but rather in *ad hoc*, pragmatic fashion, obeying the unforeseen circumstances of revolution, while displaying interesting parallels with other regimes (including the Porfirian). Revolutionary economic nationalism was, therefore, the response of a new elite to particular circumstances, conceived within a general (historical and continental) mental framework. It was neither as radical nor as innovative as often supposed, either then or since. The Revolution itself compelled a great extension of governmental intervention in the economy. The war demanded increased taxation: of mines, oil, land, cattle and so on; and this fiscal trend, evident under Madero and Huerta, continued after the peak of the fighting had passed.[1309] In addition, companies suffered arbitrary exactions, sequestrations, even outright confiscations: real estate, public utilities and railways came under military control, more for short-term, strategic than for any long-term ideological reasons. In all this, foreign interests suffered less than native (and Spanish) interests, and smaller foreign enterprises were more often driven to the wall than their bigger, corporate rivals. Indeed, while small operators were bankrupted (by the generalised economic conditions, rather than any specific 'xenophobic' persecution) the giants – Standard Oil, the Guggenheims – survived, bought out competitors, and emerged all the stronger in the 1920s.[1310]

Meanwhile, the revolutionaries learned from experience. They discovered the benefits (personal and collective) of collaboration with foreign interests; but they also became aware of the companies' resources, their capacity to insulate themselves from the sacrifices of the Revolution, and their propensity to resist 'confiscatory' tax demands for a tactical period before finally complying. The oil companies, in particular, cried 'wolf!' and predicted bankruptcy at regular intervals, but they went on producing and profiting.[1311] The oil industry, in fact, affords a good example of revolutionary policy. It was not, of course, typical; there were plenty of foreign interests which were losing money and which the government not only had little desire to control, but actively sought to 'hive off' when war left a legacy of state control.[1312] But the decade of civil war coincided with the take-off of oil production: the big investments of the 1900s began to pay off (and the profits were, as yet, lightly taxed) just as successive government became desperate for revenue; hence Madero, Huerta, then the Carrancistas increased the tax burden – a trend indicating less the radical character of the Huerta regime than the bipartisan pragmatism of such a fiscal policy. Furthermore, taxation could imply changes in the terms of the original concessions. Thus, as Lord Cowdray realised early on, the quest for governmental control and regulation obeyed fiscal motives, and in no sense threatened a termination of foreign investment. Carranza's administration, the US ambassador reported in 1917, sought to re-write the 'illegal' concessions granted by Díaz, exempt from taxation; the 'intention [is] not so much to cancel these illegal concessions as to oblige the holders in the future to fulfill the law, especially as it regards to taxes'.[1313] Now – since it was common knowledge that the companies were realising handsome profits – the tax yield could be increased: from under half a million pesos in 1912 to over twelve million in 1918, by which time oil taxation represented 11% of government revenue.[1314] The Revolution facilitated this new fiscal policy in that it brought to power new men, free from previous legal and personal commitments to the status quo; though they, too, could constitute a collaborating elite, the terms of collaboration had to be worked out afresh, and the balance of advantage could be shifted to take into account the industry's profitability. Both the trend of Porfirian policy and the example of other national oil industries suggest that such changes would have occurred, over time, *mutatis mutandis*, even in the absence of revolution. The Revolution favoured economic nationalism, but in no sense did it create it *de novo* (as it did, for example, official *agrarismo*).[1315]

Constitutionalist economic nationalism was not, of course, a simple fiscal expedient. It involved a redefinition of the terms on which foreign companies could operate in Mexico: the subsoil was reserved to the nation, thus converting mining and oil concessions from freehold to leasehold; and foreigners who sought such concessions would be considered as Mexican citizens for the purpose (i.e., the Calvo doctrine, requiring foreign holders of concessions or property to renounce diplomatic protection, was formally recognised).[1316] These changes provoked long wrangles, particularly with the oil companies, during the 1920s. But we are more concerned with the policy's origins. It did not represent the culmination of revolutionary aims (for there are surprisingly few precedents to be found, especially before 1914), or of popular demands (for 'the people' adhered to no abstract economic nationalism and generally favoured the presence of foreign business, which fostered jobs and trade).[1317] Rather, revolutionary economic nationalism, as expressed in Article 27, was the work of a small group of intellectuals and *políticos*, a minority within the minority Constituent Congress, led by Rouaix, who had studied the oil industry and was well aware of the advantage of greater control, taxation and conservation.[1318] Their drift of thought, though 'elitist' rather than 'popular', had many parallels. Their counterparts in the defunct Convention had entertained similar ideas.[1319] So, too, had counterparts elsewhere in Latin America, where the tradition of state intervention survived the era of *laissez-faire* and began a resurgence in the late nineteenth century.[1320] Spokesmen now advocated –and governments, of different political hues, instituted – controls or restrictions on foreign enterprise. In Chile, the government controlled two-thirds of the national railways by 1914; and in the 1920s, the liberal Mining Code of 1888 was substantially revised, reserving to the state the exploitation of oil deposits. In Argentina, the state launched the YPF to develop oil resources, while a 'fairly stringent law' of 1921 similarly reserved Bolivian oil resources to the state (oil, evoking 'a kind of mystique of national sovereignty', was the most extreme case; but it formed part of a general nationalist, interventionist trend, which antedated the more rigorous *desarrollo hacia adentro* of the 1930s).[1321] Central banks, too, were conceived and born by a process of natural economic development and integration, and clearly did not require social revolutions to act as midwives.[1322]

In all these cases, the Revolution probably accelerated, and sometimes gave a radical edge, to processes that were basically common and continent-wide – in a way that agrarian reform, or mass political mobilisation, were certainly not. Furthermore, there were Porfirian precedents, which tell in favour of a 'continuity' rather than 'discontinuity' explanation of revolutionary economic nationalism. Just as Sierra conceived of education policy inculcating national sentiments and integration, so, too, Científicos like Molina sought a stricter Mining Code (which was almost achieved in 1909); there was talk of oil nationalisation; and Limantour took steps to nationalise the railway system and break the American monopoly of meat packing in northern Mexico.[1323] Pablo Macedo justified initially high levels of foreign investment, arguing that it was necessary in 'new countries', but that Mexican enterprise, fostered by individual initiative, education and supportive legislation, would play an increasingly important role, as it already did in some sectors.[1324] It could have been Obregón speaking: beneath the contrasting rhetoric, Científico and

Sonoran economic policy was not so radically different; and the economic history of the 1920s (characterised by continued export-led growth and foreign investment) represented not another betrayal, but a logical outcome of the Constitutionalist/Sonoran ethos. [1325]

It is not quite enough to note the ubiquity – and thus, in a sense, the political 'neutrality' – of economic nationalist policy. Two general causal explanations may also be suggested. First, revolutionaries objected to classic enclave industries precisely because they were enclaves, not only in the economic sense of lacking linkages, but also politically, in that they were partially autonomous and besmirched the sovereignty of the Mexican state (an entity for which the Constitutionalist leaders had a high regard, especially now that they were at the head of it). This autonomy had been highlighted by the Revolution: companies, like Cananea, had successfully insulated themselves from the conflict, conserving their labour forces (even in defiance of rebel recruiting), paying wages in dollars or tokens (thus undermining Mexican paper), relying on their economic resources to tide them over until better times. In many cases, the clientelist dependency of the work force was thus enhanced, at the expense of their allegiance to the state and Revolution; in the oil fields, the companies financed the protracted Pelaecista rebellion. Such enclaves galled the Constitutionalists rather as the Oaxaqueño secession of 1915 did: both compromised the political authority of the regime, creating states within the state, which had to be reintegrated, by constitutional if not by military means. Back in 1906–7, the Cananea episode had aroused indignation not least because of the American intervention which, sanctioned by Díaz, flouted Mexican sovereignty and illustrated Cananea's 'de-nationalised' status. [1326] Now, during the Revolution, Sonorans who eagerly encouraged production in the enclaves sought at the same time to curb their autonomy: de la Huerta favoured converting Cananea from a company town into a full municipality; Calles objected to the status of Empalme as a 'private town' in fief to the Southern Pacific Railroad. [1327] (By the same token, we may note, 'radical' revolutionaries advocated foreign immigration, so long as the immigrants became Mexican citizens, and did not constitute semi-independent foreign colonies.)[1328] Article 27 – and, in some respects, Article 123 too – thus provided instruments for prising open the enclaves, without necessarily curtailing foreign investment and production. [1329]

But, aside from such political objectives, economic strategy required that the role of foreign investment in the development process be modified. Under the new order, 'foreign interests would have a place in the Mexican economy, but it would be defined by Mexicans as a necessary ingredient of true national independence'. [1330] As already suggested, with particular reference to oil, this represented less a radical new departure than a crystallisation of pre-1910 ideas, catalysed by the experience of revolution itself. As Porfirian policymakers were coming to believe, even if they were more inhibited when it came to acting upon the belief, old-style concessions, with their prodigal allocation of resources into foreign hands, were less appropriate now that Mexico had acquired an industrial base, a diverse export sector and the infrastructure of a semi-developed country. Privileged enclaves and monopolies could now be curtailed in pursuit of a more balanced, autonomous pattern of development in which the state (again blending progress with social equilibrium) would judiciously eliminate abuses, while fostering a climate of competition and initiative. This limited pragmatic economic nationalism was logically paralleled by an assertion of domestic entrepreneurial values. 'The revolutionary tendency', Pani told the First National Congress of Mexican Merchants, 'is not towards a Utopian socialistic levelling: its social ideal is to permit every man to obtain from the aggregate sum of well-being acquired by the community a part proportionate to his personal contribution of labour, intelligence and economy.'[1331] Obregón, in his more homely way, agreed: the wearers of *huaraches* and straw sombreros would not benefit if the rich were stripped of their shoes and hats; nor would it help candle-lit villages to deprive the cities of electric power; the task was to level up, not to level down.[1332] Already, it seems, the Revolution was producing its adherents of the 'trickle down' theory of social progress.[1333]

Indeed, under the imperatives of progress and competition, entrepreneurial initiative became a national virtue. Alvarado, who had cut his intellectual teeth on Samuel Smiles, longed to explode Mexico's image as a land of fly-blown shacks, bullfights, *pulquerías*, picturesque *charros* and human draught animals; he denounced the conservatism of domestic capital, its 'almost physical horror of innovation'; and the privilege and corruption which soured otherwise beneficial foreign investment. Foreign capital was vital, but it was even more vital that Mexicans themselves should be 'strong, aggressive, and innovative' in the exploitations of the country's resources; for, if not, the natural law of competition and selection would make them and their children 'the bootblacks of new masters'.[1334] National liberation, according to Hermila Galindo's presentation of the 'Carranza doctrine', required that developing countries 'assert control over their own resources and industrialise'; to which end Galindo – and other revolutionary spokespeople – called for a broad national front, a consensus of class interests, and an elimination of radical agitation in favour of patriotic solidarity (here, Galindo rebuked socialists, syndicalists and anarchists for eroding national loyalties).[1335] But the Constitutionalists went beyond exhortation. Here was an area of policy in which, unusually, practice roughly conformed to rhetoric. It was, as one *constituyente* put it, a natural aspiration to get rich; and, appropriating Guizot's slogan for themselves, the new elite practised the entrepreneurial values which they preached, producing many examples of successful innovation and profiteering.[1336]

Many of these involved the shadier side of business already mentioned: the illicit trafficking in transport, foodstuffs, city vice and real estate. But the dynamism and acquisitiveness evident here also stimulated initiatives of a more orthodox kind, sometimes conceived in high-minded, patriotic, rather than self-interested, personal terms. The Sonorans, whose entrepreneurial zeal was matched by their business opportunities, were the classic example. Obregón, the innovative *ranchero* of the 1900s, displayed 'great energy, entrepreneurial spirit and progressive ideas' in stimulating and organising chickpea cultivation in the north-west where, collaborating with American interests, he amassed a large personal fortune.[1337] De la Huerta – given to a more flamboyant entrepreneurialism (he had been an operatic tenor before 1910) – dreamed grandiose dreams and produced a spate of developmentalist schemes, even in the hard times of 1916: railways, telephones, technical schools, overseas scholarships, land reclamation and tourist resorts.[1338] Alvarado, meanwhile, carried the theory and practice of developmentalism to Yucatán where, with the cash raised by the Henequen Regulating Commission, he planned new ports, railways, steamship lines and oil exploration.[1339] Particularly in Yucatán, these projects implied a collaboration of government and private enterprise. But, with or without state participation, revolutionary entrepreneurs conceived of their individual efforts as serving the nation, as well as themselves, and thus conforming to the collective, revolutionary ethic. As the Sonoran Benjamin Hill put it to Enrique Estrada, then military commander in Sinaloa, proposing his participation in a 15m. peso irrigation scheme in the state:[1340]

I am one of the chief shareholders in this business but I can assure you that, rather than just my particular interest impelling me to cooperate in the realisation of this great enterprise, it is the desire that it will serve as an example so that great works of irrigation may be completed . . . by Mexican companies . . . not simply with the aim of making money, but fulfilling a patriotic task which deserves general acclaim. As for me, the satisfaction consists not simply in being involved in military or political matters, but also in contributing my grain of sand to . . . the progress of my country.

As the tone suggests, such ventures were undertaken not with furtive caution, but bold, self-congratulatory swagger. The press pointed to the example of 'certain military leaders' and urged the people to follow it, laying aside their arms, 'channeling their individual energies into real tasks', dedicating themselves to 'achieving, in practical terms, the progress of the Nation . . . and a reconstruction built on firm, stable bases'.[1341] The grafting generals, the generals turned landlords and the new revolutionary entrepreneurs thus operated in a climate which, with its insistence on the need for national economic development, bathed companies and consciences in an air of fragrant rectitude. Womack's quip, 'the business of the Mexican Revolution is business', though coined in 1970, contained elements of truth even in 1917.[1342]

Do we, in these statements and activities, discern the march of that famous collectivity – Latin America's equivalent of the 'rising middle class' of Whig historiography – the 'national bourgeoisie'? Plenty would agree with the formulation of the Mexican Communist Party, which saw the Sonorans as representing 'those elements which aspire to national reconstruction based on the industrialisation of the country and the creation of a strong national bourgeoisie independent of foreign influence'.[1343] This may be broadly true (though the 'independence of foreign influence' demands qualification). But it cannot therefore be argued that the Revolution served to bring this class to power, or that, putting it more starkly, it was a Revolution of the national bourgeoisie. For this to be true, the Revolution must have dismounted a previous ruling class of contrasting character: a feudal aristocracy, a *'comprador'* bourgeoisie, or some combination of the two. The Porfirian ruling class has, indeed, been depicted in these terms. But the argument is weak, and the prime differences between the pre- and post-revolutionary ruling classes (I would prefer 'elites') lie elsewhere. For, as regards strategies of development and the role of foreign interests within them, there is more kinship than antithesis. The Científicos shared with the Constitutionalists a concern for – often an obsession with – individual initiative, material improvements and economic development, which they summed up in the ubiquitous keyword 'progress'.[1344] Hence the positivistic stress on strong government and material change; the development of industry, exports and the infrastructure; the concern, too, for education (at least in the cities), sanitation, preventive medicine.[1345]

If, initially, the Porfirian 'project' conferred a pre-eminent role on foreign investment, this did not make the Porfirians parasitic *compradors*; nor was the initial role necessarily immutable. As already suggested, the Porfirians looked to a progressive Mexicanisation of productive enterprise and, by the 1900s, practical steps were being taken in that direction. Meanwhile, economic development was far from a foreign monopoly: witness the Creel–Terrazas empire, the Madero interests, the planters of Morelos and Yucatán, the *ranchero* 'petty-bourgeoisie' of Guerrero, Hidalgo, the Bajío, the industries of Monterrey or Orizaba, the bustling commercial towns of Sonora. If the bourgeoisie of the 1920s is to be deemed 'national', why not that of the 1900s? If, say, Obregón, why not Terrazas? For, though the Revolution brought changes, these were neither so profound, nor so disruptive of Mexico's economic relations with the 'core', to constitute a supposed transition from *comprador* to national bourgeois hegemony. At most, the Revolution accelerated a secular transition, one that was taking place and would take place irrespective of revolution. Furthermore, it does not seem that the Revolution derived from economic nationalist concerns, or was fuelled by the grievances of an emergent national bourgeoisie. Madero – a quintessential member of that class if it existed – premised his opposition to Díaz on non-economic, political grounds, and spoke favourably of the Porfirian economic record.[1346] And in this he spoke for most of the civilian Maderistas, whose formal statements indicate similar priorities. In the vocabulary of this discussion, the conflict between Maderistas and Porfiristas represented a division within the Mexican bourgeoisie (and petty-bourgeoisie), between political 'ins' and 'outs'; if a national bourgeoisie is to be discerned, it, too, was polarised in this fashion – Madero and Maytorena against Terrazas and Torres.

But the Revolution did not take the path foreseen by the Maderistas – or any one group. It performed functions that were unassigned and unplanned. One function, scarcely forseen by Madero, let alone by popular revolutionaries, was to stimulate the incipient economic nationalism of the late Porfiriato, thus ostensibly favouring the 'project of the national bourgeoisie'. The practical consequences were hardly impressive: foreign investment, as a proportion of national wealth, was in 1929 double what it had been in 1906.[1347] Much more important, however, were domestic social and political changes, which served to advance this 'project'. As we shall note in the concluding section, the Revolution shattered the shell of Porfirian society, breaking down constraints on economic development and releasing a flood of entrepreneurial dynamism; though in the short term the Revolution devastated the economy, in the long term it laid the groundwork for sustained future development. For, as the 1907 crisis had shown, the Porfirian pattern of development was facing serious problems on the eve of the Revolution. This is not to say the problems were insuperable: too often, the 'fundamental contradictions' which are discerned in societies on the eve of revolution – and which supposedly determine the impending débâcle – are seen only with hindsight, are to be found, *mutatis mutandis*, in other societies which do not undergo revolutions, and thus represent *ex post facto* rationalisations incapable of empirical testing.[1348] No more testable, of course, is the rival (but in my view more reasonable) assumption: that the Porfirian development strategy would have soldiered on, contradictions and all, had it not been for the avoidable political crisis of 1909–10. But to say that the Porfirian economy – which bears comparisons with other, 'contradiction'-ridden economies which did not experience revolutionary collapse – could have survived, is not to ignore the constraints on development locked within it. Societies can and do remain broadly stable over long periods despite constraints and contradictions.

The Porfirian strategy, we have noted, resembled that attempted by 'conservative modernising' regimes, analysed by Barrington Moore.[1349] They sought the benefits of economic (especially industrial) development, they embarked on programmes of political centralisation, but tried to avoid the concomitant social and political costs. Thus, Díaz and the Científicos strove to maintain the social hierarchy, above all to the advantage of the landlord class, while encouraging a rapid, traumatic form of economic development. This incurred both great, popular, rural resentment, and also more articulate, political protest on the part of the urban middle class, evidenced in Maderismo – a protest directed against Porfirian political failings rather than economic oppression and, perhaps, characteristic of 'modernising autocracies'.[1350] For, on the political front, Díaz maintained a personal dictatorship and narrow, local oligarchies clung to power, despite the growing inadequacy of such a system in an era of development and urbanisation. Even the Científicos, in their 1892 programme, realised that their economic strategy could be better served by a more flexible, institutionalised, 'modern' political structure; but Díaz would have none of it and the politics of *caciquismo* persisted. Apart from provoking opposition and ultimately revolution, such a system bred political incompetence, corruption and stagnation. Local caciques were unresponsive to the needs of growing urban communities; they neglected public order, hygiene and education; they feathered their own and their clients' nests to the detriment of other groups, including the professional and commercial classes.[1351] Entrenched oligarchies acted similarly at state level, monopolising power and freezing out competitors, thus ensuring a profitable, but inefficient, allocation of resources. The petrification of politics thus hampered development by provoking dissent, and by generalising inefficiency through the economic system, dynamic and expanding though it was. Economically progressive oligarchs, like Terrazas, still governed by means of a narrow, unrepresentative coterie of caciques.

One of the main achievements of the Revolution was the break-up of these entrenched political monopolies and their replacement by a younger, more dynamic, shifting elite which angled for some kind of 'mass' support, and which, though it created its own brand of revolutionary oligarchies, did not reproduce the narrow, mutually reinforcing political and economic monopolies characteristic of the Porfiriato. 'Sufragio Efectivo' was thus translated into a crude, illiberal form of representation; and, yet more clearly, 'No Reelección' gave the post-revolutionary polity greater flexibility and capacity for change and co-option. Favours, graft and *compadrazgo* still pervaded politics; but there was now a wider distribution of rewards, a more meritocratic system of recruitment, and a faster circulation of elites.[1352] This accorded with the *laissez-faire* economic philosophy of government and probably promoted economic efficiency and innovation; it certainly enhanced the stability of the regime, which was itself a *sine qua non* of economic development. But the crack-up of the Porfirian system implied more than just this release of new elites into business and politics. Porfirian development strategy – the Porfirian 'revolution from above' – was also flawed by major socio-economic 'contradictions', which the Porfirians were reluctant to correct: the survival, in some regions the reinvigoration, of the traditional hacienda and landlord class; of a semi-servile peonage; and of what Moore terms a 'labour-repressive' agricultural system. This in turn constricted the domestic market and thus the expansion of industry.[1353]

The Porfirians themselves, aware of agriculture's problems, conceived of solutions in narrow, technical terms, shrinking from the major surgery which the condition required, but which would have cut deep into oligarchic privilege. The revolutionaries were less inhibited; but it would be quite wrong to see the Revolution's assault on traditional landholding as some coherent blueprint. Like so much of the Revolution, it developed piecemeal, with its protagonists largely unaware of the long-term change they were initiating. The 'traditional' hacienda, particularly the central Mexican estate which catered to the domestic market, pampered by low taxes, a high tariff, cheap wages and thus easy profits, now faced a dual threat: from the entrepreneurial northern caudillos, who advocated and practised a form of dynamic, capitalist agriculture; and from peasant *agraristas*, who sought to recover or acquire land and break the hacienda's monopoly of land and labour.[1354] These were unlikely allies: Alvarado inveighed against the inertia of traditional landlords, but he had no time, either, for the kind of corporate property which peasant communities often desired.[1355] Popular *agrarismo*, however, was strong enough to establish the principle upon the national agenda, where it would be debated, championed and resisted for decades to come. The subsequent dualism of Mexican agriculture – its division into a profitable, capitalist, and a subsistence, *ejidal*, sector – thus dated back to this historic compromise. And the 'traditional' hacienda, though it fought a long rearguard action, was irreparably weakened: landlords had lost prestige, access to political power, and control over the peasantry; they now faced *agrarista* demands, incipient unionisation and the rabble-rousing of opportunist 'revolutionary' politicians.[1356] Against such threats, the best defence was often prudent, pre-emptive change: unilateral land reform (which could sometimes be achieved without damaging profitability) and a switch from 'traditional' methods (i.e., under-capitalised, labour-intensive, inefficient production) to more productive, land- and capital-intensive cultivation.[1357]

Meanwhile, the more extreme forms of peonage, which especially characterised the plantations of the south, also came under attack, more so from northern reformers than indigenous popular movements. Alvarado's boast that he had liberated the peons of Yucatán was partly justified; and those pockets of 'barbarous Mexico' which, like Catmis, survived his proconsulship were tackled by his radical successor, Carrillo Puerto, in the early 1920s.[1358] By then, the system of debt peonage and *enganche* – the subject of first Maderista, then Carrancista reforms – was also under severe attack in Chiapas, particularly in the coffee zone.[1359] Gradually, benighted southern Mexico was conforming to the northern, free wage labour model. And, from the proconsuls onwards, such 'liberal' policies obeyed political as well as social or economic ends: they offered a means to weaken the provincially jealous landed elite, to curtail their 'paternalist' control of the rural masses, and to bind the latter to the revolutionary state. 'To nationalise this state', Alvarado advised Carranza, 'the only method is to organise these Indians, creating for them real interests which they owe to the Revolution.'[1360]

A variety of conflicting motives and pressures thus determined agrarian development after the Revolution. There was no single blueprint, or 'project'; above all, the political elite was repeatedly pushed towards more radical, structural reform by the pressure of popular *agrarismo*. But, as is well known, the outcome proved to be peculiarly conducive, over time, to political stability and rapid, capitalist economic growth. Landlords were compelled to invest and modernise (some also quit agriculture and joined the ranks of the new industrial entrepreneurs).[1361] The dual agrarian system eventually met domestic needs and became a major exporter, thus reversing the chronic shortages of the late Porfiriato. Lower food prices, contrasting with the serious inflation of the 1900s, cut industry's labour costs; while increases in peasant consumption expanded the domestic market. These were long-term changes, spanning almost a generation. Their precise character, and the theoretical terms which should be used to describe them, are the subject of extensive debate.[1362] But it cannot be doubted that the unique agrarian transformation undergone in Mexico made possible both the successful institutionalisation of the Revolution, and the successful pursuit of vigorous, capitalist development. The revolutionaries were able to overcome the obstacles – above all the agrarian obstacles – which had constrained Porfirian growth; they were thus able to carry through a 'revolution from above' which did not, as in Barrington Moore's scenario, degenerate into chauvinism and fascism.[1363] It is in this respect that they may be seen as the more successful cousins of the Kuomintang, who similarly developed from an earlier, civilian liberalism, acquired a militant, nationalist ideology and a mass base, defeated (partly by incorporating) warlordism, and established a powerful, centralising, partially corrupt regime. The key difference, as this comparison suggests, was the sustained, successful, popular mobilisation which the Mexican Revolution initiated, and which was periodically renewed, especially during the Cárdenas years. For all its graft, repression and inegalitarianism, the regime had always to accommodate popular demands to a certain extent; it did not go the way of *comprador* corruption and fascism, nor did it leave too large a vacuum on the left for communism to enter in. Paradoxically, the 'project of the national bourgeoisie' flourished not least because of the strength of the popular movement; because the revolutionary elite, while actively pursuing some elements of that 'project', were also driven, perforce, to pursue others by factors beyond their control – by the 'logic of the Revolution'. The Revolution certainly brought benefits to the emergent national bourgeoisie; but, like so many of the Revolution's gifts, these were bestowed capriciously, contradictorily, upon groups who had scarcely earned them by their purposive contribution to the Revolution.

WHAT CHANGED?

A final pause for reflection – roughly from the vantage point of the mid-1920s – confirms a point already made: informal social change, unplanned and unlegislated, was more significant than formal change – discussed, codified, sometimes implemented. Now, of course, official policy and rhetoric hastened to catch up with unofficial practice: the classic case was *agrarismo*. But, as in the past, a great breach still separated constitutional theory and practice; the artificial democracy of the Porfiriato gave way to the artificial social democracy of the Sonorans. The formally liberal polity established in 1917 was characterised by rigged or violent elections, *caciquismo* and *pistolerismo*, sporadic military revolt and political assassination; ultimately, these evils were curbed at the price of bureaucratisation and corporatisation. The 'social' policies of 1917 were only gradually, haltingly, sometimes grudgingly and often cynically implemented. For eleven years, while the CROM dominated organised labour and enjoyed intimate relations with the regime, no enabling legislation translated Article 123 from a pious wish into a practical benefit for the workers. Specific favours were conferred – in the arbitration of industrial disputes, for example – but in return for industrial docility and political support; the 1920s thus saw a decline in working-class militancy, and an increasing conservatism on the part of the leadership, typified by Morones. [1364] The same was true of agrarian reform. Negligible under Carranza, land distribution accelerated under Obregón and Calles. But it served the political interests of the state (not least in its conflict with the Church) and by the end of the decade – with the Cristero rebellion defeated – Callista conservatism prevailed, the programme was declared complete, and land grants tailed off. [1365] The effects were still highly significant: in some states – Morelos, San Luis – distribution decisively affected rural social relations; elsewhere, though reform was patchy, it offered a threat to landlords and an incentive to *agraristas*, forcing the former to resist (or to attempt pre-emptive reform), encouraging the latter to mobilise and campaign. The precedents, too, were crucial. The Porfirian trend towards land concentration was reversed (this was one area of policy where discontinuity prevailed, and 1910 marked a real break) and, in the changed circumstances of the 1930s, when the Porfirian/Sonoran model of *desarrollo hacia afuera* (export-led development) broke down, agrarian reform became a key feature of the new, Cardenista model of development, in a manner unique to Mexico.

In addition, the economic nationalist provisions of the Constitution lay fallow. Protracted wrangles with the oil companies did not affect the basic character of Mexico's relations with foreign capitalism. Under the Sonorans, the country remained an exporter of primary goods and a major recipient of foreign investment – an outcome not at all surprising in view of the regime's pedigree and ethos. Again, radical new departures had to await the decade of depression.[1366] Meanwhile, the regime's boldest initiatives and greatest efforts were evident in the conflict with the Church – in which it gained a Pyrrhic victory – and, to a lesser extent, in the related field of education. And its greatest success lay in the fact that it survived, weathering recurrent army revolts, and achieved a gradual institutionalisation and demilitarisation of revolutionary politics. For over a decade, therefore, the formal policies of the regime were cautious, even conservative, still harping on the theme of reconstruction and stability. The Sonorans sought to establish a strong, stable government; to promote economic development, along conventional, capitalist lines; and to achieve a degree of social equilibrium, based on limited, guided political participation and pragmatic, even opportunist, social reforms, which implied no grand restructuring of society. Within these, their own terms of reference, they were strikingly successful – and faithful to their basic philosophy. Talk of 'betrayal' is normative nonsense.

But, in surveying the record of 1910–30, it is only natural to register a certain surprise that the towering revolutionary mountain of the 1910s strained to bring forth the political mouse of the 1920s. In part, this is a 'modern' reaction to the last of the Tocquevillean revolutions, which, like its French predecessor, displayed major continuities with the old regime. But, even more, it is an exaggerated reaction, distorted by a certain one-dimensional perspective. Historians who point to the paucity of reform in the 1920s and the conservatism of the regime are right. But this, the old revisionism turned orthodoxy, easily slides into 'statolatry': 'when all is said and done', one recent study concludes, 'all the complexities of the Mexican Revolution can be reduced to this one dimension: the state'.[1367] This is convenient, since the state is the best-reported actor in the political process; but it is misleading, since it neglects those vast areas of ocean where Leviathan did not swim. Formal policies – the doings of the state and political elite – were not co-terminous with social reality, and things often changed (or refused to change) in defiance of governmental wishes. The regime found itself accepting change *faute de mieux*, or battling vainly against inexorable change, or, if it was smart, legitimating change in the name of the Revolution and thus getting the credit. And in many cases these changes were more important, for the subsequent development of Mexico, than the halting, ambivalent reforms of government.

Major wars have been the midwives of change in the twentieth century.[1368] In Mexico's case, the war was civil, not international, but, by virtue of its 'totality', it had comparable, far-reaching, but unplanned consequences. First, the Porfirian political elite was replaced by a new revolutionary elite that was younger and more plebeian. 'The government is much darker than it was 20 years ago', Anita Brenner reckoned; 'in the whirlwind of the Revolution', some said, 'the dirt came up'.[1369] But over time, the criteria for advancement – initially military prowess, popular appeal, youth and *machismo* – necessarily changed, as warfare gave way to political stabilisation and economic reconstruction. The old criteria were no longer functional to the increasingly civilian, urban, bureaucratic society of post-revolutionary Mexico, and more appropriate criteria evolved (or were revived): wealth, education, technical and administrative expertise. Popular rebels were rarely endowed with such attributes. When a new judge was needed for the Federal court in Durango in 1915, a candidate had to be brought from Jalisco since no lawyer 'adicto a la revolución' could be found within the state.[1370] Hence, as Gutiérrez found in his electoral battle with Espinosa Mireles, the homespun heroes were likely to be passed over.[1371] Increasingly, the political elite was drawn from the university-educated, cosmopolitan, professional classes, most of them lacking individual or family claims to revolutionary status, some of them deriving from old pre-revolutionary, elite families – like the Guilléns, Añorves, and Neris of Guerrero.[1372] The transition evident in Morelos after 1940 had also occurred elsewhere in the country, often by an earlier date: 'only here and there was a veteran of the great ordeal still active, working a little through the week and then on Sunday taking buses around to see old comrades and gather signatures for a local petition. The new officials were young men, often graduates of the National University. Increasingly, they were earnest, aware, energetic and anxious . . . to keep the system functioning smoothly.'[1373] *A fortiori*, the post-revolutionary entrepreneurs, who were to play a growing part in Mexico's development, emerged from well-to-do backgrounds – often apolitical, sometimes Porfirian, less often revolutionary – and they did so because they possessed skills, attitudes (and sometimes capital) which survived the Revolution and stood them in good stead thereafter. The classic case were the Creel–Terrazas: stripped of most of their lands, and debarred from politics, they nevertheless received handsome financial compensation from the Obregón administration, which enabled them to develop their industrial interests (brewing and milling) and later return to cattle-raising. Many lesser Chihuahuan Porfiristas made a similar comeback, some into politics as well as business.[1374]

While the political elite certainly underwent change, therefore, it does not seem legitimate to talk of a new, revolutionary bourgeoisie supplanting the old, at least as regard personnel. At best, there was a syncretisation of old and new, not least through marriage. But more profound changes ensured that this hybrid elite–bourgeoisie would not comport itself like its Porfirian predecessor. The country had changed, and its rulers had to change with it; this change in attitude and behaviour – intangible and unlegislated – was of much greater consequence than any shift in personnel. There was abundant ('impressionistic') evidence that old habits of popular deference and passivity had declined. In a sense, this is all too obvious: the host of popular movements which populated the revolution by their very nature and conduct exemplified a rejection of Porfirian authority. In many regions landlords, caciques and officials had been forced to flee, had been killed or subjected to humiliation. In their place, plebeian popular *cabecillas* had seized power – men to be reckoned with while alive, and who, even after death (and their mortality was fearfully high), were invested with mythic significance. Thus, Zapata supposedly lived on (he was even said to be fighting alongside Hitler twenty years later); and lesser leaders, like Michoacán's Primo Tapia, acquired similar, charismatic appeal.[1375] Even though by the later 1910s the tide turned against the popular movement, and new dykes were built to contain its ebbing power; even though popular leaders were increasingly superseded by the literate *políticos* of the institutionalised revolution; nevertheless, observers realised that a qualitative change had taken place, and that the temper of the people – the Mexican *mentalité* we might say – had altered, and that new structures of power were demanded precisely because of that alteration.

In San José de Gracia, for example, (a solid, conservative community, only partially, belatedly disrupted by revolutionary violence), the old mores changed. The 'generation of the volcano', those who had come of age during the Revolution, seemed wild, footloose and violent, fond of displaying a swaggering *machismo*, which involved much drinking and brawling.[1376] In addition, the crime rate rose; and 'the wall of respect between bosses and workers increasingly crumbled'. So, too, at Tepoztlán, in the heart of Zapatista Morelos, the Revolution brought a new egalitarianism and an erosion of class and status differences. Men no longer 'knew their place' with deferential precision; even the old norms of dress (*huaraches* and white drawers for the peons, suits and shoes for the *gente de razón*) began to decline; in general, 'the revolution had a levelling influence, economically, socially and culturally'.[1377] This was particularly significant in areas of *agrarista* mobilisation, like Morelos. The hacienda might survive as a territorial unit, nibbled at by the official agrarian reform, but the *hacendado* could no longer rely upon his old patronal power and political contacts. In parts of Tlaxcala 'the hacienda system . . . had . . . irrevocably lost prestige and part of its control over large groups of peasants'; in San Luis, too, the *modus operandi* had to change, even if the estate survived.[1378] The agrarian protests of the revolutionary period may have been contained, as at Naranja, but this did not mean a return to the Pax Porfiriana. Protest went underground, and resurfaced, often in a new organisational guise, in the course of the 1920s. This was the case at Naranja, as well as at the Providencia Hacienda (Mexico) where, after a Zapatista outbreak in 1912, the community 'returned briefly to an uneasy tranquillity, yet agrarian unrest had begun its insidious spread. It was the signal for the gradual extinction of the hacienda.'[1379]

As a result, the Revolution left a legacy of rural violence and confrontation. Violence, to which men had become habituated between 1910 and 1920, was as much part of the system as corruption. Landlords armed hirelings, and *agraristas* resisted: in Michoacán and Hidalgo, on the Isthmus and in the

Laguna.[1380] Even in (relatively) quiet Yucatán, around 1920, city people talked apprehensively of the possibility of another Caste War: they exaggerated, but they were right to the extent that 'low-level factional *cacique* violence' remained a staple feature of rural politics for the next twenty years.[1381] And in (relatively) quiet Chiapas, too, the Revolution ushered in a 'vastly different', class-based politics, characterised by mass mobilisation, the breakdown of old social controls and the 'polarisation of *indios* versus *ladinos*, the landless versus the landed, the workers versus capitalists'.[1382] The transition from a caste-based, 'estamental' to a class society was hurried along, to the accompaniment of much violence. Landlords, thrown onto the defensive, were often responsible for the latter (to which end they could sometimes recruit 'revolutionary' *condottieri* to do their dirty work); but their *agrarista* enemies were no strangers to violence. Since the days of Díaz, popular quiescence had declined, and there were plenty of fire-arms stashed away, ready to be brought out of hiding when required.[1383] Foreigners (some of whom, like Rosalie Evans, were direct victims) were appalled at this fall from grace. The murder of two Britons near Puerto México (not, it seems, a political act) showed, the British Minister lamented, 'the deplorable extent to which the prestige of the white man had been allowed to sink during the past few years'; now (1917), the 'white man' had become 'the scorn and laughing stock of a vast number of Indians'; for an 'event of this kind would have been inconceivable in Mexico five years ago'.[1384]

Beneath the obvious, surface violence of recurrent, attempted rebellions (1923, 1927, 1929), and alongside the major campaigns of the Cristero War (1926–9), there flowed a deep undercurrent of local, agrarian violence, which some feared might rear up into another wave of revolutionary proportions.[1385] This did not occur – weariness, co-option, reform and repression all told against it – but the regime tolerated and even encouraged a degree of limited, organised violence. It armed the *agraristas* against the Cristeros and rebellious generals; it was also prepared to countenance the selective use of violence in pursuit of agrarian claims; hence, even as peasant mobilisation proceeded along 'orthodox' party, union and pressure group lines, the resort to violence was never far away and was sometimes efficacious.[1386] While the outraged British Minister, drawing upon his African past, longed to launch a punitive expedition against the killers of the two Britons, the revolutionary leaders, drawing on their past, took a more relaxed view of violence, so long as it did not challenge the government's position. They were as aware as any of the 'rebellious spirit' of the Mexican people – which was evident in urban riot and protest, as well as rural confrontation – but they sought to curb it by more subtle means than punitive expeditions (which were reserved for incorrigibles like the Yaquis).[1387] Thus, the new politics – however shocking to 'legalistic minds deeply steeped in the proprieties of parliamentary procedure' – demanded a demotic style: *políticos* could no longer afford the hauteur of their

Porfirian and Maderista predecessors; it now helped to mix with the common man, dress casually, and display a certain plebeian camaraderie.[1388] Obregón, who claimed to like talking about nothing better than the diseases of horses, was a past master of this populist style. He dressed sloppily, stressed his poor origins and larded his prolific speeches with jokes and generous tributes to the common man. And it worked: people accosted him and greeted him in the street; on the stump he showed the same rapport with 'the women of the street, with the working men he meets, and with the peasants in the country'.[1389] While this was not necessarily phoney, it was certainly prudential. Obregón hoped for a 'constant, calm effort' that would 'orient' the masses, and avert further upheavals.[1390] This involved not only individual glad-handing, but also systematic tuition: through education (especially Vasconcelos' new rural schools), through party and union organisations, through the manipulation of popular symbols (e.g., Carillo Puerto's appropriation of the cross for the Yucatecan *ligas*), and through the burgeoning industry of *indigenismo*.[1391] These are major themes which cannot be developed here. But their post-revolutionary prominence indicates official awareness of popular effervescence, which was better channeled than suppressed.

But the social change wrought by the Revolution went beyond this. The ruined haciendas which now dotted the landscape were paralleled by ruined churches, many of which, if Tepoztlán is anything to go by, were never rebuilt.[1392] Here, as in Naranja, church-going and religious fiestas appear to have declined with the Revolution – which no doubt pleased Mexico's new rulers, and perhaps persuaded them that the Catholic Church itself was ready for demolition (they erred by confusing institutional decline, which possibly occurred, with decline in belief, which did not).[1393] Sexual mores also changed, as they are wont to in wartime. Families were broken up; elope-ments, abductions and free unions became more common.[1394] The higher male mortality also had a significant effect on sex ratios, though the conse-quences are, to my knowledge, unresearched.[1395] And, while the lurid fantasies of the high-minded may not be taken literally, it cannot be doubted that venereal disease flourished along with others, as armies tramped across the country and prostitution – Puritanical efforts notwithstanding – became more blatant and uncontrolled.[1396] The wave of crime, too, which observers noted in 1915–18, was more than a passing phenomenon. Apart from the 'soaring rate of political homicides' suffered in some parts, common killings, personal attacks and robberies appear to have increased, and confronted travellers *seriatim*.[1397]

Such changes – like the net increase in graft and corruption which was alleged – are not easily measured.[1398] Geographical mobility, another major consequence of revolution, is more straightforward. Throughout the country, war, disease and economic upheaval uprooted populations. The movement of armies is obvious enough: we have noted the presence of northerners in the south and southerners in the north; and have mapped the peripatetic careers of leaders who must almost have equalled Obregón's own '8,000 kilometres on campaign'. But a multitude of civilians was on the move too. The upheaval in Morelos drove people from the villages to the mountains (in Michoacán banditry had the reverse effect, sending the people of the sierra down to lakeside communities like Huecorio); and, as times grew harder, Morelenses migrated to Guerrero or Mexico City.[1399] National statistics, including the notorious 1921 census, do not suggest a dramatic rise in spatial mobility but, given the unreliability of such statistics, they need not override the abundant evidence of local demographic shifts.[1400] Already declining communities, like Guanajuato and Zacatecas, were further depopulated by the Revolution; smaller towns, like Ocosingo (Chis.), Pineda's headquarters, were half-destroyed; Paracho (Mich.) 'was razed to the ground; its people scattered to the four winds'.[1401] There was unprecedented migration from the neighbouring ranches to San José, in the same state, and also from San José to the city; at Naranja, around 10% of the men died or emigrated.[1402] There were corresponding gains for some communities. While the nation's population (supposedly) fell by some 7% between 1910 and 1921, that of the Federal District rose by a quarter. The north-west experienced a more modest growth, as did several of the northern border ports: the municipality of Juárez grew from some 10,000 to over 24,000, thanks in part to 'the immigration from other places [in Mexico] which the revolutionary upheaval has scattered throughout the country'.[1403]

Juárez, of course, was a major port of transit to the US during years when the 'push' factors making for emigration – war, unemployment, hunger – were complemented, between 1914 and 1917, by the 'pull' of America's war-induced boom.[1404] As early as 1911, some 2,000 migrants were crossing per month to El Paso; by late 1916, though the official figure was roughly constant, unofficial emigration was reckoned to be twice as high; about half as many were passing through Nogales.[1405] All told, over 170,000 Mexicans legally entered the US between 1910 and 1919, but even a modest allowance for illegal migrants would push the figure well over a quarter of a million.[1406] A few, victims of revolutionary persecution, came with capital or commercial expertise; but the majority were poor, even destitute; their 'personal histories [had] been blown away and obliterated by five years of demoralizing and destructive warfare'. Many, the same El Paso observer noted, 'have wandered or been driven from town to town, often far from their homes'.[1407] Certainly, while many migrants were *norteños*, many others came from further south, particularly from the Bajío, whose pre-revolutionary tradition of out-migration was accentuated by events after 1910.[1408] Even small, rustic communities like San José, Naranja and Cherán produced significant numbers of *braceros*.[1409]

More conjectural, but more interesting, are the effects of such migration.

The happy assumption that travel broadened the mind and fostered national sentiments is surely too glib; it overlooks the fact that, as popular memory recalls, this was a time of tribulation, when food was scarce, families were split up, and disease was rampant.[1410] No doubt, in literate, elite circles, the experience of the Revolution enhanced an existing nationalism: 'avoir fait de grandes choses ensemble, vouloir en faire encore', Renan's definition of national sentiment, fitted well enough the pride felt by intellectuals like Pani, as Mexico's reforms became a model for the developed world; or as Mexico stood up to American pressure.[1411] But the masses, as Pani recognised, thought differently. Mass nationalism, of the kind exemplified in 1938 (with the oil expropriation) or 1970 (the World Cup), required a long process of education and propaganda, which came after rather than during the (armed) Revolution. But if spatial mobility did not necessarily generate nationalism, it certainly heightened contacts between city and countryside (evident at Tepoztlán); it broke down the isolation of rural communities (the Popoluca Indians of Veracruz were caught up in the Revolution, were forced to migrate and resettle; they served in the army, they learned Spanish); and, in more diffuse fashion, it changed attitudes to work, religion, sex.[1412] The migrants who left Paracho for America came back imbued with 'a spirit of order and enterprise', and began to compare Paracho's bad plumbing and lack of electricity with what they had witnessed north of the border.[1413] Cherán's *bracero* contingent formed the basis for the town's anti-clerical faction.[1414] Such attitudes were developed – rather than created *de novo* – by the experience of migration. But migration was only one of several factors which, neatly complementing official ideology, encouraged innovation, economic change, and social as well as spatial mobility.

People had to try new ways to make a living. At Tepoztlán they turned to charcoal-burning or, among the more entrepreneurial, cattle-dealing.[1415] The people of Milpa Alta left their cornfields for the capital, where they sold firewood and tortillas, worked as domestic servants, or engaged in petty trade.[1416] The Revolution, indeed, generated a whole range of 'peripheral money-making activities', such as the trade in jewels and other family heirlooms, whose very existence was proof of upward and downward mobility.[1417] In 1915, destitute professionals could be seen peddling goods in the Mexico City markets; in 1916, it was noted, there was a plethora of ex-domestic servants, released from once well-to-do households which could no longer keep up appearances.[1418] The exigencies of life during the Revolution thus fostered a range of new activities, making for both economic diversification and – in cases where subsistence gave way to market production – for specialisation.[1419] But the upheaval also placed a premium on energy and initiative, while simultaneously weakening the barriers of tradition, deference and ascription. Neither landlord nor village community could so easily inhibit the behaviour of the economically adventurous; the Revolution 'disposed the individual to mobility and experiment', as Gamio put it.[1420] Again, the revolutionary armies and their leaders set the example. Pharmacists, *rancheros*, and railwaymen became generals and governors, who combined political with economic self-advancement. The new elite, Blasco Ibáñez noted, contained few Quixotic idealists but plenty of 'men of hard, practical vision, who never lost sight of personal profit'.[1421] And; below — soon to be alongside — the generals were the revolutionary civilians and bureaucrats (some of whom bore military rank), to whom the future belonged: labour leaders like Morones, intellectuals like Vasconcelos and Lombardo Toledano (for whom education would afford a ladder to power), neo-Científico technocrats like Pani and Gómez Morín, as yet obscure administrators, like the future presidents Ruiz Cortines and Avila Camacho.[1422] The revolution jolted them, too, out of accustomed careers: the Lombardo Toledano family business was crippled by the currency and banking crises; most of the Gómez Morín family fortune went up in smoke during a Villista attack on Parral.[1423] Middle-class intellectuals of this type, meanwhile, were brought into contact — uncomfortable contact, as Vasconcelos and Guzmán discovered — with 'the other Mexicans'; they discovered the Indian and the agrarian question, and began to ponder how to uplift the first and solve the second.[1424]

Change, discovery and innovation were not confined to the revolutionary elite, however. Similar forces acted, often more cogently, on Porfirian families. Stripped of their wealth in many cases, debarred from politics in yet more, they were obliged to explore new avenues of advancement, where their education and expertises would still count. Some found a niche — revolutionaries complained — in Ministries like Hacienda; they have been seen as playing an important role in the emergent state bureaucracy of the 1920s.[1425] Others entered business (the Terracista recovery in Chihuahua was a classic instance) but they could not always achieve Terrazas' continuity of interests. Rather, they switched careers, most frequently from land to commerce and industry; hence they may be compared — as examples of forced economic diversification and innovation — with the Samurai of Meiji Japan, or even Pirenne's medieval *deracinés*.[1426] And this reassertion of old privilege was not confined to oligarchic families. At Tepoztlán, it was the sons of the old caciques who proved most ruthless in the exploitation of the community's timber reserves.[1427]

Lower down, too, the upheaval called forth new talents and prompted new initiatives. Off the Guerrero coast people now fished by hurling dynamite bombs into the water; in Morelos, we have noted, villagers turned to charcoal-burning and cattle-dealing (the first, initially, as an economic lifeline, the second as a source of profit); in Hidalgo's Sierra Alta the Revolution coincided with a shift from sugar to the new cashcrop, coffee, on which minor fortunes were built.[1428] It was borne in on people that society was in flux, that survival demanded struggle, but that by dint of hard work, luck and an eye for the main chance, fat pickings were to be had. The 'limited good' was perhaps no longer so limited.[1429] In this respect, the work ethic preached by Constitutionalist ideologues chimed in with reality and the example of their energetic, grafting, profiteering masters was not lost on the mass of the people. At Tepoztlán, wealth was amassed 'through hard work, thrift and self-denial', particularly in the cattle trade, in which 'only those with courage, initiative and a little capital' participated.[1430] So, too, at Paracho, the old handicrafts declined, newcomers settled and new businesses were started; returning *braceros*, including the town cacique, displayed their 'spirit of order and enterprise'.[1431] Some citizens, over time, internalised the philosophy of their masters: initiative and profit redounded to national, collective benefit; 'if an individual progresses, Mexico progresses'.[1432] Of course, the Revolution alone was not responsible for these subliminal shifts in attitude. But it decisively accelerated pre-revolutionary changes; it demolished barriers which inhibited such developments under Díaz; and it installed a government dedicated to these competitive, market values. Finally, the very devastation which it visited upon the country supplied fresh incentives to work, innovate, 'progress'. The psychology of 'reconstruction' filtered down to the lowest levels. When the new municipal president, Colonel Jesús Montoya, took office at Azteca (Mor.) in 1920, he gave guarantees to the local Zapatistas, who therefore 'believed in Montoya and went to work to improve things'; the village was cleaned up and Montoya threw open the *monte* for the villagers to exploit. 'The forest is yours', he said, 'Go on and make charcoal . . . get to work. Enough is enough! Forget the Revolution. What's done is done! Whoever is dead, is dead. Those that are left, are left! So, go on, get to work. Make charcoal and go and sell it.'[1433] It was a distillation of the current ethos: realism plus reconstruction. And the villagers responded: 'we got to work in earnest . . . The whole village became charcoal burners. We practically cut down the forests . . . .' Thus, as in other devastated, post-war societies, the ashes of destruction sprouted a collective will to rebuild, and individual opportunities to get on and prosper.[1434] These were not least among the social consequences of the Revolution.

Here, too, was a final example of the Revolution's capricious logic. Change came willy-nilly, unplanned and unforeseen, especially by the main protagonists. Madero (and I am using individuals as surrogates for social movements) had anticipated political reforms, not runaway popular rebellion; Huerta and Félix Díaz had sought, not a fierce intensification, but a quick suppression of revolutionary troubles. Popular leaders – Villa, Zapata and many others – captained parochial movements, *agrarista* and *serrano*, which found themselves acquiring strange ideological baggage, alien fellow-travellers, and responsibilities far beyond what they were able or willing to assume. Carranza and the Sonorans entered the fray fighting for local self-preservation, and were before long governing the south, signing deals with the labour unions and negotiating with the American government and the oil companies. No leaders planned – though many indirectly contributed to – the collapse of the currency, economic breakdown and the erosion of old patterns of authority and behaviour. The Constitutionalists, by virtue of winning the war of the winners, came closest to imposing their vision on the country (a Villista Mexico would have looked significantly different). But, even as the popular movement declined, and power passed to the shrewd, opportunist, grafting generals of the north, to their semi-mercenary forces, and to their increasingly prominent civilian adjutants, still this new elite confronted serious problems and narrow options. Economically, they looked to a revived capitalism, a renewal of the Porfirian model; and, though they probably did not know it and certainly had not planned it, circumstances had conspired to make such a model more viable than in the days of Díaz and the Científicos. Politically, they had to balance a 'democratic', populist appeal with the traditions of authoritarian, centralised government, and the fear of autonomous, popular movements, which they shared with preceding regimes and which the Revolution had revived rather than stifled. The masses could not be ignored; but they could be integrated into a stronger, more stable state than Díaz's; and to this end the regime took up the demands, myths and symbols of the popular movement, and wove them together with its own developmentalist *étatisme*. Here lay the genius of the revolutionary leadership: its capacity to harness the energy and grievances of the popular movement to antithetical ends – state-building and capitalist development. It was the trick the KMT failed to turn in China, and it ensured the continuation of the 'revolution from above' by other means. As for the popular movement, which had made the Revolution a genuinely 'great' or 'social' revolution, it received, at best, official reform, linked to official corruption. The *serranos* could not throw off the state; indirectly, they served to reinforce it. The *agraristas* got land – but slowly, conditionally, at the hands of burgeoning bureaucracy. And the first begetters of the whole business – the Maderista civilians of 1909–10 who, from the vantage point of 1920, seem like the innocent children of a lost age – had to settle for a sham liberalism, in return for social stability and economic development: the historic surrender required by a 'revolution from above'.[1435] By way of conclusion, we may recall Sorel's comment on the early Christian revolution:[1436]

It must be admitted that the real developments of the Revolution did not in any way resemble the enchanting pictures which created the enthusiasm among its first adepts; but without those pictures would the Revolution have been victorious?.

Notes

1 The Huerta regime

1 Manuel Calero, *Un Decenio de política mexicana* (New York, 1920), p. 130; Mariano Azuela, *Two Novels of the Mexican Revolution: The Trials of a Respectable Family and The Underdogs* (San Antonio, 1963), p. 7; John Rutherford, *Mexican Society During the Revolution: A Literary Approach* (Oxford, 1971).

2 Friedrich Katz, *Deutschland, Díaz und die mexikanische revolution* (Berlin, 1964), and *The Secret War in Mexico: Europe, the United States and the Mexican Revolution* (Chicago, 1981); cf. the revisionist view, p. 94.

3 Stronge, Mexico City, 8 Mar. 1913, FO 371/1672, 13402; Haff to Wilson, 28 May 1913, SD 812.00/7746; *Mexican Herald*, 7 Apr. 1913.

4 Body to Cowdray, 22 Feb. 1913, Cowdray Papers, box A/4, which makes clear that the Cowdray interests, while welcoming Huerta, had done nothing to assist him.

5 Price, Cordoba, 20 Mar.; Hamm, Durango, 5, 19, Mar.; Miller, Tampico, 26 Feb. 1913; SD 812.00/6565; 6789, 6976; 6634; Wilson, Tampico, 22 Feb. 1913, FO 371/1671, 13165.

6 Mariano Azuela, *The Bosses*, in *Two Novels of Mexico, The Flies, the Bosses* (Berkeley, 1956), p. 167, describes how the 'respectable element' got drunk and put a hired claque on the streets to shout 'Viva Huerta!'.

7 'Enemies of the people', memo., STA, box 84; Ernest Gruening, *Mexico and its Heritage* (New York, 1938), p. 213, citing *El País*.

8 Hector R. Olea, *Breve historia de la revolución en Sinaloa* (Mexico, 1964), pp. 58–9.

9 Petition to Gobernación, 23 Apr. 1913, AG legajo 898.

10 E. Baca Calderón in DDCC, II, p. 985.

11 C/in/c US Pacific Fleet, Guaymas, 13 Mar. 1913, SD 812.00/6974.

12 Azuela, *The Bosses*, pp. 167–8.

13 Stronge, Mexico City, 8 Mar. 1913, FO 371/1672, 13402.

14 Graham, Durango, 9 Mar.; Cummins, Gómez Palacio, 6 Mar. 1913; FO 371/1671, 14519; Miller, Tampico, 27 Apr. 1913, SD 812.00/7402.

15 Note also the reaction in Torreón: Carothers, in *United States. Investigation of Mexican Affairs: Report of a Hearing before a Sub-Committee on Foreign Relations* (2 vols., Washington, 1919–20) (referred to as 'Fall Report'), p. 1764.

16 Bonney, San Luis, 28 Mar. 1913, SD 812.00/7041.

17 John Womack, *Zapata and the Mexican Revolution* (New York, 1970), p. 160; cf. Jean Meyer, *The Cristero Rebellion. The Mexican People between Church and State, 1926–29* (Cambridge, 1976), p. 11.

18 Price, Córdoba, 20 Mar.; Alger, Mazatlán, 28 Feb. 1913; SD 812.00/6565; 6616.

19 Michael C. Meyer, *Huerta. A Political Portrait* (Lincoln, 1972), p. 69.

20 Stronge, Mexico City, 8 Mar. 1913, FO 371/1672, 13402.

21 Meyer, *Huerta*, pp. 66–7.

22 Womack, *Zapata*, pp. 161–2; Alfonso Francisco Ramírez, *Historia de la revolución en Oaxaca* (Mexico, 1970), pp. 134–5.

23 Edwards, Acapulco, 28 Apr., c/o USS Glacier, Acapulco, 5 May 1913; SD 812.00/7310, 7841; Fabela, DHRM, RRC, IV, p. 52.

24 Edwards, Juárez, 6, 7, Mar.; Hamm, Durango, 5 Mar. 1913; SD 812.00/6499, 6613, 6789.

25 Bonney, San Luis, 4 Mar. 1913, SD 812.00/6736.

26 Schmutz, Aguascalientes, 9 May; Hamm, Durango, 13 June 1913; SD 812.00/7655, 7720.

27 Stronge, Mexico City, 8 Mar. 1913, FO 371/1672, 13402.

28 Womack, *Zapata*, p. 161; Ramírez, *Oaxaca*, p. 135.

29 John Reed, *Insurgent Mexico* (New York, 1969), p. 82. Such phenomena became even commoner after 1914.

30 See vol. I, pp. 302–3.

31 Womack, *Zapata*, p. 162; Michael C. Meyer, *Mexican Rebel: Pascual Orozco and the Mexican Revolution* (Lincoln, 1967), pp. 97–8.

32 Ramírez, *Oaxaca*, pp. 134–5.

33 Womack, *Zapata*, pp. 81, 161–2.

34 *Ibid.*, pp. 163–4.

35 Wilson, Mexico City, 1 Apr. 1913, SD 812.00/7101; cf. Calvert, p. 153.

36 Womack, *Zapata*, p. 226.

37 Cf. vol. I, p. 157–8.

38 See vol. I, pp. 297–300.

39 H. L. Swain, aboard USS Minnesota, 28 May 1913, SD 812.00/7757.

40 Diebold, El Paso consul, to SRE, 19 May 1914, SRE, legajo 789, 87-R-30.

41 Hamm, Durango, 3 June 1913, SD 812.00/7857; Carothers, Torreon, 19 Mar. 1913, SD 812.00/6997, describes Campos' force as 'bandits pure and simple' who 'respect no authority'.

42 Schmutz, Aguascalientes, 9 May; Edwards, Acapulco, 28 Apr.; c/o USS Glacier, Acapulco, 5 May 1913; SD 812.00/7655; 7310; 7841; AG legajo 871 suggests similar problems, in Zacatecas and Tamaulipas, for example: no's 1467, 1490; Letcher, Chihuahua, 29 July 1913, SD 812.00/8220 on the military consequences.

43 *Mexican Herald*, 23, 30 June 1913; and see Paul J. Vanderwood, *Disorder and Progress. Bandits, Police and Mexican Development* (Lincoln, 1981), p. 177.

44 Miller, Tampico, 25 May 1913, SD 812.00/7690.

45 Harvey, Tezonapa, 14 June; Barker, Paso del Cura, 11, 16 June 1913; SD 812.00/8005.

46 *El Imparcial*, 22 Mar. 1913, for the slogan.

47 Nemesio Garcia Naranjo, *Memorias*, Monterrey, n.d., vol. VII, pp. 19–21; Womack, *Zapata*, p. 109ff.

48 Meyer, *Huerta*, p. 89.

49 Thomas Beaumont Hohler, *Diplomatic Petrel*, London, 1942, p. 184.

50 Stanley R. Ross, 'Victoriano Huerta Visto por su Compadre', *Historia Mexicana*, XII (1962–3), p. 298.

51 Cepeda to Madero, 15 Feb. 1913, and similar correspondence in Fabela, DHRM, RRM, V, pp. 88–109.

52 Charles C. Cumberland, *Mexican Revolution. The Constitutionalist Years* (Austin, 1972), p. 16; Samuel de los Santos, DDCC, I, p. 571, alleged that Cepeda went beyond grudging submission.

53 Manuel Mestre Ghigliazzi to Pino Suárez, 8 May 1912, Fabela, DHRM, RRM, III, p. 336;

same to Gobernación, 22 Feb. 1913, along with similar communications from Puebla, Jalisco, San Luis, Veracruz and Colima, in Fabela, DHRM, RRC, IV, p. 51; and Lespinasse, Frontera, 8 Mar. 1913, SD 812.00/6922.

54 Cumberland, *Constitutionalist Years*, p. 43; Jesús Romero Flores, *Historia de la revolución en Michoacán* (Mexico, 1964), p. 70; Womack, *Zapata*, p. 160; Olea, *Sinaloa*, pp. 49–50; Santos in DDCC, I, p. 571.

55 Romero Flores, *Michoacán*, p. 70.

56 Womack, *Zapata*, p. 160.

57 William H. Beezley, *Insurgent Governor: Abraham Gonzalez and the Mexican Revolution in Chihuahua* (Lincoln, 1973), pp. 155–8.

58 C/o HMS Sirius, Veracruz, 1 Mar. 1913, FO 371/1671, 13260.

59 Benjamin, p. 131.

60 Toribio Esquivel Obregón, *México y los Estados Unidos ante el derecho internacional*, Mexico, 1926, pp. 36–7, 98–101.

61 Calero, *Un decenio*, p. 128.

62 Womack, *Zapata*, pp. 160, 163; Olea, *Sinaloa*, pp. 15–16, 53.

63 Pedro López in DDCC, I, p. 317.

64 Though these existed: note the pressure on Carranza and Pesqueira to submit to Huerta, pp. 15–16.

65 Dye, Bisbee, 15 Mar.; Simpich, Nogales, 31 Mar. 1913; SD 812.00/6806, 7020.

66 Alfonso Taracena, *Venustiano Carranza* (Mexico, 1963), p. 195, citing Breceda.

67 Arnaldo Córdova, *La ideología de la revolución mexicana. La formacion del nuevo régimen* (Mexico, 1973), pp. 136, 191–4.

68 Alvaro Obregón, *Ocho mil kilómetros en campaña* (intro., F. Grajales, Mexico, 1966), p. 124.

69 *Ibid.*, pp. 35–6; Héctor Aguilar, *La Revolución Sonorense, 1910–14* (Mexico, INAH, 1975), pp. 306, 331; Alvarado to Carranza, 16 Nov. 1913, Fabela, DHRM, RRC, I, p. 14.

70 Aguilar, *Revolución Sonorense*, p. 331.

71 Taracena, *Carranza*, pp. 80–1; Francisco Urquizo, *Páginas de la revolución* (Mexico, 1954), p. 30.

72 Cumberland, *Constitutionalist Years*, p. 18.

73 Taracena, *Carranza*, pp. 85–6, 90; Santos in DDCC, I, p. 571.

74 Urquizo, *Páginas*, p. 30; Cumberland, *Constitutionalist Years*, pp. 30–1, for estimates.

75 Taracena, *Carranza*, p. 85; Isidro Fabela, *Historia diplomática de la revolución constitucionalista* (Mexico, 1958), I, pp. 219–36.

76 Junco, p. 97ff. expounded this view in 1955, when it was not well received; for a more recent version, see Kenneth J. Grieb, *The United States and Huerta* (Lincoln, 1969), pp. 31–5 and the same author's 'The Causes of the Carranza Rebellion: A Reinterpretation', *Americas*, XXV (July 1968) which, as Meyer, *Huerta*, p. 84, observes, is not as reinterpretative as all that.

77 Taracena, *Carranza*, p. 87; Holland, Saltillo, 19, 20, Feb. 1913, SD 812.00/6270, 6272.

78 Though several governors never received the circular: Ramírez, *Oaxaca*, pp. 133–4: Taracena, *Carranza*, p. 89.

79 Holland, Saltillo, 21 Feb. 1913 (twice), SD 812.00/6302, 6472. Carranza's original objection to the (technical) constitutionality of Huerta's succession was misconceived anyway: Meyer, *Huerta*, p. 68, Grieb, *The United States and Huerta*, p. 32.

80 *El Pueblo*, 20 June 1917, denied it, prompting J. R. Silliman – a confidant of Carranza, who had been present in 1913 – to confirm Holland's version: Silliman, 23 June 1917, SD 812.00/21082.

81 Holland, Saltillo, 20 Feb. 1913, SD 812.00/6286; Cumberland, *Constitutionalist Years*, pp. 19–20.

82 Meyer, *Huerta*, p. 69.

83 Holland, Saltillo, 11 Mar. 1913, SD 812.00/6968.

84 *Ibid.*, 27 Feb. 1913, SD 812.00/6512.

85 *Ibid.*, 11 Mar. 1913, SD 812.00/6968.

86 *Ibid.*; and, on the origins of the Carrancista rebellion, J. Barragán Rodríguez, *Historia del ejercito y de la revolución constitucionalista* (Mexico, 1966), I, pp. 68–94.

87 Armando María y Campos, *Múgica, crónica biográfica* (Mexico, 1939), p. 52; Cumberland, *Constitutionalist Years*, pp. 18–20.

88 Silliman, Saltillo, 4 Aug. 1913, SD 812.00/8459.

89 Silliman, Guadalajara, 23 June 1917, SD 812.00/21082.

90 María y Campos, *Múgica*, p. 55; and below, p. 105.

91 Aguilar, *Revolución Sonorense*, pp. 310–11.

92 Alvarado to Carranza, 16 Nov. 1913, Fabela, DHRM, RRC, I, pp. 149–53.

93 Aguilar, *Revolución Sonorense*, pp. 315–16, 319, 326; I. Ruiz, Banco Minero, Hermosillo, to Juan Creel, 24 Feb. 1913, STA (Creel), box 1.

94 Hostetter, Hermosillo, 26 Feb. 1913 (twice), SD 812.00/6391, 6498; Cumberland, *Constitutionalist Years*, p. 23.

95 Aguilar, *Revolución Sonorense*, pp. 316–17; 321.

96 *Ibid.*, pp. 318–19; Hostetter, Hermosillo, 1, 7 Mar. 1913, SD 812.00/6521, 6726.

97 *Ibid.*, 15 Mar. 1913, SD 812.00/6820.

98 Which caused 'much adverse comment': Bowman, Nogales, 21 Feb. 1913, SD 812.00/6313. True or not, it indicated what was expected of Huertismo.

99 Aguilar, *Revolución Sonorense*, p. 329; Cumberland, *Constitutionalist Years*, p. 25.

100 *Mexican Herald*, 7 May. 1913; *El Imparcial*, 9, 20 Mar. 1913.

101 A. M. Elias to SRE, 16 Jan. 1914; L. Pérez Verdia to same, 6 Feb. 1914, SRE, legajo 787, 86-R-10, 86-R-12.

102 Not that political opposition would prove very effective. For Maytorena's (*post hoc*) expectations, see Aguilar, *Revolución Sonorense*, p. 321, which would sum up the feelings of many Maderista civilians in 1913.

103 Cumberland, *Constitutionalist Years*, p. 26; Beezley, *Insurgent Governor*, p. 161.

104 Meyer, *Huerta*, p. 86.

105 Bonney, San Luis, 4, 28 Mar. 1913, SD 812.00/6736, 7041.

106 Raymond Th. J. Buve 'Peasant Movements, Caudillos and Land Reform during the Revolution (1910–17) in Tlaxcala, Mexico', *Boletín de Estudios Latino-americanos y del Caribe*, XVII (1975), p. 133.

107 Azuela, *The Bosses*, pp. 170–6.

108 Hanna, Monterrey, 18 Mar., 17 July 1913, SD 812.00/6770, 8206.

109 Silliman, Saltillo, 30 July 1913, SD 812.00/8330.

110 Hanna, Monterrey, 28 Mar., 17 July 1913, SD 812.00/7021, 8206.

111 Miller, Tampico, 11 Apr. 1913, SD 812.00/7353.

112 Bonney, San Luis, 28 Mar. 1913, SD 812.00/7041.

113 Cañete in DDCD, I, pp. 439–40; Sullivan, La Paz, 18 Aug. 1913, SD 812.00/8528.

114 Miller, Tampico, 20 Apr.; c/o US Navy, Tampico, 20 Mar. 1913, SD 812.00/7276; 6974.

115 Miller, Tampico, 19, 27 Mar. 1913, SD 812.00/6882, 7022.

116 A. Palomino, Havana, to SRE, 28 Feb. 1913, SRE, legajo 818, 102-R-1.

117 Elisha Ely, Tuxtepec, 20, 27 Feb. 1913, SD 812.00/6565; 6753.

118 Memo. 'para Porfirio Garza'. n.d. (1914), AG 873.

119 *Mexican Herald*, 5 May, 11 July 1913.

120 Jorge Vera Estañol, *La revolución mexicana. Origines y resultados* (Mexico, 1957), p. 292.

121 Hamm, Durango, 19, 29 Mar. 1913, SD 812.00/6976, 7098.

122 Cumberland, *Constitutionalist Years*, p. 33, n. 51.

123 *Ibid.*, pp. 33, 40, 47; Hamm, Durango, n.d., rec'd 13 June; Schmutz, Aguascalientes, 9 June 1913; SD 812.00/7720; 7855; *Mexican Herald*, 4, 14 May, 11 June, 16 July 1913.

124 Olea, *Sinaloa*, p. 52; c/o USS Buffalo, Mazatlán, 7 Apr. 1913; Canada, Veracruz 22 Jan.; Stewart, Cordoba, 16 Jan. 1914; SD 812.00/7233; 10769; 10773.

125 C/o USS Colorado, Mazatlán, 24 Mar. 1913, SD 812.00/7174.

126 Gabriel Gavira, *General de Brigada, Gabriel Gavira. Su actuación político-militar revolucionaria* (Mexico, 1933), pp. 75–6.

127 Samuel P. Huntington, *Political Order in Changing Societies* (New Haven, 1971), pp. 268–9, 306; John Rutherford, *Mexican Society During the Revolution: A Literary Approach* (Oxford, 1971), pp. 26, 193–7; James D. Cockcroft, *Intellectual Precursors of the Mexican Revolution, 1900–1913* (Austin, 1976), p. 213.

128 Rowe, Guanajuato, 30 July 1913, SD 812.00/8667.

129 Carden, Mexico City, 10 Dec. 1913, Grey Papers, FO 800/43.

130 Lozano, Laredo, to SRE, 5 Mar. 1913, SRE, legajo, 782, 84-R-10.

131 Cumberland, *Constitutionalist Years*, p. 29ff. (The author obtained access to the *Defensa Nacional* archives and is good on the 1913–14 campaigns.)

132 *Ibid.*, p. 44; Barragán, *Historia del ejército*, I, pp. 95–6, 113.

133 Calero, *Un decenio*, p. 145.

134 Lozano, Laredo, to SRE, 10 May 1913, SRE, legajo 805, 95-R-1; Vera Estañol, *Revolución mexicana*, pp. 324, 326.

135 Immigration Service Report, El Paso, 3 Oct. 1913, SD 812.00/9462.

136 Cumberland, *Constitutionalist Years*, p. 80; Urquizo, *Páginas*, pp. 150–1.

137 Cf. Robert E. Quirk, *The Mexican Revolution, 1914–15. The Convention of Aguascalientes* (New York, 1960), p. 10; Letcher, Chihuahua, 25 Aug. 1914, SD 812.00/13232, who mistakenly considers Carranza a 'lawyer'.

138 Fabela to Díaz Lombardo, 24 Jan. 1914, SRE, legajo 760, 75-R-22.

139 Aguilar, *Revolución Sonorense*, pp. 324, 326; Gonzalez Ramírez, *La revolución social de Mexico: Las ideas – la violencia* (Mexico, 1960), p. 383.

140 Dye, Moctezuma Copper Co., 15 Mar.; Bowman, Nogales, 16 Mar. 1913, SD 812.00/ 6806, 6792.

141 Hamilton Fyfe, *The Real Mexico* (London, 1914), pp. 12–13.

142 Aguilar, *Revolución Sonorense*, p. 330.

143 *Ibid.*, pp. 255–66; E. J. Dillon, *President Obregón. A World Reformer* (London, 1922), pp. 31–7; Linda B. Hall, *Alvaro Obregón, Power and Revolution in Mexico 1911–1920*, Texas A and M, 1981, pp. 19–26.

144 Dillon, *President Obregón*, p. 36.

145 *Ibid.*, pp. 41–2.

146 Hall, *Alvaro Obregón*, pp. 20–1; Barry Carr, 'Las peculiaridades del norte mexicano, 1880–1927: ensayo de interpretacion', *Historia Mexicano*, XXII (1973), pp. 320–46.

147 Obregón, *Ocho mil kilómetros*, pp. 4–5; Aguilar, *Revolución Sonorense*, p. 258.

148 Above, vol. I, p. 412.

149 Aguilar, *Revolución Sonorense*, pp. 285–7; Hall, *Alvaro Obregón*, pp. 29–36.

150 Aguilar, *Revolución Sonorense*, pp. 347, 258–9, 390–1.

151 *Ibid.*, p. 342; Obregón, *Ocho mil kilómetros*, pp. 36–9.

152 Obregon, *Ocho mil kilómetros*, pp. 47–54; Simpich, Nogales, 14 Apr. 1913, SD 812.00/7194.

153 Aguilar, *Revolución Sonorense*, pp. 338, 343, 389.

154 *Mexican Herald*, 11, 14 Apr. 1913; Obregón, *Ocho mil kilómetros*, pp. 46–54.

155 Aguilar, *Revolución Sonorense*, pp. 327, 347, 383.

156 *Ibid.*, pp. 340, 348–50, 363–4.

157 *Ibid.*, pp. 348, 431–3 (the Yaquis, of course, were a major exception).

158 *Ibid.*, pp. 372, 375–6, 378–9.

159 *Ibid.*, pp. 383–6, 440.

160 *Ibid.*, pp. 437, 441; c/o US Navy, Guaymas, 1 Oct., 1913, SD 812.00/9283.

161 *Mexican Herald*, 6 Apr. 1913.
162 Aguilar, *Revolución Sonorense*, p. 387; Azuela, *Trials*, p. 6.
163 Aguilar, *Revolución Sonorense*, pp. 387–8.
164 *Ibid.*, pp. 388–9; Cumberland, *Constitutionalist Years*, p. 38.
165 Simpich, Nogales, 14 Apr. 1913, SD 812.00/7194.
166 Aguilar, *Revolución Sonorense*, pp. 398–400.
167 Obregón, *Ocho mil kilómetros*, pp. 57–73, and Francisco J. Grajales, 'Las campanas del General Obregón', in the same volume, pp. xli–liii.
168 Cf. Hostetter, Hermosillo, 17 July, and Capt. Terhune, USS Annapolis, 26 Aug. 1913, SD 812.00/8134, 8695.
169 Cumberland, *Constitutionalist Years*, pp. 79–80; Aguilar, *Revolución Sonorense*, pp. 402, 404.
170 *Ibid.*, pp. 400, 415.
171 *Ibid.*, pp. 401, 403, 405, 407; Simpich, Nogales, n.d., rec'd 21 July; Immigration Inspection, Nogales, 25 July 1913; SD 812.00/8100; 8239.
172 Aguilar, *Revolución Sonorense*, pp. 391, 407, 410–12.
173 *Ibid.*, pp. 78, 395, 444.
174 *Ibid.*, pp. 393, 427–8; Alvarado to Carranza, 16 Nov. 1913, Fabela, DHRM, RRC, I, pp. 149–53.
175 Aguilar, *Revolución Sonorense*, pp. 364–6.
176 *Ibid.*, pp. 396, 407.
177 *Ibid.*, pp. 419, 427–9.
178 *Ibid.*, pp. 415, 420–1, 430; and pp. 409–10, 418, for relations with Obregón.
179 *Ibid.*, pp. 397, 408–9, 446.
180 *Ibid.*, pp. 394–5, 444.
181 *Ibid.*, p. 404; Obregón, *Ocho mil kilómetros*, pp. 73–9.
182 Cumberland, *Constitutionalist Years*, p. 114; Reed, *Insurgent Mexico*, p. 212.
183 Berta Ulloa, *La revolución intervenida, relaciones diplomáticas entre México y Estados Unidos (1910–1914)* (Mexico, 1971), p. 88ff.
184 Grieb, *United States and Huerta*, pp. 60–2.
185 Bliss to Scott, 10 Jan. 1914, Scott Papers, box 15.
186 Grieb, *United States and Huerta*, pp. 60–2; Quirk, *Mexican Revolution, 1914–15*, p. 44.
187 Aguilar, *Revolución Sonorense*, pp. 373–4.
188 Grieb, *United States and Huerta*, p. 60.
189 *Ibid.*, p. 61; Ulloa, *Revolución Intervenida*, p. 89; Mexican consul, El Paso, to Nogales, 9 May, and Sub-Secretary to Secretary of Foreign Relations, 27 May 1913, SRE, legajo 753, 73-R-7.
190 Cf. Grieb, *United States and Huerta*, p. xii. This is part of a more general argument concerning American influence on the Revolution: see pp. 68–70, 157, 354.
191 H. Thompson to T. Bliss, 12 Sept. 1913, Scott Papers, box 15.
192 Aguilar, *Revolución Sonorense*, p. 376.
193 Ellsworth, Cd Porfirio Díaz, 22, 27 Mar., 24, 25 Apr., 27 May, 11 June, 5 July 1913, SD 812.00/6877, 6966, 7297, 7312, 7669, 7995.
194 I. Thord-Gray, *Gringo Rebel* (Coral Gables, 1960), p. 89.
195 Memo. of W. MacKinley, 11th Cavalry, 29 Mar. 1913, SD 812.00/7150; J. Heard to T. Bliss, 20 Aug. 1913, Scott Papers, box 15.
196 Bliss to Scott, 26 Aug. 1914, Scott Papers, box 16.
197 Thord-Gray, *Gringo Rebel*, pp. 100–1.
198 Schmutz, Aguascalientes, 31 May, 15 June 1913, SD 812.00/7773, 7911.
199 Border report, Eagle Pass, 23 Aug. 1913; cf. Blocker, Cd Porfirio Díaz, 7 Oct. 1913, SD 812.00/8670, 9110, on the Federals' abundance of munitions.
200 Border report, Sierra Blanca, Feb. 1914, SD 812.00/11042.

201 Sub-Secretary to Secretary of Foreign Relations, 19 Mar. 1913, SRE, legajo 753, 73-R-8; Olea, *Sinaloa*, pp. 48–51; c/o USS Colorado, Guaymas, 24 Mar. 1913, SD 812.00/7174.

202 Olea, *Sinaloa*, pp. 52–3; Capt. Terhune, USS Annapolis, Mazatlán, 5 June 1913, SD 812.00/8695.

203 Olea, *Sinaloa*, pp. 54, 57.

204 C/o USS Colorado, Guaymas, 1 Apr. 1913, SD 812.00/7177; Thord-Gray, *Gringo Rebel*, p. 106; Gustavo Casasola, *Historia gráfica de la revolución mexicana* (Mexico, 1960), I, pp. 702–6; Jose C. Valadés, *Historia general de la revolución mexicana* (5 vols., Mexico, 1963–5), III, 188–9.

205 Alger, Mazatlán, 18 Aug., 20 Oct. 1913, SD 812.00/8477, 9583, who adds that, given sufficient arms, the rebels could at once double their fighting strength to 10,000.

206 S. Terrazas to I. Pesqueira, 22 May and to J. Jacobs, 20 June 1913, STA, box 83.

207 Martín Luis Guzmán, *Memorias de Pancho Villa*, p. 155ff. Emilio Madero's interest in Villa (and Urbina) was constant, though not always charitable; see E. Madero to Sánchez Azcona, 9 Nov., 1912, Fabela, DHRM, RRM, IV, pp. 197–8, advising against Villa's release from gaol, for fear of its effect in Chihuahua.

208 Luis Aguirre Benavides, *De Francisco I. Madero a Francisco Villa* (Mexico, 1966), pp. 43–52; cf. María y Campos, *Múgica*, p. 28 for a Porfirian example.

209 Note the coincidental escape of José Pérez Castro, the Potosino rebel: J. Bonales Sandoval to Madero, 28 Dec. 1912, Fabela, DHRM, RRM, IV, p. 263.

210 Patrick O'Hea, *Reminiscences of the Mexican Revolution* (Mexico, 1966), pp. 81–2.

211 *Ibid.*, p. 195; Reed, *Insurgent Mexico*, pp. 113–15.

212 Rutherford, *Mexican Society*, pp. 153–4.

213 Reed, *Insurgent Mexico*, p. 189.

214 Arturo Warman, *Y venimos a contradecir: los campesinos de Morelos y el estado nacional* (Mexico, 1976), pp. 104–5, 131.

215 Aguirre Benavides, *De Francisco I. Madero*, p. 44; Reed, *Insurgent Mexico*, p. 117; O'Hea, *Reminiscences*, p. 187.

216 Reed, *Insurgent Mexico*, pp. 126–8; J. Bonales Sandoval to Madero, 28 Dec. 1912, Fabela, DHRM, RRM, IV, p. 262; note Villa's later, lavish obsequies for González: Casasola, I, pp. 762–3.

217 Guzmán, *Memorias*, p. 183; Reed, *Insurgent Mexico*, p. 118; Federico Cervantes, *Francisco Villa y la revolución* (Mexico, 1960), p. 49.

218 Guzmán, *Memorias*, p. 184; Reed, *Insurgent Mexico*, pp. 158, 164.

219 E. Madero to Madero, 14 Jan., J. Sánchez Azcona to C. Patoni, 23 Jan. 1913, Fabela, DHRM, RRM, IV, pp. 330–1, 371.

220 Cumberland, *Constitutionalist Years*, pp. 26–7; though the inclusion of Chao among the 'best examples' of the 'crude and the feral' who led the Chihuahua revolution is misplaced: Chao, once a schoolmaster, read official documents to Villa, became Governor of Chihuahua, and served as unofficial emissary to Washington: Cervantes, p. 73.

221 Cervantes, *Villa*, pp. 49–50; Letcher, Chihuahua, 3 May 1913, SD 812.00/7427.

222 Cervantes, *Villa*, p. 54; Guzmán, *Memorias*, p. 186.

223 Cumberland, *Constitutionalist Years*, p. 48; S. Terrazas to J. Quevedo, 19 July 1913, STA, box 83.

224 S. Terrazas to D. Horcasitas, 18 July 1913, STA, box 83.

225 *Mexican Herald*, 9 Apr. 1913.

226 Cumberland, *Constitutionalist Years*, pp. 48–9.

227 O'Hea, *Reminiscences*, p. 90.

228 Hamm, Durango, 7 Mar., 2 Apr. 1913, SD 812.00/6750, 7357.

229 *Ibid.*, 5 Apr., n.d., rec'd 13 June 1913, SD 812.00/7358, 7720. The closure of mine, and lumber, camps swelled rebel numbers; but where mining activity continued, there was little evidence of miners leaving *en masse* for the revolution: hence the healthy figures of

production and even profit in mining zones like Sonora (*Mexican Herald*, 14 Feb. 1914, for Cananea's output), Jalisco and Oaxaca (*ibid.*, 26 Feb., 7, 23 Mar. 1914), and central Mexico (*ibid.*, 14 Feb. 1914, contrasting Pachuca with Peñoles and Aviño in Durango).

230 Hamm, Durango, n.d., rec'd 13 June 1913, SD 812.00/7720.

231 Graham, Durango, 9 Mar. 1913, FO 371/1671, 14519. As already suggested, vol. I, p. 179, the Laguna may have been witnessing the Martinez Alier phenomenon.

232 Hamm, Durango, 13 June, 27 July 1913, SD 812.00/7797, 8449.

233 Hamm, Durango, June 1913 diary, SD 812.00/8078.

234 Reed, *Insurgent Mexico*, pp. 54–5.

235 Zacatecas fell to Natera a few days earlier, but was retaken by the Federals.

236 Hamm, Durango, June 1913 diary, SD 812.00/8078; Barragán, *Historia del ejército*, I, pp. 157–8.

237 Hamm (n. 236); Barragán, *Historia del ejército*, I, pp. 159–60, citing Rouaix; Meyer, *Huerta*, pp. 94–5.

238 Cumberland, *Constitutionalist Years*, p. 42, citing General Morelos Zaragoza.

239 Rouaix, quoted in Barragán, *Historia del ejército*, I, p. 159.

240 Cobb, El Paso, 15 Sept. 1915, SD 812.00/16183.

241 Hamm, Durango, 25, 27 July 1913, SD 812.00/8310, 8449.

242 Guzmán, *Memorias*, p. 195.

243 Hamm, Durango, 23 Oct. 1913, SD 812.00/9858.

244 *Mexican Herald*, 10 Sept. 1913; Hohler, Mexico City, 24 Mar. 1914, FO 371/2026, 16251.

245 Womack, *Zapata*, pp. 239–41.

246 Wilson, Mexico City, 30 June 1913, SD 812.00/7933; *Mexican Herald*, 19 Mar. 1914; Hohler, Mexico City, 24 Mar. 1914, FO 371/2026, 10251.

247 *Mexican Herald*, 27 Nov. 1913, 25 Jan. 1914; Simmonds to Carden, 12 Feb. 1914, FO 371/2026, 13251.

248 *Mexican Herald*, 14, 22 Nov., 6 Dec. 1913, 8 Apr. 1914.

249 See pp. 115, 117, 168, 356, 358.

250 'Bloody acts of retribution were as inevitable as the recoil of a gun': Trotsky's *History of the Russian Revolution* (London, 3 vols., 1967), I, p. 246; cf. Mao's famous comment in 'Report', p. 28.

251 Carden, Mexico City, 25 June, 1 Aug. 1914, FO 371/2029, 28738; /2030, 35683.

252 D. E. Worcester and W. G. Schaeffer, *The Growth and Culture of Latin America* (Oxford, 1971), p. 379; Grieb, *United States and Huerta*, pp. 58–9.

253 Cumberland, *Constitutionalist Years*, p. 45; Hamm, Durango, 3 Aug. 1913, SD 812.00/8346.

254 Guzmán, *Memorias*, pp. 196–202.

255 General Ignacio Bravo, quoted by Cumberland, *Constitutionalist Years*, p. 46.

256 Hamm, Durango, 15 Oct., Carothers, Torreón, 11 Oct. 1913, SD 812.00/9658.

257 *Ibid.*; Aguirre Benavides, *De Francisco I. Madero*, p. 106.

258 Cumberland, *Constitutionalist Years*, p. 48; Barragán, *Historia del ejército*, I, pp. 254–8.

259 Guzmán, *Memorias*, p. 411; Barragán, *Historia del ejército*, I, p. 266.

260 Hamm, Durango, 15 Oct. 1913, SD 812.00/9658; Herman Whitaker, 'Villa – Bandit and Patriot', *The Independent*, 8 Apr. 1914.

261 Reed, *Insurgent Mexico*, p. 119.

262 See pp. 118–29, 269–71, 294–301.

263 Reed, *Insurgent Mexico*, p. 91.

264 Guzmán, *Memorias*, p. 206.

265 Schmutz, Aguascalientes, 31 May, 5, 9, 12, 15, 30 June 1913, SD 812.00/7773, 7854, 7855, 7910, 7911, 8020; Barragán, *Historia del ejército*, I, p. 514.

266 Jean Meyer, *La révolution mexicaine: 1910–1940* (Paris, 1973), p. 74.

267 *Mexican Herald*, 8 May 1913; Schmutz, Aguascalientes, 5 June 1913, SD 812.00/7854.

268 Anon. letter from Chalchihuites, 8 June 1913, SD 812.00/7911.

269 Barragán, *Historia del ejército*, I, p. 161; Casasola, *Historia gráfica*, I, p. 629; Alberto Morales Jiménez, *Hombres de la revolución* (Mexico, 1960), pp. 133–4.

270 Cumberland, *Constitutionalist Years*, p. 40; *Mexican Herald*, 19 May 1913.

271 Vasconcelos to Carranza, 19 Sept. 1913; Fabela, DHRM, RRC, I, p. 120.

272 Silliman, Saltillo, 23 May, 5 June; Bonney, San Luis, 23 June 1913; SD 812.00/7751, 7865; 8013.

273 Silliman, Saltillo, 9, 18 June 1913, SD 812.00/7866, 7996.

274 'It was not the desire of any of the chiefs of the revolution to molest Americans', he was told, 'but ... if he cared to make a voluntary offering it would be acceptable and appreciated': Silliman, Saltillo, 10 May 1913, SD 812.00/7668.

275 Bonney, San Luis, 3 May 1913, SD 812.00/7376.

276 Barragán, *Historia del ejército*, I, p. 118.

277 Bonney, San Luis, 28 May 1913, SD 812.00/7790.

278 B. Burgess, Valles, H. Tanner, Tamasopo, in Miller, Tampico, 25 May; J. Ingram, 2 July 1913; SD 812.00/7690; 8187.

279 H. Harrison, smelter manager, Cerralvo (NL), 29 Apr.; J. Shelby, Tula (Tamps.), 3 July; Bonney, San Luis, 8 Aug., 18 Dec.; A. Graham, Forlon (Tamps.), 6 Dec. 1913; SD 812.00/7394; 8183; 8270, 10466; 10350.

280 'Salida en Campaña de G. G. Sánchez', 12 July 1911, AG, legajo 898; Barragán, *Historia del ejército*, I, pp. 116–17.

281 US War Dept, border report, 23 Aug. 1913, SD 812.00/8670.

282 Shelby, Tula, 8 June; Bonney, San Luis, 28 May 1913, SD 812.00/7887; 7790.

283 Barragán, *Historia del ejército*, I, p. 119; Silliman, Saltillo, 5 June 1913, SD 812.00/7865.

284 Bonney, San Luis, 8 May 1913, SD 812.00/7675; Cumberland, *Constitutionalist Years*, p. 133, n. 60.

285 Silliman, Saltillo, 25 Nov. 1913, SD 812.00/10050.

286 *Ibid.*, 25 June, 22 Nov. 1913, SD 812.00/8073, 10032; J. Acuña to US Consul, Nogales, 23 Dec. 1913, SRE, legajo 760, 75-R-22, p. 38; Barragán, *Historia del ejército*, I, p. 171.

287 Schmutz, Aguascalientes, 19 May; Bonney, San Luis, 13 June; Silliman, Saltillo, 30 Aug. 1913; SD 812.00/7681; 7779; 8823.

288 Silliman, Saltillo, 5 June 1913, SD 812.00/7865.

289 Barragán, *Historia del ejército*, I, p. 119; Bonney, San Luis, 28 May 1913; Blocker, Cd Porfirio Díaz, 25 Jan. 1914; SD 812.00/7790; 10670.

290 Barragán, *Historia del ejército*, I, pp. 123–7, on the execution of – among others – the mayor and organiser of the *Defensa Social*, Dr Miguel Barragán ('who has no family relationship with the author of this work').

291 Bonney, San Luis, 8 May; Silliman, Saltillo, 26 Apr., 29 Dec. 1913; SD 812.00/7675, 7403, 10757.

292 H. Harrison, Cerralvo, 29 Apr. 1913, SD 812.00/7394.

293 Schmutz, Aguascalientes, 10 Nov. 1913, SD 812.00/9856.

294 Report of P. Bastanc, 31 Aug. 1913, SD 812.00/8884.

295 Silliman, Saltillo, 28 July, 28 Oct. 1913, 4 Mar. 1914; Hanna, Monterrey, 31 Oct. 1913; SD 812.00/8184, 9774, 11139; 9690. More examples will follow.

296 Silliman, Saltillo, 9, 18 June 1913, SD 812.00/7866, 7996.

297 *Ibid.*, 28 Oct. 1913, SD 812.00/9774: this coincided with the farcical presidential election.

298 Hanna, Monterrey, 17 July, 31 Oct. 1913, SD 812.00/8206, 9690; Barragan, *Historia del ejército*, I, p. 257.

299 Silliman, Saltillo, 24 June, 28 July, 28 Oct.; Hanna, Monterrey, 31 Oct. 1913; SD 812.00/8073, 8184, 9774, 9690.

300 See pp. 71, 158–61.
301 Hanna, Monterrey, 17 July 1913, SD 812.00/8206.
302 Silliman, Saltillo, 28 Oct. 1913, SD 812.00/9774.
303 *Ibid.*, 30 June 1913, SD 812.00/8074; and Fyfe, *The Real Mexico*, pp. 24–6.
304 Silliman, Saltillo, 30 June 1913, SD 812.00/8074; and vol. 1, p. 110.
305 *Ibid.*, 29 Dec. 1913, SD 812.00/10757.
306 This, despite the good harvest of 1913: Dudley Ankerson, 'The Cedillos and the Revolution in the State of San Luis Potosí 1890–1930' (Cambridge Ph.D. diss., 1981), Ch. 3, p. 28; Bonney, San Luis, 23 June 1913, SD 812.00/8013.
307 María y Campos, *Múgica*, p. 57.
308 Barragán, *Historia del ejército*, I, p. 128 Fyfe, *The Real Mexico*, p. 34; Thord-Gray, *Gringo Rebel*, p. 82.
309 Barragán, *Historia del ejército*, I, pp. 251, 254–6.
310 *Ibid.*, pp. 253–4; Fyfe, *The Real Mexico*, pp. 33–4, 40. Blanco, easy-going and affable, later entered into some shady dealings with American border interests: Canova, Mexico City, 25, 28, Aug., 19 Sept.; Rabb, Brownsville, 10 Sept. 1914; SD 812.00/13129, 13136, 13220, 13238.
311 Barragán, *Historia del ejército*, I, pp. 173–6; María y Campos, *Múgica*, pp. 65–70.
312 María y Campos, *Múgica*, p. 69.
313 *Ibid.*
314 *Ibid.*, p. 65; Barragán, *Historia del ejército*, I, p. 176.
315 Some stress Blanco's *agrarismo* as the cause of Carranza's displeasure (Adolfo Gilly, p. 89; Córdova, *Ideología*, p. 197); others (Barragán, *Historia del ejército*, I, pp. 254–6; Cumberland, *Constitutionalist Years*, p. 47) his bad relations with fellow-rebels. Certainly the north-east was riven with intra-revolutionary squabbles: Barragán, *Historia del ejército*, I, pp. 299–305, 312; Emilio Salinas to Carranza, 16 Dec. 1913, Fabela, DHRM, RRC, I, pp. 168–71. Possibly, the *agrarista* factor has been over-stressed.
316 Cumberland, *Constitutionalist Years*, pp. 47–8; Jesus to Venustiano Carranza, 12 Dec. 1913, Fabela, DHRM, RRC, I, pp. 102–3.
317 Harrison, Cerralvo, 1 May 1913, SD 812.00/7394; and below, pp. 107–8.
318 Bonney, San Luis, 28 May, 9 Sept. 1913, SD 812.00/7790, 8911; Ankerson, 'Cedillos', diss., ch. 3, p. 28.
319 Shelby, Tula, 16 May 1913, SD 812.00/7887.
320 Bonney, San Luis, 28 May 1913, SD 812.00/7790.
321 Ankerson 'Cedillos', diss., ch. 3, p. 29.
322 *Ibid.*, p. 26.
323 Miller, Tampico, and enclosures, 27 Apr., 6, 25 May 1913, SD 812.00/7402, 7422, 7690; Meade, *Valles*, p. 179; Martínez Núñez, *San Luis Potosí*, pp. 40, 43; Barragán, *Historia del ejército*, I, p. 302.
324 Miller, Tampico, 25 May 1913, SD 812.00/7690, enclosing reports from Tamasopo, Valles and San Dieguito; Ankerson 'Cedillos', diss., ch. 3, p. 29.
325 Romana Falcón, 'Saturnino Cedillo and the Mexican Revolution' (Oxford D.Phil., diss., 1983), pp. 96–107.
326 Barragán, *Historia del ejército*, I, pp. 163–8.
327 *Ibid.*, pp. 167–8.
328 Bonney, San Luis, 3, 28 Mar. 1913, SD 812.00/6738, 7041; cf. Barragán, *Historia del ejército*, I, p. 166.
329 Miller, Tampico, 18 Apr., 8 June 1913, SD 812.00/7187.
330 Martínez Núñez, *San Luis Potosí*, pp. 42–3; Ankerson 'Cedillos', diss., ch. 3, pp. 29–30.
331 Martínez Núñez, *San Luis Potosí*, pp. 41–2.
332 Moisés T. de La Peña, *El pueblo y su tierra. Mito y realidad de la reforma agraria en México* (Mexico, 1964), p. 307 (the author spent over two years with Carrera's forces).

333 Jan Bazant, *Cinco haciendas mexicanas: tres siglos de vida rural en San Luis Potosí* (Mexico, 1975), p. 182; Bonney, San Luis, 23 June 1913, SD 812.00/8013: though, Bonney argued, 'the landlord is the object of attack', 'the merchant, especially the merchant who is the agent for plantation goods' was a secondary target.

334 Bonney, 23 June 1913 (n. 333).

335 Ankerson, 'Cedillos', diss., and Falcon, 'Saturnino Cedillo', are both excellent guides to the Cedillo movement, during and after the armed revolution.

336 Gavira, *Actuación*, pp. 75–6; Canada, Veracruz, 10 Mar. 1913, SD 812.00/6862; *El Imparcial*, 15 Mar. 1913; Admiral Fletcher, Veracruz, 16 Apr. 1913, SD 812.00/7292. The Veracruzano veteran Rafael Tapia was also an early victim of Huertismo.

337 A. Rodríguez, Orizaba, 18 June; A. MacLean, Jalapa, 19 June 1913; SD 812.00/8005; note also Barragán, *Historia del ejército*, I, pp. 328–32.

338 Harvey, Tezonapa, 14 June; Trapp, Atoyac, 17 June 1913; SD 812.00/8005; de la Llave had been responsible for the killing of Camerino Mendoza: Gavira, *Actuación*, p. 75.

339 Canada, Veracruz, 26 July 1913, SD 812.00/8159.

340 Petition to A. Esteva, Dept of Labour, 29 Jan. 1914, Trabajo, 31/2/1/29; Burns, Orizaba, 11 Aug. 1913, SD 812.00/8668a.

341 Lt Gov. J. M. Camacho to alcaldes, 28 Aug. 1913, AZ, 16/134.

342 Lespinasse, Frontera, 5 Apr.; and cf. Carnahan, Aire Libre (Pue.), 25 Feb. 1913; SD 812.00/7025; 6753.

343 Manuel González Calzada, *Historia de la revolución mexicana en Tabasco* (Mexico, 1972), pp. 122, 135–6.

344 Lespinasse, Frontera, 21 Apr., 7 June, 18 July, 21, 28 Aug. 1913, SD 812.00/7213, 7724, 8269, 8646.

345 *Ibid.*, 28 Oct., 13 Nov. 1913, SD 812.00/9777, 9717; *Mexican Herald*, 10 Sept. 1913.

346 González Calzada, *Tabasco*, pp. 134, 143; Benjamin, 'Passages', p. 132; though there are discrepancies in these accounts.

347 Germon, Progreso, 20 Aug. 1914, SD 812.00/13125; Jorge Flores D., 'La vida rural en Yucatán en 1914', *Historia Mexicana*, X (1960–1).

348 Lespinasse, Frontera, 28 Mar.; Germon, Progreso, 20, 21 Aug. 1913; SD 812.00/7121; 8757, 8511.

349 Canada, Veracruz, 25 Sept. 1913, 16 Apr., 11 June 1914, SD 812.00/9211, 11742, 12312, the second enclosing reports from planters throughout the state.

350 H. Hill, La Estancia, Ver., 4 Apr. 1914, SD 812.00/11742.

351 Heather Fowler Salamini, *Agrarian Radicalism in Veracruz 1920–38* (Lincoln 1978), pp. 8–24; Falcón, *El Agrarismo*, pp. 28–31: as the brevity of these references suggests, the authors see the story of Veracruz *agrarismo* starting in the 1920s.

352 Fowler, *Agrarian Radicalism*, p. xi, quoting Horowitz.

353 Canada, Veracruz, 4 Sept. 1913, SD 812.00/8851.

354 *Ibid.*, 2 Apr. 1914, SD 812.00/11481.

355 *Jefe político*, Zongólica, to governor, n.d., Apr./May 1914, AZ, 6/51.

356 Buve, 'Peasant movements', pp. 134–5.

357 G. Pérez, Xoxocotla, to *jefe político*, Zongólica, 20 Apr. 1914, AZ, 6/51.

358 Srio de la jefatura, Zongólica, to governor, 10 Jan. 1914, AZ 9/46. The attack followed the familiar pattern: the 'professional' rebels of 'General (Raul) Ruiz' were seconded by local men.

359 A. Davenport, Aire Libre, 19 June; Canada, Veracruz, 28 Aug. 1913; SD 812.00/8005; 8852.

360 See vol. I, p. 396.

361 Miller, Tampico, 22 Sept.; Canada, Veracruz, 25 Sept.; Davenport, Aire Libre, 11 Sept. 1913; SD 812.00/9019; 9211; 9223; Davenport cites the Indians as coming from Tetela

de Ocampo, Zacapoaxtla, Tlatlauqui and Xochiapulco. On the terms of the agreement: Canada, Veracruz, 4 Dec. 1913, SD 812.00/10162.

362 Ronald Waterbury, 'Non-revolutionary peasants: Oaxaca compared to Morelos in the Mexican Revolution', *Comparative Studies in Society and History*, XVII (1975), p. 431; Ramírez, *Oaxaca*, pp. 137–48.

363 Carnahan, Teziutlán, 24 Oct. 1913, SD 812.00/9696.

364 Lind, Veracruz, 12 Dec. 1913, SD 812.00/10152.

365 Bryan to Lind, 13 Dec. 1913, SD 812.00/1015.

366 Gavira, *Actuación*, p. 99; Fowler, *Agrarian Radicalism*, p. 8; Leticia Reina, *La rebeliones campesinas en Mexico (1819–1906)* (Mexico, 1980), p. 359; Madero to Governor Levi, 17 Aug. 1912, Fabela, DHRM, RRM, IV, p. 85.

367 Gavira, *Actuación*, p. 94.

368 *Mexican Herald*, 13 May 1913; Vicente T. Mendoza, *Lírica narrativa de Mexico: el corrido* (Mexico, 1964), pp. 73–5.

369 Mendoza (n. 368); Canada, Veracruz, 2, 17 July; Miller, Tampico, 4 July 1913; SD 812.00/7950, 8162, 8069.

370 Mendoza (n. 368), p. 75. In the same month, the *Mexican Herald*, 25 July 1913, reported an Indian revolt at Chicontepec, north of Papantla; demands were made for the division of lands and the removal of officials.

371 Womack, *Zapata*, p. 162.

372 *Ibid.*, pp. 164–5; Wilson, Mexico City, 1 Apr. 1913, SD 812.00/7101, for Huerta's opinion of Leyva.

373 Womack, *Zapata*, pp. 163–6, 175.

374 *Ibid.*, p. 167. Lacking direct access to American arms supplies, the *surianos* got much of their weaponry from dead, captured or corrupt Federals.

375 L. Mix to M. Smith, 13 Mar. 1913, SD 812.00/6682.

376 Calero, *Un decenio*, p. 145; Vera Estañol, *Revolución mexicana*, pp. 326–7.

377 Womack, *Zapata*, pp. 167–8; Warman, *Y venimos a contradecir*, pp. 111, 141.

378 Oscar Lewis, *Pedro Martínez: A Mexican Peasant and his Family* (London, 1969).

379 Meyer, *Huerta*, p. 43.

380 Wilson, Mexico City, 1 Apr. 1913, SD 812.00/7101.

381 *Mexican Herald*, 23 Apr. 1913.

382 Womack, *Zapata*, pp. 174–5.

383 *Ibid.*, p. 170.

384 Oscar Lewis, *Life in a Mexican Village: Tepoztlán Restudied* (Urbana, 1963), p. 232.

385 Womack, *Zapata*, p. 170. The Amazons of Tetecala were, of course, readily incorporated into the 'Attila of the South' myth: Rutherford, *Mexican Society*, p. 151.

386 See pp. 61, 149.

387 María y Campos, *Múgica*, p. 57.

388 Womack, *Zapata*, p. 166ff.

389 María y Campos, *Múgica*, p. 172.

390 *Ibid.*, p. 178.

391 Ian Jacobs, 'Aspects of the History of the Mexican Revolution in the State of Guerrero up to 1940' (Cambridge Ph.D. diss., 1977), pp. 175–6.

392 *Ibid.*, p. 171.

393 Romero Flores, *Michoacán*, pp. 67ff.; Kirk, Manzanillo, 8 June 1913, SD 812.00/7859, notes that 'practically the entire sea-coast of Michoacán is lawless'.

394 Moisés Ochoa Campos, *Historia del estado de Guerrero* (Mexico, 1968), p. 293; Jacobs, 'Aspects', pp. 172–3.

395 Jacobs, 'Aspects', p. 176; Womack, *Zapata*, p. 180.

396 Womack, *Zapata*, pp. 181–2; cf. p. 171 for a multitude of 'adherents to the Plan of Ayala', in a dozen states, where the 'Zapatista' label meant little.

397 C/o, USS Annapolis, Mazatlán, 30 Dec. 1913, SD 812.00/10547.
398 Womack, *Zapata*, pp. 179–80.
399 William L. Sherman and Richard E. Greenleaf, *Victoriano Huerta: A Reappraisal* (Mexico, 1960), p. 101; Meyer, *Huerta*, p. 95.
400 See pp. 94–103.
401 Calero, *Un decenio*, p. 130; Katz, *Deutschland*, p. 231.
402 See vol. I, pp. 35, 102.
403 Lewis, *Pedro Martínez*, p. 129; Womack, *Zapata*, pp. 160–1; Rutherford, *Mexican Society*, pp. 156, 175–7; Francisco I. Madero, *La sucesión presidencial en 1910* (San Pedro, 1908), pp. 24, 70, 112–13.
404 Meyer, *Huerta*, pp. 140–1; Vera Estañol, *Revolución mexicana*, p. 283. Felix Díaz, intending to run for the presidency, did not hold a cabinet post.
405 Meyer, *Huerta*, p. 141; Katz, *Secret War*, p. 119.
406 *Mexican Herald*, 16 Apr. 1913.
407 Casasola, *Historia gráfica*, I, pp. 554–6, 564–6.
408 Nemesio García Naranjo, *Memorias*, VII (Monterrey, n.d.), p. 56.
409 Body to Cowdray, 1 Apr. 1913, Cowdray Papers, box A4.
410 Cravioto in DDCC, I, pp. 60–6, especially, p. 64.
411 *Mexican Herald*, 18, 24 Apr., 1 May 1913; Luis Licéaga, *Félix Díaz* (Mexico, 1958), p. 295; García Naranjo, p. 216.
412 *Mexican Herald*, 25 Apr., 1 May 1913.
413 *Ibid.*, 24 Apr. 1913.
414 *Ibid.*, 23 May, 14 June 1913.
415 *Ibid.*, 29 May, 14 June 1913; Mondragón to Díaz, 26 June 1913, Fabela, DHRM, RRC, I, 92–5; Licéaga, *Félix Díaz*, p. 300, argues this to be a forgery.
416 Licéaga, *Félix Díaz*, p. 302; Vera Estañol, *Revolución mexicana*, p. 328.
417 *Mexican Herald*, 14 June 1913; Grieb, *United States and Huerta*, p. 57.
418 Stanley R. Ross, 'Victoriano Huerta visto por su compadre', *Historia Mexicana*, XIX (1962–3), p. 302.
419 Meyer, *Huerta*, p. 143; *Mexican Herald*, 12 Sept. 1913.
420 Vera Estañol, *Revolución mexicana*, pp. 323–4.
421 Meyer, *Huerta*, pp. 144–5, quoting Valadés; *Mexican Herald*, 7, 9 May 1913.
422 García Naranjo, *Memorias*, VII, pp. 131–4.
423 Fabela to Chamber of Deputies, 25 Aug. 1913, Fabela, DHRM, RRC, I, pp. 110–15.
424 A. Ancona Albertos to Gobernación, 15 Dec. 1913, Fabela, DHRM, RRC, I, pp. 165–7.
425 Alberto J. Pani, *Apuntes autobiográficos* (Mexico, 1951), p. 187.
426 Meyer, *Huerta*, p. 145; García Naranjo, *Memorias*, VIII, pp. 135, 48.
427 Cumberland, *Constitutionalist Years*, pp. 66–7; Casasola, *Historia gráfica*, I, pp. 674–6.
428 Gruening, *Mexico and its Heritage*, p. 307; though Benjamin 'Passages', p. 133, terms him a 'staunch Maderista'.
429 Meyer, *Huerta*, p. 137.
430 Cumberland, *Constitutionalist Years*, p. 67.
431 Stronge, Mexico City, 8 Mar. 1913, FO 371/1671, 13402; Leone Moats, *Thunder in their Veins* (London, 1933), pp. 114–20; Edith O'Shaughnessy, *A Diplomat's Wife in Mexico* (New York, 1916), p. 201; *El Imparcial*, *El País*, both 27 Mar. 1913.
432 Gavira, *Actuación*, pp. 76, 78; Juchitán *jefe político*'s report, 23 Sept. 1913, in SD 812.00/9648; Casasola, *Historia gráfica*, I, p. 653; Vera Estañol, *Revolución mexicana*, p. 332. Another deputy, Edmundo Pastelín, was murdered, though in obscure circumstances: Fabela, DHRM, RRC, IV, p. 82; *Mexican Herald*, 4 July 1913.
433 Meyer, *Huerta*, pp. 138–9, mentions 35 definite cases and up to 100 unverified.
434 O'Shaughnessy, *Diplomat's Wife*, p. 179.
435 *Ibid.*, p. 7.

436 Meyer, *Huerta*, p. 138; Cumberland, *Constitutionalist Years*, p. 68.

437 Meyer, *Huerta*, pp. 146–7; Casasola, *Historia gráfica*, I, p. 676; Grieb, *United States and Huerta*, p. 105.

438 Cf. Grieb, *United States and Huerta*, p. xii: 'ultimately, the Revolution itself did not overwhelm Huerta; rather, the American government brought about his fall': an astonishing statement. Calvert and Ulloa, *Revolución intervenida*, also give detailed treatment of this question; Arthur Link, *Wilson: The New Freedom* (Princeton, 1956), is much preferable to J. M. Blum, *Woodrow Wilson and the Politics of Morality* (Boston, 1956); see pp. 89–90 for an echo of Grieb's statement.

439 Link, *Wilson*, p. 349; R. S. Baker, *Woodrow Wilson. Life and Letters* (New York, 1931), IV, pp. 55–6.

440 Some of the worst Mexican historiography relates to Mexican–American relations: e.g., Alberto María Carreño, *La diplomacia extraordinaria entre México y Estados Unidos* (Mexico, 1951), II, pp. 237–58, on this period.

441 Wilson, Mexico City, 22, 26 Feb. 1913, SD 812.00/6326, 6394; Stronge, Mexico City, 3 Mar. 1913, FO 371/1671, 13394.

442 Cf. Grieb, *United States and Huerta*, pp. 39–41; Katz, *Secret War*, pp. 156–7ff. For the views of Taft and the State Department: Ulloa, *Revolución intervenida*, p. 105; Link, *Wilson*, p. 348; W. H. Taft, 'The Democratic Record', *Yale Review*, VI/I, Oct. 1916.

443 Diary of Gen. Leonard Wood, 24 Feb. 1913, Wood Papers, box 7.

444 Theodore P. Wright, 'Free Elections in the Latin American Policy of the US', *Political Science Quarterly*, 74 (1959), pp. 89–112; cf. Robinson and Gallagher, pp. 3–4.

445 William Diamond, *The Economic Thought of Woodrow Wilson* (Baltimore, 1943), pp. 132–8.

446 Cf. Grieb, *United States and Huerta*, pp. 42–3.

447 P. A. R. Calvert, *The Mexican Revolution 1910–1914: The Diplomacy of Anglo-American Conflict* (Cambridge, 1968), ch. 5, offers a detailed account.

448 Wood Diary, 12, 13, Jan. 1914; House Diary, 3 July 1913.

449 Wood Diary, 13 June 1914; Daniels Diary, 18 Apr. 1913; House Diary, 2 May 1913; and, for widespread advocacy of recognition, House Diary, 27 Mar., 3 July, 5, 23 Sept., 7 Nov. 1913; Daniels Diary, 20 May 1913.

450 House Diary, 2 May 1913.

451 Link, *Wilson*, pp. 352–3; Ulloa, *Revolución intervenida*, pp. 108–9.

452 See the discussion in J. Edward Haley, *Revolution and Intervention: The Diplomacy of Taft and Wilson with Mexico 1910–17* (MIT, 1970), pp. 77–90, which is balanced and to the point.

453 Grieb, *United States and Huerta*, pp. 81–2, 92–3; Quirk, *Mexican Revolution*, p. 36; note also Larry D. Hill, *Emissaries to a Revolution: Woodrow Wilson's Executive Agents in Mexico* (Baton Rouge, 1973).

454 Link, *Wilson*, p. 354; Calvert, *Mexican Revolution*, p. 136; Wood Diary, 18 Nov. 1913; cf. George J. Rausch, 'Poison-Pen Diplomacy: Mexico, 1913', *Americas*, 24 (1968), pp. 272–80.

455 Hale to Bryan, 18 June 1913, SD 812.00/7798½; the fact that Bryan found it an 'extraordinary' document (to Wilson, SD 812.00/886½) suggests that it did more than confirm preconceived opinions; on the Hale mission Haley, *Revolution and Intervention*, pp. 94–5 is preferable to Rausch or Grieb, *United States and Huerta*, pp. 80–2.

456 Grieb, *United States and Huerta*, pp. 79–80; Link, *Wilson*, p. 355.

457 Grieb, *United States and Huerta*, pp. 85–7, which also shows how the American Press took up cudgels for and against Ambassador Wilson; Hale (to Bryan, 9 July 1913, SD 812.00/8203) showed perspicacity in his criticism of del Valle and evaluation of the revolution.

458 Alan Knight, 'Nationalism, Revolution and Xenophobia. The Place of Foreigners and Foreign Interests in Mexico, 1910–15' (Oxford Ph.D., diss., 1974), pp. 211–15, 219–26.

459 *Ibid.*, pp. 233–4.
460 House Diary, 11, 22 May, 30 Oct. 1913.
461 Knight, 'Nationalism, Revolution and Xenophobia', p. 222.
462 O'Shaughnessy, Mexico City, 5, 10 Aug. 1913, SD 812.00/8241, 8278.
463 Calvert, *Mexican Revolution*, p. 201; Grieb, *United States and Huerta*, p. 92.
464 Hohler, Mexico City, 6 Apr. 1914, FO 371/2027, 18393. Hohler, the British Minister, had done the diplomatic rounds at Constantinople, St Petersburg, Cairo, Tokyo and Addis Ababa; yet – or, more likely, as a result – his views were quite as biased and inaccurate as Lind's.
465 Ulloa, *Revolución intervenida*, pp. 118–19; Grieb, *United States and Huerta*, pp. 96–7.
466 Grieb, *United States and Huerta*, p. 101.
467 Knight, 'Nationalism, Revolution and Xenophobia', pp. 227–30.
468 Link, *Wilson*, pp. 360–1; J. Edward Haley, *Revolution and Intervention*, p. 103.
469 Vera Estañol, *Revolución Mexicana*, p. 334; Calero, *Un decenio*, pp. 148–9.
470 Haley, *Revolution and Intervention*, pp. 101–2; Grieb, *United States and Huerta*, pp. 104, 109.
471 Charles C. Cumberland, *Mexican Revolution. Genesis under Madero* (Austin, 1952), p. 146; *Mexican Herald*, 12 June 1913.
472 Memo. of O. Braniff, 17 July 1913, WWP, IV, 95B, box 123.
473 Meyer, *Huerta*, p. 151; *Mexican Herald*, 9, 25, 26 June 1913, Vera Estañol, *Revolución mexicana*, pp. 331–2.
474 DDCC, I, p. 88.
475 *Mexican Herald*, 26 June 1913, quoting Urrutia; Vera Estañol, *Revolución mexicana*, pp. 331–2.
476 *Mexican Herald*, 12 June 1913 and *passim*, for the politicking of summer 1913.
477 Calero, *Un decenio*, p. 128.
478 Licéaga, *Félix Díaz*, pp. 304–9.
479 García Naranjo, *Memorias*, VII, pp. 135–6.
480 O'Shaughnessy, Mexico City, 8 Oct. 1913, SD 812.00/9134.
481 Meyer, *Huerta*, p. 147; Calvert, *Mexican Revolution*, pp. 202, 232, notes that Garza Aldape had also been 'the chief advocate in Huerta's cabinet of a policy of defiance of the United States' (he had replaced Urrutia at Gobernación in September).
482 Meyer, *Huerta*, p. 148; Grieb, *United States and Huerta*, p. 106. Only one Catholic deputy was held.
483 Casasola, *Historia gráfica*, I, pp. 678–9.
484 Meyer, *Huerta*, p. 149. The *gobiernista* press applauded the dissolution of Congress – 'this aggregation of crazy men and conspirators' – as well as Huerta's decision to arrest – 'confine in a straightjacket' – these 'beings crammed full of Jean-Jacques Rousseau': *Mexican Herald*, 16 Oct. 1913, quoting *El Imparcial* and *El Independiente*.
485 Grieb, *United States and Huerta*, p. 107, quoting Nicolson: Edward I. Bell, *The Political Shame of Mexico*, p. 364, draws the same comparison.
486 Cowdray to Hayes, 13 Oct. 1913, Cowdray Papers, box A/3; Calero, p. 151; Bell, *Political Shame*, pp. 364–5, mentions a spontaneous popular demonstration in support of the imprisoned deputies, which led to bloodshed. O'Shaughnessy's comment, 11 Oct. 1913, SD 812.00/9173, that 'the people whom I have met this morning do not seem to regard the Government's action with much concern' must be considered in the light of the kind of people the American Chargé met.
487 Bryan to O'Shaughnessy, 13 Oct. 1913, SD 812.00/9180a.
488 O'Shaughnessy, Mexico City, 16 Oct. 1913, SD 812.00/9233.
489 At San Luis (Bonney, 13 Oct.) and in Tabasco (Lespinasse, 13, 18 Oct.) the coup was received unfavourably, and Lespinasse predicted renewed resistance to Huerta as a result; at Veracruz (Canada, 16 Oct.), where the state's congressional representatives were not much

liked, and at Saltillo (Silliman, 16 Oct.), there was a warmer response; the comment of a British businessman in Coahuila was typical of one school of thought, who retained faith in the iron hand: 'for my part I say bully for Huerta. It is something that should have been done long ago. Don Porfirio's system is *the* system for this country and these people and it is the only system'. See SD 812.00/9204; 9199, 9636; 9352; 9555; also 9280 and 9357 from Aguscalientes and Mazatlán.

490 Meyer, *Huerta*, pp. 152–3; Alger, Mazatlán, 20 Oct. 1913, SD 812.00/9483.
491 Schmutz, Aguascalientes, 11 Oct. 1913, SD 812.00/9357.
492 Meyer, *Huerta*, p. 152; Grieb, *United States and Huerta*, p. 109. Perhaps Huerta hoped for a powerful, popular endorsement (in which case he was disappointed); perhaps he sought to confound the opposition – though, for this, traditional electoral management would have sufficed.
493 Meyer, *Huerta*, p. 153 wonders to what extent the election was rigged; the evidence is overwhelming: see Fyfe, *The Real Mexico*, pp. 68–9; Bell, *Political Shame*, pp. 367–8; Licéaga, *Félix Díaz*, p. 310; Lind, Veracruz, 21, 26 Oct.; O'Shaughnessy, Mexico City, 25 Oct.; Davis, Guadalajara, 22 Oct. 1913; SD 812.00/9302; 9292, 9390; 9328.
494 Grieb, *United States and Huerta*, p. 109.
495 Edward, El Paso, 26 Oct.; Letcher, Chihuahua, 31 Oct.; and reports from Ensenada, Frontera, San Luis, Tampico, and Aguascalientes: SD 812.00/9398; 9495; 9409, 9410, 9429, 9477; and Casasola, *Historia gráfica*, I, pp. 688–9.
496 O'Shaughnessy, Mexico City, 3 Nov. 1913, SD 812.00/9515.
497 *Mexican Herald*, 3 Nov. 1913; Grieb, *United States and Huerta*, p. 110.
498 O'Shaughnessy, Mexico City, 3 Nov. 1913, SD 812.00/9515.
499 *Mexican Herald*, 29 Oct. 1913; Grieb, *United States and Huerta*, p. 111.
500 *Mexican Herald*, 23, 26 Oct. 1913, on the beginnings of the rift; 16, 27 Jan. 1914 and Meyer, *Huerta*, p. 169 for later arrests and closures. Some bishops, it should be noted, disavowed the Catholic press's criticism of Huerta.
501 O'Shaughnessy, Mexico City, 11 Oct. 1913, SD 812.00/9173; *El Imparcial*, 22 Mar. 1913 for the slogan.
502 Michael C. Meyer, 'The Militarisation of Mexico, 1913–14', *Americas*, 27, 1970–1, p. 294; Valadés, *Historia general*, III, p. 61; Meyer, *Huerta*, p. 98; *El Imparcial*, 16 Mar. 1914 gives an absurdly detailed breakdown, totalling 228,331.
503 Urrutia to Gobernación, 8 July 1913, AG, 'Gobernadores Estados, Asuntos Varios, 1913–14'; *Un decenio*, p. 146, cites Huerta's claim to Congress of 250,000 Federals + 12,400 rurales + 31,000 militia = 293,400.
504 'Conditions of extensive graft' were reported by an American military officer just returned from a long stay in Mexico: Wood Diary, 18 Sept. 1913; Bell, *Political Shame*, pp. 373–4, implicates Huerta's sons. See also Wilson, Mexico City, 13 July; Church, Tatahuicapa (Ver.), 9 July; Hale, 9 July 1913; c/in/c US Pacific Fleet, Mazatlán, 24 Feb. 1914; SD 812.00/8036; 8110; 8203; 11142; and Katz, *Secret War*, pp. 119, 187, quoting the pro-Huerta von Hintze.
505 See the US Military Attaché's estimate, July 1913, in Grieb, *United States and Huerta*, pp. 54–5.
506 Bonney, San Luis, 28 May 1913, SD 812.00/7790; Meyer, *Huerta*, p. 98 on pay.
507 Quoted by Hamm, Durango, 30 Nov. 1913, SD 812.00/10272.
508 Cumberland, *Constitutionalist Years*, p. 61.
509 Meyer, *Huerta*, p. 98; Bonney, San Luis, 28 May 1913, SD 812.00/7790; *Mexican Herald*, 12 June 1913.
510 J. Jiménez, Coatepec, 18 Feb. R. Pérez Jiménez, Metepec, 17 Jan. 1914, both to Dept of Labour, Trabajo, 31/2/1/34, 31/2/1/35; Meyer, *Huerta*, p. 99; D. Díaz to Carranza, from Jalapa gaol, 10 May 1916, AVC, which recounts the story of an individual given an eighteen-year sentence for homicide in 1906, who was taken from gaol and put in the army

in 1913, deserted in Morelos, and was at liberty for over a year before rashly returning to Jalapa to be arrested.

511 O'Shaughnessy, *Diplomat's Wife*, pp. 43, 67, 169; Gamio, *The Mexican Immigrant* (Chicago, 1931), pp. 6–7.

512 Admiral Fletcher, Veracruz, 26 June 1913, SD 812.00/8017; O'Shaughnessy, *Diplomat's Wife*, p. 242.

513 Cumberland, *Constitutionalist Years*, p. 62; Shanklin, Mexico City, 24 Nov.; Stadden, Manzanillo, 21 Nov. 1913; SD 812.00/9903; 9877.

514 Brown, Mazatlán, 6 June 1914, SD 812.00/12353.

515 Schmutz, Aguascalientes, 26 Mar. 1914, SD 812.00/11471; Meyer, *Huerta*, p. 99.

516 *Mexican Herald*, 20 July 1913, on the arrival of 500 Juchiteco 'volunteers' in the capital.

517 Gracey, Progreso, 22 Nov. 1913, SD 812.00/10019.

518 Above, p. 55; Canada, Veracruz, 6, 28 Aug. 1913, SD 812.00/8409, 8852.

519 Lespinasse, Frontera, 28 Nov., 8 Dec. 1913, 8 Feb. 1914, SD 812.00/10279, 10100, 11081; *jefe político*, Tuxtepec, to governor of Oaxaca, 8 May 1913, AG 66/45.

520 Cumberland, *Constitutionalist Years*, p. 62; O'Shaughnessy, *Diplomat's Wife*, pp. 57–8.

521 Sullivan, La Paz, 27 Aug.; Guyant, Ensenada, 20 Dec. 1913; SD 812.00/9654; 11081; Capt. Walter, HMS Shearwater, San Diego, 8 Jan. 1914. FO 371/2025, 4759.

522 Meyer, *Huerta*, pp. 100–1.

523 Gracey, Progreso, 18, 20 Aug. 1913, SD 812.00/8707, 8757.

524 *Mexican Herald*, 10 Oct., 22 Nov. 1913, 16 Mar. 1914, which reports the Jojutla mutineers being 'cut to bits'; according to Womack, *Zapata*, p. 183, they joined Salgado and assisted in attacks on Taxco and elsewhere.

525 As numerous observers reported; see, for example, the version of an American miner, from Ocampo, Chihuahua, in Fall to Wilson, 9 Aug. 1913. WWP, IV, 95, box 120; S. Terrazas to J. Quevedo, 19 July 1913, STA, box 83.

526 Carothers, Torreón, 12 Sept. 1913, SD 812.00/9058.

527 C/in/c US Pacific Fleet, Guaymas, 1 Oct.; Edwards, Acapulco, 19, 21 Sept.; Blocker, Cd Porfirio Díaz, 11 Sept. 1913; SD 812.00/9283, 8949; 8907.

528 Garrett, Nuevo Laredo, 30 Aug. 1913, SD 812.00/8641.

529 Stadden, Manzanillo, 25 Sept. 1913, SD 812.00/9212.

530 Knight, 'Nationalism, Revolution and Xenophobia', pp. 207–8, 237.

531 Shanklin, Mexico City, 9 Sept.; Stadden, Manzanillo, 25 Sept. 1913; SD 812.00/8771; 9212; *Mexican Herald*, 21, 29 July, 31 Aug., 4 Sept., 22 Oct. 1913; Knight, 'Nationalism, Revolution and Xenophobia', pp. 227–51, 263–5.

532 Shanklin, Mexico City, 3 Sept. 1913, SD 812.00/8682.

533 Luis González Y González, *Pueblo en vilo. Microhistoria de San Jose de Gracia* (Mexico, 1972), p. 123; Arturo Langle Ramírez, *El Militarismo de Victoriano Huerta* (Mexico, 1976), p. 58.

534 For events in 1914, see pp. 158–62.

535 See vol. I, pp. 157, 166–9.

536 Schmutz, Aguascalientes, 15 June; O'Shaughnessy, Mexico City, 17 Oct.; c/o, US Navy, Mazatlán, 21 Dec. 1913; SD 812.00/7911; 9249; 1054.

537 *Mexican Herald*, 1 May, 26 June, 27 July, 19 Aug., 6, 23, 24, 25, 26 Sept. 1913; Meyer, *Huerta*, p. 103.

538 *Mexican Herald*, 20, 25 Dec. 1913.

539 *Ibid.*, 12 June, 29 Oct., 17 Dec. 1913; Arturo Langle Ramirez, *El ejército Villista* (Mexico, 1961), pp. 50–1.

540 *Mexican Herald*, 30 Aug., 7, 9 Sept. 1913.

541 E. Creel to Banco Minero, 5 Sept. 1913, STA (E. Creel), box 1.

542 Womack, *Zapata*, p. 166.

543 *Mexican Herald*, 16, 19, 28 Feb. 1914, concerning Querétaro, Campeche and Mexico.

544 *Ibid.*, 20 July, 2 Aug., 12 Sept. 1913.

545 Womack, *Zapata*, pp. 169, 183–5; O'Shaughnessy, *Diplomat's Wife*, p. 179.

546 Womack, *Zapata*, p. 163.

547 *Mexican Herald*, 1 May 1913; Srio Gobernador, Jalapa, to alcaldes, 28 Aug. 1913, AZ.

548 Consular agent, Tuxpán, 2 Jan. 1914, on the efforts of local *jefes* to raise their contingents; Schmutz, Aguascalientes, 26 Mar. 1914, on the resentment caused, particularly among railway workers, by attempted recruitment for the state militia: SD 812.00/10634; 11471.

549 O'Shaughnessy, *Diplomat's Wife*, p. 206.

550 *El Imparcial*, 19 Mar. 1914.

551 Hamm, Durango, Apr. 1913, SD 812.00/7720; Dorador, *Mi prisión, la defensa social, y la verdad del caso* (Mexico, 1916), p. 53ff.; Matías Pazuengo, *Historia de la revolución en Durango par el General Matías Pazuengo* (Cuernavaca, 1915), p. 44; Manuel Gámiz Olivas, *Historia de la revolución en el estado de Durango* (Mexico, 1963), p. 42.

552 Rouaix, *Diccionario . . . , pp.* 144–5; Pazuengo, *Historia*, pp. 44, 52.

553 Pazuengo, *Historia*, pp. 53, 56.

554 Successively Minister of Education, Foreign Relations and Gobernación, Garza Aldape was a tough – some said crude – individual, rather after Huerta's own heart, who favoured a hard line against Congress, the US and, here, the armed rebels: Querido Moheno, *Mi actuación después de la decena trágica* (Mexico, 1939), pp. 69–71.

555 Pazuengo, *Historia*, pp. 69–71.

556 In 1914, Mariano Arrieta threatened to put all remaining ex-members of the *Defensa Social* in the front line as a protest against the Federal *leva*: Hamm, Durango, 9 Jan. 1914, SD 812.00/10654.

557 Fyfe, *The Real Mexico*, p. 80.

558 *Mexican Herald*, 4 May, 21, 29 Oct. 1913.

559 *Ibid.*, 25 Aug. 1913; S. Terrazas to I. Enriquez, 30 July 1913, STA, box 83.

560 E. Brondo Whitt, *La División del Norte (1914) por un testigo presencial* (Mexico, 1940), p. 74.

561 Barragán, *Historia del ejército*, I, pp. 126–7.

562 If this sounds like a concession to Skocpol, it is assuredly not: for it was precisely because the Huerta regime relied so heavily on outright repression – lacking, as it did, the institutional and psychological bases which underpin many other (including authoritarian) regimes – that the army's role became crucial and, ultimately, its defeat became inevitable.

563 Statement of Juan Creel and others, 3 June 1913, STA (Creel), r. 1.

564 Pazuengo, *Historia*, p. 71.

565 Knight, 'Nationalism, Revolution and Xenophobia', pp. 326–9.

566 Dept. of Justice, 17 Nov.; Guyant, Ensenada, 17 Nov. 1913; SD 812.00/9835; 9898; O'Shaughnessy, *Diplomat's Wife*, p. 218.

567 Shanklin, Mexico City, 3 Sept. 1913; SD 812.00/8682; *Mexican Herald*, 7 Sept. 1913, 13 Apr. 1915.

568 Payne, Tuxpan, 20 July 1913, SD 812.00/8244; Payne, Manager of the Oil Fields of Mexico Co., commented on the 'futility of a company attempting to organise volunteers for defence against such numbers of rebels'; his firm 'depend[ed] now, as formerly, upon neutrality, as nearly as force will permit, and diplomacy'. See also Letcher, Chihuahua, 25 Aug. 1914, SD 812.00/13232, on business' ability and preference to spend its way out of trouble.

569 *Mexican Herald*, 8, 15, 26 Nov., 15 Dec. 1913, 15, 17, 18 Mar. 1914.

570 *Ibid.*, 1, 19 Apr. 1914.

571 The *Mexican Herald*, though certainly conservative, was more independent than most of the (surviving) Mexico City press; news of Federal defeats broke sooner in its pages than elsewhere; but it was heavily dependent on official sources.

572 A. Leon Grajeda to SRE, 10 June 1913; Jose Maria Zepeda to M. Diebold, 16 July 1913; SRE, legajo 771, pp. 149, 219.

573 Consul, Naco, to SRE, 21 Feb. 1914, SRE, legajo 787, p. 55; Aguilar's masterly study contains no reference to significant counter-revolutionary movements in Sonora.

574 See vol. I, pp. 166–9, 182, 383–4.

575 Silliman, Saltillo, 29 Dec.; H. Hale to W. Davis, 18 Nov. 1913; SD 812.00/10757; 10074; *Mexican Herald*, 4 Jan. 1914.

576 S. G. Inman to A. T. Atwater, 31 Aug. 1914, SGIA, box 12.

577 Fyfe, *The Real Mexico*, p. 69; memo. of Cowdray conversation with W. H. Page, 9 Aug. 1914, Cowdray Papers, box A/3.

578 Anon. miner, Ocampo (Chih.) in Fall to Wilson, 9 Aug. 1913, WWP, IV, 95, box 120.

579 F. Von Hiller, enclosed in F. Allen, 23 Mar. 1913, SD 812.00/6891; *Mexican Herald*, 1, 15, 17 Apr., 4 Oct. 1913. Plateros was one of the chic streets of Mexico City.

580 A. Terrazas to J. Creel, 22 Dec. 1910, STA, box 84.

581 C. McNeil (British consul, Colima), enclosed in F. Allen, 23 Mar. 1913, SD 812.00/6891; note, in the same collection, H. Evans' comment on the refusal of 'the propertied classes' to back Felix Díaz, and J. B. Potter's observation that the Mexican upper classes 'are in no sense public-spirited in the Northern [sic] sense of the term'.

582 Eric R. Wolf and Edward C. Hansen, 'Caudillo Politics: A Structural Analysis', *Comparative Studies in Society and History*, IX (1966–7), pp. 178–9, for the quotation.

583 Gilbert M. Joseph, *Revolution From Without: The Mexican Revolution in Yucatán* (Yale Ph.D. diss., 1978), p. 37ff.; Womack, *Zapata*, p. 51.

584 Forman, *Brazilian Peasants*, p. 149.

585 O'Shaughnessy, *Diplomat's Wife*, pp. 92, 179; and Thomas Hohler, *Diplomatic Petrel* (London, 1942), p. 187.

586 O'Shaughnessy, *Diplomat's Wife*, p. 112 (it seems likely that 'Mr Creel-Terrazas' refers to Creel rather than Terrazas); see also Azuela, *Trials*.

587 Barrington Moore, *Social Origins of Dictatorship and Democracy, Lord and Peasant in the Making of the Modern World* (London, 1969), pp. 468–74; Manfred Hildermeier, 'Agrarian Social Protest, Populism and Economic Development: Some Problems and Results from Recent Studies', *Social History*, IV/II (May 1979), pp. 319–32, especially p. 324.

588 All these generalisations are, of course, vulnerable to further research.

589 *Mexican Herald*, 2 Apr. 1914.

590 Alfonso Ortiz Ortiz, *Episodios de la revolución en Moroleón* (Mexico, 1976), p. 11ff.

591 *Mexican Herald*, 13 June 1913.

592 See pp. 196–202, 384–6.

593 Cf. vol. I, p. 153.

594 Emile Durkheim, *The Division of Labor in Society*, New York, 1968, p. 63ff.

595 *Le Courrier du Méxique*, 17 July 1914, lists ministerial office-holders.

596 *El Imparcial*, 22 Mar. 1914; Arturo Langle Ramírez, *El militarismo de Victoriano Huerta* (Mexico, 1976), p. 73.

597 On the plight of Huerta's ministers: Vera Estañol, *Revolución mexicana*, pp. 342–5; Calero, *Un decenio*, pp. 132–7; Moheno, *Mi actuación*, pp. 43, 76, 92, 109, 158; furthermore, these ex-ministerial laments are confirmed by Bell, p. 358 ('Huerta's cabinet was made up of men whose wills counted for little') and von Hintze, quoted by Katz, *Secret War*, p. 119 (where Huerta refers to his ministers as 'pigs I would just as soon spit upon').

598 O'Shaughnessy, *Diplomat's Wife*, p. 34; Francisco Ramírez Plancarte, *La Ciudad de Mexico durante la revolución constitucionalista* (Mexico, 1941), p. 49.

599 *Mexican Herald*, 23 Dec. 1913, 4 Jan., 10 Apr., 23 May 1914; Moheno, p. 109.

600 Meyer, *Huerta*, pp. 132–3; *Mexican Herald*, 15 July 1913, 4 Mar. 1914.

601 Hohler, Mexico City, 4 Mar. 1914, FO 371/2026, 12853.

602 Bell, *Political Shame*, pp. 318–26; Moheno, *Mi actuación*, p. 16.

603 Hohler, Mexico City, 4 Mar. 1914, FO 371/2026, 12853.

604 Silliman, Saltillo, 24 June, 28 July, 28 Oct.; Hanna, Monterrey, 31 Oct. 1913; SD 812.00/8073, 8184, 9774, 9690.

605 Moheno, *Mi actuación*, p. 89; O'Shaughnessy, Mexico City, 6 Sept. 1913, SD 812.00/8937.

606 *Mexican Herald*, 9 Oct. 1913.

607 'All the accounts are most contradictory' (G. S. Spicer); 'what is one to believe?' (Sir R. Paget): minutes on Hohler, Mexico City, 7 Apr.; see also 8, 9, 11 Apr. 1914, FO 371/2026, 15519, 15675, 15853, 16093.

608 Langle Ramírez, *El militarismo*, pp. 26, 29, 39–40, 42.

609 Calero, *Un decenio*, p. 137.

610 *Mexican Herald*, 26 Apr., 5 May, 16, 26 June, 10 July 1913; Langle Ramírez, *El militarismo*, pp. 65–7.

611 González Calzada, *Tabasco*, pp. 155–8, on the views of Governor Mestre Ghigliazzi of Tabasco.

612 *Mexican Herald*, 2 June, 28 July 1913; Benjamin, 'Passages', p. 131; Womack, *Zapata*, p. 163.

613 Body to Cowdray, 13 May 1913, Cowdray Papers, box A/4 (this after a talk with de la Barra).

614 Romero Flores, *Michoacán*, p. 73; *Mexican Herald*, 12 June 1913; Vera Estañol, *Revolución mexicana*, p. 324.

615 Moheno, *Mi actuación*, p. 10. Colonel Maass was son of General Maass; the family was related to Huerta by marriage.

616 Olea, *Sinaloa*, p. 51.

617 S. G. Inman to Mrs Inman, n.d., Nov. 1913, SGIA, box 12 (the Garza Galán family had provided some of the chief bosses and politics of Porfirian Coahuila).

618 *Mexican Herald*, 6 July 1913.

619 *Ibid.*, 17 Aug., 10, 11 Nov. 1913; Vera Estañol, *Revolución mexicana*, pp. 338–9; Ciro de la Garza Treviño, *La revolución mexicana en el estado de Tamaulipas (cronología), 1885–1913* (Mexico, 1973), p. 210.

620 F. Goodchild to W. Hearn, 18 Dec. 1913, FO 371/2025, 4058; Meyer, *Huerta*, p. 101; *El Imparcial*, 14 Mar. 1914; and n. 504 above.

621 Meyer, *Huerta*, pp. 95–6.

622 UP release on the death of Urrutia – then a successful dentist in San Antonio – 1975 (reference courtesy of Mr R. del Quiaro).

623 *Mexican Herald*, 20 July, 25 Aug. 1913; Langle Ramírez, *El militarismo*, pp. 59–61, 70–3.

624 *Ibid.*, 19 Aug. 1913; Meyer, *Huerta*, p. 97, and the same author's 'Militarisation'.

625 *Mexican Herald*, 17 Mar. 1914.

626 Langle Ramírez, *El militarismo*, p. 85.

627 Meyer, *Huerta*, pp. 96, 130. Though Huerta drank a lot – chiefly brandy – the general view was that this did not evidently affect his behaviour; on only a couple of occasions was he recognisably drunk in public: García Naranjo, *Memorias*, VII, pp. 99–104; Sherman and Greenleaf, *Huerta*, p. 96.

628 Hohler, Mexico City, 24 Mar. 1914, FO 371/2026, 16247; Urrutia had an equally low opinion of the *politíco* class: Vera Estañol, *Revolución mexicana*, p. 331.

629 Vera Estañol, *Revolutión mexicana*, p. 333; Moheno, *Mi actuación*, p. 113 (both, of course, were disgruntled ex-ministers).

630 Alfred Stepan, *The Military in Politics. Changing Patterns in Brazil*, Princeton, 1974, p. 173; Huntington, *Political Order*, pp. 219, 226.

631 Moheno, *Mi actuación*, pp. 63, 77; Fyfe, *The Real Mexico*, p. 120; Calero, *Un decenio*, p. 125.

632 Hohler, Mexico City, 24 Mar. 1914, FO 371/2026, 16247: 'Huerta certainly seems a rather remarkable man', minuted Sir Ralph Paget. See also Sherman and Greenleaf, *Huerta*, pp. 97–8.

633 O'Shaughnessy, *Diplomat's Wife*, p. 12; and cf. Vera Estañol, *Revolución mexicana*, pp. 333–4.

634 Fyfe, *The Real Mexico*, p. 121.

635 Title borrowed from Eugen Weber, *Journal of Contemporary History*, 9/2, 1974, pp. 3–47.

636 Meyer, *Huerta*, pp. 156–77, especially pp. 175–7; cf. Huntington, *Political Order*, p. 269.

637 Meyer, *Huerta*, p. 176. The fact that Huerta came to power by violence (by a 'revolution' of a sort) is not at issue; Meyer – quite rightly – is trying to elucidate the basic character of the regime.

638 *Ibid.*, pp. 158–9, citing Wilkie, *Mexican Revolution*, p. 158.

639 Meyer, *Huerta*, p. 159; Wilkie, *Mexican Revolution*, p. 160. Note that the comparison is between projected expenditures: Díaz's projected 6.8% became 7.2% (1910–11); Madero's 7.3% became 7.8% (1911–12); there are no figures for Huerta's actual expenditure – a point to which I shall return.

640 Meyer, *Huerta*, pp. 160–2.

641 *Ibid.*, pp. 166–7.

642 *Ibid.*, pp. 170–2.

643 *Ibid.*, pp. 167–9, 173–4.

644 See p. 135. Meyer concedes, *Huerta*, pp. 158–9, that Wilkie's figures are 'suggestive' rather than 'conclusive'; for the sake of argument, we will also assume that they are accurate, which some would doubt.

645 Meyer, *Huerta*, pp. 159–62.

646 Only Blanquet, Minister of War and co-architect of the coup against Madero, survived the whole period of Huerta's presidency: Vera Estañol, *Revolución mexicana*, p. 350; and, on the insignificance of the education portfolio, Moheno, *Mi actuación*, p. 25.

647 Meyer, *Huerta*, pp. 166–7.

648 *Ibid.*, p. 166: F. González Roa, *El aspecto agrario de la revolución mexicana* (Mexico, 1919), pp. 245–8.

649 Meyer, *Huerta*, p. 167; we should note that, under extreme pressure, Díaz too, promised land reform and distribution: Hohler, Mexico City, 3 Apr. 1911, FO 371/1146, 14297. One desperate, off-course swallow does not make a reformist summer.

650 Moheno, *Actuación*, p. 115. As regards the *hacendados'* growing disaffection, Meyer concedes, p. 167, n. 32, that this might have been caused by Huerta's failure to quell the revolution, rather than by his 'timid threats of land reform'; which was certainly the case.

651 Wilson, Mexico City, 22, 26 Feb. 1913, SD 812.00/6326, 6394.

652 Meyer, *México y Estados Unidos*, pp. 47–50; and below, pp. 505–7.

653 Moheno, *Actuación*, pp. 118–30.

654 Canada, Veracruz, 14 Oct., 12 Nov.; Miller, Tampico, 4 Oct. 1913; SD 812.00/6363, 12, 14, 15; Cowdray to Hayes, 18 Oct., to Ryder, 18 Dec. 1913, Cowdray Papers, box A/3.

655 Cowdray to Body, 14 Mar. 1914, Cowdray Papers, box A/3.

656 Moheno, *Actuación*, p. 121; though cf. *El Imparcial*, 26 Sept. 1913.

657 Meyer, *Huerta*, pp. 170–1; Moheno, *Actuación*, pp. 32–5.

658 Moheno, *Actuación*, pp. 124–5, 131.

659 As regards the Church, I would not dissent from Meyer's view, p. 169, that 'the president believed that the church would be a useful and powerful ally as long as there was no question concerning who was in authority'; but this permitted rather more clerical support for the regime than Meyer admits: see pp. 203–4. Huertista *indigenismo* scarcely merits discussion.

660 Gracey, Progreso, 4 June; Canada, Veracruz, 25 Nov. 1913; SD 812.5045/62, 70; S. Sierra to Dept of Labour, 25 June 1913, Trabajo, 32/2/1/18.

661 Barry Carr, *El movimiento obrero y la política en México* (Mexico, 1976), I, p. 76.

662 Consul, Douglas, to SRE, 1 Aug. 1913, SRE, legajo 771, p. 239.

663 Letcher, Chihuahua, 5 Sept. 1913, SD 812.00/5051.

664 Jacinto Huitrón, *Orígenes e historia del movimiento obrero en México* (Mexico, 2nd ed., 1978), pp. 229–30; *El Sindicalista*, 30 Sept., 10 Oct. 1913, 15 Mar. 1914.

665 Carr, *Movimento obrero*, I, p. 75; Meyer, *Huerta*, p. 174.

666 *Ibid.*; Casasola, *Historia gráfica*, I, pp. 556, 566–7; Langle Ramírez, *El militarismo*, pp. 51, 63.

667 Note the expulsion from the Casa of the anarchist and railway union leaders Rafael Pérez Taylor for alleged complicity with Huerta (he was soon re-admitted): Carr, *Movimento obrero*, I, p. 76. See also Alan Knight, 'The Working Class and the Mexican Revolution c.1900–1920', *Journal of Latin American Studies*, XVI (1984).

668 Meyer, *Huerta*, p. 175.

669 Vera Estañol, *Revolución mexicana*, p. 329; and n. 597 above.

670 Meyer, *Huerta*, pp. 156–7.

671 Alejandro Martínez Jiménez, 'La educación elemental en el Porfiriato', *Historia Mexicana*, XX, (1972–3), pp. 514–530 Vera Estañol, *Revolución mexicana*, pp. 38–40, 202; James W. Wilkie, *The Mexican Revolution: Federal Expenditure and Social Change since 1910* (Berkeley, 1970).

672 Carr, *Movimento obrero*, I, pp. 43–4; Anderson, *Outcasts*, pp. 122–30, 204–11, 229–42.

673 F. González Roa, *El problema ferrocarrilero* (Mexico, 1919), pp. 35–40; Huitrón, *Orígenes*, pp. 124–5; Marrin D. Bernstein, *The Mexican Mining Industry, 1880–1950* (Albany, 1965).

674 Rutherford, *Mexican Society*, pp. 222–3; William D. Raat, 'Los intelectuales, el positivismo y la cuestión indígena', *Historia Mexicano*, XX (1971).

675 Madero to M. Urquidi, 5 Oct. 1909, Fabela, DHRM, RRM, I, p. 44.

676 Above, vol. I, pp. 2–3.

677 Meyer, *Huerta*, p. 176.

678 Alvarado, *Actuación*, p. 21; cf. Narciso Bassols, *El pensamiento político de Alvaro Obregón* (Mexico, 1976), pp. 122–9.

679 Body to Cowdray, 9 Apr. 1913, Cowdray Papers, box A/4.

680 S. G. Inman to A. R. Atwater, 9, 11 Oct. 1913, SGIA, box 12.

681 'Constitutionalism' and 'Carrancismo' will be used interchangeably, denoting – up to summer 1914 – the broad anti-Huerta movement nominally led by Carranza and, after that date, the faction led by Carranza in opposition to Villa and Zapata.

682 Córdova, *Ideología*, pp. 136, 190.

683 *Ibid.*, p. 191.

684 Taracena, *Carranza*, pp. 134–9; Cumberland, *Constitutionalist Years*, pp. 70–1; María y Campos, *Múgica*, pp. 60–2.

685 Put out by Riveros and Caballero respectively: Alger, Mazatlán, 4 Sept.; Miller, Tampico, 19 Dec. 1913; Meyer, SD 812.00/8910; 10355.

686 María y Campos, *Múgica*, p. 56.

687 Cumberland, *Constitutionalist Years*, p. 70.

688 Taracena, *Carranza*, pp. 138–9.

689 Cumberland, *Constitutionalist Years*, pp. 71–5; Meyer, *Huerta*, p. 86.

690 Fyfe, *The Real Mexico*, p. 17; Meyer, *Huerta*, pp. 93–4. Most prisoners – being rank-and-file conscripts – were in fact released, or allowed to join the rebel forces; officers, *colorados* (ex-Orozquistas) and active supporters of the Huerta regime were often executed: Brondo Whitt, *La Divisón del Norte*, pp. 48, 51, 135–6, 148–9, 154–5; Langle Ramírez, *El ejército Villista*, pp. 39, 41, 47; Gavira, *Actuación*, p. 99.

691 Cumberland, *Constitutionalist Years*, pp. 76–7; above, pp. 26, 41–2.

692 E.g., Dario Atristaín's *Notas de un ranchero* (Mexico, 1917), on revolutionary activities around Jamiltepec, where Carranza's authority did not count until mid-1914.

693 Pazuengo, *Historia*, 72, 74–5.

694 González Calzada, *Tabasco*, pp. 127, 140; Admiral Cradock, Veracruz, 20 June 1914, FO 371/2030, 32060 also describes the attempted transaction – and Greene as a 'bandit'.

695 Consul, Nogales, to SRE, 2, 3, 9, 15, 22 Aug. 1913, SRE, legajo 771, pp. 254–95;

Hostetter, Hermosillo, 13, 17 May, 13 June (twice) 1913, SD 812.00/12033, 12056, 12248, 12320.

696 Barragán, *El ejército*, I, pp. 251, 254–6; Garza Treviño, *Tamaulipas*, pp. 179–80.

697 Gavira, *Actuación*, pp. 95, 101, 111; Romero Flores, *Michoacán*, p. 104; Buve, 'Peasant movements', pp. 135–6, on Tlaxcala; Jacobs, 'Aspects', p. 170ff., on Guerrero.

698 Cumberland, *Constitutionalist Years*, p. 73.

699 Carranza to Pablo González, 15 Mar. 1914, SRE, legajo 760, p. 284.

700 Schryer, *The Ranchers of Piasaflores. The History of a Peasant Bourgeoisie in Twentieth-Century Mexico* (Toronto, 1980), pp. 72–4; Mariel to Madero, 14 Jan. 1913, Fabela, DHRM, RRM, IV, pp. 328–30; Garza Treviño, *Tamaulipas*, pp. 164, 171–2, 402–3; *Historia de la Brigada Mixta 'Hidalgo' que es a las ordenes del General Vicente Segura* (Mexico, 1917), pp. 7–8; Casasola, *Historia gráfica*, I, p. 614; S. Ramírez, San Antonio, to SRE, 16 Mar. 1914, SRE, legajo 787, p. 24.

701 González to Carranza, 14 Mar. 4, 6 Apr. and *vice versa*, 31 Mar., 5, 7, Apr. 1914, SRE, legajo 760, pp. 282, 297, 309, 311, 317, 319.

702 Gavira, *Actuación*, p. 85.

703 *Ibid.*, p. 187.

704 Olea, *Sinaloa*, p. 65.

705 Cervantes, *Francisco Villa*, p. 104; Pazuengo, *Historia*, p. 88.

706 Buve, 'Peasant movements', p. 135.

707 Cumberland, *Constitutionalist Years*, pp. 71–3.

708 *Ibid.*, pp. 129–30; Guzmán, *Memorias*, p. 188; Aguirre Benavides, *De Francisco I. Madero*, pp. 98–9, 120; Cervantes, *Francisco Villa*, p. 55; Langle Ramírez, *El ejército Villista*, pp. 37–8.

709 Barragán, *El ejército*, I, pp. 438–45; Brondo Whitt, *La División del Norte*, p. 132.

710 Barragán, *El ejército*, I, p. 444; Urquizo, *Páginas*, p. 72; Guzmán, *Memorias*, pp. 380–2; Aguirre Benavides, *De Francisco I. Madero*, p. 120.

711 Director, Sonora Land and Timber Co., to Grey, 27 Feb.; H. E. Bourchier, Chairman, British Subjects in Mexico, to Grey, 28 Feb. 1914; FO 371/2025, 8940, 9008.

712 On the Benton case and its ramifications: Guzmán, *Memorias*, pp. 254–68; Fabela, *Historia diplomática*, I, pp. 261–98; Clarence C. Clendenen, *The United States and Pancho Villa*, pp. 67–71; Villa to *New York Times* and to R. Pesqueira, 21 Feb. 1914, SRE, legajo 760, p. 216.

713 B. Carbajal y Rosas to Grey, 2 Mar. 1914, FO 371/2025, 9468; Pesqueira, Washington, to Carranza, 20, 21, Feb. 1914, SRE, legajo 760, pp. 214, 218; Fabela, *Historia diplomática*, I, p. 270.

714 Carranza to González, 1 Feb. 1914, 25 Dec. 1913, SRE, legajo 760, pp. 129, 88; Andrés García to Col E. González, 22 Nov. 1913, SRE, legajo 810, p. 313.

715 *El Correo de Chihuahua*, 5, 7, 8 June 1910; though Aguirre Benavides' qualification of Benton as a 'señor de horca y cuchillo' is a little rhetorical: *De Francisco I. Madero*, pp. 107, 109.

716 Manager, Sonora Land and Timber Co., 11 Mar. 1914, in FO 371/2025, 11026. Benton's actual killer is usually reckoned to have been Fierro, who was accomplished in such matters, rather than Villa himself: Aguirre Benavides, *De Francisco I. Madero*, p. 109; Reed, *Insurgent Mexico*, p. 56.

717 Thord-Gray, *Gringo Rebel*, p. 77; O'Hea, Gómez Palacio, 11 Mar. 1918, FO 371/3243, 60324; Barragán, *Historia del ejército*, I, pp. 30, 313.

718 Taracena, *Carranza*, p. 199.

719 Capt. Cootes, War Dept, El Paso, Dec. 1913, SD 812.00/10453.

720 Pani, *Apuntes*, pp. 189–93; O'Shaughnessy, *Diplomat's Wife*, pp. 14–18; Casasola, *Historia gráfica*, I, pp. 684–5.

721 Barragán, *Historia del ejército*, I, pp. 221–6 (a hostile version); cf. Cervantes, *Francisco Villa*, pp. 98–9.

722 Cumberland, *Constitutionalist Years*, pp. 82–3.

723 Casasola, *Historia gráfica*, 1, pp. 684–5 (though note Angeles' distinctive and fetching polo-neck).

724 Reed, *Insurgent Mexico*, p. 217.

725 Obregón, *Ocho mil kilómetros*, p. 101.

726 Guzmán, *The Eagle and the Serpent* (New York, 1965), pp. 20, 24–5; Taracena, *Carranza*, p. 198; Reed, *Insurgent Mexico*, p. 217; Thord-Gray, *Gringo Rebel*, p. 78.

727 Reed, *Insurgent Mexico*, p. 215.

728 Guzmán, *Eagle and the Serpent*, pp. 22, 26–8; Urquizo, *Páginas*, p. 61; Taracena, *Carranza*, pp. 6–8, is more charitable towards his subject's intellectual pretensions. Carranza's taste for history – of the 'Great Man', biographical school – is borne out by the contents of his personal library in Calle Río Lerma, Mexico City.

729 Obregón, *Ocho mil kilómetros*, p. 85.

730 Guzmán, *Eagle and the Serpent*, pp. 25–6, 37–9; cf. Aguilar, *Revolución Sonorense*, pp. 446–7.

731 Carranza to Julio Madero, 6 May 1913, Fabela, DHRM, RRC, 1, p. 27; Barragán, *Historia del ejército*, 1, p. 437; Carranza to S. Terrazas, 27 Dec. 1913 and Escudero to Maytorena, 12 Jan. 1914, Fabela, DHRM, 1, pp. 182, 223–6.

732 Aguilar, *Revolución Sonorense*, p. 448.

733 Pani, *Apuntes*, p. 193; Aguirre Benavides, *De Francisco I. Madero*, p. 69; Guzmán, *Eagle and the Serpent*, pp. 84–5.

734 Gavira, *Actuación*, p. 79; Barragán, *Historia del ejército*, 1, p. 254, on Calzada's dismissal of civilian *políticos*.

735 Aguirre Benavides, *De Francisco I. Madero*, pp. 96–7; Vera Estañol, *Revolución mexicana*, p. 380; Miguel Díaz Lombardo and the brothers González Garza could be added to the list.

736 Guzmán, *Memorias*, p. 272; Aguilar, *Revolución Sonorense*, pp. 132–3, 481.

737 Rafael Hernández to Villa, 2 Jan. 1914, Fabela, DHRM, RRC, 1, pp. 203–5: a closing letter, from one seeking a belated *acómodo* with the revolution; note also Ernesto Madero to Carranza, 8 Jan. 1914, same volume, pp. 206–7.

738 The phrase is Rafael Hernández's (n. 737).

739 Guzmán, *Eagle and the Serpent*, p. 12; José Vasconcelos, *Ulíses criollo* (Bloomington, 1963), 1, pp. 88–9; note Vasconcelos' impatience with what he saw as a long-drawn-out, messy, military struggle, lacking political relevance: to Carranza, 19 Sept. 1913, Fabela, DHRM, RRC, 1, pp. 118–22.

740 Such as Cabrera, whose 'prudent advice' Villa welcomed: Villa to Carranza, 23 Dec. 1913; note also Jesús Acuña to Carranza, 18 Nov. 1913, on Villa's loyalty and amenability: Fabela, DHRM, RRC, 1, pp. 178, 153–5.

741 Guzmán, *Memorias*, pp. 285–6, for Villa's opinion of the Maderista civilians (particularly acute in the case of Vasconcelos).

742 *Ibid.*, p. 284.

743 Later, when Angeles' 'treason' was consummated, some, like Obregón, *Ocho mil kilómetros*, p. 104, claimed a remarkable prescience; but suspicions were certainly in the air by mid-summer 1914: R. Pesqueira to Carranza, 1 June 1914, Fabela, DHRM, RRC, 1, pp. 281–3.

744 Eventually, Pablo González made progress; but in the autumn of 1913 Carrancista operations in the north-east had 'virtual[ly] collapse[d]': Eagle Pass Immigration report, 3 Oct. 1913, SD 812.00/9462.

745 Hamm, Durango, 15, 23 Oct. 1913; Letcher, Chihuahua, 1 Dec. 1913; SD 812.00/9658, 9858; 10126. The Federals retook Torreón early in December, the rebel garrison lacking ammunition and pulling out without resistance: Bonnet, Torreón, 16 Dec. 1913, SD 812.00/10406.

746 Cumberland, *Constitutionalist Years*, p. 50.

747 Guzmán, *Memorias*, pp. 205–15; Thord-Gray, *Gringo Rebel*; Edwards, Juárez, 18 Nov. 1913, SD 812.00/9894, reports that Villa desisted from his attack on Chihuahua because of a financial inducement from the Terrazas interests; which is unlikely (as an explanation) but revealing (as to Terracista conduct and reputation).

748 Guzmán, *Memorias*, pp. 216–20. Reed, *Insurgent Mexico*, p. 131, for similar, if not identical, accounts.

749 Aguirre Benavides, *De Francisco I. Madero*, p. 92; Ronald Atkin, *Revolution! Mexico, 1910–1920* (London, 1969), pp. 161–2.

750 Juan Medina, quoted in Guzmán, *Memorias*, p. 208.

751 Thord-Gray, *Gringo Rebel*, pp. 21–53, gives a detailed account of the battle of Tierra Blanca which, but for the author's propensity to see Apaches everywhere, is convincing; see also, Guzmán, *Memorias*, pp. 230–7; Alberto Calzadíaz Barrera, *Hechos reales de la revolución mexicana* (Mexico, 1961), I, pp. 157–9; Langle Ramírez, *El ejército Villista*, pp. 49, 50.

752 Thord-Gray, *Gringo Rebel*, pp. 36–7, where Federal numbers are put at 7,000; Guzmán and Aguirre Benavides give figures of 6,200 and 6,000 for Villa's army, as against 5,500 and 'over 6,000' for the Federals; clearly, numbers were about equal and – compared with later Villista engagements – small.

753 Aguirre Benavides, *De Francisco I. Madero*, p. 93; in what purports to be Villa's own account, in Guzmán, *Memorias*, pp. 230–7, strategic thinking is scarcely evident.

754 Thord-Gray, *Gringo Rebel*, p. 40.

755 There is general agreement, but specific variations on this point: Thord-Gray makes the commander 'an uneducated, half-breed Apache'; Barragán, *Historia del ejército*, I, pp. 269–70, in a somewhat terse, grudging account of Tierra Blanca, makes Maclovio Herrera the hero; though I. Grimaldo, *Apuntes para la historía* (San Luis, 1916), pp. 18–19, omits mentions of the charge.

756 Thord-Gray, *Gringo Rebel*, pp. 46–7.

757 *Ibid.*, p. 47.

758 *Ibid.*, p. 48; Guzmán, *Memorias*, p. 237; S. Terrazas to D. Horcasitas, 27 Nov. 1913, STA, box 83, which puts Federal casualties as high as 2,000; though no doubt an exaggeration, this may reflect losses sustained during the rout rather than the battle; for, at least in the north, the battles of the revolution were 'modern' in the sense that flight was often highly dangerous. Cf. John Keegan, *The Face of Battle* (London, 1978), pp. 314–16.

759 Meyer, *Mexican Rebel*, pp. 107–8; this disagreement was nothing new: Letcher, Chihuahua, 10 Oct. 1913, SD 812.00/9162.

760 Cumberland, *Constitutionalist Years*, p. 52; Calzadíaz Barrera, *Hechos reales*, I, p. 173.

761 Reed, *Insurgent Mexico*, p. 39 (where the trip from Chihuahua to Ojinaga is mysteriously elongated to 400 miles); Edwards, Juarez, 3 Dec. 1913, SD 812.00/10021.

762 Reed, *Insurgent Mexico*, pp. 39–41.

763 Letcher, Chihuahua, 11 Dec. 1913, SD 812.00/10167.

764 Calzadíaz Barrera, *Hechos reales*, I, 164–6; Reed, *Insurgent Mexico*, pp. 44–5; it is hard to see Ojinaga, as Meyer, *Mexican Rebel*, pp. 109–10 does, as a major turning point; Federal resistance – lasting an hour – was perfunctory.

765 Carothers, Chihuahua, 10 Feb. 1914, SD 812.00/10903.

766 C/o, Ft Sam Houston, 17 Dec. 1913; Carothers, Chihuahua, 18 Feb. 1914; SD 812.00/10247; 10917; Clendenen, *United States and Pancho Villa*, pp. 53–6.

767 Letcher, Chihuahua, 11 Dec. 1913, SD 812.00/10167; Reed, *Insurgent Mexico*, p. 119.

768 Hamm, Torreón, 19 Apr.; Edwards, Juárez, 11 Jan. 1914; SD 812.00/11703; 10511.

769 Brondo Whitt, *División del Norte*, p. 159.

770 Edwards, Juárez, 23 Dec. 1913, SD 812.00/10336.

771 Clendenen, *United States and Pancho Villa*, pp. 73–4; War Dept report, 6 Jan. 1914, SD 812.00/10467.

772 S. Terrazas to D. Bustamante, Havana, 30 Aug. 1913, STA, box 83; *Mexican Herald*, 8 Dec. 1914.

773 STA, box 84.

774 Letcher, Chihuahua, 11 Dec. 1913, SD 812.00/10167; Calzadíaz Barrera, *Hechos reales*, I, p. 168. As regards the forced circulation of Villista currency, this was no great hardship, since it was accepted in the US virtually at par: Brondo Whitt, *División del Norte*, p. 14.

775 Cf. Rutherford, *Mexican Society*, pp. 277–8; and Knight, 'Nationalism', pp. 302–9.

776 Carothers, Torreón, 11 Oct. 1913, SD 812.00/9658.

777 Silliman, Saltillo, 29 Dec. 1913, SD 812.00/10757.

778 Riaño, Spanish Ambassador, Washington, to Bryan, 7 Feb. 1914, FO 371/2025, 10802.

779 Letcher, Chihuahua, 11, 21 Dec. 1913, SD 812.00/10167, 10301.

780 Hamm, Torreón, 19 Apr. 1914, SD 812.00/11703; the same correspondent (SD 812.00/11706) also reports the assassination of Spaniards by Argumedo's retreating irregulars: an indication of the consistent Hispanophobia among plebeian troops on both sides.

781 The British vice-consul at Gómez – no friend of the revolution – was sure that members of the Spanish community 'have taken part in the political struggle'; Edwards, at Juárez, reported that 'their sympathies are quite unanimous with the Huertistas and in favor of the old regime and [they] were liberal contributors to the Huerta cause'; Hamm, at Durango, concurred. See, Cummins, Dec. 1913, FO 371/2025, 13251; Edwards, 23 Dec. 1913; Hamm, 16 Feb. 1914; SD 812.00/10336; 11028. Other examples have already been given.

782 Marte R. Gómez, *La reforma agraria en las filas Villistos* (Mexico, 1966), p. 33; Reed, *Insurgent Mexico*, p. 123 links it – not altogether implausibly – to anticlericalism. Edward (n. 781) compares anti-Spanish sentiments to popular anti-Semitism in Russia; Hohler, *Diplomatic Petrel*, pp. 171–2, makes the same comparison with Germany, and with popular attitudes towards the Syrian merchants of Egypt.

783 Cummins, Gómez, Jan. 1914; Benson to Grey, 13 Mar. 1914, transcribing report from Tlahualilo; FO 371/2025, 10096; 11732.

784 S. G. Inman to Mrs Inman, 17 Apr. 1914, SGIA, box 12.

785 Hamm, Durango, 11 Nov. 1913, SD 812.00/9989.

786 *Ibid.*; Reed, *Insurgent Mexico*, p. 122.

787 Powers, Parral, 22 Nov.; Hamm, Durango, 11 Nov. 1913; SD 812.00/10126.

788 Reed, *Insurgent Mexico*, pp. 133–4.

789 Gómez, *Reforma graria*, p. 82; but the claim was made in 1915, when Villismo faced fresh problems, and had been exposed to new influences: note Katz, *Secret War*, pp. 282–3.

790 Clendenen, *United States and Pancho Villa*, citing the *Brooklyn Eagle*.

791 Calzadíaz Barrera, *Hechos reales*, I, p. 161; N. M. Lavrov, 'La revolución mexicana de 1910–17', pp. 99, 110, where the author talks, not just of struggle and intention, but also of accomplishment: Villa 'satisfied the aspirations of the peasants, freeing them from the yoke of the latifundistas, of feudal serfdom, and of the opium of the Catholic Church'.

792 Gómez, *Reforma agraria*, pp. 28–8, 31, 123: Friedich Katz, 'Labor conditions on haciendas in Porfirian Mexico, some trends and tendencies', *Hispanic American Historical Review*, LIV (1974), p. 46, broadly agrees. The decree is mentioned in *Le Courrier du Méxique*, 18 Dec. 1914.

793 Juan Martínez Alier, *Haciendas, Plantations and Collective Farms. Agrarian Class Societies – Cuba and Peru* (London, 1977), p. 26; Rouaix, in Silva Herzog, *La cuestión de la tierra* (Mexico, 1961), I, p. 167.

794 Jesus J. Ríos to Carranza, concerning the Comisión de Agricultores de la Laguna, AVC, 11–19 Oct. 1915; memo., 'Asuntos que tratar con General Villa', STA, box 83. Zapata, and other, lesser leaders, tried similar schemes, usually with less success: Womack, *Zapata*, p. 235; Falcón, 'Cedillo', p. 120.

795 Friedrich Katz, 'Agrarian Changes in Northern Mexico in the period of Villista Rule, 1913–15', in James W. Wilkie, Michael C. Meyer and Edna Monzon de Wilkie, eds., *Contemporary Mexico: Papers of the Fourth International Congress of Mexican History* (Berkeley, 1976), p. 263.

796 Eric R. Wolf, *Peasant Wars of the Twentieth Century* (London, 1973), p. 36; Katz, *Deutschland*, pp. 242–4.

797 Katz, 'Agrarian Changes', p. 264.

798 *Ibid.*, pp. 264–6; Ríos to Carranza (n. 794) gives many examples.

799 Katz, 'Agrarian Changes', p. 267.

800 This principle is clear from both the Terrazas papers and the Ríos report; it was possible for ownerhip to remain unchanged, while a tenancy – like that of El Jabincillo, owned by Jesus Caldeŕon, but rented by the pro-Huerta Spaniard, Manuel Gutiérrez – was confiscated 'por causa política' (Ríos report).

801 Trinidad Vega, interviewed by Ximena Sepúlveda, PHO 1/126, pp. 13, 16, 45; Simón Márquez Camarena, interviewed by María Isabel Souza, PHO 1/113, pp. 12–13, 28–9, 31, 38.

802 Rouaix, *Diccionario*, pp. 369–70; Hamm, Durango, 30 Nov. 1913, SD 812.00/10272, which gives some details of this 'socialistic' measure; Gómez, *Reforma Agraria*, p. 29 is rather dismissive; Pazuengo, *Historia*, pp. 48–9.

803 Katz, 'Agrarian Changes', pp. 266–7; Katz's researches have revealed only one clear case of restitution, concerning a Creel hacienda.

804 *Ibid.*, p. 271, following Gómez.

805 *Ibid.*, p. 260.

806 Gramsci, quoted by James Joll, *Gramsci* (London, 1977), p. 95.

807 Simón Márquez Camarena, interviewed by María Isabel Souza, PHO 1/113, p. 6.

808 Huntington, *Political Order*, p. 272, n. 7.

809 'Generated' or 'released'? The historiographical – not to mention the theoretical – problems involved in attempting an answer are overwhelming. See vol. 1, p. 528.

810 Katz, 'Agrarian Changes', p. 267.

811 Pazuengo, *Historia*, pp. 48–9.

812 Reed, *Insurgent Mexico*, pp. 133–4, Katz, 'Agrarian Changes', p. 272, on the military colony scheme, Villa's 'passionate dream', which, though it could not be implemented during the war, finally took shape at Canutillo in the early 1920s.

813 Edwards, Juárez, 23 Dec. 1913, SD 812.00/10336; Reed, *Insurgent Mexico*, p. 123.

814 In their support of the Brazilian *cangaceiro*, we are told, 'members of the rural poor had turned to an individual solution to their plight as a class which . . . undercut potential for more meaningful change through mass action and revolt': Linda Lewin, 'Social Banditry in Brazil', *Past and Present*, LXXXII (1979), p. 145. But even 'mass action and revolt', if channelled through glorified social banditry – like Villismo – may not produce 'meaningful' change (if that implies durable, 'structural' reform).

815 Gómez, *Reforma Agraria*, pp. 33–4, citing Magaña; Reed, *Insurgent Mexico*, p. 124; Aguirre Benavides, *De Francisco I. Madero*, p. 105.

816 Letcher, Chihuahua, 21 Dec. 1913; Carothers, Chihuahua, 10 Feb. 1914; SD 812.00/10301; 10903; Katz, 'Agrarian Changes', p. 277, citing Almada.

817 Aguirre Benavides, *De Fransisco I. Madero*, pp. 102–3; Guzmán, *Memorias*, p. 569; Trinidad Vega, interviewed by Ximena Sepúlveda, PHO 1/126, p. 40, on Villa's (deserved) womanising reputation.

818 A list of nearly 100 names, with details, appears in STA, box 84.

819 González Galindo in DDCC, II, p. 918.

820 Gavira, *Actuación*, pp. 132–7, 178; and vol. 1, pp. 239–40.

821 Guzmán, *Memorias*, pp. 407–8.

822 The point is developed below, pp. 271–4, 299–301.

823 Calzadíaz Barrera, *Hechos reales*, I, p. 161; Reed, *Insurgent Mexico*, pp. 122, 133; Katz, *Secret War*, p. 141, and 'Agrarian Changes', p. 270.

824 Calzadíaz Barrera, *Hechos reales*, I, p. 161; Reed, *Insurgent Mexico*, p. 122.

825 Carothers, El Paso, 3 Feb. 1914, SD 812.00/10820.

826 Trinidad Vega, interviewed by Ximena Sepúlveda, Andrés Rivera Marrufo by María Isabel Souza, PHO 1/126, p. 39, /63, p. 20.

827 Jacobo Estrada Márquez, interviewed by María Alba Pastor, PHO 1/121, p. 23.

828 Gregory Mason, 'With Villa in Chihuahua', *The Outlook*, 9 May 1914.

829 Cummins, Gómez, Dec. 1913, EO 371/2025, 13251.

830 Brondo Whitt, *División del Norte*, p. 11, recounting a conversation overhead in a public park in Chihuahua; hence, perhaps, the garbled version of the Magnificat.

831 Quirk, *Mexican Revolution*, p. 27.

832 Brondo Whitt, *División del Norte*, pp. 21–2, 107–8; Reed, *Insurgent Mexico*, pp. 125–6, 133; cf. Oliver Lawson Dick, ed., *Aubrey's Brief Lives* (London, 1976), p. 219 describing the royalist Colonel Charles Cavendish.

833 Mendoza, *Lírica narrativa*, pp. 152–33, the translation from Rutherford, *Mexican Society*, p. 161; see also Reed, *Insurgent Mexico*, pp. 88–9.

834 Gracey, Progreso, 9 Feb. 1914, SD 812.00/10920.

835 Wolf, *Sons of the Shaking Earth*, pp. 208–20.

836 Reed, *Insurgent Mexico*, pp. 122, 159, 164.

837 Edwards, Juárez, 23 Dec. 1913, SD 812.00/10336; Michie to Scott, 16 Nov. 1913, Scott Papers, box 15; Aguirre Benavides, *De Francisco I. Madero*, p. 92.

838 Guzmán, *Eagle and the Serpent*, p. 97; and Oscar J. Martínez, *Border Boom Town: Ciudad Juárez Since 1848* (Austin, 1978), pp. 50–5, on revolutionary Juárez.

839 Aguirre Benavides, *De Francisco I. Madero*, pp. 106–7.

840 Katz, 'Agrarian Changes', pp. 262–3.

841 Brondo Whitt, *División del Norte*, p. 92.

842 Terrazas memo, 'Asuntos que tratar con General Villa', n.d., 1914, STA, box 84.

843 See below, pp. 459–65.

844 Wilkie, *Mexican Revolution*, pp. 24, 32, 102. These figures tally roughly with those of Ernesto Madero's budget statement to Congress, Dec. 1912, in SD 812.51/55; they show military expenditure rising from 20% of total in 1910–11 and 20% in 1911–12, to 27% (projected) in 1912–13, 31% (projected) in 1913–14.

845 Meyer, *Huerta*, p. 187; Landa y Escandón to Cowdray, 22 Dec. 1913, Cowdray Papers, box A/3 (this after a conversation with Finance Minister de la Lama). Army payrolls, of course, were padded; but the money still had to be disbursed, even if it found its way into officers' bank accounts rather than the *pelones'* pockets.

846 *Mexican Year Book*, 1984, pp. 8–9, 15–16.

847 'I have been simply dumbfounded at the financial strength of Mexico', commented an economic observer in Financial America: *Mexican Herald*, 17 Feb. 1914. Parallels with the war economies of Europe (especially Germany and Russia, 1941–5) spring to mind.

848 Gracey, Progeso, 22 Nov. 1913, SD 812.00/10019; *Mexican Herald*, 11 May 1913, 6 Apr. 1914.

849 *Mexican Herald*, 21 Oct., 13 Nov. 1913, 7 Feb. 1914.

850 In 1910 (the nadir) Yucatán exported 95m. kg. at 18.9c. per kg, total value 17.9m. pesos; by 1913, 147m. kg. were exported, at 24.4c. per kg., total value 36m. pesos; exports for the first two-thirds of 1914 were 58% up on the equivalent for the previous year: Edmundo Bolio, *Yucatán en la dictadura y la revolución* (Mexico, 1967), p. 69; *Mexican Herald*, 12 Nov. 1913, 21 Jan., 12 Mar. 1914; *Le Courrier du Méxique*, 19 Oct. 1914.

851 Gracey, Progreso, 7 Mar. 1914, SD 812.00/11159.

852 Meyer, *México y Estados Unidos*, p. 19; *Petroleum Review*, 25 Apr. 1914, gives figures of 17m. and 24m.

853 Cowdray to Bowring, 26 Dec. 1913, Cowdray Papers, box A/3; *Mexican Herald*, 26 Dec. 1913, quotes *Financial America* to the same effect.

854 *Mexican Herald*, 15, 18 Jan. 1914.

855 Lorenzo Meyer, *México y Estados Unidos en el conflicto petrolero* (Mexico, 1968), p. 19: 1914, 26m. barrels; 1915, 33m.; 1916, 41m.; 1917, 55m.

856 *Mexican Herald*, 30 Sept., 22 Nov. 1913, on Sonoran mining output.

857 See pp. 47–8.

858 *Mexican Herald*, 4 Oct. 1913; Boicort, Fénix Coal Co., 27 Apr.; Ellsworth, Cd Porfirio Díaz, 24 Apr.; border report, Eagle Pass, 23 Aug. 1913; SD 812.00/7389; 7248; which indicate that the coal mines were a strategic target; Bernstein, *Mexican Mining Industry*, p. 101, Meyer, *Huerta*, p. 179, on railway damage.

859 *Mexican Herald*, 26 Aug., 4, 24 Oct., 11 Dec. 1913, 23 Mar. 1914.

860 *Ibid.*, 4 Oct. 1913.

861 *Ibid.*, 11 Nov. 1913.

862 Based on the figures in Bernstein, *Mexican Mining Industry*, p. 101, which cannot be more than approximations. *Le Courrier du Méxique*, 27 July 1914, gives sketchier figures for 1911–13, which corroborate these relatively, if not absolutely.

863 *Mexican Herald*, 13, 17 Oct., 27 Nov., 18 Dec. 1913, 6 Feb. 1914. This did not mean that the cotton producers – if they were politically marginal, like the Tlahualilo Co., which was 'able to run with rebels, with Carrancistas and Zapatistas [sic] and every kind of "ista"' – lost out; Tlahualilo did well in 1913–14, producing over 12,000 bales, compared with 9,600 in 1914–15, 2,400 in 1916–17 (a year of drought), and 6,600 in 1917–18: J. B. Potter reports, MCETA, parcel 11.

864 *Mexican Herald*, 1, 30 Nov. 1913, 5, 8, 14 Feb. 1914; Tampico was under threat from Dec. 1913 to May 1914, when it fell.

865 *Ibid.*, 27 Sept., 7 Oct. 1913, 27 Feb., 23 Mar. 1914; Rutherford, *Mexican Society*, p. 266.

866 Silliman, Saltillo, 2 Aug. 1913, SD 812.51/87 notes the following price rises compared with 1910: rice up 41%, sugar 28%, flour 54%, meat 29%.

867 Meyer, *Huerta*, pp. 180–1; Jan Bazant, *Historia de la deuda exterior de México (1823–1946)* (Mexico, 1968), p. 180; *Mexican Herald*, 15 Feb. 1914.

868 Limantour to Cowdray, 11 Apr. 1913, Cowdray Papers, box A/3.

869 Moheno, *Actuación*, pp. 83, 108–9, 157; *Le Courrier du Méxique*, 31 July 1914, quotes Moheno.

870 Body to Murray, July 1913, Cowdray Papers, box A/3: 'financial situation very serious. Without recognition US impossible obtain funds'; see also Calvert, *Mexican Revolution*, pp. 181–5.

871 F. González Gante to Carranza, 11 May; Carranza to Díaz Lombardo, 30 May; and vice versa, 18 June 1913; Fabela, DHRM, RRC, I, pp. 31–3, 58–9, 80–4.

872 Meyer, *Huerta*, pp. 186–7; Bazant, *Deuda exterior*, p. 177.

873 Meyer, *Huerta*, p. 188; *Mexican Herald*, 13, 14, 21 Jan. 1914; O'Shaughnessy, Mexico City, 22, 26 Dec. 1913, 26 Jan. 1914, SD 812.50/104, 107, 126.

874 *Mexican Herald*, 15 Sept., 1 Oct. 1913; E. W. Kemmerer, *Inflation and Revolution: Mexico's Experience of 1912–17* (Princeton, 1940), p. 22.

875 Kemmerer, *Inflation*, pp. 9–11.

876 *Ibid.*, p. 155ff.; Bazant, *Deuda exterior*, p. 178; Meyer, *Huerta*, pp. 182–3.

877 Sandford, Monterrey, 20 Feb.; Richardson, Tlahualilo, Feb. 1914; FO 371/2026, 12805; 11752; Silliman, Saltillo, 12 Jan. 1914, SD 812.00/10633.

878 Lespinasse, Frontera, 18 Nov. 1913, SD 812.00/10073; *Mexican Herald*, 13 Jan., 9, 25 Feb. 1914; Meyer, *Huerta*, pp. 182–3.

879 *Mexican Herald*, 21 Oct., 20 Nov., 7 Dec. 1913, 15, 24 Feb. 1914; Gracey, Progreso, 31 Oct. 1913, 15 Jan. 1914, SD 812.00/9698, 10658.

880 *Mexican Herald*, 6 Oct., 20 Nov. 1913; Stadden, Manzanillo, 24 Nov. 1913; Lind, 3 Feb. 1914, SD 812.00/10778.

881 *Mexican Herald*, 6 Oct. 1913, 23, 25 Mar. 1914; Schmutz, Aguascalientes, 11 Dec. 1913, SD 812.00/10328.

882 Meyer, *Huerta*, p. 184; *Mexican Herald*, 15 Jan. 1914; Cowdray to Clive Pearson, 13 Mar. 1914, Cowdray Papers, box A/3.

883 Edwards, Acapulco, 12 Jan.; Silliman, Saltillo, 4 Mar. 1914; SD 812.00/10533, 11139.

884 Blocker, Cd Porfirio Díaz, 7 Nov. 1913; Payne, Tuxpán, 7 Jan. 1914; SD 812.00/9682; 10622.

885 Payne (n. 884).

886 *Mexican Herald*, 13 Sept. 1913; and above, pp. 1–2.

887 *Ibid.*, 26 Oct. 1913, 21 Jan. 1914.

888 House Diary, 19, 20 Jan. 1914; Canada, Veracruz, 12 Nov. 1913, SD 812.6342/14.

889 Stadden, Manzanillo, 24 Nov. 1913, 19, 24 Jan. 1914, SD 812.00/9927, 10612, 10682; Meyer, *Huerta*, p. 185.

890 Silliman, Saltillo, 12 Jan. 1914, SD 812.00/10633.

891 Lespinasse, Frontera, 26 Mar. 1914, SD 812.00/11309; E. Aranda, President of Cámara Agrícola, León, to Dept of Labour, 2 Feb. 1914; Jesus García *et al.* to same, 3 Oct. 1913; Trabajo, 32/1/2/30; 34/1/14/2.

892 Meyer, *Huerta*, p. 181: a 'number of federally supported schools' were victims of financial cuts; a measure which contrasts with Huerta's supposed educational advances.

893 Meyer, *Huerta*, p. 181; A. M. Elías, El Paso, to SRE, 15 June 1914, SRE, legajo 784, 84-R-15, p. 185.

894 Blocker, Cd Porfirio Díaz, 7 Nov. 1913; Edwards, Acapulco, 12 Jan.; Payne, Tuxpán, 7 Jan.; Silliman, Saltillo, 12 Jan.; 14 Mar. 1914; SD 812.00/9682; 10533; 10622; 10633; 11139.

895 Diebold to SRE, 28 Mar. 1914, SRE, legajo 787, 86-R-8, p. 11.

896 Guyant, Ensenada, 2, 13, 21 Jan. 1914, SD 812.00/10399, 10625, 10629.

897 F. McCaughan, Durango, May 1913, SD 812.00/7856.

898 Silliman, Saltillo, 4 Aug. 1913, SD 812.00/8459.

899 *Ibid.*, 25 Nov. 1913, SD 812.00/10050.

900 *Ibid.*, 29 Dec. 1913, SD 812.00/10757.

901 Edwards, Acapulco, 6 Nov. 1913, SD 812.00/9990.

902 Hendrick, Paris, 5 Nov.; Gerard, Berlin, 8 Dec. 1913; SD 812.00/9569, 10019; Limantour to R. Kindersley, MP, rec'd 23 Jan. 1914, FO 371/2025, 3401.

903 *Mexican Herald*, 15 Nov. 1913.

904 Though in some measure the wish was father to the thought, Lind was partially correct; his mistake was to assume that this loss of popularity would have rapid, practical consequences (above all, the fall of Huerta); but Huerta did not depend primarily on popularity for his maintenance of power – Mexico was not Minnesota. See Lind, 11, 12 Nov. 1913; O'Shaughnessy, Mexico City, 3 Nov. 1913; Boaz Long memos, 6 Nov. 1913, 4 Feb. 1914; SD 812.00/9675, 9678; 9510; 9831½, 10791.

905 Spring-Rice, Washington, 26 Jan. 1914; Hohler, memo. of conversation with Algara, Washington, 9 Feb. 1914; FO 371/2025, 3844, 8667.

906 Hohler, memo., 14 Feb. 1914, FO 371/2025, 8667.

907 Hohler, memo., 9 Feb. 1914, FO 371/2025, 8667. Wilson's own Secretary of War, Lindley Garrison, had no time for Bryan, the administration's Mexican policy, or politicians south of the border, who 'are a lot of treacherous bandits . . . the only way to make them good [being] with a big stick': House Diary, 8 May 1914.

908 Of course, a purer form of equity might have been achieved by recognising the belligerency of both sides and letting them fight it out with American arms, to the greater profit of American business; but the higher morality of such a policy is not obvious.

909 Lind, 28 Aug., on the superiority of the 'Teutonic' over the 'Latin' races; 27 Nov., 5 Dec. 1913, on the machinations of the British: SD 812.00/10487; 9931, 10077. Again, there was an element of truth here: the British Minister, Lionel Carden, was keen for Huerta,

and as anti-American as Lind was anti-British. But Carden was increasingly isolated, dreaming geopolitical fantasies, out of touch with both the Foreign Office (which recognised American local paramountcy) and British interests, like Cowdray's, which took a more pragmatic line. The whole 'Anglo-American conflict' was more myth and misunderstanding than basic enmity; by the beginning of 1914, the misunderstanding had been largely removed, and mavericks like Carden and Lind were hard put to sustain the myth in defiance of the drift of official policy. Britain now readily deferred to US policy in Mexico, even though the Foreign Office derided its *naïveté*. Katz, *Secret War*, ch. 5, is a full, recent analysis though, arguably, it exaggerates Carden's typicality and importance.

910 Lind, 14, 15 Jan. 1914, SD 812.00/10537, 1065½; Grieb *United States and Huerta*, p. 120.

911 Grieb, *United States and Huerta*, p. 121: Wilson's words.

912 Carranza to Wilson, 21 Apr. 1913, Fabela, DHRM, RRC, I, p. 22; Hale, Nogales, 12 Nov.; Maytorena to Bryan, 20 Aug.; Blocker, Cd Porfirio Díaz, 27 Aug. 1913; SD 812.00/9685; 8479; 8786.

913 See the detailed enclosures in Spring-Rice, Washington, to Grey, 14 Feb. 1914, FO 371/2025, 8667, including Cabrera's outline of policy and Hohler's memo's of talks with Cabrera, Wilson and Bryan; and note Kendrick A. Clements, 'Emissary From a Revolution: Luis Cabrera and Woodrow Wilson', *Americas*, XXXV (1979), pp. 353–71.

914 The 'European' view is here represented by Hohler; for criticism of Wilson see Calvert, *Mexican Revolution*, p. 302 ('Taft wanted to remain in the days of Diaz, Wilson in the days of Madero'); and Grieb, *United States and Huerta*, pp. 42–3 ('Wilson . . . believed that if the US swept the current caudillo away, the Mexican people would rejoice at his removal [and] establish an elective government'): both untenably simplistic.

915 Cabrera's outline, which so influenced Wilson and which the British Foreign Office deemed 'not worth reading', sought to clarify Constitutionalist policy towards property rights; it promised a 'perfectly just' land reform, involving expropriation with indemnification, offered 'careful consideration' of damage claims, and made guarded, imprecise comments on the status of foreign loans and contracts: see FO 371/2025, 8667 and Link, *Wilson*, p. 389. Ulloa, *Revolución intervenida*, pp. 92–3 and 'Carranza y el armamiento norteamericano', *Historia Mexicana*, XVII (1967), pp. 253–61, claims that Cabrera made concessions in Washington of the kind which Carranza had rejected three months before. Yet there is no evidence of Cabrera communicating formal conditions to Carranza; and my reading of the correspondence (cited by Ulloa) suggests that the US lifted the embargo without attaching conditions, vindicating Carranza's position: see R. Pesqueira to Carranza, 29 Jan., and *vice versa*, 30 Jan. 1914, SRE, legajo 760–75–21, pp. 121, 126; and Ulloa, *Revolución intervenida*, pp. 316–17.

916 Admiral Cradock, Tampico, 19 Dec.; Wilson, Tampico, 23 Dec. 1913; FO 371/2025, 2833.

917 Carothers, El Paso, 3 Feb.; Hamm, Durango, 16 Feb.; Lespinasse, Frontera, 28 Feb. 1913; SD 812.00/10820; 11028; 1115.

918 Quoted in the *Mexican Herald*, 28 Mar. 1914.

919 E. Llorente, Eagle Pass, quoted by Huertista consul, 9 Mar. 1914, SRE, legajo 784, 84-R-15, p. 73.

920 Cumberland, *Constitutionalist Years*, pp. 42, 45–6.

921 Lind, 28 Feb. 1914, SD 812.00/11011.

922 *El Imparcial*, 24 Mar. 1914; Wood Diary, 3 Mar. 1914 (Carden was in the US).

923 Lind's barrage of reports and recommendations can best be followed in the Wilson Papers, series II, boxes 103, 104, 105; see, especially, 18, 24, 25, 28 Feb.; 12, 19, Mar. 1914, deploring rebel inactivity and urging the US government 'to put an end to Huerta's saturnalia of crime and oppression'.

924 Minute of Knatchbull-Hugessen on Hohler, 23 Mar. 1914, FO 371/2028, 13004.

925 Diebold, El Paso, 20 Feb. 1914, SRE, legajo 784, 84-R-15, p. 48; Calzadíaz Barrera, *Hechos reales*, I, p. 170; Brondo Whitt, *División del Norte*, p. 34.

926 Calzadíaz Barrera, *Hechos reales*, I, p. 170; Guzmán, *Memorias*, p. 284.

927 Carothers, El Paso, 3 Feb. 1914, SD 812.00/10821 and Ramón Prida, *De la dictadura a la anarquía* (Mexico, 1958), p. 586 agree on 20,000; Langle Ramírez, *Ejército Villista*, p. 65, Aguirre Benavides, *De Francisco I. Madero*, p. 113 and Hamm, Torreón, 19 Apr. 1914, SD 812.00/11703, all estimate the army which Villa took to Torreón at 10,000; allowing for other garrisons in the north, the Division of the North must have stood at 13–14,000 (minimum); at Tierra Blanca, it will be recalled, Villa commanded some 6,000.

928 Calzadíaz Barrera, *Hechos reales*, I, pp. 172, 179–80.

929 Brondo Whitt, *División del Norte*, p. 234.

930 *Ibid.*, p. 181ff.; Guzmán, *Memorias*, p. 289; Reed, *Insurgent Mexico*, pp. 165–6, 172, 198; Calzadíaz Barrera, *Hechos reales*, I, p. 180.

931 Aguirre Benavides, *De Francisco I. Madero*, p. 92.

932 Hamm, Torreón, 13 Apr. 1914, SD 812.00/11706.

933 Reed, *Insurgent Mexico*, pp. 194–5; and cf. Brondo Whitt's description, *División del Norte*, pp. 203–4, of the peon soldiers of Zacatecas.

934 Fierro was 'Villa's best friend; and Villa loved him like a son and always pardoned him': Reed, *Insurgent Mexico*, p. 132; Aguirre Benavides, *De Francisco I. Madero*, pp. 92–3.

935 Hohler memo., 10 Feb. 1914, FO 371/2025, 8667.

936 Katz, *Deutschland*, p. 243.

937 Brondo Whitt, *División del Norte*, pp. 132, 153; Silliman, Saltillo, 14 May 1913, SD 812.00/7726; Casasola, *Historia gráfica*, I, pp. 720–3.

938 Reed, *Insurgent Mexico*, pp. 156, 163.

939 *Ibid.*, p. 170; Brondo Whitt, *División del Norte*, pp. 127, 130–1, 170, 210.

940 Reed, *Insurgent Mexico*, p. 159. Since Reed's picaresque stories sometimes invite scepticism, it is gratifying to find them corroborated: see Aguirre Benavides, *De Francisco I. Madero*, p. 113; though here the venue is Jiménez – and we are told that Villa danced the polka.

941 The garrison also contained the usual detachment of Juchitecos: see Casasola, *Historia gráfica*, I, p. 695; Brondo Whitt, *División del Norte*, p. 48 (noting that Federal prisoners were 'almost all men of the south, dirty and wretched'); and, on numbers, *El Imparcial*, 18 Mar. 1914 (14,000) and Guzmán, *Memorias*, p. 290 (10,000).

942 To date: Hamm, Torreón, 13 Apr. 1914, SD 812.00/11706.

943 Reed, *Insurgent Mexico*, p. 166. For conventional – what Keegan, *Face of Battle* (Harmondsworth, 1979), p. 40, terms 'Napierite' – accounts of the battle: Barragán, *Historia del ejército*, I, pp. 373–410; Langle Ramírez, *Ejército Villista*, pp. 57–68.

944 Reed, *Insurgent Mexico*, pp. 179–80; Guzmán, *Memorias*, pp. 310–2; *El Imparcial*, 26, 27 Mar. 1914.

945 Reed, *Insurgent Mexico*, p. 183; Brondo Whitt, *División del Norte*, p. 32.

946 Reed, *Insurgent Mexico*, pp. 155–208; Brondo Whitt, *División del Norte*, pp. 23–62.

947 Reed, *Insurgent Mexico*, p. 189.

948 Brondo Whitt, *División del Norte*, p. 37; Guzmán, *Memorias*, p. 318. Reed's account unfortunately stops at this point.

949 Guzmán, *Memorias*, p. 329; Villa to González, 14, 15, 19 Mar. 1914, SRE, legajo 760, 75-R-22, pp. 281, 284, 289.

950 Hamm, Torreón, 13 Apr. 1914, SD 812.00/11706; Cummins, Gomez, 7 Apr. 1914, FO 371/2027, 16488; Brondo Whitt, *División del Norte*, p. 62.

951 *Mexican Herald*, 9 Apr. 1914; *El Renovador*, in Fabela, DHRM, RRC, I, p. 247; Fabela to A. García, 3 Apr. 1914, SRE, legajo 760, 75-R-22, p. 314.

952 Fabela to García (n. 951); Langle Ramírez, *Ejército Villista*, pp. 66–7; Brondo Whitt, *División del Norte*, pp. 63–7, 70. The Federals were reckoned to have lost 1,000 dead, 2,000 wounded and between 1,500 and 2,000 as prisoners or deserters.

953 Guzmán, *Memorias*, p. 375; Hamm, Torreón, 19 Apr. 1914, SD 812.00/11703. Velasco was bitter against the San Pedro commanders for failing to fight their way through to the Laguna.

954 Brondo Whitt, *División del Norte*, p. 77, attributes Federal vindictiveness towards San Pedro to the town's Maderista reputation; but, by April–May 1914, other towns began to suffer in similar fashion from what appears to have been a deliberate scorched earth policy: Cumberland, *Constitutionalist Years*, p. 120, n. 26. On the significance of the battle: Barragán, *Historia del ejército*, I, pp. 431–2; Villa in Guzmán, *Memorias*, p. 365, pays a deserved tribute to Eusebio Calzada, responsible for entraining and transporting the army, post-haste, from Torreón to San Pedro.

955 Hamm, Torreón, 13 Apr. 1914, SD 812.00/11706.

956 Hohler, 11 Apr.; Carden, 4 May; and O'Shaughnessy, quoted by Spring–Rice, 14 Apr. 1913; FO 371/2026, 16093; /2028, 19917; /2027, 16485.

957 Consul, Nogales, 1 Apr. 1914, SRE, legajo 787, 86-R-12, p. 97; Lespinasse, Frontera, 13, 18 Apr. 1914, SD 812.00/11504, 12244.

958 Wightwick, Monterrey, 3 May 1914, FO 371/2029, 27317.

959 Barragán, *Historia del ejército*, I, p. 469; Cumberland, *Constitutionalist Years*, pp. 118–21. Rebel casualties at Monterrey were about 100 – or 1 in 90 of the attacking force compared with 1 in 5 at Torreón.

960 Guzmán, *Memorias*, pp. 390, 303–4.

961 *Ibid.*, pp. 398–9; Barragán, *Historia del ejército*, I, p. 479; Brondo Whitt, *División del Norte*, pp. 135–7, 155.

962 Cumberland, *Constitutionalist Years*, pp. 53–4; Obregón, *Ocho mil kilómetros*.

963 Obregón, *Ocho mil kilómetros*, p. 100; Thord-Gray, *Gringo Rebel*, p. 89; Capt. Corbett, RN, San Diego, 23 Mar. 1914, FO 371/2027, 16431, on the strength of the Federal positions, and Obregon's wisdom in bypassing them.

964 Thord-Grey, *Gringo Rebel*, pp. 107–9, 130–1; Aguilar, *Revolución Sonorense*, pp. 462–3.

965 Thord-Grey, *Gringo Rebel*, pp. 130, 133, 208.

966 *Ibid.*, p. 91. Huerta, meanwhile, approached the British Minister for information on the blockhouse system, used by the British in South Africa; concentration camps were established in Morelos; neutral observers drew the same parallel, indicating that the Boer War afforded the model for this kind of conflict. See Hohler, Mexico City, 24 Mar. 1914, FO 371/2026, 16247.

967 Thord-Grey, *Gringo Rebel*, pp. 183–91. There were more bizarre currencies: at Torreón, about the same time, sticking plasters were used: Bonney, 16 Dec. 1913, SD 812.00/10406.

968 Pazuengo, *Historia*, p. 88; Aguilar, *Revolución Sonorense*, pp. 471–3.

969 Obregón, *Ocho mil kilómetros*, pp. 104, 122; Thord-Gray, *Gringo Rebel*, p. 108.

970 Obregón, *Ocho mil kilómetros*, pp. 106–7, 131; Thord-Gray, *Gringo Rebel*, p. 181.

971 Cumberland, *Constitutionalist Years*, p. 123. Cf. Simon Collier, *From Cortés to Castro: An Introduction to the History of Latin America* (London, 1974), p. 49, attributing the 'first air raid in Latin American history' to the Bolivian air force at La Vanguardia in 1928.

972 Thord-Gray, *Gringo Rebel*, p. 200; Obregón, *Ocho mil kilómetros*, pp. 108–10; Casasola, *Historia gráfica*, I, pp. 782–3, 786.

973 Brown, Mazatlán, 6, 7, 13 May, 5 June, 15 Aug. 1914, SD 812.00/12034, 12055, 12067, 12353, 13098.

974 C/o HMS Algerine, Aug. 1914, FO 371/2031, 47873.

975 Thord-Gray, *Gringo Rebel*, pp. 228–31, 247–54; Obregón, *Ocho mil kilómetros*, pp. 115, 119–20: both actions were undertaken by the divisional vanguard, led by Generals Diéguez, Buelna and Blanco.

976 Obregón, *Ocho mil kilómetros*, p. 121.

977 Thord-Gray, *Gringo Rebel*, pp. 127, 200–1; though allowance must be made for hindsight.

978 Womack, *Zapata*, pp. 174–5, 180–3; Jacobs, 'Aspects', pp. 174–5; Edwards, Acapulco, 30 Mar. 1914, SD 812.00/11356.

979 Lind to Wilson, 14, 21, 24 Feb. 1914, WWP, series II, box 103; even before the lifting of the embargo, Lind had doubts whether 'the revolutionists will make an active campaign if they are given the chance': 7 Jan. 1914, SD 812.00/10462.

980 Lind to Wilson, 8, 12, 19 Mar. 1914, SD 812.00/11098, 11277, 11218.

981 *Ibid.*, 25, 27 Mar. SD 812.00/11277, 11313.

982 Grieb, *United States and Huerta*, pp. 123–4.

983 The details of this episode are taken from Robert E. Quirk, *An Affair of Honor: Woodrow Wilson and the Occupation of Veracruz* (New York, 1967), p. 191ff.

984 In January, three British seamen, hiring a cab, had been taken to the police station, arrested, and robbed of their money and tobacco. After a consular protest they were released, their goods returned, and the culprits 'severely punished', by order of the same General Morelos Zaragoza; this was, apparently 'a common trick of the cabmen who share in the robbery with the police': Capt. Doughty, HMS Hermione, 29 Jan. 1914, FO 371/2025, 9650; and note the same officer's report of similar incidents at Veracruz, 10 Mar. 1914, FO 371/2026, 15618.

985 Though Morelos Zaragoza denied that the boat had flown the flag: Meyer, *Huerta*, p. 195.

986 Quirk, *Affair of Honor*, p. 26.

987 Fletcher was 'decidedly of an opinion which does not correspond to ours', the President told Josephus Daniels: 11 Aug. 1913, Daniels Papers, box 12.

988 Admiral Cradock, Tampico, 19 Dec. 1913, FO 371/2025, 1194.

989 Fletcher to Rear-Admiral Fiske, 3 Feb. 1914, Daniels Papers, box 42.

990 According to Fiske, Wood Diary, 5 Jan. 1914.

991 Cradock, Tampico, 19 Dec. 1913, FO 371/2025, 2294.

992 *Ibid.*; and see Calvert, *Mexican Revolution*, pp. 281–2. Cradock and Fletcher had clashed over the question of seniority, but it seems unlikely that this would have prompted Cradock's criticism.

993 State Department researchers discovered that the US Navy had shelled Greytown (San Juan del Norte), Nicaragua, in 1854, for an alleged insult to the American consul. That was good enough. Quirk, *Affair of Honor*, p. 50.

994 *Ibid.*, p. 49. Lind was present and vocal at White House meetings during these days: Wood Diary, 18 Apr. 1914.

995 Quirk, *Affair of Honor*, p. 109 on O'Shaughnessy's disappointment.

996 *Ibid.*, pp. 53, 57, 63; Wood Diary, 18 Apr. 1914.

997 Wood Diary, 18 Apr. 1918.

998 Quirk, *Affair of Honor*, pp. 69–70, 77; House Diary, 15 Apr. 1914.

999 Wood Diary, 18 Apr. 1914: 'the military absurdity (of Lind's plan) was too apparent to require much discussion'; yet the operation was mounted with much this plan in mind.

1000 House Diary, 15 Apr. 1914.

1001 Quirk, *Affair of Honor*, pp. 85–6.

1002 Admiral Badger, Veracruz, to Daniels, 29 Apr. 1914, Daniels Papers, box 35.

1003 Quirk, *Affair of Honor*, p. 95.

1004 There was 'no cheering or running – so essential in streetfighting': Cradock, Veracruz, 29 Apr. 1914, FO 371/2029, 22879.

1005 *Ibid.*; Quirk, *Affair of Honor*, pp. 97–9.

1006 Cradock (n. 1004).

1007 'The battle-toughened marines, many of whom had seen action in the Philippines, were no respecters of person or estate', Quirk, *Affair of Honor*, pp. 100–1, notes; cf. Badger to Daniels, 29 Apr. 1914 (n. 1002) on the 'remarkable' restraint of the American forces, and citing lower casualty figures.

1008 Page to House, 27 Apr. 1914, in Burton J. Hendrick, *The Life and Letters of Walter Hines Page* (London, 1924), p. 230; *Mexican Herald*, 16 June 1914.

1009 As will become evident here, Veracruz provoked a bigger crisis than the Punitive Expedition of 1916, not least because in 1916 the Mexican government (in the main) sought to mitigate rather than exacerbate the crisis. A glance at either the Wilson papers or the American press will likewise confirm the salience of 1914: by 1916, European concerns had pushed Mexico off the front page and out of the public mind.

1010 'Nothing of much importance happened today. It was one of ordinary routine', House noted in his diary, 22 Apr. 1914, the day after the occupation.

1011 WWP, series IV, boxes 123–6. Apart from letters from numerous Socialist branches, see National Executive of the Socialist Party to Wilson, 22 Apr. 1914; John Reed to W. Phillips, 4 June; W. Kent to Wilson, 28 Apr. Many religious leaders wrote, notably Quakers; mass meetings for peace were held, e.g., at Boston on 18 Apr., with Edwin Meade and Norman Angell: 95L, box 125.

1012 Mrs H. Howard to Wilson, 23 Apr. 1914, box 124.

1013 R. Copler, Hartford, Conn., to Wilson, 26 Apr.; Carnegie to Wilson, 24 Apr., 7 May; A. Farquar, York, Pa., to Wilson, 28 Apr.; W. Gebhardt, Clinton, NJ, to Wilson, 27 Apr.; J. Kelley, Sioux City, Iowa, to Wilson, 8 May; Mayor and citizens, Norfolk, Neb. to Wilson, 1 May. The excess of 'pacifist' letters from the north-east may simply reflect that more north-easterners bothered to write to the president.

1014 Cf. Julius W. Pratt, *Expansionists of 1898: The Acquisition of Hawaii and the Spanish Islands* (Baltimore, 1936).

1015 E. Hole to Wilson, 24 Apr.; M. J. Bloomer to Wilson, 27 Apr.; H. W. Falk to Wilson, 22 Apr., reporting Wall Street opinion as being critical of the military and desirious of a mediated settlement. Katz, *Secret War*, pp. 197–8, does not produce very substantial evidence of big business interventionism.

1016 W. Sheppard to Wilson, 21 Apr. 1914, box 125.

1017 Representatives of the GAR, Wilmington, Del., 27 Apr., of Washington DC, 24 Apr., box 124; Utd Confederate Veterans, Middlesborough, Ky, 26 Apr., box 126; Col. W. Curry, Philadelphia, 16 Apr., box 121. Notwithstanding the third of these references, it is my impression that Civil War veterans were less belligerent (some fell into the 'pacifist' camp) than the later generation of veterans of the Spanish–American War, many of whom were eager, it seems, for another glorious little war.

1018 E.g., *New York Evening Journal*, 28 Apr. 1914, calling for action to halt the 'murder and robbery on our southern border'; not that atrocity stories – whose prevalence has already been noted – were confined to the American Yellow press. See *The Times* (London), 13 Apr. 1914: Federal prisoners are reported burned to death with paraffin and 'wholesale rapings are of routine occurrence'.

1019 F. Glaser to Wilson, 13 June 1914, enclosing the text of Hearst's interview with the Berlin press: strong on geopolitics, critical of 'pusilanimous pedagogues' (i.e., Wilson) and advocating strong leadership for the US (i.e., Hearst?).

1020 *Los Angeles Sunday Times*, 26 Apr. 1914; C. Ashley, Toledo, to Wilson, 1 May 1914, box 123.

1021 I.e., they were overwhelmingly 'middle' or 'upper' class; more so even than would be expected among correspondents predominantly of such type. Working-class jingoists were thin on the ground.

1022 J. B. Bailey, *Cincinnati Enquirer*, 1 May 1914: Bailey was unusual in having just left Mexico (where he had been a ship-builder); his hasty departure fired his choler against the Mexicans and warm admiration of the Germans, who had helped him escape, thus providing 'a lasting Caucasian monument', another episode in the 'battle between the cooler bloods of the world and the hot, seething, bloods of the southern countries'. Such sentiments underwrote interventionism, whether of the 'right' (as here), or the 'left' (e.g., with John Lind and Jack London).

1023 D. Barrows, Berkeley, to Redfield, 23 Apr.; A. Adams to Wilson, 22 Apr.; J. Johnston to Wilson, 11 May; boxes 123, 125.

1024 Dr S. Dabney to Wilson, 26 Apr. 1914, box 124.

1025 G. L. Maitland to Wilson, 25 Apr. 1914, box 125.

1026 M. Houston to Wilson, 18 May 1914, box 124.

1027 W. Reynolds to Wilson, 25 Apr. 1914, box 125. Cf. Hans-Ulrich Wehler, 'Industrial Growth and Early German Imperialism', in Roger Owen and Bob Sutcliffe, *Studies in the Theory of Imperialism* (London, 1972), pp. 78, 90–1.

1028 Cf. I. Boicort to Sen. J. Bristow, 27 Apr. 1913; M. Leach to Wilson, 15 July 1913; C. Jenkins to A. Shanklin, 9 Dec. 1914; SD 812.00/7389; 8109; 14073; and Dye, Bisbee, 10 June 1913, SD 812.00/7823 for the non-interventionist view. See also W. Buckley, Fall Report, pp. 830–2, and Fall himself, p. 664; and Michael C. Meyer, 'Albert B. Fall's Mexican Papers, a Preliminary Investigation', *New Mexico Historical Review*, XL (Apr. 1965).

1029 Knight, 'Nationalism', pp. 327–31; Letcher, Chihuahua, 25 Aug. 1914, SD 812.00/13232; the quote is from Dabney to Wilson (n. 1024).

1030 Haley, *Revolution and Intervention*, p. 134, largely on the strength of Lind's evidence, regards the occupation as a positive contribution to the ouster of Huerta; but he exaggerates the significance of arms and cash at the expense of intangible factors relating to prestige, politics and morale.

1031 Ulloa, *Revolucion intervenida*, p. 347; cf. Cumberland, *Constitutionalist Years*, p. 124, which suggests that the arms did not get beyond the Isthmus. For a detailed account of the whole odyssey, see Michael C. Meyer, 'The Arms of the Ypiranga', *Hispanic American Historical Review*, L (1970), pp. 543–56; Katz, *Secret War*, pp. 232–40; and Thomas Baecker, 'The Arms of the Ypiranga: the German Side', *Americas*, XXX (1973), pp. 1–17 which, along with the same author's 'Los Intereses Militares del Imperio Alemán en México, 1913–14', *Historia Mexicana*, XXIX (1972), p. 350, demonstrates that there were no devious links between Huerta and the Germans.

1032 *Mexican Herald*, 5 Mar. 1914.

1033 Accounts differ: cf. Ulloa, *Revolución intervenida*, pp. 198, 350–1; F. Villareal to Carranza, 24 Apr. 1914, Fabela, DHRM, RRC, II, pp. 59–60 (which errs in stating that a full embargo was imposed); Huertista consular reports for May 1914 in SRE, legajo 784, 84-R-15, pp. 155, 163, 165, 167; Cobb, 16 June 1914, SD 812.00/12266; and F. de la Garza to F. Sommerfeld, 27 June 1914, WWP, series II, box 111.

1034 Quirk, *Affair of Honor*, p. 116.

1035 *Ibid.*, pp. 121–55.

1036 Charles C. Cumberland, 'Huerta y Carranza ante la Ocupación de Veracruz', *Historia Mexicana*, VI (1957), pp. 534–47, reviews these events.

1037 Alger, Mazatlán, 14 Mar. 1915, SD 812.00/14681.

1038 Quirk, *Affair of Honor*, pp. 107–8; Meyer, *Huerta*, pp. 199–200.

1039 *Mexican Herald*, 25, 26 Apr., 2 May, 6 June 1914; O'Shaughnessy, *Diplomat's Wife*, pp. 289–90, 290; Carden, Mexico City, 28 Apr. 1914, FO 371/2027, 18881.

1040 Langle Ramírez, *El Militarismo*, pp. 77–85; Meyer, *Huerta*, pp. 201–2; Casasola, *Historia Gráfica*, I, p. 777.

1041 Meyer, *Huerta*, p. 201; Langle Ramírez, *El militarismo*, p. 81.

1042 Meyer, *Huerta*, p. 202.

1043 *Ibid.*; Langle Ramírez, *El militarismo*, pp. 76, 81–2.

1044 Hohler, 26 Apr. 1914, FO 371/2029, 23193.

1045 Ramírez Plancarte, *Ciudad de México*, pp. 50–1; *Mexican Herald*, 2, 14 May 1914.

1046 Will B. Davis, *Experiences and Observations of an American Consular Officer During the Recent Mexican Revolutions* (Chula Vista, 1920), pp. 18–23. Schmutz, Aguascalientes, 22 Apr. 1914, SD 812.00/11919.

1047 Davis, *Experiences*, pp. 38–9.

1048 *Mexican Herald*, 10 May 1914 (two Spaniards were also killed at El Favor; it was not a simple anti-American outburst). Note also Davis, *Experiences*, p. 23.

1049 Capt. Walter, HMS Shearwater, Acapulco, 4 May 1914, FO 371/2029, 25116.

1050 *Mexican Herald*, 26 Apr., 2, 7 May 1914, on the fate of Americans at Pachuca, El Oro and in southern Veracruz.

1051 Admiral Badger, Veracruz, 8 July 1914, SD 812.00/12576; the same officer, 3 May, SD 812.00/11836, opined that reports of Americans being endangered in Yucatán were 'greatly exaggerated'.

1052 *Mexican Herald*, 3 May 1914; Brown, Mazatlán, 10 July; Miller Tamico, 21 May 1914; SD 812/12567; 12346; Meyer, *Huerta*, pp. 200–1; according to Consul Miller's hundred page report of the Tampico 'riots' 'there was never a moment in which I thought that there was a probability of serious trouble'; he also praised the 'great fidelity with which a number of Mexican peon workers guarded the interests of their American employers who had abandoned their interests'.

1053 Simpich, Nogales, 23 Apr.; border report, Douglas, 2 May 1914; SD 812.00/11623; 11942.

1054 Hamm, Durango, 24 Apr., 4, 12 May 1914, SD 812.00/11837, 11810, 11998.

1055 Border report, Laredo, 2 May 1914, SD 812.00/11942.

1056 Cf. V. Purcell, *The Boxer Uprising* (Cambridge, 1963), pp. 125, 252.

1057 Alger, Mazatlán, 24 Apr., SD 812.00/11843; Knight, 'Nationalism, Xenophobia and Revolution', p. 250; Wightwick, Monterrey, 3 May 1914, FO 371/2029, 27317; C. Husk to H. L. Scott, 30 May 1914, Scott Papers, box 15, enclosing a fragment of the abused flag.

1058 Wightwick (n. 1057).

1059 Obregón, *Ocho mil kilómetros*, p. 111; Guzmán, *Memorias*, p. 387; Carothers, El Paso, 10 May 1914, SD 812.00/11875; Womack, *Zapata*, pp. 185–6; *Mexican Herald*, 13 May 1914; Hamm, Durango, 12 May 1914, SD 812.00/11998.

1060 Brown, Mazatlán, 4 May 1914, SD 812.00/10129, 11979.

1061 Quirk, *Affair of Honor*, p. 116; Barclay, Washington, 22 June 1914, FO 371/2030, 29611.

1062 Thord-Gray, *Gringo Rebel*, pp. 208, 216, 218, 234; Womack, *Zapata*, p. 186.

1063 Quirk, *Affair of Honor*, p. 117 cites the familiar report of Carothers – who ('behind his shiny spectacles and perpetual cigar') was dedicated to improving Villa's image (see O'Hea, *Reminiscences*, p. 98); Guzmán, *Memorias*, pp. 382–4 has a different emphasis; see also Clendenen, *United States and Pancho Villa*, p. 75; Katz, *Deutschland*, p. 318.

1064 Meyer, *Huerta*, p. 203; Luis Fernando Amaya, *La soberana convención revolucionaria, 1914–16* (Mexico, 1975), p. 21, attributes Villa's compliance to Angeles.

1065 Womack, *Zapata*, p. 186.

1066 Gonzalez, *Pueblo en vilo*, p. 123.

1067 Thord-Gray, *Gringo Rebel*, pp. 208–9, 216.

1068 Cobb to Scott, 2 May 1914, Scott Papers, box 15.

1069 Canova, Saltillo, 2 July 1914, SD 812.00/12462.

1070 Guzmán, *Memorias*, pp. 386–9.

1071 Amaya, *Soberana convención*, p. 21–2.

1072 It also made Villa dependent for his (legal) arms supply on pro-Carranza forces on the Gulf coast: L. de la Garza to Sommerfeld, 27 June 1914, WWP, series II, box 111.

1073 Obregón, *Ocho mil kilómetros*, pp. 109, 128; Casasola, *Historia gráfica*, II, pp. 788–90, 794–5; Womack, *Zapata*, p. 187.

1074 Caldwell, Zacatecas, 29 June 1914, FO 371/2030, 39909.

1075 Hohler, Mexico City, 6 Apr.; Holms, Guadalajara, 20 July 1914; FO 371/2027, 18383; /2031, 52831; Womack, *Zapata*, p. 182.

1076 Hohler, Mexico City, 4 Mar. 1914, FO 371/2026, 12853.

1077 Meyer, *Huerta*, p. 192.

1078 Carden, Mexico City, 23 Aug. 1914, FO 371/2031, 49152. Carden also blamed the rising level of corruption among the Federal leadership.

1079 Guzmán, *Memorias*, pp. 399.

1080 *Ibid.*, pp. 401–2; Brondo Whitt, *División del Norte*, p. 136; Casasola, *Historia gráfica*, II, pp. 792–3; *Mexican Herald*, 3 May 1914.

1081 Sullivan, La Paz, 18, 27 Aug. 1913, 27 March 1914, SD 812.00/8528, 8645, 11343; Thord-Gray, *Gringo Rebel*, p. 197, recalls a Federal colonel arriving by ship with 150 deserters from Baja, thus providing a great boost to morale.

1082 Canada, Veracruz, 12 May 1914, SD 812.00/11912; *Mexican Herald*, 19 May 1914; similar rumours cropped up in July: *Le Courrier du Méxique*, 2 July 1914.

1083 Cumberland, *Constitutionalist Years*, p. 120, n. 26.

1084 S. G. Inman to Mrs Inman, 28 Apr. 1914, SGIA, box 12; border report, Brownsville, 28 Apr.; Hanna, Monterrey, 26 Apr. 1914; SD 812.00/11806, 11719.

1085 Caldwell, Zacatecas, 29 June 1914, FO 371/2030, 39909.

1086 *Mexican Herald*, 12, 19 June, 13 July 1914; Romero Flores, *Michoacán*, pp. 121–2, stresses the Maderista sympathies of these landlord rebels.

1087 S. G. Inman to Mrs Inman, 12 May 1914, SGIA, box 12.

1088 Cradock, Tampico, 15, 17 May 1914, FO 371/2028, 21973, 22293.

1089 Hanna, Monterrey, 26 Apr., 1, 13 May 1914, SD 812.00/11719, 11797, 11925; the British consul, Wightwick, concurred, in his more prosaic way: 'Mr. Wightwick is evidently an admirer of the Constitutionalists' was the tart comment in Whitehall: Wightwick, Monterrey, 3 May 1914, and minutes, FO 371/2029, 27317.

1090 Holms, Guadalajara, 20 July 1914, FO 371/2031, 52831 (and Holms was no lover of the revolution).

1091 *Mexican Herald*, 24 Mar. 1914 (review of the press); Grieb, *United States and Huerta*, p. 119.

1092 *Mexican Herald*, 19 May 1914. (The *Herald* was now based in Veracruz).

1093 Grieb, *United States and Huerta*, p. 159; Spring-Rice, Washington, 27 Apr. 1914, FO 371/2028, 20023, suggests a European (Franco-Spanish) démarche.

1094 Carden, Mexico City, 27 Apr. 1914, FO 371/2027, 16485; Katz, *Secret War*, p. 200, presents an analysis heavily coloured by Von Hintze's perceptions. Only a month before, Huerta had ruled out Panamerican mediation: *El Imparcial*, 7 Mar. 1914.

1095 W. F. Buckley, Fall Report, I, p. 788. Now, even Carden admitted, 'feeling in the capital [was] generally in favour of the resignation of Huerta'; the problem was to find a way: Carden, Mexico City, 4 May 1914, FO 371/2028, 19917.

1096 Grieb, *United States and Huerta*, p. 161.

1097 *Ibid.*: Knight, 'Nationalism Xenophobia and Revolution', p. 74; and vol. I, p. 16.

1098 Rabasa to 'Nopalimpura', 21, 30 June 1914, Rabasa Papers, University of Texas, Austin. See also B. Long memo., 9 May 1914, SD 812.00/11955½ on Rabasa and his colleagues.

1099 Rabasa to 'Nopalimpura', 16, 21, 28 June 1914, Rabasa Papers.

1100 Carden, Mexico City, 13 May 1914, FO 371/2028, 21598.

1101 Anon. letter to R. H. Brand, Lazards, 17 May 1914, FO 371/371/2029, 27868; the writer (a 'personal friend' of one of Huerta's delegates at Niagara) was almost certainly Landa y Escandón (who, with Elguero, served on the board of Cowdray's Aguila Co.); in an earlier letter to Cowdray, 10 Nov. 1913, Cowdray Papers, box A/3, he had similarly urged the European powers to find an 'honourable way' for Huerta to retire.

1102 Braniff to Lansing, 16, 17 May 1914, Lansing Papers, vol. 2.
1103 Some accounts exaggerate, or antedate, the effect of the First World War. Europe's deference to American policy in Mexico began well before August 1914, and reflected longstanding economic and geopolitical realities: Mexico did not figure prominently in Wilhelmine *Weltpolitik* (as Baecker has shown); and Carden, with his maverick concern to confront the Americans, was out of step with the Foreign Office and, increasingly, with British economic interests. Europe watched Wilson, therefore, with a certain impotent chagrin: a minor anticipation of 1918–19.
1104 Grieb, *United States and Huerta*, p. 166. Katz, *Secret War*, p. 199, goes much further, seeing the Wilson administration as aiming 'to weaken the revolutionaries and to bring the new government as much as possible into the American sphere'.
1105 Grieb, *United States and Huerta*, p. 167; Lamar and Lehmann to Bryan, 13 May 1914, WWP, Series 4, box 110; Ulloa, *Revolución intervenida*, pp. 203–59, gives a full account of the talks.
1106 Rabasa to 'Nopalimpura', 3, 4, 22 June 1914, Rabasa Papers; Wilson to Page, 1 June 1914, WWP, series 4, box 110, discerned a 'Científico' cast of mind among the ABC delegates.
1107 Wilson to Lamar and Lehmann, 24 May 1914, WWP, Series 4, box 109.
1108 Urquizo, *Páginas*, p. 75; Guzmán, *Memorias*, p. 391; Pazuengo, *Historia*, pp. 98–100.
1109 Cumberland, *Constitutionalist Years*, p. 134.
1110 *Ibid.*, p. 135; Langle Ramírez, *Ejército Villista*, pp. 83–4.
1111 Amaya, *Soberana convención*, p. 24; Pazuengo, *Historia*, p. 99 illustrates the parallel.
1112 Obregón, *Ocho mil kilómetros*, p. 132.
1113 The first emanated from the Villistas, the second from the Division of the North-East, probably Villareal: Amaya, *Soberana convención*, pp. 26–8.
1114 *Ibid.*, p. 28–9.
1115 Cumberland, *Constitutionalist Years*, p. 136; Capt. José Granados to A. M. Elías, in latter to SRE, 7 July 1914, SRE, legajo 789, 87-R-28, p. 1, puts Villa's army at 25,000, with 62 cannon.
1116 Cumberland, *Constitutionalist Years*, p. 136; Langle Ramírez, *Ejército Villista*, pp. 92–4.
1117 Caldwell, Zacatecas, 29 June 1914, FO 371/2030, 39909; Brondo Whitt, *División del Norte*, pp. 206–12.
1118 Brondo Whitt, *División del Norte*, p. 209.
1119 Cumberland, *Constitutionalist Years*, p. 137, gives figures of 6,000 Federals killed to 1,000 rebels; Langle Ramírez, *Ejército Villista*, says 4,800 Federals; Caldwell (n. 1117) over 1,000 rebels: Meyer, *Huerta*, p. 208, using a Federal source, puts rebel and Federal losses about equal, which hardly seems likely.
1120 Pazuengo, *Historia*, pp. 96–7; Cumberland, *Constitutionalist Years*, p. 137.
1121 Obregón, *Ocho mil kilómetros*, pp. 134–40, claiming 2,000 Federals killed and 5,000 captured for the loss of 300 rebel troops. The battle was fought some twenty-five miles from Guadalajara (at the request of the local business community); thus sparing it the fate of Zacatecas and preserving its record of immunity from revolutionary upheaval: *Mexican Herald*, 31 May 1914.
1122 Rosa King in Hohler, Mexico City, 2 Nov. 1914, FO 371/2031, 76893.
1123 J. Bustamante to Sub-Sec. Fomento, 29 July 1914, Trabajo, 34/1/14/23.
1124 Womack, *Zapata*, pp. 187–8.
1125 Romero Flores, *Michoacán*, pp. 124–5; *Mexican Herald*, 26 June 1914; Cumberland, *Constitutionalist Years*, p. 140; Canada, Veracruz, 8, 27 July 1914, SD 812.00/12533, 12754.
1126 *Mexican Herald*, 9 July 1914; Carden, Mexico City, 7 July 1914, FO 371/2030, 30797.
1127 Cumberland, *Constitutionalist Years*, p. 138.
1128 E.g. Carden, Mexico City, 1 Aug. 1914, FO 371/2030, 35683.

1129 Moheno, *Actuación*, pp. 92–3, 107–8.
1130 Carden, Mexico City, 1, 7 July 1914, FO 371/2030, 29834, 3077.
1131 Meyer, *Huerta*, pp. 208–11.
1132 Amaya, *Soberana convención*, pp. 29–36.
1133 *Ibid.*, pp. 36–8; Cumberland, *Constitutionalist Years*, p. 148; Obregón, *Ocho mil kilómetros*, pp. 159–61.
1134 Amaya, *Soberana convención*, p. 38.

2 The revolution in power: 1 The great schism

1 Hohler, Mexico City, 25 Aug. 1914, FO 371/2031, 49155.
2 Cumberland, *Constitutionalist Years*, p. 148, n. 121; Ross, *Madero*, p. 175; Casasola, *Historia gráfica*, II, pp. 840–3; Guzmán, *Eagle and the Serpent*, p. 131; Ramírez Plancarte, *Ciudad de México*, pp. 61–4; *Le Courrier du Méxique*, 15, 20 Aug. 1914.
3 Casasola, *Historia gráfica*, II, pp. 830–1.
4 Hohler, 25 Aug. (n. 1); Carden, Mexico City, 20 Aug. 1914, FO 371/2031, 41491: the British had just been informed that Carden was to receive his passports.
5 Amaya, *Soberana convención*, p. 37.
6 Rutherford, *Mexican Society*, pp. 266–7; note Obregón's speech of 14 Apr. 1916 in Fabela, DHRM, RRC, V, p. 79.
7 Hohler, Mexico City, 25 Aug. 1914, FO 371/2031, 49155.
8 *Le Courrier du Méxique*, 18, 20 July, 2 Sept. 1914; A. Abreu Salas to R. Zubarán Capmany, 31 July 1914, Fabela, DHRM, EZ, p. 90.
9 Amaya, *Soberana convención*, p. 101.
10 Cf. Quirk, *Mexican Revolution*, p. 9: 'the revolutionaries led by Carranza were above all constitutionalists'. Amaya, *Soberana convención*, pp. 42–3, stresses Carranza's 'obsession' with legality, but in the context of agrarian reform, where Carranza disliked *de facto* expropriation; when it came to the exercise of political power, however, Carranza's legalism was less obtrusive.
11 C/o USS Maryland, Manzanillo, 23 Aug. 1914, SD 812.00/13672; C. Maldonado to S. Alvarado, 14 Feb. 1916, DHRM, RRC, V, p. 27. From a different standpoint, the *Mexican Herald*, 21 Sept. 1914, agreed.
12 C/o USS Minnesota, 9 Dec. 1914; Canada, 18 June 1915 (both Veracruz); Davis, Guadalajara, 31 Oct. 1914; SD 812.00/14047; 15344; 13720.
13 Wilson, Tampico, 27 July 1914, FO 371/2031, 47057.
14 Ramon Eduardo Ruiz, *The Great Rebellion Mexico 1905–1924* (New York, 1980), pp. 3–5.
15 Carranza to Zapata, 16 May 1913, Fabela, DHRM, EZ, p. 70 and above, p. 105.
16 Olea, *Sinaloa*, p. 65.
17 Barragán, *Historia del ejército*, I, pp. 213–8.
18 Córdova, *Ideología*, pp. 199–203. For the oddly influential analysis of 'the Carranza men . . . [as] troglodytes in the midst of the twentieth century', see Robert E. Quirk, 'Liberales y Radicales en la Revolución Mexicana', *Historia Mexicana*, II, 1953, pp. 503–28.
19 Amaya, *Soberana convención*, p. 19.
20 This view, less general and explicit than its equivalent interpretation of the Madero revolution, is sometimes qualified by a distinction made between conservative (political) revolutionaries like Carranza and radical (social) revolutionaries, like Obregón (which distinction does not affect the argument here); the view is supported and implied by several arguments – the '(petty) bourgeois' origins of the Constitutionalists; the absence of social reform pre-1914; the superficiality of paper reforms after 1914; the efficacy of such reforms as essentially conservative measures; the absence of real popular mobilisation and concomitant social change throughout.
21 Edmund Burke, *Reflections on the Revolution in France* (Harmondsworth, 1978), p. 181.

22 Manager, Refugio Mine, Zac., to H. Swain, May 1913; O'Shaughnessy, Mexico City, 17 Oct. 1913, SD 812.00/7757, 9249; for comparable fears, involving the city mob as well as the rebels: Bonney, San Luis, 18 Dec. 1913, SD 812.00/10466; Holms, Guadalajara, 11 Feb., Wilson, Tampico, 14 June, c/o HMS Algerine, Ensenada, 29 Apr. 1914, FO 371/2025, 10096; 2031, 47057; 2029, 23365.

23 O'Shaughnessy, Mexico City, 3 Feb.; Page, London, 6 May, Lansing memo., 9 May 1914, SD 812.00/10777, 11838, 11986.

24 Hamm, Durango, 27 July 1913, 9 Jan., 6, 21 Mar. 1914, SD 812.00/8449, 10654, 11223, 11353.

25 Cummins, Gómez Palacio, Dec. 1913, FO 371/2025, 13251.

26 Holms, Guadalajara, 20 July 1914, FO 371/2031, 52831.

27 *Ibid.*, where it is noted that 'local bands have joined the main body' of rebels, and that it was these 'lately allied bandits [sic]' who were most keen for reprisals.

28 Davis, Guadalajara, 28 June 1915, SD 812.00/15587.

29 Womack, *Zapata*, p. 243; note also Anita Brenner, *Idols Behind Altars* (New York, 1929), p. 218.

30 Olea, *Sinaloa*, pp. 63–4.

31 Caldwell, Zacatecas, 2 Sept. 1914, FO 371/2031, 52833; Canova, 4, 10 Aug. 1914, SD 812.00/12826, 12888. Canova, however, is somewhat more graphic than reliable: here, he confuses Melitón with Toribio Ortega (a quite different *jefe*, now dead) and compares the rebel occupation with those of Huns, Moors, Turks, and 'Morgan's freebooters'.

32 Admiral Howard, 18 Jan. 1915, SD 812.00/14239.

33 G. Anderson, El Oro, 2 June 1915, SD 812.00/15255.

34 Shelby, Tula, 9 June 1913, SD 812.00/7890.

35 Cummins, Gómez Palacio, Jan. 1914; Richardson, Tlahualilo, Feb. 1914; FO 371/2025, 10096; 2026, 11732.

36 Hamm, Durango, 25 July 1913, 6, 21 Mar. 1914, SD 812.00/8310, 11223, 11353; Pazuengo, *Historia*, p. 32.

37 Edwards, Juárez, 31 Dec., Silliman, Saltillo, 29 Dec., Hale, Tepic, 18 Dec. 1913, SD 812.00/10021, 10757, 10074.

38 Olea, *Sinaloa*, p. 74; Admiral Howard, 5 Mar. 1914, SD 812.00/11227 notes an earlier evacuation of the well-to-do, greatly fearful of the rebel Yaquis.

39 H. Harrison, Cerralvo, 29 Apr. 1913, SD 812.00/7394.

40 Anon., 8 June 1913; Bonney, San Luis, 25 June 1915; West, Chihuahua, Feb. 1915; SD 812.00/7911; 15374; 14622.

41 Funston, Veracruz, 6 May 1914, SD 812.00/11859; Hohler, Mexico City, 25 Aug. 1914, FO 371/2031, 49155; Funston to Daniels, 17 Sept. 1914, Daniels Papers, box 42.

42 *Mexican Herald*, 30 May 1914.

43 *El Demócrata*, 28 Sept. 1914; *Le Courrier du Méxique*, 1 Oct. 1914.

44 Meyer, *Huerta*, pp. 214–5.

45 Canada, Veracruz, 22 Sept., Fuller, Mexico City, 18 Sept. 1914, Wilson Papers, series IV, box 117.

46 Gavira, *Actuación*, p. 99.

47 *Ibid.*, pp. 99–100.

48 W. B. Loucks, Tabasco Plantation Co., in Fall Report, pp. 1393–4.

49 Córdova, *Ideología*, p. 192.

50 Cf. the list of 'enemies of the cause', STA, box 83; and below, pp. 272–3, 442–6.

51 Meyer, *Huerta*, p. 214; J. G. Nava to Carranza, 9 Oct. 1915, AJD, r. 3; Casasola, *Historia gráfica*, II, p. 1062; Junco, *Carranza*, pp. 113–25; Adams to Cowdray, 25 Sept. 1914, FO 371/2030, 67495.

52 Casasola, *Historia gráfica*, II, p. 844; Guzmán, *Eagle and the Serpent*, p. 185; Adams to Cowdray (n. 51). Casasús, en route from Europe to Mexico, reached Havana and was warned not to proceed: Landa y Escandón to Cowdray, 4 Nov. 1914, Cowdray Papers, box A/3.

53 W. Mitchell, Manager, Banco de Londres y México, in Fall Report, pp. 698–9.

54 Adams to Cowdray (n. 51); this, we shall note, was a provincial sport too.

55 Casasola, *Historia gráfica*, II, pp. 862–3.

56 *El Demócrata*, 10, 11, 19, 22 Oct. 1914.

57 *Ibid.*, 13, 14, 17 Oct. 1914; transcript of Rafael Cuevas y García's speech in Hohler, Mexico City, 22 Sept. 1914, FO 371/2031, 61028.

58 *Le Courrier du Méxique*, 17, 24, 25 Aug., 7 Sept. 1914. The names: *Vida Nueva, Nueva Patria* and *El Demócrata*.

59 *Le Courrier du Méxique*, 20 Aug., 8 Oct. 1914; Page, Rome, 26 Mar. 1914, SD 812.00/14701.

60 Adams to Cowdray, 23 Nov. 1914, Cowdray Papers, box A/3.

61 J. G. Nava to Carranza, 1 Dec. 1915, AVC; *El Demócrata*, 17 Dec. 1915.

62 Silliman, Mexico City, 14 Sept. 1914, SD 812.6363/136; Hohler, Mexico City, 7 Dec., S. Pearson and Son to Grey, 10 Dec. 1914, FO 371/2032, 79841, 81543; Pani, p. 222.

63 Carr, *Movimiento obrero*, I, p. 81; *Le Courrier du Méxique*, 30 Sept., 8 Oct. 1914.

64 Hanna, Monterrey, 1 June; c/o USS Minnesota, Tampico, 2 Aug., USS Chattanooga, Mazatlán, 26 Sept. 1914, SD 812.00/12192; 12819, 13672. Foreign companies were levied at Tampico, but not Monterrey.

65 B. Jiménez to J. Acuña, 22 Jan. 1915, AG 873.

66 Adams to Cowdray, 23 Nov. 1914, Cowdray Papers, box A/3; Martínez Núñez, *San Luis Potosí*, p. 47; Gemmill, Puerto México, 20 Sept. 1914, SD 812.00/13472; F. Cárdenas to Gobernación, 3 Feb. 1915, AG 873. Two years later, Raúl Dehesa was still pleading for the return of the family property: R. Dehesa to Carranza, 5 Dec. 1916, AVC.

67 Holms, Guadalajara, 20 July 1914, FO 371/2031, 52831; Davis, *Experiences*, pp. 152–3.

68 Canada, Veracruz, 3 Oct. 1914, SD 812.00/13482.

69 Gemmill, Puerto México, 20 Sept. 1914, SD 812.00/13472.

70 Canova, Mexico City, 10 Sept. 1914, SD 812.00/13220.

71 Hohler, Mexico City, 25 Aug., Watson, Mazatlán, 19 Oct. 1914, FO 371/2031, 49155, /2032, 77277; Brown, Mazatlán, 26 Sept. 1914, SD 812.00/13247; Falcón, 'Cedillo', p. 117; and cf. Olea, *Sinaloa*, p. 58.

72 Anon, memo. 'para Porfirio Garza', Zaragoza (Coa.), AG 873; Gavira, *Actuación*, p. 100; Canada, Veracruz, 10 Nov. 1914, SD 812.00/13824; Lombardo Toledano, in Wilkie, *México visto en el Siglo XX*, p. 239, recalls a Committee of Public Safety at Teziutlán in 1911 (sic).

73 Cardoso de Oliveira, 3 March, Silliman 4 Mar. 1915 (both Mexico City), SD 812.00/14488, 14497.

74 Davis, *Experiences*, pp. 82–5.

75 Hamm, Torreón, 19 Apr. 1914, SD 812.00/11703.

76 *Ibid.*, 13 Apr. 1914, SD 812.00/111706.

77 Howard, Manzanillo, 8 Nov. 1914, SD 812.00/13942; Cradock, Veracruz, 17 June 1914, FO 371/2029, 27357. Leif Adleson confirms the unpopularity of Tampico's Spaniards.

78 C/o USS New Orleans, Acapulco, 16 Feb., Silliman, Veracruz, 12 Dec. 1914, SD 812.00/11055, 13999; the reasons have been discussed, vol. I, pp. 87, 521.

79 A. Pattison, Veracruz, 17 Oct. 1914, SD 812.00/13824.

80 Pattison (n. 79); Canada, Veracruz, 21 Nov., Jenkins, Puebla, 18 Nov. 1914, SD 812.00/13857, 14073; Gerzayn Ugarte, DDCC, I, p. 314. The 'worker-peasant' character of the local rebels is well known; and these sources suggest the deliberate incitement of the ex-Maderista Governor Antonio Hidalgo, a radical, populist, former textile worker.

81 Katz, *Secret War*, pp. 256–7.

82 Che Guevara, *Reminiscences of the Cuban Revolutionary War* (Harmondsworth, 1969), pp. 90–7.

83 Fabela, DHRM, EZ, pp. 76–81, 83–6, 102–7, 305–10; Manifesto of the Conventionist

Army of the Centre, 1st and 2nd Brigades, Cedillo brothers commanding, 16 Aug. 1916, AVC.

84 See pp. 49, 372.

85 A. Burleson to Lansing, 27 July 1915, enclosing the ex-Huertista José María Lozano's plea for agrarian reform: SD 812.00/15601.

86 Fabela, DHRM, EZ, *passim*; Katz, *Secret War*, pp. 262, 606; below, pp. 465–6.

87 Simpich, Nogales, 4 Sept. 1914, SD 812.00/13147.

88 Gómez, *Reforma agraria*, p. 120.

89 D. Barrows, Chihuahua, 25 Aug. 1915, SD 812.00/15595 (I have slightly changed the order of words in the quotation).

90 Gómez, *Reforma agraria*, pp. 101–21; Katz, *Secret War*, pp. 280–1.

91 Katz, *Secret War*, p. 147, notes the waiver of rents; and see above, pp. 122–5.

92 Katz, 'Agrarian Changes', pp. 272–3. Katz mentions other factors, such as out-migration (e.g., by Villa's troops), to explain the decreased pressure on rural resources; but this must be balanced against in-migration and the economic costs of the war. In any case, land-hunger was ultimately a politico-social rather than an ecological and demographic problem.

93 A. León Grajales to SRE, 101 June 1913, SRE, legajo 771, 79-R-18, p. 149; Aguilar, *Revolución Sonorense*, pp. 380–1.

94 Simpich, Nogales, 6 Apr. 1915, SD 812.00/14863; and Katz, *Secret War*, 283–4.

95 Hamm, Durango, 21 Mar., 8 Aug. 1914, SD 812.00/11353, 12885.

96 *Mexican Herald*, 19 Nov. 1913; *El Imparcial*, 31 Mar. 1914; F. McCaughan, Durango, 14 May 1913, SD 812.00/7856.

97 Armando Bartra, *Regeneración, 1900–1918. La corriente mas radical de la revolución mexicana de 1910* (Mexico, 1977), pp. 327–8.

98 Canova, Zacatecas, 14 Aug. 1914, SD 812.00/12979; Caldwell, Zacatecas, 7 Sept. 1914, FO 371/2031, 61032, who was worried because many of the estates served as collateral for loans advanced by foreign banks.

99 J. Pattison, Bote Mines, Zacatecas to R. Kerrison, Apr. 1914, FO 371/2027, 17045.

100 *Mexican Herald*, 16 June 1914.

101 Cobb, El Paso, 14 Sept. 1916, SD 812.00/19217.

102 At Lampazos (NL) the Hacienda Dolores, belonging to the family of the old Porfirian cacique Francisco Naranjo, was among the properties seized from 'gentlemen . . . hostile to the Constitutionalist cause' and now worked by 'poor' farmers: alcalde A. Lozano to R. García, 19 July, 16 Aug., 25 Sept., 1916, Lampazos Archive, Trinity University, Texas.

103 See pp. 50–1.

104 Falcón, 'Cedillos', pp. 120–1, 174, presents valuable evidence but is somewhat ambivalent as to the degree of genuine reform. Her own material – and that of Ankerson – indicate that it was not inconsiderable.

105 *Ibid.*, pp. 102, 183, 198.

106 *Ibid.*, p. 121; and cf. Bazant, *Cinco Haciendas*, p. 182.

107 'Communal' is, in itself, ambiguous: it can refer to land owned and exploited in common by the community, especially woods (the *montes* of Morelos or Michoacán) and pastures; or to arable land, more usually farmed on an individual (family) basis, albeit owned corporately. In the latter case, the unit of production (though not the juridical status) was akin to a smallholding: both, for example, would fit Chayanov's analysis. Particularly since families – like the Zapatas – participated in both sectors, 'communal' and non-'communal', and 'communal' villages were fully acquainted with private as well as corporate property, it does not seem wise to draw the distinction – whether for individuals, families, communities, or regions – too strongly. The 'communal' Zapatas and 'smallholding' Cedillos (and their respective movements) were more similar than distinct.

108 See vol. 1, pp. 304–8.

109 Womack, *Zapata*, p. 236 and pp. 224–55 for a general picture of Morelos. D. Damián to Zapata, 29 Sept. 1914, Fabela, DHRM, EZ, pp. 126–7, on comparable attempts to get *aguardiente* distilleries into operation in Puebla.

110 Womack, *Zapata*, p. 232; Palafox to Zapata, 11 Jan. 1915, Ayaquica to Zapata, 10 May 1915, Fabela, DHRM, EZ, pp. 150, 218.

111 Womack, *Zapata*, p. 232.

112 *Ibid.*; e.g., the Ixcamilpa restitution, Apr. 1912, Fabela, DHRM, EZ, p. 66.

113 Womack, *Zapata*, p. 228.

114 See vol. I, pp. 309–15.

115 Wolf, *Peasant Wars*, p. 13; Womack, *Zapata*, p. 224.

116 Womack, *Zapata*, pp. 225–6; though cf. Palafox's scheme for railway repair and extension, Palafox to Zapata, 11 Jan. 1915, Fabela, DHRM, EZ, p. 151, which again suggests the different priorities of peasants and intellectuals.

117 Lewis, *Life in a Mexican Village: Tepoztlán*, p. 233. But cf. pp. 370–1, below.

118 J. Gómez to Zapata, 2 Oct. 1914, Fabela, DHRM, EZ, p. 128; Jacobs, 'Aspects', pp. 162–4, 180.

119 Anon. memo., from Guerrero governor's office to Carranza, Sept. 1915, AJD, r. 1.

120 According to Major Uruñuela in Edwards, Acapulco, 3 Nov. 1915, SD 812.00/16834.

121 See L. García Montoya to Zapata, 9 Oct. 1914, and numerous other examples, especially from Dolores Damián, in Fabela, DHRM, EZ, p. 129 and *passim*; Gómez, pp. 66–7, *Mexican Herald*, 1 Jan. 1915.

122 David Ronfeldt, *Atencingo: The Politics of Agrarian Struggle in a Mexican Ejido* (Stanford, 1973), p. 8.

123 *The Rosalie Evans Letters from Mexico*, ed., Daisy Caden Pettus, Indianapolis, 1926, p. 37 (henceforth: Evans).

124 Buve, 'Peasant movements', p. 137.

125 *Ibid.*, pp. 136–7; Gavira, *Actuación*, p. 107.

126 Brown, Mazatlán, 6 Dec. 1914, SD 812.00/14049.

127 *Mexican Herald*, 25 July 1913; Gómez, *Reforma agraria*, pp. 66–7; María y Campos, *Múgica*, pp. 96–9; Canada, Veracruz, 13 Apr. 1915, SD 812.00/14982; Jara to Carranza, 10 Oct. 1916, Fabela, DHRM, RRC, V, p. 179; see also Hall, *Obregón*, pp. 107–8.

128 See pp. 496, 515–7.

129 Rouaix, *Diccionario geográfico, historico y biográfico del Estado do Durango* (Mexico, 1946), pp. 369–70; Reed, *Insurgent Mexico*, pp. 76–7.

130 Zapata to Wilson, 23 Aug. 1914, Fabela, DHRM, EZ, p. 96; Amaya, *Soberana convención*, p. 28.

131 Lind, Veracruz, 25 Apr.; H. Dodge, Niagara, 25 May 1914; SD 812.00/11905; 12075.

132 Almada, *Diccionario*, p. 125; Canova, Aguascalientes, 20 Oct., c/o US Maryland, Manzanillo, 28 Aug. 1914, SD 812.00/13951, 13672; Gilbert M. Joseph, *Revolution from Without: Yucatán, Mexico and the United States, 1880–1924* (Cambridge, 1982), pp. 122–33.

133 C/o USS Sacramento, Tampico, 3 Jan. 1915, SD 812.00/14259.

134 José María Lozano in Burleson to Lansing, 27 July 1915, SD 812.00/15601.

135 E.g. R. Jiménez and others to Carranza, from Pachuca gaol, 9 May 1916, AVC: Jiménez faced the death penalty for alleged 'attacks on individual guarantees', made in support of his village's land grant, conceded by the Convention, now repudiated by the Carrancistas. Other neighbouring pueblos retained *de facto* possession of land 'illegally' acquired under the aegis of the 'ex-Convention'.

136 José Mancisidor, *Historia de la revolución mexicana* (Mexico, 1971), pp. 158–9; Hall, *Obregón*, p. 107 on Pancho Coss's Puebla *reparto*; note also Ayaquica to Zapata, 18 Nov, Fabela, DHRM, EZ, pp. 136–7, which shows that Zapatista policy, again in Puebla, was not invariably popular.

137 Cf. vol. I, pp. 137, 150, 415.
138 We have noted, pp. 4–6, the incongruous alliance of Huerta and the Orozquistas. Even twenty years later, when political fragmentation was much less marked, a radical, reformist president would still be concluding ideologically anomalous alliances: see Schryer, *Rancheros of Pisaflores*, pp. 92–4. Katz, *Secret War*, pp. 257–8, 271–2, shows great ingenuity in trying to explain revolutionary behaviour in terms of ideologically consistent positions.
139 Vicente García to junta de administración civil, Zongólica (Ver.), 10 Apr. 1917, Zongólica Archive, r. 11, f. 96, doc. 70.
140 J. Baños to E. Añorve, 9 June, I. Carmona to E. Añorve, 9 June 1911, AARD 27/74, 77; Atristaín, *Notas*, pp. 16–21.
141 Atristaín, *Notas*, p. 47.
142 Ramírez, *Oaxaca*, pp. 145–6: Baños and his cronies representing law and order.
143 Atristaín, *Notas*, pp. 34, 105. More logically, the Pozaverdeños were also linked to the Zapatistas of Guerrero.
144 *Ibid.*, pp. 134, 152.
145 *Ibid.*, pp. 32, 43, 47, 97.
146 E.g. G. Rubio to Zapata, 27 May 1915, Fabela, DHRM, EZ, pp. 226–8.
147 Atristaín, *Notas*, pp. 30, 78: Julián Blanco conferred their ranks, for what they were worth.
148 *Ibid.*, pp. 19, 32, 36, 45, 102.
149 *Ibid.*, pp. 29, 46, 92. Baños' most steadfast and useful ally was Sadot Garcés, a Jamiltepec merchant, related to the Gómez family, whose property had also suffered from the depredations of the Pozaverdeños.
150 Ramírez, *Oaxaca*, p. 146; though the same author, p. 148, recognises that Baños controlled a 'vast area' between Ometepec and Pochutla. A recent exception is the excellent thesis of Javier Garciadiego Dantan, 'Revolución Constitucionalista y Contrarrevolución (Movimientos Reaccionarios en México 1914–1920)' (Ph.D. diss., El Colegio de México, 1981), pp. 230–1.
151 The *pulque* hacienda of San Antonio Tochatlaco (Hgo) experienced no great upheavals through the late Porfiriato and early revolution (up to the end of 1914), at least judging by the continuity of the labour force; see also González, *Pueblo en vilo*, pp. 113–24, Ezio Cusi, *Memorias de un colono* (Mexico, 1969), pp. 223–4.
152 Schryer, *Rancheros de Pisaflores*, p. 74; González Calzada, *Tabasco*, pp. 142–3.
153 Schryer, *Rancheros de Pisaflores*, pp. 7, 75–6.
154 Cf. vol. I, pp. 234–40.
155 Silliman, Saltillo, 29 Dec. 1913, SD 812.00/10557.
156 Even so, Maytorena prevaricated in 1913 and impaired his revolutionary reputation; Barragán, though a rebel, vigorously opposed the agrarian pretensions of the Cedillos.
157 Urquizo, *Páginas*, p. 91; *Mexican Herald*, 13 Nov. 1914; Gruening, *Mexico and its Heritage*, pp. 436–7; *Historia de la Brigada Mixta 'Hidalgo', que es a las órdenes del General Vicente Segura* (Mexico, 1917), pp. 102–3.
158 Gavira, *Actuación*, p. 91.
159 C/o, USS Clevland, Acapulco, 11 July 1914, SD 812.00/13672.
160 Buve, 'Peasant movements', p. 138; and, a fictional version, Rutherford, *Mexican Society*, p. 253.
161 Admiral Howard, Acapulco, 18 Jan. 1915, SD 812.00/14239; Jacobs, 'Aspects', pp. 128, 132, 136; Apreza to Carranza, 1 Oct. 1915, AJD, r. 2.
162 Cf. Anna Macías, 'Women in the Mexican Revolution, 1910–20', *Americas*, XXXVII (1980), pp. 53–82.
163 C/o US Navy, Acapulco, 9 Nov. 1915, SD 812.00/16843.
164 See pp. 467–8.

165 Katz, *Secret War*, p. 257.

166 Holms, Guadalajara, 11 Dec. 1914, FO 371/2396, 9316.

167 Border reports, 31 Mar. 1917; c/o US Navy, Manzanillo, 21 Aug. 1916; SD 812.00/20793, 19063; and below, p. 396.

168 Canada, Veracruz, 12 July 1915, SD 812.00/15578.

169 Perkins, Misantla, 15 May 1915; F. K. Lane to R. Lansing, 29 Sept., 1916; SD 812.00/15352; 19410½; cf. Fowler, *Agrarian Radicalism*, pp. 4, 131.

170 Canada, Veracruz, 1 Aug. 1916, 13 Nov. 1917, SD 812.00/18987, 21525; and below, pp. 382, 390–2.

171 J. Womack, 'The Spoils of the Mexican Revolution', *Foreign Affairs*, XLVII (1970), p. 678; Fowler, *Agrarian Radicalism*, p. 131; Gruening, *Mexico and its Heritage*, pp. 617–18.

172 See pp. 386–90.

173 Javier Garciadiego Dantan, 'Revolucion constitucionalista y contrarevolución (movimientos reaccionarias en México 1914–20)' (Ph.D., El Colegio de México, 1981), pp. 97–8; Heather Fowler Salamini, 'Caciquismo and the Mexican Revolution: the case of Manuel Peláez', paper given at the Sixth Conference of Mexican and US Historians, Chicago, 1981.

174 W. F. Buckley in Fall Report, p. 840. Cf. Lorenzo Meyer, *México y Estados Unidos*, p. 72, who does not doubt that 'the Pelaecista rebellion had its origin in the conflict between Carranza and the oil companies'. Garciadiego, 'Movimentos reaccionarios', p. 98ff. corrects this misapprehension.

175 See pp. 386–8.

176 Garciadiego, 'Movimientos reaccionarios', p. 99.

177 Canada, Veracruz, 12 July; Bevan, Tampico, 18 Nov. 1915; SD 812.00/15578; 16857; Dawson, Tampico, 11 Aug. 1916 and US Naval Intelligence, 12 Apr. 1918, SD 812.00/245, 387; Wilson, Tampico, 10 Dec. 1914; Hewett, Tuxpán, 6 June 1917; FO 371/2395, 2445; /2962, 158778.

178 Cf. Fowler, *Agrarian Radicalism*, pp. 15, 163.

179 Graham, Tuxpán, 23 Dec. 1914, FO 371/2397, 23925; Garciadiego, 'Movimientos reaccionarios', p. 114.

180 Fowler, *Agrarian Radicalism*, p. 163, on the quiescence of the peasantry of Alamo.

181 See below, pp. 499–505.

182 Rutherford, *Mexican Society*, p. 288.

183 By which I mean principally the work of Jean Meyer.

184 Meyer, *Huerta*, pp. 167–9 questions and de-emphasises Catholic support for Huerta.

185 *Ibid.*, p. 169.

186 *Ibid.*, p. 168; Womack, *Zapata*, pp. 137, 139–40; and pp. 1–2.

187 Meyer, *Cristero Rebellion*, p. 11; *Mexican Herald*, 17, 18 Oct. 1913 on alleged financial help.

188 Rutherford, *Mexican Society*, pp. 289–91.

189 Meyer, *Cristero Rebellion*, p. 12; note the petition of the *vecinos* of Bachíniva to Terrazas, 28 Aug. 1889, STA, box 26, asserting that 'el [Cura] está con el pueblo y el pueblo está con él'; likewise the Velardeña riot and repression showed strong popular support for the parish priest – in a northern, 'industrial' setting: *El Correo de Chihuahua*, 14, 15, 28 Apr. 1909.

190 Obregón, *Ocho mil kilómetros*, p. 156; Hamm, Durango, 16 Feb. 1914, SD 812.00/11028.

191 Above, vol. 1, pp. 40, 254–6, 400–4.

192 González, *Pueblo en vilo*, pp. 87, 116, 123.

193 Rutherford, *Mexican Society*, p. 286.

194 I. López and vecinos to de la Barra, 22 Sept. 1911, AARD 12/35.

195 Meyer, *Cristero Rebellion*, pp. 12–13.

196 Robert E. Quirk, *The Mexican Revolution and the Catholic Church, 1910–20* (Bloomington, 1973), p. 42; Reed, *Insurgent Mexico*, pp. 61, 123; cf. O'Hea, *Reminiscences*, p. 196.

197 Quirk, *The Mexican Revolution and the Catholic Church*, pp. 51–3, 57. Jean Meyer tends to judge Villismo on its record in central Mexico (especially Michoacán) in 1914–15; but this, the briefly triumphant, 'export' Villismo, is not typical of the movement as a whole, which may be better judged in terms of its long-term, local character, exemplified in 1913–14, and after 1915.

198 Hohler, Mexico City, 24 Mar. 1914, FO 371/2026, 16251; Antonio Rius Facius, *La juventud católica y la revolución mexicana* (Mexico, 1963), pp. 51–2; O'Shaughnessy, *Diplomat's Wife*, p. 228.

199 Martínez Núñez, *San Luis Potosí*, p. 228.

200 Meyer, *Cristero Rebellion*, p. 12.

201 Pastoral letter of Mexican bishops, Nov. 1914, Conflicto Religioso, r. 9.

202 However, some Protestants – like the American missionary Samuel Inman – were certainly delighted at the progress of the Constitutionalists and the discomfiture of the Catholics; and they, too, had their conspiracy theories – concerning Huerta's regime, which he loathed, Inman believed that 'the Jesuits had planned the whole thing': Inman to Atwater, 30 Oct. 1913, SGIA, box 12.

203 Cumberland, *Constitutionalist Years*, p. 219.

204 *Ibid.*, p. 228, quoting Obregón to Carranza, Jan. 1915.

205 *Ibid.*, p. 219; *Le Courrier du Méxique*, 8 July 1914; Quirk, *The Mexican Revolution and the Catholic Church*, p. 59.

206 Cumberland, *Constitutionalist Years*, p. 224.

207 *Ibid.*, p. 222.

208 Adams to Cowdray, 24 Sept. 1914, FO 371/2031, 67495; Huitrón, *Orígines*, p. 253, 267, 280–2.

209 Gavira, *Actuación*, pp. 100l 139–40, 179–82.

210 Wightwick, Monterrey, 3 May, 18 June, 28 Sept. 1914, FO 371/2029, 27317; /2030, 33927; 2031, 68893.

211 Cumberland, *Constitutionalist Years*, p. 220.

212 *Ibid.*, p. 224; Gavira, *Actuación*, p. 179; Brondo Whitt, *División del Norte*, pp. 70, 73.

213 Wightwick reports (n. 210). This may serve as a small corrective to the view which grants the PLM credit for 'social' (i.e., labour and agrarian) reform undertaken by revolutionaries with previous PLM connections. Villareal represented perhaps the strongest individual link between the PLM and the revolution; and his major concern was (petty-bourgeois?) anti-clericalism.

214 Fernando Horcasitas, *De Porfirio Díaz a Zapata. Memoria Náhuatl de Milpa Alta* (Mexico, 1974), pp. 147–53.

215 Quirk, *Mexican Revolution and the Catholic Church*, pp. 54, 75; Cumberland, *Constitutionalist Years*, pp. 215, 227–8, rightly questions the more lurid accounts.

216 Obregón, *Ocho mil kilómetros*, p. 290; and doctor's certificate, facing p. 257.

217 *El Demócrata*, 5, 10, 11 Oct. 1914; Villareal published similar exposés in the Monterrey press: Quirk, *Mexican Revolution and the Catholic Church*, p. 55.

218 *El Demócrata*, 6 Oct. 1914.

219 See pp. 288, 293.

220 Sanford, Monterrey, 28 Sept. 1914, FO 371/2031, 68893.

221 *Le Courrier du Méxique*, 4 Sept. 1914; Gavira, *Actuación*, pp. 140–1, 179. The Durango temptress was Teresa Bracho, widow of an *hacendado* killed serving in the *Defensa Social*.

222 *Mexican Herald*, 21, 22 Feb. 1915; Quirk, *Mexican Revolution and the Catholic Church*, p. 75; Obregón, *Ocho mil kilómetros*, pp. 288–9.

223 Holms, Guadalajara, 20 July 1914, FO 371/2031, 52831; Davis, *Experiences*, pp. 40, 51, 80, 86, 116–17.

224 González, *Pueblo en vilo*, pp. 123–4.

225 Davis, Guadalajara, 31 Oct. 1914, SD 812.00/13720; S. Terrazas to F. González Garza,

27 Oct. 1914, STA, box 84, mentions the 'revolution of religious character' reported in Jalisco. It may be that the (nominally Villista) revolt of Gálvez Toscano, which took place at this time and at a place (Sahuayo) mentioned in M. Palomar y Vizcarra to Bishop Orozco y Jiménez, 23 Feb. 1915, Conflicto Religioso, r. 9, is the source – wholly or partly – of these reports. Palomar y Vizcarra, in Wilkie, *México Visto en el Siglo XX*, makes no mention of this activity, recalling that he laid low in 1914–15.

226 Calles to A. Campos, 28 Feb. 1913 in FBI report, Douglas, SD 812.00/6928.

227 Hanna, Monterrey, 7 July 1914, SD 812.00/12477.

228 Amaya, *Soberana convención*, p. 31.

229 Obregón, *Ocho mil kilómetros*, pp. 166, 181; Alfredo Aragón, *El Desarme del Ejercito Federal por la Revolución de 1913* (Paris, 1915).

230 Belt, Mexico City, 26 Sept. 1914, SD 812.00/13361; *El Demócrata*, 2 Oct. 1914.

231 Above, pp. 163–4, 168–9.

232 Brown, Mazatlán, 15 Aug. 1914; c/o US Navy, Guaymas, 1 Oct. 1914; SD 812.00/13098, 13672; Olea, *Sinaloa*, p. 73.

233 Buve, 'Peasant movements', p. 140.

234 C/o USS New Orleans, 29 Aug. 1914, SD 812.00/13672; Obregón, *Ocho mil kilómetros*, p. 181.

235 Ramírez, *Oaxaca*, p. 177; Gavira, *Actuación*, p. 105.

236 Licéaga, *Félix Díaz*, pp. 385–6; Canada, Veracruz, 29 Feb., 26 Sept., 2 Oct. 1916, SD 812.00/17409, 19476, 19552.

237 Tucson consul to Denegri, San Francisco, 21 Dec. 1914, SRE, legajo 841, 113-R-3, p. 2; E. Cota to Carranza, 22 Feb. 1916, Fabela, DHRM, RRC, v, pp. 52–9, 98–104, 118–23; and, for a recent study, see n. 280.

238 On Cantú's regime: E. Howe, El Centro, 27 Aug. 1914; Guyant, Ensenada, 7 Dec. 1914, 14 Jan., 5 June 1915; Cantú to Guyant, 17 Aug. 1915; Guyant, 27 Dec. 1915; Adjutant-General Thomas, El Centro, 22 Mar. 1916; SD 812.00/13023; 14005, 14245, 15187; 15934; 17018; 17603.

239 Admiral Caperton, Mazatlán, 7 May 1915; US Naval report, 9 Nov. 1915; SD 812.00/15055; 16843.

240 Amaya, *Soberana convención*, p. 35.

241 A joke.

242 Richard Scroop, Archbishop of York, in *Henry IV*, pt. II, act IV, scene II.

243 Carothers, El Paso, 18 Dec. 1914, SD 812.00/14061; Womack, *Zapata*, pp. 221–2.

244 Cervantes, *Francisco Villa*, pp. 59, 65; Reed, *Insurgent Mexico*, p. 81; Amaya, *Soberana convención*, p. 34.

245 F. Sommerfeld to H. Scott, 5 Sept. 1914, Scott Papers; Garrett, Laredo, 18 Aug., Funston, Veracruz, 26 Sept., border reports, Brownsville, 26 Sept., Blocker, Piedras Negras, 21 Dec. 1914, SD 812.00/12916, 13343, 13410, 14135.

246 Silliman, Mexico City, 5 Jan. 1915, SD 812.00/14146; *Mexican Herald*, 5 Jan. 1915; Villa's statement mingled praise for the old Federal Army with hints of foreign intervention.

247 Obregón, *Ocho mil kilómetros*, p. 158; Brown, Mazatlán, 6 Feb.; Blocker, Piedras Negras, 12 Mar. 1915, SD 812.00/14410, 14689.

248 Bevan, Tampico, 7 Dec. 1914, Schmutz, Aguascalientes, 23 Apr. 1915, SD 812.00/14102, 14953.

249 By 1915–16, however, when circumstances had markedly changed, some old Orozquistas re-grouped with Villa: see p. 340. It may be that there was greater, though undetectable, interchange at the level of the rank-and-file.

250 Canova, Mexico City, 25 Aug. 1914, SD 812.00/13129.

251 Womack, *Zapata*, pp. 167, 212.

252 Amaya, *Soberana convención*, p. 39; Garciadiego, 'Movimientos reaccionarios', pp. 339–40.

253 Cardoso de Oliveira, Mexico City, 25 Nov. 1914, SD 812.00/13898; Hohler, Mexico City, 28 Nov. 1914, FO 371/2031, 76670; *Mexican Herald*, 26 Nov. 1914.

254 Mexico City report, 4 Feb. 1915, in SD 812.00/14415; Hohler, Mexico City, 28 Nov. 1914, FO 371/2032, 85296, found it all 'remarkable'.

255 'Reaction', for the Carrancistas, meant conservative/Porfirian/Huertista; I shall follow their usage, in this context, without implying any specifically 'reactionary' quality analytically distinct from, say, 'conservative'.

256 *El Dictamen* (Ver.), 26 Nov. 1914.

257 *Ibid.*, 5 Feb. 1915.

258 Antonio Manero, *Por el honor y por la gloria: 50 editoriales escritos durante la lucha revolucionaria constitucionalista en Veracruz*, Mexico, 1916, pp. 164–5.

259 *El Demócrata*, 6 Oct. 1914.

260 *El Dictamen*, 5 Feb. 1915; Manero, *Por el honor*, pp. 19, 45.

261 Adams to Body, 28 Nov. 1914, Cowdray Papers, box A/3.

262 Cumberland, *Constitutionalist Years*, p. 167; Jenkins, Puebla, 7 Jan., Silliman, Mexico City, 8 Jan. 1915, SD 812.00/14285, 14169; Garciadiego, 'Movimientos reaccionarios', p. 340; H. Aguilar to Zapata, 13 Apr. 1915, Fabela, DHRM, EZ, pp. 196–200.

263 See pp. 297–302.

264 This comparison is drawn with the Porfirian regime of the 1900s; it would be less marked if drawn with the 1880s.

265 Azuela, *Trials*, p. 3.

266 Calero, *Un decenio*, pp. 171, 188, 221.

267 Vera Estañol, *Revolución mexicana*, pp. 388–9. Some of these occupational categories look suspiciously derivative of a single case: Alvarado, the pharmacist's assistant, for example, or Castro the 'tram-driver'.

268 Guzmán, *Memorias*, p. 677.

269 Cf. vol. I, p. 177.

270 Canova, Zacatecas, 4 Aug. 1914, SD 812.00/12826.

271 Hohler, Mexico City, 30 Jan. 1915, FO 371/2396, 11834.

272 F. K. Lane to R. Lansing, 29 Sept. 1916, SD 812.00/19410½; cf. Haley, *Revolution and Intervention*, pp. 160, 229.

273 C/o USS Tacoma, Tampico, 29 Apr. 1917, SD 812.00/20905.

274 Jenkins, Puebla, 7 Jan. 1915, SD 812.00/14285.

275 C/o USS Wheeling, Cd Carmen, 17 July 1916, SD 812.00/18994.

276 Simpich, Nogales, 6 Apr. 1915, SD 812.00/14863.

277 Holms, Guadalajara, 20 July 1914, FO 371/2031, 52831.

278 US Naval report, La Paz, 9 Nov. 1915, 21 Aug. 1916, SD 812.00/16843, 19063.

279 Cf. pp. 188–90, 210.

280 Joseph Richard Werne, 'Estéban Cantú y la soberanía mexicana en Baja California', *Historia Mexicana*, XXX (1980).

281 Almada, *Diccionario*, pp. 583–5; above, pp. 27–9.

282 On Alvarado – Vera Estañol's 'mancebo de bótica' (n. 267 above) – see Aguilar, *Revolución Sonorense*, pp. 132, 216, 431–2; and below, pp. 238–9, 250.

283 *Ibid.*, pp. 200–8.

284 *Ibid.*, pp. 205, 268, 272, 375.

285 John W. F. Dulles, *Yesterday in Mexico. A Chronicle of the Revolution, 1919–1936* (Austin and London, 1961), p. 20.

286 J. Ryan to H. Scott, 7 June, 16, 22 July 1915, Scott Papers, boxes 18, 19; Simpich, Nogales, 8 Mar., border reports Nogales, 14 Aug. 1915, SD 812.00/14579, 15908; Hostetter, Hermosillo, 7 July 1915, SD 812.00/15421.

287 M. Kingdom, *From Out The Dark Shadows* (San Diego, 1925), pp. 90, 102.

288 Hamm, Durango, 8, 11 Aug. 1914; Coen, Durango, 22 Jan. 1916; SD 812.00/12885, 12971; 17205.

289 Pazuengo, *Historia*, p. 110; Coen, Durango, Jan. 1916, SD 812.00/17142.
290 On Urbina's 'princely estates': Letcher, Chihuahua, 15 Sept. 1915 (twice), SD 812.00/16269, 16270; Coen, Durango, 2 Mar. 1916, SD 812.00/17422 on Contreras and the Arrietas.
291 Hamm, Durango, 21 Mar. 1914, SD 812.00/11353.
292 Canova, Zacatecas, 14 Aug. 1914, SD 812.00/12979.
293 Caldwell, Zacatecas, 7 Sept. 1914, FO 371/2031, 61032.
294 Canova, Zacatecas, 4, 10 Aug. 1914, SD 812.00/12826, 12888. Canova confuses Toribio with Melitón Ortega: the former contracted typhus at Zacatecas and returned to Chihuahua to die; Melitón, the hoodlum, died five months later at Guadalajara: Guzmán, *Memorias*, p. 798.
295 Abundio Pantoja, brother of Anastasio, 'was feared (sc. in Michoacán) for his boldness, bravery, and his excesses when drunk. His chief delight was to mount shop-counters on horseback. Needless to say, he was the terror of the Huertistas, who feared him like the devil': Alberto Oviedo Mota, *El Trágico Fin del General Gertrudis G. Sánchez* (Morelia, 1939), pt 2, p. 29.
296 Anon. memo. 'Crisis de Sonora y sus Efectos en Sinaloa', Fabela, DHRM, RRC, I, pp. 268–71; Aguilar, *Revolución Sonorense*, pp. 456–7.
297 Morales Jiménez, *Hombres de la revolución*, pp. 165–7; Keys, Rosario, Feb., Mar. 1915, SD 812.00/14229, 14784.
298 Olea, *Sinaloa*, p. 23; Guzmán, *Eagle and the Serpent*, pp. 64–5.
299 Almazán and Pedro de los Santos were comparable: see vol. I, pp. 270–2.
300 Olea, *Sinaloa*, pp. 22–3, 25–6, 91; Watson, Mazatlán, 19 Oct. 1914, FO 371/2032, 77277; Admiral Caperton, Mazatlán, 7 May 1915; Keys, Rosario, 29 Nov. 1914; SD 812.00/15055, 14014; Guzmán, *Eagle and the Serpent*, pp. 52–60.
301 Olea, *Sinaloa*, pp. 26, 64, 81.
302 Keys, Rosario, 29 May 1915, SD 812.00/15246; and cf. vol. I, p. 110.
303 Cockcroft, 'Maestros'; Bonney, San Luis, 25 June 1915, SD 812.00/15374; Vasconcelos quoted in Falcón, 'Cedillo', p. 119.
304 Quirk, *Mexican Revolution*, p. 118, refers to Gutiérrez leading forces in the triangle between Saltillo, San Luis and Concepción; which is correct, if geometrically suspect; and cf. above, pp. 43–5.
305 Cumberland, *Constitutionalist Years*, p. 175; Bonney, San Luis, 3 Nov. 1914, Jenkins, Puebla, 7 Jan. 1915, SD 812.00/13665, 14285.
306 *Mexican Herald*, 14 Dec. 1913; Cumberland (n. 305); Wilson, Tampico, 26 July; Sanford, Monterrey, 23 July; McMillan, Saltillo, 22 July 1914; FO 371/2031, 47057.
307 Quirk, *Mexican Revolution*, p. 119; Hohler, Mexico City, 3 Nov. 1914, FO 371/2031, 76897.
308 Martínez Núñez, *San Luis Potosí*, p. 50; Cumberland, *Constitutionalist Years*, p. 255.
309 Buve, 'Peasant movements', p. 137.
310 See pp. 183, 191.
311 Gómez, *Reforma agraria*, pp. 66–7; *Mexican Herald*, 1 Jan. 1915; Roberto M. y Martínez to Zapata, 7 Dec. 1914, Fabela, DHRM, EZ, pp. 137–9.
312 Martínez to Zapata (n. 311), p. 137; Falcón, 'Cedillo', pp. 56–9, 98, 112; Schryer, *Rancheros of Pisaflores*, pp. 69, 75.
313 Cravioto had been the Porfirian cacique of Hidalgo; González the leading boss of the Huasteca: Falcón, 'Cedillo', p. 48.
314 L. Spillard, Tlacotlalpam, Apr. 1915, 24 May 1915, 23 Sept. 1915; R. Perkins, Misantla, 15 May 1915; Canada, Veracruz, 12 July, 19 Aug., 6 Sept. 1915, 29 Feb. 1916; SD 812.00/14850, 15352, 16492; 15352; 15578, 16056, 16274, 17409. By late 1915, Ruiz and Casarín were fighting each other.
315 See pp. 382–3, 390–1.
316 Oviedo Mota, *El trágico fin*, I, p. 51; II, pp. 27–9; Romero Flores, *Michoacán*, pp. 66, 93–4.

317 Anon. memo. to Carranza, Sept. 1915, AJD, r. 1.

318 C/o US Pacific Fleet, 1 Oct. 1914, 18 Jan. 1915, SD 812.00/13672, 14239; Ochoa Campos, *Guerrero*, pp. 2296–8.

319 Anon. (illegible), Acapulco, to M. Méndez, 7 Feb. 1915, AJD, r. 1.

320 C/o USS Yorktown, Acapulco, 31 May 1915, SD 812.00/15296.

321 Edwards, Acapulco, 7 Aug., 3 Nov. 1915, SD 812.00/15957, 16834.

322 From Gregory Mason, *Outlook*, Nov. 1916, in Fabela, DHRM, RRC, v, p. 163.

323 For example, the various works of Friedrich Katz; or chapter one of Cockcroft, *Intellectual Precursors*, in which the author wrestles with theory much as Tobias did with the angel: valiantly but in vain.

324 E.g., Gilly, *Revolución interrumpida*, pp. 105, 122–3; N. M. Lavrov, 'La revolución mexicana de 1910–17' in Rudenko *et al.*, *Revolución mexicana*, pp. 87–125.

325 In this analysis, I am assuming that class terminology is basically informed by a Marxist/*marxisant* perspective (or, though this is never explicitly the case, a Weberian one). The point should become clear as we proceed.

326 J. H. Hexter, 'A New Framework for Social History', in *Reappraisals in History* (London, 3rd ed., 1963), p. 14.

327 E.g., Gilly, *Revolución interrumpida*, p. 105. Córdova, *Ideología*, who makes a genuine, cogent attempt to link leaders, followers, ideologies and practices, is a notable exception; he, of course, avoids dog-Marxism, and employs different categories: 'regime of privilege', 'middle classes', 'masses' and so on.

328 I, too, am guilty of conflating leaders and followers, and generalising about the latter in terms of the former. But I would plead two justifications for the occasions when this happens: (i) the sample is broad, and not confined to a handful of national caudillos; (ii) often, where it is valid, the leader stand as surrogate for the movement, e.g., it may be legitimate to talk of Zapatismo in terms of Zapata, since a congruence of character and interest united leader and led; and it makes for brevity. In many cases, however, such a conflation would be quite illicit, and I have avoided it (e.g., as regards the composition of the national coalitions, Villismo and Carrancismo).

329 In particular, concerning the nature of feudalism and capitalism, whence these terms derive their conceptual significance; it is hardly necessary to cite the abundant literature produced by Frank, Wallerstein, Laclau and others.

330 Anthony Giddens, *Capitalism and Modern Social Theory* (Cambridge, 1977), p. 37.

331 *Ibid.*, p. 164.

332 *Ibid.*, p. 38.

333 David Goodman and Michael Redclift, *From Peasant to Proletarian Capitalist Development and Agrarian Transition* (Oxford, 1981), p. 4.

334 E.g., Erik Olin Wright, *Class, Crisis and the State* (London, 1978), pp. 30–110.

335 Laclau and – with more relevance and cogency – Bartra adopt this position. For what it is worth, Zapatista manifestoes denounced 'feudal' landlords: e.g., Zapata to Wilson, 23 Aug. 1914, Fabela, DHRM, EZ, p. 97.

336 Sol Tax, *Penny Capitalism: A Guatemalan Indian Economy* (Washington, 1953); Manning Nash, 'The Social Context of Economic Choice in a Small Society', in George Dalton, ed. *Tribal and Peasant Economics* (New York, 1967), pp. 524–38, on the co-existence of market and 'tradition'.

337 See vol. 1, pp. 86, 89.

338 See vol. 1, pp. 102–4, 166–9.

339 Goodman and Redclift, *From Peasant to Proletarian*, p. 213; and pp. 195–6, 213 for the counter-argument.

340 MacFarlane, *Origins of English Individualism* (Oxford, 1978).

341 Goodman and Redclift, *From Peasant to Proletarian*, pp. 84–5.

342 Hexter, 'A New Framework', p. 16.

343 Thompson, 'Peculiarities', p. 64.

344 Lavrov, p. 120; Lobato, quoted by Albert L. Michaels and Marvin Bernstein, 'The Modernization of the Old Order: Organization and Periodization of Twentieth-Century Mexican History', in James W. Wilkie, Michael C. Meyer and Edna Monzon de Wilkie, eds., *Contemporary Mexico, Papers of the Fourth International Congress of Mexican History* (Berkeley, 1976), pp. 689–90; Carr, 'La peculiaridades'.

345 Millon, *Zapata*, p. 67; Schryer, *Rancheros of Pisaflores*, pp. 6–9, 147.

346 That is, characteristics which were revealed in their relations with other groups – followers and antagonists – and which therefore depended on the appropriate social and political context for their expression ; cf. vol. i, p. 153.

347 'Urban' as in Charles Tilly, *The Vendée* (London, 1964), pp. 9–13, 16–20.

348 Dean C. Tipps, 'Modernization Theory and the Comparative Study of Societies: A Critical Perspective', *Comparative Studies in Society and History*, xv (1973), p. 204.

349 Giddens, *Capitalism*, pp. 76–81; John G. Taylor, *From Modernization to Modes of Production* (London, 1979), pp. 6–13.

350 Alan Knight, 'Peasant and Caudillo in Revolutionary Mexico, 1910–17', in D. A. Brading, ed., *Caudillo and Peasant in the Mexican Revolution* (Cambridge, 1980), p. 44.

351 Buve, 'Peasant movements', p. 137; Atl to Carranza, 29 July 1914; Fabela, DHRM, EZ, p. 88.

352 A. Reese, Cuencamé to War Dept., 18 Sept. 1916, SD 812.00/19468.

353 Waterbury, 'Non-revolutionary peasants', pp. 431–4; and vol. i, pp. 369–82.

354 Womack, *Zapata*, p. 222; cf. Millon, *Zapata*, pp. 88–92.

355 Olea, *Sinaloa*, p. 75.

356 Bevan, Tampico, 11 Nov. 1915, SD 812.00/16813.

357 Quirk, *Mexican Revolution*, pp. 174–5; Coen, Durango, n.d., Jan., and 22 Jan. 1916, SD 812.00/171423, 17205.

358 *Ibid.*, 17 July 1915, SD 812.00/15557.

359 Pazuengo, *Historia*, p. 66; Coen, Durango, 27 Jan. 1916, SD 812.00/17237.

360 González, *Pueblo en vilo*, pp. 120–1; Douglas Butterworth, 'From Royalty to Poverty: the Decline of a Rural Mexican Community', *Human Organization*, xxix (1970), pp. 5–11.

361 Turner, *The Dynamic of Mexican Nationalism* (Chapel Hill, 1968), p. 238; and below, pp. 522–3.

362 Olea, *Sinaloa*, pp. 67, 85–6; Womack, *Zapata*, pp. 208, 219–20.

363 Gavira, *Actuación*, pp. 107, 119, 128.

364 See above, pp. 27–9, 106–9.

365 *Mexican Herald*, 13 Dec. 1914; c/o USS Dakota, Veracruz, 30 Sept. 1914, SD 812.00/13495.

366 Canada, Veracruz, 27 July 1914, SD 812.00/12754.

367 *Ibid.*, 10 Nov, SD 812.00/13824. There was a paradox here, in that Veracruz was well represented in the upper ranks of Constitutionalism (Aguilar, Jara, Gavira, Millán); it did not follow, however, that these leaders took immediate control of their own state.

368 J. Burke, Zautla, 4 Aug. 1914, SD 812.00/13306.

369 Buve, 'Peasant movements', pp. 138–9.

370 Horcasitas, *De Porfirio Díaz*, p. 123; *Mexican Herald*, 18 Dec. 1914; Jenkins, Puebla, 7 Jan. 1915, SD 812.00/14285; Gavira, *Actuación*, pp. 133, 135, 139, 142, 166.

371 *El Demócrata*, 18 Jan. 1916; and for Lind's views on Mexican, 'Latin' and 'Teuton': Lind, 28 Aug., 30 Oct. 1913, SD 812.00/10487, 9491.

372 E. Recio in DDCC, ii, p. 920.

373 S. Terrazas to Villa, 2 Dec. 1814, STA, box 84.

374 Admiral Howard, 18 Jan. 1915, SD 812.00/14239; Gavira, *Actuación*, p. 105; Obregón, *Ocho mil kilómetros*, p. 232.

375 Benjamin, 'Passages', p. 137.

376 María y Campos, *Múgica*, pp. 40–3.

377 Oviedo Mota, *El Trágico fin*, p. 24, coins the phrase (he was one himself).

378 María y Campos, *Múgica*, pp. 78–85.

379 Morales Jiménez, *Hombres de la revolución*, p. 171; J. M. Márquez, *El Veintiuno. Hombres de la Revolución y sus Hechos* (Mexico, 1916), pp. 7–9; Cobb, El Paso, 12 June 1917, SD 812.00/21039.

380 See pp. 21, 48, 51.

381 Aguilar, *Revolución Sonorense*, pp. 105, 132, 142.

382 Oviedo Mota, *El trágico fin*, p. 27.

383 US Naval report, Salina Cruz, 9 Nov. 1915, SD 812.00/16843.

384 María y Campos, *Múgica*, p. 13.

385 Salvador Alvarado, *La Reconstrucción de México: Un mensaje a los pueblos de América* (Mexico, 1919), pp. 22–3, 148, 181–2, 241, 369, 377–83.

386 Cf. vol. I, pp. 55, 66–7.

387 Aguilar, *Revolución Sonorense*, p. 105; María y Campos, *Múgica*, pp. 15–16.

388 Márquez, *El Veintiuno*, p. 13; note also Benjamin, 'Passages', p. 139.

389 Córdova, *Ideología*, pp. 199–203.

390 Hall, *Obregón*, pp. 21–4.

391 Aguilar, *Revolución Sonorense*, p. 132.

392 Meyer, *Cristero Rebellion*, p. 19, offers a suggestive parallel.

393 *Mexican Herald*, 23, 24 Jan. 1914; Ramírez, *Oaxaca*, pp. 149–52, 156; Garciadiego, 'Movimientos reaccionarios', pp. 222–3.

394 A. Ennis (American miner), aboard USS Raleigh, Salina Cruz, 29 Nov. 1916, SD 812.00/16889; *Le Courrier du Méxique*, 20 July 1914.

395 Ramírez, *Oaxaca*, p. 163; Garciadiego, 'Movimientos reaccionarios', p. 224.

396 Canada, Veracruz, 10 Nov. 1914, SD 812.00/13824; Waterbury, 'Non-revolutionary Peasants', p. 432.

397 Garciadiego, 'Movimientos reaccionarios', pp. 227, 268–9.

398 Ennis (n. 394); Quirk, *Mexican Revolution*, p. 89; Ramírez, *Oaxaca*, pp. 166–7, 194; Michael Kearney, *The Winds of Ixtepeji: World View and Society in a Zapotec Town* (New York, 1972), p. 33.

399 Canada, Veracruz, 6 July 1916, SD 812.00/18765; Garciadiego, 'Movimientos reaccionarios', p. 234.

400 Waterbury, 'Non-revolutionary Peasants', p. 432.

401 Recent work by Hernández Chávez, Benjamin and Garciadiego, on which this section is based, has greatly illuminated the history of the revolution in Chiapas.

402 Alicia Hernández Chávez, 'La defensa de los finqueros en Chiapas, 1914–20', *Historia Mexicana*, XXVIII (1979), p. 255; see also Wacher, Tuxtla, 14 Sept. 1914, FO 371/2031, 61027.

403 Benjamin, 'Passages', pp. 138–40. Land reform threatened the 'tutelage' which, Hernández Chávez argues, the landlords exercised over the Indian peons by virtue of their paternalistic protection of *ejidal* land.

404 Benjamin, 'Passages', pp. 144–6. Garciadiego stresses the role of landlords more, but recognises, and seeks to explain, the support they received from other social groups, including peons: 'Movimientos reaccionarios', pp. 161, 179–80.

405 Benjamin, 'Passages', p. 144.

406 *Ibid.*, p. 145ff.; Garciadiego, 'Movimientos reaccionarios', p. 165ff.

407 Ramírez *Oaxaca*, pp. 177–81; Garciadiego, 'Movimientos reaccionarios', p. 239; and vol. I, pp. 374–5.

408 Garciadiego, 'Movimientos reaccionarios', p. 242.

409 Gemmill, Puerto México, 30 Nov. 1914, SD 812.00/14003; cf. Gavira's version, *Actuación*, p. 109. Carbajal, in turn, was held responsible for the previous killing of the PLM veteran Hilario Salas: Gavira, *Actuación*, p. 109, *El Universal Gráfico*, 16 Jan. 1931.

410 Garciadiego, 'Movimientos reaccionarios', pp. 242–3 on Santibáñez's end; note Miguel Covarrubías, *Mexico South: The Isthmus of Tehuantepec* (Mexico, 1946), pp. 25, 29, 237–8.

411 Ramírez, *Oaxaca*, pp. 191–2. Garciadiego, 'Movimientos reaccionarios', p. 234.

412 Oaxaca consular agent in Silliman, Mexico City, 14 June 1915, SD 812.00/15220; Ramírez, *Oaxaca*, pp. 197–8.

413 Hernández Chávez, 'La defensa de los finqueros', p. 339.

414 Benjamin, 'Passages', p. 148.

415 Garciadiego, 'Movimientos reaccionarios', p. 179.

416 Luis Espinosa, DDC, II, p. 1151.

417 Garciadiego, 'Movimientos reaccionarios', pp. 235–6, 245.

418 Ennis (see n. 394); E. Ely, Tuxtepec, 11 Feb. 1916, SD 812.00/17635; on the Indians' involvement, Garciadiego, 'Movimientos reaccionarios', p. 260.

419 Garciadiego, 'Movimientos reaccionarios', pp. 236–7, 246, 248.

420 Márquez, *El veintiuno*, p. 123 and pp. 85–126 on the campaign in general.

421 Garciadiego, 'Movimientos reaccionarios', pp. 250, 254.

422 Márquez, *El veintiuno*, pp. 145–82; *El Demócrata*, 26 Nov. 1915.

423 González Calzada, *Tabasco*, pp. 142–56; Benjamin, 'Passages', p. 132.

424 Lespinasse, Frontera, 8 July 1915, SD 812.00/15434.

425 *Ibid.*, 7, 29 Aug., 8 Sept.; Canada, Veracruz, 6 Sept. 1915; SD 812.00/15690, 16070, 16180, 16274.

426 María y Campos, *Múgica*, p. 85; González Calzada, *Tabasco*, pp. 155–6 (and n. 425 sources).

427 Lespinasse, Frontera, 2 Sept. 1915, SD 812.00/16153; Alfonso Taracena, *La Verdadura revolución mexicana* (Mexico, 1960), IV, pp. 58–9 (Taracena being a Tabasqueño himself).

428 Lespinasse, Frontera, 26 May, 8 July 1915, SD 812.00/15153, 15434; González Calzada, *Tabasco*, p. 158; Hernández Chávez, 'La defensa de los finqueros', p. 160.

429 Lespinasse, Frontera, 30 Aug., 2, 3 Sept. 1915, SD 812.00/16075, 16153, 16154; Taracena, *Verdadera revolución*, IV, pp. 62–3.

430 María y Campos, *Múgica*, pp. 87–101. He also states (p. 85) that 'the most complete anarchy' reigned in Tabasco following Gil Morales' revolt, which is too strong: Múgica came less to restore order than to enforce obedience.

431 *El Demócrata*, 2 Jan. 1916; Taracena, *Verdadera revolución*, IV, pp. 71, 118, 120; González Calzada, *Tabasco*, p. 157; Carlos Martínez Assad, *El Laboratorio de la Revolución. El Tabasco Garridista* (Mexico, 1979), p. 29; Lespinasse, Frontera, 8 Sept. 1915, Canada, Veracruz, 29 Feb. 1916, SD 812.00/16180, 17410.

432 Martínez Assad, *El laboratorio*, p. 14.

433 Joseph, 'Revolution from without', pp. ii, 143, 169.

434 Capt. Scott, Progreso, 2 June, 1 July 1915, SD 812.00/15290, 15580; and above, p. 131.

435 M. J. Smith, Fall Report, pp. 874–90.

436 Germon, Progreso, 11, 14 Sept. 1914; SD 812.00/13252, 13253; Bolio, *Yucatán*, pp. 78, 81; Ramón Berzunza Pinto, 'El Constitucionalismo en Yucatán', *Historia Mexicana*, XII (1962) (which follows Bolio closely); Julio Molina Font, *Halacho* (Mexico, 1955), pp. 2–3.

437 Joseph, 'Revolution from Without', pp. 3–4.

438 C/o, USS Minnesota, Veracruz, 17 Nov., Canada, Veracruz, 10 Nov. 1914, SD 812.00/13959, 13824; Reed, *Caste War*, pp. 27–34, 86, 103–4, 258 on the secessionist tradition.

439 Young, Progreso, 12 Jan. 1915, SD 812.00/14262; Molina Font, *Halacho*, pp. 5–10; Bolio, *Yucatán*, pp. 84–5.

440 Young, Progreso, 11 Feb. 1915, SD 812.00/14454; Joseph, 'Revolution from Without', p. 5; Molina Font, *Halacho*, p. 11.

441 Córdova, *Ideología*, pp. 210–11; and below, pp. 494–516.

442 Joseph, 'Revolution from Without', pp. 68, 199; Young, Progreso, 11 Feb. 1915, SD 812.00/14454; Berzunza Pinto, 'El constitucionalismo en Yucatán'.

443 Molina Font, *Halacho*, pp. 13–17.

444 Young, Progreso, 23 Feb. 1915, SD 812.00/14561; Molina Font, *Halacho*, pp. 17–24.

445 Joseph, 'Revolution from Without', p. 5.

446 Molina Font, *Halacho*, pp. 26, 98–9; Bryan to Wilson and reply, 8 Apr.; Wilson to Bryan 12 Mar. and reply 13 Mar. 1915: Bryan Papers, box 43, book 2. Joseph, 'Revolution from Without', pp. 231–2, somewhat oddly connects Wilson's June peace initiative with this episode.

447 Bolio, *Yucatán*, pp. 93–5; Molino Font, *Halacho*, p. 27 puts Alvarado's army at 10,000.

448 Against which 'victories value little if the pay of the men [it] has lost remains and is sufficient to attract other men': quoted in Alan S. Milward, *War Economy and Society 1939–45* (London, 1977), p. xiv. This was ultimately the case with the entire Constitutionalist army.

449 Molina Font, *Halacho*, p. 24.

450 *Ibid.*, pp. 38–58; Bolio, *Yucatán*, pp. 95–101.

451 C/o, USS Des Moines, Progreso, 20 Mar., 12 Apr. 1915, SD 812.00/14819, 14961.

452 Molina Font, *Halacho*, pp. 69, 76–7, 101; Joseph, 'Revolution from Without', p. 159.

453 Joseph, 'Revolution from Without', p. 149; Molina Font, *Halacho*, pp. 66, 101, agrees.

454 Joseph, 'Revolution from Without', pp. 153, 159 and *passim*; Alvarado, *La Reconstrucción*, p. 33ff.

455 Joseph, 'Revolution from Without', pp. 197–222 gives an excellent analysis.

456 *Ibid.*, pp. 150–1, 251.

457 *Ibid.*, p. 254.

458 The phrase is lifted from Amaya, *Soberana convención*, p. 54; Amaya affords the best guide to this phase of the revolution.

459 See pp. 453–4.

460 Adams to Cowdray, 25 Sept. 1914, FO 371/2031, 67495.

461 Cumberland, *Constitutionalist Years*, p. 1512; Amaya, *Soberana convención*, p. 27.

462 Atl to Carranza, 29 July 1914, Fabela, DHRM, EZ, p. 89; Womack, *Zapata*, pp. 198–211.

463 Womack, *Zapata*, p. 207; Quirk, *Mexican Revolution*, pp. 66–7.

464 Cumberland, *Constitutionalist Years*, pp. 153–4; Quirk, *Mexican Revolution*, pp. 68–9.

465 This represents a brief paraphrase of complex negotiations, which have been well described elsewhere: Guzmán, *Memorias*, pp. 595–8; Hall, *Obregón*, pp. 59–75; and sources n. 464.

466 Caldwell, Zacatecas, 7 Sept. 1914, FO 371/2031, 61032.

467 Guzmán, *Memorias*, pp. 614–15.

468 Canova, Zacatecas, 6 Oct. 1914, SD 812.00/13518 (this was the Mexico City convention).

469 Adams to Cowdray, 24 Sept. 1914, FO 371/2031, 67495; Gavira, *Actuación*, pp. 104–5.

470 *Le Courrier du Méxique*, 24 Sept. 1914; Guzmán, *Eagle and the Serpent*, pp. 200–3; *Memorias*, p. 648.

471 Cumberland, *Constitutionalist Years*, pp. 166–7; Womack, *Zapata*, p. 212.

472 See pp. 274–5.

473 Guzmán, *Memorias*, p. 540.

474 *Ibid.*, pp. 612–32; Obregón, *Ocho mil kilómetros*, pp. 199–214; Cumberland, *Constitutionalist Years*, pp. 153–9.

475 Pershing to Wood, 15 Sept. 1914, Pershing Papers, box 215.

476 Quirk, *Mexican Revolution*, pp. 77–8.

477 *Ibid.*, pp. 79–84; Amaya, *Soberana convención*, pp. 57–8, 656–7. The Committee was an *ad hoc* group of Constitutionalist generals, based in Mexico City, which sought a compromise settlement: Lucio Blanco was its founder, and Obregón an active participant.

478 Amaya, *Soberana convención*, p. 77; Cumberland, *Constitutionalist Years*, pp. 165–6; cf. Guzmán, *Memorias*, p. 611, for the Villista view.

479 Amaya, *Soberana convención*, pp. 89–90. Fabela craftily split a motion, thus ensuring that the question of Carranza's resignation went unresolved.

480 *Ibid.*, p. 76; Cumberland, *Constitutionalist Years*, p. 166, n. 62 quotes Carranza to Villareal: 'I have no hope of good results from the conference in Aguascalientes'.

481 *Ibid.*, p. 162.

482 Amaya, *Soberana convención*, pp. 96, 99.

483 Quirk, *Mexican Revolution*, p. 95; Amaya, *Soberana convención*, pp. 77, 80–1, 99, 102; F. Barrera Fuentes, intro., *Crónicas y debates de las sesiones de la soberana convención revolucionaria*, I (Mexico, 1964), pp. 37, 73.

484 In fact, this did not turn out to be the case: see p. 257.

485 Quirk, *Mexican Revolution*, pp. 96–7; Obregón, of course, had sat out the Madero revolution, to his own subsequent chagrin: Hall, *Obregón*, p. 24. Hall's contention that Obregón was a champion of civilian against praetorian rule (pp. 69, 79) is one of the few questionable arguments in this valuable biography.

486 I do not contend that the army – in England or Mexico – faithfully represented the 'people'; rather, that it was the institution which came closest to doing so; and in some instances genuinely did. Cf. Christopher Hill, *The World Turned Upside Down, Radical Ideas during the English Revolution* (London, 1972), p. 58.

487 Amaya, *Soberana convención*, p. 61. It will be gathered that Amaya is rather fond of the revolutionary intellectuals, above all Cabrera – he of the 'implacable logic', 'masterly rhetoric', 'keen judgement' and 'telling dramatic powers': pp. 99, 102.

488 Rutherford, *Mexican Society*, pp. 86, and 78–129 generally. The author's claim that the fictional stereotype of the revolutionary intellectual is 'historically factual', displaying a 'grounding in the social realities that the novelists claim to reflect', stands up better than others in the book; novels, it seems, may be as enlightening about intellectuals as they are misleading about peasants.

489 See vol. I, pp. 400–421.

490 Guzmán, *Eagle and the Serpent*, p. 224; Amaya, *Soberana convención*, pp. 105–6.

491 Quirk, *Mexican Revolution*, p. 102; Amaya, *Soberana convención*, pp. 129–30. Not all delegates were present at any one time; 127 voted for the provisional presidency on 1 November.

492 Barrera Fuentes, *Crónicas*, p. 150; Amaya, p. 159, suggests that Gutiérrez affected a certain rustic gaucherie.

493 Canova, Aguascalientes, 20 Oct. 1914, SD 812.00/13572; Hohler, Mexico City, 20 Oct. 1914, FO 371/2031, 68897.

494 Womack, *Zapata*, p. 215 on the (military) Zapatistas' 'abdication of authority'; Olea, *Sinaloa*, p. 75.

495 Quirk, *Mexican Revolution*, p. 102.

496 Amaya, *Soberana convención*, p. 78; F. Silva in Barrera Fuentes, *Crónicas*, p. 174.

497 Womack, *Zapata*, p. 215.

498 *Ibid.*, pp. 204–5, 216; Cumberland, *Constitutionalist Years*, p. 171; Guzmán, *Memorias*, pp. 665–6. This makes nonsense of Quirk's statement that 'for most of the Zapatistas (the trip to Aguascalientes) was a journey to the utter Antipodes, for they had never before been this far from home': *Mexican Revolution*, p. 107.

499 And Eduardo Hay, veteran Anti-Re-electionist of 1909–10. See Amaya, *Soberana convención*, p. 151; Guzmán, *Eagle and the Serpent*, pp. 269, 277–9.

500 Amaya, *Soberana convención*, pp. 144–5; Silva Herzog in Wilkie, *México visto en el Siglo XX*, p. 611.

501 Womack, *Zapata*, pp. 214–17; Guzmán, *Eagle and the Serpent*, pp. 229–30.

502 Amaya, *Soberana convención*, pp. 144–8. Berlanga – 'by nature a tactless pepperpot' (Quirk, *Mexican Revolution*, p. 93) – also reminded the audience that the Plan of Ayala had originally conferred the presidency on – Pascual Orozco.

503 Womack, *Zapata*, pp. 218, and 214–19 on Angeles' sponsorship of the Zapatistas.

504 Peter H. Smith, 'The Mexican Revolution and the Transformation of Political Elites', *Boletín de Estudios Latinoamericanos y del Caribe*, XXV (1978), p. 119.

505 Quirk, *Mexican Revolution*, p. 108; Womack, *Zapata*, p. 217; Amaya, *Soberana convención*, p. 142.

506 Quirk, *Mexican Revolution*, p. 109.

507 Cockcroft, *Intellectual Precursors*, p. 71; note also (if only for the magnificent title) Gloria Villegas Moreno, 'La Militancia de la "Clase Media Intelectual" en la Revolución Mexicana: Reflexiones a propósito de la Trayectoria Teórico-Política de Antonio Díaz Soto y Gama', paper given to the Sixth Congress of Mexican and US Historians, Chicago, Sept. 1981.

508 Cockcroft, *Intellectual Precursors*, pp. 123, 190.

509 *Ibid.*, pp. 190–1, 217.

510 *El País*, 8 July 1911.

511 As already noted, the Huerta regime could tolerate a degree of apolitical, economist activity, even on the part of the Casa. Díaz Soto's efforts do not figure prominently in John M. Hart's analysis, 'The Urban Working Class and the Mexican Revolution: The Case of the Casa del Obrero Mundial', *Hispanic American Historical Review*, LVIII, 1978, pp. 1–20.

512 Womack, *Zapata*, p. 193.

513 *Ibid.*, p. 217.

514 Guzmán, *Eagle and the Serpent*, p. 230; Quirk, *Mexican Revolution*, p. 107.

515 Guzmán, *Eagle and the Serpent*, pp. 234–8; Amaya, *Soberana convención*, pp. 132–5.

516 Cumberland, *Constitutionalist Years*, p. 170.

517 Fighting continued in Sonora and along the Carrancista/Zapatista lines in Puebla and the Federal District: Amaya, pp. 122, 151, 165; for Carranza's defiance, Cumberland, *Constitutionalist Years*, p. 171.

518 Quirk, *Mexican Revolution*, pp. 101–4, 115; Amaya, *Soberana convención*, pp. 125–6; *El Demócrata*, 20 Oct. 1914.

519 Amaya, *Soberana convención*, pp. 107, 110–1, 126–8, 160–1.

520 *Ibid.*, p. 159; and above, p. 223.

521 *Ibid.*, pp. 160–1.

522 Canova, Aguascalientes, 20, 29 Oct. 1914, SD 812.00/13611, 13702.

523 Amaya, *Soberana convención*, pp. 124–5; Quirk, *Mexican Revolution*, p. 105.

524 Schmutz, Aguascalientes, 29 Oct., 4 Nov. 1914, SD 812.00/13695, 13758.

525 *Ibid.*, Cumberland, *Constitutionalist Years*, p. 173.

526 *Ibid.*, p. 174.

527 Jesús Carranza to Carranza, 3 Nov. 1914, SRE, legajo 841 113-R-2, p. 15; Quirk, *Mexican Revolution*, p. 188–9.

528 Amaya, *Soberana convención*, p. 162; *El Demócrata*, 9 Nov. 1914.

529 Amaya, *Soberana convención*, pp. 163–8; Hall, *Obregón*, pp. 91–3; Cumberland, *Constitutionalist Years*, is somewhat harsh in calling these final efforts 'puerile'; if they were not – as they seem to be – honest but desperate, they were cynical ('more for propaganda effect than anything else', Cumberland suggests) but shrewd.

530 *Ibid.*, p. 177.

531 Womack, *Zapata*, p. 218.

532 They can be found in SRE, legajo 841, 113-R-2, pp. 17–33.

533 Amaya, *Soberana convención*, pp. 162, 165, 179.

534 As even some Villistas admitted: Guzmán, *Eagle and the Serpent*, p. 228.

535 Quirk, *Mexican Revolution*, p. 126; Hall, *Obregón*, pp. 92–4.

536 Amaya, *Soberana convención*, pp. 170–1.

537 The phrase – apposite and uncontentious – comes from Cumberland, *Constitutionalist Years*, p. 151.

538 Already, the defection of the Orozquistas to Huerta blurs this distinction; as does the presence of 'last-minute' revolutionaries in both cases.

539 Terrazas to municipal presidents, 19 Jan. 1915, STA, box 84; Cumberland, *Constitutionalist Years*, pp. 189–92.

540 Lavrov, in Rudenko, *Revolución mexicana*, pp. 109, 113; Gilly, *Revolución interrumpida*, pp. 94–5; Anatol Shulgovski, *México en la encrucijada de su historia* (Mexico, 1968), p. 33.

541 Jean Meyer, *Révolution Méxicaine*, pp. 57–8, 72–4; Wolf, *Peasant Wars*, pp. 36–41 is not dissimilar.

542 Quirk, *Mexican Revolution*, pp. 74–5; and the same author's 'Liberales y Radicales', which has been taken up by Wolf, *Peasant Wars*, p. 40 and others.

543 Obregón, *Ocho mil kilómetros*, pp. 233–8; Francisco Azcona B., *Luz y Verdad. 'Pancho' Villa, el Cientificismo y la Intervención* (New Orleans, 1914); and above, pp. 213–14.

544 Amaya, *Soberana convención*, pp. 18–19, 57; though Amaya is influenced by the third school.

545 As Cumberland, *Constitutionalist Years*, pp. 162–3 more or less points out.

546 H. J. Brown to Bryan, 4 Aug. 1914, Bryan Papers, box 43, letterbook 1; a long report, based on a ten week trip to northern Mexico.

547 Carothers, El Paso, 12 Apr. 1914, SD 812.00/11755; and above, pp. 109–10, 162.

548 Calero, *Un decenio*, p. 172; Canova, Saltillo, 8 July 1914, SD 812.00/12474; Alfonso Junco, *Carranza y los orígines de su rebelión* (Mexico, 1955), pp. 31, 96–7.

549 Barragán, *Historia del ejército*, I, pp. 30, 111, 164.

550 Barragán, *Historia del ejército*, I, pp. 247–8; Cobb, Juárez, 22 Dec. 1916, SD 812.00/20207 on Murguía; José Morales Hesse, *El General Pablo González: datos para la historia, 1910–16* (Mexico, 1916), is sketchy on its subject's background.

551 Luis F. Bustamante, *De El Ebano a Torreón* (Monterrey, 1915), p. 236; Blocker, Piedras Negras, 14 Sept. 1917, SD 812.00/21281; Jenkins, Puebla, 7 Jan. 1915, SD 812.00/14285.

552 Further research – of the kind pioneered by Aguilar in the case of Sonora – would clarify these personal and regional relationships, and might explain, for example, the disproportionate revolutionary contribution of Lampazos.

553 Though the split was not perfect: Diéguez (a 'Sonoran' by adoption) went with Carranza, Treviño with the Sonorans; Pablo González, true to type, prevaricated.

554 Quirk, *Mexican Revolution*, pp. 10, 151; note Obregón's rejection of the 'Constitutionalist' label, above, p. 173.

555 For the 'conventional' definition: Knight, 'Intellectuals'.

556 Gavira, *Actuación*, pp. 184–9: as these comments show, the Veracruz faction, if powerful, was hardly united.

557 S. Terrazas to Carranza, 7 July 1914, STA, box 84.

558 At least, this is a possible interpretation: see pp. 281–2.

559 Below, pp. 299–302.

560 Guzmán, *Memorias*, p. 71; Calzadíaz Barrera, *Hechos reales*, I, pp. 22–3.

561 Guzmán, *Memorias*, p. 740; Píndaro Urióstegui Miranda, *Testimonios del Proceso Revolucionario* (Mexico, 1970), p. 92ff.

562 Cervantes, *Francisco Villa*, p. 55; Calzadíaz Barrera, *Hechos reales*, i, pp. 171–2; Brondo Whitt, *División del Norte*, pp. 34–5, 74. The long report from a 'confidential source' in the north, in Hohler, Mexico City, 20 Oct. 1914, FO 371/2031, 68895, credits Villa with '5,000 men of his own' within an army several times larger.

563 See vol. I, pp. 294–5, 319–20.

564 As befitted a popular movement with deep roots, Orozquismo survived tenaciously, in the shape of independent, local caudillos, like Campa and Salazar; in 1914, however, their power was thoroughly eclipsed by Villa's. See Meyer, *Mexican Rebel*, pp. 118–21; and below, p. 340, on their return to the fold.

565 O'Hea, quoted by Hohler, Mexico City, 17 Dec. 1914, FO 371/2395, 6623.

566 D. Barrows to B. Wheeler, 25 July 1915, SD 812.00/15595. Barrows, a professor of political science, was touring Chihuahua.

567 Schmutz, Aguascalientes, 11 Nov. 1914, SD 812.00/13914.

568 John Womack, Jr, 'The Spoils of the Mexican Revolution', *Foreign Affairs*, 48 (1970), p. 678; Cumberland, *Constitutionalist Years*, p. 182.

569 Guzmán, *Memorias*, p. 740; Letcher, Chihuahua, 25 Aug. 1914, Duval West, Mar. 1915, SD 812.00/13232, 14622.

570 Reed, *Insurgent Mexico*, pp. 160, 164; Almada, *Diccionario . . . Chihuahuenses*, p. 463; Guzmán, *Eagle and the Serpent*, pp. 277–8.

571 Cf. pp. 216–17.

572 'Nationalism' in the sense already used above, p. 232; which tended to correlate closely with other attributes, e.g., anti-clericalism.

573 The point has been discussed above, vol. 1, pp. 303–5.

574 Bustamante, *De el Ebano*, pp. 28–30; Guzmán, *Memorias*, p. 895.

575 Guzmán, *Memorias*, pp. 798–9, 840–1.

576 Aguirre Benavides, *De Francisco I. Madero*, pp. 252–3; Letcher, Chihuahua, 15 Sept. 1915, SD 812.00/16270.

577 S. Terrazas to Villa, 2 Dec. 1914, STA, box 84.

578 Holms, Guadalajara, 11 Dec. 1914, FO 371/2396, 9316.

579 M. Palomar y Vizcarra to Orozco y Jiménez, 23 Feb. 1915, Conflicto Religioso, r. 9; Duval West, Mar. 1915, SD 812.00/14622; *Mexican Herald*, 22 Oct. 1913.

580 Originally a native of Jalisco; a Sonoran by adoption.

581 See pp. 288, 312.

582 González, *Pueblo en vilo*, pp. 123–4.

583 Gruening, *Mexico and its Heritage*, pp. 436–7; Wilson, Tampico, 10 Dec. 1914, FO 371/2395, 2445; L. Spillard to Canada, 24 May 1915, SD 812.00/15353; Garciadiego, 'Movimentos reaccionarios', p. 145, n. 25; Benjamin 'Passages', p. 144.

584 Aguirre Benavides, *De Francisco I. Madero*, p. 263; Silliman, Eagle Pass, 8 Aug. 1916, SD 812.00/18931.

585 C/o USS Sacramento, Tampico, 3 Jan. 1915, SD 812.00/14259 (the currency question is explored more fully later).

586 Carranza also picked up some 'negative', anti-Villa support; but this was much less significant since, on the whole, Carrancismo inspired greater outright hostility than its genial rival.

587 'Active' participants were directly involved in the conflict – which meant, principally, fighting. Some civilians, such as Palafox, were genuinely 'active'; some, though apparently 'active' were in fact appendages of the military; the vast majority of civilians consisted of passive spectators, sympathisers and victims.

588 See pp. 289, 291, 297, 338.

589 While 'coalition' fairly describes the loose, military factions, it would be too strong for the yet looser civilian groupings. Hence 'constituency', which should be taken to mean a congeries of assorted elements, who share a rough, common allegiance: 'Dissent' or 'Middle America' are possible parallels.

590 Amaya, *Soberana convención*, pp. 52–3, 57.

591 Gavira, *Actuación*, pp. 105–6.

592 Barragán, *Historia del ejército*, II, p. 87; L. Ricketts to H. Scott, 7 Feb. 1915, Scott Papers, box 17, concluding 'Juan is an honest boy . . . but weak' (he was also an ex-employee).

593 Zuazua to González, 16 Feb. 1916, AVC.

594 Cumberland, *Constitutionalist Years*, p. 160; Obregón, *Ocho mil kilómetros*, pp. 214–15; Canova, Zacatecas, 4, 5 Oct. 1914, SD 812.00/13465, 13466.

595 For initial signs of what was soon to become a pervasive sentiment: Admiral Howard, Manzanillo, 8, 14 Nov., 7 Dec. 1914, SD 812.00/13942, 13947, 14067.

596 Hohler, Mexico City, 20 Oct. 1914, FO 371/2031, 68995, from a 'confidential source'.

597 Romero Flores, *Michoacán*, pp. 140–4; Schmutz, Aguascalientes, 20 Jan. 1915, SD 812.00/14281; Barragán, *Historia del ejército*, II, p. 124, on the case of Lucio Blanco.

598 Blocker, Piedras Negras, 5 Nov., 9 Dec. 1914, SD 812.00/13722, 14002. Dávila in fact stayed with Carranza, took Monterrey in Apr. 1915, and became Governor of San Luis: Hanna, Monterrey, 24 Apr. 1915, SD 812.00/15078.

599 Bonney, San Luis, 16 Dec. 1914, SD 812.00/13945.

600 Brown, Mazatlán, 21 Nov. 1914, SD 812.00/13945.

601 H. L. Beach, San Antonio, 30 June 1915, SD 812.00/15335.

602 Canova, Aguascalientes, 20 Oct. 1914, SD 812.00/13611.

603 See pp. 28–9.

604 Aguilar, *Revolución Sonorense*, pp. 478–85.

605 Simpich, Nogales, 28 Mar., Hostetter, Hermosillo, 13 May 1914, SD 812.00/11329, 1203.

606 Border reports, Douglas, 13 June 1914, SD 812.00/12324; Aguilar, *Revolución Sonorense*, pp. 477, 479.

607 *Ibid.*, pp. 478, 481; Hostetter, Hermosillo, 13 June 1914, SD 812.00/12320 reports Maytorena recruiting among the 'hackdrivers [and] saloon men' of Hermosillo.

608 *Ibid.*, 7, 13 June, 20 Aug. 1914, SD 812.00/12233, 12248, 13142; Carranza to Alvarado, 16 June 1914, SRE, legajo 813, 99-R-3, p. 229.

609 *El Demócrata*, 29 Oct. 1914; Aguilar, *Revolución Sonorense*, p. 481.

610 Quirk, *Mexican Revolution*, pp. 68–9; Cumberland, *Constitutionalist Years*, pp. 152–9; Hostetter, Hermosillo, 3 Aug. 1914, SD 812.00/12793.

611 Equally, the two veterans of 1910, Alvarado and Cabral, initially fell into neither camp: Alvarado was pushed towards Carrancismo; Cabral became a reluctant Villista.

612 C/o USS Raleigh, 7 Aug. 1914, SD 812.00/13151.

613 Aguilar, *Revolución Sonorense*, p. 487.

614 *Ibid.*, p. 489; Hostetter, Hermosillo, 6, 26 July 1914, SD 812.00/12422, 12720.

615 A. Hopkins, US Immigration, Tucson, to H. L. Scott, 22 July 1914; L. D. Ricketts to same, 7 Feb. 1915, Scott Papers, boxes 16, 17.

616 Aguilar, *Revolución Sonorense*, p. 487.

617 Hopkins (n. 615); F. D. Hamilton to L. D. Ricketts, 5 Nov. 1914, Scott Papers, box 16.

618 For a long (Carrancista) account of the siege of Naco, see Hill's report, 28 Mar. 1917, AVC.

619 Anon., Cananea to L. D. Ricketts, Jan. 1915, Scott Papers, box 17.

620 J. A. Ryan to H. L. Scott, 31 May 1915, Scott Papers, box 18.

621 Cf. pp. 71–2, 158–62, 281–2.

622 Simpich, Nogales, 10 Aug. 1914, SD 812.00/12803; Aguilar, *Revolución Sonorense*, p. 489.

623 Simpich, Nogales, 24 Aug.; Hostetter, Hermosillo, 15, 20 Aug., 10, 29 Sept. 1914, SD 812.00/12984; 13032, 13142, 13209, 13401.

624 Hill report (n. 618); Hamilton (n. 617).

625 Cumberland, *Constitutionalist Years*, p. 81; anon. to Carranza, 'The Sonoran Crisis and its Effects in Sinaloa', 11 June 1914; R. Pesqueira to Obregón, 5 July 1914, Fabela, DHRM, RRC, I, pp. 268–71, 303–5.

626 Olea, *Sinaloa*, pp. 76–8; Hostetter, Hermosillo, 10 Jan. 1914, SD 812.00/10592; Cervantes, *Francisco Villa*, p. 104; Pazuengo, *Historia*, pp. 86–7; Brown, Mazatlán, 23 Jan. 1915, SD 812.00/14338.

627 Keys, Rosario, 24 Mar., 29 May; c/o US Navy, Mazatlán, 7 May 1915, SD 812.00/14784, 15246, 15055; Guzmán, *Eagle and the Serpent*, pp. 52–66.

628 Gill, 'Mochis'; Olea, *Sinaloa*, pp. 81–2, 85.

629 Villa's side of the argument is given in Guzmán, *Memorias*, pp. 607, 630. The feud, dating back to the sack of Durango (see p. 39) culminated in Urbina's killing of the Arrietas' representative at Aguascalientes: *ibid.*, p. 664.

630 Pazuengo, *Historia*, pp. 98–108: though a Villista, Pazuengo was sympathetic to the Arrietas.

631 Gamiz, *Durango*, p. 54; Myles, El Paso, 1 Dec. 1914, FO 371/2032, 85701.

632 Hamm, Durango, 17 Aug., 27 Sept. 1914, 14 Apr. 1915; Brown, Mazatlan, 10 Oct. 1914, SD 812.00/12946, 13429, 14904; 13560.

633 Hamm, Durango, 12 May 1914, SD 812.00/11998, on relations with Carranza.

634 Maclovio Herrera to Domingo Arrieta, 2 Oct. 1914, Fabela, DHRM, RRC, I, pp. 369–70.

635 Bustamante, *De el Ebano*, pp. 219–20; Reed, *Insurgent Mexico*, pp. 68, 89.

636 Above, vol. I, pp. 295, 319–20.

637 Pershing, 14 Apr. 1916, SD 812.00/18072.

638 Herrera to Arrietas (n. 634); Letcher, Chihuahua, 1 Oct. 1914, SD 812.00/13431; H. R. Wagner to Scott, 8 Oct. 1914; C. Husk to same, 16 Nov. 1914; Scott Papers, box 16.

639 Guzmán, *Memorias*, pp. 562, 565, 633. Since Chao stayed loyal to Villa, this seems unlikely.

640 C. Husk to H. L. Scott, 16 Nov. 1914, Scott Papers, box 16.

641 C. Husk to H. L. Scott, 20 May 1915, Scott Papers, box 15 (Chao was the informant).

642 I.e., in the 'conventional' sense of espousing nationalist/patriotic symbols, grievances and causes; the greater 'nationalism' of the Carrancista core (as I have 'unconventionally' called it) lay in their commitment to centralised, national government. The first defined itself in terms of external enemies, the second of internal.

643 Villa to Zapata, 22 Sept. 1914, Fabela, DHRM, EZ, p. 124.

644 Hostetter, Hermosillo, 2 Aug. 1914, SD 812.00/12790.

645 C/o USS Kansas, Tampico, 30 Aug. 1914, SD 812.00/13151.

646 Letcher, Chihuahua, 1 Oct, 1914, SD 812.00/13431.

647 Border reports, Douglas, 4 Mar. 1916, SD 812.00/17513.

648 Oviedo Mota, *El trágico fin*, I, pp. 57–9, II, pp. 7, 42.

649 *Ibid.*, II, pp. 36–9.

650 Buve, 'Peasant movements', p. 138.

651 Falcon, 'Cedillo', pp. 99, 112.

652 Schryer, *Rancheros of Pisaflores*, pp. 72–5.

653 R. M. y Martínez to Zapata, 7 Dec. 1914, Fabela, DHRM, EZ, p. 139.

654 Schryer, *Rancheros of Pisaflores*, p. 74.

655 C/o US Navy, Acapulco, 11 July 1914, 18 Jan. 1915, SD 812.00/13672, 14239.

656 See pp. 194–5.

657 See n. 583.

658 Atristaín, *Notas*, pp. 97–106.

659 Urquizo, *Páginas*, p. 114.

660 See below, pp. 382–6, 391, 396–7.

661 Border reports, El Paso, 8 May 1915, SD 812.00/15029.

662 Simpich, Nogales, 1 Oct. 1914; border reports, Eagle Pass and Blocker, Piedras Negras, both 26 Sept. 1914; border reports Laredo, 3 Oct. 1914; SD 812.00/13352; 13410, 13360; 13462.

663 Schmutz, Aguascalientes, 29 Oct., Brown, Mazatlán, 12 Sept., Canova, Guanajuato, 10 Sept. 1914; Carothers, Irapuato, 22 Apr. 1915; SD 812.00/13695, 13425, 13220; 14935.

664 Carothers, 5 Feb. 1915, Bryan Papers, box 43, book 2.

665 G. Landa y Escandón to Cowdray, 4 Nov. 1914, Cowdray Papers, box A/3; Canada, Veracruz, 10 Feb. 1915, SD 812.00/14457, quoting a Mexico City source.

666 Cumberland, *Constitutionalist Years*, p. 183, n. 142; Pershing to Scott, 18 Oct. 1914, Scott Papers, box 16; Landa y Escandón to Cowdray and vice versa, 4, 10 Nov. 1914, Cowdray Papers, box A/3; Hohler, Mexico City, 30 Nov. 1914, FO 371/2032, 77190.

667 Minutes on Spring-Rice, Washington, 19 Jan. 1915 (twice) FO 371/2395, 6800, /2396, 7279. Cowdray's views, if weighty, were not infallible; in the same correspondence he predicted that the European War 'may be over by Christmas . . . or may take twelve months'.

668 *Mexican Herald* (Veracruz), 13 July 1914.

669 *Le Courrier du Méxique*, 11 Dec. 1914.

670 That is, in predictions of a Villista victory; which did not always go with pro-Villa sympathies. Still less did they imply any active commitment.

671 Benavides, *De Francisco I. Madero*, p. 234; Obregón, *Ocho mil kilómetros*, pp. 231, 268.

672 Ortiz, *Episodios*, p. 31 (Moroleón the pueblo in question).

673 Rutherford, *Mexican Society*, p. 290, n. 106. De la Barra, of course, was not deposed but served out his interim presidency; this falls within the margin of error allowed for prophecies over 200 years.

674 C/o USS Albany, Guaymas, 22 Aug. 1914, SD 812.00/13672.

675 List of 'enemies of the people', n.d., 1914, STA, box 84.

676 *Mexican Herald*, 1 July 1914; Hohler, Mexico City, 21 Dec. 1914, FO 371/2395, 6626.

677 C. Husk to H. L. Scott, 27 July 1914, Scott Papers, box 16; Hohler, Mexico City, enclosing report from N.W. Railway, Chih., 17 Dec. 1914, FO 371/2395, 6223; Blocker, Piedras Negras, 13 Jan. 1915, SD 812.00/14251; Katz, *Secret War*, p. 263.

678 Blocker, Piedras Negras, 12, 16 Mar. (twice), 26 Apr. 1915, SD 812.00/14602, 14666, 14689, 14905.

679 Hanna, Monterrey, 16, 18 Jan., 27 Mar. 1915, SD 812.00/14228, 14291, 14719 (and Hanna was far from being a 'Villista'); cf. H. Knox and N. Bagge in Fall Report, pp. 1421, 1432; and Katz, *Secret War*, p. 278.

680 Bevan, Tampico, 24 Nov. 1914, 20 Jan., 3 May, 15 June 1915, SD 812.00/13887, 14313, 15002, 15303.

681 A. Villareal, Los Angeles, to SRE, 8 Apr. 1915, SRE, legajo 841, 113-R-3, p. 137.

682 Villa's metamorphosis from bandit to saviour can be clearly followed in British consular and diplomatic records; Whitehall's opinion consistently lagged behind that of the men on the ground.

683 Davis, Guadalajara, 19 Dec. 1914, 15 Feb. 1915; Duval West, Guadalajara, 6 Mar. 1915; SD 812.00/14138, 14491; 14622; Holms, Guadalajara, 19 Dec. 1914, FO 371/2396, 9315; Guzmán, *Memorias*, pp. 747–9.

684 Riveroll in Calzadíaz Barrera, *Hechos reales*, I, p. 14; Schmutz, Agascalientes, 10 Dec. 1914, SD 812.00/14199; Carothers, Irapuato, to Bryan, 5 Feb. 1915, Bryan Papers, box 43, book 2.

685 Hanna, Monterrey, 18 Jan. 1915, SD 812.00/14291.

686 Lincoln Steffens, *The Autobiography of Lincoln Steffens* (New York, 1931), p. 715; and see, for example, Carranza's proclamation in *El Pueblo*, 12 June 1915.

687 Katz, *Secret War*, p. 276.

688 See pp. 113–4.

689 Guzmán, *Eagle and the Serpent*, pp. viii, 116–17.

690 See n. 702.

691 Katz, *Secret War*, p. 277, quotes Federico González Garza to the effect that Villista constitutionalism was belated and spurious; the point is well taken but should not be exaggerated – even belated ideological commitments (e.g., Constitutionalist agrarianism) acquire a momentum of their own.

692 Amaya, *Soberana convención*, p. 63; Cumberland, *Constitutionalist Years*, p. 162.

693 At the level of rhetoric; practice is another matter. On the sameness of factional programmes: Duval West, 5 Apr. 1915, SD 812.00/20721.

694 Fuller to Bryan, 10 Nov. 1914, Bryan Papers, box 30.

695 House, recounting a conversation with Wilson: House Diary, 27 Apr. 1914.

696 SD 812.00/19, 30 Aug. 1914.

697 *El Demócrata*, 6 Nov. 1914.

698 Quirk, *Mexican Revolution*, pp. 9–10.

699 Canova, Torreón and Zacatecas, 25 July, 10 Aug. 1914, SD 812.00/12650, 12888; R. V.

Pesqueira to Obregón, 5 July 1914, Fabela, DHRM, RRC, 1, p. 303 on the danger of *ernestismo* (from Ernesto Madero), which threatened to ensnare Villa and make Angeles 'lord and master of the Revolution'.

700 Letcher, Chihuahua, 25 Aug. 1914, SD 812.00/13232.

701 Guzmán, *Eagle and the Serpent*, pp. 117–18.

702 Vasconcelos, *A Mexican Ulysses*, pp. 70, 87, 90–1, 94. Vasconcelos' dislike of plebeian caudillos (and faith in education) went further: 'given ten more years of Madero's schools', he claimed, rather implausibly, 'men like Orozco and Pancho Villa would never have appeared again in our history'. It should be remembered that Juan Banderas, another plebeian caudillo, was looking to shoot Vasconcelos about this time, over a disputed legal fee.

703 Canova, Aguascalientes, 21 Oct. 1914, SD 812.00/13633: the interlocutor was Antonio Villareal, who later, reluctantly, threw in his lot with Carranza.

704 G. H. Pound to H. L. Scott, 10 Aug. 1915, Scott Papers, box 19; Katz, 'Agrarian Changes', pp. 262–3.

705 Body to Riba, 24 Sept. 1914, Cowdray Papers, box A/3: Miguel Díaz Lombardo was recommended. The company's role in this was, again, passive but receptive.

706 Pershing to Scott, 10 Oct. 1914, Scott Papers, box 16.

707 S. Terrazas to Villa, 29 Oct. 1914, STA, box 84.

708 Guzmán, *Memorias*, p. 640; Hohler, Mexico City, 11 Sept. 1914, FO 371/2031, 56920; cf. Calero, p. 171.

709 Quirk, *Mexican Revolution*, pp. 176–7.

710 Guzmán, *Memorias*, pp. 597, 892; Hohler, Mexico City, 11 Sept. 1914 (n. 708); Vera Estañol, *Revolución mexicana*, p. 408; memo. of 4 Mar. 1914 in STA, box 84.

711 Guzmán, *Eagle and the Serpent*, p. 279.

712 Carothers, Irapuato, to Bryan, 5 Feb. 1915, Bryan Papers, box 43, book 2.

713 Guzmán, *Memorias*, pp. 188, 537–8.

714 Hohler, Mexico City, 21 Dec. 1914, FO 371/2395, 6626.

715 Pershing to Bliss, 2 June 1914, Pershing Papers, box 26, on Carothers' influence.

716 Katz, *Secret War*, p. 278; Terrazas to Villa, 27 Feb. 1915, STA, box 84; Bryan to Wilson, 21 Dec. 1914, Bryan Papers, box 43, book 2.

717 Guzmán, *Memorias*, pp. 537–8.

718 Carothers, Irapuato, to Bryan, 5 Feb. 1915, Bryan Papers, box 43, book 2.

719 Caldwell, Zacatecas, 22 Oct. 1914, FO 371/2031, 71957.

720 Hanna, Monterrey, 18 Jan. 1915, SD 812.00/14291; Sommerfeld to Scott, 18 Feb. 1915, Scott Papers, box 17.

721 Clendenen, *United States and Pancho Villa*, p. 152.

722 Above all by General Hugh Scott, famous for his sign-language conversations with the Hopi Indians, who now liaised with a different primitive, Pancho Villa, instructing him in the conventions of war: Clendenen, *United States and Pancho Villa*, pp. 158–9.

723 Note also the cases of Damy and Carrasco, Silva Herzog and the Cedillos: Knight, 'Intellectuals'.

724 Clendenen, *United States and Pancho Villa*, p. 143; Hamm, Durango, 4 June 1913, SD 812.00/8078.

725 Brondo Whitt, *Division du Norte*, p. 78.

726 Guzmán, *Eagle and the Serpent*, p. 299; Vasconcelos, *A Mexican Ulysses*, p. 116.

727 Katz, *Secret War*, p. 262 asserts that 'with few exceptions, all peasant leaders or peasant movements in northern Mexico sided with Villa'. In part, the truth of this statement derives from Villa's dominance of the north, which necessarily brought him a majority of peasant (as well as landlord, worker, business and clerical) support. Nevertheless, there were popular leaders and movements (which, depending on the definition being used, could qualify as 'peasant') which adhered to Carrancismo: Carrasco, Coss, the Arrietas, the

Herreras, Hurtado. The balance of peasant support certainly favoured Villa; but not unanimously. Furthermore, there is no reason to exclude consideration of the rest of the country, where no noticeable imbalance was evident; and which – I would argue – shows that the Carranza–Villa schism followed pragmatic, local (rather than class) allegiances.

728 Berta Ulloa, *Historia de la revolución mexicana, Período 1914–17, IV, La revolución escindida* (Mexico, 1979), p. 15.

729 Guzmán, *Memorias*, p. 725.

730 N. Bagge, in Fall Report, p. 1433; and Manuel Gamio, *The Life Story of the Mexican Immigrant* (Chicago, 1931), p. 7.

731 Womack, *Zapata*, pp. 12, 14–15.

732 Ulloa, *Revolución escindida*, pp. 13–16: a good, concise portrait.

733 Canova, Saltillo, 2 July 1914, SD 812.00/12462.

734 See p. 172.

735 Blocker, Piedras Negras, 26 Sept. 1914, SD 812.00/13360.

736 Womack, *Zapata*, p. 210; though it is hardly valid to argue, as Womack does, that Carranza was 'politically obsolete': he attained national power, held it for five years, and outlived Zapata (just). Not that 'political obsolescence' is any more a vice than political modernity is a virtue.

737 Rutherford, *Mexican Society*, pp. 155, 166.

738 Brown, Mazatlán, 12 Sept., Keys, Rosario, n.d., rec'd 16 Nov., 29 Nov. 1914, SD 812.00/13425, 13777, 14014.

739 Hostetter, Hermosillo, 6 July, 3 Aug. 1914, SD 812.00/12422, 12734.

740 Cumberland, *Constitutionalist Years*, p. 179; Sandford, Monterrey, 28 Sept. 1914, FO 371/2031, 68893.

741 Cf. Gunther E. Rothenberg, 'The Habsburg Army in the First World War', in Robert A. Kann *et al.*, eds., *The Habsburg Empire in World War I* (New York, 1977), pp. 83–4. Robert Graves makes the same point in *Goodbye To All That*.

742 Romero Flores, *Michoacán*, pp. 61, 91–2; Amaya, *Soberana convención*, pp. 199–200.

743 Larry M. Grimes, *The Revolutionary Cycle in the Literary Production of Martín Luis Guzmán* (Cuernavaca, 1969), p. 43; Cardoso de Oliveira, Mexico City, 22 Mar. 1915, SD 812.00/14668.

744 Guzmán, *Memorias*, p. 765; Obregón, *Ocho mil kilómetros*, p. 169; Amaya, *Soberana convención*, p. 180.

745 Guzmán, *Eagle and the Serpent*, pp. 310–11.

746 Vasconcelos, *A Mexican Ulysses*, p. 107; for a critical view of Vasconcelos' Villista flirtation, very different from his own, see Vito Alessio Robles, *Desfile sangriento. Mis andanzas con nuestro Ulíses* (Mexico, 1979) (first ed., 1938), pp. 182–7.

747 Pani, *Apuntes*, p. 221.

748 Bonney, San Luis, 25 June 1915, SD 812.00/15374; Martínez Núñez, *San Luis Potosi*, p. 61; Amaya, *Soberana convención*, pp. 223–4, 315.

749 Torreón consular report in Hohler, Mexico City, 17 Dec. 1914, FO 371/2395, 6623.

750 Aguirre Benavides, *De Francisco I. Madero*, pp. 91–2.

751 Carothers, El Paso, 17 Oct. 1916, SD 812.00/19596.

752 Guzmán, *Memorias*, p. 867; *Eagle and the Serpent*, p. 307.

753 Amaya, *Soberana convención*, pp. 223–4; Cumberland, *Constitutionalist Years*, p. 163.

754 Ulloa, *Revolución escindida*, p. 81.

755 Schmutz, Aguascalientes, 11 Nov. 1914, 3, 10 May 1915, SD 812.00/13914, 14997, 15032, on the 'great pretence of cordiality' shown to Americans by the Villistas – until the spring of 1915.

756 See pp. 304–6.

757 Hence Womack's image of 'rowdy' Villismo: 'Spoils', pp. 678.

758 Cf. the discussion of social banditry above, vol. I, pp. 352–63.

759 Guzmán, *Eagle and the Serpent*, p. 311; Bliss to Pershing, 23 Jan. 1915, Pershing Papers, box 26.

760 Hohler, Mexico City, 8 Jan. 1915, FO 371/2396, 12746.

761 Eugenia Meyer *et al.*, 'La vida con Villa en la Hacienda de Canutillo', DEAS, Mexico, 1974.

762 I am referring to centralised, national, bureaucratic government, of the kind which increasingly prevailed in Mexico after 1920.

763 Ankerson, 'Saturnino Cedillo', pp. 151, 153–4, 158, 160–8; Falcón, 'Cedillo', pp. 199, 231, 280, 313, 328, 352, 381.

764 L. Whitehead, 'The State and Sectional Interests: the Bolivian case', *European Journal of Political Research*, III (1975), pp. 115–16.

765 Of course, the political outcome had important implications for economic development; but it did not avert a hypothetical, radical (Villista) alternative; nor (though the argument is more plausible) did it bring to power (a fraction of?) the 'national bourgeoisie', committed to a specific 'project'. See below, pp. 512–13.

766 Cumberland's estimate, *Constitutionalist Years*, p. 163.

767 E.g., Grajales, 'Las campañas', p. lxxv; Meyer, *Révolution Mexicaine*, p. 56.

768 Cumberland, *Constitutionalist Years*, p. 183; Urquizo, *Páginas*, pp. 90–5.

769 Cumberland, *Constitutionalist Years*, pp. 179, 187; Hall, *Obregón*, pp. 103–4.

770 Adams to Cowdray, 23 Nov. 1914, Cowdray Papers, box A/3; *Mexican Herald*, 1 Dec. 1914.

771 Adams (n. 770); Hohler, Mexico City, 23 Nov. 1914, FO 371/2032, 85240. For the complicated negotiations leading up to the American evacuation (promised in September but not effected until November) see Quirk, *Affair of Honor*, pp. 156–71; Hohler, Mexico City, 28 Nov. 1914, FO 371/2031, 76632; Fabela, DHRM, RRC, II, p. 180ff.

772 Obregón, *Ocho mil kilómetros*, pp. 227–8.

773 Adams to Body, 28 Nov. 1914; Cowdray Papers, box A/3; Hohler, Mexico City, 28 Nov. 1914, FO 371/2032, 85296; *Le Courrier du Méxique*, 25 Nov. 1914.

774 *Mexican Herald*, 26 Nov. 1914.

775 Womack, *Zapata*, pp. 200–1; Quirk, *Mexican Revolution*, pp. 139–45; Guzmán, *Memorias*, pp. 725–8; and Ulloa, *Revolución escindida*, pp. 44–6, which differs slightly.

776 Casasola, *Historia gráfica*, II, pp. 926–8; Clendenen, *United States and Pancho Villa*, pp. 134–5, suggests that this 'was probably the greatest number of troops assembled at one time and place on the American continent since the American Civil War'.

777 Womack, *Zapata*, p. 219; Adams to Cowdray, 11 Jan. 1915, Cowdray Papers, box A/3.

778 Adams to Body (n. 773); *Mexican Herald*, 29 Nov. 1914.

779 Hohler, Mexico City (n. 773); *Mexican Herald*, 26 Nov. 1914.

780 Canova, Mexico City, 8 Dec. 1914, SD 812.00/14048.

781 Aguirre Benavides, *De Francisco I. Madero*, p. 252.

782 Womack, 'Spoils', p. 678; Vasconcelos, *A Mexican Ulysses*, p. 196.

783 Quirk, *Mexican Revolution*, p. 144; Canova, Mexico City, 15 Dec. 1914, SD 812.00/14018 – which unfairly includes Mateo Almanza in the wild bunch.

784 F. Cortina (hotel manager) to Zapata, 29 Dec. 1914, AG, Archivo Zapata, 4; Quirk, *Mexican Revolution*, pp. 207–8; Canova, Mexico City, 16 Dec. 1914, SD 812.00/14097.

785 Canova, 16, 17 Dec. 1914, SD 812.00/14097, 14122; Aguirre Benavides, *De Francisco I. Madero*, p. 216; Guzmán, *Memorias*, pp. 737–8; *El Demócrata*, 7 Dec. 1915 (a belated obituary).

786 Womack, *Zapata*, p. 222; Aguirre Benavides, *De Francisco I. Madero*, p. 219.

787 Quirk, *Mexican Revolution*, pp. 139, 144. Like the hero of his story, Womack is only too keen to quit the corrupt metropolis and get back to the lush fields of Morelos; hence the Zapatista occupation of the capital gets short shrift, and incidents like this are passed over.

788 Canova, Mexico City, 14 Dec. 1914, SD 812.00/14008; Cumberland, *Constitutionalist Years*, p. 185.

789 Hanna, Monterrey, 16 Jan. 1915, SD 812.00/14361.

790 Davis, Guadalajara, 10 Jan. 1915, SD 812.00/14266: though the mood fluctuated; after another bout of Diéguez, the Villistas were again welcomed back.

791 M. Palomar y Vizcarra to Orozco y Jiménez, 23 Feb. 1915, Conflicto Religioso, r. 9.

792 Bonney, San Luis, 25 June 1915, SD 812.00/15374: this, it should be said, came after Urbina's serious defeat at El Ebano.

793 Canova, Mexico City, 16, 18 Dec. 1914, SD 812.00/14097, 14043; Adams to Cowdray, 11 Jan. 1915, Cowdray Papers, box A/3.

794 Silliman, Mexico City, 14 Dec. 1914, SD 812.00/14010.

795 Amaya, *Soberana convención*, pp. 183–4.

796 Vasconcelos, *A Mexican Ulysses*, p. 106.

797 Cumberland, *Constitutionalist Years*, pp. 185–6.

798 Hohler, Mexico City, 18 Jan. 1915, FO 371/2396, 21711.

799 Hall, *Obregón*, p. 105; Amaya, *Soberana convención*, pp. 185–6, 193–7; Palafox to Zapata, 18 Jan. 1915, Fabela, DHRM, EZ, pp. 152–4; Quirk, *Mexican Revolution*, pp. 165–7.

800 Cumberland, *Constitutionalist Years*, p. 192; Quirk, *Mexican Revolution*, pp. 173–6.

801 Vasconcelos, pp. 114–19; cf. Alessio Robles, *Misandanzas*, pp. 186–7.

802 *Mexican Herald*, 17 Jan. 1915; *Soberana converción*, pp. 197–8, 202, 232.

803 Amaya, *Soberana convención*, pp. 187, 233–4; Quirk, *Mexican Revolution*, pp. 203–4, 206, 234.

804 Amaya, *Soberana convención*, pp. 190–1, 213–15, 241–2, 258, 286; Quirk, *Mexican Revolution*, p. 213.

805 Amaya, *Soberana convención*, pp. 455–8.

806 *Ibid.*, p. 216; Quirk, *Mexican Revolution*, p. 236.

807 Hohler, Mexico City, 21 Dec. 1914, 9 Feb. 1915, FO 371/2395, 6626, /2397, 26993.

808 Amaya, *Soberana convención*, p. 299.

809 *Ibid.*, p. 233.

810 *Ibid.*, pp. 230, 239, 264, 273–4.

811 *Ibid.*, pp. 206, 285; Quirk, *Mexican Revolution*, pp. 206–7.

812 Amaya, *Soberana convención*, pp. 233–4; Quirk, *Mexican Revolution*, p. 205.

813 Hohler, Mexico City, 26 Jan. 1915, FO 371/2397, 23922; Amaya, *Soberana convención*, p. 436.

814 Quirk, *Mexican Revolution*, pp. 204, 231, 238.

815 *Ibid.*, pp. 242, 244; Cardoso de Oliveira, Mexico City, 27 Mar. 1915, SD 812.00/14721.

816 Silliman, Mexico City, 7 Dec. 1914, SD 812.00/13971.

817 Guzmán, *Memorias*, p. 745; and cf. Pani, *Apuntes*, p. 224.

818 Womack, *Zapata*, pp. 222–3; Cumberland, *Constitutionalist Years*, pp. 187–8; Guzmán, *Eagle and the Serpent*, p. 307.

819 Adams to Cowdray, 11 Jan. 1915, Cowdray Papers, box A/3; cf. Millon, *Zapata*, p. 88 for an unconvincing alternative view.

820 Womack, *Zapata*, p. 239; Amaya, *Soberana convención*, p. 217; Quirk, *Mexican Revolution*, p. 210.

821 Quirk, *Mexican Revolution*, pp. 180–99; Cumberland, *Constitutionalist Years*, pp. 193–6; *Mexican Herald*, 3 Feb. 1915; and below, pp. 314–17.

822 Quirk, *Mexican Revolution*, p. 195.

823 Guzmán, *Memorias*, p. 746.

824 On the siege, agreement and subsequent evacuation of Naco: report of B. Hill, 28 Mar. 1917, AVC; Quirk, *Mexican Revolution*, pp. 158–65; Obregón, *Ocho mil kilómetros*, pp. 266–7.

825 Border reports, Nogales, 1, 8 May 1915, SD 812.00/15012, 15029.

826 Quirk, *Mexican Revolution*, p. 165; *Mexican Herald*, 10 Jan. 1915; Blocker, Piedras 17 Jan., Hanna, Monterrey, 16 Jan. 1915, SD 812.00/14251, 14361.

827 Obregón, *Ocho mil kilómetros*, p. 294; Grimaldo, *Apuntes*, pp. 23–4, which suggests that Herrera was killed (accidentally) by his own troops.

828 Obregón, *Ocho mil kilómetros*, p. 294.

829 Blocker, Piedras Negras, 12 Mar. 1915, SD 812.00/14593; cf. Guzmán, *Memorias*, p. 747, on Angeles' appreciation of Tampico's importance; Alger, Mazatlán, 22 Apr. 1915, SD 812.00/14986, on the campaign for the Fuerte Valley garbanzo crop.

830 Bustamante, *De el Ebano*, p. 6ff.; Clendenen, *United States and Pancho Villa*, pp. 145–6.

831 Bustamante, *De el Ebano*, p. 157.

832 Bonney, San Luis, 25 June 1915, SD 812.00/15374.

833 Romero Flores, *Michoacán*, pp. 145–7; Guzmán, *Memorias*, pp. 797, 807; Obregón, *Ocho mil kilómetros*, pp. 259–62; Davis, Guadalajara, 16, 19 Jan. 1915, SD 812.00/14478, 14482.

834 Davis, Guadalajara, 15, 24 Feb. 1915, SD 812.00/14491, 14531.

835 Carothers, Irapuato, 22 Apr., Davis, Guadalajara, 25 Mar., 20 Apr., 8 May 1915, SD 812.00/14935, 14798, 15039, 15152.

836 Keys, Rosario, 6 Jan., 20 Feb., 26 Mar. 1915, SD 812.00/14270, 14429, 14784; Obregón, *Ocho mil kilómetros*, p. 253.

837 Obregón, *Ocho mil kilómetros*, p. 295.

838 Silva Herzog, *Breve Historia*, pp. 137–41; Mancisidor, *Historia de la Revolución mexicana*, pp. 260–1; cf. Quirk, *Mexican Revolution*, pp. 151–2, who is more sceptical.

839 Silva Herzog, *Breve Historia*, p. 138; Cumberland, *Constitutionalist Years*, p. 232.

840 Cumberland, *Constitutionalist Years*, p. 212ff.; above, pp. 49, 191, 206–7, 250.

841 Amaya, *Soberana convención*, pp. 212–17, 238–41.

842 Córdova, *Ideología*, p. 205.

843 Cf. Fabela, DHRM, RRC, IV, p. 112ff.

844 Quirk, *Mexican Revolution*, pp. 151–2; Cumberland, *Constitutionalist Years*, p. 232.

845 Mancisidor, *Historia de la revolución mexicana*, p. 284; Córodva, *Ideología*, p. 204; and cf. DDCC, p. 1084.

846 Hall, *Obregón*, pp. 107–8. As already suggested, any manifesto required not only publicity, but also 'muscle': that is, there had to be a reasonable supposition that its authors could implement it. See above, p. 193.

847 Cumberland, *Constitutionalist Years*, pp. 220–1.

848 Quirk, *Mexican Revolution*, p. 188; Ulloa, *Revolución Escindida*, pp. 111–13.

849 *Mexican Herald*, 21, 22 Feb. 1915.

850 *Ibid.*, 23 Feb., 2, 4, 9 Mar. 1915; Hall, *Obregón*, pp. 113–14.

851 *Mexican Herald*, 5, 6, 20 Feb. 1915; Silliman, Mexico City, 8, 12 Feb. 1915, SD 812.00/14371, 14385.

852 *Mexican Herald*, 18, 23 Feb., 6 Mar. 1915; Ulloa, *Revolución escindida*, p. 79.

853 *Mexican Herald*, 11 Feb. 1915; Pani, *Apuntes*, pp. 227–7; Cardoso de Oliveira to Bryan and vice versa, 2, 6 Mar. 1915, SD 812.00/14472, 14501.

854 Quirk, *Mexican Revolution*, p. 190.

855 *Ibid.*, p. 196. Obregón's denunciation – including foreign merchants – has been taken as further proof of Carrancista xenophobia: e.g., Ulloa, *Revolución escindida*, p. 111, Hall, *Obregón*, pp. 115–16. Both Obregón and Carranza, however, carefully qualified what they said: 'I am not an enemy of foreigners but of infamies'; 'we should accustom ourselves to like foreigners, not to fear them' (Obregón in *Mexican Herald*, 26 Feb. 1915); note also Carranza to Wilson, Ulloa, *Revolución escindida*, pp. 121–3. It is further clear that Obregón's attack was directed against the Mexico City merchant houses – a distinct, politically involved group – not foreign interests in general: Obregón, *Ocho mil kilómetros*, pp. 285–6.

856 Casasola, *Historia gráfica*, II, pp. 991–2; Obregón, *Ocho mil kilómetros*, p. 290; Cumberland, *Constitutionalist Years*, p. 197.

857 See pp. 410–11, 416–7.

858 Carr, *Movimiento obrero*, I, pp. 80–1; Rosendo Salazar and José Escobedo, *Las pugnas de la gleba* (Mexico, 1923), p. 83; Ulloa, *Revolución escindida*, pp. 113–14.

859 Carr, *Movimiento obrero*, I, pp. 81–2; Davis, Guadalajara, 7 Nov. 1914, SD 812.50/3; S. Corona *et al.* to A. Valero, 24 Sept. 1914, Trabajo, 31/2/9/14.

860 Womack, *Zapata*, p. 193; Carr, *Movimiento obrero*, I, pp. 82–3; Amaya, *Soberana convención*, pp. 258–67.

861 R. González Garza to Unión de Forjadores, 10 Apr. 1915, Trabajo, 34/3/14/33; Amaya, *Soberana convención*, pp. 199–200; *Mexican Herald*, 13 Dec. 1914.

862 E. Baca Calderón in DDCC, II, p. 858; *Trabajo y Producción*, 11 Feb. 1917; A. Pacheco to M. López Jiménez, 30 Jan. 1915, Trabajo, 34/1/14/28; *Mexican Herald*, 22 Mar. 1915.

863 Salazar, *Las pugnas*, pp. 93–4; Huitrón, *Orígines*, p. 250.

864 Silliman, Mexico City, 8, 12 Feb. 1915, SD 812.00/14371, 14385; Casasola, II, p. 988.

865 Salazar, *Las pugnas*, p. 98.

866 *Ibid.*, p. 128.

867 Amaya, *Soberana convención*, p. 259, quoting Rafael Pérez Taylor.

868 Salazar, *Las pugnas*, p. 112.

869 Cumberland, *Constitutionalist Years*, p. 255.

870 Amaya, *Soberana convención*, p. 223; F. Pacheco *et al.*, to Zapata, 31 Oct. 1915, Fabela, DHRM, EZ, p. 255.

871 Cf. vol. I, pp. 127, 140.

872 Huitrón, *Orígenes*, p. 253; Salazar, *Las pugnas*, pp. 150–1; *El Sindicalista*, p. 31 Jan. 1914; and vol. I, pp. 63, 132.

873 Huitrón, *Orígines*, pp. 215–27; Hart, 'The Urban Working Class', pp. 4–6; Barry Carr, 'The Casa del Obrero Mundial, Constitutionalism and the Pact of February 1915', in Elsa Cecilia Frost *et al.*, eds., *El trabajo y los trabajadores en la historia de México* (Mexico and Arizona, 1979).

874 Pérez Taylor, Salazar and Julio Quintero were all poetasters. See: Huitrón, *Orígines*, p. 214; Linda B. Hall, *Alvaro Obregón. Power and Revolution in Mexico, 1911–20* (Texas A and M, 1981), p. 110 on Obregón's *veladas*.

875 Hall, *Obregón*, p. 110; Obregón, *Ocho mil kilometros*, pp. 258, 287; Knight, 'Working Class'.

876 *Revolución Social*, 9, 30 May 1915; Hall, *Obregón*, p. 112.

877 Womack, *Zapata*, p. 245; director, 6th dirección to Secretary of Labour, 8 Aug. 1914 Trabajo, 34/1/14/22; Hohler, Mexico City, 9 Mar. 1915, SD 812.00/2404, 182348.

878 A. Pacheco to M. López Jiménez, 30 Jan. 1915, Trabajo, 34/1/14/28; Ruiz, *Labor*, p. 50.

879 Hart, 'The Urban Working Class', p. 13; Carr, *Movimiento obrero*, I, pp. 84–5.

880 Huitrón, *Orígines*, p. 258; Salazar, *Las pugnas*, p. 92.

881 Cf. E. P. Thompson, 'Peculiarities', p. 71.

882 Carr, *Movimiento obrero*, I, pp. 88–9; Ruiz, *Labor*, p. 51. Atl, a radical painter, influential in Mexico City labour circles, was prominent in Carrancista relief in the capital, won over the Casa to the pact, and edited its paper, *Vanguardia*, 'with a certain paranoiac brilliance'. Some said he was the son of the Spanish freethinker Ferrer; others, an 'East Indian wizard . . . adept in many black arts'; a reference, perhaps, to his political skill, which greatly exceeded his artistic. See S. Bonsal to American Red Cross, 28 Aug. 1915, Bonsal Papers, box 6; and Hall, *Obregón*, pp. 110–33.

883 Salazar, *Las pugnas*, pp. 97–101.

884 *Ibid.*, pp. 111–12, 148; *Mexican Herald*, 11 Feb. 1915.

885 *Mexican Herald*, 13 Feb. 1915.

886 *Ibid.*, 7 Mar. 1915, refers to 7,000 worker-recruits leaving the capital; Carr, *Movimiento*

obrero, I, pp. 89. mentions estimates between 4,000 and 8,000; Salazar, *Las pugnas*, p. 119, prefers 4,200.

887 Pani, *Apuntes*, p. 229; cf. Obregón, *Ocho mil kilómetros*, p. 289.

888 Bustamante, *De el Ebano*, pp. 26, 45; Obregón, *Ocho mil kilómetros*, p. 327 (figures of 700 out of 6,000 and 1,400 out of 15,000 respectively).

889 Bustamente, *De el Ebano*, pp. 50, 72–3; Obregón, *Ocho mil kilómetros*, p. 327; M. R. Clark, *Organised Labor in Mexico* (Chapel Hill, 1934), p. 33; Jean Meyer, 'Les ouvriers dans la révolution mexicaine, les bataillons rouges', *Annales, E.S.C.*, XXV/1 (1970), gives a total of only sixty-six 'Red' deaths in battle.

890 Gavira, *Actuación*, p. 119.

891 Douglas W. Richmond, 'El nacionalismo de Carranza y los cambios socio-economicos, 1915–20', *Historia Mexicana*, XXVI (1976), pp. 124–5.

892 Flores Magón, quoted by Nieto, in Amaya, *Soberana convención*, p. 263.

893 Zapitista Manifesto 'Pueblo!', n.d., 1915, Fabela, DHRM, EZ, pp. 146–7.

894 Carl von Clausewitz, *On War*, ed., A. Raport (London, 1968), p. 137.

895 Francisco Grajales, 'Las campañas', p. lxxix.

896 Obregón, *Ocho mil kilómetros*, pp. 292–8.

897 Grajáles, 'Las campañas', p. lxxxii; Guzmán, *Memorias*, p. 851; Hall, *Obregón*, p. 124.

898 Gavira, *Actuación*, p. 118; de Szyszlo, *Dix milles kilomètres*, p. 226.

899 Scott to F. McCoy, 30 Apr. 1915, Scott Papers, box 18.

900 Guzmán, *Memorias*, p. 847.

901 *Ibid.*, p. 848; Obregón, *Ocho mil kilómetros*, p. 296; Womack, *Zapata*, pp. 243–4.

902 Guzmán, *Memorias*, p. 850.

903 Quirk, *Mexican Revolution*, p. 220; *Mexican Herald*, 8 Apr. 1915.

904 Cumberland, *Constitutionalist Years*, p. 200 follows the trend in asserting that Villa outnumbered Obregón by three to one, which hardly seems credible; cf. Grajales, 'Las campañas', p. lxxxiii; Guzmán, *Memorias*, p. 850; Hall, *Obregón*, pp. 123–4, 129.

905 These are rough estimates, based on different versions. In June 1915 González Garza asserted that 60,000 had died in the Villa–Carranza conflict to date: Taracena, *Verdadera revolución*, IV, p. 11.

906 Barragán, *Historia del ejército*, II, p. 354 argues convincingly that León, not Celaya, was crucial; cf. Quirk, *Mexican Revolution*, p. 226; Cumberland, *Constitutionalist Years*, p. 202.

907 Grajales, 'Las campañas', p. lxxxi.

908 Obregón, *Ocho mil kilómetros*, p. 323; *Mexican Herald*, 10 Apr. 1915.

909 Obregón, *Ocho mil kilómetros*, p. 323.

910 *Ibid.*, p. 324.

911 Guzmán, *Memorias*, p. 835; Grajales, 'Las campañas', p. lxxxvii.

912 Obregón, *Ocho mil kilómetros*, pp. 301–2, 323–4; Hall, *Obregón*, p. 127.

913 Villa also complained that his artillery shells, manufactured in Chihuahua, were defective: Guzmán, *Memorias*, pp. 856–8; Obregón, *Ocho mil kilómetros*, pp. 301, 325.

914 *Mexican Herald*, 10 Apr. 1915; even Carothers to Bryan, 9 Apr. 1915, admitted it was a 'repulse': SD 812.00/14897. Villa (Guzmán, *Memorias*, pp. 861–2) admitted 2,000 casualties against 2,500 Carrancista losses; Obregón, *Ocho mil kilómetros*, pp. 302–5 admitted only 922 against 5,300.

915 Obregón, *Ocho mil kilómetros*, pp. 310, 327; Guzmán, *Memorias*, p. 879; *Mexican Herald*, 15 Apr. 1915; Romero Flores, *Michoacán*, p. 149.

916 Scott to McCoy, 30 Apr. 1915, Scott Papers, box 18; Carothers to Bryan (n. 914).

917 Calzadíaz Barrera, *Hechos reales*, I, p. 49.

918 Ricketts to Scott, 1 Apr. 1915, Scott Papers, box 18; Schmutz, Aguascalientes, 23 Apr. 1915, SD 812.00/14953.

919 Grajales, 'Las campañas', pp. xciv–v; *Mexican Herald*, 14 Apr. 1915; Clendenen, *United States and Pancho Villa*, p. 166, shows that the American press was no less misleading.

920 Gavira, *Actuación*, pp. 188–9; Guzmán, *Memorias*, pp. 883–5.

921 There was a suspicion that Obregón did not entirely trust Amaro and his men – recent converts to Carrancismo, whose record in Michoacán was hardly unblemished: Romero Flores, *Michoacán*, pp. 148–9.

922 Obregón, *Ocho mil kilómetros*, pp. 315, 327; Grajales, 'Las campañas', p. xcvi; Guzmán, *Memorias*, p. 888. Obregón claimed 4,000 Villistas killed and 6,000 taken prisoner; Villa admitted over 3,000 casualties and heavy loss of matériel.

923 González Garza finally reported a 'truce' at Celaya, necessitated by flooding: *Mexican Herald*, 18–24 Apr. 1915.

924 Carothers, Irapuato, 16, 22 Apr.; Cobb, El Paso, 5 May 1915; SD 812.00/14898, 14935; 14973.

925 Grajales, 'Las campañas', p. ciii.

926 Guzmán, *Memorias*, pp. 909–10.

927 *Ibid.*, Carothers, 18 Dec. 1914, SD 812.00/14061.

928 Obregón, *Ocho mil kilómetros*, p. 364.

929 *Ibid.*, pp. 347–8.

930 Gavira, *Actuación*, pp. 122–3.

931 Obregón, *Ocho mil kilómetros*, pp. 370–1.

932 Of the battle; Obregón's survival obviously had important consequences for Mexico's political future.

933 Aguilar, *Revolución Sonorense*, pp. 12–13.

934 Obregón, *Ocho mil kilómetros*, pp. 373–8; Grajales, 'Las campañas', p. cxvi; Hall, *Obregón*, pp. 135–6. Again, with the fall of León, the city mob set about looting, while at Aguascalientes the well-to-do feared the 'usual mob rule' if Villa were driven out: Gavira, *Actuación*, p. 125; Schmutz, Aguascalientes, 17 June 1915, SD 812.00/15292.

935 Bonney, San Luis, 10 July 1915, SD 812.00/15407; Gavira, *Actuación*, p. 127.

936 Obregón, *Ocho mil kilómetros*, pp. 408–10; Schmutz, Aguascalientes, 10, 17 June, SD 812.00/15257, 15292.

937 Obregón, *Ocho mil kilómetros*, p. 407 gives figures of 1,500 Villistas killed and wounded, 2,000 taken prisoner, 5,000 dispersed; Gavira, *Actuación*, p. 129 on the Villista *suave-qui-peut*.

938 Grajales, 'Las campañas', pp. cxxvii–iii.

939 Hall, *Obregón*, pp. 134–5.

940 Córdova, *Ideología*, p. 264, n. 2, citing R. García.

3. The revolution in power: 2. Reconstruction

1 Louis G. Kahle, 'Robert Lansing and the recognition of Venustiano Carranza', *Hispanic American Historical Review*, XXXVIII (1958), pp. 353–72; Lansing's memo., 'The Conference in regard to Mexico', 10 Oct. 1915, Lansing Papers, Confidential Notes and Memo's, vol. 1, argues that the US must recognise 'and do what we can to strengthen the Carrancista faction', less out of sympathy or conviction than a desire to achieve stability and frustrate supposed German subversion in Mexico.

2 From the Monterrey press alone: *El Constitucional*, 4 May; *El Reformista*, 8 May; *El Liberal*, 27 Aug. 1917: AVC, file 112/159; Fabela, DHRM, RRC, v, pp. 304; note also *El Demócrata*, 4 Nov. 1916 (PLC manifesto); Alvarado, *Reconstrucción*; and the commitment to co-operate in the 'great work of national reconstruction', given to Cándido Aguilar by Ursulo Galván – the latter Communist leader – on behalf of the Veracruz Union of Public Cleaning Workers: 23 June 1916, AVC.

3 I stress contemporary, as against secular. In similar manner, the Punitive Expedition is sometimes given excessive attention.

4 There are less scholarly monographs on this later period; and, as a glance at either the *New*

York Times or the British Foreign Office indexes will confirm, Mexico attracted much less international interest after 1915 (for reasons, of course, that were often external to the Revolution).

5 In this respect, 1920 marks no decisive break: much of the general analysis included in this final chapter is relevant to the 1920s too.

6 Meyer, *Cristero Rebellion*, p. 17.

7 Border reports, Nogales, 1 May; Coen, Durango, 30 Apr.; c/o USS Colorado, Manzanillo, 18 Apr., 1915; SD 812.00/15012; 14976; 14891.

8 Bevan, Tampico, 8 May; Bonney, San Luis, 25 June; Blocker, Piedra Negras, 21, 25 May 1915; SD 812.00/15018; 15374; 15047, 15110.

9 O'Hea, Gómez Palacio, 4 June 1915, SD 812.00/15307.

10 Carothers, El Paso, 22, 31 July; Cobb, Chihuahua, 1 Aug.; Letcher, Chihuahua, 31 July, 1 Aug. 1915; SD 812.00/15518, 15606; 15605; 15654, 15607; Clendenen, *United States and Pancho Villa*, pp. 160–2, 183–6. Under a Villista decree of Mar. 1915, mining properties which had been abandoned, or on which taxes had not been paid, were liable to confiscation; Carranza, it should be noted, issued similar decrees, with particular reference to oil.

11 Letcher, Chihuahua, 29 Sept. 1915, SD 812.00/16449, notes only five major foreign enterprises still working in the state (two mines, a lumber and woollen textile mill, and a hydro-electric plant); *United States and Pancho Villa*, p. 186, on Scott's appeasement of Villa, helped by the miners' donation of 1,000 tons of coal.

12 Reed, *Insurgent Mexico*, p. 120; Cobb, El Paso, 19 July; Letcher, Chihuahua, 3 Aug., 29 Sept.; Schmutz, Aguascalientes, 8 Sept.; Hanna, Monterrey, 6 Oct. 1915; SD 812.00/15489; 15702; 16449; 16327; 16469.

13 Cobb, El Paso, 22 July 1915, SD 812.00/15519.

14 Carothers, El Paso, 31 July, 5 Aug. 1915, SD 812.00/15606, 15656; Katz, *Secret War*, pp. 285–6 and p. 282, where this is seen – perhaps too schematically – as a 'new turn' in Villa's 'social policy', designed to 'expand his social base'.

15 Letcher, Chihuahua, 3 Aug.; Coen, Durango, 22 July, 30 Aug. 1915; SD 812.00/15702; 15586, 16165.

16 Bonney, San Luis, 25 June 1915, SD 812.00/15374.

17 *Ibid.*, 10 July 1915, SD 812.00/15407; Gov. Siurob to Carranza, 16 Sept. 1915, AJD, r. 1; Obregón, *Ocho mil kilómetros*, pp. 417–27 minimises the military significance of Fierro's expedition.

18 Hanna, Monterrey, 24 May; Letcher, Chihuahua, 29 Sept. 1915; SD 812.00/15078; 16449. Here the Villistas rather than the canaille seem to have been the culprits.

19 Coen, Durango, 8 July 1915, SD 812.00/15462.

20 D. Barrows to B. Wheeler, 25 July; Letcher, Chihuahua, 3 Aug., 24 Sept.; Cobb, El Paso, 2 Oct. 1915; SD 812.00/15598; 15702, 16449; 16353.

21 Cobb, El Paso, 21 Sept. 1915, SD 812.00/16254.

22 Alberto Calzadíaz Barrera, *El Fin de la Division del Norte* (Mexico, 1965), pp. 147–9. In the absence of *soldaderas*, one observer commented, 'there are certain results ... which it is not desirable to dwell upon': O'Hea, Gómez Palacio, 11 Jan. 1917, FO 371/2959, 41521.

23 Border report, Marfa, 21 Aug. 1915, SD 812.00/16054.

24 *Ibid*; Coen, Durango, 16 July; Cobb, El Paso, 7 Sept. 1915; SD 812.00/15464, 16071.

25 Cobb, El Paso, 16 Oct. 1915, Cobb, SD 812.00/16503.

26 Obregón, *Ocho mil kilómetros*, pp. 436–8, 442–5; Carothers, Juárez, 9 Oct. 1915, SD 812.00/16441.

27 Letcher, Chihuahua, 7 Oct. 1915, SD 812.00/16524.

28 'Not much given to discussion', the inscrutable Yaqui remained inscrutable and 'no-one has had the temerity to approach him on the subject': border report, Douglas, 16 Oct. 1915, SD 812.00/16600. Maytorena urged his old lieutenant not to co-operate: Katz, *Secret War*, p. 284.

29 J. Ryan to H. L. Scott, 31 May 1915, Scott Papers, box 18; Border reports, Douglas, 2, 23 Oct. 1915, SD 812.00/16457, 16667.

30 Clendenen, *United States and Pancho Villa*, p. 209.

31 Border report, Douglas, 16 Oct. 1915, SD 812.00/16600.

32 The Villistas suffered 300 casualties: Cobb, El Paso, 9, 11 Nov. 1915, SD 812.00/16749, 16771.

33 Cobb, El Paso, 11 Nov.; Carothers, Douglas, 11 Nov. 1915; SD 812.00/16771; 16749; Clendenen, *United States and Pancho Villa*, p. 214; Obregón, *Ocho mil kilómetros*, pp. 460–2.

34 Obregón, *Ocho mil kilómetros*, pp. 463–4, 481–3. Buelna, captaining the Villistas of Sinaloa, was also beaten.

35 Clendenen, *United States and Pancho Villa*, p. 214; Calzadíaz Barrera, *El Fin*, pp. 163, 167–9.

36 Cobb, El Paso, 8 Aug. 1914, SD 812.00/12914, counted some 50,000 Villista troops between Juárez and Aguascalientes; and, as the accounts of the Bajío battles indicate, this number had increased by 1915.

37 Cobb, El Paso, 30 Sept.; Letcher, Chihuahua, 29 Sept.; Edwards, El Paso, 24 Oct. 1915; SD 812.00/16334; 16449; 16583; which give figures of 10, 11 and 9,000.

38 Border report, Marfa, 21 Aug.; Carothers, Douglas, 25 Oct. 1915; SD 812.00/16054; 16588.

39 Edwards, Juárez, 9 Jan. 1916, SD 812.00/17073; Obregón, *Ocho mil kilómetros*, p. 475.

40 Rivera Marrufo interview, PHO 1/63, p. 19.

41 Though in many cases, it may be presumed, *gente* followed *jefe*.

42 Coen, Durango, 13 July 1915, SD 812.00/15507.

43 *Ibid.*, 6 Mar. 1917, SD 812.00/20638; Caldwell, Zacatecas, 8 Jan. 1917, FO 371/2959, 41521; Pazúengo, *Historia*, p. 3 establishes Cuevas' veteran status.

44 Coen, Durango, 17 July 1915, 22 Jan. 1916, SD 812.00/15557, 17205.

45 Letcher, Chihuahua, 9 Sept. 1915, SD 812.00/16164; the whole question of banditry is taken up later.

46 In which they were encouraged by an amnesty offered by Obregón after Celaya: Canada, Veracruz, 15 July 1915, SD 812.00/15577, citing the text from *El Pueblo*.

47 Obregón, p. 431; Calzadíaz Barrera, *El Fin*, p. 61; Coen, Durango, 17 Aug. 1915, SD 812.00/15928. Following Natera's defection the Villista Banda took the Natera family hostage; so the Arrietas seized Orestes Pereyra's wife.

48 Admiral Howard, USS Colorado, 30 June 1915; Cobb, El Paso, 2 Aug. 1915; SD 812.00/15653; 15618; Cobb, 4 Aug. 1915 in Scott Papers, box 19.

49 Cobb, El Paso, 3 Sept., 14, 16 Oct. 1915, SD 812.00/16029, 16473, 16503.

50 Obregón, *Ocho mil kilómetros*, pp. 472–3.

51 Cobb, El Paso, 1 Feb.; Letcher, Chihuahua, 9 Feb. 1916; SD 812.00/17190; 17268; *El Demócrata*, 10 Feb. 1916.

52 Calzadíaz Barrera, *El Fin*, pp. 58, 188.

53 *Ibid.*, pp. 66–70, which blames Fierro; cf. Carothers, 10 Sept.; Letcher, 9, 15 Sept.; Cobb, 15 Sept. 1915; SD 812.00/16100; 16164, 16270; 16183.

54 Letcher, Chihuahua, 15 Sept. 1915, SD 812.00/16270, citing *La Nueva Era*, 14 Sept. 1915.

55 Border report, Douglas, 26 Feb. 1916, SD 812.00/17358, on the execution of (amnestied) Villista prisoners *en route* to the Tres Marías islands (the inclusion of Urbalejo, however, is mistaken).

56 Cobb, El Paso, 11 Sept. 1915, SD 812.00/16123; Calzadíaz Barrera, *El Fin*, pp. 186, 195.

57 Calzadíaz Barrera, *El Fin*, pp. 57, 59; Katz, *Secret War*, p. 594, n. 69.

58 Letcher, Chihuahua, 17 Oct. 1916, SD 812.00/19596; Almada, *Diccionario Sonorense*, pp. 125, 460–1.

59 Davis, Guadalajara, 4 Nov. 1915, SD 812.00/16835.

60 *El Demócrata*, 3 Feb. 1916; Taracena, *Verdadera revolución*, v, p. 201.

61 Letcher, Chihuahua, 7 Oct. 1915; Cobb, El Paso, 7 Jan.; Blocker, Piedras Negras, 23 Mar. 1916; SD 812.00/16524; 17061; 17650.

62 Letcher, Chihuahua, 9 Feb. 1916, SD 812.00/17268; Almada, *Diccionario Chihuahuense*, p. 9.

63 O'Hea, Gómez Palacio, 11 July 1916, SD 812.00/18811. Note the later death of Zapata.

64 O'Hea's report in Cobb, 16 Jan. 1918, SD 812.00/20410.

65 Davis, Guadalajara, 26 Sept. 1915, SD 812.00/16537; A. Medina to Carranza, 1 Mar. 1916, AVC.

66 Rivera Marrufo interview, PHO 1/63, p. 15.

67 Letcher, Chihuahua, 9 Feb. 1916, SD 812.00/17268.

68 See pp. 284, 363, 382.

69 Cobb, El Paso, 30 June, 26 July 1915, SD 812.00/15339, 15545.

70 Border report, Fort Bliss, 12 Dec. 1915, SD 812.00/16979.

71 Carothers, El Paso, 1 Sept. 1915, SD 812.00/15997, on Villa's ill temper and suspicions concerning 'better elements' like Angeles, Llorente and Díaz Lombardo.

72 Cf. Katz, *Secret War*, p. 284: where Villa's new radicalism is possibly exaggerated, and the inability of 'conservatives' like Angeles and Maytorena to tolerate such radicalism is over-emphasised; the history of the revolution is full of individuals (like Carranza) who tolerated a degree of (often rhetorical) radicalism – *faute de mieux*, or because they could thereby better control it. Had not Angeles coaxed the Zapatistas to Aguascalientes, thus helping to radicalise the Convention? Then, as in 1915, ideology took second place to pragmatism.

73 Carothers, El Paso, 3 Aug. 1915, SD 812.00/15626. Carothers had been – and to some extent still was – sympathetic to Villa, so these reports must carry weight.

74 *Ibid.*, 16 Oct. 1915, SD 812.00/16502; Katz, *Secret War*, p. 286.

75 Cobb, El Paso, 11 Sept. 1915, SD 812.00/16123.

76 Calzadíaz Barrera, *El Fin*, pp. 89–92 on the death of Fierro; Estrada Márquez interview, PHO 1/121, p. 12, on Estrada.

77 Calzadíaz Barrera, *El Fin*, pp. 173, 182–3; Rivera Marrufo interview, PHO 1/63, pp. 13, 24; Taracena, *Veradera revolución*, IV, p. 172; and below, pp. 345, 358.

78 Cobb, El Paso, 15 Nov. 1915, SD 812.00/16790; Estrada Márquez interview, PHO 1/121, pp. 12–13.

79 Letcher, Chihuahua, 9 Feb. 1916, SD 812.00/17268.

80 Calzadíaz Barrera, *El Fin*, pp. 86, 152, 167, 183, indicates the continued importance of *serranos* in these campaigns; see also Rivera Marrufo interview PHO 1/63, pp. 11, 33.

81 Pershing, 14 Apr.; Dr W. Stell, Cd Guerrero, 30 Oct. 1916; SD 812.00/18072, 19972.

82 Estrada Márquez interview, PHO 1/121, pp. 30–2; and pp. 438–9.

83 Border report, Douglas, 4 Mar. 1916, SD 812.00/17513; and p. 283.

84 Border report, Douglas, 29 Jan. 1916, SD 812.00/17239; Calzadíaz Barrera, *El Fin*, pp. 93, 163.

85 *El Demócrata*, 2 Feb. 1916; border report, Douglas, 29 June 1916, SD 812.00/18899.

86 Border reports, Nogales, 21 Oct., 23 Dec. 1916; Chapman, Nogales, 17 Feb. 1917; SD 812.00/19706, 20235; 20557.

87 J. Galusha, Albuquerque, to Scott, 12 Apr. 1915, Scott Papers, box 180; Bevan, Tampico, 18 Nov. 1915, SD 812.00/16857; see also Ralph H. Vigil, 'Revolution and Confusion: The Peculiar Case of José Inés Salazar', *New Mexico Historical Review*, LII (1978), pp. 145–70.

88 Edwards, Juárez, 18 Sept.; Cobb, El Paso, 19 Sept. 1916; SD 812.00/19212; 19225; Almada, *Diccionario Chihuahuense*, pp. 437, 476–7.

89 Carothers, El Paso, 27 Oct. 1916, SD 812.00/19669.

90 *Ibid.*; Dr W. Stell, Cd Guerrero, 30 Oct.; Blocker, Piedras Negras, 13 Nov. 1916; SD 812.00/19972; 19852; Almada, *Diccionario Chihuahuense*, p. 477.

91 Katz, *Secret War*, p. 309, argues that Villa's guerrilla expertise was newly acquired, which surely underestimates both his early revolutionary career and previous bandit past. On Carrancista military ineptitude see pp. 389–90, 396, 456–9.

92 Cobb, El Paso, 27 Jan.; Letcher, Chihuahua, 9 Feb. 1916; SD 812.00/17164; 17268.

93 María Isabel Souza, 'Porqué Con Villa?' (INAH, unpublished), pp. 12–13; Estrada Márquez interview, PHO 1/121, p. 35.

94 G. Patton to B. Patton, 28 Jan. 1917, Patton Papers, box 8, telling the story of how Villa burned a mother and child – alleged to be spies – with paraffin; other examples will follow.

95 Márquez Camarena interview, PHO 1/113, pp. 34–6.

96 Anon. report, Torreón, 3 Jan. 1917, FO 371/2959, 60652.

97 Pershing to L. Wood, 10 Sept. 1916, Pershing Papers, box 215.

98 Or, as Thomas Hohler, drawing on his far-flung imperial experience, put it: 'Villa's career is that of a dog in rabies, a Mad Mullah, a Malay running amok': 11 Jan. 1917, FO 371/2959, 41521.

99 Schmutz, Aguascalientes, 10 May 1915, SD 812.00/15032.

100 *Ibid.*, 21 May, 5, 7, 11 June 1915, SD 812.00/15086, 15195, 15244, 15186.

101 Coen, Durango, 25 June 1915, SD 812.00/15361 (Coen owned the hacienda). This shift in Villista policy is traced in Necah S. Furman, '*Vida Nueva*: A Reflection of Villista Diplomacy, 1914–15', *New Mexico Historical Review*, LIII (1978), pp. 171–92.

102 Haley, *Revolution and Intervention*, pp. 162–3.

103 *Ibid.*, pp. 153–62, on the 'welter of intrigue, prejudice and misinformation' which surrounded Wilson, and the 'wildly inappropriate' policies urged upon him (not least by Leon Canova: see Katz, *Secret War*, pp. 303–5).

104 Haley, *Revolution and Intervention*, p. 165.

105 For the Villista reaction see Villa to Wilson, 11 June, to Lansing, 12 June, and Carothers, El Paso, 18 June 1915, SD 812.00/15289, 15294, 15263.

106 Schmutz, Aguascalientes, 5 June; Letcher, Chihuahua, 1 Aug. (twice); Coen, Durango, 1 Sept. 1915; SD 812.00/15195; 15607, 15610; 16178.

107 In the opinion of many, American policy still leaned towards Villa: Cobb, El Paso, 7 Sept. 1915, SD 812.00/16071.

108 C. Folsom, El Paso, to Lansing, 29 Nov. 1915, SD 812.00/16903; see also Katz, *Secret War*, pp. 306–7.

109 Cf. Calvert, *Mexican Revolution*, p. 289. Canova, Chief of the Mexican Bureau of the State Department, certainly sought a conservative, compromise settlement of the revolution (a 1915 version of the 1911 *transacción*, which would guarantee American interests in Mexico); and, to this end, he was supported by some American business and Mexican *émigré* groups. But Wilson – and, of course, Carranza – spurned Canova's project. Furthermore, there is no direct evidence that even this project contained the far-reaching annexationist aims denounced by Villa (though Katz hypothesises that 'in all probability' it did). In my view, Villa's allegations were sufficiently shopworn not to require any basis in fact. See Katz, *Secret War*, pp. 303–7; and the same author's *Pancho Villa y el ataque a Columbus, Nuevo Mexico* (Chihuahua, 1979), pp. 38–42 (English version: 'Pancho Villa and the Attack on Columbus, New Mexico', *American Historical Review*, LXXXII (1978), pp. 101–30).

110 Carothers, El Paso, 25, 31 Oct.; Funston, Nogales, 30 Nov. 1915; SD 812.00/16066, 16653; 16893.

111 Clendenen, *United States and Pancho Villa*, pp. 234–5; border report, Columbus, 28 Aug. 1915, SD 812.00/16054.

112 There is a considerable literature on the 1915–16 border troubles, much of which tends to exaggerate their importance from the point of view of the revolution. See, for example, Charles C. Cumberland, 'Border Raids in the Lower Rio Grande Valley, 1915', *South-Western Historical Quarterly*, LVII (1954), pp. 285–311; Charles H. Harris III and Louis R.

Sadler, 'The Plan of San Diego and the Mexican–United States War Crisis of 1916: A Reexamination', *Hispanic American Historical Review*, LVIII (1978), pp. 381–408; pp. 382–3, n. 5 and Katz, *Secret War*, p. 607, both provide good bibliographies.

113 'The Carrancista people are most anxious to have these troubles stopped and I believe they are trying to do all they can to help': Johnson, Matamoros, 21 Sept. 1915; see also Garret, Laredo, 26, 28 Aug.; Dept. of Justice report, 9 Sept. 1915; SD 812.00/16289; 15929, 15946; 16194. The Negro revolution was reported in 1913: Hanna, Monterrey, 28 Nov., Silliman, Saltillo, 1 Dec. 1913; SD 812.00/9960; 10001; Theodore Roosevelt's preparations for rebellion were reported in *El Demócrata*, 12 Nov. 1916.

114 The suggestion is made by Harris and Sadler, 'Plan of San Diego', pp. 388–9.

115 As A. J. P. Taylor has rightly reminded us, war plans are not necessarily evidence of warlike intentions; and, even though President Wilson had set his face against the interventionist lobby, the Carrancistas would have been quite justified in seeing American intervention as a contingent possibility (perhaps under Republican auspices).

116 So a 'very reliable source' informed General Hugh Scott: Clayton, Monterrey, to Scott, 9 Aug. 1915, Scott Papers, box 19. The subsequent American court proceedings had their funny side, too: one plotter was charged with conspiring to steal 'certain property of the United States, to wit, the states of Texas, Oklahoma, New Mexico, Arizona, Colorado and California'.

117 Bevan, Tampico, 18 Nov. 1915; Williams, Torreón, 6 Jan.; Cobb, El Paso, 23 Feb. 1916; SD 812.00/16857; 17237; 17330.

118 Border report, Fort Bliss, 17 Jan. 1916, SD 812.00/17152; Clendenen, *United States and Pancho Villa*, pp. 225–7.

119 Around the turn of the year Villa left Madera, heading south with a small band; he was in the general vicinity of Cusihuaráchic in mid-January before returning north: Edwards, El Paso, 12 Dec. 1915, 9 Jan. 1916; Cobb, El Paso, 5, 27 Jan. 1916; SD 812.00/16942, 17073; 17055, 17164.

120 Col. H. Slocum to H. Scott, 17 Jan. 1916, Scott Papers, box 21.

121 An additional factor, which will be considered shortly, was the presence on the border of both Victoriano Huerta and Pascual Orozco (June 1915–Jan. 1916).

122 Clendenen, *United States and Pancho Villa*, pp. 234–9; Cobb, El Paso, 3 Mar. 1916, SD 812.00/17340.

123 The attackers numbered between 400 and 500; their casualties have been put as high as 160 and as low as a dozen. See: Cobb, El Paso, 9 Mar. 1916, SD 812.00/17277; Clendenen, *United States and Pancho Villa*, pp. 236–46; Mancisidor, *Historia de la Revolución*, p. 298; Michael L. Tate, 'Pershing's Punitive Expedition: Pursuer of Bandits or Presidential Panacea?', *Americas*, XXXII (1975), pp. 51–2.

124 Katz, *Deutschland*, pp. 338–50; James A. Sandos, 'German Involvement in Northern Mexico, 1915–16: A New Look at the Columbus Raid', *Hispanic American Historical Review*, L (1970), pp. 70–88.

125 Bernstorff to Bethmann Hollweg, 4 Apr. 1916, in Katz, *Deutschland*, p. 346.

126 Lansing memo., 10 Oct. 1915 (see fn. 1); *Revolution and Intervention*, p. 184.

127 Bernstorff to Foreign Office and minute, 28 Mar. 1916, Katz, *Deutschland*, p. 346.

128 Katz, *Deutschland*, p. 344, on Sommerfeld who, German-born, had lived in Mexico since the early 1900s, dabbling in business and 'sponging on the German community', before linking up with first Madero then Villa: see Letcher, Chihuahua, 25 Aug. 1914, SD 812.00/13232. Sommerfeld had connections with German agents in the US but, as Katz admits, it is pure conjecture to infer from these a German initiative behind the Columbus raid. The evidence for Rauschbaum (Sandos, 'German involvement', pp. 70–1) appears to be two contemporary (1960s) interviews; one with the lady in charge of the South-Western Reference Room of El Paso Public Library.

129 Clendenen, *United States and Pancho Villa*, p. 219.

130 Border report, Columbus, 28 Aug. 1915, SD 812.00/16054.

131 Cobb, El Paso, 31 May 1915, SD 812.00/15099.

132 Alberto Calzadíaz Barrera, *Porqué Villa atacó a Columbus (intriga internacional)* (Mexico, 1972), p. 111.

133 *Ibid.*, p. 158; Clendenen, *United States and Pancho Villa*, pp. 245–6 (where Rabel appears as Revel).

134 Funston to Cols. Dodd and Slocum, 10 Mar. 1916, WWP, box 142; cf. *El Demócrata*, 12 Mar. 1916. Once inside Mexico Pershing also formed a low opinion of the 'weak and puerile' efforts of the Carrancistas to police the north: to Wood, 21 Oct. 1916, Pershing Papers, box 215.

135 Edwards, Juárez, 9 Mar. 1916, SD 812.00/17889.

136 House Diary, 29 Mar. 1916. The mobilisation as well as the subsequent campaign revealed America's lack of 'preparedness': Clendenen, *United States and Pancho Villa*, pp. 287–8, 294–5.

137 Cobb, El Paso, 9 Mar. 1916, SD 812.00/17385; Lansing memo's, 11 July, 10 Oct. 1915, 9 Jan., n.d., Sept. 1916, Confidential Notes and Memo's, vol. I; Katz, *Secret War*, p. 311.

138 House Diary, 17 Mar. 1916; F. K. Lane (Secretary of the Interior) to Wilson, 13 Mar. 1916, in A. W. Lane and L. H. Lane, eds., *The Letters of Franklin K. Lane* (Boston, 1922), p. 204.

139 Vasconcelos – hardly a Gringophile – argued that Wilson's response was unavoidable and moderate: J. Fred Rippy, José Vasconcelos and Guy Stevens, *American Policies Abroad: Mexico* (Chicago, 1928), pp. 128–9.

140 House Diary, 17 Mar. 1916.

141 J. P. Tumulty, *Woodrow Wilson As I Knew Him* (New York, 1921), pp. 154–6.

142 House Diary, 17, 29 Mar. 1916; Haley, *Revolution and Intervention*, pp. 192–5.

143 Clendenen, *United States and Pancho Villa*, p. 250; Haley, *Revolution and Intervention*, pp. 190–1.

144 Haley, *Revolution and Intervention*, p. 192; Clendenen, *United States and Pancho Villa*, p. 254; War Dept press release, 10 Mar.; Secretary of War to Chief of Staff, 16 Mar. 1916; WWP, series II, boxes 142, 143; Lansing to consuls, 10 Mar. 1916, SD 812.00/17426a.

145 Haley, *Revolution and Intervention*, p. 194; Clendenen, *United States and Pancho Villa*, p. 256.

146 *El Demócrata*, 12, 14, 15, 16, 20, 21, 23 Mar. 1916.

147 Clendenen, *United States and Pancho Villa*, pp. 256–7.

148 Pershing, 17, 23 Apr. 1916, SD 812.00/17903, 17984; Pershing to F. Carpenter, 19 June 1916, Pershing Papers, box 40.

149 'There is no basis for [the expedition] if the restrictions placed upon [it] be taken into account': Pershing to Wood, 10 Sept. 1916, Pershing Papers, box 215. The same letter mentions the greater co-operation now shown by the Mexican population, attributable to 'the kindly treatment received at our hands'. The Patton diary, 25 Mar. 1916, Patton papers, box 1, notes that the *pacíficos* of El Valle 'seemed to be quite friendly' and were prepared to sell supplies to the Americans; so, too, were the rural police of Casas Grandes: see Jacinto Treviño's report, 14 Aug. 1916, AG 85/53.

150 Patton Diary, 14 May 1916; Patton to B. Patton, 17 May 1916; Patton Papers, boxes 1, 8.

151 Clendenen, *United States and Pancho Villa*, p. 276: for neither the first nor the last time, word went out that Villa was dead; which Pershing himself doubted: Pershing to Crowder, 15 June 1916, Pershing Papers, box 56.

152 The Mayor of Columbus had already offered a $5,000 reward the day of the raid; this $50,000, however, was a freelance offer made by a serving officer which Pershing was 'not at liberty to publish . . . to the world'. It was hoped that Consul Letcher of Chihuahua would deploy his 'secret service workers' in response to this incentive; Letcher confessed that he had no such workers and his 'activities in this direction are somewhat limited': see

Pershing memo. to B. Foulois and Letcher to Pershing, both 6 Apr. 1916, Foulois Papers, Library of Congress, box 34.

153 Patton to 'Papa', 28 Sept. 1916, Patton Papers, box 8.

154 David Lawrence, *The True Story of Woodrow Wilson* (New York, 1924), p. 106.

155 Fabela, DHRM, EZ, p. 278; Lefaivre, Mexico City, 21 Apr. 1916, AAE, Mex. Pol. Int., N.S., XIII, n. 27.

156 This was the final, in respects clearest, case of this syndrome.

157 *El Demócrata*, 27 Mar. 1916 (and throughout the month); Lefaivre, Mexico City, 4 Apr. 1916, AAE, Mex. Pol. Int., N.S. XIII, n. 24.

158 Schmutz, Aguascalientes, 13 Apr.; Bowman, Frontera, 20 Apr. 1916; SD 812.00/17930; 17949.

159 Dawson, Tampico, 14 Mar.; Edwards, Acapulco, 24 Mar.; Carothers, El Paso, 12 Apr. 1916; SD 812.00/17573; 17638; 17881.

160 Edwards, Juárez, 24 Mar.; Letcher, Chihuahua, 24 Mar. 1916; SD 812.00/17620; 17641.

161 'There is little or no general public sentiment with regard to [the] possibilities created by [the] presence [of] our troops on Mexican territory. What sentiment may be developed later . . . will depend entirely on inspiration received by [the] people from [the] authorities': Murray, Mexico City, 23 Mar. 1916, SD 812.00/17615.

162 Carothers, El Paso, 22, 24 Mar. 1916, SD 812.00/17583, 17609; Hall, *Obregón*, p. 148.

163 Murray, Mexico City (n. 161).

164 Rodgers, Querétaro and Mexico City, 31 Mar., 15 Apr.; Coen, Durango, 14 Apr. 1916; SD 812.00/17710, 17872; 17873. The first of these also refers to Carrancista concern at the 'political effect' of continued tolerance of the expedition.

165 House Diary, 6 Apr. 1916. On American public opinion: Tate, 'Pershing's Punitive Expedition', pp. 58–9.

166 Pershing, 14 Apr. 1916, SD 812.00/17870; Clendenen, *United States and Pancho Villa*, pp. 266–7.

167 Carothers, El Paso, 14 Apr. 1916, SD 812.00/17863, reported an attack on the Alvarado Co., countenanced by the authorities; for reports of anti-American sentiment, see Bonney San Luis, 13 Apr.; Rodger, Mexico City, 19 Apr. 1916; SD 812.00/17845; 17925.

168 E.g., Blocker, Piedras Negras, 15, 24 Apr.; Simpich, Nogales, 14 Apr.; Hanna, Monterrey, 15 Apr.; USS Kentucky, Veracruz, 15 Apr. 1916; SD 812.00/17876, 17879; 17860; 17880; 17995.

169 Aguilar to Arredondo, 12 Apr. 1916, SD 812.00/17865.

170 Rodgers, Mexico City, 21 Apr.; D. C. Brown, 22 Apr. 1916; SD 812.00/17951, 17973.

171 On the restraining influence of Obregón and other Carrancista officers, including Treviño, de la Garza and Laveaga, see Edwards, Juárez, 14 Apr.; Hanna, Monterrey, 20, 29 Apr.; Coen, Durango, 3 May 1916; SD 812.00/17852; 17989, 18025; 18141.

172 Clendenen, *United States and Pancho Villa*, pp. 272–5; Haley, *Revolution and Intervention*, pp. 201–10. Carranza himself may also have had an interest in compromising Obregón's reputation: Hall, *Obregón*, p. 148.

173 Haley, *Revolution and Intervention*, p. 207; Silliman, Saltillo, 15 May 1916, SD 812.00/18176; *El Demócrata*, 9 May 1916; Tate, 'Pershing's Punitive Expedition', p. 63.

174 Clendenen, *United States and Pancho Villa*, p. 276; Haley, *Revolution and Intervention*, p. 210, calls Carranza's note of 22 May 'rambling and abusive'. In spiking a possible agreement between Generals Scott and Obregón, Carranza was also playing domestic politics, by averting an Obregonista diplomatic triumph: Hall, *Obregón*, pp. 151–2.

175 Haley, *Revolution and Intervention*, p. 212.

176 Silliman, Saltillo, 5 June; Carothers, El Paso, 7 June; Hanna, Monterrey, 7 June 1916; SD 812.00/18321; 18341; 18342.

177 Clendenen, *United States and Pancho Villa*, p. 276; Silliman, Saltillo, 7 June; Guyant, Progreso, 15 June; Blocker, Piedras Negras, 16 June 1916; SD 812.00/18344; 18441; 18445.

178 Carothers, El Paso, 12, 17 June 1916, SD 812.00/18397, 18472.

179 Blocker, Piedras Negras, 16, 18 June; Canada, Veracruz, 18 June 1916; SD 812.00/18445, 18452; 18474.

180 Rodgers, Mexico City, 18 June 1916, SD 812.00/18457; Haley, *Revolution and Intervention*, p. 214.

181 Haley, *Revolution and Intervention*, p. 212; cf. Clendenen, *United States and Pancho Villa*, p. 278.

182 Clendenen, *United States and Pancho Villa*, pp. 278–81; Tate, 'Pershing's Punitive Expedition', pp. 65–6.

183 Hanna, Monterrey, 7 June; Rodgers, Mexico City, 19 June; USS Nebraska, Veracruz, 12 June 1916; SD 812.00/18342; 18485; 18558.

184 Silliman, Saltillo, 5 June 1916, SD 812.00/18321.

185 Coen, Durango, 15 June 1916, SD 812.00/18488.

186 Blocker, Piedras Negras, 16 June 1916, SD 812.00/18445.

187 *Ibid.*, 22, 23 June; USS Annapolis, Mazatlán, 22 June; Cobb, El Paso, 27 June 1916; SD 812.00/18358, 18591; 18453; 18597.

188 USS Nebraska, Veracruz, 2 July 1916, SD 812.00/18119.

189 Silliman, 22 June; Blocker, 6 July (both Eagle Pass); SD 812.00/18540; 18662.

190 Cobb, El Paso, 8 July 1916, SD 812.00/18739.

191 Wilson reciprocated, and spurned the advice of those – like Pershing – who favoured extending American military operations in northern Mexico: Haley, *Revolution and Intervention*, pp. 217, 220; Rodgers, Mexico City, 28 June 1916 (twice), SD 812.00/18593, 18607; *El Demócrata*, 27 June 1916.

192 Blocker, Eagle Pass, 12 July; Dawson, Tampico, 6 July; Garret, Nuevo Laredo, 30 July 1916; SD 812.00/18743; 18771; 18819.

193 Haley, *Revolution and Intervention*, pp. 227–44.

194 Tate, 'Pershing's Punitive Expedition', pp. 67–71; Katz, *Secret War*, pp. 311–12, sees this as 'the greatest concession to American business interests in Mexico in the history of Wilsonian diplomacy'. This being true (and I believe it is), and the outcome of the policy being what it was (the unconditional withdrawal of the expedition and, in Katz's words, 'one of the greatest triumphs of Carranza's career'), it must be concluded that Wilsonian diplomacy was in no sense a faithful and effective instrument of American big business (which is also true).

195 Haley, *Revolution and Intervention*, pp. 236–7.

196 Patton's letters to his wife give a bleak picture of life with the expedition in the latter part of 1916; e.g., 11 Jan. 1917 on the level of desertion: Patton Papers, box 8.

197 Rodgers, Mexico City, 8 July 1916, SD 812.00/18674; *El Demócrata*, 11, 16 Sept. 1916.

198 Cabrera, in particular, wanted to float 'some financial plans' Rodgers, 8 July 1916, SD 812.00/18674. There was an influential body of Carrancista opinion which favoured a closer political, diplomatic and economic liaison with the US, in the interests of domestic reconstruction and stability – if they could get it on acceptable terms; which, in the event, they could not. See Katz, *Secret War*, p. 317.

199 Rodgers, Mexico City, 21 July 1916, SD 812.00/18767. Note the *volte-face* of *El Demócrata*: 16 Sept. (Mexican delegates explain 'vast' reform programme); 17 Sept. (denial of American reports that the talks go beyond the simple question of withdrawal). See also Haley, *Revolution and Intervention*, p. 230ff.

200 Tate, 'Pershing's Punitive Expedition', p. 62; Haley, *Revolution and Intervention*, p. 219; Jusserand, Washington, 30 June, 7 July 1916, AAE, Mex. Pol. Int., N.S., XIII, no's 405, 430 on public and official opinion; note, in particular, the conciliatory role of Gompers and

the AFL: Robert F. Smith, *United States and Revolutionary Nationalism in Mexico 1916–32* (Chicago, 1972), pp. 53–4. The US Government's belief that it could exert a 'strong hold' over Mexico 'owing to the lack of food in that country' proved to be another illusion: de Bunsen, Washington, 22 Nov., Thurstan, Mexico City, 14 Dec. 1917, FO 371/2964, 221012, 235682.

201 Katz, *Secret War*, pp. 312, 314; Smith, *United States and Revolutionary Nationalism*, pp. 61–2.

202 Patton to B. Patton, 25, 28 Jan. 1917, Patton Papers, box 8.

203 Clendenen, *United States and Pancho Villa*, p. 251, where the discussion of the expedition's objectives seems somewhat confused.

204 Pershing to Crowder, 15 June 1916, Pershing Papers, box 56. Thereafter, Pershing chafed at the restrictions placed upon him, which rendered his presence in Mexico pointless; and he hankered for a solution 'along the lines on which we proceeded in Cuba': Pershing to Theodore Roosevelt and vice versa, 24 May, 6 June 1916, Pershing Papers, box 177 (the phrase is Roosevelt's). In the light of these (and other) interventionist opinions, it is hard to accept Smith's argument that 'there was not much difference between Wilson and his critics': *United States and Revolutionary Nationalism*, p. 67.

205 Calzadíaz Barrera, *El Fin*, pp. 195–6.

206 Williams, Torreón, 3 Dec. 1915, 6 Jan. 1916; Coen, Durango, 22 Jan., 11 Feb. 1916; SD 812.00/16965, 17237; 17205, 17294.

207 Cobb, El Paso, 14 Apr.; Rodgers, Mexico City, 19 Apr. 1916, SD 812.00/17854; 17925.

208 *El Demócrata*, 2 Feb., 2 Mar. 1916; O'Hea, Gómez Palacio, 18 Apr. and n.d., July 1916, SD 812.00/18141, 18853.

209 Coen, Durango, 3, 6 May 1916, SD 812.00/18141, 18157.

210 Parker, Mexico City, 7 Apr. 1916, SD 812.00/17782.

211 Coen, Durango, 15 June 1916, SD 812.00/18435.

212 Atkin, *Revolution!*, p. 290, quotes the American press on the variety of deaths Villa was supposed to have suffered during 1916; his list omits the alleged poisoning by a wily Japanese doctor, reported by Pershing to Carothers, 30 Aug. 1916, Pershing Papers, box 40; anon. report, Torreón, 3 Jan. 1917, FO 371/2959, 60652, describes Villa's condition.

213 O'Hea, Gómez Palacio, 11 July; Blocker, Piedras Negras, 7 Nov. 1916; SD 812.00/18811; 19763; Taracena, *Verdadera revolución*, V, p. 103. This atrocity was not only well attested, but also followed precedent: see Benjamin, 'Passages', p. 125, on the Tuxtlecos' mutilation of Chamula rebels in 1911.

214 Cobb, El Paso, 20 July 1916, SD 812.00/18791.

215 Cobb, El Paso, 18 Sept.; Edwards, El Paso, 18 Sept. 1916; SD 812.00/19205, 19212; Taracena, *Verdadera revolución*, IV, p. 235. It was now that Salazar and other prisoners were sprung from Chihuahua prison.

216 Caldwell, Zacatecas, 8 Jan. 1917, FO 371/2959, 41521; and Cobb, El Paso, 25 Sept.; Carothers, El Paso, 7 Nov. 1916; SD 812.00/19295; 19846; on Villista shortages.

217 Carothers, El Paso, 13 July; Cobb, El Paso, 25 Sept., 3 Oct. 1916; SD 812.00/18716; 19295, 19403; Patton to 'Papa', 20 Sept. 1916, Patton Papers, box 8.

218 Calzadíaz Barrera, *El Fin*, p. 198; Cobb, El Paso, 8 Mar. 1916, SD 812.00/1736.

219 Pershing, 30 Sept. 1916; Cobb, El Paso, 24 Oct. 1916; SD 812.00/19416; 19630.

220 Blocker, Piedras Negras, 14 Oct. 1916 (twice), SD 812.00/19529, 19583.

221 Carothers, El Paso, 1, 3, 6 Nov. 1916, SD 812.00/19719, 19734, 19749.

222 *El Demócrata*, 25 Nov. 1916; Edwards, El Paso, 27 Nov. 1916, SD 812.00/19966.

223 O'Hea, Gómez Palacio, 11 Jan. 1917, FO 371/2959, 45121.

224 *Ibid.*, and anon, Torreón, 3 Jan. 1917, FO 371/2959, 60652.

225 Taracena, *Verdadera revolución*, V, pp. 27–8; DDCC, II, pp. 39, 101, for unusual Carrancista references to the Torreón débâcle and the press silence which enveloped it; Carrancista consul, Presidio, 25 Dec. 1916, AVC, on the Ojinaga revival.

226 Coen, Durango, 6 Mar.; Blocker, Piedras Negras, 14 Mar. 1917; SD 812.00/20638; 20649.

227 Taracena, *Verdadera revolución*, v, pp. 59–60.

228 Cobb, El Paso, 16, 17 Mar.; Carothers, Cobb, El Paso, 28 Mar., 1 Apr. 1917; SD 812.00/20658, 20664; 20724, 20734.

229 Cobb, El Paso, 17 Apr., 3 May; Edwards, El Paso, 30 Apr. 1917; SD 812.00/20801, 20877; 20857.

230 Edwards, Juárez, 23 May; Cobb, El Paso, 15 Nov. 1917; SD 812.00/20933; 20958; 21462; Taracena, *Verdadera revolución*, v, p. 177.

231 American military intelligence reported such incidents 'nearly every week': Clendenen, *United States and Pancho Villa*, p. 307; Dale, Chihuahua, 10 May 1918, FO 371/3244, 97566 reported 'absolute anarchy and chaos' in the state (allow for consular hyperbole) and ubiquitous local defence groups.

232 Clendenen, *United States and Pancho Villa*, pp. 309–12.

233 Murguía was also reported as having executed over forty officers for collusion with Villa: Cobb, El Paso, 5 Apr., 1 May 1917, SD 812.00/20754, 20861.

234 Taracena, *Verdadera revolución*, v, p. 60; O'Hea, Gómez Palacio, 2 Oct. 1918; Dale, Chihuahua, 23 Jan. 1919; FO 371/3247, 187177; 3827, 33183.

235 Anon. report, Torreón, 3 Jan. 1917, FO 371/2959, 60652; Coen, San Antonio, 26 July 1917, SD 812.00/21159.

236 Dale, Chihuahua, 31 Jan. 1919, FO 371/3827, 38516; which also mentions Carrancista desertions.

237 Clendenen, *United States and Pancho Villa*, p. 309 (though the source is not impeccable).

238 E.g., Funston, 24 Oct. 1916, SD 812.00/19819.

239 Taracena, *Verdadera revolución*, v, p. 103, vi, p. 146; Gavira, *Actuación*, pp. 201–4; Casasola, *Historia gráfica*, ii, pp. 1342–3; Calero, *Un decenio*, pp. 224–8.

240 Murguía to Carranza, 13 Dec. 1916, in Cumberland, *Constitutionalist Years*, pp. 324–5.

241 See pp. 437–9.

242 O'Hea, Gómez Palacio, 4 Jan. 1918, FO 371/3242, 30946.

243 Cf. Barrington Moore, *Injustice. The Social Bases of Obedience and Revolt* (London, 1978), pp. 73, 78–80.

244 Above, vol. i, pp. 277, 315, 318, 378.

245 O'Hea, Gómez Palacio, 4 Jan. 1918, FO 371/3242, 30946.

246 Hanna, Monterrey, 23 Sept. 1916, SD 812.00/19262.

247 Taracena, *Verdadera revolución*, v, p. 85.

248 Cobb, El Paso, 3 May 1917, SD 812.00/20877.

249 Routinisation – and its usual concomitants, military graft and corruption – were less apparent in Chihuahua than in other theatres; the war against Villa, especially when conducted by Murguía, had too much needle.

250 See pp. 492–3.

251 Paulino Fontes to H. P. Fletcher, 17 Sept. 1918, Fletcher Papers, Library of Congress, box 5.

252 Womack, *Zapata*, p. 268.

253 Obregón, *Ocho mil kilómetros*, pp. 442–6.

254 Williams, Torreón, 3 Dec. 1915; Coen, Durango, 30 Apr. 1916; SD 812.00/16965; 18157.

255 Coen, Durango, 3 May 1916, SD 812.00/18141.

256 Coen, Durango and San Antonio, 3 May, 13 June 1916, SD 812.00/18141, 18488.

257 Coen, Durango, received 29 Aug. 1916, SD 812.00/19042.

258 *Ibid.*, and 30 Apr. 1916, SD 812.00/18157; Reece, Cuencamé, 18 Sept. 1916, SD 812.00/19468.

259 H. Potter in Williams, Torreón, 6 Jan. 1916, SD 812.00/17237.

260 Anon. report from Torreón in Hanna, Monterrey, 12 Jan. 1917, SD 812.00/20271.

261 'There is no doubt that in this city [Durango] and surrounding country the pueblo is entirely against the Carrancistas, that is, the military. They have been robbed and robbed and are still being robbed': Coen, Durango, 30 Apr. 1916, SD 812.00/18157.

262 O'Hea, Gómez Palacio, 4 Jan. 1918, FO 371/3242, 30946.

263 Coen, Durango, 11 Feb., 1 Mar., n.d., received 29 Aug. 1916, 16 Feb., 6 Mar. 1917, SD 812.00/17294, 17337, 19042, 20545, 20638; Taracena, *Verdadera revolución*, v, pp. 113–14, 135.

264 O'Hea, Gómez Palacio, 1 Oct. 1918, FO 371/3247, 183112.

265 Bonney, San Luis, 8 Nov.; Bevan, Tampico, 11 Nov. 1915; SD 812.00/16779; 16813; Obregón, *Ocho mil kilómetros*, p. 432, states that a deal was struck, which the Cedillos subsequently broke.

266 Bevan, Tampico, 11 Nov. 1915, SD 812.00/16813.

267 Magdaleno Cedillo, for example, had 200 at Cerritos, Saturnino 180 north of San Bartolo: Bonney, San Luis, 29 Mar. 1916, SD 812.00/17730.

268 Garret, Nuevo Laredo, 20 Sept. 1016, SD 812.00/19239; Falcón, 'Cedillo', pp. 128–9.

269 Manifiesto del Ejercito Convencionista del Centro, Cd del Maíz, 16 Aug. 1916, AVC.

270 Garret, Nuevo Laredo, 23 Oct. 1916; Dawson, Tampico, 7 Dec. 1917; SD 812.00/19681; 21557; Falcón, 'Cedillo', p. 130.

271 Blocker, Eagle Pass, 11 Oct. 1916, SD 812.00/19544; Dawson, Tampico, 7 Dec. 1917, SD 812.00/21557, reports that the Cedillos' 'influence in the country is accentuated by the friendly attitude of the civilian population'.

272 Ankerson, 'Saturnino Cedillo', p. 145; Taracena, *Verdadera revolución*, v, p. 173; Cockcroft, 'El maestro de primaría'.

273 Border report, 6 Sept. 1917, SD 812.00/21254.

274 The title of Womack, *Zapata*, ch. 8.

275 *Ibid.*, p. 244, 248. Huerta, it will be remembered, had tried first to snuff out the *suriano* rebellion before turning to the more serious threat in the north; the Carrancistas made no such error, ignoring Zapata while they first defeated Villa.

276 Schryer, *Rancheros of Pisaflores*, p. 75; *Historia de la Brigada Mixta Hidalgo*, pp. 15, 103.

277 Womack, *Zapata*, pp. 248–9, 252.

278 Edwards, Acapulco, 25 Jan. 1915, SD 812.00/17256: de la O led 3,000 men.

279 Womack, *Zapata*, pp. 247, 253.

280 *Ibid.*, p. 253; *El Demócrata*, 15 May 1916.

281 Womack, *Zapata*, pp. 261–3.

282 *Ibid.*, p. 266, which suggests that Zapata might have borrowed this tactic from Villa. It is hardly necessary to suppose this: the similarities displayed by Zapatismo and Villismo in 1915–20 are many, and denote a common, basic character, rather than conscious plagiarism.

283 González to Carranza, 17 June 1916, AJD; Womack, *Zapata*, p. 266.

284 D. G. Lamadrid, Security Service, to Secretary of War, 18 July 1916; F. Ortiz Borbolla to Secretary of Gobernación, 16 May 1916; AG 59/23; 75/1. Some of these were Zapatistas in the strict sense (like de la O), some were not.

285 Womack, *Zapata*, pp. 266–7, 269–70.

286 Manuel Lárraga to Secretary of War, 19 July 1916, AJD; Womack, *Zapata*, pp. 271–000.

287 Womack, *Zapata*, pp. 312–13.

289 A. Cabrera, Governor of Puebla, to Carranza, 17 Dec. 1918, AJD.

299 Womack, *Zapata*, p. 268, quoting Juan Espinosa Barreda.

290 *Ibid.*, pp. 268–9; Warman, *Y Vcenimos a contradecir*, pp. 166–7, 141–2, 147, which adds oral evidence.

291 *El Demócrata*, 14 Nov. 1916.

292 Gobernación agent to Acuña, 7 Oct. 1915, AVC, concerning Jara's threat to burn

Chimalhuacán which, the local Indians claimed, sheltered none of de la O's Zapatistas, and only '*gente tranquila*'.

293 Womack, *Zapata*, pp. 257, 260; González to Carranza, 7 Feb. 1917, AJD.

294 Womack, *Zapata*, p. 260.

295 *El Demócrata*, 11 Mar., 16 May, 16 Nov. 1916 (all from editorials).

296 E.g., Luis Navarro, at Querétaro, in DDCC, ii, p. 1984.

297 Hill to Carranza, 29 Dec. 1916; Carranza to González, 9 Feb. 1917; AJD.

298 Horcasitas, *De Porfirio Díaz*, pp. 145–7.

299 Warman, *Y venimos a contradecir*, p. 147.

300 *El Demócrata*, 16 Nov. 1916.

301 Lewis, *Pedro Martínez*, p. 156.

302 Womack, *Zapata*, pp. 262, 265–6, 274, 319; Fabela, DHRM, EZ, p. 262.

303 Martín Sosa, Amatitlán, to Zapata, 17 Apr. 1915, Archivo del Gral Emiliano Zapata, varios asuntos, legajo 6.

304 Womack, *Zapata*, p. 261.

305 Cristóbal Flores to Zapata, 5 July 1917, Archivo del Gral Emiliano Zapata; Eufemio to Emiliano Zapata, 11 Mar., and petition of San Miguel Huepalcalco to Eufemio Zapata, 9 Mar. 1916, Fabela, DHRM, EZ, pp. 262–4.

306 Womack, *Zapata*, pp. 281, 305; Zapata to municipal presidents, 30 Mar. 1916, Fabela, DHRM, EZ, pp. 268–9.

307 Fabela, DHRM, RRC, v, pp. 315, 394; see also n. 288, 309.

308 Warman, *Y venimos a contradecir*, p. 147.

309 Cabrera to Carranza, 17 Dec. 1916, AJD; González to Carranza, 27 Mar. 1916, AVC; Jacobs, *Ranchero Revolt*, p. 101.

310 Eufemio to Emiliano Zapata, 11 Mar. 1916; Fabela, DHRM, EZ, p. 262; the individual in question was Vicente Rojas.

311 Cf. vol. i, p. 355.

312 See pp. 394–5.

313 Fabela, DHRM, EZ, p. 303.

314 Womack, *Zapata*, p. 314.

315 *Ibid.*, pp. 262, 285–6; Taracena, *Verdadera revolución*, v, p. 88.

316 For Zapata, Palafox seemed 'too intransigent and bigoted', it was said; being gay did not help either, in the lusty *machismo* of Morelos. See W. Gates to H. L. Hall, 26 Apr. 1919, Fletcher Papers, box 6; Womack, *Zapata*, p. 306; Fabela, DHRM, EZ, pp. 310–11.

317 Womack, *Zapata*, pp. 287, 295. The poacher turned gamekeeper was Sidronio Camacho.

318 E. J. Hobsbawm, *Bandits* (Harmonsworth, 1972), pp. 50–1.

319 Though Hobsbawm, *ibid.*, p. 108, considers Zapatismo – in complete contrast to Villismo – to be 'entirely unbandit-like'; a dichotomisation which it is hard to sustain.

320 Womack, *Zapata*, p. 319.

321 Fabela, DHRM, EZ, pp. 311–14.

322 Womack, *Zapata*, pp. 325–9.

323 SD 812.00/pp. 330, 335.

324 Hobsbawm, *Bandits*, p. 51.

325 Womack, *Zapata*, pp. 310–12.

326 Emigdio Martínez to Zapata, 1 Oct. 1914; Fortino Ayaquica to Zapata, 10 Mar. 1915; Archivo del Gral Emiliano Zapata.

327 Martín Sosa to Zapata, 17 Apr. 1915, Archivo del Gral Emiliano Zapata, puts the current price of maize as between 50c. and 1 peso a cuartillo (a little over a litre), while Zapatista soldiers received 2 pesos a day, ordinary peons somewhat less. A peon's daily wage could thus purchase two or three litres of maize, compared with six or more in the 1900s: Lewis, *Tepoztlán*, pp. 93–5.

328 Francisco Pacheco *et al.* to Zapata, 31 Oct. 1915, Fabela, DHRM, EZ, pp. 254–6; and pp. 233–4 in the same volume.

329 Womack, *Zapata*, pp. 274, 304.

330 *Ibid.*, p. 311.

331 Lewis, *Pedro Martínez*, p. 171.

332 Womack, *Zapata*, p. 370.

333 *Ibid.*, pp. 263, 273, 284, 292–3, 296, 301–2.

334 *Ibid.*, pp. 299–300. The evidence for Zapata's belief in imminent American intervention, it should be noted, comes from William Gates; and Gates it was who imparted this belief in the first place. Zapata's appeals for revolutionary unity, which Womack attributes to this belief, could have derived from his desperate need for allies.

335 María y Campos, *Múgica*, p. 301.

336 *Ibid.*, pp. 283–4, 288.

337 *Ibid.*, pp. 297–8, 302–4.

338 *Ibid.*, pp. 288–90; Taracena, *Verdadera revolución*, VI, pp. 145–6.

339 Womack, *Zapata*, pp. 291, 338–9.

340 Alvarado to Carranza, 25 Jan. 1916, Fabela, DHRM, RRC, V, pp. 22–3.

341 Hewett, Tuxpan, 5, 15, July 1917, FO 371/2962, 172054, 172652; Charles W. Hamilton, *Early Oil Tales of Mexico* (Houston, 1966), pp. 82–6.

342 Obregón, *Ocho mil kilómetros*, pp. 461–2, 466–7.

343 *Ibid.*, pp. 478–83; US Naval report, Topolobampo, Nov. 1915; Border report, Douglas, 26 Feb. 1916; SD 812.00/16843; 17358. The latter (which is not wholly accurate) reports the subsequent killing of Bachomo.

344 Obregón, *Ocho mil kilómetros*, p. 471; cf. Hall, 'Alvaro Obregón and the Agrarian Movement', pp. 132–3, 138, which presents a rosier picture.

345 Memo. of conversation with H. A. Sibbet, vice-president of the Richardson Construction Co., 6 Oct. 1915; Border report, Douglas, 19 Feb. 1916; SD 812.00/16843; 17335.

346 The decree was rescinded within weeks. Simpich, Nogales, 27 Dec. 1915, 29 Jan. 1916; border reports, Douglas, 26 Feb. 1916; SD 812.00/17023, 17282; 17358.

347 Simpich, Nogales, 15 Mar.; c/o USS Chattanooga, Guaymas, 10 Mar. 1916; SD 812.00/17480; 17769; Francisco Serrano report, in Obregón to Carranza, 25 Mar. 1916, AVC.

348 Border reports, Nogales, 22 Apr.; Douglas, 16 Sept. 1916; SD 812.00/18043; 19458. Note – as in the case of Villa – the summer campaigning; the sign of the late-revolutionary predator.

349 Hostetter, Hermosillo, 7 June; border report, Nogales, 20 May 1916; SD 812.00/18420; 18284.

350 Border reports, Nogales, 15 Sept., 14 Oct.; Doherty, Nogales, 16 Oct. 1916; SD 812.00/19427, 19654; 19546.

351 Border reports, Douglas, 29 June; Nogales, 14 Oct. 1916; SD 812.00/18899, 19654.

352 Border reports, Douglas, 18 Nov.; Nogales, 11 Nov. 1916; SD 812.00/20008; 19952; *El Demócrata*, 2 Nov. 1916, citing General Mateo Muñoz.

353 Lawton, Nogales, 16 Oct. 1916, SD 812.00/21382.

354 *Ibid.*; Simpich, Guaymas, 20 Nov. 1917, SD 812.00/21508.

355 Carleton Beals, *Mexican Maze* (Philadelphia, 1931), pp. 179, 182.

356 Cumberland, *Constitutionalist Years*, p. 407; Hall, *Obregón*, p. 234.

357 Dulles, *Yesterday in Mexico*, pp. 311–2; Moisés Gonzalez Navarro, *Raza y Tierra* (Mexico, 1970), p. 238.

358 Thord Grey, *Gringo Rebel*, p. 216; Alfonso Fabila, *Las tribus Yaquis de Sonora: su cultura y anhelada autodeterminación* (Mexico, 1940), p. 180.

359 Hence Calles' withdrawal of Mexican citizenship from these troublesome natives; or Cándido Aguilar's disparaging comment, when the Agua Prieta rebellion won Yaqui

support in 1920: 'are the Yaquis, with the thirst for vengeance of their race, with their readiness for any rebellion whatsoever – are they to be taken as indicators of national opinion?': Aguilar to F. Montes, 17 Apr. 1920, Fabela, DHRM, RRC, VI, p. 103.

360 Fabila, *Las tribus Yaquis*, p. 103.

361 See pp. 200–1.

362 Guyant, Progreso, 2 May 1916, SD 812.00/18114; Benjamin, 'Passages', pp. 156–7.

363 Meyer, *Huerta*, pp. 214–15 for a long list.

364 As in the days of Huerta, much of the consular correspondence, which can be read in the SRE archive, with published examples in Fabela, DHRM, RRC, concerns émigré plots and propaganda; the SD files also contain many FBI reports.

365 Statement to Dept. of Justice agent by José Vasconcelos (no less), 30 June 1915, SD 812.001/39.

366 Meyer, *Huerta*, pp. 213–29 and the same author's 'The Mexican–German Conspiracy of 1915', *Americas*, XXIII (1966), pp. 76–89; and George J. Rausch Jr, 'The Exile and Death of Victoriano Huerta', *Hispanic American Historical Review*, XLII (1962), pp. 133–51.

367 Meyer, 'Mexican–German Conspiracy'; Katz, *Deutschland*, pp. 339–40 and *Secret War*, p. 328ff.

368 Captain von Rintelen, *The Dark Invader, War-time Reminiscences of a German Naval Intelligence Officer* (London, 1937).

369 Rausch, *Exile and Death*, pp. 136–7, which follows Barbara W. Tuchman, *The Zimmermann Telegram* (London, 1959); cf. Grieb, *United States and Huerta*, pp. 183–5, which is more sceptical about German involvement.

370 Katz, *Deutschland*, p. 341.

371 Meyer, *Huerta*, pp. 217–18. Many of Huerta's backers were members of the Mexican Peace Assembly, an *émigré* organisation formed in February 1915: see T. Esquivel Obregón to Wilson, 8 Mar. 1915, SD 812.00/14576. Arguing that they were 'much more counter-revolutionary than the Huerta presidency itself', Meyer dismisses their modest, paper reformism of 1915 as 'hollow'; the modest paper reformism of 1913–14 deserves the same, sceptical treatment.

372 Meyer, *Mexican Rebel*, pp. 131–5, which goes into the contentious details of Orozco's death.

373 Meyer, *Huerta*, pp. 227–9; Rausch, 'Exile and Death', pp. 150–1.

374 Cf. Meyer, *Huerta*, p. 229: 'the [Felicista] movement was easily crushed'. While deflating Felicismo, Meyer – and Rausch – exaggerate both the actual and the potential significance of Huerta's conspiracy.

375 Schmutz, Aguascalientes, 23 Apr. 1915, SD 812.00/17.

376 G. Morgan to Scott, 23 Apr. 1915, Scott Papers, box 18. As already noted, there was also a degree of American support for the *émigré* counter-revolutionaries: Katz, *Secret War*, p. 316.

377 Liceaga, *Félix Díaz*, is a flattering biography, good on personal detail, useless on general interpretation. See also Katz, *Deutschland*, p. 340.

378 Henderson, *Félix Díaz*, pp. 120–3.

379 *Ibid.*, p. 126; Licéaga, *Félix Díaz*, p. 364ff.

380 In Veracruz, hopes were pinned on Díaz even before his inauspicious return to Mexico: S. Bonsal, Report to the American Red Cross of Conditions in Mexico, June–Aug. 1915 (dated 28 Aug. 1915), Bonsal Papers, box 6, p. 21.

381 Taracena, *Verdadera revolución*, IV, p. 218; Garciadiego, 'Movimientos reaccionarios', p. 245.

382 Garciadiego, 'Movimientos reaccionarios', pp. 246–7.

383 Licéaga, *Félix Díaz*, pp. 389–93.

384 *El Demócrata*, 8 Nov. 1916; Taracena, *Verdadera revolución*, V, pp. 35, 192.

385 Garciadiego, 'Movimientos reaccionarios', p. 182; Benjamin, 'Passages', pp. 149–50.

386 For the Plan and its accompanying manifesto see Fabela, DHRM, RRC, V, pp. 46–51, 62–6; and Licéaga, *Félix Díaz*, pp. 421–6, for *émigré* denunciations of the new Constitution.

387 Manifesto al Pueblo Mexicano, by Félix Díaz *et al.*, 1 Oct. 1918, in Fabela, VI, pp. 63–80.

388 *Ibid.*, p. 64.

389 Some (by no means all) Carrancistas were pro-German: see Katz, *Secret War*, pp. 346–7, 448–53. Others, like Palavicini and Rouaix, were pro-Ally.

390 Plan of Tierra Colorada, art. 9, in Fabela, DHRM, RRC, V, p. 48. Henderson, *Félix Díaz*, p. 130 stretches matters when he describes the 'bulk of the Plan' as being 'devoted to the agrarian situation'; in fact, it takes up about a quarter of the document.

391 Fabela, DHRM, RRC, V, p. 49.

392 'The [Mexican Peace] Assembly initiates in the first line of its program the SUBDIVISION OF THE LAND, along with other popular reforms': Esquivel Obregón to Wilson, 8 Mar. 1915, SD 812.00/14576; and p. 192 above.

393 Licéaga, *Félix Díaz*, pp. 438–9.

394 Fabela, DHRM, RRC, VI, pp. 65–6.

395 *Ibid.*, p. 65; cf. Zapata's Carta Abierta al Señor Carranza, n.d., in Fabela, DHRM, EZ, pp. 305–10.

396 Robles to Wilson, 8 Oct. 1916, SD 812.00/20415.

397 Licéaga, *Félix Díaz*, p. 540; Taracena, *Verdadera revolución*, V, p. 139.

398 Licéaga, *Félix Díaz*, pp. 377, 393; Taracena, *Verdadera revolución*, IV, p. 182, V, p. 139.

399 Licéaga, *Félix Díaz*, pp. 396, 406, 410, 414–15; and for *émigré* Felicista activities, Henderson, *Félix Díaz*, pp. 134–7.

400 Licéaga, *Félix Díaz*, pp. 457, 486–8, 529–33.

401 Garciadiego, 'Movimientos reaccionarios', p. 245.

402 Licéaga, *Félix Díaz*, pp. 482–3; Taracena, *Verdadera revolución*, VI, p. 115; Henderson, *Félix Díaz*, p. 137.

403 Licéaga, *Félix Díaz*, pp. 488, 535. If anything, Cíntora was a Chavista and/or a Villista: see Jesus Síntoira (sic) to Villa, 3 Feb. 1917, Fabela, DHRM, RRC, V, p. 237; and below, p. 398.

404 Though his brother was a Felicista *émigré*: Henderson, *Félix Díaz*, p. 141.

405 Note the length and complexity of the National Reorganising Army's dispositions for these states in Licéaga, *Félix Díaz*, pp. 486–8; Henderson, *Félix Díaz*, p. 138; Fowler, *Agrarian Radicalism*, p. 15, concludes from the *New York Times* that, 'Veracruz was the state with the greatest number of recorded incidences of violence in 1919 and 1920.'

406 Canada, Veracruz, 14 June 1917, SD 812.00/21058; Henderson, *Félix Díaz*, p. 129.

407 Canada, Veracruz, 2 Oct. 1916, 9 Nov. 1917; Spillard, Naranjal, 20 Sept. 1915; SD 812.00/19552, 21481; 16492; Licéaga, *Félix Díaz*, pp. 385–8, 480, 525; Garciadiego, 'Movimientos reaccionarios', p. 243. It was ironic that Santibáñez, the killer of Jesús Carranza, should meet retribution at the hands of Félix Díaz.

408 L. Ostien to Lansin, from Chiapas, 13 Sept. 1916; Canada, Veracruz, 26 Sept. 1916, 14 June 1914; SD 812.00/19260; 19476, 21058; Stevenson, Tapachula, 21 July; Gemmill, Puerto Mexico, 15 Mar. 1917; FO 371/2962, 172060; 2966, 88697.

409 This was a constant theme at Querétaro: e.g., DDCC, II, pp. 920–35.

410 Benjámin, 'Passages', pp. 156–60.

411 US Military Attaché report in Barclay, Washington, 14 Feb. 1918, FO 371/3242, 35522.

412 Canada, Veracruz, 1 Aug., 6 Dec. 1917; USS Huntington, Salina Cruz, 10 Dec. 1916, SD 812.00/18987, 21525; 20276.

413 Taracena, *Verdadera revolución*, VI, p. 13.

414 Joseph, *Revolution From Without*, pp. 95–8.

415 William B. Taylor, *Landlord and Peasant in Colonial Oaxaca* (Stanford, 1972), pp. 198–9.

416 Gavira, *Actuación*, pp. 96, 98, 108; Canada, Veracruz, 11 Sept. 1916, 4 May 1917; c/o,

US Navy, Salina Cruz, 9 Nov. 1915; SD 812.00/19256, 20917; 16843; Hohler, Mexico City, 18 July 1917, FO 371/2962, 166713; F. Mariel to Aguilar, 4 Jan. 1916, AVC.

417 Canada, Veracruz, 13 Nov. 1917, SD 812.00/21491.

418 Benjamin, 'Passages', p. 159.

419 Canada, Veracruz, 6 Dec. 1917, SD 812.00/21525.

420 Aguilar to Millán, 13 May 1916, AVC.

421 *Ibid.* Not that Aguilar himself was above suspicion: see Bonsal Report (n. 380), p. 17.

422 Cf. vol. I, pp. 117, 307, 368–82.

423 Canada, Veracruz, 6 Dec. 1917, SD 812.00/21583; anon. to S. Yépez, 2 May 1916, AVC; Henderson, *Félix Díaz*, p. 140.

424 Almazán returned, via Guatemala, to the north; Robles was captured and shot in Apr. 1917. His later career is recounted in Luis Espinosa, *Defección del General José Isabel Robles en la Sierra de Ixtlán, Oaxaca* (Mexico, n.d.), pp. 5–61.

425 See pp. 201–2.

426 Cowdray to Ryder, 11 Sept. 1914, Ryder to Body, 2 Jan. 1915, Cowdray Papers, box A/3; Hohler memo. in Spring-Rice, Washington, 1 Mar. 1917, FO 371/2959, 60106; US Naval Intelligence, 12 Apr. 1918, SD 812.6363/387.

427 Spillard, Naranjal, 25 May and in Canada, Veracruz, 25 Sept. 1915; c/o USS Kentucky, Veracruz, 26 Jan.; Canada, Veracruz, 2 Oct. 1916; SD 812.00/15352, 16492; 17229; 19552.

428 Hamilton, *Oil Tales*, pp. 170–2.

429 C/o USS Nashville, Veracruz, 26 Jan. 1917; Dawson, Tampico, 6 Dec. 1917; SD 812.6363/259, 332; Garcíadiego, 'Movimientos reaccionarios', pp. 117, 134–5.

430 On the German threat (often more imagined than real): Katz, *Secret War*, pp. 342–3, 383, 396, 415, 430.

431 Manifesto of 5 May 1917 in Walker, Washington, 7 Aug. 1917, SD 812.6363/303.

432 Walker to Auchincloss, 9 Sept. 1917, SD 812.6363/312 (Walker was an employee of Doheny's Mexican Petroleum Co.). See also Smith, *United States and Revolutionary Nationalism*, pp. 100–5; and Dennis J. O'Brien, 'Petróleo e intervención: relaciones entre los Estados Unidos y México 1917–18', *Historia Mexicana*, XXVII (1977), pp. 103–40.

434 The importance of Mexican oil for the Allied war effort has often been exaggerated. In the course of 1917, the British war effort absorbed 5½m. tons of American oil, ½m. tons of Mexican; a complete shutdown of Mexican production would have required an increase of only 9% in American output to meet the shortfall: Grey to Barclay, 5 Feb. 1918, FO 371/3242, 21258. J. Body, working for Cowdray in Mexico, argued that 'all the fuel oil and otherwise that the Allies need could be obtained in the States irrespective of Mexico and even if Mexican crude were unobtainable': Body to Cowdray, 22 May 1917, Cowdray Papers, box A/4. When, at the same time, Body advocated a coup against the Carranza regime, he did so for business rather than patriotic motives; just as the British Admiralty, two years before, preferred to contract with American rather than British oil suppliers (see Katz, *Secret War*, pp. 178–9, 467). Company and national policy thus diverged, even in wartime; and company spokesmen who invoked vital national interests, or strategic necessity, should not always be credited.

434 Cf. Raymond Aron, *The Imperial Republic. The United States and the World 1945–73* (London, 1975), which argues this point.

435 Grey to Spring-Rice, 13 Mar.; Hohler memo., in Grey, 1 Mar. 1917; FO 371/2959, 52769; 60106; O'Brien, 'Petróleo e intervención', pp. 118–19; Garciadiego, 'Movimientos reaccionarios', pp. 117–18, 120.

436 Thurstan, Mexico City, 17 Apr. 1917; Hohler, Mexico City, 20 Feb. 1918; FO 371/2959, 79679; 3242, 43257; Katz, *Secret War*, pp. 463, 465, 474, 477.

437 Hohler, Mexico City, 20 Feb. 1918, FO 371/3242, 43257; American official circles were

strongly divided over the wisdom of intervention: O'Brien, 'Petroleo e intervención', pp. 129–30.

438 The German military attaché in Washington (the later Chancellor, von Papen) planned a sabotage campaign against the Tampico wells in 1915–16, but nothing came of it (possibly because the German Admiralty doubted the campaign's utility); again, in 1917, the German military's plans for sabotage were overruled by the German Minister, Eckardt, who feared a rupture with Carranza and favoured more subtle economic penetration: Katz, *Secret War*, pp. 342–3, 395–8. German policy is more notable for its internal fragmentation than for its direct impact on events in Mexico.

439 O'Brien, 'Petróleo e intervención', pp. 114, 117, n. 18. Canova combined suspicion of the British, contempt for his own Ambassador, and a cordial hostility to Carranza: on his erratic career and opinions, see Katz, 'Pancho Villa y el ataque a Columbus', pp. 40–7; Louis M. Teitelbaum, *Woodrow Wilson and the Mexican Revolution 1913–1916* (New York, 1967), pp. 163, 379.

440 Greene to Paddleford, 2 Feb. 1918, SD 812.6363/389.

441 Smith, *United States and Revolutionary Nationalism*, p. 118.

442 Hewett, Tuxpán, 5 Feb. 1918, FO 371/3242, 41499.

443 Greene to Paddleford, 17 Feb. 1918, SD 812.6363/389; Grey to Reading, 12 Feb., to Spring-Rice, 8 Jan., FO 371/3242, 28287; Katz, *Secret War*, pp. 471–2, 484, 486 dates Cowdray's change of heart to late 1917.

444 Smith, *United States and Revolutionary Nationalism*, p. 119ff.; O'Brien, 'Petróleo e intervención', p. 134, sees American anxiety giving way to optimism, and belligerence to diplomacy, in the latter part of 1918.

445 Garciadiego, 'Movimientos reaccionarios', p. 139.

446 Katz, *Secret War*, pp. 554, 557, 562–3, 568–78.

447 This raises again the perplexing question of the relationship between Pelaecismo and the agrarian movements which had characterised this same region during the Porfiriato and early Revolution. The comments of Adalberto Tejeda – the later, *agrarista* governor of Veracruz – conveyed in anon. to Jara, 22 Mar. 1916, AVC, indicate the continued importance of land seizures and agrarian violence; but it is not clear whether the aggrieved villagers became spectators, supporters, or victims of Pelaecismo. Fowler, 'Caciquismo and the Mexican Revolution' is aware of the problem, but offers no answers.

448 Dudley Ankerson, verbal communication; Garciadiego, 'Movimientos reaccionarios', notes certain loose regional alliances, but confirms that Pelaecismo was rooted in the locality: p. 138.

449 To the extent that oil exploration was curbed, some manpower might have been released for Pelaecista recruitment; production workers would not have found it easy to double up as *guerrilleros*: Naval Intelligence report, 12 Apr. 1918, SD 812.6363/387.

450 US Military Attaché report in Barclay, Washington, 14 Feb. 1918, FO 371/3242, 35522.

451 Garciadiego, 'Movimientos reaccionarios', p. 119.

452 Hewett, Tuxpán, 1 Apr. 1918, SD 812.6363/392.

453 Dawson, Tampico, 19 Feb. 1918, SD 812.6363/344.

454 Pulsford, Tampico, 4 Sept. 1918, FO 371/371/3246, 174257.

455 Garciadiego, 'Movimentos reaccionarios', pp. 129, 132.

456 Most reports suggest that Peláez could count on 5–6,000 men, though only half this number could be supplied with arms: Barclay, Washington, 14 Feb. 1918, FO 371/3242, 35522.

457 On Carrancista numbers, failings and abuses: Pulsford, Tampico, 11 June 1917; Hewett, Tampico, 20 Feb. 1917, 26 Jan. 1918; Greene, Huasteca Co., 1 Mar. 1918; FO 371/2962, 143982; 2960, 79890, 3242, 41501; 3243, 70846; Dawson, Tampico, 25 Feb. 1918 and Greene to Paddleford, 17 Feb. 1918, SD 812.6363/349, 389. These observers, it should be added, were not well disposed towards Carrancismo.

458 Garciadiego, 'Movimientos reaccionarios', p. 123, counts five successive Carrancista commanders in the space of a year.
459 Hewett, Tuxpan, 1 Apr. 1917, FO 371/2960, 96567.
460 *Ibid.*, 1 Feb. 1918, FO 371/3242, 58153.
461 *Ibid.*, and memo. of Hohler, Mexico City, 20 Feb. 1918, FO 371/3242, 58153, 43257.
462 Garciadiego, 'Movimientos reaccionarios', pp. 130–4.
463 *Ibid.*, p. 153, n. 112; Licéaga, *Félix Díaz*, pp. 469–70.
464 Licéaga, *Félix Díaz*, pp. 596, 609.
465 Canada, Veracruz, 14 Oct. 1916, 6 Dec. 1917, SD 812.00/19698, 21583; Barclay, Washington, 21 Feb. 1918, FO 371/3242, 43261, gives comparable, though smaller figures.
466 Licéaga, *Félix Díaz*, pp. 520–1, states that Felicista operations were further extended in 1919; this seems unlikely. 1916, 1917, 1918, appear to have been the years of greatest rebel activity.
467 S. Bonsal report (n. 380); L. Spillard, Naranjal, 24 May 1915, SD 812.00/15352.
468 E. Ely, Tuxtepec, 11 Feb. 1916, SD 812.00/17365; Benjamin, 'Passages', p. 157; Garciadiego, 'Movimientos reaccionarios', pp. 181–5.
469 Licéaga, *Félix Díaz*, p. 433; Hutchinson, Veracruz, 29 Dec. 1917, FO 371/3242, 20158; Canada, Veracruz, 29 Feb. 1916, SD 812.00/17409; Henderson, *Félix Díaz*, pp. 139–40.
470 Canada, Veracruz, 29 Feb. 1916, SD 812.00/17409; c/o USS Kentucky, Veracruz, 10 Feb. 1916, SD 812.00/17310; Benjamin, 'Passages', p. 157.
471 S. Bonsal report (n. 380).
472 Canada, Veracruz, 19 Aug. 1915, SD 812.00/16056.
473 Gruening, *Mexico and its Heritage*, p. 320, corroborates Licéaga, *Félix Díaz*, p. 643.
474 Decree of 28 Aug. 1917 in Licéaga, *Félix Díaz*, p. 443; Garciadiego, 'Movimientos reaccionarios', p. 183.
475 US military intelligence report in Barclay, Washington, 26 July 1918, FO 371/3245, 136688; Benjamin, 'Passages', p. 159; Garciadiego, 'Movimientos reaccionarios', pp. 190–1.
476 Elsee, Frontera, 16 June 1917; Sparks, Puerto Mexico, 3 Jan., 4 Mar. 1918; FO 371/2962, 158767; 3242, 41478, 3243, 71329; though cf. Garciadiego, 'Movimientos reaccionarios', p. 186.
477 Benjamin, 'Passages', p. 160.
478 Canada, Veracruz, 29 Feb. 1916, SD 812.00/17409.
479 C/o USS Kentucky, 6 Apr. 1916; Canada, Veracruz, 28 May 1917; SD 812.00/17921; 20950; Licéaga, *Félix Díaz*, pp. 464, 506; Taracena, *Verdadera revolución*, VI, p. 48.
480 Bonsal report (n. 380), p. 17; Stacpoole, Orizaba, 31 Mar. 1918, FO 371/3243, 75797.
481 Canada, Veracruz, 20, 21 Nov., 26 Dec. 1916, SD 812.00/19927, 19928, 20145; Hutchinson, Veracruz, 29 Dec. 1917, FO 371/3242, 20158.
482 Licéaga, *Félix Díaz*, p. 541. Was this the advice of a tired old man, looking for quick, conventional victories?
483 Taracena, *Verdadera revolución*, VI, pp. 8, 85; Henderson, *Félix Díaz*, p. 139.
484 Taracena, *Verdadera revolución*, VI, p. 101; Casasola, *Historia gráfica*, II, pp. 1305–7.
485 Taracena, *Verdadera revolución*, VI, pp. 110, 167, 184, 190, 192; Henderson, *Félix Díaz*, pp. 141–2; Garciadiego, 'Movimientos reaccionarios', p. 255.
486 Benjamin, 'Passages', pp. 158, 160.
487 Taracena, *Verdadera revolución*, VI, pp. 197, 202; Licéaga, *Félix Díaz*, pp. 604–7.
488 Taracena, *Verdadera revolución*, VI, p. 152; León Medel y Alvarado, *Historia de San Andrés Tuxtla* (Mexico, 1963), II, p. 86.
489 H. B. C. Pollard, *A Busy Time in Mexico* (London, 1913), pp. 17, 30–1; Juan Tavera, 5th Rural Corps, Pijijiapam, to Gobernación, 29 May 1908, AG, 653.
490 See vol. I, p. 355.

491 Womack, *Zapata*, p. 274.

492 Porfirio del Castillo in DDCC, 1, p. 339.

493 Governor Machorro to Obregón, 23 Aug.; military commander, Tlaxcala, to Gobernación, 10 Oct. 1916; AG 85/65; 69/31. This region, on the south-eastern slopes of the Malintzi, is peripheral to Buve's study of the state.

494 Womack, *Zapata*, pp. 352, 376.

495 Apart from Friedrich's well-researched case of Naranja, note also that of the Hacienda La Orilla, seized from its owners in 1912 and still in rebel hands in 1916 (M. Barre de St Leu to Gobernación, 9 Aug. 1916, AG 71/23); that of the *finca* El Pilón, taken over by a 'Zapatista horde' (Agustín Barragán to Carranza, 4 Aug. 1916, AVC); that of Los Reyes Ecuandereo, where the *indios comuneros* complained that their agrarian demands had incurred the wrath of landlords, military and *casiques* (sic) (Francisco Herrero to Carranza, 18 Aug. 1916, AVC); and the cases mentioned by Díaz Soto y Gama, 'La Revolución Agraria en Michoacán', *El Universal*, 23 July 1953.

496 See vol. 1, pp. 199–200, 259–61.

497 Dickinson, San Luis, 12 Dec. 1916; Silliman, Guadalajara, 5 Apr.; Glenn, Guanajuato, 16 May 1917; SD 812.00/20069; 20759; 20963.

498 *El Demócrata*, 17, 18 Nov. 1915, 3, 12 Feb., 3 Nov. 1916.

499 J. Ambrosius to Gobernación, 27 Oct. 1915, AG 84/35.

500 Jean Meyer, *La Cristiada* (Mexico, 1973), 1, p. 106, n. 102; Garciadiego, 'Movimientos reaccionarios', p. 94, n. 98.

501 H. C. Cummins, Mexico City, 23 Apr. 1918, FO 371/3244, 87167, enclosing account of Charles Furber (Furber's brother, Percy, had his own adventures in the oil district, which have been recorded; the family's name was – briefly – preserved in the settlement of Furbero, now San Miguel).

502 Garciadiego, 'Movimientos reaccionarios', pp. 72–3, where Spanish support for the rebels is also noted.

503 E. J. Hobsbawm, *Primitive Rebels. Studies in Archaic Forms of Social Movement in the Nineteenth and Twentieth Centuries* (Manchester, 1974), p. 18.

504 Hobsbawm, *Bandits*, p. 22. Garciadiego, however, is prepared to see Chavismo as a form of social banditry, its leader as a Mexican *haiduk*: 'Movimientos reaccionarios', pp. 76, 93.

505 Gov. Siurob, Gto, to Carranza, 16 Sept. 1915, AJD.

506 *Ibid.*, which notes in particular the inefficiency of Carrancista troops brought into the state from outside.

507 González, *Pueblo en vilo*, pp. 125–7; Garciadiego, 'Movimientos reaccionarios', pp. 28–9, correlates the rise and fall of Chavismo with the dearth of 1915–16 and the recovery of 1919.

508 Aguirre Valles report, 11 Sept. 1917; F. Dávila to Secretary of War, 20 July 1918; AJD; note also Summerlin, Mexico City, 9 Jan. 1918, SD 812.00/21660; and Garciadiego's useful map, 'Movimientos reaccionarios', p. 85.

509 C. Bernaldo de Quirós, *El bandolerismo en España y México* (Mexico, 1959), pp. 383–8.

510 González, *Pueblo en vilo*, p. 125.

511 It is also clear that the bandits were local men, not outside interlopers.

512 Taracena, *Verdadera revolución*, V, pp. 190, 225–7; González, *Pueblo en vilo*, pp. 128,130; Summerlin, Mexico City, 12 Feb. 1918, SD 812.00/21751; A. Alcocer to Carranza, 6 Feb. 1918, AVC; Garciadiego, 'Movimientos reaccionarios', p. 63.

513 Taracena, *Verdadera revolución*, V, pp. 227–8.

514 Romero Flores, *Michoacán*, p. 151; Cusi, *Memorias*, p. 216; *Excelsior*, 27 July 1918, in Thurstan, Mexico City, 30 July 1918, FO 371/3245, 148790; Garciadiego, 'Movimientos reaccionarios', pp. 70–3.

515 Doherty, Nogales, 4 Dec. 1916, SD 812.00/20059.

516 The treacherous execution of Pantoja and several of his officers (the work, it seems, of

Amaro) helped determine Chávez García's conversion to Villismo and banditry: Oviedo Mota, *El trágico fin*, II, pp. 38–9; and, for further details of his and his colleagues' backgrounds, see Governor of Jalisco to Carranza, 14 Dec. 1917, AJD; Thurstan, Mexico City, 9 Sept. 1918, FO 371/3246, 170916; and Garciadiego, 'Movimientos reaccionarios', pp. 42–3, 93, n. 96.

517 González, *Pueblo en vilo*, p. 131; Cusi, *Memorias*, p. 120; Taracena, *Verdadera revolución*, V, pp. 199–200.

518 Dávila to Secretary of War, 20 July 1918, AJD; Taracena, *Verdadera revolución*, V, p. 213; Fabela, DHRM, RRC, V, p. 400; Garciadiego, 'Movimientos reaccionarios', p. 51.

519 González, *Pueblo en vilo*, pp. 129–30.

520 Taracena, *Verdadera revolución*, V, p. 199.

521 *Ibid.*, pp. 190, 228, 234–5, 253; González, *Pueblo en vilo*, pp. 130–1; Garciadiego, 'Movimientos reaccionarios', pp. 57, 61.

522 Taracena, *Verdadera revolución*, V, p. 190; González, *Pueblo en vilo*, p. 130.

523 Garciadiego, 'Movimientos reaccionarios', 75–6, 93, n. 88.

524 González, *Pueblo en vilo*, pp. 128–9; Luis Navarro, DDCC, II, pp. 1080–1.

525 González, *Pueblo en vilo*, p. 128; Taracena, *Verdadera revolución*, V, pp. 181, 228, 253; Womack, *Zapata*, p. 301, calls him a Felicista, which is odd.

526 Cusi, *Memorias*, p. 208.

527 Meyer, *Cristero Rebellion*, pp. 112, 124; Taracena, *Verdadera revolución*, IV, p. 189, V, p. 149; Garciadiego, 'Movimientos reaccionarios', p. 81, stresses Chavista Catholicism – in my view overmuch.

528 Oviedo Mota, *El trágico fin*, p. 40; Garciadiego, 'Movimientos reaccionarios', pp. 56–7.

529 Garciadiego, 'Movimientos reaccionarios', p. 61.

530 *Ibid.*, pp. 57–8, 61–2, 74–5. There was no contact between Chavismo and Zapatismo.

531 Thurstan, Mexico City, 30 July 1918, FO 371/3245, 148790, citing *Excelsior*. Chávez's campaigns were contained within the rectangle formed by Tacámbaro, Acámbaro, Degollado and Cotija. On boltholes: Garciadiego, 'Movimientos reaccionarios', p. 64.

532 *Excelsior* (n. 531).

533 Paul Friedrich, *Agrarian Revolt in a Mexican Village* (Englewood Cliffs, 1970), p. 69. Tapia's comment is neither wholly clear nor error-free, but it seems probable that Chávez García is the subject.

534 Garciadiego, 'Movimientos reaccionarios', pp. 67–9, 76 on the myth. Of course, Chavismo was not monolithic: as already suggested, it may have changed over time, and incorporated contrasting elements (some more 'professional' than others). This guarded conclusion relates to the broad character of 'mature' Chavismo, and is no doubt vulnerable to further research.

535 Hugh M. Hamill, *The Hidalgo Revolt; Prelude to Mexican Independence* (Gainesville, 1966), pp. 48, 89, 140, 176.

536 González, *Pueblo en vilo*, p. 130; Taracena, *Verdadera revolución*, V, p. 213; Garciadiego, 'Movimientos reaccionarios', pp. 48, 52–3, 58, 63.

537 Garciadiego, 'Movimientos reaccionarios', pp. 52–8.

538 González, *Pueblo en vilo*, pp. 128, 130–1.

539 *Ibid.*, pp. 127–8; Meyer, *Cristero Rebellion*, pp. 124–5.

540 Ortiz, *Episodios*, pp. 24, 32–3, 42–3.

541 González, *Pueblo en vilo*, p. 128.

542 *Ibid.*, pp. 128–9.

543 For the confusion evident to local observers: Cusi, *Memorias*, p. 215.

544 Garciadiego, 'Movimientos reaccionarios', p. 66; King, Mexico City, 25 Nov. 1918, FO 371/3247, 205361.

545 Garciadiego, 'Movimientos reaccionarios', pp. 70, 74.

546 Taracena, *Verdadera revolución*, VI, p. 150.

547 Beals, *Mexican Maze*, pp. 205–13.

548 *Viz.*, Enrique Ramírez, leader of La Piedad's defence force: Garciadiego, 'Movimientos reaccionarios', p. 88, n. 36.

549 See pp. 524–6.

550 *Jefe político*, Tepic, to Gobernación, 27 Oct. 1916, AG 81/21; Brown, Mazatlán, 8 Jan. 1916, SD 812.00/17113; M. Trueba *et al.* to Governor Cepeda, 28 Aug. 1916, AG 71/72; A. Sánchez to Carranza, 21 Dec. 1916, AVC.

551 Stevenson, Tapachula, 21 July 1917, FO 371/2962, 172060; Lt Col Martínez to municipal president, 29 Apr. 1917, Lampazos Archive, r. 225; Secretary of War to Carranza, 2 May 1916, AVC.

552 Secretary of ayuntamiento and municipal president to Governor De la Garza, 28, 30 Jan. 1917, Lampazos Archive, r. 225. Other bandits had been known to enter the town; the fatal incident formed part of a long struggle between the bandits and the municipal authorities.

553 *El Demócrata*, 19 Nov. 1916.

554 A report of the Belgian Minister, 5 July 1918, in Hohler, Mexico City, 30 July 1918, FO 371/3245, 139785, gave figures – taken from the press – of 10,137 crimes notified to the Federal District authorities between January and June 1918; of these, 3,905 were violent. Such figures, however, were not thought to be authoritative; no more were those produced during the Porfiriato. It seems likely, however, that the Revolution reversed a trend whereby crime rates, during the Porfiriato, had tended to fall: Moises González Navarro, *Historia Moderna de Mexico, El Porfiriato, La Vida Social* (Mexico, 1970), pp. 426–8.

555 *El Demócrata*, 20, 24 Mar., 6 May 1916.

556 The Belgian Minister's figures suggest a high proportion of crimes of violence, comparable to the 40% noted by González Navarro, *Vida Social*, p. 426, for the 1870s and 1880s (see n. 554). On night-life: V. Blasco Ibáñez, *Mexico in Revolution* (New York, 1920), pp. 192–7; on rape, pp. 333, 394, 406.

557 Belgian Minister's report (n. 554).

558 Moore, La Paz, 22 June 1917; Hutchinson, Veracruz, 3 June 1918; Stacpoole, Orizaba, 23 May 1918; FO 371/2962, 166760; 3245, 122580; 3244, 112172.

559 Norton, Durango, 17 May, 2 Aug. 1917, FO 371/2962, 138794, 17248.

560 Blocker, Piedras Negras, 31 Jan. 1916, SD 812.00/17223. Such an incident (of the kind readily cited out of context to indicate popular 'xenophobia') in fact reflected the prevailing level of crime (officially defined), which was in turn linked to destitution. The same is broadly true of the stabbing of the German Chargé d'Affaires in Chapultepec Park which, fortunately, had a happy ending ('[he] being a fat man, the poniard did not reach any vital organ'): Hohler, *Diplomatic Petrel*, p. 202.

561 *El Demócrata*, 22 Mar., 1 Nov. 1916; F. Tovar to Gov. Machorro, 13 Oct. 1916, AG 82/53; concerning robberies at Querétaro and Apam.

562 *El Demócrata*, 19 Sept., 22 Nov. 1916.

563 *Ibid.*, 4, 5, 7, 8 Mar. 1916.

564 E.g., *El Demócrata*, 6 Sept. 1916, on the execution of a captain, before a 'numerous crowd', and in front of the Mexico City shop he had allegedly robbed. On the Mixcoac robberies: H. P. Fletcher report, 27 Jan. 1918, Fletcher Papers, Library of Congress, box 5.

565 *El Demócrata*, 8 Sept. 1916; Blasco Ibáñez, *Mexico in Revolution*, pp. 189–90; Bernaldo de Quirós, *El bandolerismo*, p. 391; Taracena, *Verdadera revolucion*, IV, p. 77.

566 Taracena, *Verdadera revolución*, IV, pp. 55, 121, 130; VI, pp. 68, 70–4, 76–9, 82.

567 *Ibid.*, VI, pp. 67–8 on General José Cavazos' allegations of Manuel Avila Camacho's participation in a major jewel robbery; and below, pp. 510–11.

568 J. G. Nava to Carranza, 9 Dec. 1915, AVC.

569 C/o USS Kentucky, Tampico, 25 Oct. 1916, SD 812.00/19772.

570 Governor of Guanajuato to Carranza, 16 Sept. 1915, AJD.

571 C/o, USS Kentucky, Veracruz, 14 Jan. 1916, SD 812.00/17151.

572 *El Demócrata*, 25 Nov. 1916.

573 DDCC, II, pp. 273–4, 347.

574 For a revisionist review of the economic history of the revolutionary decade see John Womack Jr, 'The Mexican Economy During the Revolution, 1910–1920: Historiography and Analysis', *Marxist Perspectives*, I (1978), pp. 80–123.

575 G. Pound to H. L. Scott, 6 Nov. 1915, Scott Papers, box 143; memo. of Hohler in Spring-Rice to Grey, 16 July 1917 and Cummins, Mexico City, 23 Aug. 1917, FO 371/2962, 158278, 172778, on the primacy of economic and financial questions.

576 Guzmán, *Memorias*, pp. 365, 429; Obregón, *Ocho mil kilómetros*, pp. 296, 418, 429.

577 Illegible, Hymans-Michael Scrap Co., to D. Dillon, 13 Oct. 1915; AVC; Bonsal report (n. 380); Womack, *Zapata*, p. 286.

578 O'Hea, Gómez Palacio, 11 Jan. 1917, FO 371/2959, 37114.

579 G. Bergman, Jalapa, 16 July 1918, FO 371/3245, 135921.

580 Pani, *Apuntes*, pp. 235, 239–40, on the demilitarisation of the railways: in one instance, disgruntled railwaymen sabotaged the brakes of the car in which Pani slept and rolled it down an incline into a path of a scheduled passenger train; but the train was late, and Pani's car ground to a halt, enabling the occupants to sound the alarm.

581 According to Taracena, *Verdadera revolución*, VI, pp. 43–4; see also Gov. Siurob to Carranza, 16 Sept. 1915, AJD; Bonney, San Luis, 13 Apr. 1915, SD 812.50/7.

582 See also Blasco Ibáñez, *Mexico in Revolution*, pp. 130–1.

583 Pani, *Apuntes*, pp. 237–9, on Cedillista and Zapatista attacks.

584 E.g., the appeal of the Laguna planter Pedro Lavín to Carranza in C. Rochin to Carranza, 8 May 1916, AVC.

585 Blocker, Piedras Negras, 31 Jan. 1916, SD 812.00/17223.

586 C/o USS Wheeling, Cd Carmen, 14 June 1916; Dickinson, San Luis, 16 Nov. 1916; SD 812.00/18722; 19891.

587 Pani, *Apuntes*, p. 185; Kemmerer, *Inflation and Revolution*, pp. 30–1.

588 *Ibid.*, p. 33, suggests 33m.

589 Silliman, Mexico City, 19 Sept., Canova, Mexico City, 25 Aug. 1914, SD 812.002/44, SD 812.00/13129.

590 Canova (n. 589); Silliman, Mexico City, 4 Feb. 1915, SD 812.00/14352; Zapata to R. González Garza, 9 Feb. 1915, Fabela, DHRM, EZ, pp. 183–4.

591 Brown, Mazatlán, 16 Jan. 1915, SD 812.00/14339.

592 Kemmerer, *Inflation and Revolution*, pp. 40–1, which puts Carrancista issue at 283m.; cf. US Naval report, Guaymas, 9 Nov. 1915, SD 812.00/16843, which suggests between 300 and 400m. See also Ulloa, *Revolución Escindida*, pp. 216–23.

593 See pp. 133–4, 147, 560 n.967.

594 Brown (n. 591).

595 Cardoso de Oliveira, Mexico City, 18 July 1915; see also Silliman, Mexico City, 6, 8 Feb.; Davis, Guadalajara, 2 Feb.; Silliman, Veracruz, 15 July 1915; SD 812.00/15473; 14356; 14371; 14486; 15454.

596 G. Pound to H. L. Scott, 6 Nov. 1915, Scott Papers, box 143.

597 Kemmerer, *Inflation and Revolution*, pp. 44–6.

598 C/o, USS Kentucky, 14 Jan. 1916, SD 812.00/17151.

599 C/o, USS Marietta, Veracruz, 23 Mar. 1916, SD 812.00/17729.

600 W. McCaleb in Fall Report, p. 737; see also the resumé in Thurstan, Mexico City, 13 Aug. 1918, FO 371/3245, 151945, which details the decline of the peso between 1913 and 1916 and estimates total paper issue at 5,000m.

601 Douglas W. Richmond, 'The First Chief and Revolutionary Mexico: the Presidency of

Venustiano Carranza, 1915–20' (Ph.D. diss., University of Washington, 1976), p. 33; Krauze, *Caudillos culturales*, pp. 114–15.

602 Doherty, Nogales, 4 Dec.; Dickinson, San Luis, 8 Dec.; Hostetter, Los Angeles, 26 Dec. 1916; Silliman, Guadalajara, 5 Apr.; border report, Nogales, 31 Mar. 1917; SD 812.00/20059; 20112; 20191; 20759; 20793.

603 E.g., Lespinasse, Frontera, 8 July 1915, SD 812.00/15434.

604 *El Demócrata*, 2, 5 May 1916.

605 *Ibid.*, 15 May 1916.

606 *Ibid.*, 6, 16 May 1916; note also the boast of the same governor, in his annual *informe*, of the quantity of money withdrawn, *ibid.*, 13 Nov. 1916.

607 Fabela, DHRM, RRC, v, p. 314.

608 *El Demócrata*, 6 Mar. 1916.

609 *Ibid.*, 5 May 1916. Three months later, after the *infalsificable* issue, Cabrera was still blaming 'reactionaries' for the currency depreciation: Taracena, *Verdadera revolución*, v, p. 128.

610 Gov. Machorro to Carranza, 12 Aug. 1916; AVC; Barron to Carranza, 9 May 1916, AVC.

611 *El Demócrata*, 22 Nov. 1916.

612 *Ibid.*, 4 May 1916.

613 *Ibid.*, 13 Nov. 1916; Lt Col Octavio Hidalgo to municipal president, Barrón Escandón, Tlaxcala, 10 Nov. 1916, AG 69/44.

614 Rutherford, *Mexican Society*, p. 253; Moats, *Thunder in their veins*, p. 171; and see Enrique Krauze, *Caudillos culturales en la revolución mexicana* (Mexico, 1976), pp. 37–8 on the efforts of the young Lombardo Toledano to defend the family patrimony against the great, impersonal forces of the revolutionary economy, above all the bank confiscation and hyper-inflation.

615 See pp. 524–5.

616 Alfredo Damy, Quila (Sin.) to Carranza, 8 Aug. 1916, AVC, on the currency problem and its effects on the poor.

617 Pacheco to Zapata, 31 Oct. 1915, Fabela, DHRM, EZ, p. 255.

618 Though – another warning against simple stereotypes and reminder, perhaps, of the Martínez Alier phenomenon – even some industrial workers petitioned for land; and some (significantly, in the Orizaba region) were successful: Governor Jara to Carranza, 10 Nov. 1916, Fabela, DHRM, RCC, v, p. 179, on the grants to workers of the Cocolapán, El Yute and Cerritos factories.

619 US Naval report, Manzanillo, 9 Nov. 1915, SD 812.00/16843.

620 Donald, Aguascalientes, 6 Oct. 1917, FO 371/21361.

621 For example: C. Kurtz, Guanajuato Reduction and Mines Co., 15 Dec. 1916, SD 812.00/20097.

622 C/o USS Yorktown, Topolobampo, 15 Oct. 1916, SD 812.00/19679.

623 Simpich, Nogales, 10 Sept.; c/o USS Wheeling, Progreso, 20 Apr., 12 Sept. 1916; SD 812.00/19121; 18156, 19338; Joseph, 'Revolution From Without', pp. 155, 210.

624 Simpich (n. 623); Blocker, Piedras Negras, 17 Nov. 1915, 12 Sept. 1916, SD 812.00/16841, 19152. Both sources mention a certain antagonism between the companies and the local authorities, while clearly discounting any popular hostility.

625 Casasola, *Historia gráfica*, II, pp. 1123, 1149, 1150, 1222, 1244–5, 1247, 1249, 1250, 1254, 1263, 1267, 1273, 1275, 1278, 1351, 1371; note also Teitelbaum, *Woodrow Wilson*, pp. 286–7.

626 González Roa, *El Aspecto Agrario*, p. 186; Bulnes, *El verdadero Díaz* p. 236.

627 Silliman, Saltillo, 2 Aug. 1913, SD 812.51/87.

628 *Mexican Herald*, 4 Apr. 1915.

629 Stewart to de Bunsen, 12 Mar. 1918, FO 371/3242; 46189; See also, Richmond, 'The First Chief', p. 66.

630 Thurstan, Mexico City, 14 Dec. 1917, FO 371/2964, 235682; Cravioto in DDCC, II, p. 223.

631 Schmutz and Berly, Aguascalientes, 16 Dec. 1915, 26 Feb., 22 July, 9 Sept. 1916, SD 812.00/16993, 17326, 18830, 19201.

632 *Mexican Herald*, 5, 21 July 1915; Taracena, *Verdadera revolución*, IV, pp. 34–6; see also Ulloa, *Revolución escindida*, pp. 220–1, for figures from Chihuahua.

633 *Jefe político*, Tepic, to Gobernación, 27 Oct. 1916, AG 81/21; c/o USS Buffalo, Mazatlán, 20 Dec. 1916, SD 812.00/20268.

634 Elsee, Frontera, 16 June 1917, FO 371/2962, 158767; cf. González Roa, *El Aspecto Agrario*, pp. 167–8.

635 González Roa, *El Aspecto Agrario*, p. 165, following Esquivel Obregón.

636 Alberto Pani, *La Higiene en Mexico* (Mexico, 1916), pp. 67–8.

637 USS Marietta, Tampico, 29 Mar. 1916, SD 812.00/17921.

638 J. B. Potter, 11 Apr. 1916, SD 812.00/17822; replies to Dept of Labour circular from Governors of Zacatecas, 12 Sept., and San Luis, 7 June 1916, Trabajo, 31/3/5/34. In Aguascalientes (1917) some peons were receiving two or three litres of corn per day, and no cash wage: Katz, *Secret War*, p. 287.

639 González Roa, *El Aspecto Agrario*, pp. 170–1.

640 Coen, Durango, 19 Aug., n.d., rec'd 29 Aug. 1916, 28 July 1917, SD 812.00/19056, 19042, 21161.

641 Gov. Triana to Carranza, 14 June 1916, AG 86/7; Bonsal report (n. 380); E. Espinosa Arriaga to Carranza, 12 Aug. 1916, AVC.

642 O'Hea, Gómez Palacio, 4 Jan. 1918, FO 371/3242, 30946.

643 Silliman, Eagle Pass, 29 July; Hanna, Monterrey, 4 Aug. 1916; SD 812.00/18821; 18853; Triana to Carranza (n. 641).

644 Cobb, El Paso, 14 Sept. 1916, SD 812.00/19217.

645 Doherty, Nogales, 4 Dec. 1916; border report, Del Rio, 13 Jan.; Hanna, Monterrey, 22 Feb.; Blocker, Eagle Pass, 23 Feb., 22 May, 4 June 1917; SD 812.00/20059; 20459, 20551; 20576, 20937, 20992.

646 Fall Report, testimony of S. Conger, p. 741. Cf. Richmond, 'El Nacionalismo de Carranza', p. 110, where the worst is said to be over by 1917 (wrong), thanks in particular to the efforts of Carranza (wrong).

647 Border report, Piedras Negras, 23 Aug.; Coen, Durango, 27 Aug. 1917; SD 812.00/21222; 21235.

648 Fletcher, Mexico City, 3 Oct.; Donald, Aguascalientes, 6 Oct. 1917; SD 812.00/21320; 21361. Beans, the other staple food, were also in short supply.

649 O'Hea, Gómez Palacio, 12 Nov. 1917, FO 371/2964, 244149.

650 González, *Pueblo en vilo*, p. 127.

651 L. D. Ricketts to H. L. Scott, 13 Apr. 1915, Scott Papers, box 18; E. Martínez, Jonacatepec, 1 Oct. 1914. M. Sosa, Amatitlán, 17 Apr. 1915, both to Zapata, Archivo del Gral E. Zapata.

652 Canada, Veracruz, 27 May 1916, SD 812.00/18282.

653 J. Rogers to H. P. Fletcher, 28 Apr. 1916, Fletcher Papers, box 4.

654 Col. Manuel Bauche Alcalde to Carranza, 17 Apr. 1917, AVC. The supplicant, facing bankruptcy and a family bereavement, received 1,000 pesos (silver) from the First Chief.

655 Simpich, Nogales, 8 Mar. 1915, SD 812.00/14579.

656 Davis, Guadalajara, 4 Nov. 1915, SD 812.00/16853.

657 Cobb, El Paso, 14 Apr., 14 Sept. 1916; Hanna, Monterrey, 16 July 1916; Simpich, Nogales, 23 Aug. 1916; SD 812.00/17854, 19217; 18736; 19112; petition to Carranza from Sta María Magdalena Cuayucatepec (Pue.), 2 Feb. 1915, AVC.

658 Bonsal report (n. 380).

659 Bonney, San Luis, 13 Apr. 1915, SD 812.50/7.

660 Davis, Guadalajara, 9 Dec. 1915, SD 812.00/17008.

661 Silliman, Saltillo, 3 May 1916, SD 812.00/18113; Thurstan, Mexico City, 27 Sept. 1918, FO 371/3247, 183019.

662 Berly, Aguascalientes, 8 July 1916, SD 812.00/18737; Cano in DDCC, II, p. 850; Thurstan (n. 661).

663 Ulloa, *Revolución escindida*, pp. 153–6; *Mexican Herald*, 20, 22 May 1915.

664 Border report, Mission, 9 Apr., Nogales, 23 Aug. 1916; Hanna, Monterrey, 29 July 1916; SD 812.00/17908, 19112; 18820.

665 Guyant, Progreso, 11 June; Bowman, Frontera, 9 June 1916; SD 812.00/18484; 18383; see also Silliman, Saltillo, 12 June 1916, SD 812.00/18398 and Falcón, 'Cedillo', p. 158, on food riots and robberies in San Luis, 1916.

666 Bowman, Frontera, 10 June 1916, SD 812.00/18386.

667 'There is naturally more or less privation', a spokesman conceded, '[but] there is nothing in the way of starvation or suffering'; reports to this effect were much exaggerated. See Ramon P. de Negri, *Official Statement Regarding the Food Situation in Mexico City* (San Francisco, 1915), p. 19.

668 *El Demócrata*, 23 Mar., 7 Sept. 1916.

669 *Ibid.*, 3, 9 May 1916; Blocker, Piedras Negras, 14 June 1916, SD 812.00/18489.

670 Pani, *Apuntes*, p. 227; *El Demócrata*, 4, 6, 12 Sept. 1916.

671 Governor Siurob to Carranza, 16 Sept. 1915, AJD: the points, made in 1915, were all the more valid a year later.

672 *El Demócrata*, 19 Sept. 1916.

673 *Ibid.*, 21 Mar. 1916.

674 Pani, *Apuntes*, p. 229; and Ulloa, *Revolución escindida*, on Conventionist measures.

675 The fears, if 'objectively' mistaken or exaggerated, were 'subjectively' real, in that the Constitutionalists genuinely entertained them; the alleged improvement in food supplies, however, was at once contradicted by the press itself.

676 *El Demócrata*, 7 May 1917.

677 See pp. 498, 500, 526.

678 Smith, *United States and Revolutionary Nationalism*, pp. 112–15.

679 Charles C. Cumberland, *Mexico, The Struggle for Modernity* (London, 1968), p. 372.

680 *Ibid.*; and note the figures in Richmond, 'The First Chief', p. 66, which tally, and bring out the fact that 1910 was a bad year anyway. Ruiz, *Great Rebellion*, p. 275 uses contemporary figures which differ – in the case of 1910 dramatically.

681 Cumberland, *Modernity*, p. 247.

682 Canada, Veracruz, 29 Feb. 1915, SD 812.00/17409; Cumberland, *Constitutionalist Years*, p. 398.

683 Governor Siurob to Carranza, 16 Sept. 1915, AJD.

684 See pp. 459–61.

685 Hewitt, Tuxpán, 13 May, 14 June 1918, FO 371/3244, 108160, /3245, 128549; A. Parry to Carranza, 20 Dec. 1916, AVC.

686 J. R. Ambrosius to Governor Siurob, Gro, 27 Oct. 1915, AG 84/35; C. Rochín to Carranza 8, 9, May 1916; José de Vizcaya to Carranza, 3 Aug. 1916; AVC. Note also the case of Col. Pablo Rodríguez (to Carranza, 7 May 1916): granted permission to export 10,000 hides at a time when such exports had been banned, Rodríguez was caught by a new decree which, by allowing export on payment of duty, deprived him of his anticipated profits (against which he had incurred 'heavy obligations'); accordingly, he requested tax exemption on the import of tobacco instead.

687 Weber, *Theory of Social and Economic Organization*, pp. 346–58.

688 *Jefe político*, Tepic, to Gobernación, 27 Oct. 1916, AG 81/21.

689 J. G. Nava to Carranza, 9 Dec. 1915, AVC

690 Pani, *La Higiene*, argues, with impressive detail, that the Federal capital was 'the most unhealthy city in the world', see p. 19.

691 *El Demócrata*, 6 Sept. 1916: an unusual piece of muckraking (if the phrase may be allowed) from the official press.

692 Bonsal report (n. 380), p. 10; Stevenson, Tapachula, 15 Oct. 1917, FO 371/2964, 233209; Lewis, *Pedro Martínez*, p. 171.

693 See the report of the Oficina de Bienes Intervenidos, Cd Jiménez (Chih.), 9 Oct. 1916, in Trabajo 31/3/5/3; *jefe político*, Tepic to Gobernación, 27 Oct. 1916, AG 81/21.

694 Norton, Durango, 17 May 1917, FO 371/2962, 138794; Arnulfo Sánchez, Tejamen, to Carranza, 10 Aug. 1916, AVC, on local conditions. On the Porfirian death rate: González Navarro, *Vida Social*, pp. 42–6.

695 Thurstan, Mexico City, 9 Feb. 1917, FO 371/2959, 60669.

696 *Ibid.*, where Thurstan's exaggerated – and apparently uncertain – estimate of the 1910 population of Zacatecas requires correction (he gives 35,000–40,000).

697 Moisés González Navarro, *Población y sociedad en México (1900–1970)* (Mexico, 2 vols., 1974), I, cuadro IV, facing p. 52.

698 Cumberland, *Constitutionalist Years*, p. 398.

699 William H. McNeil, *Plagues and People* (Oxford, 1977), p. 220; J. C. Cloudsley-Thompson, *Insects: A History* (London, 1976), pp. 102–3.

700 Carden, Mexico City, 15 July 1914, FO 371/2030, 32196; Cumberland, *Constitutionalist Years*, p. 137.

701 *Mexican Herald*, 18 Feb. 1915; Ulloa, *Revolución escindida*, p. 160.

702 Parker, Mexico City, 13 Dec. 1915, SD 812.00/16948; *El Demócrata*, 8 Feb., 23 Mar., 10 May, 23 Nov. 1916.

703 Thurstan, Mexico City, 14 Sept. 1918, FO 371/3246, 170921.

704 J. G. Nava to Carranza, 9 Dec. 1915, AVC.

705 Berly, Aguascalientes, 19 Aug.; Montague, El Paso, 30 Aug.; MacBurn, US Treasury, 27 Sept. 1916; SD 812.00/19056; 19083; 19321; Oviedo Mota, *El trágico fin*, II, p. 40.

706 Dickinson, San Luis, 21 Oct. 1916, 8 Jan. 1917; border report, Nogales, 28 Oct. 1916; Coen, Durango and San Antonio, 17 Nov. 1916, 16 Feb. 1917; SD 812.00/19604, 20241; 19804; 19901, 20545; Falcón, 'Cedillo', p. 130. A few observers distinguished between typhus and typhoid (whether correctly or not we do not know), most did not and probably could not; I have not aimed for a degree of diagnostic precision unwarranted by the sources.

707 Berly, Aguascalientes, 19 Aug. 1916, SD 812.00/19056; *El Demócrata*, 11 Nov. 1916; José María Rodríguez in DDCC, II, p. 654.

708 Gonzalez Navarro, *Población y sociedad*, I, pp. 348–50.

709 Oficina de Bienes Intervenidos, Cd Jiménez (Chih.), 9 Oct. 1916, Trabajo, 31/3/5/3; Patton Diary, 31 Mar. 1916, Patton Papers, box 1; O'Hea, Gómez Palacio, 3 Feb. 1917, FO 371/2959, 70100; Canada, Veracruz, 27 May 1916, SD 812.00/18282; Lewis, *Pedro Martínez*, pp. 139, 155–6.

710 C. Aguilar to J. Barragán, 17 Jan. 1917, AVC. The same report also mentions typhus and smallpox.

711 J. MacBurn, US Treasury, 27 Sept. 1916, SD 812.00/19321; Stevenson, Tapachula, 15 Oct. 1917, FO 371/2964, 233209.

712 Clarence Senior, *Land Reform and Democracy* (Gainesville, 1958), p. 76.

713 Dale, Chihuahua, 15 Oct., 1, 15 Nov. 1918, FO 371/3247, 191665, 205360, 207328.

714 González Navarro, *Población y sociedad*, I, pp. 348–50.

715 Taracena, *Verdadera revolución*, VI, p. 45; Womack, *Zapata*, p. 310.

716 A. J. P. Taylor, *English History 1914–1945* (Oxford, 1975), p. 155; González Navarro, *Población y sociedad*, I, p. 350, considers this estimate (300,000 dead) too high; cf. González, *Pueblo en vilo*, p. 132, n. 34, which cites an estimate of 500,000. Richard Collier, *The Plague of the Spanish Lady: The Influenza Pandemic of 1918–19* (London, 1974), pp. 305–6, gives a lower death rate for India (40 per 1,000) but a slightly higher one for Mexico (23 per 1,000), which represents the third highest in the world.

717 Chihuahua appears to be the only state with demographic figures for 1910–21: though these register a near 100% increase in mortality for 1918 (38 deaths per 1,000, compared with 20 for 1910, 21 for 1921) the remaining years of the revolution seem strangely static: 19 per 1,000 in 1916, 21 per 1,000 in 1917. For these, and the dubious San Pedro figures, see González Navarro, *Población y sociedad*, I, pp. 297–8, 349.

718 Taracena, *Verdadera revolución*, VI, p. 45.

719 González Navarro, *Población y sociedad*, i, pp. 349–50.

720 *Ibid.*, which suggests around 14 per 1,000 for Nuevo León, and about half that for Mexico City. At Orizaba some 20–25 were dying per day; over a month this would mean a death rate of some 20 per 1,000: Stacpoole, Orizaba, 30 Nov. 1918, FO 371/3247, 213867. San José de Gracia lost only 4 per 1,000: González, *Pueblo en vilo*, pp. 131–2.

721 Taracena, *Verdadera revolución*, VI, p. 45; King, Mexico City, 25 Nov. 1918, FO 371/3247, 205361; Casasola, *Historia gráfica*, II, p. 1295.

722 Womack, *Zapata*, p. 311.

723 King (n. 721).

724 Womack, *Zapata*, p. 328.

725 González, *Pueblo en vilo*, p. 132.

726 Wounds and pneumonia may also have helped. See Taracena, *Verdadera revolución*, VI, pp. 52–3; Oviedo Mota, *El trágico fin*, pp. 40, 46.

727 James Joll, *Europe Since 1870* (London, 1976), pp. 30–1. On Porfirian public health policy – and its awareness of foreign models – see González Navarro, *Vida social*, pp. 102–34, and n. 733 below.

728 Wilson, Tampico, 13 Apr. 1914, FO 371/2029, 23192.

729 *El Demócrata*, 2 Feb., 23 Mar., 10 Sept. 1916; see also the report of F. Valenzuela to the Consejo Superior de Salubridad, 3 Oct. 1916, AG 22/9; and J. Araujo to Gobernación, 13 Sept. 1916, AG 58/22.

730 *El Demócrata*, 6, 9 Mar., 16 Nov. 1916; G. Cordero to Gobernación, 31 Aug. 1916, AG 71/8 on health measures in Hidalgo; *jefe político* Tepic to Gobernación, 27 Oct. 1916, AG 81/21.

731 *El Demócrata*, 18 Mar. 1916.

732 Classically bureacratic in the sense of depending on rational procedures carried out by salaried officials – not, as in the case of food supply, on the 'irrational' initiatives of 'patrimonial retainers'. On the Guanajuato scheme: *El Demócrata*, 4 Sept. 1916.

733 Pani, *La higiene*, pp. 87–8 (on Vienna and Brussels). This combination of shared (international) trends and specific (Mexican) stimuli will also be noted in the formulation of economic nationalist policies.

734 See pp. 501–3.

735 *El Demócrata*, 10 May 1916; Alvarado, *Actuación*, p. 55.

736 Gavira, *Actuación*, pp. 180–1; *El Demócrata*, 5 Mar. 1916.

737 *Revolución social*, 27 Feb. 1915.

738 *Ibid.*, 17 June 1915; Salazar, *Las pugnas*, pp. 152–3. Ramón Eduardo Ruiz, *Labor and the Ambivalent Revolutionaries, Mexico 1911–23* (Baltimore, 1976), p. 48 somewhat anticipates and exaggerates the Casa's national effort; cf. Carr, 'Casa', p. 605.

739 J. García Núñez to Gobernación, 2 May 1915, AG 80/23; Salazar, *Las Pugnas*, pp. 125–7; Huitrón, *Orígines*, p. 283.

740 Huitrón, *Orígines*, pp. 280, 284, 289; Carr, 'Casa', p. 623; Joseph, *Revolution From Without* (book), pp. 109–10.

741 C. J. Reynaud, Río Blanco, to Trabajo, 12 Feb. 1915, Trabajo 31/2/1/14; Silliman, Veracruz, 19 Mar. 1915, SD 812.77/215.

742 *Revolución social* (Orizaba), 1, 30 May 1915.

743 Carr, 'Casa', p. 624.

744 Jenkins, Puebla, 10 Feb. 1915, SD 812.00/13824; Ruiz, *Labor*, p. 53.

745 Zubarán Capmany, quoted by Silliman, Veracruz, 16 Mar. 1915, SD 812.00/14610.

746 Ruiz, *Labor*, p. 53; Carr, 'Casa', p. 624, which notes that the Casa's recruits came from the ranks of the tram workers and brewery employees, rather than the textile operatives; see also A. Pacheco to M. López Jiménez, 9 May 1915, Trabajo, 34/1/14/28.

747 R. Díaz to M. López Jiménez, 22 Mar. 1915, Trabajo, 32/1/1/14; Canada, Veracruz, 13 Apr. 1915, SD 812.00/14982.

748 D. Galindo to M. López Jiménez, 22 Mar. 1915, Trabajo, 32/2/1/15.

749 Some, around Orizaba, even petitioned, with apparent success, for land grants. See J. García *et al*. to Trabajo, 3 Oct. 1914, Trabajo, 34/1/14/2; and above, p. 620 n.618. The political left – the Casa, the diminutive Partido Obrero Socialista – was similarly divided: Barry Carr, 'Marxism and Anarchism in the Formation of the Mexican Communist Party, 1910–19', *Hispanic American Historical Review*, LXIII (1983), p. 285.

750 A. Pacheco to M. López Jiménez, 30 Jan. 1915, Trabajo, 34/1/14/28.

751 See pp. 316–20.

752 Amaya, *Soberana convención*, pp. 259–60, 263–7.

753 Carr, 'Casa', p. 627.

754 See pp. 433–4, 471.

755 US Naval report, Veracruz, 9 Dec. 1914; Canada, Veracruz, 10 Nov. 1014, SD 812.00/14047; 13824, on supposed Constitutionalist incitement to strike.

756 Bevan, Tampico, 29 June 1915, SD 812.00/15367.

757 USS Marietta, Tampico, 3 May 1916; Blocker, Piedras Negras, 27, 28 Nov. 1916; SD 812.00/18156; 19964, 19976; Gov. Machorro to Carranza, 16 Aug. 1916, AJD.

758 Carr, 'Casa', pp. 618–19.

759 Cumberland, *Constitutionalist Years*, p. 26.

760 *Ibid.*; Canova, Mexico City, 10 Sept. 1914, SD 812.00/18156; Davis, Guadalajara, 7 Nov. 1914, SD 812.50/3.

761 M. Triana to Gobernación, 14 June 1916, AG, 86/7; *El Demócrata*, 3 Feb., 7 Mar. 1916; Hall, *Obregón*, pp. 197–8.

762 See pp. 470–1.

763 *Jefe político*, Tepic, to Gobernación, 27 Oct. 1916, AG 81/21.

764 *El Demócrata*, 25, 29 Nov. 1915, 26 Jan. 1916; Schmutz, Aguascalientes, 6 Mar.; Hanna, Monterrey, 27 Oct.; Rodgers, Mexico City, 12 Nov. 1916; SD 812.00/17476; 19664; 19847.

765 USS Kentucky, Veracruz, 10 Feb.; Canada, Veracruz, 29 Feb.; USS Marietta, 3 May 1916; SD 812.00/17310; 17410; 18156; *El Demócrata*, 2, 3 Feb. 1916; Huitrón, *Orígines*, pp. 292–3; Cobb, El Paso, 8, 15 Feb.; Edwards, Juárez, 24 Nov. 1916; SD 812.00/17345, 17280; 19950.

766 USS Kentucky, Veracruz, 31 May; border report, Laredo, 20 May 1916; SD 812.00/18367; 18284; Thurstan, Mexico City, 24 Nov. 1916, SD 812.00/19943.

767 Stacpoole, Orizaba, 30 Nov. 1918, FO 371/3247, 213867.

768 *El Demócrata*, 3 Mar. 1916: the speaker was Agustín Rosete, President of the Unión de Resistencia de Obreros.

769 Hobsbawm, *Primitive Rebels*, pp. 108, 124.

770 S. Rivas and L. Mendiola, Sociedad Mutua de Obreros Aquiles Serdán, Cananea, to Chamber of Deputies, Hermosillo, 27 Sept. 1919, in Trabajo 34/2/8.

771 J. Nolasco and R. Pimentel, CIDO–Mutua, Sociedad Cooperativa, Río Blanco, to Trabajo, 16 Feb. 19120, Trabajo, 34/2/8.

772 Hanna, Monterrey, 19 Dec. 1917, SD 812.00/21585; Husk, Santa Barbara, to Scott, 12 May 1915, Scott Papers, box 18.

773 Ruiz, *Labor*, p. 46.

774 Gruening, *Mexico and its Heritage*, p. 343; *Mexican Year Book*, 1922, p. 280.

775 Joseph, *Revolution From Without*, pp. 102–10.

776 See pp. 250, 506–8.

777 Meyer, *México y Estados Unidos*, p. 19.

778 R. Campbell, Mexico City, 9 Jan. 1918, FO 371/3242, 38000.

779 USS Marietta, Tampico, 2 Apr. 1916, SD 812.00/17903.

780 Gruening, *Mexico and its Heritage*, p. 342.

781 F. Garzall to Carranza, 8 May 1916, AVC.

782 F. Garzall to Carranza, 17 Feb. 1917, AVC.

783 Blocker, Piedras Negras, 28 Nov. 1916, 8 Jan. 1917, SD 812.00/19976, 20261.

784 See pp. 465–7, 489.

785 USS Marietta, Tampico, 30 Mar. 1916, SD 812.00/17921.

786 USS Marietta, Veracruz, 23 Mar. 1916, SD 812.00/17729.

787 A. Millán to C. Aguilar, 23 Mar. 1917, AVC. The 'gentleman' in question was Herón Proal, 'the anarchist tailor from Hidalgo', organiser of a regional labour confederation in 1916 and later – more successfully – of the Veracruz tenants' strike of 1922: Fowler, *Agrarian Radicalism*, pp. 26, 32.

788 USS Marietta, Tampico, 5 Apr. 1916, SD 812.00/17921; and Ruiz, *Labor*, p. 53.

789 USS Marietta (n. 788).

790 USS Marietta, Tampico, 11 May 1916, SD 812.00/18271. A strike by the lightermen had led to picketing, scabbing and violence; the strikers' protest was directed particularly against American managers and Jamaican blacklegs.

791 Anti-Americanism and economic nationalism did not necessarily correlate (positively); indeed, they may have correlated negatively. Rebel leaders – like Nafarrette – who were unresponsive, brusque or hostile towards Americans (*ergo*, anti-American) were often indifferent to the question of American economic penetration, keen to maintain business activity, and tough on the (foreign-employed) working class. Conversely, leaders – like Pastor Rouaix – who exuded responsibility and reasonableness went on to become the architects of economic nationalist legislation (and related labour reform); see Knight, 'Nationalism, Xenophobia and Revolution', pp. 150–6, 274–98.

792 USS Annapolis, Tampico, 26 Sept. 1917, SD 812.00/21362; Col. Pedro Chapa, commanding earlier in 1916, had also taken a tough line with union leaders: Dawson, Tampico, 2 Mar. 1916, SD 812.00/17448.

793 Salazar, *Las pugnas*, pp. 148–50.

794 Joseph, *Revolution From Without*, pp. 110–1.

795 Lawton, Nogales, 12 Sept. 1917, SD 812.00/21282.

796 Caballero to Carranza, 15 Nov. 1916, AVC; border report, Laredo, 20 May 1916, SD 812.00/18284.

797 Lux, Veracruz, 29 Dec. 1915; USS Marietta, Tampico, 31 Mar. 1916; SD 812.00/17058; 17921.

798 US Naval report, Salina Cruz, 6 Nov. 1915; border report, Nogales, 8 Mar. 1916; SD 812.00/168430 17592.

799 USS Petrel, Tampico, 27 June 1915, SD 812.00/15496.

800 Ruiz, *Labor*, p. 54.

801 Carranza to Sub-Secretary of Railways, 28 Nov. 1915; to C. Aguilar, 27 Jan. 1916; AJD; see also *El Demócrata*, 2 Feb. 1916.

802 *El Demócrata*, 12 Sept. 1916; Salazar, *Las pugnas*, p. 133.

803 J. G. Nava to R. Múzquiz, 15, 23, 27 Oct. 1915, SRE, legajo 794, 88-R-31, pp. 14, 71, 181.

804 Salazar, *Las pugnas*, pp. 153–4.

805 Ruiz, *Labor*, pp. 55–6; Córdova, *La ideología*, pp. 212–13; cf. Richmond, 'First Chief', pp. 95–6, where this bizarre apologia runs full tilt into reality.

806 Salazar, *Las pugnas*, p. 166; Carr, 'Casa', p. 629; USS Buffalo, Mazatlán, 30 Sept. 1916, SD 812.00/19571.

807 See p. 106.

808 Barrón to Carranza, 3 Aug. 1916, AVC; see also his article in *El Demócrata*, 6 Aug. 1916. Barrón readily named names (such as Dr Atl's) and called for the recently closed *Acción Mundial* to be reopened as a Constitutionalist paper – under his (Barrón's) editorship. On Barrón's career: Cosio Villegas, *Vida política*, II, pp. 694, 748.

809 The text of the decree, dated 1 Aug. 1916 can be found in AVC, doc. 10097; see also Salazar, *Las pugnas*, pp. 205–7.

810 Salazar, *Las pugnas*, pp. 167–9; *El Demócrata*, 19 Jan. 1916.

811 Alvarado, *La reconstrucción*, I, p. 269; see also Córdova, *La ideología*, p. 211.

812 *El Demócrata*, 11 Mar. 1916.

813 *Ibid*.

814 *Ibid*., 19 Sept. 1916: 'this function of moderating, compensating and harmonizing rights is the highest function appertaining to the State, and, in the opinion of contemporary civilization, it is the fundamental reason for the existence of governments'.

815 Ruiz, *Labor*, p. 57; Carr, 'Casa', p. 616.

816 Ruiz, *Labor*, p. 70; Carr, *Movimiento Obrero*, I, p. 135, on continued unrest.

817 *Germinal*, 19 Aug. 1917. For examples of harassment: *Germinal*, 21 July 1917, *Palanca Obrera* (Torreón), 9 Sept. 1917.

818 *Evolución* (Zac.), 1 Oct. 1917; Carr, 'Marxism and Anarchism', p. 290.

819 *El Obrero Libre* (Coatepec, Ver.), 26 Dec. 1917.

820 USS Nebraska, Veracruz, 7 Sept. 1916; Blocker, Piedras Negras, 17 Feb. 1917; SD 812.00/19221; 20533.

821 José Neira *et al.* of the Asociación de Obreros Industriales de la Revolución Mexicana, Río Blanco, to Gral Francisco Villa, 15 Dec. 1916, AJD (the same letter is enclosed in Manuel González to Villa, 12 Feb. 1917, SRE legajo 816, 101-R-2).

822 DDCC, II, pp. 846, 848–50.

823 See pp. 487–8.

824 The present analysis focuses on 1915–20 and, obviously enough, the 1920s witnessed new developments; most of the major trends of the 1920s, however, can be discerned during the Carrancista presidency – some in embryo, some surprisingly mature. Agua Prieta, in other words, did not mark a fundamental rupture (though it is a convenient place to stop).

825 Meyer, *Cristero Rebellion*, p. 20.

826 See vol. I, pp. 100, 429–31.

827 Lefaivre, Mexico City, 14 May 1916, AAE, Mex. Pol. Int., N.S. XIII, B/25/1, n. 33, Simpich, Nogales, 6 Apr. 1915, SD 812.00/14863.

828 Mendoza, *Lírica narrativa*, pp. 41–2 (no date is given).

829 US Naval report, La Paz, 7 May 1915, SD 812.00/15055; Elsee, Frontera, 16 June 1917, FO 371/2962, 158767.

830 Lewis, *Pedro Martínez*, pp. 155–6; Bonsal report (n. 380), p. 17; Schmutz, Aguascalientes, 5 June 1915, SD 812.00/15194.

831 Coen, Durango, 31 Mar. 1916, SD 812.00/17756; Husk, Parral, to Scott, 12 May 1915, Scott Papers, box 18.

832 See pp. 83–4.

833 *El Demócrata*, 5 Sept. 1916; Pablo González to Carranza, 27 Mar. 1916; AVC; Fabela, DHRM, RRC, V, p. 315; and above, pp. 401–2.

834 Petition from San Lorenzo Teotipilco to Carranza, 10 Jan. 1916, AVC; Oscar Schmieder, *The Settlements of the Tzapotec and Mije Indians* (Berkeley, 1930), p. 30; Ian Jacobs, *Ranchero Revolt. The Mexican Revolution in Guerrero* (Austin, 1982), p. 101; Taracena, *Verdadera revolución*, VI, pp. 9, 35.

835 A. Millán to F. Múgica, 20 May 1919 in María y Campos, *Múgica*, p. 136; *El Dictamen*, 22 Aug. 1917 in Fabela, DHRM, RRC, V, pp. 299–300; Fowler, 'Revolutionary caudillos', p. 185.

836 Bonsal report (n. 380), p. 19; Hewett, Tuxpán, 26 Sept. 1917, FO 371/2964, 222284; Gov. Machorro to Carranza, 16 Aug. 1916, AJD.

837 Cobb, El Paso, 15 Feb. 1916, conveying report of an American miner from Chalchihuites, SD 812.00/17347; *El Demócrata*, 19 Sept. 1916.

838 Coen, Durango, 25 Mar. 1916, SD 812.00/17733.

839 The character and failings of the Carrancista army will be considered shortly. In the particular case of Chihuahua, Pershing was a scathing, if partisan, critic: 'this *de facto* outfit is impotent', he wrote to Wood, 21 Oct. 1916, 'it is pitiful to see their weak and puerile efforts. Unless very superior in numbers, these government troops are all afraid of Villa': Pershing Papers, box 215.

840 Katz, *Secret War*, pp. 324–5, sees the Chihuahua *defensas sociales* as middle-class associations, though the point is not proven. It presupposes a degree of class polarisation and continued, popular support for Villa after 1915 which may not be warranted.

841 Ximena Sepúlveda Otaiza, *La Revolución en Bachíniva* (Mexico, 1975), p. 11.

842 Cobb, El Paso, 13 Jan. 1916, SD 812.00/17092; Taracena, *Verdadera revolución*, v, p. 103, VI, p. 124.

843 Chihuahua report in Hohler, Mexico City, 15 May 1918, FO 371/3244, 97566.

844 Gruening, *Mexico and its Heritage*, pp. 410–11; and above, n. 835.

845 Machorro Narváez in DDCC, II, pp. 99.

846 Davis, Guadalajara, 20, 23 Oct. 1915, SD 812.00/16780, 16783. Two months later Davis again reported that 'the general sentiment of the peaceable peon and general citizen is very strongly in favor of the Villa cause': 9 Dec. 1915, SD 812.00/17008. The character of this residual Villismo will be explored shortly.

847 Brereton, Aguascalientes, 29 Oct.; Alger, Mazatlán, 4 Nov.; Bevan, Tampico, 11 Nov. 1915; SD 812.00/16800; 16796; 16813.

848 E.g., *El Demócrata*, 4 Mar., 4 Nov. 1916.

849 Parker, Mexico City, 23 Mar.; Cobb, El Paso, 20 Apr. 1916; SD 812.00/17615; 17935; see also USS Marietta, 14, 23, Mar. 1916, SD 812.00/17637, 17729.

850 Silliman, 8 June 1914, SD 812.44/C23/1; cf. Richmond, 'First Chief', p. iv.

851 Urquizo, *Páginas*, pp. 149–50 (Urquizo was a Carrancista *adicto*).

852 Blasco Ibáñez, *Mexico in Revolution*, p. 166; Lefaivre, Mexico City, 22 Apr. 1916, AAE, Mex. Pol. Int., N.S., XIII, n. 28.

853 Womack, *Zapata*, p. 221.

854 D. G. Lamadrid to Carranza, 17 Mar. 1916, AVC; Rutherford, *Mexican Society*, p. 166.

855 *Ibid*. There is plenty of evidence not only of press censorship, but also of positive press campaigns to exalt Carranza; note, for example, Calixto Maldonado to Alvarado, 1 Oct. 1916, AJD.

856 Bonney, San Luis, 29 Dec. 1915, SD 812.00/17052 (Bonney was one of the most balanced and perceptive of American consular officials).

857 Cf. Obregón, *Ocho mil kilómetros*, p. 447 and Davis, Guadalajara, 19 Feb., 7 Mar. 1916, SD 812.00/17659, 17666. On his occasional departures from military narrative, Obregón does not convince.

858 Rutherford, *Mexican Society*, p. 165. When government troops looked to invoke the charisma of a caudillo it was to Obregón, not Carranza, that they turned: hence they attacked Torreón (Jan. 1917) to cries of 'Viva Obregón': O'Hea, Gómez Palacio, 11 Jan. 1917, FO 371/2959, 41521. Carranza's cronies, of course, feared and resented Obregón's elevation to 'demi-God' status: L. Rivas Iruz to Carranza, 4 May 1916, AVC.

859 Womack, *Zapata*, p. 210; Quirk, *Mexican Revolution*, pp. 9–10.

860 O'Hea, Gómez Palacio, 1 Oct. 1918, FO 371/3247, 18312.

861 See the report of F. Thompson, who managed an American colony in southern Sinaloa, in USS Denver, San Diego, 20 Apr. 1916, SD 812.00/18063.

862 Continental Mexican Rubber Co. representative, Torreón, 29 Mar. 1916; USS Nashville, Tampico, 26 Nov. 1916; SD 812.00/17792; 20065; Gavira, *Actuación*, p. 147.

863 J. G. Nava to Carranza, 9 Dec. 1915, AVC. In the bars of Tepic (1917) it was even worse: 'at night, when the *pelados* get drunk with the soldiers themselves they cry "death to old whiskers and his bad government"': border report, 31 Mar. 1917, SD 812.00/20793.

864 Pershing to Wood, 10 Sept. 1916, Pershing Papers, box 215; O'Hea, enclosed in Cobb, El Paso, 23 Feb. 1916; border report, Nogales, 3 May 1916; USS Albany, Manzanillo, 7 Mar. 1917; border report, 31 Mar. 1917; SD 812.00/17342; 18177; 20705; 20793.

865 Useful lists of Carrancista governors and military commanders are to be found in Obregón to Carranza, 24 Mar. 1916, AVC, and Funston to State Department, 9 Sept. 1916, SD 812.00/19168.

866 Alvarado, *Actuación*, pp. 17, 53.

867 Gavira, *Actuación*, pp. 132–47.

868 *Ibid.*, p. 144.

869 Taracena, *Verdadera revolución*, IV, pp. 134–5.

870 *El Demócrata*, 6 Sept. 1916; cf. Fabela, DHRM, RRC, V, p. 425 – *El Demócrata*, harping on the theme of 'reaction' again.

871 *El Demócrata*, 14, 16, 23, 26 Mar. 1916; Taracena, *Verdadera revolución*, IV, pp. 87–91, 113, 158, 163.

872 *El Demócrata*, 15 Nov. 1915.

873 Taracena, *Verdadera revolución*, IV, pp. 75–82; J. G. Nava to Carranza, 9 Oct. 1915; AVC; Junco, *Carranza*, pp. 117–25.

874 Fabela, DHRM, RRC, V, pp. 317, 321–2; Taracena, *Verdadera revolución*, IV, mentions mob acclamation of the death of García Granados.

875 Múgica to Alvarado, 29 Aug. 1916, in María y Campos, *Múgica*, p. 102.

876 *El Demócrata*, 2 Mar. 1916; Taracena, *Verdadera revolución*, IV, pp. 95, 103, 104, 242.

877 Manuel Zapata to Aguilar, 16 Apr. 1917, AVC.

878 Salvador Moreno to Carranza, 12 May 1916, AVC.

879 Taracena, *Verdadera revolución*, IV, p. 115; *El Demócrata*, 17 Dec. 1915.

880 *El Demócrata*, 24 Mar. 1916; D. G. Lamadrid to G. Ugarte, 16 Dec. 1915; employees of Dirección General del Catastro to Carranza, 31 Jan. 1916; AVC.

881 *El Demócrata*, 4, 7, 16 Mar. 1916; Gavira, *Actuación*, pp. 177–9.

882 Among Gavira's victims at San Luis was Jesus Silva Herzog, later a luminary of the official left, then a young journalist on *La Patria*, against whom 'irrefutable proof' was brought of his hostility to Constitutionalism. A court-martial sentenced him to three years gaol, which Gavira increased to eight; in fact, he served much less: Gavira, *Actuación*, pp. 134–5; and, for the victim's version, Wilkie, *México visto en el siglo XX*, pp. 614–18.

883 Múgica to Alvarado, 29 Aug. 1916, in María y Campos, *Múgica*, p. 100.

884 P. de la Garza to Carranza, 15 Dec. 1916, AVC.

885 F. Montalvo to G. Ugarte, 19 Mar. 1917, AVC.

886 F. Cuevas to Carranza, 2 Aug. 1916, AVC.

887 Rutherford, *Mexican Society*, pp. 167–8; on the manufacture of personal myths, note also Schryer, *Rancheros of Pisaflores*, p. 69; Warman, *Y venimos a contradecir*, p. 161.

888 This is not to say that Stalinism – whether in the mild, Mexican version or the full-blown original – lacked all justification, given the prevailing circumstances.

889 *El Demócrata*, 3, 5, Feb. 1916.

890 J. G. Nava, 2 Dec. 1915; E. Sandoval, 31 Jan. 1916; H. Barrón, 3 Aug. 1916; all to Carranza, AVC; reports of the Agencia Confidencial to Gobernación, 26, 28 Oct., 2 Nov. 1915, AJD. Gavira, *Actuación*, pp. 168, 171, comments on the usefulness of his spy/secret police network in the hostile ambience of Chihuahua (he found women particularly efficient: another aspect of 'women in the revolution' which recent studies have overlooked).

891 J. M. Sáenz to Carranza, 8 May 1916, AVC.

892 Affidavit of D. Johnson, 7 Aug. 1916, AVC.

893 In which respect (official) Constitutionalist expropriations clearly differed from those of

'mature' agrarian movements, like Zapatismo or Cedillismo. Even so, such 'political' confiscations could – given the breadth of landlord support for the old regime – have an important, if not always permanent effect on rural land tenure and class relations.

894 See pp. 180–2, 459–65.

895 Secretary of Gobernación to Hacienda, 31 July 1915, AG 60/33. These 'urban' properties included several *ranchos* and fractions of *ranchos*; eleven were unclassified as regards ownership. Several (non-clerical) properties were simply deemed confiscated 'by order of the state governor', 'by order of General Pablo González', or 'for infringing the orders of the headquarters of the Army Corps of the East', without further explanation.

896 Sub-Secretary of Gobernación to Gov. Castro, Pue., 14 Oct., to Gov. Cepeda, Mex., 5 Sept., to Sub-Secretary of Hacienda, 6 Sept. 1916, AG 78/48, 85/6, 85/36.

897 *El Pueblo*, 21 Sept. 1917, in Fabela, DHRM, RRC, v, p. 395.

898 Taracena, *Verdadera revolución*, v, p. 72; see the draft addressed to Manuel Aguirre Berlanga, 3 Apr. 1917, AVC.

899 Carranza to Gov. Dávila, SLP, 27 Jan. 1916, AVC, ordering the closure of *La Patria* (Silva Herzog's paper) and the arrest of its staff; and Fabela, DHRM, RRC, v, p. 384.

900 Taracena, *Verdadera revolución*, vi, pp. 110–13. Diéguez's comment was directed specifically at René Capistrán Garza, later president of the Catholic youth movement (ACJM).

901 *El Demócrata*, 11 Mar. 1916 (banning of a Catholic book on civics); Taracena, *Verdadera revolución*, vi, p. 191, on theatre censorship.

902 *El Demócrata*, 10, 12 Nov. 1916, which also rebuts *El Pueblo*'s claim to be profit-making.

903 *Ibid.*, 5 Sept. 1916; Taracena, *Verdadera revolución*, v, pp. 82, 225.

904 See n. 157, 158; Taracena, *Verdadera revolución*, v, p. 53 (though there were diplomatic reasons for playing down publicity of the telegram: Katz, *Secret War*, pp. 362–7).

905 Katz, *Secret War*, pp. 446–8, 458.

906 Taracena, *Verdadera revolución*, v, p. 200.

907 Manero, *Por el honor*, pp. 12, 14, 34, 44–5.

908 Gregorio A. Velázquez, 'El Señor Carranza y su Acción Heróica dentro de México', in Fabela, DHRM, RRC, vi, pp. 150–217, especially pp. 150–2.

909 Palavicini, intro. to Manero, *Por el honor*, p. 5 (admittedly, Palavicini was a journalist himself).

910 C. Maldonado to S. Alvarado, 1 Oct. 1916, AJD.

911 Taracena, *Verdadera revolución*, v, p. 72.

912 Thurstan, Mexico City, 16 Apr.; Cummins, Mexico City, 22 June 1917; FO 371/2960, 96568; 2962, 148197.

913 Maldonado to Alvarado (n. 910).

914 Cummins, Mexico City, 13 Mar. 1919, FO 371/3827, 40943.

915 Knight, 'Peasant and Caudillo', especially pp. 51–8.

916 Rodgers, Mexico City, 28 July 1916, SD 812.00/18815.

917 See pp. 490–3.

918 Silliman, Veracruz, 16, 17, 18, 19 June 1915; Murray, Mexico City, 27 Mar. 1916; Rodgers, Mexico City, 15 May, 10 June 1916; SD 812.002/59, 60, 62; 66; 69, 70; Rodgers, Mexico City, 28 July 1916, SD 812.00/18815; Hall, *Obregón*, p. 142; Cumberland, *Constitutionalist Years*, p. 333.

919 Lux, 26 Jan., Canada, 11 Sept. 1916, both Veracruz, SD 812.00/17232, 19256; Aguilar to Millán, 13 May 1916, AVC.

920 Cobb, El Paso, 8 Jan., 14 July, 6 Nov., 18 Dec.; Rodgers, Mexico City, 12 Nov.; Carothers, Juárez, 18 Dec. 1916; SD 812.00/17098, 18732, 19755, 20093; 19847; 20099.

921 Treviño to Carranza, 25 Mar. 1917, AVC.

922 Border report, Nogales, 15 Jan. 1916, SD 812.00/17152; Gavira, *Actuación*, pp. 167–8, 183; border report, Nogales, 14 Oct. 1916, SD 812.00/19654; Jacobs, *Ranchero Revolt*, pp. 104–5.

923 Summerlin, Mexico City, 30 Jan. 1918, SD 812.00/21711; Jacobs, *Ranchero Revolt*, pp. 106–7.

924 Buve, 'Peasant movements', pp. 142–3; A. Machorro to Carranza, 12 Aug. 1916, AVC; Mariscal to Pablo González, 12 May 1916, AVC; USS Denver, Acapulco, 3 June 1916, SD 812.00/18495. At Ometepec, scene of the 1911 jacquerie, the 'illiterate bandolero and mountaineer' Manuel Hernández installed himself as boss, defended his fief against Zapatista threats, and governed in arbitrary, populist style, alarming the local well-to-do, who engineered his overthrow and execution in 1919. But that was not the end of the local popular challenge. I am endebted to Asgar Simonsen for this information.

925 J. B. Body, Mexico City, 29 Apr. 1917, FO 371/2960, 102949. Examples will follow.

926 Cf. Douglas W. Richmond, 'Carranza: The Authoritarian Populist as Nationalist President' in George Wolfskill and Douglas W. Richmond, eds., *Essays on the Mexican Revolution: Revisionist Views of the Leaders* (Austin, 1979), pp. 57, 66, on Carranza's 'well-run machine' staffed by obedient and idealistic generals. Manero, Velázquez and their fellow-hacks did not labour in vain!

927 Gavira, *Actuación*, p. 162. Obregón vs. Treviño cannot be explained in terms of Sonora vs. Coahuila, since Obregón's local protégé and Treviño's replacement was another Coahuilan, Murguía.

928 See pp. 476–7.

929 Angus W. McDonald Jr., *The Urban Origins of Rural Revolution: Elites and Masses in Hunan Province, China, 1911–27* (Berkeley, 1978), p. 318.

930 Obregón's defence of the military's right to determine the revolutionary settlement was quite compatible with both an aversion to praetorianism ('the unbridled ambitions of an odious militarism') and a long-term commitment to civilian political institutions; the military, in other words, should eschew factionalism, participate in the post-revolutionary settlement, and, in doing so, convert their own (legitimate) military power into civilian political – and economic – power, as Obregón himself did. Hence the champion of the military in 1914–15 became – along with Calles and Amaro – an architect of demilitarisation in the 1920s. See Hall, *Obregón*, pp. 68–9, 143.

931 Border report, Nogales, 5 Aug. 1916, SD 812.00/19038, relaying the comments of Rodolfo Garduño, one-time jefe político of Hermosillo. The elections in question had been held in Jalisco, Tepic and Sinaloa.

932 Alvarado to Carranza, 26 Sept. 1916, Fabela, DHRM, RRC, v, p. 133.

933 J. G. Nava to Carranza, 2 Dec. 1915 (twice), AVC, reporting anti-military oratory in San Luis; Courget, Mexico City, 6 Dec. 1916, AAE, Mex. Pol. Int., N.S. XIII, n. 113, quoting Palavicini.

934 Hall, *Obregón*, p. 170.

935 Introduction to Manero, *Por el honor*, p. 5.

936 Canada, Veracruz, 7 May 1915, SD 812.00/15068; Silliman, Veracruz, 16 June 1915, SD 812.00/59; Hall, *Obregón*, p. 142.

937 Canada and Silliman, both 18 June 1915, SD 812.002/61, 62.

938 Silliman, Mexico City, 12 Feb. 1916, SD 858.29/23; *El Demócrata*, 5, 7 Nov. 1916.

939 Katz, *Secret War*, p. 459.

940 Cumberland, *Constitutionalist Years*, p. 362; Hall, *Obregón*, pp. 143–4.

941 DDCC, II, pp. 243–4; Rutherford, *Mexican Society*, p. 216; cf. Madero *Sucesión presidencial*, pp. 30–61, 87, 169–70.

942 DDCC, II, p. 1017, the words of Modesto González Galindo.

943 *Excelsior*, 29 June 1918; Taracena, *Verdadera revolución*, VI, p. 44.

944 *El Universal*, 18 Apr. 1917; Cummins, Mexico City, 22 June 1917, FO 371/2962, 148197.

945 Taracena, *Verdadera revolución*, VI, pp. 44, 214. Banderas had also been out for the blood of

Vasconcelos, who had allegedly swindled him out of a legal fee: Alessio Robles, *Mis andanzos*, p. 186.

946 Rutherford, *Mexican Society*, p. 216; Rodgers, Mexico City, 10 June 1916, SD 812.002/70.

947 Canada, Veracruz, 7 May 1915 (relaying an anon. report), SD 812.00/15068; Green, Huasteca Petroleum Co., 1 Mar. 1918, in FO 371/3243, 70846.

948 Hall, *Obregón*, p. 148.

949 Cummins, Mexico City, 14 Dec. 1917, FO 371/2964, 237691; Summerlin, Mexico City, 14, 16, 21 Dec. 1917, 14 Jan. 1918, SD 812.00/21547, 21558, 21579, 21650.

950 F. Cárdenas to Gobernación, 3 Feb. 1915, AG 873; Terrazas memo., 'Asuntos que tratar con Gral Villa', STA, box 84 (Villista abuses); and, on the 'numberless complaints' registered against the military at Lampazos, see *alcalde* to state governor, 11 Aug. 1915, 1 Feb. 1916, Lampazos Archive, r. 860.

951 Schmutz, Aguascalientes, 4 May 1916, SD 812.00/18132; Cobb, El Paso, 3 Oct. 1916, SD 812.00/19403; municipal agent, Ocotlán, to Gov. Machorro, 10 Sept. 1916, AG 58/17; Stacpoole, Orizaba, 28 Feb. 1918, FO 371/3243, 58877.

952 Harrison, Guadalajara, 15 May 1917, FO 371/2962, 138791: the reference was specifically to La Unión de Tula.

953 *El Demócrata*, 12 Feb. 1916 (forced recruitment), 3 May 1916 (sequestering); DDCC, ii, pp. 945–7, 1083–4, on drunkenness and popular antipathy to the troops; Gobernación to War Dept, 18 Sept. 1916, AG 71/72, concerning soldiers' robbery from sharecroppers on the Xico Hacienda (Mex.).

954 O'Hea, Gómez Palacio, 17 Apr. 1917, FO 371/2960, 107192; Gral Carlos Osuna to Carranza, 13 May 1916, AVC; and press reports, 29 May 1916, AVC, doc. 12949.

955 Blocker, Eagle Pass and Piedras Negras, 12 Nov. 1915, 29 Sept. 1916, SD 812.00/16806, 19356.

956 Jacbos, 'Rancheros', p. 90.

957 *Ibid.*, p. 91 notes that a second generation of Figueroas recovered power, not as independent caciques but loyal clients of the new revolutionary state: see also the same author's *Ranchero Revolt*, p. 130ff.

958 Coen, Durango, 22 Jan., 11 Feb. 1916, SD 812.00/17205, 17294; Gavira, *Actuación*, p. 202, characteristically blames conservative machinations.

959 Coen, Durango, 2 Mar., 3 May 1916, SD 812.00/17422, 18141.

960 *Ibid.*, 3 May, 13 June 1916, SD 812.00/18141, 18488.

961 Coen, San Antonio, 28 July 1917, SD 812.00/21161; Gámiz, *Durango*, p. 61; Rouaix, *Diccionario*, pp. 38–40.

962 Cobb, El Paso, 22, 23 Mar., 3 Oct.; Funston, Ft Sam Houston, 10 Apr.; Pershing, 14 Apr. 1916; SD 812.00/17583, 17596, 17843; 17808, 18072. Despite the family's anti-American reputation, Pershing found Luis Herrera to be 'rather formal and reticent' – illiterate, but not hostile; while his father, as mayor of Parral, calmed an anti-American demonstration.

963 Grimaldo, *Apuntes*, p. 13; and above, p. 358.

964 See Falcón, 'Cedillo', pp. 230–40, 280, 311.

965 Cumberland, *Constitutionalist Years*, p. 212 (based on a presidential *informe*); Richmond, 'First Chief', p. 186, cites an American estimate of 184,000 (1918). Wilkie, *Federal Expenditure*, pp. 102–3, puts (official) military expenditure at between half and two-thirds of total government expenditure between 1917 and 1920. J. MacLachlan, military attaché, Washington, 17 Dec. 1918, FO 371/3826, 472, put it as high as 85%.

966 Coen, Durango, 11 Feb. 1916, SD 812.00/17294; Alvarado to Carranza, 1 Mar. 1916, Fabela, DHRM, RRC, v, p. 67; anon. memo., Guerrero, n.d., late 1915, AJD. Richmond, 'First Chief', pp. 186–7, suggests that official rosters should be deflated by 35–40% to allow for padded payrolls.

967 Rutherford, *Mexican Society*, p. 218.

968 Aguilar, 'Relevant Tradition', pp. 115–17.

969 O'Hea, Gómez Palacio, 12 Nov. 1917, FO 371/2964, 244149.

970 Cobb, El Paso, 24 Oct.; Coen, Durango, 17 Nov. 1916; SD 812.00/19630; 19901; Taracena, *Verdadera revolución*, IV, p. 220; O'Hea, Gómez Palacio, 11 Jan. 1917, FO 371/2959, 1521. Coen, Durango, 22 July 1915, SD 812.00/15586 noted that three-quarters of the Villista troops sent to stop the Carrancista advance at Pedriceña were mere adolescents.

971 To police Guanajuato, the state governor told Carranza, 'we only lack arms: soldiers we have aplenty': Siurob to Carranza, 16 Sept. 1915, AJD. Stephen Bonsal encountered 'Indians' joining the army in Veracruz, where they received two pesos a day; when asked why they were joining up they replied: 'pa' comer tenemos' ('we gotta eat'): Bonsal report (n. 380), p. 21.

972 Coen, Durango, 17 Nov. 1916; US Naval reports, Salina Cruz and La Paz, 9 Nov. 1915; SD 812.00/19907; 16843.

973 Obregón, *Ocho mil kilómetros*, pp. 338, 348.

974 Lawton, Nogales, 15 Nov. 1918, SD 812.00/21490.

975 Trinidad Vega and Rivera Marrufo interviews, PHO 1/126, pp. 47–53, /63, p. 19.

976 Border report, Laredo, 25 Mar. 1916; Blocker, Piedras Negras, 11 Oct. 1916; SD 812.00/17754; 19544; Patton Diary, 25 Mar. 1916, Patton Papers, box 1.

977 Edwards, Juárez, 14 Jan.; Letcher, Chihuahua, 9 Feb. 1916; SD 812.00/17095; 17268.

978 Lárraga to Secretary of War, 19 June 1916, AJD; Lewis, *Pedro Martínez*, p. 155.

979 Anon. memo., Guerrero, to Carranza, n.d., late 1915, AJD.

980 In one Saltillo garrison of 400 men, 324 were reckoned to have syphilis; a higher ratio even than that among the Mexico City clergy (cf. DDCC, II, p. 652; Obregón, *Ocho mil kilómetros*, p. 290). Allegations of rampant hereditary syphilis (by, for example, Bulnes, *El verdadero Díaz*, p. 423, or Senator Fall, González Navarro, *Población y Sociedad*, I, pp. 375–6) may be treated sceptically, but it is worth noting that recorded deaths from syphilis, though small in absolute terms, doubled in relative incidence between 1903 and 1922 (whether this reflected a *pro rata* increase in the disease, or improved diagnosis cannot be said): see González Navarro, p. 371.

981 Over a hundred so-called Carrancistas mutinied and turned 'Villista' at Salta Barranca, southern Veracruz, when ordered to leave the region to fight in the Bajío; they included one detachment of peons and sugar mill workers who had joined the army on the understanding that 'under no circumstances would they be compelled or even asked to leave the town, the object of the formation of this garrison being purely for local defence': Spillard, Ingenio San Francisco, 24 May 1915, SD 812.00/15352; Siurob to Carranza, 16 Sept. 1915, AJD.

982 Pershing to Roosevelt, 24 May 1916, Pershing Papers, box 177; J. B. Potter to Lansing, 11 Apr. 1916, enclosing Tlahualilo report, SD 812.00/17822; note also Gavira, *Actuación*, pp. 194–6, on problems of pay, drink and desertion.

983 Gov. Machorro to Carranza, 16 Aug. 1916, AJD; Gral Francisco Mariel to Aguilar, 4 Jan. 1916, AVC.

984 O'Hea, Gómez Palacio, 10 Jan. 1917, FO 371/2959, 41521; DDCC, II, p. 100; border report, Nogales, 23 Aug. 1916, SD 812.00/19112.

985 Cobb, El Paso, 3 Oct. 1916, SD 812.00/19403; other cases have been cited.

986 Hall, *Obregón*, pp. 156–9.

987 US naval report, Guaymas, 30 June 1915, SD 812.00/15653; cf. Gavira, *Actuación*, p. 196.

988 Alger, Mazatlán, 21 Feb.; Coen, Durango, 22 Jan. 1916; SD 812.00/17454; 17205.

989 Blocker, Piedras Negras, 11 Oct., 1916, SD 812.00/19544; O'Hea, Gómez Palacio, 11 Jan. 1917, FO 371/2959, 41521.

990 Richmond, 'First Chief', pp. 31–3; *El Demócrata*, 2 Nov. 1916.

991 Berly, Aguascalientes, 25 Nov.; British consular report, Torreón, in Hanna, Monterrey, 4 Dec. 1916; SD 812.00/20023; 20013.

992 Cobb, El Paso, 23 Mar. 1917, SD 812.00/20699; Hewett, Tuxpan, 5 July 1917; O'Hea, Gómez Palacio, 27 May 1918; FO 371/2962, 172054; 3244, 112184. The Chinese again suffered from specific exactions: USS Annapolis, Topolobampo, 20 Nov. 1916, SD 812.00/20051.

993 Guzmán, *Eagle and the Serpent*, p. 186.

994 'When governments attempt to do more than they have ever done without the organisation to do it properly . . . corruption grows in volume': Joel Hurstfield, *Freedom and Corruption in Elizabethan England* (London, 1973), pp. 148–9.

995 See pp. 510–11, 524–6.

996 Blasco Ibáñez, *Mexico in Revolution*, pp. 84–5; Ruiz, *Great Rebellion*, pp. 377–781; Fabela, DHRM, EZ, pp. 305–8; Liceaga, *Félix Díaz*, pp. 491–2.

997 Lincoln Steffens, *The autobiography of Lincoln Steffens* (2 vols., New York, 1931), p. 732.

998 Taracena, *Verdadera revolución*, v, p. 28; Canada, Veracruz, 28 May 1915, SD 812.00/15341 (citing *La Vanguardia*); DDCC, II, pp. 1083–4.

999 J. B. Body to M. de Bunsen, 7 Dec. 1917, FO 371/2964, 236721, quoting Nieto. 'The army establishments are honeycombed with graft', the new American Ambassador reckoned (Fletcher to Lansing, 28 Aug. 1917, Fletcher Papers, box 4); Bonsal (n. 380) claimed that four successive military commanders at Orizaba had left the posting decidedly richer.

1000 Murguía to Carranza, 18 Mar. 1916, AVC (but note Treviño to Murguía, 24 Mar. 1917, AVC, alleging Murguía's graft, examples of which will follow); Guillermo Boils, *Los militares y la política en México, 1915–1974* (Mexico, 1975), p. 60.

1001 Blocker, Piedras Negras, 14 Sept. 1917, SD 812.00/21821.

1002 Womack, *Zapata*, p. 313; King, Mexico City, 25 Nov. 1918, FO 371/3247, 205361.

1003 Anon. memo., Guerrero, to Carranza, late 1915, AJD, indicts Mariscal who, in turn, to González, 12 May 1916, AVC, tells how a subordinate general, Cipriano Lozano, was killed by mutineers whose pay and rations he had withheld; Gavira, *Actuación*, pp. 96, 98, 108; Canada, Veracruz, 11 Sept. 1916; Cobb, El Paso, 20 Aug. 1916; Edwards, Juárez, 23 Sept. 1916; Cobb, El Paso, 4 June 1917, 23 Aug. 1917, 13 Feb. 1918; SD 812.00/19256; 19003; 19275; 20981, 21341, 21736; Hohler, Mexico City, 18 July 1917; King, Mexico City, 25 Nov. 1918; Hewett, Tuxpán, 13 May, 14 June 1918; FO 371/2962, 166713; 3247/205361; 3244/108160, 3245/128549.

1004 Davidson, Guaymas, 12 Sept. 1918, FO 371/3246, 174353; Cobb, El Paso, 10 July 1917; Lawton, Nogales, 15 Jan. 1918; SD 812.00/21172; 21668, are less charitable in their interpretation of Obregón's operations than Hall, *Obregón*, pp. 188, 200–2; Obregón to Fletcher, 15 Dec. 1917, Fletcher Papers, box 5, enlisting American support for the deal.

1005 DDCC, II, p. 1081; Benjamin, 'Passages', p. 159. Alvarado himself is not implicated; in Yucatán he had honestly striven to curtail corruption: Joseph, *Revolution From Without*, p. 113.

1006 Womack, *Zapata*, p. 260.

1007 Parker, Mexico City, 23 July, 12 Oct. 1916, SD 812.00/17615, 19530.

1008 Womack, *Zapata*, pp. 260, 268.

1009 Brown, Mazatlán, 16 Jan.; US naval report, Salina Cruz, 9 Nov.; Davis, Guadalajara, 4 Dec. 1915; SD 812.00/14339; 16843; 17258.

1010 Parry to Carranza, 20 Dec. 1916, AVC.

1011 Lowery, 7 Dec. 1915, in Davis, Guadalajara, 9 Dec. 1915, SD 812.00/17008.

1012 Cusi, *Memorias*, p. 224.

1013 Lowery (n. 1011). Amaro's corruption was well-known: Garciadiego, 'Movimientos reaccionarios', p. 78.

1014 Womack, *Zapata*, p. 261.

1015 US naval report, Salina Cruz, 9 Nov. 1915, SD 812.00/16843.

1016 O'Hea, Gómez Palacio, 12 Nov. 1917, FO 371/1964, 244149; J. G. Nava to Carranza, 9 Dec. 1915, AVC; W. Mitchell in Fall, p. 697; Blocker, Piedras Negras, 6 Mar. 1916; Edwards, Juárez, 23 Sept. 1916; Cobb, El Paso, 20, 23 Aug. 1916, 4 June 1917, 13 Feb. 1918; SD 812.00/17380; 19275; 19003, 19027, 20981, 21736.

1017 Governor Siurob to Carranza, 16 Sept. 1915, AJD.

1018 J. G. Nava to Carranza, 2 Jan. 1916, AVC.

1019 Border report, Nogales, 23 Aug.; Cobb, El Paso, 8 Feb. 1916; SD 812.00/19112; 17325; interview with G. Bergman, Arbuckle Bros., Jalapa, 16 July 1918, FO 371/3245, 135921; note also Mitchell in Fall Report, p. 697.

1020 Parker, Mexico City, 18 Nov. 1915, SD 812.00/16818.

1021 Canada, Veracruz, 4 May 1917, SD 812.00/20917; Gral Antonio Medina to Carranza, 1 Mar. 1916, AVC.

1022 *El Pueblo*, 10 Sept. 1917 in Fabela, DHRM, RRC, V, p. 347; and see below, pp. 502–3.

1023 Womack, *Zapata*, p. 342.

1024 Terrazas, 'Asuntos que tratar con Gral Villa', n.d., late 1914, STA, box 84; Guzmán, *Eagle and the Serpent*, p. 97; Terrazas ms., n.d., 1915, STA, box 84.

1025 Richmond, 'First Chief', p. 132; Blocker, Piedras Negras, 7 Feb. 1916, 8 Jan., 4 June 1917, SD 812.00/20511, 20261, 20992.

1026 Gral Carlos Vidal to Carranza, 28 Feb. 1917, AJD; *jefe político*, Ensenada, to Gobernación, 1 July 1912 (sic), AG 65/11. Though the second reference dates back to the Maderista period, it is a particularly good example of the problems of Puritanical officialdom, confronting – as they saw it – a mounting tide of prostitution, alcoholism and degeneracy; it illustrates, too, the permanence of these issues within the revolutionary 'discourse', Maderista and Carrancista. On the similar problems of Vidal's peninsular neighbour Alvarado, see Joseph, *Revolution From Without*, pp. 105–6.

1027 Blocker, Piedra Negras, 14 June 1917, SD 812.00/20992.

1028 Border report, Douglas, 22 Jan. 1917, SD 812.00/20512; *La Montaña*, Cananea, 20 Apr. 1917, AVC, doc. 12890, notes the failure of prohibition in Sonora.

1029 Border report, Douglas, 3 Feb. 1917, SD 812.00/20536.

1030 Alger, Mazatlán, 21 Feb. 1916, SD 812.00/17454.

1031 J. G. Nava to Carranza, 1, 2, Dec. 1915, AVC.

1032 State Department weekly report, 27 Jan. 1918, Fletcher Papers, box 6; Thurstan, Mexico City, 27 Sept. 1918, FO 371/3247, 183019; *El Demócrata*, 10 Sept. 1916, at which time newspaper adverts for races, raffles and concerts 'con objeto de colectar fondos para la amortización de la deuda nacional' were not infrequent e.g., *El Demócrata*, 3 Sept. 1916.

1033 *El Demócrata*, 10 May 1916; King, Mexico City, 4 Dec. 1918, FO 371/3247, 213868.

1034 DDCC, I, pp. 939–40, 954–7.

1035 This was not the end of the story: the battle between Puritanism and corruption continued through the 1920s and into the 1930s, above all in the Tabasco of Garrido Canabál: on his campaigns against drink and related vices, see Carlos Martínez Assad, *El laboratorio de la revolución El Tabasco garridista* (Mexico, 1979), pp. 44, 54, 75, 143–6.

1036 Múgica to Alvarado, 29 Aug. 1916, María y Campos, *Múgica*, p. 102; Katz, *Secret War*, p. 291.

1037 Richmond, 'El Nacionalismo', p. 120; Hans-Werner Tobler, 'Las paradojas del ejército revolucionario: su papel en la reforma agraria mexicana, 1920–1935', *Historia Mexicana*, XXI (1971), p. 73, n. 55.

1038 Hector Aguilar Camín, 'The Relevant Tradition: Sonoran Leaders in the Revolution', in D. A. Brading, ed., *Caudillo and Peasant in the Mexican Revolution*, Cambridge, 1980, pp. 112–14; Palavicini in DDCC, II, p. 538.

1039 J. Williams, Cerro de San Pedro, SLP, 19 June 1915, SD 812.00/15563.

1040 Aguilar, 'Relevant Tradition', pp. 119–20.

1041 Hall, 'Alvaro Obregón and the agrarian movement', pp. 134–6; Tobler, 'Las paradojas', p. 72, n. 53; and above, n. 1004.

1042 Aguilar, 'Relevant Tradition', p. 121; Hill to Carranza, 1 Aug. 1916, AVC.

1043 Cobb, El Paso, 14 June 1917, 12 Feb. 1918, SD 812.00/20981, 21736.

1044 Katz, *Secret War*, p. 253; Córdova, *Ideología*, p. 263.

1045 Katz, *Secret War*, pp. 287–8; Richmond, 'First Chief', p. 57 notes thirty-six cases in the Carranza Archive; e.g., Hacienda to Carranza, 16 Mar. 1916, Manuel Martínez to Carranza, 1 Jan. 1917, AVC: *El Demócrata*, 3, 6, 11 Mar. 1916 also reports *devoluciones* in Veracruz, Chihuahua and Sonora.

1046 US naval report, Mazatlán, 9 Nov. 1915, SD 812.00/16843; border report, Nogales, 3 Feb. 1917, SD 812.00/20536.

1047 Schmutz, Aguascalientes, Dec. 1915, SD 812.00/17034; Rojas Nieto, *La destrucción de la hacienda en Aguascalientes*, pp. 119, 134.

1048 Bonney, San Luis, 7 Mar. 1916, SD 812.00/17477.

1049 J. Baranda to Carranza, 17, 29 July 1916 and G. Calzada to Carranza, n.d., 1917, AJD; Richmond, 'First Chief', p. 60; note also Katz, *Secret War*, p. 290, on the case of Guillermo Muñoz.

1050 Katz, *Secret War*, p. 261 rightly stresses the centre's initiative. On the El Salado case, Urbano Flores to Carranza, 9 Dec. 1916, AVC.

1051 Múgica to Alvarado, 29 Aug. 1916 and vecinos of Jonuta to Múgica, 28 Oct. 1917, María y Campos, *Múgica*, p. 101, 104.

1052 O'Hea, Gómez Palacio, 19 Apr. 1916, SD 812.00/18011.

1053 Flores to Carranza, 29 Dec. 1916, AVC; cf. Schryer, *Rancheros of Pisaflores*, pp. 69, 75.

1054 Raymond Buve, 'State governors and peasant mobilisation in Tlaxcala', in Brading, *Caudillo and Peasant*, pp. 230–3.

1055 Womack, *Zapata*, p. 353.

1056 *Ibid.*, p. 352.

1057 F. Thompson, manager of an American colony, Sinaloa, 20 Apr. 1916, SD 812.00/18063.

1058 Joseph, *Revolution From Without*, pp. 130–3; María y Campos, *Múgica*, pp. 99–101; and pp. 471, 475, 489.

1059 Simpson, *The ejido*, p. 609 gives figures of 180,000 hectares, which had been distributed to some 48,000 recipients; McBride, *Land Systems*, p. 165, offers a regional breakdown (omitting Morelos), in which the predominance of the central Mexican states is obvious: of 243 recipient pueblos, 140 were located in Puebla, Tlaxcala, Hidalgo, Veracruz and Mexico state.

1060 Katz, *Secret War*, p. 293, quoting one of Cowdray's representatives.

1061 Hans-Werner Tobler, 'Alvaro Obregón und die Anfänge der Mexikanischen Agrarreform, Agrarpolitik und Agrarkonflikt, 1920–1924', *Jahrbuch fur Geschichte von Staat, Wirtschaft und Gesellschaft Latein Amerikas*, VIII (1971), pp. 325, 327.

1062 That is, the tendency for agricultural production to fall with the threat and actuality of land redistribution.

1063 Joseph, *Revolution From Without*, pp. 126–33.

1064 Cantabria, locked in a bitter struggle with local villagers, was a supplier of maize to the government: C. Rochín to Carranza, 9 May 1916, AVC; on Slade, see María y Campos, *Múgica*, p. 102.

1065 The revaluation of land taxes was a progressive measure, as well as a budgetary necessity, and it followed familiar Maderista precedents; but it was an alternative rather than a complement to expropriation. See Lawton, Nogales, 16 July; Coen, Durango, 4 Aug. 1917; SD 812.00/21141; 21178 and A. Baird, Cía Explotadora de Terrenos y Maderas de Sonora to Carranza, 4 Aug. 1916, AJD Machorro to Carranza, 26 Aug. 1916, AJD on the tax strike.

1066 A reinforced deference (similar to that evident in the foreign enclaves) seems to have characterised Aguascalientes, where *agrarismo* had never flourished: Katz, *Secret War*, p. 287. Elsewhere, a selective 'paternalism' for some (usually *acasillados*) accompanied resistance to and repression of villagers: e.g., Margolies, *Princes*, pp. 35, 39, Ronfeldt, *Atencingo*, pp. 12–15, and Friedrich, *Agrarian Revolt*, pp. 90, who notes that at Naranja 'local *hacendados* systematically refused to employ anyone associated with land reform'.

1067 Katz, *Secret War*, p. 296; Tobler's examples (n. 1037, 1061) tend to bear this out.

1068 J. G. Nava to Carranza 1, 2, 15 Dec. 1915, AVC; Gavira, *Actuación*, pp. 136, 143.

1069 Grimaldo, *Apuntes*, pp. 34–5.

1070 Nava (n. 1068); Gavira, *Actuación*, p. 154; Gruening, *Mexico and its Heritage*, pp. 149–50.

1071 Falcon, 'Cedillo', pp. 133–5.

1072 DDCC, II, p. 918.

1073 San Lorenzo Teotipilco petition to Carranza, 10 Jan. 1916, AVC.

1074 *Ibid.*, and cf. vol. I, p. 223.

1075 Santa Maria Magdalena Cuayucatepec petition to Carranza, 12 Jan. 1916, AVC.

1076 Evans, *Letters*, pp. 42–4, 127–8, 249–51.

1077 Friedrich, p. 99; Apolinar Martínez Múgica, *Primo Tapia semblanza de un revolucionario michoacano* (Mexico, 1946), pp. 41–2.

1078 Tobler, 'Las paradojas', pp. 56–79; Gruening, *Mexico and its Heritage*, p. 145; Fowler, *Agrarian Radicalism*, pp. 37–9.

1079 Benjamin, 'Passages', p. 170; Womack, *Zapata*, pp. 378–81, 384.

1080 Amaya, *Soberana convención*, pp. 99–100; E. V. Niemeyer Jr, *Revolution at Querétaro: The Mexican Constitutional Convention of 1916–1917* (Austin, 1974), pp. 26–7.

1081 Niemeyer, *Revolution at Querétaro*, pp. 32, 36.

1082 Cravioto in DDCC, II, p. 223.

1083 Niemeyer, *Revolution at Querétaro*, ch. 5; Cumberland, *Constitutionalist Years*, pp. 341–60.

1084 Cumberland, *Constitutionalist Years*, pp. 347–8; Ruiz, *Labor*, p. 69. The French Minister considered Article 123 to be 'la loi ouvrière probablement la plus avancée qui existe de nos jours': Couget, Mexico City, 8 Feb. 1917, AAE, Mex. Pol. Int., N.S., XIV, n. 22.

1085 Córdova, *La Ideología*, pp. 228–9.

1086 *Ibid.*, p. 230; DDCC, II, pp. 990–1, 1146.

1087 Cf. Palavicini in DDCC, II, p. 39 and p. 101.

1088 Cano in DDCC, II, p. 850.

1089 Martínez de Escobar in DDCC, II, pp. 879–80; Maldonado to Alvarado, 1 Oct. 1916, AJD.

1090 *El Demócrata*, 3, 5, Feb. 1916.

1091 On the flexibility of the 'moderates' see Peter H. Smith, 'La política dentro de la revolución: el congreso constituyente de 1916–17', *Historia Mexicana*, XXII (1972–3), pp. 372–3. The *constituyente* was Cano (DDCC, II, p. 826); Niemeyer, *Revolution at Querétaro*, p. 101, finds Article 123 'incredible'. Pani, reviewing the 'transcendental' labour and anti-clerical reforms, notes that they were won 'with the blood of an illiterate, ignorant people, *incapable of understanding the significance of such reforms*' (my italics): Pani to Carranza, 12 Mar. 1919, in Alberto Pani, *Cuestiones diversas* (Mexico, 1922), pp. 65–7. The 'revolution at Querétaro' was very much a 'revolution from above'.

1092 Niemeyer, *Revolution at Querétaro*, pp. 33–5; cf. Cumberland, *Constitutionalist Years*, p. 331.

1093 On irregularities: DDCC, I, pp. 127, 197–9, 217; Jesus Navarro Rodríguez, of Club 'Belisario Domínguez', La Piedad (Mich.) to Gobernación, 15 Nov. 1916, alleging that the electoral returns of five districts were fixed by a variety of frauds, at the behest of the local municipal president: AG 69/20.

1094 Niemeyer, *Revolution at Querétaro*, p. 34.

1095 Cumberland, *Constitutionalist Years*, p. 331; returns from DDCC, I, pp. 126–373.

1096 DDCC, I, p. 127. At Veracruz, the official ticket got 714 out of 1,100 votes cast in a city of 50,000; the election was held amid calm and indifference, with only 'a weak section of the working-class party' taking an interest: A. Brouzet, Veracruz, 23 Oct. 1916, AAE, Mex. Pol. Int., N.S., XIV, N. 64.

1097 BERLY, AGUASCALIENTES, 28 OCT. 1916, SD 812.00/19767; NIEMEYER, *Revolution at Querétaro*, p. 35.

1098 Parker, Mexico City, 10 Oct. 1916, SD 812.00/19487.

1099 Carr, *Movimiento obrero*, I, p. 126; Ruiz, *Labor*, p. 68: cf. Córdova, *Ideología*, p. 231.

1100 DDCC, II, pp. 282, 323, 412, 473, 663–4, 678, 751, 772, 824, 825, 926, 998–9.

1101 *Ibid.*, pp. 44, 282, 519, 520, 687, 772, 824, 925, 972, 1006. The working-class press, however, does not seem to have followed events at Querétaro with any real interest. *Trabajo y Producción*, the organ of the Unión Minera Mexicana, did not comment upon the work of the constituent congress until 25 Mar. 1917 – well after its deliberations had ended.

1102 William P. Glade and Charles W. Anderson, *The Political Economy of Mexico* (Madison, 1968), pp. 208–9, citing Merle Simmons.

1103 Quirk, 'Liberales y radicales', p. 525, which is followed by Córdova, *Ideología*, p. 219.

1104 Smith, 'La política', p. 383; both Niemeyer, *Revolution at Querétaro*, p. 42 and Cumberland, *Constitutionalist Years*, pp. 358–9 suggest a broader cross-section than in fact pertained.

1105 Smith (n. 1104); Niemeyer, *Revolution at Querétaro*, pp. 32–3, 205.

1106 Niemeyer, *Revolution at Querétaro*, p. 39; DDCC, II, p. 847.

1107 Smith (n. 1104), p. 383; Niemeyer, *Revolution at Querétaro*, pp. 263–7; on Nafarrete, Fall Report, p. 833 and border report, Brownsville, 25 Nov. 1916, SD 812.00/20041, where it is suggested that Nafarrete was elected, at Carranza's instigation, to get him away from the border.

1108 Niemeyer, *Revolution at Querétaro*, p. 223; cf. Hall, *Obregón*, p. 168.

1109 Maldonado to Alvarado, 14 Feb. 1916, Fabela, DHRM, RRC, V, p. 31.

1110 Niemeyer, *Revolution at Querétaro*, pp. 45–6; Pastor Rouaix, *Génesis de los Artículos 27 y 123 de la Constitución Política de 1917* (Mexico, 1959), p. 63.

1111 Niemeyer, *Revolution at Querétaro*, p. 151; Rouaix, *Génesis*, p. 61. Hidalgo, though an ex-governor, was a genuinely popular revolutionary.

1112 Niemeyer, *Revolution at Querétaro*, pp. 42–3; DDCC, II, pp. 306–8.

1113 Quirk, 'Liberales y Radicales' appears to have been influential; Rouaix, *Génesis*, p. 63, is more qualified.

1114 Martínez Escobar in DDCC, II, p. 880.

1115 Niemeyer, *Revolution at Querétaro*, pp. 55–9; though, as Carranza's address to the Congress makes clear, his position was not one of uncritical acceptance of the 1857 document: Fabela, DHRM, RRC, V, pp. 199–220.

1116 *El Demócrata*, 3, 5 Feb. 1916.

1117 Niemeyer, *Revolution at Querétaro*, pp. 119–21; Córdova, *Ideología*, p. 232; Cumberland, *Constitutionalist Years*, p. 357.

1118 Niemeyer, *Revolution at Querétaro*, pp. 122–6, 131; Palavicini in DDCC, II, p. 1056.

1119 Niemeyer, *Revolution at Querétaro*, pp. 138, 141–58; on the intellectual antecedents and rationale: Córdova, *Ideología*, pp. 224–9.

1120 Niemeyer, *Revolution at Querétaro*, p. 164; Cumberland, *Constitutionalist Years*, p. 352.

1121 Niemeyer, *Revolution at Querétaro*, p. 164.

1122 Cumberland, *Constitutionalist Years*, p. 352.

1123 Niemeyer, *Revolution at Querétaro*, p. 214; DDCC, II, p. 1140; Cumberland, *Constitutionalist Years*, p. 358.

1124 Cf. Ruiz, *Great Rebellion*, p. 143, who imposes his own, arbitrary criteria and sees anti-clericalism as 'camouflage' for the failure of social reform, hence 'essentially irrelevant' to an analysis of the 'Revolution'.

1125 It may be questioned how reliable the relevant sources are. Some accounts rely heavily on the (considerably later) reminiscences and rationalisations of participants, like Rouaix, Portes Gil, Bojórquez; Hall, *Obregón*, p. 171, following Bojórquez, even suggests that the official account was doctored – by the 'moderates'.

1126 Smith, 'La política', pp. 375–81.

1127 Joseph, *Revolution from Without*, pp. 110, 112 and note Alvarado to Carranza, 26 Sept. 1916, Fabela, DHRM, RRC, v, p. 133; DDCC, i, p. 922; Benjamin, 'Passages', p. 156.

1128 Hall, *Obregón*, p. 172, on the formation and influence of the Partido Liberal Constitucionalista, which had a strong Sonoran presence among the leadership.

1129 Parker, Querétaro, 6 Dec. 1916, 11 Jan. 1917, SD 812.00/20033, 20258; Couget, Mexico City, 30 Oct., 2, 6 Dec. 1916, AAE, Mex. Pol. Int., N.S., xiv, n. 92, 113, 117 on the civil–military polarisation.

1130 Hall, *Obregón*, p. 176.

1131 DDCC, ii, pp. 922–3.

1132 Thurstan, Mexico City, 30 Nov. 1916, SD 812.00/19990 conveys the impression; but, as the French Minister admitted, 'one is very badly informed in Mexico [City] of what is happening and, above all, what is being thought at Querétaro': Couget, 6 Dec. 1916, AAE, Mex. Pol. Int., N.S., xiv, n. 118.

1133 DDCC, ii, p. 923.

1134 DDCC, i, pp. 480–7, 569–74.

1135 *El Demócrata*, 25 Nov. 1916. It cannot be inferred from this that there was unanimous enthusiasm for the 'social' provisions: rather, a keen minority confronted a 'floating' majority, who had no desire to oppose (or to be seen to oppose) these fine-sounding but also long-term aspirations; the clerical question, on the other hand, engaged strong feelings on either side and was amenable to prompt action. This is borne out by the history not only of the Congress, but also of post-revolutionary reform.

1136 Niemeyer, *Revolution at Querétaro*, p. 213; Cumberland, *Constitutionalist Years*, p. 341.

1137 Chester Lloyd Jones, *Mexico and its Reconstruction* (New York, 1921), p. 52; cf. Taracena, *Verdadera revolución*, v, p. 61.

1138 Cummins, Mexico City, 22 June 1917, FO 371/2962, 148197.

1139 Adams to Body, 1 June 1917, Cowdray Papers, box A/4; Cumberland, *Constitutionalist Years*, p. 363.

1140 Cumberland, *Constitutionalist Years*, pp. 370–1; examples will be given.

1141 Richmond, 'First Chief', p. 260; Taracena, *Verdadera revolución*, v, p. 61.

1142 J. Padilla González to Carranza, 18 Jan. 1917, AVC, representing the ex-Conventionist officers grouped in the Partido Nacional Regenerador; many other examples are to be found in the Carranza archive.

1143 Thurstan, Mexico City, 19 Mar. 1917, FO 371/2960, 79896; Fletcher, Mexico City, 13 Mar. 1917, SD 812.00/20696; Edwards, Juárez, 12 Mar.; USS Albany, Mazatlan, 7 Mar.; USS Pittsburgh, Manzanillo, 15 Feb. 1917; SD 812.00/20633; 20705; 20652.

1144 The French Minister reported 'general indifference': Couget, Mexico City, 17 Sept. 1916, AAE, Mex. Pol. Int., N.S., xiv, n. 64; cf. *El Demócrata*, 2, 4 Sept. 1916.

1145 Hence the blanket 'election' of an official Carrancista slate was common: e.g., border report, Nogales, 25 Aug. 1916, SD 812.00/19112; on Villar's blackballing, Canada, Veracruz, 4 Sept. 1916, SD 812.00/19221.

1146 Blocker, Piedras Negras, 5 Sept.; USS Raleigh, Guaymas, 19 Sept. 1916; SD 812.00/19130; 19348.

1147 Canada (n. 1145) and Couget (n. 1144) agree; Bowman, Frontera, 12 May 1916, SD 812.00/18246; USS Pittsburgh, Manzanillo, 15 Feb. 1917, SD 812.00/20652.

1148 Particularly the gubernatorial conflicts, which will be discussed shortly.

1149 Berly, 9 Sept., Donald, 13 Nov. 1916, both Aguascalientes, SD 812.00/19201, 21483; for later electoral history, Berly, 19 May, 23 June, Donald, 2 Oct. 1917, SD 812.00/20938, 21081, 21352.

1150 F. Zuazua to Carranza, 19 Dec. 1916; AVC; L. Herrera to Aguilar, 10 Jan. 1917, AVC: Coen, San Antonio, 4 Aug. 1917, SD 812.00/21178.

1151 Doherty, Nogales, 1, 23 Oct.; War Dept interview with F. Elías, 17 Oct. 1916; SD 812.00/19372, 19625; 19612.

1152 Canada (n. 1145).

1153 Hewett, Tuxpán, 11 Mar. 1917, FO 371/2960, 96559.

1154 Canada, Veracruz, 13, 18 Dec. 1917, SD 812.00/21682, 21590.

1155 USS Buffalo, Mazatlán, 16 Sept., 20 Dec. 1916, SD 812.00/19393, 20268.

1156 Dawson, Tampico, 15 Sept. 1916, SD 812.00/19346.

1157 Stacpoole, Orizaba, 31 Dec. 1917, 31 Jan. 1918, FO 371/3242, 30954, 41502.

1158 Club 'Unión Fraternal', San Miguel del Soldado, to Carranza, 2 Jan.; Club 'Cuauhtémoc', Tlacolula, 5 Jan.; Club 'Allende', Coacoazintla, 7 Jan.; Club 'Nicolás Bravo', Tonoyán, 10 Jan.; 'Club Progresista Veracruzano 1910', Veracruz, 14 Jan. 1917; all AVC.

1159 Canada, Veracruz, 16 Apr., 4 May 1917, SD 812.00/20842, 20917, where, however, it is suggested that Gavira enjoyed greater support in the towns, Aguilar in the countryside. If true, this could have reflected the respective backgrounds of the candidates (Gavira an urban artisan, Aguilar an hacienda manager), or, more likely, the greater propensity of urban voters to oppose the official candidate.

1160 Stacpoole, Orizaba, 31 May 1917, FO 371/2962, 138798.

1161 Gavira, *Actuación*, pp. 184–7; Hutchison, Veracruz, 5 June 1917, FO 371/2962, 143987.

1162 Bowman, Frontera, 3 May 1917, SD 812.00/20971; Richmond, 'First Chief', pp. 261–2.

1163 D. A. Jiménez to Aguilar, 27 Jan. 1917, AVC.

1164 Cumberland, *Constitutionalist Years*, pp. 365, 369; Robertson, Monterrey, 28 May 1917, SD 812.00/20944.

1165 Cumberland, *Constitutionalist Years*, p. 365; Falcón, 'Cedillo', p. 134; Cobb, El Paso, 20 Apr. 1917, SD 812.00/20834.

1166 Silliman, Guadalajara, 2 June 1917, SD 812.00/20974; Richmond, 'First Chief', p. 263; María y Campos, *Múgica*, pp. 124–9.

1167 Cumberland, *Constitutionalist Years*, p. 370, lists nineteen states, of which fourteen acquired loyalist governors (the Carrancista 'addiction' of González, Aguascalientes, may be questioned; and, *a fortiori*, the independence of Ortiz Rubio).

1168 Of Cumberland's nineteen, the genuine revolutionary military included Arrieta, Mariscal, Flores, Diéguez, Barragán, Iturbe, Calles, Aguilar and Estrada; if my point about Ortiz Rubio (n. 1167) is conceded, all Cumberland's 'independent' governors are to be found in this group. Carrancista 'addiction' thus correlated with civilian status.

1169 Donald, Aguascalientes, 2 Oct. 1917, SD 812.00/21352.

1170 Caldwell, Zacatecas, 15 June 1917, FO 371/2962, 143984.

1171 Cobb, El Paso, 12 June; Coen, San Antonio, 28 July 1917; SD 812.00/21039; 21161; Norton, Durango, 19 Oct. 1916; O'Hea, Gómez Palacio, 11 Mar. 1918; FO 371/2966, 17240; 3243/60324.

1172 Hall, *Obregón*, p. 185.

1173 Hostetter, Los Angeles, 26 Dec. 1916, SD 812.00/20191.

1174 Border report, Nogales, 3 Feb. 1917, SD 812.00/20536.

1175 Richmond, 'First Chief', p. 241.

1176 Border report, Nogales, 28 June; Lawton, Nogales, 16 July 1917; SD 812.00/21120; 21141.

1177 Cumberland, *Constitutionalist Years*, pp. 370–1; Doherty, Nogales, 14 May; border report, Nogales, 27 Jan. 1917; SD 812.00/20911; 20512.

1178 Cumberland, *Constitutionalist Years*, p. 366.

1179 Border report, Nogales, 5 May 1917, SD 812.00/20931.

1180 Border report, Nogales, 5 May; Chapman, Mazatlán, 10 July 1 Aug. 1917; SD 812.00/20931; 21103, 21201.

1181 Border report, Nogales, 23 Dec. 1916; USS Buffalo, Mazatlán, 20 Dec. 1916, 23 Apr. 1917; Keys, Rosario, 3 Aug. 1917; SD 812.00/20235; 20268, 20905; 21220.

1182 Chapman, Mazatlán, 7 June 1917, SD 812.00/21030.

1183 Chapman, Mazatlán, 10 July (twice), 13 July, 1 Aug. 1917, SD 812.00/21103, 21125, 21111, 21201.

1184 Cumberland, *Constitutionalist Years*, p. 368; Casasola, *Historia gráfica*, II, p. 1254.

1185 Hanna, Monterrey, 20 July 1917, SD 812.00/21128.

1186 Ogston, Galveston, 20 Apr. 1918, FO 371/3243, 81765; Cumberland, *Constitutionalist Years*, p. 369; Cobb, El Paso, 19 Apr.; Dawson, Tampico, 17 Aug. 1917; Scholes, N. Laredo, 19 Jan. 1918; SD 812.00/10895; 21230; 21677.

1187 Hewett, Tampico, 11 Jan. 1918, FO 371/3242, 41474; Cumberland, *Constitutionalist Years*, p. 370.

1188 Cummins, Mexico City, 25 Mar. 1918, FO 371/3243, 55054.

1189 Scholes, N. Laredo, 19 Jan. 1918, SD 812.00/21677.

1190 Cumberland, *Constitutionalist Years*, pp. 363–70.

1191 O'Hea, Gómez Palacio, 11 Mar. 1918, FO 371/3243, 60324; and Gruening, *Mexico and its Heritage*, p. 417.

1192 On Espinosa Mireles, cf. Cumberland, *Constitutionalist Years*, p. 388 and Carr, *Movimiento obrero*, I, pp. 130, 162, n. 19; Falcón, 'Cedillo', pp. 139, 166, 177–8, 181; Jacobs, 'Rancheros', pp. 89–91.

1193 Cf. the counter-factual alternative of a Villista Mexico, above, pp. 299–301.

1194 Cumberland, *Constitutionalist Years*, pp. 366–7.

1195 Blocker, Piedras Negras, 23 Feb., 21 Apr. (twice) 1917, SD 812.00/20576, 10817, 20843.

1196 Blocker, Piedras Negras, 6, 14 Sept. 1917, SD 812.00/21245, 21281.

1197 Blocker, Piedras Negras, 17 Feb., 21 Apr. 1917, SD 812.00/20533, 20817.

1198 *Trabajo y Producción*, 18 Feb. 1917 endorses Espinosa and urges workers to join the political struggle; Carr, *Movimiento obrero*, I, p. 130.

1199 Blocker, Piedras Negras, 15 Mar. 1917, SD 812.00/20685.

1200 Silliman, Saltillo, 3 May 1916, SD 812.00/18113 had noted the erection of new private houses in the city, 'probably the most pretentious of them . . . belonging to General Luis Gutiérrez'; Blocker, Piedras Negras, 14 Sept. 1917, SD 812.00/21281, on Carranza's offer; cf. vol. I, p. 308.

1201 Blocker (n. 1200).

1202 Blocker, Piedras Negras, 13 Nov., 13 Dec. 1917, SD 812.00/21478, 21570.

1203 Blocker, Piedras Negras, 11, 12 Dec. 1917, 10 Jan. 1918, SD 812.00/21535, 21539, 21652.

1204 Blocker, Piedras Negras, 10 Jan. 1918, SD 812.00/21652.

1205 Cf. Gruening, *Mexico and its Heritage*, pp. 413–17.

1206 Carranza to Aguilar, 27 Jan., to López de Lara, 22 Mar. 1916, AJD.

1207 Cf. Cumberland, *Constitutionalist Years*, p. 388 and Carr, *Movimiento obrero*, I, p. 130; Ruiz, *Labor*, p. 71; *Lucha Social* (Saltillo) 11 Apr. 1918.

1208 Carr, *Movimiento obrero*, I, pp. 132–5. *Lucha Social*, 1 May 1918 lists 108 delegates, of whom 69 came from the north-east: 39 from the host state, Coahuila, 16 from Nuevo León, and 15 from Tamaulipas.

1209 Carr, *Movimiento obrero*, p. 133; Cumberland, *Constitutionalist Years*, p. 389.

1210 M. Jasso in *Trabajo y Producción*, 4 Feb. 1917; Huitrón, *Orígenes*, pp. 299–300, expresses his disgust.

1211 *El Pequeño Grande* (Doña Cecilia), 26 Jan., 8 Feb. 1919, 10 July 1921.

1212 Harvey A. Levenstein, *Labor Organizations in the United States and Mexico* (New York, 1971), p. 65.

1213 Carr, *Movimiento obrero*, I, p. 134.

1214 *Mexican Herald*, 27 June 1915, prints Morones' denunciation of all government.

1215 On the growth of the CROM and opposition of the railwaymen: Carr, *Movimiento obrero*, I, pp. 134, 178, 192–4; on the oil workers, Leif Adleson, 'Coyuntura y consciencia: factores convergentes en la fundación de los sindicatos petroleros de Tampico durante la década de 1920', in Elsa Cecilia Frost *et al.*, eds., *El Trabajo y los trabajadores en la historia de México* (Mexico and Arizona, 1979), pp. 632–61.

1216 Carr, *Movimiento obrero*, pp. 134–5, 142–3; Aguilar, 'Relevant tradition', pp. 104–5.

1217 Above all, the CROM was recognised as the sole, central representative of organised labour, and was given an effective lien on the ministerial posts of Labour (a new post) and Agriculture. See Carr, *Movimiento obrero*, I, pp. 143–4, Hall, *Obregón*, p. 217.

1218 Obregón launched his presidential bid with a statement that was solidly political and 'referred only briefly to the economic problems of the country': Hall, *Obregón*, p. 212.

1219 Adams to Body, June 1917, Cowdray Papers, box A/4; and, a year later, the 'radicals' were reported to be 'bitterly disappointed and disillusioned': Thurstan, Mexico City, 7 Aug. 1918, FO 371/3246, 153090.

1220 Ruiz, *Labor*, pp. 70–2; Cumberland, *Constitutionalist Years*, pp. 385–6.

1221 Cumberland, *Constitutionalist Years*, pp. 382–3; for premonitory rumblings of dissent, see Múgica to Alvarado, 29 Aug. 1916, María y Campos, *Múgica*, pp. 101–3; DDCC, II, p. 1085. See also n. 1059 above.

1222 Ronfeldt, *Atencingo*, pp. 17–18; Senior, *Land Reform*, pp. 65–6; Joseph, *Revolution From Without*, p. 292 offer local illustrations of this point.

1223 Cummins, Mexico City, 12 July 1917, FO 371/2962, 138581; Inman in Fall Report, p. 9; Adams to Body, 1 June 1917, Cowdray Papers, box A/4, where it is stated that the President wished for a better understanding with foreign interests 'but ... no longer controls the policy of the government and is quite unable personally to revoke any of the confiscatory clauses of the new Constitution'.

1224 Quirk, *Mexican Revolution and the Catholic Church*, pp. 103, 111; Meyer, *Cristero Rebellion*, p. 15.

1225 Katz, *Secret War*, pp. 534–6.

1226 Cummins, Mexico City, 13 Mar. 1919, FO 371/3827, 40943, reported 'violent' press attacks, which Carranza 'seems afraid to suppress'; Fletcher to Long, 28 May 1919, Fletcher Papers, box 6, on expectations of political upheaval; see also Hall, *Obregón*, pp. 192–3. Late 1919 saw heightened tension with the US following a consular kidnapping: Charles C. Cumberland, 'The Jenkins Case and Mexican–American Relations', *Hispanic American Historical Review*, XXXI (1951), pp. 596–607.

1227 Obregón, *Ocho mil kilómetros*, pp. 550–64.

1228 Córdova, *Ideología*, p. 218.

1229 Hall, *Obregón*, pp. 209, 227, 240–1; Womack, *Zapata*, pp. 340, 357–8.

1230 Cumberland, *Constitutionalist Years*, p. 404; Dulles, *Yesterday in Mexico*, p. 22.

1231 Hall, *Obregón*, p. 216.

1232 Córdova, *Ideología*, p. 265, n. 4 citing Mena Brito; Dulles *Yesterday in Mexico*, p. 22.

1233 In this respect, Obregón's emphasis on his civilian status and outspoken 'antimilitarist stance' (Hall, *Obregón*, pp. 214–15) had some justification.

1234 Hall, *Obregón*, pp. 205, 209, 223, 228.

1235 *Ibid.*, pp. 233, 242; Dulles, *Yesterday in Mexico*, pp. 23, 27.

1236 Hall, *Obregón*, pp. 184–6, on his decision not to run in 1917: 'this is the time of unbridled ambitions', he had then confided in Gavira, 'it's best to let them display themselves like hungry dogs, squabbling over a bone' (Gavira, *Actuación*, p. 183). He was right: many of the 'electoral' victors of 1917–18 lost out in 1920; and the 1920–4 presidential term held out more enticements than its truncated, troubled predecessor.

1237 Hall, *Obregón*, pp. 209–10, 220–2.

1238 *Ibid.*, pp. 214, 221–2, 225–6; Dulles, *Yesterday in Mexico*, pp. 20, 23–4.

1239 Hall, *Obregón*, pp. 199–200, 228, 243.

1240 Dulles, *Yesterday in Mexico*, pp. 29–34; Garciadiego, 'Movimientos reaccionarios', pp. 132–4, 194–9, 257–60; Benjamin, 'Passages', pp. 165–7.

1241 Cumberland, *Constitutionalist Years*, p. 412.

1242 Gruening, *Mexico and its Heritage*, p. 314.

1243 Dulles, *Yesterday in Mexico*, pp. 38–46.

1244 *Ibid.*, p. 64; Garciadiego, 'Movimientos reaccionarios', p. 134; Benjamin, 'Passages', pp. 166, 170ff.

1245 Dulles, *Yesterday in Mexico*, pp. 66–70; Meyer *et al.*, 'La Vida con Villa'.

1246 Womack, *Zapata*, p. 359ff.

1247 Ankerson, 'Saturnino Cedillo', pp. 145–6.

1248 Córdova, *Ideología*, pp. 238–41. The electoral politics of 1917–20, which we have briefly sketched, set the style for the 1920s: see Gruening's valuable resumé, *Mexico and its Heritage*, pp. 399–492, especially the comments on p. 481.

1249 Córdova, *Ideología*, p. 288.

1250 *Ibid.*, pp. 198–204, 218, 264, 314, 318; and Obregón, *Ocho mil kilómetros*, p. 579.

1251 Alvarado to Carranza, 25 Jan. 1916, Fabela, DHRM, RRC, V, pp. 21–3, on the need to 'organise' the 200,000 Indians of Yucatán – 'very intelligent Indians, very apt for organisation' – in order to 'nationalise' the state; Katz, *Secret War*, pp. 286–7, quotes Federico González Garza on the Convention's failure to undertake a land reform which – on the lines of the French Revolution – 'would have created new interests which would have helped to sustain the new regime'.

1252 See pp. 215–17 and vol. I, pp. 264–7.

1253 Obregón, *Ocho mil kilómetros*, p. 567; Benjamin, 'Passages', p. 139; Schryer, *Rancheros of Pisaflores*, pp. 15, 69; Warman, *Y venimos a contradecir*, p. 158 all reflect aspects of populist rhetoric.

1254 The *étatiste*, instrumental character of official *agrarismo* has been illustrated by many recent studies: see Womack, *Zapata*, pp. 374–9; Schryer, *Rancheros of Pisaflores*, pp. 93–4; Friedrich, *Agrarian Report*, pp. 91–2, 141; Ankerson, 'Saturnino Cedillo', pp. 163–4; Meyer, *Cristero Rebellion*, pp. 107–10; and – not so recent – Beals, *Mexican Maze*, p. 211.

1255 Tocqueville, *L'Ancien Régime*, pp. 4–5.

1256 Obregón, *Ocho mil kilómetros*, p. 569.

1257 *Ibid.*, pp. 573, 578–80, 586–7; Alvarado, *Reconstrucción*, I, pp. 61–7, 80–4, 160–3, 340; Córdova, *Ideología*, pp. 311–22; Joseph, *Revolution From Without*, pp. 101–2.

1258 See pp. 206–8.

1259 Meyer, *Cristiada*, I, pp. 71–83; Rius Facius, *La juventud católica*, pp. 72–87; Quirk, *Mexican Revolution and the Catholic Church*, pp. 52–112.

1260 DDCC, I, p. 693; note also Meyer, *Cristiada*, I, p. 84.

1261 DDCC, II, p. 1058 (Múgica again).

1262 Friedrich, *Agrarian Revolt*, p. 121; Múgica in DDCC, II, p. 665.

1263 Rutherford, *Mexican Society*, notes that novels written during (not about) the Maderista period ignore the clerical question; he is right, but wrong to conclude that this indicates the 1910 revolution's 'genteel nature': pp. 194, 280, 288. See also vol. I, pp. 400–3.

1264 Rutherford, *Mexican Society*, p. 288.

1265 Friedrich, *Agrarian Revolt*, pp. 54, 120 on clerical support for embattled landlords; M. Palomar y Vizcarra to Orozco y Jiménez, 23 Feb. 1915, Conflicto Religioso, r. 9, lamenting the dissolution of the Federal Army; and above, pp. 2, 203–4.

1266 Richmond, 'Carranza: The Authoritarian Populist as Nationalist President' manages to combine two; note also Quirk, 'Liberales y Radicales'; Meyer, *Cristero Rebellion*, pp. 14–15, 24ff.

1267 Niemeyer, *Revolution at Querétaro*, p. 221, offers a definition of jacobinism which is helpful, but raises the question, why 'jacobin' at all?

1268 Córdova, *Ideología*, p. 216; Jose C. Valadés, *Alamán Estadista e Historiador* (Mexico, 1977), pp. 383–7.

1269 William P. Glade and Charles W. Anderson, *The Political Economy of Mexico* (Madison, 1963), pp. 40–1, quoting Fuentes.

1270 Obregón, *Ocho mil kilómetros*, p. 568; Fabela, DHRM, RRC, V, p. 304; DDCC, II, pp. 989, 1047; note also Gómez Morín's championship of 'businesslike' government, and Lombardo Toledano's homilies on the 'sanctity of individual work': Krauze, *Caudillos culturales*, pp. 140, 175.

1271 See pp. 525–6. Germany, Japan and, perhaps, the Soviet Union are obvious examples of collective, post-war commitments to work and reconstruction. As far as I know, there have been no studies of post-revolutionary Mexican society couched in these terms; nor are comparative/sociological theories to hand. William H. Form and Charles P. Loomis, 'The Persistence and Emergence of Social and Cultural Systems in Disasters', *American Sociological Review*, XXI (1956), pp. 180–5, addresses the question, but reads like a parody of the Parsonian method.

1272 DDCC, II, p. 184.

1273 Niemeyer, *Revolution at Querétaro*, p. 61.

1274 *Ibid.*, pp. 67, 74–5; DDCC, II, pp. 1028–9, 1948; Quirk, *Mexican Revolution and the Catholic Church*, p. 71, illustrates that the liberal intellectuals of the Convention entertained similar ideas.

1275 Niemeyer, *Revolution at Querétaro*, p. 75; note also Alvarado's concern for racial vigour: *Reconstrucción*, I, pp. 148, 339, 377–83.

1276 DDCC, II, p. 630; Fabela, DHRM, RRC, V, p. 381; Obregón, *Ocho mil kilómetros*, pp. 567, 576; for post-revolutionary examples, note Martínez Assad, *El laboratorio*, pp. 61–81 and Joseph, *Revolution From Without*, pp. 107–8, 196, 214–16.

1277 DDCC, II, p. 1047; Niemeyer, *Revolution at Querétaro*, p. 91; Rius Facius, *La juventud católica*, pp. 274–5.

1278 González Navarro, *Vida social*, pp. 536, 562, 571–6, 579–81, 598; Meyer, *Cristero Rebellion*, pp. 2–3.

1279 Meyer, *Cristero Rebellion*, p. 24; see also *La Cristiada*, I, p. 84, on the ideology of the *constituyentes*.

1280 Fall Report, testimony of Inman and Lill, pp. 5–7, 27, 666; Rius Facius, *La juventud católica*, p. 95; Francis McCullagh, *Red Mexico* (London, 1928), pp. 332–3; even Palavicini inveighed against Protestant influence in Mexico – not least the YMCA: Niemeyer, *Revolution at Querétaro*, pp. 71–2.

1281 *From Max Weber: Essays in Sociology*, ed., H. H. Gerth and C. Wright Mills (London, 1974), pp. 62–3, 284.

1282 C. Hill, 'Protestantism and the Rise of Capitalism' in *Society and Puritanism in Pre-Revolutionary England* (London, 1966), pp. 97–100. Note also the cases in post-revolutionary Mexico: Lewis, *Pedro Martínez*, pp. 25–6, 233–69; Schryer, *Rancheros of Pisaflores*, pp. 82, 96, 120, 122. Global parallels are abundant, from the Bolivian revolution to African proto-nationalism.

1283 David E. Apter, 'Political Organisation and Ideology' in Wilbert E. Moore and Arnold S. Feldman, *Labor Commitment and Social Change in Developing Areas* (New York, 1960), pp. 326, 328, 331, 347.

1284 Niemeyer, *Revolution at Querétaro*, pp. 182, 187, 192–3; DDCC, II, pp. 620, 646–7, 825, 948–50.

1285 Thompson, 'Time, Work-Discipline and Industrial Capitalism', *Past and Present*, XXXVIII (1907), pp. 50–1; the Carrancista agent Nava was disgusted by the cessation of work, constant peals of bells and religious processions which characterised Aguascalientes at the feast of San Juan de los Lagos: such 'rancid customs', he wrote to Carranza (9 Dec. 1915, AVC), should be extirpated. At Veracruz, Bonsal noted, bells rang out for victories or the 'name days' (días onomásticos) of generals: 'don't say saint's day in Carranzaland' (n. 380); in Hidalgo and elsewhere they were busy stripping villages, haciendas, streets, squares, parks and buildings of saintly, clerical, bestial and other 'frivolous' names, replacing them with 'abstract titles such as: Liberty, Concord, Independence, Constitution, etc' (*El Demócrata*, 9 Mar. 1916). Ultimately, in Yucatán, San Lunes became *lunes rojo* – a day of Socialist enlightenment; while in Tabasco, saints' days gave way to the Feast of Work, of Progress, or of the Orange: Joseph, *Revolution From Without*, p. 222; Martínez Assad, *El laboratorio*, p. 125.

1286 USS Raleigh, Guaymas, 19 Sept. 1916, SD 812.00/19348; Ryan to Scott, 22 July 1915, Scott Papers, box 19, praises Calles' clean-up of the 'vile resort' of Naco; *El Demócrata*, 4, 5 Mar. 1916, which alleges Catholic profiteering in the *pulque* trade; Blocker, Eagle Pass, 8 Jan. 1917, SD 812.00/20261.

1287 *El Demócrata*, 29 Nov. 1915, 2 Jan. 1916; *Jefe político*, Tepic, 27 Oct. 1916, AG 21/81; Joseph, *Revolution From Without*, pp. 105–6; María y Campos, *Múgica*, p. 93.

1288 González Navarro, *Vida social*, pp. 416–20; R. J. MacHugh, *Modern Mexico* (London, 1914), p. 133, averred that 'so long as *pulque*-drinking continues, it is doubtful if the people of Mexico can ever attain to any high stage of development' (MacHugh was a *Daily Telegraph* reporter).

1289 Niemeyer, *Revolution at Querétaro*, p. 182; DDCC, II, p. 825.

1290 *El Demócrata*, 2, 8 Feb., 8, 24 Mar., 15 May, 4, 16 Nov. 1916; *Orientación* (Hermosillo), 7 Sept. 1917, Fabela, DHRM, RRC, v, p. 361.

1291 DDCC, II, p. 651.

1292 Martínez Assad, *El laboratorio*, *passim*; note also Krauze, *Caudillos culturales*, pp. 180–1, on Lombardo Toledano's unsuccessful campaigns against bullfights and booze while Governor of Puebla.

1293 *El Demócrata*, 10 Sept. 1916; and, by 1918, the traditional gambling joints of Villa de Guadalupe were thriving, despite government disapproval: State Department weekly report, 27 Jan. 1918, Fletcher Papers, box 6.

1294 Alvarado, *Actuación*, p. 66.

1295 E. V. Niemeyer, 'Anti-clericalism in the Mexican Constitutional Convention of 1916–17', *Americas*, XI (1954), p. 33; DDCC, II, pp. 875–6, 888–9, 1028–9, 1031, 1045–6.

1296 DDCC, II, pp. 992, 995, 1049–50.

1297 Rius Facius, *La juventud católica*, p. 42ff.; Bailey, *Viva Cristo Rey!*, pp. 27–36.

1298 Meyer, *Cristero Rebellion*, pp. 22–3.

1299 Quirk, *Mexican Revolution and the Catholic Church*, p. 111; Rius Facius, *La juventud católica*, pp. 147–8; *El Republicano* (Guadalajara), 19 Sept. 1917, Fabela, DHRM, RRC, v, p. 398.

1300 Rius Facius, *La juventud católica*, pp. 145–6.

1301 Meyer, *Cristero Rebellion*, pp. 14–15; Quirk, *Mexican Revolution and the Catholic Church*, pp. 107–11.

1302 As the Mexico-watcher Prof. R. B. Brinsmade communicated to Dearing of the State Department, Madero's 'general views of the [economy] are eminently sound and nothing need be feared from him along the lines of socialism or half-baked radicalism' – which proved true: Knight, 'Nationalism', pp. 120–41; Brinsmade to Dearing, 12 Aug. 1911, SD 812.50/1.

1303 Knight, 'Nationalism, Xenophobia and Revolution', pp. 275–98: bouquets for Obregón, Alvarado, Calles, Villa, Aguilar, Caballero, González, Rouaix, the Arrietas and others.

1304 Fall and Buckley in Fall Report, pp. 827, 874; Smith, *United States and Revolutionary*

Nationalism, p. 88; transcript of interview with 'Mr X' (a henequen buyer), 31 Oct. 1919, Buckley Papers, File 114, which argues that 'the socialist movement in Yucatán was the first experiment station for the whole Bolshevik movement in the world'.

1305 Pani to Carranza and vice versa, 26 Feb., 8 Apr. 1919 in Pani, *Cuestiones Diversas*, on the value of European (French) capital; Ruiz, *Great Rebellion*, pp. 383–8.

1306 Alvarado, *Reconstrucción*, I, pp. 7–8, 44, 63, 71, 83, 146–51. In practice, too, Alvarado's *política alcista* – high price policy – only succeeded while the war-induced boom went on; in 1919 the market collapsed, and with it Alvarado's Regulating Commission; neither the structure of henequen production nor the essentials of Yucatán's economic relations with International Harvester were substantially altered by the brief boom of 1915–18. See Joseph's excellent analysis in *Revolution From Without*, pp. 133–82.

1307 Obregón, *Ocho mil kilómetros*, pp. 560, 580; DDCC, II, pp. 665–6; note also Lill in Fall Report, p. 666. All agreed, however, on a bar to Chinese immigration.

1308 Coen, Durango, 11 Feb.; Cobb, El Paso, 20 Aug.; Berly, Aguascalientes, 5 Aug. 1916; SD 812.00/17294; 19003; 18994; Chester Lloyd Jones and George Wythe, 'Economic Conditions in Mexico' (sent to Morrow, 1928), SD 812.50/161.

1309 Abundant examples are to be found in SD 812.00 (general file) and 812.6363 (oil). E.g., 812.00/16818, 16896, 17343, 17347, 17729, 17802, 18025, 18253, 18991, 19140, 19152, 19164, 20536, 21141, 21178 (covering the period 1915–17).

1310 Jones and Wythe (n. 1308) noted how 'the disturbed conditions . . . have hastened the tendency for properties to be concentrated in comparatively few hands'; see also Ronfeldt, *Atencingo*, p. 9 (the acquisition of the Jenkins empire in Puebla); Bernstein, *Mexican Mining Industry*, pp. 100–11, 118–20; George Sweet Gibb and Evelyn H. Knowlton, *History of Standard Oil Company (NJ) The Resurgent Years, 1911–27* (New York, 1956), pp. 88, 360.

1211 Meyer, *México y Estados Unidos*, pp. 47–50, 68; Smith, *United States and Revolutionary Nationalism*, p. 101; Miller, Tampico, 2 July 1914, SD 812.6363/124 offers a long account of taxation and company responses to date.

1312 E.g., the coal mines and certain public utilities: see pp. 429–30.

1313 Cowdray to Body, 9 Apr. 1912, 5 Feb. 1913, Cowdray Papers, box A/4; Fletcher to State Department, 13 Mar. 1917, Fletcher Papers, box 4. Meyer, *México y Estados Unidos*, p. 32, also points out that the new tax schedules also served to encourage refining within Mexico.

1314 DDCC, II, p. 1089; Meyer, *México y Estados Unidos*, p. 31.

1315 Knight, 'The Political Economy of Revolutionary Mexico', forthcoming in C. Lewis and C. Abel, eds., *Economic Imperialism in Latin America*.

1316 Smith, *United States and Revolutionary Nationalism*, pp. 73–4, 117.

1317 Knight, 'Nationalism, Xenophobia and Revolution', pp. 82–92, 183, 187–8, 192–4, 275–7, 283–4, 289, 325–6.

1318 Smith, *United States and Revolutionary Nationalism*, pp. 77–8; Rouaix, *Génesis*, pp. 39–43, 57.

1319 *Mexican Herald*, 12 May 1915; Amaya, *Soberana convención*, pp. 215, 240–1, 459–60; Fabela, DHRM, *La Convención*, II, pp. 339, 350, 357–9.

1320 William P. Glade, *The Latin American Economies: A Study of their Institutional Evolution* (New York, 1969), pp. 227, 233–5, 242, 244–5, 326–30, 350.

1321 *Ibid.*, pp. 317, 327–30, 350; Herbert S. Klein, *Parties and Political Change in Bolivia 1880–1952* (Cambridge, 1969), pp. 78–9. As already suggested (in the context of labour), there was also a parallel 'extension of the area of state intervention . . . beyond the narrow limits set by orthodox liberalism', in response to the 'social question': James O. Morris, *Elites, Intellectuals, and Consensus: A Study of the Social Question and the Industrial Relations System in Chile* (Ithaca, 1966), pp. 150–2.

1322 Glade, *Latin American Economies*, p. 380. By 'natural' I mean 'following a common pattern'. The notion of establishing a central bank was in the air in 1918 (when the British representative, reviewing the financial state of the country, dismissed it as a 'revolutionary dream'); championed, in particular, by Gómez Morín, the reform had to await the return of the banks – expropriated in 1915–16 – to private hands (1921) and the settlement of foreign claims against Mexico (1923). The Banco de México was finally set up, under Pani's financial leadership, in 1925: see Thurstan, Mexico City, 24 Aug. 1918, FO 371/3245, 146522; Krauze, *Caudillos culturales*, pp. 114–18; Dulles, *Yesterday in Mexico*, pp. 283–5; José Iturriaga de la Fuente, *La Revolución Hacendaria* (Mexico, 1976), pp. 44, 141, 154.

1323 González Navarro, *Vida social*, p. 605; Smith, *United States and Revolutionary Nationalism*, pp. 8–12; and note the comparison of Porfirian and revolutionary economic nationalism in Fernando González Roa, *El Aspecto Agrario*, reprinted in *Problemas Agrícolas e Industriales de México*, V (1953), pp. 111–12.

1324 González Navarro, *Vida social*, p. 157.

1325 Knight, 'Political Economy of Revolutionary Mexico'.

1326 Anderson, *Outcasts*, pp. 112–14.

1327 Border reports, Nogales, 23 Aug., 18 Nov. 1916, SD 812.00/19912, 20008; and González Roa (n. 1323), p. 110, on revolutionary antipathy to foreign landholdings that seemed to constitute a state within the state.

1328 Múgica, in DDCC, II, pp. 665–6; note, again, the Porfirian precedent: González Navarro, *Vida Social*, pp. 157–8.

1329 Tannenbaum, *Peace By Revolution*, pp. 234–5, 261, sees revolutionary labour legislation working in this fashion.

1330 Smith, *United States and Revolutionary Nationalism*, p. 76.

1331 *Ibid.*, p. 77.

1332 Obregón, *Ocho mil kilómetros*, pp. 571, 578.

1333 Wilkie, *Federal Expenditure and Social Change*, pp. 259–61; Hansen, *Politics of Mexican Development*, pp. 87–8.

1334 Alvarado, *Reconstrucción*, I, pp. 7, 62–3, 338, 369.

1335 Hermila Galindo, cited by Smith, *United States and Revolutionary Nationalism*, pp. 82–3.

1336 DDCC, I, p. 270.

1337 Aguilar, 'Relevant Tradition', p. 121.

1338 Hostetter, Hermosillo, 2, 7 June 1916; border report, Nogales, 23 Aug. 1916; SD 812.00/18409, 18420; 19112.

1339 Guyant, Progreso, 15 May 1916, SD 812.00/18239; Joseph, *Revolution From Without*, pp. 146–7.

1340 Hill to Estrada, 3 Aug. 1920, in Aguilar, 'Relevant Tradition', p. 121; note also Hill to Carranza, 1 Aug. 1916, AVC, seeking a range of tax concessions for an agricultural enterprise, and couched in similar terms (the government's responsibility to 'stimulate entrepreneurs' and Hill's desire to 'collaborate in my own small sphere of action' in the country's development).

1341 *El Reformista* (Monterrey), 8 May 1917, press resume, AVC.

1342 Womack, 'Spoils', p. 677.

1343 *El Machete*, 13 Aug. 1927, quoted by Aguilar, 'Relevant Tradition', p. 122; Aguilar seems to agree with this formulation.

1344 Above, vol. I, pp. 23, 41.

1345 González Navarro, *Vida social*, pp. 112, 157, 416; Córdova, *Ideología*, pp. 39–86 (a good summary of Porfirian ideology which, e.g., pp. 69–70, is less convincing as an analysis of Porfirian reality); cf. the interesting argument of Gerald Theisen, 'La mexicanización de la industria en la época de Porfirio Díaz', *Foro Internacional*, XII (1972), pp. 497–506.

1346 Madero, *La sucesión presidencial*, pp. 143, 220–1, 237.

1347 Leopoldo Solís, *La realidad económica mexicana: retrovisión y perspectivas* (Mexico, 1971), pp. 96, 108.

1348 'An explanation based only on cases where something happened is quite likely to attribute importance to conditions which are actually quite common in cases where nothing happened': Tillys, *Rebellious Century*, p. 12.

1349 See vol. I, pp. 35–6, 102.

1350 David Apter, *Politics of Modernization* (Chicago, 1967), pp. 25, 37, 402–5.

1351 See vol. I, pp. 30–1, 36, 56–7.

1352 Gruening, *Mexico and its Heritage*, pp. 481–2; Peter H. Smith, *Labyrinths of Power: Political Recruitment in Twentieth-Century Mexico* (Princeton, 1979), is a rich source.

1353 Above, vol. I, pp. 102, 134–5.

1354 Brading, *Haciendas and Ranchos*, pp. 206–7.

1355 Alvarado, *Reconstrucción*, I, pp. 62, 115–16, 127–8, 155.

1356 Buve, 'Peasant movements', pp. 148–9; Benjamin, 'Passages', p. 179; Margolies, *Princes*, pp. 35, 39; Evans, *Letters*, pp. 40, 62–3, 149–50, 154, 194, 198.

1357 Brading, *Haciendas and Ranchos*, p. 210; Ronfeldt, *Atencingo*, pp. 18–32, analyses a later example.

1358 Joseph, *Revolution From Above*, pp. 103–4, 214.

1359 Benjamin, 'Passages', pp. 171–8, 189–90.

1360 Alvarado to Carranza, 25 Jan. 1916, Fabela, DHRM, RRC, V, pp. 22–3.

1361 Glade and Anderson, *Political Economy*, pp. 68–9: we shall return to this point in conclusion.

1362 Goodman and Redclift, *From Peasants*, p. 185ff.

1363 Moore, *Social Origins*, p. 442.

1364 Carr, *Movimiento obrero*, II, pp. 25–9, 41–4.

1365 Gruening, *Mexico and its Heritage*, pp. 49–50, 144, 167; Womack, *Zapata*, pp. 377–8; Lewis, *Tepoztlán*, p. 116; Friedrich, *Agrarian Revolt*, pp. 94, 101; Meyer, *Cristero Rebellion*, pp. 108–9; Tzvi Medin, *Ideología y praxis política de Lázaro Cárdenas* (Mexico, 1980), pp. 25–6.

1366 Miguel S. Wionczek, *El nacionalismo mexicano y la inversión extranjera* (Mexico, 1967), pp. 6, 185–94; Solís, *Realidad económica*, pp. 94–9. It may be argued that in Mexico – as in other 'peripheral' economies – symptoms of depression antedated 1929 by up to three years; but the failure of *desarrollo hacia afuera* cannot be pushed back as far as the Revolution.

1367 Jacobs, *Ranchero Revolt*, p. 167.

1368 Arthur Marwick, *War and Social Change in the Twentieth Century* (London, 1974); Gordon Wright, *The Ordeal of Total War, 1939–45* (New York, 1968), pp. 234–62.

1369 Brenner, *Idols*, p. 29; Norman S. Hayner, 'Differential Social Change in a Mexican Town', *Social Forces*, XXVI (1948), p. 386.

1370 Coen, Durango, 8 July 1915, SD 812.00/15462.

1371 Above, p. 486; as a witness of that gubernatorial conflict generalised: 'few of these (sc. popular, military leaders) ultimately survived into . . . the immediate post-insurrection period . . . and other men strode across the graves of these turbulent and homespun, but mostly well-meaning patriots to grasp the administrative powers that should have been their reward': O'Hea, *Reminiscences*, p. 16.

1372 Jacobs, *Ranchero Revolt*, pp. 167–8. Jacobs is dealing with a regional elite; cf. Warman, *Y venimos a contradecir*, pp. 158–9, on local equivalents; and Roderic Ai Camp, *Mexican Political Biographies, 1935–75* (Tucson, 1976), which supplies ample evidence of this trend at national level.

1373 Womack, *Zapata*, pp. 384–5.

1374 Mark Wasserman, 'Persistent Oligarchs: Vestiges of the Porfirian Elite in Revolutionary Chihuahua, Mexico 1920–1935', Sixth Conference of Mexican and US Historians Paper,

Chicago, Sept. 1981. Examples of elite survival and recuperation may be found in Flavia Derossi, *The Mexican Entrepreneur* (Paris, 1971), pp. 22–3, 157, 259; and Larissa Adler Lomnitz and Marisol Pérez, 'The History of a Mexican Urban Family', *Journal of Family History* (1978), pp. 392–409.

1375 Lewis, *Tepotzlán*, p. 46; Friedrich, *Agrarian Revolt*, p. 131.

1376 González, *Pueblo en vilo*, pp. 133, 137–8.

1377 Lewis, *Tepotzlán*, pp. xxvi, 51, 206, 429–30, 443.

1378 Buve, 'Peasant Movements', pp. 148–9; Bazant, *Cinco Haciendas*, pp. 183–4; cf. Hayner, 'Differential Social Change', pp. 384–5; Evans, *Letters*, pp. 71, 78, 154.

1379 Friedrich, *Agrarian Revolt*, pp. 51–7, 78ff.; Margolies, *Princes*, pp. 35, 37–40.

1380 Friedrich, *Agrarian Revolt*, p. 139; Schryer, *Rancheros of Pisaflores*, pp. 78–84, 90–2; Senior, *Land Reform*, p. 186; Tobler, 'Alvaro Obregón', p. 351. *Agrarismo, hacendados* lamented, had supplanted religion; Brenner, *Idols*, pp. 225–6.

1381 Joseph, *Revolution From Without*, p. 207.

1382 Benjamin, 'Passages', pp. 162, 167, 169–70, 177–9ff.

1383 E.g., Schryer, *Rancheros of Pisaflores*, p. 79.

1384 Thurstan, Mexico City, 20 Mar. 1917, EO 371/2966, 88967; 'the Indians', Rosalie Evans complained, '. . . are no longer apathetic, they are insolent and aggressive'; hence 'men are doing now what a few years ago they would have been incapable of': *Letters*, pp. 40, 63.

1385 Tobler, 'Alvaro Obregón', pp. 327–30, 341.

1386 Ronfeldt, *Atencingo*, pp. 233–4, makes the point for later years; it was no less valid in the 1920s and 1930s. Indeed, the high incidence of 'official' rebellion (1923, 1927, 1929) and government counter-measures gave popular, agrarian violence a degree of legitimacy and tactical opportunity which, in later, more peaceful times would be lacking: for a good example, see Fowler, *Agrarian Radicalism*, pp. 42–5.

1387 DDCC, II, p. 830.

1388 Beals, *Cherán*, p. 110; cf. Schryer, *Rancheros of Pisaflores*, p. 15.

1389 Blasco Ibáñez, *Mexico in Revolution*, pp. 55, 59, 65; Hall, *Obregón*, pp. 214, 222–3, 225–7.

1390 Obregón, *Ocho mil kilómetros*, p. 579.

1391 Knight, 'Intellectuals'.

1392 A. F. Tschiffely, *Tschiffely's Ride* (London, 1952), pp. 232, 259, 263 notes the ruined haciendas; on the physical and institutional effects of the Revolution upon the Church, see Beals, *Mexican Maze*, pp. 125–6; Lewis, *Tepoztlán*, pp. 260–1; Huxley, *Beyond the Mexique Bay* (London, 1959), pp. 208–9; González, *Pueblo en vilo*, p. 126; and cf. DDCC, II, pp. 1507–8, where Múgica sees iconoclasm as refutation of popular clericalism.

1393 Friedrich, *Agrarian Revolt*, p. 121; Meyer, Cristero Rebellion, p. 44, on Calles' strategy.

1394 Friedrich, *Agrarian Revolt*, p. 49; Beals, *Cherán*, p. 178; Brondo Whitt, *División del Norte*, p. 127; González Navarro, *Población y sociedad*, I, pp. 90–1; González, *Pueblo en vilo*, p. 126.

1395 Hayner, 'Differential Social Change', p. 385, notes that the male:female ratio shifted from 0.84 to 0.76 between 1910 and 1921.

1396 *Ibid.*, p. 389; and above, n. 980. The growth of prostitution was probably most marked along the border, where it had developed 'in scandalous fashion' by 1912, at Mexicali; and where Tijuana became (1920) 'a mecca of prostitutes, booze-sellers, gamblers and other American vermin': *jefe político*, Ensenada, to Gobernación, 1 July 1912, AG 65/11; Martínez, p. 58, quoting an American Methodist source. The number of official brothels in Mexico City fell by half during the Revolution (from 91 to 47); very probably this reflected a weakening of official supervision rather than objective decline.

1397 Schryer, *Rancheros of Pisaflores*, pp. 76–95; Friedrich, *Agrarian Revolt*, pp. 75–6, 108–10, 115; González, *Pueblo en vilo*; pp. 125–6, 133, 136. On continued political violence, note

Gruening, *Mexico and its Heritage*, pp. 435–6, 474–5, 488–9; and, more generally, *Beyond the Mexique Bay*, pp. 173–4; Tschiffely, *Ride*, pp. 225, 233, 235, 262; and Manuel Gómez Morín, *1915* (Mexico, 1927), pp. 18–20.

1398 Hayner, 'Differential Social Change', p. 386.

1399 Lewis, *Tepoztlán*, p. 446, *Pedro Martínez*, pp. 150, 156; Horcasitas, *De Porfirio Díaz*, pp. 165–9; Michael Belshaw, *A Village Economy: Land and People of Huecorio* (New York and London, 1967), p. 290.

1400 In 1910 84.66% of all Mexicans were natives of the state/territory in which they resided; by 1921 this had fallen only to 83.65%: González Navarro, *Población y Sociedad*, cuadro 3, facing p. 52. The one spectacular demographic shift evident in these figures relates to Tamaulipas, where the percentage of 'natives' fell from 87.86 to 68.86; the result, not of revolution, but of oil.

1401 Above, p. 420; Benjamin, 'Passages', p. 171; Beals, *Mexican Maze*, p. 206.

1402 González, *Pueblo en vilo*, p. 132; Friedrich, *Agrarian Revolt*, pp. 76, 139.

1403 Secretario de Gobierno, Chihuahua, to Trabajo, 1 July 1916, Trabajo 31/3/5.

1404 Martínez, *Border Boom Town*, pp. 44–5; Manuel Gamio, *Mexican Immigration to the United States* (New York, 1971; first pub., 1930), pp. 23–7, notes the growth of migration to new centres in the mid-West and East, encouraged by war industries.

1405 Martínez, *Border Boom Town*, p. 41; border report, Nogales, 21 Oct. 1916, SD 812.00/19706.

1406 Martínez, *Border Boom Town*, p. 41; González Navarro, *Población y sociedad*, I, p. 35 cites American census figures showing an increase in Mexican residents of 266,000; a Mexican estimate, in the same source, puts total Mexican out-migration during the Revolution at half a million.

1407 Martínez, *Border Boom Town*, p. 44, quoting an El Paso charity spokesman.

1408 Hohler, Washington, 26 June 1918, FO 371/3245, 120679; Gamio, *Mexican Immigration*, pp. 13, 21, shows that 54% of all money orders sent from the US to Mexico (1926) went to the states of Michoacán, Guanajato and Jalisco.

1409 Friedrich, *Agrarian Revolt*, pp. 67–8; Gonzalez, *Pueblo en vilo*, pp. 135, 137; Beals, *Cherán*, p. 12.

1410 González, *Pueblo en vilo*, p. 127; Lola Romanucci-Ross, *Conflict, Violence and Morality in a Mexican Village* (Palo Alto, 1973), pp. 15–18; cf. Turner, *Dynamic of Mexican Nationalism*, pp. 121–4.

1411 Pani to Carranza, 12 Mar. 1919, in Pani, *Cuestiones diversas*, pp. 65–7; Córdova, *Ideología*, pp. 254–8; Manero, *Por el honor*, pp. 157–60, 164.

1412 Lewis, *Tepoztlán*, p. 443; Foster, *A Primitive Mexican Economy*, pp. 14–15.

1413 Beals, *Mexican Maze*, 208.

1414 Beals, *Cherán*, pp. 119–20.

1415 Lewis, *Tepoztlán*, pp. 177–8, *Pedro Martínez*, pp. 174–5.

1416 Horcasitas, *De Porfirio Díaz*, pp. 165–9.

1417 Rutherford, *Mexican Society*, p. 306.

1418 *Ibid.*, p. 307; Rodgers to Fletcher, 31 May 1916, Fletcher Papers, box 4; Krauze, *Caudillos culturales*, p. 58.

1419 Hence it is legitimate to see the Revolution as an agent of 'modernization', conceived in Parsonian terms, even before the 'institutional' revolution got under way: see Glade and Anderson, *Political Economy*, pp. 50–1. That is not to say that 'modernization' offers the best – still less the only – conceptualisation of the revolutionary process.

1420 Gamio, *The Mexican Immigrant*, p. 1; and *Mexican Immigration*, p. 128, where transnational migration is said to foster nationalism.

1421 Blasco Ibáñez, *Mexico in Revolution*, p. 8.

1422 Krauze, *Caudillos culturales*, pp. 98, 104–6, 137–40, 161.

1423 *Ibid.*, pp. 37, 44.

1424 *Ibid.*, pp. 50, 66, 104, 163, 189; Gómez Morín, *1915*, pp. 7–8, 9–10.

1425 Múgica to Alvarado, 29 Aug. 1916, in María y Campos, *Múgica*, p. 102; Glade and Anderson, *Political Economy*, p. 114.

1426 *Ibid.*, p. 45; Derossi, *The Mexican Entrepreneur*, p. 157.

1427 Lewis, *Tepoztlán*, pp. 117–18, *Pedro Martínez*, p. 176.

1428 US Naval report, Acapulco, 9 Nov. 1915, SD 812.00/16843; Schryer, *Rancheros of Pisaflores*, p. 37. One must say 'coincided' rather than 'caused', since Schryer stresses that it was international demand rather than 'political upheavals' which brought about the shift; it would seem plausible, however, that the peons' ability to set up as coffee-cultivating tenants (which gave the region 'a reputation as [one] where landless peasants could improve their circumstances') was linked to the political mobilisation – and 'upheaval' – of the revolutionary and post-revolutionary period.

1429 Foster, 'Peasant Society', pp. 293–315.

1430 Lewis, *Tepoztlán*, p. 178; Brenner, *Idols*, pp. 185–6, notes how the Revolution inculcated 'the highest respect for work'.

1431 Beals, *Mexican Maze*, pp. 207–8.

1432 Belshaw, *A Village Economy*, p. 340.

1433 Lewis, *Pedro Martínez*, p. 174.

1434 *Ibid.*, p. 175; cf. Wright, *Ordeal of Total War*, p. 235.

1435 Moore, *Social Origins*, p. 437.

1436 George Sorel, *Reflections on Violence* (New York, 1961), p. 125.

Bibliography

Archival Sources

Mexico

Archivo General de la Nación: Archivo de Gobernación (various legajos, plus unclassified files: Convención revolucionaria y Correspondencia con Francisco I. Madero; Relaciones con los Estados; Archivo del Gral E. Zapata).

    Departamiento de Trabajo.

Museo de Antropología e Historia

    Conflicto Religioso

    Archivo Jorge Denegri

    Archivo Francisco I. Madero

    Serie Sonora

    San Antonio Tochatlaco

    Archivo Zongólica

Condumex

    Archivo Venustiano Carranza

    Archivo Ramón Corral

    Archivo Francisco León de la Barra

Secretaria de Relaciones Exteriores: Archivo de Relaciones Exteriores

Biblioteca de México: Archivo Alfredo Robles Domínguez

United States

Library of Congress: Papers of Stephen Bonsal; William Jennings Bryan; Josephus Daniels; Henry P. Fletcher; Benjamin Foulois; Edward House; Samuel Guy Inman; Robert Lansing; George Patton; John J. Pershing; Hugh L. Scott; Woodrow Wilson; Leonard Wood.

State Department: Records relating to the internal affairs of Mexico, 1910–29.

Bancroft Library, Berkeley: Silvestre Terrazas Archive.

University of Texas, Austin: Papers of William F. Buckley; Emilio Rabasa.

Trinity University, San Antonio: Mexican municipal archives (Lampazos).

Europe

Public Record Office, London: Foreign Office Papers; Grey Papers.

Science Museum, London: Cowdray Papers.

Kleinwort Benson Archive, Speen, Newbury: Mexican Cotton Estates of Tlahualilo Papers.

Quai d'Orsay, Paris: Archives du Ministère des Affaires Etrangères.

Instituut voor Sociale Geschiednis, Amsterdam: Mexican press collection.

Newspaper Sources:

Le Courrier du Mexique (Mexico City); *El Demócrata* (Mexico City); *El Dictamen* (Veracruz); *El Correo de Chihuahua* (Chihuahua); *El Diario del Hogar* (Mexico City); *El Imparcial* (Mexico City); *La Nueva Era* (Parral); *The Mexican Herald* (Mexico City and Veracruz); *El País* (Mexico City); *The Times* (London); *The New York Times* (New York).

Books and articles

Aguilar Camín, Héctor, 'The Relevant Tradition: Sonoran Leaders in the Revolution', in D. A. Brading, ed., *Caudillo and Peasant in the Mexican Revolution* (Cambridge, 1980).
  La Revolución Sonorense, 1910–1914 (Mexico, INAH, 1975).
Aguirre, Manuel J., *Cananea* (Mexico, 1958).
Aguirre Benavides, Luis, *De Francisco I. Madero a Francisco Villa* (Mexico, 1966).
Alessio Robles, Vito, *Desfile sangriento. Mis andanzas con nuestro Ulíses* (Mexico, 1979).
Alperovich, M. S., and Rudenko, B. T., *La revolución mexicana de 1910–1917 y la política de los Estados Unidos* (Mexico, 1960).
Alvarado, Salvador, *Actuación revolucionaria del General Salvador Alvarado en Yucatán* (Mexico, 1955).
  La reconstrucción de México: Un mensaje a los pueblos de América (2 vols., Mexico, 1919).
Amaya, Luis Fernándo, *La soberana convención revolucionaria, 1914–16* (Mexico, 1975).
Ankerson, Dudley, 'The Cedillos and the Revolution in the state of San Luis Potosí, 1890–1938' (Cambridge Ph.D. diss., 1981).
  'Saturnino Cedillo: a Traditional Caudillo in San Luis Potosí', in Brading, ed., *Caudillo and Peasant in the Mexican Revolution* (Cambridge, 1980).
Atristaín, Dario, *Notas de un ranchero* (Mexico, 1917).
Azuela, Mariano, *Obras completas* (3 vols., Mexico, 1958–60).
  Two Novels of Mexico: The Flies; The Bosses, transl., Leslie B. Simpson (Berkeley, 1956).
  Two Novels of the Mexican Revolution: The Trials of a Respectable Family and The Underdogs by Mariano Azuela, transl., F. K. Hendricks and B. Berler (San Antonio, 1963).
Baecker, Thomas, 'The Arms of the Ypiranga: the German side', *Americas*, XXX (1973), pp. 1–17.
  'Los intereses militares del imperio alemán en México, 1913–14', *Historia Mexicana*, XXII (1972), pp. 347–62.
Bailey, David C., *Viva Cristo Rey! The Cristero Rebellion and Church–State Conflict in Mexico* (Austin, 1974).
Barragán Rodríguez, Juan, *Historia del ejército y de la revolución constitucionalista* (2 vols., Mexico, 1966).
Barrera Fuentes, Florencio, *Crónicas y debates de las sesiones de la soberana convención revolucionaria* (Mexico, 1964).
Bartra, Armando, *Regeneración, 1900–1918, La corriente más radical de la revolución mexicana de 1910* (Mexico, 1977).
Bassols, Narciso, *El pensamiento político de Alvaro Obregón* (Mexico, 1976).
Bazant, Jan, *Cinco haciendas mexicanas: tres siglos de vida rural en San Luis Potosí* (Mexico, 1975).
  Historia de la deuda exterior de México (1823–1946) (Mexico, 1968).
Beals, Carleton, *Mexican Maze* (Philadelphia, 1931).
Beals, Ralph L., *Cherán: A Sierra Tarascan Village* (New York, 1973).
Beezley, William H., *Insurgent Governor: Abraham González and the Mexican Revolution in Chihuahua* (Lincoln, 1973).
Bell, Edward I., *The Political Shame of Mexico* (New York, 1914).
Bellingeri, Marco, 'L'economia del latifondo in Messico. L'hacienda San Antonio Tochatlaco dal 1880 al 1920', *Annali della Fondazione Luigi Einaudi*, X (1976), pp. 287–428.
Bernaldo de Quirós, C., *El bandolerismo en España y México* (Mexico, 1959).

Bernstein, Marvin D., *The Mexican Mining Industry, 1880–1950: A Study of the Interaction of Politics, Economics, and Technology* (Albany, 1965).
Blasco Ibáñez, Vicente, *Mexico in Revolution* (New York, 1920).
Blok, Anton, 'The Peasant and the Brigand: Social Banditry Reconsidered', *Comparative Studies in Society and History*, XIV (1972), pp. 494–503.
Boils, Guillermo, *Los militares y la política en México, 1915–74* (Mexico, 1975).
Brading, D. A., ed., *Caudillo and Peasant in the Mexican Revolution* (Cambridge, 1980).
  Haciendas and Ranchos in the Mexican Bajío León 1700–1860 (Cambridge, 1978).
Brenner, Anita, *Idols Behind Altars* (New York, 1929).
Brondo Whitt, E., *La división del norte (1914) por un testigo presencial* (Mexico, 1940).
Bustamante, Luis F., *De el Ebano a Torreón* (Monterrey, 1915).
Buve, Raymond Th. J., 'Peasant Movements, Caudillos and Land Reform during the Revolution (1910–17) in Tlaxcala, Mexico', *Boletín de Estudios Latino-americanos y del Caribe*, XVIII (1975), pp. 112–52.
Calero, Manuel, *Un decenio de política mexicana* (New York, 1920).
Calvert, P. A. R., *The Mexican Revolution 1910–1914: The Diplomacy of Anglo-American Conflict* (Cambridge, 1968).
Calzadíaz Barrera, Alberto, *Hechos reales de la revolución mexicana* (vol. I, Mexico, 1961).
  El fin de la división del norte (Mexico, 1965).
  Porqué Villa atacó a Columbus (Mexico, 1972).
Carr, Barry, 'The Casa del Obrero Mundial, Constitutionalism and the Pact of February 1915', in Elsa Cecilia Frost *et al.*, eds., *El trabajo y los trabajadores en la historia de México* (Mexico and Arizona, 1979).
  El movimiento obrero y la política en México (2 vols., Mexico, 1976).
  'Las peculiaridades del norte mexicano, 1880–1927: ensayo de interpretación', *Historia Mexicana*, XXII (1973), pp. 320–46.
Casasola, Gustavo, *Historia gráfica de la revolución mexicana* (5 vols., Mexico, 1967).
Cervantes, Federico, *Francisco Villa y la revolución* (Mexico, 1960).
Chase, Stuart, *Mexico, A Study of Two Americas* (New York, 1931).
Clark, Marjorie Ruth, *Organised Labor in Mexico* (Chapel Hill, 1934).
Clendenen, Clarence C., *The United States and Pancho Villa: A Study in Unconventional Diplomacy* (New York, 1961).
Córdova, Arnaldo, *La ideología de la revolución mexicana. La formación del nuevo régimen* (Mexico, 1973).
Covarrubias, Miguel, *Mexico South. The Isthmus of Tehuantepec* (Mexico, 1946).
Coy, Peter, 'A Watershed in Mexican Rural History: Some Thoughts on the Reconciliation of Conflicting Interpretations', *Journal of Latin American Studies*, III (1971), pp. 39–57.
Cumberland, Charles C., *Mexican Revolution The Constitutionalist Years* (Austin, 1972).
  Mexico The Struggle for Modernity (London, 1968).
  'Huerta y Carranza ante la ocupación de Veracruz', *Historia Mexicana*, VI, 1957, pp. 534–47.
  'The Sonoran Chinese and the Mexican Revolution', *Hispanic American Historical Review*, XL (1960), pp. 191–211.
Cusi, Ezio, *Memorias de un colono* (Mexico, 1969).
Diario de los debates del congreso constituyente, 1916–17 (2 vols., Mexico, 1960).
Dillon, E. J., *President Obregón. A World Reformer* (London, 1922).
Dorador, Silvestre, *Mi prisión, la defensa social, y la verdad del caso* (Mexico, 1916).
Dulles, John W. F., *Yesterday in Mexico. A Chronicle of the Revolution 1919–1936* (Austin and London, 1961).
Duncan, Kenneth and Rutledge, Ian, *Land and Labour in Latin America. Essays on the Development of Agrarian Capitalism in the Nineteenth and Twentieth Centuries* (Cambridge, 1977).
La economía mexicana en cifras (Mexico, Nacional Financiera, 1978).

Esquivel Obregón, Toribio, *México y Estados Unidos ante el derecho internacional* (Mexico, 1926).

Estadísticas económicas del Porfiriato (Mexico, El Colegio de Mexico, 1956).

Evans, Rosalie, *The Rosalie Evans Letters from Mexico* (ed., Daisy Caden Pettus, Indianapolis, 1926).

Fabela, Isidro, ed., *Documentos históricos de la revolución mexicana, revolución y régimen constitucio-nalista* (4 vols., Mexico, 1960–3).

    Documentos históricos de la revolución mexicana. Emiliano Zapata, El Plan de Ayala y su política agraria (Mexico, 1970).

    Historia diplomática de la revolución constitucionalista (2 vols., Mexico, 1959).

Fabila, Alfonso, *Las tribus Yaquis de Sonora: su cultura y anhelada autodeterminación* (Mexico, 1940).

Falcón, Romana, *El agrarismo en Veracruz. La etapa radical (1928–1935)* (Mexico, 1977).

    'The Rise and Fall of Military Caciquismo in Revolutionary Mexico: the Case of San Luis Potosí' (Oxford Ph.D. diss., 1983).

Fall Report: see US Senate.

Flores D., Jorge, 'La vida rural en Yucatán en 1914', *Historia Mexicana,* x (1960–1), pp. 470–83.

Foster, George M., *A Primitive Mexican Economy* (Seattle and London, 1942).

Fowler Salamini, Heather, *Agrarian Radicalism in Veracruz 1920–38* (Lincoln, 1978).

    'Caciquismo and the Mexican Revolution: the Case of Manuel Peláez', paper presented at the Sixth Conference of Mexican and US Historians, Chicago, September 1981.

Friedrich, Paul, *Agrarian Revolt in a Mexican Village* (Englewood Cliffs, 1970).

Frost, Elsa Cecilia, *et al.*, eds., *El trabajo y los trabajadores en la historia de México* (Mexico and Arizona, 1979).

Gamio, Manuel, *The Life Story of the Mexican Immigrant* (Chicago, 1931).

    Mexican Immigration to the United States (New York, 1971; first published 1930).

    La población del valle de Teotihuacán (Mexico, 1922).

Gamiz Olivas, Manuel, *Historia de la revolución en el estado de Durango* (Mexico, 1963).

García, Mario T., *Desert Immigrants. The Mexicans of El Paso 1880–1920* (Yale, 1981).

García Naranjo, Nemesio, *Memorias* (vol. VII, Monterrey, n.d.).

Garciadiego Dantan, Javier, 'Revolución constitucionalista y contrarrevolución (Movimientos reaccionarios en México 1914–20)' (Ph.D., El Colegio de México, 1981).

Garza Treviño, Ciro de la, *La revolución mexicana en el estado de Tamaulipas (Cronología), 1885–1913* (Mexico, 1973).

Gavira, Gabriel, *General de Brigada Gabriel Gavira. Su actuación político-militar revolucionaria* (Mexico, 1933).

Gill, Mario, 'Mochis, fruto de un sueño imperialista', *Historia Mexicana,* v (1955), pp. 303–20.

Gilly, Adolfo, *et al.*, *Interpretaciones de la Revolución Mexicana* (Mexico, 1980).

    La revolución interrumpida, Mexico 1910–40. Una guerra campesina por la tierra y el poder (Mexico, 1971).

Glade, William P., *The Latin American Economies, a Study of their Institutional Evolution* (New York, 1963).

Glade, William P., and Anderson, Charles W., *The Political Economy of Mexico* (Madison, 1968).

Gómez, Marte R., *La reforma agraria en las filas Villistas* (Mexico, 1966).

González Calzada, Manuel, *Historia de la revolución mexicana en Tabasco* (Mexico, 1972).

González y González, Luis, *Pueblo en vilo. Microhistoria de San José de Gracia* (Mexico, 1972).

González Navarro, Moisés, *Historia Moderna de México. El Porfiriato. La Vida Social* (Mexico, 1970).

    Población y sociedad en México (1900–1970) (2 vols., Mexico, 1974).

González Roa, F., *El aspecto agrario de la revolución mexicana* (Mexico, 1919).

Goodman, David and Redclift, Michael, *From Peasant to Proletarian: Capitalist Development and Agrarian Transition* (Oxford, 1981).

Grajales, Francisco J., see Obregón.

Greene, Graham, *The Lawless Roads* (Harmondsworth, 1971; first published 1939).

Grieb, Kenneth J., 'The Causes of the Carranza Rebellion: a Reinterpretation', *Americas*, XXV (1968), pp. 25–32.

The United States and Huerta (Lincoln, 1969).

Grimaldo, I., *Apuntes para la historia* (San Luis, 1916).

Gruening, Ernest, *Mexico and its Heritage* (New York, 1928).

Guerra, F.-X., 'La révolution mexicaine: d'abord une révolution minière?', *Annales, E.S.C.*, XXXVI / 5 (1981), pp. 785–814.

Guzmán, Martín Luis, *The Eagle and the Serpent* (New York, 1965).

Memorias de Pancho Villa (Mexico, 1964).

Haley, J. Edward, *Revolution and Intervention. The Diplomacy of Taft and Wilson with Mexico 1910–17* (MIT, 1970).

Hall, Linda B., 'Alvaro Obregón and the agrarian movement, 1912–20' in Brading, ed., *Caudillo and Peasant in the Mexican Revolution* (Cambridge, 1980).

Alvaro Obregón. Power and Revolution in Mexico, 1911–20 (Texas A and M, 1981).

Hart, John M., *Anarchism and the Mexican Working Class, 1869–1931* (Austin, 1978).

'The Urban Working Class and the Mexican Revolution: the Case of the Casa del Obrero Mundial', *Hispanic American Historical Review*, LVIII (1978), pp. 1–20.

Henderson, Peter V. N., *Félix Díaz, the Porfirians, and the Mexican Revolution* (Lincoln, 1981).

Hendrick, Burton J., *The Life and Letters of Walter Hines Page* (London, 1924).

Hernández Chávez, Alicia, 'La defensa de los finqueros en Chiapas, 1914–20', *Historia Mexicana*, XXVIII (1979), pp. 335–69.

Hill, Larry D., *Emissaries to a Revolution: Woodrow Wilson's Executive Agents in Mexico* (Baton Rouge, 1973).

Hilton, Rodney, *et al.*, *The Transition From Feudalism to Capitalism* (London, 1978).

Historia de la Brigada Mixta 'Hidalgo' que es a las órdenes del General Vicente Segura (Mexico, 1917).

Hobsbawm, E. J., *Bandits* (Harmondsworth, 1972).

Hohler, Thomas Beaumont, *Diplomatic Petrel* (London, 1942).

Horcasitas, Fernando, *De Porfirio Díaz a Zapata. Memoria Náhuatl de Milpa Alta* (Mexico, 1974).

Huitrón, Jacinto, *Orígines e historia del movimiento obrero en México* (Mexico, 1978).

Huntington, Samuel P., *Political Order in Changing Societies* (New Haven, 1971).

Huxley, Aldous, *Beyond the Mexique Bay* (London, 1955).

Jacobs, Ian, 'Aspects of the History of the Mexican Revolution in the State of Guerrero up to 1940' (Cambridge Ph.D. diss., 1977).

Ranchero Revolt. The Mexican Revolution in Guerrero (Austin, 1982).

'Rancheros of Guerrero: the Figueroa Brothers and the Revolution', in Brading, ed., *Caudillo and Peasant in the Mexican Revolution* (Cambridge, 1980).

Jones, Chester Lloyd, *Mexico and its Reconstruction* (New York, 1921).

Joseph, Gilbert M., 'Revolution from Without: the Mexican Revolution in Yucatán' (Yale, Ph.D. diss., 1978).

Revolution from Without: Yucatán, Mexico and the United States, 1880–1924 (Cambridge, 1982).

Junco, Alfonso, *Carranza y los orígenes de su rebelión* (Mexico, 1955).

Katz, Friedrich, 'Agrarian changes in northern Mexico in the period of Villista rule, 1913–15', in James W. Wilkie, Michael C. Meyer and Edna Monzón de Wilkie, eds., *Contemporary Mexico Papers of its Fourth International Congress of Mexican History* (Berkeley, 1976).

Deutschland, Díaz und die mexikanische Revolution (Berlin, 1964).

'Pancho Villa and the attack on Columbus, New Mexico', *American Historical Review*, LXXXIII (1978), pp. 101–30.

The Secret War in Mexico; Europe, The United States and the Mexican Revolution (Chicago, 1981).

Kearney, Michael, *The Winds of Ixtepeji: World View and Society in a Zapotec Town* (New York, 1972).

Kemmerer, E. J., *Inflation and Revolution: Mexico's Experience of 1912–17* (Princeton, 1940).

King, Rosa, *Tempest Over Mexico* (Boston, 1935).

Kingdom, M., *From Out the Dark Shadows* (San Diego, 1925).

Knight, Alan, 'Intellectuals in the Mexican Revolution', paper presented at the Sixth Conference of Mexican and US Historians, Chicago, September, 1981.

'The political economy of revolutionary Mexico 1900–40', in C. Abel and C. Lewis. eds., *Latin America, Economic Imperialism and the State. The Political Economy of the External Connection from Independence to the Present* (London, 1985), pp. 288–317.

'Nationalism, Xenophobia and Revolution: The Place of Foreigners and Foreign Interests in Mexico, 1910–15' (Oxford Ph.D. diss., 1974).

'La révolution mexicaine: révolution minière ou révolution serrano?', *Annales, E.S.C.*, XXXVIII / 2 (1983), pp. 449–59.

'The working class and the Mexican Revolution, c. 1900–1920', *Journal of Latin American Studies*, XVI (1984), pp. 51–79.

Krauze, Enrique, *Caudillos culturales en la revolución mexicana* (Mexico, 1976).

Langle Ramírez, Arturo, *El ejército Villista* (Mexico, 1961).

El militarismo de Victoriano Huerta (Mexico, 1976).

Lewis, Oscar, *Life in a Mexican Village: Tepoztlán Restudied* (Urbana, 1963).

Pedro Martínez: A Mexican Peasant and his Family (London, 1969).

Liceaga, Luis, *Félix Díaz* (Mexico, 1958).

Lieuwen, Edwin, *Mexican Militarism: the Political Rise and Fall of the Revolutionary Army, 1910–40* (Albuquerque, 1968).

Link, Arthur S., *Wilson: The New Freedom* (Princeton, 1956).

Lister, Florence C. and Robert H., *Chihuahua, Storehouse of Storms* (Albuquerque, 1966).

Lozoya, Jorge Alberto, *El ejército mexicano, 1911–65* (Mexico, 1970).

Macías, Anna, 'Women in the Mexican Revolution, 1910–20', *Americas*, XXXVII (1980), pp. 53–82.

Mancisidor, José, *Historia de la Revolución Mexicana* (Mexico, 1971).

Manero, Antonio, *Por el honor y por la gloria: 50 editoriales escritos durante la lucha revolucionaria constitucionalista en Veracruz* (Mexico, 1916).

Margolies, Barbara Luise, *Princes of the Earth. Subcultural Diversity in a Mexican Municipality* (Washington DC, 1975).

María y Campos, Armando, *Múgica, crónica biográfica* (Mexico, 1939).

Martínez, Oscar J., *Border Boom Town: Ciudad Juárez since 1848* (Austin, 1978).

Martínez Alier, Juan, *Haciendas, Plantations and Collective Farms. Agrarian Class Societies – Cuba and Peru* (London, 1977).

Martínez Núñez, Eugenio, *La revolución en el estado de San Luis Potosí* (Mexico, 1964).

McBride, George M., *The Land Systems of Mexico* (New York, 1923).

Meade, Joaquín, *Historia de Valles* (Mexico, 1970).

Mendieta y Núñez, Lucio, *Efectos sociales de la reforma agraria en tres comunidades ejidales de la República Mexicana* (Mexico, 1960).

El problema agrario de México (Mexico, 1966).

Mendoza, Vicente T., *El corrido de la revolución mexicana* (Mexico, 1956).

Lírica narrativa de México: el corrido (Mexico, 1964).

Mexican Year Book (London, 1914).

Mexican Year Book (Los Angeles, 1922).

Meyer, Eugenia *et al.*, *La vida con Villa en la Hacienda de Canutillo* (Mexico, 1974).

Meyer, Jean, *The Cristero Rebellion. The Mexican People Between Church and State, 1926–29* (Cambridge, 1976).

La Cristiada (3 vols., Mexico, 1973).

La révolution mexicaine: 1910–1940 (Paris, 1973).

'Les ouvriers dans la révolution mexicaine: les bataillons rouges', *Annales, E.S.C.*, XXV / 1 (1970), pp. 30–55.

Meyer, Lorenzo, *México y Estados Unidos en el conflicto petrolero* (Mexico, 1968).

Meyer, Michael C., *Huerta. A Political Portrait* (Lincoln, 1972).

Mexican Rebel: Pascual Orozco and the Mexican Revolution (Lincoln, 1967).

'The militarisation of Mexico, 1913–14', *Americas*, XXVII (1970–1), pp. 293–306.

Migdal, Joel S., *Peasants, Politics and Revolution* (Princetown, 1974).

Millon, Robert P., *Zapata: The Ideology of a Peasant Revolutionary* (New York, 1969).

Moats, Leone, *Thunder in their Veins* (London, 1933).

Moheno, Querido, *Mi actuación después de la decena trágica* (Mexico, 1939).

Moore, Barrington, *Injustice. The Social Bases of Obedience and Revolt* (London, 1978).

Social Origins of Dictatorship and Democracy. Lord and Peasant in the Making of the Modern World (London, 1969).

Morales Jiménez, Alberto, *Hombres de la Revolución* (Mexico, 1960).

Morgan, A. L., 'Industry and Society in the Mexico City Area, 1875–1920' (CNAA Ph.D. diss., 1984).

Nahmad, Salomon, *Los mixes* (Mexico, 1965).

Niemeyer, E. V., *Revolution at Querétaro: The Mexican Constitutional Convention of 1916–17* (Austin, 1974).

Obregón, Alvaro, *Ocho mil kilómetros en campaña* (intro., F. Grajales, Mexico, 1966).

O'Brien, Dennis J., 'Petroleo e intervención: relaciones entre los Estados Unidos y México, 1917–18', *Historia Mexicana*, XXVII (1977), pp. 103–41.

Ochoa Campos, Moisés, *Historia del estado de Guerrero* (Mexico, 1968).

O'Hea, Patrick, *Reminiscences of the Mexican Revolution* (Mexico, 1966).

Olea, Hector R., *Breve historia de la revolución en Sinaloa* (Mexico, 1964).

Olivera Sedano, Alicia, *Aspectos del conflicto religioso de 1926 a 1929. Sus antecedentes y consecuencias* (Mexico, 1966).

Ortiz Ortiz, Alfonso, *Episodios de la revolución en Moroleón* (Mexico, 1976).

O'Shaughnessy, Edith, *A Diplomat's Wife in Mexico* (New York, 1916).

Oviedo Mota, Alberto, *El trágico fin del General Gertrudis G. Sánchez* (Morelia, 1939).

Paige, Jeffery M., *Agrarian Revolution: Social Movements and Export Agriculture in the Underdeveloped World* (New York, 1978).

Palavicini, Félix F., *Mi vida revolucionaria* (Mexico, 1937).

Pani, Alberto, J., *Apuntes autobiográficos* (Mexico, 1951).

Pazuengo, Matías, *Historia de la revolución en Durango por el General Matías Pazuengo* (Cuernavaca, 1915).

Peña, Moisés T. de la, *El pueblo y su tierra. Mito y realidad de la reforma agraria en México* (Mexico, 1964).

Popkin, Samuel L., *The Rational Peasant. The Political Economy of Rural Society in Vietnam* (Berkeley, 1979).

Quijano Obregón, Aníbal, 'Contemporary peasant movements' in Seymour Martin Lipset and Aldo Solari eds., *Elites in Latin America* (Oxford, 1970).

Quirk, Robert E., *An Affair of Honor: Woodrow Wilson and the Occupation of Veracruz* (New York, 1967).

'Liberales y radicales en la revolución mexicana', *Historia Mexicana*, II (1953), pp. 503–28.

The Mexican Revolution, 1914–15. The Convention of Aguascalientes (New York, 1960).

The Mexican Revolution and the Catholic Church, 1910–29 (Bloomington, 1973).

Ramírez, Alfonso Francisco, *Historia de la revolución en Oaxaca* (Mexico, 1970).

Ramírez Plancarte, Francisco, *La Ciudad de México durante la revolución constitucionalista* (Mexico, 1941).

Redfield, Robert, *A Village That Chose Progress: Chan Kom Revisited* (Chicago and London, 1970).

Reed, John, *Insurgent Mexico* (New York, 1969).

Reed, Nelson, *The Caste War of Yucatán* (Stanford, 1964).

Reynolds, Clark W., *The Mexican Economy. Twentieth-Century Structure and Growth* (Yale, 1970).

Richmond, Douglas W., 'The First Chief and Revolutionary Mexico: the Presidency of Venustiano Carranza, 1915–20' (Ph.D. diss., University of Washington 1976).

'El nacionalismo de Carranza y los cambios socio-económicos, 1915–20', *Historia Mexicana*, XXVI (1976), pp. 107–31.

Venustiano Carranza's Nationalist Struggle, 1893–1920 (Lincoln, 1983).

Ríus Facius, Antonio, *La juventud católica y la revolución mexicana* (Mexico, 1963).

Rojas Nieto, Luisa Beatriz, *La destrucción de la hacienda en Aguascalientes, 1910–31* (Mexico, 1976).

Romero Flores, Jesús, *Historia de la revolución en Michoacán* (Mexico, 1964).

Ronfeldt, David, *Atencingo: The Politics of Agrarian Struggle in a Mexican Ejido* (Stanford, 1973).

Ross, Stanley R., 'Victoriano Huerta visto por su compadre', *Historia Mexicana*, XII (1962–3), pp. 296–321.

Rouaix, Pastor, *Génesis de los artículos 27 y 123 de la constitución política de 1917* (Mexico, 1959).

Rudenko, B. T., Lavrov, N. M., and Alperovich, M. S., *La revolución mexicana: cuatro estudios soviéticos* (Mexico, 1978).

Ruiz, Ramón Eduardo, *The Great Rebellion. Mexico 1905–1924* (New York, 1980).

Labor and the Ambivalent Revolutionaries Mexico 1911–23 (Baltimore, 1976).

Rutherford, John, *Mexican Society During the Revolution: A Literary Approach* (Oxford, 1971).

Salazar, Rosendo, and Escobedo, José, *Las pugnas de la gleba* (Mexico, 1923).

Sánchez Azcona, Juan, *Apuntes para la historia de la revolución mexicana* (Mexico, 1961).

Schmieder, Oscar. *The Settlements of the Tzapotec and Mije Indians* (Berkeley, 1930).

Schmitt, Karl M., *Mexico and the United States, 1821–1973: Conflict and Co-existence* (New York, 1974).

Schryer, Frans J., *The Rancheros of Pisaflores. The History of a Peasant Bourgeoisie in Twentieth-Century Mexico* (Toronto, 1980).

Sherman, William L., and Greenleaf, Richard E., *Victoriano Huerta: A Reappraisal* (Mexico, 1960).

Silva Herzog, Jesús, *La cuestión de la tierra* (4 vols., Mexico, 1961).

Breve historia de la revolución mexicana (2 vols., Mexico, 1969).

Simpson, Eyler N., *The Ejido, Mexico's Way Out* (Chapel Hill, 1937).

Skocpol, Theda, *States and Social Revolutions: A Comparative Analysis of France, Russia and China* (Cambridge, 1980).

Smith, Peter H., *Labyrinths of Power: Political Recruitment in Twentieth Century Mexico* (Princeton, 1979).

'The Mexican Revolution and the transformation of political elites', *Boletín de Estudios Latinoamericanos y del Caribe*, XXV (1978), pp. 3–20.

Smith, Robert F., *The United States and Revolutionary Nationalism in Mexico, 1916–32* (Chicago, 1972).

Sotelo Inclán, Jesús, *Raíz y razón de Zapata* (Mexico, 1943).

Tannenbaum, Frank, *Peace by Revolution: Mexico After 1910* (New York, 1966).

'La revolución agraria mexicana', *Problemas Agrícolas e Industriales de México*, IV (1952).

Taracena, Alfonso, *Venustiano Carranza* (Mexico, 1963).

La verdadera revolución mexicana (vols. I-V, Mexico, 1960).

Teitelbaum, Louis M., *Woodrow Wilson and the Mexican Revolution, 1913–16* (New York, 1967).

Thord-Grey, I., *Gringo Rebel* (Coral Gables, 1960).

Tilly, Charles, Tilly, Louise, and Tilly, Richard, *The Rebellious Century, 1830–1930* (Cambridge, 1975).

Tobler, Hans Werner, 'Alvaro Obregón und die Anfänge der mexikanischen Agrarreform. Agrarpolitik und Agrarkonflikt, 1921–24', *Jahrbuch für Geschichte von Staat, Wirtschaft und Gesellschaft Lateinamerikas*, VIII (1971), pp. 310–56.

'Las pardojas del ejército revolucionario: su papel en la reforma agraria mexicana, 1920–35', *Historia Mexicana*, XXI (1971), pp. 38–79.

Tocqueville, Alexis de, *L'Ancien Régime* (Oxford, 1962).

Turner, Frederick C., *The Dynamic of Mexican Nationalism* (Chapel Hill, 1968).

Ulloa, Berta, 'Carranza y el armamiento norteamericano', *Historia Mexicana*, XVII (1967), pp. 253–61.

Historia de la Revolución Mexicana, Periodo 1914–17, IV La revolución escindida (Mexico, 1979).

La Revolución intervenida: relaciones diplomáticas entre México y Estados Unidos (1910–1914) (Mexico, 1971).

Urquizo, Francisco, *Páginas de la revolución* (Mexico, 1956).

United States Senate. Investigation of Mexican Affairs: Report of a Hearing before a Sub-Committee on Foreign Relations (2 vols., Washington, 1919–20) (referred to as 'Fall Report').

Valadés, José C., *Historia general de la Revolución Mexicana* (5 vols., Mexico, 1963–5).

Vanderwood, Paul J., *Disorder and Progress. Bandits, Police and Mexican Development* (Lincoln, 1981).

Vasconcelos, José, *A Mexican Ulysses: An Autobiography* (transl., W. R. Crawford, Bloomington, 1963).

Vázquez de Knauth, Josefina, *Nacionalismo y educación en México* (Mexico, 1970).

Vera Estañol, Jorge, *La revolución mexicana. Orígines y resultados* (Mexico, 1957).

Warman, Arturo, *Y venimos a contradecir: los campesinos de Morelos y el estado nacional* (Mexico, 1976).

Waterbury, Ronald, 'Non-revolutionary Peasants: Oaxaca Compared to Morelos in the Mexican Revolution', *Comparative Studies in Society and History*, XVII (1975), pp. 410–42.

Whetten, Nathan, *Rural Mexico* (Chicago, 1948).

White, Robert A., 'Mexico: the Zapata Movement and the Revolution', in Landsberger, ed., *Latin American Peasant Movements*.

Wilkie, James W., Meyer, Michael C., and Monzón de Wilkie, Edna, eds., *Contemporary Mexico, Papers of the Fourth International Congress of Mexican History* (Berkeley, 1976).

Wilkie, James W., *The Mexican Revolution: Federal Expenditure and Social Change since 1910* (Berkeley, 1970).

Wilkie, James W., and Monzón de Wilkie, Edna, *México visto en el siglo XX: entrevistas de historia oral* (Mexico, 1969).

Wilson, Henry Lane, *Diplomatic Episodes in Mexico, Belgium and Chile* (New York, 1927).

Wolf, Eric R., 'On peasant rebellions', in T. Shanin, ed., *Peasants and Peasant Societies* (Harmondsworth, 1971).

Peasant Wars of the Twentieth Century (London, 1973).

Wolf, Eric R., and Hansen, Edward C., 'Caudillo Politics: a Structural Analysis', *Comparative Studies in Society and History*, IX (1966–7), pp. 168–79.

Womack, John, *Zapata and the Mexican Revolution* (New York, 1970).

Zuno, José G., *Historia de la revolución en el estado de Jalisco* (Mexico, 1964).

Index